EXPLORING MARKETING RESEARCH

NINTH EDITION

William G. Zikmund
Oklahoma State University

Barry J. Babin
University of Southern Mississippi

THOMSON
™
SOUTH-WESTERN

Australia · Brazil · Canada · Mexico · Singapore · Spain · United Kingdom · United States

THOMSON

SOUTH-WESTERN

Exploring Marketing Research, Ninth Edition
William G. Zikmund, Barry J. Babin

VP/Editorial Director:
Jack W. Calhoun

Publisher:
Neil Marquardt

Developmental Editor:
Ohlinger Publishing Services

Marketing Manager:
Nicole C. Moore

Content Project Manager:
Robert Dreas

Marketing Communications Manager:
Sarah Greber

Manager of Technology, Editorial:
Peggy Buskey

Technology Project Manager:
Kristen Meere

Sr. 1st Print Buyer:
Diane Lohman

Production House:
Interactive Composition Corporation

Printer:
Courier Corp.
Kendallville, Indiana

Art Director:
Stacy Shirley

Internal and Cover Designer:
Craig Ramsdell

Cover Images:
® Getty Images/Taxi/James Porto

Photography Manager:
Deanna Ettinger

Photo Researcher:
Susan Van Etten

Library of Congress Control Number:
2006923594

For more information about our products,
contact us at:
Thomson Learning Academic Resource
Center
1-800-423-0563

Thomson Higher Education
5191 Natorp Boulevard
Mason, OH 45040
USA

To my wonderful children: my dear little girl, Amie, and that awesome dude, James.

BRIEF CONTENTS

Preface, xv

Part 1 Introduction, 1
1. The Role of Marketing Research, 2
2. Information Systems and Knowledge Management, 26
3. The Marketing Research Process, 47
4. The Human Side of Marketing Research: Organizational and Ethical Issues, 72

Part 2 Beginning Stages of the Research Process, 102
5. Problem Definition: Jump-Starting the Research Process, 103
6. Qualitative Research Tools, 128
7. Secondary Data Research in a Digital Age, 159

Part 3 Research Designs for Collecting Primary Data, 184
8. Survey Research: An Overview, 185
9. Survey Research: Basic Methods of Communication with Respondents, 207
10. Observation, 236
11. Experimental Research: An Overview, 255
12. Test-Markets and Experimental Design, 284

Part 4 Measurement Concepts, 307
13. Measurement, 308
14. Attitude Measurement, 329
15. Questionnaire Design, 352

Part 5 Sampling and Fieldwork, 401
16. Sampling Designs and Sampling Procedures, 402
17. Determination of Sample Size: A Review of Statistical Theory, 429
18. Fieldwork, 460

Part 6 Data Analysis and Presentation, 477
19. Editing and Coding: Transforming Raw Data into Information, 478
20. Basic Data Analysis: Descriptive Statistics, 501
21. Univariate Statistical Analysis, 523
22. Bivariate Statistical Analysis: Differences Between Two Variables, 545
23. Bivariate Statistical Analysis: Measures of Association, 575
24. Introducing Multivariate Statistical Analysis, 596
25. Communicating Research Results: Research Report, Oral Presentation, and Research Follow-Up, 623

Part 7 Comprehensive Cases with Computerized Databases, 648

Appendix: Statistical Tables, 665 • Glossary of Frequently Used Symbols, 673

Glossary, 674 • Endnotes, 685

Index, 693

CONTENTS

CONTENTS

PART 1
INTRODUCTION

Preface, xv

Chapter 1 The Role of Marketing Research, 2

Introduction, 3

The Nature of Marketing Research, 4
Marketing Research Defined, 5
Applied and Basic Marketing Research, 6

Research Snapshot Good Fat and Bad Fat, 6
The Scientific Method, 7

The Marketing Concept, 7
Customer Orientation, 8
Long-Run Profitability, 9
A Cross-Functional Effort, 9
Keeping Customers and Building Relationships, 10
*Marketing Research: A Means for Implementing
    the Marketing Concept, 11*

Research Snapshot Harley-Davidson Goes Abroad, 11

**The Managerial Value of Marketing Research for Strategic
Decision Making, 12**
Identifying and Evaluating Opportunities, 13
Analyzing and Selecting Target Markets, 13
Planning and Implementing a Marketing Mix, 14

Research Snapshot Business Class Success?, 15

Research Snapshot Disney Distribution, 16
Analyzing Marketing Performance, 18

When is Marketing Research Needed?, 19
Time Constraints, 19

Research Snapshot Swifter or Swiffer?, 19
Availability of Data, 20
Nature of the Decision, 20
Benefits versus Costs, 20

Marketing Research in the Twenty-First Century, 21
Communication Technologies, 21
Global Marketing Research, 21

Research Snapshot "Jacques" Daniels, 22

Summary, 22
Key Terms and Concepts, 23
Questions for Review and Critical Thinking, 24
Research Activities, 24

Video Case 1.1 Krispy Kreme, 24
Video Case 1.2 Ben & Jerry's, 25

Chapter 2 Information Systems and Knowledge
Management, 26

Introduction, 27
Information, Data, and Intelligence, 27

The Characteristics of Valuable Information, 27
Relevance, 28
Quality, 28
Timeliness, 29
Completeness, 29

Knowledge Management, 29
Global Information Systems, 30

Research Snapshot RFID Technology Gets
Cheaper—Marketing Knowledge Grows, 30

Decision Support Systems, 31
Databases and Data Warehousing, 32
Input Management, 32

Research Snapshot Are Marketers
Clairvoyant?, 32
Computerized Data Archives, 35

Research Snapshot Staying Home at
Home Depot, 35

Research Snapshot We Are Resetting Our Clocks to Real
Time, 36
Networks and Electronic Data Interchange, 38

The Internet and Research, 38
What Exactly is the Internet?, 39
How is the Internet Useful in Research?, 39
Navigating the Internet, 40

Interactive Media and Environmental Scanning, 40
Information Technology, 41
Intranets, 42
Internet2, 42

Summary, 43
Key Terms and Concepts, 44
Questions for Review and Critical Thinking, 44
Research Activities, 44

Case 2.1 Harvard Cooperative Society, 45
Video Case 2.2 Wine.com, 45
Video Case 2.3 IBM: Enterprise Resource Planning, 46

Chapter 3 The Marketing Research Process, 47

Introduction, 48
Decision Making, 48
   Certainty, 49
   Uncertainty, 49
   Ambiguity, 49

Types of Marketing Research, 50
   Exploratory Research, 51
   Descriptive Research, 51

Research Snapshot Cute, Funny, or Sexy? What Makes a Mascot Tick?, 52
   Causal Research, 53

Research Snapshot Whines for Wines, 53
   Uncertainty Influences the Type of Research, 57

Stages in the Research Process, 58
   Alternatives in the Research Process, 59
   Defining the Research Objectives, 59

Research Snapshot Nothing So Practical as Theory?, 63
   Planning the Research Design, 64
   Sampling, 65

Research Snapshot Rolling Rock, 66
   Gathering Data, 67
   Processing and Analyzing Data, 67
   Drawing Conclusions and Preparing a Report, 68

The Research Program Strategy, 68

Summary, 69
Key Terms and Concepts, 69
Questions for Review and Critical Thinking, 70

Research Activities, 70

Video Case 3.1 Black Forest Motors/Mercedes-Benz, 71
Video Case 3.2 Fisher-Price Rescue Heroes, 71

Chapter 4 The Human Side of Marketing Research: Organizational and Ethical Issues, 72

Who Does the Research?, 73
Organizational Structure of Marketing Research, 74
   Marketing Research Jobs, 75
   The Director of Marketing Research as a Manager, 76
   Sources of Conflict between Marketing Management and Marketing Research, 77

Research Snapshot Marketing Research Pays, 78
   Reducing the Conflict between Management and Researchers, 80

Research Snapshot "Seat-of-the-Pants" Marketing, 80
   Cross-Functional Teams, 82

Research Suppliers and Contractors, 83
   Syndicated Service, 83
   Standardized Research Services, 83
   Limited Research Service Companies and Custom Research, 84

Research Snapshot Finding Häagen-Dazs in China, 84
Ethical Issues in Marketing Research, 85
   Ethical Questions Are Philosophical Questions, 86
   General Rights and Obligations of Concerned Parties, 86
   Rights and Obligations of the Research Participant, 87

Research Snapshot Kidstuff can be Complicated!, 90
   Rights and Obligations of the Researcher, 91

Research Snapshot Is it Right, or Is it Wrong?, 92
Research Snapshot Power Selling: An Ethical Dilemma?, 94
   Rights and Obligations of the Client Sponsor (User), 97
   Privacy, 98
   Privacy on the Internet, 98
   A Final Note on Ethics, 98

Summary, 99
Key Terms and Concepts, 100
Questions for Review and Critical Thinking, 100
Research Activities, 101

Case 4.1 Global Eating, 101
Case 4.2 Big Brother is Watching?, 101

PART 2
BEGINNING STAGES OF THE RESEARCH PROCESS

Chapter 5 Problem Definition: Jump-Starting the Research Process, 103

The Nature of Marketing Problems, 104
   Importance of Starting with a Good Problem Definition, 104
   Problem Complexity, 104

Research Snapshot Good Answers, Bad Questions?, 105
The Problem-Definition Process, 107
   Problems Mean Gaps, 107
   The Problem-Definition Process Steps, 108
   Understand the Business Decision, 108

Research Snapshot Gaming and Planning: How to get It Right, 108
Research Snapshot Opportunity Is a "Fleeting" Thing, 111
   Identifying the Relevant Issues from the Symptoms, 112
   Writing Managerial Decision Statements and Corresponding Research Objectives, 112
   Determine the Unit of Analysis, 114
   Determine Relevant Variables, 114
   Write Research Objectives and Questions, 117

Research Snapshot Pricing Turbulence, 117

Clarity in Research Questions and Hypotheses, 118

How Much Time Should Be Spent on Problem Definition?, 119

The Research Proposal, 119
The Proposal as a Planning Tool, 119
The Proposal as a Contract, 121
Anticipating Outcomes, 123

Summary, 124
Key Terms and Concepts, 125
Questions for Review and Critical Thinking, 125
Research Activities, 126

Case 5.1 E-ZPass, 126
Case 5.2 Cane's Goes International, 127
Case 5.3 Mario Lagasto's Italian Restaurant, 127
Video Case 5.4 Burton Snowboards, 127

Chapter 6 Qualitative Research Tools, 128

What is Qualitative Research?, 129
Describing Qualitative Research, 129
Qualitative "versus" Quantitative Research, 130

Research Snapshot Surprises at P&G!, 131

Research Snapshot Listening—Here's Johnny!, 132

Qualitative Research Orientations, 135
Phenomenology, 136

Research Snapshot "When Will I Ever Learn?", 136
Ethnography, 137
Grounded Theory, 138
Case Studies, 138

Research Snapshot It's Like Riding a Bike!, 139

Common Techniques Used in Qualitative Research, 140
What is a Focus Group Interview?, 141

Research Snapshot Overworked and Overpaid? Ethical Issues in Choosing Focus Group Respondents, 144
Depth Interviews, 149
Conversations, 150
Free-Association/Sentence Completion Method, 151

Research Snapshot Let the Computer do Your Reading!, 152

Exploratory Research in Science and in Practice, 153
Misuses of Exploratory and Qualitative Research , 153

Summary, 155
Key Terms, 156

Questions for Review and Critical Thinking, 156
Research Activities, 157

Case 6.1. Disaster and Consumer Value, 157
Video Case 6.2 Upjohn's Rogaine, 157
Video Case 6.3 Goya, 158
Video Case 6.4 Edward Jones, 158

Chapter 7 Secondary Data Research in a Digital Age, 159

Secondary Data Research, 160
Advantages, 160
Disadvantages, 160

Typical Objectives for Secondary-Data Research Designs, 163
Fact-Finding, 163

Research Snapshot New Trends—Music for Mobile Phones, 164
Model Building, 165
Data Mining, 168
Database Marketing and Customer Relationship Management, 169

Research Snapshot Mining Data from Blogs, 169

Sources of Secondary Data, 170
Sources of Internal and Proprietary Data, 170
External Data: The Distribution System, 171
Information as a Product and Its Distribution Channels, 171

Research Snapshot Pulte Homes Builds on Its Customer Data, 171

Research Snapshot Associations See Half-Empty Beer Stein, 176

Research Snapshot Fandango and Nielsen Keeping an Eye on Moviegoers, 177

Single-Source Data-Integrated Information, 178

Sources for Global Research, 178

Research Snapshot Around the World of Data, 179

Summary, 180
Key Terms and Concepts, 181
Questions for Review and Critical Thinking, 181
Research Activities, 182

Case 7.1 Demand for Gas Guzzlers, 182
Video Case 7.2 FedEx Corporation, 182

PART 3
RESEARCH DESIGNS FOR COLLECTING PRIMARY DATA

Chapter 8 Survey Research: An Overview, 185

The Nature of Surveys, 186
Survey Objectives: Type of Information Gathered, 186
Advantages of Surveys, 187

Errors in Survey Research, 187

Research Snapshot Measuring Demand for HDTV, 187
Random Sampling Error, 188
Systematic Error, 188

Respondent Error, 189
Nonresponse Error, 189

Research Snapshot Overestimating Patient Satisfaction, 189
Response Bias, 190

Research Snapshot My Opinion? It Depends on Your Words, 191

Administrative Error, 193
Data-Processing Error, 193

Sample Selection Error, 194
Interviewer Error, 194
Interviewer Cheating, 194

Rule-of-Thumb Estimates for Systematic Error, 194

What Can Be Done to Reduce Survey Error?, 195

Classifying Survey Research Methods, 195

Research Snapshot The "Mere-Measurement" Effect, 195
Structured and Disguised Questions, 196
Temporal Classification, 196

**Total Quality Management and Customer
Satisfaction Surveys, 198**
What Is Quality?, 198
Internal and External Customers, 199
Implementing Total Quality Management, 199

Research Snapshot Fairfax Library's Survey for
Satisfaction, 199

Summary, 203
Key Terms and Concepts, 203
Questions for Review and Critical Thinking, 204
Research Activities, 204

Case 8.1 SAT and ACT Writing Tests, 205
Case 8.2 Turner's Department Store, 205
Video Case 8.3 The Walker Information Group, 206

**Chapter 9 Survey Research: Basic Methods
of Communication with Respondents, 207**

Media Used to Communicate with Respondents, 208
Human Interactive Media and Electronic Interactive Media, 208
Noninteractive Media, 208

Personal Interviews, 209
Advantages of Personal Interviews, 209

Research Snapshot M:Metrics Finds Consumers on the Web
and on the Phone, 209

Research Snapshot General Social Survey Goes
Face-to-Face, 210
Disadvantages of Personal Interviews, 211
Door-to-Door Interviews and Shopping Mall Intercepts, 212

Research Snapshot Matters of Taste, 213
Global Considerations, 214

Telephone Interviews, 214
Characteristics of Telephone Interviews, 214
Central Location Interviewing, 217
Computer-Assisted Telephone Interviewing, 217

Research Snapshot Automating Phone Surveys
of Teens, 217
Computerized Voice-Activated Telephone Interview, 218
Global Considerations, 218

Self-Administered Questionnaires, 218
Mail Questionnaires, 219
Response Rates, 220
Increasing Response Rates for Mail Surveys, 221
Global Considerations, 224

**Self-Administered Questionnaires Using Other Forms
of Distribution, 224**
Fax Surveys, 225

E-Mail Surveys, 225
Internet Surveys, 226

Research Snapshot Personalizing E-mail Invitations, 227
Kiosk Interactive Surveys, 230
Survey Research That Mixes Modes, 230

Selecting the Appropriate Survey Research Design, 230

Pretesting, 232

Ethical Issues in Survey Research, 232

Summary, 232
Key Terms and Concepts, 233
Questions for Review and Critical Thinking, 233
Research Activities, 234

Case 9.1 National Do Not Call Registry, 234
Case 9.2 Royal Bee Electric Fishing Reel, 235

Chapter 10 Observation, 236

Observation in Marketing Research, 237
What Can Be Observed?, 237
The Nature of Observation Studies, 238

Observation of Human Behavior, 238

Research Snapshot This Trend Brought to You by DDB
SignBank, 238
Complementary Evidence, 239
Direct Observation, 240

Research Snapshot Hand Washing Overreported, Says
Observational Research, 241
Combining Direct Observation and Interviewing, 242
Ethical Issues in the Observation of Humans, 242

Observation of Physical Objects, 243

Content Analysis, 244

Mechanical Observation, 244
Television Monitoring, 244

Research Snapshot Mobiltrak Reads Radios, 245
Monitoring Website Traffic, 246
Scanner-Based Research, 247

Research Snapshot Klipmart Watches Ad Viewership
Online, 247

Research Snapshot IRI Scanner Data Link Sales
to Laws, 248
Measuring Physiological Reactions, 249

Summary, 250
Key Terms and Concepts, 251
Questions for Review and Critical Thinking, 251

Case 10.1 Mazda and Syzygy, 252
Case 10.2 Texas Instruments and E-Lab, 252
Case 10.3 Tulsa's Central Business District (A), 253

**Chapter 11 Experimental Research:
An Overview, 255**

The Nature of Experiments, 256

An Illustration: Does Color Cause Preference?, 256
Independent Variables, 257
Experimental Outcome , 258
Independent Variable Main Effects and Interaction, 258

Basic Issues in Experimental Design, 259
Manipulation of the Independent Variable, 259

Research Snapshot Does Promotion Cause
Intoxication?, 260
Selection and Measurement of the Dependent Variable, 261
Selection and Assignment of Test Units, 262

Demand Characteristics, 265
What are Demand Characteristics?, 265
Experimenter Bias and Demand Effects, 265
Hawthorne Effect, 266
Reducing Demand Characteristics, 266

Establishing Control, 268
Problems Controlling Extraneous Variables, 268

Ethical Issues in Experimentation, 268

Fundamental Questions in Experimentation, 269
Basic versus Factorial Experimental Designs, 269
Laboratory Experiments, 269
Field Experiments, 270
Between-Subjects Designs, 271

Research Snapshot The Hidden in Hidden Valley Ranch, 271

Issues of Experimental Validity, 272
Internal Validity, 272

Research Snapshot Celling Experiments, 273
External Validity, 275
Trade-Offs Between Internal and External Validity, 275

Classification of Experimental Designs, 276
Symbolism for Diagramming Experimental Designs, 276
Three Examples of Quasi-Experimental Designs, 276
Three Alternative Experimental Designs, 277
Time Series Designs, 279
Complex Experimental Designs, 280

Summary, 281
Key Terms and Concepts, 281
Questions for Review and Critical Thinking, 282
Research Activities , 282

Case 11.1 Examining Product Failure at No-Charge Electronics, 282
Case 11.2 Tooheys, 283

Chapter 12 Test-Markets and Experimental
Design, 284

Using Test-Markets, 285
Effective Uses of Test-marketing, 285
Advantages of Test-marketing, 287

Research Snapshot Test-marketing Channels, 287
Disadvantages of Test-marketing, 288

Research Snapshot The Fast-Food Tests Race On!, 288

Research Snapshot Testing all the Circuits is Costly at
Circuit City, 289
When Not to Test-market, 290

Selecting a Test-Market, 291
U.S. Test-market Cities, 291
International Test-markets, 292
Factors to Consider in Test-market Selection, 293

Estimating Sales Volume: Some Problems, 294
Overattention, 295
Unrealistic Store Conditions, 295
Reading the Competitive Environment Incorrectly, 295
Incorrect Volume Forecasts, 295
Time Lapse, 295

Projecting Test-Market Results, 296
Consumer Surveys, 296
Straight Trend Projections, 296
Ratio of Test Product Sales to Total Company Sales, 296
Market Penetration × Repeat-Purchase Rate, 296

Alternative Test-Market Methods, 297
Standard and Control Methods, 297
High-Technology Systems Using Scanner Data, 298
Simulated Test-markets, 298
Virtual-Reality Simulations, 299

Research Snapshot Testing in a Virtual World, 299

Complex Experimental Designs, 300
Completely Randomized Design, 300
Randomized-block Design, 301
Factorial Designs, 301

Research Snapshot A Lethal Interaction, 303
Latin Square Design, 304

Summary, 305
Key Terms and Concepts, 305
Questions for Review and Critical Thinking, 305
Research Activities, 306

Case 12.1 Bueno Chiles Rellenos, 306

PART 4
MEASUREMENT CONCEPTS

Chapter 13 Measurement, 308

What Do I Measure?, 309
Concepts, 311
Operational Definitions, 311

Research Snapshot Measuring Yahoo! Impact, 312

Levels of Scale Measurement, 313
Nominal Scale, 313
Ordinal Scale, 315

Interval Scale, 315
Ratio Scale, 316
Mathematical and Statistical Analysis of Scales, 316

Research Snapshot Football Follies, 317

Index Measures, 319
Indexes and Composites, 319
Computing Scale Values, 320

Three Criteria for Good Measurement, 321
Reliability, 321

Research Snapshot Recoding Made Easy, 321
Validity, 323
Reliability versus Validity, 324
Sensitivity, 324

Summary, 325
Key Terms and Concepts, 325
Questions for Review and Critical Thinking, 326
Research Activities, 326

Case 13.1 FlyAway Airways, 327

Chapter 14 Attitude Measurement, 329
Attitudes in Marketing Research, 330
Attitudes as Hypothetical Constructs, 330
Importance of Measuring Attitudes, 330
Techniques for Measuring Attitudes, 331

Research Snapshot This Hypothetical Construct Is a
Four-Letter Word, 331
Attitude Rating Scales, 332
Simple Attitude Scales, 332
Category Scales, 332
Method of Summated Ratings: The Likert Scale, 333

Research Snapshot Attitudes of the Rich, 333
Semantic Differential, 335
Numerical Scales, 337
Stapel Scale, 337
Constant-Sum Scale, 337
Graphic Rating Scales, 338

Research Snapshot A Measuring Stick for Website
Usability, 338
Thurstone Interval Scale, 340

Research Snapshot How Much Is a Healthy
Home Worth?, 340
Measuring Behavioral Intention, 341
Behavioral Differential, 342

Ranking, 342
Paired Comparisons, 342

Sorting, 343

Randomized Response Questions, 343

Other Methods of Attitude Measurement, 344

**Selecting a Measurement Scale: Some Practical
Decisions, 345**
Ranking, Sorting, Rating, or Choice Technique?, 345
Monadic or Comparative Scale?, 345
What Type of Category Labels, If Any?, 346
How Many Scale Categories or Response Positions?, 346
Balanced or Unbalanced Rating Scale?, 346

Research Snapshot Skip the Pâté, We're Ordering
Thai Food, 346
*Use a Scale That Forces a Choice among Predetermined
Options?, 347*
Single Measure or an Index Measure?, 347

Summary, 348
Key Terms and Concepts, 348

Questions for Review and Critical Thinking, 349
Research Activities, 349

Case 14.1 Roeder-Johnson Corporation, 350
Case 14.2 Ha-Pah-Shu-Tse, 350
Case 14.3 Attitudes toward Technology and Lifestyle, 351

Chapter 15 Questionnaire Design, 352
**Questionnaire Quality and Design:
Basic Considerations, 353**
What Should Be Asked?, 353
Questionnaire Relevancy, 353
Questionnaire Accuracy, 354

How Should Questions Be Phrased?, 354
*Open-Ended Response versus Fixed-Alternative
Questions, 354*

Research Snapshot Corporate Reputations: Consumers Put
Johnson & Johnson on Top, 356
Types of Fixed-Alternative Questions, 357
*Phrasing Questions for Self-Administered, Telephone, and Personal
Interview Surveys, 358*

The Art of Asking Questions, 359
Avoid Complexity: Use Simple, Conversational Language, 359
Avoid Leading and Loaded Questions, 359

Research Snapshot What to Do with the Clubhouse?, 360
Avoid Ambiguity: Be as Specific as Possible, 362
Avoid Double-Barreled Items, 362
Avoid Making Assumptions, 363
*Avoid Burdensome Questions That May Tax the Respondent's
Memory, 363*

Research Snapshot Who's *Really* Doing the
Housework?, 364
What Is the Best Question Sequence?, 365

Research Snapshot What Citizens (Don't) Know about
Climate Change, 366
What Is the Best Layout?, 368
Traditional Questionnaires, 368
Internet Questionnaires, 373

How Much Pretesting and Revising Are Necessary?, 377

Research Snapshot Pretesting the CAHPS Hospital
Survey, 378

Designing Questionnaires for Global Markets, 379

Summary, 380
Key Terms and Concepts, 380
Questions for Review and Critical Thinking, 381
Research Activity, 382

Case 15.1 Agency for Healthcare Research and Quality, 382
Case 15.2 Canterbury Travels, 387
Case 15.3 McDonald's Spanish Language Questionnaire, 389
Case 15.4 Schönbrunn Palace in Vienna, 390

**Appendix 15A   Question Wording and Measurement Scales
for Commonly Researched Topics, 391**
Questions About Advertising, 391
Questions About Ownership and Product Usage, 393
Questions About Goods and Services, 394
Questions About Demographics, 398

PART 5
SAMPLING AND FIELDWORK

Chapter 16 Sampling Designs and Sampling Procedures, 402

Sampling Terminology, 403

Why Sample?, 403
Pragmatic Reasons, 403
Accurate and Reliable Results, 404
Destruction of Test Units, 405

Research Snapshot William's Census Was Ahead of Its Time, 405

Practical Sampling Concepts, 406
Defining the Target Population, 406
The Sampling Frame, 407

Research Snapshot George Gallup's Nation of Numbers, 407
Sampling Units, 409

Random Sampling and Nonsampling Errors, 409
Random Sampling Error, 410
Systematic Sampling Error, 410
Less than Perfectly Representative Samples, 410

Probability versus Nonprobability Sampling, 411

Nonprobability Sampling, 411
Convenience Sampling, 411
Judgment Sampling, 412
Quota Sampling, 412

Research Snapshot American Kennel Club Tries to Keep Pet Owners Out of the Doghouse, 413
Snowball Sampling, 414

Probability Sampling, 414
Simple Random Sampling, 414
Systematic Sampling, 415
Stratified Sampling, 415
Proportional versus Disproportional Sampling, 416
Cluster Sampling, 417
Multistage Area Sampling, 418

Research Snapshot Who's at Home? Different Ways to Select Respondents, 418

What Is the Appropriate Sample Design?, 420
Degree of Accuracy, 421
Resources, 421
Time, 422
Advance Knowledge of the Population, 422
National versus Local Project, 422

Research Snapshot Reactions to Handbills in Hong Kong, 422

Internet Sampling Is Unique, 423
Website Visitors, 423
Panel Samples, 423
Recruited Ad Hoc Samples, 424
Opt-in Lists, 424

Summary, 425
Key Terms and Concepts, 425
Questions for Review and Critical Thinking, 426

Case 16.1 Who's Fishing?, 427
Case 16.2 Scientific Telephone Samples, 427
Case 16.3 Action Federal Savings and Loan Corporation, 428

Chapter 17 Determination of Sample Size: A Review of Statistical Theory, 429

Review of Basic Terminology, 430
Descriptive and Inferential Statistics, 430
Sample Statistics and Population Parameters, 430

Making Data Usable, 430
Frequency Distributions, 431
Proportions, 431
Measures of Central Tendency, 432

Research Snapshot The Well-Chosen Average, 433
Measures of Dispersion, 434

Research Snapshot Are Incomes Growing? It Depends What You Measure, 435

The Normal Distribution, 438

Population Distribution, Sample Distribution, and Sampling Distribution, 441

Central-Limit Theorem, 443

Estimation of Parameters, 445
Point Estimates, 446
Confidence Intervals, 447

Research Snapshot Measuring Viewership . . . with Confidence, 447

Sample Size, 449
Random Error and Sample Size, 449
Factors in Determining Sample Size for Questions Involving Means, 450

Research Snapshot Target and Wal-Mart Shoppers Really Are Different, 450
Estimating Sample Size for Questions Involving Means, 451
The Influence of Population Size on Sample Size, 452
Factors in Determining Sample Size for Proportions, 452

Research Snapshot Slone Survey Finds That Most of Us Use Medications, 453
Calculating Sample Size for Sample Proportions, 454
Determining Sample Size on the Basis of Judgment, 455
Determining Sample Size for Stratified and Other Probability Samples, 456

A Reminder about Statistics, 456

Summary, 457
Key Terms and Concepts, 457
Questions for Review and Critical Thinking, 458
Research Activities, 458

Case 17.1 Pointsec Mobile Technologies, 459
Case 17.2 Coastal Star Sales Corporation (A), 459

Chapter 18 Fieldwork, 460

The Nature of Fieldwork, 461

Who Conducts the Fieldwork?, 461

Research Snapshot Interviewing for Horizon Research Services, 461

In-House Training for Inexperienced Interviewers, 462
Making Initial Contact and Securing the Interview, 462
Asking the Questions, 464

Research Snapshot Questioning and Probing on an Electronic Bulletin Board, 464
Probing when No Response Is Given, 465

Research Snapshot Probing for Deeper Meaning at Olson Zaltman Associates, 465
Recording the Responses, 466
Terminating the Interview, 467

Principles of Good Interviewing, 467
The Basics, 467
Required Practices, 469

Research Snapshot Interviewers at Work: Jerusalem and Canberra, 469

Fieldwork Management, 470
Briefing Session for Experienced Interviewers, 471
Training to Avoid Procedural Errors in Sample Selection, 471

Supervision of Fieldworkers, 472

Research Snapshot Total Quality Management for Interviewing, 472
Sampling Verification, 473
Interviewer Cheating, 473
Verification by Reinterviewing, 474

Summary, 474
Key Terms and Concepts, 475
Questions for Review and Critical Thinking, 475
Research Activity, 475

Case 18.1 Thomas and Dorothy Leavey Library, 476
Case 18.2 Margaret Murphy O'Hara, 476

PART 6
DATA ANALYSIS AND PRESENTATION

Chapter 19 Editing and Coding: Transforming Raw Data into Information, 478

Stages of Data Analysis, 479

Editing, 480
Field Editing, 480
In-House Editing, 481
Editing for Consistency, 481

Research Snapshot Do you Have Integrity?, 481
Editing for Completeness, 483
Editing Questions Answered Out of Order, 484
Facilitating the Coding Process, 484
Pitfalls of Editing, 484
Pretesting Edit, 485

Coding, 485
Coding Qualitative Responses, 485
The Data File, 488
Code Construction, 488
Precoding Fixed-Alternative Questions, 489

Research Snapshot I Ain't Missing You, 489
More on Coding Open-Ended Questions, 490
Devising the Coding Scheme, 492
Code Book, 494
Editing and Coding Combined, 494
Computerized Survey Data Processing, 494

Research Snapshot Verbastat, 494
Error Checking, 495

Summary, 496
Key Terms and Concepts, 496

Questions for Review and Critical Thinking, 496
Research Activity, 497

Case 19.1 U.S. Department of the Interior Heritage Conservation and Recreation Service, 497
Case 19.2 Shampoo 9–10, 498

Chapter 20 Basic Data Analysis: Descriptive Statistics, 501

The Nature of Descriptive Analysis, 502

Tabulation, 503

Cross-Tabulation, 504
Contingency Tables, 504
Percentage Cross-Tabulations, 506

Research Snapshot Contingent Personalities, 506
Elaboration and Refinement, 507
How Many Cross-Tabulations?, 507
Quadrant Analysis, 508

Data Transformation, 509
Simple Transformations, 509
Problems with Data Transformations, 509
Index Numbers, 511

Calculating Rank Order, 512

Research Snapshot Wine Index Can Help Retailers, 512

Tabular and Graphic Methods of Displaying Data, 513

Computer Programs for Analysis, 514
Statistical Packages, 514
Computer Graphics and Computer Mapping, 516

Interpretation, 517

Summary, 518
Key Terms and Concepts, 519
Questions for Review and Critical Thinking, 519
Research Activities, 520

Case 20.1 Body on Tap, 520
Case 20.2 Downy-Q Quilt, 521

Chapter 21 Univariate Statistical Analysis, 523

Hypothesis Testing, 524
The Hypothesis-Testing Procedure, 524

Research Snapshot F-22 Target Tests, 525
An Example of Hypothesis Testing, 527
Type I and Type II Errors, 530

Choosing the Appropriate Statistical Technique, 531
Type of Question to Be Answered, 531
Number of Variables, 531

Research Snapshot The Law and Type I and
Type II Errors, 531
Level of Scale of Measurement, 532
Parametric versus Nonparametric Hypothesis Tests, 532

Research Snapshot Living in a Statistical Web, 532

The t-Distribution, 533
Calculating a Confidence Interval Estimate Using
the t-Distribution, 535
Univariate Hypothesis Test Using the t-Distribution, 536

The Chi-Square Test for Goodness-of-Fit, 537

Research Snapshot Art for Girls and Boys, 539

Hypothesis Test of a Proportion, 540
Additional Applications of Hypothesis Testing, 541

Summary, 541
Key Terms and Concepts, 542
Questions for Review and Critical Thinking, 542
Research Activities, 543

Case 21.1 Quality Motors, 544
Case 21.2 Coastal Star Sales Corporation (B), 544

Chapter 22 Bivariate Statistical Analysis: Differences Between Two Variables, 545

What Is the Appropriate Test of Difference?, 546
Cross-Tabulation Tables: The χ^2 Test for Goodness-of-Fit, 546
The t-Test for Comparing Two Means, 550
Independent Samples t-Test, 550

Research Snapshot Chi-Training, 550

Research Snapshot Expert "T-eeze", 553
Paired-Samples t-Test, 555

The Z-Test for Comparing Two Proportions, 556
Analysis of Variance (ANOVA), 557
What Is ANOVA?, 557
Simple Illustration of ANOVA, 558
Partitioning Variance in ANOVA, 559
The F-Test, 560

Research Snapshot More than One-Way, 561
Practically Speaking, 562

Summary, 563
Key Terms and Concepts, 563
Questions for Review and Critical Thinking, 564
Research Activities, 566

Case 22.1 Old School versus New School Sports Fans, 566

Appendix 22A Manual Calculation of an F-Statistic, 568
Appendix 22B ANOVA for Complex Experimental
Designs, 571
Factorial Designs, 572
ANOVA for a Factorial Experiment, 572
Partitioning the Sum of Squares for a Two-Way
ANOVA, 573

Chapter 23 Bivariate Statistical Analysis: Measures of Association, 575

The Basics, 576
Simple Correlation Coefficient, 577
An Example, 578
Correlation, Covariance, and Causation, 578
Coefficient of Determination, 579
Correlation Matrix, 580

Research Snapshot What Makes Attractiveness?, 581

Regression Analysis, 582
The Regression Equation, 582
Parameter Estimate Choices, 582
Visual Estimation of a Simple Regression Model, 584
Ordinary Least-Squares Method of Regression
Analysis (OLS), 585

Research Snapshot Size and Weight, 590

Summary, 591
Key Terms and Concepts, 591
Questions for Review and Critical Thinking, 592
Research Activities, 593

Case 23.1 International Operations at CarCare Inc., 593

Appendix 23A Arithmetic Behind OLS, 594

Chapter 24 Introducing Multivariate Statistical Analysis, 596

The Nature of Multivariate Analysis, 597
What Is Multivariate Data Analysis?, 597
The "Variate" in Multivariate, 597

Classifying Multivariate Techniques, 598
Dependence Techniques, 598
Interdependence Techniques, 598
Influence of Measurement Scales, 598

Analysis of Dependence, 600
Multiple Regression Analysis, 600

Research Snapshot Too Much of a Good Thing!, 602
ANOVA (n-way) and MANOVA, 605
Discriminant Analysis, 605

Research Snapshot How to Get MANOVA Results?, 606

Analysis of Interdependence, 608
Factor Analysis, 608
Cluster Analysis, 612
Multidimensional Scaling, 614

Summary, 615
Key Terms and Concepts, 616
Questions for Review and Critical Thinking, 616
Research Activities, 617

Case 24.1 The Utah Jazz, 619
Case 24.2 How Do We Keep Them?, 621

Appendix 24A Getting Factor Results with SAS or SPSS, 622

Chapter 25 Communicating Research Results: Research Report, Oral Presentation, and Research Follow-Up, 623
Insights from the Communications Model, 624

Research Snapshot Sloppy Numbers in the Crosshairs of Dow Jones Newspaper Fund's Director, 625

The Report in Context, 626

Report Format, 626

Tailoring the Format to the Project, 627
The Parts of the Report, 628

Research Snapshot Research ROI, 630

Research Snapshot Dr. Zemel's Valuable Data, 631

Effective Use of Graphic Aids, 632
Tables, 633
Charts, 633

The Oral Presentation, 639

Research Snapshot Noah's Law of Slide Presentations, 640

The Research Follow-Up, 642

Reports on the Internet, 642

Research Snapshot Online Reports: Easy to Get, Easy to Ignore, 642

Summary, 643
Key Terms and Concepts, 643
Questions for Review and Critical Thinking, 644
Research Activity, 644

Case 25.1 Annenberg Public Policy Center, 645

A Final Note on Marketing Research, 647

PART 7
COMPREHENSIVE CASES WITH COMPUTERIZED DATABASES

Case 1: Running the Numbers: Does It Pay?, 649
Case 2: Employees Federal Credit Union, 650
Case 3: University Van Pool, 654
Case 4: Values and the Automobile Market, 657

Case 5: Say It Ain't So! Is this the Real Thing?, 659
Case 6: TABH, INC., Automotive Consulting, 661
Case 7: Survey on Americans and Dietary Supplements, 662

Appendix: Statistical Tables, 665

Glossary of Frequently Used Symbols, 673

Glossary, 674

Endnotes, 685

Index, 693

PREFACE

PREFACE PREFACE

Why a needle in a haystack on the cover? This image presents a graphic analogy to the research process from many perspectives. How do you find the needle? Where do you start? Clearly, it would be helpful if you could discover better places to start searching and better techniques to help direct the search.

Similarly, imagine trying to find a single piece of market information from the Internet. Like the needle, this information may well be hidden beneath piles and piles of irrelvant stuff! Or how about trying to find a key piece of market information that may be hidden in the mind of a consumer or some employee who isn't consciously aware of all his or her reasons for some preference or some behavior and, consequently, can't identify or talk about it? How do you go about finding this information that could be so crucial to making a good market decision?

Searching for the needle is very much like searching for answers to market problems. Both can be very well hidden. And both need to be discovered for you to succeed.

Using an X-ray monitor would be a great way to find the needle. But your real-world success is probably more dependent on the ability to wield an effective research process than an X-ray monitor. And that's where this text comes in: *Exploring Marketing Research* equips students with the knowledge and skills involved in this basic research process that will simplify and provide more accuracy to their search for market intelligence.

Chapter 3 introduces this process, which includes six stages. Researchers must first work together with decision makers to decide why they are looking for that metaphorical needle; the next two stages plot out the way to go about finding the needle. Next are two stages that focus on the actual search for the needle. The process concludes when the market researcher communicates the benefits of finding "pointed" information that can help mend problems or create something really new and special to the decision maker. Success in this process usually merits the researcher a reward that is a bit more valuable than that needle!

New to Exploring Marketing Research

To ensure that students are able to conduct market research with an understanding of all the latest theories and techniques available to them, the ninth edition is substantially revised and updated. Certainly, the field of marketing research is dynamic both in terms of the demands placed on it by business and in terms of the technological advances that provide more tools for the researcher's toolbox.

The Internet is revolutionizing information systems, ways of gathering secondary data, survey processes, sampling, questionnaire design, qualitative analysis, and communication of results. Practically every chapter includes significant coverage of Internet related topics, and most chapters also include review questions and activities that get students involved with the Internet in a relevant way.

In addition to greater currency and attention given to the Internet, other key features added to the ninth edition include

- All New Chapter Vignettes—Each chapter opens with a story relevant to the material featured in that particular chapter. Some of these vignettes involve famous brands and companies, so the reader may well be familiar with some of the topics. Other vignettes involve "slice of life" stories describing a businessperson's struggle to make smart decisions and demonstrate how research is intertwined with this struggle.
- A Simplified Approach and Style—The boxed material, chapter objectives, and end-of-chapter materials are now presented in a simplified form that allows greater focus on the truly important information. Boxed materials highlight Research Snapshots that cover ethical angles of research, provide illustrations of research in practice, and offer relevant tips or detailed examples. The chapter learning objectives ensure an important coherence and structure to the chapters that culminate with the end-of-chapter materials.

     This deliberate approach has been taken to emphasize significant content material and issues, which will reinforce positive student learning outcomes. Moreover, this simplified approach continues into the analytical chapters, which now deemphasize statistical theory and detail and focus more on practical statistical application.

- Increased Coverage on International Business Issues—The examples and illustrations make much greater use of international business. Readers of this book may end up working outside the United States or Canada, so the increased international examples will increase awareness of research issues beyond North America and open up domestic students to global dynamics. This is a particularly important addition to the text since cultural and language barriers often present challenges for the researcher.

- New Case Materials—Nearly all chapters include at least one new end-of-chapter case; several new end-of-book cases have also been added. Many of the revised and new end-of-chapter materials focus on Internet issues or ethical issues associated with marketing research. New and updated video cases provide great opportunities to get into real-world business situations that involve marketing research.

- Greater Attention to Qualitative Research—More and more companies are benefitting from qualitative research. In response to this important phenomenon, Chapter 6 is essentially a new chapter that focuses much more directly on qualitative research philosophies and methodologies. Phenomenology, grounded theory, ethnography, and case study approaches are now all covered. Qualitative research is also now featured in other chapters throughout the book. For example, the chapter on coding now provides a clear illustration of how qualitative data can be coded.

     In addition, significant coverage is now given to the ways that new technology, including Internet technology, is affecting qualitative research. The end-of-chapter materials as well as seven end-of-book cases provide more attention to qualitative research applications.

Organization of the Book

The organization of the ninth edition of *Exploring Marketing Research* follows the logic of the marketing research process itself. The book is organized into seven parts, and each part presents the basic research concepts for one of the stages in the research process; each part also discusses how these concepts relate to decisions about conducting specific projects.

Part 1: Introduction emphasizes the interplay between research and business and how the importance and scope of research varies with the type of business orientation that characterizes a company. Included in this discussion is an overview of computerized data management and information systems, an overview of the entire marketing research process, and an explanation of how all of this is changing due to the Internet.

Without high ethical standards, no business is good. Thus, the introductory materials also include an emphasis on business ethics and the special ethical problems associated with marketing research.

Part 2: Beginning Stages of the Research Process covers the essentials involved in starting to study business problems. This part emphasizes decision making, problem definition, and the process of how the business problem must be translated into research questions and/or research hypotheses. Research proposals are covered in some detail, and the reader is encouraged to see these as the written agreement that helps put the decision maker and the researcher on the same page.

Chapter 6 emphasizes qualitative research applications. One role played by qualitative research is helping to separate business problem symptoms from true issues that can be attacked with marketing research. However, qualitative research extends far beyond problem definition; it allows greater potential for discovery as well as deeper and potentially more meaningful explanations in marketing research.

Part 2 concludes with a detailed discussion of secondary data and emphasizes its increasing importance in an increasingly data-rich world.

Part 3: Research Designs for Collecting Primary Data examines some topics most closely associated with marketing research. For example, the chapters describe issues related to planning, conducting, and administering surveys. Surveys remain a mainstay for collecting consumer and employee opinion.

Additionally, Part 3 includes two chapters that deal specifically with market experiments. As such, this part emphasizes test-marketing, which is also synonymous with marketing research in many ways.

Part 4: Measurement Concepts are critical to research. This part of the text discusses the basics of measurement theory. Key topics include descriptions of the different levels of scale measurement and how this affects the interpretation of results. Basic ways to measure human attitudes and practical matters dealing with questionnaire design are also discussed. An increased emphasis is placed on the use of new technologies for conducting interviews. For instance, how does asking a question in an electronic format change options for respondents and the researcher? Topics such as these are highlighted in Part 4.

Part 5: Sampling and Fieldwork explains the difference between a population and a sample. The reasons why sampling is needed and why it can be used to confidently allow predictions about larger numbers of people are covered. The fieldwork process is also discussed including the importance of supervision of fieldwork. Sloppy sampling and a lack of field supervision lead to error.

Part 6: Data Analysis and Presentation covers important processes necessary in translating raw data into market intelligence. Included among these topics, the data must be edited and coded. The coded data are then ready for analysis. Some of the most commonly used methods for analyzing data are also presented. For instance, basic descriptive statistics are discussed as ways of portraying key results like central tendency.

Inferential statistics are also discussed, including often-used univariate and bivariate approaches such as *t*-tests. Multivariate statistical approaches are also introduced so that the reader has an awareness of techniques that can analyze many variables simultaneously. Additionally, this part discusses communication both in the form of a written report and an oral communication. Here again is another area that is being shaped by technological advances.

Part 7: Comprehensive Cases with Computerized Databases make up the last section of the book. These cases provide materials that challenge students to apply and integrate the concepts they have learned throughout the text. Instructors will find that these cases provide some flexibility either to expand or simplify the assignment to suit the demands of varying course assignments.

The new cases likewise provide more variety and include some that involve analysis of internal marketing problems as well as an opportunity to use qualitative research. When quantitative data are included, they can be easily analyzed with basic statistical tools like SPSS. Excel files are also included with the same data. These files can be read directly by statistical programs like SAS or other programs.

Superior Pedagogy

More than other marketing research textbooks, the ninth edition of *Exploring Marketing Research* addresses students' need to comprehend all aspects of the marketing research process. The following features facilitate learning throughout the book:

- **Learning Objectives.** Each chapter begins with a concise list of learning objectives that emphasize the major areas of competency the student should achieve before proceeding to the next chapter. Chapter material is clearly linked to the learning objectives, and the end-of-chapter materials emphasize questions and activities relevant to these key competencies.
- **Opening Chapter Vignettes.** The opening vignettes describe marketing research challenges in actual businesses. They frame the material that follows and provide context to the subject matter. Instructors and students are invited to extend these stories with updated current events or with war stories of their own.
- **Research Snapshots.** All of the box materials now share a common title, Research Snapshots. The boxes explore marketing research processes in a variety of modern businesses situations, ranging from natural disasters to international food. The boxes also illustrate some research techniques and applications in a step-by-step fashion.
- **Writing Style.** An accessible, interesting writing style continues as a hallmark of this book. With a careful balance between theory and practice and a sprinkling of interesting examples and anecdotes, the writing style clarifies and simplifies the market research process. In addition, the text offers a comprehensive treatment of important and current topics.
- **Statistical Approach.** A short review of statistical theory in Chapter 17 provides students with an overview of the basic aspects of statistics. Because this text stresses managerial applications more than statistical theory, students are given some basic tools to perform common data analysis. More sophisticated data analysis approaches are left for further reference. Thus, the readers can learn how to test simple hypotheses involving differences between means or relationships among variables. Cross-tabulation, *t*-tests, ANOVA, and regression are covered in sufficient depth to allow a student to use these techniques.

  In addition, easy-to-follow, click-through sequences can walk a student through a few of the most basic approaches to producing statistical results.
- **Key terms.** Learning the vocabulary of marketing research is essential to understanding the topic, and *Exploring Marketing Research* facilitates this with key terms. First, key concepts are boldfaced and completely defined when they first appear in the textbook. Second, all key terms and concepts are listed at the end of each chapter, and many terms are highlighted in a marginal glossary. Third, a glossary summarizing all key terms and definitions appears at the end of the book for handy reference. A glossary of frequently used symbols is also included.
- **Ethics questions.** Identified by a special icon, **ETHICS**, ethics questions are included in most chapters. Among the compelling issues students are asked to explore is redefining the right to privacy in light of new technology. The ethical issues also provide a great opportunity for building critical thinking skills.
- **Internet questions.** Internet questions also are identified by a special icon, **'NET**. Nearly all chapters include multiple questions and research activities that illustrate advances in Internet applications common to marketing research.
- **Research Activities.** The end-of-chapter materials include a few real-world research activities intended to provide actual research experience for the student. Most provide an opportunity for the student to gain experience with multiple content areas. Some involve ethical aspects of research, and some involve Internet usage.
- **Cases.** Extensive cases and video cases taken from real-life situations illustrate marketing research concepts and build knowledge and research skills. These cases offer students the opportunity to participate actively in the decision-making process, one of the most effective forms of learning. The video cases portray actual research activities for brands and companies, such as Fisher-Price, Wine.com, Krispy Kreme, Federal Express, Goya Foods, and Burton Snowboards. Seven additional cases at the end of the text provide students with real-life opportunities to apply the knowledge and skills they have learned from multiple areas of the text.

Comprehensive Instructor Resources

It is important for any text to develop comprehensive supplemental materials to support instructors in their vital teaching function. Because of this pedagogical philosophy, the extensive learning package provided with *Exploring Marketing Research* includes a Test Bank, a computerized Test Bank (ExamView Testing Software), a comprehensive Instructor's Manual and Transparency Masters, PowerPoint presentation slides, data sets for several cases, a comprehensive video library, and online marketing resources (available on the web at www.thomsonedu.com/marketing/zikmund).

- The Instructor's Resource CD-ROM (ISBN: 0-324-36097-5) contains valuable instructor resources on one easy-to-use CD-ROM: the Test Bank, ExamView Testing Software, the Instructor's Manual, PowerPoint presentation slides, and data sets for cases.
- The Test Bank (ISBN: 0-324-34348-5), originally written by Thomas Quirk of Webster University, has been carefully rewritten to provide a variety of questions covering every major concept in the textbook. All the questions have been scrutinized to eliminate ambiguity and to provide varying levels of difficulty. Each question is identified with a page number from the textbook where the answer may be located.
- ExamView is an easy-to-use automated testing program that allows instructors to create exams by using provided questions, modifying questions, or adding new questions.
- The Instructor's Manual with Transparency Masters (ISBN: 0-324-53598-8), prepared by Laurie Babin of The University of Southern Mississippi, were designed to ease lecture preparation by offering detailed and comprehensive lecture outlines, solutions to all assignments, and transparency masters. The solution to each case and video case includes the objectives of the case, a brief summary of the case, and recommended questions and solutions. The Instructor's Manual is available both on the Instructor's Resource CD-ROM and at www.thomsonedu. com/marketing/zikmund on the instructor's portion of the website.
- PowerPoint Presentation Slides, prepared by Charlie T. Cook, Jr. of the University of West Alabama, summarize and illustrate key concepts in each chapter. These slides are available both on the Instructor's Resource CD-ROM and at www.thomsonedu.com/marketing/zikmund, where they can be downloaded.
- Data are provided that match several end-of-chapter exercises and different case analyses. The data are provided both in EXCEL files, allowing great flexibility to be used with many programs, and in SPSS files, which are ready to use with either the student or full version of SPSS. Students may download the data sets at www.thomsonedu.com/marketing/zikmund by clicking on the textbook and then on "Data Sets." Data sets are also available on the Instructor's Resource CD-ROM.
- Video DVD (ISBN: 0-324-53904-5) consists of eleven chapter video cases. Brand new video cases correspond with new video segments. The video cases guide students through marketing research issues faced by a variety of well-known companies, such as Mercedes-Benz, Krispy Kreme, and the successful e-commerce business Wine.com. Discussion questions related to the video cases are included in the Instructor's Manual.
- Web Resources at www.thomsonedu.com/marketing/zikmund provide the latest information about what's new and what's cool in marketing research. The site features links to other research-related sites, tips about using the supplemental video library, and much more.

Resources for Students

To promote learning and competency, it is also important to provide students with well-crafted resources. In addition to covering the latest information technology (described above), the ninth edition includes the following student resources:

- The Dedicated Website www.thomsonedu.com/marketing/zikmund, developed especially for the new edition, includes chapter quizzes that allow students to test and retest their knowledge of chapter concepts. Each chapter has a quiz to encourage retesting. In addition, the website features downloadable flash cards of key terms, the very best online marketing research resources available, and much more.

- SPSS (ISBN: 0-324-53741-7) brings affordable, professional statistical analysis and modeling tools to a student's own PC. SPSS 14.0 for Windows Student Version includes an easy-to-use interface and comprehensive online help that lets students learn statistics, not software. SPSS 14.0 is available as an optional bundle with the new edition.

Acknowledgments

Certainly, no list of acknowledgments will be complete. So many people have assisted in this project. Chief among these would be to the late Bill Zikmund for carrying the weight of this project for each of the eight previous editions. I am privileged to be able to carry the project along into hopefully many more editions as the premier marketing research text. Also, thanks go to some of my team here at the University. My graduate assistants Melanie Gardner and Christina Chung have helped with research for this text and helped share some of the workload on other endeavors freeing up time for me to spend on this project. Thanks also to Betty Dickerson and Janice Prescott for helping to manage my crazy schedule. My family also has had to put up with less elaborate dinners and many evenings and weekends working around my writing time. Also, thanks go to all the great faculty who mentored me during my days in the Ph.D. program at LSU. Most notable among these are Joseph F. Hair, Jr. and the late William R. Darden.

Special thanks go to all the good people at Thomson Publishing who helped make this project possible. Thanks to my publisher, Neil Marquardt, for motivating the whole team to stay on schedule. Thanks to Nicole Moore for creative inspirations and marketing support. Also, a special thanks to Erin Curtis and Joanne Vickers at Ohlinger Publishing Services. They provided tremendous support through the writing and production process, including assistance with proofing, permissions, photos, and exhibits. Thanks also to Karen Hill for assistance with research and editing.

Many colleagues contributed ideas for this book. They made many suggestions that greatly enhanced this book. For their insightful reviews of the manuscript for the ninth or previous editions of *Exploring Marketing Research*, I would like to thank the following:

Karen Goncalves
Nichols College

Carol Bienstock
Radford University

Steven V. Cates
Averett University

Stephanie Noble
The University of Mississippi

Bob Lauman
Webster University

Natalie Wood
St. Joseph's University

Robert Jaross
Florida International University

Terry Paul
The Ohio State University

Mike Parent
Utah State University

Stephen Batory
Bloomsburg University

Michael R. Hyman
New Mexico State University

Rick Saucier
St. John's University

Xin Zhao
University of Utah

Gerald Albaum
University of Oregon

William Bearden
University of South Carolina

Joseph A. Bellizzi
Arizona State University–West

James A. Brunner
University of Toledo

F. Anthony Bushman
San Francisco State University

Thomas Buzas
Eastern Michigan University

Roy F. Cabaniss
Huston-Tillotson College

Michael d'Amico
University of Akron

Ron Eggers
Barton College

H. Harry Friedman
City University of New York–Brooklyn

Ron Goldsmith
Florida State University

Larry Goldstein
Iona College

Sanjay Mishra
University of Kansas

David Gourley
Arizona State University

G. M. Naidu
University of Wisconsin–Whitewater

Jim Grimm
Illinois State University

Charles Prohaska
Central Connecticut State University

Al Gross
Robert Morris College

Alan Sawyer
University of Florida

Don Heinz
University of Wisconsin

Robert Schaffer
California State University–Pomona

Craig Hollingshead
Texas A&M University–Kingsville

Leon G. Schiffman
City University of New York–Baruch

Victor Howe
University of Kentucky

K. Sivakumar
Lehigh University

Roy Howell
Texas Tech University

Mark Speece
Central Washington University

Rhea Ingram
Columbus State University–Georgia

Harlan Spotts
Western New England College

P. K. Kannan
University of Maryland

Wilbur W. Stanton
Old Dominion University

Susan Kleine
Arizona State University

Bruce L. Stern
Portland State University

David B. Klenosky
Purdue University

James L. Taylor
University of Alabama

C. S. Kohli
California State University–Fullerton

Gail Tom
California State University–Sacramento

Jerome L. Langer
Assumption College

Deborah Utter
Boston College

James H. Leigh
Texas A&M University

David Wheeler
Suffolk University

Larry Lowe
Bryant College

Richard Wilcox
Carthage College

Karl Mann
Tennessee Technological University

Margaret Wright
University of Colorado

Charles R. Martin
Wichita State University

Clifford E. Young
University of Colorado–Denver

Marlys Mason
Oklahoma State University

William Lee Ziegler
Bethune-Cookman College

Tom K. Massey
University of Missouri–Kansas City

Thanks also to all of the students who have inspired me and reinforced the fact that I made a great career decision about two decades ago. Thanks also to my close colleagues Mitch Griffin, Dave Ortinau, and Jim Boles for their continued support and insight.

Barry J. Babin
The University of Southern Mississippi
April 2006

In Remembrance

William G. Zikmund (1943-2002)

A native of the Chicago area, William G. Zikmund was a professor of marketing at Oklahoma State University and died shortly after completing the previous edition. He received a Ph.D. in business administration with a concentration in marketing from the University of Colorado.

Before beginning his academic career, Professor Zikmund worked in marketing research for Conway/Millikin Company (a marketing research supplier) and Remington Arms Company (an extensive user of marketing research). Professor Zikmund also has served as a marketing research consultant to several business and nonprofit organizations. During his academic career, Professor Zikmund published dozens of articles and papers in a diverse group of scholarly journals, ranging from the *Journal of Marketing* to the *Accounting Review* to the *Journal of Applied Psychology*. In addition to *Exploring Marketing Research*, Professor Zikmund authored *Essentials of Marketing Research*, *Business Research Methods*, *Marketing*, *Effective Marketing*, and a work of fiction, *A Corporate Bestiary*.

Professor Zikmund was a member of several professional organizations, including the American Marketing Association, the Academy of Marketing Science, the Association for Consumer Research, the Society for Marketing Advances, the Marketing Educators' Association, and the Association of Collegiate Marketing Educators. He served on the editorial review boards of the *Journal of Marketing Education*, *Marketing Education Review*, *Journal of the Academy of Marketing Science*, and *Journal of Business Research*.

Part 1
Introduction

©PHIL KNOTT/PYMCA/JUPITER IMAGES

CHAPTER 1
The Role of Marketing Research

CHAPTER 2
Information Systems and Knowledge Management

CHAPTER 3
The Marketing Research Process

CHAPTER 4
The Human Side of Marketing Research: Organizational and Ethical Issues

CHAPTER 1
THE ROLE OF MARKETING RESEARCH

After studying this chapter, you should

1. Understand how marketing research contributes to business success
2. Know how to define marketing research
3. Understand the difference between basic and applied marketing research
4. Understand how marketing research activities can be used to address decisions in each marketing mix dimension
5. Be able to integrate marketing research results into the strategic planning process
6. Know when marketing research should and should not be conducted
7. Appreciate the way that technology and internationalization are changing marketing research

Chapter Vignette: "If it Quacks Like a Duck?"

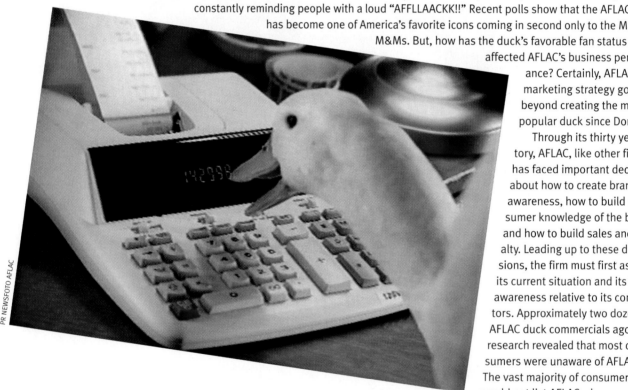

PR NEWSFOTO AFLAC

"If you're hurt and you miss work": This is the tag line for one of the most popular U.S. advertising campaigns—for AFLAC Insurance. The tag line is accompanied by the familiar Peking duck constantly reminding people with a loud "AFFLLAACKK!!" Recent polls show that the AFLAC duck has become one of America's favorite icons coming in second only to the Mars M&Ms. But, how has the duck's favorable fan status affected AFLAC's business performance? Certainly, AFLAC's marketing strategy goes beyond creating the most popular duck since Donald!

Through its thirty year history, AFLAC, like other firms, has faced important decisions about how to create brand awareness, how to build consumer knowledge of the brand, and how to build sales and loyalty. Leading up to these decisions, the firm must first assess its current situation and its brand awareness relative to its competitors. Approximately two dozen AFLAC duck commercials ago, research revealed that most consumers were unaware of AFLAC. The vast majority of consumers would not list AFLAC when prompted to name insurance companies. Instead, names like Allstate, State Farm, and Prudential proved more familiar. Not surprisingly, these companies enjoyed greater market share. Based on this research, AFLAC decided to invest in a national television campaign to build awareness of the brand name—"AFFLLAAACCK!!" The phonic similarity to "QUACK" proved successful.

Today, AFLAC has built great awareness of its name, but this hasn't necessarily translated into business success. Despite the tag line, fewer than 30 percent of consumers who recognize the name know that AFLAC specializes in supplemental disability insurance. This accounts for over three-fourths of AFLACs nearly $14 billion dollar annual revenue. Thus, while the initial research suggested the need for building awareness, their more recent research is addressing difficulties in creating the right "knowledge" of AFLAC. What communication medium is best for building knowledge? Can knowledge be built in the same way as awareness? Will knowledge lead to increased intentions to do business with AFLAC? What role does personal selling play in building knowledge? All of these are questions that should be answered. Marketing research will be directed toward answering these questions. The answers will then be used to try and erase the knowledge deficit faced by AFLAC. If the answers are half as effective as those that lead to the AFLAC duck, the company should enjoy tremendous success. Thus, for AFLAC, as for many firms, marketing research is an important tool in shaping business strategy.[1]

Introduction

The recent history of AFLAC demonstrates the need for information in making informed decisions addressing key issues faced by all competitive businesses. Research can provide that information. Without it, business decisions involving product promotion, distribution, pricing, and the product design itself are made in the dark.

We open with two examples illustrating how business decisions require intelligence and how research can provide that intelligence. The following focus specifically on how marketing research encourages innovation in the form of new products or improvements in existing goods and services. Imagine yourself in the role of brand manager as you read these examples and think about the information needs you may have in trying to build success for your brand.

Jelly Belly brand sells fifty varieties of jelly beans, with the number growing every year. Some flavors came from suggestions of visitors to Jelly Belly's website. In return for filling out an interactive questionnaire, visitors had samples sent to them. Jelly Belly received a great response to this offer. Researchers categorized the suggestions, grouping them by similar flavors. Some suggestions were put back on the Web so that people could vote for the flavor they most wanted to see introduced. The company received some really off-the-wall flavor ideas. Among the strangest are flavors such as Dill Pickle, Taco, Persimmon Pudding, Blackened Plantain, and Cream of Wheat.[2]

More recently, Jelly Belly is trying to capitalize on consumers' desires to have a healthy snack without giving up tasty treats. Survey research suggests that consumers would respond favorably to food and drink products containing additives that will make them more healthy and/or energetic.[3] As a result, Jelly Belly has introduced "Sport Beans." Sport Beans contain added enzymes, carbohydrates, and vitamins all designed to provide added energy and alertness. In addition, following up on the Harry Potter craze, Jelly Belly's research suggested that kids would indeed go for *vomit, booger,* or *earthworm* flavored beans, among other similarly interesting flavors. So, the decision was made to launch Bertie Botts Every Flavor Beans in Canada and the United States. More research is needed before deciding to launch this product internationally.

The coffee industry, after years of the "daily grind," has proved quite dynamic over the past decade. After years of steady

Jelly Belly brand's market research has capitalized on consumers' desires to produce fifty varieties of jelly beans as well as recipes on how to create snacks with them.

decline, research on consumers' beverage purchases show that coffee sales began rebounding around 1995. Telephone interviews with American consumers estimated that there were 80 million occasional coffee drinkers and 7 million daily upscale coffee drinkers in 1995. By 2001, estimates suggested there were 161 million daily or occasional U.S. coffee drinkers and 27 million daily upscale coffee drinkers.[4]

Coffee drinking habits have also changed. In 1991 there were fewer than 450 coffeehouses in the United States. Today, it seems like places such as Starbucks, Second Cup, The Coffee Bean, Tea Leaf, and Gloria Jean's are virtually everywhere in the United States and Canada. There are more than nine thousand Starbucks stores alone today, with plans for over twenty thousand more.[5] While locating these outlets requires significant formal research, Starbucks also is market testing new concepts aimed at other ways a coffee shop can provide value to consumers. One concept that has survived testing thus far is the addition of free, in-store high-speed wireless Internet access. Thus, you can have hot coffee in a hot spot! After Starbucks *barristas* began reporting that customers were asking clerks what music was playing in the stores, Starbucks began testing the sales of CDs containing their in-store music. Concepts still being tested include a lunch menu and limited wine service. The research that underlies the introduction of these value-added concepts could first include simply asking a consumer or a small group of consumers for their reaction to the concept. Survey research and then actual in-store tests may follow. However, had Starbucks simply asked consumers the question, "Are you willing to pay three dollars for a cup of coffee?" back in 1985, we would likely not be discussing them today. So, the research underlying such decisions can be multilayered.

These examples illustrate the need for information in making informed business decisions. Jelly Belly provides consumers with the incentive of free samples of jelly beans in return for ideas about desirable new bean flavors. The statistics about coffee demonstrate how research can track trends that may lead to new business opportunities. Also, it is clear to see how research can be used to examine new concepts in progressively more complex stages, setting the stage for a more successful product introduction. These are only the tip of the iceberg when it comes to the types of marketing research that are conducted every day. This chapter introduces basic concepts of marketing research and describes how research can play a crucial role in successful marketing and business success in general.

The Nature of Marketing Research

In its essence, business is very simple. Companies need to produce benefits that people want to buy! That means that consumers must view the company as providing valuable bundles of benefits. There are many factors that can affect this value, and successful companies are those that understand the value equation. With this in mind, there are several key questions, the answers to which help provide this understanding.

1. *What do we sell?*
   This includes not only the benefits that are easily seen, but also the more emotional benefits such as the comfort and relaxation of enjoying a cup of gourmet coffee in a pleasant atmosphere or the novelty of trying a booger jelly bean.

2. *How do consumers view our company?*
   All too often, companies define themselves too narrowly based only on the physical *product* they sell. A key question involves whom the customers will do business with if they do not choose your company. For instance, how is Starbucks viewed relative to its competitors? Who are the competitors? Does Starbucks compete more directly with Maxwell House, Seattle Drip, or something completely outside the coffee arena like a local lounge? Are we viewed more or less favorably relative to the competition?

3. *What does our company/product mean?*
   What knowledge do people have of the company and its products? Do they know how to use them? Do they know all the different needs the company can address? What does our packaging and promotion communicate to consumers? The opening chapter vignette described AFLAC's problem in creating consumer knowledge now that it has consumer awareness.

4. *What do consumers desire?*

How can the company make the lives of its customers better, and how can it do this in a way that is not easily duplicated by another firm? Part of this lies in uncovering the things that customers truly desire, but which they can often not put into words.

Answering these questions requires information. Marketing research's function is to supply information that helps answer these questions, thereby leading to more informed and more successful business decision making. With useful information, decisions can be made with less risk.

It's been said that "every business issue ultimately boils down to an information problem":[6] Can the right information be delivered? Research thus seeks to deliver accurate and precise information that can make marketing strategy and management more effective.[7] Marketing research attempts to supply accurate information that reduces the uncertainty in decision making. Very often, decisions are made with little information for various reasons, including insufficient time to conduct research or management's belief that enough is already known. Relying on seat-of-the-pants decision making—decision making without research—is like betting on a long shot at the racetrack because the horse's name is appealing. Occasionally there are successes, but in the long run intuition without research leads to losses. Marketing research helps decision makers shift from intuitive information gathering to systematic and objective investigating.

Marketing Research Defined

Marketing research is the application of the scientific method in searching for the truth about marketing phenomena. These activities include defining marketing opportunities and problems, generating and evaluating marketing ideas, monitoring performance, and understanding the marketing process. Marketing research is more than conducting surveys.[8] This process includes idea and theory development, problem definition, searching for and collecting information, analyzing data, and communicating the findings and their implications.

This definition suggests that marketing research information is not intuitive or haphazardly gathered. Literally, *research* (re-search) means "to search again." The term connotes patient study and scientific investigation wherein the researcher takes another, more careful look at the data to discover all that is known about the subject. Ultimately, all findings are tied back to marketing theory.

The definition also emphasizes, through reference to the scientific method, that any information generated should be accurate and objective. The researcher should be personally detached and free of bias attempting to find truth. Research isn't performed to support preconceived ideas but to test them. If bias enters into the research process, the value of the research is considerably reduced. We will discuss this further in a subsequent chapter.

Clearly, our definition makes it clear that marketing research is relevant to all aspects of the marketing mix. Research can facilitate managerial decision making in all aspects of the firm's marketing mix: product, pricing, promotion, and distribution. By providing the necessary information on which to base marketing mix decisions, marketing research can decrease the risk of making a wrong decision in each area.

Finally, this definition of marketing research is limited by one's definition of *marketing*. Although research in the marketing area of a for-profit corporation like AFLAC clearly is marketing research, marketing research also includes efforts that assist nonprofit organizations such as the American Heart Association, the San Diego Zoo, the Boston Pops Orchestra, or a parochial school. Each of these organizations exists to satisfy social needs, and each requires marketing skills to produce and distribute their products and services. The federal government also performs many functions that are similar, if not identical, to those of for-profit business organizations. Governments can use research in much the same way as managers at Starbucks or General Motors. For instance, the FDA is an important user of marketing research, employing it to address the way people view and use various food and drugs. One such study commissioned and funded research to address the question of how consumers used the risk summaries that are included with all drugs sold in the United States.[9] This book explores marketing research as it applies to all organizations and institutions engaging in some form of marketing activity.

Marketing research
The application of the scientific method in searching for the truth about marketing phenomena. These activities include defining marketing opportunities and problems, generating and evaluating marketing ideas, monitoring performance, and understanding the marketing process.

RESEARCHSNAPSHOT

Good Fat and Bad Fat

American consumers can be seen every day scouring nutrition labels. Most likely, the item they show the most interest in recently is the amount of fat. The Food and Drug Administration (FDA) is concerned that consumers get information that is not only accurate, but that also conveys the proper message to achieve a healthy diet. But all fat is not created equal. In particular, dieticians warn of the dangers associated with excess amounts of trans-fats; diet nutrition labels break fats into saturated and unsaturated fats. Among numerous factors that complicate the interpretation of the nutrition label, trans-fat (hydrogenated) is technically a nonsaturated fat, but it acts more like a saturated fat when consumed. So, where should it be

placed? The FDA cannot address this problem intelligently without marketing research addressing questions like.

1. If trans-fats are listed as a saturated fat, would consumers' beliefs about

their consumption become more negative?

2. If the saturated fat amount includes a specific line indicating the amount of "saturated fat" that is really trans-fat, would consumers become more confused about their diet?

3. If all amounts of fat are given equal prominence on the label, will consumer attitudes toward the different types of fats be the same?

Making this even more complicated is the fact that some consumer segments, such as teenagers in this case, may actually use the nutrition labels to select the brands that are least nutritious rather than most nutritious. So, they may actually seek out the one with the worst proportion of trans-fats!

Sources: "Health Labels are in the Eye of the Beholder," Vol. 40 (January), 80. Hunter, B.T. (2003), "Labeling Transfat is Tricky," Consumers' Research Magazine, 86 (July), 8–10.

©SUSAN VAN ETTEN

Applied and Basic Marketing Research

Applied marketing research
Research conducted to address a specific marketing decision for a specific firm or organization.

Basic marketing research
Research conducted without a specific decision in mind that usually does not address the needs of a specific organization. It attempts to expand the limits of marketing knowledge in general and is not aimed at solving a particular pragmatic problem.

One useful way to describe research is based on the specificity of its purpose. **Applied marketing research** is conducted to address a specific marketing decision for a specific firm or organization. The opening vignette describes a situation in which AFLAC may use applied marketing research to decide how to best create knowledge of its supplemental disability insurance products.

Basic marketing research is conducted without a specific decision in mind, and it usually does not address the needs of a specific organization. It attempts to expand the limits of marketing knowledge in general, and as such it is not aimed at solving a particular pragmatic problem. Basic research can be used to test the validity of a general marketing theory (one that applies to all of marketing) or to learn more about some market phenomenon. For instance, a great deal of basic marketing research addresses the ways in which retail atmosphere influences consumers' emotions and behavior.[10] From such research, we can learn how much the physical place creates value for consumers relative to the actual product consumed. This basic research does not examine the problem from any single retail or service provider's perspective. However, Starbucks' management may become aware of such research and use it to design applied research studies examining questions about its store designs. Thus, the two types of research are not completely independent.

Sometimes researchers use different terms to represent the same distinction. Some reserve the term *marketing* research to refer to basic research. Then, the term *market* research is used to capture applied research addressing the needs of a firm within a particular market. While the distinction is very useful in describing research, there are very few aspects of research that apply to only basic or only applied research. The focus of this text is more on applied research—studies that are undertaken to answer questions about specific problems or to make decisions about particular courses of action or policies. In addition, we will use the term *marketing research* more generally to refer to either type of research. Applied research is emphasized in this text because most students will be oriented toward the day-to-day practice of marketing management, and most students and researchers will be exposed to short-term, problem-solving research conducted for businesses or nonprofit organizations.

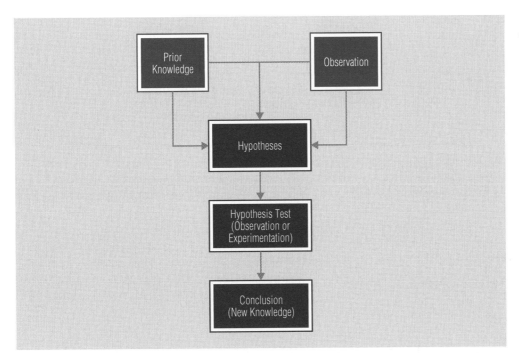

EXHIBIT 1.1
A Summary of the Scientific Method

The Scientific Method

All marketing research, whether basic or applied, involves the scientific method. **The scientific method** is the way researchers go about using knowledge and evidence to reach objective conclusions about the real world. The scientific method is the same in social sciences such as marketing and in physical sciences such as physics. In this case, it is the way we come to understand marketing phenomena.

Exhibit 1.1 briefly illustrates the scientific method. In the scientific method, there are multiple routes to developing ideas. When the ideas can be stated in researchable terms, we reach the hypothesis stage. The next step involves testing the hypothesis against empirical evidence (facts from observation or experimentation). The results either support a hypothesis or do not support a hypothesis. From these results, new knowledge is acquired.

In basic research, testing these prior conceptions or hypotheses and then making inferences and conclusions about the phenomena leads to the establishment of general laws about the phenomena. Use of the scientific method in applied research ensures objectivity in gathering facts and testing creative ideas for alternative marketing strategies. The essence of research, whether basic or applied, lies in the scientific method. Much of this book deals with scientific methodology. Thus, the techniques of basic and applied research differ largely in degree rather than in substance.

The scientific method
The way researchers go about using knowledge and evidence to reach objective conclusions about the real world.

The Marketing Concept

In all of business strategy, there are only a few business orientations (see Exhibit 1.2). A firm can be **product-oriented**. A product-oriented firm prioritizes decision making in a way that emphasizes technical superiority in the product. Thus, input from technicians and experts in the field are very important in making critical decisions. A firm can be **production-oriented**. Production orientation means that the firm prioritizes efficiency and effectiveness of the production processes in making decisions. Here, input from engineers and accounting becomes important as the firm seeks to drive costs down. Production-oriented firms are usually very large firms manufacturing products in very large quantities. In both of these orientations, marketing research may take a backseat.

Product-oriented
Describes a firm that prioritizes decision making in a way that emphasizes technical superiority in the product.

Production-oriented
Describes a firm that prioritizes efficiency and effectiveness of the production processes in making decisions.

EXHIBIT 1.2 **Business Marketing Orientations**

Product-Oriented Firm

Prioritizes decision making that emphasizes
the physical product design, trendiness or
technical superiority

Example

The fashion industry makes clothes in styles
and sizes that few can adopt.

Little consumer research

Production-Oriented Firm

Prioritizes efficiency and effectiveness of
the production processes in making decisions

Example

U.S. auto industry's assembly-line process
is intent on reducing costs of production as
low as possible.

Little consumer research

Marketing-Oriented Firm

Focuses on how the firm provides value
to customers

Example

Well known hotel chains are designed to
address the needs of travelers, particularly
business travelers.

Much consumer research

Marketing concept
A central idea in modern
marketing thinking that focuses
on how the firm provides value
to customers more than on the
physical product or production
process.

Marketing orientation
The corporate culture existing
for firms adopting the
marketing concept. It
emphasizes customer
orientation, long-term
profitability over short-term
profits, and a cross-functional
perspective.

Customer-oriented
Describes a firm in which all
decisions are made with a
conscious awareness of their
effect on the consumer.

TOTHEPOINT

*The aim of marketing
is to know your
customer so well that
when your prospects
are confronted with
your product, it fits
them so exactly that it
sells itself.*

—Peter Drucker

In contrast, marketing research is a primary tool enabling implementation of a marketing orientation.[11] The **marketing concept** is a central idea in modern marketing thinking that focuses more on how the firm provides value to customers than on the physical product or production process. It has evolved over time as product- and production-oriented firms respond to changes in the competitive and economic environments. When a firm adapts the marketing concept, it develops **marketing orientation**. It calls on management to

1. Be **customer-oriented**—meaning that all firm decisions are made with a conscious awareness of their effect on the consumer
2. Emphasize long-run profitability rather than short-term profits or sales volume
3. Adopt a cross-functional perspective, meaning that marketing is integrated across other business functions

Customer Orientation

According to the marketing concept, the consumer is at the center of the operation, the pivot point about which the business moves to achieve the balanced best interests of all concerned. According to this philosophy, the firm creates products and services with consumers' needs in mind. Many marketing theorists and marketing managers believe that the creation of value for consumers is the justification for a firm's existence. Therefore, unlike the other two orientations, marketing research addressing consumer desires, beliefs, and attitudes becomes essential.

Yoplait Go-Gurt, yogurt packaged in a three-sided tube designed to fit in kids' lunchboxes, had more than $100 million in sales its first year on the market. The development of Go-Gurt clearly illustrates a consumer orientation. The company's consumer research about eating regular yogurt at school showed that moms and kids in their "tweens" wanted convenience and portability. Some brands, like Colombo Spoon in a Snap, offered the convenience of having a utensil as part of the packaging/delivery system. However, from what Yoplait marketers learned about consumers, they thought kids would eat more yogurts if they could "lose the spoon" and eat yogurt anywhere, anytime. Moms and kids participating in a taste test were invited to sample different brand-on-the-go packaging shapes—long tubes, thin tubes, fat tubes, and other shapes—without being told how to handle the packaging. One of the company's researchers said, "It was funny to see the moms fidget around, then daintily pour the product onto a spoon, then into their mouths. The kids instantly jumped on it. They knew what to do."[12] Squeezing Go-Gurt from the tube was a big plus. The kids

EXHIBIT 1.3
Long-Run Profitability

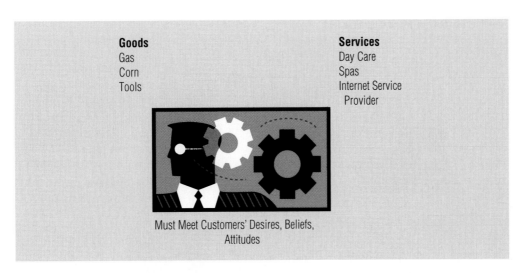

Goods
Gas
Corn
Tools

Services
Day Care
Spas
Internet Service
  Provider

Must Meet Customers' Desires, Beliefs,
Attitudes

loved the fact that the packaging gave them permission to play with their food, something parents always tell them not to do. Go-Gurt is a fun, convenient product that allows consumers the freedom to eat whenever and wherever they want. Yoplait realized that knowledge of consumers' needs, coupled with product research and development, leads to successful marketing strategies and that industry leadership—indeed, corporate survival—depends on satisfying consumers.

Long-Run Profitability

Customer orientation does not mean slavery to consumers' every fleeting whim. Implicit in the marketing concept is the assumption of the continuity of the firm. Thus, the firm must eventually experience profitability to survive (see Exhibit 1.3). As popular as Starbucks is, it would probably be even more popular if the average price for a cup of coffee was thirty cents instead of three dollars. However, the production costs of the coffee and the labor costs associated with maintaining the Starbucks atmosphere greatly exceed that figure. Thus, Starbucks would likely have failed had it attempted to satisfy the desire for low prices. In contrasts to a production orientation, Starbucks succeeds with perhaps the highest cost profile of all national coffee chains.

The second aspect of the marketing concept argues against profitless volume or sales volume for the sake of volume alone. Sometimes, the best decision for a customer and the best decision in the long-run for the firm is the sale that is not made. For instance, a parts supplier might be able to mislead a customer about the relative quality of the parts he or she sells and make an immediate sale. However, when the parts begin to fail sooner than expected, it is fairly certain the customer will not do business with this firm again. If instead the salesperson for the supplier had been honest and suggested another supplier, he or she may be able to find another opportunity to do business with that firm.

A Cross-Functional Effort

Marketing personnel do not work in a vacuum, isolated from other company activities. The actions of people in areas such as production, credit, and research and development may affect an organization's marketing efforts. Similarly, the work of marketers will affect activities in other departments. Problems are almost certain to arise from lack of an integrated, company-wide effort. The marketing concept stresses a cross-functional perspective to achieve consumer orientation and long-term profitability. The first panel of Exhibit 1.4 illustrates a firm in which every department works independently; it is not cross-functional and, consequently, not marketing-oriented. The second panel illustrates a firm in which marketing personnel work cross-functionally with other departments to achieve long-term profitability.

EXHIBIT 1.4 **Isolation versus Cross-functionality of Marketing in a Firm**

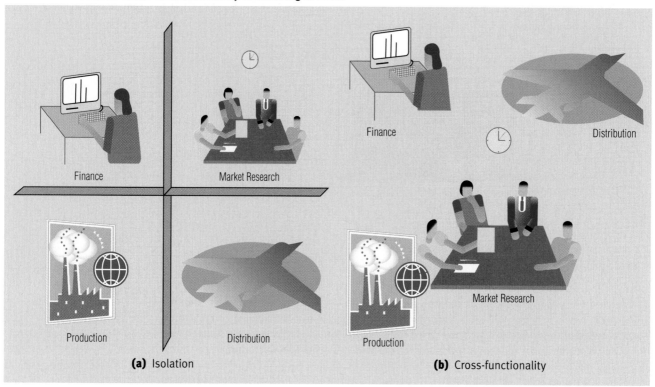

(a) Isolation   **(b)** Cross-functionality

Problems occur when the marketing department views focusing on consumer needs as its sole responsibility. Indeed, other functional areas' goals may conflict with customer satisfaction or long-term profitability. For instance, the engineering department may want long lead times for product design, with simplicity and economy as major design goals. Marketing, however, may prefer short lead times and more complex designs with custom components and optional features for multiple models. The finance department may want fixed budgets, strict spending justifications, and prices that cover costs, whereas the marketing department may seek flexible budgets, liberal spending rationales, and below-cost prices to develop markets quickly.

Similar differences in outlook may be found in other functional areas of the organization, and these may be sources of serious conflicts. When a firm lacks organizational procedures for communicating marketing information and coordinating marketing efforts, the effectiveness of its marketing programs will suffer. Marketing research findings produce some of the most crucial marketing information; thus, such research is management's key tool for finding out what customers want and how best to satisfy their needs. It is vital, then, that management conducts marketing research, that researchers produce valid and reliable results, and that those results be communicated to decision makers so that they can help shape the firm's marketing strategy.

Marketing-oriented firms visualize a chain of customers within the production/delivery system.[13] An accountant who prepares a report for a sales manager should view the manager as a customer who will use the information to make decisions that will benefit external customers who buy the company's products. Every employee should contribute to quality improvement and providing value to customers.

Keeping Customers and Building Relationships

Relationship marketing
Communicates the idea that a major goal of marketing is to build long-term relationships with the customers contributing to their success.

Marketers often talk about getting customers, but keeping customers is equally important. Effective marketers work to build long-term relationships with their customers. The term **relationship marketing** communicates the idea that a major goal of marketing is to build long-term relationships

RESEARCHSNAPSHOT

Harley-Davidson Goes Abroad

Before Harley-Davidson goes overseas, it must perform considerable research on that market. It may find that consumers in some countries, such as France or Italy, have a strong preference for more economical and practical motor bikes. There, people may prefer a Vespa Wasp to a Harley Hog! Other times, they may find that consumers have a favorable attitude toward Harley-Davidson and that it could even be a product viewed as very prestigious. Harley recently considered doing business in India based on trend analysis showing a booming economy. Favorable consumer opinion and a booming economy were insufficient to justify distributing Harleys in India. The problem? Luxury imports would be subject to very high duties which would make them cost-prohibitive to nearly all Indian consumers. Thus, although research on the market was largely positive, Harley's research on the political operating environment eventually determined its decision. Instead, Harley may direct its effort more toward the U.S. women's market for bikes. Research shows that motorcycle ownership among U.S. women has nearly doubled since 1990 to approximately 10 percent. Product research suggests that Harley may need to design smaller and sportier bikes to satisfy this market's desires.

Sources: Asia-Africa Intelligence Wire (2005), "Harley Davidson Rules Out India Foray for Near Future," (September 2), Akron Beacon Journal (2005), "Women Kick it Into Gear," (May 22).

with the customers contributing to their success. Once an exchange is made, effective marketing stresses managing the relationships that will bring about additional exchanges. Effective marketers view making a sale not as the end of a process but as the start of the organization's relationship with a customer. Satisfied customers will return to a company that has treated them well if they need to purchase the same product in the future. If they need a related item, satisfied customers know the first place to look.

Total quality management is a business philosophy that has much in common with the marketing concept. It embodies the belief that the management process must focus on integrating customer-driven quality throughout the organization. The philosophy underlying the implementation of total quality management was clearly articulated by a Burger King executive: "The customer is the vital key to our success. We are now looking at our business through the customers' eyes and measuring our performance against their expectations, not ours."[14] A company that employs a total quality strategy must evaluate itself through the eyes of the customer.

Obviously, the marketing concept and total quality management are closely intertwined. In a company that practices total quality management, manufacturing's orientation toward lowest-cost productivity should harmonize with marketing's commitment to quality products at acceptable prices. For example, if Ford Motor Company advertises that "Quality Is Job One," the production department must make sure that every automobile that comes off the assembly line will meet consumers' quality specifications. The notion that quality improvement is every employee's job must be integrated throughout the organization so that marketing and production will be in harmony. If this notion conflicts with manufacturing's desire to allow for variations from quality standards, the firm must implement statistical quality controls and other improvements in the manufacturing operation to improve its systems and increase productivity.

Chapter 8 discusses the measurement of quality, customer satisfaction, and value in detail. Throughout this book, however, we will explain how marketing research can help a company achieve the goal of creating valuable experiences for customers.

Marketing Research: A Means for Implementing the Marketing Concept

Home building used to be a business completely dominated by local construction contractors. If a customer wanted a home that would provide maximum satisfaction, a customer home at a custom price was the only option. Today, there is another option. Several home builders are going national. In doing so, they have implemented market-driven design processes that integrate research into the

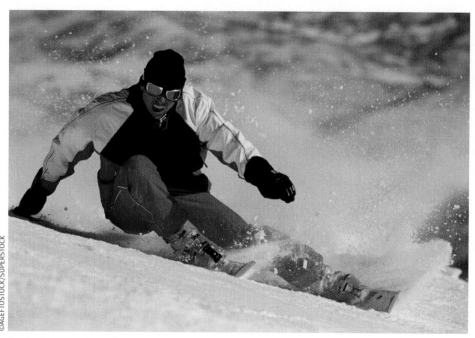

Fun in the snow depends on weather trends, equipment, and clothing—all subjects for a market researcher.

home designs. The research tracks consumers' actual living patterns to build homes with maximum livability. Thus, rather than "wasting space" on things like hallways that add little or even distract from a home's livability, that space is cannibalized, allowing more space allocated to the places where families really "live." In addition, research shows that consumers will make use of outdoor living areas if they are properly designed. Thus, the homes often include covered porches or lanais in place of less used indoor space like a formal living room.[15]

David Weekley also directs considerable attention to service after the sale. Research indicates that after-sale service could be a significant source of referrals. As a result, each David Weekley home comes with a ten-year warranty. Before any appliances are placed in Weekley homes, they must be proven to be durable enough to have a good chance of lasting the length of the warranty. Consistent with the research, over 30 percent of Weekley home owners refer new customers to the company. Thus, David Weekley has been tremendously successful with this model and offers both affordability and a custom feel. It is now the nation's largest home building firm.[16]

Marketing research can also help prevent commercialization of products that are not consumer-oriented. Sometimes ideas that look like technological breakthroughs in the laboratory fall flat when presented to consumers. For example, a powdered pain reliever was supposed to be a soothing remedy because it was to be mixed with milk. It did not soothe customers, however. Research showed that the public thought this great step forward was actually a step backward in convenience. Someone forgot to consider the consumer benefit.

By improving efficiency, research also facilitates profitability. For instance, during the introduction of a new product, accurate forecasting of the product's potential sales volume is an essential basis for estimating its profitability. A firm considering the introduction of a cat snack that contains hairball medicine might rely on a test market experiment to determine the optimal price for this new concept. Extensive testing should be done to ensure that the marketing program is fine-tuned to maximize the firm's profitability while satisfying consumers.

Analysis of data may also be a form of marketing research that can increase efficiency. Marketing representatives from Exxon Chemical Company used laptop computers to present a complex set of calculations to sales prospects to show them the advantage of Exxon products over competitors' products. Such analysis of research data improves the salesperson's batting average and the firm's efficiency.

Because of the importance of integrating company efforts, a marketing researcher must be knowledgeable not only about marketing research but about the entire spectrum of marketing activities.

The Managerial Value of Marketing Research for Strategic Decision Making

Effective marketing management requires research. DirectTV, the direct-broadcast satellite television service, uses marketing research to determine which kinds of programming to add to its lineup of channels. A company executive says, "Research has driven every aspect of our business decisions."[17] At Ford Motor Company, research is so fundamental that the company hardly makes any significant decision without the benefit of some kind of marketing research. The prime managerial value of marketing research comes from the reduced uncertainty that results from information and facilitates decision making about marketing strategies and tactics to achieve an organization's strategic goals.

Developing and implementing a marketing strategy involves four stages:

1. Identifying and evaluating market opportunities
2. Analyzing market segments and selecting target markets
3. Planning and implementing a marketing mix that will provide value to customers and meet organizational objectives
4. Analyzing firm performance

Identifying and Evaluating Opportunities

One job that marketing research can perform is monitoring the competitive environment for signals indicating a business opportunity. A mere description of some social or economic activity, such as trends in consumer purchasing behavior, may help managers recognize problems and identify opportunities for enriching marketing efforts. In some cases, this research can motivate a firm to take action to address consumer desires in a way that is beneficial to both the customers and to the firm.

At times, evaluating opportunities may involve something as mundane as tracking weather trends. Consumers have a physical need to maintain some degree of physical comfort. Thus, changes in the temperature patterns may create business opportunities for utility companies, appliance companies, and even beverage companies as more consumers will select a hot beverage like hot chocolate when the weather is cold and dreary. Companies can also adjust their logistic distribution patterns based on the weather. When Hurricane Katrina hit the Gulf Coast of the United States, several chainsaw companies (such as Poulan) and companies that manufacture generators (such as Honda) began directing inventory toward those areas even before the hurricane actually struck. As a result, many home supply stores like Home Depot and Lowe's were able to maintain inventories of these vital products despite an increase in demand of over 1,000 percent! Thus, the misfortune of a hurricane created a business opportunity that also provided real value to consumers. In this case, the businesses and the consumers all benefited from the fact that firms scan the opportunity for trends.

The purpose of a research study on running shoes was to investigate the occasions or situations associated with product use—that is, when individuals wore running shoes. The researchers found that most owners of running shoes wore the shoes while walking, not running. Also, most of this walking was part of a normal daily activity like shopping or commuting to work. Many of the people who wore running shoes for routine activities considered the shoes an alternative to other casual shoes. This research ultimately led to a shift in design and production toward walking shoes designed for comfortable, everyday walking and casual wear.[18]

Market opportunities may be evaluated using many performance criteria. For example, the performance criterion of market demand typically is estimated using marketing research techniques. Estimates of market potential or predictions about future environmental conditions allow managers to evaluate opportunities. Accurate sales forecasts are among the most useful pieces of planning information a marketing manager can have. Complete accuracy in forecasting the future is not possible, because change is constantly occurring in the marketing environment. Nevertheless, objective forecasts of demand or changing environments may be the foundations on which marketing strategies are built.

Analyzing and Selecting Target Markets

The second stage of marketing strategy development is to analyze market segments and select target markets. Marketing research is a major source of information for determining which characteristics of market segments distinguish them from the overall market. Such research can help "locate" or describe a market segment in terms of demographic and characteristics. Geo-demographics can be important to study and track in this effort. **Geo-demographics** refers to information describing the demographic profile of consumers in a particular geographic region. The company may learn that consumers in a particular postal code within a region tend to be middle-aged, have multiple children over the age of twelve, and have college degrees and white-collar jobs. Once the company knows the geo-demographics of a market segment, it can effectively communicate with those customers by choosing media that reach that particular profile. For example, *Architectural Digest* is a magazine that is read predominantly by consumers with very high social status in the most exclusive zip codes in the United States.

Geo-demographics
Refers to information describing the demographic profile of consumers in a particular geographic region.

Planning and Implementing a Marketing Mix

Using the information obtained in the two previous stages, marketing managers plan and execute a marketing-mix strategy. Marketing research may be needed to support specific decisions about any aspect of the marketing mix. For instance, the research can evaluate an alternative course of action. For example, advertising research might investigate whether an actress like Julia Roberts or a singer like Mariah Carey would make a better spokesperson for a specific brand of hair coloring. Research might be conducted involving test ads with each celebrity examining questions such as whether or not attitudes toward the brand are higher for Julia or for Mariah and how much each celebrity is liked, but also, perhaps not as obviously, how much credibility each celebrity would have based on the beliefs consumers have about whether or not each would really use the product.

It is essential that an overall research plan involve all elements of marketing strategy. In other words, once the research identifies a target market and media that can be used in promotion, it needs to determine what benefits are required to create value for the customers, what price is most appropriate and, not to be overlooked, what channels of distribution will best reach the consumer. The integration of all of this research leads to effective brand management.[19] The following examples highlight selected types of research that might be conducted for each element of the marketing mix.

PRODUCT RESEARCH

Product research takes many forms and includes studies designed to evaluate and develop new products and to learn how to adapt existing product lines. Concept testing exposes potential customers to a new product idea to judge the acceptance and feasibility of the concept. Product testing reveals a product prototype's strengths and weaknesses or determines whether a finished product performs better than competing brands or according to expectations. Brand-name evaluation studies investigate whether a name is appropriate for a product. Package testing assesses size, color, shape, ease of use, and other attributes of a package. Product research encompasses all applications of marketing research that seek to develop product attributes that will add value for consumers.

Before Cheetos became the first major brand of American snack food to be made and marketed in China, product taste tests revealed that traditional cheese-flavored corn puffs Cheetos did not appeal to Chinese consumers. So the company conducted consumer research with 600 different flavors to learn which flavors would be most appealing. Among the flavors Chinese consumers tested and disliked were ranch dressing, nacho, Italian pizza, Hawaiian barbecue, peanut satay, North Sea crab, chili prawn, coconut milk curry, smoked octopus, caramel, and cuttlefish. Research did show that consumers liked some flavors. So, when Cheetos were introduced in China, they came in two flavors: savory American cream and zesty Japanese steak.[20] So, the result was essentially cheeseless Cheetos.

PRICING RESEARCH

Pricing
Involves finding the amount of monetary sacrifice that best represents the value customers perceive in a product after considering various market constraints.

In many ways, pricing research represents typical marketing research. Many test markets address the question of how consumers will respond to a product offering two different prices. **Pricing** involves finding the amount of monetary sacrifice that best represents the value customers perceive in a product after considering various market constraints. Most organizations conduct pricing

RESEARCHSNAPSHOT

Business Class Success?

If you've ever checked the price of business-class airfare on a flight overseas, you were probably surprised at the price. A discounted round-trip coach ticket from Atlanta to Paris in peak season often costs just over one thousand dollars. That same business class ticket would often cost between five and ten thousand dollars! Typically, these flights take place in the larger passenger aircraft flown such as a Boeing 747 or a Boeing 777. A Boeing 777 can seat up to 450 passengers. However, by including three dozen business-class seats, the capacity drops to under 400 passengers.

Thus, it is easy to see that a great deal of research must assess both the product design (what service and product attributes make up a business-class experience) and pricing (in both coach and business class) to determine the best configuration of the aircraft. Research shows that business-class travelers prioritize the comfort of the seat and the ability to be able to lie flat during the flight, the quality of food, and convenience of boarding as attributes that make up the business-class experience.

Recently, a few start-up airlines have been trying to capitalize on this concept by starting "discount" business-class only airlines. Maxjet estimates that consumers will exchange a little comfort for a reduction in price. They plan on configuring Boeing 737s (smaller than typical trans-ocean carriers) with 102 business-class seats that will not quite lay flat—and no coach seats! The result is a business-class only airline with cross-Atlantic fares ranging between $1600 and $3800, less than half of traditional business-class fares. Taking the concept to an even smaller scale, some airlines are experimenting with business-class service on Citation Excel jets configured for only seven passengers.

Sources: McCarnety, Scott (2005), "Start-Up Airlines Fly Only Business Class," The Wall Street Journal (September 20), D1; Pitock, Todd (2005), "Getting There," Forbes, 176 (September), 30–32.

©AMIT BHARGAVA/BLOOMBERG NEWS/LANDOV

---

research. Starbucks may seem expensive now, but if the price doubled, would Starbucks lose many customers? At AFLAC, how much are consumers willing to pay each month for every one dollar of supplementary disability insurance? Pricing research also investigates the way people respond to pricing tactics. How do consumers respond to price reductions in one form or another? How much are people willing to pay for some critical product attribute? Do consumers view prices and/or quantity discounts as fair in a given category?[21] Do price gaps among national brands, regional brands, and private labels exist?[22] Most importantly, research also addresses the way consumers determine perceived value.

Pricing research addresses consumer quality perceptions by its very nature. A great deal of research addresses consumer reactions to low prices and documents the fact that, in quite a few instances, prices can actually be too low. In other words, sales can actually decrease with lower prices instead of increasing.[23]

Recently, Wal-Mart test marketed a Starbucks-type coffee shop called Medina's Kicks.[24] A Kicks coffee shop was set up in a Texas Wal-Mart store. They are testing prices relative to the nearby Starbucks. At prices 25 percent below Starbucks, sales remain relatively low while Starbucks remains popular. By lowering the price, they may also have lowered the perceived product quality. By raising the price, might quality perceptions improve and get consumers to think the coffee may be more similar to Starbucks? These are typical pricing questions.

▥ DISTRIBUTION RESEARCH

Distribution involves the marketing channels that will physically "distribute" products from a producer to a consumer. A **marketing channel** is a network of interdependent institutions that perform the logistics necessary for consumption to occur. Some channels are very short and involve only a producer and a consumer, and some are very long involving much transportation, wholesale, and retail firms. It may be somewhat obvious why the term **supply chain** is sometimes used to refer to a channel of distribution. Distribution is necessary to remove the separations between buyers and sellers (see Exhibit 1.5).

Distribution research is typified by studies aimed at selecting retail sites or warehouse locations. A survey of retailers or wholesalers may be conducted because the actions of one channel member

Marketing channel
A network of interdependent institutions that perform the logistics necessary for consumption to occur.

Supply chain
Another term for a channel of distribution, meaning the link between suppliers and customers.

RESEARCHSNAPSHOT

Disney Distribution

Typically, when we think of distribution images, tractor-trailer trucks and railroad cars loaded with industrial or consumer products come to mind. But research questions involving distribution are just as important for companies that sell "soft" goods as for those that sell more tangible products like refrigerators. Entertainment companies like Disney are currently facing a rapidly changing consumer environment. The change is driven largely by advances in digital and electronic technology. One key distribution decision they face is whether or not to stop distributing motion pictures on film and begin releasing them to theaters solely in a digital format. Disney researchers analyzed the potential cost savings associated with such a move and estimate a savings of a billion dollars per year. However, it is also estimated that they will have to subsidize theaters on the order of approximately 100 thousand dollars per auditorium to help finance the new equipment required to show digital movies. Disney is also facing key marketing questions involving the timing and format of movie distribution. Video delivery is possible through many technologies today. Also, movie piracy is occurring faster and on a larger scale than ever. Thus, Disney is considering releasing movies directly to consumers at the same time that they release them to theaters. In addition, they are examining the effect of distributing movies to be downloaded onto iPods or mobile phones. These issues spawn many questions involving pricing and product design since a movie filmed for the "big screen" may not translate well to a two-inch iPod screen! Clearly, marketing research will be involved in addressing these questions.

Sources: Marr, Merissa (2005), "In Shakeup, Disney Rethinks How It Reaches Audiences," The Wall Street Journal (October 1), A1; Marr, Merissa (2005), "A Cineplex Pitch: Hey Hollywood, Make Better Movies to Lure Crowds," The Wall Street Journal (August 19), B2; Wingfield, Nick and Ethan Smith (2005), "Video Comes to the iPod," The Wall Street Journal (October 13), B1.

©DAVID YOUNG-WOLFF/PHOTOEDIT

EXHIBIT 1.5
Distribution Channels

can greatly affect the performance of other channel members. Distribution research often is needed to gain knowledge about retailers' and wholesalers' operations and to learn their reactions to a manufacturer's marketing policies. It may also be used to examine the effect of just-in-time ordering systems or exclusive distribution on product quality. Research focused on developing and improving the efficiency of marketing channels is extremely important.

Golden Books traditionally distributed its small hardcover children's books with golden spines to book retailers like Waldenbooks or B. Dalton Booksellers. When it researched where its customers would prefer to purchase Golden Books, the company learned that mass merchandisers, grocery stores, and drug stores would be just as popular as the upscale stores as distribution channels. Today, publishing companies like Golden Books face the possibility of new and shorter marketing channels that would allow home delivery via the Internet. Not only does this mean reduced time from production to consumption, but it also allows the books to come alive through interactivity. Should Golden Book abandon its more traditional marketing channels and focus its resources on this new delivery option?

Similarly, other companies are faced with key decisions involving distribution in a new and more technologically advanced operating environment. Television technology has advanced greatly. As a result, more and more consumers are building home theaters. These home theaters include increasingly more affordable technologies such as flat-screen, high-definition televisions and sound systems that rival those found in movie theaters. How will this affect the traditional channels of distribution for motion pictures, such as production studios, entertainment companies, theater groups/cooperatives, and individual theaters? Also, prescription drugs can now be purchased via the Internet. For the consumer, this marketing channel bypasses the traditional doctor's visit and local pharmacy. For the pharmaceutical firm, is it wise to take advantage of this channel? By removing the family doctor from the channel of distribution, does the drug seem to be less effective, and if so, is the brand's reputation harmed? Marketing research is needed to examine related issues including whether or not the product is equally effective through both the new and traditional marketing channel. Research results may both help firms make the distribution decision and help policy makers decide on the limits that should be placed on prescription drug distribution options.

PROMOTION RESEARCH

Promotion is the communication function of the firm responsible for informing and persuading buyers. Promotion research investigates the effectiveness of advertising, premiums, coupons, sampling, discounts, public relations, and other sales promotions. However, among all of these, firms spend more time, money, and effort on advertising research.

The marketing research findings of Zales, a large jewelry retailer, helped in the creation of advertising with large, one-word headlines that simply asked, "Confused?," "Nervous?," or "Lost?" The advertisements overtly acknowledged the considerable emotional and financial risks that consumers face in jewelry purchases. Research had shown that typical consumers felt unable to determine the relative quality of various jewelry items, believed jewelry purchases were expensive, and needed reassurance about their purchases, especially because they often purchased jewelry for someone else. This promotion helped communicate an effective message of empathy with the consumer.

Similarly, a business in transition must effectively communicate its meaning. As AT&T's business shifts from that of a pure long-distance provider into that of a distanceless cable, Internet, and wireless communication specialist, it is trying to make sure its image changes too. But research showed its brand name still conjured up the image of an old-fashioned telephone company.[25] Marketing research also indicates great familiarity with the blue-and-white striped globe that served as AT&T's logo. A survey found 75 percent unaided recognition among the broad consumer market, 77 percent recognition among 18- to 24-year-olds, and 80 percent recognition among "high-value, active networkers"—consumers spending seventy-five dollars or more per month on long-distance and wireless services. Because of this high level of recognition, AT&T produced numerous TV commercials featuring an animation of the logo bouncing around, giving fun, high-intensity demonstrations of the various ways the company is transforming itself in the broadband-enabled world, accompanied by voice-over explanations of these new services. Future research may even consider placing the logo on iPod sites or even as a product placement in video games as a

Promotion
The communication function of the firm responsible for informing and persuading buyers.

Promotion research
Investigates the effectiveness of advertising, premiums, coupons, sampling, discounts, public relations, and other sales promotions.

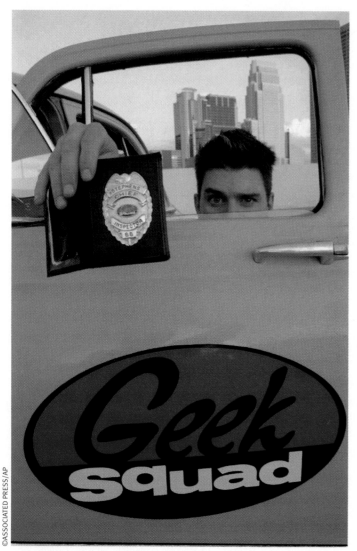

Best Buy has re-invented the traditional Geek image and made it work for them.

Integrated marketing communication
Means that all promotional efforts (advertising, public relations, personal selling, event marketing, and so forth) should be coordinated to communicate a consistent image.

Integrated marketing mix
The effects of various combinations of marketing-mix elements on important outcomes.

Total value management
Trying to manage and monitor the entire process by which consumers receive benefits from a company.

way of further transforming AT&T's image from "Ma Bell" into a modern technology service provider.[26]

Media research helps businesses make decisions about whether television, newspapers, magazines, or other media alternatives are best suited to convey the intended message. Choices among media alternatives may be based on research that shows the proportion of consumers in each market segment that a particular advertising vehicle can reach.

▥ THE INTEGRATED MARKETING MIX

Marketing today focuses increasingly on the fact that different promotional decisions should not be made in isolation. Instead, the concept of **integrated marketing communication** is adopted, meaning that all promotional efforts (advertising, public relations, personal selling, event marketing, and so forth) should be coordinated to communicate a consistent image. Likewise, more generally marketing firms realize that the elements of the marketing mix itself must work together. For instance, a change in price can affect the quality of the product, which may also influence decisions about distribution. From a research standpoint, the **integrated marketing mix** means that research studies often investigate effects of various combinations of marketing mix elements on important outcomes like sales and image. Research suggests that consumer-oriented firms are particularly oriented toward integrating all aspects of their marketing into a single message.[27]

Best Buy, a U.S.-based electronic and appliance retailer, recently showed the success of integrating sales and service with promotion. You'll find a Geek in every Best Buy. The Geeks are technology experts (i.e., "computer geeks") that provide knowledgeable sales advice and technical service. To be a Geek, you have to look like a Geek! Their attire is carefully coordinated: white socks with black shoes, black pants that are just a little too short, a white sport shirt, and a narrow black tie. Today, the Geeks have become prominent in Best Buy television ads, and they even provide in-home set-up and technical service. The Geeks are transforming Best Buy in the minds of consumers.[28] Companies that integrate the use of consistent spokespeople, such as the Geeks, across marketing elements enjoy more favorable brand images among consumers and are better able to communicate relevant information.[29]

Analyzing Marketing Performance

After a marketing strategy has been implemented, marketing research may serve to inform managers whether planned activities were properly executed and are accomplishing what they were expected to achieve. In other words, marketing research may be conducted to obtain feedback for evaluation and control of marketing programs. This aspect of marketing research is especially important for successful **total value management**, which attempts to manage the entire process by which a consumer receives benefits from a company.

Performance-monitoring research refers to research that regularly, sometimes routinely, provides feedback for evaluation and control of marketing activity. For example, most firms continuously monitor wholesale and retail activity to ensure early detection of sales declines and other anomalies. In the grocery and drug industries, sales research may use Universal Product Codes (UPCs) on packages read by electronic cash registers and computerized checkout counts to provide valuable market-share information to store and brand managers interested in the retail sales

RESEARCHSNAPSHOT

Swifter or Swiffer?

Procter & Gamble (P&G) performs a great deal of consumer research. When P&G set out on a research project aimed at designing a better mop, meaning a better mopping experience, consumers' reactions were interpreted as indicating that they didn't want any mop at all. They didn't want to mop! Mopping was too time-consuming, boring, and messy. They wanted to throw away their mops. The result? A mop you throw away! We know it today as a Swiffer. The chemically treated cloths pick up dirt like a magnet and then can be neatly and easily discarded. This same research led to disposable replacements for cleaning cloths and for toilet brushes. Thus, research examining how current products can be improved led to key product developments. All of these products continue to perform very well for P&G.

Sources: Ellison, Sarah (2005), "Studying Messy Habits to Sweep Up a Market," The Wall Street Journal (July 14), B1–B4; Neff, Jack (2005), "Swiffer by Another Name," Advertising Age, 76 (15), 11.

volumes of their products. Market-share analysis and sales analysis are the most common forms of performance-monitoring research. Almost every organization compares its current sales with previous sales and with competitors' sales. However, analyzing marketing performance is not limited to the investigation of sales figures.

Marketing metrics refer to quantitative ways of monitoring and measuring marketing performance. Research is needed to determine marketing metrics that allow a firm to know whether the resources invested in marketing activities have met their quantitative business goals. Marketing metrics allow the firm to assess the return on investment (ROI) associated with marketing activities. Performance monitoring research conducted by the ACNielsen firm suggests that only 18 percent of television commercials return a positive ROI for the companies advertised.[30]

When analysis of marketing performance indicates that things are not going as planned, marketing research may be required to explain why something went wrong. Detailed information about specific mistakes or failures is frequently sought. If a general problem area is identified, breaking down industry sales volume and a firm's sales volume into different geographical areas may explain specific problems. Exploring problems in greater depth may indicate which managerial judgments were erroneous.

Performance-monitoring research
Refers to research that regularly, sometimes routinely, provides feedback for evaluation and control of marketing activity.

Marketing metrics
Quantitative ways of monitoring and measuring marketing performance.

When is Marketing Research Needed?

The need to make intelligent, informed decisions ultimately motivates marketing research. Not every decision requires marketing research. Thus, when confronting a key decision, a marketing manager must initially decide whether or not to conduct marketing research. The determination of the need for marketing research centers on (1) time constraints, (2) the availability of data, (3) the nature of the decision to be made, and (4) the value of the research information in relation to costs.

Time Constraints

Systematic research takes time. In many instances management believes that a decision must be made immediately, allowing no time for research. Decisions sometimes are made without adequate information or thorough understanding of market situations. Although making decisions without researching a situation is not ideal, sometimes the urgency of a situation precludes the use of research.

The urgency with which managers often want to make decisions often conflicts with the marketing researchers' desire for rigor in following the scientific method.

Availability of Data

Often managers already possess enough information to make sound decisions without additional marketing research. When they lack adequate information, however, research must be considered. This means that data need to be collected from an appropriate source. If a potential source of data exists, managers will want to know how much it will cost to get the data.

If the data cannot be obtained, or it cannot be obtained in a timely fashion, this particular research project should not be conducted. For example, many African nations have never conducted a population census. Organizations engaged in international business often find that data about business activity or population characteristics that are readily available in the United States are nonexistent or sparse in developing countries. Imagine the problems facing marketing researchers who wish to investigate market potential in places like Uzbekistan, Yugoslavian Macedonia, and Rwanda.

Nature of the Decision

The value of marketing research will depend on the nature of the managerial decision to be made. A routine tactical decision that does not require a substantial investment may not seem to warrant a substantial expenditure for marketing research. For example, a computer company must update its operator's instruction manual when it makes minor product modifications. The research cost of determining the proper wording to use in the updated manual is likely to be too high for such a minor decision. The nature of the decision is not totally independent of the next issue to be considered: the benefits versus the costs of the research. In general, however, the more strategically or tactically important the decision, the more likely it is that research will be conducted.

Benefits versus Costs

There are both costs and benefits to conducting marketing research. Earlier we discussed some of the managerial benefits of marketing research. Of course, conducting research to obtain these benefits requires an expenditure of money. In any decision-making situation, managers must identify alternative courses of action and then weigh the value of each alternative against its cost. Marketing research can be thought of as an investment alternative. When deciding whether to make a decision without research or to postpone the decision in order to conduct research, managers should ask three questions:

1. Will the payoff or rate of return be worth the investment?
2. Will the information gained by marketing research improve the quality of the marketing decision enough to warrant the expenditure?
3. Is the proposed research expenditure the best use of the available funds?

For example, *TV-Cable Week* was not test-marketed before its launch. Although the magazine had articles and stories about television personalities and events, its main feature was program listings, channel by channel, showing the exact programs a particular subscriber could receive. To produce a custom magazine for each individual cable television system in the country required developing a costly computer system. Because that development necessitated a substantial expenditure, one that could not be scaled down for research, conducting research was judged to be an unwise investment. The value of the research information was not positive because its cost exceeded its benefits. Unfortunately, pricing and distribution problems became so compelling after the magazine was launched that the product was a marketing failure. Nevertheless, without the luxury of hindsight, managers made a reasonable decision not to conduct research. They analyzed the cost of the information (that is, the cost of test-marketing) relative to the potential benefits of the information. Exhibit 1.6 outlines the criteria for determining when to conduct marketing research.

EXHIBIT 1.6 **Determining When to Conduct Marketing Research**

Time Constraints		Availability of Data		Nature of the Decision		Benefits versus Costs		
Is sufficient time available before a decision will be made?	Yes →	Can the decision be made with what is already known?	Yes →	Is the decision of considerable strategic or tactical importance?	Yes →	Does the value of the research information exceed the cost of conducting research?	Yes →	Conduct Marketing Research
No ↓		No ↓		No ↓		No ↓		

Do Not Conduct Marketing Research

Marketing Research in the Twenty-First Century

Marketing research, like all business activity, continues to change. Changes in communication technologies and the trend toward an ever more global marketplace have played a large role in many of these changes.

Communication Technologies

Virtually everyone is "connected" today. Increasingly, many people are "connected" nearly all the time. Within the lifetime of the typical undergraduate college senior, the way information is exchanged, stored, and gathered has been revolutionized completely. Today, the amount of information formally contained in an entire library can rest easily in a single personal computer.

The speed with which information can be exchanged has also increased tremendously. During the 1970s, exchanging information overnight from anywhere in the continental United States was heralded as a near miracle of modern technology. Today, we can exchange information from nearly anywhere in the world to nearly anywhere in the world almost instantly. Internet connections are now wireless, so one doesn't have to be tethered to a wall to access the World Wide Web. Our mobile phones and handheld data devices can be used not only to converse, but also as a means of communication that can even involve marketing research data. In many cases, technology also has made it possible to store or collect data for lower costs than in the past. Electronic communications are usually less costly than regular mail—and certainly less costly than a face-to-face interview—and cost about the same amount no matter how far away a respondent is from a researcher. Thus, the expressions "time is collapsing" and "distance is disappearing" capture the tremendous revolution in the speed and reach of our communication technologies.

Changes in computer technology have made for easier data collection and data analysis. As we discuss in a later chapter, many consumer household panels now exist and can be accessed via the Internet. Thus, there is less need for the time and expense associated with regular mail survey approaches. Furthermore, the computing power necessary to solve complicated statistical problems is now easily accessible. Again, as recently as the 1970s, such computer applications required expensive mainframe computers found only in very large corporations, major universities, and large governmental/military institutions. Researchers could expect to wait hours or even longer to get results from a statistical program involving 200 respondents. Today, even the most basic laptop computers can solve complicated statistical problems involving thousands of data points in practically a nanosecond.

Global Marketing Research

Marketing research has become increasingly global as more and more firms take advantage of markets that have few, if any, geographic boundaries. Some companies have extensive international marketing research operations. Upjohn conducts marketing research in 160 different countries.

RESEARCHSNAPSHOT

"Jacques" Daniels

Sales of U.S. distilled spirits have declined over the last 10 to 15 years as more Americans turn to wine or beer as their beverage of choice. As a result, companies like Bacardi and Brown-Forman, producers of Jack Daniels, have pursued market development strategies involving increased efforts to expand into international markets. The Brown-Forman marketing budget for international ventures includes a significant allocation for marketing research. By doing research before launching the product, Brown-Forman can learn product usage patterns within a particular culture. Some of the findings from this research indicate

1. Japanese consumers use Jack Daniels (JD) as a dinner beverage. A party of four or five consumers in a restaurant will order and drink a bottle of "JD" with their meal.

2. Australian consumers mostly consume distilled spirits in their homes. Also in contrast to Japanese consumers, Australians prefer to mix JD with soft drinks or other mixers. As a result of this research, JD launched a mixture called "Jack and Cola" sold in 12 ounce bottles all around Australia. The product has been very successful.
3. British distilled spirit consumers also like mixed drinks, but they usually partake in bars and restaurants.
4. In China and India, consumers more often chose counterfeit or "knock-offs" to save money. Thus, innovative research approaches have addressed questions related to the way the black market works and how they can better educate consumers about the differences between the real thing and the knock-offs.

The result is that of all Jack Daniels sold is now sold outside of the United States.

Sources: Swibel, Mathew (2005), "How Distiller Brown-Forman Gets Rich by Exploiting the Greenback's Fall—and Pushing its Brands Abroad," Forbes, 175 (8), 152–155.

ACNielsen International, known for its television ratings, is the world's largest marketing research company. Two-thirds of its business comes from outside the United States.[31] Starbucks can now be found in nearly every developed country on the earth. AFLAC offers its products on multiple continents.

Companies that conduct business in foreign countries must understand the nature of those particular markets and judge whether they require customized marketing strategies. For example, although the fifteen nations of the European Union share a single formal market, marketing research shows that Europeans do not share identical tastes for many consumer products. Marketing researchers have found no such thing as a typical European consumer; language, religion, climate, and centuries of tradition divide the nations of the European Union. Scantel Research, a British firm that advises companies on color preferences, found inexplicable differences in Europeans' preferences in medicines. The French prefer to pop purple pills, but the English and Dutch favor white ones. Consumers in all three countries dislike bright red capsules, which are big sellers in the United States. This example illustrates that companies that do business in Europe must research throughout Europe to adapt to local customs and buying habits.[32]

Even companies that produce brands that are icons in their own country are now doing research internationally. The Real World Research box discusses how Brown-Forman, the parent company of Jack Daniels (the classic American "Sour Mash" or Bourbon Whiskey), are now interviewing consumers in the far corners of the world.[33] The internationalization of research places greater demands on marketing researchers and heightens the need for research tools that allow us to **cross-validate** research results, meaning that the empirical findings from one culture also exist and behave similarly in another culture. The development and application of these international research tools are an important topic in basic marketing research.[34]

Cross-validate
To verify that the empirical findings from one culture also exist and behave similarly in another culture.

Summary

There were seven learning objectives in this chapter. After reading the chapter, the student should be competent in each area described by a learning objective.

1. **Explain why marketing research is essential to business success.** While many business decisions are made "by the seat of the pants" or based on a manager's intuition, this type of decision making

carries with it a large amount of risk. By first researching an issue and gathering intelligence on customers, competitors, and the market, a company can make a more informed decision. The result is less risky decision making.

Marketing research is the intelligence-gathering function in business. The intelligence includes information about customers, competitors, economic trends, employees, and other factors that affect marketing success. This intelligence assists in decisions ranging from long-range planning to near-term tactical decisions.

2. Define marketing research. Marketing research is the application of the scientific method in searching for truth about marketing phenomena. The research must be conducted systematically, not haphazardly. It must be objective to avoid the distorting effects of personal bias. Marketing research can be rigorous, but the rigor is always traded off against the resource and time constraints that go with a particular business decision.

3. Identify the difference between applied and basic research. Applied marketing research seeks to facilitate managerial decision making. Basic or pure research seeks to increase knowledge of theories and concepts. Both are important. Applied research is more often the topic in this text.

4. Explain how marketing research is relevant to product, pricing, promotion, and distribution decisions. Businesses can make more accurate decisions about the marketing mix by using marketing research results. The chapter provides examples of studies involving each dimension of the marketing mix. Thus, marketing research is useful in a tactical sense.

5. Discuss how marketing research helps the firm develop and implement strategy. Marketing research is a means of implementing the marketing concept, the most central idea in marketing. The marketing concept says that a firm must be oriented both toward consumer satisfaction and toward long-run profitability (rather than toward short-run sales volume). Organizations need to focus both on creating and on keeping customers. Marketing research can help implement the marketing concept by identifying consumers' problems and needs, improving efficiency, and evaluating the effectiveness of marketing strategies and tactics.

The development and implementation of a marketing strategy consist of four stages: (1) identifying and evaluating opportunities, (2) analyzing market segments and selecting target markets, (3) planning and implementing a marketing mix that will provide value to customers and meet the objectives of the organization, and (4) analyzing firm performance. Marketing research helps in each stage by providing information for strategic decision making.

6. Identify the situations that call for market research and those that don't. Marketing managers determine whether marketing research should be conducted based on (1) time constraints, (2) availability of data, (3) the nature of the decision to be made, and (4) the benefit of the research information versus its cost.

7. Describe how technology and internationalization are affecting the way research is conducted and used. Technology has changed almost every aspect of marketing research. Modern computer and communications technology makes data collection, study design, data analysis, data reporting, and practically all other aspects of research easier and better. Furthermore, as more companies do business outside their own borders, companies are doing research in an international marketplace. This places a greater emphasis on research that can assess the degree to which research tools can be applied and interpreted the same way in difference cultures. Thus, research techniques often must cross-validate results.

Key Terms and Concepts

Marketing research	Customer-oriented	Integrated marketing communication
Applied marketing research	Relationship marketing	Integrated marketing mix
Basic marketing research	Geo-demographics	Total value management
The scientific method	Pricing	Performance-monitoring research
Product-oriented	Marketing channel	Marketing metrics
Production-oriented	Supply chain	Cross-validate
Marketing concept	Promotion	
Marketing orientation	Promotion research	

Questions for Review and Critical Thinking

1. Is it possible to make sound marketing decisions without marketing research? What advantages does research offer to the decision maker over seat-of-the-pants decision making?
2. Define a marketing orientation and a product orientation. Under which strategic orientation is there a greater need for marketing research?
3. Name some products that logically might have been developed with the help of marketing research.
4. Define *marketing research* and describe its task.
5. Which of the following organizations are likely to use marketing research? Why? How?
   a. Manufacturer of breakfast cereals
   b. Manufacturer of nuts, bolts, and other fasteners
   c. The Federal Trade Commission
   d. A hospital
   e. A company that publishes marketing textbooks
6. An automobile manufacturer is conducting research in an attempt to predict the type of car design consumers will desire in the year 2020. Is this basic or applied research? Explain.
7. What is the definition of an *integrated marketing mix?* How might this affect the research a firm conducts?
8. Comment on the following statements:
   a. Marketing managers are paid to take chances with decisions. Marketing researchers are paid to reduce the risk of making those decisions.
   b. A marketing strategy can be no better than the information on which it is formulated.
   c. The purpose of research is to solve marketing problems.
9. List the conditions that help a researcher decide when marketing research should or should not be conducted.
10. How have technology and internationalization affected marketing research?
11. **'NET** How do you believe the Internet has facilitated research? Try to use the Internet to find the total annual sales for Starbucks and for AFLAC. You can use the *Business Resource Center* tools that accompany the text to help with this.
12. What types of tools does the marketing researcher use more given the ever increasing internationalization of marketing?

Research Activities

1. **'NET** Suppose you owned a jewelry store in Denton, Texas. You are considering opening a second store just like your current store. You are undecided on whether to locate the new store in another location in Denton, Texas, or in Birmingham, Alabama. Why would you decide to have some marketing research done before making the decision? Should the research be conducted? Go to http://www.census.gov. Do you think any of this information would be useful in the research?

2. Visit the Business Resource Center (via the Internet). Use it to find recent examples of news articles involving the use of marketing research in making decisions about each element of the marketing mix.
3. Using the Business Resource Center, find an article illustrating an example of an applied marketing research study involving some aspect of technology. How does it differ from a basic research study also focusing on a similar aspect of technology?

Video Case 1.1 Krispy Kreme

Krispy Kreme began a storefront business in 1937 when Vernon Rudolph bought a secret raised-doughnut recipe from a French chef. Since then, hundreds of the signature green-roofed shops have sprung up across the United States. Krispy Kreme would even like to expand into countries like Canada, Spain, Japan, Great Britain, and Australia.

The company credits its success to quality products, clean stores, and good relationships with customers in the community. No one seems able to define specifically what makes the Krispy Kreme doughnut taste so much better than any other brand, but everyone agrees that it has something to do with "the hot donut experience." Company marketing managers explain that their bottom-line focus in every store is on what they do best: offer good donuts and good coffee. Their product, they maintain, crosses all socioeconomic and geographical boundaries, and they don't bombard their customers with any other messages.

Krispy Kreme stores are more than just clean. The "donut theater" allows customers to watch donuts being made through glass windows; they can even see the baked donuts going through what the company has termed the "glazing waterfall." All of this invites customers into the production experience and assures them of a quality product.

Krispy Kreme also works hard to develop relationships with its customers and to be a positive force in communities where stores are located. It has helped to raise millions for fundraising events by generously donating donuts to charitable projects; in fact, it was one of the first companies in the United States to get involved in fundraising. Community-relationship programs are specifically family-oriented. For example, they encourage kids to get good grades; students who bring in good report cards receive a free donut for every A grade they earn. The company sponsors local sports teams. It invites groups of children to take tours of its sites, which can include the kids making their own donuts.

Questions

1. To succeed in the global market, what market research should Krispy Kreme undertake?
2. What market research activities does Krispy Kreme engage in to determine where to build a site?
3. Krispy Kreme is currently facing criticism from low-carb diet practitioners that have lowered sales. How can market research help it deal with this problem?

Video Case 1.2 Ben & Jerry's

 Ben & Jerry's Homemade, Inc., the Vermont-based manufacturer of ice cream, frozen yogurt, and sorbet, was founded in 1978 in a renovated gas station in Burlington, Vermont, by childhood friends Ben Cohen and Jerry Greenfield, with a $12,000 investment ($4,000 of which was borrowed).[35] They soon became popular for their innovative flavors, made from fresh Vermont milk and cream. The company currently distributes ice cream, low-fat ice cream, frozen yogurt, sorbet, and novelty products nationwide, as well as in selected foreign countries, in supermarkets, grocery stores, convenience stores, franchised Ben & Jerry's scoop shops, restaurants, and other venues.

Ben & Jerry's product strategy is to differentiate its super-premium brand from other ice cream brands. The brand image reflects high quality, uniqueness, and a bit of amusement. Its all-natural flavors have unique names. For example, "Chubby Hubby" has chunks of chocolate-covered, peanut-butter-filled pretzels in a rich vanilla malt ice cream with deep ripples of fudge and peanut butter. Other names in the company's line of ice creams include Cherry Garcia, Bovinity Divinity, Dilbert Totally Nuts, New York Super Fudge Chunk, Chunky Monkey, and From Russia with Buzz.

The new product development process and flavor naming process are a top priority at Ben & Jerry's. For example, Phish Food ice cream was developed as a unique product with a fun name associated with the band Phish. Ben Cohen had been a neighbor of members of Phish since the band's early years as favorites on the local music scene. When Ben & Jerry's suggested mixing up a Phish ice cream to celebrate their shared Vermont roots, the band agreed. So Ben & Jerry's concocted a chocolate ice cream with chewy marshmallow nougat, a thick caramel swirl, and a school of fudge fish in every pint. Most marshmallow variegates disappear into nothingness. The company took great pains to make sure that the marshmallow was the way it was meant to be. With Phish Food you can see, taste, and feel the white streaks of marshmallow. The Phish Food package is a departure from traditional Ben & Jerry's graphics. The pint container is designed with images from Phish's concert light show, featuring Phish band members Trey Anastasio, Mike Gordon, Jon Fishman, and Page McConnell on the pint lid along with Ben and Jerry.

Question

What role does marketing research play in new product development and brand name development for a company like Ben & Jerry's?

CHAPTER 2
INFORMATION SYSTEMS AND KNOWLEDGE MANAGEMENT

After studying this chapter, you should

1. Know and distinguish the concepts of data, information, and intelligence.
2. Understand the four characteristics that describe data.
3. Know the purpose of research in assisting marketing operations.
4. Know what a decision support system is and does.
5. Recognize the major categories of databases.

Chapter Vignette: Data for Doughnuts!

Who makes the best doughnut in America? Which doughnut firm does the best marketing? These are two different questions to some extent. There is more to selling doughnuts than making a great doughnut.

Krispy Kreme is the market-share leader among U.S. doughnut firms, operating hundreds of stores in practically every state in the nation; it also has operations in several foreign countries, including South Korea! Although consumers may first think of the neon-laced doughnut shops when they think of Krispy Kreme, the fact is that the bulk of Krispy Kreme's revenue is generated from doughnut sales outside of its own stores. Krispy Kremes can be found in thousands of convenience and grocery stores and at practically every super store in the United States. Thus, there is a great deal of data to keep track of in terms of where doughnuts are delivered and where they are sold. Collecting these data manually would involve thousands of phone calls each time the data were needed. Clearly, this would be a labor intensive process, particularly considering that the decisions made based on these data include many day-to-day operational decisions.

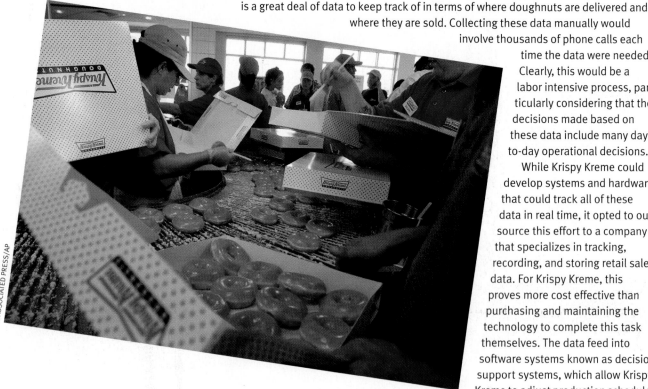

©ASSOCIATED PRESS/AP

While Krispy Kreme could develop systems and hardware that could track all of these data in real time, it opted to outsource this effort to a company that specializes in tracking, recording, and storing retail sales data. For Krispy Kreme, this proves more cost effective than purchasing and maintaining the technology to complete this task themselves. The data feed into software systems known as decision support systems, which allow Krispy Kreme to adjust production schedules to meet demand, adjust pricing, manage billing processes, and even track inventory-shrinkage trends. Thus, if a store's employees or customers are indulging in the Krispy Kremes without purchasing them, the system lets the executives at Krispy Kreme know. Furthermore, when Krispy

Kreme needs additional data, the information provider may very well already have the data available in a data warehouse. Thus, the data provide knowledge that greatly assists Krispy Kreme marketing managers in day-to-day operational matters.[1]

Introduction

Krispy Kreme's use of an outside firm to manage its information illustrates the sometimes sophisticated way in which modern marketing firms integrate data into their decision processes. Many of the decisions that used to be made with guesswork are now supplemented with "intelligence" either automatically delivered by some computer software or drawn from a data warehouse.

Doughnut companies aren't alone in this effort. Imagine all the information that passes through a single Home Depot store each day. Every customer transaction, every empty shelf, every employee's work schedule—right down to the schedule to clean restrooms—creates potentially valuable information that can be used by researchers and decision makers. Considering that Home Depot operates thousands of stores, obviously, Home Depot needs a data depot!

Like Krispy Kreme, Home Depot has outsourced the storage and management of data inventories. In this case, IBM manages the data, allowing it to be integrated into management strategy and tactics. Data from cash registers, time clocks, shelf counts, and much more are all compiled, analyzed, and either fed automatically into management systems or supplied in the form of a research report. In a way, this type of marketing research is automatic![2]

This chapter discusses knowledge management and the role decision support systems play in helping firms make informed marketing decisions. The chapter also introduces the concept of global information systems and sources of data that exist beyond the walls of any business. Modern data technology allows businesses to more easily integrate research into marketing strategy and operations.

Information, Data, and Intelligence

In everyday language, terms like *information* and *data* are often used interchangeably. Researchers use these terms in specific ways that emphasize how useful each can be. Data are simply facts or recorded measures of certain phenomena (things or events). Information is data formatted (structured) to support decision making or define the relationship between two facts. Market intelligence is the subset of data and information that actually has some explanatory power enabling effective decisions to be made. So, there is more data than information, and more information than intelligence.

Think again about the thousands upon thousands of unsummarized facts recorded by Home Depot each day. Each time a product is scanned at checkout, that fact is recorded and becomes data. Each customer's transactions are simultaneously entered into the store's computerized inventory system. The inventory system structures the data in such a way that a stocking report can be generated and orders for that store can be placed. Thus, the automated inventory system turns data into information. Further, the information from each store's sales and inventory records may be harvested by analysts tracking sales trends. The analysts may analyze the trends and prepare reports that help Home Depot buyers get the right products into each store or to even suggest places for new Home Depot locations. Thus, the analyst has now completed the transformation of data into intelligence. Exhibit 2.1 helps to illustrate the distinction between data, information, and intelligence.

Data
Facts or recorded measures of certain phenomena (things).

Information
Data formatted (structured) to support decision making or define the relationship between two facts.

Market intelligence
The subset of data and information that actually has some explanatory power enabling effective decisions to be made.

The Characteristics of Valuable Information

Not all data are valuable to decision makers. Useful data become information and help a marketing manager make decisions. Useful data can also become intelligence. Four characteristics help determine how useful data may be: relevance, quality, timeliness, and completeness.

EXHIBIT 2.1
Data, Information, Intelligence

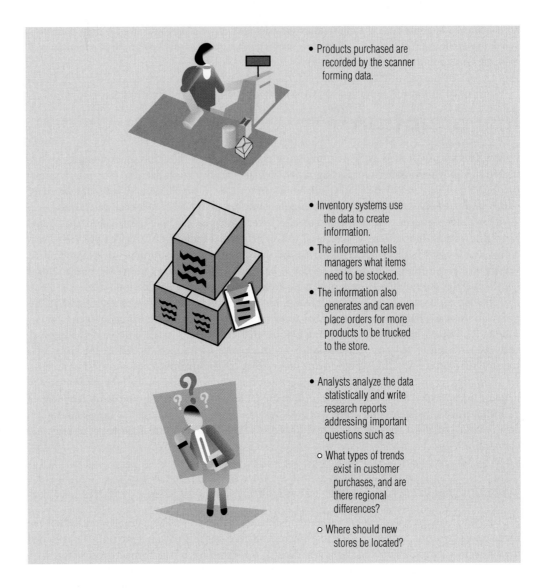

- Products purchased are recorded by the scanner forming data.

- Inventory systems use the data to create information.
- The information tells managers what items need to be stocked.
- The information also generates and can even place orders for more products to be trucked to the store.

- Analysts analyze the data statistically and write research reports addressing important questions such as

  o What types of trends exist in customer purchases, and are there regional differences?

  o Where should new stores be located?

Relevance

Relevance
The characteristics of data reflecting how pertinent these particular facts are to the situation at hand.

Relevance is the characteristics of data reflecting how pertinent these particular facts are to the situation at hand. Put another way, the facts are logically connected to the situation. Unfortunately, irrelevant data and information often creep into decision making. One particularly useful way to distinguish relevance from irrelevance is to think about how things change. Relevant data are facts about things that can be changed, and if they are changed, it will materially alter the situation. So, this simple question becomes important:

Will a change in the data coincide with a change in some important outcome?

American consumers' dietary trends are relevant to Krispy Kreme. If American diets become more health-conscious, then it can be expected that sales of doughnuts will be affected. This may lead Krispy Kreme to rethink its product offering. However, information on French consumers' wine preference is probably irrelevant since it is difficult to think how a change in wine preferences will affect U.S. doughnut preferences.

Quality

Data quality
The degree to which data represent the true situation.

Data quality is the degree to which data represent the true situation. High-quality data are accurate, valid, and reliable. High-quality data represent reality faithfully. If a consumer were to replace the product UPC from one drill at Home Depot with one from a different drill, not only would the consumer be acting unethically, but it would also mean that the data collected at the checkout counter would be inaccurate. Therefore, to the extent that the cash register is not actually recording the products that consumers take out of the stores, its quality is lowered. Sometimes, researchers will try to obtain the same data from multiple data sources as one check on its quality.[3] Data quality is a critical issue in marketing research, and it will be discussed throughout this text.

Timeliness

Marketing is a dynamic field in which out-of-date information can lead to poor decisions. Marketing information must be timely—that is, provided at the right time. Computerized information systems can record events and dispense relevant information soon after the event. A great deal of marketing information becomes available almost at the moment that a transaction occurs. **Timeliness** means that the data are current enough to still be relevant.

Computer technology has redefined standards for timely information. For example, if a marketing executive at Home Depot wishes to know the sales volume of any store worldwide, detailed information about any of thousands of products can be instantly determined. At Home Depot, the point-of-sale checkout system uses UPC scanners and satellite communications to link individual stores to the headquarters' computer system, from which managers can retrieve and analyze up-to-the-minute sales data on all merchandise in each store.

Timeliness
Means that the data are current enough to still be relevant.

Completeness

Information completeness refers to having the right amount of information. Marketing managers must have sufficient information about all aspects of their decisions. For example, a researcher investigating Eastern European markets may plan to analyze four former Soviet-bloc countries. Population statistics and information on inflation rates may be available on all four countries. However, information about disposable personal income may be available for only three of the countries. If information about disposable personal income or other economic characteristics cannot be obtained, the information is incomplete. Often incomplete information leads decision makers to conduct marketing research.

Information completeness
Having the right amount of information.

Knowledge Management

Who has the best pizza in town? The answer to this question requires knowledge. Indeed, you, as a consumer, have stored knowledge about many products. You know the best restaurants, best theaters, best movies, and so forth. All of this knowledge helps you make decisions as a consumer. Much of it is based on personal research involving product trials or searchers for information. From a consumer's perspective, knowledge is simply what you have stored in memory. It helps you, as a consumer, make decisions.

Organizations can use knowledge in a similar way. Knowledge is accumulated not just from a single individual, however, but from salespeople, managers, customer reports, and custom-ordered research. All of this *data* forms the organization's memory. Put another way, this is the firm's knowledge. From a company's perspective, **knowledge** is a blend of previous experience, insight, and data that forms organizational memory. It provides a framework that can be thoughtfully applied when assessing a marketing problem. Marketing researchers and decision makers use this knowledge to help create solutions to strategic and tactical problems. Thus, knowledge is a key resource and a potential competitive advantage.[4]

Knowledge management is the process of creating an inclusive, comprehensive, easily accessible organizational memory, which can be called the organization's *intellectual capital*.[5] The purpose of knowledge management is to organize the intellectual capital of an organization in a formally structured way for easy use. Knowledge is presented in a way that helps employees comprehend and act on that information and make better decisions in all areas of the marketing mix. Knowledge management systems are particularly useful in making data available across the functional areas of the firm. Thus, marketing knowledge and financial knowledge can be integrated. Recent

Knowledge
A blend of previous experience, insight, and data that forms organizational memory.

Knowledge management
The process of creating an inclusive, comprehensive, easily accessible organizational memory, which is often called the organization's *intellectual capital*.

RESEARCHSNAPSHOT

RFID Technology Gets Cheaper—Marketing Knowledge Grows

Radio frequency identification (RFID) tags have been used by large organizations for several years now. The U.S. military makes great use of RFIDs in tracking the whereabouts of virtually all kinds of products both big and small. Logistics officers can instantly track the whereabouts of Humvees and MREs (Meals Ready to Eat). Information from the tag is transmitted to computer servers and then directly into a GTN (Global Tracking Network). Equipment and supplies can then be ordered and dispatched to needed locations with a minimal of human contact. Product consumption (ammunition, food, water, computer printers, and so forth) can

also be tracked in real time. The Marines can know in real time if personnel in a desert use more food and water than personnel in a jungle.

Wal-Mart is pushing suppliers to adopt the technology.

Not only can Wal-Mart use them in logistical operations, but the potential exists to "go into" consumers homes and track how much and the way consumers actually consume products. Potentially, decision support systems (DSS) could tie ordering to customer consumption. However, the costs of RFIDs make it impractical for many suppliers.

Alien Technology Corporation recently announced a drop in the price of RFID tags. Now, when a company orders a million or more, the unit cost for an RFID is 12.9¢. Although this is a "basic" RFID tag, it still can store 96 bits of information. Analysts predict that the price of RFID tags will continue to drop. By 2008, the cost may drop to about 5¢, at which point the use of RFID technology in marketing research and business operations should soar.

Sources: Clark, Don (2005), "Alien Cuts Radio ID Tag Price to Spur Adoption by Retailiners," The Wall Street Journal (September 12), D4. Ferguson, R.B. (2004), "Marines Deploy RFID," e-Week, 21 (November 15), 37.

COURTESY, DIVISION OF PUBLIC AFFAIRS, UNITED STATES MARINE CORPS, DEPARTMENT OF DEFENSE, USA

Global information system

An organized collection of computer hardware, software, data, and personnel designed to capture, store, update, manipulate, analyze, and immediately display information about worldwide business activity.

TOTHEPOINT

An immense and ever-increasing wealth of knowledge is scattered about the world today; knowledge that would probably suffice to solve all the mighty difficulties of our age, but it is dispersed and unorganized. We need a sort of mental clearing house for the mind: a depot where knowledge and ideas are received, sorted, summarized, digested, clarified and compared.[21]

—H. G. Wells

research demonstrates how knowledge management systems are particularly useful in new product development and introduction.[6]

The firm's sales force plays a particularly useful role in the knowledge management process. Salespeople are in a key position to have a lot of knowledge about customers and the firm's capabilities. Thus, they are tools both for accumulating knowledge and for turning it into useful information.[7] Market-oriented organizations generally provide both formal and informal methods through which the knowledge gained by salespeople can be entered into a data warehouse to assist all decision makers, not just the sales force.

Global Information Systems

Increased global competition and technological advances in interactive media have given rise to global information systems. A **global information system** is an organized collection of computer hardware, software, data, and personnel designed to capture, store, update, manipulate, analyze, and immediately display information about worldwide business activities. A global information system is a tool for providing past, present, and projected information on internal operations and external activity. Using satellite communications, high-speed microcomputers, electronic data interchanges, fiber optics, data storage devices, and other technological advances in interactive media, global information systems are changing the nature of business.

Consider a simple example. At any moment, United Parcel Service (UPS) can track the status of any shipment around the world. UPS drivers use handheld electronic clipboards called delivery information acquisition devices (DIADs) to record appropriate data about each pickup or delivery. The data are then entered into the company's main computer for record-keeping and analysis. A satellite telecommunications system allows UPS to track any shipment for a customer.

RFID stands for radio frequency identification. It is a new technology that places a tiny chip, which can be woven onto a fabric, onto virtually any product, allowing it to be tracked anywhere in the world. This can provide great insight into the different distribution channels around the world and, potentially, to the different ways consumers acquire and use products. The U.S. military uses RFID technology to assist in its logistics, and Wal-Mart is one of the leading proponents of the technology as it can greatly assist in its global information system.[8]

With so much diverse information available in a global information system, organizations have found it necessary to determine what data, information, and knowledge are most useful to particular business units.

Decision Support Systems

Marketing research can be described in many ways. One way is to categorize research based on the four possible functions it serves in business:

1. Foundational—answers basic questions such as what consumer segments should be served and with what types of products.
2. Testing—addresses things like new product concepts or promotional ideas. How effective will they be?
3. Issues—examines how specific issues impact the firm. The way organizational structure impacts employee outcomes or the impacts of advertising spending are issues that can be researched.
4. Performance—this type of research monitors specific metrics including financial statistics like profitability and delivery times. They are critical in real-time management and in "what-if" types of analyses examining the potential impact of a change in policy.

Of these, it is the performance category that is of most interest to decision support systems. The metrics that are monitored can be fed into automated decision-making systems, or they can trigger reports that are delivered to managers. These form the basis of a decision support system and best typify the way marketing research assists managers with day-to-day operational decisions.

A marketing **decision support system (DSS)** is a system that helps decision makers confront problems through direct interaction with computerized databases and analytical software programs. The purpose of a decision support system is to store data and transform them into organized information that is easily accessible to marketing managers. Doing so saves managers countless hours so that decisions that might take days or even weeks otherwise can be made in minutes using a DSS.

Modern decision support systems greatly facilitate **customer relationship management (CRM)**. A CRM system is the part of the DSS that addresses exchanges between the firm and its customers. It brings together information about customers including sales data, market trends, marketing promotions and the way consumers respond to them, customer preferences, and more. A CRM system describes customer relationships in sufficient detail so that managers, salespeople, customer service representatives, and perhaps the customers themselves can access information directly, match customer needs with satisfying product offerings, remind customers of service requirements, and know what other products a customer has purchased.

Casinos track regular customers' behavior via "player's cards" that are swiped each time a consumer conducts a transaction. This information is fed automatically into a CRM system that creates tailor made promotional packages. The promotion may be unique to a specific customer's preferences as tracked by their own pattern of behavior. You may notice when visiting certain websites that they seem to be able to predict your behavior. The Research Snapshot box titled, "Are Marketers Clairvoyant?" tells how a CRM may be behind this clairvoyance.

Exhibit 2.2 illustrates a decision support system. Raw, unsummarized data are input to the DSS. Data collected in marketing research projects are a major source of this input, but the data may be purchased or collected by accountants, sales managers, production managers, or company employees other than marketing researchers. Effective marketers spend a great deal of time and effort collecting information for input into the decision support system. Useful

Decision support system (DSS)
A computer-based system that helps decision makers confront problems through direct interaction with databases and analytical software programs.

Customer relationship management (CRM)
Part of the DSS that addresses exchanges between the firm and its customers.

EXHIBIT 2.2
Decision Support System

RESEARCHSNAPSHOT

Are Marketers Clairvoyant?

A business traveler checks into a Wyndham hotel and finds his favorite type of pillow, favorite snacks, and a one of his favorite types of wine waiting upon arrival. Another customer daydreams of a recent golf vacation to Hawaii and wishes she could do it again. Later that day, an e-mail from Travelocity arrives with a great package deal to visit the same resort. Yet another consumer visits Barnesandnoble.com and a pop-up displays a new novel by his favorite author. Using a system called *active data warehousing,* the companies integrate data with research results that allow them to predict consumer preferences and even cyclical usage patterns quite accurately. Modern technology gives these firms a big advantage in the marketplace. Firms that don't adapt the technology may have a much harder time serving their customers. The latest technologies even provide ways for customers to voluntarily enter data or block certain data from being transmitted to the companies they do business with.

Sources: Schwarz, E. (2003), "Data Warehouses Get Active," Infoworld (December 8), 12. Watson, Richard T. (2004), "I am My Own Database," Harvard Business Review, 82 (November), 18–19.

information is the output of a DSS. A decision support system requires both databases and software. For firms operating across national borders, the DSS becomes part of its global information system.

Databases and Data Warehousing

Database
A collection of raw data arranged logically and organized in a form that can be stored and processed by a computer.

A **database** is a collection of raw data arranged logically and organized in a form that can be stored and processed by a computer. A customer mailing list is one type of database. Population characteristics may be recorded by state, county, and city in another database. Modern computer technology makes both the storage and retrieval of this information easy and convenient. The population data needed to do a retail site analysis may have meant days, possibly weeks, in a library. Today, the information is just a few clicks away.

Data warehousing
The process allowing important day-to-day operational data to be stored and organized for simplified access.

Data warehousing is the process allowing important day-to-day operational data to be stored and organized for simplified access. More specifically, a **data warehouse** is the multitiered computer storehouse of current and historical data. Data warehouse management requires that the detailed data from operational systems be extracted, transformed, placed into logical partitions (for example daily data, weekly data, etc.), and stored in a consistent manner. Organizations with data warehouses may integrate databases from both inside and outside the company. Managing a data warehouse effectively requires considerable computing power and expertise. As a result, data warehouse companies exist that provide this service for companies in return for a fee.[9] Data warehousing allows for sophisticated analysis, such as data mining, discussed in Chapter 7.

Data warehouse
The multitiered computer storehouse of current and historical data.

Input Management

How does data end up in a data warehouse where it can be used by a decision support system? In other words, how is the input managed? Input includes all the numerical, text, voice, and image data that enter the DSS. Systematic accumulation of pertinent, timely, and accurate data is essential to the success of a decision support system.

DSS managers, systems analysts, and programmers are responsible for the decision support system as a whole, but many functions within an organization provide input data. Marketing researchers, accountants, corporate librarians, sales personnel, production managers, and many others within the organization help to collect data and provide input for the DSS. Input data can also come from external sources.

EXHIBIT 2.3 Five Major Sources of Marketing Input for Decision Support Systems

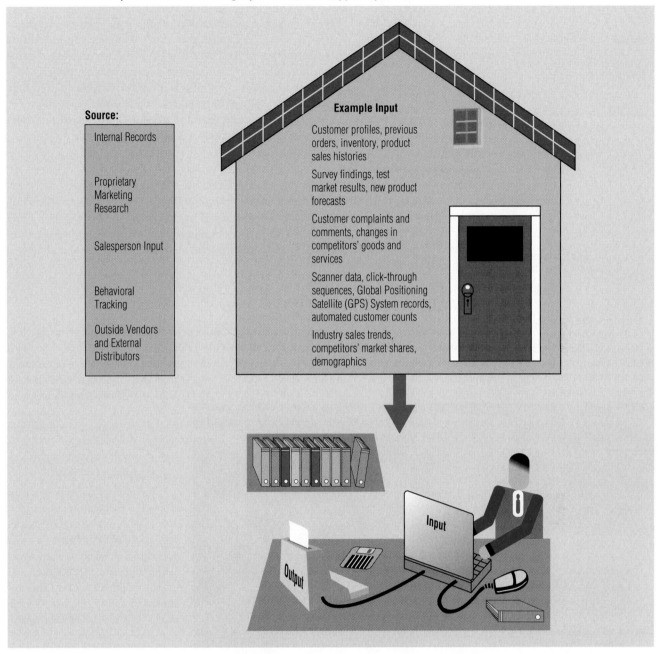

Exhibit 2.3 shows five major sources of data input: internal records, proprietary marketing research, salesperson input, behavioral tracking, and outside vendors and external distributors of data. Each source can provide valuable input.

INTERNAL RECORDS

Internal records, such as accounting reports of sales and inventory figures, provide considerable data that may become useful information for marketing managers. An effective data collection system establishes orderly procedures to ensure that data about costs, shipments, inventory, sales, and other aspects of regular operations are routinely collected and entered into the computer.

■ PROPRIETARY MARKETING RESEARCH

Proprietary marketing research
The gathering of new data to investigate specific problems.

Marketing research has already been defined as a broad set of procedures and methods. To clarify the DSS concept, consider a narrower view of marketing research. **Proprietary marketing research** emphasizes the company's gathering of new data. Few proprietary marketing research procedures and methods are conducted regularly or continuously. Instead, research projects conducted to study specific company problems generate data; this is proprietary marketing research. Providing managers with nonroutine data that otherwise would not be available is a major function of proprietary marketing research. Earlier, we discussed four categories of research. Proprietary marketing research may involve either the "testing" and/or "issues" types of research.

■ SALESPERSON INPUT

Salespeople work in firms' external environments, so they commonly provide essential marketing data. Sales representatives' reports frequently alert managers to changes in competitors' prices and new product offerings. It also may involve the types of complaints salespeople are hearing form customers. As trends become evident, this data may become marketing intelligence, leading to a change in product design or service delivery.

Scanner data
The accumulated records resulting from point of sale data recordings.

■ BEHAVIORAL TRACKING

GPS devices, like those used in automobile navigation systems, allow management to track delivery personnel or even actual customer behavior.

Modern technology provides new ways of tracking human behavior. Global positioning satellite (GPS) systems allow management to track the whereabouts of delivery personnel at all times. This is the same system that provides directions through an automobile's navigation system. For example, if your delivery person takes a quick break for nine holes of golf or decides to stop at Neil's Bar for a couple of beers mid-afternoon, management can spot these as deviations from the appropriate delivery route are noted. Thus, it can help track which employees are doing their jobs well.

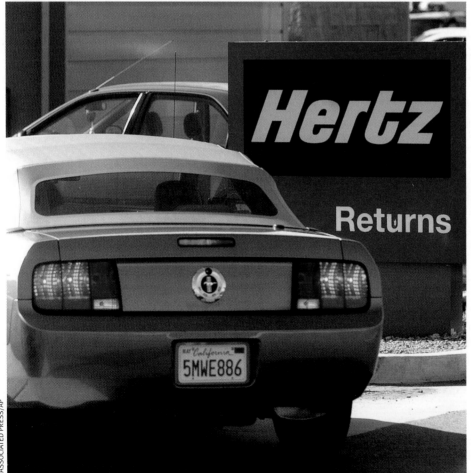

Technology also allows firms to track actual customer behavior. While it's possible that GPS tracking data of customers is also sometimes possible, as the photograph suggests, the Internet also greatly facilitates customer behavior tracking. For instance, Google tracks the "click-through" sequence of customers. Therefore, if a customer is searching for information on refrigerators, and then goes to BestBuy.com, Google can track this behavior and use the information to let BestBuy know how important it is to advertise on Google and even automate pricing for advertisers.[10]

Purchase behavior can also be tracked at the point of sale. **Scanner data** refers to the accumulated records resulting from point of sale data recordings. In other words, each time products are scanned at a

RESEARCHSNAPSHOT

Staying Home at Home Depot

The DSS of any organization is no better than the quality of the data input to its data warehouse. How can firms make sure that the input remains relevant and retains a "high-touch" component in a "high-tech" world?

Home Depot has always tried to make sure its executives "stay in touch" by requiring them to spend a substantial amount of time on the sales floor of a Home Depot store, which means that one of the folks in the bright orange apron helping you choose the right flush valve may well be a six-figure executive. Thus, the people who decide what should go into the data warehouse and how the DSS will use it maintain an appreciation for the types of decisions faced by Home Depot store managers each and every day. Home Depot even asks outside suppliers who may

be involved in information technology (IT) design to spend a few days in an actual Home Depot store. Thus, as Home Depot implements key innovations in its data networks, the people helping it to do so understand what the information needs of employees really are. Even Home Depot's outside directors meet with middle managers and conduct store visits so that they can provide more meaningful advice to senior executives. Part of this advice concerns the data needs of Home Depot managers.

Do you think such a plan would be similarly successful for a company like Krispy Kreme?

Sources: Alberts, Brad (2001), "Home Depot's Special Projects Support Team Powers Information Management for Business Needs," Journal of Organizational Excellence, 21 (Winter), 3–15; Lublin, Joanne (2005), "Home Depot Board Gains Insight from Trenches," The Wall Street Journal (October 10), B3.

©SUSAN VAN ETTEN

checkout counter, the information can be stored. The term *single-source* data refers to a system's ability to gather several types of interrelated data, such as type of purchase, use of a sales promotion, or advertising frequency data, from a single source in a format that will facilitate integration, comparison, and analysis.

OUTSIDE VENDORS AND EXTERNAL DISTRIBUTORS

Outside vendors and external distributors market information as their products. Many organizations specialize in the collection and publication of high-quality information. One outside vendor, the ACNielsen Company, provides television program ratings, audience counts, and information about the demographic composition of television viewer groups. Other vendors specialize in the distribution of information. Public libraries have always purchased information, traditionally in the form of books, and they have served as distributors of this information.

Media representatives often provide useful demographic and lifestyle data about their audiences. *Advertising Age, The Wall Street Journal, Sales and Marketing Management,* and other trade- and business-oriented publications are important sources of information. These publications keep managers up-to-date about the economy, competitors' activities, and other aspects of the marketing environment.

Companies called *data specialists* record and store certain marketing information. Computer technology has changed the way many of these organizations supply data, favoring the development of computerized databases.

Computerized Data Archives

Historically, collections of organized and readily retrievable data were available in printed form at libraries. The *Statistical Abstract of the United States,* which is filled with tables of statistical facts, is a typical example. In recent years, the *Statistical Abstract* has become available electronically. Users can purchase it via CD-ROM or access it via the Internet. The entire 2000 census as well as projections through the current year is available in print, CD-ROM, and via the Internet at http://www.census.gov. More and more data are available in digitized form every day.

RESEARCHSNAPSHOT

We Are Resetting Our Clocks to Real Time

Imagine a world in which time seems to vanish and space seems completely malleable, where the gap between need or desire and fulfillment collapses to zero, where distance equals a microsecond in lapsed connection time—a virtual world created at your command. Imagine a world in which everything you do, from work to education, is clothed as an entertainment-like experience, veiled by technology so subtle and transparent that you have no idea it is there at all. Habits, attitudes, opinions, preferences, expectations, demands, perceptions, and needs all adapt unwittingly to an environment in which immediacy rules.

All of this may sound like material for a science fiction thriller. But it is very nearly the world we are living in today.

Technology is transforming our existence in profound ways, and the pace of change is speeding up, not slowing down. Almost all technology today is focused on compressing to zero the amount of time it takes to acquire and use information, to learn, to make decisions, to initiate action, to deploy resources, to innovate. When action and response are simultaneous, we are in *real time*.

The change in our consciousness of time is the creation of ubiquitous programmable technology producing results at the click of a mouse or the touch of a button or key. Real time occurs when time and distance vanish, when action and response are simultaneous.

©OWAKI-KULLA/CORBIS

Source: McKenna, Regis (1997), Real Time. Boston: Harvard Business School Press.

Numerous computerized search and retrieval systems and electronic databases are available as subscription services or in libraries. Just as a student can query the school library to find information for a term paper without leaving home, data acquisition for businesses has also become far more convenient in recent years. Today, business people access online information search and retrieval services, such as Dow Jones News Retrieval and Bloomberg Financial Markets, without leaving their offices. In fact, some information services can be accessed from remote locations via digital wireless devices.

Modern library patrons can command a computer to search indexes and retrieve databases from a range of vendors. Just as wholesalers collect goods from manufacturers and offer them for sale to retailers who then provide them to consumers, many information firms serve as data wholesalers. **Data wholesalers** put together consortia of data sources into packages that are offered to municipal, corporate, and university libraries for a fee. Information consumers then access the data through these libraries. Some of the better known *databases* include Wilson Business Center, Hoovers, PROQUEST, INFOTRAC, DIALOG (Dialog Information Services, Inc.), LEXIS-NEXIS, and Dow Jones News Retrieval Services. These databases provide all types of information including recent news stories and data tables charting statistical trends.

Data wholesalers
Companies that put together consortia of data sources into packages that are offered to municipal, corporate, and university libraries for a fee.

DIALOG, for example, maintains more than 600 databases. A typical database may have a million or more records, each consisting of a one- or two-paragraph abstract that summarizes the major points of a published article along with bibliographic information. One of the DIALOG databases, ABI/INFORM, abstracts significant articles in more than 1,000 current business and management journals. Many computerized archives provide full-text downloads of published articles about companies and various research topics.

Exhibit 2.4 illustrates the services provided by two popular vendors of information services that electronically index numerous databases. For a more extensive listing, see the *Gale Directory of Databases*.[11]

Several types of databases from outside vendors and external distributors are so fundamental to decision support systems that they deserve further explanation. The following sections discuss statistical databases, financial databases, and video databases in slightly more detail.

STATISTICAL DATABASES

Statistical databases contain numerical data for market analysis and forecasting. Often demographic, sales, and other relevant marketing variables are recorded by geographical area. Geographic

EXHIBIT 2.4 **Vendors of Information Services and Electronic Indexing**

Vendors	Selected Databases	Type of Data
DIALOG	ABI/INFORM	Summaries and citations from over 1,000 academic management, marketing, and general business journals with full text of more than 500 of these publications
	ASI (American Statistics Index)	Abstracts and indexes of federal government statistical publications
	PROMT (The Predicast Overview of Markets and Technologies)	Summaries and full text from 1,000 U.S. and international business and trade journals, industry newsletters, newspapers, and market research studies; information about industries and companies, including the products and technologies they develop and the markets in which they compete
	Investext	Full text of over 2 million company, industry, and geographic research reports written by analysts at more than 600 leading investment banks, brokerage houses, and consulting firms worldwide
Dow Jones News Retrieval	Business Newsstand	Articles from *New York Times, Los Angeles Times, Washington Post*, and other leading newspapers and magazines
	Historical Market Data Center	Historical data on securities, dividends, and exchange rates
	Web Center	Information obtained from searches of corporate, industry, government, and news websites

information systems use these *geographical databases* and powerful software to prepare computer maps of relevant variables. Companies such as Claritas, Urban Decision Systems, and CACI all offer geographic/demographic databases that are widely used in industry.

One source for these huge data warehouses is scanner data. Substituting mechanized record-keeping like optical scanners for human record-keeping results in greater accuracy and more rapid feedback about store activity.

One weakness of scanner data is that not all points of sale have scanner technology. For instance, many convenience stores lack scanner technology, as do most vending machines. Thus, those purchases go unrecorded. The Universal Product Code, or UPC, contains information on the category of goods, the manufacturer, and product identification based on size, flavor, color, and so on. This is what the optical scanner actually reads. If a large percentage of a brand's sales occur in environments without the ability to read the UPC code, the marketer should be aware that the scanner data may not be representative.

FINANCIAL DATABASES

Competitors' and customers' financial data, such as income statements and balance sheets, may interest managers. These are easy to access in financial databases. CompuStat publishes an extensive financial database on thousands of companies, broken down by industry and other criteria. To illustrate the depth of this pool of information, CompuStat's Global Advantage offers extensive data on 6,650 companies in more than thirty countries in Europe, the Pacific Rim, and North America.

VIDEO DATABASES

Video databases and streaming media are having a major impact on the marketing of many goods and services. For example, movie studios provide clips of upcoming films and advertising agencies

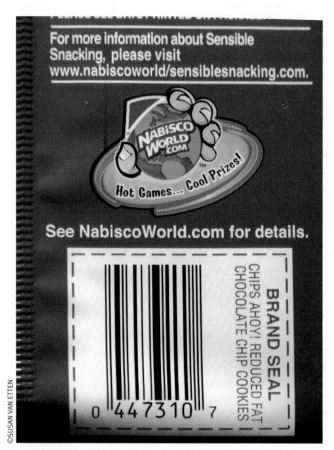

Statistical information has its limitations. When a product is sold in an environment that cannot read scanner data, important information about that product is not available for marketing analysis and forecasting.

put television commercials on the Internet (see http://www .adcritic.com). McDonald's maintains a digital archive of television commercials and other video footage to share with its franchisers around the world. The video database enables franchisers and their advertising agencies to create local advertising without filming the same types of scenes already archived. Just imagine the value of digital video databases to advertising agencies' decision support systems.

Networks and Electronic Data Interchange

Individual personal computers can be connected through networks to other computers. Networking involves linking two or more computers to share data and software.

Electronic data interchange (EDI) systems integrate one company's computer system directly with another company's system. Much of the input to a company's decision support system may come through networks from other companies' computers. Companies such as Computer Technology Corporation and Microelectronics market data services that allow corporations to exchange business information with suppliers or customers. For example, every evening Wal-Mart transmits millions of characters of data about the day's sales to its apparel suppliers. Wrangler, a supplier of blue jeans, for instance, shares the data and a model that interprets the data. Wrangler also shares software applications that act to replenish stock in Wal-Mart stores. This DSS lets Wrangler's managers know when to send specific quantities of specific sizes and colors of jeans to specific stores from specific warehouses. The result is a learning loop that lowers inventory costs and leads to fewer stockouts.

Electronic data interchange (EDI)
Type of exchange that occurs when one company's computer system is integrated with another company's system.

The Internet and Research

When most readers of this book were born, the Internet had yet to enter the everyday vocabulary. In fact, few people outside of a small number of universities and the U.S. Department of Defense had any clue as to what the Internet might be. In the 1960s, mainframe computers revolutionized research by allowing researchers to use research techniques involving large numbers of mathematical computations that previously would have been impossible or, at the least, impractical. In the 1980s, the mainframe computing power of the 1960s, which was available primarily in large universities, government agencies, and very large companies, was transformed into something that could go on nearly every businessperson's desktop. The personal computer (PC) and simple operating systems like DOS and eventually Windows revolutionized many business applications by making computing power relatively inexpensive and convenient. Today, the widespread usage of the Internet is perhaps the single biggest change agent in marketing research. Since most readers are no doubt experienced in using the Internet, we highlight a few terms and facts about the Internet that are especially useful in understanding marketing research.

In the following pages we discuss the World Wide Web and how to use the Internet for research. However, keep in mind that the Internet is constantly changing. The description of the Internet, especially home page addresses, may be out of date by the time this book is published. Be aware that the Internet of today will not be the Internet of tomorrow.

What Exactly is the Internet?

The **Internet** is a worldwide network of computers that allows users access to data, information, and feedback from distant sources. It functions as the world's largest public library, proving access to a seemingly endless range of data. Many people believe the Internet is the most important communications medium since television.

The Internet began in the 1960s as an experimental connection between computers at Stanford University, the University of California at Santa Barbara, the University of California at Los Angeles, and the University of Utah, in conjunction with the Department of Defense.[12] The Department of Defense was involved because it wanted to develop a communications network that could survive nuclear war. The Internet gradually grew into a nationwide network of connected computers, and now it is a worldwide network often referred to as the "information superhighway."

The Internet has no central computer; instead, each message sent bears an address code that lets a sender forward a message to a desired destination from any computer linked to the Net. Many benefits of the Internet arise because the Internet is a collection of thousands of small networks, both domestic and foreign, rather than a single computer operation.

A domain is typically a company name, institutional name, or organizational name associated with a host computer. A **host** is where the content for a particular website physically resides and is accessed. For example, *Forbes* magazine's Internet edition is located at http://forbes.com. The "com" indicates this domain is a commercial site. George State University can be virtually reached at http://www.gsu.edu. Educational sites end in "edu." The United States Marine Corps can be found at http://www.marines.mil, and many government sites, such as the U.S. House of Representatives, end with "gov," as in http://www.house.gov. Many nonprofit organizations end in "org," as in http://www.ams-web.org, the web home for the Academy of Marketing Science. Web addresses outside the United States often end in abbreviations for their country such as "ca," "de," or "uk" for Canada, Germany (Deutschland), and the United Kingdom, respectively.

Internet
A worldwide network of computers that allows users access to information from distant sources.

Host
Where the content for a particular website physically resides and is accessed.

How is the Internet Useful in Research?

The Internet is useful to researchers in many ways. In fact, more and more applications become known as the technology grows and is adopted by more and more users. The Internet is particularly useful as a source of available data and as a way of collecting data.

ACCESSING AVAILABLE DATA

The Internet allows instantaneous and effortless access to a great deal of information. Noncommercial and commercial organizations make a wealth of data and other resources available on the Internet. For example, the U.S. Library of Congress provides full text of all versions of House and Senate legislation and full text of the *Congressional Record*. The Internal Revenue Service makes it possible to download an income tax form. Thomson Learning (http://thomsonlearning.com) and its South-Western college division (http://www.thomsonedu.com) have online directories that allow college professors to access information about the company and its textbooks. The Gale Research Database, which can be accessed through the Business Resource Center made available to users of this text, provides basic statistics and news stories on literally thousands of companies worldwide. Thus, information that formally took a great deal of time and effort to obtain is now available with a few clicks. Further, since it can often be electronically downloaded or copied, it isn't necessary for a person to transcribe the data. Therefore, it is available in a more error-free form.

COLLECTING DATA

The Internet is also revolutionizing the way researchers collect data. Later in this text, we discuss in more detail the use of web-based surveys. In other words, questionnaires can be posted on a website and respondents can be invited to go to the particular URL and participate in the survey. This cuts down on the expense associated with traditional mail surveys and also reduces error since the data can be automatically recorded rather than transcribed from a paper form into an electronic format.

TOTHEPOINT

*The Net is 10.5 on
the Richter scale of
economic change.*

—Nicholas Negroponte

Furthermore, when a consumer uses the World Wide Web, his or her usage leaves a record that can be traced and observed. For instance, we can know how many pages were visited at some shopping site before a purchase was made. We can know if products were abandoned in the "virtual cart" without a purchase being made. Online auctions provide another mechanism to track consumers' behavior. Prototype products can be offered for sale in an online auction to help assist with product design, forecasting demand, and setting an appropriate price.[13]

Navigating the Internet

**World Wide Web
(WWW)**
A portion of the Internet that is
a system of computer servers
that organize information into
documents called web pages.

The **World Wide Web (WWW)** refers specifically to that portion of the Internet made up of servers that support a retrieval system that organizes information into documents called web pages. World Wide Web documents, which may include graphic images, video clips, and sound clips, are formatted in programming languages, such as HTML (HyperText Markup Language) and XML (Extensible Markup Language) that allow for displaying, linking, and sharing of information on the Internet.

Content providers
Parties that furnish information
on the World Wide Web.

Parties that furnish information on the World Wide Web are called **content providers**. Content providers maintain websites. A website consists of one or more web pages with related information about a particular topic; for example, a university website might include pages about its mission, courses, and faculty (see http://www.gsu.edu, for example). The introductory page or opening screen is called the home page because it provides basic information about the purpose of the document along with a menu of selections or links that lead to other screens with more specific information. Thus, each page can have connections, or hyperlinks, to other pages, which may be on any computer connected to the Internet. People using the World Wide Web may be viewing information that is stored on a host computer or on a machine halfway around the world.

**Uniform Resource
Locator (URL)**
A website address that web
browsers recognize.

Most web browsers also allow the user to enter a **Uniform Resource Locator (URL)** into the program. The URL is really just a website address that web browsers recognize. Many websites allow any user or visitor access without previous approval. However, many commercial sites require that the user have a valid account and password before access is granted.

Search engine
A computerized directory that
allows anyone to search the
World Wide Web for information
using a keyword search.

One of the most basic research tools available via the Internet is a search engine. A **search engine** is a computerized directory that allows anyone to search the World Wide Web for information based on a keyword search. A **keyword search** takes place as the search engine searches through millions of web pages for documents containing the keywords. Some of the most comprehensive and accurate search engines are:

Keyword search
Takes place as the search
engine searches through
millions of web pages for
documents containing the
keywords.

Yahoo!	http://www.yahoo.com
Google	http://www.google.com
Hotbot	http://www.hotbot.com
Go network	http://www.go.com
Excite	http://www.excite.com
Lycos	http://www.lycos.com
Ask Jeeves	http://www.ask.com
WebCrawler	http://www.webcrawler.com

Google revolutionized search engines by changing the way the search was actually conducted. It searches based on a mathematical theory known as *graph theory*.[14] Google greatly improved the accuracy and usefulness of the search results obtained from a keyword search. Exhibit 2.5 illustrates the Google interface and expanded Google options. For instance, if one clicks on Google Scholar, a search of basic research papers on any given topic indicated by the keywords can be performed.

Interactive Media and Environmental Scanning

Interactive medium
A medium, such as the Internet,
that a person can use to
communicate with and interact
with other users.

The Internet is an **interactive medium** because users click commands and often get customized responses. So the user and equipment can have a continuing conversation. Two or more individuals who communicate one-to-one via e-mail using an Internet service provider are also using interactive

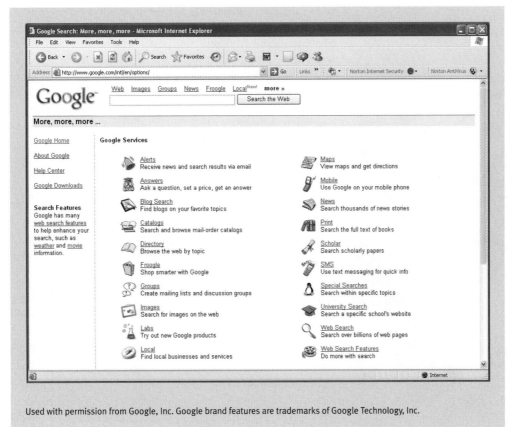

Used with permission from Google, Inc. Google brand features are trademarks of Google Technology, Inc.

EXHIBIT 2.5
The Google Web Interface

media. So are individuals who communicate with many senders and receivers via bulletin boards or chat rooms. Because of its vastness, the Internet is an especially useful source for scanning many types of environmental changes. **Environmental scanning** entails all information gathering designed to detect changes in the external operating environment of the firm. These things are usually beyond the control of the firm, but they still can have a significant impact on firm performance.

Ford Motor Company maintains an Internet-based relationship marketing program that, among other things, helps the automaker scan its environment using the Internet. Its dealer website creates a centralized communication service linking dealers via an Internet connection. Its buyer website allows prospective buyers to visit a virtual showroom and to get price quotes and financial information. Its owner website allows an owner who registers and supplies pertinent vehicle information to get free e-mail and other ownership perks. A perk might be a free Hertz upgrade or an autographed photo of one of the Ford-sponsored NASCAR drivers. In return, Ford collects data at all levels, which allow managers to scan for trends and apply what they learn at a local level.

Information Technology

Data and information can be delivered to consumers or other end users via either **pull technology** or **push technology**. Conventionally, consumers request information from a web page and the browser then determines a response. Thus, the consumer is essentially asking for the data. In this case, it is said to be pulled through the channel. The opposite of pull is push. Push technology sends data to a user's computer without a request being made. In other words, software is used to guess what information might be interesting to consumers based on the pattern of previous responses.

Smart information delivery (known by a variety of technical names, including *push phase technology*) allows a website, such as the Yahoo portal, to become a one-on-one medium for each individual user. Today's information technology uses "smart agents" or "intelligent agents" to deliver customized content to a viewer's desktop. **Smart agent software** is capable of learning

Environmental scanning
Entails all information gathering designed to detect changes in the external operating environment of the firm.

Pull technology
Consumers request information from a web page and the browser then determines a response; the consumer is essentially asking for the data.

Push technology
Sends data to a user's computer without a request being made; software is used to guess what information might be interesting to consumers based on the pattern of previous responses.

Smart agent software
Software capable of learning an Internet user's preferences and automatically searching out information in selected websites and then distributing it.

©DAVID YOUNG-WOLFF/PHOTOEDIT

The iPod offers one example of how modern technology makes it possible to store and deliver information. Various models can capture, store, and deliver hundreds of songs to their owners.

Cookies
Small computer files that a content provider can save onto the computer of someone who visits its website.

Intranet
A company's private data network that uses Internet standards and technology.

an Internet user's preferences and automatically searching out information and distributing the information to a user's computer. My Yahoo! and MyExcite are portal services that personalize web pages. Users can get stock quotes relevant to their portfolios, news about favorite sports teams, local weather, and other personalized information. Users can customize the sections of the service they want delivered. With push technology, pertinent content is delivered to the viewer's desktop without the user having to do the searching.

Cookies, in computer terminology, are small computer files that record a user's web usage history. If a person looks up a weather report by keying in a zip code into a personalized web page, the fact that the user visited the website and the zip code entered are recorded in the cookie. This is a clue that tells where the person lives (or maybe where he or she may be planning to visit). Websites can then direct information to that consumer based on information in the cookie. So, someone in College Station, Texas, may receive pop-up ads for restaurants in College Station. Information technology is having a major impact on the nature of marketing research. We will explore this topic in several places throughout this book.

Intranets

An **Intranet** is a company's private data network that uses Internet standards and technology.[15] The information on an Intranet—data, graphics, video, and voice—is available only inside the organization or to those individuals whom the organization deems as appropriate participants. Thus, a key difference between the Internet and an Intranet is that security software programs, or "firewalls," are installed to limit access to only those employees authorized to enter the system. Intranets then serve as secure knowledge portals that contain substantial amounts of organizational memory and can integrate it with information from outside sources. The challenge in designing an Intranet is making sure that it is capable of delivering relevant data to decision makers. Research suggests that relevance is a key in getting knowledge workers to actually make use of company Intranets.[16]

The Intranet can be extended to include key consumers as a source of valuable research. Their participation in the Intranet can lead to new product developments. Texas Instruments has successfully established an Intranet that integrated communications between customers and researchers leading to the introduction and modification of its calculators.[17] An Intranet lets authorized users, possibly including key customers, to look at product drawings, employee newsletters, sales figures, and other kinds of company information.

Internet2

As we mentioned earlier, information technology changes rapidly. As sophisticated as the Internet and Intranets are today, new technologies, such as Internet2, will dramatically enhance researchers' ability to answer marketing problems in the future.

Internet2 (http://www.internet2.edu/) is a collaborative effort involving just over 200 universities, government entities including the military, and sixty corporate organizations in the United States. The project hopes to recreate some of the cooperative spirit that created the Internet originally. Internet2 users are limited to those involved with the affiliate organizations. The hope is to create a faster, more powerful Internet by providing multimodal access, employing more wireless technologies, and building in global trading mechanisms. Right now, the Internet2 is a research tool for the universities and organizations involved in its development.[18]

Summary

1. Distinguish between the concepts of data, information, and intelligence. Increased global competition and technological advances in interactive media have spurred development of global information systems. A global information system is an organized collection of computer hardware, software, data, and personnel designed to capture, store, update, manipulate, analyze, and immediately display information about worldwide business activity.

From a research perspective, there is a difference between data, information, and intelligence. Data are simply facts or recorded measures of certain phenomena (things); information is data formatted (structured) to support decision making or define the relationship between two facts. Market intelligence is the subset of data and information that actually has some explanatory power enabling effective decisions to be made.

2. Describe the four characteristics that explain the usefulness of data. The usefulness of data to management can be described based on four characteristics: relevance, quality, timeliness, and completeness. Relevant data have the characteristic of pertinence to the situation at hand. The information is useful. The quality of information is the degree to which data represent the true situation. High-quality data are accurate, valid, and reliable. High-quality data represent reality faithfully and present a good picture of reality. Timely information is obtained at the right time. Computerized information systems can record events and present information soon after a transaction takes place, improving timeliness. Complete information is the right quantity of information. Marketing managers must have sufficient information to relate all aspects of their decisions together.

3. Identify the purpose of research in assisting marketing operations. A computer-based marketing decision support system helps decision makers confront problems through direct interactions with databases and analytical models. A DSS stores data and transforms them into organized information that is easily accessible to marketing managers.

4. Explain what a decision support system is and what it does. A database is a collection of raw data arranged logically and organized in a form that can be stored and processed by a computer. Marketing data come from four major sources: internal records, proprietary marketing research, marketing intelligence, and outside vendors and external distributors. Each source can provide valuable input. Because most companies compile and store many different databases, they often develop data warehousing systems. Data warehousing is the process allowing important day-to-day operational data to be stored and organized for simplified access. More specifically, a data warehouse is the multitiered computer storehouse of current and historical data. Data warehouse management requires that the detailed data from operational systems be extracted, transformed, and stored (warehoused) so that the various database tables from both inside and outside the company are consistent. All of this feeds into the decision support system that automates or assists business decision making.

Numerous database search and retrieval systems are available by subscription or in libraries. Computer-assisted database searching has made the collection of external data faster and easier. Marketers refer to many different types of databases.

Although personal computers work independently, they can connect to other computers in networks to share data and software. Electronic data interchange (EDI) allows one company's computer system to join directly to another company's system.

5. Identify the major categories of databases. The Internet is a worldwide network of computers that allows users access to information and documents from distant sources. It is a combination of a worldwide communication system and the world's largest public library. The World Wide Web is a system of thousands of interconnected pages, or documents, that can be easily accessed with web browsers and search engines.

An Intranet is a company's private data network that uses Internet standards and technology. The information on an Intranet—data, graphics, video, and voice—is available only inside the organization. Thus, a key difference between the Internet and an Intranet is that "firewalls," or security software programs, are installed to limit access to only those employees authorized to enter the system.

A company uses Internet features to build its own Intranet. Groupware and other technology can facilitate the transfer of data, information, and knowledge. In organizations that practice knowledge management, Intranets function to make the knowledge of company experts more accessible throughout their organizations.

Key Terms and Concepts

Data
Information
Market intelligence
Relevance
Data quality
Timeliness
Information completeness
Knowledge
Knowledge management
Global information system
Decision support system (DSS)

Customer relationship management (CRM)
Database
Data warehousing
Data warehouse
Proprietary marketing research
Scanner data
Data wholesalers
Electronic data interchange (EDI)
Internet
Host
World Wide Web (WWW)

Content provider
Uniform Resource Locator (URL)
Search engine
Keyword search
Interactive medium
Environmental scanning
Pull technology
Push technology
Smart agent software
Cookies
Intranet

Questions for Review and Critical Thinking

1. What is the difference between data, information, and intelligence?
2. What are the characteristics of useful information?
3. What is the key question distinguishing relevant data from irrelevant data?
4. Define *knowledge management*. What is its purpose within an organization?
5. What types of databases might be found in the following organizations?
   a. Holiday Inn
   b. A Major University Athletic Department
   c. Anheuser-Busch
6. What type of operational questions could a delivery firm like FedEx expect to automate with the company's decision support system?
7. What makes a decision support system successful?
8. What is data warehousing?
9. **'NET** How does data warehousing assist decision making? Visit http://www.kbb.com. While there, choose two cars that you might consider buying and compare them. Which do you like the best? What would you do now? What are at least three pieces of data that should be stored in a data warehouse somewhere based on your interaction with *Kelly Blue Book?*

10. **'NET** Give three examples of computerized databases that are available at your college or university library.
11. **'NET** What is the difference between the Internet and an Intranet?
12. Suppose a retail firm is interested in studying the effect of lighting on customer purchase behavior. Which of the following pieces of information is the least relevant and why?
    a. Amount of natural light in the store
    b. The compensation system for store salespeople
    c. The color of the walls in the store
    d. The type of lighting: fluorescent or incandescent
13. **'NET** Imagine the data collected by eBay each day. List at least five types of data that are collected through the daily operations. Describe each in terms of it illustrating data, information, or intelligence. Make sure you list at least one of each.
14. How could New Balance, a maker of athletic shoes, use RFID technology to collect data?
15. **'NET** The Spider's Apprentice is a website that provides many useful tips about using search engines. Go to http://www.monash.com/spidap.html, then click on The Spider's Apprentice to learn the ins and outs of search engines.

Research Activities

1. **'NET** To learn more about data warehousing, go to http://www.datawarehousing.org.
2. **'NET** Use the Internet to see if you can find information to answer the following questions:
   a. What is the weather in Denver today?
   b. What are four restaurants in the French Quarter in New Orleans?
   c. What is the population of Brazil?

Case 2.1 Harvard Cooperative Society

From his office window overlooking the main floor of the Harvard Cooperative Society, CEO Jerry Murphy can glance down and see customers shopping.[19] They make their way through the narrow aisles of the crowded department store, picking up a sweatshirt here, trying on a baseball cap there, checking out the endless array of merchandise that bears the Harvard University insignia.

Watching Murphy, you can well imagine the Coop's founders, who started the store in 1882, peering through the tiny window-panes to keep an eye on the shop floor. Was the Harvard Square store attracting steady traffic? Were the college students buying enough books and supplies for the Coop to make a profit? Back then, it was tough to answer those questions precisely. The owners had to watch and wait, relying only on their gut feelings to know how things were going from minute to minute.

Now, more than a hundred years later, Murphy can tell you, down to the last stock-keeping unit, how he's doing at any given moment. His window on the business is the PC that sits on his desk.

All day long it delivers up-to-the-minute, easy-to-read electronic reports on what's selling and what's not, which items are running low in inventory and which have fallen short of forecast. In a matter of seconds, the computer can report gross margins for any product or supplier, and Murphy can decide whether the margins are fat enough to justify keeping the supplier or product on board. "We were in the 1800s, and we had to move ahead," he says of the $55 million business.

Questions

1. What is a decision support system? What advantages does a decision support system have for a business like the Harvard Cooperative Society?
2. How would the decision support system of a business like the Harvard Cooperative Society differ from that of a major corporation?
3. Briefly outline the components of the Harvard Cooperative Society's decision support system.

Video Case 2.2 Wine.com

Wine.com advertises itself as the "world's largest wine store." With over 14,000 fine wines in its website inventory, it probably is.

The company was launched in the nineties as an e-commerce venture by Peter Granoff, one of the nation's leading wine experts with over twenty years of wine-selling experience, and Robert Olson, an expert in the computer industry. The two were talking over a glass of wine about recent trends in the wine industry that threatened both small producers and consumers when they had a brainstorm about how to get a broad variety of fine wines into the retail market. They took their initial program to a couple of wineries and asked if the producers thought their idea would work.

With positive feedback, they "went live," first building their site and then advertising it in appropriate channels both online and offline. Wine.com is one of the first merchants to get started as a purely e-commerce business. A positive aspect of web selling is that it collapses the geography of the retail base, but a challenging reality for this product is that it has a narrow market segment—adults who drink wine and are willing to spend time in choosing the wine they drink.

Granoff explains that marketing initiatives are the important key to branding their company on and off the web. The company has a multimillion dollar advertising campaign. It maintains active affiliate programs with other online products and other e-commerce ventures like Amazon.com. It advertises extensively on television and radio and in print media like *Food & Wine* and *The Wall Street Journal*.

Wine itself has a "passionate customer base," and the company does its best to find the best wines for its customers. Experts review

hundreds of samples of wine each month. Wine.com educates consumers about fine wines, helps them find the perfect bottle of wine for a reasonable price, and then delivers the wine directly to their doorsteps. The website is designed to put people at ease and to de-mystify the process of selecting a wine. The wine retailer also retains a full-time customer-support staff that provides the individual attention that customers would expect in a brick-and-mortar wine shop. Customers can contact the company online, through e-mail, and by phone. When customers put in an order, they immediately receive an automated confirmation of their order.

Granoff identifies the metrics that are the best indicators of Wine.com's success: a branding proposition that is working, a customer acquisition model that is working, retention rates that are where they need to be, and a high-visibility public relations and advertising program.

The costs and complexity of the infrastructure in an e-commerce wine business are challenging. Their revenues are ramping between 300 to 500 percent every year, so Wine.com must rethink their fundamental business processes every four to six months. "The speed of the ramp, more than anything else, cuts across everything that we do," says Granoff. And it's the speed of the ramp "that is so exciting."

Questions

1. What suggestions might you have for Wine.com's customer relationship management?
2. In the future, Wine.com wants to expand to Australia, Asia, South Africa, and countries in Europe. How could a global information system help the company?

Video Case 2.3 IBM: Enterprise Resource Planning

 By centralizing information and making it more widely available, IBM's ERP (Enterprise Resource Planning) system has the potential to make companies much more competitive and responsive.[20] Here is what IBM says about ERP:

ERP solutions are effective at streamlining business processes that cut across the functional areas of your business. ERP brings together fragmented operations, often replacing a multiplicity of legacy systems. By sharing common information across an integrated set of application modules, ERP can speed up transactions. For instance, ERP can consolidate financial records, allowing you to close the books faster and more accurately.

ERP can help you better manage your inventory, driving dramatic cost savings. ERP can map customer orders to your production plans, helping to improve the cycle time to respond to customer demand. And ERP can help eliminate process duplication, wait times, and information errors, yielding productivity improvements for your professionals. In addition, the regimen of an ERP implementation forces you to look at how you run your business—your processes, practices, and procedures. ERP implementations are a great opportunity to institutionalize a number of changes, many of which you may have been considering for some time.

While ERP is very good at driving improvements, its focus is inward, within your own enterprise. However, if your company's top challenges involve relationships with your customers or trading partnerships with your suppliers, you may want to consider other solutions—either implemented individually or together with an ERP solution. Also, given the time it takes to fully deploy an ERP solution, you may want to consider a phased approach that includes these additional areas. This will ensure that the solution you implement meets your needs for the coming years, not just your immediate problem.

IBM offers industry expertise to know what it takes to differentiate your business. Plus, IBM offers solution expertise spanning ERP, e-commerce, supply chain, customer relationship management, business intelligence, and more, to help you decide the combination that's best for your business.

Question

Different companies use different terminology for global information systems and decision support systems. After viewing the video, explain how IBM's ERP system parallels the book's definition and explanation of global information systems and decision support systems.

LEARNING OUTCOMES

CHAPTER 3
THE MARKETING RESEARCH PROCESS

After studying this chapter, you should

1. Be able to define decision making and understand the role research plays in making decisions
2. Classify marketing research as either exploratory research, descriptive research, or causal research
3. Be able to list the major phases of the marketing research process and the steps within each
4. Understand the concepts of theory and hypothesis and the critical role they play in research
5. Be able to explain the difference between a research project and a research program

Chapter Vignette: The Changing Educational Market

Students seeking a higher education enjoy many more choices than did their parents. Universities offer new degree programs in varied and specific fields including areas like sports marketing and gaming management. However, it isn't simply the fields of study that may be new, but also the manner of study. Options for nontraditional students who have difficulty attending day classes or devoting years of study to obtaining a degree have grown exponentially. The University of Phoenix, Strayer University, and Nova Southeast typify institutions that specialize in catering to those seeking a nontraditional degree program. These competitive pressures have led even the most traditional universities to rethink the traditional "sage on the stage" approach and conventional academic calendars.

The market for the MBA degree is particularly competitive. Students pursue their MBA either traditionally, in weekend only programs, at night school, online, or in some combination. Over a quarter of a million U.S. students alone attend MBA classes of one form or another at any given time. In urban areas, such as the Dallas-Fort Worth, Texas, area, there are sometimes a dozen or more institutions offering an MBA. In smaller communities too, universities are facing decisions about their MBA offerings:

- How much should they adapt to the changing market?
- Should they offer courses online?
- If so, who are they competing with?
- Should they offer a weekend program?
- Should they offer classes in multiple locations?
- Is demand sufficient? That is, are there enough potential students to make this financially feasible?
- Is there a potential perceived product quality difference between a traditional and a nontraditional MBA program?
- Can they better accomplish the mission of university with an online MBA program?

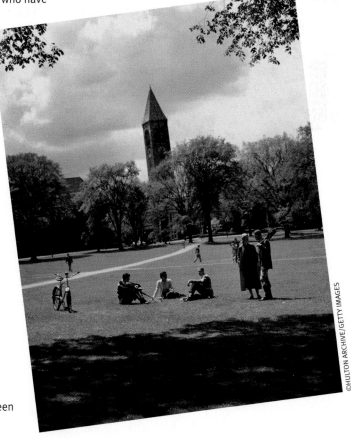
©HULTON ARCHIVE/GETTY IMAGES

The competitive MBA market typifies the landscape of many marketing firms. Clearly, universities could benefit from marketing research addressing some of these key questions. Each university maintains its own academic standard while still trying to attract enough students to make its MBA program feasible. The competitive landscape is filled with both potential opportunities and potential problems. Decisions made by university faculty and administrators will determine how successfully each school deals with the changing marketplace.

Introduction

This chapter focuses on the relationship between business decisions and marketing research. Business success is determined directly by the quality of decisions made by key personnel. Researchers contribute to decision making in several key ways. These include

1. Helping to better define the current situation
2. Defining the firm—determining how consumers, competitors, and employees view the firm
3. Providing ideas for product improvements or possible new product development
4. Testing ideas that will assist in implementing the marketing mix strategy for the firm
5. Examining how correct a certain marketing theory is in a given situation

The chapter introduces the types of research that allow researchers to provide input to key decision makers. Product design is also discussed because effective design depends on marketing research. Last but not least, the chapter discusses stages in the marketing research process.

Decision Making

A college student makes many decisions that affect the future. These include important strategic decisions like whether to go to college or not. If the answer is yes, then a decision is faced about where to attend. Furthermore, the student must decide what subject to major in, what electives to take, which instructors to sign up for, whether to belong to a fraternity or sorority, how much to work outside of school, and so forth. The student may seek out data provided by other students, parents, or various media sources. These data may be critical in reaching decisions. Indeed, the answers to each of these questions shape a student's future, ultimately determine how successful he or she will be, and shape the way he or she is viewed by others.

Likewise, businesses face decisions that shape the future of the organization, its employees, and its customers. In each case, the decisions are brought about as the firm either seeks to capitalize on some opportunity or to lessen any potential negative impacts related to some market problem. A **market opportunity** is a situation that makes some potential competitive advantage possible. Thus, the discovery of some underserved market segment presents such an opportunity. For example, eBay capitalized on the opportunity presented by technological advances to do much the same thing that is done at a garage sale but on a very, very large scale.

A **market problem** is a situation that makes some significant negative consequence more likely. An impending natural disaster can present a problem for many firms as they face potential loss of property and personnel and the possibility that their operations, and therefore their revenue, will be interrupted. Problems are usually not as obvious as they may seem. In fact, they usually are not easily observable. Instead, problems are inferred from **symptoms**, which are observable cues that serve as a signal of a problem because they are caused by that problem. A drop in market share is generally only a symptom of a market problem and not the problem itself. Research may help identify what is causing this symptom so that decision makers can actually attack the problem, not just the symptom. Patients don't usually go the doctor and point out their problem (like an ulcer). Instead, they point out symptoms (upset stomach). Similarly, decision makers usually hear about symptoms and often need help from research to identify and attack problems. Whether facing an opportunity or a problem, businesses need quality information to deal effectively with these situations.

Market opportunity
A situation that makes some potential competitive advantage possible.

Market problem
A situation that makes some significant negative consequence more likely.

Symptoms
Observable cues that serve as a signal of a problem because they are caused by that problem.

Formally defined, **decision making** is the process of developing and deciding among alternative ways of resolving a problem or choosing from among alternative opportunities. A decision maker must recognize the nature of the problem or opportunity, identify how much information is currently available and how reliable it is, and determine what information is needed to better deal with the situation. Every decision-making situation can be classified based on whether it best represents a problem or an opportunity and on whether it represents a situation characterized by complete certainty or absolute ambiguity.

©SUSAN VAN ETTEN

Can you identify symptoms that may indicate problems for these businesses? What market problems might they signify?

Decision making
The process of developing and deciding among alternative ways of resolving a problem or choosing from among alternative opportunities.

Certainty

Complete certainty means that the decision maker has all information needed to make an optimal decision. This includes the exact nature of the marketing problem or opportunity. For example, an advertising agency may need to know the demographic characteristics of subscribers to magazines in which it may place a client's advertisements. The agency knows exactly what information it needs and where to find the information. If a manager is completely certain about both the problem or opportunity and future outcomes, then research may not be needed at all. However, perfect certainty, especially about the future, is rare.

Uncertainty

Uncertainty means that the manager grasps the general nature of desired objectives, but the information about alternatives is incomplete. Predictions about forces that shape future events are educated guesses. Under conditions of uncertainty, effective managers recognize that spending additional time to gather data that clarify the nature of a decision is needed. For instance, a university may understand that there is an objective of increasing the number of MBA students, but it may not know whether an online, weekend, or off-site MBA program is the best way to accomplish the objective. Marketing decisions generally involve uncertainty, particularly when a company is seeking different opportunities.

Ambiguity

Ambiguity means that the nature of the problem itself is unclear. Objectives are vague and decision alternatives are difficult to define. This is by far the most difficult decision situation, but perhaps the most common.

Marketing managers face a variety of problems and decisions. Complete certainty and predictable future outcomes may make marketing research a waste of time. However, under conditions of uncertainty or ambiguity, marketing research becomes more attractive to the decision makers. Decisions also vary in terms of importance, meaning that some may have great impact on the welfare of the firm and others may have negligible impact. The more important, ambiguous, or uncertain a situation is, the more likely it is that additional time must be spent on marketing research.

EXHIBIT 3.1
Describing Decision-Making
Situations

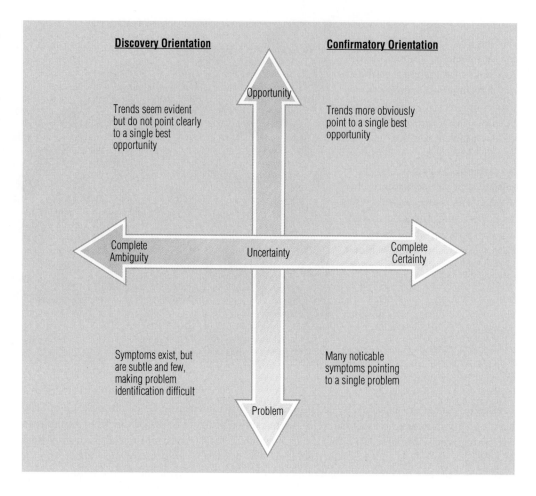

PROBLEMS AND OPPORTUNITIES

Exhibit 3.1 depicts decision situations characterized by the nature of the decision and the degree of ambiguity.[1] Under problem-focused decision making and conditions of high ambiguity, symptoms may not clearly point to some problem. Indeed, they may be quite vague or subtle, indicating only small deviations from normal conditions. For instance, a fast-food restaurant may be experiencing small changes in the sales of its individual products, but no change in overall sales. Such a symptom may not easily point to a problem such as a change in consumer tastes. As ambiguity is lessened, the symptoms are clearer and are better indicators of a problem. A large and sudden drop in overall sales may suggest the problem that the restaurant's menu does not fare well compared to competitors' menus. Thus, a menu change may be in order.

Similarly, in opportunity-oriented research, ambiguity is characterized by marketplace and environmental trends that do not suggest a clear direction. As the trends become larger and clearer, they are more diagnostic, meaning they point more clearly to a single opportunity.

Types of Marketing Research

Marketing research can reduce uncertainty. It also helps focus decision making. Sometimes marketing researchers know exactly what their marketing problems are and can design careful studies to test specific hypotheses. A university may face a problem with an out-of-date curriculum. Awareness of this problem could be based on input from employers, students, and alumni. The problem could even be contributing to low enrollment. How should the faculty and administration decide to address this problem? They may devise a careful test exploring which of three new curricula can be implemented to improve this perception. This type of research is problem-oriented and seems relatively unambiguous. The marketing research may culminate with researchers preparing a report suggesting the relative effect of each alternative curriculum on enrollment. The decision should follow relatively directly from the research.

In more ambiguous circumstances, management may be totally unaware of a marketing problem. Alternatively, the company may be scanning the environment for opportunities. For example, a small undergraduate university in a mid-sized Colorado town may consider adding an online MBA program. University administrators may have little idea as to how this would affect the image of their school among current students, employers, alumni, or faculty. They also may not know exactly what programs would be most desired by its current or potential customer bases. Some preliminary research may be necessary to gain insights into the nature of such a situation. Without it, the situation may remain too ambiguous to make more than a seat-of-the-pants decision. Marketing research is almost certainly needed.

Marketing research can be classified on the basis of either technique or purpose. Experiments, surveys, and observational studies are just a few common research techniques. Classifying research by its purpose shows how the nature of a decision situation influences the research methodology. The following section introduces the three types of marketing research:

1. Exploratory
2. Descriptive
3. Causal

Matching the particular decision situation with the right type of research is important in obtaining useful research results.

Exploratory Research

Exploratory research is conducted to clarify ambiguous situations or discover ideas that may be potential business opportunities. Exploratory research is *not* intended to provide conclusive evidence from which to determine a particular course of action. In this sense, exploratory research is not an end unto itself. Usually it is conducted with the expectation that more research will be needed to provide more conclusive evidence. Using exploratory research can sometimes also make the difference in determining the usefulness of other related research. Rushing into detailed surveys before it is clear exactly what decisions need to be made can waste time, money, and effort by providing irrelevant information.

Exploratory research is particularly useful in new product development.[2] Sony and Honda have each been instrumental in developing robot technology.[3] Making a functional robot that can move around, perform basic functions, carry out instructions, and even carry on a conversation isn't really a problem. What Sony and Honda have to research is what market opportunities may exist based on robot technology. Research can allow consumers to interact with robots as a form of exploratory research. The results suggest that consumers interact much more when the robot has human qualities, including the ability to walk on two legs. Researchers noticed that people will actually talk to the robot (which can understand basic oral commands) more when it has human qualities. In addition, consumers do seem entertained by a walking, talking, dancing robot. Thus, this has allowed each company to form more specific research questions focusing on the relative value of a robot as an entertainment device or as a security guard.

In our university example, it could be that exploratory research is needed to help identify concerns about nontraditional course delivery for business classes. This exploratory research should include open-ended interviews with faculty, students, and alumni. By doing so, specific hypotheses can be developed that test the relative attractiveness of alternative curricula to students, the effect of online instruction on job satisfaction and on alumni quality perceptions.[4] These hypotheses may be tested by either or both of the remaining two research types.

Descriptive Research

The major purpose of **descriptive research**, as the name implies, describes characteristics of objects, people, groups, organizations, or environments. Put more simply, descriptive research tries to "paint a picture" of a given situation. Marketing managers frequently need to determine

Exploratory research
Conducted to clarify ambiguous situations or discover ideas that may be potential business opportunities.

Descriptive research
Describes characteristics of objects, people, groups, organizations, or environments; tries to "paint a picture" of a given situation.

RESEARCHSNAPSHOT

Cute, Funny, or Sexy? What Makes a Mascot Tick?

Has the Pillsbury Doughboy ever changed? How old should the Brawny (paper towel) man be? What should the M&Ms characters be named? These questions all have many possible answers. In truth, a lot of research goes into these kinds of questions. It often begins with exploratory research. For instance, focus groups involving female consumers revealed a considerable amount of intimate discussion about the Brawny man. Thus, it seemed that a sexy Brawny man would yield a better response than a humorous or intelligent Brawny man.

Mr. Peanut, the icon for Planter's Peanuts, has actually changed very little since his introduction in the 1920s. He looks good for his age. Again, exploratory research suggests generally positive comments about Mr. Peanut, so only minor changes in the color scheme have been introduced. A few years ago, exploratory research led to some further tests of a Mr. Peanut in Bermuda shorts, but the tests proved overwhelmingly negative, sending Planters back to a more original peanut!

Similarly, simple exploratory research simply asked a few consumers for their reactions to the Mars M&M characters. Mars was interested in discovering names for the characters. They found that most consumers simply referred to them by their colors. This piece of information became useful in shaping future research and marketing strategy.

Sources: Voight, Joan (2003), "Mascot Makeover: The Risky Business of Tampering with Brand Icons," Adweek (July 7), 20–26; Elliot, Stuart (2004), "Updating a venerable character, or tarnishing a sterling reputation?" The New York Times, (March 19), C5.

who purchases a product, portray the size of the market, identify competitors' actions, and so on. Descriptive research addresses *who, what, when, where,* and *how* questions.

Descriptive research often helps describe market segments. For example, marketing researchers used simple descriptive surveys to describe consumers who are heavy consumers (buy a lot) of organic food products. The resulting report showed that these consumers tend to live in coastal cities with populations over 500,000, with the majority residing on the West Coast. The most frequent buyers of organic foods are affluent men and women ages 45–54 (36 percent) and 18–34 (35 percent).[5] Interestingly, consumers who buy organic foods are not very brand-oriented—81 percent of them cannot name a single organic brand. Research such as this helps high-quality supermarkets such as Whole Foods make location decisions. Over half of Whole Foods' food products are organic.

Descriptive research about consumers who buy organic food has paid off for the Whole Foods chain of stores.

Similarly, the university considering the addition of an online MBA program might benefit from descriptive research profiling the market and the potential customers. Online customers are not identical to the traditional MBA student. They tend to be older than the average 24-year-old traditional student, instead averaging about 30 years of age. Also, they tend to live in rural communities, be more introverted, and expect a higher workload than traditional students. Another key statistic is that the dropout rate for online students is significantly higher than for traditional MBA students. Nearly 14 percent of online students drop before completing a course as compared to 7.2 percent

RESEARCHSNAPSHOT

Whines for Wines

Greg Norman is best known for performance on the golf course. However, he is actually one of the most successful businesspeople to come out of sports. Among his many ventures, Norman is a well-respected vintner. Norman Estates gained fame in the wine trade with Australian wines that offered considerable quality at a fair price. More recently, Norman Estates is expanding its portfolio by purchasing vineyard properties and production capacity in California. As Norman Estates and other wineries consider diversifying production beyond their traditional boundaries, descriptive research can be vital in making these key decisions.

Descriptive research details what wine consumers like to drink in terms of where the wine is from and where the consumers are located. Consumers around the world form geographic segments with preferences for wines from certain areas. American consumers, for instance, have contributed to the growing slump in French wine sales by switching increasingly from French wines to Australian- and American-made wines. In particular, French wines at low and moderate prices have

suffered, whereas higher price French wine sales remain steady. In addition, wine sales in the United States and in the United Kingdom are relatively strong compared to wine sales in France and Germany.

All of these descriptive results may allow Greg Norman a better understanding of the international wine market and therefore make better decisions about where to grow and produce wine. Do you think the choice to expand to California rather than France seems like a good decision?

Sources: Orth, U.R., M.M. Wolf, and T. Dodd (2005), "Dimensions of Wine Region Equity and their Impact on Consumer Preferences," Journal of Product and Brand Management, 14 (2), 88–97; Conibear, Helena (2005), "World-wide Consumption Trends," AIM-Digest, http://www.aim-digest.com/gateway/pages/trends/articles/trends.htm, accessed November 24, 2005.

©THE IMAGE BANK/GETTY IMAGES

for traditional in-class students. For this and other reasons, online students are much more costly to serve.[6]

Accuracy is critically important in descriptive research. If a descriptive study estimates a university's demand for its MBA offering by even a few students, it can mean the difference between the program sustaining itself or being a drain on already scarce resources. For instance, if a cohort group of twenty-five students is predicted, but only fifteen students actually sign up, the program will likely not generate enough revenue to sustain itself. Therefore, it is easy to see that descriptive research forecasting sales revenue and costs or describing consumer attitudes, satisfaction, and commitment must be accurate or decision making will suffer.

Unlike exploratory research, descriptive studies are conducted with a considerable understanding of the situation being studied. This understanding, which may have been developed in part from exploratory research, directs the study toward specific issues. Later, we will discuss the role of research questions and hypotheses. These statements help greatly in designing and implementing a descriptive study. Without these, the researcher would have little or no idea of what questions to ask.

Survey research typifies a descriptive study. Many surveys try to answer questions such as "why are brand A's sales lower than brand B's sales?" In other words, a **diagnostic analysis** seeks to diagnose reasons for market outcomes and focuses specifically on the beliefs and feelings consumers have about and toward competing products. A research study trying to diagnose slumping French wine sales might ask consumers their beliefs about the taste of French, Australian, and American wines. The results might indicate a deficiency in taste, suggesting that consumers do not believe French wines taste as fruity as do the others. Descriptive research can sometimes provide an explanation by diagnosing differences among competitors, but descriptive research does not provide direct evidence of causality.

Diagnostic analysis
Seeks to diagnose reasons for market outcomes and focuses specifically on the beliefs and feelings consumers have about and toward competing products.

Causal Research

If a decision maker knows what causes important outcomes like sales and employee satisfaction, then he or she can shape firm decisions in a positive way. Causal inferences are very powerful because they lead to greater control. **Causal research** allows causal inferences to be made. That

Causal research
Allows causal inferences to be made; seeks to identify cause-and-effect relationships.

is, causal research seeks to identify cause-and-effect relationships. When something *causes* an effect, it means it brings it about or makes it happen. The effect is the outcome. Rain causes grass to get wet. Rain is the cause and wet grass is the effect.

Exploratory and/or descriptive research usually precedes causal research. In causal studies, researchers typically have a good understanding of the phenomena being studied. Because of this, the research can make an educated prediction about the cause and effect relationships that will be tested. Although greater knowledge of the situation is a good thing, it doesn't come without a price. Causal research designs can take a long time to implement. Also, they often involve intricate designs that can be very expensive. Thus, even though managers may often want the assurance that causal inferences can bring, they are not always willing to spend the time and money it takes to get them.

▓ CAUSALITY

Ideally, managers want to know how a change in one event (say, using a new product logo) will change another event of interest, like sales. Causal research attempts to establish that when we do one thing, another thing will follow. A **causal inference** is just such a conclusion. While we use the term "cause" all the time in everyday language, scientifically establishing something as a cause is not so easy. A causal inference can only be supported when very specific causal evidence exists. Three critical pieces of causal evidence are

1. Temporal Sequence
2. Concomitant Variance
3. Nonspurious Association

Temporal Sequence

Temporal sequence deals with the time order of events. In other words, having an *appropriate causal order of events,* or temporal sequence, is one criterion for causality. The cause must occur before the effect. It would be difficult for a restaurant manager to blame a decrease in sales on a new chef if the drop in sales occurred before the new chef arrived. If advertising causes sales, the advertising must appear before the change in sales.

Concomitant Variation

Concomitant variation occurs when two events "covary," meaning they vary systematically. In causal terms, concomitant variation means that when a change in the cause occurs, a change in the outcome also is observed. Correlation, which we discuss in a later chapter, is often used to represent concomitant variation. Causality cannot possibly exist when there is no systematic variation between the variables. For example, if a retail store never changes its employees' vacation policy, then the vacation policy cannot possibly be responsible for a change in customer satisfaction. There is no correlation between the two events. On the other hand, if two events vary together, one event may be causing the other. If a university increases its number of online MBA course offerings and experiences a decrease in enrollment in its traditional in-class MBA offerings, the online course offerings may be causing the decrease. But, the systematic variation alone doesn't guarantee it.

Nonspurious Association

Nonspurious association means any covariation between a cause and an effect is true and not simply due to some other variable. A spurious association is one that is not true. Often, a causal inference cannot be made even though the other two conditions exist because both the cause and effect have some common cause; that is, both may be influenced by a third variable. For instance, a city worker notices an alarming trend. On days when a large number of ice cream cones are sold at Virginia Beach, more people drown. So, when ice cream sales go up, so does drowning. Should the city decide to ban ice cream? This would be silly because the concomitant variation observed between ice cream consumption and drowning is spurious. On days when the beach is particularly crowded, more ice cream is sold and more people drown. So, the number of people at the beach, being associated with both, may cause both. Exhibit 3.2 illustrates the concept of spurious association.

Establishing evidence of nonspuriousness can be difficult. If a researcher finds a third variable that is related to both the cause and effect, causing a significant drop in the correlation between the

Causal inference
A conclusion that when one thing happens, another specific thing will follow.

Temporal sequence
One of three criteria for causality; deals with the time order of events—the cause must occur before the effect.

Concomitant variation
One of three criteria for causality; occurs when two events "covary," meaning they vary systematically.

Nonspurious association
One of three criteria for causality; means any covariation between a cause and an effect is true and not simply due to some other variable.

EXHIBIT 3.2 **The Spurious Effect of Ice Cream**

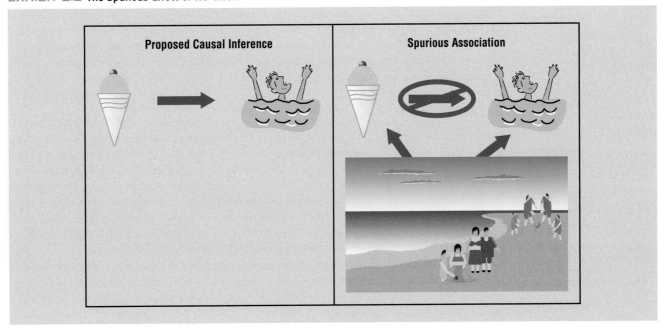

cause and effect, then a causal inference becomes difficult to support. Although the researcher would like to rule out the possibility of any alternative causes, it is impossible to observe the effect of all variables on the correlation between the cause and effect. Therefore, the researcher must use theory to identify the most likely "third" variables that would relate significantly to both the cause and effect. The research must control for these variables in some way, as we will see in Chapter 11. In addition, the researcher should use theory to make sure that the cause-and-effect relationship truly makes sense.

In summary, causal research should do all of the following:

1. Establish the appropriate causal order or sequence of events
2. Measure the concomitant variation between the presumed cause and the presumed effect
3. Examine the possibility of spuriousness by considering the presence of alternative plausible causal factors

DEGREES OF CAUSALITY

In everyday language, we often use the word "cause" in an absolute sense. For example, a warning label used on cigarette packages claims "smoking causes cancer." Is this true in an absolute sense? **Absolute causality** means the cause is necessary and sufficient to bring about the effect. Thus, if we find only one smoker who does not eventually get cancer, the claim is false. Although this is a very strong inference, it is impractical to think that we can establish absolute causality in the behavioral sciences.

Why do we continue to do causal research then? Well, although managers may like to be able to draw absolute conclusions, they can often make very good decisions based on less powerful inferences. **Conditional causality** means that a cause is necessary but not sufficient to bring about an effect. This is a weaker causal inference. One way to think about conditional causality is that the cause can bring about the effect, but it cannot do so alone. If other conditions are right, the cause can bring about the effect. We know there are other medical factors that contribute to cancer. For instance, lifestyle and diet are also both plausible causes of cancer. Thus, if one smokes and has a diet and lifestyle that promote cancer, smoking could be a considered a conditional cause of cancer. However, it we can find someone who has contracted cancer and never smoked, the causal inference would be proven wrong.

Contributory causality may be the weakest form of causality, but it is still a useful concept. A cause need be neither necessary nor sufficient to bring about an effect. However, causal evidence

Absolute causality
Means the cause is necessary and sufficient to bring about the effect.

Conditional causality
Means that a cause is necessary but not sufficient to bring about an effect.

Contributory causality
Means that a cause need be neither necessary nor sufficient to bring about an effect.

can be established using the three types of evidence shown on the previous page. For any outcome, there may be multiple causes. So, an event can be a contributory cause of something so long as the introduction of the other possible causes does not eliminate the correlation between it and the effect. This will become clearer when we discuss ways to test relationships later in the text. Smoking then can be a contributory cause of cancer so long as the introduction of other possible causes does not cause both smoking and cancer.

▄ EXPERIMENTS

Experiment
A carefully controlled study in which the researcher manipulates a proposed cause and observes any corresponding change in the proposed effect.

Experimental variable
Represents the proposed cause and is controlled by the researcher by manipulating it.

Manipulation
Means that the researcher alters the level of the variable in specific increments.

Test-market
An experiment that is conducted within actual market conditions.

Marketing *experiments* hold the greatest potential for establishing cause-and-effect relationships. An **experiment** is a carefully controlled study in which the researcher manipulates a proposed cause and observes any corresponding change in the proposed effect. An **experimental variable** represents the proposed cause and is controlled by the researcher by manipulating it. **Manipulation** means that the researcher alters the level of the variable in specific increments. So, managers often want to make decisions about the price and distribution of a new product. In other words, both price and the type of retail outlet in which a product is placed are considered potential causes of sales. A study can be designed which manipulates both the price and distribution.

Suppose a company produces a new video game box called the Wee Box. They may manipulate price by offering it for $100 among some consumers and $200 among others. Retail distribution may be manipulated by selling the Wee Box at discount stores in some consumer markets and at specialty electronic stores in others. The retailer can examine whether price and distribution cause sales by comparing the sales results in each of the four conditions created. Exhibit 3.3 illustrates this study. We will say much more about manipulations and experimental designs in Chapters 11 and 12.

An experiment like the one described above may take place in a test-market. Test-marketing is a frequently used form of marketing experimentation. A **test-market** is an experiment that is conducted within actual market conditions. Anheuser-Busch test-marketed a "not-so-soft soft drink" named Chelsea. The two experimental variables manipulated were the alcohol level and degree of sweetness. Anheuser-Busch first introduced Chelsea to the test-market as a sweet drink with a slight alcoholic content—about 0.4 percent. A Virginia nurses' association and some religious groups strongly criticized the company and the new product. These critics suggested that Anheuser-Busch had introduced a product that might encourage children to become beer drinkers. They contended that Chelsea was packaged like beer and looked, foamed, and poured like it. Later, Anheuser-Busch reintroduced the product as a soft drink with only "a trace of alcohol" as a "natural alternative" to soft drinks, with not-so-sweet and stylish attributes. Similar problems

EXHIBIT 3.3 Testing for Causes with an Experiment

WEE BOX SALES BY CONDITION		
	HIGH PRICE	LOW PRICE
SPECIALTY DISTRIBUTION	Peoria, Illinois: Retail Price: $200 Retail Store: Best Buy	Des Moines, Iowa: Retail Price: $100 Retail Store: Best Buy
GENERAL DISTRIBUTION	St. Louis, Missouri: Retail Price $200 Retail Store: Big Cheap-Mart	Kansas City, Missouri: Retail Price: $100 Retail Store: Big Cheap-Mart

Assuming that Wee Box consumers are the same in each of these cities, the extent to which price and distribution cause sales can be examined by comparing the sales results in each of these 4 conditions.

occurred in the second experiment. Therefore, the reduction in alcohol did not cause a more favorable impression of Chelsea.

Most basic scientific studies in marketing (for example, the development of consumer behavior theory) ultimately seek to identify cause-and-effect relationships. One often associates science with experiments. To predict a relationship between, say, price and perceived quality of a product, causal studies often create statistical experiments with controls that establish contrast groups.

Uncertainty Influences the Type of Research

The most appropriate type and the amount of research needed are determined in part by how much uncertainty surrounds the marketing situation motivating the research. Exhibit 3.4 contrasts the types of research and illustrates that exploratory research is conducted during the early stages of decision making. At this point, the decision situation is usually highly ambiguous and management is very uncertain about what actions should be taken. When management is aware of the problem but lacks some knowledge, descriptive research is usually conducted. Causal research requires sharply defined problems.

Each type of research also produces a different type of result. In many ways, exploratory research is the most productive since it should yield large numbers of ideas. It is discovery-oriented and as such, unstructured approaches can be very successful. Too much structure in this type of research may lead to more narrowly focused types of responses that could stifle creativity. Thus, although it is productive, its results usually need further testing and evaluation before they can be made actionable. At times, managers do take managerial action based only on exploratory research results. Sometimes, management may not be able to or may not care to invest the time and resources needed to conduct further research. Decisions made based only on exploratory research can be more risky since exploratory research does not test ideas among a scientific sample.[7] For instance, a business school professor may ask a class of current MBA students for ideas about an online program. Although the students may provide many ideas that sound very good, even the best of them has not been tested on a sample of potential online MBA students.

EXHIBIT 3.4 **Characteristics of Different Types of Marketing Research**

	Exploratory Research	**Descriptive Research**	**Causal Research**
Amount of Uncertainty Characterizing Decision Situation	Highly ambiguous	Partially defined	Clearly defined
Key Research Statement	Research question	Research question	Research hypothesis
When Conducted?	Early stage of decision making	Later stages of decision making	Later states of decision making
Usual Research Approach	Unstructured	Structured	Highly Structured
Examples	"Our sales are declining for no apparent reason" "What kinds of new products are fast-food customers interested in?"	"What kind of people patronize our stores compared to our primary competitor?" "What product features are most important to our customers?"	"Will consumers buy more products in a blue package?" "Which of two advertising campaigns will be more effective?"
Nature of Results	Discovery oriented, productive, but still speculative. Often in need of further research.	Can be confirmatory although more research is sometimes still needed. Results can be managerially actionable.	Confirmatory oriented. Fairly conclusive with managerially actionable results often obtained.

Forward linkage
Implies that the earlier stages of the research process influence the later stages.

Backward linkage
Implies that later steps influence earlier stages of the research process.

Descriptive research is usually focused around one or more fairly specific research questions. It is usually much more structured, and for many common types of marketing research, it can yield managerially actionable results. For example, descriptive research is often used to profile a market segment both demographically and psychographically. Results like this can greatly assist firms in deciding when and where to offer their goods or services for sale.

Causal research is usually very tightly focused around a small number of research hypotheses. Experimental methods require tight control of research procedures. Thus, causal research is highly structured to produce specific results. Causal research results are often managerially actionable since they suggest that if management changes the value of a "cause," some desirable effect will come about. So, by changing a package's color, i.e., the cause, from orange to blue, higher sales occur.

Stages in the Research Process

Marketing research, like other forms of scientific inquiry, involves a sequence of highly interrelated activities. The stages of the research process overlap continuously, and it is somewhat of an oversimplification to state that every research project has exactly the same ordered sequence of activities. Nevertheless, marketing research often follows a general pattern. The stages are

1. Defining the research objectives
2. Planning a research design
3. Planning a sample
4. Collecting the data
5. Analyzing the data
6. Formulating the conclusions and preparing the report

Research is sometimes directly actionable. The results may also suggest ideas for new studies.

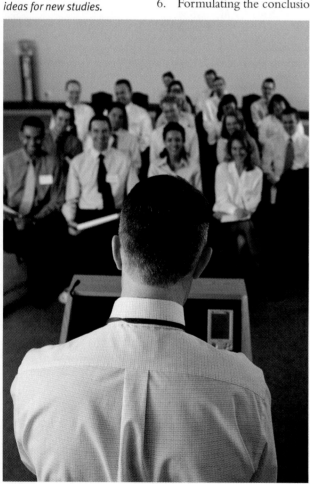

Exhibit 3.5 portrays these six stages as a cyclical or circular-flow process. The circular-flow concept is used because conclusions from research studies can generate new ideas and knowledge that can lead to further investigation. Thus, there is a dashed connection between *conclusions and reporting* and *defining the research objectives*. Notice also, though, that management is in the center of the process. The research objectives cannot be properly defined without managerial input. After all, it is the manager who ultimately has to make the decision. It is also the manager who may ask for additional research once a report is given.

In practice, the stages overlap somewhat from a timing perspective. Later stages sometimes can be completed before earlier ones. The terms *forward linkage* and *backward linkage* reflect the interrelationships between stages. **Forward linkage** implies that the earlier stages influence the later stages. Thus, the research objectives outlined in the first stage affect the sample selection and how the way data are collected. The sample selection question affects the wording of questionnaire items. For example, if the research concentrates on respondents with low educational levels, the questionnaire wording will be simpler than if the respondents were college graduates.

Backward linkage implies that later steps influence earlier stages of the research process. If it is known that the data will be collective via e-mail, then the sampling should include those with e-mail access. A very important example of backward linkage is the knowledge that the executives who will read the research report are looking for specific results. The professional researcher anticipates executives' needs for information throughout the planning process, particularly during the analysis and reporting.

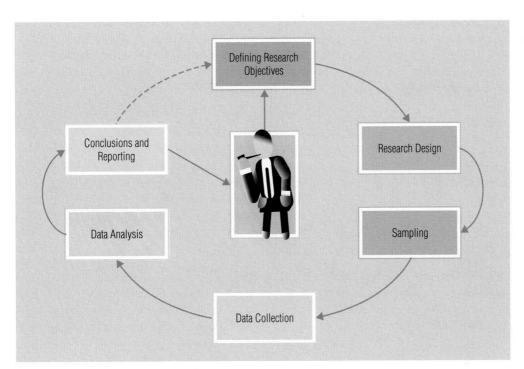

EXHIBIT 3.5
**Stages of the Research
Process**

Alternatives in the Research Process

The researcher must choose among a number of alternatives during each stage of the research process. The research process can be compared to a map. It is important to remember that there is no single right or best path for all journeys. The road one takes depends on where one wants to go and the resources (money, time, labor, and so on) available for the trip. The map analogy is useful for the marketing researcher because there are several paths that can be followed at each stage. When there are severe time constraints, the quickest path may be most appropriate. When money and human resources are plentiful, the appropriate path may be quite different.

The following sections briefly describe the six stages of the research process. (Each stage is discussed in greater depth in later chapters.) Exhibit 3.6 shows the decisions that researchers must make in each stage. This discussion of the research process begins with research objectives, because most research projects are initiated to remedy managers' uncertainty about some aspect of the firm's marketing program.

Defining the Research Objectives

Exhibit 3.6 shows that the research process begins with **research objectives**. Research objectives are the goals to be achieved by conducting research. In consulting, the term **deliverables** is often used to describe the objectives to a research client. The genesis of the research objectives lies in the type of decision situation faced. The objectives may involve exploring some new product within a new market. Alternatively, they may involve testing the effect of some policy change on service quality. Different types of objectives lead to different types of research designs.

In applied or market research, the objectives cannot be listed until there is an understanding of the decision situation. This understanding must be shared between the actual decision maker and the lead researcher. We often describe this understanding as a problem statement. In general usage, the word *problem* suggests that something has gone wrong. This isn't always the case before research gets started. Actually, the research objective may be to simply clarify a situation, define an opportunity, or monitor and evaluate current operations. The research objectives cannot be developed until managers and researchers have agreed on the actual business "problem" that will be addressed by the research. Thus, they set out to "discover" this problem through a series of interviews and through a document called a research proposal.

Research objectives
The goals to be achieved by
conducting research.

Deliverables
The term used often in
consulting to describe research
objectives to a research client.

EXHIBIT 3.6 **Flowchart of the Marketing Research Process**

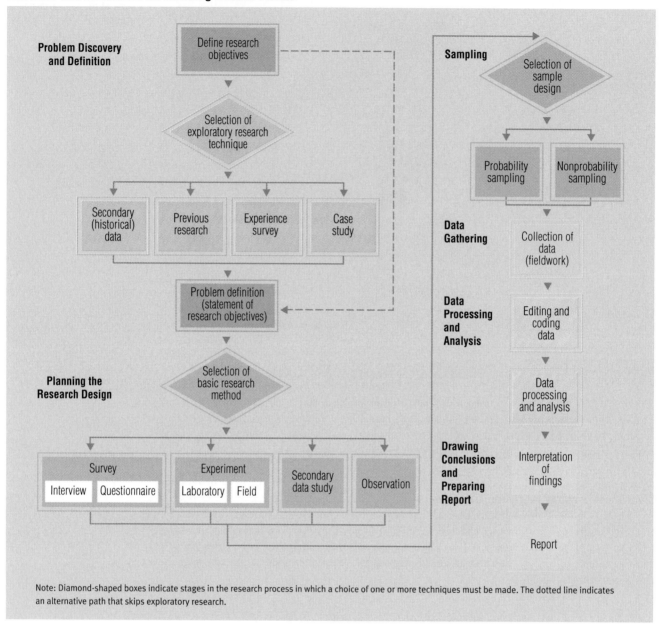

Note: Diamond-shaped boxes indicate stages in the research process in which a choice of one or more techniques must be made. The dotted line indicates an alternative path that skips exploratory research.

It should be noted that this process is oriented more toward *discovery* than *confirmation*. Managers and researchers alike may not have a clear-cut understanding of the situation at the outset of the research process. Managers may only be able to list symptoms that could indicate a problem. Sales may be declining, but management may not know the exact nature of the problem. Thus, the problem statement often is made only in general terms; what is to be investigated is not yet specifically identified.

■ DEFINING THE MANAGERIAL DECISION SITUATION

In marketing research, the adage "a problem well defined is a problem half solved" is worth remembering. This adage emphasizes that an orderly definition of the research problem lends a sense of direction to the investigation. Careful attention to problem definition allows the researcher to set the proper research objectives. If the purpose of the research is clear, the chances of collecting necessary and relevant information and not collecting surplus information will be much greater.

Albert Einstein noted that "the formulation of a problem is often more essential than its solution."[8] This is good advice for marketing managers. Managers naturally concentrate on finding the right answer rather than asking the right question. They also want one solution quickly rather than having to spend time considering many possible solutions. Properly defining a problem can be more difficult than solving it. In marketing research, if data are collected before the nature of the marketing problem is carefully thought out, they probably will not allow useful results.

Marketing research must have clear objectives and definite designs. Unfortunately, little or no planning goes into the formulation of many research problems. Consider the case of the Ha-Pah-Shu-Tse brand of Indian fried bread mix (the name "Ha-Pah-Shu-Tse" comes from the Pawnee Indian word for red corn). The owner of the company, Mr. Ha-Pah-Shu-Tse, thought that his product, one of the few Native American food products available in the United States, was not selling because it was not widely advertised. He wanted a management consulting group to conduct some research concerning advertising themes. However, the management consultants pointed out to the Ha-Pah-Shu-Tse family that using the family name on the bread mix might be a foremost source of concern. They suggested that consumer behavior research to investigate the brand image might be a better initial starting point, rather than advertising copy research. Family management agreed.

Defining the decision situation must precede the research objectives. Frequently the marketing researcher will not be involved until line management has discovered that some information about a particular aspect of the marketing mix is needed. Even at this point the exact nature of the situation may be poorly defined. Once a problem area has been discovered, the marketing researcher and management together can begin the process of precisely defining it.

Frequently, research is conducted without a clear definition of the research's objectives. Too many researchers forget that the best place to begin a research project is at the end. Knowing what is to be accomplished determines the research process. An error or omission in problem objectives is likely to be a costly mistake that cannot be corrected in later stages of the process. Chapter 5 discusses problem objectives in greater detail.

▪ EXPLORATORY RESEARCH

Exploratory research can be used to help identify the decisions that need to be made. The preliminary activities undertaken can yield results that place the situation into a more easily researched context. Exploratory research can progressively narrow the scope of the research topic and help transform ambiguous problems into well-defined ones that yield specific research objectives. By investigating any existing studies on the subject, talking with knowledgeable individuals, and informally investigating the situation, the researcher can progressively sharpen the concepts. After such exploration, the researcher should know exactly which data to collect during the formal phases of the project and how to conduct the project. Exhibit 3.6 indicates that managers and researchers must decide whether to use one or more exploratory research techniques. As Exhibit 3.6 indicates, this stage is optional.

The marketing researcher can employ techniques from four basic categories to obtain insights and gain a clearer idea of the problem: previous research, pilot studies, case studies, and experience surveys. These are discussed in detail in Chapter 6. This section will briefly discuss previous research and focus group interviews, the most popular type of pilot study.

Previous Research

As a general rule, researchers should first investigate previous research to see whether or not others may have addressed the same research problems previously to gain a better understanding of the area. Previous research reports should be searched within the company's archives. In addition, some firms specialize in providing various types of research reports, such as economic forecasts. The *Census of Population* and the *Survey of Current Business* are each examples of previous research conducted by an outside source.

The library contains a wealth of information. Studies forming a literature review can be found in the library.

©DIGITAL VISION/GETTY IMAGES

Previous research may also exist in the public domain. A **literature review** is a directed search of published works, including periodicals and books, that discusses theory and presents empirical results that are relevant to the topic at hand. A literature survey is common in applied market research studies but it is a fundamental requirement of a basic (i.e., marketing) research report. Literature reviews are conducted using traditional library research tools. The Internet and modern electronic search engines available through most university libraries have made literature reviews simpler to do and allowed them to be done in less time.

Suppose, for example, that a bank is interested in determining the best site for additional automated teller machines. A logical first step would be to investigate the factors that bankers in other parts of the country consider important. By reading articles in banking journals, management might quickly discover that the best locations are inside supermarkets located in residential areas where people are young, highly educated, and earning higher-than-average incomes. These data might lead the bank to investigate census information to determine where in the city such people live. Reviewing and building on the work already compiled by others is an economical starting point for most research.

Pilot Studies

Almost all consumers take a test drive before buying a car. A pilot study serves a similar purpose for the researcher. A **pilot study** is a small-scale research project that collects data from respondents similar to those that will be used in the full study. It can serve as a guide for a larger study or examine specific aspects of the research to see if the selected procedures will actually work as intended. Pilot studies are critical in refining measures and reducing the risk that the full study will be fatally flawed. This is particularly true for experimental research, which depends critically on valid manipulations of experimental variables.[9] Pilot studies also often are useful in fine-tuning research objectives. Pilot studies are sometimes referred to as pretests. A **pretest** is a very descriptive term indicating a small-scale study in which the results are only preliminary and intended only to assist in design of a subsequent study.

Focus group interviews are sometimes used as a pilot study. A **focus group** interview brings together six to twelve people in a loosely structured format. The technique is based on the assumption that individuals are more willing to talk about things when they are able to do so within a group discussion format. Focus group respondents sometimes feed on each other's comments to develop ideas that would be difficult to express in a different interview format. Focus groups are discussed much more in Chapter 6.

For example, suppose a consultant is hired by Carrefour to research the way consumers react to sales promotions. Carrefour is second in size only to Wal-Mart, operating nearly 11,000 stores in twenty-nine countries. Carrefour began in France over forty-five years ago and pioneered the discount hypermarket format. More specifically, the researcher may be asked to help management decide whether or not the size of promotions should vary with national culture. In other words, the basic research question is whether or not culture influences consumer perceptions of sales promotions.[10] A pretest may be needed to examine whether or not differences in currency might interfere with these perceptions, or whether or not the different terms that refer to promotions and discounts can be translated into the languages of each culture. For example, is a discount expressed in Korean won interpreted the same way as a discount expressed in euros? Each euro equals about $1.18, whereas a single dollar is worth about 1,050 won.[11]

Exploratory research need not always follow a structured design. Because the purpose of exploratory research is to gain insights and discover new ideas, researchers may use considerable creativity and flexibility. Some companies perform exploratory research routinely as part of environmental scanning. If the conclusions made during this stage suggest marketing opportunities, the researcher is in a position to begin planning a formal, quantitative research project.

▓ STATING RESEARCH OBJECTIVES

After identifying and clarifying the problem, with or without exploratory research, the researcher must formally state the research objectives. This statement delineates the type of research that is needed and what intelligence may result that would allow the decision maker to make informed choices. The statement of research objectives culminates the process of clarifying the managerial decision into something actionable.

RESEARCHSNAPSHOT

Nothing So Practical as Theory?

Theory and marketing practice do come together. First, students learn theory in their formal education. Business professors consider it good practice to blend theory and practice in their teaching. Business professionals use these theories to help shape their thinking about different business situations.

Neurology, psychobiology, anthropology, economics, and social psychology all offer relevant theories that can help explain marketing problems. Recently, structuration theory has been proposed as a way of explaining marketing communication outcomes. The theory suggests that more focus should be placed on the communication exchanges between buyers and sellers and that if one can understand the goals of the buyer and seller involved in a communication interaction, then the outcome of the

interaction can be predicted. Studies using theory of this type may assist electronic communication design in better placements of pop-up ads and hyperlinks and can also assist face-to-face sales exchanges in better predicting when a consumer is actually ready to buy.

©MICHAEL NEWMAN/PHOTOEDIT

Sources: Green, Paul E. (2004), "Theory, Practice both have Key MR Roles," Marketing News, 38 (September 15), 40–44; Schultz, Don (2005), "Accepted Industry Truths Not Always Acceptable," Marketing News, 39 (October 15), 6; Stewart, D. T. (2005), "Traditional Ad Research Overlooks Interactions," Marketing News, 39 (November 15), 26–29.

A written decision statement expresses the business situation to the researcher. The research objectives try to directly address the decision statement or statements, as the case may be. As such, the research objectives represent a contract of sorts that commits the researcher to producing the needed research. This is why they are expressed as deliverables in applied market research. Research objectives drive the rest of the research process. Indeed, before proceeding, the researcher and managers must agree that the objectives are appropriate and will produce relevant information.

■ WHAT IS A THEORY?

Ultimately, theory plays a role in determining the appropriate research objectives. A **theory** is a formal, logical explanation of some events that includes predictions of how things relate to one another. A theory is built through a process of reviewing previous findings of similar studies, simple logical deduction, and knowledge of applicable theoretical areas. For example, if a web designer is trying to decide what color the background of the page should be, the researcher may first consult previous studies examining the effects of color on package design and retail store design. He or she may also find theories that deal with the wavelength of different colors or theories that explain retail atmospherics. This may lead to specific predictions that predict blue as a good background color.[12]

While it may seem that theory is only relevant to academic or basic marketing research, theory plays a role in understanding practical research as well. Before setting research objectives, the researcher must be able to describe the business situation in some coherent way. Without this type of explanation, the researcher would have little idea of where to start. Ultimately, the logical explanation helps the researcher know what variables need to be included in the study and how they may relate to one another. The Research Snapshot box above illustrates how theory and practice come together in marketing research.

Theory
A formal, logical explanation of some events that includes predictions of how things relate to one another.

■ WHAT IS A HYPOTHESIS?

A **hypothesis** is a formal statement explaining some outcome. Hypotheses (pl.) must be testable. In other words, when one states a hypothesis, it should be written as a proposition. For example, using our opening vignette as an example, the researcher may use theoretical reasoning to develop the following hypothesis:

H1: The more hours per week a prospective student works, the more favorable the attitude toward online MBA class offerings.

Hypothesis
A formal statement explaining some outcome.

EXHIBIT 3.7
Example Decision Statements, Research Objectives, and Research Hypotheses

Decision Statement:	Research Objectives:	Hypotheses:
What should be the retail price for product X?	Forecast sales for product X at three different prices.	Sales will be higher at $5.00 than at $4.00 or at $6.99.
What things should we invest in to improve our service quality?	Identify the top factors that contribute to customers' service quality perceptions.	Cleanliness is related positively to customers' service quality perceptions. Crowding is related negatively to customers' service quality perceptions.
Should we invest in a training program to reduce role conflict among our employees?	Determine how much role conflict influences employee job satisfaction.	Role conflict is related positively to job satisfaction.

In its simplest form, a hypothesis is a guess. A sales manager may hypothesize that the sales-people who are highest in product knowledge will be the most productive. An advertising manager may hypothesize that if consumers' attitudes toward a product change in a positive direction, there will be an increase in consumption of the product.

Empirical testing
Means that something has been examined against reality using data.

We often apply statistics to data to empirically test hypotheses. **Empirical testing** means that something has been examined against reality using data. When the data are consistent with a hypothesis, we say the hypothesis is *supported*. When the data are inconsistent with a hypothesis, we say the hypothesis is *not supported*. We are often tempted to say that we prove a hypothesis when the data conform to the prediction; this isn't really true. Because our result is based on statistics, there is always the possibility that our conclusion is wrong. Now, at times we can be very, very confident in our conclusion, but from an absolute perspective, statistics cannot prove a hypothesis is true.

Exhibit 3.7 illustrates how decision statements are linked to research objectives, which are linked to research hypotheses. Although the first two objectives each have one hypothesis, notice that the third has two. In reality, most research projects will involve more than one research objective, and each of these may often involve more than one hypothesis. Think about how you might go about trying to test the hypothesis listed in Exhibit 3.7.

Planning the Research Design

Research design
A master plan that specifies the methods and procedures for collecting and analyzing the needed information.

After the researcher has formulated the research problem, he or she must develop the research design as part of the research design stage. A **research design** is a master plan that specifies the methods and procedures for collecting and analyzing the needed information. A research design provides a framework or plan of action for the research. Objectives of the study determined during the early stages of research are included in the design to ensure that the information collected is appropriate for solving the problem. The researcher also must determine the sources of information, the design technique (survey or experiment, for example), the sampling methodology, and the schedule and cost of the research.

■ SELECTION OF THE BASIC RESEARCH METHOD

Here again, the researcher must make a decision. Exhibit 3.6 shows four basic design techniques for descriptive and causal research: surveys, experiments, secondary data, and observation. The objectives of the study, the available data sources, the urgency of the decision, and the cost of obtaining the data will determine which method should be chosen. The managerial aspects of selecting the research design will be considered later.

Survey
A research technique in which a sample is interviewed in some form or the behavior of respondents is observed and described in some way.

The most common method of generating primary data is the survey. Most people have seen the results of political surveys by Gallup or Harris Online, and some have been respondents (members of a sample who supply answers) to marketing research questionnaires. A **survey** is a research technique in which a sample is interviewed in some form or the behavior of respondents is observed and described in some way. The term *surveyor* is most often reserved for civil engineers who describe some piece of property using a transit. Similarly, marketing researchers describe some market segment using a questionnaire. The task of writing a list of questions and designing the format of the printed or written questionnaire is an essential aspect of the development of a survey research design.

Research investigators may choose to contact respondents by telephone or mail, on the Internet, or in person. An advertiser spending nearly $2.5 million for thirty seconds of commercial time during the Super Bowl may telephone people to quickly gather information concerning their responses to the advertising. A forklift truck manufacturer trying to determine a cause for low sales in the wholesale grocery industry might choose a mail questionnaire because the appropriate executives are hard to reach by telephone. A manufacturer of a birth control device for men might determine the need for a versatile survey method wherein an interviewer can ask a variety of personal questions in a flexible format. While personal interviews are expensive, they are valuable because investigators can use visual aids and supplement the interviews with observations. Each of these survey methods has advantages and disadvantages. A researcher's task is to find the most appropriate way to collect the needed information.

The objective of many research projects is merely to record what can be observed—for example, the number of automobiles that pass by a proposed site for a gas station. This can be mechanically recorded or observed by humans. Research personnel known as mystery shoppers may act as customers to observe actions of sales personnel or do comparative shopping to learn prices at competing outlets. A mystery shopper is paid to pretend to be a customer and gather data about the way employees behave and the way they are treated in general. How often are store policies followed? How often are they treated courteously? Mystery shoppers can be valuable sources for observational data.

The main advantage of the observation technique is that it records behavior without relying on reports from respondents. Observational data are often collected unobtrusively and passively without a respondent's direct participation. For instance, the ACNielsen Company uses a "people meter" attached to television sets to record the programs being watched by each household member. This eliminates the possible bias of respondents stating that they watched the president's State of the Union address rather than a situation comedy on another station.

Observation is more complex than mere "nose counting," and the task is more difficult than the inexperienced researcher would imagine. Several things of interest, such as attitudes, opinions, motivations, and other intangible states of mind, simply cannot be observed.

THE "BEST" RESEARCH DESIGN

It is argued that there is no single best research design. As such, the researcher often has several alternatives that can accomplish the stated research objectives. Consider the researcher who must forecast sales for the upcoming year. Some commonly used forecasting methods are surveying executive opinion, collecting sales force composite opinions, surveying user expectations, projecting trends, and analyzing market factors. Any one of these may yield a reliable forecast.

The ability to select the most appropriate research design develops with experience. Inexperienced researchers often jump to the conclusion that a survey methodology is usually the best design because they are most comfortable with this method. When Chicago's Museum of Science and Industry wanted to determine the relative popularity of its exhibits, it could have conducted a survey. Instead, a creative researcher familiar with other research designs suggested a far less expensive alternative: an unobtrusive observation technique. The researcher suggested that the museum merely keep track of the frequency with which the floor tiles in front of the various exhibits had to be replaced, indicating where the heaviest traffic occurred. When this was done, the museum found that the chick-hatching exhibit was the most popular. This method provided the same results as a survey but at a much lower cost.

Sampling

Although the sampling plan is outlined in the research design, the sampling stage is a distinct phase of the research process. For convenience, however, we will treat the sample planning and the actual sample generation processes together in this section.

If you take your first bite of a steak and conclude that it needs salt, you have just conducted a sample. **Sampling** involves any procedure that draws conclusions based on measurements of a

TOTHEPOINT

You cannot put the same shoe on every foot.

—Publius Syrus

Sampling
Involves any procedure that draws conclusions based on measurements of a portion of the population.

RESEARCHSNAPSHOT

Rolling Rock

Making a mark in the U.S. beer market can be difficult. American consumers tend to favor milder beers at lower price points. Some argue that most beers taste very similar. Taste tests do reveal that similarly positioned beers do taste very much the same. However, the taste rankings do not correspond to market share. For instance, Stroh's fared very well in the taste tests, but it is hardly a market leader. Rolling Rock rated twelfth out of twelve beers tasted. Tasters said it tasted a bit like canned corn. Clearly, there is something more to a successful beer than taste.

For many years Rolling Rock beer was a regional brand in western Pennsylvania. Its signature package was a longneck green bottle with a white painted label featuring icons such as a horsehead, a steeplechase, the number "33," and a legend about the beer being brought to you "from the glass-lined tanks of Old Latrobe." The brand, now marketed by Labatt USA, expanded nationally during the 1980s by focusing on core consumers who purchased specialty beers for on-premise consumption and who were willing to pay higher prices than for national brands such as Budweiser.

As years went by, packaging options expanded to include bottles with ordinary paper labels for take-home consumption, often packaged in 12-packs. In the mid-1990s, in response to a competitive explosion from microbrews, Rolling Rock offered a number of line extensions, such as Rock Bock and amber Rock Ice. They failed. Sales stagnated. In New York and other crucial markets, price reductions to the level of Budweiser and Miller became inhibiting aspects of its marketing program. Marketing executives held the view that the longneck painted bottle was the heart of the brand. However, earlier efforts to develop cheaper imitations of the painted-label look had not achieved success.

Rolling Rock executives decided to conduct a massive consumer study, recruiting consumers at shopping malls and other venues to view "live" shelf sets of beer—not just specialty beer, but beer at every price range from subpremiums and up. Consumers given money to spend in the form of chips were exposed to "old-bundle" packages (the old graphics and the paper-label stubbies) and "new-bundle" packages (two new graphics approaches, including the one ultimately selected, and painted-label longnecks) at a variety of price points and asked to allocate chips to their next ten purchases. Some were even invited to take the "new-bundle" packages home with them for follow-up research.

As the marketing executives had hoped, the results did not leave any room for interpretation: Not only did the new packages meet with consumers' strong approval, but consumers consistently indicated that they would be willing to pay more for the brand in those packages. In fact, not only were they willing to pay more; they *expected* to pay more, particularly among consumers already familiar with the Rock. In three regions, the Northeast, Southeast, and West, purchase-intent among users increased dramatically both at prices 20 cents higher per 12-pack and at prices 40 cents higher per 12-pack. The increase in purchase intent was milder in the Midwest, but there Rock already commanded a solid premium over Bud and other premium beers. The sole exception to that trend was in the brand's core markets in Pennsylvania and Ohio, where Rock has never entirely escaped its shot-and-a-beer origins, but even there, purchase intent declined by only 2 percent at each of the higher prices.

Sources: Gerry Khermouch, "Sticking Their Neck Out," BrandWeek, November 9, 1998, pp. 25–34. © 2006 VNU Business Media, Inc. Used with permission from Brandweek. © 1998–1999 VNU Business Media Inc.; Consumer Reports (2001), "Which Brew for You?" (August), 10–17.

©SUSAN VAN ETTEN

portion of the population. In other words, a sample is a subset from a larger population. If certain statistical procedures are followed, a researcher need not select every item in a population because the results of a good sample should have the same characteristics as the population as a whole. Of course, when errors are made, samples do not give reliable estimates of the population.

A famous example of error due to sampling is the 1936 *Literary Digest* fiasco. The magazine conducted a survey and predicted that Republican Alf Landon would win over Democrat Franklin D. Roosevelt by a landslide in that year's presidential election. This prediction was wrong—and the error was due to sample selection. The post–mortems showed that *Literary Digest* had sampled its readers as well as telephone subscribers. In 1936, these people were not a representative cross-section of voters, because a disproportionate number of them were Republicans.

In 2004, early "exit polls" led many to believe that John Kerry would win the U.S. Presidential election.[13] The "exit polls" were performed early on election day and done mostly in highly urban areas in the Northeast, areas that are predominantly democratic. The resulting sample of voters responding to the early exit polls did not represent the entire U.S. population, and Kerry lost to Bush by over 3 million votes, or about 3 percent of all votes cast. Thus, the accuracy of predictions from research depends on getting a sample that really matches the population.

The first sampling question to ask is "Who is to be sampled?" The answer to this primary question requires the identification of a *target population*. Defining this population and determining the sampling units may not be so easy. If, for example, a savings and loan association surveys people who already have accounts for answers to image questions, the selected sampling units will not represent *potential* customers. Specifying the target population is a crucial aspect of the sampling plan.

The next sampling issue concerns sample size. How big should the sample be? Although management may wish to examine every potential buyer of a product or service, doing so may be unnecessary as well as unrealistic. Typically, larger samples are more precise than smaller ones, but proper probability sampling can allow a small proportion of the total population to give a reliable measure of the whole. A later discussion will explain how large a sample must be in order to be truly representative of the universe or population.

The final sampling decision is how to select the sampling units. Simple random sampling may be the best known type, in which every unit in the population has an equal and known chance of being selected. However, this is only one type of sampling. For example, a cluster-sampling procedure may reduce costs and make data gathering procedures more efficient. If members of the population are found in close geographical clusters, a sampling procedure that selects area clusters rather than individual units in the population will reduce costs. Rather than selecting 1,000 individuals throughout the United States, it may be more economical to first select twenty-five counties and then sample within those counties. This will substantially reduce travel, hiring, and training costs. In determining the appropriate sampling plan, the researcher will have to select the most appropriate sampling procedure for meeting the established study objectives. Chapter 16 provides a full discussion of sampling.

Gathering Data

The data gathering stage begins once the sampling plan has been formalized. Data gathering is the process of gathering or collecting information. Data may be gathered by human observers or interviewers, or they may be recorded by machines as in the case of scanner data.

Obviously, the many research techniques involve many methods of gathering data. Surveys require direct participation by research respondents. This may involve filling out a questionnaire or interacting with an interviewer. In this sense, they are obtrusive. **Unobtrusive methods** of data gathering are those in which the subjects do not have to be disturbed for data to be collected. They may even be unaware that research is going on at all. For instance, a simple count of motorists driving past a proposed franchising location is one kind of data gathering method. However the data are collected, it is important to minimize errors in the process. For example, the data gathering should be consistent in all geographical areas. If an interviewer phrases questions incorrectly or records a respondent's statements inaccurately (not verbatim), major data collection errors will result.

Unobtrusive methods
Methods in which research respondents do not have to be disturbed for data to be gathered.

Processing and Analyzing Data

▪ EDITING AND CODING

After the fieldwork has been completed, the data must be converted into a format that will answer the marketing manager's questions. This is part of the data processing and analysis stage. Here, the information content will be mined from the raw data. Data processing generally begins with editing and coding the data. Editing involves checking the data collection forms for omissions, legibility, and consistency in classification. The editing process corrects problems such as interviewer errors (an answer recorded on the wrong portion of a questionnaire, for example) before the data are transferred to the computer.

Before data can be tabulated, meaningful categories and character symbols must be established for groups of responses. The rules for interpreting, categorizing, recording, and transferring the data to the data storage media are called codes. This coding process facilitates computer or hand tabulation. If computer analysis is to be used, the data are entered into the computer and verified. Computer-assisted (online) interviewing is an example of the impact of technological change on the research process. Telephone interviewers, seated at computer terminals, read survey questions displayed on the monitor. The interviewer asks the questions and then types in the respondents' answers. Thus, answers are collected and processed into the computer at the same time, eliminating intermediate steps that could introduce errors.

▨ DATA ANALYSIS

Data analysis
The application of reasoning to
understand the data that have
been gathered.

Data analysis is the application of reasoning to understand the data that have been gathered. In its simplest form, analysis may involve determining consistent patterns and summarizing the relevant details revealed in the investigation. The appropriate analytical technique for data analysis will be determined by management's information requirements, the characteristics of the research design, and the nature of the data gathered. Statistical analysis may range from portraying a simple frequency distribution to more complex multivariate analyses approaches, such as multiple regression. Later chapters will discuss three general categories of statistical analysis: univariate analysis, bivariate analysis, and multivariate analysis.

Drawing Conclusions and Preparing a Report

One of the most important jobs that a researcher performs is communicating the research results. This is the final stage of the research project, but it is far from the least important. The conclusions and report preparation stage consists of interpreting the research results, describing the implications, and drawing the appropriate conclusions for managerial decisions. These conclusions should fulfill the deliverables promised in the research proposal. In addition, it's important that the researcher consider the varying abilities of people to understand the research results. The report shouldn't be written the same way to a group of PhDs as it would be to a group of line managers.

All too many applied market research reports are overly complicated statements of technical aspects and sophisticated research methods. Frequently, management is not interested in detailed reporting of the research design and statistical findings, but wishes only a summary of the findings. If the findings of the research remain unread on the marketing manager's desk, the study will have been useless. The importance of effective communication cannot be overemphasized. Research is only as good as its applications.

Now that we have outlined the research process, note that the order of topics in this book follows the flowchart of the research process presented in Exhibit 3.4. Keep this flowchart in mind while reading later chapters.

The Research Program Strategy

Our discussion of the marketing research process began with the assumption that the researcher wished to collect data to achieve a specific marketing objective. When the researcher has only one or a small number of research objectives that can be addressed in a single study, that study is referred to as a **research project**. We have emphasized the researcher's need to select specific techniques for solving one-dimensional problems, such as identifying market segments, selecting the best packaging design, or test-marketing a new product.

Research project
A single study that addresses
one or a small number of
research objectives.

However, if you think about a firm's marketing mix activity in a given period of time (such as a year), you'll realize that marketing research is not a one-shot activity—it is a continuous process. An exploratory research study may be followed by a survey, or a researcher may conduct a specific research project for each aspect of the marketing mix. If a new product is being developed, the different types of research might include market potential studies to identify the size and characteristics of the market; product usage testing to record consumers' reactions to prototype products; brand name and packaging research to determine the product's symbolic connotations; and test-marketing the new product. Thus, when numerous related studies come together to address issues about a single company, we refer to this as a **research program**. Because research is a continuous process, management should view marketing research at a strategic planning level. The program strategy refers to a firm's overall plan to use marketing research. It is a planning activity that places a series of marketing research projects in the context of the company's marketing plan.

Research program
Numerous related studies that
come together to address
multiple, related research
objectives.

The marketing research program strategy can be likened to a term insurance policy. Conducting marketing research minimizes risk and increases certainty. Each research project can be seen as a series of term insurance policies that makes the marketing manager's job a bit safer.

Summary

1. Define decision making and understand the role research plays in making decisions. Decision making occurs when managers choose among alternative ways of resolving problems or pursuing opportunities. Decision makers must recognize the nature of the problem or opportunity, identify how much information is available, and recognize what information they need. Every marketing decision can be classified on a continuum ranging from complete certainty to absolute ambiguity. Research is a way that managers can become informed about the different alternatives and make an educated guess about which alternative, if any, is the best to pursue.

2. Classify marketing research into one of three types. Exploratory, descriptive, and causal research are three major types of marketing research projects. The clarity with which the decision situation is defined determines whether exploratory, descriptive, or causal research is most appropriate. When the decision is very ambiguous, or the interest is on discovering ideas, exploratory research is most appropriate. Descriptive research attempts to paint a picture of the given situation by describing characteristics of objects, people, or organizations. Causal research identifies cause-and-effect relationships. Or, in other words, what change in "Y" will occur when there is some change in "X"? Three conditions must be satisfied to establish evidence of causality: 1) temporal sequence—the cause must occur before the effect; 2) concomitant variation—a change in the cause is associated with a change in the effect; and 3) nonspurious association—the cause is true and not eliminated by the introduction of another potential cause.

3. List the major phases of the marketing research process. The six major phases of the research process are 1) defining the research objectives, 2) planning the research design, 3) sampling, 4) data gathering, 5) data processing and analysis, and 6) drawing conclusions and report preparation. Each stage involves several activities or steps. For instance, in planning the research design, the researchers must decide which type of study will be done and, if needed, recruit participants and design and develop experimental stimuli. Quite often research projects are conducted together as parts of a research program. Such programs can involve successive projects that monitor an established product or a group of projects undertaken for a proposed new product to determine the optimal form of various parts of the marketing mix.

4. Distinguish between the concepts of theory and hypothesis. A *hypothesis* is a formal statement explaining some outcome. It is stated in a way that it is testable. A *theory* is a formal, logical explanation of some events that includes predictions of how things relate to one another. A theory is built through a process of reviewing previous findings of similar studies, simple logical deduction, and knowledge of applicable theoretical areas. The explanations in a theory are often in the form of hypotheses. They are extremely useful in research because they give the research an idea of what to expect prior to testing. As such, they also help to identify the variables that need to be included in the study.

5. Explain the difference between a research project and a research program. A *research project* addresses one of a small number of research objectives that can be included in a single study. In contrast, a *research program* represents a series of studies addressing multiple research objectives. Many marketing activities require an ongoing research task of some type.

Key Terms and Concepts

Market opportunity	Conditional causality	Focus group
Market problem	Contributory causality	Theory
Symptoms	Experiment	Hypothesis
Decision making	Experimental variable	Empirical testing
Exploratory research	Manipulation	Research design
Descriptive research	Test-market	Survey
Diagnostic analysis	Forward linkage	Sampling
Causal research	Backward linkage	Unobtrusive method
Causal inference	Research objectives	Data analysis
Temporal sequence	Deliverables	Research project
Concomitant variation	Literature review	Research program
Nonspurious association	Pilot study	
Absolute causality	Pretest	

Questions for Review and Critical Thinking

1. List five ways that marketing research can contribute to effective business decision making.
2. Define *market opportunity, market problem,* and *symptoms.* Given an example of each as it applies to a university business school.
3. Consider the following list, and indicate and explain whether each best fits the definition of a problem, opportunity, or symptom:
   a. A 12.5 percent decrease in store traffic for a children's shoe store in a medium sized city mall.
   b. FedEx's fuel costs increase 100 percent between 2005 and 2006.
   c. A furniture manufacturer and retailer in North Carolina reads a research report indicating consumer trends toward Australian Jara and Kari wood. The export of these products is very limited and very expensive.
   d. Marlboro reads a research report written by the U.S. FDA. It indicates that the number of cigarette smokers in sub-Saharan Africa is expected to increase dramatically over the next decade.
4. What are the three types of marketing research? Indicate which type each item in the list below illustrates. Explain your answers.
   a. Establishing the relationship between advertising and sales in the beer industry
   b. Identifying target market demographics for a shopping center located in Omaha, Nebraska
   c. Estimating the 5-year sales potential for Cat-Scan machines in the Ark-La-Tex (Arkansas, Louisiana, and Texas) region of the United States
   d. Testing the effect of the inside temperature of a clothing store on sales of outerwear
   e. Discovering the ways that people who live in apartments actually use vacuum cleaners, and identifying cleaning tasks for which they do not use a vacuum
5. Describe the type of research evidence that allows one to infer causality.
6. What is an experimental manipulation? A marketing researcher is hired by a specialty retail firm. The retailer is trying to decide what level of lighting and what temperature it should maintain in its stores. How can the researcher manipulate these experimental variables within a causal design?
7. A market researcher gives a presentation to a music industry executive. After considering the results of a test-market examining whether or not lowering the price of in-store CDs will lower the number of illicit downloads of the same music, the executive claims: "The test-market was conducted in eight cities. In two of the cities, lowering the price did not decrease illicit downloading. Therefore, lowering the price does not decrease this behavior, and we should not decide to lower prices based on this research." Comment on the executive's conclusion. What type of inference is being made? Will the decision not to lower prices be a good one?
8. Do the stages in the research process seem to follow the scientific method?
9. Why is the "define research objectives" of the research process probably the most important stage?
10. Suppose Auchan (http://www.auchan.fr), a hypermarket chain based out of France, was considering opening three hypermarkets in the midwestern United States. What role would theory play in designing a research study to track how the shopping habits of consumers from the United States differ from those in France and from those in Japan? What kind of hypothesis might be examined in a study of this topic?
11. Define research project and research program. Referring to the question immediately above, do you think a research project or a research program is needed to provide useful input to the Auchan decision makers?
12. What type of research design would you recommend in the situations below? For each applied market research project, what might be an example of a "deliverable"? Which do you think would involve actually testing a research hypothesis?
    a. The manufacturer and marketer of flight simulators and other pilot training equipment wish to forecast sales volume for the next five years.
    b. A local chapter of the American Lung Association wishes to identify the demographic characteristics of individuals who donate more than $500 per year.
    c. A major petroleum company is concerned with the increased costs of marketing regular leaded gasoline and is considering dropping this product.
    d. A food company researcher wishes to know what types of food are carried in brown-bag lunches to learn if the company can capitalize on this phenomenon.
    e. A researcher wishes to identify who plays bingo.

Research Activities

1. **'NET** Look up information about the online MBA programs at the University of Phoenix (http://www.phoenix.edu/online_learning). Compare it to the traditional MBA program at your university. Suppose each was looking to expand the numbers of students in their programs, how might the research design differ for each?
2. **'NET** Use a web browser to go to the Gallup Organization's home page at (http://www.gallup.com). The Gallup home page changes regularly. However, it should provide an opportunity to read the results of a recent poll. For example, a poll might break down American's sympathies toward Israel or the Palestinians based on numerous individual characteristics such as political affiliation or religious involvement. After reading the results of a Gallup poll of this type, learn how polls are conducted (hint: see Frequently Asked Questions). You may need to click on the Frequently Asked Questions List (FAQ) to find this information. List the various stages of the research process and how they were (or were not) followed in Gallup's project.
3. Any significant business decision requires input from a research project. Write a brief essay either defending this statement or refuting it.

Video Case 3.1 Black Forest Motors/Mercedes-Benz

Mercedes-Benz entered the United States market in the late 1950s and dominated the foreign luxury car scene during the 1970s and 1980s until other luxury cars like Lexus and Infiniti appeared on stage. And then their sales began to drop substantially—other car companies could offer comparable products for lesser prices. At this point, Mercedes knew it faced a real challenge.

Robert Wilshaw, market manager of the Chicago Region of Mercedes-Benz of North America, affirms that the company met this challenge squarely. New company strategies led to the development of a customer-value triad that highlights perceived goods quality, perceived service quality, and value-based prices.

Mercedes was always regarded as the leader in engineering and design, but their engineers were given two new guidelines. Rule 1 states, "Build the best car in the world," and Rule 2 adds, "Build a more affordable car without breaking rule number one."

Dealerships are a key element in Mercedes' quest to provide quality service. Black Forest Motors in northern Michigan is the premier dealership in this geographic area. Robert S. Chan, the principal, sums up his dealership's relationship with his customer base: "To our customers, we are Mercedes-Benz." This means offering customers "a no-excuses product. . . . [a car] that is as perfect as man can make a machine." But it also means offering high-quality, reliably consistent service that keeps customers coming back. When interviewed, Chan's customers confirm the organization's commitment to "world-class service."

Noting that, in today's market, economics can be as important as engineering, Wilshaw says that Mercedes has proved that it can now build a premier product that can be priced lower than those of their competitors, and they have driven this message into the market place. He adds that the company's price-sensitive strategies have maximized perceived customer value and led to successful new product introductions, which, in turn, have continued to increase overall customer satisfaction.

Question

1. What market research should be done to develop a program that could persuade more customers in the luxury car market to buy Mercedes-Benz? Define the problem, and explain the types of research that would be necessary to develop such a program.

Video Case 3.2 Fisher-Price Rescue Heroes

Fisher-Price's action-figure collection Rescue Heroes, as well as the CBS television show with the same name, is popular with boys ages three and older. The Rescue Heroes characters' mission is to help and rescue with courage, perseverance, resourcefulness, and nonviolent problem solving. The product line consists of action figures (such as Jake Justice Police Officer, Wendy Waters Firefighter, and Rocky Canyon Mountain Ranger), vehicles (for example, Rescue Heroes Quick Response Helicopter), and command centers. Additional details about the characters may be found online at http://www.fisher-price.com/us/rescueheroes/.

Fisher-Price uses marketing research extensively in its new product development process. Rescue Heroes went from an identified need to a commercial product line with the help of a multistage research program. Though exploratory research, the company learned that there was a gap in toys available for preschool and early elementary school boys. Little boys liked the idea of action figures that their older brothers and friends played with, but those toys were difficult for them to understand and handle. The findings led Fisher-Price to coin the term KAGO—"Kids Are Getting Older"—meaning younger children want more grown-up toys.

Research with mothers indicated their toy preferences. The mothers liked the idea of imaginative play with action figures, but they clearly did not want their young children playing with toys that had violent overtones. As a result of these research findings and creative thinking, Fisher-Price came up with the idea of age-appropriate action figures. After much marketing research, the company learned that young boys had trouble with the figures toppling over. The product concept was refined so that the new action figures would have wide feet for stability.

During the marketing research process, Fisher-Price's researchers conduct focus group interviews to test new toy concepts. They interview both kids and moms in search of ideas for toys that have play value—the tangible features and intangible allure that entice a child to interact with and have fun with a toy. Fisher-Price tried versions of the action-figure line in its play laboratory, a large nursery overflowing with toys that is different from ordinary nurseries because there is a wall of one-way mirrors and microphones dangle from the ceiling so that researchers can observe how children are using the toys.

Fisher-Price conducted extensive in-home testing around the country. After the boys played with the toys at home, researchers interviewed the parents about price and asked if they would buy the toys.

Questions

1. Using the flowchart in Exhibit 3.4, outline the steps in the research process that you would recommend that Fisher-Price take in evaluating an idea for a new toy.
2. What type of outcome might Fisher-Price expect from its exploratory research efforts?
3. Describe the program strategy for Rescue Heroes. How did the early research projects influence subsequent research objectives?

CHAPTER 4
THE HUMAN SIDE OF MARKETING RESEARCH: ORGANIZATIONAL AND ETHICAL ISSUES

After studying this chapter, you should

1. Know when research should be conducted externally and when it should be done internally
2. Be familiar with the types of jobs, job responsibilities, and career paths available within the marketing research industry
3. Understand the often conflicting relationship between marketing management and researchers
4. Be able to define ethics and understand how it applies to marketing research
5. Know and appreciate the rights and obligations of a) research respondents—particularly children, b) marketing researchers, and c) research clients or sponsors
6. Know how to avoid a conflict of interest in performing marketing research

Chapter Vignette: Researching Online Auctions—Do's and Don'ts Are Not Always Clear

Auctions are certainly not new. However, auctions are no longer relegated to estate sales, livestock yards, or art sales; eBay and competing websites have brought the consumer auction to the masses. Consumers can bid on practically any product imaginable. The NCAA BCS Football Championship Game is sold out each year. But, you can always bid for tickets on eBay. A lucky owner of tickets for this game can sell tickets to the highest bidder. In 2004, loyal Louisiana State University Tiger fans were willing to bid and pay more than $600 for a ticket with a face value of about $60.

©ASSOCIATED PRESS/AP

Recently, there has been considerable interest in understanding why consumers have flocked to online auctions in such large numbers.[1] The research can help web designers and online auction companies decide how to design their sites to enhance the experience for consumers. When questioned, consumers often talk about how they can get a good price by participating in an auction, or they can get something they might not be able to otherwise. However, could it be that emotional reasons involved in competing to "win" the auctions are equally as important?

When consumers are unable or unwilling to voice their emotional or psychological reasons for behavior, some researchers have turned to hypnosis. Hypnosis relaxes the inhibitions of consumers and can get them to behave in a manner that may more accurately reflect their true thoughts, emotions, and behavior.[2] A researcher may consider using hypnosis to study online auctions. Research participants could be recruited and asked to participate in a real online auction on eBay. Half of the participants will participate in the auction while a researcher looks on. The other half will do the same thing, but only after being induced into a hypnotic state by a member of the research team.

When preparing the report, the researcher notices that, indeed, those in the hypnotic state reported experiencing more emotions and more feelings of competitiveness than did other participants. Hypnotized respondents also placed more bids, purchased more goods, and had higher average price offers than did the others. Although the results appear to be valuable to the client, the researcher is beginning to have some reservations about the research approach used. Is the use of hypnosis ever ethical marketing research?[3] If so, would this situation qualify as one in which there are no ethical issues in the use of hypnosis? Questions like these continue to plague the researcher. Compounding this problem is the fact that the research client wanted the research report completed by yesterday. The researcher suspects that the company already has a tactical plan for redesigning their web operations. It isn't clear that the research results would ever be used anyway.

Who Does the Research?

The vignette described above involves one company hiring an outside company to provide results from a research project. Although this is very typical, many companies have their own employees perform research projects and research programs. Thus, research is sometimes performed in-house, meaning that employees of the company that will benefit from the research project actually perform the research. In other cases, the research is performed by an **outside agency**, meaning that the company that will benefit from the research results hires an independent, outside firm to perform a research project.

While it would seem that **in-house research** would usually be of higher quality because of the increased knowledge of the researchers conducting the studies, there are several reasons why employees of the firm may not always be the best people to do the job. When the firm facing a decision encounters one of the following situations, they should consider having the research performed by an outside agency:

- An outside agency often can provide a fresh perspective. Creativity is often hindered by too much knowledge. When a firm is seeking new ideas, particularly in discovery-oriented research, an outsider is not constrained by the groupthink that often affects a company employee. In other words, employees who spend so much time together in their day-to-day work activities begin to act and think alike to a large degree. History is filled with stories of products that remained unsuccessful commercially for years until someone from outside the company discovered a useful application. The technology for a microwave oven was invented in the 1940s by a company called Raytheon. Raytheon worked on radar systems for the Allied military in World War II. Not until someone from another company, Amana, tested the concept of using microwaves in a kitchen appliance did it become a commercial success.
- An outside agency often can be more objective. When a firm is facing a particularly sensitive situation that may even impact a large number of jobs within the company, it may be difficult for researchers to be objective. Alternatively, if a particular chief executive within the firm is in love with some new idea, researchers may feel a great deal of pressure to present results that are supportive of the concept. In these cases, outside researchers may be a good choice. Since they don't have to work for the company and interact with the players involved on a daily basis, they are less concerned about presenting results that may not be truly welcome.
- An outside agency may have special expertise. When a firm needs research requiring a particular expertise that some outside agency specializes in, it may be a good idea to use that firm to conduct the research. For example, if a company is searching for new ideas about how to use its website, an online focus group interview may be needed. While this is a skill that may not be prevalent within the company, there are several research firms that specialize in this particular type of research. Thus, the outside agency may have greater competency in this specific area.

Likewise, there are conditions that make in-house research more attractive as well, as in the following situations:

- If the research project needs to be completed very quickly, chances are that in-house researchers can get started more quickly and get quicker access to internal resources that can help get the project done in short order.
- If the research project will require the close collaboration of many other employees from diverse areas of the organization, then in-house research may be preferable. The in-house

Outside agency
An independent research firm contracted by the company that actually will benefit from the research.

In-house research
Research performed by employees of the company that will benefit from the research.

TOTHEPOINT

To manage a business is to manage its future; and to manage the future is to manage information.

—Marion Harper

research firms can usually gain cooperation and can more quickly ascertain just who needs to be interviewed and where those people can be found.

- A third reason for doing a project in-house has to do with economy. In-house research can almost always be done more cheaply than that done by an outside research firm.
- If secrecy is a major concern, then the research is best done in-house. Even though the outside firm might be trusted, it may take slightly less care in disguising its research efforts. Thus, other companies may pick up on signals in the marketplace that suggest the area of research for a firm. (See Exhibit 4.1.)

This chapter focuses on the human side of research. We first discuss the internal working of a research unit within a large company. We then turn to the different types of options that exist when dealing with an outside agency. All of this is wrapped up by a discussion of the many ways in which ethics and research come together.

Organizational Structure
of Marketing Research

According to the American Marketing Association, 76 percent of organizations reported having formal marketing research departments. Consumer products companies, manufacturers, and retailers are most likely to have an in-house marketing research department.[4] Larger companies also are more likely to have marketing research departments.

The placement of marketing research within a firm's organizational structure and the structure of the research department itself vary substantially, depending on the firm's acceptance of the marketing concept and its stage of marketing research sophistication. A marketing research department can easily become isolated with poor organizational placement. Researchers may lack a voice in executive committees when they have no continuous relationship with marketing management. This can occur when the research department is positioned at an inappropriately low level. Given the critically important nature of the intelligence coming out of a research department, it should be placed relatively high in the organizational structure to ensure that senior management is well informed. Research departments should also be linked with a broad spectrum of other units within the organization. Thus, they should be positioned to provide credible information both upstream and downstream within the marketing organization.

Research departments that perform a staff function must wait for management to request assistance. Often the term "client" is used by the research department to refer to line management for whom services are being performed. The research department responds to clients' requests and is responsible for the design and execution of all research. It should function like an internal consulting organization that develops action-oriented, data-based recommendations.

Marketing Research Jobs

Marketing research organizations themselves consist of layers of employees. Each employee has certain specific functions to perform based on his or her area of expertise and experience. A look at these jobs not only describes the potential structure of a research organization, but it also provides insight into the types of careers available in marketing research.

▣ SMALL FIRMS

While it is difficult to precisely define the boundaries between small firms, mid-sized firms, and large firms, generally speaking,

government statistics usually consider firms with fewer than 100 employees to be small. In small firms, the vice president of marketing may be in charge of all significant marketing research. This officer generally has a sales manager collect and analyze sales histories, trade association statistics, and other internal data. Small marketing companies usually have few resources and special competencies to conduct large-scale, sophisticated research projects. An advertising agency or a firm that specializes in marketing research will be contracted if a large-scale survey is needed. At the other extreme, a large company like Procter & Gamble may staff its research departments with more than 100 people.

▣ MID-SIZED FIRMS

Mid-sized firms can be thought of as those with between 100 and 500 employees. In a mid-sized marketing firm, the research department might be organized as shown in Exhibit 4.2. Someone usually holds the position of **director of marketing research**. This person provides leadership in research efforts and integrates all staff-level research activities. (This position will be discussed in greater detail in the next section.)

When market research departments grow, they begin to specialize by product or business unit. This happened in the Marriot Corporation, which now has a specific director of marketing research for its lodging facilities.

Director of marketing research
This person provides leadership in research efforts and integrates all staff-level research activities into one effort. The director plans, executes, and controls the firm's marketing research function.

EXHIBIT 4.2
Structure of a Medium-Sized Research Department

Research analyst
A person responsible for client contact, project design, preparation of proposals, selection of research suppliers, and supervision of data collection, analysis, and reporting activities.

Research assistants
Research employees who provide technical assistance with questionnaire design, data analyses, and similar activities.

Manager of decision support systems
Employee who supervises the collection and analysis of sales, inventory, and other periodic customer relationship management (CRM) data.

Forecast analyst
Employee who provides technical assistance such as running computer programs and manipulating data to generate a sales forecast.

A **research analyst** is responsible for client contact, project design, preparation of proposals, selection of research suppliers, and supervision of data collection, analysis, and reporting activities. Normally, the research analyst is responsible for several projects simultaneously covering a wide spectrum of the firm's organizational activities. He or she works with product or division management and makes recommendations based on analysis of collected data.

Research assistants (or associates) provide technical assistance with questionnaire design, data analyses, and so forth. Another common name for this position is *junior analyst*. The **manager of decision support systems** supervises the collection and analysis of sales, inventory, and other periodic customer relationship management (CRM) data. Sales forecasts for product lines usually are developed using analytical and quantitative techniques. Sales information is provided to satisfy the planning, analysis, and control needs of decision makers. The manager of decision support systems may be assisted by a **forecast analyst** who provides technical assistance, such as running computer programs and manipulating data to forecast sales.

Personnel within a planning department may perform the marketing research function in a mid-sized firm. At times, they may outsource some research functions. The planner may design research studies and then contract with outside firms that supply research services such as interviewing or data processing. They can combine the input from these outside agencies with their own work to write research reports.

▓ LARGE RESEARCH FIRMS

As marketing research departments grow, they tend to specialize by product or strategic business unit. Major firms can be thought of as those with over 500 employees. Marriott Corporation has a director of marketing research for lodging (for example, Marriott Hotels and Resorts, Courtyard by Marriott, and Fairfield Inn) and a director of marketing research for contract services and restaurants (for example, Roy Rogers, Big Boy, and Senior Living Services). Each business unit's research director reports to the vice president of corporate marketing services. Many large organizations have managers of customer quality research who specialize in conducting surveys to measure consumers' satisfaction with product quality.

Exhibit 4.3 illustrates the organization of a major firm's marketing research department. Within this organization, the centralized marketing research department conducts research for all the division's product groups. This is typical of a large research department that conducts much of its own research, including fieldwork. The director of marketing research reports to the vice president of marketing.

Other positions within a major firm's research department may include director of data collection (field supervisor), manager of quantitative research, focus group moderator, and manager of data processing. These are not shown in Exhibit 4.3. Even large firms sometimes outsource some research functions or even an entire project from time to time. For now, we turn our attention to the job of director of marketing research and the interface between the marketing research department and other departments.

The Director of Marketing Research as a Manager

A director of marketing research plans, executes, and controls the firm's marketing research function. This person typically serves on company executive committees that identify competitive opportunities and formulate marketing strategies. The various directors from each functional area generally make up this committee (such as finance, sales, production, and so forth). The director of marketing research provides the research perspective during meetings. For instance, the researcher can provide input as to what types of market intelligence can be feasibly obtained given the decision being discussed. Marketing research directors typically face problems like these:

- Skilled research professionals like conducting research better than managing people. They pride themselves on being hands-on researchers. However, a director is a manager and spends more time in meetings and managing than actually conducting research.
- The research management role often is not formally recognized.

EXHIBIT 4.3 Organization of the Marketing Research Department in a Large Firm

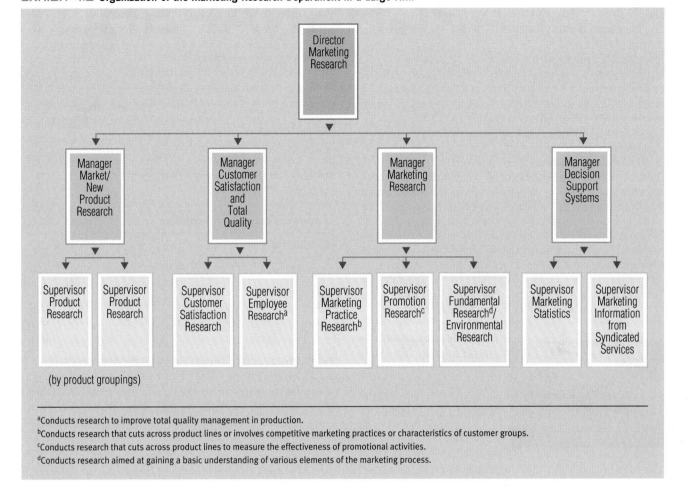

aConducts research to improve total quality management in production.
bConducts research that cuts across product lines or involves competitive marketing practices or characteristics of customer groups.
cConducts research that cuts across product lines to measure the effectiveness of promotional activities.
dConducts research aimed at gaining a basic understanding of various elements of the marketing process.

- Outstanding research professionals often have trouble delegating responsibility. The pride that comes with being a knowledgeable researcher makes it difficult to give up control. They may genuinely feel "I can do it better myself." As a result, they delegate only elementary or tedious tasks to subordinates. The subordinates can sometimes become disenchanted and thus become unhappy with their work.
- Finally, research is often seen as a hodgepodge of techniques available to answer individual, unrelated questions. According to this view, a research operation encompasses an array of more or less equal projects, each handled by a project director. Hence, many firms view a full-time director as unnecessary.[5]

Sources of Conflict between Marketing Management and Marketing Research

In principle, the functions of marketing research should merge harmoniously with the objectives of marketing management for the benefit of both parties. In practice, the relationship between the marketing research department and the users of marketing research frequently is characterized by misunderstanding and conflict.

■ RESEARCH THAT IMPLIES CRITICISM

A product manager who requests a survey of dealer loyalty will not be happy if the survey finds that the dealers are extremely critical. Similarly, a sales manager who informally projects a 5 percent increase in sales will not like hearing from the research department that the market potential

RESEARCHSNAPSHOT

Marketing Research Pays

Marketing research can pay! Careers in marketing research can be very lucrative. This is particularly true if one has the right attributes. These attributes include being a good people person as well as having good quantitative skills and a good education. The fastest career tracks in marketing research are for those with at least a master's degree.

The prospects of finding a job remain good. Marketing researchers have long been in greater demand than the supply can address. The salaries also can be very lucrative. The 2002 U.S. Department of Labor Salary Survey suggests that marketing research analysts' salaries are generally between $40,000 and $80,000. These are for actual research analysts and not research directors. Beginning research employees, with little or no experience, generally enter the firm as a survey researcher. Those salaries are considerably less, generally between $20,000 and $40,000. However, they require no significant work experience.

Job opportunities in marketing research exist outside the United States as well. The salaries also are lucrative in other countries. The chart below shows salaries for non-managerial marketing research positions in the United States, Australia, Japan, and the

United Kingdom. For comparison purposes, salaries for non-mangerial sales employees also are provided. The salaries are expressed in thousands of U.S. dollars and reflect the latest available statistics. As can be seen, research jobs compare very favorably. In addition, researchers that move into research director positions see a substantial increase in pay. Perhaps you'll give marketing research a try?

Common Currency ($)	Australia	UK	Japan	United States
Sales Market Analysts				
High	44.78	122.81	82.82	55.00
Low	33.58	61.40	41.41	35.00
Marketing Research				
High	55.97	78.95	82.82	76.30
Low	48.51	43.86	49.69	38.76

Sources: Enright, A. (2005), "Carve out a Niche," Marketing News (November 15), 17; Fellman, M.W. (1998), "Survey: Employment Levels Critically Low in MR Industry," Marketing News, 322 (June 8), 12; U.S. Department of Labor (2006), "Wages, Benefits and Earnings," http://www.bls.gov/bls/wages.htm. Accessed May 2, 2006. Robert Walters (2006), "Market Research Search Results," http://www.robertwalters.com. Accessed January 20, 2006.

©PHOTODISC/GETTY IMAGES

indicates sales volume should be up by 20 percent. In each of these situations, marketing research presents information that implies criticism of a line executive's decision. In personal life, a sure way to lose a friend is to be openly critical of him or her. Things are no different in business.

MONEY

Research budgets are a source of conflict between management and researchers. Financial managers often see research as a cost rather than as an investment or a way of lowering risk. Successful decisions that are supported by research are seldom attributed to the marketing researcher. Thus, as is often true in many areas of business, managers often want to spend as little as possible on research. In contrast, researchers often vigorously resist cutting corners in conducting research. For instance, they may feel that a large random sample is necessary to adequately address a research question using descriptive research. This approach can be very expensive and sometimes time consuming. Inevitably, management's desire to save money and the researcher's desire to conduct rigorous research conflict. Successful research projects often are those that are based on compromise. This may involve working within a budget that will produce meaningful results and sacrifice precision and rigor minimally.

TIME

Researchers say, "Good research takes time!" Managers say, "Time is money!" Like oil and water, these two views do not go together easily. A look back at the research process in the last chapter makes it clear that it can take some time to complete a research project. Simply planning one can involve days, if not weeks, of study and preparation. For instance, conducting a literature review or a review of previous studies can take weeks. Without them, the researcher may not be able to develop specific research hypotheses that would direct the project very specifically toward the current issue. Other times, the researcher may wish to interview more people than time can allow or take the time to use a more sophisticated data analysis approach.

The more quickly the research project is done, the less likely it is to be successful. This doesn't mean it can't provide valuable information. It simply is not as certain that a quickly put-together study will provide valuable answers as would a more deliberately planned project. When studies are rushed, the following sources of error become more prominent than they would be otherwise:

- Conducting a study that is needed. Taking more time to perform a literature search, including through company and industry reports, may have provided the needed intelligence without a new study.
- Addressing the wrong issue. Taking more time to make sure the decision statement is well defined and that the research questions that follow will truly address relevant issues can lessen the chance that the research goes in the wrong direction.
- Sampling difficulties. Correctly defining, identifying, and contacting a truly representative sample is a difficult and time consuming task. However, in some types of research, the quality of results depends directly on the quality of the sample.
- Inadequate data analysis. The researcher may analyze the data quickly and without the rigor that would otherwise be taken. Therefore, certain assumptions may not be considered, and important information within the data is simply not discovered.

Sometimes a marketing researcher will have to submit to the time pressure and do a quick-and-dirty study. A sudden event can make it necessary to acquire data quickly—but rush jobs can sometimes be avoided with proper planning of the research program. If it is necessary to conduct a study under severe time limitations, the researcher is obligated to point this out to management. The research report and presentation should include all the study limitations, including those that resulted from a shortage of time or money.

INTUITIVE DECISION MAKING

The fact of the matter is that managers are decision makers. They are action-oriented, and they often rely on gut reaction and intuition. Many times their intuition serves them well, so it isn't surprising that they sometimes do not believe a research project will help improve their decision making. At other times, they resist research because it just may provide information that is counter to their intuition or their desires. They particularly abhor being held back while waiting for some research report.

If managers do use research, they often request simple projects that will provide concrete results with certainty. Researchers tend to see problems as complex questions that can be answered only within probability ranges. One aspect of this conflict is the fact that a research report provides findings, but cannot make decisions. Decision-oriented executives may unrealistically expect research to make decisions for them or provide some type of guarantee that the action they take will be correct. While research provides information for decision making, it does not always remove all the uncertainties involved in complex decisions. Certain alternatives may be eliminated, but the research may reveal new aspects of a problem. Although research is a valuable decision-making tool, it does not relieve the executive of the decision-making task.

Presentation of the right facts can be extremely useful. However, decision makers often believe that researchers collect the wrong facts. Many researchers view themselves as technicians who generate numbers using sophisticated mathematical and statistical techniques; they may spend more time on technical details than on satisfying managerial needs. Each person who has a narrow perspective of another's job is a partial cause of the problem of generating limited or useless information.

The following two advertising approaches typify poor decision-making that could have been avoided through focused research:

1. An Internet retailer (Send.com) used a television ad to try to stimulate more gift purchasing among its customers. The spot centers on several men on the golf course drinking champagne. The "punch line" comes when one of the guys is hit in the groin. The voice over exclaims, "He just got hit in the little giver!"
2. Another company that registers Internet domains ran the following ad: Two men in a locker-room shower are talking casually with each other. One says, "I didn't know you could get one that long." The other replies, "Yes, it only cost me 60 bucks and lasts for two years." The tagline: "Longer domain names now available."

TOTHEPOINT

Someone's sitting in the shade today because someone planted a tree a long time ago.

—Warren Buffett

RESEARCHSNAPSHOT

"Seat-of-the-Pants" Marketing

Often, the term "seat of the pants" is used to refer to intuitive decision making. Marketing decision makers of all types rely on seat-of-the-pants decision making for numerous reasons. Some say that it is just more fun to make decisions that way instead of letting research guide your choice. Others simply are in too much of a hurry to wait for results from a thorough market research project.

In recent years, place marketing, or the marketing of geographical destinations like cities or tourist areas, has become very prevalent. City planners seek to develop an area economically by attracting industries and people to their area. This provides a steady job and economic base. Place marketing efforts have been successful in attracting automobile manufacturing plants, high-tech firms, retail developments, professional sports teams, and even retirees. However, for every effort that succeeds, there are many that fail. Even though the stakes are very high, city planners and political officials seldom conduct research prior to implementing a specific place marketing program. Instead, they fly by the "seat of the pants"! The more successful programs are generally backed by months, if not years, of well-planned research.

Do seat-of-the-pants decisions have a better than average success rate? Another way to look at this would be to ask if an informed decision maker can somehow make his or her own luck. Although this is an interesting research proposition, and there is a role for intuition in decision making, place marketers appear better served by hiring research professionals to provide information that reduces the reliance on luck.

Sources: Ulaga, Wolfgang, Arun Sharma, and R. Krishnan (2002), "Plant Location and Place Marketing: Understanding the Process from the Business Customer's Perspective," Industrial Marketing Management, 31 (August), 393–401; Lemons, Bob (2002), "Ad Pearls of Wisdom Help Guide the Way," Marketing News, 36 (October 28), 10; Brown, Stephen (2005), "Fortune Favors the Brand," Marketing Research, 17 (Summer), 22–27.

©RACHEL EPSTEIN/THE IMAGE WORKS

Welcome to RIGBY
Birthplace of Television
Philo T. Farnsworth
Easy off -- Easy on!

Both of these are the types of punch lines that a male ad executive may find funny and entertaining; however, the audience for these ads is not all male. Had research been used to test these ideas prior to spending the money to produce the ads and buy the spots, it would have revealed that men didn't respond as favorably as expected to these ads and women found them boorish.[6] Thus, intuition has its limits as a replacement for informed market intelligence.[7]

■ FUTURE DECISIONS BASED ON PAST EXPERIENCE

Managers wish to predict the future, but researchers measure only current or past events. In 1957, Ford introduced the Edsel, one of the classic marketing failures of all time. One reason for the Edsel's failure was that the marketing research conducted several years before the car's introduction indicated a strong demand for a medium-priced car for the "man on his way up." By the time the car was introduced, however, consumer preference had shifted to two cars, one being a small import for the suburban wife. Not all research information is so dated, but all research describes what people have done in the past. In this sense, researchers use the past to predict the future.

Reducing the Conflict between Management and Researchers

Given the conflicting goals of management and research, it is probably impossible to completely eliminate the conflict. However, when researchers and decision makers work more closely together, there will be less conflict. The more closely they work together, the better the communication between decision makers and researchers. In this way, business decision makers will better understand the information needs and work requirements of researchers. It will allow for better planning of research projects and a greater appreciation for the role that research plays in minimizing the riskiness of business decision making. Exhibit 4.4 lists some common areas of conflict between research and management. Many of these can be avoided through improved understanding of the other's position.

With closer cooperation, managers are more involved with projects from the beginning. Early involvement increases the likelihood that managers will accept and act on the results. Researchers'

EXHIBIT 4.4 Areas of Conflict Between Top Management and Marketing Researchers

Area of Potential Conflict	Top Management's Position	Marketing Researcher's Position
Research responsibility	Marketing researchers lack a sense of accountability. The sole function of the marketing researcher is to provide information.	The responsibility for research should be explicitly defined, and this responsibility should be consistently followed. The researcher should be involved with top management in decision making.
Research personnel	Marketing researchers are generally poor communicators who lack enthusiasm, skills, and imagination.	Top managers are anti-intellectual. Researchers should be hired, judged, and compensated on the basis of their research capabilities.
Budget	Research costs too much. Since the marketing research department's contribution is difficult to measure, budget cuts in the department are defensible.	"You get what you pay for." Research must have a continuing, long-term commitment from top management.
Assignments	Projects tend to be overengineered and not executed with a sense of urgency. Researchers have a ritualized, staid approach.	Top managers make too many nonresearchable or emergency requests and do not allocate sufficient time or money.
Problem definition	The marketing researcher is best equipped to define the problem; it is sufficient for the top manager to give general direction. Top managers cannot help it if circumstances change. The marketing researcher must appreciate this and be willing to respond to changes.	Researchers are often not given all the relevant facts about situations, which often change after research is under way. Top managers are generally unsympathetic to this widespread problem.
Research reporting	Most reports are dull, use too much jargon and too many qualifiers, and are not decision-oriented. Reports too often are presented after a decision has been made.	Top managers treat research reports superficially. Good research demands thorough reporting and documentation. Top managers give insufficient time to prepare good reports.
Use of research	Top managers should be free to use research as they see fit. Changes in the need for and timing of research are sometimes unavoidable.	Top managers' use of research to support a predetermined position or to confirm or excuse past decisions represents misuse. Also, it is wasteful to request research and then not use it after it has been conducted.

Based on John G. Keane, "Some Observations on Marketing Research in Top Management Decision Making," Journal of Marketing, October 1969, p. 13.

responsibility should be made explicit by a formal job description. Better planning and an annual statement of the research program for the upcoming year will help minimize emergency assignments, which usually waste resources and demoralize personnel.

Marketing researchers likewise will come to understand management's perspective better. Researchers enhance company profits by encouraging better decisions. The closer together managers and researchers work, the more researchers realize that managers sometimes need information urgently. Thus, they should try to develop cost-saving research alternatives and realize that sometimes a quick-and-dirty study is necessary, even though it may not be as scientifically rigorous as might be desired. Sometimes, quick-and-dirty studies still provide usable and timely information. In other words, they should focus on results.

Perhaps most important is more effective communication of the research findings and research designs. The researchers must understand the interests and needs of the users of the research. If the researchers are sensitive to the decision-making orientation of management and can translate research performance into management language, organizational conflict will diminish.

A **research generalist** can effectively serve as a link between management and the research specialist. The research generalist acts as a problem definer, an educator, a liaison, a communicator,

Research generalist
An employee who serves as a link between management and research specialists. The research generalist acts as a problem definer, an educator, a liaison, a communicator, and a friendly ear.

EXHIBIT 4.5
Two-Way Improvement

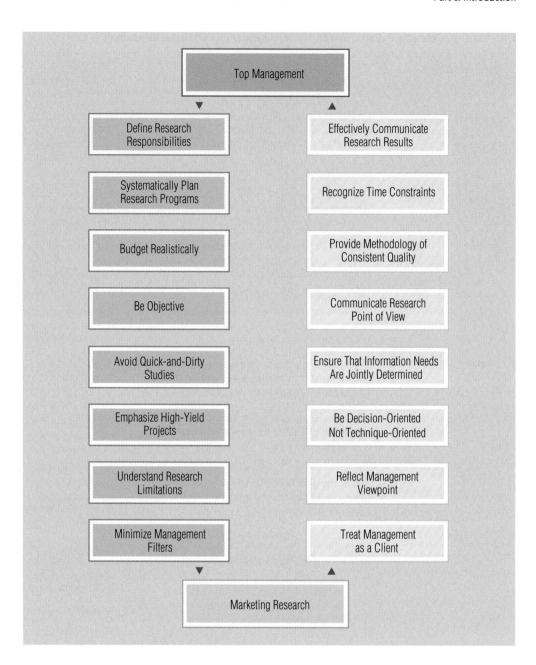

and a friendly ear. This intermediary could work with specialists who understand management's needs and demands. The student of marketing research who has a business degree seems most suited for this coordinating function.

Several strategies for reducing the conflict between management and research are possible. Managers generally should plan the role of research better, and researchers should become more decision-oriented and improve their communication skills (see Exhibit 4.5).[8]

Cross-Functional Teams

Cross-functional teams
Employee teams composed of individuals from various functional areas such as engineering, production, finance, and marketing who share a common purpose.

Marketing orientation was discussed in Chapter 1. In a truly marketing-oriented organization, all employees are involved in the intelligence-gathering and dissemination process. Therefore, employees from different areas of the organization are more likely to communicate and act on marketing information in marketing-oriented firms.

Thus, employees are more likely to discuss market information between different functional areas in a marketing-oriented firm. **Cross-functional teams** are composed of individuals from various functional areas such as engineering, production, finance, and marketing who share a common purpose. Cross-functional teams help organizations focus on a core business process, such as customer service or new-product development. Working in teams reduces the tendency for employees to focus single-mindedly on an isolated functional activity. Cross-functional teams help employees increase customer value since communication about their specific desires and opinions are better communicated across the firm.

At trendsetting organizations, many marketing research directors are members of cross-functional teams. New-product development, for example, may be done by a cross-functional team of engineers, finance executives, production personnel, marketing managers, and marketing researchers who take an integrated approach to solve a problem or exploit opportunities. In the old days, marketing research may not have been involved in developing new products until long after many key decisions about product specifications and manufacturing had been made. Now marketing researchers' input is part of an integrated team effort. Researchers act both as business consultants and as providers of technical services. Researchers working in teams are more likely to understand the broad purpose of their research and less likely to focus exclusively on research methodology.

The effective cross-functional team is a good illustration of the marketing concept in action. It reflects an effort to satisfy customers by using all the organization's resources. Cross-functional teams are having a dramatic impact on views of the role of marketing research within the organization.

Research Suppliers and Contractors

As mentioned in the beginning of the chapter, there are times when it makes good sense to obtain marketing research from an outside organization. In these cases, marketing managers must interact with **research suppliers**, who are commercial providers of marketing research services. Marketing research is carried out by firms that may be variously classified as marketing research consulting companies, such as Burke or Market Facts, Inc.; advertising agencies, such as J. Walter Thompson; suppliers of syndicated research services, such as Roper Starch Worldwide; as well as interviewing agencies, universities, and government agencies.

Research suppliers
Commercial providers of marketing research services.

Syndicated Service

No matter how large a firm's marketing research department is, some projects are too expensive to perform in-house. A **syndicated service** is a marketing research supplier that provides standardized information for many clients in return for a fee. They are a sort of supermarket for standardized research results. For example, J. D. Power and Associates sells research about customers' ratings of automobile quality and their reasons for satisfaction. Most automobile manufacturers and their advertising agencies subscribe to this syndicated service because the company provides important industry-wide information it gathers from a national sample of thousands of car buyers. By specializing in this type of customer satisfaction research, J. D. Power gains certain economies of scale.

Syndicated service
A marketing research supplier that provides standardized information for many clients in return for a fee.

Syndicated services can provide expensive information economically to numerous clients because the information is not specific to one client but interests many. Such suppliers offer standardized information to measure media audiences, wholesale and retail distribution data, and other forms of data.

Standardized Research Services

Standardized research service companies develop a unique methodology for investigating a business specialty area. Several research firms, such as Retail Forward (http://www.retailforward.com), provide location services for retail firms. The Research Snapshot Box on the following page illustrates an interesting application for which an outside location service company may be particularly useful. Research suppliers conduct studies for multiple, individual clients using the same methods.

Standardized research service
Companies that develop a unique methodology for investigating a business specialty area.

ACNielsen (http://www.acnielsen.com) collects information throughout the new-product development process, from initial concept screening through test-marketing. The BASES system

RESEARCHSNAPSHOT

Finding Häagen-Dazs in China

Ice cream lovers needn't worry if they are sent on a business trip to China. **Häagen-Dazs** ice cream shops first appeared in Shanghai, China, in 1996 and now there are dozens of **Häagen-Dazs** ice cream shops in coastal China, with plans for hundreds more. Clearly, many firms would like to follow **Häagen-Dazs** into China. China is expected to be the world's largest consumer market by 2020. However, where should an ice cream shop be located in China? While location decisions can be difficult enough within the borders of one's own country, imagine trying to decide where to put a shop in a huge, unfamiliar country.

Fortunately, standardized research companies like Retail Forward have resources deployed all around the world that can synthesize Geographic Information System (GIS) information with survey research and other information to assist firms with location decisions in China and in other developing countries. Since U.S.-based retail firms may lack the necessary connections and knowledge (expertise) to efficiently conduct research in faraway places, the use of an outside research provider not only saves time and money, but also yields higher quality results than an in-house study. Imagine how difficult language barriers could be when dealing with the Chinese consumer market.

And, as difficult as identifying good retail locations seems in China, other top emerging retail nations include India, Russia, and the Ukraine. As in China, American and European firms may find that using a research supplier to help with retail location issues in these countries is wiser than doing the research themselves.

Sources: China Business Review (2004), "Häagen-Dazs in China," 31 (Jul/Aug), 22. Hall, Cecily (2005), "Spanning the Retail Globe," WWD: Women's Wear Daily, 190 (7/21), 11.

©CHINA FEATURES/CORBIS SYGMA

"Doing research in a foreign country is often better done by an outside agency with resources in those places."

©RHODA SIDNEY/PHOTOEDIT

can evaluate initiatives relative to other products in the competitive environment. For example, a client can compare its Day-After Recall scores with average scores for a product category.

Even when a firm could perform the research task in-house, research suppliers may be able to conduct the project at a lower cost, faster, and relatively more objectively. A company that wishes to quickly evaluate a new advertising strategy may find an ad agency's research department is able to provide technical expertise on copy development research that is not available within the company itself. Researchers may be well advised to seek outside help with research when conducting research in a foreign country in which the necessary human resources and knowledge to effectively collect data are lacking. The Research Snapshot box above illustrates this situation.

Limited Research Service Companies and Custom Research

Limited-service research suppliers specialize in particular research activities, such as syndicated service, field interviewing, data warehousing, or data processing. Full-service research suppliers sometimes contract these companies for ad hoc marketing research projects. The client usually controls these marketing research agencies or management consulting firms, but the research supplier handles most of the operating details of **custom research** projects. These are projects that are tailored specifically to a client's unique needs. A custom research supplier may employ individuals with titles that imply relationships with clients, such as *account executive* or *account group manager,* as well as functional specialists with titles such as *statistician, librarian, director of field services, director of tabulation and data processing,* and *interviewer.*

EXHIBIT 4.6 **Top 20 Global Research Organizations**

Organization	Headquarters	Website	Employees	Revenue (millions)
VNU NV	Haarlem, Netherlands	www.vnu.com	35,611	$3,429
Taylor Nelson Sofres, PLC	London, U.K.	www.tns-global.com	12,731	$1,721
IMS Health Inc.	Fairfield, Conn., U.S.	www.imshealth.com	6,400	$1,569.0
The Kantar Group	Fairfield, Conn., U.K.	www.kantargroup.com	7,200	$1,136.3
GfK Group	Nuremberg, Germany	www.gfk.com	5,539	$835.5
Ipsos Group SA	Paris, France	www.ipsos.com	4,660	$753.2
Information Resources Inc.	Chicago, U.S.	www.infores.com	2,765	$572.8
Synovate	London, U.K.	www.synovate.com	4,252	$499.3
NOP World	London, U.K.	www.nopworld.com	1,672	$407.1
Westat Inc.	Rockville, Md., U.S.	www.westat.com	1,800	$397.8
Arbitron Inc.	New York, U.S.	www.arbitron.com	929	$296.6
INTAGE Inc.	Tokyo, Japan	www.intage.co.jp	1,350	$246.2
Harris Interactive Inc.	Rochester, N.Y., U.S.	www.harrisinteractive.com	856	$208.9
Maritz Research	Fenton, Mo., U.S.	www.maritzresearch.com	526	$185.3
Video Research Ltd.	Tokyo, Japan	www.videor.co.jp	373	$177.2
J.D. Power and Associates	Westlake Village, Calif., U.S.	www.jdpa.com	787	$167.6
Opinion Research Corp.	Princeton, N.J., U.S.	www.opinionresearch.com	1,538	$147.5
The NPD Group Inc.	Port Washington, N.Y., U.S.	www.npd.com	750	$139.2
Market & Opinion Research Int'l	London, U.K.	www.mori.com	441	$81.0
Lieberman Research Worldwide	Los Angeles, U.S.	www.lrwonline.com	300	$77.7

Exhibit 4.6 lists the top twenty suppliers of global research and their revenues in 2004.[9] Most provide various services ranging from designing activities to fieldwork. The services they can provide are not covered in detail here because they are discussed throughout the book, especially in the sections on fieldwork. However, here we briefly consider some managerial and human aspects of dealing with research suppliers. Clearly, the exhibit reveals that research is big business. Its growth will continue as data availability increases and as businesses desire more precision in their decision making. Therefore, attractive career opportunities are numerous for those with the right skills and desires.

Custom research
Research projects that are tailored specifically to a client's unique needs.

Ethical Issues in Marketing Research

As in all human interactions, ethical issues exist in marketing research. Our earlier discussion of organizational politics and the use of pseudo-research to bolster one's position within the organization introduced a situation where ethics can come into play. This book considers various ethical issues concerning fair business dealings, proper research techniques, and appropriate use of research results in other chapters. The remainder of this chapter addresses society's and managers' concerns about the ethical implications of marketing research.

Ethical Questions Are Philosophical Questions

Ethical questions are philosophical questions. There are several philosophical theories that address how one develops a moral philosophy and how behavior is affected by morals. These include theories about cognitive moral development, the bases for ethical behavioral intentions, and opposing moral values.[10] While ethics remain a somewhat elusive topic, what is clear is that not everyone involved in business, or in fact involved in any human behavior, comes to the table with the same ethical standards or orientations.[11]

Marketing ethics is the application of morals to behavior related to the exchange environment. Generally, good ethics conforms to the notion of "right," and a lack of ethics conforms to the notion of "wrong." Highly ethical behavior can be characterized as being fair, just, and acceptable.[12] Ethical values can be highly influenced by one's moral standards. **Moral standards** are principles that reflect beliefs about what is ethical and what is unethical. More simply, they can be thought of as rules distinguishing right from wrong. The Golden Rule, "Do unto others as you would have them do unto you," is one such ethical principle.

An **ethical dilemma** simply refers to a situation in which one chooses from alternative courses of actions, each with different ethical implications. Each individual develops a philosophy or way of thinking that is applied to resolve the dilemmas they face. Many people use moral standards to guide their actions when confronted with an ethical dilemma. Others adapt an ethical orientation that rejects absolute principles. Their ethics are based more on the social or cultural acceptability of behavior. If it conforms to social or cultural norms, then it is ethical. From a moral theory standpoint, idealism is a term that reflects the degree to which one accepts moral standards as a guide for behavior. **Relativism** is a term that reflects the degree to which one rejects moral standards in favor of the acceptability of some action. This way of thinking rejects absolute principles in favor of situation-based evaluations. Thus, an action that is judged ethical in one situation can be deemed unethical in another. In contrast, **idealism** is a term that reflects the degree to which one bases one's morality on moral standards. Someone who is an ethical idealist will try to apply ethical principles like the golden rule in all ethical dilimmas.

For example, a student may face an ethical dilemma when taking a test. Another student may arrange to exchange multiple choice responses to a test via electronic text messages. This represents an ethical dilemma because there are alternative courses of action each with differing moral implications. An ethical idealist may apply a rule that cheating is always wrong and therefore would not be likely to participate in the behavior. An ethical relativist may instead argue that the behavior is acceptable because a lot of the other students will be doing the same. In other words, the consensus is that this sort of cheating is acceptable, so this student would be likely to go ahead and participate in the behavior. Marketing researchers, marketing managers, and even consumers face ethical dilemmas practically every day. The following sections describe how this can occur.

General Rights and Obligations of Concerned Parties

Everyone involved in marketing research can face an ethical dilemma. For this discussion, we can divide those involved in research into three parties:

1. The people actually performing the research, who can also be thought of as the "doers"
2. The research client, sponsor, or the management team requesting the research, who can be thought of as "users" of marketing research
3. The research participants, meaning the actual research respondents or subjects

Each party has certain rights and obligations toward the other parties. Exhibit 4.7 diagrams these relationships.

Marketing ethics
The application of morals to behavior related to the exchange environment.

Moral standards
Principles that reflect beliefs about what is ethical and what is unethical.

Ethical dilemma
Refers to a situation in which one chooses from alternative courses of actions, each with different ethical implications.

Relativism
A term that reflects the degree to which one rejects moral standards in favor of the acceptability of some action. This way of thinking rejects absolute principles in favor of situation-based evaluations.

Idealism
A term that reflects the degree to which one bases one's morality on moral standards.

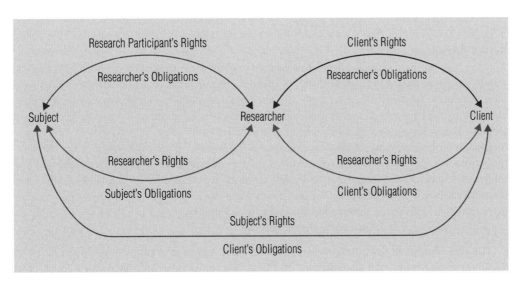

EXHIBIT 4.7
Interaction of Rights and Obligations

Like the rest of business, research works best when all parties act ethically. Each party depends on the other to do so. A client depends on the researcher to be honest in presenting research results. The researcher depends on the client to be honest in presenting the reasons for doing the research and in describing the business situation. Each is also dependent on the research participant's honesty in answering questions during a research study. Thus, each is morally obligated toward the other. Likewise, each also has certain rights. The following section elaborates on the obligations and rights of each party.

Rights and Obligations of the Research Participant

Most marketing research is conducted with the research participant's consent. In other words, the participation is active. Traditional survey research requires that a respondent voluntarily answer questions in one way or another. This may involve answering questions on the phone, responding to an e-mail request, or even sending a completed questionnaire by regular mail. In these cases, **informed consent** means that the individual understands what the researcher wants him or her to do and consents to the research study. In other cases, research participants may not be aware that they are being monitored in some way. For instance, a research firm may monitor superstore purchases via an electronic scanner. The information may assist in understanding how customers respond to promotions. However, no consent is provided since the participant is participating passively. The ethical responsibilities vary depending on whether participation is active or passive.

Informed consent
When an individual understands what the researcher wants him or her to do and consents to the research study.

▦ THE OBLIGATION TO BE TRUTHFUL

When someone willingly consents to participate actively, it is generally expected that he or she will provide truthful answers. Honest cooperation is the main obligation of the research participant. In return for being truthful, the subject has the right to expect confidentiality. **Confidentiality** means that information involved in the research will not be shared with others. When the respondent truly believes that confidentiality will be maintained, then it becomes much easier to respond truthfully, even about potentially sensitive topics. Likewise, the researcher and the researcher sponsor also may expect the respondent to maintain confidentiality. For instance, if the research involves a new food product from Nabisco, then they may not want the respondent to discuss the idea for fear that the idea may fall into the competition's hands. Thus, confidentiality is a tool to help ensure truthful responses.

Confidentiality
The information involved in a research will not be shared with others.

■ PARTICIPANT'S RIGHT TO PRIVACY

Active Research

Americans relish their privacy. Hence, the right to privacy is an important issue in marketing research. This issue involves the participant's freedom to choose whether to comply with the investigator's request. Traditionally, researchers have assumed that individuals make an informed choice. However, critics have argued that the old, the poor, the poorly educated, and other underprivileged individuals may be unaware of their right to choose. They have further argued that an interviewer may begin with some vague explanation of a survey's purpose, initially ask questions that are relatively innocuous, and then move to questions of a highly personal nature. It has been suggested that subjects be informed of their right to be left alone or to break off the interview at any time. Researchers should not follow the tendency to "hold on" to busy respondents. However, this view definitely is not universally accepted in the research community.

The privacy issue is illustrated by these questions:

- "Is a telephone call that interrupts family dinner an invasion of privacy?"
- "Is an e-mail requesting response to a 30-minute survey an invasion of privacy?"

Generally, interviewing firms practice common courtesy by trying not to interview late in the evening or at other inconvenient times. However, the computerized random phone number interview has stimulated increased debate over the privacy issue. As a practical matter, respondents may feel more relaxed about privacy issues if they know who is conducting the survey. Thus, it is generally recommended that field interviewers indicate that they are legitimate researchers and name the company they work for as soon as someone answers the phone. For in-person surveys, interviewers should wear official name tags and provide identification giving their name and the names of their companies.

Do Not Call legislation
Restricts any telemarketing effort from calling consumers who either register with a no-call list or who request not to be called.

Research companies should adhere to the principles of the "Do Not Call" policy and should respect consumers' "Internet privacy." **Do Not Call legislation** restricts any telemarketing effort from calling consumers who either register with a no-call list in their state or who request not to be called. Legislators aimed these laws at sales-related calls. However, legislation in several states, including California, Louisiana, and Rhode Island, has extended this legislation to apply to "those that seek marketing information." Thus, the legislation effectively protects consumers' privacy from researchers as well as salespeople.[13]

Consumers often are confused about the difference between telemarketing efforts and true marketing research. Part of this is because telemarketers sometimes disguise their sales efforts by opening the conversation by saying they are doing research. The resulting confusion contributes to both increased refusal rates and lower trust. In 1980, a public opinion poll found that 19 percent of Americans reported having refused to participate in a marketing survey within the past year. Today, that number approaches 50 percent. In 2001, only 40 percent of Americans either agreed or strongly agreed that marketers will protect their privacy. That number is down from 50 percent in 1995.[14]

Companies using the Internet to do marketing research also face legislative changes. Much of this legislation is aimed at making sure consumers are properly notified about the collection of data and to whom it will be distributed. Researchers should make sure that consumers are given a clear and easy way to either consent to participation in active research or to easily opt out. Furthermore, companies should ensure that the information consumers send via the Internet is secure.[15]

Passive Research

Passive research involves different types of privacy issues. Generally, it is believed that unobtrusive observation of public behavior in places such as stores, airports, and museums is not a serious invasion of privacy. This belief is based on the fact that the consumers are indeed anonymous in that they are never identified by name nor is any attempt made to identify them. They are "faces in the crowd." As long as the behavior observed is typical of behavior commonly conducted in public, then there is no invasion of privacy. In contrast, recording behavior that is not typically conducted in public would be a violation of privacy. For example, hidden cameras recording people (without consent) taking showers at a health club, even if ultimately intended to gather information to help improve the shower experience, would be considered inappropriate.

Technology has also created new ways of collecting data passively that have privacy implications. Researchers are very interested in consumers' online behavior. For instance, the paths that consumers take while browsing the Internet can be extremely useful in understanding what kinds of information are most valued by consumers. Much of this information can be harvested and entered into a data warehouse. Researchers sometimes have legitimate reasons to use this data, which can improve consumers' ability to make wise decisions. In these cases, the researcher should gain the consumers' consent in some form before harvesting information from their web usage patterns. Furthermore, if the information will be shared with other companies, a specific consent agreement is needed. This can come in the form of a question to which consumers respond yes or no, as in the following example:

From time to time, the opportunity to share your information with other companies arises and this could be very helpful to you in offering your desirable product choices. We respect your privacy, however, and if you do not wish us to share this information, we will not. Would you like us to share your information with other companies?
- *Yes, you can share the information*
- *No, please keep my information private*

Not all of these attempts are legitimate. Most readers have probably encountered spyware on their home computer. **Spyware** is software that is placed on your computer without consent or knowledge while using the Internet. This software then tracks your usage and sends the information back through the Internet to the source. Then, based on these usage patterns, the user will receive push technology advertising, usually in the form of pop-up ads. Sometimes, the user will receive so many pop-up ads that the computer becomes unusable. The use of spyware is illegitimate because it is done without consent and therefore violates the right to privacy and confidentiality.

Spyware
Software placed on a computer without consent or knowledge of the user.

Legislators are increasingly turning their attention to privacy issues in data collection. When children are involved, researchers have a special obligation to insure their safety. COPPA, the Children's Online Privacy Protection Act, was enacted into U.S. federal law on April 12, 2000. It defines a child as anyone under the age of thirteen. Anyone engaging in contact with a child through the Internet is obligated to obtain parental consent and notification before any personal information or identification can be provided by a child. Therefore, a researcher collecting a child's name, phone number, or e-mail address without parental consent is violating the law. While the law and ethics do not always correspond, in this case, it is probably pretty clear that a child's personal information shouldn't be collected. The Research Snapshot box on the following page further explains how conducting research with children is ethically complex.

◼ DECEPTION IN RESEARCH DESIGNS AND THE RIGHT TO BE INFORMED

Experimental Designs

Experimental manipulations often involve some degree of deception. In fact, without some deception, a researcher would never know if a research subject was responding to the actual manipulation or to their perception of the experimental variable. This is why researchers sometimes use a placebo.

A **placebo** is a false experimental effect used to create the perception of a true effect. Imagine two consumers, each participating in a study of the effect of a new herbal supplement on hypertension. One consumer receives a packet containing the citrus-flavored supplement, which is meant to be mixed in water and drunk with breakfast. The other also receives a packet, but in this case the packet contains a mixture that will simply color the water and provide a citrus flavor. The second consumer also believes he or she is drinking the actual supplement. In this way, the psychological effect is the same on both consumers, and any actual difference in hypertension must be due to the actual herbs contained in the supplement. Interestingly, experimental subjects often display some placebo effect in which the mere belief that some treatment has been applied causes some effect.

Placebo
A false experimental effect used to create the perception that some effect has been administered.

This type of deception can be considered ethical. Primarily, researchers conducting an experiment must generally (1) gain the willful cooperation of the research subject and (2) fully explain the actual experimental variables applied following the experiment's completion. Every experiment should include a **debriefing** session in which research subjects are fully informed and provided a chance to ask any questions that they may have about the experiment.

Debriefing
Research subjects are fully informed and provided with a chance to ask any questions they may have about the experiment.

RESEARCHSNAPSHOT

Kidstuff can be Complicated!

Children may be small in stature but they are big in the business world. Over half of all purchases in the United States are made for family consumption. Many of these are products for children. These purchases involve fast food, school supplies, clothing, automobile-related items, sports equipment, computers, software, and video games, just to name a few. Thus, there is a big need for research involving children.

Research with children complicates research ethics even further. Today, issues involving consent and confidentiality are complicated by a child's increased vulnerability. For instance, should a child be allowed to consent to participating in research without parental consent? The age of consent for marketing research isn't clear. However, to be safe, most standard research conducted with children under the age of sixteen should only be done with parental consent. When the research involves matters that are for "mature audiences," such as human

©DAVID KATZENSTEIN/CORBIS

sexuality or alcohol consumption, then parental consent should be sought for anyone under the age of eighteen.

Clearly, children under a certain age should only be interviewed in the presence of a parent. However, will the child respond the same way when a parent is present as when alone? Imagine asking a fourteen-year-old if he or she enjoys smoking cigarettes. How might a parent's presence change the response?

There are other issues as seemingly innocuous as providing the child an incentive for participation. It is possible that even a simple incentive like a chocolate bar might not meet with the approval of a parent.

Doing research with children can yield extremely useful information. However, it is also more risky than doing research with adults. When in doubt, researchers should consider how they would like to see their own child treated and then go even further to make sure that there are no ethical problems with the use of children in research.

Sources: Ahuja, R. D., M. Walker, and R. Tadepalli (2001), "Paternalism, Limited Paternalism and the Pontius Pilate Plight When Researching Children," Journal of Business Ethics, 32 (July), 81–92; Clegg, A. (2005), "Out of the Mouths of Babes," Marketing Week, (6/23), 43.

Descriptive Research

Researchers sometimes will even withhold the actual research questions from respondents in simple descriptive research. A distinction can thus be made between deception and discreet silence. For instance, sometimes providing the actual research question to respondents is simply providing them more information than they need to give a valid response. A researcher may ask questions about the perceived price of a product when his or her real interest is in how consumers form quality impressions.

Research aimed at marketing employees also sometimes involves deception. For instance, employees are sometimes passive respondents in observational research involving a mystery shopper. **Mystery shoppers** are employees of a research firm that are paid to "pretend" to be actual shoppers. A mystery shopper would rarely identify him or herself as anything other than a customer. However, since most employees perform their jobs in public, and perform behaviors that are easily observable, research using mystery shoppers is not considered an invasion of an employee's privacy.

Mystery shoppers
Employees of a research firm that are paid to pretend to be actual shoppers.

■ PROTECTION FROM HARM

Researchers should do everything they can to make sure that research participants are not harmed by participating in research. Most marketing research does not expose participants to any harm. However, the researcher should consider every possibility. For example, if the research involves tasting food or drink, the possibility exists that a research participant could have a severe allergic reaction. Similarly, researchers studying retail and workplace atmospherics often manipulate odors by injecting certain scents into the air.[16] The researcher is sometimes in a difficult situation. He or she has to somehow find out what things the subject is allergic to, without revealing the actual experimental conditions. One way this may be done is by asking the subjects to provide a list of potential allergies ostensibly as part of a separate research project.

Other times, research may involve some potential psychological harm. This may come in the form of stress or in the form of some experimental treatment that questions some strongly held conviction. For instance, a researcher studying helping behavior may lead a subject to believe that another person is being harmed in some way. In this way, the researcher can see how much a subject can withstand before doing something to help another person. In reality, the other person is usually a research confederate simply pretending to be in pain. Three key questions that can determine whether a research participant is being treated unethically as a result of experimental procedures are:

1. Has the research subject provided consent to participate in an experiment?
2. Is the research subject to substantial physical or psychological trauma?
3. Can the research subject be easily returned to his or her initial state?

The issue of consent is tricky in experiments because the researcher cannot reveal exactly what the research is about ahead of time or the validity of the experiment will be threatened. In addition, experimental research subjects are usually provided some incentive to participate. We will have more on this later in the book, but ethically speaking, the incentives should always be noncoercive. In other words, a faculty member seeking volunteers should not withhold a student's grade if he or she does not participate in an experiment. Thus, the volunteer should provide consent without fear of harm for saying no and with some idea about any potential risk involved.

If the answer to the second question is yes, then the research should not be conducted. If the answer to the second question is no and consent is obtained, then the manipulation does not present an ethical problem, and the researcher can proceed.

The third question is really helpful in understanding how far one can go in applying manipulations to a research subject. If the answer to the third question is no, then the research should not be conducted. The opening vignette of this chapter discussed the use of hypnosis in marketing research. If the hypnotic state would cause the participant severe trauma, or if he or she cannot be easily returned to the prehypnotic state, then the research procedure should not be used. If, for instance, the consumer makes a large number of purchases under hypnosis, going deeply into debt, returning him or her to the original state may be difficult. If so, the application of hypnosis is probably inappropriate. If the answer to this question is yes, then the manipulation is ethical.

Many research companies and practically all universities now maintain a **human subjects review committee**. This is a committee that carefully reviews a proposed research design to try to make sure that no harm can come to any research participant. A side benefit of this committee is that it can also review the procedures to make sure no legal problems are created by implementing the particular design.

Human subjects review committee
Carefully reviews proposed research design to try to make sure that no harm can come to any research participant.

Rights and Obligations of the Researcher

Marketing research firms and marketing research departments should practice good business ethics. Researchers are often the focus of discussions of business ethics because of the necessity that they interact with the public. Several professional organizations have written and adopted codes of ethics for their researchers, including the American Marketing Association, the European Society for Opinion and Market Research, and the Marketing Research Society.[17] Exhibit 4.8 presents the Code of Ethics of the American Marketing Association.

In addition, the researchers have rights. In particular, once a research consulting firm is hired to conduct some research, they have the right to cooperation from the sponsoring client. In addition, the researchers have the right to be paid for the work they do as long as it is done professionally. Sometimes, the client may not like the results. But not liking the results is no basis for not paying. In addition, the client should pay the researcher in full and in a timely manner.

THE PURPOSE OF RESEARCH IS RESEARCH

Mixing Sales and Research

Consumers sometimes agree to participate in an interview that is purported to be pure research, but it eventually becomes obvious that the interview is really a sales pitch in disguise. This is unprofessional at best and fraudulent at worst. The Federal Trade Commission (FTC) has indicated that it is illegal to use any plan, scheme, or ruse that misrepresents the true status of a person seeking admission to a prospect's home, office, or other establishment. No research firm or basic marketing

RESEARCHSNAPSHOT

Is it Right, or Is it Wrong?

Sometimes, the application of research procedures to research participants can present significant ethical issues that cannot be easily dismissed by a single researcher alone. This is where a peer review process takes place. A Human Subjects Research Committee consists of a panel of researchers (and sometimes a legal authority) who carefully review the proposed procedures to identify any obvious or non-obvious ethical or legal issues. In fact, any research supported by U.S. federal funds must be subject to a peer review of this type. The peer review process for grants is described at this website: http://grants.nih.gov/grants/peer/peer.htm.

Most business research is innocuous and affords little opportunity for substantial physical or psychological trauma. However, companies involved in food marketing, dietary supplements or programs and exercise physiology and pharmaceuticals, among others, do conduct consumer research with such possibilities. Academic researchers also sometimes conduct research with significant risks for participants. Consider research examining how some dietary supplement might make exercise more enjoyable, thus creating a better overall health and psychological effect. Clearly, a peer review by knowledgeable researchers is needed before proceeding with such research.

As it isn't possible to completely eliminate risk from research, a human subjects review is a good safety net. Deaths have been attributed to lack of or the breakdown of the human subjects review. Some of these have brought negative publicity to well-known universities including the University of Pennsylvania and Johns Hopkins University. At other times, the risk to research participants is not obvious. For example, recently several researchers were interested in surveying through personal interviews victims of Hurricane Katrina. The results of the research may help public entities better serve victims, allow companies to respond with more appropriate goods and services, and help build psychological theory about how consumers make decisions under conditions of high personal trauma and stress. However, is it ethical to survey participants standing in the rubble of their home? Is it ethical to survey participants who are in the process of searching for or burying relatives that did not survive the disaster? Clearly, a thorough review of the procedures involved in such situations is called for.

Corporate human subjects committees are also becoming common. These reviews also consider the possibility of legal problems with experimental or survey procedures. In addition, as technology blurs the line between research and sales, they also should review the ethics of "research" that may somehow blend with sales. In addition, research conducted on animals also needs a critical review.

Sources: Glenn, David (2005), "Lost (and Found) in the Flood," Chronicle of Higher Education, 52 (10/7), A14–A19; Putney, S. B. and S. Gruskin (2002), "Time, Place and Consciousness: Three Dimensions of Meaning for U.S. Institutional Review Boards," American Journal of Public Health, 92 (July), 1067–1071.

©JEFF GREENBERG/PHOTOEDIT

researcher should engage in any sales attempts. Applied market researchers working for the sponsoring company should also avoid overtly mixing research and sales. However, the line is becoming less clear with increasing technology.

Research That Isn't Research

Consider the following typical exchange between a product manager and a marketing researcher. The manager wants to hire the firm to do a test-market for a new product:

Researcher: *What if the test results are favorable?*
Product manager: *Why, we'll launch the product nationally, of course.*
Researcher: *And if the results are unfavorable?*
Product manager: *They won't be. I'm sure of that.*
Researcher: *But just suppose they are.*
Product manager: *I don't think we should throw out a good product just because of one little market test.*
Researcher: *Then why test?*
Product manager: *Listen, Smith, this is a major product introduction. It's got to have some research behind it.*

It's probably pretty easy to see what is actually going on here. The product manager really wants research that will justify a decision that already has been made. If the test-market's results contradict the decision, the product manager will almost certainly disregard the research. This isn't really research so much as it is **pseudo-research** because it is conducted not to gather information for marketing decisions but to bolster a point of view and satisfy other needs.

The most common type of pseudo-research is performed to justify a decision that has already been made or that management is already strongly committed to. A media company may wish to

Pseudo-research
Conducted not to gather information for marketing decisions but to bolster a point of view and satisfy other needs.

EXHIBIT 4.8 Code of Ethics of the American Marketing Association

The American Marketing Association, in furtherance of its central objective of the advancement of science in marketing and in recognition of its obligations to the public, has established these principles of ethical practice of marketing research for the guidance of its members.

In an increasingly complex society, marketing research is more and more dependent upon marketing information intelligently and systematically obtained. The consumer is the source of much of this information. Seeking the cooperation of the consumer in the development of information, marketing management must acknowledge its obligation to protect the public from misrepresentation and exploitation under the guise of research.

Similarly, the research practitioner has an obligation to the discipline he practices and to those who provide support for his practice—an obligation to adhere to basic and commonly accepted standards of scientific investigation as they apply to the domain of marketing research.

It is the intent of this code to define ethical standards required of marketing research in satisfying these obligations.

Adherence to this code will assure the user of marketing research that the research was done in accordance with acceptable ethical practices. Those engaged in research will find in this code an affirmation of sound and honest basic principles that have developed over the years as the profession has grown. The field interviewers who are the points of contact between the profession and the consumer will also find guidance in fulfilling their vitally important role.

For Research Users, Practitioners, and Interviewers

1. No individual or organization will undertake any activity that is directly or indirectly represented to be marketing research, but that has as its real purpose the attempted sale of merchandise or services to some or all of the respondents interviewed in the course of the research.
2. If a respondent has been led to believe, directly or indirectly, that he or she is participating in a marketing research survey and that his or her anonymity will be protected, the respondent's name shall not be made known to anyone outside the research organization or research department, or used for anything other than research purposes.

For Research Practitioners

1. There will be no intentional or deliberate misrepresentation of research methods or results. An adequate description of

methods employed will be made available upon request to the sponsor of the research. Evidence that fieldwork has been completed according to specifications will, upon request, be made available to buyers of research.
2. The identity of the survey sponsor and/or the ultimate client for whom a survey is being done will be held in confidence at all times, unless this identity is to be revealed as part of the research design. Research information shall be held in confidence by the research organization or department and not used for personal gain or made available to any outside party unless the client specifically authorizes such release.
3. A research organization shall not undertake studies for competitive clients when such studies would jeopardize the confidential nature of client-agency relationships.

For Users of Marketing Research

1. A user of research shall not knowingly disseminate conclusions from a given research project or service that are inconsistent with or not warranted by the data.
2. To the extent that there is involved in a research project a unique design involving techniques, approaches, or concepts not commonly available to research practitioners, the prospective user of research shall not solicit such a design from one practitioner and deliver it to another for execution without the approval of the design originator.

For Field Interviewers

1. Research assignments and materials received, as well as information obtained from respondents, shall be held in confidence by the interviewer and revealed to no one except the research organization conducting the marketing study.
2. No information gained through a marketing research activity shall be used, directly or indirectly, for the personal gain or advantage of the interviewer.
3. Interviews shall be conducted in strict accordance with specifications and instructions received.
4. An interviewer shall not carry out two or more interviewing assignments simultaneously unless authorized by all contractors or employers concerned.

Members of the American Marketing Association will be expected to conduct themselves in accordance with provisions of this code in all of their marketing research activities.

"AMA Adopts New Code of Ethics," *Marketing News*, September 11, 1987, pp. 1, 10. Reprinted with permission of the American Marketing Association.

sell advertising space on Internet search sites. Even though they strongly believe that the ads will be worth the rates they will charge advertisers, they may not have the hard evidence to support this view. Therefore, the advertiser's sales force may provide feedback indicating customer resistance to moving their advertising from local radio to the Internet. The advertising company may then commission a study for which the only result they care to find is that the Internet ads will be effective. In this situation, a researcher should walk away from the project if it appears that management strongly desires the research to support a predetermined opinion only. While it is a fairly easy matter for an outside researcher to walk away from such a job, it is another matter for an in-house researcher to refuse such a job. Thus, avoiding pseudo-research is a right of the researcher but an obligation for the manager.

Occasionally, marketing research is requested simply to pass blame for failure to another area. A product manager may deliberately request a research study with no intention of paying attention to the findings and recommendations. The manager knows that the particular project is in trouble but plays the standard game to cover up for his or her mismanagement. If the project fails, marketing

RESEARCHSNAPSHOT

Power Selling: An Ethical Dilemma?

The line between research and sales isn't always clear. A market researcher for a large utility company routinely collects programmatic data on customer satisfaction. The data warehouse that results contains information about power usage (and outages), appliance ownership, billing, consumer demographics, and geographic location, as well as customer perceptions of quality and

satisfaction. Certainly, this information is useful in helping the power company monitor how well it is doing with its customers. However, the power company also is in the business of selling appliances and service programs that can

help reduce energy costs. The researcher's manager asks if it is possible to identify customers with low satisfaction and then target them with sales pitches aimed at providing the customer with appliances and programs that will reduce their bills, and hopefully create more satisfaction. What should the researcher do?

Also, technology is making the line between research and sales less clear. It is very likely that research data collected by companies we transact with online could be used to push products toward us that we may truly like. This is the point of push technology. What makes this ethical or not ethical? With consent, it is clearly ethical. What other ethical challenges may be faced as the technology to collect consumer information continues to develop?

research will become the scapegoat. The ruse may involve a statement something like this: "Well, research should have identified the problem earlier!"

Push Polls

Push poll
Telemarketing under guise of research.

Politicians have concocted a particular type of pseudo-research as a means of damaging opposing candidates' reputations. A **push poll** is telemarketing under the guise of research. Its name derives from the fact that the purpose of the poll is to push consumers into a pre-determined response. For instance, thousands of potential voters can be called and asked to participate in a survey. The interviewer then may ask loaded questions that put a certain spin on a candidate.

Service Monitoring

Occasionally, the line between research and customer service isn't completely clear. For instance, Toyota may survey all of its new car owners after the first year of ownership. While the survey appears to be research, it may also provide information that could be used to correct some issue with the customer. For example, if the research shows that a customer is dissatisfied with the way the car handles, Toyota could follow up with the specific customer. The follow-up could result in changing the tires of the car, resulting in a smoother and quieter ride, as well as a more satisfied customer. Should a pattern develop showing other customers with the same opinion, Toyota may need to switch the original equipment tires used on this particular car.

In this case, both research and customer service are involved. Since the car is under warranty, there would be no selling attempt. Researchers are often asked to design satisfaction surveys. These may identify the customer so they may be contacted by the company. Such practice is acceptable as long as the researcher allows the consumer the option of either being contacted or not being contacted. In other words, the customer should be asked whether it is okay for someone to follow up in an effort to improve their satisfaction. There are actually situations in which a customer could be made more satisfied by purchasing some product. The Research Snapshot box above describes such a situation. Here, the ethics are less clear than is the service-monitoring example used above.

Push polls, selling under the guise of research, and pseudo-research are all misrepresentations of the true purpose of research and should be avoided. It is important that researchers understand the difference between research and selling.

■ OBJECTIVITY

The need for objective scientific investigation to ensure accuracy is stressed throughout this book. Researchers should maintain high standards to be certain that their data are accurate. Furthermore, they must not intentionally try to prove a particular point for political purposes.

MISREPRESENTATION OF RESEARCH

It should go without saying, but research results should not be misrepresented. This means, for instance, that the statistical accuracy of a test should be stated precisely and the meaning of findings should not be understated or overstated. Both the researcher and the client share this obligation. There are many ways that research results can be reported in a less than full and honest way. For example, a researcher may present results showing a relationship between advertising spending and sales. However, the researcher may also discover that this relationship disappears when the primary competitors' prices are taken into account. In other words, the relationship between advertising spending and sales is made spurious by the competitors' prices (see Chapter 3). Thus, it would be questionable to say the least to report a finding suggesting that sales could be increased by increasing ad spending without also mentioning the spurious nature of this finding.

Honesty in Presenting Results

Misrepresentation can also occur in the way results are presented. For instance, charts can be created that make a very small difference appear very big. Likewise, they can be altered to make a meaningful difference seem small. Exhibit 4.9 illustrates this effect. Each chart presents exactly the same data. The data represent consumer responses to service quality ratings and satisfaction ratings.

EXHIBIT 4.9
How Results Can Be Misrepresented in a Report or Presentation

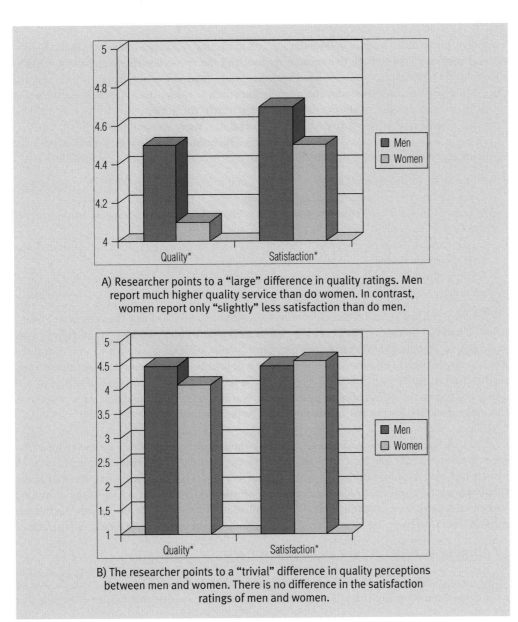

A) Researcher points to a "large" difference in quality ratings. Men report much higher quality service than do women. In contrast, women report only "slightly" less satisfaction than do men.

B) The researcher points to a "trivial" difference in quality perceptions between men and women. There is no difference in the satisfaction ratings of men and women.

Both quality and satisfaction are collected on a 5-point strongly-disagree-to-strongly-agree scale. In frame A, the chart appears to show meaningful differences between men and women, particularly for the service-quality rating. However, notice that the scale range is shown as 4 to 5. In frame B, the researcher presents the same data but shows the full scale range (1 to 5). Now, the differences are reported as trivial.

All charts and figures should reflect fully the relevant range of values reported by respondents. If the scale range is from 1 to 5, then the chart should reflect a 1 to 5 range unless there is some value that is simply not used by respondents. If no or only a very few respondents had reported a 1 for their service quality or satisfaction rating, then it may be appropriate to show the range as 2 to 5. However, if there is any doubt, the researcher should show the full scale range.

Honesty in Reporting Errors

Likewise, any major error that has occurred during the course of the study should not be kept secret from management or the sponsor. Hiding errors or variations from the proper procedures tends to distort or shade the results. Similarly, every research design presents some limitations. For instance, the sample size may be smaller than ideal. The researcher should point out the key limitations in the research report and presentation. In this way, any factors that qualify the findings can be understood. The decision maker needs this information before deciding on any risky course of action.

▓ CONFIDENTIALITY

Confidentiality comes into play in several ways. The marketing researcher often is obligated to protect the confidentiality of both the research sponsor and the research participant. In fact, business clients value marketing researchers' confidentiality more than any other attribute of a research firm.[18] Imagine a researcher conducting a test-market for a new high-tech Apple iPod device that allows interactive video. Just after conducting the research, the same researcher is contacted by Samsung. Samsung, who has yet to develop video capability, wants research that addresses whether or not there is a market for iPod video of any type. The researcher is now in a difficult position. Certainly, an ethical dilemma exists presenting multiple choices to the researcher, including

- Agreeing to do the research for Samsung and using some results from the Apple study to prepare a report and recommendation for Samsung
- Agreeing to sell the new concept to Samsung without doing any additional research. In other words, provide Apple's company secrets to Samsung
- Conducting an entirely new project for Samsung without revealing any of the results or ideas from the Apple study
- Turning down the chance to do the study without revealing any information about Apple to Samsung

Which is the best choice? Obviously, both of the first two options violate the principle of maintaining client confidentiality. Thus, both are unethical. The third choice, conducting an entirely new study, may be an option. However, it may prove nearly impossible to do the entire project as if the Apply study had never been done. Even with the best of intentions, the researcher may inadvertently violate confidentiality with Apple. The last choice is the best option from a moral standpoint. It avoids any potential **conflict of interest**. In other words, actions that would best serve one client, Samsung, would be detrimental to another client, Apple. Generally, it is best to avoid working for two direct competitors.

Conflict of interest
Occurs when one researcher works for two competing companies.

Likewise, the researcher must also predict any confidentiality agreement with research participants. For instance, a researcher conducting a descriptive research survey may have identified each participant's e-mail address in the course of conducting the research. After seeing the results, the client may ask for the e-mail addresses as a logical prospect list. However, as long as the researcher assured each participant's confidentiality, the e-mail addresses cannot ethically be provided to the firm. Indeed, a commitment of confidentiality also helps build trust among survey respondents.[19]

▓ DISSEMINATION OF FAULTY CONCLUSIONS

The American Marketing Association's marketing research Code of Ethics states that "a user of research shall not knowingly disseminate conclusions from a given research project or service that are inconsistent with or not warranted by the data." A dramatic example of a violation of this principle occurred in an advertisement of a cigarette smoker study. The advertisement compared two brands and stated that "of those expressing a preference, over 65 percent preferred" the advertised brand to a competing brand. The misleading portion of this reported result was that most of the respondents did *not* express a preference; they indicated that both brands tasted about the same. Thus, only a very small percentage of those studied actually revealed a preference, and the results were somewhat misleading. Such shading of results violates the obligation to report accurate findings.

TOTHEPOINT

He uses statistics as a drunken man uses a lamppost—for support rather than illumination.

—Andrew Lang

Rights and Obligations of the Client Sponsor (User)

▨ ETHICAL BEHAVIOR BETWEEN BUYER AND SELLER

The general business ethics expected between a purchasing agent and a sales representative should hold in a marketing research situation. For example, if a purchasing agent has already decided to purchase a product from a friend, it would be unethical for that person to solicit competitive bids from others because they have no chance of being accepted. Similarly, a client seeking research should only seek bids from firms that have a legitimate chance of actually doing the work. In addition, any section on the ethical obligation of a research client would be remiss not to mention that the user is obligated to pay the provider the agreed upon wage and pay within the agreed upon time.

▨ AN OPEN RELATIONSHIP WITH RESEARCH SUPPLIERS

The client sponsor has the obligation to encourage the research supplier to objectively seek out the truth. To encourage this objectivity, a full and open statement of the decision situation, a full disclosure of constraints in time and money, and any other insights that assist the researcher should be provided. This means that the researcher will be provided adequate access to key decision makers. These decision makers should agree to openly and honestly discuss matters related to the situation. Finally, this means that the client is open to actually using the research results. Time is simply too valuable to ask a researcher to perform a project when the results will not be used.

▨ AN OPEN RELATIONSHIP WITH INTERESTED PARTIES

Conclusions should be based on data—not conjecture. Users should not knowingly disseminate conclusions from a research project in a manner that twist them into a position that cannot be supported by the data. Twisting the results in a self-serving manner or to support some political position poses serious ethical questions. A user may also be tempted to misrepresent results while trying to close a sale. Obviously, this is also morally inappropriate.

    Advocacy research—research undertaken to support a specific claim in a legal action or to represent some advocacy group—puts a client in a unique situation. Researchers often conduct advocacy research in their role as an expert witness. For instance, a researcher may be deposed to present evidence showing that a "knock-off" brand diminishes the value of a better known name brand. In conventional research, attributes such as sample size, profile of people actually interviewed, and number of questions asked are weighed against cost in traditional research. However, a court's opinion on whether research results are reliable may be based exclusively on any one specific research aspect. Thus, the slightest variation from technically correct procedures may be magnified by an attorney until a standard marketing research project no longer appears adequate in a judge's eyes. How open should the client be in the courtroom?

    The ethics of advocacy research present a number of serious issues that can lead to an ethical dilemma:

Advocacy research
Research undertaken to support a specific claim in a legal action or represent some advocacy group.

- Lawyers' first responsibility is to represent their clients. Therefore, they might not be interested as much in the truth as they are in evidence that supports their client's position. Presenting accurate research results may harm the client.
- A researcher should be objective. However, he or she runs the risk of conducting research that does not support the desired position. In this case, the lawyer may ask the researcher if the results can somehow be interpreted in another manner.

- Should the lawyer (in this case a user of research) ask the researcher to take the stand and present an inaccurate picture of the results?

Ethically, the attorney should certainly not put the researcher on the stand and encourage an act of perjury. The attorney may hope to ask specific questions that are so limited that taken alone, they may appear to support the client. However, this is risky because the opposing attorney likely also has an expert witness that can suggest questions for cross-examination. Returning to our branding example, if the research does not support an infringement of the known brand's name, then the brand name's attorney should probably not have the researcher take the stand.

Advocacy researchers do not necessarily bias results intentionally. However, attorneys rarely submit advocacy research evidence that does not support their clients' positions.

The question of advocacy research is one of objectivity: Can the researcher seek out the truth when the sponsoring client wishes to support its position at a trial? The ethical question stems from a conflict between legal ethics and research ethics. Although the courts have set judicial standards for marketing research methodology, perhaps only the client and individual researcher can resolve this question.

Privacy

People believe the collection and distribution of personal information without their knowledge is a serious violation of their privacy. The privacy rights of research participants create a privacy obligation on the part of the research client. Suppose a database marketing company is offering a mailing list compiled by screening millions of households to obtain brand usage information. The information would be extremely valuable to your firm, but you suspect those individuals who filled out the information forms were misled into thinking they were participating in a survey. Would it be ethical to purchase the mailing list? If respondents have been deceived about the purpose of a survey and their names subsequently are sold as part of a user mailing list, this practice is certainly unethical. The client and the research supplier have the obligation to maintain respondents' privacy.

Consider another example. Sales managers know that a marketing research survey of their business-to-business customers' buying intentions includes a means to attach a customer's name to each questionnaire. This confidential information could be of benefit to a sales representative calling on a specific customer. A client wishing to be ethical must resist the temptation to identify those accounts (that is, those respondents) that are the hottest prospects.

Privacy on the Internet

Privacy on the Internet is a controversial issue. A number of groups question whether website questionnaires, registration forms, and other means of collecting personal information will be kept confidential. Many marketers argue that their organizations don't need to know who the user is because the individual's name is not important for their purposes. However, they do want to know certain information (such as demographic characteristics or product usage) associated with an anonymous profile. For instance, a web advertiser could reach a targeted audience without having access to identifying information. Of course, unethical companies may violate anonymity guidelines. Research shows that consumers are sensitive to confidentiality notices before providing information via a website. Over 80 percent of consumers report looking for specific privacy notices before they will exchange information electronically. In addition, over half believe that companies do not do enough to ensure the privacy of personal information.[20] Thus, research users should not disclose private information without permission from the consumers who provided that information.

A Final Note on Ethics

Certainly, there are researchers who would twist results for a client or who would fabricate results for personal gain. However, these are not professionals. When one is professional, one realizes that one's actions not only have implications for oneself but also for one's field. Indeed, just a few unscrupulous researchers can give the field a bad name. Thus, researchers should maintain the highest integrity in their work to protect our industry. Research participants should also play their role, or else the data they provide will not lead to better products for all consumers. Finally, the research users must also follow good professional ethics in their treatment of researchers and research results. When all three parties participate with integrity, consumers in general, and society overall, gain the most benefit from professional marketing research.

Summary

1. Know when research should be conducted externally and when it should be done internally. The company who needs the research is not always the best company to actually perform the research. Sometimes it is better to use an outside supplier of some form. An outside agency is better when a fresh perspective is needed, when it would be difficult for inside researchers to be objective, and when the outside firm has some special expertise. In contrast, it is better to do the research in-house when it needs to be done very quickly, when the project requires close collaboration of many employees within the company, when the budget for the project is limited, and when secrecy is a major concern. The decision to go outside or stay inside for research depends on these particular issues.

2. Be familiar with the types of jobs, job responsibilities, and career paths available within the marketing research industry. A marketing research function may be organized in any number of ways depending on a firm's size, business, and stage of research sophistication. Marketing research managers must remember they are managers, not just researchers.

Marketing research offers many career opportunities. Entry-level jobs may involve simple tasks such as data entry or performing survey research. A research analyst may be the next step on the career path. This position may involve project design, preparation of proposals, data analysis, and interpretation. Whereas there are several intermediate positions that differ depending on whether one works for a small or large firm, the director of marketing research is the chief information officer in charge of marketing information systems and research projects. The director plans, executes, and controls the marketing research function.

3. Understand the often conflicting relationship between marketing management and researchers. Researchers and managers have different and often conflicting goals. Some of the key sources of conflict include money, time, intuition, and experience. Managers want to spend the least amount of money on research possible, have it done in the shortest period of time conceivable, and believe that intuition and experience are good substitutes for research. Researchers will exchange greater expense for more precision in the research, would like to take more time to be more certain of results, and are hesitant to rely on intuition and experience. Better communication is a key to reducing this conflict. One tool that can be useful is the implementation of cross-functional teams.

4. Be able to define ethics and understand how it applies to marketing research. Marketing ethics is the application of morals to behavior related to the exchange environment. Generally, good ethics conforms to the notion of "right" and a lack of ethics conforms to the notion of "wrong." Those involved in marketing research face numerous ethical dilemmas. Researchers serve clients or, put another way, the doers of research serve the users. It is often easy for a doer to compromise professional standards in an effort to please the user. After all, the user pays the bills. Given the large number of ethical dilemmas involved in research, ethics is highly applicable to marketing research.

5. Know and appreciate the rights and obligations of a) research participants, b) marketing researchers, and c) the research client or sponsor. Each party involved in research has certain rights and obligations. These are generally interdependent in the sense that one party's right often leads to an obligation for another party. While the rights and obligations of all three parties are important, the obligation of the researcher to protect research participants is particularly important. Experimental manipulations can sometimes expose subjects to some form of harm or involve them in a ruse. The researcher must be willing to fully inform the subjects of the true purpose of the research during a debriefing. The researcher must also avoid subjecting participants to undue physical or psychological trauma. In addition, it should be reasonably easy to return an experimental subject to his or her original, pre-experiment condition.

6. Know how to avoid a conflict of interest in performing marketing research. A conflict of interest occurs when a researcher is faced with doing something to benefit one client at the expense of another client. One good way to avoid a conflict of interest is to avoid getting involved with multiple projects involving competing firms.

Key Terms and Concepts

Outside agency
In-house research
Director of marketing research
Research analyst
Research assistants
Manager of decision support systems
Forecast analyst
Research generalist
Cross-functional teams
Research suppliers

Syndicated service
Standardized research service
Custom research
Marketing ethics
Moral standards
Ethical dilemma
Relativism
Idealism
Informed consent
Confidentiality

Do Not Call Legislation
Spyware
Placebo
Debriefing
Mystery shoppers
Human subjects review committee
Pseudo-research
Push poll
Conflict of interest
Advocacy research

Questions for Review and Critical Thinking

1. What are the conditions that make in-house research preferable? What are the conditions that make outside research preferable?
2. Read a recent news article from *The Wall Street Journal* or other key source that deals with a new-product introduction. Would you think it would be better for that firm to do research in-house or to use an outside agency? Explain.
3. What might the organizational structure of the research department be like for the following organizations?
   a. A large advertising agency
   b. A founder-owned company that operates a 20-unit restaurant chain
   c. Your university
   d. An industrial marketer with four product divisions
   e. A large consumer products company
4. What problems do marketing research directors face in their roles as managers?
5. What are some of the basic causes of conflict between management and marketing research?
6. Comment on the following situation: A product manager asks the research department to forecast costs for some basic ingredients (raw materials) for a new product. The researcher asserts that this is not a research job; it is a production forecast.
7. What is the difference between research and pseudo-research? Cite several examples of each.
8. **ETHICS** What are marketing ethics? How are marketing ethics relevant to research?
9. **ETHICS** What is the difference between ethical relativism and ethical idealism? How might a person with an idealist ethical philosophy and a person with a relativist ethical philosophy differ with respect to including a sales pitch at the end of a research survey?
10. **ETHICS** What obligations does a researcher have with respect to confidentiality?
11. How should a marketing researcher help top management better understand the functions and limitations of research?
12. **ETHICS** List at least one research obligation for researcher participants (respondents), marketing researchers, and research clients (sponsors)?
13. **ETHICS** What is a conflict of interest in a research context? How can such conflicts of interest be avoided?
14. **ETHICS** What key questions help resolve the question of whether or not research participants serving as subjects in an experiment are treated ethically?
15. Identify a research supplier in your area and determine what syndicated services and other functions are available to clients.
16. **'NET** Use the Internet to find at least five marketing research firms that perform survey research. List and describe each firm briefly.
17. What actions might the marketing research industry take to convince the public that marketing research is a legitimate activity and that firms that misrepresent their intentions and distort findings to achieve their aims are not true marketing research companies?
18. **ETHICS** Comment on the ethics of the following situations:
    a. A food warehouse club advertises "savings up to 30 percent" after a survey showed a range of savings from 2 to 30 percent below average prices for selected items.
    b. A radio station broadcasts the following message during a syndicated rating service's rating period: "Please fill out your diary (which lists what media the consumer has been watching or listening to)."
    c. A sewing machine retailer advertises a market test and indicates that the regular price will be cut to one-half for three days only.
    d. A researcher tells a potential respondent that an interview will last ten minutes rather than the thirty minutes he or she actually anticipates.
    e. A respondent tells an interviewer that she wishes to cooperate with the survey, but her time is valuable and, therefore, she expects to be paid for the interview.
    f. When you visit your favorite sports team's home page on the web, you are asked to fill out a registration questionnaire before you enter the site. The team then sells your information (team allegiance, age, address, and so on) to a company that markets sports memorabilia via catalogs and direct mail.
19. **ETHICS** Comment on the following interview:

Interviewer:	*Good afternoon, sir. My name is Mrs. Johnson, and I am with Counseling Services. We are conducting a survey concerning Memorial Park. Do you own a funeral plot? Please answer yes or no.*
Respondent:	*(pauses)*
Interviewer:	*You do not own a funeral plot, do you?*
Respondent:	*No.*
Interviewer:	*Would you mind if I sent you a letter concerning Memorial Park? Please answer yes or no.*
Respondent:	*No.*
Interviewer:	*Would you please give me your address?*

20. **ETHICS** Try to participate in a survey at a survey website such as http://www.mysurvey.com or http://www.themsrgroup.com. Write a short essay response about your experience with particular attention paid to how the sites have protections in place to prevent children from providing personal information.

Research Activities

1. Find the mission statement of Burke, Inc. (http://www.burke.com). What career opportunities exist at Burke? Would you consider it a small, mid-sized, or large firm?

2. **'NET – ETHICS** One purpose of the United Kingdom's Market Research Society is to set and enforce the ethical standards to be observed by research practitioners. Go to its website at http://www.marketresearch.org.uk. Click on its code of conduct and evaluate it in light of the AMA's code.

Case 4.1 Global Eating

Barton Boomer, director of marketing research for a large research firm, has a bachelor's degree in marketing from Michigan State University. He joined the firm nine years ago after a one-year stint as a marketing research trainee at the corporate headquarters of a western packing corporation. Barton has a wife and two children. He earns $60,000 a year and owns a home in the suburbs. He is typical of a marketing research analyst. He is asked to interview an executive with a local restaurant chain, Eats-R-Wee. Eats-R-Wee is expanding internationally. The logical two choices for expansion are either to expand first to other nations that have values similar to those in the market area of Eats-R-Wee or to expand to the nearest geographical neighbor. During the initial interviews, Mr. Big, Vice President of Operations for Eats-R-Wee, makes several points to Barton.

- "Barton, we are all set to move across the border to Ontario and begin our international expansion with our neighbor to the north, Canada. Can you provide some research that will support this position?"

- "Barton, we are in a hurry. We can't sit on our hands for weeks waiting to make this decision. We need a comprehensive research project completed by the end of the month."

- "We are interested in how our competitors will react. Have you ever done research for them?"

- "Don't worry about the fee; we'll pay you top money for a "good" report."

Marla Madam, Barton's Director of Marketing Research, encourages Barton to get back in touch with Mr. Big and tell him that the project will get underway right away.

Question

Critique this situation with respect to Barton's job. What recommendations would you have for him? Should the company get involved with the research? Explain your answers.

Case 4.2 Big Brother is Watching?

Technology is making our behavior more and more difficult to keep secret. Right at this very moment, there is probably some way that your location can be tracked in a way that researchers could use the information. Do you have your mobile phone with you? Is there an RFID tag in your shirt, your backpack, or some other personal item? Are you in your car, and does it have a GPS (Global Positioning Satellite) device? All of these are ways that your location and movements might be tracked.

For instance, rental cars can be tracked using GPS. Suppose a research firm contracts with an insurance firm to study the way people drive when using a rental car. A customer's every movement is then tracked. So, if the customer stops at a fast-food restaurant, the researcher knows. If the customer goes to the movie when he or she should be on a sales call, the researcher knows. If the customer is speeding, the researcher knows.

Clearly, modern technology is making confidentiality more and more difficult to maintain. While legitimate uses of this type of technology may assist in easing traffic patterns and providing better locations for service stations, shopping developments, and other retailers, at what point does the collection of such information become a concern? When would you become concerned about having your whereabouts constantly tracked?

Question

Suppose a GIS research firm is approached by the state legislature and asked to provide data about vehicle movement within the state for all cars with a satellite tracking mechanism. Based on the movement of the cars over a certain time, the police can decide when a car was speeding. They intend on using this data to send speeding tickets to those who moved too far, too fast. If you are the research firm, would you supply the data? Discuss the ethical implications of the decision.

Part 2
Beginning Stages of the Research Process

CHAPTER 5
Problem Definition: Jump-Starting the Research Process

CHAPTER 6
Qualitative Research Tools

CHAPTER 7
Secondary Data Research In a Digital Age

CHAPTER 5
PROBLEM DEFINITION:
JUMP-STARTING THE RESEARCH PROCESS

After studying this chapter, you should be able to

1. Explain why proper "problem definition" is essential to useful marketing research
2. Know how to recognize problems
3. Translate managerial decision statements into relevant research objectives
4. Translate research objectives into research questions and/or research hypotheses
5. Outline the components of a research proposal
6. Construct dummy tables as part of a research proposal

Chapter Vignette: Mario Lagasto's "Advertising" Problem

James Michael, owner of a small market research firm in Columbus, Ohio, sits over a bowl of spaghetti and meatballs and a glass of Chianti Classico at Mario Lagasto's Italian Restaurant. James isn't there just for lunch; he is there discussing Lagasto's current business situation with Mario Lagasto, the restaurant's owner. James finishes only about a third of the spaghetti and half of the wine, and says, "Thanks for the lunch. It seems that I remember the house red being a lovely Barbera d'Asti."

Mario replies, "Ah, yes, from Cascina Ballarin to be exact. But, we had to move that to our reserve list. Our new comptroller has really helped us control our costs."

James asks, "Well, let's get down to business. What seems to be the problem? People certainly love Italian food."

Mario explains that his sales, which have grown every year since he opened the restaurant in 1990, have actually dropped over the last twelve months. Yet, the suburban neighborhood has continued to grow. "I was sitting at home and I realized that all the downtown restaurants have dramatically increased their television advertising and on top of this, the city's downtown revival campaign is everywhere!" He continued, "I've been using the same advertising for years: a few spots on local radio, an occasional newspaper spot, and a billboard on the main highway across from the restaurant. When I see the fancy advertising run by my competitors, it is clear that I have an advertising problem. I want you to tell me what I can do to make my advertising more effective!"

©ROYALTY FREE/CORBIS

Once the interview is complete, James informs Mario that he will go back and prepare a proposal that will describe how he may be able to help Lagasto's get back on track.

Once back in the office, James begins to scribble some notes. He begins to study the advertising of both Lagasto and his competitors. He realizes that some of the neighborhood competitors, including the big chain Italian restaurants like Olive Garden, have always had a large promotional budget, including television ads. The advertising deficit isn't new. He tries to identify all the things that have changed since Lagasto's sales trends turned downward. Does Mario really have an advertising problem? Is it a problem with competitive positioning? Is it a problem with a change in the external operating environment? Has Mario just missed out on some growth opportunities? Then, just as hunger starts to set in, he remembers the rather average spaghetti and meatballs and red wine he had for lunch. He thinks about how it is has changed from what he remembers. Maybe James' hunger has led to a discovery!

The Nature of Marketing Problems

Importance of Starting with a Good Problem Definition

Chapter 3 discussed some basics of translating a business situation into specific research objectives. Thus, it is the first stage in the research process introduced in Chapter 3. While it is tempting to skip this step and go directly to designing a research project, the chances that a research project will prove useful are directly related to how well the research objectives correspond to the true business "problem." Clearly, the easiest thing for James to do in the opening vignette is to start designing a study of Lagasto's advertising effectiveness. This seems to be what Mario wants. Is it what Mario needs, however?

This chapter looks at this important step in the research process more closely. Some useful tools are described that can help translate the business situation into relevant, actionable research objectives. Research too often takes the blame for business failures when the real failure was really management's view of its own company's situation. The Research Snapshot box on page 105 describes some classic illustrations involving companies as big and successful as Coca-Cola, RJ Reynolds, and Ford. While the researcher has some say in what is actually studied, remember that the client (either management or an outside sponsor) is the research customer and the researcher is serving the client's needs through research. In other words, when the client fails to understand their situation or insists on studying an irrelevant problem, the research is very likely to fail, even if it is done perfectly.

Translating a business situation into something that can be researched is somewhat like translating one language into another. It begins by coming to a consensus on a decision statement or question. A **decision statement** is a written expression of the key question(s) that a research user wishes to answer. It is the reason that research is being considered. It must be well stated and relevant. As discussed in Chapter 3, the researcher translates this into research terms by rephrasing the decision statement into one or more research objectives. These are expressed as deliverables in the research proposal. The researcher then further expresses these in precise and scientific research terminology by creating research hypotheses from the research objectives.

In this chapter, we use the term *problem definition*. Realize that sometimes this is really opportunity seeking. For simplicity, the term **problem definition** is adapted here to refer to the process of defining and developing a decision statement and the steps involved in translating it into more precise research terminology, including a set of research objectives. If this process breaks down at any point, the research will almost certainly be useless or even harmful. It will be useless if it presents results that simply are deemed irrelevant and do not assist in decision making. It can be harmful both because of the wasted resources and because it may misdirect the company in a poor direction.

Ultimately, it is difficult to say that any one step in the research process is most important. However, formally defining the problem to be attacked by research by developing decision statements and translating them into actionable research objectives must be done well or the rest of the research process is misdirected. Even a good road map is useless unless you know just where you are going. All of the roads can be correctly drawn, but they still don't get you where you want to be. Similarly, even the best research procedures will not overcome poor problem definition.

Decision statement
A written expression of the key question(s) that the research user wishes to answer.

Problem definition
The process of defining and developing a decision statement and the steps involved in translating it into more precise research terminology, including a set of research objectives.

Problem Complexity

Ultimately, the quality of marketing research in improving business decisions is limited by the quality of the problem definition stage. This is far from the easiest stage of the research process. Indeed,

RESEARCHSNAPSHOT

Good Answers, Bad Questions?

It's amazing, but sometimes even the most successful companies make huge blunders. These blunders often are based on a misunderstanding of exactly what the brand and/or product means to consumers. Some of the famous, or infamous, examples of such blunders include RJR's introduction of Premier "Smokeless" Cigarettes, Ford's introduction of the Edsel in the 1950s, and most famous (or infamous) of all, Coca-Cola's introduction of New Coke as a replacement for regular "old" Coke.

Volumes have been written about each of these episodes. One does have to wonder, how did these great companies do such apparently dumb things? The blame is often placed at the foot of marketing research: "Research should have revealed that product was a loser." However, researchers address the questions they are asked to address by management. Certainly, the researchers play a role in framing any decision situation into something that can be addressed by a pointed research question. The decision makers, management, almost always start the process by asking research for input. Hopefully, the dialogue that results will lead to a productive research question that will provide useful results, but it isn't always the case.

Hindsight certainly is clearer than foresight. It seems almost unthinkable that Coke could have based its decision to replace a product with a century-long success record without considering the emotional meaning that goes along with drinking a "Coke." However, management considered Coke to be a beverage, not a brand. Thus, the focus was on the taste of Coke. Thus, researchers set about trying to decide if New Coke, which was more similar to Pepsi, tasted better than the original Coke. A great deal of very careful research suggested clearly that it did taste better. If the key question was taste, New Coke was preferred over old Coke by more consumers. In fact, there was considerable evidence that already showed a taste preference for Pepsi over old Coke. Interestingly, Coke appeared to view itself as its primary competitor. At least two very important questions were never asked or were addressed insufficiently:

1. Do consumers prefer New Coke over Pepsi?
2. When people know what they are drinking, do they still prefer New Coke to old Coke?

For a taste test to be valid, it is should be done "blindly," meaning that the taster doesn't know what he or she is drinking. Only then can one assess taste without being psychologically influenced by knowing the brand. So, Coke and Pepsi conducted a blind taste test. This is certainly a good research practice—if the question is taste. The Coke research correctly answered the taste question. The big problem is that since management didn't realize that most of the meaning of Coke is psychological, and since they were so convinced that their old product was "inferior," the dialogue between management and researchers never produced more useful questions.

In the case of Ford's Edsel, a postmortem analysis suggests that research actually indicated many of the problems that ultimately led to its demise. The name, Edsel, was never tested by research, even though hundreds of other possibilities were.

Similarly, the idea of a smokeless cigarette seemed appealing. Marketing research addressed the question, "What is the attitude of smokers and nonsmokers toward a smokeless cigarette?" Nonsmokers loved the idea. Smokers, particularly those who lived with a nonsmoker, also indicated a favorable attitude. However, as we know, the product failed miserably. If you take the "smoke" out of "smoking," is it still the same thing? This question was never asked. Would someone who would try a smokeless cigarette replace their old brand with this new brand? Again, this wasn't asked.

Today, it is possible that some famous company could be making a very similar mistake. Consider Macy's. Macy's has acquired many regional and local department stores around the country over the past few years. Clearly, Macy's is a very recognizable name brand that brings with it considerable "equity." How important is it for Macy's to ask, "What is the best name for this department store?" If the acquisition involves taking over a local retail "institution," is a name change always a good thing? Certainly, it seems to be a good question to which research could probably provide a good answer!

Sources: Gibson, Larry (2003), "Why the New Coke Failed," Marketing Research, 15 (Summer); 52. Advertising Age (2005), "Is Macy's the New Coke?" 76 (9/26), 24.

©DANNY LEHMAN/CORBIS

it can be the most complex. Exhibit 5.1 helps to illustrate factors that influence how complex the process can be.

▦ SITUATION FREQUENCY

Many business situations are cyclical. Cyclical business situations lead to recurring business problems. These problems can even become routine. In these cases, it is easy to define problems and identify the types of research that are needed. In some cases, problems are so routine that they can be solved without any additional research. Recurring problems can even be automated through a company's DSS.

EXHIBIT 5.1
Defining Problems Can Be Difficult

EXHIBIT 5.1
Defining Problems Can Be Difficult

Pricing problems often occur routinely. Just think about how the price of gas fluctuates when several stations are located within sight of each other. One station's prices definitely affect the sales of the other stations as well as of the station itself. Similarly, automobile companies, airline companies, and computer companies, to name just a few, face recurring pricing issues. Because these situations recur so frequently, addressing them becomes routine. Decision makers know how to communicate them to researchers and researchers know what data are needed.

Most pricing decisions in the airline industry are automated based on sophisticated demand models. The models take into account fluctuations in travel patterns based on the time of the year, time of the day, degree of competition for that particular route, and many other factors. At one time, these decisions were based on periodic research reports. Now, the information is simply fed into a decision support system that generates a pricing schedule. It is interesting that one factor that is not very important in many of these pricing decisions is the cost involved in flying someone from point A to point B. Indeed, some passengers pay a fare much higher than the actual costs and others pay a fare much lower than the actual costs involved in getting them to their desired destination.

DRAMATIC CHANGES

When a sudden change in the business situation takes place, it can be easier to define the problem. For example, if Lagasto's business had fallen sharply in a two-month period, the key factors to study could be isolated by identifying other factors that have changed in that same time period. For example, it could be that road construction began in a nearby feeder road just over two months ago. This may lead to questions about how much traffic time and patterns influence sales at the restaurant.

In contrast, when changes are very subtle and take effect over a long period of time, it can be more difficult to define the actual decision and research problems. Consumer tastes often change slowly. The American diet evolves slowly. Detecting trends that would permanently affect one particular food market segment can be difficult. If Americans are slowly increasing their preference toward a lighter diet, traditional Italian foods may be selected less often. However, it may be difficult to detect the beginning of such a trend and even more difficult to know whether such a trend is relatively permanent or simply a temporary fad.

HOW WIDESPREAD ARE THE SYMPTOMS?

The more scattered any symptoms are, the more difficult it is to put them together into some coherent problem statement. In contrast, firms may sometimes face situations in which multiple symptoms exist, but they are all pointing to some specific business area. For instance, an automobile manufacturing company may exhibit symptoms such as increased complaints about a car's handling, increased warranty costs due to repairs, higher labor costs due to inefficiency, and lower performance ratings by consumer advocates such as *Consumer Reports*. All of these symptoms point to production as a likely problem area. This may lead to research questions that deal with supplier-manufacturer relationships, job performance, job satisfaction, supervisory support, and performance. Although having a lot of problems in one area may not sound very positive, it can be very helpful in pointing out the direction that is most in need of attention and improvement.

In contrast, when the problems are more widespread, it can be very difficult to develop useful research questions. If consumer complaints dealt with the handling and the appearance of the car, and these were accompanied by symptoms including consumer beliefs that gas mileage could be better and that dealerships did not have a pleasant environment, it may be more difficult to put these scattered symptoms together into one or a few related research questions. Later in the chapter, we'll discuss some tools for trying to analyze symptoms in an effort to find some potential common cause.

SYMPTOM AMBIGUITY

Ambiguity is almost always unpleasant. People simply are uncomfortable with the uncertainty that comes with ambiguity. Similarly, an environmental scan of a business situation may lead to many symptoms, none of which seem to point in a clear and logical direction. In this case, the problem area remains vague and the alternative directions are difficult to ascertain.

A retail store may face a situation in which sales and traffic are up, but margins are down. They may have decreased employee turnover, but lower job satisfaction. In addition, there may be several issues that arise with their suppliers, none of which is clearly positive or negative. In this case, it may be very difficult to sort through the evidence and reach a definitive decision statement or list of research objectives.

The Problem-Definition Process

Problems Mean Gaps

A **problem** occurs when there is a difference between the current conditions and a more preferable set of conditions. In other words, a gap exists between the way things are now and a way that things could be better. The gap can come about in a number of ways:[1]

> **Problem**
> Occurs when there is a difference between the current conditions and a more preferable set of conditions.

1. Business performance is worse than expected business performance. For instance, sales, profits, and margins could be below targets set by management. This is a very typical type of problem analysis. Think of all the new products that fail to meet their targeted goals. Trend analysis would also be included in this type of problem. Management is constantly monitoring key performance variables. Previous performance usually provides a benchmark forming expectations. Sales, for example, are generally expected to increase a certain percentage each year. When sales fall below this expectation, or particularly when they fall below the previous year's sales, management usually recognizes that they have a potential problem on their hands.

2. Actual business performance is less than possible business performance. Realization of this gap first requires that management have some idea of what is possible. This may form a research problem in and of itself.[2] Opportunity-seeking often falls into this type of problem-definition process. Many American and European Union companies have redefined what possible sales levels are based upon the expansion of free markets around the world. China's Civil Aviation Administration has relaxed requirements opening the Chinese air travel market to private airlines.[3] Suddenly, the possible market size for air travel has increased significantly, creating opportunities for growth.

3. Expected business performance is greater than possible business performance. Sometimes, management has unrealistic views of possible performance levels—either too high or too low. One key problem with new product introductions involves identifying realistic possibilities for sales. While you may have heard the old adage that 90 percent of all new products fail, how

RESEARCHSNAPSHOT

©DARMA/CORBIS

Gaming and Planning: How to Get It Right

Imagine how difficult it could be to make accurate predictions about video game console sales. Consider that Sony's PlayStation 2 game console has sold over 100 million units in less than six years and that Nintendo 64 (http://www. nintendo.com) has sold over 120 million units in about the same time. What would you forecast sales of the Microsoft XBox 360

(http://www.xbox.com) or the new and "revolutionary" Sony PlayStation 3 (http://www.playstation.com) to be? In particular, consider that PlayStation 3 will follow the XBox 360, with Nintendo's new "Revolution" being introduced at about the same time, plus there is increased competition from other platforms and from non-console gaming opportunities. Should Sony expect to sell 20 million consoles in the first year? Would the PlayStation 3 be a failure if it sold only 8 million consoles in the first year and only 75 million in six years? Or, would it be a case of meeting the possible sales ceiling but perhaps not meeting expectations? Although only Sony knows the true sales forecast for the PlayStation 3, it would be easy to see how the "possible" sales could be lower than the forecasted expectations.

many of the failures had a realistic sales ceiling? In other words, did the company know the possible size of the market? In this case, the problem is not with the product but with the plan. Some product "failures" may actually have been successful if management had a more accurate idea of the total market potential. The Research Snapshot box above illustrates this point.[4] Management can close this gap through decision making. Researchers help managers make decisions by providing relevant input.

The Problem-Definition Process Steps

The problem-definition process involves several interrelated steps as shown in Exhibit 5.2. Sometimes, the boundaries between each step aren't exactly clear. But generally, completing one step leads to the other and by the time the problem is defined, each of these steps has been addressed in some way. The steps are

1. Understand the business situation—identify key symptoms
2. Identify key problem(s) from symptoms
3. Write managerial decision statement and corresponding research objectives
4. Determine the unit of analysis
5. Determine the relevant variables
6. Write research questions and/or research hypotheses

A separate section deals with each stage below.

Understand the Business Decision

Situation analysis
The gathering of background information to familiarize researchers and managers with the decision-making environment.

A **situation analysis** involves the gathering of background information to familiarize researchers and managers with the decision-making environment. It is a way of formally documenting the problem-definition process. Gaining an awareness of marketplace conditions and an appreciation of the situation often requires exploratory research. Some exploratory research techniques covered in Chapter 6 can be helpful in problem definition. The situation analysis begins with an interview between the researcher and management.

■ INTERVIEW PROCESS

The researcher must enter a dialogue with the key decision makers in an effort to fully understand the situation that has motivated a research effort. This process is critical and the researcher should be granted access to all individuals who have specific knowledge of or insight into this situation.

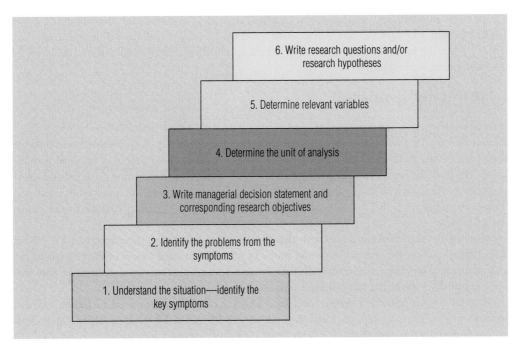

EXHIBIT 5.2
The Problem-Definition Process

Researchers working with marketing managers who want the information "yesterday" often get little assistance when they ask, "What are your objectives for this study?" Nevertheless, even decision makers who have only a gut feeling that marketing research might be a good idea benefit greatly if they work with the marketing researcher to articulate precise research objectives.[5] Even when there is good cooperation, seldom can key decision makers express the situation in research terms:

Despite a popular misconception to the contrary, objectives are seldom clearly articulated and given to the researcher. The decision maker seldom formulates his objectives accurately. He is likely to state his objectives in the form of platitudes which have no operational significance. Consequently, objectives usually have to be extracted by the researcher. In so doing, the researcher may well be performing his most useful service to the decision maker.[6]

Researchers may often be tempted to accept the first plausible problem statement offered by management. For instance, in the opening vignette, it is clear that Mario believes there is an advertising problem. However, it is very important that the researcher not blindly accept a convenient problem definition for expediency's sake. In fact, research demonstrates that people who are better problem solvers generally reject problem definitions as given to them. Rather, they take information provided by others and re-associate it with other information in a creative way. This allows them to develop more innovative and more effective decision statements.[7]

There are many ways to discover problems and spot opportunities. There is certainly much art involved in translating scattered pieces of evidence about some business situation into relevant problem statements and then relevant research objectives. While there are other sources that address creative thinking in detail, some helpful hints that can be useful in the interview process include

1. Develop many alternative problem statements. These can emerge from the interview material or from simply rephrasing decision statements and problem statements.
2. Think about potential solutions to the problem.[8] Ultimately, for the research to be actionable, some plausible solution must exist. After pairing decision statements with research objectives, think about the solutions that might result. This can help make sure any research that results is useful.
3. Make lists. Use free-association techniques to generate lists of ideas. The more ideas, the better. Use interrogative techniques to generate lists of potential questions that can be used in the interview process. **Interrogative techniques** simply involve asking multiple what, where, who, when, why, and how questions. They can also be used to provoke introspection, which can assist with problem definition.

Interrogative techniques
Asking multiple what, where, who, when, why, and how questions.

4. Be open-minded. It is very important to consider all ideas as plausible in the beginning stages of problem solving. One sure way to stifle progress is to think only like those intimately involved in the business situation or only like those in other industries. Analogies can be useful in thinking more creatively.

IDENTIFYING SYMPTOMS

Interviews with key decision makers also can be one of the best ways to identify key problem symptoms. Recall that all problems have symptoms just as human disease is diagnosed through symptoms. Once symptoms are identified, then the researcher must probe to identify possible causes of these changes. **Probing** is an interview technique that tries to draw deeper and more elaborate explanations from the discussion. This discussion may involve potential problem causes. This probing process will likely be very helpful in identifying key variables that are prime candidates for study.

One of the most important questions the researcher can ask during these interviews is, "What has changed?" Then, the researcher should probe to identify potential causes of the change. At the risk of seeming repetitive, it is important that the researcher repeat this process to make sure that some important change has not been left out.

In addition, the researcher should look for changes in company documents, including financial statements and operating reports. Changes may also be identified by tracking down news about competitors and customers. Exhibit 5.3 provides a summary of this approach.

Think back to the opening vignette. Often, multiple interviews are necessary to identify all the key symptoms and gain a better understanding of the actual business situation. On a follow up interview, the dialogue between James and Mario may proceed as follows:

James: Mario, as you suggested, the downward sales trend began twelve months ago. Aside from the advertising you mentioned earlier, what other changes have occurred inside of your business within the past year?

Mario: Just a few things. Although sales are down, our profits haven't suffered very much. Since we hired the comptroller just over a year ago, we've effectively managed our costs by changing suppliers and dropping some of the more costly items from our menu.

James (probing): Such as changing the house red? Tell me, what led to this decision?

Mario: The Barbera d'Asti that we served costs us almost $15 per bottle. Customers don't like to pay more than $5 per glass for a house wine, so we were doing little more than breaking even on it. Besides, the Olive Garden and Macaroni Grill serve a jug wine for their house red. They always have.

James: Have you noticed changes in your customers?

Mario: Other than the fact that they are coming less often, no! They are the same faces that I have seen for years. They tend to come from the nearby neighborhoods.

EXHIBIT 5.3
What Has Changed?

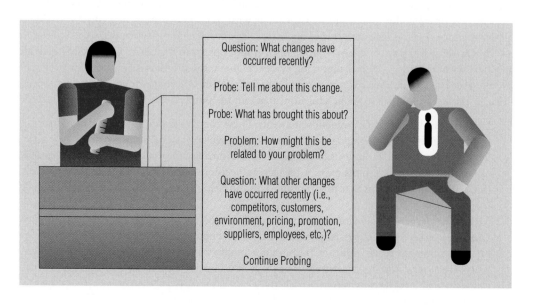

RESEARCHSNAPSHOT

Opportunity Is a "Fleeting" Thing

Have non-European automotive companies missed out on European opportunities? Europe represents a nearly $17 million annual market for new automobiles. Traditionally, the thinking is that European's prefer smaller or "light-cars." Thus, European car companies like BMW and Audi were slow to enter the SUV market. Mercedes entered the SUV market rather early on, but the emphasis was on the American market. American and Japanese companies offered little more than a token effort at selling SUVs in Europe. Thus, the SUV wars were fought in America where total volume reached 4 million shortly after 2000. Europeans were left with fewer choices if an SUV struck their fancy.

As a result, pre-2000 SUV sales in Europe were almost non-existent. However, SUV sales in Europe have increased dramatically since then. By 2004, European SUV sales have reached 16.5 million units, about one in twenty of all new units sold in Europe. Today, Nissan, Toyota, Land Rover, and Suzuki are major players in the European SUV market. Expectations are that Opel, Renault, Volkswagen, Mercedes, and Audi will show sales growth as they introduce new models for the 2006–2008 model years. In hindsight, could it be that several prominent automobile companies missed opportunities in Europe because they failed to know how big the market truly was?

Looking at this from the opposite direction, the tiny (by U.S. standards) two-seater SMART (http://www.smartusa.com) car is planned to be introduced in the United States. Importers hope to sell 15,000 units in the first year. What do you think the opportunity for the SMART car is here in the United States? Word is there may even be SMART SUV—a miniature version of an American icon.

Sources: Crain, K.C. (2005), "Analyst Sees Sales Decline for Light Vehicles in 2005," Automotive News, 79 (1/24), 111; Meiners, Jena (2004), "SUV Sales in Europe will Peak in 2008," Automotive News Europe, 9 (6/28); Llanos, Miguel (2004), "Europe's 'Smart' Cars Coming to U.S.," MSNBC News, (8/31), http:www.msnbc.msn.com/id/5217861/.

©ALASTAIR MILLER/BLOOMBERG NEWS.LANDOV

James: Have the complaints or comments changed?

Mario: Not to speak of. A few commented on removing an item or two from the menu. A couple about the wine change, but they can still get the Barbera on our reserve list for just $42 a bottle.

James: Has there been a change in personnel?

Mario: Yes, we've had more than the usual share of turnover. I've turned over most personnel decisions to the comptroller. We've had trouble maintaining good kitchen help.

James: Have you noticed any changes to the competitors that you have not already mentioned?

Mario: Most of the nearby places are doing the same things they have done for years. The chain Italian restaurants have the same promotions each year and their menu doesn't change very much.

In the *change interview,* the researcher is trying to identify possible changes in the customers, the competitors, the internal conditions of the company, and the external environment. The interplay between things that have changed and things that have stayed the same can often lead to key research factors. Before preparing the proposal, James and Mario agree that the real decision faced is not as narrow as an advertising problem; rather, the decision involves finding ways in which Mario can return sales to their previous level. In this case, James is beginning to suspect that one key factor is that the food and beverage quality have suffered as a result of cost-cutting measures. Perhaps this has been noticed by more than a few customers.

Almost any situation can be framed from a number of different perspectives. A pricing problem may be rephrased as a brand image problem. People expect high quality products to have higher prices. A quality problem may be rephrased as a packaging problem. For example, a potato chip company thought that a quality differential between their potatoes and their competitors was the cause for the symptom showing sliding market share. However, one of the research questions that eventually resulted dealt with consumer preferences for packaging. In the end, research suggested that consumers prefer a foil package because it helps the chips stay fresher longer. Thus, the key gap turned out to be a package gap![9]

Researchers should make sure that they have uncovered all possible relevant symptoms and considered their potential causes. Perhaps more interview time with key decision makers asking why people choose Coke would have helped identify some of the less tangible aspects of the Coke-Pepsi-New Coke battle. It can help avoid mistakes later.

TOTHEPOINT

The real voyage of discovery consists not in seeking new landscapes, but in having new eyes.

—Marcel Proust

Identifying the Relevant Issues from the Symptoms

Anticipating the many influences and dimensions of a problem is impossible for any researcher or executive. The interview process above is extremely useful in translating the decision situation into a working problem definition by focusing on symptoms. The probing process discussed on pages 110–111 begins this process. However, the researcher needs to be doubly certain that the research attacks real problems and not superficial symptoms.

For instance, when a firm has a problem with advertising effectiveness, the possible causes of this problem may be low brand awareness, the wrong brand image, use of the wrong media, or perhaps too small a budget. Certain occurrences that appear to be the problem may be only symptoms of a deeper problem. Exhibit 5.4 illustrates how symptoms can be translated into a problem and then a decision statement.

Writing Managerial Decision Statements and Corresponding Research Objectives

The situation analysis ends once researchers have a clear idea of the managerial objectives from the research effort. Decisions statements capture these objectives in a way that invites multiple

EXHIBIT 5.4 Symptoms Can Be Confusing

	Firm's Situation	Symptoms	Probable Problem	Decision Statement
RESEARCH ACTION	Conduct Situation Analysis including interviews with key decision makers		Consider results of probing and apply creative processes	Express in actionable terms and make sure decision makers are in agreement
SITUATION 1	22-year-old neighborhood swimming association seeks research help	• Declining Membership for 6 years • Increased attendance at new water park • Less frequent usage among members	Swim facility is outdated and does not appeal to younger families. Younger families and children have a negative image of pool. Their "old market" is aging.	What things can be done to energize new markets and create a more favorable attitude toward the association?
SITUATION 2	Manufacturer of palm-sized computer with wireless Internet access believes B2B sales are too low	• Distributors complain prices are too high • Business users still use larger computers	• Business users do not see advantages of smaller units • Advantages are not outweighed by costs • Transition costs may be a drawback for B2B customers more than for B2C customers	What things can be done to improve competitive positioning of the new product in B2B markets?
SITUATION 3	A new micro-brewery is trying to establish itself	• Consumers seem to prefer national brands over the local microbrew products • Many customers order national brands within the microbrew itself • Some customers hesitant to try new microbrew flavors	Is there a negative flavor gap? Do consumers appreciate the micro-brew approach and the full beer tasting (as opposed to drinking) experience?	How can we encourage more consumers to come to the microbrew and try our products? Should we redesign the brewery to be more inviting?

solutions. Multiple solutions are encouraged by using plural nouns to describe solutions. In other words, a decision statement that says in what "ways" a problem can be solved is better than one that says in what "way" a problem can be solved. Ultimately, research may provide evidence showing results of several ways a problem can be attacked.

Decision statements must be translated into research objectives. At this point, the researcher is starting to visualize what will need to be measured and what type of study will be needed. Exhibit 5.5 extends the examples from Exhibit 5.4, showing research objectives that correspond to each decision statement. Note that each research objective states a corresponding, potential result(s) of the research project. Thus, in some ways, it is stating the information that is needed to help make the decision. Once the decision statement is written, the research essentially answers the question, "What information is needed to address this situation?"

Referring back to the opening vignette, the analysis of the symptoms has led to the conclusion that there is a loyalty problem. Perhaps customers used to eat at the restaurant more frequently because it was seen as more unique and of higher quality than the chain restaurants. In other

EXHIBIT 5.5 Translating Decision Statements

	Decision Statement	Research Objectives	Research Questions	Research Hypotheses
RESEARCH ACTION	Express in actionable terms and make sure decision makers are in agreement	Expresses potential research results that should aid decision-making	Ask a question that corresponds to each research objective	Specific statement explaining relationships, usually involving two variables, and including the direction of the relationship
SITUATION 1	What things can be done to energize new markets and create a more favorable attitude toward the association?	Determine reasons why families may choose to join or not join a "swim club."	How do the type of facilities and pricing relate to family attitudes toward a swim facility?	Child-friendly *pool designs* are positively related to *attitudes toward the facility.* Flexible *pricing policies* are positively related to *attitudes toward the facility.*
SITUATION 2	What product features can be improved and emphasized to improve competitive positioning of the new product in B2B markets?	List actions that may overcome the objections (switching costs) of B2B customers toward adoption of the new product.	What are the factors that most lead to perceptions of high switching costs?	*Perceived difficulty* in learning how to use the new device is related to *switching costs.* *Price* is positively related to *switching costs.* *Knowledge* of new product is positively related to *switching costs.*
SITUATION 3	How can we encourage more consumers to come to the microbrew and try our products? Should we redesign the brewery to be more inviting?	Describe how situational factors influence beer consumption and consumer attitudes toward beer products. List factors that will improve attitudes toward the microbrewery.	Do situational factors (such as time of day, food pairings, or environmental factors) relate to taste perceptions of beer?	Microbrew beer is *preferred* when consumed *with food.* An exciting *atmosphere* will improve consumer *attitudes toward the microbrew.*

words, there is gap between how frequently we expect good customers to return and how often they have been returning over the past year. They eventually agree on the following decision statement:

In what ways can Mario Lagasto's Restaurant build customer loyalty *so that revenues increase through more frequent* patronage *and* higher average tickets?

What information or data will be needed to help answer this question? Obviously, we'll need to study customer loyalty, restaurant patronage, and customer spending behavior. James needs to find out what things might cause customer loyalty, patronage, and spending to increase. Thinking back to the interview, James knows that there have been several changes in the restaurant itself, many related to saving costs. Saving costs on food preparation and quality sounds like a good idea; however, if it harms customer loyalty even slightly, it probably isn't worthwhile. Thus, the corresponding research objectives are stated as follows:

- Determine what key variables relate to customer loyalty among competing restaurants, meaning 1) how committed the customer is emotionally to the restaurant and 2) how frequently the customer visits one restaurant relative to the competition.
- Profile customers that spend significantly more than average each time they visit Lagasto's restaurant.

These research objectives are the deliverables of the research project. A research study will be conducted that (1) shows how much each of several key variables relates to customer commitment and patronage frequency and (2) provides a description of the type of customer that spends the most money.

The researcher should reach a consensus agreement with the decision maker regarding the overall decision statement(s) and research objectives. If the decision maker agrees that the statement captures the situation well and understands how the research objectives, if accomplished, will help address the situation, then the researcher can proceed. The researcher should make every effort to insure that the decision maker understands what a research project can deliver. If there is no agreement on the decision statement or research objectives, more dialogue between decision makers and researchers is needed.

Determine the Unit of Analysis

Unit of analysis
A study indicates what or who should provide the data and at what level of aggregation.

The **unit of analysis** for a study indicates what or who should provide the data and at what level of aggregation. Researchers specify whether an investigation will collect data about individuals (such as customers, employees, and owners), households (families, extended families, and so forth), organizations (businesses and business units), departments (sales, finance, and so forth), geographical areas, or objects (products, advertisements, and so forth). In studies of home buying, for example, the husband/wife dyad typically is the unit of analysis rather than the individual because many purchase decisions are made jointly by husband and wife.

Researchers who think carefully and creatively about situations often discover that a problem can be investigated at more than one level of analysis. Determining the unit of analysis, although relatively straightforward in most projects, should not be overlooked during the problem-definition stage of the research.

Determine Relevant Variables

▦ WHAT IS A VARIABLE?

Variable
Anything that varies or changes from one instance to another; can exhibit differences in value, usually in magnitude or strength, or in direction.

What things should be studied to address a decision statement? Researchers answer this question by identifying key variables. A **variable** is anything that varies or changes from one instance to another. Variables can exhibit differences in value, usually in magnitude or strength, or in direction. In research, a variable is either observed or manipulated, in which case it is an experimental variable.

The converse of a variable is a `constant`. A constant is something that does not change. Constants are not useful in addressing research questions. Since constants don't change, management isn't very interested in hearing the key to the problem is something that won't or can't be changed. In causal research, it can be important to make sure that some potential variable is actually held constant while studying the cause and effect between two other variables. In this way, a spurious relationship can be ruled out. At this point however, the notion of a constant is more important in helping to understand how it differs from a variable.

Constant
Something that does not change; is not useful in addressing research questions.

TYPES OF VARIABLES

There are several key terms that help describe types of variables. The *variance* in *variables* is captured either with numerical differences or by an identified category membership. In addition, different terms describe whether a variable is a potential cause or an effect.

A `continuous variable` is one that can take on a range of values that correspond to some quantitative amount. Consumer attitude toward different airlines is a variable that would generally be captured by numbers, with higher numbers indicating a more positive attitude than lower numbers. Each attribute of airlines' services, such as safety, seat comfort, and baggage handling can be numerically scored in this way. Sales volume, profits, and margin are common business metrics that represent continuous variables.

A `categorical variable` is one that indicates membership in some group. The term `classificatory variable` is sometimes also used and is generally interchangeable with *categorical variable*. Categorical variables sometimes represent quantities that take on only a small number of values (one, two, or three). However, categorical variables more often simply identify membership.

For example, people can be categorized as either male or female. A variable representing biological sex describes this important difference. The variable values can be an "M" for membership in the male category and an "F" for membership in the female category. Alternatively, the researcher could assign a "0" for men and a "1" for women. In either case, the same information is represented.

A common categorical variable in consumer research is adoption, meaning the consumer either did or did not purchase a new product. Thus, the two groups, purchase or not purchase, comprise the variable. Similarly, turnover, or whether an employee has quit or not, is a common organizational variable.

In descriptive and causal research, the terms *dependent variable* and *independent variable* describe different variable types. This distinction becomes very important in understanding how business processes can be modeled by a researcher. The distinction must be clear before one can correctly apply certain statistical procedures like multiple regression analysis. In some cases, however, such as when only one variable is involved in a hypothesis, the researcher need not make this distinction.

A `dependent variable` is a process outcome or a variable that is predicted and/or explained by other variables. An `independent variable` is a variable that is expected to influence the dependent variable in some way. Such variables are independent in the sense that they are determined outside of the process being studied. That is another way of saying that dependent variables do not change independent variables.

For example, average customer loyalty may be a dependent variable that is influenced or predicted by an independent variable such as perceptions of restaurant food quality, service quality, and customer satisfaction. Thus, a process is described by which several variables together help create and explain how much customer loyalty exists. In other words, if we know how a customer rates the food quality, service quality, and satisfaction with a restaurant, then we can predict that customer's loyalty toward that restaurant. Note that this does not mean that we can predict food quality or service quality with customer loyalty.

Continuous variable
A variable that can take on a range of values that correspond to some quantitative amount.

Categorical variable
A variable that indicates membership in some group.

Classificatory variable
Another term for a categorical variable because it classifies units into categories.

Dependent variable
A process outcome or a variable that is predicted and/or explained by other variables.

Independent variable
A variable that is expected to influence the dependent variable in some way.

Several variables describe child consumers. Their biological sex is a categorical variable; how much they weigh and how often they go out to eat are continuous variables.

©ERIKO SUGITA/REUTERS/CORBIS

Dependent variables are conventionally represented by the letter Y. Independent variables are conventionally represented by the letter X. If research involves two dependent variables and two or more independent variables, subscripts may also be used to indicate Y_1, Y_2 and X_1, X_2, and so on.

Ultimately, theory is critical in building processes that include both independent and dependent variables (see Chapter 3). Managers and researchers must be careful to identify relevant and actionable variables. *Relevant* means that a change in the variable matters and *actionable* means that a variable can be controlled by managerial action. Superfluous variables are those that are neither relevant nor actionable and should not be included in a study. Theory should help distinguish relevant from superfluous variables.

The process of identifying the relevant variables overlaps with the process of determining the research objectives. Typically, each research objective will mention a variable or variables to be measured or analyzed. As the translation process proceeds through research objectives, research questions, and research hypotheses, it is usually possible to emphasize the variables that should be included in a study (as in Exhibits 5.5 and 5.6).

Exhibit 5.6 includes some common marketing research hypotheses and a description of the key variables involved in each. In the first case, a regional grocery chain is considering offering a delivery service that would allow consumers to purchase groceries via the store website. They have conducted a trial of this in one market and have conducted a survey in that area. In the second case,

EXHIBIT 5.6 **Common Marketing Problems, Corresponding Research Hypotheses, and Variable Descriptions**

Managerial Decision	Research Question(s)	Research Hypotheses	Categorical Variable(s)	Continuous Variable(s)
Retail grocer considering web-based delivery service	Is there sufficient demand? Will delivery influence customer perceptions of quality? Will delivery service (new retail form) cannibalize current business?	*Projected sales volume* will exceed $5 M annually. *Retail form* influences *quality perceptions* such that web (in-store) customers perceive lower (higher) quality. Web customers express lower *intentions to visit store* than other customers.	Retail Form (independent variable)—classifies respondents based on whether they shopped (1) in-store or (2) via the web (delivery).	Sales Volume—dollar amount based on a test trial in one geographic market (i.e., Phoenix/Scottsdale). Intentions to visit store (dependent variable)—the percentage likelihood that a survey respondent would visit the store within the next 7 days.
What market segments should be served?	Does nationality matter? Will French and German consumers express interest in our product? Does the attitude toward Korean companies influence purchase intentions?	*French* consumers have more *interest in purchasing our product* than *German* consumers. *Attitude toward Korean companies* is related positively to *product purchase intenterest*.	Nationality (independent variable)—represents which country a survey respondent lives in: (1) France (2) Germany	Attitude toward Korean companies (independent variable)—ratings scale that describes how favorably survey respondents view Korean companies (quality, reputation, value; higher scores mean better attitude) Product purchase interest—ratings scale that shows how interested a consumer is in buying the Korean product (higher scores = more interest)

RESEARCHSNAPSHOT

Pricing Turbulence

A heavy equipment distributor sought out research because it believed there was an opportunity to increase revenues by raising prices. After several weeks of discussion, interviews, and proposal reviews, they settled on a decision question that asked, "In what ways could revenues be increased by altering pricing policies across customers?" A research project was conducted that offered the following deliverables: (1) demonstrate how much customer characteristics and environmental characteristics influence price elasticity and (2) identify market segments based on price elasticity. This led to several hypotheses including the following:

H1: The desired delivery time for equipment is negatively related to price sensitivity.
H2: The degree of market turbulence is negatively related to price sensitivity.

In addition, a research question specifically addressing market segments was asked:

RQ1: Are there market segments that can be identified based on customers' desired benefits or environmental characteristics?

In other words, the more critical a piece of heavy equipment is to a company, the less concerned they are with the price.

Similarly, customers are less concerned with price in markets that are more turbulent, meaning there are ever-changing environmental, competitive, and political pressures.

A study of heavy equipment purchasers around the world supported both hypotheses. For business segments where delivery time is of critical importance, higher prices can be charged without the fear of losing business. Similarly, in turbulent international markets, customers have other important concerns that make them less sensitive to equipment price and more sensitive to reliability and service. In the end, the heavy equipment company was able to build customer characteristic data into a DSS system that automated prices.

Interestingly, management did not express any concerns about either market segments or market turbulence in the initial interviews. Thus, this research succeeded because good research objectives, questions, and hypotheses were developed before any study was implemented.

Sources: Smith, M.F., I. Sinha, R. Lancianai, and H. Forman (1999), "Role of Market Turbulence in Shaping Pricing," Industrial Marketing Management, 28 (November), 637–649; Peters, G. (2005), "Combating Too Much Information," Industrial Distribution, 94 (December), 22.

ASSOCIATED PRESS/AP

a Korean automobile company is considering offering one of its models for sale in Europe. The company has also conducted a survey in two key European auto markets.

Write Research Objectives and Questions

Both managers and researchers expect problem-definition efforts to result in statements of research questions and research objectives. At the end of the problem-definition stage, the researcher should prepare a written statement that clarifies any ambiguity about what the research hopes to accomplish. This completes the translation process.

Research questions express the research objectives in terms of questions that can be addressed by research. For example, one of the key research questions involved in the opening vignette is "Are *consumer perceptions* of food quality, price, and atmosphere related to *customer loyalty*?" Hypotheses are more specific than research questions. One key distinction between research questions and hypotheses is that hypotheses can generally specify the direction of a relationship. In other words, when an independent variable goes up, we have sufficient knowledge to predict that the dependent variable should also go up (or down as the case may be). One key research hypothesis for Lagasto's is:

Food quality perceptions *are related positively to* customer commitment *toward a restaurant.*

At times, a researcher may suspect that two variables are related but have insufficient theoretical rationale to support the relationship as positive or negative. In this case, hypotheses cannot be offered. At times in research, particularly in exploratory research, a proposal can only offer research questions. Research hypotheses are much more specific and therefore require considerably more

Research questions
Express the research objectives in terms of questions that can be addressed by research.

theoretical support. In addition, research questions are interrogative, whereas research hypotheses are declarative.

Clarity in Research Questions and Hypotheses

Research questions make it easier to understand what is perplexing managers and to indicate what issues have to be resolved. A research question is the researcher's translation of the marketing problem into a specific inquiry.

A research question can be too vague and general, such as "Is advertising copy 1 better than advertising copy 2?" Advertising effectiveness can be variously measured by sales, recall of sales message, brand awareness, intention to buy, recognition, or knowledge, to name a few possibilities. Asking a more specific research question (such as, "Which advertisement has a higher day-after recall score?") helps the researcher design a study that will produce useful results. Research question answers should provide input that can be used as a standard for selecting from among alternative solutions. Problem definition seeks to state research questions clearly and to develop well-formulated, specific hypotheses.

A sales manager may hypothesize that salespeople who show the highest job satisfaction will be the most productive. An advertising manager may believe that if consumers' attitudes toward a product are changed in a positive direction, consumption of the product also will increase. Hypotheses are statements that can be empirically tested.

A formal hypothesis has considerable practical value in planning and designing research. It forces researchers to be clear about what they expect to find through the study, and it raises crucial questions about data required. When evaluating a hypothesis, researchers should ensure that the information collected will be useful in decision making. Notice how the following hypotheses express expected relationships between variables:

- There is a positive relationship between *buying on the Internet* and the presence of *younger children* in the home.
- *Sales* are lower for salespeople in regions that receive less *advertising support*.
- Consumers will experience *cognitive dissonance* after the decision to *adopt* a TiVo personal video recorder.
- *Opinion leaders* are more affected by mass media communication *sources* than are non-leaders.
- Among non-exporters, the degree of perceived importance of overcoming barriers to exporting is related positively to general interest in exporting (export intentions).[10]

Management is often faced with a "go/no go" decision. In such cases, a research question or hypothesis may be expressed in terms of a meaningful barrier that represents the turning point in such a decision. In this case, the research involves a **managerial action standard** that specifies a specific performance criterion upon which a decision can be based. If the criterion to be measured (for example, sales or attitude changes) turns out to be higher than some predetermined level, management will do *A*; if it is lower, management will do *B*.[11] In Exhibit 5.6, the specified sales volume of $5 million represents a managerial action standard for the retail grocery chain.

Managerial action standard
A specific performance criterion upon which a decision can be based.

Research objectives also should be limited to a manageable number. Fewer study objectives make it easier to ensure that each will be addressed fully. It becomes easy to lose focus with too many research objectives.

Exhibit 5.7 summarizes how a decision statement (corresponding to a marketing problem) leads to research objectives that become a basis for the research design. Once the research has been conducted, the results may show an unanticipated aspect of the problem and suggest a need for additional research to satisfy the main objective. Accomplished researchers who have had the experience of uncovering additional aspects of a marketing problem after finishing fieldwork recommend designing studies that include questions designed to reveal the unexpected.

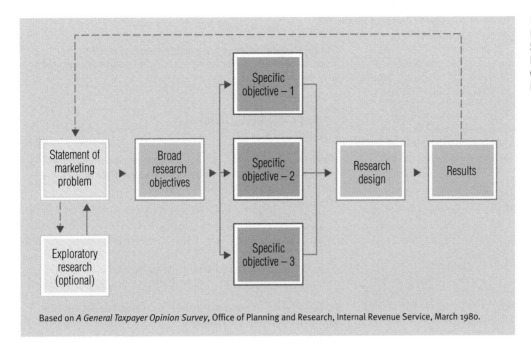

EXHIBIT 5.7
Influence of Decision Statement of Marketing Problem on Research Objectives and Research Designs

Based on *A General Taxpayer Opinion Survey*, Office of Planning and Research, Internal Revenue Service, March 1980.

How Much Time Should Be Spent on Problem Definition?

Budget constraints usually influence how much effort is spent on problem definition. Marketing situations can be complex and numerous variables may be relevant. Searching for every conceivable cause and minor influence is impractical. The more important the decision faced by management, the more resources should be allocated toward problem definition. While not a guarantee, allowing more time and spending more money will help make sure the research objectives that result are relevant and can demonstrate which influences management should focus on.

Marketing managers, being responsible for decision making, may wish the problem-definition process to proceed quickly. Researchers who take a long time to produce a set of research objectives can frustrate managers. However, the time taken to identify the correct problem is usually time well spent.

The Research Proposal

The **research proposal** is a written statement of the research design. It always includes a statement explaining the purpose of the study (in the form of research objectives or deliverables) and a definition of the problem, often in the form of a decision statement. A good proposal systematically outlines the particular research methodology and details procedures that will be used during each stage of the research process. Normally a schedule of costs and deadlines is included in the research proposal. The research proposal becomes the primary communication document between the researcher and the research user.

Exhibit 5.8 illustrates an abbreviated proposal for a short research project conducted for the Internal Revenue Service (IRS) that explores public attitudes toward a variety of tax-related issues.

Research proposal
A written statement of the research design.

The Proposal as a Planning Tool

Preparation of a research proposal forces the researcher to think critically about each stage of the research process. Vague plans, abstract ideas, and sweeping generalizations about problems or procedures must become concrete and precise statements about specific events. Data requirements and

EXHIBIT 5.8 An Abbreviated Version of a Research Proposal for the IRS

Current Situation

Public perception of the IRS appears to be extremely negative. The IRS is the brunt of jokes, and the public avoids contact with any IRS entity. As a result, taxpayers are more inclined to cheat on their returns and many services provided by the IRS to assist taxpayers in preparing their tax returns and to help them understand ways they can avoid paying unnecessary taxes and penalties go unused. In addition, negative attitude lessens the Service's ability to effectively lobby for policy changes. The key decision faced by the IRS due to this situation can be stated as,

What steps could be taken to effectively improve consumer perceptions of the IRS and help design more user-friendly services?

Purpose of the Research

The general purpose of the study is to determine the taxpaying public's perceptions of the role of the IRS in administering the tax laws. In defining the limits of this study, the IRS identified the study areas to be addressed. A careful review of those areas led to the identification of the following specific research objectives:

1. To identify the extent to which taxpayers cheat on their returns, their reasons for doing so, and approaches that can be taken to deter this kind of behavior
2. To determine taxpayers' experience and level of satisfaction with various IRS services
3. To determine what services taxpayers need
4. To develop an accurate profile of taxpayers' behavior relative to the preparation of their income tax returns
5. To assess taxpayers' knowledge and opinions about various tax laws and procedures

Research Design

The survey research method will be the basic research design. Each respondent will be interviewed in his or her home. The personal interviews are generally expected to last between 35 and 45 minutes, although the length will vary depending on the previous tax-related experiences of the respondent. For example, if a respondent has never been audited, questions on audit experience will not be addressed. Or, if a respondent has never contacted the IRS for assistance, certain questions concerning reactions to IRS services will be skipped.

Some sample questions that will be asked are

Did you or your spouse prepare your federal tax return for (year)?
- Self
- Spouse
- Someone else

Did the federal income tax package you received in the mail contain all the forms necessary for you to fill out your return?
- Yes
- No
- Didn't receive one in the mail
- Don't know

If you were calling the IRS for assistance and no one was able to help you immediately, would you rather get a busy signal or be asked to wait on hold?
- Busy signal
- Wait on hold
- Neither
- Don't know

During the interview a self-administered questionnaire will be given to the taxpayer to ask certain sensitive questions, such as

Have you ever claimed a dependent on your tax return that you weren't really entitled to?
- Yes
- No

Sample Design

A survey of approximately 5,000 individuals located in 50 counties throughout the country will provide the database for this study. The sample will be selected on a probability basis from all households in the continental United States.

Eligible respondents will be adults over the age of 18. Within each household an effort will be made to interview the individual who is most familiar with completing the federal tax forms. When there is more than one taxpayer in the household, a random process will be used to select the taxpayer to be interviewed.

Data Gathering

The fieldworkers of a consulting organization will conduct the interviews.

Data Processing and Analysis

Standard editing and coding procedures will be utilized. Simple tabulation and cross-tabulations will be utilized to analyze the data.

Report Preparation

A written report will be prepared, and an oral presentation of the findings will be made by the research analyst at the convenience of the IRS.

Budget and Time Schedule

Any complete research proposal should include a schedule of how long it will take to conduct each stage of the research and a statement of itemized costs.

research procedures must be specified clearly so others may understand their exact implications. All ambiguities about why and how the research will be conducted must be clarified before the proposal is complete.

The researcher submits the proposal to management for acceptance, modification, or rejection. Research clients (management) evaluate the proposed study with particular emphasis on whether or not it will provide useful information, and whether it will do so within a reasonable resource budget. Initial proposals are almost always revised after the first review.

The proposal helps managers decide if the proper information will be obtained and if the proposed research will accomplish what is desired. If the marketing problem has not been adequately translated into a set of specific research objectives and a research design, the client's assessment of the proposal will help ensure that the researchers revise it to meet the client's information needs.

An effective proposal communicates exactly what information will be obtained, where it will be obtained, and how it will be obtained. For this reason, it must be explicit about sample selection, measurement, fieldwork, and data analysis. For instance, most proposals involving descriptive research include a proposed questionnaire (or at least some sample questions).

The format for the IRS research proposal in Exhibit 5.8 follows the six stages in the research process outlined in Chapter 3. At each stage, one or more questions must be answered before the researcher can select one of the various alternatives. For example, before a proposal can be completed, the researcher needs to know what is to be measured. A simple statement like "market share" may not be enough; market share may be measured by auditing retailers' or wholesalers' sales, using trade association data, or asking consumers what brands they buy. What is to be measured is just one of many important questions that must be answered before setting the research process in motion. This issue will be addressed in greater detail in Chapter 13. For now, Exhibit 5.9 presents an overview of some of the basic questions that managers and researchers typically must answer when planning a research design.

The Proposal as a Contract

When the research will be conducted by a consultant or an outside research supplier, the written proposal serves as that person's bid to offer a specific service. Typically, a client solicits several competitive proposals, and these written offers help management judge the relative quality of alternative research suppliers.

A wise researcher will not agree to do a research job for which no written proposal exists. The proposal also serves as a contract that describes the product the research user will buy. In fact, the proposal is in many ways the same as the final research report without the actual results. Misstatements and faulty communication may occur if the parties rely only on each individual's memory of what occurred at a planning meeting. The proposal creates a record, which greatly reduces conflicts that might arise after the research has been conducted. Both the researcher and the research client should sign the proposal indicating agreement on what will be done.

The proposal then functions as a formal, written statement of agreement between marketing executives and researchers. As such, it protects the researcher from criticisms such as, "Shouldn't we have had a larger sample?" or "Why didn't you use a focus group approach?" As a record of the researcher's obligation, the proposal also provides a standard for determining whether the actual research was conducted as originally planned.

Suppose in our Italian restaurant case, following the research, Mario is unhappy with the nature of the results because they indicate that customers report higher loyalty toward other restaurants. This is something that Mario may not wish to face. In his despair, he complains to James saying,

"What I really wanted was an advertising study, yet you provide results indicating my food is no good! Why should I pay you?"

James can refer back to the research proposal, which is signed

Congress fights about everything . . . including how to spend taxpayers' money on federal research grants.

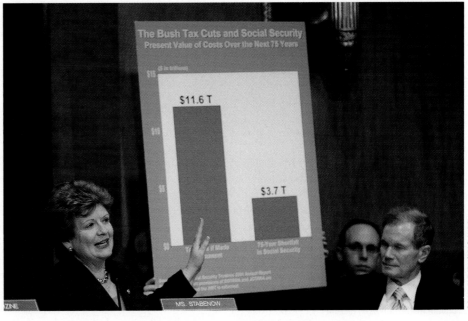

EXHIBIT 5.9 **Basic Points Addressed by Research Proposals**

Decisions to Make	Basic Questions
Problem definition	What is the purpose of the study? How much is already known? Is additional background information necessary? What is to be measured? How? Can the data be made available? Should research be conducted? Can a hypothesis be formulated?
Selection of basic research design	What types of questions need to be answered? Are descriptive or causal findings required? What is the source of the data? Can objective answers be obtained by asking people? How quickly is the information needed? How should survey questions be worded? How should experimental manipulations be made?
Selection of sample	Who or what is the source of the data? Can the target population be identified? Is a sample necessary? How accurate must the sample be? Is a probability sample necessary? Is a national sample necessary? How large a sample is necessary? How will the sample be selected?
Data gathering	Who will gather the data? How long will data gathering take? How much supervision is needed? What procedures will data collectors need to follow?
Data analysis and evaluation	Will standardized editing and coding procedures be used? How will the data be categorized? Will computer or hand tabulation be used? What is the nature of the data? What questions need to be answered? How many variables are to be investigated simultaneously? What are the criteria for evaluation of performance?
Type of report	Who will read the report? Are managerial recommendations requested? How many presentations are required? What will be the format of the written report?
Overall evaluation	How much will the study cost? Is the time frame acceptable? Is outside help needed? Will this research design attain the stated research objectives? When should the research begin?

by Mario. He can point right to the deliverables described above showing that Mario agreed to a study involving customer loyalty and the restaurant characteristics that lead to loyalty. The proposal certainly protects the researcher in this case. In most cases like this, after the initial emotional reaction to unflattering results, the client comes around and realizes the report contents include information that will be helpful. Realize too that the proposal protects Mario in case James produced a study that addresses only research objectives not included in the proposal.

In basic research efforts, a formal proposal serves much the same purpose. **Funded marketing research** generally refers to basic research usually performed by academic researchers and supported by some public or private institution. Most commonly, researchers pursue federal government grants. A very detailed proposal is usually needed for federal grants, and the agreement for funding is predicated on the research actually delivering the results described in the proposal.

Funded marketing research
Refers to basic research usually performed by academic researchers that is financially supported by some public or private institution as in federal government grants.

One important comment needs to be made about the nature of research proposals. Not all proposals follow the same format. A researcher can adapt his or her proposal to the target audience or situation. An extremely brief proposal submitted by an organization's internal marketing research department to its own marketing executives bears little resemblance to a complex proposal submitted by a university professor to a federal government agency to research a basic consumer issue.

Anticipating Outcomes

As mentioned above, the proposal and the final research report will contain much of the same information. The proposal describes the data collection, measurement, data analysis, and so forth, in future tense. In the report, the actual results are presented. In this sense, the proposal anticipates the research outcome.

Experienced researchers know that research fails more often because the problem-definition process breaks down or because the research client never truly understood what a research project could or couldn't do. While it probably seems as though the proposal should make this clear, any shortcoming in the proposal can contribute to a communication failure. Thus, any tool that helps communication become as clear as can be is valued very highly.

▦ DUMMY TABLES

One such tool that is perhaps the best way to let management know exactly what kind of results will be produced by research is the *dummy table*. **Dummy tables** are placed in research proposals and are exact representations of the actual tables that will show results in the final report with one exception: The results are hypothetical. They get the name because the researcher fills in, or "dummies up," the tables with likely but fictitious data. Dummy tables include the tables that will present hypothesis test results. In this way, they are linked directly to research objectives.

Dummy tables
Tables placed in research proposals that are exact representations of the actual tables that will show results in the final report with the exception that the results are hypothetical (fictitious).

A research analyst can present dummy tables to the decision maker and ask, "Given findings like these, will you be able to make a decision?" If the decision maker says yes, the proposal may be accepted. However, if the decision maker cannot see how results like those in the dummy tables will help make the needed decision(s), it may be back to the drawing board. In other words, the client and researcher need to rethink what research results are necessary to solve the problem. Sometimes, examining the dummy tables may reveal that a key variable is missing or that some dependent variable is really not relevant. In other words, the marketing problem is clarified by deciding on action standards or performance criteria and recognizing the types of research findings necessary to make specific decisions.

▦ EXAMPLE DUMMY TABLE

Exhibit 5.10 shows a dummy table taken from the research proposal for Mario Lagasto's Italian Restaurant. From it, Mario can see that it shows what things most determine how often a customer chooses a restaurant over its top competitors. If the results turn out as shown in the dummy table, it would suggest that Mario needs to emphasize food quality, a pleasant atmosphere, service quality, and wine and beverage quality to restore loyalty. In contrast, results like these would suggest that customers are not price sensitive. Price would not determine loyalty according to results like these.

Such results would indicate that the emphasis on cost control, to the extent that it lowers prices, reduces food or beverage quality, or harms the atmosphere and service quality, is misplaced and harmful. In addition, results like these would suggest that Mario's strengths are things that are not very important. Although these results would suggest Mario is second overall in terms of consumer price perceptions, this variable does not determine loyalty. Looking at the table, Mario can see how the results could be used.

While some tables may require some additional explanation from the researcher, every effort should be made to allow tables to stand alone and be interpreted by someone who is not an experienced researcher. In other words, the user should be able to understand the results and surmise implications that the results imply. When the final report is compiled, these tables will be included with the results replaced with the actual research results.

EXHIBIT 5.10 **A Dummy Table for Mario Lagasto**

Regression Table: Results Showing which Variables Determine Restaurant Customer's Loyalty (Patronage Frequency)

Independent Variable	Standardized Regression Coefficient	Rank (Importance in Determining Frequency)	Mean Score Rank (How Lagasto's Ranks Compared to Ten Closest Competitors)
Food Quality	.50**	1	6
Pleasant Atmosphere	.45**	2	7
Service Quality	.30**	3	5
Wine and Beverage Quality	.25**	4	8
Convenience of Location	.15*	5	3
Advertising	.05	6	4
Menu Prices	−.05	7	2

* P-VALUE < .001
** P-VALUE < .05

Summary

1. Problem Definition is Essential to Marketing Research. Problem definition is the process of defining and developing a decision statement and the steps involved in translating it into more precise research terminology, including a set of research objectives. While it is difficult to point to any particular research stage as the most important, a strong case can be made for this, the first stage. If this step falls apart, the entire research design is misguided. Effective problem definition helps make sure the research objectives are relevant and useful—meaning the results will actually be used. If problem definition is glossed over or done poorly, the results are likely irrelevant and potentially harmful.

2. Know How to Recognize Problems. Problems and opportunities are usually associated with differences. The differences can occur because of changes in some situation, or they can occur because expectations were unrealistic. Problems occur when there is a difference, or gap, between the current situation and a more ideal situation. One very common type of gap is when business performance does not match the expectations of performance in that dimension. In addition, opportunities exist when actual performance in some area does not match the potential performance. Research can supply information to help close the gap. Thus, problems are noticed by spotting these gaps. While many of these gaps may just be symptoms, further steps are taken to make sure that research addresses relevant issues, not just symptoms.

3. Translate Decision Objectives into Relevant Research Hypotheses. The problem-definition process outlined in the chapter can help make sure that the research objectives are relevant. A situation analysis is helpful in this regard. In particular, interviews that identify symptoms and then probe the respondent for potential causes of these symptoms are helpful. One tool to help in this process is the "what has changed?" technique. The research objectives, once written, also indicate what variables are likely needed in the study.

4. Translate Research Objectives into Research Questions and/or Research Hypotheses. Research questions simply restate the research objectives in the form of a question. When the researcher has sufficient theoretical reasoning to make a more specific prediction that includes the direction of any predicted relationship, the research question can be translated into one or more research hypotheses.

5. Outline the Components of a Research Proposal. The research proposal is a written statement of the research design that will be followed in addressing a specific problem. The research proposal allows managers to evaluate the details of the proposed research and determine if alterations are needed. Most research proposals include the following sections: decision description, purpose of the research including the research objectives, research design, sample design, data gathering and/or fieldwork techniques, data processing and analysis, budget, and time schedule.

6. Construct Dummy Tables. Dummy tables are included in research proposals and look exactly like the real tables that will be included in the final research report. However, they cannot actually contain results since the study has not yet been done. So, they include hypothetical results that look as much as possible like the actual results. These tables are a very good tool for communicating the value of a research project to management because they provide a real sense for implications that may result from the research.

Key Terms and Concepts

Decision statement
Problem definition
Problem
Situation analysis
Interrogative techniques
Probing
Unit of analysis

Variable
Constant
Continuous variable
Categorical variable
Classificatory variable
Dependent variable
Independent variable

Research questions
Managerial action standard
Research proposal
Funded marketing research
Dummy tables

Questions for Review and Critical Thinking

1. What is a *decision statement?* How does the focus on an irrelevant decision affect the research process?
2. Define *problem recognition.* How is this process like translating text from one language into another? What role does "probing" play in this process?
3. List and describe four factors that influence how difficult the problem-definition process can be.
4. What are three types of gaps that exist, indicating that research may be needed to assist a business in making some decision?
5. Examine an article in *The Wall Street Journal* or a similar source that discusses a business situation of a company in the electronics or defense industry. Identify a problem that exists with the company. Develop some research objectives that you believe correspond to the problem.
6. What is a situation analysis? How can it be used to separate symptoms from actual problems?
7. Define unit of analysis in a marketing research context.
8. Recall the concept of marketing orientation from the first chapter. If a company was conducting research investigating whether companies that are marketing-oriented outperformed companies that were production-oriented, what would the appropriate unit of analysis be?
9. Find some business journal articles that deal with culture and international expansion. Find one that lists some hypotheses. What kinds of decisions might be assisted by the results of testing these hypotheses?
10. List and describe at least four terms that can describe the nature of a variable.
11. For each of the following variables, explain why it should be considered either continuous or categorical:
    a. Whether or not a university played in a football bowl game during 2006
    b. The average wait time a customer has before being served in a full-service restaurant

    c. Letter grades of A, B, C, D, or F
    d. The job satisfaction of a company's salespeople
    e. A consumer's age
12. Write at least three examples of hypotheses that involve a managerial action statement. Provide a corresponding decision statement for each.
13. What are the major components of a research proposal? How does a research proposal assist the researcher?
14. The chapter provides an example dummy table for the Lagasto's restaurant vignette. Provide another example dummy table that corresponds to this same situation.
15. Evaluate the following statements of marketing problems. For each provide a decision statement and corresponding research objectives:
    a. A farm implement manufacturer: Our objective is to learn the most effective form of advertising so we can maximize product line profits.
    b. An employees' credit union: Our problem is to determine the reasons why employees join the credit union, determine members' awareness of credit union services, and measure attitudes and beliefs about how effectively the credit union is operated.
    c. The producer of a television show: We have a marketing problem. The program's ratings are low. We need to learn how we can improve our ratings.
    d. A soft-drink manufacturer: The marketing problem is that we do not know if our bottlers are more satisfied with us than our competitors' bottlers are with them.
    e. A women's magazine: Our problem is to document the demographic changes that have occurred in recent decades in the lives of women and to put them in historical perspective; to examine several generations of American women through most of this century, tracking their roles as students, workers, wives, and mothers and noting the changes in timing,

sequence, and duration of these roles; to examine at what age and for how long a woman enters various stages of her life: school, work, marriage, childbearing, divorce. This will be accomplished by analyzing demographic data over several generations.

f. A manufacturer of fishing boats: The problem is to determine sales trends over the past five years by product category and to determine the seasonality of unit boat sales by quarters and by region of the country.

g. The inventor of a tension-headache remedy (a cooling pad that is placed on the forehead for up to four hours): The purpose of this research is (1) to identify the market potential for the product, (2) to identify what desirable features the product should possess, and (3) to determine possible advertising strategies/channel strategies for the product.

16. Comment on the following statements and situations:
   a. "The best marketing researchers are prepared to rethink and rewrite their proposals."
   b. "The client's signature is an essential element of the research proposal."

17. You have been hired by a group of hotel owners, restaurant owners, and other people engaged in businesses that benefit from tourism on South Padre Island, Texas. They wish to learn how they can attract a large number of college students to their town during spring break. Define the marketing decision statement.

18. You have been hired by a local Big Brothers and Big Sisters organization to learn how they can increase the number of males who volunteer to become Big Brothers to fatherless boys. Define your research objectives.

Research Activities

1. 'NET Examine the website for International Communications Research (http://icrsurvey.com).[12] What services do they seem to offer that fall into the problem-definition process?

2. Consider the current situation within your local university music department. Assuming it stages musical productions to which audiences are invited and for which tickets are sold, describe the marketing situation it faces. Prepare a research proposal that would help it address a key decision. Make sure it includes at least one dummy table.

Case 5.1 E-ZPass

In the 1990s, a task force was formed among executives of seven regional transportation agencies in the New York–New Jersey area.[13] The mission of the task force was to investigate the feasibility and desirability of adopting electronic toll collection (ETC) for the interregional roadways of the area. Electronic toll collection is accomplished by providing commuters with small transceiver (tags) that emit a tuned radio signal. Receivers placed at tollbooths are able to receive the radio signal and identify the commuter associated with the particular signal. Commuters establish ETC accounts that are debited for each use of a toll road or facility, thus eliminating the need for the commuter to pay by cash or token. Because the radio signal can be read from a car in motion, ETC can reduce traffic jams at toll plazas by allowing tag holders to pass through at moderate speeds.

At the time the New York and New Jersey agencies were studying the service, electronic toll collection was already being used successfully in Texas and Louisiana. Even though several of the agencies had individually considered implementing ETC, they recognized that independent adoption would fall far short of the potential benefits achievable with an integrated interregional system.

The task force was most interested in identifying the ideal configuration of service attributes for each agency's commuters, and determining how similar or different these configurations might be across agencies. The task force identified a lengthy list of attributes that was ultimately culled to six questions:

- How many accounts are necessary and what statements will be received?
- How and where does one pay for E-ZPass?
- What lanes are available for use and how they are controlled?
- Is the tag transferable to other vehicles?
- What is the price of the tag and possible service charge?
- What are other possible uses for the E-ZPass tag (airport parking, gasoline purchases, and so forth)?

From a marketing researcher's perspective, it also seemed important to assess commuter demand for the service. However, the task force was not convinced that it needed a projection of demand, because it was committed to implementing ETC regardless of initial commuter acceptance. The task force considered its primary role to be investigating commuters' preferences for how the service should be configured *ideally*.

Questions

1. Evaluate the problem-definition process. Has the problem been defined adequately so that a relevant decision statement can be written?

2. What type of research design would you recommend for this project?

3. What research questions might be tested?

4. What might a dummy table include in this research proposal?

Case 5.2 Cane's Goes International

Raising Cane's is a fast-food chicken finger establishment based in Baton Rouge, Louisiana. Cane's restaurants are popular throughout the Gulf South. Cane's recently has been approached by people interested in opening Cane's restaurants in other countries. The best contact is an Australian. However, Cane's has also been approached about outlets in Montreal, Quebec, and in Monterey, Mexico. Cane's prepares high-quality fried chicken fingers and has a limited menu consisting of fingers, fries, slaw, and lemonade (http://www.raisingcanes.com).

1. Write a decision statement for Raising Cane's.
2. Write corresponding research objectives and research questions.
3. What role would a proposal play in assisting this research effort and in assisting Cane's in improving their business situation?

Case 5.3 Mario Lagasto's Italian Restaurant

Based on the case scenario described throughout this chapter, prepare a research proposal that addresses this situation.

Video Case 5.4 Burton Snowboards

Burton Snowboards, headquartered in Burlington, Vermont, is the leading global designer and manufacturer of snowboards; they also market snowboard equipment and accessory lines, such as cold-weather clothing. The company was founded in 1977 by Jake Burton, the inventor of modern snowboarding, in his garage. His philosophy for the company is to do whatever is in the best interest of the snowboarder.

This means that Burton Snowboards does not compromise the quality of any of its products, using the best materials and technological advances, for example, to redesign its snowboards. The result is that Burton controls about 40 percent of the world market in snowboards. Jake Burton still holds the company privately and has opened offices in Austria and Japan.

The company's success is based on gathering information about factors in the external business environment, which include social trends, demographic trends, technological trends, and trends in global competition. Social trends are most important; for many consumers, snowboarding is a way of life that influences the way they talk and dress, the products they buy, and the activities they engage in.

Demographic trends refer to information about people's preferences for snowboarding equipment according to their age range and gender. Technological trends involve learning innovations that can be used to develop new and better products. Amy Barrett, PR specialist, affirms: "Every year we're redesigning every single product we have."

Knowing the competition from similar companies around the world is also important at Burton. "We definitely like to think of ourselves as innovators, not imitators," says Barry Dugan, team and promotions manager.

This is a fun industry, and employee commitment to the joy of the sport runs high. Emmett Manning, a factory store manager, sums up the feelings of Burton employees when he says, "We're a company of snowboards, and we're very passionate about it. . . . Success is knowing that there's going to be another snowfall and that we're going to go snowboarding."

Questions

1. Imagine a hypothetical marketing question such as this: Should Burton develop a line of snowboards targeted exclusively to women between the ages of twenty and thirty? Develop the appropriate research questions and research objectives for this question.
2. Suppose that Burton executives are wondering about how they can best tailor products so that they are acceptable in markets in Europe and Asia. Define the research problem and determine relevant variables for this situation.

CHAPTER 6
QUALITATIVE RESEARCH TOOLS

After studying this chapter, you should be able to

1. List and understand the differences between qualitative research and quantitative research
2. Understand the role of qualitative research in exploratory research designs
3. Describe the basic categories of qualitative research
4. Prepare a focus group interview outline
5. Recognize technological advances in the application of qualitative research approaches
6. Recognize common qualitative research tools and know the advantages and limitations of their use
7. Know the risks associated with acting on only exploratory results

Chapter Vignette: What's in the Van?

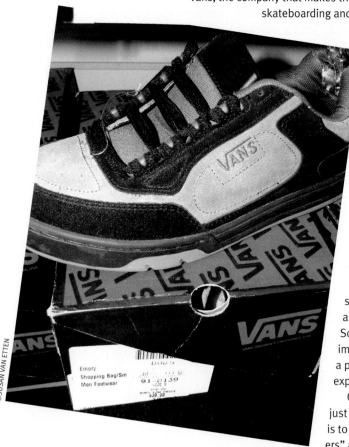

©SUSAN VAN ETTEN

Is this shoe too cool? That was really the question asked by VF Corporation when they acquired Vans, the company that makes the shoe shown here.[1] Vans traditionally are synonymous with skateboarding and skateboard culture. Readers that are unfamiliar with skateboarding may well have never heard of the company. However, a reader that is part of the skateboard culture is probably looking down at his or her Vans right now!

Former Vans CEO Gary Schoenfield points out that a decade before the acquisition (a $396 million deal), Vans was practically a dead brand.[2] However, the last ten years has seen a revival in skateboard interest and Vans has remained the number one skateboard shoe provider. Now, the incoming management team has been given the task of deciding how to raise Vans sales to $500 million per year.

Where will the growth come from? Should the company define itself as a "skateboard footwear" company, a "lifestyle" company, or as the icon for the skate culture? Answering this question will require a deeper interpretation of the meaning of the "Van."

Skateboarding is a dynamic activity. A study by Board-Trac suggests that today over one in four skateboarders is female, as opposed to fewer than one in ten as recently as 2000.[3] So, what exactly is in the mind and heart of a "boarder"? Two important research questions involve "What is the meaning of a pair of Vans?" and "What things define the skateboarding experience?"

Questions like these call for qualitative research methods.[4] Not just any researcher is "fit" for this job. One way to collect this data is to hire young, energetic research employees to become "boarders" and immerse themselves into the culture.

They may have to "Kasper" like a "flatland techer" while probing for meaning among the discussion and activities of the other boarders. Here, Vans may find that their brand helps identify a boarder and make them feel unique in some ways. If so, Vans may want to investigate increasing their product line beyond shoes and simple apparel.

Depth interviews of Vans wearers in which people describe in detail why they wear Vans will also be useful. Vans shouldn't be surprised if they find a significant portion of their shoes are sold to people like Mr. Samuel Teel, a retired attorney from Toledo, Ohio. Sam is completely unaware of the connection between Vans and skateboarding. He likes them because he doesn't have to bend to tie his shoes! Maybe there are some secondary segments that could bring growth to Vans. But, marketing to them could complicate things—who knows?

What is Qualitative Research?

Describing Qualitative Research

Chemists sometimes use the term *qualitative analysis* to mean research that determines what some compound is made of. In other words, the focus is on the inner meaning of the chemical—its *qualities*. As the word implies, qualitative research is interested more in *qualities* than quantities. Therefore, qualitative research is not about applying specific numbers to measure variables or using statistical procedures to numerically specify a relationship's strength.

Qualitative marketing research is research that addresses marketing objectives through techniques that allow the researcher to provide elaborate interpretations of market phenomena without depending on numerical measurement. Its focus is on discovering true inner meanings and new insights. Qualitative research is very widely applied in practice. There are many research firms that specialize in qualitative research.

Qualitative research is less structured than most quantitative approaches. It does not rely on self-response questionnaires containing structured response formats. Instead, it is more **researcher-dependent** in that the researcher must extract meaning from unstructured responses, such as text from a recorded interview or a collage representing the meaning of some experience, such as skateboarding. The researcher interprets the data to extract its meaning and converts it to information.

▓ USES OF QUALITATIVE RESEARCH

Mechanics can't use a hammer to fix everything that is broken. Instead, the mechanic has a toolbox from which a tool is matched to a problem. Marketing research is the same. The researcher has many tools available and the research design should try to match the best tool to the research objective. Also, just as a mechanic is probably not an expert with every tool, each researcher usually has special expertise with a small number of tools. Not every researcher has expertise with tools that would comprise qualitative research.

Generally, the less specific the research objective, the more likely that qualitative research tools will be appropriate. Also, when the emphasis is on a deeper understanding of motivations or on developing novel concepts, qualitative research is very appropriate. The following list represents common situations that often call for qualitative research:[5]

1. When it is difficult to develop specific and actionable decision statements or research objectives. For instance, if after several interviews with the research client the researcher still can't determine what needs to be measured, then qualitative

Qualitative marketing research
Research that addresses marketing objectives through techniques that allow the researcher to provide elaborate interpretations of market phenomena without depending on numerical measurement; its focus is on discovering true inner meanings and new insights.

Researcher-dependent
Research in which the researcher must extract meaning from unstructured responses such as text from a recorded interview or a collage representing the meaning of some experience.

Qualitative researchers can learn about the skating experience by becoming immersed in the culture.

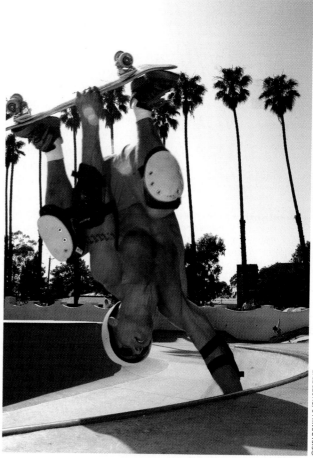

research approaches may help with problem definition. Perhaps several previous studies of the same topic have not proven particularly useful.

2. When the research objective is to develop an understanding of some phenomena in great detail and in much depth. Qualitative research tools are aimed at discovering the primary themes indicating human motivations and the documentation of activities is usually very complete.

3. When the research objective is to learn how consumers use a product in its natural setting or to learn how to express some concept in colloquial terms. A survey can probably ask many useful questions, but watching how someone actually experiences a product will usually be more insightful. Qualitative research produces many product improvement ideas.

4. When some behavior the researcher is studying is particularly context-dependent—meaning the reasons something is liked or some behavior is performed depends very much on the particular situation surrounding the event. Understanding why Vans are liked is probably difficult to understand properly outside the skating environment.

5. When a fresh approach to studying some problem is needed. This is particularly the case when quantitative research has been less than satisfying. Qualitative tools can yield unique insights, many of which may lead to new product ideas.

Each situation also describes a situation that may require an exploratory orientation. In Chapter 3, we defined exploratory research as appropriate in ambiguous situations or when new insight is needed. In the last chapter, we indicated that exploratory research approaches are sometimes needed just to reach the appropriate decision statement and research objectives. While equating qualitative research with exploratory research is an oversimplification, the application of qualitative tools can help clear up ambiguity and provide innovative ideas.

Qualitative "versus" Quantitative Research

In social science, one can find many debates about the superiority of qualitative research over quantitative research or vice versa.[6] We'll begin by saying that this is largely a superfluous argument in either direction. The truth is that qualitative research can accomplish research objectives that quantitative research cannot. Similarly truthful, but no more so, quantitative research can accomplish objectives that qualitative research cannot. The key to successfully using either is to match the right approach to the right research context.

Many good research projects combine both qualitative and quantitative research. For instance, developing valid survey measures requires first a deep understanding of the concept to be measured and a description of the way these ideas are expressed in everyday language. Both of these are tasks best suited for qualitative research. However, validating the measure formally to make sure it can reliably capture the intended concept will likely require quantitative research.[7] Also, qualitative research may be needed to separate symptoms from problems and then quantitative research can follow up to test relationships among relevant variables. The Research Snapshot box on the following page describes one such situation.[8]

Quantitative marketing research

Marketing research that addresses research objectives through empirical assessments that involve numerical measurement and analysis.

Quantitative marketing research can be defined as marketing research that addresses research objectives through empirical assessments that involve numerical measurement and analysis approaches. Qualitative research is more apt to stand on its own in the sense that it requires less interpretation. For example, quantitative research is quite appropriate when a research objective involves a managerial action standard. For example, a salad dressing company considered changing its recipe.[9] The new recipe was tested with a sample of consumers. Each consumer rated the product using numeric scales. Management established a rule that a majority of consumers rating the new product higher than the old product would have to be established with 90 percent confidence before replacing the old formula. A project like this can involve both quantitative measurement in the form of numeric rating scales and quantitative analysis in the form of applied statistical procedures.

■ CONTRASTING QUALITATIVE AND QUANTITATIVE METHODS

Exhibit 6.1 illustrates some differences between qualitative and quantitative research. Certainly, these are generalities and exceptions may apply. However, it covers some of the key distinctions.

RESEARCHSNAPSHOT

Surprises at P&G!

With literally thousands of products to manage, Procter & Gamble (P&G) finds itself in the situation to conduct qualitative research almost daily. P&G doesn't introduce a product that hasn't been reviewed from nearly every possible angle. Likewise, before taking a product to a new country, P&G has probably combined qualitative research techniques to discover potential problems or opportunities for marketing the product. So we can be sure that a product modification like Tide Kick or a laundry detergent made just for the French market, Le Croix Plus, has been "focus grouped."

At times, P&G seeks outside help for its research. Such was the case when P&G wanted a study of its marketing problems. The researchers selected began by applying qualitative research techniques including depth interviews, observational techniques (shadowing), and focus groups on P&G managers and marketing employees. These interviews gave the researchers the idea that perhaps P&G was suffering more from a management problem than from a marketing problem. It helped form a general research question that asked whether any marketing problems were really due to low morale among the marketing employees. After a lot of qualitative interviews with dozens and dozens of P&G employees, a quantitative study followed up these findings and supported this idea and led to suggestions for improving marketing morale!

Sources: Nelson, Emily (2002), "Focus Groupies: P&G Keeps Cincinnati Busy with all its Studies," The Wall Street Journal-Eastern Edition, 239 (1/24), A1; Stengel, J.R., A.L. Dixon, and C.T. Allen (2003), "Listening Begins at Home," Harvard Business Review (November), 106–116.

©AMY ETRA/PHOTOEDIT

EXHIBIT 6.1
Comparing Qualitative and Quantitative Research

Qualitative Research	Research Aspect	Quantitative Research
Discover Ideas, Used in Exploratory Research with General Research Objects	Common Purpose	Test Hypotheses or Specific Research Questions
Observe and Interpret	Approach	Measure and Test
Unstructured, Free-Forms	Data Collection Approach	Structured Response Categories Provided
Researcher Is Intimately Involved. Results Are Subjective.	Researcher Independence	Researcher Uninvolved Observer. Results Are Objective.
Small Samples—Often in Natural Settings	Samples	Large Samples to Produce Generalizable Results (Results that Apply to Other Situations)
Exploratory Research Designs	Most Often Used	Descriptive and Causal Research Designs

RESEARCHSNAPSHOT

ASSOCIATED PRESS/AP

Listening—Here's Johnny!

While there are many successful talk shows, the king of them all remains the late Johnny Carson. Johnny made the talk format popular in more than twenty years as host of NBC's *The Tonight Show*. What was the secret to Johnny's success? According to Johnny, it was listening. He was a terrific listener.

Well, Johnny would have also been a terrific qualitative researcher. Listening is one of the most important attributes for effective qualitative research. Two researchers may "hear" an adolescent consumer talk about smoking with her friends. One realizes this may be important in indicating the social aspects of smoking, the other is thinking about the next topic while the respondent talks and misses the chance to follow up on this point. Sometimes, silence promotes good listening.

Listening is equally as valuable in interviews with clients. Sometimes, in-depth interview techniques are needed to glean the best research objectives from the discussion. As in sales, listening is as valuable to a qualitative marketing researcher as is a strong throwing arm to a major league pitcher.

Sources: Foden, Atfiol (2003), "Do You Hear What I Hear?" Marketing News, 37 (3/3); Henderson, N.R. (2002), "The Many Faces of Consumer Research," Marketing Research, 14 (Summer), 13–17.

Quantitative researchers direct a considerable amount of activity toward measuring concepts with scales that either directly or indirectly provide numeric values. The numeric values can then be used in statistical computations and hypothesis testing. As will be described in detail later, this process involves comparing numbers in some way. In contrast, qualitative researchers are more interested in observing, listening, and interpreting. As such, the researcher is intimately involved in the research process and in constructing the results. For these reasons, qualitative research is said to be more **subjective**, meaning that the results are researcher-dependent. Different researchers may reach different conclusions based on the same interview. In contrast, when a survey respondent provides a commitment score on a quantitative scale, it is thought to be more objective because the number will be the same no matter what researcher is involved in the analysis.

Subjective Results are researcher-dependent, meaning different researchers may reach different conclusions based on the same interview.

Qualitative research seldom involves samples with hundreds of respondents. Instead, a handful of consumers are usually the source of qualitative data. This is perfectly acceptable in discovery-oriented research. All ideas would still have to be tested before adopted. Does a smaller sample mean that qualitative research is cheaper than qualitative? Perhaps not. Although fewer respondents have to be interviewed, the greater researcher involvement in both the data collection and analysis can drive up the costs of qualitative research.

Given the close relationship between qualitative research and exploratory designs, it should not be surprising that qualitative research is most often used in exploratory designs. Small samples, interpretive procedures that require subjective judgments, and the unstructured interview format all make traditional hypotheses testing difficult with qualitative research. Thus, these procedures are not best suited for drawing definitive conclusions such as results from causal designs involving experiments. These disadvantages for drawing inferences, however, become advantages when the goal is to draw out potential explanations because the researcher spends more time with each respondent and is able to explore much more ground due to the flexibility of the procedures.

▨ QUALITATIVE APPROACHES TO EXPLORATORY RESEARCH

When researchers have limited experience or knowledge about a research issue, exploratory research is a useful step. Exploratory research, which often involves qualitative methods, can be an essential first step to a more rigorous, conclusive, confirmatory study by reducing the chance of beginning with an inadequate, incorrect, or misleading set of research objectives.

Philosophically, research can be considered as either exploratory or confirmatory. Confirmatory research tests hypotheses. The results of these tests help decision making by suggesting a specific course of action. Exploratory research, on the other hand, takes a different approach. For instance, exploratory research may well be needed to develop the ideas that lead to research hypotheses in the first place.

Most exploratory research designs produce **qualitative data**. These data are not characterized by numbers and instead are textual, visual, or oral. The focus of qualitative research is not on numbers but on stories, visual portrayals, meaningful characterizations, interpretations, and other expressive descriptions. Exploratory designs do not usually produce **quantitative data**, which represent phenomena by assigning numbers in an ordered and meaningful way.

For example, a quantitative researcher may search for numbers that indicate economic trends. This may lead to hypothesis tests concerning how much the economy influences movie consumption. An exploratory researcher is more likely to adopt a qualitative approach that might involve trying to develop a deeper understanding of how families are impacted by changing economic times and why people suffering economically spend scarce resources on movie consumption. This may lead to the development of a hypothesis, but would not test one.

Most exploratory research does not produce quantitative data. This chapter focuses mostly on qualitative research in the context of an exploratory research design. Exploratory research may be a single formal investigation or a series of informal studies.

Some types of qualitative studies can be conducted very quickly. Others take a very long time. For example, a single focus group analysis involving a large bottling company's sales force can likely be conducted and interpreted in a matter of days. This would provide faster results than most descriptive or causal designs. However, other types of qualitative research, such as a participant-observer study aimed at understanding skateboarding, could take months to complete. A qualitative approach can but does not necessarily save time.

IDEA GENERATION

Exploratory research plays a big role in new product development, including developing and screening new product ideas. Exhibit 6.2 shows the new product development process and describes how marketing research is involved at each step.[10] Exploratory research is particularly useful in idea generation and screening by producing multiple ideas and then narrowing the choices down to a small number of alternatives. In this process, exploratory research may indicate that some new product ideas are unworkable.

Qualitative research can generate ideas for new products, advertising copy, promotional ideas, and product improvements in numerous ways. Researchers using qualitative approaches can ask consumers to describe their product experiences in great detail. This data can reveal the consumer needs that a product can truly address. For example, a consumer may be asked to describe their dog food experiences. When a customer is asked what he or she wants in a dog food, the reply likely will be "Something that is good for the dog." Once the consumer is encouraged to continue, however, we may learn that the dog food "smells bad in the refrigerator" and "is messy to clean up." Thus, the interview reveals that needs related to dog food that are not entirely centered on the dog.

Technology can also assist in this effort. For example, automobile marketers have consumers design their dream cars using computerized design systems similar to those used by automotive designers. This exploratory research might generate ideas that would never have occurred to the firm's own designers.[11]

CONCEPT TESTING

Research's main role in idea screening is concept testing. **Concept testing** is a frequently performed type of exploratory research representing many similar research procedures all having the same purpose: to screen new, revised, or repositioned ideas. Although the term *testing* is used, concept testing approaches are largely qualitative. Typically, respondents are presented with a written statement, pictorial representation, or some other idea description form and asked for comments.

Qualitative data
Data that are not characterized by numbers, and instead are textual, visual, or oral; focus is on stories, visual portrayals, meaningful characterizations, interpretations, and other expressive descriptions.

Quantitative data
Represent phenomena by assigning numbers in an ordered and meaningful way.

TOTHEPOINT

The cure for boredom is curiosity. There is no cure for curiosity.

—Dorothy Parker

Concept testing
A frequently performed type of exploratory research representing many similar research procedures all having the same purpose: to screen new, revised, or repositioned ideas.

EXHIBIT 6.2
**The Role of Research in the
New Product Development
(NPD) Process**

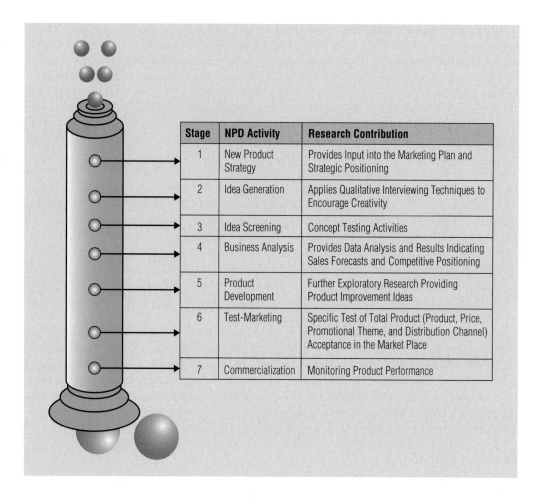

Stage	NPD Activity	Research Contribution
1	New Product Strategy	Provides Input into the Marketing Plan and Strategic Positioning
2	Idea Generation	Applies Qualitative Interviewing Techniques to Encourage Creativity
3	Idea Screening	Concept Testing Activities
4	Business Analysis	Provides Data Analysis and Results Indicating Sales Forecasts and Competitive Positioning
5	Product Development	Further Exploratory Research Providing Product Improvement Ideas
6	Test-Marketing	Specific Test of Total Product (Product, Price, Promotional Theme, and Distribution Channel) Acceptance in the Market Place
7	Commercialization	Monitoring Product Performance

The questions almost always include whether the idea is likeable, whether it would be useful, and whether it seems new. Respondents then are provided an opportunity to elaborate on the idea orally, in writing, or through some visual communication. Concept testing allows an initial evaluation prior to the commitment of any additional research and development, manufacturing, or other company resources. Perhaps just as importantly, the qualitative analysis of respondent comments provides themes that can be used to improve the product.

Concept testing processes work best when they not only identify ideas with the most potential, but they also lead to important refinements. Beiersdorf, the German company that produces Nivea skin care products (http://www.beiersdorf.com, http://www.nivea.com), like all consumer product firms, is constantly developing and screening new product ideas. One idea included a blemish hiding skin crème that worked by reflecting light from the blemish causing it to "disappear." During concept testing, most consumers were interested but asked questions about its moisturizing abilities. As a result, the product was introduced by emphasizing both its ability to hide blemishes and to moisturize the skin.[12]

Likewise, if Vans introduces snowboarding and biking products as a way of increasing sales revenues, those products will have to undergo concept screening. Will consumers respond favorably to the ideas of a Vans Cushioned Snowboard or Vans Biking Shoes? What does the Vans idea mean to snowboarders or bikers? Clearly, concept testing including probing interview techniques will be helpful in this effort.

Many ideas may not get evaluated unfavorably overall, but may contain flaws pointed out through concept-testing procedures. Aside from vanishing skin crème, Procter & Gamble marketed Enviro-Paks first in Europe and Canada. Enviro-Paks are a soft plastic refill pouch of detergents, fabric softeners, and other cleaning products. Given the successful introduction in these important markets, they decided to consider introducing the product in the United States. Concept testing

EXHIBIT 6.3 **Concept Statements for Two Seafood Products**

Squid Concept Alternative 1: CALAMARIOS	Squid Concept Alternative 2: SCLAM CHOWDER
CALAMARIOS[a] are a new and different seafood product made from tender, boneless North Atlantic squid. The smooth white body (mantle) of the squid is thoroughly cleaned, cut into thin, bite-sized rings, then frozen to seal in the flavor. To cook CALAMARIOS, simply remove them from the package and boil them for only 8 minutes. They are then ready to be used in a variety of recipes.	SCLAM CHOWDER is a delicious new seafood soup made from choice New England clams and tasty, young, boneless North Atlantic squid. Small pieces of clam are combined with bite-sized strips of squid and boiled in salted water until they are soft and tender. Sautéed onions, carrots, and celery are then added together with thick, wholesome cream, a dash of white pepper, and a sprinkling of fresh parsley. The entire mixture is then cooked to perfection, bringing out a fine, natural taste that will make this chowder a favorite in your household.
For example, CALAMARIOS can be combined with noodles, cheese, tomatoes, and onions to make "Baked CALAMARIOS Cacciatore." Or CALAMARIOS can be marinated in olive oil, lemon juice, mint, and garlic and served as a tasty squid salad. CALAMARIOS also are the prime ingredient for "Calamari en Casserole" and "Squid Italienne." You may simply want to steam CALAMARIOS, lightly season them with garlic, and serve dipped in melted butter. This dish brings out the fine flavor of squid. A complete CALAMARIOS recipe book will be available free of charge at your supermarket.	SCLAM CHOWDER is available canned in your supermarket. To prepare, simply combine SCLAM CHOWDER with 1½ cups of milk in a saucepan, and bring to a boil. After the chowder has reached a boil, simmer for 5 minutes and then serve. One can makes two to three servings of this hearty, robust seafood treat. Considering its ample nutrition and delicious taste, SCLAM CHOWDER is quite a bargain at $3.89 per can.
CALAMARIOS are both nutritious and economical. Squid, like other seafood, is an excellent source of protein. CALAMARIOS can be found at your supermarket priced at $6.50 per pound. Each pound you buy is completely cleaned and waste-free.	Both clams and squid are high in protein, so high in fact that SCLAM CHOWDER makes a healthy meal in itself, perfect for lunches as well as with dinner. Instead of adding milk, some will want to add a cup of sour cream and use liquid chowder as an exquisite sauce to be served on rice, topped with grated Parmesan cheese.
Because of their convenient versatility, ample nutrition, and competitive price, we hope you will want to make CALAMARIOS a regular item on your shopping list.	However you choose to serve it, you are sure to find SCLAM CHOWDER a tasty, nutritious, and economical seafood dish.

[a]Calamari is the Italian word for squid.

Glen L. Urban and John R. Hauser, *Design and Marketing of New Products* (Englewood Cliffs, NJ: Prentice Hall, 1980.) © 1980 Prentice Hall, Inc.

with American consumers, however, indicated that they preferred refill packaging that was different and that would be more convenient to use.

Exhibit 6.3 shows excellent concept statements for two seafood products made from squid. The statements portraying the intangibles (brand image, product appearance, name, and price) and a description of the product simulate reality. The product idea is clearly conveyed to the subject.

Qualitative Research Orientations

Qualitative research can be performed in many ways using many techniques. Orientations to qualitative research are very much influenced by the different fields of study involved in research. These orientations are each associated with a category of qualitative research. The major categories of qualitative research include

1. Phenomenology—originating in philosophy and psychology
2. Ethnography—originating in anthropology
3. Grounded theory—originating in sociology
4. Case studies—originating in psychology and in business research

Precise lines between these approaches are difficult to draw and a particular qualitative research study may involve elements of two or more approaches. However, each category does reflect a somewhat unique approach to human inquiry and approaches to discovering knowledge. Each will

RESEARCHSNAPSHOT

"When Will I Ever Learn?"

A hermeneutic approach can be used to provide insight into car shopping experiences. The approach involved a small number of consumers providing relatively lengthy stories about recent car shopping experiences. The goal is trying to discover particular reasons why certain car models are eliminated from consideration. The consumer tells a story of comparing a Ford and a GM (General Motors) minivan. She describes the two vehicles in great detail and ultimately concludes, "We might have gone with the Ford instead because it was real close between the Ford and the GM." The Ford was cheaper, but the way the door opened suggested difficulties in dealing with kids and groceries and the like, and so she purchased the GM model. The researcher in this story goes on to interpret the plotline of the story as having to do with her responsibility for poor consumption outcomes. Consider the following passage:

"It has got GM defects and that is really frustrating. I mean the transmission had to be rebuilt

after about 150 miles . . . and it had this horrible vibration problem. We took a long vacation where you couldn't go over sixty miles an hour because the thing started shaking so bad. . . . I told everybody,' Don't buy one of these things.' We should have known because our Buick—the Buick that is in the shop right now—its transmission lasted about 3,000 miles. My husband's parents are GM people and they had one go bad. I keep thinking, When I am going to learn? I think this one has done it. I don't think I will ever go back to GM after this."[13]

The research concludes that a hermeneutic link exists between the phrase "When I am going to learn?" and the plot of self-responsibility. The resulting behavior including no longer considering GM products and the negative word-of-mouth behavior are ways of restoring esteem given the events.

Source: Journal of Marketing Research by /Winer, Russ. Copyright 1997 by Am Marketing Assn (AMA) (CHIC). Reproduced with permission of Am Marketing Assn (AMA) (CHIC) in the format Textbook via Copyright Clearance Center.

be described briefly below, followed by a description of some of the more common qualitative techniques used to generate qualitative data.

Phenomenology

▣ WHAT IS A PHENOMENOLOGICAL APPROACH TO RESEARCH?

Phenomenology
A philosophical approach to studying human experiences based on the idea that human experience itself is inherently subjective and determined by the context in which people live.

Phenomenology represents a philosophical approach to studying human experiences based on the idea that human experience itself is inherently subjective and determined by the context in which people live.[14] The phenomenological researcher focuses on how a person's behavior is shaped by the relationship he or she has with the physical environment, objects, people, and situations. Phenomenological inquiry seeks to describe, reflect upon, and interpret experiences.

Researchers with a phenomenological orientation rely largely on conversational interview tools. When conversational interviews are face to face, they are recorded either with video or audiotape and then interpreted by the researcher. The phenomenological interviewer is careful to avoid asking direct questions when at all possible. Instead, the research respondent is asked to tell a story about some experience. In addition, the researcher must do everything possible to make sure a respondent is comfortable telling his or her story. One way to accomplish this is to become a member of the group (for example, becoming a skateboarder in the scenario described earlier in this chapter). Another way may be to avoid having the person use his or her real name. This might be particularly necessary in studying potentially sensitive topics including smoking, shoplifting, or employee theft.

Therefore, a phenomenological approach to studying the meaning of Vans may require considerable time. The researcher may first spend weeks or months fitting in with the person or group of interest to establish a comfort level. During this time, careful notes of conversations are made. If an interview is sought, the researcher would likely not begin by asking a skateboarder to describe his or her shoes. Rather, asking for favorite skateboard incidents or talking about what makes a skateboarder unique may generate productive conversation. Generally, the approach is very unstructured as a way of avoiding leading questions and to provide every opportunity for new insights.

■ WHAT IS HERMENEUTICS?

The term hermeneutics is important in phenomenology. Hermeneutics is an approach to understanding phenomenology that relies on analysis of texts in which a person tells a story about him or herself.[15] Meaning is then drawn by connecting text passages to one another or to themes expressed outside the story. These connections are usually facilitated by coding the key meanings expressed in the story. While a full understanding of hermeneutics is beyond the scope of this text, some of the terminology is used when applying qualitative tools. For instance, a hermeneutic unit refers to a text passage from a respondent's story that is linked with a key theme from within this story or provided by the researcher.[16] These passages are an important way in which data are interpreted.

Computerized software exists to assist in coding and interpreting texts and images. Atlas-Ti is one such software package that adopts the term hermeneutic unit in referring to groups of phrases that are linked with meaning. Hermeneutic units and computerized software are also very appropriate in grounded theory approaches. One useful component of computerized approaches is a word counter. The word counter will return counts of how many times words were used in a story. Often, frequently occurring words suggest a key theme. The research snapshot above demonstrates the use of hermeneutics in interpreting a story about a consumer shopping for a car.

Ethnography

■ WHAT IS ETHNOGRAPHY?

Ethnography represents ways of studying cultures through methods that involve becoming highly active within that culture. Participant-observation typifies an ethnographic research approach. Participant-observation means the researcher becomes immersed within the culture that he or she is studying and draws data from his or her observations. A *culture* can be either a broad culture, like American culture, or a narrow culture, like urban gangs or skateboarding enthusiasts.[17]

Organizational culture would also be relevant for ethnographic study.[18] At times, researchers have actually become employees of an organization for an extended period of time. In doing so, they become part of the culture and over time other employees come to act quite naturally around the researcher. The researcher may observe behaviors that the employee would never reveal otherwise. For instance, a researcher investigating the ethical behavior of salespeople may have difficulty getting a car salesperson to reveal any potentially deceptive sales tactics in a traditional interview. However, ethnographic techniques may result in the salesperson letting down his or her guard, resulting in more valid discoveries about the car-selling culture.

■ OBSERVATION IN ETHNOGRAPHY

Observation plays a key role in ethnography. Researchers today sometimes ask households for permission to place video cameras in their home. In doing so, the ethnographer can study the

Hermeneutics
An approach to understanding phenomenology that relies on analysis of texts through which a person tells a story about him or herself.

Hermeneutic unit
Refers to a text passage from a respondent's story that is linked with a key theme from within this story or provided by the researcher.

Ethnography
Represents ways of studying cultures through methods that involve becoming highly active within that culture.

Participant-observation
Ethnographic research approach where the researcher becomes immersed within the culture that he or she is studying and draws data from his or her observations.

Ethnographic (participant-observation) approaches may be useful to understanding how children obtain value from their experiences with toys.

consumer in a "natural habitat" and use the observations to test new products, develop new product ideas, and develop marketing strategies in general.[19]

Ethnographic study can be particularly useful when a certain culture is comprised of individuals who cannot or will not verbalize their thoughts and feelings. For instance, ethnography has advantages for discovering insights among children since it does not rely largely on their answers to questions. Instead, the researcher can simply become part of the environment, allow the children to do what they do naturally, and record their behavior.[20]

The opening vignette describing a participant-observer approach to leaning about skateboarding culture represents an ethnographic approach. Here, the researcher would draw insight from observations and personal experiences with the culture.

Grounded Theory

WHAT IS GROUNDED THEORY?

Grounded theory is probably applied less often in business research than is either phenomenology or ethnography.[21]

Grounded theory
Represents an inductive investigation in which the researcher poses questions about information provided by respondents or taken from historical records; the researcher asks the questions to him or herself and repeatedly questions the responses to derive deeper explanations.

Grounded theory represents an inductive investigation in which the researcher poses questions about information provided by respondents or taken from historical records. The researcher asks the questions to him or herself and repeatedly questions the responses to derive deeper explanations. Grounded theory is particularly applicable in highly dynamic situations involving rapid and significant change. Two key questions asked by the grounded theory researcher are "What is happening here?" and "How is it different?"[22] The distinguishing characteristic of grounded theory is that it does not begin with a theory but instead extracts one from whatever emerges from an area of inquiry.[23]

HOW IS GROUNDED THEORY USED?

Consider a company that approaches a researcher to study whether or not its sales force is as effective as it has been over the past five years. The researcher uses grounded theory to discover a potential explanation. A theory is inductively developed based on text analysis of dozens of sales meetings that had been recorded over the previous five years. By questioning the events discussed in the sales interviews and analyzing differences in the situations that may have led to the discussion, the researcher is able to develop a theory. The theory suggests that with an increasing reliance on e-mail and other technological devices for communication, the salespeople do not communicate with each other informally as much as they did five years previously. As a result, the salespeople had failed to bond into a close-knit "community."[24]

Computerized software also can be useful in developing grounded theory. In our Vans example, the researcher may interpret skateboarders' stories of good and bad skating experiences by questioning the events and changes described. These may yield theories about the role that certain brands play in shaping a good or bad experience. Alternatively, grounded theorists often rely on visual representations. Thus, the skateboarder could develop collages representing good and bad experiences. Just as with the text, questions can be applied to the visuals in an effort to develop theory.

Case Studies

WHAT ARE CASE STUDIES?

Case studies
The documented history of a particular person, group, organization, or event.

Case studies simply refer to the documented history of a particular person, group, organization, or event. Typically, a case study may describe consumers' acceptance or rejection of a particular product. Alternatively, case studies may describe the events of a specific company introducing a new product or dealing with some management crisis. Textbook cases typify this kind of case study. Clinical interviews of individual consumers can represent a case study. These may focus on their experiences with certain brands or products.

Themes
Identified by the frequency with which the same term (or a synonym) arises in the narrative description.

RESEARCHSNAPSHOT

It's Like Riding a Bike!

Schwinn has long relied on observational research in their exploratory research studies. Here is a description of a case study documented from observational techniques:

We had a very successful dealer on the West Coast. So it occurred to me that we'd go out and find out how he's doing it. So we go out. The guy's got a nice store out in Van Nuys. We sit in the back room and we listen. The first customers come in, a man and a woman with a boy about nine or ten years old. The dad says, "Which one is it?" The son says, "This one over here." Dad looks at it. He says to the clerk, "How much is it?" The clerk says, "$179.95." The father says, "Okay, we'll take it." It blew the whole bit [there were no magic sales approaches]. Suddenly it dawned on us that it's not what they say, it's the atmosphere of the store. Here was not Joe's old, dirty bike shop—it was a beautiful store on the main street. A big sign was in front, "Valley Cyclery," inside [were] fluorescent lights, carpeting on the floor, stereo music, air-conditioning, and a beautiful display of bicycles. It was like a magnet. People came in. So, we've tried to introduce that idea to other dealers. Put a bigger investment into your store and see what happens. Some of them did, and it happened [sales improved].

More recently, researchers documented with photographs the way that most people use their bicycles. Although the vast majority of bikes available for sale are multispeed racing or mountain bikes, even a cursory observation of the photos suggested that most people clearly do not race on their bikes nor use them off-road. As a result, Schwinn reintroduced the Cruiser with much success. The Cruiser is the 1950ish touring bike with the big cushioned seat and fenders. Observation is like riding a bike—once you learn, you shouldn't ever forget!

Sources: Burch, Ray (1973), "Marketing Research: Why It Works, Why It Doesn't Work," speech to the Chicago Chapter of the American Marketing Association, 1973 reprinted with permission of the Chicago Chapter of the American Marketing Association; Curry, A. and M. Silver (2004), "One Speed is Enough," U.S. News and World Report, 136 (May 10), 67–68.

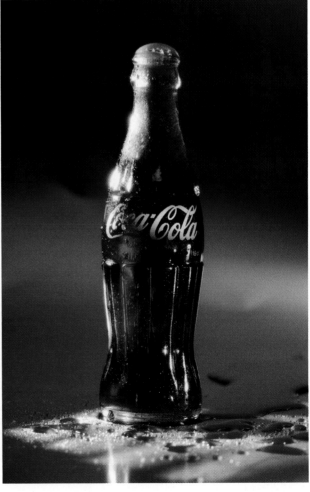

Qualitative research reveals that products that are perceived as "authentic" offer more value for consumers.

The case studies can then be analyzed for important themes. **Themes** are identified by the frequency with which the same term (or a synonym) arises in the narrative description. The themes may be useful in discovering variables that are relevant to potential explanations.

▶ HOW ARE CASE STUDIES USED?

Case studies are commonly applied in business. For instance, case studies of brands that sell "luxury" products helped provide insight into what makes up a prestigious brand. A marketing researcher carefully conducted case studies (no pun intended) of higher end wine labels (such as Penfold's Grange) including the methods of production and marketing. This analysis suggested that a key ingredient to a prestige brand may well be authenticity. When consumers know something is authentic, they attach more esteem to that product or brand.[25]

Case studies often overlap with one of the other categories of qualitative research. The Research Snapshot box above illustrates how observation was useful in discovering insights leading to important marketing changes.

A primary advantage of the case study is that an entire organization or entity can be investigated in depth with meticulous attention to detail. This highly focused attention enables the researcher to carefully study the order of events as they occur or to concentrate on identifying the relationships among functions, individuals, or entities. Conducting a case study often requires the cooperation of the party whose history is being studied. This freedom to search for whatever data an investigator deems important makes the success of any case study highly dependent on the alertness, creativity, intelligence, and motivation of the individual performing the case analysis.

Common Techniques Used in Qualitative Research

Qualitative researchers apply a nearly endless number of techniques. These techniques overlap more than one of the categories previously discussed, although each category may display a preference for certain techniques. Exhibit 6.4 lists characteristics of some common qualitative research techniques. Each is then described.

EXHIBIT 6.4 **Common Qualitative Research Tools**

Tool	Description	Type of Approach (Category)	Key Advantages	Key Disadvantages
Focus Group Interviews	Small group discussions led by a trained moderator	Ethnography, Case Studies	• Can be done quickly • Gain multiple perspectives • Flexibility	• Results dependent on moderator • Results do not generalize to larger population • Difficult to use for sensitive topics • Expensive
Depth Interviews	One-on-one, probing interview between a trained researcher and a respondent	Ethnography, Grounded Theory, Case Studies	• Gain considerable insight from each individual • Good for understanding unusual behaviors	• Results dependent on researcher's interpretation • Results not meant to generalize • Very expensive
Conversations	Unstructured dialogue recorded by a researcher	Phenomenology, Grounded Theory	• Gain unique insights from enthusiasts • Can cover sensitive topics • Less expensive than depth interviews or focus groups	• Easy to get off course • Interpretations are very researcher-dependent
Semi-Structured Interviews	Open-ended questions, often in writing, that ask for short essay-type answers from respondents	Grounded theory, ethnography	• Can address more specific issues • Results can be easily interpreted • Cost advantages over focus groups and depth interviews	• Lack the flexibility that is likely to produce truly creative or novel explanations
Word Association/ Sentence Completion	Records the first thoughts that come to a consumer in response to some stimulus	Grounded theory, case studies	• Economical • Can be done quickly	• Lack the flexibility that is likely to produce truly creative or novel explanations
Observation	Recorded notes describing observed events	Ethnography, grounded theory, case studies	• Can be inobtrusive • Can yield actual behavior patterns	• Can be very expensive with participant-observer series
Collages	Respondent assembles pictures that represent their thoughts/feelings	Phenomenology, Grounded theory	• Flexible enough to allow novel insights	• Highly dependent on the researcher's interpretation of the collage
Thematic Apperception/ Cartoon Tests	Researcher provides an ambiguous picture and respondent tells about the story	Phenomenology, Grounded theory	• Projective, allows to get at sensitive issues • Flexible	• Highly dependent on the researcher's interpretation

What is a Focus Group Interview?

The focus group interview is so widely used that many advertising and research agencies do nothing but focus group interviews. In that sense, it is wrongly synonymous with qualitative research. A **focus group interview** is an unstructured, free-flowing interview with a small group of people, usually between six and ten. Focus groups are led by a trained moderator who follows a flexible format encouraging dialogue among respondents. Common focus group topics include employee programs, brand meanings, problems with products, advertising themes, or new-product concepts.

The group meets at a central location at a designated time. Participants may range from consumers talking about hair coloring, petroleum engineers talking about problems in the "oil patch," children talking about toys, or employees talking about their jobs. A moderator begins by providing some opening statement to broadly steer discussion in the intended direction. Ideally, discussion topics emerge at the group's initiative, not the moderator's. Consistent with phenomenological approaches, moderators should avoid direct questioning unless absolutely necessary.

Focus group interview
An unstructured, free-flowing interview with a small group of around six to ten people. Focus groups are led by a trained moderator who follows a flexible format encouraging dialogue among respondents.

ADVANTAGES OF FOCUS GROUP INTERVIEWS

Focus groups allow people to discuss their true feelings, anxieties, and frustrations, as well as the depth of their convictions, in their own words. While other approaches may also do much the same, focus groups offer several advantages:

1. Relatively fast
2. Easy to execute
3. Allow respondents to piggyback off each other's ideas
4. Provide multiple perspectives
5. Flexibility to allow more detailed descriptions
6. High degree of scrutiny

Piggyback
A procedure in which one respondent stimulates thought among the others; as this process continues, increasingly creative insights are possible.

Focus group facilities typically include a comfortable room for respondents, recording equipment, and a viewing room via a two-way mirror.

Speed and Ease

In an emergency situation, three or four group sessions can be conducted, analyzed, and reported in a week or so. The large number of research firms that conduct focus group interviews makes it easy to find someone to conduct the research. Practically every state in the United States contains multiple research firms that have their own focus group facilities. Companies with large research departments likely have at least one qualified focus group moderator so that they need not outsource the focus group.

Piggybacking and Multiple Perspectives

Furthermore, the group approach may produce thoughts that would not be produced otherwise. The interplay between respondents allows them to **piggyback** off of each other's ideas. In other words, one respondent stimulates thought among the others and, as this process continues, increasingly creative insights are possible. A comment by one individual

©CHRIS DAVIS/GAMMA-LIAISON/GETTY IMAGES

often triggers a chain of responses from the other participants. The social nature of the focus group also helps bring out multiple views as each person shares a particular perspective.

Flexibility

The flexibility of focus group interviews is advantageous, especially when compared with the more structured and rigid survey format. Numerous topics can be discussed and many insights can be gained, particularly with regard to the variations in consumer behavior in different situations. Responses that would be unlikely to emerge in a survey often come out in group interviews: "*If* it is one of the three brands I sometimes use and *if* it is on sale, I buy it; otherwise, I buy my regular brand" or "*If* the day is hot and I have to serve the whole neighborhood, I make Kool-Aid; otherwise, I give them Dr Pepper or Coke."

If a researcher is investigating a target group to determine who consumes a particular beverage or why a consumer purchases a certain brand, situational factors must be included in any interpretations of respondent comments. For instance, in the situation above, the fact that a particular beverage is consumed must be noted. It would be inappropriate to say that Kool-Aid is preferred in general. The proper interpretation is situation-specific. On a hot day the whole neighborhood gets Kool-Aid. When the weather isn't hot, the kids may get nothing, or if only a few kids are around, they may get lucky and get Dr Pepper. Thus, Kool-Aid can be interpreted as appropriate for satisfying large numbers of hot kids while Dr Pepper is a treat for a select few.

Scrutiny

A focus group interview allows closer scrutiny in several ways. First, the session can be observed by several people, as it is usually conducted in a room containing a two-way mirror. The respondents and moderator are on one side, and an invited audience that may include both researchers and decision makers is on the other. If the decision makers are located in another city or country, the session may be shown via a live video hookup. Either through live video or a two-way mirror, some check on the eventual interpretations is provided through the ability to actually watch the research being conducted. Second, focus group sessions are generally recorded on audio or videotape. Later, detailed examination of the recorded session can offer additional insight and help clear up disagreements about what happened.

▓ FOCUS GROUP ILLUSTRATION

Imagine the differences in reactions to legislation further restricting smoking behavior that would be found among a group of smokers compared to a group of nonsmokers.

Focus groups often are used for concept screening and concept refinement. The concept may be continually modified, refined, and retested until management believes it is acceptable. While RJR's

initial attempts at smokeless cigarettes failed in the United States, Philip Morris is developing a smokeless cigarette for the U.K. market. Focus groups are being used to help understand how the product will be received and how it might be improved.[26] The voluntary focus group respondents are presented with samples of the product and then they discuss it among themselves. The interview results suggest that the key product features that must be conveyed are the fact that it produces no ashes, no side smoke, and very little odor. These beliefs are expected to lead to a positive attitude. Focus group respondents show little concern about how the cigarette actually functioned.

Smokers believe they will use the product if nonsmokers are not irritated by being near someone using the "electronic cigarette." Thus, the focus groups are useful in refining the product and developing a theory of how it should be marketed.

GROUP COMPOSITION

The ideal size of the focus group is six to ten people. If the group is too small, one or two members may intimidate the others. Groups that are too large may not allow for adequate participation by each group member.

Homogeneous groups seem to work best because they allow researchers to concentrate on consumers with similar lifestyles, experiences, and communication skills. The session does not become rife with too many arguments and different viewpoints stemming from diverse backgrounds. Also, from an ethnographic perspective, the respondents should all be members of a unique and identifiable culture. Vans may benefit from a focus group interview comprised only of skateboard enthusiasts. Perhaps participants can be recruited from a local skate park.

When the Center for Disease Control and Prevention tested public service announcements about AIDS through focus groups, it discovered that single-race groups and racially diverse groups reacted differently. By conducting separate focus groups, the organization was able to gain important insights about which creative strategies were most appropriate for targeted versus broad audiences.

For example, a typical homogeneous group might be made up of married, full-time homemakers with children at home. The researcher may find that including first-time mothers in a group with women who have three or four children reduces the new mothers' participation. Instead of giving their opinion, they become more interested in listening to the more experienced mothers for advice. Although they may differ in their opinions, they defer to the more experienced mothers. Therefore, researchers may consider interviewing first-time mothers and experienced mothers in separate groups.

Researchers who wish to collect information from different types of people should conduct several focus groups. A diverse overall sample may be obtained by using different groups even though each group is homogeneous. For instance, in discussing household chores, four groups might be used:

1. Married Men
2. Married Women
3. Single Men
4. Single Women

Although each group is homogenous, by using four groups, researchers obtain opinions from a wide degree of respondents. Similarly, a rule of thumb is that four focus group sessions, each in a different city, can satisfy exploratory research needs dealing with common consumer product or possible employee development issues.

ENVIRONMENTAL CONDITIONS

A focus group session may typically take place at the research agency in a room specifically designed for this purpose. Research suppliers that specialize in conducting focus groups operate from commercial facilities that have videotape cameras in observation rooms behind two-way mirrors and microphone systems connected to tape recorders and speakers to allow greater scrutiny as discussed above. Refreshments are provided to help create a more relaxed atmosphere conducive to a free exchange of ideas. More open and intimate reports of personal experiences and sentiments can be obtained under these conditions.

THE FOCUS GROUP MODERATOR

Exhibit 6.5 is a partial transcript of a focus group interview. Notice how the moderator insures that everyone gets a chance to speak and how he or she contributes to the discussion.

There are several qualities that a good moderator must possess:

1. The moderator must develop rapport with the group to promote interaction among all participants. The moderator should be someone who is really interested in people, who listens

Moderator
A person who leads a focus group interview and insures that everyone gets a chance to speak and contribute to the discussion.

RESEARCHSNAPSHOT

Overworked and Overpaid? Ethical Issues in Choosing Focus Group Respondents

Focus groups are one of the most sought after services provided by research firms. What is a research supplier's responsibility when recruiting individuals to participate in a focus group? Practically every focus group interview requires that respondents be selected based on some relevant characteristic. For example, if the topic involves parochial school education, the group should probably not include non-parents or non-parents with no plans of having children or ever putting a child through school. Consumers that fit the desired profile sometimes make poor focus group participants. When a researcher finds good focus group participants, he or she may be tempted to use them over and over again. Is this appropriate? Should respondents be recruited because they will freely offer a lot of discussion without being overbearing or because they have the desired characteristics given the focus group topic? This is a question the focus group planner may well face.

For example, a research client observed a focus group interview being conducted by a research supplier that had previously performed several other projects for the client, each dealing with a quite unique topic. During the interview, the client noticed that some focus group respondents looked familiar.

©SPENCER GRANT/PHOTO EDIT

A few days later, the client reviewed video recordings of the session alongside videotapes from two previous focus groups outsourced to the same company. She found that eight of the ten respondents in the latest focus group had appeared in one of the previous interviews as well. She was furious and considered whether or not she should pay for the interview or bother having a report prepared.

The focus group researcher had taken this approach to make sure the session went smoothly. The moderator solicited subjects who in the past had been found to be very articulate and talkative. In this case, the focus group respondents are more or less "professional," paid participants. It is questionable whether such "professional respondents" can possibly offer relevant opinions on all these topics. The question is, has the research firm acted in an ethical manner?

EXHIBIT 6.5 **What Happens in a Focus Group**

"My company is interested in finding out how people feel about different products and services," the moderator tells the semicircle of women. "In this group situation, what we're doing is exploring how you feel. Today we're interested in talking about restaurants and eating out."

The women have been told that someone "from a market research company" is listening to them, but they don't know which franchiser is the sponsor.

When the moderator displays the first card on the easel beside her, a card reading "McDonald's, Jack in the Box, Carl's Jr., Burger King, Wendy's," she asks, "What do you think of these restaurants?"

"The only one I really enjoy going to is Carl's Jr.," says Anne, a bright-faced woman in her early twenties who wears athletic shorts and flip-flops. "I don't know what Burger King does to their hamburgers, but I always get indigestion."

"You get indigestion at Burger King?" the moderator asks solicitously.

Anne nods. "It looks great when they bring it to you, but as soon as I start eating it, and especially when I finish, I get this awful feeling. . . ."

"I think it looks great on TV," says Nancy, whose hair has been frosted with two colors, for a total of three. "The lettuce is so crispy, you know—"

"Oh yeah, and it's these huge hamburgers," says Laura.

"But then you get it and it's all crushed together," Anne says ruefully.

"I think the worst is Jack in the Box," says Victoria, a very thin woman who lives in Reseda, near a block that she contends houses one of every food franchise in the world. "The meat doesn't taste like meat. It tastes . . . low-grade. Fatty. The last time I ate there—I had a coupon for it and we were close by and this friend of mine hadn't tried it—" she explains quickly, "it was terrible. I've heard that Wendy's—I haven't been there yet, but everybody who goes there thinks it's terrific."

"Really?" Nancy looks a little funny at Victoria. "Wendy's?"

"I've been there," Anne says. "It's terrible."

"Is it terrible?" Victoria asks sheepishly, retreating from the group's conclusion that she's been taking restaurant advice from a pack of cretins out there in Reseda.

"Oh, my daughter is the hamburger addict of the world, and she couldn't finish it," Nancy says. "It ran all down—it was so greasy—"

"I like Burger King," says Marlene, who has had nine children during her 25-year marriage, "and I like Carl's Jr." She smiles nicely, relishing the impending heresy: "McDonald's I could vomit from." The women laugh. "I like Jack in the Box Super Tacos."

"Charlie Hass on Advertising," New West Magazine, November 5, 1979, pp. 32–39.

carefully to what others have to say, and who can readily establish rapport, gain people's confidence, and make them feel relaxed and eager to talk.

2. The moderator must be a good listener. Careful listening is especially important because the group interview's purpose is to stimulate spontaneous responses. Without good listening skills, the moderator may direct the group in an unproductive direction.

3. The moderator must try not to interject his or her own opinions. Good moderators usually say less rather than more. They can stimulate productive discussion with generalized follow-ups such as, "Tell us more about that incident," or "How are your experiences similar or different from the one you just heard?" The moderator must be particularly careful not to ask leading questions such as "You do like cornflakes, don't you?"

4. The moderator must be able to control discussion without being overbearing. The moderator's role is also to focus the discussion on the areas of concern. When a topic is no longer generating fresh ideas, the effective moderator changes the flow of discussion. The moderator does not give the group total control of the discussion, but he or she normally has prepared questions on topics that concern management. However, the timing of these questions in the discussion and the manner in which they are raised are left to the moderator's discretion. The term *focus group* thus stems from the moderator's task. He or she starts out by asking for a general discussion but usually *focuses* in on specific topics during the session.

PLANNING THE FOCUS GROUP OUTLINE

Focus group researchers use a discussion guide to help control the interview and guide the discussion into product areas. A **discussion guide** includes written introductory comments informing the group about the focus group purpose and rules and then outlines topics or questions to be addressed in the group session. Thus, the discussion guide serves as the focus group outline. Some discussion guides will have only a few phrases in the entire document. Others may be more detailed. The amount of content depends on the nature and experience of the researcher and the complexity of the topic.

A cancer center that wanted to warn the public about the effects of the sun used the discussion guide in Exhibit 6.6. The marketing researchers had several objectives for this question guide:

- The first question was very general, asking that respondents describe their feelings about being out in the sun. This opening question aimed to elicit the full range of views within in the group. Some individuals might view being out in the sun as a healthful practice, whereas others view the sun as deadly. The hope is that by exposing the full range of opinions, respondents would be motivated to fully explain their own position. This was the only question asked specifically of every respondent. Each respondent had to give an answer before free discussion began. In this way, individuals experience a nonthreatening environment encouraging their free and full opinion. A general question seeking a reaction serves as an effective icebreaker.

- The second question asks whether participants could think of any reason they should be warned about sunlight exposure. This question was simply designed to introduce the idea of a warning label.

- Subsequent questions were asked and became increasingly specific. They were first asked about possible warning formats that might be effective. Respondents are allowed to react to any formats suggested by any other respondent. After this discussion, the moderator will introduce some specific formats the cancer center personnel have in mind.

- Finally, the "bottom-line" question is asked: "What format would be most likely to induce people to take protective measures?" There would be probing follow-ups of each opinion so that a respondent couldn't simply say something like "The second one." All focus groups finish up with a catch-all question asking for any comments including any thoughts they wanted passed along to the sponsor (which in this case was only then revealed as the Houston-based cancer center).

Researchers who planned the outline established certain objectives for each part of the focus group. The initial effort was to break the ice and establish rapport within the group. The logical flow of the group session then moved from general discussion about sunbathing to more focused discussion of types of warnings about danger from sun exposure.

Discussion guide
A focus group outline that includes written introductory comments informing the group about the focus group purpose and rules and then outlines topics or questions to be addressed in the group session.

EXHIBIT 6.6 Discussion Guide for A Focus Group Interview

Thank you very much for agreeing to help out with this research. We call this a focus group; let me explain how it works, and then please let me know if something isn't clear.

This is a discussion, as though you were sitting around just talking. You can disagree with each other, or just comment. We do ask that just one person talk at a time, because we tape-record the session to save me from having to take notes. Nothing you say will be associated with you or your church—this is just an easy way for us to get some people together.

The subject is health risk warnings. Some of you may remember seeing a chart in a newspaper that gives a pollen count or a pollution count. And you've heard on the radio sometimes a hurricane watch or warning. You've seen warnings on cigarette packages or cigarette advertising, even if you don't smoke. And today we're going to talk about warnings about the sun. Before we start, does anybody have a question?

1. OK, let's go around and talk about how often you spend time in the sun, and what you're likely to be doing. (FOR PARENTS): What about your kids—do you like them to be out in the sun?
2. OK, can you think of any reason that somebody would give you a warning about exposure to the sun?

(PROBE: IS ANY SUN EXPOSURE BAD, OR ONLY A CERTAIN DEGREE OF EXPOSURE, AND IF SO, WHAT IS IT? OR IS THE SUN GOOD FOR YOU?)

3. What if we had a way to measure the rays of the sun that are associated with skin problems, so that you could find out which times of the day or which days are especially dangerous? How could, say, a radio station tell you that information in a way that would be useful?
4. Now let me ask you about specific ways to measure danger. Suppose somebody said, "We monitored the sun's rays at noon, and a typical fair-skinned person with unprotected skin will burn after 40 minutes of direct exposure." What would you think?
5. Now let me ask you about another way to say the same kind of thing. Suppose somebody said, "The sun's rays at noon today measured 10 times the 8 A.M. baseline level of danger." What would you think?
6. OK, now suppose that you heard the same degree of danger expressed this way: "The sun's rays at noon today measured 8 on a sun danger scale that ranges from 1 to 10." What would you think?
7. What if the danger scale wasn't in numbers, but words? Suppose you heard, "The sun's rays at noon showed a moderate danger reading," or "The sun's rays showed a high danger reading." What would you think?
8. And here's another possibility: What if you heard "Here's the sun danger reading at noon today—the unprotected skin of a typical fair-skinned person will age the equivalent of 1 hour in a 10-minute period."
9. OK, what if somebody said today is a day to wear long sleeves and a hat, or today is a day you need sunscreen and long sleeves? What would you think?
10. OK, here's my last question. There are really three things you can do about sun danger: You can spend less time in the sun, you can go out at less dangerous times of day, like before 10 in the morning or after 4 in the afternoon, and you can cover your skin by wearing a hat or long sleeves, or using protective sunscreen lotion. Thinking about yourself listening to the radio, what kind of announcement would make you likely to do one or more of those things? (PARENTS: WHAT WOULD MAKE YOU BE SURE THAT YOUR CHILD WAS PROTECTED?)
11. And what would you be most likely to do to protect yourself? (YOUR CHILD?)
12. Before we break up, is there anything else you think would be useful for M. D. Anderson's people to know? Do you have any questions about any aspect of this interview?

OK, thank you very much for your help.

Betsy D. Gelb and Michael P. Eriksen, "Market Research May Help Prevent Cancer," Marketing Research, September 1991, p. 46. Published by American Marketing Association. Reprinted with Permission.

In general, the following steps should be used to conduct an effective focus group discussion guide:

1. Welcome and introductions should take place first.
2. Begin the interview with a broad icebreaker that does not reveal too many specifics about the interview. Sometimes, this may even involve respondents providing some written story or their reaction to some stimulus like a photograph, film, product, or advertisement.
3. Questions become increasingly more specific as the interview proceeds. However, the moderator will notice that a good interview will cover the specific question topics before they have to be asked. This is preferable as respondents are clearly not forced to react to the specific issue; it just emerges naturally.
4. If there is a very specific objective to be accomplished, such as explaining why a respondent would either buy or not buy a product, that question should probably be saved for last.
5. A debriefing statement should provide respondents with the actual focus group objectives and answering any questions they may have. This is also a final shot to gain some insight from the group.

FOCUS GROUPS AS DIAGNOSTIC TOOLS

Focus groups are perhaps the predominant means by which marketing researchers implement exploratory research designs. Focus groups also can be helpful in later stages of a research project, particularly when the findings from surveys or other quantitative techniques raise more questions than they answer. Managers who are puzzled about the meaning of survey research results may use focus groups to better understand what consumer surveys indicate. In such a situation, the focus group supplies diagnostic help after quantitative research has been conducted.

Focus groups are also excellent diagnostic tools for spotting problems with ideas. For instance, idea screening is often done with focus groups. An initial concept is presented to the group and then they are allowed to comment on it in detail. This usually leads to lengthy lists of potential product problems and some ideas for overcoming them. Mature products can also be "focused-grouped" in this manner.

VIDEOCONFERENCING AND STREAMING MEDIA

The videoconferencing industry has grown dramatically in recent years. As our ability to communicate via telecommunications and videoconferencing links has improved in quality, the number of companies using these systems to conduct focus groups has increased. With videoconference focus groups, marketing managers can stay home and watch on television rather than having to take a trip to a focus group facility.

Focus Vision Network of New York is a marketing research company that provides videoconferencing equipment and services. The Focus Vision system is modular, allowing for easy movement and an ability to capture each group member close up. The system operates via a remote keypad that allows observers in a far-off location to pan the focus group room or zoom in on a particular participant. Managers viewing at remote locations can even send the moderator messages during the interview. For example, while new product names were being tested in one focus group, an observant manager contacted the moderator with an idea and the moderator then asked respondents for a reaction to the new name on the spot.[27]

Streaming media consist of multimedia content such as audio or video that is made available in real time over the Internet or a corporate Intranet. This new technology for digital media delivery allows researchers to "broadcast" focus groups that can be viewed online. Offsite managers view the focus group using a media player like Microsoft Media Player. Like videoconferencing, this saves a trip to a focus group facility. Traditionally, the quality of streaming video has been far lower than videoconferencing. However, the quality difference is fast disappearing as streaming technology improves.

Streaming media
Consist of multimedia content such as audio or video that is made available in real time over the Internet or a corporate Intranet.

INTERACTIVE MEDIA AND ONLINE FOCUS GROUPS

Internet applications of qualitative exploratory research are growing rapidly and involve both formal and informal applications. Formally, the term **online focus group** refers to a qualitative research effort in which a group of individuals provides unstructured comments by entering their remarks into an electronic, Internet display board of some type. Participants use a keyboard and mouse to make their remarks during a chat-room session or in the form of a blog. Because respondents enter their comments into the computer, transcripts of verbatim responses are available immediately after the group session. Online groups can be quick and cost-efficient. However, because there is less interaction between participants, group synergy and snowballing of ideas may be diminished.

Several companies have established a form of informal, "continuous" focus group by establishing an Internet blog for that purpose.[28] We might call this technique a **focus blog** when the intention is to mine the site for business research purposes. General Motors, American Express, and Lego all have used ideas harvested from their focus blogs. The Lego blog can be found at http://www.bricksonthebrain.com. While online focus group respondents are generally paid $100 or more to show up and participate for ninety minutes, bloggers and online focus group respondents often participate for absolutely no fee at all! Thus, technology provides some cost advantages over traditional focus group approaches.[29]

Online focus group
A qualitative research effort in which a group of individuals provides unstructured comments by entering their remarks into an electronic Internet display board of some type.

Focus blog
A type of informal, "continuous" focus group established as an Internet blog for the purpose of collecting qualitative data from participant comments.

TOTHEPOINT

Necessity, mother of invention.

—William Wycherley

ONLINE VERSUS FACE-TO-FACE FOCUS GROUP TECHNIQUES

A research company can facilitate a formal online focus group by setting up a private, electronic chat room for that purpose. Participants in formal and informal online focus groups feel that their anonymity is very secure. Often respondents will say things in this environment that they would never say otherwise. For example, a lingerie company was able to get insights into how it could design sexy products for larger women. Online, these women freely discussed what it would take "to feel better about being naked."[30] One can hardly imagine how difficult such a discussion might be face to face. Increased anonymity can be a major advantage for a company investigating sensitive or embarrassing issues.

Because participants do not have to be together in the same room at a research facility, the number of participants in online focus groups can be larger than in traditional focus groups. Twenty-five participants or more is not uncommon for the simultaneous chat-room format. Participants can be at widely separated locations, even in different time zones, because the Internet does not have geographical restrictions. Of course, a major disadvantage is that often the researcher does not exercise as much control in precisely who participates. In other words, a person could very easily not match the desired profile or even answer screening questions in a misleading way simply to participate.

A major drawback with online focus groups is that moderators cannot see body language and facial expressions (bewilderment, excitement, interest, and so forth). Thus, they cannot fully interpret how people are reacting. Also, moderators' ability to probe and ask additional questions on the spot is reduced in online focus groups. Research that requires focus group members to actually touch something (such as a new easy-opening packaging design) or taste something is not generally suitable for an online format.

DISADVANTAGES OF FOCUS GROUPS

Focus groups offer many advantages. Like practically every other research technique, the focus group has some limitations and disadvantages too. Problems with focus groups include those discussed below.

First, focus groups require objective, sensitive, and effective moderators. It is very difficult for a moderator to remain completely objective about most topics. In large research firms, the moderator may be provided only enough information to effectively conduct the interview, no more. The focus group interview shouldn't reduce to only the moderator's opinion. Also, without a good moderator, one or two participants may dominate a session, yielding results that are really the opinion of one or two people, not the group. The moderator has to try very hard to make sure that all respondents feel comfortable giving their opinions and even a timid respondent's opinion is given due consideration. While many people, even some with little or no background to do so, conduct focus groups, good moderators become effective through a combination of good people skills (which cannot be taught), training (in qualitative research), and experience.

Second, some unique sampling problems arise with focus groups. Researchers often select focus group participants because they have similar backgrounds and experiences or because screening indicates that the participants are more articulate or gregarious than the typical consumer (see the Research Snapshot box on page 144). Such participants may not be representative of the entire target market. Thus, focus group results are not intended to be representative of a larger population.

Third, although not so much an issue with online formats where respondents can remain anonymous, traditional face-to-face focus groups may not be useful for discussing sensitive topics. A focus group is a social setting and usually involves people with little to no familiarity with each other. Therefore, issues that people normally do not like to discuss in public may also prove difficult to discuss in a focus group.

Fourth, focus groups do cost a considerable amount of money, particularly when they are not conducted by someone employed by the company desiring the focus group. As research projects go, there are many more expensive approaches, including a full-blown mail survey using a national random sample. This may costs thousands of dollars to conduct and thousands of dollars to analyze and disseminate. Focus group prices vary regionally, but the following figures provide a rough guideline:

Renting Facilities and Equipment	$500
Paying Respondents ($100/person)	$1,000
Researcher Costs	
• Preparation	$750
• Moderating	$1,000
• Analysis and Report Preparation	$1,500
Miscellaneous Expenses	$250

Thus, a client can expect a professional focus group to cost $5,000 or more. Most marketing topics will call for multiple focus groups. There is some cost advantage in this, as some costs will not change proportionately just because there are multiple interviews. Preparation costs may be the same for one or more interviews; the analysis and report preparation will likely only increase slightly because two or three interviews are included instead of one.

Depth Interviews

An alternative to a focus group is a depth interview. A **depth interview** is a one-on-one interview between a professional researcher and a research respondent. Depth interviews are much the same as a psychological, clinical interview, but with a different purpose. The researcher asks many questions and follows up each answer with probes for additional elaboration. An excerpt from a depth interview is given in Exhibit 6.7.

Like focus group moderators, the interviewer's role is critical in a depth interview. He or she must be a highly skilled individual who can encourage the respondent to talk freely without influencing the direction of the conversation. Probing questions are critical.

Laddering is a term used for a particular approach to probing, asking respondents to compare differences between brands at different levels. What usually results is that the first distinctions are attribute-level distinctions, the second are benefit-level distinctions, and the third are at the value or motivation level. Laddering can then distinguish two brands of skateboarding shoes based on a) the materials they are made of, b) the comfort they provide, and c) the excitement they create.

Depth interview
A one-on-one interview between a professional researcher and a research respondent conducted about some relevant business or social topic.

Laddering
A particular approach to probing asking respondents to compare differences between brands at different levels that produces distinctions at the attribute level, the benefit level, and the value or motivation level.

EXHIBIT 6.7 Excerpt from a Depth Interview

An interviewer (I) talks with Marsha (M) about furniture purchases. Marsha indirectly indicates she delegates the buying responsibility to a trusted antique dealer. She has already said that she and her husband would write the dealer telling him the piece they wanted (e.g., bureau, table). The dealer would then locate a piece that he considered appropriate and would ship it to Marsha from his shop in another state.

M: ... We never actually shopped for furniture since we state what we want and (the antique dealer) picks it out and sends it to us. So we never have to go looking through stores and shops and things.
I: You depend on his (the antique dealer's) judgment?
M: Uh, huh. And, uh, he happens to have the sort of taste that we like and he knows what our taste is and always finds something that we're happy with.
I: You'd rather do that than do the shopping?
M: Oh, much rather, because it saves so much time and it would be so confusing for me to go through stores and stores looking for things, looking for furniture. This is so easy that I just am very fortunate.

I: Do you feel that he's a better judge than . . .
M: Much better.
I: Than you are?
M: Yes, and that way I feel confident that what I have is very, very nice because he picked it out and I would be doubtful if I picked it out. I have confidence in him, (the antique dealer) knows everything about antiques, I think. If he tells me something, why I know it's true—no matter what I think. I know he is the one that's right.

This excerpt is most revealing of the way in which Marsha could increase her feeling of confidence by relying on the judgment of another person, particularly a person she trusted. Marsha tells us quite plainly that she would be doubtful (i.e., uncertain) about her own judgment, but she "knows" (i.e., is certain) that the antique dealer is a good judge, "no matter what I think." The dealer once sent a chair that, on first inspection, did not appeal to Marsha. She decided, however, that she must be wrong, and the dealer right, and grew to like the chair very much.

From Donald F. Cox, Ed. *Risk Taking and Information Handling in Consumer Behavior* (Boston: Division of Research, Harvard Business School, © 1967), pp. 65–66. Reprinted with Permission.

Each depth interview may last more than an hour. Thus, it is a time-consuming process if multiple interviews are conducted. Not only does the interview have to be conducted, but each interview produces about the same amount of text as does a focus group interview. This has to be analyzed and interpreted by the researcher. A third major issue stems from the necessity of recording both surface reactions and subconscious motivations of the respondent. Analysis and interpretation of such data are highly subjective, and it is difficult to settle on a true interpretation.

Depth interviews provide more insight into a particular individual than do focus groups. In addition, since the setting isn't really social, respondents are more likely to discuss sensitive topics than are those in a focus group. Depth interviews are particularly advantageous when some unique or unusual behavior is being studied. For instance, depth interviews have been usefully applied to reveal characteristics of adolescent behavior, ranging from the ways they get what they want from their parents to shopping, smoking, and shoplifting.[31]

Depth interviews are similar to focus groups in many ways. The costs are similar if only one to two interviews are conducted. However, if a dozen or more interviews are included in a report, the costs are higher than focus group interviews due to the increased interviewing and analysis time.

Conversations

Conversations
An informal qualitative data-gathering approach in which the researcher engages a respondent in a discussion of the relevant subject matter.

Holding **conversations** in qualitative research is an informal data-gathering approach in which the researcher engages a respondent in a discussion of the relevant subject matter. This approach is almost completely unstructured and the researcher enters the conversation with few expectations. The goal is to have the respondent produce a dialogue about his or her lived experiences. Meaning will be extracted from the resulting dialogue.

A conversational approach to qualitative research is particularly appropriate in phenomenological research and for developing grounded theory. In our Vans experience, the researcher may simply tape-record a conversation about becoming a "skater." The resulting dialogue can then be analyzed for themes and plots. The result may be some interesting and novel insight into the consumption patterns of skaters, for example, if the respondent said,

"I knew I was a real skater when I just had to have Vans, not just for boarding, but for wearing."

This theme may connect to a right-of-passage plot and show how Vans play a role in this process.

Technology is also influencing conversational research. Online communications such as the reviews posted about book purchases at http://www.barnesandnoble.com can be treated as a conversation. Companies may discover product problems and ideas for overcoming them by analyzing these computer-based consumer dialogues.[32]

A conversational approach is advantageous because each interview is usually inexpensive to conduct. Respondents often need not be paid because they are enthusiasts in a product area. They are relatively effective at getting at sensitive issues once the researcher establishes a rapport with them. Conversational approaches, however, are prone to produce little relevant information since little effort is made to steer the conversation. Additionally, the data analysis is very much researcher-dependent.

SEMI-STRUCTURED INTERVIEWS

Semi-structured interviews usually come in written form and ask respondents for short essay responses to specific open-ended questions. Respondents are free to write as much or as little as they want. The questions would be divided into sections, typically, and within each section, the opening question would be followed by some probing questions. When these are performed face to face, there is room for less structured follow ups.

The advantages to this approach include an ability to address more specific issues. Responses are usually easier to interpret than other qualitative approaches. Since the researcher can simply prepare the questions in writing ahead of time, and if in writing, the questions are administered without the presence of an interviewer, semi-structured interviews can be relatively cost-effective.

Some researchers interested in studying car salesperson stereotypes used qualitative semi-structured interviews to map consumers' cognitions (memory). The semi-structured interview began with a free-association task:

List the first five things that come into your mind when you think of a "car salesman."

This was followed up with a probing question:

Describe the way a typical "car salesman" looks.

This was followed with questions about how the car salesperson acts and how the respondent feels in the presence of a car salesperson. The results led to research showing how the information that consumers process differs in the presence of a typical car salesperson, as opposed to a less typical car salesperson.[33]

Free-Association/Sentence Completion Method

Free-association techniques simply record a respondent's first cognitive reactions (top-of-mind) to some stimulus. The Rorschach or inkblot test typifies the free-association method. Respondents view an ambiguous figure and are asked to say the first thing that comes to their mind. Free-association techniques allow researchers to map a respondent's thoughts or memory.

The sentence completion method is based on free-association principles. Respondents simply are required to complete a few partial sentences with the first word or phrase that comes to mind. For example:

People who drink beer are _____.
A man who drinks a dark beer is _____.
Imported beer is most liked by _____.
The woman in the commercial _____.

Answers to sentence-completion questions tend to be more extensive than responses to word-association tests. Although the responses lack the ability to probe for meaning as in other qualitative techniques, they are very effective in finding out what is on a respondent's mind. They can also do so in a quick and very cost-effective manner. Free-association and sentence-completion tasks are sometimes used in conjunction with other approaches. For instance, they can sometimes be used as effective icebreakers in focus group interviews.

OBSERVATION

Throughout this chapter, we have described how observation can be a very important qualitative tool. The participant-observer approach typifies how observation can be used to explore various issues. Meaning is extracted from field notes. **Field notes** are the researchers' descriptions of what actually happens in the field. These notes then become the text from which meaning is extracted.

Observation may also take place in visual form. Researchers may observe consumers in their home, as mentioned above, or try to gain knowledge from photographic records of one type or another. Observation can either be very inexpensive, such as when a research associate sits and simply observes behavior, or it can be very expensive, as in most participant-observer studies. Observational research is keenly advantageous for gaining insight into things that respondents cannot or will not verbalize.

COLLAGES

Marketing researchers sometimes have respondents prepare a collage to represent their experience with some good, service, or brand. The collages are then analyzed for meaning much in the same manner as text dialogues are analyzed. Computer software can even be applied to help develop potential grounded theories from the visual representations.

Harley-Davidson commissioned research in which collages depicting feelings about Harley-Davidson were compared based on whether the respondent was a Harley owner or an owner of a

Free-association techniques
Record respondents' first (top-of-mind) cognitive reactions to some stimulus.

Field notes
The researcher's descriptions of what actually happens in the field; these notes then become the text from which meaning is extracted.

RESEARCHSNAPSHOT

Let the Computer do Your Reading!

Computerized qualitative analysis is now commonly used. Two commonly used programs are Atlas-Ti and NVivo. These can save a lot of time by helping to identify themes and connections within text. In fact, today's programs can even assist in interpreting videotapes and photographs for meaning.

Computerized analysis of depth interviews with service providers and their customers revealed interesting key themes dealing with the friendship or bond that forms between them. Some of the themes that emerged included the feeling that meetings were more like get-togethers with a friend, the feeling

that the service provider wants to give something back to a client, and the belief that one can share one's true thoughts and feelings with a client. On the not-so-positive side, a

theme that also emerged was that sometimes the friendships are not mutual. Comments like, "I thought she would never leave" or "Won't he give me a break?" would be consistent with that theme.

There are many software programs that can assist with basic qualitative interpretation. Some are available as freeware. AnSWR is available from the U.S. Centers for Disease Control (http://www.cdc.gov/hiv/software/answr.htm) as is EZ-Text (http://www.cdc.gov/hiv/software/ez-text.htm). Transana will read video and audio tape data and is available from the Wisconsin Center for Education Research (http://www.transana.org). Commercial programs will normally have a student or trial version available free of charge or at reduced rates.

Source: Journal of Marketing by /Bolton, Ruth N. Copyright 1999 by Am Marketing Assn (AMA) (CHIC) in the format Textbook via Copyright Clearance Center.

competitor's brand. The collages of "Hog" owners revealed themes of artwork and the freedom of the great outdoors. These themes did not emerge in the non-Hog groups. This led to confirmatory research which helped Harley continue its growth, appealing more specifically to its diverse market segments.[34]

Like sentence completion and word association, collages are often used within some other approach, such as a focus group or a depth interview. Collages offer the advantage of flexibility but are also very much subject to the researcher's interpretations.

▦ THEMATIC APPERCEPTION TEST (TAT)

Thematic apperception test (TAT)
A test that presents subjects with an ambiguous picture(s) in which consumers and products are the center of attention; the investigator asks the subject to tell what is happening in the picture(s) now and what might happen next.

A **thematic apperception test (TAT)** presents subjects with an ambiguous picture(s) in which consumers and products are the center of attention. The investigator asks the subject to tell what is happening in the picture(s) now and what might happen next. Hence, themes (*thematic*) are elicited on the basis of the perceptual-interpretive (*apperception*) use of the pictures. The researcher then analyzes the contents of the stories that the subjects relate.

The picture or cartoon stimulus must be sufficiently interesting to encourage discussion but ambiguous enough not to disclose the nature of the research project. Clues should not be given to the character's positive or negative predisposition. A pretest of a TAT investigating why men might purchase chainsaws used a picture of a man looking at a very large tree. The research respondents were homeowners and weekend woodcutters. They almost unanimously said that they would get professional help from a tree surgeon to deal with this situation. Thus, early in pretesting, the researchers found out that the picture was not sufficiently ambiguous. The tree was too large and did not allow respondents to identify with the tree-cutting task. If subjects are to project their own views into the situation, the environmental setting should be a well-defined, familiar problem, but the solution should be ambiguous.

Frequently, the TAT consists of a series of pictures with some continuity so that stories may be constructed in a variety of settings. The first picture might portray two people discussing a product in a supermarket; in the second picture, a person might be preparing the product in the kitchen; the final picture might show the product being served at the dinner table. A TAT might include several ambiguous pictures of a skateboarder and then show him or her heading to the store. This might reveal ideas about the brands and products that fit the role of skateboarder.

Picture frustration
A version of the TAT using a cartoon drawing in which the respondent suggests a dialogue in which the characters might engage.

A **picture frustration** version of the TAT uses a cartoon drawing in which the respondent suggests a dialogue in which the characters might engage. Exhibit 6.8 is a purposely ambiguous illustration of an everyday occurrence. The two office workers are shown in a situation and the

EXHIBIT 6.8
**Picture Frustration Version
of TAT**

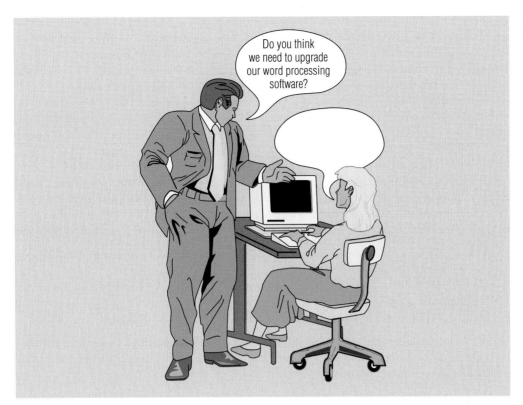

respondent is asked what the woman might be talking about. This setting could be used for discussions about products, packaging, the display of merchandise, store personnel, and so on.

PROJECTIVE RESEARCH TECHNIQUES

A TAT represents a projective research technique. A **projective technique** is an indirect means of questioning enabling respondents to project beliefs and feelings onto a third party, an inanimate object, or a task situation. Projective techniques usually encourage respondents to describe a situation in their own words with little prompting by the interviewer. Individuals are expected to interpret the situation within the context of their own experiences, attitudes, and personalities and to express opinions and emotions that may be hidden from others and possibly themselves. All projective techniques are particularly useful in studying sensitive issues.

There is an old story about asking a man why he purchased a Mercedes. When asked directly why he purchased a Mercedes, he responds that the car holds its value and does not depreciate much, that it gets better gas mileage than you'd expect, or that it has a comfortable ride. If you ask the same person why a neighbor purchased a Mercedes, he may well answer, "Oh, that status seeker!" This story illustrates that individuals may be more likely to give true answers (consciously or unconsciously) to disguised questions, and a projective technique provides a way of disguising just who is being described.

Projective technique
An indirect means of questioning enabling respondents to project beliefs and feelings onto a third party, an inanimate object, or a task situation.

Exploratory Research in Science and in Practice

Misuses of Exploratory and Qualitative Research

Any research tool can be misapplied. Exploratory research cannot take the place of conclusive, confirmatory research. Thus, since many qualitative tools are best applied in exploratory design, they are likewise limited in the ability to draw conclusive inferences—test hypotheses. One of the biggest drawbacks is the subjectivity that comes along with "interpretation." In fact, sometimes the term *interpretive* research is used synonymously with qualitative research. When only one researcher interprets the meaning of what a single person said in a depth interview or similar technique, one should be very cautious before major marketing decisions are made based on these results. Is the result replicable, meaning the same conclusion would be reached based on another researcher's interpretation?

Indeed, some qualitative methodologies were generally frowned upon for years based on a few early and public misapplications during what became known as the "motivational research" era. While many of the ideas produced during this time had some merit, as can sometimes be the case, too few researchers did too much interpretation of too few respondents. Compounding this, marketers were quick to act on the results, believing that the results peaked inside one's subliminal consciousness and therefore held some type of extra power. Thus, often the research was flawed based on poor interpretation, and the decision process was flawed because the deciders acted prematurely. Projective techniques and depth interviews were frequently used in the late 1950s and early 1960s, producing some interesting and occasionally bizarre reasons for consumers' purchasing behavior:

- A woman is very serious when she bakes a cake because unconsciously she is going through the symbolic act of giving birth.
- A man buys a convertible as a substitute mistress and a safer (and potentially cheaper) way of committing adultery.
- Men who wear suspenders are reacting to an unresolved castration complex.[35]

About two decades later, researchers for McCann-Erickson advertising agency interviewed low-income women using a form of TAT involving story completion regarding attitudes toward insecticides. Themes noted included:

- The joy of victory over roaches (watching them die or seeing them dead)
- Using the roach as a metaphor through which women can take out their hostility of men (women generally referred to roaches as "he" instead of "she" in their stories).[36]

Certainly, some useful findings resulted. Even today, we have the Pillsbury Doughboy as evidence that useful ideas were produced. In many of these cases, interpretations were either misleading or too ambitious (taken too far). However, many companies became frustrated when decisions based upon motivational research approaches proved poor. Thus, marketing researchers moved away from qualitative tools during the late 1960s and 1970s. Today, however, qualitative tools have won acceptance once again as researchers realize they have greater power in discovering insights that would be difficult to capture in typical survey research (which is limited as an exploratory tool).

SCIENTIFIC DECISION PROCESSES

Objectivity and replicability are two characteristics of scientific inquiry. Are focus groups objective and replicable? Would three different researchers all interpret focus group data identically? How should a facial expression or nod of the head be interpreted? Have subjects fully grasped the idea or concept behind a nonexistent product? Have respondents overstated their interest because they tend to like all new products? Many of these questions reduce to a matter of opinion that may vary from researcher to researcher and from one respondent group to another. Therefore, a focus group, or a depth interview, or TAT alone does not best represent a complete scientific inquiry.

However, if the thoughts discovered through these techniques survive preliminary evaluations and are developed into research hypotheses, they can be further tested. These tests may involve survey research or an experiment testing an idea very specifically (in other words, if a certain slogan is more effective than another; for example, if Diet, Vanilla, or Cherry Dr Pepper is liked better than Diet Pepsi, and so forth). Thus, exploratory research approaches using qualitative research tools are very much a *part* of *scientific* inquiry.

An exploratory research design is the most productive design, meaning the tools used produce more discoveries than do other research designs. A company cannot determine the most important product benefits until all benefits obtained from consuming the product are known.

Before making a *scientific* decision, a research project should include a confirmatory study using objective tools and an adequate sample in terms of both size and how well it represents a population. But, is a *scientific* decision approach always used or needed?

In practice, many marketing decisions are based solely on the results of focus group interviews or some other exploratory result. The primary reasons for this are (1) time, (2) money, and (3) emotion.

TIME

Sometimes, researchers simply are not given enough time to follow up on exploratory research results. Marketing companies feel an increasingly urgent need to get new products to the market faster. Thus, a seemingly good idea generated in a focus group (like Diet, Vanilla, or Cherry Dr Pepper) is simply not tested with a more conclusive study. The risk of delaying a decision may be seen as greater than the risk of proceeding without completing the scientific process. Thus, although the researcher may wish to protest, there may be logical reasons for such action. The decision makers should be aware, though, that the conclusions drawn from exploratory research designs are just that—exploratory. Thus, there is less likelihood of good results from the decision than if the research process had involved further testing.

MONEY

Similarly, researchers sometimes do not follow up on exploratory research results because they believe the cost is too high. Realize that thousands of dollars may have already been spent on qualitative research. Managers who are unfamiliar with research will be very tempted to wonder, "Why do I need yet another study?" and "What did I spend all that money for?" Thus, they choose to proceed based only on exploratory results. Again, the researcher has fulfilled the professional obligation as long as the tentative nature of any ideas derived from exploratory research has been relayed through the research report.

Again, this isn't always a bad approach. If the decision itself does not involve a great deal of risk or if it can be reversed easily, the best course of action may be to proceed to implementation instead of investing more money in confirmatory research. Remember, research shouldn't be performed if it will cost more than it will return.

EMOTION

Time, money, and emotion are all related. Decision makers sometimes become so anxious to have something resolved, or they get so excited about some novel discovery resulting from a focus group interview, they may act rashly. Perhaps some of the ideas produced during the motivational research era sounded so enticing that decision makers got caught up in the emotion of the moment and proceeded without the proper amount of testing. Thus, as in life, when we fall in love with something, we are prone to act irrationally. The chances of emotion interfering in this way are lessened, but not reduced, by making sure multiple decision makers are involved in the decision process.

In conclusion, we began this section by suggesting that exploratory, qualitative research cannot take the place of a confirmatory study. However, a confirmatory study cannot take the place of an exploratory, qualitative study either. While confirmatory studies are best for testing specific ideas, a qualitative study is needed to develop ideas and practical theories.

Summary

1. List and understand the differences between qualitative research and quantitative research. The chapter emphasized that any argument about the overall superiority of qualitative versus quantitative research is misplaced. Rather, each approach has advantages and disadvantages that make it appropriate in certain situations. The most noticeable difference is the relative absence of numbers in qualitative research. Qualitative research relies more on researchers' subjective interpretations of text or other visual material. In contrast, the numbers produced in quantitative research are objective in the sense that they don't change simply because someone else computed them. Qualitative research involves small samples while quantitative research usually uses large samples. Qualitative procedures are generally more flexible and produce deeper and more elaborate explanations than quantitative research.

2. Understand the role of qualitative research in exploratory research designs. The high degree of flexibility that goes along with most qualitative techniques makes it very useful in exploratory research designs. Therefore, exploratory research designs most often involve some qualitative research technique.

3. Describe the basic categories of qualitative research. Phenomenology is a philosophical approach to studying human experiences based on the idea that human experience itself is inherently subjective and determined by the context within which a person experiences something. It lends itself well to conversational research. Ethnography represents ways of studying cultures through methods that include high involvement with that culture. Participant-observation is a common ethnographic approach. Grounded theory represents inductive qualitative investigation in which the researcher continually poses questions about a respondent's discourse in an effort to derive a deep explanation of their behavior. Collages are sometimes used to develop grounded theory. Case studies simply are documented histories of a particular person, group, organization, or event.

4. Prepare a focus group interview outline. A focus group outline should begin with introductory comments followed by a very general opening question that does not lead the respondent. More specific questions should be listed until a blunt question directly pertaining to the study objective is included. It should conclude with debriefing comments and a chance for question-and-answers with respondents.

5. Apply technological advances in the application of qualitative research approaches. Videoconferencing and online chat rooms are more economical ways of trying to do much the same as traditional focus group interviews. Some companies have even established a focus blog that is a source for continuous commentary on a company. While they are certainly cost advantageous, there is less control over who participates.

6. Recognize common qualitative research tools and know the advantages and limitations of their use. The most common qualitative research tools include the focus group interview and the depth interview. The focus group has some cost advantage per respondent because it would take ten times as long to conduct the interview portion(s) of a series of depth interviews compared to one focus group. However, the depth interview is more appropriate for discussing sensitive topics.

7. Know the risks associated with acting on only exploratory results. Companies do make decisions using only exploratory research. There are several explanations for this behavior. The researcher's job is to make sure that decision makers understand the increased risk that comes along with basing a decision only on exploratory research results.

Key Terms

Qualitative marketing research	Participant-observation	Depth interview
Researcher-dependent	Grounded theory	Laddering
Quantitative marketing research	Case studies	Conversations
Subjective	Themes	Free-association techniques
Qualitative data	Focus group interview	Field notes
Quantitative data	Piggyback	Thematic apperception test (TAT)
Concept testing	Moderator	Picture frustration
Phenomenology	Discussion guide	Projective technique
Hermeneutics	Streaming media	Replicable
Hermeneutic unit	Online focus group	
Ethnography	Focus blog	

Questions for Review and Critical Thinking

1. Define *qualitative* and *quantitative* research. Compare and contrast the two approaches.
2. Why do exploratory research designs rely so much on qualitative research techniques?
3. Why do causal designs rely so much on quantitative research techniques?
4. What are the basic categories (orientations) of qualitative research?
5. Of the four basic categories of qualitative research, which do you think is most appropriate for a qualitative approach designed to

better define a marketing situation prior to conducting confirmatory research?
6. How might ethnography be used in concept testing?
7. What type of exploratory research would you suggest in the following situations?
   a. A product manager suggests development of a non-tobacco cigarette blended from wheat, cocoa, and citrus.
   b. A research project has the purpose of evaluating potential brand names for a new insecticide.

c. A manager must determine the best site for a convenience store in an urban area.

d. An advertiser wishes to identify the symbolism associated with cigar smoking.

8. What are the key differences between a focus group interview and a depth interview?

9. **'NET** Visit some websites for large companies like Honda, Qantas Airlines, Target, Tesco, and Marriot. Is there any evidence that they are using their Internet sites in some way to conduct a continuous online focus blog or intermittent online focus groups?

10. What is *laddering?* How might it be used in trying to understand which fast-food restaurant customers prefer?

11. Comment on the following remark by a marketing consultant: "Qualitative exploration is a tool of marketing research and a stimulant to thinking. In and by itself, however, it does not constitute market research."

12. **ETHICS** A researcher tells a manager of a wine company that he has some "cool focus group results" suggesting that respondents like the idea of a screw-cap to top wine bottles. Even before the decision maker sees the report, the manager begins purchasing screw-caps and the new bottling equipment. Comment on this situation.

13. A packaged goods manufacturer receives many thousands of customer letters a year. Some are complaints, some are compliments. They cover a broad range of topics. Are these letters a possible source for exploratory research? Why or why not?

Research Activities

1. **'NET** How might the following organizations use an Internet chat room for exploratory research?
   a. A zoo
   b. A computer software manufacturer
   c. A video game manufacturer

2. Go back to the opening vignette. What if Vans approached you to do a focus group interview that explored the idea of offering casual attire (off-board) aimed at their primary segment (skateboarders) and offering casual attire for male retirees like Samuel Teel? How would you recommend the focus group(s) proceed? Prepare a focus group outline(s) to accomplish this task.

3. Interview two people about their exercise behavior. In one interview, try to use a semi-structured approach by preparing questions ahead of time and trying to have the respondent complete answers for these questions. With the other, try a conversational approach. What are the main themes that emerge in each? Which approach do you think was more insightful? Do you think there were any "sensitive" topics that a respondent was not completely forthcoming about?

Case 6.1. Disaster and Consumer Value

After September 11, 2001, U.S. consumers showed a desire to tone down their consumer activities. They ordered simpler foods in restaurants and spent more time at home. Therefore, a lot of marketing campaigns began emphasizing down-home themes.[37]

At some point after a disaster, it is time to get back to business. But, major catastrophic events are likely to leave permanent changes on consumers and employees in those areas. Suppose you are approached by the owner of several delicatessens and full-service wine stores in the Gulf Coast area. It is January 2006, and they want to get back to business. But they are uncertain about whether they should simply maintain the same positioning they had previous to Hurricane Katrina and Hurricane Rita. They would like to have a report from you within eighty days.

1. How could each classification of qualitative research be used here?
2. What qualitative research tool(s) would you recommend be used and why?
3. Where would you conduct any interviews and with whom would you conduct them?
4. **ETHICS** Are there ethical issues that you should be sensitive to in this process? Explain.
5. What issues would arise in conducting a focus group interview in this situation?
6. Prepare a focus group outline.

Video Case 6.2 Upjohn's Rogaine

The Upjohn Company, based in Kalamazoo, Michigan, manufactures and markets pharmaceuticals and health-related products.[38] With over 19,000 employees and distribution in over thirty countries, from Australia to Zaire, its annual sales top $1 billion. Upjohn is constantly developing and marketing new products. One recent example is Rogaine.

Originally developed as an antihypertension drug, Rogaine was shown in clinical tests to encourage moderate hair growth on some balding male volunteers. Thereafter, Upjohn quickly applied to the U.S. Food and Drug Administration (FDA) for the right to market the drug as a hair-growth product in the United States.

Questions

1. Define Rogaine's marketing problem from a marketing research perspective.
2. What type of exploratory marketing research should Rogaine conduct?

Video Case 6.3 Goya

 "If it is Goya, it has to be good." This is the motto created by the founder of Goya in 1936 when he and his wife emigrated from Spain to New York in to order to establish a food products company that would serve the numbers of Spanish immigrants to the United States. It also describes the current philosophy of a company that is known for its wide assortment of Latin/Hispanic food products, ranging from beans and rice to condiments to beverages to salsa to cooking oils. Robert Unanue, the founder's grandson, is the president of this preeminent Hispanic family-owned business.

Joe Perez, vice president of purchasing, attributes the success of Goya to the fact that it consistently offers a quality product at a fair price to all of its consumers. He notes that Goya makes over 1,200 different food products that appeal to Hispanics and Latinos in North America as well as people in South American countries, such as Peru, Columbia, and Uruguay, and Caribbean countries, such as Cuba, Costa Rica, and Puerto Rico. As another company official notes, the Hispanic market is very diverse.

Consequently, Goya's marketing efforts are sensitive to both the similarities and differences among these populations. As Andy Nenoya, executive vice president and chief of operations, says, the company works at the "micro-market" level. One result is that Goya uses "standard neutral Spanish terms" that every consumer in every country can understand. Another result of marketing research is that the company provides products for every generation of consumer, from the older generation who, for example, might prefer a bulk bag of dry beans, to the younger generations, who prefer frozen and canned products because of various, competing commitments in their lives and limited time for food preparation.

Beginning in the late 1970s and early 1980s, Goya also started the "Americanization" of their products into the mainstream U.S. food market. This involves a reeducation of the population to convince them that Goya products work well in such meal-time staples as spaghetti and beef stew and, on their own, offer an interesting diversity to meal choices. The company does not want to compromise the integrity of their products, but they do want U.S. consumers to be aware that their products are low in fat and cholesterol and have a variety of flavors that make food more interesting and enjoyable.

Their efforts have been successful in all market segments, and Goya is experiencing continuous growth. "Nobody has the breadth of products that we have or the distribution throughout the country that we have," affirms Nenoya.

Questions

1. Any exploratory research endeavors should take into account the wide diversity of consumers for Goya products. Identify the relevant factors that might be similar among this consumer population and the factors that might identify relevant differences in this population.
2. What information would a Goya focus group composed of non-Hispanic individuals in the United States want to learn?

Video Case 6.4 Edward Jones

 Edward Jones is one of the largest investment firms in the United States with over 4,000 branch offices in this country, Canada, and the United Kingdom. It is the only major brokerage firm that exclusively targets individual investors and small businesses, and it has nearly 6 million clients.

Edward Jones' philosophy is to offer personalized services to individual clients starting with a one-on-one interview. During the interview, investment representatives seek to identify each client's specific goals for investing. Richard G. Miller, one such representative, says that he needs to thoroughly understand what a client wants before he can build an investment strategy for that person. His initial conversation starts with, "Hey, how are you?" Gregory L. Starry, another representative, confirms the Edward Jones philosophy: "Most of my day is spent talking with and meeting clients [rather than placing stock trades]."

Only after learning these goals do the representatives design an investment strategy that will provide a client with income, growth, and safety. Each client's goals also evolve over time. Young people are focused on earning enough money to make a down payment on their first home or to buy a car. Clients in the thirty-five to forty-five age range are concerned about getting their children through school and about their own retirement. Those in retirement want to make sure that they have an adequate income level. Miller notes, "It's not the timing in the market, but the time in the market" that will help clients achieve their goals.

Questions

1. Many people in minority groups, including African Americans, Hispanic Americans, Asian Americans, and Native Americans, do not invest. What exploratory research should Edward Jones do to develop the minority market?
2. Another group with low investment activity includes those who stopped their education at the high school level. What factors should Edward Jones representatives consider in designing focus groups with these potential clients?

CHAPTER 7
SECONDARY DATA RESEARCH IN A DIGITAL AGE

After studying this chapter, you should be able to

1. Discuss the advantages and disadvantages of secondary data
2. Define types of secondary data analysis conducted by marketing managers
3. Identify various internal and proprietary sources of secondary data
4. Give examples of various external sources of secondary data
5. Describe the impact of single-source data and globalization on secondary data research

Chapter Vignette: Pentagon Recruits with Databases

In a nation with an all-volunteer military, finding recruits is an ongoing need. The project is especially challenging in wartime, when more service members are necessary but the costs of serving are too daunting for many citizens. One way that the Department of Defense meets this challenge is by reviewing data that exist in a variety of sources. Its Joint Advertising, Market Research & Studies (JAMRS) project operates over a dozen research initiatives that make data available to military recruiters in all branches of the U.S. armed services.[1] Some involve data collection, but many apply already-existing data (secondary data) to the task of recruitment.

One of these efforts is a service called Population Representation (Pop Rep). For the past three decades, JAMRS has been gathering data on applicants and service members, including their age, race or ethnicity, gender, marital status, and education level. Recruiters can visit the JAMRS website to obtain reports showing which characteristics are associated with particular areas of service and performance levels. This information can help them target candidates for recruitment.

JAMRS also pays for data from third-party research firms. For example, it uses the PRIZM market segmentation data gathered and sold by Claritas, a marketing research firm. The PRIZM data describe the purchasing and media behavior of many market segments. Recruiters can use the data to identify the activities of potential recruits that live in their region—for example, to identify the magazines they read. This information can help local recruiters or branches of the military target messages likely to appeal to particular groups of young men and women. Many people know that recruits are most likely to come from households with lower-middle incomes or below in rural areas and small towns. However, the PRIZM data go much deeper, showing, for example, that U.S. Army recruits often come from households that listen to Spanish-language radio and that prospective Marines tend to read *Outdoor Life* and enjoy fishing and hunting.

Another JAMRS service is called its Recruit Market Information System (RMIS). This web-based computer application allows recruiting professionals to search a database that combines the Pentagon's own data about recruits and additional data purchased to aid recruiters. For example, recruiters can look up population statistics and the number of contracts signed by new recruits to determine geographic areas in which recruitment is strong. The military also uses data from schools, including names, ages, grades, and e-mail addresses of students aged sixteen to twenty-five.

For the Defense Department, recruiting would no doubt be far more difficult and far less effective without access to secondary data, in this case, data gathered for purposes other than military recruitment. But the data are useful only with careful analysis and interpretation. This chapter discusses how to conduct research with secondary data in a digital age. An appendix listing sources of secondary data is available on this book's website at http://www.thomsonedu.com/marketing/zikmund. Many sources can also be found using Internet search engines.

Secondary Data Research

Secondary data
Data that have been previously collected for some purpose other than the one at hand.

Research projects often begin with **secondary data**, which are gathered and recorded by someone else prior to (and for purposes other than) the current project. Secondary data usually are historical and already assembled. They require no access to respondents or subjects.

Advantages

The primary advantage of secondary data is their availability. Obtaining secondary data is almost always faster and less expensive than acquiring primary data. This is particularly true when researchers use electronic retrieval to access data stored digitally. In many situations, collecting secondary data is instantaneous.

Consider the money and time saved by researchers who obtained updated population estimates for a town during the interim between the 2000 and 2010 censuses. Instead of doing the fieldwork themselves, researchers could acquire estimates from a firm dealing in demographic information or from sources such as Claritas or PCensus. As in this example, the use of secondary data eliminates many of the activities normally associated with primary data collection, such as sampling and data processing.

Secondary data are essential in instances when data cannot be obtained using primary data collection procedures. For example, a manufacturer of farm implements could not duplicate the information in the *Census of Agriculture* because much of the information there (for example, amount of taxes paid) might not be accessible to a private firm.

Disadvantages

An inherent disadvantage of secondary data is that they were not designed specifically to meet the researchers' needs. Thus, researchers must ask how pertinent the data are to their particular project. To evaluate secondary data, researchers should ask questions such as these:

- Is the subject matter consistent with our problem definition?
- Do the data apply to the population of interest?
- Do the data apply to the time period of interest?
- Do the secondary data appear in the correct units of measurement?
- Do the data cover the subject of interest in adequate detail?

Even when secondary information is available, it can be inadequate. Consider the following typical situations:

- A researcher interested in forklift trucks finds that the secondary data on the subject are included in a broader, less pertinent category encompassing all industrial trucks and tractors. Furthermore, the data were collected five years earlier.
- An investigator who wishes to study individuals earning more than $100,000 per year finds the top category in a secondary study reported at $75,000 or more per year.
- A brewery that wishes to compare its per-barrel advertising expenditures with those of competitors finds that the units of measurement differ because some report point-of-purchase expenditures with advertising and others do not.
- Data from a previous warranty card study show where consumers prefer to purchase the product but provide no reasons why.

The most common reasons why secondary data do not adequately satisfy research needs are (1) outdated information, (2) variation in definition of terms, (3) different units of measurement, and (4) lack of information to verify the data's accuracy. Furthermore, in our rapidly changing environment, information quickly becomes outdated. Because the purpose of most studies is to predict the future, secondary data must be timely to be useful.

Every primary researcher has the right to define the terms or concepts under investigation to satisfy the purpose of his or her primary investigation. This practice provides little solace, however, to the investigator of the African-American market who finds secondary data reported as "percent nonwhite." Variances in terms or variable classifications should be scrutinized to determine whether differences are important. The populations of interest must be described in comparable terms. Researchers frequently encounter secondary data that report on a population of interest that is similar but not directly comparable to their population of interest. For example, Arbitron reports its television audience estimates by geographical areas known as ADIs (Areas of Dominant Influence). An ADI is a geographic area consisting of all counties in which the home market commercial television stations receive a preponderance of total viewing hours. This unique population of interest is used exclusively to report television audiences. The geographic areas used in the census of population, such as Metropolitan Statistical Areas, are not comparable to ADIs.

Units of measurement may cause problems if they do not conform exactly to a researcher's needs. For example, lumber shipments in millions of board-feet are quite different from billions of ton-miles of lumber shipped on freight cars. Head-of-household income is not the same unit of measure as total family income. Often the objective of the original primary study may dictate that the data be summarized, rounded, or reported. When that happens, even if the original units of measurement were comparable, aggregated or adjusted units of measurement are not suitable in the secondary study.

When secondary data are reported in a format that does not exactly meet the researcher's needs, data conversion may be necessary. **Data conversion** (also called *data transformation*) is the process of changing the original form of data to a format more suitable for achieving a stated research objective. For example, sales for food products may be reported in pounds, cases, or dollars. An estimate of dollars per pound may be used to convert dollar volume data to pounds or another suitable format.

Data conversion
The process of changing the original form of the data to a format suitable to achieve the research objective; also called data transformation.

Another disadvantage of secondary data is that the user has no control over their accuracy. Although timely and pertinent secondary data may fit the researcher's requirements, the data could be inaccurate. Research conducted by other persons may be biased to support the vested interest of the source. For example, media often publish data from surveys to identify the characteristics of their subscribers or viewers, but they will most likely exclude derogatory data from their reports. If the possibility of bias exists, the secondary data should not be used.

Investigators are naturally more prone to accept data from reliable sources such as the U.S. government. Nevertheless, the researcher must assess the reputation of the organization that gathers the data and critically assess the research design to determine whether the research was correctly implemented. Unfortunately, such evaluation may be impossible without full information that explains how the original research was conducted.

Researchers should verify the accuracy of the data whenever possible. **Cross-checks** of data from multiple sources—that is, comparison of the data from one source with data from

Cross-checks
The comparison of data from one source with data from another source to determine the similarity of independent projects.

EXHIBIT 7.1
Evaluating Secondary Data

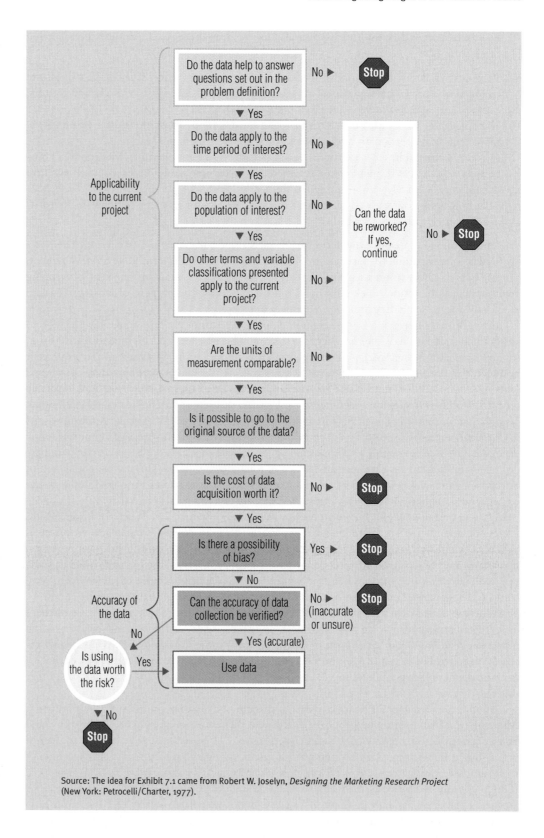

Source: The idea for Exhibit 7.1 came from Robert W. Joselyn, *Designing the Marketing Research Project* (New York: Petrocelli/Charter, 1977).

another—should be made to determine the similarity of independent projects. When the data are not consistent, researchers should attempt to identify reasons for the differences or to determine which data are most likely to be correct. If the accuracy of the data cannot be established, the researcher must determine whether using the data is worth the risk. Exhibit 7.1 illustrates a series of questions that should be asked to evaluate secondary data before they are used.

Broad Objective	Specific Research Example
Fact-finding	Identifying consumption patterns Tracking trends
Model building	Estimating market potential Forecasting sales Selecting trade areas and sites
Database marketing	Enhancing customer databases Developing prospect lists

EXHIBIT 7.2
Common Research Objectives for Secondary-Data Studies

Typical Objectives for Secondary-Data Research Designs

It would be impossible to identify all the purposes of marketing research using secondary data. However, some common marketing problems that can be addressed with secondary research designs are useful. Exhibit 7.2 shows three general categories of research objectives: fact-finding, model building, and database marketing.

Fact-Finding

The simplest form of secondary-data research is fact-finding. A restaurant serving breakfast might be interested in knowing what new products are likely to entice consumers. Secondary data available from National Eating Trends, a service of the NPD Group, show that the most potential may be in menu items customers can eat on the go.[2] According to data from the survey of eating trends, take-out breakfasts have doubled over the past few years, and they have continued to surpass dine-in breakfast sales for over a decade. These trends make smoothies and breakfast sandwiches sound like a good bet for a breakfast menu. Also, NPD found that 41 percent of breakfast sandwiches are consumed by people in their cars and 24 percent of people polled take them to work. These findings suggest that the sandwiches should be easy to handle. But what to put on the biscuit or bun? Another research firm, Market Facts, says almost half of consumers say they would pay extra for cheese. These simple facts would interest a researcher who was investigating the market for take-out breakfasts. Fact-finding can serve more complex purposes as well.

Secondary-data research supports the fact that breakfast sandwiches are at the top of the menu.

RESEARCHSNAPSHOT

New Trends—Music for Mobile Phones

Until a few years ago, selling music involved recordings on CDs, but marketing researchers have lately been tracking the newer practice of selling tunes to serve as ringtones. According to business-news sources, consumers spent $4 billion on ringtones in 2004. Strategy Analytics, a marketing research firm, forecasted that mobile music would generate $9 billion in sales by 2010. So far, the most popular song category is hip-hop, but videogame themes and movie themes also sell well.

Ringtones are profitable for music sellers. Almost one-third of the ringtones sold in 2004 were song clips known as mastertones or true tones, and consumers were paying more for ringtones ($2.49) than for an entire song downloaded to an MP3 player. The music companies, such as Sony and EMI, get royalties of up to 50 percent for mastertones. In this environment, Sony BMG skipped the traditional approach of CD singles and MTV videos when Cassidy released an album in 2005; instead, the company made a 25-second sample of Cassidy's song "I'm a Hustla" and released it as a ringtone. Coldplay's song "Speed of Sound" was available as a ringtone from Cingular before the album went on sale.

Predicting trends for a new product is difficult. In the case of ringtones, the landscape may quickly shift as mobile-phone makers introduce models that play entire songs. Paying $2.49 for a ringtone will seem too expensive when consumers can play a whole song on their phone for less money.

Sources: Based on Matthew Maier, "Digital Entertainment: Can Cell Phones Save the Music Business?" Business 2.0, September 2005, downloaded from InfoTrac at http://www.galenet.com; Sue Marek, "Ringing in the New Year," Wireless Week, January 1, 2006, http://www.galenet.com; "Music Marketing Gets Digital Tune-Up," Financial Express, January 28, 2006, http://www.galenet.com; and "Top Polyphonic Ringtones of 2005," Wireless Week, January 15, 2006, http://www.galenet.com.

IDENTIFICATION OF CONSUMER BEHAVIOR FOR A PRODUCT CATEGORY

A typical objective for a secondary research study might be to uncover all available information about consumption patterns for a particular product category or to identify demographic trends that affect an industry. For example, a company called Servigistics offers software that will scan a company's own parts inventory data and compare it with marketing objectives and competitors' prices to evaluate whether the company should adjust prices for its parts. Kia Motors tried using this service in place of the usual method of marking up cost by a set fraction. By considering secondary data including internal inventory data and external data about competitors' prices, it was able to make service parts a more profitable segment of its business.[3] This example illustrates the wealth of factual information about consumption and behavior patterns that can be obtained by carefully collecting and analyzing secondary data.

TREND ANALYSIS

Market tracking
The observation and analysis of trends in industry volume and brand share over time.

Marketers watch for trends in the marketplace and the environment. **Market tracking** is the observation and analysis of trends in industry volume and brand share over time. Scanner research services and other organizations provide facts about sales volume to support this work.

Almost every large consumer goods company routinely investigates brand and product category sales volume using secondary data. This type of analysis typically involves comparisons with competitors' sales or with the company's own sales in comparable time periods. It also involves industry comparisons among different geographic areas. Exhibit 7.3 shows the trend in cola market share relative to the total carbonated soft-drink industry.

ENVIRONMENTAL SCANNING

In many instances, the purpose of fact-finding is simply to study the environment to identify trends. Environmental scanning entails information gathering and fact-finding designed to detect indications of environmental changes in their initial stages of development. As mentioned in Chapter 2, the Internet can be used for environmental scanning; however, there are other means, such as periodic review of contemporary publications and reports. For example, environmental scanning

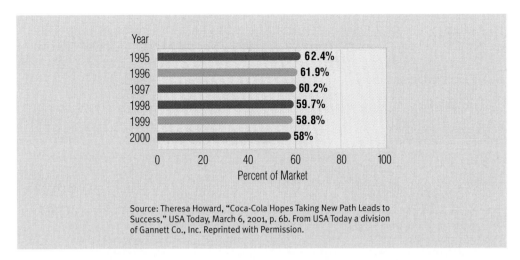

EXHIBIT 7.3
Cola's Share of the Carbonated Soft-Drink Market

Source: Theresa Howard, "Coca-Cola Hopes Taking New Path Leads to Success," USA Today, March 6, 2001, p. 6b. From USA Today a division of Gannett Co., Inc. Reprinted with Permission.

has shown many marketers that consumer demand in China is skyrocketing. In the case of beauty products such as cosmetics, Chinese authorities in the early 1990s stopped discouraging the use of makeup, and sales of these products took off—hitting $524 million in 2005 and expected to grow by over one-third, reaching $705 million by 2009. Marketers including Procter & Gamble, L'Oréal, and Shiseido have captured a sizable share of this market by realizing the potential and developing products to get into the market early.[4]

A number of online information services, such as Factiva and LexisNexis, routinely collect news stories about industries, product lines, and other topics of interest that have been specified by the researcher. As we mentioned in Chapter 2, push technology is an Internet information technology that automatically delivers content to the researcher's or manager's desktop. Push technology uses "electronic smart agents," custom software that filters, sorts, prioritizes, and stores information for later viewing.[5] This service frees the researcher from doing the searching. The true value of push technology is that the researcher who is scanning the environment can specify the kinds of news and information he or she wants, have it delivered to his or her computer quickly, and view it at leisure.

Model Building

The second general objective for secondary research, model building, is more complicated than simple fact-finding. **Model building** involves specifying relationships between two or more variables, perhaps extending to the development of descriptive or predictive equations. Models need not include complicated mathematics, though. In fact, decision makers often prefer simple models that everyone can readily understand over complex models that are difficult to comprehend. For example, market share is company sales divided by industry sales. Although some may not think of this simple calculation as a model, it represents a mathematical model of a basic relationship.

We will illustrate model building by discussing three common objectives that can be satisfied with secondary research: estimating market potential, forecasting sales, and selecting sites.

Model building
The use of secondary data to help specify relationships between two or more variables; can involve the development of descriptive or predictive equations.

ESTIMATING MARKET POTENTIAL FOR GEOGRAPHIC AREAS

Marketers often estimate market potential using secondary data. In many cases exact figures may be published by a trade association or another source. However, when the desired information is unavailable, the researcher may estimate market potential by transforming secondary data from two or more sources. For example, managers may find secondary data about market potential for a country or other large geographic area, but this information may not be broken down into smaller geographical areas, such as by metropolitan area, or in terms unique to the company, such as sales territory. In this type of situation, researchers often need to make projections for the geographic area of interest.

An extended example will help explain how secondary data can be used to calculate market potential. Suppose a brewing company is looking for opportunities to expand sales by exporting

Country	(1) Population Projection for 2010 (thousands)	(2) Annual per Capita Beer Consumption (liters)	(3) Market Potential Estimate (k liters)
Czech Republic	10,158	157	1,594,806
Germany	82,701	125	10,337,625
Japan	128,457	51	6,551,307
Spain	43,993	80	3,519,440

Source: Population data from Population Division of the Department of Economic and Social Affairs of the United Nations Secretariat, World Population Prospects: The 2004 Revision and World Urbanization Prospects; The 2003 Revision, http://esa.un.org/unpp, accessed February 9, 2006. Consumption data from "Spanish Beer Producers Face Flatter Times," http://just-drinks.com, March 1, 2005, downloaded from Business & Company Resource Center, http://galenet.galegroup.com; and "China Ranked Largest Beer Consumer in 2004," Kyodo News International, December 15, 2005, http://galenet.galegroup.com.

or investing in other countries. Managers decide to begin by estimating market potential for the Czech Republic, Germany, Japan, and Spain. Secondary research uncovered data for per capita beer consumption and population projections for the year 2005. The data for the four countries appear in Exhibit 7.4.

To calculate market potential for the Czech Republic in 2010, multiply that country's population in the year 2010 by its per capita beer consumption:

$$10,158,000 \text{ people} \times 157 \text{ liters/person} = 1,594,806,000 \text{ liters}$$

In the Czech Republic, the market potential for beer is 1,594,806,000 liters. To get a sense of the expected sales volume, the marketer would have to multiply this amount by the price per liter at which beer typically sells in the Czech Republic. As Exhibit 7.4 reveals, Japan's population is much higher, so its market potential is greater, even though the average Czech drinks much more beer.

Of course, the calculated market potential for each country in Exhibit 7.4 is a rough estimate. One obvious problem is that not everyone in a country will be of beer-drinking age. If the marketer can get statistics for each country's projected *adult* population, the estimate will be closer. Also, the marketer will want to consider whether each country is experiencing growth or decline in the demand for beer to estimate whether consumption habits are likely to be different in 2010. For example, beer consumption is barely growing in Europe and Japan, but it is expanding in Latin America (at about 4 percent a year) and even faster in China (by at least 6 percent a year).[6] Perhaps this information will cause the marketer to investigate market potential in additional countries where more growth is expected.

FORECASTING SALES

Marketing managers need information about the future. They need to know what company sales will be next year and in future time periods. Sales forecasting is the process of predicting sales totals over a specific time period.

Accurate sales forecasts, especially for products in mature, stable markets, frequently come from secondary-data research that identifies trends and extrapolates past performance into the future. Marketing researchers often use internal company sales records to project sales. A rudimentary model would multiply past sales volume by an expected growth rate. A researcher might investigate a secondary source and find that industry sales are expected to grow by 10 percent; multiplying company sales volume by 10 percent would give a basic sales forecast.

Exhibit 7.5 illustrates trend projection using a moving average projection of growth rates. Average ticket prices for a major-league baseball game are secondary data from Team Marketing Report (http://www.teammarketing.com/fci.cfm). The moving average is the sum of growth

EXHIBIT 7.5
Sales Forecast Using Secondary Data and Moving Averages

Year	Average Ticket Price ($)	Percentage Rate of Growth (Decline) from Previous Year	3-Year Moving Average Rate of Growth (Decline)
1994	10.45	—	—
1995	10.65	+1.9	—
1996	11.20	+5.1	—
1997	12.36	+10.4	+5.8
1998	13.59	+10.0	+8.5
1999	14.91	+9.7	+10.0
2000	16.67	+11.9	+10.5
2001	18.99	+13.9	+11.8
2002	18.30	+3.8	+9.9
2003	19.01	+3.4	+7.0
2004	19.82	+3.9	+3.7
2005	21.17	+6.3	+4.5

Forecast of average ticket price for 2006: $21.17 + ($21.17 × .045) = $22.12

rates for the past three years divided by 3 (number of years). The resulting number is a forecast of the percentage increase in ticket price for the coming year. Using the three-year average growth rate of 4.5 percent for the 2003, 2004, and 2005 sales periods, we can forecast the average ticket price for 2006 as follows:

$$\$21.17 + (\$21.17 \times .045) = \$22.12$$

Moving average forecasting is best suited to a static competitive environment. More dynamic situations make other sales forecasting techniques more appropriate.

Statistical trend analysis using secondary data can be much more advanced than this simple example. Many statistical techniques build forecasting models using secondary data. This chapter emphasizes secondary-data research rather than statistical analysis. Chapter 23, Bivariate Analysis: Measures of Association, and Chapter 24, Multivariate Analysis, explain more sophisticated statistical model-building techniques for forecasting sales.

ANALYSIS OF TRADE AREAS AND SITES

Marketing managers examine trade areas and use **site analysis techniques** to select the best locations for retail or wholesale operations. Secondary-data research helps managers make these site selection decisions. Some organizations, especially franchisers, have developed special computer software based on analytical models to select sites for retail outlets. The researcher must obtain the appropriate secondary data for analysis with the computer software.

The **index of retail saturation** offers one way to investigate retail sites and to describe the relationship between retail demand and supply.[7] It is easy to calculate once the appropriate secondary data are obtained:

$$\text{Index of retail saturation} = \frac{\text{Local market potential (demand)}}{\text{Local market retailing space}}$$

Site analysis techniques
Techniques that use secondary data to select the best location for retail or wholesale operations.

Index of retail saturation
A calculation that describes the relationship between retail demand and supply.

EXHIBIT 7.6
**Secondary Data for
Calculating an Index of Retail
Saturation**

1. Population	261,785
2. Annual per capita shoe sales	$54.43
3. Local market potential (line 1 × line 2)	$14,249,000
4. Square feet of retail space used to sell shoes	94,000 sq. ft.
5. Index of retail saturation (line 3/line 4)	152

For example, Exhibit 7.6 shows the relevant secondary data for shoe store sales in a five-mile radius surrounding a Florida shopping center. These types of data can be purchased from vendors of market information such as Urban Decision Systems. First, to estimate local market potential (demand), we multiply population by annual per capita shoe sales. This estimate, line 3 in Exhibit 7.6, goes in the numerator to calculate the index of retail saturation:

$$\text{Index of retail saturation} = \frac{\$14,249,000}{94,000} = 152$$

The retailer can compare this index figure with those of other areas to determine which sites have the greatest market potential with the least amount of retail competition. An index value above 200 is considered to indicate exceptional opportunities.

Data Mining

Large corporations' decision support systems often contain millions or even hundreds of millions of records of data. These complex data volumes are too large to be understood by managers. Consider, for example, Capital One, a consumer lending company with nearly 50 million customer accounts, including credit cards and auto loans. Suppose the company collects data on customer purchases, and each customer makes five transactions in a month, or sixty per year. With 50 million customers and decades of data (the company was founded in 1988), it's easy to see how record counts quickly grow beyond the comfort zone for most humans.[8]

Two points about data volume are important to keep in mind. First, relevant marketing data are often in independent and unrelated files. Second, the number of distinct pieces of information each data record contains is often large. When the number of distinct pieces of information contained in each data record and data volume grow too large, end users don't have the capacity to make sense of it all. Data mining helps clarify the underlying meaning of the data.

The term **data mining** refers to the use of powerful computers to dig through volumes of data to discover patterns about an organization's customers and products. It is a broad term that applies to many different forms of analysis. For example, **neural networks** are a form of artificial intelligence in which a computer is programmed to mimic the way that human brains process information. One computer expert put it this way:

A neural network learns pretty much the way a human being does. Suppose you say "big" and show a child an elephant, and then you say "small" and show her a poodle. You repeat this process with a house and a giraffe as examples of "big" and then a grain of sand and an ant as examples of "small." Pretty soon she will figure it out and tell you that a truck is "big" and a needle is "small." Neural networks can similarly generalize by looking at examples.[9]

Market-basket analysis is a form of data mining that analyzes anonymous point-of-sale transaction databases to identify coinciding purchases or relationships between products purchased and other retail shopping information.[10] Consider this example about patterns in customer purchases: Osco Drugs mined its databases provided by checkout scanners and found that when men go to its drugstores to buy diapers in the evening between 6:00 p.m. and 8:00 p.m., they sometimes

Data mining
The use of powerful computers to dig through volumes of data to discover patterns about an organization's customers and products; applies to many different forms of analysis.

Neural network
A form of artificial intelligence in which a computer is programmed to mimic the way that human brains process information.

Market-basket Analysis
A form of data mining that analyzes anonymous point-of-sale transaction databases to identify coinciding purchases or relationships between products purchased and other retail shopping information.

RESEARCHSNAPSHOT

Mining Data from Blogs

One way to find out what people are thinking these days is to read what they are posting on their blogs. But with tens of millions of blogs available on the Internet, there is no way to read them all. One solution: data-mining software designed for the blogosphere.

Umbria Communications, based in Boulder, Colorado, offers a program called Buzz Report, which searches 13 million blogs, looking for messages related to particular products and trends. Marketers can buy the service to find out what people are saying about their new products, or they can explore unmet needs in areas they might consider serving. Not only does Buzz Report identify relevant blogs, but it also has a language processor that can identify positive and negative messages and analyze word choices and spelling to estimate the writer's age range and sex. The company's CEO, Howard Kaushansky, says the program can even recognize sarcasm.

Most of Umbria's clients are large makers of consumer products, including Sprint and Electronic Arts. U.S. Cellular used Buzz Report to learn that teenage users of cell phones are particularly worried about using more than their allotted minutes, fearing that parents would take the extra amount from their allowance. Such knowledge is useful for developing new service plans and marketing messages.

Sources: Based on Bridget Finn, "Consumer Research: Mining Blogs for Marketing Insight," Business 2.0, September 2005, downloaded from InfoTrac at http://www.galenet.com; Justin Martin, "Blogging for Dollars," Fortune, December 12, 2005, http://www.galenet.com.

©BANANASTOCK/JUPITER IMAGES

walk out with a six-pack of beer as well. Knowing this behavioral pattern, supermarket managers may consider laying out their stores so that these items are closer together.[11]

A data-mining application of interest to marketers is known as **customer discovery**, which involves mining data to look for patterns identifying who is likely to be a valuable customer. For example, a larger provider of business services wanted to sell a new product to its existing customers, but it knew that only some of them would be interested. The company had to adapt each product offering to each customer's individual needs, so it wanted to save money by identifying the best prospects. It contracted with a research provider called DataMind to mine its data on sales, responses to marketing, and customer service to look for the customers most likely to be interested in the new product. DataMind assigned each of the company's customers an index number indicating their expected interest level, and the selling effort was much more efficient as a result.[12]

When a company knows the identity of the customer who makes repeated purchases from the same organization, an analysis can be made of sequences of purchases. The use of data mining to detect sequence patterns is a popular application among direct marketers, such as catalog retailers. A catalog merchant has information for each customer, revealing the sets of products that the customer buys in every purchase order. A sequence detection function can then be used to discover the set of purchases that frequently precedes the purchase of, say, a microwave oven. As another example, a sequence of insurance claims could lead to the identification of frequently occurring medical procedures performed on patients, which in turn could be used to detect cases of medical fraud.

Data mining requires sophisticated computer resources, and it is expensive. That's why companies like DataMind, IBM, Oracle, Information Builders, and Acxiom Corporation offer data-mining services. Customers send the databases they want analyzed and let the data-mining company do the "number crunching."

Customer discovery
Involves mining data to look for patterns identifying who is likely to be a valuable customer.

Database Marketing and Customer Relationship Management

As we have already mentioned, a CRM (customer relationship management) system is a decision support system that manages the interactions between an organization and its customers. A CRM maintains customer databases containing customers' names, addresses, phone numbers, past purchases, responses to past promotional offers, and other relevant data such as demographic and

Database marketing
The use of customer databases
to promote one-to-one
relationships with customers
and create precisely targeted
promotions.

financial data. **Database marketing** is the practice of using CRM databases to develop one-to-one relationships and precisely targeted promotional efforts with individual customers. For example, a fruit catalog company CRM contains a database of previous customers, including what purchases they made during the Christmas holidays. Each year the company sends last year's gift list to customers to help them send the same gifts to their friends and relatives.

Because database marketing requires vast amounts of CRM data compiled from numerous sources, secondary data are often acquired for the exclusive purpose of developing or enhancing databases. The transaction record, which often lists the item purchased, its value, customer name, address, and zip code, is the building block for many databases. This may be supplemented with data customers provide directly, such as data on a warranty card, and by secondary data purchased from third parties. For example, credit services may sell databases about applications for loans, credit card payment history, and other financial data. Several companies, such as Donnelley Marketing (with its BusinessContentFile and ConsumerContentFile services) and Claritas (with PRIZM), collect primary data and then sell demographic data that can be related to small geographic areas, such as those with a certain zip code. (Remember that when the vendor collects the data, they are primary data, but when the database marketer incorporates the data into his or her database, they are secondary data.)

Now that some of the purposes of secondary-data analysis have been addressed, we turn to a discussion of the sources of secondary data.

Sources of Secondary Data

Chapter 2 classified secondary data as either internal to the organization or external. Modern information technology makes this distinction seem somewhat simplistic. Some accounting documents are indisputably internal records of the organization. Researchers in another organization cannot have access to them. Clearly, a book published by the federal government and located at a public library is external to the company. However, in today's world of electronic data interchange, the data that appear in a book published by the federal government may also be purchased from an online information vendor for instantaneous access and subsequently stored in a company's decision support system.

Internal data should be defined as data that originated in the organization, or data created, recorded, or generated by the organization. **Internal and proprietary data** is perhaps a more descriptive term.

**Internal and proprietary
data**
Secondary data that originate
inside the organization.

Sources of Internal and Proprietary Data

Most organizations routinely gather, record, and store internal data to help them solve future problems. An organization's accounting system can usually provide a wealth of information. Routine documents such as sales invoices allow external financial reporting, which in turn can be a source of data for further analysis. If the data are properly coded into a modular database in the accounting system, the researcher may be able to conduct more detailed analysis using the decision support system. Sales information can be broken down by account or by product and region; information related to orders received, back orders, and unfilled orders can be identified; sales can be forecast on the basis of past data. Other useful sources of internal data include salespeoples' call reports, customer complaints, service records, warranty card returns, and other records.

Researchers frequently aggregate or disaggregate internal data. For example, a computer service firm used internal secondary data to analyze sales over the previous three years, categorizing business by industry, product, purchase level, and so on. The company discovered that 60 percent of its customers represented only 2 percent of its business and that nearly all of these customers came through telephone directory advertising. This simple investigation of internal records showed that, in effect, the firm was paying to attract customers it did not want.

Internet technology is making it easier to research internal and proprietary data. Often companies set up Intranets so that employees can use web tools to store and share data within the organization. And just as Google's search software lets people search the entire World Wide Web,

RESEARCHSNAPSHOT

Pulte Homes Builds on Its Customer Data

The biggest home builder in the United States, Pulte Homes, owes its success in part to its use of internal data about its customers. As the company has grown (it now builds at a rate of one hundred homes a day), it has collected data about its home buyers in twenty-eight states. Chief operating officer Richard Dugas set up a market segmentation team to study the data and identify market segments for the company's homes. Analyzing its over 500,000 buyers, the team identified eleven groups of customers, including first-time buyers (called "starters") and single parents returning to the housing market ("restarters").

Now when the company considers a purchase of land, it first evaluates whether the area will serve a segment with good potential in that part of the country. For example, a large parcel in Huntley, Illinois, northwest of Chicago, turned out to be a great location for a retirement community, attracting people who wanted to live not too far from their previous homes in metropolitan Chicago. In New Jersey, the company paid for land that other developers had ignored, recognizing that it was in a desirable location for baby boomers, near cultural and other activities they cared about. Customer data also influenced Pulte's withdrawal from Mexico, where the fastest growing segment of housing sales is only around $30,000.

Customer data also help Pulte save money. Analysis of its database showed that 80 percent of its customers, across all customer groups, tended to buy the same options, such as countertops, carpets, and flooring. The company slashed the number of floor plans and began to standardize options. With costs down, the company wins, and so do its customers.

Sources: Based on Thomas Mucha, "The Builder of Boomtown," Business 2.0, September 2005, downloaded from InfoTrac at http://www.galenet.com; "Mexico: Pulte pulls out of Mexico," The America's Intelligence Wire, December 28, 2005.

©PHOTOGRAPHER'S CHOICE GETTY IMAGES

Google is offering the enterprise search, which is essentially the same technology in a version that searches a corporate Intranet. The enterprise search considers not only how often a particular document has been viewed but also the history of the user's past search patterns, such as how often that user has looked at particular documents and for how long. In addition, other companies have purchased specialized software, such as Autonomy, which searches internal sources plus such external sources as news government websites.[13]

External Data: The Distribution System

External data are generated or recorded by an entity other than the researcher's organization. The government, newspapers and journals, trade associations, and other organizations create or produce information. Traditionally, this information has been in published form, perhaps available from a public library, trade association, or government agency. Today, however, computerized data archives and electronic data interchange make external data as accessible as internal data. Exhibit 7.7 illustrates some traditional and some modern ways of distributing information.

External data
Data created, recorded, or generated by an entity other than the researcher's organization.

Information as a Product and Its Distribution Channels

Because secondary data have value, they can be bought and sold like other products. And just as bottles of perfume or plumbers' wrenches may be distributed in many ways, secondary data also flow through various channels of distribution. Many users, such as the Fortune 500 corporations, purchase documents and computerized census data directly from the government. However, many small companies get census data from a library or another intermediary or vendor of secondary information.

▇ LIBRARIES

Traditionally, libraries' vast storehouses of information have served as a bridge between users and producers of secondary data. The library staff deals directly with the creators of information, such as the federal government, and intermediate distributors of information, such as abstracting and

EXHIBIT 7.7
**Information as a Product and
Its Distribution Channels**

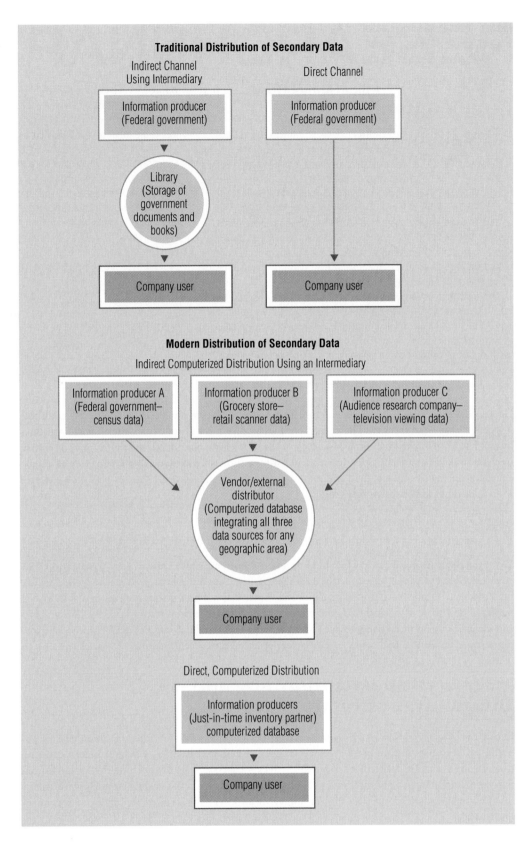

Traditional Distribution of Secondary Data

Indirect Channel
Using Intermediary

Direct Channel

Information producer
(Federal government)

Information producer
(Federal government)

Library
(Storage of
government
documents and
books)

Company user

Company user

Modern Distribution of Secondary Data

Indirect Computerized Distribution Using an Intermediary

Information producer A
(Federal government–
census data)

Information producer B
(Grocery store–
retail scanner data)

Information producer C
(Audience research company–
television viewing data)

Vendor/external
distributor
(Computerized database
integrating all three
data sources for any
geographic area)

Company user

Direct, Computerized Distribution

Information producers
(Just-in-time inventory partner)
computerized database

Company user

indexing services. The user need only locate the appropriate secondary data on the library shelves. Libraries provide collections of books, journals, newspapers, and so on for reading and reference. They also stock many bibliographies, abstracts, guides, directories, and indexes, as well as offer access to basic databases.

The word *library* typically connotes a public or university facility. However, many major corporations and government agencies also have libraries. A corporate librarian's advice on sources of industry information or the United Nations librarian's help in finding statistics about international markets can be invaluable.

THE INTERNET

Today, of course, much secondary data is conveniently available over the Internet. Its creation has added an international dimension to the acquisition of secondary data. For example, Library Spot, at http://www.libraryspot.com, provides links to online libraries, including law libraries, medical libraries, and music libraries. Its reference desk features links to calendars, dictionaries, encyclopedias, maps, and other sources typically found at a traditional library's reference desk.

Chapter 2 discussed how to access and use the Internet. Exhibit 7.8 lists some of the more popular Internet addresses where secondary data may be found.

VENDORS

The information age offers many channels besides libraries through which to access data. Many external producers make secondary data available directly from the organizations that produce the data or through intermediaries, which are often called *vendors*. Vendors such as Factiva now allow managers to access thousands of external databases via desktop computers and telecommunications systems. Hoovers (http://www.hoovers.com) specializes in providing information about thousands of companies' financial situations and operations.

PRODUCERS

Classifying external secondary data by the nature of the producer of information yields five basic sources: publishers of books and periodicals, government sources, media sources, trade association sources, and commercial sources. The following section discusses each type of secondary data source.

Books and Periodicals

Some researchers consider books and periodicals found in a library to be the quintessential secondary data source. A researcher who finds books on a topic of interest obviously is off to a good start.

Professional journals, such as the *Journal of Marketing, Journal of Marketing Research, Journal of the Academy of Marketing Science, The Journal of Business Research, Journal of Advertising Research, American Demographics,* and *The Public Opinion Quarterly,* as well as commercial business periodicals such as *The Wall Street Journal, Fortune,* and *BusinessWeek,* contain much useful material. *Sales and Marketing Management's Survey of Buying Power* is a particularly useful source of information about markets. To locate data in periodicals, indexing services such as the *ABI/INFORM and Business Periodicals Index* and *The Wall Street Journal Index* are very useful. Guides to data sources also are helpful. For example, *American Statistical Index and Business Information Sources* is a very valuable source. Most university libraries provide access to at least some of these databases. Some can also be accessed through the Business Resource Center (www.thomson.com).

Government Sources

Government agencies produce data prolifically. Most of the data published by the federal government can be counted on for accuracy and quality of investigation. Most students are familiar with the U.S. *Census of Population,* which provides a wealth of data.

The *Census of Population* is only one of many resources that the government provides. Banks and savings and loan companies rely heavily on the *Federal Reserve Bulletin* and the *Economic Report of the President* for data relating to research on financial and economic conditions. Builders and contractors use the information in the *Current Housing Report and Annual Housing Survey* for their research. The *Statistical Abstract of the United States* is an extremely valuable source of information about the social, political, and economic organizations of the United States. It abstracts data available in hundreds of other government publications and serves as a convenient reference to more specific statistical data.

TOTHEPOINT

The man who does not read good books has no advantage over the man who cannot read them.

—Mark Twain

EXHIBIT 7.8 **Selected Internet Sites for Secondary Data**

Name	Description	URL
Yahoo!	Portal that serves as a gateway to all kinds of sites on the Web.	http://www.yahoo.com
CEOexpress	The 80/20 rule applied to the Internet. A series of links designed by a busy executive for busy executives.	http://www.ceoexpress.com
The New York Public Library Home Page	Library resources and links available online.	http://www.nypl.org
Census Bureau	Demographic information from the U.S. Census Bureau.	http://www.census.gov
Statistical Abstract of the United States	Highlights from the primary reference book for government statistics.	http://www.census.gov/statab/www
STAT-USA/Internet	A comprehensive source of U.S. government information that focuses on economic, financial, and trade data.	http://www.stat-usa.gov/
Advertising Age magazine	Provides content on marketing media, advertising, and public relations.	http://www.adage.com
Inc.com	*Inc.* magazine's resources for growing a small business.	http://www.inc.com
The Wall Street Journal Online	Provides a continually updated view of business news around the world.	http://online.wsj.com
CNN Money	Provides business news, information on managing a business and managing money, and other business data.	http://money.cnn.com
NAICS—North American Industry Classification System	Describes the new classification system that replaced the SIC system.	http://www.census.gov/epcd/www/naics.html
MapQuest	Allows users to enter an address and zip code and see a map.	http://www.mapquest.com
Brint.com: The BizTech Network	Business and technology portal and global network for e-business, information, technology, and knowledge management.	http://www.brint.com

The federal government is a leader in making secondary data available on the Internet. Visit FedWorld (http://www.fedworld.gov) for a central access point and links to many of these important documents. STAT-USA/Internet is another authoritative and comprehensive source of U.S. government information that focuses on economic, financial, and trade data. It contains the following types of information:

- More than 18,000 market research reports on individual countries and markets compiled by foreign experts at U.S. embassies

- Economic data series, current and historical, such as gross domestic product, balance of payment, and merchandise trade
- Standard reference works, such as the *Economic Report of the President,* the *Budget of the United States Federal Government,* and the *World Factbook*
- Worldwide listings of businesses interested in buying U.S. products

The STAT-USA/Internet web address is http://www.stat-usa.gov. However, only subscribers who pay a fee have access to this service.

State, county, and local government agencies can also be useful sources of information. Many state governments publish state economic models and forecasts, and many cities have metropolitan planning agencies that provide data about the population, economy, transportation system, and so on. These are similar to federal government data but are more current and are structured to suit local needs.

Many cities and states publish information on the Internet. Many search engines have directory entries that allow easy navigation to a particular state's website. A researcher using Yahoo!, for example, needs only to click Regional Information to find numerous paths to information about states.

Media Sources

Information on a broad range of subjects is available from broadcast and print media. *CNN Financial News* and *BusinessWeek* are valuable sources for information on the economy and many industries. Media frequently commission research studies about various aspects of Americans' lives, such as financial affairs, and make reports of survey findings available to potential advertisers free of charge. Data about the readers of magazines and the audiences for broadcast media typically are profiled in media kits and advertisements.

Information about special-interest topics may also be available. *Hispanic Business* reports that the number of Hispanic-owned companies in the United States is expected to grow at a rate of 55 percent between 2004 and 2010, reaching 3.2 million firms, with revenue growth for the period of 70 percent. According to the magazine, most of these firms are located in twenty states, with over half in California and Florida. For researchers willing to pay a modest $85, *Hispanic Business* offers a more detailed report about Hispanic-owned businesses.[14]

Data such as these are plentiful because the media like to show that their vehicles are viewed or heard by advertisers' target markets. These types of data should be evaluated carefully, however, because often they cover only limited aspects of a topic. Nevertheless, they can be quite valuable for research, and they are generally available free of charge.

Trade Association Sources

Trade associations, such as the Food Marketing Institute or the American Petroleum Institute, serve the information needs of a particular industry. The trade association collects data on a number of topics of specific interest to firms, especially data on market size and market trends. Association members have a source of information that is particularly germane to their industry questions. For example, the Newspaper Advertising Bureau (NAB) has catalogued and listed in its computer the specialized sections that are currently popular in newspapers. The NAB has surveyed all daily, Sunday, and weekend newspapers in the United States and Canada on their editorial content and has stored this information, along with data on rates, circulation, and mechanical requirements, in its computer for advertisers' use.

Commercial Sources

Numerous firms specialize in selling and/or publishing information. For example, the Polk Company publishes information on the automotive field, such as average car values and new-car purchase rates by zip code. Many of these organizations offer information in published formats and as CD-ROM or Internet databases. The following discussion of several of these firms provides a sampling of the diverse data that are available.

Market-Share Data A number of syndicated services supply either wholesale or retail sales volume data based on product movement. Information Resources, Inc., collects market-share data using Universal Product Codes (UPC) and optical scanning at retail store checkouts. INFOSCAN is a syndicated store tracking service that collects scanner data weekly from more than 32,000

RESEARCHSNAPSHOT

Associations See Half-Empty Beer Stein

Trade associations that track beer consumption habits include the Beer Institute as well as the Distilled Spirits Council of the United States, makers of competing products. The latter group recently shared data showing that beer sales have recently declined as a percentage of the market for alcoholic beverages. In 1999, 56 percent of alcoholic beverages sold in the United States were beer, but the percentage dropped to 53 percent. At the same time, sales of spirits grew three percentage points, from 28 to 31 percent.

Third-party research data lend support to this trend. Simmons Research found that the share of white males aged 21 to 29 who drink regular

domestic beer fell from 49 percent in 1999 to 4 percent in 2004. Morgan Stanley measured growth in sales of beer, but at a slower pace than sales of wine and spirits.

The Beer Institute publishes statistics about beer consumption on its website, breaking down the numbers by product type and state. The institute recorded an overall downturn in beer sales from 2002 to 2003. Sales grew only slightly in the following year. Beer companies have plenty of data indicating they need a fresh strategy if they want to avoid crying in their beverages.

Sources: Based on James B. Arndofer, "The Death of Beer," Advertising Age, vol. 76, pp. 1–59, May 2, 2005; and Beer Institute, "Industry Update" and "Monthly Statistical Updates," http://www.beerinstitute.org, accessed February 7, 2006.

©TAXI JAPAN/GETTY IMAGES

supermarket, drug, and mass merchandiser outlets across the United States. Sales in France, Germany, Greece, Italy, the Netherlands, Spain, and the United Kingdom also are tracked by INFOSCAN.

Although it is best known for its television rating operations, ACNielsen also has a scanner-based marketing and sales information service called ScanTrack. This service gathers sales and marketing data from a sample of more than 4,800 stores representing more than 800 retailers in fifty major U.S. markets. As part of Nielsen's Retail Measurement Service, auditors visit the stores at regular intervals to track promotions to customers, retail inventories, displays, brand distribution, out-of-stock conditions, and other retail marketing activity. Scanner data allow researchers to monitor sales data before, during, and after changes in advertising frequency, price changes, distribution of free samples, and similar marketing tactics.

Wal-Mart operates its own in-store scanner system called RetailLink. Key suppliers can have online access to relevant data free of charge.[15] The *Market Share Reporter* is produced each year, made available for sale, and provides market share data for most industries.

Many primary data investigations use scanner data to measure the results of experimental manipulations such as altering advertising copy. For example, scanning systems combined with consumer panels are used to create electronic test-markets. Systems based on UPCs (bar codes) and similar technology have been implemented in factories, warehouses, and transportation companies to research inventory levels, shipments, and the like.

Demographic and Census Updates A number of firms, such as CACI Marketing Systems and Urban Information Systems, offer computerized U.S. census files and updates of these data broken down by small geographic areas, such as zip codes. Many of these research suppliers provide in-depth information on minority customers and other market segments.

Consumer Attitude and Public Opinion Research Many research firms offer specialized syndicated services that report findings from attitude research and opinion polls. For example, Yankelovich provides custom research, tailored for specific projects, and several syndicated services. Yankelovich's public opinion research studies, such as the voter and public attitude surveys that appear in *Time* and other news magazines, are a source of secondary data. One of the firm's services is the *Yankelovich MONITOR,* a syndicated annual census of changing social values and an analysis of how they can affect consumer marketing. The *MONITOR* charts the growth and spread of new social values, characterizes the types of customers who support the new values and those who continue to support traditional values, and outlines the ways in which people's values affect purchasing behavior.

Harris/Interactive is another public opinion research firm that provides syndicated and custom research for business. One of its services is its ABC News/Harris survey. This survey, released three

Chapter 7: Secondary Data Research in a Digital Age

RESEARCHSNAPSHOT

Fandango and Nielsen Keeping an Eye on Moviegoers

Fandango, which sells movie tickets online, never set out to be a research firm. But in 2002, MGM contacted Fandango to ask for demographic data about customers who bought tickets to war movies. That was the first sign that the company's data were as valuable as its ticket sales. By looking at purchase data for its 1.7 million registered users, Fandango can tell moviemakers a lot about who is choosing particular movies. It also can use the e-mail addresses (of those who choose to accept e-mail) as a pool of subjects for opinions about movie ideas and ads. Buying histories can help researchers verify that people who offer an opinion about a particular movie actually spent the money to see it.

ACNielsen set out to offer a similar service when it partnered with MovieTickets.com, which like Fandango sells tickets online. Supplementing Nielsen's research asking consumers about their awareness of and interest in particular movies, this partnership will investigate actual movie viewing. Nielsen asks customers of MovieTickets.com questions related to their choice of movies and their opinions about movies they saw. In some cases, the surveys will ask the same questions about different movies to provide a standard set of data available for sale. The company also researches particular movies to fulfill requests from inidividual clients.

Sources: Based on Geoff Keighley, "Puppet's Got a Brand-New Bag," Business 2.0, October 2005, downloaded from InfoTrac at http://www.galenet.com; Kate Kelly, "Nielsen Venture to Mine for Data on Moviegoers," The Wall Street Journal, January 17, 2006, http://online.wsj.com.

©STONE+/GETTY IMAGES

---

times per week, monitors the pulse of the American public on topics such as inflation, unemployment, energy, attitudes toward the president, elections, and so on.

Consumption and Purchase Behavior Data NPD's *National Eating Trends* (NET) is the most detailed database available on consumption patterns and trends for more than 4,000 food and beverage products. This is a syndicated source of data about the types of meals people eat and when and how they eat them. The data, called *diary panel data,* are based on records of meals and diaries kept by a group of households that have agreed to record their consumption behavior over an extended period of time.

National Family Opinion (NFO), Marketing Research Corporation of America (MRCA), and many other syndicated sources sell diary panel data about consumption and purchase behavior. Since the advent of scanner data, diary panels are more commonly used to record purchases of apparel, hardware, home furnishings, jewelry, and other durable goods, rather than purchases of nondurable consumer packaged goods. More recently, services have been tracking consumer behavior online, collecting data about sites visited and purchases made over the Internet.

Advertising Research Advertisers can purchase readership and audience data from a number of firms. W. R. Simmons and Associates measures magazine audiences; Arbitron measures radio audiences; ACNielsen Media Measurement estimates television audience ratings. By specializing in collecting and selling audience information on a continuing basis, these commercial sources provide a valuable service to their subscribers.

Assistance in measuring advertising effectiveness is another syndicated service. For example, Roper Starch Worldwide measures the impact of advertising in magazines. Readership information can be obtained for competitors' ads or the client's own ads. Respondents are classified as noted readers, associated readers, or read-most readers.

Burke Marketing Research provides a service that measures the extent to which respondents recall television commercials aired the night before. It provides product category norms, or average DAR (Day-After Recall) scores, and DAR scores for other products.

An individual advertiser would be unable to monitor every minute of every television program before deciding on the appropriate ones in which to place advertising. However, numerous clients, agencies, television networks, and advertisers can purchase the Nielsen television ratings service.

EXHIBIT 7.9
Examples of Single-Source Databases

CACI Marketing Systems http://www.caci.com	Provides industry-specific marketing services, such as customer profiling and segmentation, custom target analysis, demographic data reports and maps, and site evaluation and selection. CACI offers demographics and data on businesses, lifestyles, consumer spending, purchase potential, shopping centers, traffic volumes, and other statistics.
PRIZM by Claritas Corporation http://www.claritas.com	PRIZM which stands for Potential Rating Index for Zip Markets, is based on the "birds-of-a-feather" assumption that people live near others who are like themselves. PRIZM combines census data, consumer surveys about shopping and lifestyle, and purchase data to identify market segments. Colorful names such as Young Suburbia, Shot Guns, and Pickups describe 40 segments that can be identified by zip code. Claritas also has a lifestyle census in the United Kingdom (http://www.claritas.co.uk).
MRI Cable Report—Mediamark Research Inc. http://www.mediamark.com	Integrates information on cable television viewing with demographic and product usage information.

Single-Source Data-Integrated Information

ACNielsen Company offers data from both its television meters and scanner operations. The integration of these two types of data helps marketers investigate the impact of television advertising on retail sales. In other ways as well, users of data find that merging two or more diverse types of data into a single database offers many advantages.

PRIZM by Claritas Corporation, CACI, ClusterPlus by SMI, Mediamark Research Inc., and many other syndicated databases report product purchase behavior, media usage, demographic characteristics, lifestyle variables, and business activity by geographic area such as zip code. Although such data are often called *geodemographic,* they cover such a broad range of phenomena that no one name is a good description. These data use small geographic areas as the unit of analysis.

Single-source data
Diverse types of data offered by a single company; usually integrated on the basis of a common variable such as geographic area or store.

The marketing research industry uses the term **single-source data** for diverse types of data offered by a single company. Exhibit 7.9 identifies three major marketers of single-source data.

Sources for Global Research

As business has become more global, so has the secondary data industry. The Japan Management Association Research Institute, Japan's largest provider of secondary research data to government and industry, maintains an office in San Diego. The Institute's goal is to help U.S. firms access its enormous store of data about Japan to develop and plan their business there. The office in San Diego provides translators and acts as an intermediary between Japanese researchers and U.S. clients.

Secondary data compiled outside the United States have the same limitations as domestic secondary data. However, international researchers should watch for certain pitfalls that frequently are associated with foreign data and cross-cultural research. First, data may simply be unavailable in certain countries. Second, the accuracy of some data may be called into question. This

RESEARCHSNAPSHOT

Around the World of Data

With the Internet, we can quickly go around the world and find data. Many countries have websites that summarize basic characteristics with data tables. Here are just a few of the many websites that make finding data about different parts of the world easier:

- United States
  http://www.stat-usa.gov
- South Africa
  http://www.statssa.gov.za
- Australia
  http://www.nla.gov.au/oz/stats.html

- Japan
  http://portal.stat.go.jp/Pubstat/topE.html
- U.K.
  http://www.statistics.gov.uk
- France
  http://www.insee.fr
- South America
  http://www.unicef.org/sowco6/statistics/statistics.php
- United Nations
  http://www.un.org/esa
- Norway
  http://www.ssb.no

is especially likely with official statistics that may be adjusted for the political purposes of foreign governments. Finally, although economic terminology may be standardized, various countries use different definitions and accounting and recording practices for many economic concepts. For example, different countries may measure disposable personal income in radically different ways. International researchers should take extra care to investigate the comparability of data among countries.

The U.S. government and other organizations compile databases that may aid international marketers. For example, *The European Union in the US* (http://www.eurunion.org/) reports on historical and current activity in the European Union providing a comprehensive reference guide to information about laws and regulations. The *European Union in the U.S.* profiles in detail each European Union member state, investment opportunities, sources of grants and other funding, and other information about business resources.

The U.S. government offers a wealth of data about foreign countries. The CIA's *World Factbook* and the *National Trade Data Bank* are especially useful. Both can be accessed using the Internet. The National Trade Data Bank (NTDB), the U.S. government's most comprehensive source of world trade data, illustrates what is available.

The National Trade Data Bank was established by the Omnibus Trade and Competitiveness Act of 1988.[16] Its purpose was to provide "reasonable public access, including electronic access" to an export promotion data system that was centralized, inexpensive, and easy to use.

The U.S. Department of Commerce has the responsibility for operating and maintaining the NTDB and works with federal agencies that collect and distribute trade information to keep the NTDB up-to-date. The NTDB has been published monthly on CD-ROM since 1990. Over one thousand public and university libraries offer access to the NTDB through the Federal Depository Library system.

The National Trade Data Bank consists of 133 separate trade- and business-related programs (databases). By using it, small- and medium-sized companies get immediate access to information that until now only Fortune 500 companies could afford.

Topics in the NTDB include export opportunities by industry, country, and product; foreign companies or importers looking for specific products; how-to market guides; demographic, political, and socioeconomic conditions in hundreds of countries; and much more. NTDB offers one-stop shopping for trade information from more than twenty federal sources. You do not need to know which federal agency produces the information: All you need to do is consult NTDB.

Some of the specific information that can be obtained from the NTDB are listed in Exhibit 7.10.

EXHIBIT 7.10
Examples of Information Contained in the NTDB

Agricultural commodity production and trade

Basic export information

Calendars of trade fairs and exhibitions

Capital markets and export financing

Country reports on economic and social policies and trade practices

Energy production, supply, and inventories

Exchange rates

Export licensing information

Guides to doing business in foreign countries

International trade terms directory

How-to guides

International trade regulations/agreements

International trade agreements

Labor, employment, and productivity

Maritime and shipping information

Market research reports

Overseas contacts

Overseas and domestic industry information

Price indexes

Small business information

State exports

State trade contacts

Trade opportunities

U.S. export regulations

U.S. import and export statistics by country and commodity

U.S. international transactions

World Fact Book

World minerals production

Summary

1. Discuss the advantages and disadvantages of secondary data. Secondary data are data that have been gathered and recorded previously by someone else for purposes other than those of the current researcher. The chief advantage of secondary data is that they are almost always less expensive to obtain than primary data. Generally they can be obtained rapidly and may provide information not otherwise available to the researcher. The disadvantage of secondary data is that they were not intended specifically to meet the researcher's needs. The researcher must examine secondary data for accuracy, bias, and soundness. One way to do this is to cross-check various available sources.

2. Define types of secondary data analysis conducted by marketing managers. Secondary research designs address many common marketing problems. There are three general categories of secondary research objectives: fact-finding, model building, and database marketing. A typical fact-finding study might seek to uncover all available information about consumption patterns for a particular product category or to identify business trends that affect an industry. Model building is more complicated; it involves specifying relationships between two or more variables. The practice of database marketing, which involves maintaining customer databases with customers' names, addresses, phone numbers, past purchases, responses to past promotional offers, and other relevant data such as demographic and financial data, is increasingly being supported by marketing research efforts.

3. Identify various internal and proprietary sources of secondary data. Managers often get data from internal proprietary sources such as accounting records. Data mining is the use of powerful computers to dig through volumes of data to discover patterns about an organization's customers and products. It is a broad term that applies to many different forms of analysis.

4. Give examples of various external sources of secondary data. External data are generated or recorded by another entity. The government, newspaper and journal publishers, trade associations, and other organizations create or produce information. Traditionally this information has been distributed in published form, either directly from producer to researcher, or indirectly through intermediaries such as public libraries. Modern computerized data archives, electronic data interchange, and the Internet have changed the distribution of external data, making them almost as accessible as internal data. *Push technology* is a term referring to an Internet information technology that automatically delivers content to the researcher's or manager's desktop. This service helps in environmental scanning.

5. Describe the impact of single-source data and globalization on secondary data research. The marketing of multiple types of related data by single-source suppliers has radically changed the nature of secondary-data research. Businesses can measure promotional efforts and related buyer behavior by detailed customer characteristics. As business has become more global, so has the secondary-data industry. International researchers should watch for pitfalls that can be associated with foreign data and cross-cultural research, such as problems with the availability and reliability of data.

Key Terms and Concepts

Secondary data	Site analysis techniques	Customer discovery
Data conversion	Index of retail saturation	Database marketing
Cross-checks	Data mining	Internal and proprietary data
Market tracking	Neural network	External data
Model building	Market-basket analysis	Single-source data

Questions for Review and Critical Thinking

1. Secondary data have been called the first line of attack for marketing researchers. Discuss this description.
2. Suppose you wish to learn about the size of the soft-drink market, particularly root beer sales, growth patterns, and market shares. Indicate probable sources for these secondary data.
3. What is *push technology?*
4. Identify some typical research objectives for secondary-data studies.
5. How might a marketing researcher doing a job for a company such as Pulte Homes (http://www.pultehomes.com) or David Weekley Homes (http://www.davidweekley.com/) use secondary data and data mining?
6. What would be a source for the following data?
    a. Population, average income, and employment rates for Oregon
    b. Maps of U.S. counties and cities
    c. Trends in automobile ownership
    d. Divorce trends in the United States
    e. Median weekly earnings of full-time, salaried workers for the previous five years
    f. Annual sales of the top ten fast-food companies
    g. Top ten websites ranked by number of unique visitors
    h. Attendance at professional sports events
7. Suppose you are a marketing research consultant and a client comes to your office and says, "I must have the latest information on the supply of and demand for Maine potatoes within the next 24 hours." What would you do?
8. Find the following data in the *Survey of Current Business:*
    a. U.S. gross domestic product for the first quarter of 2004
    b. Exports of goods and services for the fourth quarter of 2004
    c. Imports of goods and services for the fourth quarter of 2004
9. **ETHICS** A newspaper reporter finds data in a study that surveyed children that reports that a high percentage of children can match cartoon characters with the products they represent. For instance, they can match cereal with Captain Crunch and Ronald McDonald with a Big Mac. The reporter used this to write a story about the need to place limits on the use of cartoon characters. However, the study also provided data suggesting that matching the cartoon character and the product did not lead to significantly higher consumption. Would this be a proper use of secondary data?

Research Activities

1. Use secondary data to learn the size of the U.S. golf market and to profile the typical golfer.
2. **'NET** Where could a researcher working for the U.S. Marine Corps (http://www.marines.com) find information that would identify the most productive areas of the United States in which to recruit? What would you recommend?
3. **'NET** POPClocks estimate the U.S. and world populations. Go to the Census Bureau home page (http://www.census.gov), navigate to the population section, and find today's estimate of the U.S. and world populations.
4. **'NET** Try to find the U.S. market share for the following companies within thirty minutes:
   a. Home Depot
   b. Burger King
   c. Marlboro
   d. Was this a difficult task? If so, why do you think it is this difficult?
5. **'NET** Use the Internet to learn what you can about Indonesia.
   a. Check the corruption index for Indonesia at http://www.transparency.org.
   b. What additional kinds of information are available from the following sources?

- Go to http://freetheworld.com/member.html and view info for Indonesia.
- Visit the CIA's *World Factbook* at http://www.cia.gov/cia/publications/factbook.
- Go to Google, Yahoo! Search, or another search engine, and use "Indonesia" as a search word.

6. **'NET** Go to Statistics Norway at http://www.ssb.no. What data, if any, can you obtain in English? What languages can be used to search this website? What databases might be of interest to the business researcher?
7. **'NET** Go to Statistics Canada at http://www.statcan.ca. What languages can be used to search this website? What databases might be of interest to the business researcher?
8. **'NET** Suppose you were working for a company that wanted to start a business selling handmade acoustic guitars that are reproductions of classic vintage guitars. Pricing is a big part of the decision. Secondary information is available via the Internet. Use eBay (http://ebay.com) to identify four key brands of acoustic guitars by studying the vintage acoustic guitars listed for sale. Since the company wishes to charge premium prices, they will model after the most expensive brand. What brand seems to be associated with the highest prices?

Case 7.1 Demand for Gas Guzzlers

In fall 2005, Hurricanes Katrina and Rita churning in the Gulf of Mexico damaged oil rigs and refineries, contributing to a spike in oil prices. Many observers expressed confidence that those events were the long-expected trigger that would kill off demand for SUVs and other gas-guzzling vehicles.[17] They were only partly right.

In the months leading up to the hurricanes, sales of SUVs had already been falling, according to data from *Automotive News*. Automakers had been shifting ad dollars away from these products. CNW Market Research said that in August 2005, consumers had for the first time placed fuel economy ahead of performance when ranking factors for choosing a new vehicle. When gas prices approached three dollars a gallon in September 2005, marketers felt sure that fuel economy would remain a top concern. Advertisers began creating more ads featuring vehicles' gas mileage.

But by the end of the year, attitudes were shifting again. The National Automobile Dealers Association surveyed consumers

visiting its website for information about car purchases, and it learned they ranked price as most important, followed by make and model, then performance. Fuel economy ranked last, with 3 percent considering it most important and 11 percent considering it least important. What's a carmaker to do? General Motors gathers data from the shoppers who visit websites such as www.kbb.com to look up information, and it is analyzing the data to identify the price of fuel at which car buyers adjust their priorities.

Questions
1. From the standpoint of an automobile company, what sources of information in this article offer secondary data?
2. Suggest two or three other sources of data that might be of interest to auto companies interested in forecasting demand.
3. Online or at your library, look for information about recent trends in SUV purchases. Report what you learned, and forecast whether SUV sales are likely to recover or continue their decline. What role do gas prices play in your forecast?

Video Case 7.2 FedEx Corporation

FedEx's two key descriptors explain its success: relationship-focused and data-intensive.

The company was started by Frederick W. Smith in 1973. Smith had an idea about the coming computerization of society, based on an essay written he was a student at Yale University. (He received a below-average grade on the essay.)* His idea caused

him to speculate about a then-existing need in U.S. economy for a reasonably priced and reliable package air delivery system.

Today, Smith's idea has literally taken off. As the world's largest air and ground express transportation company, FedEx handles 3.2 million packages and deliveries each day to 210 countries worldwide.

The company's marketing efforts are directed at building 100 percent satisfaction-guaranteed relationships with its customers.

*Interview: Frederick W. Smith, http://www.achievement.org/autodoc/page, accessed April 26, 2005.

What it aims to provide for its varied customer base is true reliability and peace of mind in shipping, so customers know that FedEx can be depended on.

Jeff Wyne, manager of marketing, notes that it's important "to understand what your customer wants . . . and needs from you as a supplier." And he adds that it's also important "to anticipate customer needs." One example of how FedEx does this is to offer various shipping channels. Customers, whether large corporations or individuals, have a variety of shipping options from free delivery-service software they can download onto their own computers to shipping centers where non-technically oriented customers can take in their packages for delivery.

FedEx has also been at the forefront in using technology to respond to its customer base. For example, FedEx will install a server directly on-site for companies who have a large number of transactions and require high speed. FedEx has also become known as "the warehouse in the sky" because it can connect production and transportation operations such that companies do not have to stockpile products on their sites. FedEx can communicate with both parties so that parts are manufactured and delivered at properly appropriate times.

Jeff Wyne says, "I think that what has made [FedEx] so successful is that it's been able to make so many other businesses successful."

Questions

1. How can FedEx use its current customer database to determine or anticipate future customer needs and/or demands?
2. If you were responsible for converting FedEx's technology-resistant consumers into consumers who were comfortable using some of the corporation's automation channels, what market research would you need, and how would you obtain it?

Part 3
Research Designs for Collecting Primary Data

©JOHN LUND/THE IMAGE BANK/GETTY IMAGES

CHAPTER 8
Survey Research: An Overview

CHAPTER 9
Survey Research: Basic Methods of Communication with Respondents

CHAPTER 10
Observation

CHAPTER 11
Experimental Research: An Overview

CHAPTER 12
Test-Markets and Experimental Design

CHAPTER 8
SURVEY
RESEARCH:
AN OVERVIEW

After studying this chapter, you should be able to

1. Define surveys, and explain their advantages
2. Describe the type of information that may be gathered in a survey
3. Identify sources of error in survey research
4. Distinguish among the various categories of surveys
5. Discuss the importance of survey research to total quality management programs

Chapter Vignette: Intuit Gets Answers to Satisfy Customers

Intuit, maker of Quicken, QuickBooks, and Turbo Tax software for accounting and tax preparation, has enjoyed years of growth and profits, thanks in part to its efforts to learn what customers want.[1] One of its most important marketing research tools is called a "net promoter survey." That survey is extremely simple. Researchers simply ask customers, "On a scale of 0 to 10 [with 10 being most likely], how likely is it that you would recommend our product to your friends or colleagues?"

Customers who respond with a 9 or 10 are called "promoters," and customers who respond with 0 through 6 are called "detractors." Subtracting the percentage of respondents who are detractors from the percentage who are promoters yields the net promoter score.

Intuit's CEO, Steve Bennett—who says he believes that "anything that can be measured can be improved"—encourages the ongoing collection of net promoter scores as a way to improve products and customer service and thereby build revenues and profits. Of course, making improvements requires that the company not only know *whether* customers are satisfied or dissatisfied but also know

why. To learn more, the company asks survey respondents who are promoters to go online and provide more detailed opinions. For example, Intuit learned that claiming rebates was an annoying process (the company has simplified it) and that discount stores were offering some products for less than the prices offered online to frequent buyers (the company plans to adjust prices).

For even more in-depth information, Intuit supplements survey research with direct observation of customers. One year the company sent hundreds of employees, including CEO Bennett, to visit customers as they worked at their computers. The observers learned that a significant number of small-business owners were struggling with the accounting know-how they needed to use QuickBooks and were mystified by terms such as *accounts payable* and *accounts receivable*.

In response, the company introduced QuickBooks: Simple Start Edition, which replaces the financial jargon with simple terms like *cash in* and *cash out*. In the first year after its launch, Simple Start Edition sold more copies than any other accounting software except the standard QuickBooks.

The purpose of survey research is to collect primary data—data gathered and assembled specifically for the project at hand. This chapter, the first of two on survey research, defines the subject. It also discusses typical research objectives that may be accomplished with surveys and various advantages of the survey method. The chapter explains many potential errors that researchers must be careful to avoid. Finally, it classifies the various survey research methods.

The Nature of Surveys

Respondents
People who verbally answer an interviewer's questions or provide answers to written questions.

Sample survey
A more formal term for a survey.

Often research entails asking people—called **respondents**—to provide answers to written or spoken questions. These questionnaires or interviews collect data through the mail, on the telephone, online, or face-to-face. Thus, a survey is defined as a method of collecting primary data based on communication with a representative sample of individuals. Surveys provide a snapshot at a given point in time. The more formal term, **sample survey**, emphasizes that the purpose of contacting respondents is to obtain a representative sample of the target population.

Survey Objectives: Type of Information Gathered

The type of information gathered in a survey varies considerably depending on its objectives. Typically, surveys attempt to describe what is happening or to learn the reasons for a particular marketing activity.

Identifying characteristics of target markets, measuring consumer attitudes, and describing consumer purchasing patterns are common survey objectives. Most marketing surveys have multiple objectives; few gather only a single type of factual information. Questions about product use and desirable features help with product development and advertising messages. Demographic information and information on media exposure might also be collected in the survey to help plan a market segmentation strategy. A survey commissioned by eBay learned that almost 60 percent of respondents receive unwanted gifts, and 15 percent of them had sold an unwanted gift online, suggesting a possible source of demand for eBay's auction services.[2] In addition, the survey indicated that selling unwanted gifts online was twice as common among 25- to 34-year-olds. Although consumer surveys are a common form of marketing research, not all survey research is conducted with the ultimate consumer. Frequently, studies focus on wholesalers, retailers, or industrial buyers.

Because most survey research is descriptive research, the term *survey* is most often associated with quantitative findings. Although most surveys are conducted to quantify certain factual information, some aspects of surveys may also be qualitative. In new-product development, a survey often has a qualitative objective of refining product concepts. Stylistic, aesthetic, or functional changes may be made on the basis of respondents' suggestions. Evaluating the qualitative nature of advertising may also be an objective of survey research, as in the following story told to advertiser Michael Arlen about testing a rough commercial for AT&T:

We called it "Fishing Camp." The idea was this: These guys go off to a fishing camp in the north woods, somewhere far away, where they're going to have a terrific time together and do all this great fishing, only what happens is that it rains all the time and the fishing is a bust. Mind you, this was a humorous ad. The emphasis was on the humor. Anyway, the big moment occurs when the fishing guys are talking on the phone to their jealous friends back home—who naturally want to know how great the fishing is—and what you see are the fishing guys, huddled in this cabin, with the rain pouring down outside, and one of the guys is staring at a frying pan full of hamburgers sizzling on the stove while he says into the phone, "Boy, you should see the great trout we've got cooking here."[3]

However, much to the advertisers' astonishment, when they tested the advertisement and gave subjects a questionnaire, respondents recalled that what was cooking was trout. To counteract this

RESEARCHSNAPSHOT

Measuring Demand for HDTV

For companies that sell high-definition televisions—retailers and manufacturers alike—it's important to forecast demand and to know which market segments are most likely to buy products. Survey research is helping to provide both types of information.

Marketers have been optimistic about HDTV's future, in part because they expect demand to be stimulated by new video game systems such as Sony's PlayStation 3 and Microsoft's Xbox 360, both of which display games in high definition. They assume that gamers who buy a PlayStation 3 or Xbox 360 will want to upgrade their television to take advantage of the new games' graphics.

Survey research has provided mixed support for this outlook. Several months before the release of the Xbox 360 and a year before the launch date for PlayStation 3, marketing research firm NPD asked consumers without an HDTV what was holding them

back from the purchase. Far more said price (29 percent) than a lack of HD games to play (2 percent). Still, when the research focuses on gamers who buy the latest technology, the interest seems to be high. QTX Research conducts weekly surveys of gamers' purchase intentions.

In one of those surveys, 15 percent of gamers with an Xbox 360 (or those with plans to buy one) said they intended to purchase an HDTV. These enthusiasts may be the people HDTV sellers should be talking to.

Source: Wall Street Journal. Online [Only Staff-Produced Materials May Be Used] by Nick Wingfield. Copyright 2006 by Dow Jones & Co Inc. Reproduced with permission of Dow Jones & Co Inc in the format Textbook via Copyright Clearance Center.

©PHOTODISC/GETTY IMAGES

misimpression, said the advertiser, "We ended up making it, but what we had to do was, when we came to that segment, we put the camera almost *inside* the frying pan, and in the frying pan we put huge, crude chunks of hamburger that were so raw they were almost red."

Although most marketing surveys are descriptive, they can also be designed to provide insights about causal explanations or to explore ideas.

Advantages of Surveys

Surveys provide a quick, inexpensive, efficient, and accurate means of assessing information about a population. The examples given earlier illustrate that surveys are quite flexible and, when properly conducted, extremely valuable to the manager.

As we discussed in Chapter 1, marketing research has proliferated since the general adoption of the marketing concept. The growth of survey research is related to the simple idea that to find out what consumers think, you need to ask them.[4]

Over the last fifty years and particularly during the last two decades, survey research techniques and standards have become quite scientific and accurate. When properly conducted, surveys offer managers many advantages. However, they can also be used poorly when researchers do not follow research principles, such as careful survey and sample design. Sometimes even a well-designed and carefully executed survey is not helpful because the results are delivered too late to inform decisions.

The disadvantages of specific forms of survey data collection—personal interview, telephone, mail, Internet, and other self-administered formats—are discussed in Chapter 9. However, errors are common to all forms of surveys, so it is appropriate to describe them generally.

Errors in Survey Research

A manager who is evaluating the quality of a survey must estimate its accuracy. Exhibit 8.1 outlines the various forms of survey error. They have two major sources: random sampling error and systematic error.

EXHIBIT 8.1 Categories of Survey Errors

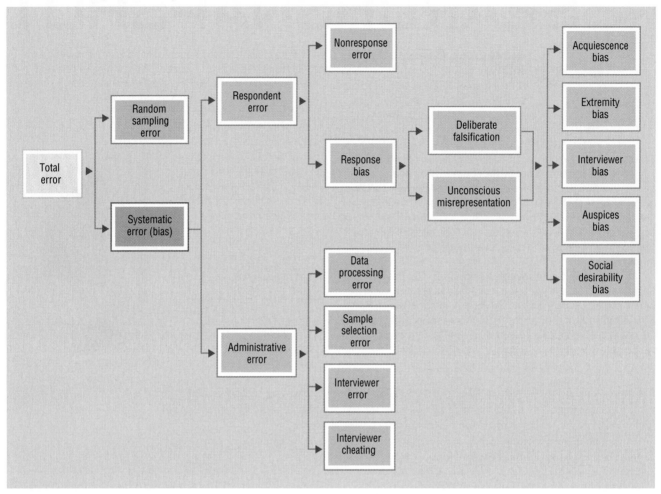

Random Sampling Error

Most surveys try to portray a representative cross-section of a particular target population. Even with technically proper random probability samples, however, statistical errors will occur because of chance variation in the elements selected for the sample. These statistical problems are unavoidable without very large samples (>400). However, the extent of **random sampling error** can be estimated. Chapters 16 and 17 will discuss these errors and ways they can be estimated in more detail.

Random sampling error
A statistical fluctuation that occurs because of chance variation in the elements selected for a sample.

Systematic error
Error resulting from some imperfect aspect of the research design that causes respondent error or from a mistake in the execution of the research.

Sample bias
A persistent tendency for the results of a sample to deviate in one direction from the true value of the population parameter.

Systematic Error

The other major source of survey error, **systematic error**, results from some imperfect aspect of the research design or from a mistake in the execution of the research. Because systematic errors include all sources of error other than those introduced by the random sampling procedure, these errors or biases are also called *nonsampling errors*. A **sample bias** exists when the results of a sample show a persistent tendency to deviate in one direction from the true value of the population parameter. The many sources of error that in some way systematically influence answers can be divided into two general categories: respondent error and administrative error.

RESEARCHSNAPSHOT

Overestimating Patient Satisfaction

When companies conduct surveys to learn about customer satisfaction, they face an important challenge: whether the responses come from a cross-section of customers. Maybe just the happiest or most angry customers choose not to participate. This problem also occurs when the "customers" are the patients of a health-care provider.

To investigate this issue, a group of researchers in Massachusetts studied data from patient satisfaction surveys that rated 6,681 patients' experiences with 82 primary-care physicians (internists and family practitioners) at a health maintenance organization. These ratings represented response rates ranging from 11 to 55 percent, depending on the physician being rated. The researchers compared their information about response rates with a set of simulated data for which they knew the underlying distribution of responses. They found that the actual data closely matched simulated data in which responses

were biased so that responses were more likely when satisfaction was higher.

The researchers concluded that there was a significant correlation between the response rate and average (mean) satisfaction rating. In other words, more-satisfied patients were more likely to complete and return the survey. If the HMO were to use the data to evaluate how satisfied patients are with their doctors, it would overestimate satisfaction. Also, it would have less information about its lower-performing doctors. The researchers therefore concluded that it is important to follow up with subjects to encourage greater response from less-satisfied patients.

Source: Based on Kathleen M. Mazor, Brian E. Clauser, Terry Field, Robert A. Yood, and Jerry H. Gurwitz, "A Demonstration of the Impact of Response Bias on the Results of Patient Satisfaction Surveys," Health Services Research, October 2002, downloaded from Business & Company Resource Center at http://galenet.galegroup.com.

©PHOTODISC/GETTY IMAGES

Respondent Error ◀

Surveys ask people for answers. If people cooperate and give truthful answers, a survey will likely accomplish its goal. If these conditions are not met, nonresponse error or response bias, the two major categories of **respondent error**, may cause sample bias.

Respondent error
A category of sample bias resulting from some respondent action or inaction such as nonresponse or response bias.

Nonresponse Error

Few surveys have 100 percent response rates. But a researcher who obtains a 1 percent response to a five-page e-mail questionnaire concerning various brands of spark plugs may face a serious problem. To use the results, the researcher must be believe that consumers who responded to the questionnaire are representative of consumers who did not respond. The statistical differences between a survey that includes only those who responded and a survey that also included those who failed to respond are referred to as **nonresponse error**. This problem is especially acute in mail and Internet surveys, but nonresponse also threatens telephone and face-to-face interviews.

People who are not contacted or who refuse to cooperate are called **nonrespondents**. A nonresponse occurs if no one answers the phone at the time of both the initial call and a subsequent callback. The number of **no contacts** in survey research has been increasing because of the proliferation of answering machines and growing use of caller ID to screen telephone calls.[5] A parent who must juggle the telephone and a half-diapered child and refuses to participate in the survey because he or she is too busy also is a nonresponse. **Refusals** occur when people are unwilling to participate in the research. A research team reviewed fifty mail surveys of pediatricians conducted by the American Academy of Pediatrics (AAP) between 1994 and 2002 and found that response rates declined over the period studied. In the early years of the study period, an average 70 percent of pediatricians returned completed surveys; the response rate fell to an average 63 percent in the second half of the period.[6] No contacts and refusals can seriously bias survey data. In the case of the pediatricians, the researchers found little difference in the response rates attributable to differences in such easy-to-measure variables as age, sex, and type of membership in the AAP, leaving them to wonder whether the cause of refusals was some unknown but important difference among these doctors.

Nonresponse error
The statistical differences between a survey that includes only those who responded and a perfect survey that would also include those who failed to respond.

Nonrespondents
People who are not contacted or who refuse to cooperate in the research.

No contacts
People who are not at home or who are otherwise inaccessible on the first and second contact.

Refusals
People who are unwilling to participate in a research project.

Many e-mail addresses are actually inactive. Inactive e-mails contribute to low response rates.

Self-selection bias
A bias that occurs because people who feel strongly about a subject are more likely to respond to survey questions than people who feel indifferent about it.

Response bias
A bias that occurs when respondents either consciously or unconsciously tend to answer questions with a certain slant that misrepresents the truth.

Because of this problem, researchers investigate the causes of nonresponse. For example, a study analyzed a large database collected by AT&T and found that the effort required to participate in an ongoing study contributes to the problem.[7] People tend not to respond to questions that are difficult to answer. When they are asked to participate in a long-term panel, the rate of nonresponse to individual items grows over time, and eventually some people stop participating altogether. However, eventually it becomes easier to keep answering the same kinds of panel questions, and nonresponse rates level off.

Comparing the demographics of the sample with the demographics of the target population is one means of inspecting for possible biases in response patterns. If a particular group, such as older citizens, is underrepresented or if any potential biases appear in a response pattern, additional efforts should be made to obtain data from the underrepresented segments of the population. For example, personal interviews may be used instead of telephone interviews for the underrepresented segments.

After receiving a refusal from a potential respondent, an interviewer can do nothing other than be polite. The respondent who is not at home when called or visited should be scheduled to be interviewed at a different time of day or on a different day of the week.

With a mail survey, the researcher never really knows whether a nonrespondent has refused to participate or is just indifferent. Researchers know that those who are most involved in an issue are more likely to respond to a mail survey. **Self-selection bias** is a problem that frequently plagues self-administered questionnaires. In a restaurant, for example, a customer on whom a waiter spilled soup, a person who was treated to a surprise dinner, or others who feel strongly about the service are more likely to complete a self-administered questionnaire left at the table than individuals who are indifferent about the restaurant. Self-selection biases distort surveys because they overrepresent extreme positions while underrepresenting responses from those who are indifferent. Several techniques will be discussed later for encouraging respondents to reply to mail and Internet surveys.

Response Bias

A **response bias** occurs when respondents tend to answer questions with a certain slant. People may consciously or unconsciously misrepresent the truth. If a distortion of measurement occurs because respondents' answers are falsified or misrepresented, either intentionally or inadvertently, the resulting sample bias will be a response bias. When researchers identify response bias, they should include a corrective measure.

▦ DELIBERATE FALSIFICATION

Occasionally people deliberately give false answers. It is difficult to assess why people knowingly misrepresent answers. A response bias may occur when people misrepresent answers to appear intelligent, conceal personal information, avoid embarrassment, and so on. For example, respondents may be able to remember the total amount of money spent grocery shopping, but they may forget the exact prices of individual items that they purchased. Rather than appear ignorant or unconcerned about prices, they may provide their best estimate and not tell the truth—namely, that they cannot remember. Sometimes respondents become bored with the interview and provide answers just to get rid of the interviewer. At other times respondents try to appear well informed by providing the answers they think are expected of them. On still other occasions, they give answers simply to please the interviewer.

RESEARCHSNAPSHOT

My Opinion? It Depends on Your Words

It's hard to capture the nuances of a person's opinion with a simple survey question. Word choices seem to shape some respondents' answers. Carl Bialik, a columnist for *The Wall Street Journal,* observed this problem when he looked at responses to public-opinion polls exploring differences of opinion about activities of the National Security Agency. Bialik concluded that opinions varied based on the wording of the questions.

One pollster, Rasmussen Reports, asked, "Should the National Security Agency be allowed to intercept telephone conversations between terrorism suspects in other countries and people living in the United States?" Almost two-thirds of respondents said yes. But in a Gallup survey for *USA Today* and CNN, only 51 percent favored the NSA's wiretapping of "telephone conversations between U.S. citizens living in the United States and suspected terrorists living in other countries without getting a court order allowing it to do so."

One source of the difference might be the language "people" in the first poll and "U.S. citizens" in the second. A *Wall Street Journal*/NBC poll found 53 percent favoring the wiretapping program when it involved "American citizens in the United States," while more (56 percent) favored the program in a *Washington Post*/ABC poll asking about "some people in the United States." Scott Rasmussen, president of Rasmussen Reports, also hypothesizes that results of polls investigating this issue also may be swayed by whether the questions mention the lack of search warrants for the wiretaps. In these examples, the word choices shape which aspects of a complex issue the respondents focus on.

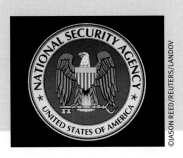

Source: Wall Street Journal. Online [Only Staff-Produced Materials May Be Used] by Carl Bialik. Copyright 2006 by Dow Jones & Co Inc. Reproduced with permission of Dow Jones & Co Inc in the format Textbook via Copyright Clearance Center.

©JASON REED/REUTERS/LANDOV

One explanation for conscious and deliberate misrepresentation of facts is the so-called average-person hypothesis. Individuals may prefer to be viewed as average, so they alter their responses to conform more closely to their *perception* of the average person. Average-person effects have been found in response to questions about such topics as savings account balances, car prices, voting behavior, and hospital stays.

■ UNCONSCIOUS MISREPRESENTATION

Even when a respondent is consciously trying to be truthful and cooperative, response bias can arise from the question format, the question content, or some other stimulus. For example, bias can be introduced by the situation in which the survey is administered. The results of two in-flight surveys concerning aircraft preference illustrate this point. Passengers flying on B-747s preferred B-747s to L-1011s (74 percent versus 19 percent), while passengers flying on L-1011s preferred L-1011s to B-747s (56 percent versus 38 percent). The difference in preferences appears to have been largely a function of the aircraft the respondents were flying on when the survey was conducted, although sample differences may have been a factor. A likely influence was the respondent's satisfaction with the plane on which he or she was flying when surveyed. In other words, in the absence of any strong preference, the respondent may simply have identified the aircraft traveled on and indicated that as his or her preference.[8]

Respondents who misunderstand questions may unconsciously provide biased answers. Or, they may be willing to answer but unable to do so because they have forgotten the exact details. Asking "When was the last time you attended a concert?" may result in a best-guess estimate because the respondent has forgotten the exact date.

A bias may also occur when a respondent has not thought about an unexpected question. Many respondents will answer questions even though they have given them little thought. For example, in most investigations of consumers' buying intentions, the predictability of the intention scales depends on how close the subject is to making a purchase. The intentions of subjects who have little knowledge of the brand or the store alternatives being surveyed and the intentions of subjects who have not yet made any purchase plans cannot be expected to predict purchase behavior accurately.

In many cases consumers cannot adequately express their feelings in words. The cause may be questions that are vague or ambiguous. Researchers may ask someone to describe his or her frustration when using a computer. The problem is, the researcher may be interested in software problems while the respondent is thinking of hardware issues. Language differences also may be a source of misunderstanding. A survey in the Philippines found that, despite seemingly high toothpaste usage, only a tiny percentage of people responded positively when asked, "Do you use toothpaste?" As it turned out, people in the Philippines tend to refer to toothpaste by using the brand name Colgate. When researchers returned and asked, "Do you use Colgate?" the positive response rate soared.

As the time following a purchase or a shopping event increases, people become more likely to underreport information about that event. Time lapse influences people's ability to precisely remember and communicate specific factors.

Unconscious misrepresentation bias may also occur because consumers unconsciously avoid facing the realities of a future buying situation. Housing surveys record that Americans overwhelmingly continue to aspire to own detached, single-family dwellings (preferably single-level, ranch-type structures that require two to five times the amount of land per unit required for attached homes). However, builders know that *attached* housing purchases by first buyers are more common than respondents expect.

▓ TYPES OF RESPONSE BIAS

Response bias falls into four specific categories: acquiescence bias, extremity bias, interviewer bias, and social desirability bias. These categories overlap and are not mutually exclusive. A single biased answer may be distorted for many complex reasons, some distortions being deliberate and some being unconscious misrepresentations.

Acquiescence Bias

Acquiescence bias
A tendency for respondents to agree with all or most questions asked of them in a survey.

Some respondents are very agreeable. They seem to agree to practically every statement they are asked about. A tendency to agree with all or most questions is known as **acquiescence bias**. This bias is particularly prominent in new-product research. Questions about a new-product idea generally elicit some acquiescence bias because respondents give positive connotations to most new ideas. For example, consumers responded favorably to survey questions about pump baseball gloves (the pump inserts air into the pocket of the glove providing more cushioning). However, when these expensive gloves hit the market, they sat on the shelves. When conducting new-product research, researchers should recognize the high likelihood of acquiescence bias.

Another form of acquiescence is evident in some people's tendency to disagree with all questions. Thus, acquiescence bias is a response bias due to the respondents' tendency to concur with a particular position.

Extremity Bias

Extremity bias
A category of response bias that results because some individuals tend to use extremes when responding to questions.

Some individuals tend to use extremes when responding to questions; others consistently avoid extreme positions and tend to respond more neutrally. Response styles vary from person to person, and extreme responses may cause an **extremity bias** in the data.[9]

Interviewer Bias

Interviewer bias
A response bias that occurs because the presence of the interviewer influences respondents' answers.

Response bias may arise from the interplay between interviewer and respondent. If the interviewer's presence influences respondents to give untrue or modified answers, the survey will be marred by **interviewer bias**. Many homemakers and retired people welcome an interviewer's visit as a break in routine activities. Other respondents may give answers they believe will please the interviewer rather than the truthful responses. Respondents may wish to appear intelligent and wealthy—of course they read *Scientific American* rather than *Playboy*.

The interviewer's age, sex, style of dress, tone of voice, facial expressions, or other nonverbal characteristics may have some influence on a respondent's answers. If an interviewer smiles and makes a positive statement after a respondent's answers, the respondent will be more likely to give similar responses. In a research study on sexual harassment against saleswomen, male interviewers might not yield as candid responses from saleswomen as female interviewers would.

Many interviewers, contrary to instructions, shorten or rephrase questions to suit their needs. This potential influence on responses can be avoided to some extent if interviewers receive training and supervision that emphasize the necessity of appearing neutral.

If interviews go on too long, respondents may feel that time is being wasted. They may answer as abruptly as possible with little forethought.

Social Desirability Bias

A **social desirability bias** may occur either consciously or unconsciously because the respondent wishes to create a favorable impression or save face in the presence of an interviewer. Incomes may be inflated, education overstated, or perceived respectable answers given to gain prestige. In contrast, answers to questions that seek factual information or responses about matters of public knowledge (zip code, number of children, and so on) usually are quite accurate. An interviewer's presence may increase a respondent's tendency to give inaccurate answers to sensitive questions such as "Did you vote in the last election?," "Do you have termites or roaches in your home?," or "Do you color your hair?"

The social desirability bias is especially significant in the case of research that addresses sensitive or personal topics, including respondents' sexual behavior. A group of researchers recently evaluated responses to questions about homosexual sexual activity, collected by NORC's long-running General Social Survey.[10] The researchers found that over time, as attitudes toward homosexual conduct have softened, the frequency of repeated female-female sexual contacts increased dramatically, suggesting the possibility that reporting levels have been subject to social desirability bias. However, the researchers noted that rates of male-male sexual contact were fairly steady over the period and that the rate of change for female-female sexual contact persisted even when adjusted for measures of greater tolerance. This evidence suggests that the data reflect more phenomena than mere social desirability bias.

The more people are susceptible to interpersonal influence, the more likely a response bias will occur. One example of this can be found in adolescents' buying behavior.

Social desirability bias
Bias in responses caused by respondents' desire, either conscious or unconscious, to gain prestige or appear in a different social role.

Administrative Error

The result of improper administration or execution of the research task is called an **administrative error**. Administrative errors are caused by carelessness, confusion, neglect, omission, or some other blunder. Four types of administrative error are data-processing error, sample selection error, interviewer error, and interviewer cheating.

Administrative error
An error caused by the improper administration or execution of the research task.

Data-Processing Error

Processing data by computer, like any arithmetic or procedural process, is subject to error because data must be edited, coded, and entered into the computer by people. The accuracy of data processed by computer depends on correct data entry and programming. **Data-processing error** can be minimized by establishing careful procedures for verifying each step in the data-processing stage.

Data-processing error
A category of administrative error that occurs because of incorrect data entry, incorrect computer programming, or other procedural errors during data analysis.

One problem with web-based surveys is that there is no way of knowing who exactly responded to the questionnaire.

Sample Selection Error

Many kinds of error involve failure to select a representative sample. **Sample selection error** is systematic error that results in an unrepresentative sample because of an error in either the sample design or the execution of the sampling procedure. Executing a sampling plan free of procedural error is difficult. A firm that selects its sample from the phone book will have some systematic error, because unlisted numbers are not included. Stopping respondents during daytime hours in shopping centers excludes working people who shop by mail, Internet, or telephone. In other cases, researchers interview the wrong person. Consider a political pollster who uses random-digit dialing to select a sample, rather than a list of registered voters. Unregistered 17-year-olds may be willing to give their opinions, but they are the wrong people to ask because they cannot vote.

Sample selection error
An administrative error caused by improper sample design or sampling procedure execution.

Interviewer Error

Interviewers' abilities vary considerably. **Interviewer error** is introduced when interviewers record answers but check the wrong response or are unable to write fast enough to record answers verbatim. Also, selective perception may cause interviewers to misrecord data that do not support their own attitudes and opinions.

Interviewer error
Mistakes made by interviewers failing to record survey responses correctly.

Interviewer Cheating

Interviewer cheating occurs when an interviewer falsifies entire questionnaires or fills in answers to questions that have been intentionally skipped. Some interviewers cheat to finish an interview as quickly as possible or to avoid questions about sensitive topics.

Interviewer cheating
The practice of filling in fake answers or falsifying questionnaires while working as an interviewer.

If interviewers are suspected of faking questionnaires, they should be told that a small percentage of respondents will be called back to confirm whether the initial interview was actually conducted. This practice should discourage interviewers from cheating. The term *curb-stoning* is sometimes used to refer to interviewers filling in responses for respondents that do not really exist.

Rule-of-Thumb Estimates for Systematic Error

The techniques for estimating systematic, or nonsampling, error are less precise than many sample statistics. Researchers have established experience-based, conservative rules of thumb based on experience to estimate systematic error. In the case of consumer research, experienced researchers might determine that only a certain percentage of people who say they will definitely buy a new product actually do so. Evidence for a mere-measurement effect (see the Research Snapshot box on the following page) suggests that in some situations, researchers might conclude that respondents' own buying behavior will exaggerate overall sales. Thus, researchers often present actual survey

RESEARCHSNAPSHOT

The "Mere-Measurement" Effect

Will you eat high-fat food this week? Will you floss your teeth? Researchers have found that answering survey questions like these can actually shift your behavior. This influence, called the mere-measurement effect, means that simply answering a question about intentions will increase the likelihood of the underlying behavior—*if* the behavior is seen as socially desirable. If the behavior is considered undesirable, answering the question tends to decrease the likelihood of the behavior.

To test this, a group of business school professors conducted a series of surveys in which certain subjects were asked about their intentions to eat fatty food or to floss. In follow-up surveys, they found that subjects ate less fatty food and flossed more often if they were asked about those behaviors. However, the mere-measurement effect did not occur if the surveys indicated that they were sponsored by groups that would be likely to want to persuade the subjects (in this case, the American Fruit Growers Association and the Association of Dental Products Manufacturers). In fact, subjects *decreased* their frequency of flossing if they took the supposedly manipulative survey that asked about flossing. Follow-up experiments verified that changes to behavior were genuine, not merely a survey bias.

The researchers propose that the mere-measurement effect occurs because subjects of a survey generally do not think the questions are an attempt to persuade them. If they receive information that puts them on their guard against persuasion, the mere-measurement effect is lessened and sometimes even generates the opposite behavior. Their results suggest a need for caution when surveys attempt to predict future behavior.

Source: Patti Williams, Gavan J. Fitzsimons, Lauren G. Block, "When Consumers Do Not Recognize "Benign" Intention Questions as Persuasion Attempts, "© 2004 by Journal of Consumer Research, Inc., Vol. 31, December 2004. All rights reserved. Reprinted with permission by The University of Chicago Press."

©GARY SALTER/ZEFA/CORBIS

findings *and* their interpretations of estimated purchase response based on estimates of nonsampling error. For example, one pay-per-view cable TV company surveys geographic areas it plans to enter and estimates the number of people who indicate they will subscribe to its service. The company knocks down the percentage by a "ballpark 10 percent" because experience in other geographic areas has indicated that there is a systematic upward bias of 10 percent on this intentions question.

What Can Be Done to Reduce Survey Error?

Now that we have examined the sources of error in surveys, you may have lost some of your optimism about survey research. Don't be discouraged! The discussion emphasized the bad news because it is important for marketing managers to realize that surveys are not a panacea. There are, however, ways to handle and reduce survey errors. For example, Chapter 15 on questionnaire design discusses the reduction of response bias; Chapters 16 and 17 discuss the reduction of sample selection and random sampling error. Indeed, much of the remainder of this book discusses various techniques for reducing bias in marketing research. The good news lies ahead!

Classifying Survey Research Methods

Now that we have discussed some advantages and disadvantages of surveys in general, we turn to a discussion of classification of surveys according to several criteria. Surveys may be classified based on the method of communication, the degrees of structure and disguise in the questionnaire, and the time frame in which the data are gathered (temporal classification). Chapter 9 classifies surveys according to method of communicating with the respondent, covering topics such as personal interviews, telephone interviews, mail surveys, and Internet surveys. The classifications based on structure and disguise and on time frame will be discussed in the remainder of this chapter.

Structured and Disguised Questions

In designing a questionnaire (or an *interview schedule*), the researcher must decide how much structure or standardization is needed.[11] A **structured question** limits the number of allowable responses. For example, the respondent may be instructed to choose one alternative response such as "under 18," "18–35," or "over 35" to indicate his or her age. An **unstructured question** does not restrict the respondent's answers. An open-ended, unstructured question such as "Why do you shop at Wal-Mart?" allows the respondent considerable freedom in answering.

The researcher must also decide whether to use **undisguised questions** or **disguised questions**. A straightforward, or undisguised, question such as "Do you have dandruff problems?" assumes that the respondent is willing to reveal the information. However, researchers know that some questions are threatening to a person's ego, prestige, or self-concept. So, they have designed a number of indirect techniques of questioning to disguise the purpose of the study.

Questionnaires can be categorized by their degree of structure and degree of disguise. For example, interviews in exploratory research might use *unstructured-disguised* questionnaires. The projective techniques discussed in Chapter 6 fall into this category. Other classifications are *structured-undisguised, unstructured-undisguised,* and *structured-disguised.* These classifications have two limitations: First, the degree of structure and the degree of disguise vary; they are not clear-cut categories. Second, most surveys are hybrids, asking both structured and unstructured questions. Recognizing the degrees of structure and disguise necessary to meet survey objectives will help in the selection of the appropriate communication medium for conducting the survey.

Temporal Classification

Although most surveys are for individual research projects conducted only once over a short time period, other projects require multiple surveys over a long period. Thus, surveys can be classified on a temporal basis.

CROSS-SECTIONAL STUDIES

Early in 2006, *The Wall Street Journal* teamed up with Harris Interactive to ask people about their New Year's resolutions.[12] The survey asked people whether they had made resolutions the year before, which resolutions they had succeeded in keeping, and what they had resolved for the coming year. The results indicated that 43 percent of men and 52 percent of women made resolutions for 2006, even though less than half had kept their resolutions from the year before. This was a **cross-sectional study** because it collected the data at a single point in time. Such a study samples various segments of the population to investigate relationships among variables by cross-tabulation. Most marketing research surveys fall into this category, particularly those that deal with market segmentation.

The typical method of analyzing a cross-sectional survey is to divide the sample into appropriate subgroups. For example, if a winery expects income levels to influence attitudes toward wines, the data are broken down into subgroups based on income and analyzed to reveal similarities or differences among the income subgroups.

LONGITUDINAL STUDIES

In a **longitudinal study** respondents are questioned multiple points in time. The purpose of longitudinal studies is to examine continuity of response and to observe changes that occur over time. Many syndicated polling services, such as Gallup, conduct regular polls. For example, the Bureau of Labor Statistics conducts the National Longitudinal Survey of Youth, interviewing the same sample of individuals repeatedly since 1979. (Respondents, who were "youth" at the beginning of the study, are now in their forties.) Research scientist Jay Zagorsky recently analyzed the longitudinal data from that study to determine that those who married and stayed with their spouse accumulated almost twice as much wealth as single and divorced people in the study.[13] The *Yankelovich MONITOR* has been tracking American values and attitudes for more than thirty

EXHIBIT 8.2
Longitudinal Research from a Harris Poll

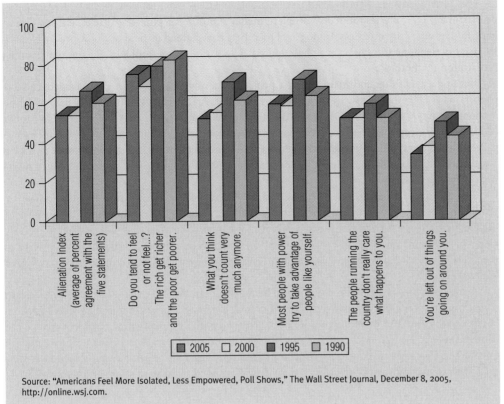

Source: "Americans Feel More Isolated, Less Empowered, Poll Shows," The Wall Street Journal, December 8, 2005, http://online.wsj.com.

years. This survey is an example of a longitudinal study that uses successive samples; its researchers survey several different samples at different times. Longitudinal studies of this type are sometimes called *cohort studies,* because similar groups of people who share a certain experience during the same time interval (cohorts) are expected to be included in each sample. Exhibit 8.2 illustrates the results of a longitudinal study by Harris Interactive, which since 1966 has been asking five questions related to powerlessness and isolation to create an "alienation index."

In applied marketing research, a longitudinal study that uses successive samples is called a **tracking study** because successive waves are designed to compare trends and identify changes in variables such as consumer satisfaction, brand image, or advertising awareness. These studies are useful for assessing aggregate trends but do not allow for tracking changes in individuals over time.

Conducting surveys in waves with two or more sample groups avoids the problem of response bias resulting from a prior interview. A respondent who was interviewed in an earlier survey about a certain brand may become more aware of the brand or pay more attention to its advertising after being interviewed. Using different samples eliminates this problem. However, researchers can never be sure whether the changes in the variable being measured are due to a different sample or to an actual change in the variable over time.

Consumer Panel

A longitudinal study that gathers data from the same sample of individuals or households over time is called a **consumer panel**. Consider the packaged-goods marketer that wishes to learn about brand-switching behavior. A consumer panel that consists of a group of people who record their purchasing habits in a diary over time will provide the manager with a continuous stream of information about the brand and product class. Diary data that are recorded regularly over an extended period enable the researcher to track repeat-purchase behavior and changes in purchasing habits that occur in response to changes in price, special promotions, or other aspects of marketing strategy.

TOTHEPOINT

Time is but the stream I go a-fishing in.
—Henry David Thoreau

Tracking study
A type of longitudinal study that uses successive samples to compare trends and identify changes in variables such as consumer satisfaction, brand image, or advertising awareness.

Consumer panel
A longitudinal survey of the same sample of individuals or households to record their attitudes, behavior, or purchasing habits over time.

Panel members may be contacted by telephone, in a personal interview, by mail questionnaire, or by e-mail. Typically respondents complete media exposure or purchase diaries and mail them back to the survey organization. If the panel members have agreed to field test new products, face-to-face or telephone interviews may be required. The nature of the problem dictates which communication method to use.

Because establishing and maintaining a panel is expensive, panels often are managed by contractors who offer their services to many organizations. A number of commercial firms, such as National Family Opinion (NFO), Inc., Market Research Corporation of America, and Consumer Mail Panels, Inc., specialize in maintaining consumer panels. In recent years Internet panels have grown in popularity. Because clients of these firms need to share the expenses with other clients to acquire longitudinal data at a reasonable cost, panel members may be asked questions about a number of product classes.

The first questionnaire a panel member is asked to complete typically includes questions about product ownership, product usage, pets, family members, and demographic data. The purpose of such a questionnaire is to gather the behavioral and demographic data that will be used to identify heavy buyers, difficult-to-reach customers, and so on for future surveys. Individuals who serve as members of consumer panels usually are compensated with cash, attractive gifts, or the chance to win a sweepstakes.

Marketers whose products are purchased by few households find panels an economical means of reaching respondents who own their products. A two-stage process typically is used. A panel composed of around 15,000 households can be screened with a one-question statement attached to another project. For example, a question in an NFO questionnaire screens for ownership of certain uncommon products, such as snowmobiles and motorcycles. This information is stored in a database. Then households with the unusual item can be sampled again with a longer questionnaire.

Total Quality Management and Customer Satisfaction Surveys

Total quality management
A business philosophy that emphasizes market-driven quality as a top organizational priority.

Total quality management is a business strategy that emphasizes market-driven quality as a top priority. Total quality management involves implementing and adjusting the firm's business activities to assure customers' satisfaction with the quality of goods and services.

Many U.S. organizations adopted total quality management in the 1980s when an increase in high-quality foreign competition challenged their former dominance. Today companies continue to recognize the need for total quality management programs. Executives and production workers are sometimes too far removed from the customer. Companies need a means to bridge this gap with feedback about quality of goods and services. This means marketing research. Of course, these programs are not the exclusive domain of marketing researchers. However, in an organization driven by the quality concept, marketing research plays an important role in the management of total product quality.

What Is Quality?

Organizations used to define quality by engineering standards. Most companies no longer see quality that way. Some managers say that having a quality product means that the good or service conforms to consumers' requirements, that the product is acceptable. Effective executives who subscribe to a total quality management philosophy, however, believe that the product's quality must go beyond acceptability for a given price range. Rather than merely being relieved that nothing went wrong, consumers should experience some delightful surprises or reap some unexpected benefits. In other words, quality assurance is more than just meeting minimum standards. The level of quality is the degree to which a good or service corresponds to buyers' expectations.

Obviously, an S-type Jaguar does not compete with a Nissan Altima. Buyers of these automobiles are in different market segments, and their expectations of quality differ widely. Nevertheless, managers at Jaguar and Nissan try to establish the quality levels their target markets expect and then to produce and market products that continually surpass expectations.

RESEARCHSNAPSHOT

Fairfax Library's Survey for Satisfaction

In Fairfax, Virginia, the Fairfax County Public Library (FCPL) uses surveys to gather data and improve the satisfaction of library users and the community at large—the taxpayers who pay the library's bills. Like most libraries, FCPL has long gathered usage data such as circulation statistics and number of patrons who visit each day, but it has more recently focused on outcomes including satisfaction with specific services and the library overall.

Every spring, FCPL posts a ten-question survey on its website. This Web Site User Survey asks users how easy the site is to navigate, what additional online services they would like, and whether they are satisfied with the website. Periodically, the library conducts face-to-face and telephone surveys of library users. These surveys gather descriptive information about visitors and ask what services they use, how aware they are of particular services, and how satisfied they are. Answers help the library correct problems and set budget priorities.

In a recent telephone survey, the library called a sample of community members to investigate whether changes it had made to its information services had affected use of the library. Answers to thirty-three questions helped the library pinpoint what services were being used and what attitudes they held toward the library. FCPL's librarians were pleased to learn that even nonusers of the library viewed it as a valuable part of the community.

Source: Based on Edwin S. Clay III and Patricia Bangs, "Beyond Numbers," Library Journal, January 1, 2006, downloaded from InfoTrac at http://www.galenet.com.

©PHOTODISC/GETTY IMAGES

Internal and External Customers

Organizations that have adopted the total quality management philosophy believe that a focus on customers must include more than external customers. Like Arbor, Inc., they believe that everyone in the organization has customers:

Every person, in every department, and at every level, has a customer. The customer is anyone to whom an individual provides service, information, support, or product. The customer may be another employee or department (internal) or outside the company (external).[14]

Total quality management programs work most effectively when every employee knows exactly who his or her customers are and what output internal and external customers expect. Also, it is important to know how customers perceive their needs are being met. All too often differences between perceptions and reality are not understood.

Implementing Total Quality Management

Implementing a total quality management program requires considerable survey research. A firm must routinely ask customers to rate it against its competitors. It must periodically measure employee knowledge, attitudes, and expectations. It must monitor company performance against benchmark standards. It must determine whether customers found any delightful surprises or major disappointments. In other words, a total quality management strategy expresses the conviction that to improve quality, an organization must regularly conduct surveys to evaluate quality improvement.

Exhibit 8.3 illustrates the total quality management process. The exhibit shows that overall tracking of quality improvement requires longitudinal research. The process begins with a *commitment and exploration stage,* during which management makes a commitment to total quality assurance and marketing researchers explore external and internal customers' needs and beliefs. The research must discover what product features customers value, what problems customers are having with the

EXHIBIT 8.3 **Longitudinal Research for Total Quality Management**

Time	Marketing Research Activity with External Consumers (Customers)	Marketing Management Activity	Marketing Research Activity with Internal Consumers (Employees)
Time 1 — Commitment and exploration stage	Exploratory study to determine the quality the customer wants, discover customer problems, and identify the importance of specific product attributes.	Establish marketing objective that the customer should define quality.	Exploratory study to determine (1) whether internal customers, such as service employees, are aware of the need for service quality as a major means to achieve customer satisfaction and (2) whether they know the quality standards for their jobs. Establish whether employees are motivated and trained. Identify road blocks that prevent employees from meeting customer needs.
Time 2 — Benchmarking stage	Benchmarking study to measure overall satisfaction and quality ratings of specific attributes.	Identify brand's position relative to competitors' satisfaction and quality rating; establish standards for customer satisfaction.	Benchmarking to measure employees' actual performance and perceptions about performance.
Time 3 — Initial quality improvement stage	Tracking wave 1 to measure trends in satisfaction and quality ratings.	Improve quality; reward performance.	Tracking wave 1 to measure and compare what is actually happening with what should be happening. Establish whether the company is conforming to its quality standards.
Time 4 — Continuous quality improvement	Tracking wave 2 to measure trends in satisfaction and quality ratings.	Improve quality; reward performance.	Tracking wave 2 to measure trends in quality improvement.

product, what aspects of product operation or customer service have disappointed customers, what the company is doing right, and what the company may be doing wrong.

After internal and external customers' problems and desires have been identified, the *benchmarking stage* begins. Research must establish quantitative measures that can serve as benchmarks or points of comparison against which to evaluate future efforts. The surveys must establish initial measures of overall satisfaction, of the frequency of customer problems, and of quality ratings for specific attributes. Researchers must identify the company's or brand's position relative to competitors' quality positions. For example, when Anthony Balzarini became food-service manager at Empire Health Services in Spokane, Washington, he became responsible for serving meals to the patients of the company's two hospitals, plus retail food service (sales to visitors and employees who eat in the hospitals). He began tracking quality according to several measures, including satisfaction scores on patient surveys and sales volume and revenue on the retail side. Sales measurements include comparing the average sale with other locations, including restaurants, in the Spokane area.[15]

The *initial quality improvement* stage establishes a quality improvement process within the organization. Management and employees must translate quality issues into the internal vocabulary of the organization. The company must establish performance standards and expectations for improvement. For Balzarini, this stage include training food-service employees in providing patient service. He began holding meetings twice daily to identify any problems to be resolved. Managers were each assigned to one floor of the hospital and charged with building a close working relationship with the nursing staff there. They are expected to visit their floor every week and conduct fifteen interviews with patients to learn about what they like and dislike. On the retail side, the manager is expected to revise menus every twelve weeks to offer more variety. Waste is literally weighed and categorized to identify which types of food are rejected by patients and customers.

After managers and employees have set quality objectives and implemented procedures and standards, the firm continues to track satisfaction and quality ratings in successive waves. The purpose of tracking wave 1 is to measure trends in satisfaction and quality ratings. Marketing researchers determine whether the organization is meeting customer needs as specified by quantitative standards. At one of Empire's two hospitals, one of the food-service managers learned that a patient on a liquid diet disliked the broth he was being served. An investigation showed that the recipe had been changed, and a taste test confirmed that the original recipe was superior, so the hospital switched back to the original recipe.

The next stage, *continuous quality improvement,* consists of many consecutive waves with the same purpose—to improve over the previous period. Continuous quality improvement requires that management allow employees to initiate problem solving without a lot of red tape. Employees should be able to initiate proactive communications with consumers. In tracking wave 2, management compares results with those of earlier stages. Quality improvement management continues. At Empire, improvements have been reflected in rising patient satisfaction scores and growing sales in retail operations.

Management must also reward performance. At Empire, Balzarini set up a program called "You Rock." Any employee who observes an excellent action by another employee, beyond mere job requirements, acknowledges the good work with a card awarding points redeemable in the hospitals' retail areas. Balzarini also sends weekly thank-you cards to workers who showed outstanding performance.

Exhibit 8.3 shows that total quality management programs measure performance against *customers'* standards—not against standards determined by quality engineers within the company. All changes within the organization are oriented toward improvement of customers' perceptions of quality. The exhibit indicates the need for integration of establishing consumer requirements, quantifying benchmark measures, setting objectives, conducting marketing research studies, and making adjustments in the organization to improve quality. Continuous quality improvement is an ongoing process.

The activities outlined in Exhibit 8.3 work for marketers of both goods and services. However, service products and customer services offered along with goods have some distinctive aspects. We will first discuss the quality of goods and then consider the quality of services.

In general, marketers of consumer and industrial goods track customer satisfaction to investigate customer perceptions of product quality by measuring perceptions of the product characteristics listed in Exhibit 8.4.[16] These studies measure whether a firm's perceptions about product characteristics conform to customers' expectations and how these perceptions change over time. For example, any customer satisfaction survey will investigate a good's performance by asking, "How well does the product perform its core function?" To determine the quality of a recycling lawn mower, a researcher might ask, "How well does the mower cut grass and eliminate the need for bagging clippings?" The researcher may ask questions to determine whether the product's quality of performance was a delightful surprise, something well beyond expected performance. Similar questions will cover the other major product characteristics.

Measuring service quality involves comparing expectations with performance. Consumers who perceive high service quality believe service providers matched their expectations. Time after time, studies have shown differences between what customers expected and what the service frontline, contact personnel delivered. Marketers who stress service quality strategies focus on the service encounter because service quality depends on what takes place during the service encounter.

EXHIBIT 8.4 Quality Dimensions for Goods and Services

Quality Dimension	Characteristic	Example
Goods		
Performance	The product performs its core function.	A razor gives a close shave.
Features	The product has auxiliary dimensions that provide secondary benefits.	A motor oil comes in a convenient package.
Conformance with specifications	There is a low incidence of defects.	A vineyard never sells spoiled wine.
Reliability	The product performs consistently.	A lawn mower works properly each time it is used.
Durability	The economic life of the product is within an acceptable range.	A motorcycle runs fine for many years.
Serviceability	The system for servicing the product is efficient, competent, and convenient.	A computer software manufacturer maintains a toll-free phone number staffed by technical people who can answer questions quickly and accurately.
Aesthetic design	The product's design makes it look and feel like a quality product.	A snowmobile is aerodynamic.
Services		
Access	Contact with service personnel is easy.	A visit to the dentist does not involve a long wait.
Communication	The customer is informed and understands the service and how much it will cost.	A computer technician explains needed repairs without using overly technical terms.
Competence	The service providers have the required skills.	A tax accountant has a CPA certification.
Courtesy	Personnel are polite and friendly.	Bank tellers smile and wish the customer a "good day" at the close of each transaction.
Reliability	The service is performed consistently and personnel are dependable.	Employees of the office cleaning service arrive on schedule every Friday evening after working hours.
Credibility	Service providers have integrity.	The doctor who is performing a heart transplant is trustworthy and believable.

Source: Adapted from David A. Aaker, *Managing Brand Equity* (New York: Macmillan, 1991), pp. 90–95.

In organizations that wish to improve service quality, managers must identify and analyze customer service needs and then establish specifications for the level of service. They must then train frontline personnel and give them the responsibility for quality service. Frontline personnel need to be motivated and encouraged to deliver the service according to these specifications. Finally, regular surveys with both external customers and internal employees measure results against standards.

Marketers investigate service quality to measure customer satisfaction and perceived quality in terms of the service attributes listed in Exhibit 8.4. Considerations in the actual measurement of quality of goods and service delivery are further addressed in Chapters 13, 14, and 15.

Summary

1. Define surveys, and explain their advantages. The survey is a common tool for asking respondents questions. Surveys can provide quick, inexpensive, and accurate information for a variety of objectives. The term *sample survey* is often used because a survey is expected to obtain a representative sample of the target population.

2. Describe the type of information that may be gathered in a survey. The typical survey is a descriptive research study with the objective of measuring awareness, product knowledge, brand usage behavior, opinions, attitudes, and so on.

3. Identify sources of error in survey research. Two major forms of error are common in survey research. The first, random sampling error, is caused by chance variation and results in a sample that is not absolutely representative of the target population. Such errors are inevitable, but they can be predicted using the statistical methods discussed in later chapters on sampling. The second major category of error, systematic error, takes several forms. Nonresponse error is caused by subjects' failing to respond to a survey. This type of error can be reduced by comparing the demographics of the sample population with those of the target population and making a special effort to contact underrepresented groups. In addition, response bias occurs when a response to a questionnaire is falsified or misrepresented, either intentionally or inadvertently. There are four specific categories of response bias: acquiescence bias, extremity bias, interviewer bias, and social desirability bias. An additional source of survey error comes from administrative problems such as inconsistencies in interviewers' abilities, cheating, coding mistakes, and so forth.

4. Distinguish among the various categories of surveys. Surveys may be classified according to methods of communication, by the degrees of structure and disguise in the questionnaires, and on a temporal basis. Questionnaires may be structured, with limited choices of responses, or unstructured, to allow open-ended responses. Disguised questions may be used to probe sensitive subjects. Surveys may consider the population at a given moment or follow trends over a period of time. The first approach, the cross-sectional study, usually is intended to separate the population into meaningful subgroups. The second type of study, the longitudinal study, can reveal important population changes over time. Longitudinal studies may involve contacting different sets of respondents or the same ones repeatedly. One form of longitudinal study is the consumer panel. Consumer panels are expensive to conduct, so firms often hire contractors who provide services to many companies, thus spreading costs over many clients.

5. Discuss the importance of survey research to total quality management programs. Total quality management is the process of implementing and adjusting a firm's business strategy to assure customers' satisfaction with the quality of goods or services. The level of quality is the degree to which a good or service corresponds to buyers' expectations. Marketing research provides companies with feedback about the quality of goods and services. Implementing a total quality management program requires considerable survey research, conducted routinely, to ask customers to rate a company against its competitors. It also measures employee attitudes and monitors company performance against benchmark standards. After identifying customer problems and desires, the firm tracks satisfaction and quality ratings in successive waves. Total quality management research is an ongoing process for continuous quality improvement that works for both marketers of goods and service providers.

Key Terms and Concepts

Respondents
Sample survey
Random sampling error
Systematic error
Sample bias
Respondent error
Nonresponse error
Nonrespondents
No contacts
Refusals

Self-selection bias
Response bias
Acquiescence bias
Extremity bias
Interviewer bias
Social desirability bias
Administrative error
Data processing error
Sample selection error
Interviewer error

Interviewer cheating
Structured question
Unstructured question
Undisguised questions
Disguised questions
Cross-sectional study
Longitudinal study
Tracking study
Consumer panel
Total quality management

Questions for Review and Critical Thinking

1. Name several nonbusiness applications of survey research.
2. What is *self-selection bias?*
3. Do surveys tend to gather qualitative or quantitative data? What types of information are commonly measured with surveys?
4. Give an example of each type of error listed in Exhibit 8.1.
5. In a survey, chief executive officers (CEOs) indicated that they would prefer to relocate their businesses to Atlanta (first choice), San Diego, Tampa, Los Angeles, or Boston. The CEOs who said they were going to build the required office space in the following year were asked where they were going to build. They indicated they were going to build in New York, Los Angeles, San Francisco, or Chicago. Explain the difference.
6. What potential sources of error might be associated with the following situations?
   a. In a survey of frequent fliers age fifty and older, researchers concluded that price does not play a significant role in airline travel because only 25 percent of the respondents check off price as the most important consideration in determining where and how they travel, while 35 percent rate price as being unimportant.
   b. A survey of voters finds that most respondents do not like negative political ads—that is, advertising by one political candidate that criticizes or exposes secrets about the opponent's "dirty laundry."
   c. Researchers who must conduct a 45-minute personal interview decide to offer $10 to each respondent because they believe that people who will sell their opinions are more typical than someone who will talk to a stranger for 45 minutes.
   d. A company's sales representatives are asked what percentage of the time they spend making presentations to prospects, traveling, talking on the telephone, participating in meetings, working on the computer, and engaging in other on-the-job activities.
   e. A survey comes with a Water Hardness Packet to test the hardness of the water in a respondent's home. The packet

includes a color chart and a plastic strip to dip into hot water. The respondent is given instructions in six steps on how to compare the color of the plastic strip with the color chart that indicates water hardness.

7. A sample of 14-year-old school children is asked if they have ever smoked a cigarette. The students are asked to respond orally in the presence of other students. What types of error might enter into this process?
8. A survey conducted by the National Endowment for the Arts asked, "Have you read a book within the last year?" What response bias might arise from this question?
9. Name some common objectives of cross-sectional surveys.
10. Give an example of a political situation in which longitudinal research might be useful. Name some common objectives for a longitudinal study in a business situation.
11. What are the advantages and disadvantages of using consumer panels?
12. Page through your local newspaper to find some stories derived from survey research results. Was the study's methodology appropriate? Could the research have been termed *advocacy research?*
13. Suppose you are the marketing research director for your state's tourism bureau. Assess the state's information needs, and identify the information you will collect in a survey of tourists who visit your state.
14. **ETHICS** A researcher sends out 2,000 questionnaires via email. Fifty are returned because the addresses are inaccurate. Of the 1,950 delivered questionnaires, 100 are completed and e-mailed back. However, 40 of these respondents wrote that they did not want to participate in the survey. The researcher indicates the response rate was 5.0 percent. Is this the right thing to do?
15. **'NET** Located at the University of Connecticut, the Roper Center is the largest library of public opinion data in the world. An online polling magazine and the methodology and findings of many surveys may be found at http://www.ropercenter. uconn.edu. Report on an article or study of your choice.

Research Activities

1. **'NET** Go to Survey Monkey (http://www.surveymonkey.com). Then, visit http://www.mysurvey.com. What is the difference between the two websites in terms of the services they provide to users?
2. **'NET** The National Longitudinal Surveys (NLS) conducted by the Bureau of Labor Statistics provide data on the labor force experience (current labor force and employment status, work history, and characteristics of current or last job) of five groups of the U.S. population. Go to http://www.bls.gov/opub/hom/homtoc.htm to

learn about the objectives and methodology for this study. How accurate do you believe the information reported here really is? What sources of error might be present in the data?

3. Ask a small sample of students at your local university to report their GPA. Then, try to find the average GPA of students at your school. If you have to, ask several professors to give their opinion. Does it seem that the student data are subject to error? Explain.

Case 8.1 SAT and ACT Writing Tests

The SAT and ACT college entrance exams once were completely multiple-choice, but both tests recently began including an essay portion (which is optional for the ACT). Some researchers have investigated how the essay tests are used by one group they serve: the admissions offices of the colleges that look at test results during the selection process.[17]

Early survey research suggests that some admissions officers harbor doubts about the essay tests. ACT, Inc. reported that among the schools it surveyed, only about one-fifth are requiring that applicants take the writing portion of the exam. Another one-fifth merely recommend (but don't require) the essay.

Kaplan, Inc., which markets test preparation services, conducted surveys as well. Kaplan asked 374 colleges whether they would be using the SAT writing test in screening candidates. Almost half (47 percent) said they would not use the essay at all. Another 22 percent said they would use it but give it less weight than the math and verbal SAT scores.

Kaplan also surveys students who take the exams for which it provides training. On its website, the company says, "More than 25 percent of students ran out of time on the essay!"

Questions

1. What survey objectives would ACT have in asking colleges how they use its essay test? What objectives would Kaplan have for its survey research?
2. If you were a marketer for the College Board (the SAT's company) or ACT, Inc., what further information would you want to gather after receiving the results described here?
3. What sources of error or response bias might be present in the surveys described here?

Case 8.2 Turner's Department Store

Turner's had been in business for forty-seven years. The first store was located downtown, but the organization had been expanding over the years. The local department store chain operated ten department stores and junior department stores, ranging in size from 10,000 to 60,000 square feet. All stores were located in a single metropolitan area with a population of approximately 600,000 people. The firm's volume strength was in soft goods, although it also handled housewares and small appliances in all stores as well as major appliances in some stores. Price savings on name brands were the primary emphasis of Turner's merchandising strategy.

Turner's was considering its first major venture into survey research. Mr. Clay Turner, executive vice president, had indicated that "we want to find out what customers and noncustomers think about us and to learn what directions we may take to gain a bigger share of the market." He sent a list of research needs (see Case Exhibit 8.2–1) to several marketing research consultants.

Questions

1. Has the marketing research problem been adequately defined?
2. What type of survey would you recommend?
3. What sources of survey error are most likely in this project?
4. Prepare a brief research proposal for this project.

Note: Names are fictitious to ensure confidentiality.

CASE EXHIBIT 8.2–1 Research Needs for Turner's Department Stores

We're not looking for praise or compliments, but as honest an appraisal as possible. The questions contained here are merely suggestions and may be amplified, condensed, or changed as need be to arrive at a summary that can be acted on.

What Turner's wants to know is "How do people look upon Turner's, and what should we do to merit more of their patronage?" We will appreciate having from you

1. Your suggested questionnaire
2. Sampling size or sizes
3. Degree of expected accuracy
4. Cost or costs
5. Time frame in which the study may be completed
6. Type of summary or summaries to be presented on completion
7. Recommendations for action

Perhaps the study should encompass all or part of the following:

1. A sampling sufficient to give an overall picture
2. The sampling to be divided as equally as possible among people who shop frequently at Turner's and those who shop at Turner's occasionally, seldom, or never

3. The sampling to be done at various income levels, as equitably as possible in relationship of the specific income levels to the total, perhaps
   $8,000–$15,000
   $15,000–$35,000
   $35,000–$55,000
   $55,000–$75,000
   Over $75,000
4. The sampling to be done by age level breakdown: under 25, 25–35, 35–44, over 44
5. The sampling to include family composition: ages of children, if any, and number of boys and girls
6. To determine from those who shop often or occasionally at Turner's, what departments they depend on. (Examples: men's apparel; women's apparel, sportswear, hosiery, accessories; cosmetics and fragrances; men's, women's, and children's shoes; costume jewelry; fabrics, linens, sheets, towels, bedspreads, draperies; small appliances; major appliances; housewares; giftware; china; glassware; lamps; radios and televisions; boys', girls', infants' wear.)

(continued)

CASE EXHIBIT 8.2-1 **Research Needs for Turner's Department Stores** (*continued*)

7. Some idea of readership of Turner's newspaper advertising, preferably among various income levels.
8. How people perceive us in relation to other local retail firms (Sears, Macy's, JC Penney's, Kmart, Bloomingdale's);
    Turner's merchandise is most like: _____
    Turner's fashions are most like: _____
    Turner's prices are most like: _____
    Turner's stores look most like: _____
    Turner's advertising is most like: _____
    Turner's prices are as low or lower than: _____
9. Turner's salespeople are: helpful _____ courteous _____ discourteous _____ not helpful _____
10. Of those who do not shop at Turner's: "I would shop more at Turner's if _____ ."
11. Turner's advertising is: informative _____ not informative _____ sometimes honest _____ not accurate _____
12. Do you think Turner's carries a large number of well-known brands?
13. Among those who shop often at Turner's: Do you shop most at the nearest Turner's store? Or do you go to another Turner's? Which one?
14. When you go to Turner's with a specific purchase in mind, do you usually find it in stock? (This applies particularly to everyday items such as hosiery, underwear, jeans, housewares, small appliances, etc.)
15. If the respondent has a Turner's charge account: Is charge authorization prompt?
16. When did you last shop at Turner's? (A week ago, a month ago, 3 months ago)
17. If the respondent has previously shopped at Turner's, but no longer does so, is it because of a bad experience? Credit? Exchange, refund, or adjustment of a merchandise purchase?
18. Turner's values are: _____ excellent _____ good _____ fair _____ poor
19. Turner's carries: some irregulars and seconds _____ many irregulars and seconds _____ all first quality
20. I believe seconds and irregulars offer excellent value: yes _____ no _____

Video Case 8.3 The Walker Information Group

The Walker Information Group is one of the fifteen largest marketing research companies in the world. The Walker Group's total revenue tops that of such well-known names as J. D. Power and Associates, Roper, and Yankelovich Partners. Walker's clients include many Fortune 500 and Blue Chip industry leaders such as Cummins Engine Company, Lenscrafters, Continental Cablevision, Florida Power and Light, and Oglethorpe Power Corporation.

The Indianapolis-based company was founded in 1939 as a field interviewing service by Tommie Walker, mother of Frank Walker, the current chairman and chief executive officer of the organization. In the 1920s Tommie Walker's late husband worked for a bank that was considering sponsoring an Indianapolis radio show featuring classical music. The bank wanted to know who was listening to this show. Tommie was hired to do the interviewing, and she threw herself into the work. After that, referrals brought her more interviewing work for surveys. During an interview with a woman whose husband was a district sales manager for the A&P grocery chain, she learned that A&P was looking for a surveyor in the Midwest. A&P's sales manager liked Tommie, but wouldn't hire anyone without a formal company, a field staff, and insurance. Tommie founded Walker Marketing Research on October 20, 1939, and her business with A&P lasted seventeen years.

Today, the Walker Group specializes in business, health care, and consumer research, as well as database marketing. The company is organized into six strategic business units.

Walker Market Research and Analysis conducts traditional market research services that range from questionnaire design and data collection to advanced analysis and consultation. Walker has expertise in helping companies measure how their actions are perceived by the audiences most important to them, and how these perceptions affect their image, reputation, corporate citizenship, recruiting, sales, and more.

Data Source is a business unit that primarily is concerned with data collection and processing data. It specializes in telephone data collection.

Customer Satisfaction Measurement (CSM), as the name implies, specializes in measuring customer satisfaction and in helping clients improve their relationship with customers.

CSM Worldwide Network spans more than fifty countries. It is the first international network of professional research and consulting businesses dedicated to customer satisfaction measurement and management. The CSM Worldwide Network assures that multicountry customer satisfaction research is consistent by taking into account local conditions and cultural norms. Network members are trained to use consistent methods that allow standardization and comparability of information from country to country.

Walker Direct designs and develops databases and implements direct-marketing programs that help generate leads for businesses and raise funds for nonprofit organizations.

Walker Clinical is a health-care product use research company. Walker helps pharmaceutical, medical-device, and consumer-product manufacturers test how well new products work and how customers like them.

Questions

1. What type of custom survey research projects might Walker Market Research and Analysis conduct for its clients?
2. What stages are involved in conducting a survey? For which stages might a client company hire a research supplier like Walker Marketing Research and Analysis? Data Source?
3. What is the purpose of customer satisfaction measurement?
4. What measures, other than findings from surveys, might a company use to evaluate the effectiveness of a total quality management program?

CHAPTER 9
SURVEY RESEARCH: BASIC METHODS OF COMMUNICATION WITH RESPONDENTS

After studying this chapter, you should be able to

1. Summarize ways researchers gather information through interviews
2. Compare the advantages and disadvantages of conducting door-to-door, mall intercept, and telephone interviews
3. Evaluate the advantages and disadvantages of distributing questionnaires through the mail, the Internet, and by other means
4. Discuss the importance of pretesting questionnaires
5. Describe ethical issues that arise in survey research

Chapter Vignette: LinkedIn Surveys Customers Where They Are: Online

"It's not what you know but who you know" is a saying that may exaggerate, but most people agree with the idea that having a network of friends and colleagues can help them get a job, make a sale, and meet other objectives. Thanks to the Internet, more and more networking is happening online, sometimes through services like LinkedIn.[1] The 5 million members of this network have registered and provided facts about their work history, interests, and individuals they know. This last category of information is the key to how LinkedIn works; rather than making information available to everyone, the service lets you contact the people you already know and ask for an introduction to someone *they* know.

©PHOTODISC/GETTY IMAGES

LinkedIn grows through referrals, not advertising, so the company's marketing challenges involve identifying ways to make the site more attractive and useful. At one point, LinkedIn was considering ways to attract members to sign up for more features. Cofounder Konstantin Guericke thought users might like to add photographs to their profiles, but he wasn't sure whether users would value that service, so he decided to conduct a user survey.

Where best to reach users of an online service? On the Internet, of course. Guericke envisioned a survey that identified a set of possible new features for LinkedIn and asked users to choose the ideas they liked. For this simple survey instrument, he went to a service called Zoomerang, which provided the software for LinkedIn to prepare the online survey, send it to LinkedIn subscribers, and tally the results. LinkedIn quickly learned that half of its users wanted to be able to post photos, but far more (80 percent) wanted a search function that would help them look for people they had once worked with. Just a month later, LinkedIn added a search feature and other services the survey identified as popular.

Media Used to Communicate with Respondents

During most of the twentieth century, obtaining survey data involved inviting individuals to answer questions asked by human interviewers (interviews) or questions they read themselves (questionnaires). Interviewers communicated with respondents face-to-face or over the telephone, or respondents filled out self-administered paper questionnaires, which were typically distributed by mail. These media for conducting surveys remain popular with marketing researchers. However, as we mentioned in Chapters 2 and 7, digital technology is having a profound impact on society in general and on marketing research in particular. Its greatest impact is in the creation of new forms of communications media.

Human Interactive Media and Electronic Interactive Media

When two people engage in a conversation, human interaction takes place. Human interactive media are a personal form of communication. One human being directs a message to and interacts with another individual (or a small group). When most people think of interviewing, they envision two people engaged in a face-to-face dialogue or a conversation on the telephone.

Electronic interactive media allow marketers to reach a large audience, personalize individual messages, and interact using digital technology. To a large extent, electronic interactive media are controlled by the users themselves. No other human need be present. Survey respondents today are not passive audience members. They are actively involved in a two-way communication using electronic interactive media.

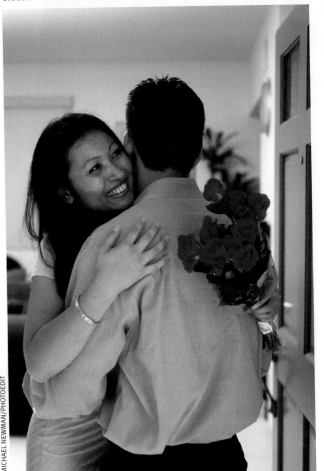

Electronic dating services have become a popular, successful example of electronic interactive media.

©MICHAEL NEWMAN/PHOTOEDIT

The Internet is radically altering many organizations' research strategies, providing a prominent example of the new electronic interactive media. Consumers determine what information they will be exposed to by choosing what sites to visit and by blocking or closing annoying pop-up ads. Electronic interactive media also include CD-ROM and DVD materials, touch-tone telephone systems, touch-screen interactive kiosks in stores, and other forms of digital technology.

Noninteractive Media

The traditional questionnaire received by mail and completed by the respondent does not allow a dialogue or an exchange of information providing immediate feedback. So, from our perspective, self-administered questionnaires printed on paper are noninteractive. This fact does not mean that they are without merit, just that this type of survey is less flexible than surveys using interactive communication media.

Each technique for conducting surveys has merits and shortcomings. The purpose of this chapter is to explain when researchers should use different types of surveys. The chapter begins with a discussion of surveys that use live interviews. Then we turn to noninteractive, self-administered questionnaires. Finally, we explain how the Internet and digital technology are dramatically changing survey research.

RESEARCHSNAPSHOT

M:Metrics Finds Consumers on the Web and on the Phone

Cellphones are used for so much more than simply sending and receiving phone calls. Marketers who peddle these phones or deliver content ("mobile media") to them want to know how consumers are using them. Some of these marketers are getting answers from M:Metrics.

M:Metrics combines data from monitoring software installed on phones in a sample group with monthly interviews of cellphone owners. Where to find these consumers, who may not even have a landline listed in the phone directory? M:Metrics uses an online survey. For some types of products, getting a representative group of users online might be difficult. But cellphone owners aren't likely to be technologically backward, so it's not too hard to put together the monthly sample of more than 20,000 consumers.

What can M:Metrics' customers learn? The combination of monitoring and survey results provides demographic and usage data. For one thing, those data show that games are important.

About one-third of men and a similar share of women play games on their phones at least once a month. About as many sent and received text messages. Other popular activities include retrieving news or information with a web browser and buying ringtones. Most visited mobile-media sites include ESPN Sports News, Yahoo!, and Google.

Sources: Based on Michael Myser, "Market Research: How M:Metrics Is Making Mobile Content Count," Business 2.0, downloaded from InfoTrac at http://www.galenet.com; M:Metrics, "M:Metrics Reports that in Battle of Portals Yahoo! Has Early Lead in Mobile Domain," news release, January 30, 2006, www.mmetrics.com; and M:Metrics, "Mobile Market Measurement," "Services" page of M:Metrics website, http://www.mmetrics.com, accessed February 14, 2006.

©DIGITAL VISION/GETTY IMAGES

Personal Interviews

To conduct interviews, the researcher may communicate with individuals in person by going door-to-door or intercepting them in shopping malls, or interviews may take place over the telephone. Traditionally, researchers have recorded interview results using paper and pencil, but computers are increasingly supporting survey research. In this section, we examine the general characteristics of face-to-face personal interviews, then compare the characteristics of door-to-door personal interviews and personal interviews conducted in shopping malls. The next section examines telephone interviews.

Although the history of marketing research is sketchy, gathering information through face-to-face contact with individuals goes back many years. Periodic censuses were used to set tax rates and aid military conscription in the ancient empires of Egypt and Rome.[2] During the Middle Ages, the merchant families of Fugger and Rothschild prospered in part because their far-flung organizations enabled them to get information before their competitors could.[3] Today, survey researchers typically present themselves in shopping centers and street corners throughout the United States and announce, "Good afternoon, my name is _____. I am with _____ Marketing Research Company, and we are conducting a survey on _____."

A **personal interview** is a form of direct communication in which an interviewer asks respondents questions face-to-face. This versatile and flexible method is a two-way conversation between interviewer and respondent.

Personal interview
Face-to-face communication in which an interviewer asks a respondent to answer questions.

Advantages of Personal Interviews

Marketing researchers find that personal interviews offer many unique advantages. One of the most important is the opportunity for feedback.

RESEARCHSNAPSHOT

General Social Survey Goes Face-to-Face

Are you happy? If you believe you have more problems than you once did, you have some company in the United States. In 2004 the Chicago-based National Opinion Research Center (NORC) asked 1,340 people about negative life events and compared their answers with responses to the same questions in 1991. The share of people reporting at least one significant negative life event rose from 88 percent in 1991 to 92 percent in 2004. Problems most often involved inability to afford health care, growing bills to pay, unemployment, and difficulties with relationships. Of course, many people are happy in spite of their problems.

The people who described negative life events were a sub-sample of NORC's General Social Survey. In that survey, NORC has been gathering data through personal interviews since 1972. The center conducted the survey once a year until 1994, when it began gathering data every two years. The survey includes topics on behaviors such as alcohol and marijuana use and membership in institutions, as well as attitudes on a variety of subjects, including crime and punishment, confidence in institutions, and race relations. The study's goals include observing trends in American society, many of which are relevant to marketers. For example, the study has found strong trends toward greater support for racial equality and civil liberties.

The General Social Survey takes ninety minutes on average to complete, yet NORC's research team has achieved response rates of 70 percent and higher. For a survey of this length and to obtain high participation, personal interviews are important, even though this interview format is relatively expensive.

©BRAND X PICTURES/JUPITER IMAGES

Sources: Based on Sharon Jayson, "Unhappiness Has Risen in the Past Decade," USA Today, January 9, 2006, http://www.usatoday.com; and National Opinion Research Center (NORC), "General Social Survey: GSS Study Description" and "General Social Survey: Study FAQs," Projects page of NORC website, http://www.norc.org, accessed February 14, 2006.

OPPORTUNITY FOR FEEDBACK

Personal interviews provide the opportunity for feedback and clarification. For example, if a consumer is reluctant to provide sensitive information, the interviewer may offer reassurance that his or her answers will be strictly confidential. Personal interviews offer the lowest chance that respondents will misinterpret questions, because an interviewer who senses confusion can clarify the instruction or questions. Circumstances may dictate that at the conclusion of the interview, the respondent be given additional information concerning the purpose of the study. This clarification is easily accomplished with a personal interview. If the feedback indicates that some question or set of questions is particularly confusing, the researcher can make changes that make the questionnaire easier to understand.

PROBING COMPLEX ANSWERS

Another important characteristic of personal interviews is the opportunity to follow up by probing. If a respondent's answer is too brief or unclear, the researcher may request a more comprehensive or clearer explanation. In probing, the interviewer asks for clarification with standardized questions such as "Can you tell me more about what you had in mind?" (See Chapter 6 on qualitative research for an expanded discussion of probing.) Although interviewers are expected to ask questions exactly as they appear on the questionnaire, probing allows them some flexibility. Depending on the research purpose, personal interviews vary in the degree to which questions are structured and in the amount of probing required. The personal interview is especially useful for obtaining unstructured information. Skilled interviewers can handle complex questions that cannot easily be asked in telephone or mail surveys.

LENGTH OF INTERVIEW

If the research objective requires an extremely lengthy questionnaire, personal interviews may be the only option. A general rule of thumb on mail surveys is that they should not exceed six pages, and telephone interviews typically last less than ten minutes. In contrast, a personal interview can be much longer, perhaps an hour and a half. However, the longer the interview, no matter what the form, the more the respondent should be compensated for their time and participation. Researchers should also be clear about how long participation should take in the opening dialog requesting participation. Online surveys should include a completion meter that shows the progress a respondent has made toward completing the task.

COMPLETENESS OF QUESTIONNAIRE

The social interaction between a well-trained interviewer and a respondent in a personal interview increases the likelihood that the respondent will answer all the items on the questionnaire. The respondent who grows bored with a telephone interview may terminate the interview at his or her discretion simply by hanging up the phone. Self-administration of a mail questionnaire requires even more effort by the respondent. Rather than write lengthy responses, the respondent may fail to complete some of the questions. Item nonresponse—failure to provide an answer to a question—is least likely to occur when an experienced interviewer asks questions directly.

Item nonresponse
Failure of a respondent to provide an answer to a survey question.

PROPS AND VISUAL AIDS

Interviewing respondents face-to-face allows the investigator to show them new product samples, sketches of proposed advertising, or other visual aids. When Lego Group wanted to introduce new train model sets for its famous building bricks, the company targeted adults who build complex models with its product. The company invited adults who were swapping ideas at the Lego website to visit the New York office, where they viewed ideas and provided their opinions. The respondents wound up rejecting all the company's ideas, but they suggested something different: the Santa Fe Super Chief set, which sold out within two weeks, after being advertised only by enthusiastic word of mouth.[4] This research could not have been done in a telephone interview or mail survey.

Marketing research that uses visual aids has become increasingly popular with researchers who investigate film concepts, advertising problems, and moviegoers' awareness of performers. Research for movies often begins by showing respondents videotapes of the prospective cast. After the movie has been produced, film clips are shown and interviews conducted to evaluate the movie's appeal, especially which scenes to emphasize in advertisements.

HIGH PARTICIPATION

Although some people are reluctant to participate in a survey, the presence of an interviewer generally increases the percentage of people willing to complete the interview. Respondents typically are required to do no reading or writing—all they have to do is talk. Many people enjoy sharing information and insights with friendly and sympathetic interviewers. People are often more hesitant to tell a person "no" face-to-face than they are over the phone or through some impersonal contact.

Disadvantages of Personal Interviews

Personal interviews also have some disadvantages. Respondents are not anonymous and as a result may be reluctant to provide confidential information to another person. Suppose a survey asked top executives, "Do you see any major internal instabilities or threats (people, money, material, and so on) to the achievement of your marketing objectives?" Many managers may be reluctant to answer this sensitive question honestly in a personal interview in which their identities are known.

INTERVIEWER INFLUENCE

Some evidence suggests that demographic characteristics of the interviewer influence respondents' answers. For example, one research study revealed that male interviewers produced larger amounts of interviewer variance than female interviewers in a survey in which 85 percent of the respondents were female. Older interviewers who interviewed older respondents produced more variance than other age combinations, whereas younger interviewers who interviewed younger respondents produced the least variance.

Differential interviewer techniques may be a source of bias. The rephrasing of a question, the interviewer's tone of voice, and the interviewer's appearance may influence the respondent's answer. Consider the interviewer who has conducted 100 personal interviews. During the next one, he or she may lose concentration and either selectively perceive or anticipate the respondent's answer. The interpretation of the response may differ somewhat from what the respondent intended. Typically, the public thinks of the person who does marketing research as a dedicated scientist. Unfortunately, some interviewers do not fit that ideal. Considerable interviewer variability exists. Cheating is possible; interviewers may cut corners to save time and energy, faking parts of their reports by dummying up part or all of the questionnaire. Control over interviewers is important to ensure that difficult, embarrassing, or time-consuming questions are handled properly.

■ LACK OF ANONYMITY OF RESPONDENT

Because a respondent in a personal interview is not anonymous and may be reluctant to provide confidential information to another person, researchers often spend considerable time and effort to phrase sensitive questions to avoid social desirability bias. For example, the interviewer may show the respondent a card that lists possible answers and ask the respondent to read a category number rather than be required to verbalize sensitive answers.

■ COST

Personal interviews are expensive, generally substantially more costly than mail, Internet, or telephone surveys. The geographic proximity of respondents, the length and complexity of the questionnaire, and the number of people who are nonrespondents because they could not be contacted (not-at-homes) will all influence the cost of the personal interview.

Door-to-Door Interviews and Shopping Mall Intercepts

Personal interviews may be conducted at the respondents' homes or offices or in many other places. Increasingly, personal interviews are being conducted in shopping malls. Mall intercept interviews allow many interviews to be conducted quickly. Often, respondents are intercepted in public areas of shopping malls and then asked to come to a permanent research facility to taste new food items or to view advertisements. The locale for the interview generally influences the participation rate, and thus the degree to which the sample represents the general population.

■ DOOR-TO-DOOR INTERVIEWS

Door-to-door interviews
Personal interviews conducted at respondents' doorsteps in an effort to increase the participation rate in the survey.

The presence of an interviewer at the door generally increases the likelihood that a person will be willing to complete an interview. Because **door-to-door interviews** increase the participation rate, they provide a more representative sample of the population than mail questionnaires. For example, response rates to mail surveys are substantially lower among Hispanics whether the questionnaire is printed in English or Spanish.[5] People who do not have telephones, who have unlisted telephone numbers, or who are otherwise difficult to contact may be reached using door-to-door interviews. However, door-to-door interviews may underrepresent some groups and overrepresent others based on the geographic areas covered.

Door-to-door interviews may exclude individuals who live in multiple-dwelling units with security systems, such as high-rise apartment dwellers, or executives who are too busy to grant personal interviews during business hours. Other people, for security reasons, simply will not open the door when a stranger knocks. Telephoning an individual in one of these subgroups to make an appointment may make the total sample more representative. However, obtaining a representative sample of this security-conscious subgroup based on a listing in the telephone directory may be difficult. For these reasons, door-to-door interviews are becoming a thing of the past.

■ CALLBACKS

Callbacks
Attempts to recontact individuals selected for a sample who were not available initially.

When a person selected to be in the sample cannot be contacted on the first visit, a systematic procedure is normally initiated to call back at another time. **Callbacks**, or attempts to recontact individuals selected for the sample, are the major means of reducing nonresponse error. Calling

RESEARCHSNAPSHOT

Matters of Taste

Asking an opinion is easy to do over the phone or online, but not if you want people's reactions to a new food, wine, or perfume. For those opinions, you probably want people to sample the new product first. And for best results, they need to try it away from odors that could mask or alter the experience. As a result, researchers arrange for sensory evaluations to take place along with personal interviews, often using the mall intercept format.

By listening to consumers drawn from a mall intercept, marketers can hear the way consumers react to a product. Sometimes researchers simply want to know whether consumers like the product; in other situations, they are trying to meet objectives such as maintaining the same taste after substituting a new ingredient. Sartori Foods uses a chart it calls the Italian Cheese Flavor Wheel to ask consumers to describe various cheeses. The chart matches consumer-friendly terms like *nutty, buttery,* and *creamy* with terms useful in the industry (for example, *aromatic amino acids* and *sulfur compounds*). Other research projects involve a specialized set of subjects who have been trained to discuss wine, cheese, or perfume using technical language.

For sensory research, finding qualified participants is more complicated than for other kinds of interviews. Besides knowing whether individuals buy the category of product, researchers want to eliminate anyone who has a cold, smokes, or has other conditions that could interfere with taste and smell. Sometimes the problem goes beyond screening. A team of researchers who traveled to Venezuela for research discovered that the hosts of the testing room had beautified it with a fresh coat of paint—and the paint odor made the room unusable.

Sources: Based on Claudia D. O'Donnell, "Tips for Sensory Tests," Prepared Foods, January 2005, downloaded from InfoTrac at http://www.galenet.com; Fran LaBell, "International Sensory Tests: When in Rome," Prepared Foods, February 2002, downloaded from Business & Company Resource Center, http://galenet.galegroup.com; and Paula Frank, "Sensory Analysis: An Invaluable Tool," Dairy Field, January 2002, http://galenet.galegroup.com.

©FOODPIX/JUPITER IMAGES

back a sampling unit is more expensive than interviewing the person the first time around, because subjects who initially were not at home generally are more widely dispersed geographically than the original sample units. Callbacks in door-to-door interviews are important because not-at-home individuals (for example, working parents) may systematically vary from those who *are* at home (nonworking parents, retired people, and the like).

■ MALL INTERCEPT INTERVIEWS

Personal interviews conducted in shopping malls are referred to as **mall intercept interviews,** or *shopping center sampling.* Interviewers typically intercept shoppers at a central point within the mall or at an entrance. The main reason mall intercept interviews are conducted is because their costs are lower. No travel is required to the respondent's home; instead, the respondent comes to the interviewer, and many interviews can be conducted quickly in this way.

A major problem with mall intercept interviews is that individuals usually are in a hurry to shop, so the incidence of refusal is high—typically around 50 percent. Yet, the commercial marketing research industry conducts more personal interviews in shopping malls than it conducts door-to-door.

In a mall interview, the researcher must recognize that he or she should not be looking for a representative sample of the total population. Each mall has its own target market's characteristics, and there is likely to be a larger bias than with careful household probability sampling. However, personal interviews in shopping malls are appropriate when the target group is a special market segment such as the parents of children of bike-riding age. If the respondent indicates that he or she has a child of this age, the parent can then be brought into a rented space and shown several bikes. The mall intercept interview allows the researcher to show large, heavy, or immobile visual materials, such as a television commercial. A mall interviewer can give an individual a product to take home to use and obtain a commitment that the respondent will cooperate when recontacted later by telephone. Mall intercept interviews are also valuable when activities such as cooking and tasting of food must be closely coordinated and timed to follow each other. They may also be appropriate when a consumer durable product must be demonstrated. For example, when videocassette

Mall intercept interviews
Personal interviews conducted in a shopping mall.

recorders and DVD players were innovations in the prototype stage, the effort and space required to set up and properly display these units ruled out in-home testing.

Global Considerations

Willingness to participate in a personal interview varies dramatically around the world. For example, in many Middle Eastern countries women would never consent to be interviewed by a man. And in many countries the idea of discussing grooming behavior and personal-care products with a stranger would be highly offensive. Few people would consent to be interviewed on such topics.

The norms about appropriate business conduct also influence businesspeople's willingness to provide information to interviewers. For example, conducting business-to-business interviews in Japan during business hours is difficult because managers, strongly loyal to their firm, believe that they have an absolute responsibility to oversee their employees while on the job. In some cultures when a businessperson is reluctant to be interviewed, a reputable third party may be asked to intervene so that an interview may take place.

Telephone Interviews

Good evening, I'm with a nationwide marketing research company. Are you watching television tonight?
A: Yes.
Did you see 60 minutes on CBS?
A: "Click"

Telephone interviews
Personal interviews conducted by telephone, the mainstay of commercial survey research.

For several decades, **telephone interviews** have been the mainstay of commercial survey research. The quality of data obtained by telephone may be comparable to the quality of the data collected in personal interviews. Respondents are more willing to provide detailed and reliable information on a variety of personal topics over the telephone than with personal interviews. Telephone surveys can provide representative samples of the general U.S. population in the United States. Conducting telephone interviews may be less possible in developed nations, although the widespread adoption of mobile phones is certain changing the telephone interview landscape. Additionally, the recent no-call laws discussed earlier limit the ability to generate a representative sample.

Characteristics of Telephone Interviews

Telephone interviews have several distinctive characteristics that set them apart from other survey techniques. These characteristics present significant advantages and disadvantages for the researcher.

■ SPEED

One advantage of telephone interviewing is the speed of data collection. While data collection with mail or personal interviews can take several weeks, hundreds of telephone interviews can be conducted literally overnight. When the interviewer enters the respondents' answers directly into a computerized system, the data processing speeds up even more.

■ COST

As the cost of personal interviews continues to increase, telephone interviews are becoming relatively inexpensive. The cost of telephone interviews is estimated to be less than 25 percent of the cost of door-to-door personal interviews. Travel time and costs are eliminated. However, the typical Internet survey is less expensive than a telephone survey.

ABSENCE OF FACE-TO-FACE CONTACT

Telephone interviews are more impersonal than face-to-face interviews. Respondents may answer embarrassing or confidential questions more willingly in a telephone interview than in a personal interview. However, mail and Internet surveys, although not perfect, are better media for gathering extremely sensitive information because they seem more anonymous. Some evidence suggests that people provide information on income and other financial matters only reluctantly, even in telephone interviews. Such questions may be personally threatening for a variety of reasons, and high refusal rates for this type of question occur with each form of survey research.

Although telephone calls may be less threatening because the interviewer is not physically present, the absence of face-to-face contact can also be a liability. The respondent cannot see that the interviewer is still writing down the previous comment and may continue to elaborate on an answer. If the respondent pauses to think about an answer, the interviewer may not realize it and may go on to the next question. Hence, there is a greater tendency for interviewers to record no answers and incomplete answers in telephone interviews than in personal interviews.

COOPERATION

One trend is very clear. In the last few decades, telephone response rates have fallen. Analysis of response rates for the long-running Survey of Consumer Attitudes conducted by the University of Michigan found that response rates fell from a high of 72 percent to 67 percent during the period from 1979 to 1996 and then even faster after 1996, dropping to 60 percent.[6] Lenny Murphy of data collection firm Dialtek says he has observed a decline in survey response rates from a typical range of 30 to 40 percent in the past down to below 20 percent.[7] Fewer calls are answered because more households are using caller ID and answering machines to screen their calls, and many individuals do not pick up the phone when the display reads "out of area" or when an unfamiliar survey organization's name and number appear on the display. Also, more phone lines are dedicated to fax machines and computers. However, the University of Michigan study found that the rate of refusal actually grew faster in the more recent period than the rate of not answering researchers' calls.

One way researchers can try to improve response rates is to leave a message on the household's telephone answering machine or voice mail. However, many people will not return a call to help someone conduct a survey. Using a message explicitly stating that the purpose of the call is not sales related may improve responses. Other researchers simply hope to reach respondents when they call back, trying callbacks at different times and on different days.

Further complicating the situation is the use of wireless mobile phone services.[8] Regulations by the Federal Communications Commission make it illegal for researchers to use automated dialing equipment to call mobile phones. Even if researchers dial the calls by hand, they may not contact anyone who would have to pay for the call—that is, most cellphone users. So far, only a small share of U.S. households (less than 4 percent) have given up their landlines, but those numbers are growing, and they include a sizable segment of young adults. Worse for marketers, consumers may keep their phone numbers when they change to a new phone company, so many consumers who have abandoned landlines for cellphones may be keeping a phone number that marketers may no longer dial without penalty.

Other countries may not adopt laws restricting calls to mobile phones. In addition, consumers in other countries are more open to responding to research delivered by voice or by text messaging. Thus, the mobile phone may be a better interview tool outside of the United States than in the United States.

Refusal to cooperate with interviews is directly related to interview length. A major study of survey research found that interviews of 5 minutes or less had a refusal rate of 21 percent; interviews of between 6 and 12 minutes had 41 percent refusal rates; and interviews of 13 minutes or more had 47 percent rates. In unusual cases, a few highly interested respondents will put up with longer interviews. A good rule of thumb is to keep telephone interviews approximately 10 to 15 minutes long. In general, 30 minutes is the maximum amount of time most respondents will spend unless they are highly interested in the survey subject.

Another way to encourage participation is to send households an invitation to participate in a survey. The invitation can describe the purpose and importance of the survey and the likely duration of the survey. The invitation can also encourage subjects to be available and reassure them that the caller will not try to sell anything. In a recent study comparing response rates, the rates were highest among households that received an advance letter, somewhat lower when the notice came on a postcard, and lowest when no notice was sent.[9]

INCENTIVES TO REPOND

Respondents should receive some incentive to respond. Research addresses different types of incentives. For telephone interviews, test-marketing involving different types of survey introduciton suggests that not all introductions are equally effective. A financial incentive or some significant chance to win a desirable prize will produce a higher telephone response rate than a simple assurance that the research is not a sales pitch, a more detailed description of the survey or an assurance of confidentiality.[10]

REPRESENTATIVE SAMPLES

Practical difficulties complicate obtaining representative samples based on listings in the telephone book. About 95 percent of households in the United States have landline telephones. People without phones are more likely to be poor, aged, rural, or living in the South. Unlisted phone numbers and numbers too new to be printed in the directory are a greater problem. People have unlisted phone numbers for two reasons:

- They have recently moved
- They prefer to have unlisted numbers for privacy

Individuals whose phone numbers are unlisted because of a recent move differ slightly from those with published numbers. The unlisted group tends to be younger, more urban, and less likely to own a single-family dwelling. Households that maintain unlisted phone numbers by choice tend to have higher incomes. And, as previously mentioned, a number of low-income households are unlisted by circumstance.

Random digit dialing
Use of telephone exchanges and a table of random numbers to contact respondents with unlisted phone numbers.

The problem of unlisted phone numbers can be partially resolved through the use of random digit dialing. Random digit dialing eliminates the counting of names in a list (for example, calling every fiftieth name in a column) and subjectively determining whether a directory listing is a business, institution, or legitimate household. In the simplest form of random digit dialing, telephone exchanges (prefixes) for the geographic areas in the sample are obtained. Using a table of random numbers, the last four digits of the telephone number are selected. Telephone directories can be ignored entirely or used in combination with the assignment of one or several random digits. Random digit dialing also helps overcome the problem due to new listings and recent changes in numbers. Unfortunately, the refusal rate in commercial random digit dialing studies is higher than the refusal rate for telephone surveys that use only listed telephone numbers.

CALLBACKS

An unanswered call, a busy signal, or a respondent who is not at home requires a callback. Telephone callbacks are much easier to make than callbacks in personal interviews. However, as mentioned, the ownership of telephone answering machines is growing, and their effects on callbacks need to be studied.

LIMITED DURATION

Respondents who run out of patience with the interview can merely hang up. To encourage participation, interviews should be relatively short. The length of the telephone interview is definitely limited.

LACK OF VISUAL MEDIUM

Because visual aids cannot be used in telephone interviews, this method is not appropriate for packaging research, copy testing of television and print advertising, and concept tests that require

RESEARCHSNAPSHOT

Automating Phone Surveys of Teens

Automatic telephone surveys are a good way to reach all members of the family, not just the head of the household. What if you wanted to ask questions about holiday shopping, what's for dinner, or what kind of vacation the family would like? A short telephone survey may be the answer. One advantage is that no "real person" has to hear the answers to potentially sensitive quesitons.

Computer-assisted telephone interviewing (CATI) and computerized self-interviewing, in which the subjects listened to pre-recorded questions and then responded by entering answers with the telephone's keypad, have been used to ask the "teen" in the house about smoking. The researchers predicted that the young people would be more likely to say they smoke in the self-administered survey than in response to a live interviewer, because pressing keys on the keypad would feel more confidential.

The interviewers were right. In the self-administered survey, the teens were more likely to say they had smoked in the past thirty days or, if they had not smoked, to lack a firm commitment not to smoke in the future. Many of them indicated a parent was present while they answered the questions, and when they did, their responses were less likely to indicate smoking desire or susceptibility. This pattern suggests that they might be under-reporting their smoking behavior. These findings encourage researchers to be attentive to confidentiality when working with teenage subjects.

Sources: Stores (2001), "Survey: Consumers Say 'Yes' To Holiday Shopping," (December), 83 (12), 18; also based on Moskowitz, Joel M. (2004), "Assessment of Cigarette Smoking and Smoking Susceptibility among Youth: Telephone Computer-Assisted Self-Interviews versus Computer-Assisted Telephone Interviews," Public Opinion Quarterly, 68 (Winter), 565–587.

©IMAGE SOURCE/GETTY IMAGES

visual materials. Likewise, certain attitude scales and measuring instruments, such as the semantic differential (see Chapter 13), require the respondent to see a graphic scale, so they are difficult to use over the phone.

Central Location Interviewing

Research agencies or interviewing services typically conduct all telephone interviews from a central location. Such **central location interviewing** allows firms to hire a staff of professional interviewers and to supervise and control the quality of interviewing more effectively. When telephone interviews are centralized and computerized, an agency or business can benefit from additional cost economies.

Central location interviewing
Telephone interviews conducted from a central location using wats lines at fixed charges.

Computer-Assisted Telephone Interviewing

Advances in computer technology allow responses to telephone interviews to be entered directly into the computer in a process known as **computer-assisted telephone interviewing (CATI)**. Telephone interviewers are seated at computer terminals. Monitors display the questionnaires, one question at a time, along with precoded possible responses to each question. The interviewer reads each question as it appears on the screen. When the respondent answers, the interviewer enters the response directly into the computer, and it is automatically stored in the computer's memory. The computer then displays the next question on the screen. Computer-assisted telephone interviewing requires that answers to the questionnaire be highly structured. If a respondent gives an unacceptable answer (that is, one not precoded and programmed), the computer will reject it.

Computer-assisted telephone interviewing systems include telephone management systems that select phone numbers, dial the numbers automatically, and perform other labor-saving functions. These systems can automatically control sample selection by randomly generating names or fulfilling a sample quota. A computer can generate an automatic callback schedule. A typical call management system might schedule recontact attempts to recall no answers after two hours and busy numbers after ten minutes and allow the interviewer to enter a more favorable time slot (day and hour) when a respondent indicates that he or she is too busy to be interviewed. Software

Computer-assisted telephone interviewing (CATI)
Technology that allows answers to telephone interviews to be entered directly into a computer for processing.

systems also allow researchers to request daily status reports on the number of completed interviews relative to quotas. CATI interviews can also be conducted by a pre-recorded voice with the respondent answering by punching buttons on the phone.

Computerized Voice-Activated Telephone Interview

Technological advances have combined computerized telephone dialing and voice-activated computer messages to allow researchers to conduct telephone interviews without human interviewers. However, researchers have found that computerized voice-activated telephone interviewing works best with very short, simple questionnaires. One system includes a voice-synthesized module controlled by a microprocessor. With it the sponsor is able to register a caller's single response such as "true/false," "yes/no," "like/dislike," or "for/against." This type of system has been used by television and radio stations to register callers' responses to certain issues. One system, Telsol, begins with an announcement that the respondent is listening to a recorded message. Many people are intrigued by the idea of talking to a robot or a computer, so they stay on the line. The computer then asks questions, leaving blank tape in between to record the answers. If respondents do not answer the first two questions, the computer disconnects and goes to the next call. With this process, the entire data collection process can be automated because a recorded voice is used to both ask the questions and record answers.

Global Considerations

Different cultures often have different norms about proper telephone behavior. For example, business-to-business researchers have learned that Latin American businesspeople will not open up to strangers on the telephone. So, researchers in Latin America usually find personal interviews more suitable than telephone surveys. In Japan, respondents consider it ill-mannered if telephone interviews last more than twenty minutes.

Self-Administered Questionnaires

Many surveys do not require an interviewer's presence. Marketing researchers distribute questionnaires to consumers through the mail and in many other ways (see Exhibit 9.1). They insert questionnaires in packages and magazines. They may place questionnaires at points of purchase or in high-traffic locations in stores or malls. They may even fax questionnaires to individuals. Questionnaires can be printed on paper, but they may be posted on the Internet or sent via e-mail. No matter

EXHIBIT 9.1
Self-Administered Questionnaires Can Be Either Printed or Electronic

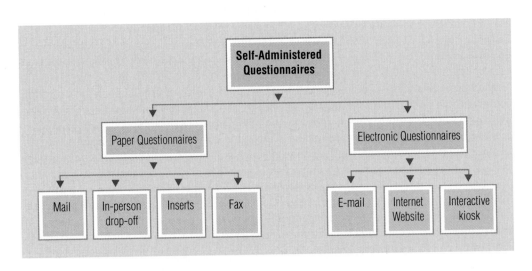

how the **self-administered questionnaires** are distributed, they are different from interviews because the respondent takes responsibility for reading and answering the questions.

Self-administered questionnaires present a challenge to the marketing researcher because they rely on the clarity of the written word rather than on the skills of the interviewer. The nature of self-administered questionnaires is best illustrated by explaining mail questionnaires.

Mail Questionnaires

A **mail survey** is a self-administered questionnaire sent to respondents through the mail. This paper-and-pencil method has several advantages and disadvantages.

▓ GEOGRAPHIC FLEXIBILITY

Mail questionnaires can reach a geographically dispersed sample simultaneously because interviewers are not required. Respondents (such as farmers) who are located in isolated areas or those (such as executives) who are otherwise difficult to reach can easily be contacted by mail. For example, a pharmaceutical firm may find that doctors are not available for personal or telephone interviews. However, a mail survey can reach both rural and urban doctors who practice in widely dispersed geographic areas.

▓ COST

Mail questionnaires are relatively inexpensive compared with personal interviews, though they are not cheap. Most include follow-up mailings, which require additional postage and printing costs. And it usually isn't cost-effective to try to cut costs on printing—questionnaires photocopied on low-grade paper have a greater likelihood of being thrown in the wastebasket than those prepared with more expensive, high-quality printing. The low response rates contribute to the high cost.

▓ RESPONDENT CONVENIENCE

Mail surveys and other self-administered questionnaires can be filled out when the respondents have time, so respondents are more likely to take time to think about their replies. Many hard-to-reach respondents place a high value on convenience and thus are best contacted by mail. In some situations, particularly in business-to-business marketing research, mail questionnaires allow respondents to collect facts, such as sales statistics, that they may not be able to recall without checking. Being able to check information by verifying records or, in household surveys, by consulting with other family members should provide more valid, factual information than either personal or telephone interviews would allow. A catalog retailer may use mail surveys to estimate sales volume for catalog items by sending a mock catalog as part of the questionnaire. Respondents would be asked to indicate how likely they would be to order selected items. Using the mail allows respondents to consult other family members and to make their decisions within a reasonable timespan.

▓ ANONYMITY OF RESPONDENT

In the cover letter that accompanies a mail or self-administered questionnaire, marketing researchers almost always state that the respondents' answers will be confidential. Respondents are more likely to provide sensitive or embarrassing information when they can remain anonymous. For example, personal interviews and a mail survey conducted simultaneously asked the question "Have you borrowed money at a regular bank?" Researchers noted a 17 percent response rate for the personal interviews and a 42 percent response rate for the mail survey. Although random sampling error may have accounted for part of this difference, the results suggest that for research on personal and sensitive financial issues, mail surveys are more confidential than personal interviews.

Anonymity can also reduce social desirability bias. People are more likely to agree with controversial issues, such as extreme political candidates, when completing self-administered questionnaires than when speaking to interviewers on the phone or at their doorsteps.

Self-administered questionnaires
Surveys in which the respondent takes the responsibility for reading and answering the questions.

Mail survey
A self-administered questionnaire sent to respondents through the mail.

■ ABSENCE OF INTERVIEWER

Although the absence of an interviewer can induce respondents to reveal sensitive or socially un-desirable information, this lack of personal contact can also be a disadvantage. Once the respondent receives the questionnaire, the questioning process is beyond the researcher's control. Although the printed stimulus is the same, each respondent will attach a different personal meaning to each question. Selective perception operates in research as well as in advertising. The respondent does not have the opportunity to question the interviewer. Problems that might be clarified in a personal or telephone interview can remain misunderstandings in a mail survey. There is no interviewer to probe for additional information or clarification of an answer, and the recorded answers must be assumed to be complete.

Respondents have the opportunity to read the entire questionnaire before they answer individual questions. Often the text of a later question will provide information that affects responses to earlier questions.

■ STANDARDIZED QUESTIONS

Mail questionnaires typically are highly standardized, and the questions are quite structured. Questions and instructions must be clear-cut and straightforward. Ambiguous questions only create additional error. Interviewing allows for feedback from the interviewer regarding the respondent's comprehension of the questionnaire. An interviewer who notices that the first fifty respondents are having some difficulty understanding a question can report this fact to the research analyst so that revisions can be made. With a mail survey, however, once the questionnaires are mailed, it is difficult to change the format or the questions.

■ TIME IS MONEY

If time is a factor in management's interest in the research results, or if attitudes are rapidly changing (for example, toward a political event), mail surveys may not be the best communication medium. A minimum of two or three weeks is necessary for receiving the majority of the responses. Follow-up mailings, which usually are sent when the returns begin to trickle in, require an additional two or three weeks. The time between the first mailing and the cut-off date (when questionnaires will no longer be accepted) normally is six to eight weeks. In a regional or local study, personal interviews can be conducted more quickly. However, conducting a national study by mail might be substantially faster than conducting personal interviews across the nation.

■ LENGTH OF MAIL QUESTIONNAIRE

Mail questionnaires vary considerably in length, ranging from extremely short postcard questionnaires to multipage booklets that require respondents to fill in thousands of answers. A general rule of thumb is that a mail questionnaire should not exceed six pages in length. When a questionnaire requires a respondent to expend a great deal of effort, an incentive is generally required to induce the respondent to return the questionnaire. The following sections discuss several ways to obtain high response rates even when questionnaires are longer than average.

Response Rates

All questionnaires that arrive via bulk mail are likely to get thrown away. Questionnaires that are boring, unclear or too complex are even more likely to get thrown in the wastebasket. A poorly designed mail questionnaire may be returned by less than 5 percent of those sampled (that is, a 5 percent response rate). The basic calculation for obtaining a **response rate** is to count the number of questionnaires returned or completed, then divide the total by the number of eligible people who were contacted or requested to participate in the survey. Typically, the number in the denominator is adjusted for faulty addresses and similar problems that reduce the number of eligible participants.

Response rate
The number of questionnaires returned or completed divided by the number of eligible people who were asked to participate in the survey.

The major limitations of mail questionnaires relate to response problems. Respondents who complete the questionnaire may not be typical of all people in the sample. Individuals with a special interest in the topic are more likely to respond to a mail survey than those who are indifferent.

A researcher has no assurance that the intended subject is the person who fills out the questionnaire. The wrong person answering the questions may be a problem when surveying corporate executives, physicians, and other professionals, who may pass questionnaires on to subordinates to complete. This probably is not unique to snail mail surveys since electronic surveying suffers similarly.

Evidence suggests that cooperation and response rates rise as home value increases. Also, if the sample has a high proportion of retired and well-off householders, response rates will be lower. Mail survey respondents tend to be better educated than nonrespondents. If they return the questionnaire at all, poorly educated respondents who cannot read and write well may skip open-ended questions to which they are required to write out their answers. Rarely will a mail survey have a 50 percent or greater response rate. However, the use of follow-up mailings and other techniques may increase the response rate to an acceptable percentage. The lower the response rate, the greater the concern that the resulting sample will not adequately represent the population.

Increasing Response Rates for Mail Surveys

Nonresponse error is always a potential problem with mail surveys. Individuals who are interested in the general subject of the survey are more likely to respond than those with less interest or little experience. Thus, people who hold extreme positions on an issue are more likely to respond than individuals who are largely indifferent to the topic. To minimize this bias, researchers have developed a number of techniques to increase the response rate to mail surveys. For example, almost all surveys include postage-paid return envelopes. Using a stamped return envelope instead of a business reply envelope increases response rates even more.[11] Designing and formatting attractive questionnaires and wording questions so that they are easy to understand also help ensure a good response rate. However, special efforts may be required even with a sound questionnaire. Several of these methods are discussed in the following subsections.

COVER LETTER

A **cover letter** that accompanies a questionnaire or is printed on the first page of the questionnaire booklet is an important means of inducing a reader to complete and return the questionnaire. Exhibit 9.2 illustrates a cover letter and some of the points considered by a marketing research professional to be important in gaining respondents' attention and cooperation. The first paragraph of the letter explains why the study is important. The basic appeal alludes to the social usefulness of responding. Two other frequently used appeals are asking for help ("Will you do us a favor?") and the egotistical appeal ("Your opinions are important!"). Most cover letters promise confidentiality, invite the recipient to use an enclosed postage-paid reply envelope, describe any incentive or reward for participation, explain that answering the questionnaire will not be difficult and will take only a short time, and describe how the person was scientifically selected for participation.

A personalized letter addressed to a specific individual shows the respondent that he or she is important. Including an individually typed cover letter on letterhead rather than a printed form is an important element in increasing the response rate in mail surveys.[12]

Cover letter
Letter that accompanies a questionnaire to induce the reader to complete and return the questionnaire.

MONEY HELPS

The respondent's motivation for returning a questionnaire may be increased by offering monetary incentives or premiums. Although pens, lottery tickets, and a variety of premiums have been used, monetary incentives appear to be the most effective and least biasing incentive. Money attracts attention and creates a sense of obligation. Perhaps for this reason, monetary incentives work for all income categories. Often, cover letters try to boost response rates with messages such as "We know that the attached dollar cannot compensate you for your time but please accept it as a token of our appreciation." Response rates increase dramatically when the monetary incentive is to be sent to a charity of the respondent's choice rather than directly to the respondent.

EXHIBIT 9.2
Example of Cover Letter for Household Survey

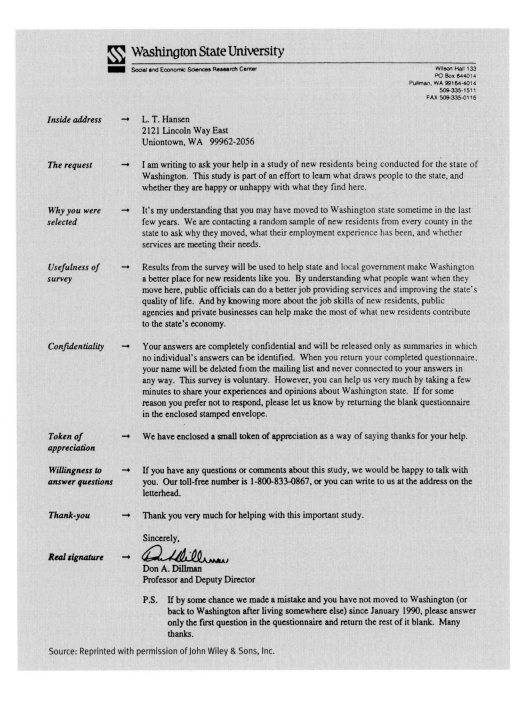

Source: Reprinted with permission of John Wiley & Sons, Inc.

INTERESTING QUESTIONS

The topic of the research—and thus the point of the questions—cannot be manipulated without changing the definition of the marketing problem. However, certain interesting questions can be added to the questionnaire, perhaps at the beginning, to stimulate respondents' interest and to induce cooperation. By including questions that are of little concern to the researchers but that the respondents want to answer, the researchers may give respondents who are indifferent to the major questions a reason for responding.

FOLLOW-UPS

Most mail surveys generate responses in a pattern like that shown in Exhibit 9.3, which graphs the cumulative response rates for two mail surveys. The response rates are relatively high for the first two weeks (as indicated by the steepness of each curve), then the rates gradually taper off.

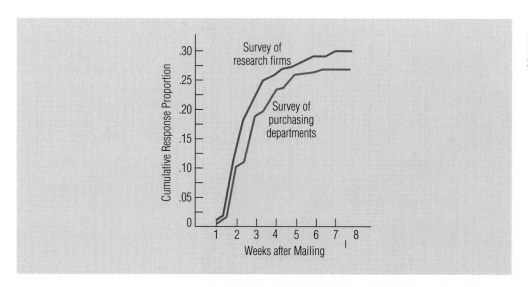

EXHIBIT 9.3
**Plots of Actual Response
Patterns for Two Commercial
Surveys**

After responses from the first wave of mailings begin to trickle in, most studies use a follow-up letter or postcard reminder, which request that the questionnaire be returned because a 100 percent return rate is important. A follow-up may include a duplicate questionnaire or may merely be a reminder to return the original questionnaire. Multiple contacts almost always increase response rates. The more attempts made to reach people, the greater the chances of their responding.[13]

Both of the studies in Exhibit 9.3 used follow-ups. Notice how the cumulative response rates picked up around week four.

ADVANCE NOTIFICATION

Advance notification, by either letter or telephone, that a questionnaire will be arriving has been successful in increasing response rates in some situations. ACNielsen has used this technique to ensure a high cooperation rate in filling out diaries of television watching. Advance notices that go out closer to the questionnaire mailing time produce better results than those sent too far in advance. The optimal lead time for advance notification is three days before the mail survey is to arrive.

SURVEY SPONSORSHIP

Auspices bias may result from the sponsorship of a survey. One business-to-business marketer wished to conduct a survey of its wholesalers to learn their stocking policies and their attitudes concerning competing manufacturers. A mail questionnaire sent on the corporate letterhead very likely would have received a much lower response rate than the questionnaire actually sent, which used the letterhead of a commercial marketing research firm. Sponsorship by well-known and prestigious organizations such as universities or government agencies may also significantly influence response rates. A mail survey sent to members of a consumer panel will receive an exceptionally high response rate because panel members have already agreed to cooperate with surveys.

OTHER TECHNIQUES

Numerous other devices have been used for increasing response rates. For example, the type of postage (commemorative versus regular stamp), envelope size, color of the questionnaire paper, and many other factors have been varied in efforts to increase response rates. Each has had at least limited success in certain situations; unfortunately, under other conditions each has failed to increase

©ASSOCIATED PRESS/AP

Mail surveys can reach a geographically dispersed sample and are relatively inexpensive. One disadvantage is the length of time involved in getting responses back. Response rates themselves also offer a challenge to surveyors.

response rates significantly. The researcher should consider his or her particular situation. For example, the researcher who is investigating consumers faces one situation; the researcher who is surveying corporate executives faces quite another.

▌ KEYING MAIL QUESTIONNAIRES WITH CODES

A marketing researcher planning a follow-up letter or postcard should not disturb respondents who already have returned the questionnaire. The expense of mailing questionnaires to those who already have responded is usually avoidable. One device for eliminating those who have already responded from the follow-up mailing list is to mark the questionnaires so that they may be keyed to identify members of the sampling frame who are nonrespondents. Blind keying of questionnaires on a return envelope (systematically varying the job number or room number of the marketing research department, for example) or a visible code number on the questionnaire has been used for this purpose. Visible keying is indicated with statements such as "The sole purpose of the number on the last page is to avoid sending a second questionnaire to people who complete and return the first one." Ethical researchers key questionnaires only to increase response rates, thereby preserving respondents' anonymity.

Global Considerations

Researchers conducting surveys in more than one country must recognize that postal services and cultural circumstances differ around the world. Some of the issues to consider are the reliability of mail delivery, literacy rates, and trust that researchers can and will provide confidentiality. In some cases, hand delivery of surveys or door-to-door interviewing may be necessary. In other cases, consumers (especially women or children) might be discouraged from talking to an interviewer who is not a family member, so mailed questionnaires would be superior to interviews.

Self-Administered Questionnaires Using Other Forms of Distribution

Many forms of self-administered, printed questionnaires are very similar to mail questionnaires. Airlines frequently pass out questionnaires to passengers during flights. Restaurants, hotels, and other service establishments print short questionnaires on cards so that customers can evaluate the service. *Tennis Magazine, Advertising Age, Wired,* and many other publications have used inserted questionnaires to survey current readers inexpensively, and often the results provide material for a magazine article.

Many manufacturers use their warranty or owner registration cards to collect demographic information and data about where and why products were purchased. Using owner registration cards is an extremely economical technique for tracing trends in consumer habits. Again, problems may arise because people who fill out these self-administered questionnaires differ from those who do not.

Extremely long questionnaires may be dropped off by an interviewer and then picked up later. The **drop-off method** sacrifices some cost savings because it requires traveling to each respondent's location.

Fax Surveys

With fax surveys, potential survey respondents receive and/or return questionnaires via fax machines.[14] A questionnaire inserted in a magazine may instruct the respondent to clip out the questionnaire and fax it to a certain phone number. In a mail survey, a prepaid-postage envelope places little burden on the respondent. But faxing a questionnaire to a long-distance number requires that the respondent pay for the transmission of the fax. Thus, a disadvantage of the **fax survey** is that only respondents with fax machines who are willing to exert the extra effort will return questionnaires. Again, people with extreme opinions will be more likely to respond.

To address this disadvantage, marketers may use faxing as one of several options for replying to a survey. Recently, the journal *American Family Physician* carried a reader survey that gave respondents the option of either returning the reply by fax or visiting the journal's website to answer the same questions online.[15] For busy physicians who likely have access to office equipment, this approach would improve the response rate.

Fax machines can also be used to distribute questionnaires. These fax surveys reduce the sender's printing and postage costs and can be delivered and returned faster than traditional mail surveys. Questionnaires distributed via fax can deal with timely issues. Although few households have fax machines, when the sample consists of organizations that are likely to have fax machines, the sample coverage may be adequate.

E-Mail Surveys

Questionnaires can be distributed via e-mail, but researchers must remember that some individuals cannot be reached this way. Certain projects do lend themselves to **e-mail surveys**, such as internal surveys of employees or satisfaction surveys of retail buyers who regularly deal with an organization via e-mail. The benefits of incorporating a questionnaire in an e-mail include the speed of distribution, lower distribution and processing costs, faster turnaround time, more flexibility, and less handling of paper questionnaires. The speed of e-mail distribution and the quick response time can be major advantages for surveys dealing with time-sensitive issues.

Not much academic research has been conducted on e-mail surveys. Nevertheless, some researchers have argued that many respondents feel they can be more candid in e-mail than in person or on the telephone, for the same reasons they are candid on other self-administered questionnaires. Yet, in many organizations employees know that their e-mails are not secure and "eavesdropping" by a supervisor could possibly occur. Further, maintaining respondents' anonymity is difficult, because a reply to an e-mail message typically includes the sender's address. Researchers designing e-mail surveys should assure respondents that their answers will be confidential.

Not all e-mail systems have the same capacity: Some handle color and graphics well; others are limited to text. The extensive differences in the capabilities of respondents' computers and e-mail software limit the types of questions and the layout of the e-mail questionnaire. For example, the display settings for computer screens vary widely, and wrap-around of lines may put the questions and the answer choices into strange and difficult-to-read patterns.[16] Many novice e-mail users find it difficult to mark answers in brackets on an e-mail questionnaire and/or to send a completed questionnaire using the e-mail Reply function. For this reason, some researchers give respondents the option to print out the questionnaire, complete it in writing, and return it via regular mail. Unless the research is an internal organizational survey, this alternative, of course, requires the respondent to pay postage.

In general, the guidelines for printed mail surveys apply to e-mail surveys. However, some differences exist, because the cover letter and the questionnaire appear in a single e-mail message.

Drop-off method
A survey method that requires the interviewer to travel to the respondent's location to drop off questionnaires that will be picked up later.

Fax survey
A survey that uses fax machines as a way for respondents to receive and return questionnaires.

E-mail surveys
Surveys distributed through electronic mail.

A potential respondent who is not immediately motivated to respond, especially one who considers an unsolicited e-mail survey to be spam, can quickly hit the Delete button to remove the e-mail. This response suggests that e-mail cover letters should be brief and the questionnaires relatively short. The cover letter should explain how the company got the recipient's name and should include a valid return e-mail address in the "FROM" box and reveal who is conducting the survey. Also, if the e-mail lists more than one address in the "TO" or "CC" field, all recipients will see the entire list of names. This lack of anonymity has the potential to cause response bias and nonresponse error. When possible, the e-mail should be addressed to a single person. (The blind carbon copy, or BCC, field can be used if the same message must be sent to an entire sample.)

E-mail has another important role in survey research. E-mail letters can be used as cover letters asking respondents to participate in an Internet survey. Such e-mails typically provide a password and a link to a unique website location that requires a password for access.

Internet Surveys

Internet survey
A self-administered
questionnaire posted on a
website.

An **Internet survey** is a self-administered questionnaire posted on a website. Respondents provide answers to questions displayed onscreen by highlighting a phrase, clicking an icon, or keying in an answer. Like every other type of survey, Internet surveys have both advantages and disadvantages.

SPEED AND COST-EFFECTIVENESS

Internet surveys allow marketers to reach a large audience (possibly a global one), personalize individual messages, and secure confidential answers quickly and cost-effectively. These computer-to-computer self-administered questionnaires eliminate the costs of paper, postage, and data entry, as well as other administrative costs. Once an Internet questionnaire has been developed, the incremental cost of reaching additional respondents is minimal. So, samples can be larger than with interviews or other types of self-administered questionnaires. Even with large samples, surveys that used to take many weeks can be conducted in a week or less.

VISUAL APPEAL AND INTERACTIVITY

Surveys conducted on the Internet can be interactive. The researcher can use more sophisticated lines of questioning based on the respondents' prior answers. Many of these interactive surveys utilize color, sound, and animation, which may help to increase respondents' cooperation and willingness to spend time answering the questionnaires. The Internet is an excellent medium for the presentation of visual materials, such as photographs or drawings of product prototypes, advertisements, and movie trailers. Innovative measuring instruments that take advantage of the ability to adjust backgrounds, fonts, color, and other features have been designed and applied with considerable success.

RESPONDENT PARTICIPATION AND COOPERATION

Participation in some Internet surveys occurs because computer users intentionally navigate to a particular website where questions are displayed. For example, a survey of more than 10,000 visitors to the Ticketmaster website helped Ticketmaster better understand its customer purchase patterns and evaluate visitor satisfaction with the site. In some cases, individuals expect to encounter a survey at a website; in others, it is totally unexpected. In some instances, the visitor cannot venture beyond the survey page without providing information for the organization's "registration" questionnaire. When the computer user does not expect a survey on a website and participation is voluntary, response rates are low. And, as with other questionnaires that rely on voluntary self-selection, participants tend to be more interested in or involved with the subject of the research than the average person.

For many other Internet surveys, respondents are initially contacted via e-mail. Often they are members of consumer panels who have previously indicated their willingness to cooperate. When

RESEARCHSNAPSHOT

Personalizing E-mail Invitations

When inviting people to participate in a study, researchers should address them by name. A recent study testing e-mail invitations to a web survey supported this widely held view.

The researcher set up an Internet survey to ask university students a set of questions about marriage and divorce. The objective was not to learn about their attitudes, but to measure their response rates to different kinds of invitations. One set of students received an e-mail invitation addressing them as "Dear student," while the other half received invitations addressing them by first and last name. Both invitations requested that the students visit the website where they could take the survey. A week later, both sets of students received a reminder e-mail, using the same experimental treatment regarding use of their names.

When students were invited by name, they were significantly more likely to visit the website and log in to take the survey.

However, the use of a name was not associated with whether the students finished taking the survey once they had begun.

The researcher also wondered whether students would think the survey was less confidential when the research team contacted them by name. To test this, the survey included questions about the frequency of their sexual activity—a topic that might produce a tendency to bias answers in a socially desirable direction. The research results did not indicate a social desirability bias. Do you think they weren't worried about privacy or didn't care whether their sexual activity met social norms?

Source: Heerwegh, Dirk (2005), "Effects of Personal Salutations in E-mail Invitations to Participate in a Web Survey," Public Opinion Quarterly, 69 (Winter), 588–598.

panel members receive an e-mail invitation to participate, they are given logon instructions and a password. This security feature prevents access by individuals who are not part of the scientifically selected sample. Assigning a unique password code also allows the researchers to track the responses of each respondent, thereby identifying any respondent who makes an effort to answer the questionnaire more than once.

Panel members also need an incentive to respond. A study of German consumers showed that nothing beat financial incentives. In other words, the best way to get responses was to simply pay consumers for participating in surveys.[17]

Ideally, the **welcome screen** contains the name of the research company and information about how to contact the organization if the respondent has a problem or concern. A typical statement might be "If you have any concerns or questions about this survey or if you experience any technical difficulties, please contact [name of research organization]."

Welcome screen
The first web page in an Internet survey, which introduces the survey and requests that the respondent enter a password or pin.

REPRESENTATIVE SAMPLES

The population to be studied, the purpose of the research, and the sampling methods determine the quality of Internet samples, which varies substantially. If the sample consists merely of those who visit a web page and voluntarily fill out a questionnaire, then it is not likely to be representative of the entire U.S. population, because of self-selection error. However, if the purpose of the research is to evaluate how visitors feel about a website, randomly selecting every 100th visitor may accomplish the study's purpose. Scientifically drawn samples from a consumer panel or samples randomly generated in other ways also can be representative.

Of course, a disadvantage, albeit ever decreasing, of Internet surveys is that many individuals in the general population cannot access the Internet. Even among people with Internet access, not all of them have the same level of technology. Many people with low-speed Internet connections (low bandwidth) cannot quickly download high-resolution graphic files. Many lack powerful computers or software that is compatible with advanced features programmed into many Internet questionnaires. Some individuals have minimal computer skills. They may not know how to navigate through and provide answers to an Internet questionnaire. For example, the advanced audio- and video-streaming technology of RealPlayer or Windows Media Player software can be used to incorporate a television commercial and questions about its effectiveness into an Internet survey.

However, some respondents might find downloading the file too slow or even impossible, others might not have the RealPlayer or Windows Media Player software, and still others might not know how to use the streaming media software to view the commercial.

For the foreseeable future, Internet surveys sampling the general public should be designed with the recognition that problems may arise for the reasons just described. Thus, photographs, animation, or other cutting-edge technological features created on the researcher's/web designer's powerful computer may have to be simplified or eliminated so that all respondents can interact at the same level of technological sophistication.

Because Internet surveys can be accessed anytime (24/7) from anywhere, they can reach certain hard-to-reach respondents, such as doctors. Chapter 16 discusses sampling techniques for Internet surveys.

ACCURATE REAL-TIME DATA CAPTURE

The computer-to-computer nature of Internet surveys means that each respondent's answers are entered directly into the researcher's computer as soon as the questionnaire is submitted. In addition, the questionnaire software may be programmed to reject improper data entry. For example, on a paper questionnaire a respondent might incorrectly check two responses even though the instructions call for a single answer. In an Internet survey, this mistake can be interactively corrected as the survey is taking place. Thus, the data capture is more accurate than when humans are involved.

Real-time data capture allows for real-time data analysis. A researcher can review up-to-the-minute sample size counts and tabulation data from an Internet survey in real time.

CALLBACKS

When the sample for an Internet survey is drawn from a consumer panel, those who have not completed the survey questionnaire can be easily recontacted. Computer software can simply automatically send e-mail reminders to panel members who did not visit the welcome page. Computer software can also identify the passwords of respondents who completed only a portion of the questionnaire and send those people customized messages. Sometimes such e-mails offer additional incentives to those individuals who terminated the questionnaire with only a few additional questions to answer, so that they are motivated to comply with the request to finish the questionnaire.

PERSONALIZED AND FLEXIBLE QUESTIONING

Computer-interactive Internet surveys are programmed in much the same way as computer-assisted telephone interviews. That is, the software that is used allows questioning to branch off into two or more different lines depending on a respondent's answer to a filtered question. The difference is that there is no interviewer. The respondent interacts directly with software on a website. In other words, the computer program asks questions in a sequence determined by the respondent's previous answers. The questions appear on the computer screen, and answers are recorded by simply pressing a key or clicking an icon, thus immediately entering the data into the computer's memory. Of course, these methods avoid labor costs associated with data collection and processing of paper-and-pencil questionnaires.

This ability to sequence questions based on previous responses is a major advantage of computer-assisted surveys. The computer can be programmed to skip from question 6 to question 9 if the answer to question 6 is no. Furthermore, responses to previous questions can lead to questions that can be personalized for individual respondents (for example, "When you cannot buy your favorite brand, Revlon, what brand of lipstick do you prefer?"). Often the respondent's name appears in questions to personalize the questionnaire. Fewer and more relevant questions speed up the response process and increase the respondent's involvement with the survey.

A related advantage of using a web survey is that it can prompt respondents when they skip over a question. In a test comparing telephone and Internet versions of the same survey, the rate of item nonresponse was less for the Internet version, which issued a prompt for each item that was left blank.[18] This was likely not a simple matter of motivation, because the rate of respondents who actually took the web version was less than for the telephone version, even though the researchers offered a larger incentive to those who were asked to go online. (An earlier telephone screening had verified that everyone who was asked to participate had a computer.)

The ability to customize questions and the low cost per recipient also help researchers keep surveys short, an important consideration for boosting responses.[19] Jakob Nielsen, a consultant on Internet usability with the Nielsen Norman Group, emphasizes that "quick and painless" surveys generate the highest response and urges researchers to keep surveys as short as possible. He suggests that if the research objectives call for a long survey, the questions can be divided among several questionnaires, with each version sent to a different group of respondents.

Designers of Internet questionnaires can be creative and flexible in the presentation of questions by using a variety of **dialog boxes**, or windows that prompt the respondent to enter information. Chapter 15 discusses software issues, the design of questions, and questionnaire layouts for Internet surveys.

Dialog boxes
Windows that open on a computer screen to prompt the user to enter information.

RESPONDENT ANONYMITY

Respondents are more likely to provide sensitive or embarrassing information when they can remain anonymous. The anonymity of the Internet encourages respondents to provide honest answers to sensitive questions.

RESPONSE RATES

The methods for improving response rates for an Internet survey are similar to those for other kinds of survey research. A personalized invitation may be important. In many cases, the invitation is delivered via e-mail. The respondents may not recognize the sender's address, so the message's subject line is critical.[20] The subject line should refer to a topic likely to interest the audience, and legal as well as ethical standards dictate that it may not be deceptive. Thus, the line might be worded in a way similar to the following: "Please give your opinion on [subject matter of interest]." Researchers should avoid gimmicks like dollar signs and the word *free,* either of which is likely to alert the spam filters installed on most computers.

As mentioned earlier, with a password system, people who have not participated in a survey in a predetermined period of time can be sent a friendly e-mail reminder asking them to participate before the study ends. This type of follow-up, along with preliminary notification, interesting early questions, and variations of most other techniques for increasing response rates to mail questionnaires, is recommended for Internet surveys.

Unlike mail surveys, Internet surveys do not offer the opportunity to send a physical incentive, such as a dollar bill, to the respondent. Incentives to respond to a survey must be in the form of a promise of a future reward—for example, "As a token of appreciation for completing this survey, the sponsor of the survey will make a sizable contribution to a national charity. You can vote for your preferred charity at the end of the survey." Although some researchers have had success with promising incentives, academic research about Internet surveys is sparse, and currently there are few definitive answers about the most effective ways to increase response rates.

SECURITY CONCERNS

Many organizations worry that hackers or competitors may access websites to discover new product concepts, new advertising campaigns, and other top-secret ideas. Respondents may worry whether personal information will remain private. So may the organizations sponsoring the research. Recently, McDonald's conducted quality-control research in England and Scotland, automating the transmittal of data with a system in which consultants used handheld devices and sent the numbers to headquarters as e-mail messages. The system saved hours of work, but the company worried that confidential information could be compromised. McDonald's therefore purchased software that encrypted the data and allowed the handhelds to be remotely wiped clean of data if they were lost or stolen.[21]

As in the experience of McDonald's, no system can be 100 percent secure, but risks can be minimized. Many research service suppliers specializing in Internet surveying have developed password-protected systems that are very secure. One important feature of these systems restricts access and prevents individuals from filling out a questionnaire over and over again.

Kiosk Interactive Surveys

A computer with a touch screen may be installed in a kiosk at a trade show, at a professional conference, in an airport, or in any other high-traffic location to administer an interactive survey. Because the respondent chooses to interact with an on-site computer, self-selection often is a problem with this type of survey. Computer-literate individuals are most likely to complete these interactive questionnaires. At temporary locations such as conventions, these surveys often require a fieldworker to be at the location to explain how to use the computer system. This personal assistance is an obvious disadvantage.

Survey Research That Mixes Modes

Mixed-mode survey
Study that employs any combination of survey methods.

For many surveys, research objectives dictate the use of some combination of telephone, mail, e-mail, Internet, and personal interview. For example, the researcher may conduct a short telephone screening interview to determine whether respondents are eligible for recontact in a more extensive personal interview. Such a **mixed-mode survey** combines the advantages of the telephone survey (such as fast screening) and those of the personal interview. A mixed-mode survey can employ any combination of two or more survey methods. Conducting a research study in two or more waves, however, creates the possibility that some respondents will no longer cooperate or will be unavailable in the second wave of the survey.

Several variations of survey research use cable television channels. For example, a telephone interviewer calls a cable subscriber and asks him or her to tune in to a particular channel at a certain time. An appointment is made to interview the respondent shortly after the program or visual material is displayed. NBC uses this type of mixed-mode survey to test the concepts for many proposed new programs.

Selecting the Appropriate Survey Research Design

Earlier discussions of research design and problem definition emphasized that many research tasks may lead to similar decision-making information. There is no best form of survey; each has advantages and disadvantages. A researcher who must ask highly confidential questions may use a mail survey, thus sacrificing speed of data collection to avoid interviewer bias. If a researcher must have considerable control over question phrasing, central location telephone interviewing may be appropriate.

To determine the appropriate technique, the researcher must ask several questions: Is the assistance of an interviewer necessary? Are respondents interested in the issues being investigated? Will cooperation be easily attained? How quickly is the information needed? Will the study require a long and complex questionnaire? How large is the budget? The criteria—cost, speed, anonymity, and so forth—may differ for each project.

Exhibit 9.4 summarizes the major advantages and disadvantages of typical door-to-door, mall intercept, telephone, mail, and Internet surveys. It emphasizes the typical types of surveys. For example, a creative researcher might be able to design highly versatile and flexible mail questionnaires, but most researchers use standardized questions. An elaborate mail survey may be far more expensive than a short personal interview, but generally this is not the case.

EXHIBIT 9.4 **Advantages and Disadvantages of Typical Survey Methods**

	Door-to-Door Personal Interview	**Mall Intercept Personal Interview**	**Telephone Interview**	**Mail Survey**	**Internet Survey**
Speed of data collection	Moderate to fast	Fast	Very fast	Slow; researcher has no control over return of questionnaire	Instantaneous; 24/7
Geographic flexibility	Limited to moderate	Confined, possible urban bias	High	High	High (worldwide)
Respondent cooperation	Excellent	Moderate to low	Good	Moderate; poorly designed questionnaire will have low response rate	Varies depending on website; high from consumer panels
Versatility of questioning	Quite versatile	Extremely versatile	Moderate	Not versatile; requires highly standardized format	Extremely versatile
Questionnaire length	Long	Moderate to long	Moderate	Varies depending on incentive	Moderate; length customized based on answers
Item non-response rate	Low	Medium	Medium	High	Software can assure none
Possibility for respondent misunderstanding	Low	Low	Average	High; no interviewer present for clarification	High
Degree of interviewer influence on answers	High	High	Moderate	None; interviewer absent	None
Supervision of interviewers	Moderate	Moderate to high	High, especially with central-location interviewing	Not applicable	Not applicable
Anonymity of respondent	Low	Low	Moderate	High	Respondent can be either anonymous or known
Ease of callback or follow-up	Difficult	Difficult	Easy	Easy, but takes time	Difficult, unless e-mail address is known
Cost	Highest	Moderate to high	Low to moderate	Lowest	Low
Special features	Visual materials may be shown or demonstrated; extended probing possible	Taste tests, viewing of TV commercials possible	Fieldwork and supervision of data collection are simplified; quite adaptable to computer technology	Respondent may answer questions at own convenience; has time to reflect on answers	Streaming media software allows use of graphics and animation

Note: The emphasis is on *typical* surveys. For example, an elaborate mail survey may be far more expensive than a short personal interview, but this generally is not the case.

Pretesting

Pretesting
Screening procedure that involves a trial run with a group of respondents to iron out fundamental problems in the survey design.

A researcher who is surveying 3,000 consumers does not want to find out after the questionnaires have been completed or returned that most respondents misunderstood a particular question, skipped a series of questions, or misinterpreted the instructions for filling out the questionnaire. To avoid problems such as these, screening procedures, or *pretests,* are often used. **Pretesting** involves a trial run with a group of respondents to iron out fundamental problems in the instructions or design of a questionnaire. The researcher looks for such obstacles as the point at which respondent fatigue sets in and whether there are any particular places in the questionnaire where respondents tend to terminate. Unfortunately, this stage of research is sometimes eliminated because of costs or time pressures.

Broadly speaking, three basic ways to pretest exist. The first two involve screening the questionnaire with other research professionals, and the third—the one most often called pretesting—is a trial run with a group of respondents. When screening the questionnaire with other research professionals, the investigator asks them to look for such problems as difficulties with question wording, leading questions, and bias due to question order. An alternative type of screening might involve a client or the research manager who ordered the research. Often, managers ask researchers to collect information, but when they see the questionnaire, they find that it does not really meet their needs. Only by checking with the individual who has requested the questionnaire does the researcher know for sure that the information needed will be provided. Once the researcher has decided on the final questionnaire, data should be collected with a small number of respondents (perhaps 100) to determine whether the questionnaire needs refinement.

TOTHEPOINT

Practice is the best of all instructors.

—Publius Syrus,
Circa 42 BC

Ethical Issues in Survey Research

Chapter 4 mentioned that the American Marketing Association's code of ethics expresses researchers' obligation to protect the public from misrepresentation and exploitation under the guise of marketing research. Many ethical issues apply to survey research, such as respondents' right to privacy, the use of deception, respondents' right to be informed about the purpose of the research, the need for confidentiality, the need for honesty in collecting data, and the need for objectivity in reporting data. You may wish to reexamine Chapter 4's coverage of these issues now that various survey research techniques have been discussed.[22]

Summary

1. Summarize ways researchers gather information through interviews. Interviews can be categorized based on the medium used to communicate with respondents. Interviews can be conducted door-to-door, in shopping malls, or on the telephone. Traditionally, interviews have been recorded using paper and pencil, but survey researchers are increasingly using computers. Personal interviews are a flexible method that allows researchers to use visual aids and various kinds of props. However, the presence of an interviewer may influence subjects' responses.

2. Compare the advantages and disadvantages of conducting door-to-door, mall intercept, and telephone interviews. Door-to-door personal interviews can get high response rates, but they are more costly to administer than other types of surveys. When a sample need not represent the entire country, mall intercept interviews may reduce costs. Telephone interviewing has the advantage of providing data fast and at a lower cost per interview. However, not all households have telephones, and not all telephone numbers are listed in directories. This causes problems in obtaining a representative sample, so researchers often use random digit dialing. Absence of face-to-face contact and inability to use visual materials also limit telephone interviewing. Computer-assisted telephone interviewing from central locations can improve the efficiency of certain kinds of telephone surveys.

3. Evaluate the advantages and disadvantages of distributing questionnaires through the mail, the Internet, and other means. Traditionally, self-administered questionnaires have been distributed by mail, but self-administered questionnaires also may be dropped off to individual respondents, distributed from central locations, or administered via computer. Mail questionnaires generally are less expensive than telephone or personal interviews, but they also introduce a much larger chance of nonresponse error. Several methods can be used to encourage higher response rates. Mail questionnaires must be more structured than other types of surveys and cannot be changed if problems are discovered in the course of data collection. The Internet and other interactive media provide convenient ways for organizations to conduct surveys. Internet surveys are quick and cost-effective, but not everyone has Internet access. Because the surveys are computerized and interactive, questionnaires can be personalized and data can be captured in real time. Some privacy and security concerns exist, but the future of Internet surveys looks promising.

4. Discuss the importance of pretesting questionnaires. Pretesting a questionnaire on a small sample of respondents is a useful way to discover problems while they can still be corrected. Pretests may involve screening the questionnaire with other research professionals or conducting a trial run with a set of respondents.

5. Describe ethical issues that arise in survey research. Researchers must protect the public from misrepresentation and exploitation. This obligation includes honesty about the purpose of a research project and protection of subjects' right to refuse to participate or to answer particular questions. Researchers also should protect the confidentiality of participants and record responses honestly.

Key Terms and Concepts

Personal interview	Computer-assisted telephone	E-mail surveys
Item nonresponse	interviewing (CATI)	Internet survey
Door-to-door interview	Self-administered questionnaires	Welcome screen
Callbacks	Mail survey	Dialog boxes
Mall intercept interviews	Response rate	Mixed-mode survey
Telephone interviews	Cover letter	Pretesting
Random digit dialing	Drop-off method	
Central location interviewing	Fax survey	

Questions for Review and Critical Thinking

1. What type of communication medium would you use to conduct the following surveys? Why?
   a. Survey of the buying motives of industrial engineers
   b. Survey of the satisfaction levels of rental car users
   c. Survey of television commercial advertising awareness
   d. Survey of top corporate executives
2. A publisher offers college professors one of four best-selling mass-market books as an incentive for filling out a ten-page mail questionnaire about a new textbook. What advantages and disadvantages does this incentive have?
3. "Individuals are less willing to cooperate with surveys today than they were fifty years ago." Comment on this statement.
4. What do you think should be the maximum length of a self-administered email questionnaire?
5. Do most surveys use a single communication mode (for example, the telephone), as most textbooks suggest?
6. A survey researcher reports that "205 usable questionnaires out of 942 questionnaires delivered in our mail survey converts to a 21.7 percent response rate." What are the subtle implications of this statement?
7. Evaluate the following survey designs:
   a. A researcher suggests mailing a small safe (a metal file box with a built-in lock) without the lock combination to respondents, with a note explaining that respondents will be called in a few days for a telephone interview. During the telephone interview, the respondent is given the combination and the safe may be opened.
   b. A shopping mall that wishes to evaluate its image places packets including a questionnaire, cover letter, and stamped return envelope in the mall where customers can pick them up if they wish.
   c. An e-mail message is sent to individuals who own computers, asking them to complete a questionnaire on a website. Respondents answer the questions and then have the opportunity to play a slot-machine game on the website. Each respondent is guaranteed a monetary incentive but has the option to increase it by playing the slot-machine game.
   d. A mall intercept interviewing service is located in a regional shopping center. The facility contains a small room for television and movie presentations. Shoppers are used as sampling units. However, mall intercept interviewers recruit additional subjects for television commercial experiments by offering them several complimentary tickets for special sneak previews. Individuals contacted at the mall are allowed to bring up to five guests. In some cases the complimentary tickets are offered through ads in a local newspaper.
   e. *Time* magazine opts to conduct a mail survey rather than a telephone survey for a study to determine the demographic characteristics and purchasing behavior of its subscribers.
8. What type of research studies lend themselves to the use of e-mail for survey research? What are the advantages and disadvantages of using e-mail?
9. **ETHICS** Comment on the ethics of the following situations:
   a. A researcher plans to use invisible ink to code questionnaires to identify respondents in a distributor survey.
   b. A political action committee conducts a survey about its cause. At the end of the questionnaire, it includes a request for a donation.

c. A telephone interviewer calls at 1 p.m. on Sunday and asks the person who answers the phone to take part in an interview.

d. An industrial marketer wishes to survey its own distributors. It invents the name "Mountain States Marketing Research" and sends out a mail questionnaire under this name.

e. A questionnaire is printed on the back of a warranty card included inside the package of a food processor. The questionnaire includes a number of questions about shopping behavior, demographics, and customer lifestyles. At the bottom of the warranty card is a short note in small print that says "Thank you for completing this questionnaire. Your answers will be used for marketing studies and to help us serve you better in the future. You will also benefit by receiving important mailings and special offers from a number of organizations whose products and services relate directly to the activities, interests, and hobbies in which you enjoy participating on a regular basis. Please indicate if there is some reason you would prefer not to receive this information."

10. **ETHICS** How might the marketing research industry take action to ensure that the public believes that telephone surveys and door-to-door interviews are legitimate activities and that firms that misrepresent and deceive the public using marketing research as a sales ploy are not true marketing researchers?

11. Why is the mobile phone likely to be an ineffective way of reaching potential respondents in America?

12. The American Testing Institute (also known as the U.S. Testing Authority) mails respondents what it calls a "tele-vision" survey. A questionnaire is sent to respondents, who are asked to complete it and mail it back along with a check for $14.80. In return for answering eight questions on viewing habits, the institute promises to send respondents one of twenty prizes ranging in value from $200 to $2,000—among which are video recorders, diamond watches, a lifetime supply of film, color televisions, and two nights of hotel accommodations at a land development resort community. The institute lists the odds of winning as 1 in 150,000 on all prizes except the hotel stay, for which the odds are 149,981 out of 150,000. During a three-month period, the institute sends out 200,000 questionnaires. What are the ethical issues in this situation?

13. **'NET** Go to the Pew Internet and American Life page at http://www.pewinternet.org. Several reports based on survey research will be listed. Select one of the reports. What were the research objectives? What were the first three questions on the survey?

14. **'NET** Go to the NPD Group Web site (http://www.npd.com) and click on the Store link. What types of custom and syndicated survey research services does the company offer?

15. **'NET** Go to the CASRO (Council of American Survey Research Organizations) home page (http://www.casro.org). Select "About CASRO." What are the key aspects of this research organization's mission?

Research Activities

1. **'NET** Visit this web site: http://www.zoomerang.com. What unique service does this company offer? Then visit this site: http://www.websurveyor.com. How does this service differ from zoomerang? Create a short survey and email it to ten of your friends without any advanced notice. At the end of the survey, ask them if they would have responded had they not noticed the survey came from you. What is the response rate? What would it have been if the respondent did not know you?

Case 9.1 National Do Not Call Registry

Citizens' annoyance with phone calls from salespeople prompted Congress to pass a law setting up a National Do Not Call Registry. The registry was soon flooded with requests to have phone numbers removed from telemarketers' lists. By law, salespeople may not call numbers listed on this registry. The law makes exceptions for charities and researchers. However, a recent poll suggests that even though phone calls from researchers may be legal, they are not always well received.[23]

In late 2005, Harris Interactive conducted an Internet survey in which almost 2,000 adults answered questions about the National Do Not Call Registry. About three-quarters of the respondents said they had signed up for the registry, and a majority (61 percent) said they had since received "far less" contact from telemarketers. In addition, 70 percent said that since registering, they had been contacted by someone "who was doing a poll or survey" and wanted them to participate. But apparently respondents weren't sure whether this practice was acceptable. Only one-fourth (24 percent) of respondents said they knew that researchers "are allowed to call," and over half (63 percent) weren't sure about researchers' rights under the law.

Questions

1. Was an online survey the best medium for a poll on this subject? What were some pros and cons of conducting this poll online?

2. How might the results have differed if this poll had been conducted by telephone?

3. As a researcher, how would you address people's doubts about whether pollsters may contact households listed on the Do Not Call Registry?

Case 9.2 Royal Bee Electric Fishing Reel

Royal Barton started thinking about an electric fishing reel when his father had a stroke and lost the use of an arm. To see that happen to his dad, who had taught him the joys of fishing and hunting, made Barton realize what a chunk a physical handicap could take out of a sports enthusiast's life. Being able to cast and retrieve a lure and experience the thrill of a big bass trying to take your rig away from you were among the joys of life that would be denied Barton's father forever.

Barton was determined to do something about it, if not for his father, then at least for others who had suffered a similar fate. So, after tremendous personal expense and years of research and development, Barton perfected what is sure to be the standard bearer for all future freshwater electric reels. Forget those saltwater jobs, which Barton refers to as "winches." He has developed something that is small, compact, and has incredible applications.

He calls it the Royal Bee. The first word is obviously his first name. The second word refers to the low buzzing sound the reel makes when in use.

The Royal Bee system looks simple enough and probably is if you understand the mechanical workings of a reel. A system of gears ties into the gears of the spool, and a motor in the back drives the gears attached to the triggering system.

All gearing of the electrical system can be disengaged so that you can cast normally. But pushing the button for "Retrieve" engages two gears. After the gears are engaged, the trigger travels far enough to touch the switch that tightens the drive belt, and there is no slipping. You cannot hit the switch until the gears are properly engaged. This means that you cast manually, just as you would normally fish, then you reengage the reel for the levelwind to work. And you can do all that with one hand!

The system works on a 6-volt battery that you can attach to your belt or hang around your neck if you are wading. If you have a boat with a 6-volt battery, the reel can actually work off of the battery. There is a small connector that plugs into the reel, so you could easily use more than one reel with the battery. For instance, if you have two or three outfits equipped with different lures, you just switch the connector from reel to reel as you use it. A reel with the Royal Bee system can be used in a conventional manner. You do not have to use it as an electric reel unless you choose to do so.

Barton believes the Royal Bee may not be just for handicapped fishermen. Ken Cook, one of the leading professional anglers in the country, is sold on the Royal Bee. After he suffered a broken arm, he had to withdraw from some tournaments because fishing with one hand was difficult. By the time his arm healed, he was hooked on the Royal Bee because it increased bassing efficiency. As Cook explains, "The electric reel has increased my efficiency in two ways. One is in flipping, where I use it all the time. The other is for fishing topwater, when I have to make a long cast. When I'm flipping, the electric reel gives me instant control over slack line. I can keep both hands on the rod. I never have to remove them to take up slack. I flip, engage the reel, and then all I have to do is push the lever with my thumb to take up slack instantly."

Cook's reel (a Ryobi 4000) is one of several that can be converted to the electric retrieve. For flipping, Cook loads his reel with 20-pound test line. He uses a similar reel with lighter line when fishing a surface lure. "What you can do with the electric reel is eliminate unproductive reeling time," Cook says.

A few extra seconds may not mean much if you are out on a neighborhood pond just fishing on the weekend. But it can mean a lot if you are in tournament competition, where one extra cast might keep you from going home with $50,000 tucked in your pocket. "Look at it this way," Cook explains. "Let's suppose we're in clear water and it's necessary to make a long cast to the cover we want to fish with a topwater lure. There's a whole lot of unproductive water between us and the cover. With the electric reel, I make my long cast and fish the cover. Then, when I'm ready to reel in, I just press the retrieve lever so the battery engages the necessary gears, and I've got my lure back ready to make another cast while you're still cranking."

When Royal Barton retired from his veterinary supply business, he began enjoying his favorite pastimes: hunting, fishing, and developing the Royal Bee system. He realized he needed help in marketing his product, so he sought professional assistance to learn how to reach the broadest possible market for the Royal Bee system.

Questions

1. What marketing problem does Royal Barton face? What are his information needs? Outline some survey research objectives for a research project on the Royal Bee system.
2. What type of survey—personal interview, telephone interview, or mail survey—should be selected?
3. What sources of survey error are most likely to occur in a study of this type?
4. What means should be used to obtain a high response rate?

CHAPTER 10
OBSERVATION

LEARNING OUTCOMES

After studying this chapter, you should be able to

1. Discuss the role of observation as a marketing research method
2. Describe the use of direct observation and contrived observation
3. Identify ethical issues in observation studies
4. Explain the observation of physical objects and message content
5. Describe major types of mechanical observation
6. Summarize techniques for measuring physiological reactions

Chapter Vignette: Neuroco Peers into the Consumer's Brain

When Hewlett-Packard was developing advertisements for its digital photography products, the firm wanted to ensure its ad images would evoke the desired response. For guidance, the company turned to Neuroco and its high-tech research method, known as neuromarketing.[1] Neuroco researchers showed subjects a pair of photos of the same woman, and about half of them preferred each picture. Then Neuroco measured the electrical activity in the brains of subjects looking at the same images, and the analysis showed a definite preference for one of the pictures in which the woman's smile was a little warmer.

Neuroco's approach uses a technology called *quantified electroencephalography (QEEG)*. Subjects wear light and portable EEG equipment that records brain activity; software presents the data in computer maps that display activity levels in areas of the brain. Researchers can then evaluate whether the person is attentive and whether brain activity signifies emotional involvement or analytical thinking. QEEG is more flexible than the better-known use of functional magnetic resonance imaging (fMRI), which has provided many advances in brain research but requires all subjects to lie still in a large, noisy machine. With QEEG, the measuring equipment can travel with subjects as they walk around a store or watch advertisements.

Consider a young woman demonstrating a Neuroco study by shopping with electrodes discreetly attached to her head. Neuroco chief scientist David Lewis observes a computer screen showing a map of her brain waves in red and green, with the colors signaling levels of alpha-wave activity. The zigzag pattern tells Lewis that this shopper is alert but not engaged in making purchase decisions. As the woman walks into a store's shoe department, however, the pattern changes when she picks up a pair of stiletto heels. An explosion of brain activity occurs, then the woman heads for the cash register, decision made.

As this example illustrates, observation can provide significant insights to marketers, and advances in observation technology are literally providing a view of what is happening in customers' brains. This chapter introduces the observation method of data gathering in marketing research.

Observation in Marketing Research

In marketing research, **observation** is a systematic process of recording behavioral patterns of people, objects, and occurrences as they happen. No questioning or communicating with people is needed. Researchers who use observation method data collection either witness and record information while watching events take place or take advantage of some tracking system such as checkout scanners or Internet activity records. These tracking systems can observe and provide data such as whether or not a specific consumer purchased more products on discount or at regular price or how much time a consumer spent viewing a particular web page before either exiting or clicking through to the next page.

Observation becomes a tool for scientific inquiry when it meets several conditions:

- The observation serves a formulated research purpose.
- The observation is planned systematically.
- The observation is recorded systematically and related to general propositions rather than simply reflecting a set of interesting curiosities.
- The observation is subjected to checks or controls on validity and reliability.[2]

Observation
The systematic process of recording the behavioral patterns of people, objects, and occurrences as they are witnessed.

What Can Be Observed?

Observational studies gather a wide variety of information about behavior. Exhibit 10.1 lists seven kinds of observable phenomena: physical actions, such as shopping patterns (in-store or via a web interface) or television viewing; verbal behavior, such as sales conversations; expressive behavior, such as tone of voice or facial expressions; spatial relations and locations, such as traffic patterns; temporal patterns, such as amount of time spent shopping or driving; physical objects, such as the amount of newspapers recycled; and verbal and pictorial records, such as the content of advertisements. (Investigation of secondary data also uses observation, but that subject was described in Chapter 7 and is not extensively discussed in this chapter.)

The observation method may be used to describe a wide variety of behavior, but cognitive phenomena such as attitudes, motivations, and preferences cannot be observed. As a result, observation research cannot provide an explanation of why a behavior occurred or what actions were intended. Another limitation is that the observation period generally is short. Observing behavior patterns that occur over a period of several days or weeks generally is too costly or even impossible.

TOTHEPOINT

Where observation is concerned, chance favors only the prepared mind.

—Louis Pasteur

EXHIBIT 10.1
What Can Be Observed

Phenomenon	Example
Physical action	A shopper's movement pattern in a store
Verbal behavior	Statements made by airline travelers while waiting in line
Expressive behavior	Facial expressions, tones of voices, and other forms of body language
Spatial relations and locations	How close visitors at an art museum stand to paintings
Temporal patterns	How long fast-food customers wait for their orders to be served
Physical objects	What brand-name items are stored in consumers' pantries
Verbal and pictorial records	Bar codes on product packages

RESEARCHSNAPSHOT

This Trend Brought to You by DDB SignBank

Extending the practice of observation beyond what can clearly be done scientifically, such as counting the number of tomato soup cans in a pantry or measuring the time spent watching television, some researchers have tried to catalog behaviors that may signal the beginning of important trends. This practice, called *trend spotting,* is controversial because the observations are subjective and unsystematic. In spite of the criticism, marketers are increasingly turning to trend spotters, so researchers have an incentive to develop this method's capabilities.

Starting in its office in Copenhagen, Denmark, giant ad agency DDB Worldwide has created a service called DDB SignBank, which invites all of DDB's staff throughout the world, plus other targeted groups such as members of youth organizations, to submit their observations to managers appointed as SignBankers. Staff members are directed to identify consumer behaviors, rather than comments gathered from other research methods, that might signal a new trend in the society or culture. The Sign-Bankers classify the observations and enter them into a corporate database. The database is updated each day, and account teams at the agency can search it for signs related to their clients' advertising objectives.

The idea behind SignBank, developed by sociologist Eva Steensig, is that the size of the database (which contained thirty thousand signs at a recent count) will allow patterns to emerge in the sheer number of observations. The data may be most useful as a source of ideas to test more rigorously. Anthon Berg, a Scandinavian brand of chocolate, used SignBank data to identify new occasions for which to promote chocolate and new uses for chocolate in health and beauty treatments.

Source: Based on Matthew Creamer, "DDB Collects 'Signs' to Identify Trends," Advertising Age, December 5, 2005, downloaded from http://www.adage.com, June 16, 2006; Eric Pfanner, "On Advertising: Do I Spot a Trend?" International Herald Tribune, January 1, 2006, www.iht.com; and DDB Worldwide, "DDB Worldwide Introduces DDB SignBank, a New Consumer Knowledge Model," news release, November 29, 2005, http://www.ddbneedham.dk.

©GENE BLEVINS/REUTERS/LANDOV

The Nature of Observation Studies

Marketing researchers can observe people, objects, events, or other phenomena using either human observers or machines designed for specific observation tasks. Human observation best suits a situation or behavior that is not easily predictable in advance of the research. Mechanical observation, as performed by supermarket scanners or traffic counters, can very accurately record situations or types of behavior that are routine, repetitive, or programmatic.

Human or mechanical observation is generally *unobtrusive,* meaning no communication with a respondent takes place. For example, rather than asking customers how much time they spend shopping in the store, a supermarket manager might observe and record the intervals between when shoppers enter and leave the store. The unobtrusive or nonreactive nature of the observation method often generates data without a subject's knowledge. A situation in which an observer's presence is known to the subject involves **visible observation**. A situation in which a subject is unaware that observation is taking place is **hidden observation**. Hidden, unobtrusive observation minimizes respondent error. Asking subjects to participate in the research is not required when they are unaware that they are being observed.

The major advantage of observation studies over surveys, which obtain self-reported data from respondents, is that the data are free from distortions, inaccuracies, or other response biases due to memory error, social desirability bias, and so on. The data are recorded when the actual behavior takes place.

Visible observation
Observation in which the observer's presence is known to the subject.

Hidden observation
Observation in which the subject is unaware that observation is taking place.

Observation of Human Behavior

Whereas surveys emphasize verbal responses, observation studies emphasize and allow for the systematic recording of nonverbal behavior. Toy manufacturers such as Fisher Price use the observation technique because children often cannot express their reactions to products. By observing

EXHIBIT 10.2 Nonverbal Communication: Status and Power Gestures

Behavior	Between People of Equal Status		Between People of Unequal Status		Between Men and Women	
	Intimate	**Nonintimate**	**Used by Superior**	**Used by Subordinate**	**Used by Men**	**Used by Women**
Posture	Relaxed	Tense (less relaxed)	Relaxed	Tense	Relaxed	Tense
Personal space	Closeness	Distance	Closeness (optional)	Distance	Closeness	Distance
Touching	Touch	Don't touch	Touch (optional)	Don't touch	Touch	Don't touch
Eye gaze	Establish	Avoid	Stare, ignore	Avert eyes, watch	Stare, ignore	Avert eyes
Demeanor	Informal	Circumspect	Informal	Circumspect	Informal	Circumspect
Emotional expression	Show	Hide	Hide	Show	Hide	Show
Facial expression	Smile	Don't smile	Don't smile	Smile	Don't smile	Smile

Source: Reprinted with permission of Simon & Schuster Adult Publishing Group, from *Body Politics* by Nancy C. Henley. Copyright © 1977 by Prentice-Hall, Inc.

children at play with a proposed toy, doll, or game, marketing researchers may be able to identify the elements of a potentially successful product. Toy marketing researchers might observe play to answer the following questions:

- How long does the child's attention stay with the product?
- Does the child put the toy down after two minutes or twenty minutes?
- Are the child's peers equally interested in the toy?

Behavioral scientists have recognized that nonverbal behavior can be a communication process by which meanings are exchanged among individuals. Head nods, smiles, raised eyebrows, and other facial expressions or body movements have been recognized as communication symbols. Observation of nonverbal communication may hold considerable promise for the marketing researcher. For example, a hypothesis about customer-salesperson interactions is that the salesperson would signal status based on the importance of each transaction. In low-importance transactions, in which potential customers are plentiful and easily replaced (say, a shoe store), the salesperson may show definite nonverbal signs of higher status than the customer. When customers are scarce, as in big-ticket purchase situations (real estate sales), the opposite should be true, with the salesperson showing many nonverbal indicators of deference. One way to test this hypothesis would be with an observation study using the nonverbal communication measures shown in Exhibit 10.2.

Of course, researchers would not ignore verbal behavior. In fact, in certain observation studies, verbal expression is very important.

Complementary Evidence

The results of observation studies may amplify the results of other forms of research by providing *complementary evidence* concerning individuals' "true" feelings. Focus group interviews often are conducted behind one-way mirrors from which marketing executives observe as well as listen to what is occurring. This additional source allows for interpretation of nonverbal behavior such as facial expressions or head nods to supplement information from interviews.

For example, in one focus group session concerning women's use of hand lotion, researchers observed that all the women's hands were above the table while they were casually waiting for the session to begin. Seconds after the women were told that the topic was to be hand lotion, all their hands were placed out of sight. This observation, along with the group discussion, revealed the women's anger, guilt, and shame about the condition of their hands. Although they felt they were expected to have soft, pretty hands, their housework required them to wash dishes, clean floors, and do other chores that were hard on their hands.

When focus group behavior is videotaped, observation of the nonverbal communication symbols can add even more to marketers' knowledge of the situation.

Direct Observation

Direct observation
A straightforward attempt to observe and record what naturally occurs; the investigator does not create an artificial situation.

Direct observation can produce detailed records of what people actually do during an event. The observer plays a passive role, making no attempt to control or manipulate a situation, instead merely recording what occurs. Many types of data can be obtained more accurately through direct observation than by questioning. For example, recording traffic counts or observing the direction of traffic flows within a supermarket can help managers design store layouts that maximize the exposure of departments that sell impulse goods. A manufacturer can determine the number of facings, shelf locations, display maintenance, and other characteristics that improve store conditions. If directly questioned in a survey, most shoppers would be unable to accurately portray the time they spent in each department. The observation method, in contrast, could determine this without difficulty.

With the direct observation method, the data consist of records of events made as they occur. An observation form often helps keep researchers' observations consistent and ensures that they record all relevant information. A respondent is not required to recall—perhaps inaccurately—an event after it has occurred; instead, the observation is instantaneous.

In many cases, direct observation is the most straightforward form of data collection—or the only form possible. A produce manager for Auchan (a France-based hypermart firm) may periodically gather competitive price information from Carrefour (also a France-based hypermart firm) stores within competing areas. Both Carrefour and Auchan can monitor each other's promotions by observing promotions posted on the competitor's website (see http://www.Auchan.fr and http://www.carrefour.fr, for example). In other situations, observation is the most economical technique. In a common type of observation study, a shopping center manager may observe the license plate (tag) numbers on cars in its parking lot. These data, along with automobile registration information, provide an inexpensive means of determining where customers live.

Certain data may be obtained more quickly or easily using direct observation than by other methods—gender, race, and other respondent characteristics can simply be observed. Researchers investigating a diet product may use observation when selecting respondents in a shopping mall. Overweight people may be prescreened by observing pedestrians, thus eliminating a number of screening interviews.

In a quality-of-life survey, researchers asked respondents a series of questions that were compiled into an index of well-being. But interviewers also used direct observation because the researchers wanted to investigate the effect of weather conditions on people's answers. The researchers quickly and easily observed and recorded outside weather conditions on the day of the interviews, as well as the temperature and humidity in the building in which the interviews were conducted.[3]

Response latency
The amount of time it takes to make a choice between two alternatives; used as a measure of the strength of preference.

Recording the decision time necessary to make a choice between two alternatives is a relatively simple, unobtrusive task easily accomplished through direct observation. The choice time recorded as a measure of the strength of the preference between alternatives is called **response latency**. This measure is based on the hypothesis that the longer a decision maker takes to choose between two alternatives, the closer the two alternatives are in terms of preference. In contrast, making a quick decision presumably indicates a considerable psychological distance between alternatives—that is, the choice is obvious. A computer can record decision times, so the response

RESEARCHSNAPSHOT

Hand Washing Overreported, Says Observational Research

People know that hand washing is a fundamental way to stay healthy, not to mention simple good manners. So, when you ask them, most people say they faithfully wash their hands. But according to observational research, what people say about this behavior is not what they necessarily do.

The American Society for Microbiology and the Soap and Detergent Association together arranged for a nationwide study of hand washing by U.S. adults. In an online survey by Harris Interactive, 91 percent of adults said they always wash their hands after using a public restroom. Men were somewhat less likely to make this claim—88 percent, versus 94 percent of women. The researchers followed up on the survey results by observing adults in public restrooms in Atlanta, Chicago, New York City, and San Francisco. A tally of the percentage who washed their hands found that only 83 percent did so. Keep in mind that some of the people observed to wash their hands might be people who would claim to do it only some of the time; so, the difference between the proportion of people who say they wash their hands and those who are observed doing it is probably more than the 8 percentage points observed. The difference

between reporting of hand washing and actual hand washing was greater for the men (about a 16 percent difference) than for the women (12 percent).

This research showing a divide between what individuals believe they should be doing and what they actually do could help the American Society for Microbiology and government agencies to craft messages aimed at improving citizens' health. In addition, soap marketers may want to learn more about what keeps individuals from washing their hands (Is it inconvenient? Are public sinks a turnoff?), even while being prepared for some response bias.

Source: Based on Harris Interactive, "Many Adults Report Not Washing Their Hands When They Should, and More People Claim to Wash Their Hands than Who Actually Do," news release, December 14, 2005, http://www.harrisinteractive.com; Soap and Detergent Association (SDA), "Women Better at Hand Hygiene Habits, Hands Down," news release, September 21, 2005, www.cleaning101.com; SDA, "Hand Washing Survey Fact Sheet," 2005, http://www.cleaning101.com, accessed February 24, 2006; and Harris Interactive, "A Survey of Hand Washing Behavior (2005 Findings)," September 2005, accessed at "2005 ASM/SDA Hand Hygiene Survey Results," http://www.cleaning101.com (SDA website), February 24, 2006.

©M. THOMSEN/ZEFA/CORBIS

latency measure is gaining popularity now that computer-assisted data collection methods are becoming more common.

ERRORS ASSOCIATED WITH DIRECT OBSERVATION

Although direct observation involves no interaction with the subject, the method is not error-free; the observer may record events subjectively. The same visual cues that may influence the interplay between interviewer and respondent (e.g., the subject's age or sex) may come into play in some direct observation settings, such as when the observer subjectively attributes a particular economic status or educational background to a subject. A distortion of measurement resulting from the cognitive behavior or actions of the witnessing observer is called **observer bias**. For example, in a research project using observers to evaluate whether sales clerks are rude or courteous, fieldworkers may be required to rely on their own interpretations of people or situations during the observation process.

Also, accuracy may suffer if the observer does not record every detail that describes the persons, objects, and events in a given situation. Generally, the observer should record as much detail as possible. However, the pace of events, the observer's memory, the observer's writing speed, and other factors will limit the amount of detail that can be recorded.

Interpretation of observation data is another potential source of error. Facial expressions and other nonverbal communication may have several meanings. Does a smile always mean happiness? Does the fact that someone is standing or seated next to the president of a company necessarily indicate the person's status?

SCIENTIFICALLY CONTRIVED OBSERVATION

Most observation takes place in a natural setting, but sometimes the investigator intervenes to create an artificial environment in order to test a hypothesis. This approach is called **contrived observation**. Contrived observation can increase the frequency of occurrence of certain behavior

Observer bias
A distortion of measurement resulting from the cognitive behavior or actions of a witnessing observer.

TOTHEPOINT

What we see depends mainly on what we look for.

—Sir John Lubbock

Contrived observation
Observation in which the investigator creates an artificial environment in order to test a hypothesis.

patterns, such as employee responses to complaints. An airline passenger complaining about a meal or service from the flight attendant may actually be a researcher recording that person's reactions. If situations were not contrived, the research time spent waiting and observing would expand considerably. A number of retailers use observers called *mystery shoppers* to visit a store and pretend to be interested in a particular product or service. After leaving the store, the "shopper" evaluates the salesperson's performance.

Combining Direct Observation and Interviewing

Some research studies combine visible observation with personal interviews. During or after in-depth observations, individuals are asked to explain their actions.[4] For example, direct observation of women applying hand and body lotion identified two kinds of users. Some women slapped on the lotion, rubbing it briskly into their skin. Others caressed their skin as they applied the lotion. When the women were questioned about their behavior, the researchers discovered that women who slapped the lotion on were using the lotion as a remedy for dry skin. Those who caressed their skin were more interested in making their skin smell nice and feel soft.

Even if fashion companies could learn a lot about the types of problems consumers typically have when purchasing and wearing clothes, would observation through two-way mirrors be appropriate?

Ethical Issues in the Observation of Humans

Observation methods introduce a number of ethical issues. Hidden observation raises the issue of the respondent's right to privacy. Suppose a research firm is approached by a company interested in acquiring information about how women put on their bras by observing behavior in a spa dressing area. The researcher considers approaching spas in several key cities about placing small cameras inconspicuously to observe women getting dressed. Obviously, such a situation raises an ethical question. While to some extent the dressing room is an area where women often do dress where others can observe them, women do not expect to have their dressing behavior recorded. Therefore, unless a way can be found to have some women consent to such observation, this observational approach is unethical.

Some people might see contrived observation as entrapment. To *entrap* means to deceive or trick into difficulty, which clearly is an abusive action. The problem is one of balancing values. If the researcher obtains permission to observe someone, the subject may not act naturally. So, at times there is a stront temptation to observe without obtaining consent. In other times, such as monitoring mall traffic, obtaining consent just to observe people walking through the mall would be difficult.

So, when should researchers feel comfortable collecting observational data? While exceptions exist to every rule, here are three questions that can help address this question:

1. Is the behavior being observed commonly performed in public where it is expected that others can observe the behavior?
2. Is the behavior performed in a setting in which the anonymity of the person being observed is assured (meaning there is no way to identify individuals)?
3. Has the person agreed to be observed?

If the answer to the first two questions is yes, then there is not likely a violation of privacy in collecting observational research data. If the answer to the third question is yes, then gathering the data also is likely to be ethical.

Observation of Physical Objects

Physical phenomena may be the subject of observation study. Physical-trace evidence is a visible mark of some past event or occurrence. For example, the wear on library books indirectly indicates which books are actually read (handled most) when checked out. A classic example of physical-trace evidence in a nonprofit setting was erosion on the floor tiles around the hatching-chick exhibit at Chicago's Museum of Science and Industry. These tiles had to be replaced every six weeks; tiles in other parts of the museum did not need to be replaced for years. The selective erosion of tiles, indexed by the replacement rate, was a measure of the relative popularity of exhibits.

Clearly, a creative marketing researcher has many options for determining the solution to a problem. The story about Charles Coolidge Parlin, generally recognized as one of the founders of commercial marketing research, counting garbage cans at the turn of the twentieth century illustrates another study of physical traces.

Parlin designed an observation study to persuade Campbell's Soup Company to advertise in the *Saturday Evening Post*. Campbell's was reluctant to advertise because it believed that the *Post* was read primarily by working people who would prefer to make soup from scratch, peeling the potatoes and scraping the carrots, rather than paying ten cents for a can of soup. To demonstrate that rich people weren't the target market, Parlin selected a sample of Philadelphia garbage routes. Garbage from each specific area of the city that was selected was dumped on the floor of a local National Guard Armory. Parlin had the number of Campbell's soup cans in each pile counted. The results indicated that the garbage from the rich people's homes didn't contain many cans of Campbell's soup. Although they may not have made soup from scratch themselves, their housekeepers may have. The garbage piles from the blue-collar area showed a larger number of Campbell's soup cans. This observation study was enough evidence for Campbell's. They advertised in the *Saturday Evening Post*.[5]

The method used in this study has since been used in a scientific project at the University of Arizona in which aspiring archaeologists have sifted through garbage for over thirty years. They examine soggy cigarette butts, empty milk cartons, and half-eaten Big Macs in an effort to understand modern life.

What is most interesting about the garbage project is that observations can be compared with the results of surveys about food consumption—and garbage does not lie. This type of observation can correct for overreporting consumption of healthful items and underreporting of, say, cigarette or alcohol consumption.

Another application of observing physical objects is to count and record physical inventories through retail or wholesale audits. This method allows researchers to investigate brand sales on regional and national levels, market shares, seasonal purchasing patterns, and so on. Marketing research suppliers offer audit data at both the retail and the wholesale levels.

An observer can record physical-trace data to discover information a respondent could not recall accurately. For example, measuring the number of ounces of a liquid bleach used during a test provides precise physical-trace evidence without relying on the respondent's memory. The accuracy of respondents' memories is not a problem for the firm that conducts a pantry audit. The pantry audit requires an inventory of the brands, quantities, and package sizes in a consumer's home rather than responses from individuals. The problem of untruthfulness or some other form of response bias is avoided. For example, the pantry audit prevents the possible problem of respondents erroneously claiming to have purchased prestige brands. However, gaining permission to physically check consumers' pantries is not easy, and the fieldwork is expensive. In addition, the brand in the pantry may

TOTHEPOINT

What would you rather believe? What I say, or what you saw with your own eyes?

—Groucho Marx

Picking through the garbage on the side of the road can reveal behaviors of fast-food customers.

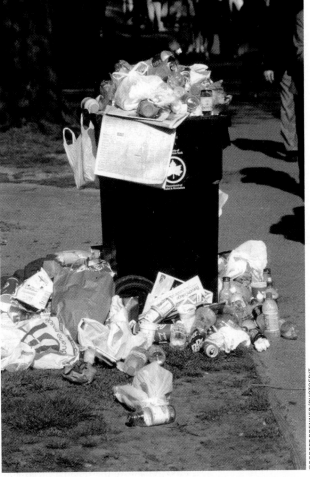

not reflect the brand purchased most often if consumers substituted it because they had a coupon, the usual brand was out of stock, or another reason.

Content Analysis

Content analysis
The systematic observation and quantitative description of the manifest content of communication.

Besides observing people and physical objects, researchers may use **content analysis**, which obtains data by observing and analyzing the contents or messages of advertisements, newspaper articles, television programs, letters, and the like. This method involves systematic analysis as well as observation to identify the specific information content and other characteristics of the messages. Content analysis studies the message itself and involves the design of a systematic observation and recording procedure for quantitative description of the manifest content of communication. This technique measures the extent of emphasis or omission of a given analytical category. For example, content analysis of advertisements might evaluate their use of words, themes, characters, or space and time relationships. Another topic of content analysis is the frequency with which women, African-Americans, or ethnic minorities appear in mass media.

Content analysis might be used to investigate questions such as whether some advertisers use certain themes, appeals, claims, or deceptive practices more than others or whether recent consumer-oriented actions by the Federal Trade Commission have influenced the contents of advertising. A cable television programmer might do a content analysis of network programming to evaluate its competition. Every year researchers analyze the Super Bowl telecast to see how much of the visual material is live-action play and how much is replay, or how many shots focus on the cheerleaders and how many on spectators. Content analysis also can explore the information content of television commercials directed at children, the company images portrayed in ads, and numerous other aspects of advertising.

Study of the content of communications is more sophisticated than simply counting the items; it requires a system of analysis to secure relevant data. After one employee role-playing session involving leaders and subordinates, researchers analyzed videotapes to identify categories of verbal behaviors (e.g., positive reward statements, positive comparison statements, and self-evaluation requests). Trained coders, using a set of specific instructions, then recorded and coded the leaders' behavior into specific verbal categories.

Mechanical Observation

In many situations, the primary—and sometimes the only—means of observation is mechanical rather than human. Video cameras, traffic counters, and other machines help observe and record behavior. Some unusual observation studies have used motion-picture cameras and time-lapse photography. An early application of this observation technique photographed train passengers and determined their levels of comfort by observing how they sat and moved in their seats. Another time-lapse study filmed traffic flows in an urban square and resulted in a redesign of the streets. Similar techniques may help managers design store layouts and resolve problems in moving people or objects through spaces over time.

Television Monitoring

Television monitoring
Computerized mechanical observation used to obtain television ratings.

Perhaps the best-known marketing research project involving mechanical observation and computerized data collection is ACNielsen's **television monitoring** system for estimating national television audiences. Nielsen Media Research uses a consumer panel and a monitoring device called a PeopleMeter to obtain ratings for television programs nationwide.[6] The Nielsen PeopleMeter gathers data on what each television in a household is playing and who is watching it at the time. Researchers attach electronic boxes to television sets and remote controls to capture information on program choices and the length of viewing time. Nielsen matches the signals captured through these devices with its database of network broadcast and cable program schedules so that it can identify the specific programs being viewed.

RESEARCHSNAPSHOT

Mobiltrak Reads Radios

Mobiltrak, a research firm based in Herndon, Virginia, uses a device that can observe what is playing on cars' stereos. The company installs observation equipment the size of a shoebox on towers located at heavily traveled intersections. Sensors on the equipment measure the level of electronic radiation emitted by the radio of each car as it passes by. Each radio station in the area broadcasts at a particular frequency, and the radio emits a level of radiation that corresponds to the station's frequency. Unless the drivers notice the small devices, they don't know that they are being observed.

The ease of mechanical data collection lets Mobiltrak collect tens of thousands of observations every month. Mobiltrak's equipment translates the data it collects into information about the stations being played. The data describe the volume of traffic listening to each station, not the stations being played by individual vehicles or any demographic data about the vehicles' drivers or passengers.

By paying a subscription fee to Mobiltrak, radio stations in the company's service areas can obtain data about their listeners. They can use the data to sell advertising time to businesses located where the most listeners are driving. In addition, advertisers can pay for data collected at particular locations. For example, Home Depot, which has used Mobiltrak, can find out which stations people are listening to as they travel on roads leading past one of the company's stores. An auto dealer who signed up for MobilTrak data discovered that the two popular—and expensive—stations on which he had been buying advertising time were not the stations people tended to listen to on the streets near his dealership.

Source: Based on "Lucas Conley, "At 1600 Pennsylvania Avenue, of Course, It's 'Rush Limbaugh,'" Fast Company, February 2005, issue 91 (Feb), page 29; Dina ElBoghdady, The Washington Post, October 25, 2004, http://www.washingtonpost.com; and Bear Stearns, "iBiquity and Mobiltrak: Bringing Radio into the Digital Age," Equity Research, February 8, 2005, http://www.bearstearns.com.

When a television in the panel household is turned on, a red light on the PeopleMeter periodically flashes to remind viewers to indicate who is watching. The viewer then uses a remote control to record who is watching. One button on the control is assigned to each member of the household and a separate visitor button is used for potential guests. The household member presses his or her button to indicate the sex and age of the person who is watching. Knowing who in the family is watching allows executives to match television programs with demographic profiles.

Each night, Nielsen's computers automatically retrieve the data stored in the PeopleMeter's recording box. In this way, Nielsen gathers daily estimates of when televisions are in use, which channels are used, and who is viewing each program. The panel includes more than five thousand households, selected to be representative of the U.S. population. For local programming, Nielsen uses additional panels equipped with recording devices but not People Meters to record viewer demographics. (Nielsen uses surveys to record demographic data for local programming.)

Critics of the PeopleMeter argue that subjects in Nielsen's panel grow bored over time and do not always record when they begin or stop watching television. Arbitron, best known for measuring radio audiences, has attempted to answer this objection with its own

Traffic cameras that monitor speeding on major highways are becoming commonplace in Europe, Australia, and even in some parts of the United States. Would car companies learn anything from the observed behavior?

measuring system, which it calls the Portable People Meter.[7] The Portable People Meter, which occupies about 4 cubic inches and weighs less than 3 ounces, reads inaudible codes embedded in audio signals to identify their source. Study participants wear or carry the meter throughout the day, and it automatically picks up codes embedded in whatever radio and television signals they encounter. At the end of the day, the participant inserts the meter into a "base station," which extracts the data collected, sends it to a household hub, and recharges the battery. The household hub then sends the data to Arbitron's computer over phone lines. To encourage cooperation, the meter has a motion sensor connected to a green light signaling that the meter senses it is being carried. Each participant is awarded points for the amount of time the meter is on. Total points are displayed in the base station and used to determine the size of the incentive paid to each participant. Arbitron's meter simplifies the participants' role and collects data on exposure to radio and television programming outside the home. However, the device records only signals that the radio or television system embeds using Arbitron's equipment.

Other devices gather data about the viewing of advertisements. The TiVo digital television recorder, so far used by only a small percentage of the population, collects detailed viewing data, such as what commercials people skip by using fast-forward. The PreTesting Company sets up contrived observational studies in which viewers equipped with a remote control are invited to watch any of three prerecorded channels playing different programs and advertisements, including the client's ads to be tested.[8] The system records the precise points at which the viewer changes the channel. By combining the results from many participants, the company arrives at a Cumulative Zapping Score, that is, the percentage of viewers who had exited the client's advertisement by each point in the ad. So that viewing behavior will be more natural, subjects are told they are evaluating the programming, not the ads.

Monitoring Website Traffic

Computer technology makes gathering detailed data about online behavior easy and inexpensive. The greater challenges are to identify which measures are meaningful and to interpret the data correctly. For instance, most organizations record the level of activity at their websites. They may count the number of *hits*—mouse clicks on a single page of a website. If the visitor clicks on many links, that page receives multiple hits. Similarly, they can track *page views,* or single, discrete clicks to load individual pages of a website. Page views more conservatively indicate how many users visit each individual page on the website and may also be used to track the path or sequence of pages that each visitor follows.

▓ CLICK-THROUGH RATES

Click-through rate
Proportion of people who are exposed to an Internet ad who actually click on it's hyperlink to enter the website; click-through rates are generally very low.

A **click-through rate** (CTR) is the percentage of people who are exposed to an advertisement who actually click on the corresponding hyperlink which takes them to the company's web site. Counting hits or page views can suggest the amount of interest or attention a website is receiving, but these measures are flawed. First, hits do not differentiate between a lot of activity by a few visitors and a little activity by many visitors. In addition, the researcher lacks information about the meaning behind the numbers. If a user clicks on a site many times, is the person finding a lot of useful or enjoyable material, or is the user trying unsuccessfully to find something by looking in several places? Additionally, some hits are likely made by mistake. The consumers may have had no intention of clicking through the ad or may not have known what they were doing when they clicked on the ad.

A more refined count is the number of *unique visitors* to a website. This measurement counts the initial access to the site but not multiple hits on the site by the same visitor during the same day or week. Operators of websites can collect the data by attaching small files, called *cookies,* to the computers of visitors to their sites and then tracking those cookies to see whether the same visitors return. Some marketing research companies, notably Jupiter Research and Nielsen//NetRatings, specialize in monitoring this type of Internet activity. A typical approach is to install a special tracking program on the personal computers of a sample of Internet users who agree to participate in the research effort. Nielsen//NetRatings has its software installed in thirty thousand computers in homes and workplaces. Internet monitoring enables these companies to identify the popularity of websites. In recent years, accurate measurement of unique visitors has become more difficult,

RESEARCHSNAPSHOT

Klipmart Watches Ad Viewership Online

As bandwidth widens, more and more computer users are going online to download audio and video content. Providers of that content are earning revenues through a combination of user fees and advertising. This situation is creating demand for information about how many people are seeing Internet ads and whether they are paying attention. Klipmart not only provides video content online but also is finding ways to measure the behavior of computer users—in particular, their viewership of ads using video.

Klipmart sets up tests in which computer users are presented with 30-second video ads as they perform other tasks. The company's equipment then measures how long the users spend watching each advertisement. The assumption is that a 30-second ad is too long for a computer user, so the company can get an upper limit of viewers' interest in the ads by seeing how many seconds out of the 30 the viewers keep watching. Early results suggest that the length of time spent viewing an online video ad averages 21 seconds but varies according to what the

user is trying to accomplish. Users stayed with an ad the longest—an average of 22.5 seconds—when they were waiting for the download of a home video. They were least patient, clicking away from the ad after 19 seconds, if they were downloading a finance video. The results surprised some people, who expected that computer users would exit advertisements within a few seconds.

Klipmart also can measure the user's interaction with an advertisement. Data from Klipmart indicate that users interact more with ads that contain more interactive elements.

©ELISA CINCINELLI/INDEX STOCK IMAGERY

Source: Based on Zachary Rodgers, "What's the Optimal Length for Video Ads?" ClickZ Internet Advertising News, October 4, 2005, http://www.clickz.com; Klipmart, "About Us" and "Research," http://www.klipmart.com, accessed February 6, 2006.

because over half of computer users have deleted cookies and many users block cookies to make themselves anonymous.[9]

As online advertising has become more widespread, marketing research has refined methods for measuring the effectiveness of the advertisements. The companies that place these ads can keep count of the click-through rate (CTR). Applying the CTR to the amount spent on the advertisement gives the advertiser a *cost per click*. These measures have been hailed as a practical way to evaluate advertising effectiveness. However, marketers have to consider that getting consumers to click on an ad is rarely the ad's objective. Companies are more often advertising to meet short- or long-term sales goals.

Google has benefited from CTR research indicating that the highest click-through rates tend to occur on pages displaying search results. (Not surprisingly, someone who searches for the term *kayaks* is more likely to be interested in an advertisement offering a good deal on kayaks.) The company showed Vanguard, for example, that its banner ads cost the financial firm less than fifty cents per click and generated a 14 percent click-through rate. That CTR is far above typical response rates for direct-mail advertising, but it does not indicate whether online clicks are as valuable in terms of sales.[10]

Scanner-Based Research

Lasers performing optical character recognition and barcode technology like the universal product code (UPC) have accelerated the use of mechanical observation in marketing research. Chapter 7 noted that a number of syndicated services offer secondary data about product category movement generated from retail stores using scanner technology.

This technology allows researchers to investigate questions that are demographically or promotionally specific. Scanner research has investigated the different ways consumers respond to price promotions and the effects of those differences on a promotion's profitability. One of the primary means of implementing this type of research is through the establishment of a **scanner-based consumer panel** to replace consumer purchase diaries. In a typical scanner panel, each household is assigned a barcoded card, like a frequent-shopper card, which members present to the clerk at the

scanner-based consumer panel
A type of consumer panel in which participants' purchasing habits are recorded with a laser scanner rather than a purchase diary.

RESEARCHSNAPSHOT

IRI Scanner Data Link Sales to Laws

Many popular cold and allergy medicines, including products sold under the brand names Dimetapp, Sudafed, and Triaminic, contain a decongestant called pseudoephedrine (PSE). The product is widely used and has been available over the counter for years. However, some states have recently restricted how these medicines may be sold, because individuals have used this legal medicine to extract ingredients for making the illegal drug methamphetamine. For example, Oklahoma and Illinois have required that drugs containing PSE be removed from store shelves and sold only at pharmacy counters.

Information Resources, Inc., used store scanner data to investigate whether such laws have brought about a decline in sales of PSE-containing medicines. IRI began measuring sales in Oklahoma and Illinois stores before the laws took effect and for months afterward. In Oklahoma, where all PSE-containing drugs had to be moved into the pharmacy, stores cut the selection of these products by one-third when they had to move the drugs. In addition, the volume of PSE products sold declined after the law went into effect, while the sales volume of non-PSE cold and allergy medicines increased. However, the situation actually provided an opportunity for drugstores, which saw an increase in PSE sales, while the overall sales decline hit grocery stores hardest (because many lack pharmacies).

In Illinois, only single-ingredient PSE products had to be moved, and the impact on sales was less dramatic. Sales of PSE products continued to grow, although sales of non-PSE alternatives grew faster. IRI used other data to further explain the trends in Illinois. For example, Illinois experienced a strong allergy season, and compliance with the law was reportedly poor in urban areas of that state. This mix of results shows that scanner data, especially combined with other data, can provide detailed information for making decisions that apply to the situations faced by particular store categories or geographic areas.

Source: Based on Information Resources, Inc., "Legislation Placing Pseudoephedrine Products behind the Counter Has Dramatic Effect on Sales According to IRI Study," news release, June 6, 2005, http://www.infores.com; and National Library of Medicine, National Institutes of Health, "Drug Information: Pseudoephedrine (Systemic)," Medline Plus, http://www.nlm.nih.gov/medlineplus, last updated December 14, 1998.

©PHOTODISC/GETTY IMAGES

register. The household's code number is coupled with the purchase information recorded by the scanner. In addition, as with other consumer panels, background information about the household obtained through answers to a battery of demographic and psychographic survey questions can also be coupled with the household code number.

Aggregate data, such as actual store sales as measured by scanners, are available to clients and industry groups. Data may also be aggregated by product category. To interpret the aggregated data, researchers can combine them with secondary research and panel demographics. For instance, data from Information Resources Inc. (IRI) have indicated a downward trend in sales of hair-coloring products. Demographic data suggest that an important reason is the aging of the population; many consumers who dye their hair reach an age at which they no longer wish to cover their gray hair. A smaller segment of the population is at an age where consumers typically begin using hair coloring.[11]

Data from scanner research parallel data provided by a standard mail diary panel, with some important improvements:

1. The data measure observed (actual) purchase behavior rather than reported behavior (recorded later in a diary).
2. Substituting mechanical for human record-keeping improves accuracy.
3. Measures are unobtrusive, eliminating interviewing and the possibility of social desirability or other bias on the part of respondents.
4. More extensive purchase data can be collected, because all UPC categories are measured. In a mail diary, respondents could not possibly reliably record all items they purchased. Because all UPC-coded items are measured in the panel, users can investigate many product categories to determine loyalty, switching rates, and so on for their own brands as well as for other companies' products and locate product categories for possible market entry.
5. The data collected from computerized checkout scanners can be combined with data about advertising, price changes, displays, and special sales promotions. Researchers can scrutinize them with powerful analytical software provided by the scanner data providers.

Scanner data can show a marketer week by week how a product is doing, even in a single store, and track sales in response to local ads or promotions. Also, several organizations have developed scanner panels, such as Information Resources Inc. Behavior Scan System, and expanded them into electronic test-market systems. These issues are discussed in greater detail in Chapter 12.

Advances in bar-code technology have led to **at-home scanning systems** that use handheld wands to read UPC symbols. Consumer panelists perform their own scanning *after* they have taken home the products. This advance makes it possible to investigate purchases made at stores that lack in-store scanning equipment.

At-home scanning systems
Systems that allow consumer panelists to perform their own scanning after taking home products, using handheld wands that read UPC symbols.

Measuring Physiological Reactions

Marketing researchers have used a number of other mechanical devices to evaluate consumers' physical and physiological reactions to advertising copy, packaging, and other stimuli. Researchers use such means when they believe consumers are unaware of their own reactions to stimuli such as advertising or that consumers will not provide honest responses. Four major categories of mechanical devices are used to measure physiological reactions: (1) eye-tracking monitors, (2) pupilometers, (3) psychogalvanometers, and (4) voice-pitch analyzers.

A magazine or newspaper advertiser may wish to grab readers' attention with a visual scene and then direct it to a package or coupon. Or a television advertiser may wish to identify which selling points to emphasize. Eye-tracking equipment records how the subject reads a print ad or views a television commercial and how much time is spent looking at various parts of the stimulus. In physiological terms, the gaze movement of a viewer's eye is measured with an **eye-tracking monitor**, which measures unconscious eye movements. Originally developed to measure astronauts' eye fatigue, modern eye-tracking systems need not keep a viewer's head in a stationary position. The devices track eye movements with invisible infrared light beams that lock onto a subject's eyes. The light reflects off the eye, and eye-movement data are recorded while another tiny video camera monitors which magazine page is being perused. The data are analyzed by computer to determine which components in an ad (or other stimuli) were seen and which were overlooked. Eye-tracking monitors have recently been used to measure the way subjects view e-mail and web marketing messages. OgilvyOne has used this technology to learn that people often skip over more than half of the words in e-mail advertising, especially words on the right side of the message. Interestingly, consumers generally ignore the word *free*.[12]

Eye-tracking monitor
A mechanical device used to observe eye movements; some eye monitors use infrared light beams to measure unconscious eye movements.

Pupilometer
A mechanical device used to observe and record changes in the diameter of a subject's pupils.

Other physiological observation techniques are based on a common principle: that adrenaline is released when the body is aroused. This hormone causes the heart to enlarge and to beat harder and faster. These changes increase the flow of blood to the fingers and toes. The blood vessels dilate, and perspiration increases, affecting the skin's electrical conductivity. Other physical changes following the release of adrenaline include dilation of the pupils, more frequent brain wave activity, higher skin temperature, and faster breathing. Methods that measure these and other changes associated with arousal can apply to a variety of marketing questions, such as subjects' reactions to advertising messages or product concepts.

Physiological responses to advertising can be recorded with a device like this one.

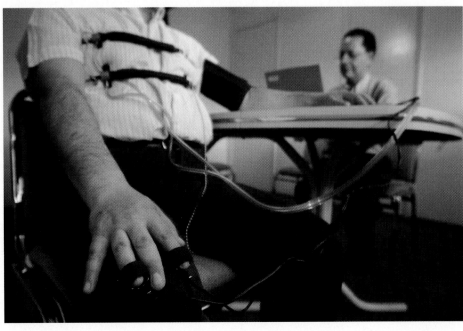

©ASSOCIATED PRESS/AP

A **pupilometer** observes and records changes in the diameter of a subject's pupils. A subject is instructed to look at a screen on which an advertisement or other stimulus is projected. When the brightness and distance of the stimulus from the subject's eyes are held constant, changes in pupil size may be interpreted as changes in cognitive activity that result from the stimulus, rather than from eye dilation and constriction in response to light intensity, distance from the object, or other physiological reactions to the conditions of observation. This method of research is based on the assumption that increased pupil size reflects positive attitudes toward and interest in advertisements.

A **psychogalvanometer** measures galvanic skin response (GSR), a measure of involuntary changes in the electrical resistance of the skin. This device is based on the assumption that physiological changes, such as increased perspiration, accompany emotional reactions to advertisements, packages, and slogans. Excitement increases the body's perspiration rate, which increases the electrical resistance of the skin. The test is an indicator of emotional arousal or tension.

Voice-pitch analysis is a relatively new physiological measurement technique that gauges emotional reactions as reflected in physiological changes in a person's voice. Abnormal frequencies in the voice caused by changes in the autonomic nervous system are measured with sophisticated, audio-adapted computer equipment. Computerized analysis compares the respondent's voice pitch during warm-up conversations (normal range) with verbal responses to questions about his or her evaluative reaction to television commercials or other stimuli. This technique, unlike other physiological devices, does not require the researcher to surround subjects with mazes of wires or equipment.

All of these devices assume that physiological reactions are associated with persuasiveness or predict some cognitive response. This assumption has not yet been clearly demonstrated. No strong theoretical evidence supports the argument that such a physiological change is a valid measure of future sales, attitude change, or emotional response. Another major problem with physiological research is the *calibration,* or sensitivity, of measuring devices. Identifying arousal is one thing, but precisely measuring *levels* of arousal is another. In addition, most of these devices are expensive. However, as a prominent researcher points out, physiological measurement is coincidental: "Physiological measurement isn't an exit interview. It's not dependent on what was remembered later on. It's a live blood, sweat, and tears, moment-by-moment response, synchronous with the stimulus."[13]

Each of these mechanical devices has another limitation: The subjects are usually placed in artificial settings, such as watching television in a laboratory rather than at home, and they know they are being observed.

Summary

1. Discuss the role of observation as a marketing research method. Observation is a powerful tool for the marketing researcher. Scientific observation is the systematic process of recording the behavioral patterns of people, objects, and occurrences as they are witnessed. Questioning or otherwise communicating with subjects does not occur. A wide variety of information about the behavior of people and objects can be observed. Seven kinds of phenomena are observable: physical actions, verbal behavior, expressive behavior, spatial relations and locations, temporal patterns, physical objects, and verbal and pictorial records. Thus, both verbal and nonverbal behavior may be observed. Observation may not, however, be used for cognitive phenomena. Attitudes, motivations, expectations, intentions, and preferences are not observable; only overt behavior of short duration can be observed.

2. Describe the use of direct observation and contrived observation. Human observation, whether direct or contrived, is commonly used when the situation or behavior to be recorded is not easily predictable in advance of the research. It may be unobtrusive, and many types of data can be obtained more accurately through direct observation than by questioning respondents. Direct observation involves watching and recording what naturally occurs, without creating an artificial situation. For some data, observation is the most direct or the only method of collection. For example, researchers can measure response latency, the time it takes individuals to choose between alternatives. Observer bias may be a problem in correctly perceiving the behaviors being observed. Observation can also be contrived by creating the situations to be observed. This can reduce the time and expense of obtaining reactions to certain circumstances.

3. Identify ethical issues in observation studies. Contrived observation, hidden observation, and other observation research designs have the potential to involve deception. For this reason, these methods often raise ethical concerns about subjects' right to privacy and right to be informed.

Psychogalvanometer
A device that measures galvanic skin response, a measure of involuntary changes in the electrical resistance of the skin.

Voice-pitch analysis
A physiological measurement technique that records abnormal frequencies in the voice that are supposed to reflect emotional reactions to various stimuli.

4. Explain the observation of physical objects and message content. Physical-trace evidence serves as a visible record of past events. Researchers may examine whatever evidence provides such a record, including inventory levels, the contents of garbage cans, or the items in a consumer's pantry. Content analysis obtains data by observing and analyzing the contents of the messages in written or spoken communications.

5. Describe major types of mechanical observation. Mechanical observation uses a variety of devices to record behavior directly. It may be an efficient and accurate choice when the situation or behavior to be recorded is routine, repetitive, or programmatic. National television audience ratings are based on mechanical observation (for example, PeopleMeters) and computerized data collection. Website traffic may be measured electronically. Scanner-based research provides product category sales data recorded by laser scanners in retail stores. Many syndicated services offer secondary data collected through scanner systems.

6. Summarize techniques for measuring physiological reactions. Physiological reactions, such as arousal or eye movement patterns, may be observed using a number of mechanical devices. Eye-tracking monitors identify the direction of a person's gaze, and a pupilometer observes and records changes in the diameter of the pupils of subjects' eyes, based on the assumption that a larger pupil signifies a positive attitude. A psychogalvanometer measures galvanic skin response as a signal of a person's emotional reactions. Voice-pitch analysis measures changes in a person's voice and associates the changes with emotional response.

Key Terms and Concepts

Observation
Visible observation
Hidden observation
Direct observation
Response latency
Observer bias

Contrived observation
Content analysis
Television monitoring
Click-through rate
Scanner-based consumer panel
At-home scanning systems

Eye-tracking monitor
Pupilometer
Psychogalvanometer
Voice-pitch analysis

Questions for Review and Critical Thinking

1. Yogi Berra, former New York Yankee catcher, said, "You can observe a lot just by watching." How does this fit in with the definition of scientific observation?
2. What are the advantages and disadvantages of observation studies relative to surveys?
3. Under what conditions are observation studies most appropriate?
4. **ETHICS** The chapter showed a photograph of a traffic monitoring camera. Do you think the use of these cameras to issue speeding tickets is ethical? What types of behavior might cameras like these capture that would help automobile designers produce products that better match our needs as drivers?
5. A multinational fast-food corporation plans to locate a restaurant in La Paz, Bolivia. Secondary data for this city are sketchy and outdated. How might you determine the best location using observation?
6. Discuss how an observation study might be combined with a personal interview.
7. **'NET** Click-through rates for advertisements placed in websites are usually very, very low (less than 1 percent). What types of error might exist in using click-through rate data as a measure of an ad's success?
8. Outline a research design using observation for each of the following situations:
   a. A bank wishes to collect data on the number of customer services and the frequency of customer use of these services.

   b. A state government wishes to determine the driving public's use of seat belts.
   c. A researcher wishes to know how many women have been featured on *Time* covers over the years.
   d. A fast-food franchise wishes to determine how long a customer entering a store has to wait for his or her order.
   e. A magazine publisher wishes to determine exactly what people look at and what they pass over while reading one of its magazines.
   f. A food manufacturer wishes to determine how people use snack foods in their homes.
   g. An overnight package delivery service wishes to observe delivery workers beginning at the moment when they stop the truck, continuing through the delivery of the package, and ending when they return to the truck.
9. What is a scanner-based consumer panel?
10. What are the major types of mechanical observation?
11. **ETHICS** Comment on the ethics of the following situations:
   a. During the course of telephone calls to investors, a stockbroker records respondents' voices when they are answering sensitive investment questions and then conducts a voice pitch analysis. The respondents do not know that their voices are being recorded.
   b. A researcher plans to invite consumers to be test users in a simulated kitchen located in a shopping mall and then to

videotape their reactions to a new microwave dinner from behind a two-way mirror (one that an observer behind the mirror can see through but the person looking into the mirror sees only the reflection).

c. A marketing researcher arranges to purchase the trash from the headquarters of a major competitor. The purpose is to sift through discarded documents to determine the company's strategic plans.

12. What is a psychogalvanometer?

13. **'NET** William Rathje, a researcher at the University of Arizona, Department of Anthropology, has become well-known for the "Garbage Project." The project involves observational research. Use http://www.ask.com to find information about the garbage project at the University of Arizona. What is the name of the book that describes some of the key findings of the Garbage Project? How do you think it involves observational research?

14. **'NET** The Internet is filled with webcams. For example, Pebble Beach Golf Club has several webcams (http://www.pebblebeach.com). How could a researcher use webcams like these to collect behavioral data?

Case 10.1 Mazda and Syzygy

When Mazda Motor Europe set out to improve its website, the company wanted details about how consumers were using the site and whether finding information was easy. Mazda hired a research firm called Syzygy to answer those questions with observational research.[14] Syzygy's methods include the use of an eye-tracking device that uses infrared light rays to record what areas of a computer screen a user is viewing. For instance, the device measured the process computer users followed in order to look for a local dealer or arranging a test drive. Whenever a process seemed confusing or difficult, the company looked for ways to make the website easier to navigate.

To conduct this observational study, Syzygy arranged for sixteen subjects in Germany and the United Kingdom to be observed as they used the website. The subjects in Germany were observed with the eye-tracking equipment. As the equipment measured each subject's gaze, software recorded the location on the screen and graphed the data. Syzygy's results included three-dimensional contour maps highlighting the "peak" areas where most of the computer users' attention was directed.

Questions

1. What could Mazda learn from eye-tracking software that would be difficult to learn from other observational methods?

2. What are the shortcomings of this method?

3. Along with the eye-tracking research, what other research methods could help Mazda assess the usability of its website? Summarize your advice for how Mazda could use complementary methods to obtain a complete understanding of its website usability.

Case 10.2 Texas Instruments and E-Lab

E-Lab, LLC is a business research and design firm in Chicago that specializes in observing people, identifying patterns in behavior, and developing an understanding of why these patterns exist.[15] The company then uses the knowledge that it gains as a framework in the product development process. Texas Instruments (TI) used E-Lab to investigate the mobility, connectivity, and communications needs of law enforcement officers, which led to ideas for a set of computing and communications products. As part of its product development research, TI's Advanced Integrated Systems Department and E-Lab researchers spent 320 hours shadowing police officers in three Texas police departments. Shadowing involves asking questions while observing. Researchers walked foot patrols, rode in patrol cars, and pedaled with bike patrols. They spent time with crowd control, narcotics, homicide, dispatch, and juvenile teams. They recorded their observations and interviews on paper, digital camera, and video.

A number of interesting findings emerged from all this research. First, police officers are very social, so it was important that any product TI developed should enhance socialization rather than detract from it. For example, an in-car computing and communications device should be able to access a database that lists names and numbers of experts on the force so officers can call or e-mail the experts directly. Second, police officers are not driven by procedure. That told TI that the procedures for an investigation should reside in the device and that the device should prompt the officer at each step in the process. And third, officers rely on informal information about people and activities on their beats. This information may be kept on scraps of paper, on a spreadsheet back in the office, or in the police officer's head. Business researchers concluded that any device that TI develops should have a place to compile and share informal information.

Questions

1. Identify the research design used by E-Lab.

2. Compare this research design with a survey research design. What advantages, if any, did this research design have over a survey?

Case 10.3 Tulsa's Central Business District (A)

The metropolitan Tulsa Chamber of Commerce recognized that there was a critical gap between the availability of timely information about the central business district (CBD) and the need for this information for investment decision making, commercial marketing efforts, and the continued pursuit of the goal of downtown revitalization. The Chamber of Commerce undertook four separate research projects to gather information about the CBD. One project was a physical inventory of the existing downtown commercial base. The objectives of the study were to determine what types of establishments were operating in the CBD and the number of vacancies there and to generally profile the commercial geography of the CBD. The researchers found that the central business district was based on the U.S. Bureau of the Census classification scheme. The CBD was identified as the area encompassed by the inner dispersal loop (a system of expressways),

which corresponded identically with census tract 25 (see Case Exhibit 10.3–1).

A team of ten pedestrian fieldworkers covered each block in the inner dispersal loop. The fieldworkers used the observation form in Case Exhibit 10.3–2 to record the company name, address, primary business activity, estimated frontage, and other relevant information about each building site or office. Fieldworkers recorded Standard Industrial Classification (SIC) codes for retailers. SIC codes for all other establishments were recorded by research assistants after the data were collected. All the data were identified by census block.

Questions

1. Evaluate this research design.
2. What changes, if any, would you make in the observation form?
3. What problems would you expect in the data collection stage?
4. What techniques would you use to analyze the data?

CASE EXHIBIT 10.3–1 **Census Blocks in Census Tract 25**

Source: U.S. Bureau of the Census.

CASE EXHIBIT 10.3-2 **Observation Study Recording Form**

Company Name _____

_____

Address: _____

Tulsa, Oklahoma

Activities: ___ 1 Vacant ___ 2 Retail ___ 3 Wholesale ___ 4 Manufacturing

___ 5 Service ___ 6 Other (Specify) _____

Retail SIC: ___ 52 ___ 53 ___ 54 ___ 55 ___ 56 ___ 57 ___ 58 ___ 59 ___ 60

Other Activities (describe): _____

_____

Is the Building: ___ 1 For Sale? ___ 2 For Rent?

Leasable Space: _____

Realtor's Name: _____

Realtor's Phone: _____

Rent (per sq. foot)

Is the Building Being: ___ 1 Restored? ___ 2 Remodeled?

Estimated Frontage (Feet): _____

Estimated Number of Stories: _____

Comments: _____

_____

_____

CHAPTER 11
EXPERIMENTAL RESEARCH:
AN OVERVIEW

After studying this chapter, you should be able to

1. Create an experimental, independent variable through a valid experimental manipulation of its value
2. Understand and minimize the systematic experimental error
3. Know ways of minimizing experimental demand characteristics
4. Avoid unethical experimental practices
5. Understand the advantages of a between-subjects experimental design
6. Weigh the trade-off between internal and external validity

Chapter Vignette: The Color of Fish

Marketing managers often like to show off by proving that their brand is superior to a competitor's offering. When Brand "X" managers claim that customers prefer its product over Brand "Y's" product, they had best be prepared to defend that claim in court. As a result, lawyers often need marketing research. This vignette describes just such a situation.

Sea Snapper brand gourmet frozen fish products claimed in advertising that their fish sticks are preferred more than two to one over the most popular brand, Captain John's.[1] The advertisements all include a definitive statement indicating that research existed which substantiated this claim.

Captain John's reaction was *war;* or at least legal war. They decided to sue Sea Snapper claiming that the advertisements include false claims based on faulty research. In court, the research is described in great detail. Sea Snapper conducted taste tests involving four hundred consumers who indicated that they regularly ate frozen food products. Two hundred tasted Sea Snapper premium fish sticks and the other two hundred tasted Captain John's premium fish sticks. Consumer preference was measured with a 100-point rating scale. The results showed the average preference score for Sea Snapper was 78.2 compared to 39.0 for Captain John's. Case closed?

Captain John's attorney hires a marketing research firm to assist in the lawsuit. They claim that the research is faulty because the procedures were improperly conducted. First, it turns out that Sea Snapper fish sticks were always presented to consumers on a blue plate while Captain John's were always presented to consumers on an orange plate. Second, the Sea Snapper products used in the experiment were taken directly from the Sea Snapper kitchens to the testing facility, while the Captain John's products were purchased at a local warehouse store. Therefore, because the research is invalid, the claims are invalid and Sea Snapper should stop making the claims and pay for any damages to Captain John's in the form of lost sales and damaged image. Who will win this lawsuit?

©STOCK FOOD/GETTY IMAGES

The Nature of Experiments

Most students are familiar with scientific experiments from studying physical sciences like physics and chemistry. The term *experiment* typically conjures up an image of a chemist surrounded by bubbling test tubes and Bunsen burners. Behavioral and physical scientists have used experimentation far longer than have marketing researchers. Nevertheless, both social scientists and physical scientists use experiments for much the same purpose.

As described in Chapter 3, experiments are widely used in causal research designs. Experimental research allows a researcher to control the research situation so that *causal* relationships among variables may be evaluated. The marketing experimenter manipulates one or more independent variables and holds constant all other possible independent variables while observing effects on dependent variables. Events may be controlled in an experiment to a degree not possible in a survey.

Independent variables are expected to determine the outcomes of interest. In an experiment, they are controlled by the researcher through manipulations. Dependent variables are the outcomes of interest to the researcher and the decision makers. A simple example would be thinking about how changes in price would influence sales. Price would be an independent variable and sales would be a dependent variable. In our opening vignette, the brand (Sea Snapper or Captain John's) would be an experimental independent variable and the 100-point ratings scale indicating liking would be the important dependent variable.

The researcher's goal in conducting an experiment is to determine whether changing an experimental independent variable causes changes in an important dependent variable. Sea Snapper's preference claim is based on the brand causing preference. In other words, when a consumer is presented with Sea Snapper brand instead of Captain John's, it causes him or her to rate the product higher. If everything else is the same each time a consumer tried the product in the experiment, then a causal inference is supported.

A famous marketing experiment investigated the influence of brand name on consumers' taste perceptions. An experimenter manipulated whether consumers preferred the taste of beer in labeled or unlabeled bottles. One week respondents were given a six-pack containing bottles labeled only with letters (A, B, C). The following week, respondents received another six-pack with brand labels (like Budweiser, Coors, Miller, and so forth). The experimenter measured reactions to the beers after each tasting. In every case, the beer itself was the same. So, every person involved in the experiment drank the very same beer. Therefore, the differences observed in taste, the key dependent variable, could only be attributable to the difference in labeling. When the consumers participating in the experiment expressed a preference for the branded beer, the conclusion is that brand name does influence consumers' taste perceptions.

An Illustration: Does Color Cause Preference?

The next two chapters deal with marketing experiments. Marketing experiments can best be illustrated through examples like this one. We will refer back to this example through the next two chapters.

Here, let's take a look at an experiment investigating how color and lights might influence shoppers. This particular research is highly relevant for those involved in retail management and design. The key decisions center around ways color and lighting can be changed to produce favorable consumer reactions. A corresponding research question is, "What is the effect of color and lighting on shopper patronage (meaning how much someone would shop in the store)?"[2]

Over two hundred female consumers were recruited to participate in the experiment. Participants in experimental research are referred to as **subjects** rather than respondents. This is because the experimenter subjects them to some experimental treatment. Each subject in this experiment was simply asked to provide responses to a "new fashion store" concept. The store would sell women's clothing and accessories to the fashion-minded professional woman.

Subjects
The sampling units for an experiment, usually human respondents who provide measures based on the experimental manipulation.

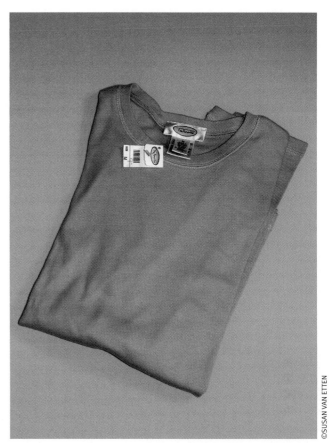

©SUSAN VAN ETTEN

Independent Variables

An experiment can capture whether or not color can cause differences in consumer preference for products.

The experiment involved two relevant independent variables. Fictitious store environments were created for the experiment. Four different hypothetical stores were created. The only thing that differed between the four was the predominant store color and the type of lighting. Thus, the two key independent variables were color and lighting.

Each consumer participating in the experiment (subject) responded to one new store description. The color independent variable was created by describing the new store as predominantly blue or predominantly orange. Similarly, the lighting independent variable was created by describing the store as either having bright or soft lights. Exhibit 11.1 illustrates the four different experimental conditions created by the experimenter. An **experimental condition** refers to one of the possible levels of an experimental variable manipulation.

Subjects were assigned to one of four condition groups. Each group was assigned a store with one of the four color and lighting combinations as shown in the exhibit. Thus, all participants within a group received the same description. Subjects in different groups received different descriptions. By analyzing differences between the groups, the researcher can see what effects occur due to the two experimentally controlled independent variables.

Experimental condition
One of the possible levels of an experimental variable manipulation.

		Color	
		Blue	**Orange**
Lighting:	Soft	¼ of Participants	¼ of Participants
	Bright	¼ of Participants	¼ of Participants

EXHIBIT 11.1
Experimental Conditions in Color and Lighting Experiment

EXHIBIT 11.2
Consumer Average Patronage Scores in Each Condition

		Color		
		Blue	**Orange**	
Lighting:	Soft	148.5	140.1	**144.7**
	Bright	159.1	122.6	**140.4**
		153.8	**131.8**	

Experimental Outcome

The key outcome, or dependent variable, in this example is a subject's perception of how much he or she would patronize the store. In this case, a rating scale asking how much each participant thought they would actually visit and buy things at the store was created. The possible scores ranged from 0 to 300. A higher score means higher patronage.

Exhibit 11.2 shows the average for each experimental condition. The results show that among experimental subjects who rated a blue store, an average patronage score of 153.8 was reported, which is considerably higher than the average of 131.8 reported by subjects who rated an orange store. The lighting experimental variable however, doesn't seem to have much of an effect. Average scores for the soft and bright lighting condition are not that different. Subjects in the soft lighting condition reported an average of 144.7 and subjects in the bright lighting condition reported only a slightly lower average of 140.4.

Thus, the conclusion at this point seems to be that changing a store's color can change consumer patronage. A blue store is more likely to be patronized by a consumer than is an orange store. Lighting doesn't seem to make much difference. Or does it?

Independent Variable Main Effects and Interaction

Main effect
The experimental difference in dependent variable means between the different levels of any single experimental variable.

Interaction effect
Differences in dependant variable means due to a specific combination of independent variables.

Color does seem to matter. But, maybe lighting shouldn't be dismissed so quickly. The researcher must examine both the effects of each experimental variable considered alone and the effects due to combinations of variables. A **main effect** refers to the experimental difference in means between the different levels of any single experimental variable. In this case, there are potential main effects for color and for lighting, but only the differences associated with color are significant. An **interaction effect** is due to a specific combination of independent variables. In this case, it's possible that the combination of color and lighting creates effects that are not clearly represented in the main effects.

Experimental results are often shown with a line graph as shown in Exhibit 11.3. Main effects are illustrated when the lines are at different heights as is the case here. Notice the blue line is

EXHIBIT 11.3
Experimental Graph Showing Results within Each Condition

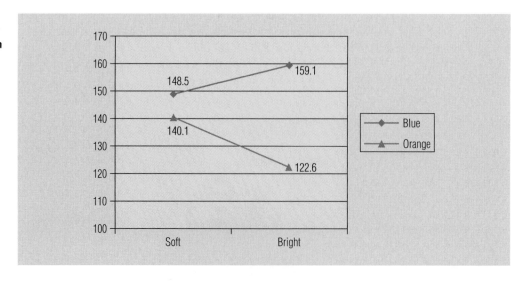

higher than the orange line. When the lines have very different slopes, an interaction is likely present. In this case, the combination of lights and color is presenting an interaction leading to the following interpretation.

The best possible reaction occurs when the store has a blue color with bright lights and the worst combination occurs when the store is orange with bright lights. In contrast, the means are essentially the same for either color when the lights are soft. So, lights may indeed matter. When the lights are soft, there is little difference in patronage between a blue and orange store. But, when the lights are bright, there is quite a difference between blue and orange.

Basic Issues in Experimental Design

Experimental design is a major research topic. In fact, there are courses and books devoted only to that topic.[3] Here, an introduction into experimental design is provided. A student should be able to design and implement basic experimental designs with this introduction. Fortunately, most experimental designs in marketing are relatively simple.

Experimental designs involve no less than four important design elements. These issues include (1) manipulation of the independent variable, (2) selection and measurement of the dependent variable, (3) selection and assignment of experimental subjects, and (4) control over extraneous variables.[4] Each is discussed below.

Manipulation of the Independent Variable

Recall from Chapter 3, the thing that makes independent variables special in experimentation is that the researcher actually creates his or her values. This is how the researcher manipulates, and therefore controls, independent variables. In our color experiment, the researcher manipulated the values of the color independent variable by assigning it a value of either blue or orange. Experimental independent variables are hypothesized to be causal influences. Therefore, experiments are very appropriate in causal designs.

An **experimental treatment** is the term referring to the way an experimental variable is manipulated. For example, the opening vignette manipulated the brand with an experimental treatment assigning consumers to taste either Sea Snapper or Captain John's fish sticks. Thus, there were two levels (or values) of the brand variable. A medical researcher may manipulate an experimental variable by treating some subjects with one drug and the other subjects with a separate drug. In the retail atmosphere experiment, the color treatment was either blue or orange and the lighting treatment was either bright or soft lights. Experimental variables often involve treatments with more than two levels. For instance, prices of $1.29, $1.69, and $1.99 might represent treatments in a pricing experiment examining how price affects sales.

Experimental variables like these can not only be described as independent variables, but they also can be described as a *categorical variable* because they take on a value to represent some classifiable or qualitative aspect. Color, for example, is either orange or blue. Advertising copy style is another example of a categorical or classificatory variable that might be manipulated in an experiment. In

Experimental treatment
The term referring to the way an experimental variable is manipulated.

A lot of marketing research involves experiments that manipulate different elements of physical environments.

©THOMAS MICHAEL CORCORAN/PHOTOEDIT

RESEARCHSNAPSHOT

Does Promotion Cause Intoxication?

One of the most pressing issues on college campuses is over-indulgence of alcohol. What are all of the factors that lead to the abuse of alcohol among undergraduate college students? Cultural influences such as the rite of passage can be identified in qualitative research. However, when it comes to setting policies that govern the sale of alcohol on and near universities, decision makers need to know what controllable practices cause drunkenness among college students and what behaviors are caused by drunkenness.

If heavy price promotion leads to drunkenness, which leads to detrimental behaviors, bars may reconsider their use and policy makers may consider restricting the types of promotions allowable if they wish to maintain their license to sell alcoholic beverages. These decision questions have led to numerous market experiments. For instance, the type of price promotion used by bars can be manipulated either in the field or in a lab experiment by exposing some subjects to an ad with one type of promotion and exposing others to a different type of promotion. This may allow a test of the causal influence of promotion on alcohol consumption. These studies show results like those shown in the chart titled "Mean Number of Drinks":

Mean Number of Drinks

This experiment involves an experimental manipulation varying the promotion over three levels. One-third of the student-subjects were exposed to each condition. The results show that reduced price drinks do lead to an increase in the number of drinks that a student estimates he or she would drink. This effect looks to be slightly larger among men than among women, although

women simply estimate they will drink less than men no matter what the experimental condition.

An experiment can also be used to show potentially negative results of too much drinking among college students. Researchers have designed simple experiments to examine how likely over-drinking is to lead a women to experience an unwanted sexual encounter. An experimental variable can be created that manipulates the amount of alcohol a student-subject actually consumes. This experiment can be performed in a lab environment, and one experimental condition could involve non-alcoholic drinking and another could involve heavy drinking and then asking subjects how likely they would be to consent to or actively resist unwanted sexual advances. A similar experiment showed results like those depicted in the chart below:

These results show that although self-reported consent is low in both cases (on a 1 – 5 scale with 5 indicating probable consent), it is slightly higher in the intoxicated case. There appears to be very little difference in self-reported aggressive resistance. Thus, the manipulation did not seem to affect the means on aggressive resistance. Other experiments looked at different interactions that have further implications for policy makers.

Thus, experimental manipulations like these are very helpful in implementing causal designs studying drinking related behaviors.

Sources: Christie, J., D. Fisher, J. Kozup, S. Smith, S. Burton, and E. Creyer (2001), "The Effects of Bar-Sponsored Alcohol Beverage Promotions Across Binge and Non-binge Drinkers," Journal of Public Policy and Marketing, 20 (Fall), 240–253; Davis, K.C., W. H. George, and J. Norris (2004), "Women's Responses to Unwanted Sexual Advances: The Role of Alcohol and Inhibition Conflict," Psychology of Women Quarterly, 28 (December), 333–343.

other situations an independent variable may truly be a *continuous variable*. When this is the case, the researcher must select appropriate levels of that variable as experimental treatments. For example, lighting can actually be varied over any level from no brightness onward. Before conducting the experiment, the researcher decides on levels that would be relevant to study. The levels should be noticeably different and realistic.

EXPERIMENTAL AND CONTROL GROUPS

In perhaps the simplest experiment, an independent variable is manipulated over two treatment levels resulting in two groups, an experimental group and a control group. An **experimental group** is one in which an experimental treatment is administered. A **control group** is one in which no experimental treatment is administered. For example, consider an experiment studying how advertising affects sales. In the experimental group, the advertising budget may be set at $200,000. In the control condition, advertising may remain at zero or may not change from its current level. By holding conditions constant in the control group, the researcher controls for potential sources of error in the experiment. Sales (the dependent variable) in the two treatment groups are compared at the end of the experiment to determine whether the level of advertising (the independent variable) had any effect. Note that this simple experiment can only produce a main effect.

SEVERAL EXPERIMENTAL TREATMENT LEVELS

The advertising/sales experiment with one experimental and one control group may not tell the advertiser everything he or she wishes to know. If the advertiser wished to understand the functional nature of the relationship between sales and advertising at several treatment levels, additional experimental groups with advertising expenditures of $250,000, $500,000, and $1 million might be studied. This experiment may still involve a control variable. By analyzing more groups each with a different treatment level, a more precise result may be obtained than in the simple experimental group–control group experiment described above. This design also can produce only a main effect.

MORE THAN ONE INDEPENDENT VARIABLE

An experiment can also be made more complicated by including the effect of another experimental variable. Our extended example involving retail atmosphere would typify a still relatively simple two-variable experiment. Since there are two variables, each with two different levels, four experimental groups are obtained. Often, the term **cell** is used to refer to a treatment combination within an experiment. The number of cells involved in any experiment can be easily computed as follows:

$$K = (T_1)(T_2)..(T_m)$$

where K = the number of cells, T_1 = the number of treatment levels for experimental group number one, T_2 = the number of treatment levels for experimental group number two, and so forth through the mth experimental group (T_m). In this case, since there are two variables each with two levels, the computation is quite simple:

$$K = 2 \times 2 = 4 \; cells$$

Including multiple variables allows a comparison of experimental treatments on the dependent variable. Since there are more than two experimental variables, this design involves both main effects and interactions. We will return to the topic of multiple variable experiments when in Chapter 12.

Selection and Measurement of the Dependent Variable

Selecting dependent variables is crucial in experimental design. Unless the dependent variables are relevant and truly represent an outcome of interest, the experiment will not be useful. Sometimes, the logical dependent variable is fairly obvious. If researchers introduce a new cinnamon,

Experimental group
A group of subjects to whom an experimental treatment is administered.

Control group
A group of subjects to whom no experimental treatment is administered.

Cell
Refers to a specific treatment combination associated with an experimental group.

pink grapefruit tea mix in a test-market, sales volume is most likely to be a key dependent variable. However, if researchers are experimenting with different forms of advertising copy appeals, defining the dependent variable may be more difficult. For example, measures of advertising awareness, recall, changes in brand preference, or sales might be possible dependent variables. In the retail atmosphere example, retail patronage was the key dependent variable. However, other potential dependent variables might include perceived product quality, excitement, or price perceptions.

Choosing the right dependent variable is part of the problem definition process. Like the problem definition process in general, it sometimes is considered less carefully than it should be. The experimenter's choice of a dependent variable determines what type of answer is given to assist managers in decision making.

Consider how difficult it can be to select the right dependent variable in a test-market. While sales are almost certainly important, when should sales be measured? The amount of time needed for effects to become evident should be considered in choosing the dependent variable. Sales may be measured several months after the experiment to determine if there were any carryover effects. Changes that are relatively permanent or longer lasting than changes generated only during the period of the experiment should be considered. Repeat purchase behavior may be important too since some consumers may try a product once but then never choose that product again. Consumers often try a "loser" once, but they do not buy a "loser" again and again.

The introduction of the original Crystal Pepsi illustrates the need to think beyond consumers' initial reactions. When Crystal Pepsi, a clear cola, was introduced, the initial trial rate was high, but only a small percentage of customers made repeat purchases. The brand never achieved high repeat sales within a sufficiently large market segment. Brand awareness, trial purchase, and repeat purchase are all possible dependent variables in an experiment. The dependent variable therefore should be considered carefully. Thorough problem definition will help the researcher select the most important dependent variable(s).

Selection and Assignment of Test Units

Test units
The subjects or entities whose responses to the experimental treatment are measured or observed.

Test units are the subjects or entities whose responses to the experimental treatment are measured or observed. Individual consumers, employees, organizational units, sales territories, market segments, brands, stores, or other entities may be the test units. People are the most common test units in most marketing and consumer behavior experiments. In our unit retail atmospherics example, individual consumers are the test units.

■ SAMPLE SELECTION AND RANDOM SAMPLING ERRORS

As in other forms of marketing research, random sampling errors and sample selection errors may occur in experimentation. For example, experiments sometimes go awry even when a geographic area is specially chosen for a particular investigation. A case in point was the experimental testing of a new lubricant for outboard motors by Dow Chemical Company. The lubricant was tested in Florida. Florida was chosen because researchers thought the hot, muggy climate would provide the most demanding test. In Florida the lubricant was a success. However, the story was quite different when the product was sold in Michigan. Although the lubricant sold well and worked well during the summer, the following spring Dow discovered the oil had congealed, allowing the outboard motors, idle all winter, to rust. The rusting problem never came to light in Florida, where the motors were in year-round use. Thus, sample selection error occurs because of flaws in procedures used to assign experimental test units. Florida conditions made the experiment irrelevant in Michigan.

Systematic or nonsampling error
Occurs if the sampling units in an experimental cell are somehow different than the units in another cell, and this difference affects the dependent variable.

Systematic or nonsampling error may occur if the sampling units in an experimental cell are somehow different than the units in another cell, and this difference affects the dependent variable. For example, suppose some professors are interested in testing the effect of providing snacks during exams on student's scores. The experimental variable is snacks, manipulated over three levels: (1) fruit, (2) cookies, and (3) chocolate. The test units in this case are individual students. When the professors conduct the experiment, for convenience, they decide to give all of the 8 a.m. classes chocolate for a snack, all of the 1 p.m. classes get fruit, and all of the 7 p.m. classes get cookies. While this type of procedure is often followed, if our tastes and digestive systems react differently to different foods at different times of the day, systematic error is introduced into the experiment. Furthermore, because the night classes contain students who are older on average, the professors may reach the conclusion that students perform better when they eat cookies, when it may really be due to the fact that students who are older perform better no matter what they are fed.

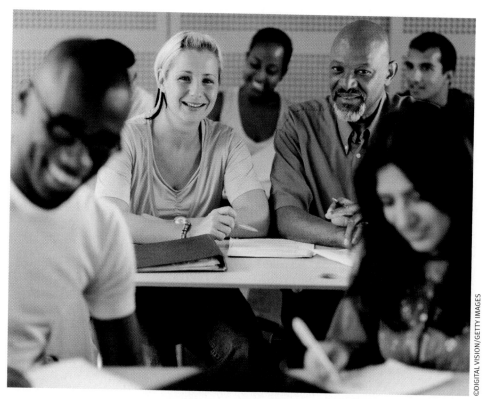

Although experiments are often administered in groups, if all groups are not the same, then systematic error is introduced.

▮ RANDOMIZATION

Randomization—the random assignment of subject and treatments to groups—is one device for equally distributing the effects of extraneous variables to all conditions. The presence of nuisance variables will not be eliminated, but they will be controlled because they are likely to exist to the same degree in every experimental cell. Thus, all cells would be expected to yield similar average scores on the dependent variables if it were not for the experimental treatments administered in a particular cell. In other words, the researcher would like to set up a situation where everything in every cell is the same except for the experimental treatment. Random assignment of subjects allows the researcher to make this assumption.

Randomization
The random assignment of subject and treatments to groups; it is one device for equally distributing the effects of extraneous variables to all conditions.

▮ MATCHING

Random assignment of subjects to the various experimental groups is the most common technique used to prevent test units from differing from each other on key variables; it assumes that all characteristics of the subjects have been likewise randomized. Matching the respondents on the basis of pertinent background information is another technique for controlling systematic error by assigning subjects in a way that their characteristics are the same in each group. This is best thought of in terms of demographic characteristics. If a subject's sex is expected to influence dependent variable responses, as in a taste test, then the researcher may make sure that there are equal numbers of men and women in each experimental cell. In general, if a researcher believes that certain extraneous variables may affect the dependent variable, he or she can make sure that the subjects in each group are the same on these characteristics.

For example, in a taste test experiment for a dog food, it might be important to match the dogs in various experimental groups on the basis of age or breed. That way, the same number of Basset Hounds and Dobermans will test formula A, formula B, and formula C. While matching can be a useful approach, the researcher can never be sure that sampling units are matched on all characteristics. Here, for example, even though breeds can be matched, it is difficult to know if all dogs live in the same type of environment (indoors, outdoors, spacious, cramped, with table scraps or without, and so on).

▮ REPEATED MEASURES

Experiments in which an individual subject is exposed to more than one level of an experimental treatment are referred to as **repeated measures** designs. Although this approach has

Repeated measures
Experiments in which an individual subject is exposed to more than one level of an experimental treatment.

advantages, including being more economical since the same subject provides more data than otherwise, it has several drawbacks that can limit its usefulness. We will discuss these in more detail later.

CONTROL OVER EXTRANEOUS VARIABLES

The fourth decision about the basic elements of an experiment concerns control over extraneous variables. This is related to the various types of experimental error. In Chapter 8 we classified total survey error into two basic categories: random sampling error and systematic error. The same dichotomy applies to all research designs, but the terms *random (sampling) error* and *systematic error* are more frequently used when discussing experiments.

EXPERIMENTAL CONFOUNDS

We have already discussed how systematic error can occur when the extraneous variables or the conditions of administering the experiment are allowed to influence the dependent variables. When this occurs, the results will be confounded because the extraneous variables have not been controlled or eliminated. The results can be confounded by an extraneous cause. A **confound** in an experiment means that there is an alternative explanation beyond the experimental variables for any observed differences in the dependent variable. Once a potential confound is identified, the validity of the experiment is severely questioned.

Recall from the opening vignette that the experimental procedures involved a taste test. Sea Snapper fish sticks were always presented on a blue plate and Captain John's fish sticks were always presented on an orange plate. Since the color of the plates coincides with the assignment of the brand, there is no way of knowing from these results whether any observed differences in liking are due to the brand or the color of the plate. The plate's color is confounding the explanation that the difference in brands is responsible for the difference in liking.

In a simple experimental group–control group experiment, if subjects in the experimental group are always administered treatment in the morning and subjects in the control group always receive the treatment in the afternoon, a systematic error occurs. In such a situation, time of day represents a confound. In a training experiment the sources of constant error might be the persons who do the training (line or external specialists) or whether the training is conducted on the employees' own time or on company time. These and other characteristics of the training may have an impact on the dependent variable and will have to be taken into account:

The effect of a constant error is to distort the results in a particular direction, so that an erroneous difference masks the true state of affairs. The effect of a random error is not to distort the results in any particular direction, but to obscure them. Constant error is like a distorting mirror in a fun house; it produces a picture that is clear but incorrect. Random error is like a mirror that has become cloudy with age; it produces a picture that is essentially correct but unclear.[5]

EXTRANEOUS VARIABLES

Most students of marketing realize that the marketing mix variables—price, product, promotion, and distribution—interact with uncontrollable forces in the market, such as competitors' activities and consumer trends. Thus, marketing experiments are subject to the effect of extraneous variables. Since extraneous variables can produce confounded results, they must be identified before the experiment if at all possible.

Cigarette smoking has been a topic of much debate and research. Does cigarette advertising cause young people to smoke? Although this is an often asked question, it is far from settled. One of the primary reasons for the inconclusiveness of this debate is the failure for most of the research to control for extraneous variables.[6] For instance, consider a study in which two groups of U.S. high school students are studied over the course of a year. One is exposed to a greater percentage of foreign television media in which American cigarettes are more often shown in a flattering and glamorous light. In fact, the programming includes cigarette commercials. The other group is a control group in which their exposure to media is not controlled. At the end of the year, the experimental group reports a greater frequency and incidence of cigarette smoking. Did the increased media exposure involving cigarettes cause smoking behavior?

While the result seems plausible at first, the careful researcher may ask the following questions:

- Was the demographic makeup of the two groups the same? While it is clear that the ages of the two groups are likely the same, it is well known that different ethnic groups have different smoking rates. Approximately 28 percent of all high school students report smoking, but the rate is higher among Hispanic teens, for example.[7] Therefore, if one group contained more Hispanics or Asians, we might expect it to report different smoking rates than otherwise. Similarly, smoking varies with social class.
- How did the control group fill the time consumed by the experimental group in being exposed to the experimental treatment? Could it be that it somehow dissuaded them from smoking? Perhaps they were exposed to media with more anti-smoking messages?
- Were the two groups of the same general achievement profiles? Those who are high in the need for achievement may be less prone to smoke than are other students.
- Although it is a difficult task to list all possible extraneous factors, some that even sound unusual can sometimes have an effect. For example, did the students have equally dispersed birthdays? Researchers have even shown that smoking rates correspond to one's birthday, meaning that different astrological groups have different smoking rates.[8]

Because an experimenter does not want extraneous variables to affect the results, he or she must control or eliminate such variables. It is always better to spend time thinking about how to control for possible extraneous variables before the experiment since often there is nothing that can be done to salvage results after a confounding effect is identified.

Demand Characteristics

What are Demand Characteristics?

The term **demand characteristic** refers to an experimental design element that unintentionally provides subjects with hints about the research hypothesis. Researchers cannot reveal the research hypotheses to subjects before the experiment or else they can create a confounding effect. Think about the retail atmospherics experiment. If the subjects were told before they participated that they were going to be involved in an experiment to see if they liked stores that were predominantly orange or predominantly blue, the researcher would never be sure if their responses to the dependent variable were really due to the differences in the experimental stimuli or due to the fact that the subjects were trying to provide a "correct" response. In addition, once subjects know the hypotheses, there is little hope that they will respond naturally.

So, knowledge of the experimental hypothesis creates a confound. This particular type of confound is known as a **demand effect**. Demand characteristics make demand effects very likely.

Demand characteristic
Experimental design element or procedure that unintentionally provides subjects with hints about the research hypothesis.

Demand effect
Occurs when demand characteristics actually affect the dependent variable.

Experimenter Bias and Demand Effects

Demand characteristics are aspects of an experiment that *demand* (encourage) that the subjects respond in a particular way. Hence, they are a source of systematic error (see Exhibit 11.4). If participants recognize the experimenter's expectation or demand, they are likely to act in a manner consistent with the experimental treatment. Even slight nonverbal cues may influence their reactions.

Prominent demand characteristics are often presented by the person administering experimental procedures. If an experimenter's presence, actions, or comments influence the subjects' behavior or sway the subjects to slant their answers to cooperate with the experimenter, the

EXHIBIT 11.4
**By Smiling or Looking
Solemn, Experimenters Can
Modify Subjects' Behavior**

experiment has introduced *experimenter bias*. When subjects slant their answers to cooperate with the experimenter, they are exhibiting behaviors that might not represent their behavior in the marketplace. For example, if subjects in an advertising experiment understand that the experimenter is interested in whether they changed their attitudes in accord with a given advertisement, they may answer in the desired direction. Acting in this manner reflects a demand effect rather than a true experimental treatment effect.

Hawthorne Effect

A famous management experiment illustrates a common demand characteristic. Researchers were attempting to study the effects on productivity of various working conditions, such as hours of work, rest periods, lighting, and methods of pay, at the Western Electric Hawthorne plant in Cicero, Illinois. The researchers found that workers' productivity increased whether the work hours were lengthened or shortened, whether lighting was very bright or very dim, and so on. The surprised investigators realized that the workers' morale was higher because they were aware of being part of a special experimental group. This totally unintended effect is now known as the **Hawthorne effect** because researchers realize that people will perform differently when they know they are experimental subjects.[9]

Hawthorne effect
People will perform differently from normal when they know they are experimental subjects.

If subjects in a laboratory experiment interact (i.e., are not relatively isolated), their conversations may produce joint decisions rather than a desired individual decision. For this reason, social interaction generally is restricted in laboratory experiments.

Reducing Demand Characteristics

Although it is practically impossible to eliminate demand characteristics from experiments, there are steps that can be taken to reduce them. Many of these steps make it difficult for subjects to know what the researcher is trying to find out. Some or all of these may be appropriate in a given experiment.

1. Use an experimental disguise.
2. Isolate experimental subjects.
3. Use a "blind" experimental administrator.
4. Administer only one experimental treatment level to each subject.

▦ EXPERIMENTAL DISGUISE

Subjects taking place in the experiment can be told that the purpose of the experiment is somewhat different than the actual purpose. Most often, they are simply told less than the complete "truth" about what is going to happen. For instance, in the retail atmosphere study above, subjects were told that they would be asked to react to a new retail store concept. This really is true, but they were not told anything about color, lighting, or any other potential experimental effect.

In other cases, more deceit may be needed. Psychologists studying how much pain one person may be willing to inflict on another might use a ruse telling the subject that they are actually interested in the effect of pain on human performance. The researcher tells the actual subject to administer a series of questions to another person (who is actually a research assistant) and to provide them with an increasingly strong electric shock each time an incorrect answer is given. In reality, the real dependent variable has something to do with how long the actual subject will continue to administer shocks before stopping.

A placebo is an experimental deception involving a false treatment. A **placebo effect** refers to the corresponding effect in a dependent variable that is due to the psychological impact that goes along with knowledge of the treatment. A placebo is particularly important when the experimental variable involves physical consumption of some product. The placebo should not be different in any manner that is actually noticeable by the research subject. If someone is told that a special food additive will suppress appetite, and they are supposed to sprinkle it on their dinner before eating as part of an experiment, another group should receive a placebo that looks exactly like the actual food additive but actually is some type of inert compound. Both groups are likely to show some difference in consumption compared to someone undergoing no effect. The difference in the actual experimental group and the placebo group would represent the true effect of the additive.

Placebo effects exist in marketing research. For example, when subjects are told that an energy drink is sold at a discount price, they believe it is significantly less effective than when it is sold at the regular, non-discounted price.[10] Later, we will return to the ethical issues involved in experimental deception.

Placebo effect
The effect in a dependent variable associated with the psychological impact that goes along with knowledge of some treatment being administered.

▦ ISOLATE EXPERIMENTAL SUBJECTS

Researchers should minimize the extent to which subjects are able to talk about the experimental procedures with each other. Although it may be unintentional, discussion among subjects may lead them to guess the experimental hypotheses. For instance, it could be that different subjects received different treatments. The experimental integrity will be higher when each only knows enough to participate in the experiment.

▦ USE A "BLIND" EXPERIMENTAL ADMINISTRATOR

When possible, the people actually administering the experiment may not be told the experimental hypotheses. The advantage is that if they do not know what exactly is being studied, then they are less likely to give off clues that result in demand effects. Like the subjects, when there is some reason to expect that their knowledge may constitute a demand characteristic, administrators best know only enough to do their job.

▦ ADMINISTER ONLY ONE EXPERIMENTAL CONDITION PER SUBJECT

When subjects know more than one experimental treatment condition, they are much more likely to guess the experimental hypothesis. So, even though there are cost advantages to administering multiple treatment levels to the same subject, it should be avoided when possible. For example, in the retail atmospherics example, if subjects responded first to a blue retail store concept, and then saw the same store that was exactly the same except the walls had become orange, then he or she is very likely to know that the researcher is interested in color.

Establishing Control

The major difference between experimental research and descriptive research is an experimenter's ability to control variables by either holding conditions constant or manipulating the experimental variable. If the color of beer causes preference, a brewery experimenting with a new clear beer must determine the possible extraneous variables other than color that may affect an experiment's results and attempt to eliminate or control those variables. Marketing theory tell us that brand image and packaging design are important factors in beer drinkers' reactions. Therefore, the researcher may wish to control the influence of these variables. He or she may eliminate these two extraneous variables by packaging the test beers in plain brown packages without any brand identification.

Constancy of conditions
Means that subjects in all experimental groups are exposed to identical conditions except for the differing experimental treatments.

When extraneous variables cannot be eliminated, experimenters may strive for **constancy of conditions**. This means that subjects in all experimental groups are exposed to identical conditions except for the differing experimental treatments. The principle of matching discussed earlier helps make sure that constancy is achieved.

A supermarket experiment involving four test products shows the care that must be taken to hold all factors constant. The experiment required that all factors other than shelf space be kept constant throughout the testing period. In all stores the shelf level that had existed before the tests began was to be maintained throughout the test period. Only the *amount* of shelf space (the treatment) was changed. One problem involved store personnel accidentally changing shelf level when stocking the test products. This deviation from the constancy of conditions was minimized by auditing each store four times a week. In this way, any change could be detected in a minimum amount of time. The experimenter personally stocked as many of the products as possible, and the cooperation of stock clerks also helped reduce treatment deviations.

If an experimental method requires that the same subjects be exposed to two or more experimental treatments, an error may occur due to the *order of presentation*. For instance, if subjects are examining the effects of different levels of graphical interface on video game enjoyment, and they are asked to view each of four different levels, the order in which they are presented may influence enjoyment. Subjects might perform one level simply because it follows a very poor level. **Counterbalancing** attempts to eliminate the confounding effects of order of presentation by requiring that one fourth of the subjects be exposed to treatment A first, one fourth to treatment B first, one fourth to treatment C first, and finally one fourth to treatment D first. Likewise, the other levels are counterbalanced so that the order of presentation is rotated among subjects.

Counterbalancing
Attempts to eliminate the confounding effects of order of presentation by requiring that one fourth of the subjects be exposed to treatment A first, one fourth to treatment B first, one fourth to treatment C first, and finally one fourth to treatment D first.

Problems Controlling Extraneous Variables

In marketing experiments it is not always possible to control every possible extraneous variable. For example, competitors may bring out a product during the course of a test-market. This form of competitive interference occurred in a Boston test-market for Anheuser-Busch's import beer, Wurzburger Hofbrau. During the test, Miller Brewing Company introduced its own brand, Munich Oktoberfest, and sent eight salespeople out to blitz the Boston market. A competitor who learns of a test-market experiment may knowingly change its prices or increase advertising to confound the test results. This brings us to ethical issues in experimentation.

Ethical Issues in Experimentation

Ethical issues with experimentation were discussed in Chapter 4. There, the question of deception was raised. Although deception is necessary in most experiments, when subjects can be returned to their prior condition through debriefing, then the experiment is probably consistent with high moral standards. When subjects have been injured significantly or truly psychologically harmed, debriefing will not return them to their formal condition and the experiment should not proceed. Therefore, some additional commentary on debriefing is presented.

Debriefing experimental subjects by communicating the purpose of the experiment and the researcher's hypotheses about the nature of consumer behavior is expected to counteract negative effects of deception, relieve stress, and provide an educational experience for the subject.

Proper debriefing allows the subject to save face by uncovering the truth for himself. The experimenter should begin by asking the subject if he has any questions or if he found any part of the experiment odd, confusing, or disturbing. This question provides a check on the subject's suspiciousness and effectiveness of manipulations. The experimenter continues to provide the subject cues to the deception until the subject states that he believes there was more to the experiment than met the eye. At this time the purpose and procedure of the experiment [are] revealed.[11]

Additionally, there is the issue of test-markets and efforts extended toward interfering with a competitor's test-market. The research snapshot dealing with Hidden Valley Ranch salad dressings described just such a situation. When a company puts a product out for public consumption, they should be aware that competitors may also now freely consume the product. When attempts to interfere with a test-market are aimed solely at invalidating test results or they are aimed at infringing on some copyright protection, those acts are ethically questionable.

Fundamental Questions in Experimentation

Basic versus Factorial Experimental Designs

In *basic experimental designs* a single independent variable is manipulated to observe its effect on a single dependent variable. However, we know that complex marketing dependent variables such as sales, product usage, and preference are influenced by several factors. The simultaneous change in independent variables such as price and advertising may have a greater influence on sales than if either variable is changed alone. *Factorial experimental designs* are more sophisticated than basic experimental designs and allow for an investigation of the interaction of two or more independent variables. Factorial experiments are discussed further in a section on complex experimental designs in Chapter 12.

Laboratory Experiments

A marketing experiment can be conducted in a natural setting (a field experiment) or in an artificial or laboratory setting. In social sciences, the actual laboratory may be a behavioral lab, which is somewhat like a focus group facility. However, it may simply be a room or classroom dedicated to collecting data, or it can even take place in one's home.

In a **laboratory experiment** the researcher has more complete control over the research setting and extraneous variables. For example, subjects are recruited and brought to an advertising agency's office, a research agency's office, or perhaps a mobile unit designed for research purposes. They are exposed to a television commercial within the context of a program that includes competitors' ads among the commercials shown. They are then allowed to purchase either the advertised product or one of several competing products in a simulated store environment. Trial purchase measures are thus obtained. A few weeks later, subjects are contacted again to measure their satisfaction and determine repeat purchasing intention. This laboratory experiment gives the consumer an opportunity to "buy" and "invest." In a short timespan, the marketer is able to collect information on decision making. Our retail atmospheric experiment also illustrates a laboratory experiment.

Other laboratory experiments may be more controlled or artificial. For example, a **tachistoscope** allows a researcher to experiment with the visual impact of advertising, packaging, and so on by controlling the amount of time a subject is exposed to a visual image. Each stimulus (for example, package design) is projected from a slide to the tachistoscope at varying exposure lengths

Laboratory experiment
The researcher has more complete control over the research setting and extraneous variables.

Tachistoscope
Device that controls the amount of time a subject is exposed to a visual image.

EXHIBIT 11.5
The Artificiality of Laboratory versus Field Experiments

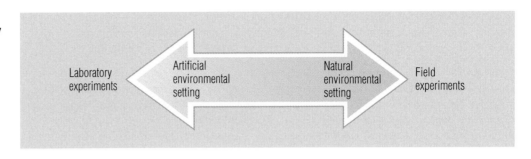

Laboratory experiments — Artificial environmental setting — Natural environmental setting — Field experiments

(1/10 of a second, 2/10, 3/10, and so on). The tachistoscope simulates the split-second duration of a customer's attention to a package in a mass display.

Field Experiments

Field experiments Research projects involving experimental manipulations that are implemented in a natural environment.

Field experiments are research projects involving experimental manipulations that are implemented in a natural environment. They can be useful in fine-tuning marketing strategies and determining sales forecasts for different marketing mix designs. Test-markets are field experiments. Betty Crocker's Squeezit (a 10 percent fruit juice drink in a squeeze bottle) was so successful in a test-market that production could not keep up with demand. As a result, the product's national introduction was postponed until production capacity could be increased.

McDonald's conducted a field experiment testing the Triple Ripple, a three-flavor ice cream product. The product was dropped because the experiment revealed distribution problems reduced product quality and limited customer acceptance. In the distribution system the product would freeze, defrost, and refreeze. Solving the problem would have required each McDonald's city to have a local ice cream plant with special equipment to roll the three flavors into one. A naturalistic setting for the experiment helped McDonald's executives realize the product was impractical.

The naturally occurring noise that exists in the field can interfere with experimental manipulations.

Experiments vary in their degree of artificiality and control. Exhibit 11.5 shows that as experiments increase in naturalism, they begin to approach a pure field experiment. As they become more artificial, they approach a pure laboratory experiment.

In field experiments, a researcher manipulates experimental variables but cannot possibly control all the extraneous variables. An example is NBC's research on new television programs. Viewers who subscribe to a cable television service are asked to watch a cable preview on their home television sets at a certain time on a certain cable channel. While the program is being aired, telephone calls from the viewers' friends cannot be controlled. In contrast, an advertising professor may test some advertising effect by showing subjects advertising in a classroom setting. Here, there are no phone calls and little to distract the subject. Which produces a better experiment?

Generally, subjects know when they are participating in a

RESEARCHSNAPSHOT

The Hidden in Hidden Valley Ranch

A few years ago, Hidden Valley Ranch (HVR) conducted a field market experiment to examine how effective three new flavors of salad dressings would be in the marketplace. Thus, there were three levels of the experimental variable, each representing a different flavor. Tests like this can be expensive. HVR had to produce small batches of each flavor, get them bottled, and ship them to their sales representatives, who then had to stock the dressings in the participating retail stores. All of this is very expensive.

So, the first day of the test was consumed with sales reps placing the products in the salad dressing sections of retail stores. The second day, each rep went back to each store to record the number of sales for each flavor. By the third day, all of the bottles of all flavors had sold! Amazing! Was every flavor a huge success? Actually, one of HVR's competitors had sent its sales reps around beginning on the second day of the test to buy every bottle of the new HVR dressings in every store it had been placed in. Thus, HVR was unable to produce any valid sales data (the dependent variable) and the competitor was able to break down the dressing in its labs and determine the recipe.

This illustrates one risk that comes along with field tests. Once a product is available for sale, there are no secrets. Also, you risk espionage of this type that can render the experiment invalid.

©SUSAN VAN ETTEN

laboratory experiment. Performance of certain tasks, responses to questions, or some other form of active involvement is characteristic of laboratory experiments. In field experiments, as in test-markets, subjects do not even know they have taken part in an experiment. Ethically, consent should be sought before having someone participate in an experiment. However, with field experiments the consent is implied since subjects are not asked to do anything departing from their normal behavior to participate in the experiment. All precautions with respect to safety and confidentiality should be maintained.

Field experiments involving new products or promotions are often conducted in a retail store. These are known as controlled store tests. The products are put into stores in a number of small cities or into selected supermarket chains. Product deliveries are made not through the traditional warehouse but by the research agency, so product information remains confidential. The Research Snapshot box above describes such a test. While they can be less expensive than a full-blown market test, they also have drawbacks because of the relatively small sample of stores and the limitations on the type of outlet where the product is tested. Thus, their results may not generalize to all consumers in a population.

Between-Subjects Designs

A basic question faced by the researchers involves how many treatments a subject should receive. For economical reasons, the researcher may wish to apply multiple treatments to the same subject. For instance, in the retail atmosphere experiment, each subject could rate each combination of colors and lighting. Thus, four observations on the dependent variable can be obtained from a single subject. Such a design is called a **within-subjects design**. Within-subjects designs involve repeated measures because with each treatment the same subject is measured.

In contrast, the researcher could decide that each person will receive only one treatment combination. This is referred to as a **between-subjects design**. Each dependent variable is measured only once for every subject. Exhibit 11.6 illustrates this point.

Between-subjects designs are usually advantageous although they are usually more costly. The validity of between-subjects designs is usually higher because by applying only one treatment combination to one subject, demand characteristics are greatly reduced. In addition, as we will see later, statistical analysis of between subjects designs are simpler than within-subjects designs. This also means the results are easier to report and explain to management.

Within-subjects design
Involves repeated measures because with each treatment the same subject is measured.

Between-subjects design
Each subject receives only one treatment combination.

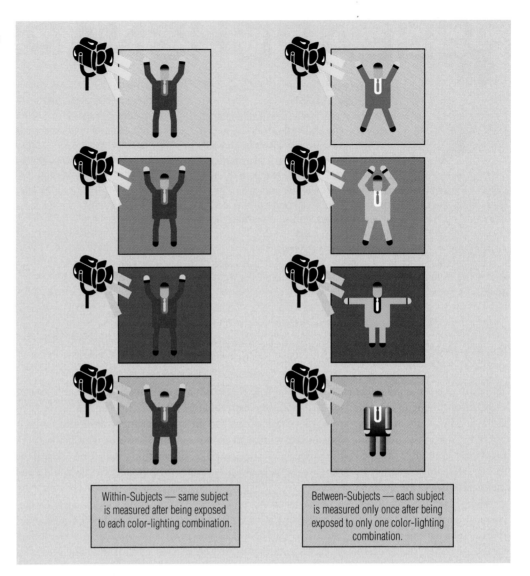

Within-Subjects — same subject
is measured after being exposed
to each color-lighting combination.

Between-Subjects — each subject
is measured only once after being
exposed to only one color-lighting
combination.

Issues of Experimental Validity

An experiment's quality is judged by two types of validity. These are known as internal and external validity.

Internal Validity

Internal validity
Exists to the extent that an experimental variable is truly responsible for any variance in the dependent variable.

Internal validity exists to the extent that an experimental variable is truly responsible for any variance in the dependent variable. In other words, does the experimental manipulation truly cause changes in the specific outcome of interest? If the observed results were influenced or confounded by extraneous factors, the researcher will have problems making valid conclusions about the relationship between the experimental treatment and the dependent variable.

Thus, a lab experiment enhances internal validity because it maximizes control of outside forces. If we wish to know whether a certain odor causes increased productivity among service workers, we may set up a task in a room with a tightly controlled airflow so we can be sure that the specific odor exists in the air in the amount and intensity desired. We can also control temperature, lighting, density, sounds, and many other factors that would be difficult or impossible to control outside of a lab environment. If the only thing that varies from subject to subject is the odor, then

RESEARCHSNAPSHOT

Celling Experiments

More and more marketing researchers are finding ways to conduct experiments with mobile phone technology. For instance, advertising appeals can be delivered via text message or voicemail. Advertisers can manipulate the size of a discount offered for a brief period of time and then track to see whether the subject takes advantage of the discount. For instance, advertisers in Hong Kong, where consumers are more receptive to advertising via mobile phones, can send a short text blast to all consumers near a Starbucks. They can then have the consumer send back a reply to activate a discount at that store. In this way, they might be able to test whether a free cookie or a half-price latte is a better incentive and results in more patronage.

However, conducting experiments in this manner threatens internal validity in several ways. Although the large number of

mobile phones in use has made them more practical for doing research, and their increased flexibility in delivering messages has provided more capability for doing research, it is nearly impossible to control for extraneous variables. Is the subject in a car, on a train, in a meeting, alone, or with others? Many factors like these might interfere with experimental results. Despite the weaknesses, the convenience and technological advantages will likely lead to more rather than less "celling" experiments.

Sources: Long, J., K. Tomak, and A. B. Whinston (2003), "Calling All Customers," Marketing News, (January 20), p. 18; Grapentine, T. (2005), "Don't Cell Yourself Short," Marketing Research, 17 (Fall), 5.

©PHOTODISC/GETTY IMAGES

we can safely say that any differences in performance must be attributable to human reactions to the scent.

MANIPULATION CHECKS

Internal validity depends in large part on successful manipulations. Manipulations should be carried out in a way that varies the experimental variable over meaningfully different levels. If the levels are too close together, the experiment may lack the power necessary to observe differences in the dependent variable. In a pricing experiment, it may be that manipulating the price of an automobile over two levels, $24,800 and $24,600, would not be successful in creating truly different price categories.

The validity of manipulations can often be checked with a **manipulation check**. If a drug is administered in different dosages that should affect blood sugar levels, the researcher could actually measure blood sugar level after administering the drug to make sure that the dosages were different enough to produce a change in blood sugar. In marketing, the manipulation check is often conducted by asking a survey question or two. In the pricing example above, subjects may be asked a question about how low they believe the price of the car to be. A valid manipulation would produce substantially different average responses to that question in a "high" and "low" price group. Manipulation checks should always be administered after dependent variables in self-response format experiments. This keeps the manipulation check item from becoming a troublesome demand characteristic.

Extraneous variables can jeopardize internal validity. The six major ones are *history, maturation, testing, instrumentation, selection,* and *mortality.*

Manipulation check
A validity test of an experimental manipulation to make sure that the manipulation does produce differences in the independent variable.

HISTORY

A **history effect** occurs when some change other than the experimental treatment occurs during the course of an experiment that affects the dependent variable. A common history effect occurs when competitors change their marketing strategies during a test marketing experiment. History effects are particularly prevalent in repeated measures experiments that take place over an extended time. If we wanted to assess how much a change in recipe improves individual subjects' consumption of a food product, we would first measure their consumption and then compare it with consumption after the change. Since several weeks may pass between the first and second measurement, there are many things that could occur that would also influence subjects' diets.

History effect
Occurs when some change other than the experimental treatment occurs during the course of an experiment that affects the dependent variable.

Although it may sound extreme, examining the effect of some dietary supplement on various health-related outcomes may require that a subject be confined during the experiment's course. This may take several weeks. Without confining the subject in something like a hospital setting, there would be little way of controlling food and drink consumption, exercise activities, and other factors that may also affect the dependent variables.

Cohort effect
Refers to a change in the dependent variable that occurs because members of one experimental group experienced different historical situations than members of other experimental groups.

A special case of the history effect is the **cohort effect**, which refers to a change in the dependent variable that occurs because members of one experimental group experienced different historical situations than members of other experimental groups. For example, two groups of managers used as subjects may be in different cohorts because one group encountered different experiences over the course of an experiment. If the experimental manipulation involves different levels of financial incentives and performance is the dependent variable, one group may be affected by an informative article appearing in a trade magazine during the experiment. Since the other group participated prior to this group, members of that group could not benefit from the article. Therefore, the possibility exists that the article rather than the change in incentive is truly causing differences in performance.

MATURATION

Maturation effects
Effects that are a function of time and the naturally occurring events that coincide with growth and experience.

Maturation effects are effects that are a function of time and the naturally occurring events that coincide with growth and experience. Experiments taking place over longer timespans may see lower internal validity as subjects simply grow older or more experienced. Suppose an experiment were designed to test the impact of a new compensation program on sales productivity. If this program were tested over a year's time, some of the salespeople probably would mature as a result of more selling experience or perhaps gain increased knowledge. Their sales productivity might improve because of their knowledge and experience rather than the compensation program.

TESTING

Testing effects
A nuisance effect occurring when the initial measurement or test alerts or primes subjects in a way that affects their response to the experimental treatments.

Testing effects are also called *pretesting effects* because the initial measurement or test alerts or primes subjects in a way that affects their response to the experimental treatments. Testing effects only occur in a before-and-after study. A before-and-after study is one requiring an initial baseline measure be taken before an experimental treatment is administered. So, before-and-after experiments are a special case of a repeated measures design. For example, students taking standardized achievement and intelligence tests for the second time usually do better than those taking the tests for the first time. The effect of testing may increase awareness of socially approved answers, increase attention to experimental conditions (that is, the subject may watch more closely), or make the subject more conscious than usual of the dimensions of a problem.

INSTRUMENTATION

Instrumentation effect
A nuisance that occurs when a change in the wording of questions, a change in interviewers, or a change in other procedures causes a change in the dependent variable.

A change in the wording of questions, a change in interviewers, or a change in other procedures used to measure the dependent variable causes an **instrumentation effect**, which may jeopardize internal validity. If the same interviewers are used to ask questions for both before and after measurement, some problems may arise. With practice, interviewers may acquire increased skill in interviewing, or they may become bored and decide to reword the questionnaire in their own terms. To avoid this problem, new interviewers are hired, but different individuals are also a source of extraneous variation due to instrumentation variation. There are numerous other sources of instrument decay or variation. Again, instrumentation effects are problematic with any type of repeated measures design.

SELECTION

The selection effect is a sample bias that results from differential selection of respondents for the comparison groups, or sample selection error, discussed earlier.

▥ MORTALITY

If an experiment is conducted over a period of a few weeks or more, some sample bias may occur due to the **mortality effect (sample attrition)**. Sample attrition occurs when some subjects withdraw from the experiment before it is completed. Mortality effects may occur if subjects drop from one experimental treatment group disproportionately from other groups. Consider a sales training experiment investigating the effects of close supervision of salespeople (high pressure) versus low supervision (low pressure). The high-pressure condition may misleadingly appear superior if those subjects who completed the experiment did very well. If, however, the high-pressure condition caused more subjects to drop out than the other conditions, this apparent superiority may be due to the fact that only very determined and/or talented salespeople stuck with the program.

Mortality effect (sample attrition)
Occurs when some subjects withdraw from the experiment before it is completed.

External Validity

External validity is the accuracy with which experimental results can be generalized beyond the experimental subjects. External validity is increased when the subjects comprising the sample truly represent some population and when the results extend to market segments or other groups of people. The higher the external validity, the more researchers and managers can count on the fact that any results observed in an experiment will also be seen in the "real world" (marketplace, workplace, sales floor, and so on).

External validity
Is the accuracy with which experimental results can be generalized beyond the experimental subjects.

For instance, to what extent would results from our retail atmosphere experiment, which represents a simulated shopping experiment, transfer to a real-world retail store in a shopping mall, downtown mall, or lifestyle center? Can one extrapolate the results from a tachistoscope to an in-store shopping situation? Lab experiments are associated with low external validity because the limited set of experimental conditions, holding all else constant, do not adequately represent all the influences existing in the real world. In other words, the experimental situation may be too artificial. When a study lacks external validity, the researcher will have difficulty repeating the experiment with any change in subjects, settings, or time.

▥ STUDENT SURROGATES

Basic researchers often use college students as experimental subjects.[12] Convenience, time, money, and a host of other practical considerations often lead to using students as research subjects. This practice is widespread in academic studies. Some evidence shows that students are quite similar to household consumers, but other evidence indicates that they do not provide sufficient external validity to represent most consumer or employee groups. This is particularly true when students are used as substitutes or surrogates for businesspeople.

The issue of external validity should be seriously considered because the student population is likely to be atypical. Students are easily accessible, but they often are not representative of the total population. This is not always the case, however, and when behaviors are studied for which students have some particular expertise, then they are certainly appropriate. For instance, the Research Snapshot box on page 260 is an example where students are very appropriate.

Trade-Offs Between Internal and External Validity

Naturalistic field experiments tend to have greater external validity than artificial laboratory experiments. Marketing researchers often must trade internal validity for external validity. A researcher who wishes to test advertising effectiveness by manipulating treatments via a split-cable experiment has the assurance that the advertisement will be viewed in an externally valid situation, the subjects' homes. However, the researcher has no assurance that some interruption (for example, a telephone call) will not have some influence that will reduce the internal validity of the experiment. Laboratory experiments with many controlled factors usually are high in internal validity, while field experiments generally have less internal validity, but greater external validity. Ideally, results from lab experiments would be followed up with some type of field test.

Classification of Experimental Designs

An experimental design may be compared to an architect's plans for a building. The basic requirements for the structure are given to the architect by the prospective owner. Several different plans may be drawn up as options for meeting the basic requirements. Some may be more costly than others. One may offer potential advantages that another does not.

There are various types of experimental designs. If only one variable is manipulated, the experiment has a **basic experimental design**. If the experimenter wishes to investigate several levels of the independent variable (for example, four price levels) or to investigate the interaction effects of two or more independent variables, the experiment requires a *complex,* or *statistical,* experimental design.

Basic experimental design
An experimental design in which only one variable is manipulated.

Symbolism for Diagramming Experimental Designs

The work of Campbell and Stanley has helped many students master the subject of basic experimental designs.[13] The following symbols will be used in describing the various experimental designs:

X = *exposure of a group to an experimental treatment*
O = *observation or measurement of the dependent variable; if more than one observation or measurement is taken, subscripts (that is, O_1, O_2, etc.) indicate temporal order*
$\boxed{R}$ = *random assignment of test units; $\boxed{R}$ symbolizes that individuals selected as subjects for the experiment are randomly assigned to the experimental groups*

The diagrams of experimental designs that follow assume a time flow from left to right. Our first example will make this clearer.

Three Examples of Quasi-Experimental Designs

Quasi-experimental designs do not involve random allocation of subjects to treatment combinations. In this sense, they do not qualify as true experimental designs because they do not adequately control for the problems associated with loss of internal validity. However, they are used particularly when it is the only way to implement a study.

Quasi-experimental designs
Experimental designs that do not involve random allocation of subjects to treatment combinations.

ONE-SHOT DESIGN

The one-shot design, or *after-only design,* is diagrammed as follows:

$X \qquad O_1$

Suppose that during a very cold winter an automobile dealer finds herself with a large inventory of cars. She decides to experiment for the month of January with a promotional scheme. She offers a free trip to New Orleans with every car sold. She experiments with the promotion (X = experimental treatment) and measures sales (O_1 = measurement of sales after the treatment is administered).

This one-shot design is a case study of a research project fraught with problems. Subjects or test units participate because of voluntary self-selection or arbitrary assignment, not because of random assignment. The study lacks any kind of comparison or any means of controlling extraneous influences. There should be a measure of what will happen when the test units have not been exposed to X to compare with the measures of when subjects have been exposed to X. Nevertheless, under certain circumstances, even though this design lacks internal validity, it is the only viable choice.

ONE-GROUP PRETEST–POSTTEST DESIGN

Suppose a real estate franchiser wishes to provide a training program for franchisees. If the franchiser measures subjects' knowledge of real estate selling before (O_1) they are exposed to the experimental treatment (X) and then measures real estate selling knowledge after (O_2) they are exposed to the treatment, the design will be as follows:

O_1 X O_2

In this example the trainer is likely to conclude that the difference between O_2 and O_1 ($O_2 - O_1$) is the measure of the influence of the experimental treatment. This one-group pretest–posttest design offers a comparison of the same individuals before and after training. Although this is an improvement over the one-shot design, this research still has several weaknesses that may jeopardize internal validity. For example, if the time lapse between O_1 and O_2 was a period of several months, the trainees may have matured as a result of experience on the job (maturation effect). History effects may also influence this design. Perhaps some subjects dropped out of the training program (mortality effect). The effect of testing may also have confounded the experiment.

Although this design has a number of weaknesses, it is used in marketing research. Remember, the cost of the research is a consideration in most business situations. While there will be some problems of internal validity, the researcher must always take into account questions of time and cost.

STATIC GROUP DESIGN

In a static group design each subject is identified as a member of either an experimental group or a control group (for example, exposed or not exposed to a commercial). The experimental group is measured after being exposed to an experimental treatment, and the control group is measured without having been exposed to this experimental treatment:

Experimental group: X O_1
Control group: O_2

The results of the static group design are computed by subtracting the observed results in the control group from those in the experimental group ($O_1 - O_2$). A major weakness of this design is its lack of assurance that the groups were equal on variables of interest before the experimental group received the treatment. If the groups were selected arbitrarily by the investigator, or if entry into either group was voluntary, systematic differences between the groups could invalidate the conclusions about the effect of the treatment. Random assignment of subjects may eliminate problems with group differences. If groups are established by the experimenter rather than existing as a function of some other causation, the static group design is referred to as an *after-only design with control group.*

On many occasions, an after-only design is the only possible option. This is particularly true when conducting use tests for new products or brands. Cautious interpretation and recognition of the design's shortcomings may make this design valuable.

Three Alternative Experimental Designs

In a formal scientific sense, the three designs just discussed are not pure experimental designs. Subjects for the experiments were not selected from a common pool of subjects and randomly assigned to one group or another. In the following discussion of three basic experimental designs, the symbol $\boxed{R}$ to the left of the diagram indicates that the first step in a true experimental design is the randomization of subject assignment.

PRETEST–POSTTEST CONTROL GROUP DESIGN (BEFORE–AFTER WITH CONTROL)

A pretest–posttest control group design, or *before–after with control group design,* is the classic experimental design:

Experimental group: $\boxed{R}$ O_1 $\quad X \quad$ O_2
Control group: $\boxed{R}$ O_3 $\qquad$ O_4

As the diagram indicates, the subjects in the experimental group are tested before and after being exposed to the treatment. The control group is tested at the same two times as the experimental group, but subjects are not exposed to the experimental treatment. This design has the advantages of the before–after design with the additional advantages gained by its having a control group. The effect of the experimental treatment equals

$$(O_2 - O_1) - (O_4 - O_3)$$

If there is brand awareness among 20 percent of the subjects ($O_1 = 20$ percent, $O_3 = 20$ percent) before an advertising treatment and then 35 percent awareness in the experimental group ($O_2 = 35$ percent) and 22 percent awareness in the control group ($O_4 = 22$ percent) after exposure to the treatment, the treatment effect equals 13 percent:

$$(0.35 - 0.20) - (0.22 - 0.20) = (0.15) - (0.02) = 0.13 \; or \; 13\%$$

The effect of all extraneous variables is assumed to be the same on both the experimental and the control groups. For instance, since both groups receive the pretest, no difference between them is expected for the pretest effect. This assumption is also made for effects of other events between the before and after measurements (history), changes within the subjects that occur with the passage of time (maturation), testing effects, and instrumentation effects. In reality there will be some differences in the sources of extraneous variation. Nevertheless, in most cases assuming that the effect is approximately equal for both groups is reasonable.

However, a testing effect is possible when subjects are sensitized to the subject of the research. This is analogous to what occurs when people learn a new vocabulary word. Soon they discover that they notice it much more frequently in their reading. In an experiment the combination of being interviewed on a subject and receiving the experimental treatment might be a potential source of error. For example, a subject exposed to a certain advertising message in a split-cable experiment might say, "Ah, there is an ad about the product I was interviewed about yesterday!" The subject may pay more attention than normal to the advertisement and be more prone to change his or her attitude than in a situation with no interactive testing effects. This weakness in the before–after with control group design can be corrected (see the next two designs).

Testing the effectiveness of television commercials in movie theaters provides an example of the before–after with control group design. Subjects are selected for the experiments by being told that they are going to preview several new television shows. When they enter the theater, they learn that a drawing for several types of products will be held, and they are asked to complete a product preference questionnaire (see Exhibit 11.7). Then a first drawing is held. Next, the television pilots and commercials are shown. Then the emcee announces additional prizes and a second drawing. Finally, subjects fill out the same questionnaire about prizes. The information from the first questionnaire is the before measurement, and that from the second questionnaire is the after measurement. The control group receives similar treatment except that on the day they view the pilot television shows, different (or no) television commercials are substituted for the experimental commercials.

POSTTEST-ONLY CONTROL GROUP DESIGN (AFTER-ONLY WITH CONTROL)

In some situations pretest measurements are impossible. In other situations selection error is not anticipated to be a problem because the groups are known to be equal. The posttest-only control group design, or *after-only with control group design,* is diagrammed as follows:

Experimental group: $\boxed{R}$ $\quad X \quad$ O_1
Control group: $\boxed{R}$ $\qquad$ O_2

The effect of the experimental treatment is equal to $O_2 - O_1$.

EXHIBIT 11.7 **Product Preference Measure in an Experiment**

We are going to give away a series of prizes. If you are selected as one of the winners, which brand from each of the groups listed below would you truly want to win?

Special arrangements will be made for any product for which bulk, or one-time, delivery is not appropriate.

Indicate your answers by filling in the box like this: ■

Do not "X," check, or circle the boxes please.

Cookies			Allergy Relief Products		
(A 3-month supply, pick ONE.)			(A year's supply, pick ONE.)		
NABISCO OREO	☐	(1)	ALLEREST	☐	(1)
NABISCO OREO DOUBLE STUFF	☐	(2)	BENADRYL	☐	(2)
NABISCO NUTTER BUTTER	☐	(3)	CONTAC	☐	(3)
NABISCO VANILLA CREMES	☐	(4)	TAVIST–D	☐	(4)
HYDROX CHOCOLATE	☐	(5)	DRISTAN	☐	(5)
HYDROX DOUBLES	☐	(6)	SUDAFED	☐	(6)
NABISCO COOKIE BREAK	☐	(7)	CHLOR–TRIMETON	☐	(7)
NABISCO CHIPS AHOY	☐	(8)			
KEEBLER E.L. FUDGE	☐	(9)			
KEEBLER FUDGE CREMES	☐	(10)			
KEEBLER FRENCH VANILLA CREMES	☐	(11)			

Suppose the manufacturer of an athlete's-foot remedy wishes to demonstrate by experimentation that its product is better than a competing brand. No pretest measure about the effectiveness of the remedy is possible. The design is to randomly select subjects, perhaps students, who have contracted athlete's foot and randomly assign them to the experimental or the control group. With only the posttest measurement, the effects of testing and instrument variation are eliminated. Furthermore, researchers make the same assumptions about extraneous variables described above—that is, that they operate equally on both groups, as in the before–after with control group design.

COMPROMISE DESIGNS

True experimentation is often simply not possible. The researcher may compromise by approximating an experimental design. A compromise design is one that falls short of assigning subjects or treatments randomly to experimental groups.

Consider a situation in which a researcher would ideally implement a pretest–posttest control group design to study the effect of training on employee performance. In this case, subjects may not be able to be assigned randomly to the experimental and control group because the researcher cannot take workers away from their work groups. Thus, one entire work group is used as the experimental group and a separate work group is used as a control group. The researcher has no assurance that the groups are equivalent. The situation has forced a compromise to experimental integrity.

The alternative to the compromise design when random assignment of subjects is not possible is to conduct the experiment *without* a control group. Generally this is considered a greater weakness than using groups that have already been established. When the experiment involves a longitudinal study, circumstances usually dictate a compromise with true experimentation.

Time Series Designs

Many marketing experiments may be conducted in a short period of time (a few hours, a week, or a month). However, a marketing experiment investigating long-term structural changes may require a **time series design**. Time series designs are quasi-experimental because they generally do not allow the researcher full control over the treatment exposure or influence of extraneous variables. When experiments are conducted over long periods of time, they are most vulnerable to

Time series design
Used for an experiment investigating long-term structural changes.

EXHIBIT 11.8
**Selected Time Series
Outcomes**

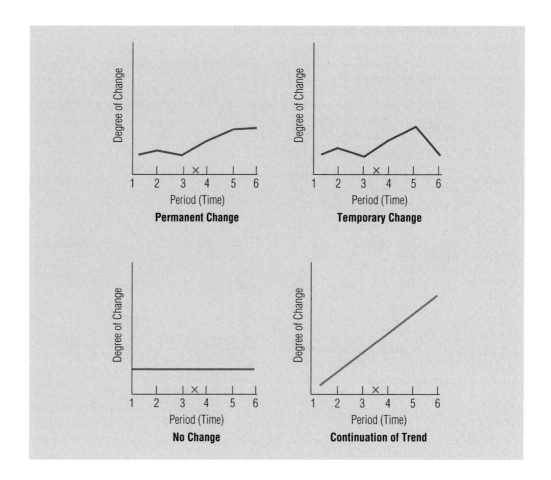

history effects due to changes in population, attitudes, economic patterns, and the like. Although seasonal patterns and other exogenous influences may be noted, the experimenter can do little about them when time is a major factor in the design.

Political tracking polls provide an example. A pollster normally uses a series of surveys to track candidates' popularity. Consider the candidate who plans a major speech (the experimental treatment) to refocus the political campaign. The simple time series design can be diagrammed as follows:

$$O_1 \qquad O_2 \qquad O_3 \qquad X \qquad O_4 \qquad O_5 \qquad O_6$$

Several observations have been taken to identify trends before the treatment (X) is administered. After the treatment has been administered, several observations are made to determine if the patterns *after* the treatment are similar to those *before*. If the longitudinal pattern shifts after the political speech, the researcher may conclude that the treatment had a positive impact on the pattern. Of course, this time series design cannot give the researcher complete assurance that the treatment caused the change in the trend. Problems of internal validity are greater than in more tightly controlled before-and-after designs for experiments of shorter duration.

One unique advantage of the time series design is its ability to distinguish temporary from permanent changes. Exhibit 11.8 shows some possible outcomes in a time series experiment.

Complex Experimental Designs

Complex experimental designs are statistical designs that isolate the effects of confounding extraneous variables or allow for manipulation of more than one independent variable in the experiment. *Factorial designs, Latin square designs, completely randomized designs,* and *randomized block designs,* as well as statistical discussions of these techniques, are covered in Chapter 12, on complex experimental designs, and Chapter 22, on tests of differences.

Summary

1. Create an experimental, independent variable through a valid experimental manipulation of its value. Independent variables are created through manipulation in experiments rather than through measurement. The researcher creates unique experimental conditions that represent unique levels of an independent variable. In our extended example, the researcher manipulated the color independent variable by creating a retail store concept that varied over two levels—blue and orange. The levels should be different enough to represent meaningful categories of the dependent variable. If the two colors studied were orange and burnt orange, consumers may react too similarly to expect any differences in the dependent variable.

2. Understand and minimize the systematic experimental error. Systematic experimental error occurs because sampling units (research subjects) in one experimental cell are different from those in another cell in a way that affects the dependent variable. In an experiment involving how people respond to color, the researcher would not want to have all males in one color group and all females in another. Randomization is an important way of minimizing systematic experimental error. If research subjects are randomly assigned to different treatment combinations, then the differences among people that exist naturally within a population should also exist within each experimental cell.

3. Know ways of minimizing experimental demand characteristics. Demand characteristics are experimental procedures that somehow inform the subject about the actual research purpose. Demand effects can result from demand characteristics. When this happens, the results are confounded. Demand characteristics can be minimized by following these simple rules: using an experimental disguise, isolating experimental subjects, using a "blind" experimental administrator, and administering only one experimental treatment combination to each subject.

4. Avoid unethical experimental practices. Experiments involve deception. Additionally, research subjects are sometimes exposed to stressful or possibly dangerous manipulations. Every precaution should be made to insure that subjects are not harmed. Debriefing subjects about the true purpose of the experiment following its conclusion is important for the ethical treatment of subjects. If debriefing can restore subjects to their pre-experimental condition, the experimental procedures are likely consistent with ethical practice. If subjects are affected in some way that makes it difficult to return them to their prior condition, then the experimental procedures probably go beyond what is considered ethical.

5. Understand the advantages of a between-subjects experimental design. A between-subjects design means that every subject receives only one experimental treatment combination. The main advantages of between-subjects designs are the reduced likelihood of demand effects and simpler analysis and presentation.

6. Weigh the trade-off between internal and external validity. Lab experiments offer higher internal validity because they maximize control of extraneous variables. High internal validity is a good thing because we can be more certain that the experimental variable is truly the cause of any variance in the dependent variable. Field experiments maximize external validity because they are conducted in a more natural setting meaning that the results are more likely to generalize to the actual business situation. The increased external validity comes at the expense of internal validity.

Key Terms and Concepts

Subjects
Experimental condition
Main effect
Interaction effect
Experimental treatment
Experimental group
Control group
Cell
Test units
Systematic or nonsampling error
Randomization
Repeated measures

Confound
Demand characteristic
Demand effect
Hawthorne effect
Placebo effect
Constancy of conditions
Counterbalancing
Laboratory experiment
Tachistoscope
Field experiments
Within-subjects design
Between-subjects design

Internal validity
Manipulation check
History effect
Cohort effect
Maturation effects
Testing effects
Instrumentation effect
Mortality effect (sample attrition)
External validity
Basic experimental design
Quasi-experimental designs
Time series design

Questions for Review and Critical Thinking

1. Define *experimental condition, experimental treatment,* and *experimental group.* How are these related to the implementation of a valid manipulation?
2. A tissue manufacturer that has the fourth-largest market share plans to experiment with a 50¢ off coupon during November and a buy one, get one free coupon during December. The experiment will take place at Target stores in St. Louis and Kansas City. Sales will be recorded by scanners from which mean tissue sales for each store for each month can be computed and interpreted.
   a. What are the independent variable and the dependent variable?
   b. Prepare a "dummy" table (covered in Chapter 5) that would describe what the results of the experiment would look like.
3. What is the difference between a *main effect* and an *interaction* in an experiment? In question 2, what will create a main effect? Is an interaction possible?
4. In what ways might the design in question 2 yield systematic or nonsampling error?
5. What purpose does the random assignment of subjects serve?
6. Why is an experimental confound so damaging to the conclusions drawn from an experiment?
7. What are demand characteristics? How can they be minimized?
8. **ETHICS** Suppose researchers were experimenting with how much more satisfied consumers are with a "new and improved" version of some existing product. How might the researchers design a placebo within an experiment testing this research question? Is using such a placebo ethical or not?
9. If a company wanted to know whether to implement a new management training program based on how much it would improve ROI in its southwest division, would you recommend a field or lab experiment?
10. **'NET** Suppose you wanted to test the effect of three different email requests inviting people to participate in a survey posted on the Internet. One simply contained a hyperlink with no explanation, the other said if someone participated $10 would be donated to charity, and the other said if someone participated he or she would have a chance to win $1,000. How would this experiment be conducted differently based on whether it was a between-subjects or within-subjects design? What are the advantages of a between-subjects design?
11. What is a manipulation check? How does it relate to internal validity?
12. **ETHICS** What role does debriefing play in ensuring that experimental procedures are consistent with good ethical practice?

Research Activities

1. Consider the situation of a researcher approached by Captain John's in the opening vignette.
   a. Provide a critique of the procedures used to support the claim that Sea Snapper's product is superior. Prepare it in a way that it could be presented as evidence in court.
   b. Design an experiment that would provide a more valid test of the research question, "Do consumers prefer Sea Snapper fish sticks compared to Captain John's fish sticks?"
2. Conduct a taste test involving some soft drinks with a group of friends. Pour them several ounces of three popular soft drinks and simply label the cups A, B, and C. Make sure they are blind to the actual brands. Then, let them drink as much as they want and record how much of each they drink. You may also ask them some questions about the drinks. Then, allow other subjects to participate in the same test, but this time, let them know what the three brands are. Record the same data and draw conclusions. Does brand knowledge affect behavior and attitudes about soft drinks?

Case 11.1 Examining Product Failure at No-Charge Electronics

 No-Charge Electronics owner Buzz Auphf needs to know how much product failure affects customer loyalty. Buzz contacts David Handy, a local market researcher, and they ultimately decide on examining a research question asking, "How do current customers react to different levels of product failure?" David designs the following experiment to examine the causal effect of product failure on customer purchase intentions, satisfaction, and loyalty.

The experiment is implemented via e-mail using a sample of current and prospective customers. Three free mp3 movies are provided as an incentive to participate. Subjects are asked to click through to an Internet site to download a product that will enhance their computer's graphics capability. In the low-failure condition, after the subjects click to the site, there is no change in the graphics of their computers. In the high-failure condition, once they click through to the site, the subjects' computers go into an infinite loop of obscene graphical images until a message arrives indicating that a severe virus has infected their computer and some files may be permanently damaged. This goes on for forty-five minutes with no remedy. At that time, a debriefing message pops up telling subjects that it was all part of an experiment and that their computer should now function properly. Prepare a position statement either agreeing or disagreeing that the experiment is consistent with good ethical practice.

Case 11.2 Tooheys

Sixty-six willing Australian drinkers helped a Federal Court judge decide that Tooheys didn't engage in misleading or deceptive advertising for its 2.2 beer. The beer contains 2.2 percent alcohol, compared to 6 percent for other beers leading to a claim that could be interpreted as implying it was non-alcoholic.

Volunteers were invited to a marathon drinking session after the Aboriginal Legal Service claimed Tooheys' advertising implied beer drinkers could imbibe as much 2.2 as desired without becoming legally intoxicated. Drunken driving laws prohibit anyone with a blood-alcohol level above 0.05 from getting behind the wheel in Australia.

So, an experiment was conducted to see what happens when a lot of 2.2 is consumed. But the task wasn't easy or that much fun. Some subjects couldn't manage to drink the required 10 "middies," an Aussie term for a beer glass of 10 fluid ounces, over the course of an hour.

Thirty-six participants could manage only nine glasses. Four threw up and were excluded. Two more couldn't manage the "minimum" nine glasses and had to be replaced.

Justice J. Beaumont observed that consuming enough 2.2 in an hour to reach the 0.05 level was "uncomfortable and therefore an unlikely process." Because none of the ads mentioned such extreme quantities, he ruled they couldn't be found misleading or deceptive.[14]

Questions

1. Would a lab experiment or a field experiment be more "valid" in determining whether Tooheys could cause a normal beer consumer to become intoxicated? Explain.
2. Describe an alternate research design that would have higher validity.
3. Is the experiment described in this story consistent with good ethical practice? Likewise, comment on how the design described in part 2 would be made consistent with good ethical practices.
4. Is validity or ethics more important?

CHAPTER 12
TEST-MARKETS AND EXPERIMENTAL DESIGN

After studying this chapter, you should be able to

1. Know the basics of test-marketing, including how experimental manipulations can be used to test marketing strategies in a real world setting
2. Recognize the appropriate uses of test-marketing
3. List the advantages and disadvantages of test-marketing
4. Use manipulations to implement a completely randomized experimental design, a randomized-block design, and a factorial experimental design
5. Display experimental results using graphical charts

Chapter Vignette: Imported Lights!

Heineken, the Dutch beer that many Americans mistake as German, is the leading selling European import beer in the United States. Whereas Anheuser-Busch and Miller Brewing Company have long been differentiated marketers, offering a portfolio of beer products each for a slightly different taste, Heineken has won its position almost entirely with the product in the familiar green can.

In more recent years, Heineken has enjoyed some success with a second label, Amstel Light, but they continue to struggle with the decision of whether or not to offer a premium light beer under the Heineken label itself. Finally, after noticing a trend among American consumers to trade up to brands perceived as higher in quality, Heineken commissioned a test-market of Heineken Premium Light in 2005.[1] The test-market addressed research questions related not only to whether or not Heineken Premium Light (HPL) would sell, but also where potential sales would come from. If HPL simply cannibalizes traditional Heineken sales, then it may not be wise to introduce the product. The test-market also addressed issues related to promotion. What promotional appeal would do the most to create favorable attitudes about HPL?

Researchers for Heineken selected four locations for the experiment. Consumers in Providence, Rhode Island; Tampa, Florida; Dallas, Texas; and Phoenix, Arizona, would be included in the test-market. The light beer would be sold in all the traditional retail outlets alongside traditional Heineken. Key dependent variables include sales of Heineken Light, sales of Heineken, sales of Amstel Light, and sales of domestic light beers such as Bud Light and Miller Lite.

Heineken researchers revealed several key findings in a presentation to company executives:

1. HPL did cannibalize Amstel Light, but not as much as expected. A slight repositioning of Amstel can minimize cannibalization.
2. The introduction of HPL lowered Heineken sales in only one test-market city. So, fears of cannibalization are reduced.
3. HPL sales were associated with slightly lower sales among domestic light beers.
4. HPL sales were overall equal or above expectations in three of four cities. HPL sales were higher than expected among ethnic market segments.

The presentation and report led Heineken to introduce the beer throughout the United States in 2006. An advertising budget of $40 million was allocated to spread the word about Heineken Light. The ad theme that tested best appeared to be consistent with their current advertising theme. Thus, the test-market proved vital to the decision to launch Heineken Light.

In the meantime, German beer maker Becks has introduced a premium light beer with only sixty-four calories. Grolsch Light has been introduced in five states and Corona Light is being introduced with a $10 million ad campaign of its own.

Using Test-Markets

Test-marketing involves scientific testing and controlled field experimentation. As such, test-marketing goes well beyond merely "trying something out in the marketplace." Just because a product is introduced in a small marketing area before deciding whether to do a national launch does not mean a test-market has been conducted. Those who underestimate the need for a rigorous approach to test-marketing often "succeed" in their test-market but fail in their product launch. Test-marketing is the most prominent type of field experiment.

Chapter 3 briefly introduced test-marketing. Recall that a *test-market* is a market experiment conducted in an actual product market, meaning under real-world conditions. While we most often think of test-markets in conjunction with a decision about the viability of some newly developed product, they are equally useful in examining other elements of marketing strategy. Even though test-markets are not "small scale" research projects, they do test-marketing questions under a smaller scale than the entire market. So, before implementing a marketing strategy throughout the United States or Europe, test cities such as Tampa, Florida, and Frankfurt, Germany, may be used to represent the way consumers in other cities might react.

Effective Uses of Test-marketing

Test-marketing has three broad primary uses in marketing research. Each use can be broken down more specifically to look at some issue in close detail. The three broad uses are

1. Forecasting the success of a newly developed product.
2. Testing hypotheses about different options for marketing mix elements.
3. Identifying weaknesses in product designs or marketing strategies.

▨ FORECASTING NEW PRODUCT SUCCESS

Test-markets have long been used as a pilot test for a new product introduction. While test-markets can be complicated to implement, the basic idea is simple. A product can be marketed on a small scale under actual market conditions and the results used to forecast the success or failure once the product is introduced on a large scale. The opening vignette described how Heineken is using a test-market to forecast the success of Heineken Premium Light (HPL) beer.

Companies using test-markets should realize that a new product concept also involves issues like advertising, pricing, supply chains, and retail placement. These issues may also be manipulated within a test-market. Estimates can then be made about the optimal advertising level, the need for product sampling, retail channel fit, or perhaps even advertising and retail channel selection interaction. Test-marketing permits evaluation of the entire new product concept, not just the physical good itself.

A marketing manager for Life Savers candies vividly portrays this function of experimentation in the marketplace:

A market test may be likened to an orchestra rehearsal. The violinists have adjusted their strings, the trumpeters have tested their keys, and the drummer has tightened his drums. Everything is ready to go. But all these instruments have not worked in unison. So a test-market is like an orchestra rehearsal where you can practice with everything together before the big public performance.[2]

A researcher conducting a test-market may evaluate not only new product's sales as a dependent variable, but also existing products' sales as relevant dependent variables, as seen in the HPL vignette. In this way, test-marketing allows a firm to determine whether a new offering will cannibalize sales from existing products, meaning that consumers are choosing the new offering as a replacement for another product offered by the same company.

For example, Nabisco's cracker business is mature. The company has many brands, and to add positively to overall sales, a new product must tap just the right market segment. Concept testing may suggest that a new cheese flavored saltine is a great concept. But a test-market may show that the consumers who are actually buying the new product are already Nabisco Cheese Nips fans. Rather than buying more Nabisco products, they are actually substituting the lower priced cheese saltines for the old product. Thus, Nabisco may decide not to proceed with the new product. Test-marketing provides the most effective examination of cannibalization prior to full-scale production.

TESTING THE MARKETING MIX

Test-markets are not confined to studying new products or product modifications. They also are equally useful as a field experiment manipulating different marketing plans for existing products. Any element of the marketing mix can be examined with a test-market.

As we all know, retailers rely heavily on weekly flyers distributed through newspapers or through direct mail. This is particularly true in France, where retail advertising is restricted by law in many ways, including the ability to advertise on television. In France, the average French household receives over 12 kg (26.4 lbs) of retail flyers annually![3] Yet, many have little idea about the effectiveness of different approaches. Should the flyers simply promote low price, or should they emphasize products related to a specific theme? In fact, different flyer styles can significantly affect not only sales, but retailer image too.[4]

Test-marketing can provide an effective way of estimating the effect of a different flyer approach. Interestingly, Staples recently tested the effect of several different flyer approaches on sales. Different flyers were tested in different market areas. Prior to the test, top managers at Staples were given a chance to guess which flyer would produce the most positive effect. Results of the test showed how valid "expert" opinion can sometimes be. The consensus pick for the best flyer came in dead last in the market test![5] Thus, although a test-market can be timely and expensive, even for an existing offering, the advantages of a field test can prevent mistakes in decision making.

IDENTIFYING PRODUCT WEAKNESSES

Test-market experimentation also allows identification of previously undetected product or marketing plan weaknesses. The weaknesses can then be dealt with before the company commits to the actual sales launch. Although often this use of test-markets is accidental, in the sense that it isn't the reason for conducting the test-markets, huge sums of resources can be saved by spotting problems before the full-scale marketing effort begins. Often, this use of test-marketing occurs when a product underperforms in at least one location. Researchers can then follow up

---

Cannibalize
When consumers choose a new offering as a replacement for another product offered by the same company.

TOTHEPOINT

You cannot create experience. You must undergo it.

—Albert Camus

Test-marketing can be used to determine the impact of different promotional approaches on sales and brand image.

RESEARCHSNAPSHOT

Test-marketing Channels

Traditionally, most construction material companies have focused their advertising on B2B efforts by targeting their sales and promotional efforts at construction material wholesalers, retailers, and contractors. The emphasis as a result was often centered around price in one way or another.

Construction products today are changing the way these products are sold and promoted. They are going right to the end-consumers in a classic pull strategy. The hope is that by advertising and selling directly to consumers, they will demand that contractors use a certain material and that home centers stock these products. Both Hardi Plank siding products and Georgia-Pacific drywall products have seen success in communicating emotionally about the importance of building and repairing one's home "right."

GP has test-marketing advertising campaigns aimed squarely at end-consumers in Atlanta, Minneapolis, Tampa, Charlotte, and Raleigh-Durham, North Carolina. The campaigns include commercials that address consumers' fears about mold in their homes. They tout drywall products that can "stop feeding the mold." Similarly, Hardi Plank ads show how their products can help homeowners relax without fear of rotting or constant repainting. Both companies are excited about the results of marketing directly to consumers. However, the building industry is slow to change and most building product companies continue to target business markets.

Sources: Lovel, J. (2005), "New GP Ads Take Drywall to the Masses," Adweek, 46 (8/8), 11; Rodriguez, Dennis. (2004), "Shea Homes," Professional Builder, 69 (Mid-December), 34.

©PHOTONICA/GETTY IMAGES

with other research approaches to try and reveal the reason for the lack of performance. Once identified, product modifications can be made that address these reasons specifically.

McDonald's test-marketed pizza periodically for years. The first test-market provided lower than expected sales results. The reasons for the underperformance included a failure to consider learned competitors' reactions and problems associated with the small, single portion pizza, which was the only way McPizza was sold. Additionally, McPizza didn't seem to bring any new customers to McDonald's. In the next round of test-marketing, the marketing strategy repositioned the pizza, shifting to a 14-inch pizza that was only sold from about 4 p.m. until closing. With still underwhelming results, McDonalds test-marketed "Pizza Shoppes" within the test McDonald's where employees could be seen assembling ingredients on ready-made pizza dough. Although the concept is still alive, McDonald's has shied away from pizza for the U.S. adult market. A McPizza Happy Meal remains as a sole pizza concept with promise for American stores. Pizza-like products, however, exist and succeed at many McDonald's locations in other nations.

Note that just because a product fails its market test, the test-market can't be considered a failure. In most cases, this represents an important *research success*. Encountering problems in a test-market either properly leads the company to introduce the new product or to make the planned change in marketing strategy. Thus, a huge mistake is likely avoided. In addition, test-market results may lead management to make adjustments that will turn the poor test-market results into a market success. The managerial experience gained in test-marketing can be extremely valuable, even when the performance results are disappointing.

Advantages of Test-marketing

This discussion of test-marketing should make it clear that test-markets are advantageous in ways that are very difficult to match with other research approaches. The key advantage of test-marketing is the real-world setting in which the experiment is performed. Although focus groups and surveys also can be useful in describing what people may like in a new product, the actual behavior of consumers in a real test-market location is far more likely to lead to accurate projections.

A second advantage of test-marketing is that the results are usually easily communicated to management. Although the experiment itself can be difficult to implement for a host of reasons, most of which are related to small-scale or temporary marketing, the data analysis is usually very

RESEARCHSNAPSHOT

The Fast-Food Tests Race On!

Fast-food companies are among the leaders in test-marketing. Wendy's has had some of the most successful new sandwich launches ever, including the Big Bacon Classic. As consumer tastes change, the fast-food companies have to try to keep up.

By the time this book is published, Wendy's, McDonald's, and Burger King will have completed test-markets of new products, each trying to be the first to capitalize on the latest consumer trends. Wendy's is testing fancy deli-style sandwiches such as the Frescata, Roasted Turkey with Basil Pesto, and a Sun-Dried Tomato Chicken sandwich. Not to be outdone,

McDonald's is testing more traditional deli-style sub sandwiches in Columbus, Ohio; Louisville, Kentucky; Richmond, Virginia; and Rockford, Illinois. Will consumers accept these types of non-traditional fast-food offerings from typical fast-food restaurants?

Burger King on the other hand, is reaching toward a different segment. They are test-marketing Chicken Fries. Chicken fries are thin strips of fried, battered all-white meat chicken. Who will win the fast-food race?

Sources: Restaurants and Institutions (2005), "Menu Matters," 115 (7/1), 22; Restaurant and Institutions (2004), "Toast of the Town," 114 (9/15), 13; Garber, Amy (2003), "McDonald's Seeks Green with New Salads, Blasts Legal Setback," Nation's Restaurant News, 37 (5/12), 4.

simple. Very often, the same procedures used in any simple experiment can be used with test-markets. As we will see, this relies heavily on comparing means in some way. Researchers find marketing managers much more receptive to these types of results than they may be to results drawn from complicated mathematical models or qualitative approaches relying on deep subjective interpretation.

Disadvantages of Test-marketing

Test-markets also have disadvantages. While the power of test-markets in providing accurate predictions are apparently such that companies would use test-markets for all major marketing changes, this is hardly the case. The disadvantages are such that test-markets are used less frequently than one might think.

COST

Test-marketing is very expensive. Consider that for most new products, companies have to actually create production facilities on a small scale, develop distribution within selected test-market cities, arrange media coverage specific to those locations, and then have systems and people in place to carefully monitor market results. All of this leads to high cost overall and very high unit costs. Heineken is faced with all these issues in test-marketing HPL. As a result, each six-pack can cost several times over the actual selling price. However, when HPL is introduced throughout the United States, the economies of scale that come with full-scale marketing will leave unit costs below the selling price.

Test-marketing a packaged-goods product typically costs millions. As with other forms of marketing research, the value of the information must be compared with the research costs. The expense of test-marketing certainly is a primary reason why marketing managers refuse to use the approach. Although they do reduce error in decision making, they are not perfect and certainly some risk remains in basing decisions on test-market results. If they were risk-free, managers would use them far more frequently. Because they are not risk-free and so expensive, managers may decide to make go or no-go decisions based on less expensive techniques that are often less accurate.

Exhibit 12.1 illustrates the magnitude of costs typically associated with getting a single new product through the new product pipeline and into the marketplace,[6] where success is still not guaranteed. As can be seen from the chart, the research approaches used for early product testing are relatively inexpensive per idea tested. Once the test-marketing stage is reached however, testing an idea can cost millions. Thus, managers like to be somewhat certain that a new product idea is good before they commit to a test-market. Therefore, products that are test-marketed are usually

RESEARCHSNAPSHOT

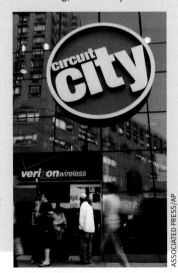

Testing all the Circuits is Costly at Circuit City

Circuit City is among the most successful electronic retailers in the United States. Every year, the retailer is involved in many research projects. One of the frequent topics for research involves the company's retail store design, or atmosphere. A test-market of a store concept can be very expensive; however, it can provide data not only on potential store sales, but also on the expense associated with operating a store and on how the concept comes together with advertising to create an improved store image.

Circuit City has spent millions test-marketing redesigns of its store atmosphere. Recent tests involved an energy saving design and a design that reduces the perceived density in a store to allow consumers a greater sense of freedom while shopping. One test-market involved redesigning over twenty stores, about half in Washington, D.C., the other half in Chicago. The cost to redesign each store was originally estimated at just over $2.5 million. After some additional screening, Circuit City was able to simplify the redesign process to about $1 million per store. In addition, the company tested two different advertising approaches, one in each market. Thus, the total cost of the test-market exceeded $20 million. The result, greater confidence that Circuit City had the design right!

Sources: Heller, Laura. (2001), "Circuit City Saves on New Look," DSN Retailing Today, 40 (10/22), 3–4; Chain Store Age (2005), "Circuit City Goes Green with LEED Project," 81 (January), 77.

ASSOCIATED PRESS/AP

expected to succeed. In this sense, the test-market can be thought of as the last line of defense against a marketing blunder.

The Research Snapshot box above illustrates how the expense associated with test-marketing can be even higher, particularly when it involves designing a physical service or retail environment.[7]

TIME

Test-markets cost more than just money. Test-markets cannot be put together overnight. Simply planning a test-market usually takes months. Actually implementing one takes much longer. On top of the time for planning and implementation, researchers also must decide how long is long enough. In other words, when is the amount of data collected sufficient to have confidence in drawing valid conclusions?

EXHIBIT 12.1 The Risks and Costs Associated with Product Development Research

Testing Procedure	Number of Ideas Considered	Number That Survive	Approximate Cost of Testing	Total Expense
Initial Idea Screening	80	8	$50	$4,000
Concept Testing	8	4	$4,000	$32,000
Product Development	4	2	$250,000	$1,000,000
Test-Marketing	2	1	$2,500,000	$5,000,000
Initial Full Launch	1	1	$10,000,000	$10,000,000
				$16,036,000

Sources: Ding, M. and J. Eliashberg (2002), "Structuring the New Product Development Principle," Management Science, 48 (March) 343–363; P. Kotler (1997), *Marketing Management: Analysis, Planning and Control* (Upper Saddle River, NJ: Prentice Hall), p. 310.

The appropriate time period for a test-market varies depending on the research objectives. Sometimes, as in Procter & Gamble's testing of its unique new products Febreze, Dryel, and Fit Fruit & Vegetable Wash, the research takes several years. In other situations, as in P&G's testing of Encaprin pain reliever (a product that ultimately failed in national distribution), the time period may be shorter. HPL's test-markets lasted less than a year, relatively short by most standards.

Thus, even a quickly planned and implemented test-market can cost the firm a year or more in time. During this time, competitors are also trying to gain competitive advantage. The fear that competitors may make a big move first puts added pressure on marketing managers to move quickly. For this reason, the time costs associated with test-markets are a primary reason for forgoing them.

How long should a test-market be? Test-markets should be long enough for consumers to become aware of the product, have a chance to purchase it, consume it, and repurchase it at least one more time. Thus, it must be longer than the average purchase cycle for that particular product. A test-market that is too short may overestimate sales, because typically the early adopters are heavy users of the product. Thus, projections are based on consumers who are far from average.

Time must be allowed for sales to settle down from their initial honeymoon level. In addition, the share and sales levels must be allowed to stabilize. After the introduction of a product, peaks and troughs will inevitably stem from initial customer interest and curiosity as well as from competitive product retaliation.[8]

Thus, the time required for test-marketing depends on the product. The purchase cycle for chewing gum is much shorter than a bottle of shampoo. After high initial penetration and when the novelty of the product has stabilized, the researcher may make an estimate of market share. The average test-market requires about twelve months.

LOSS OF SECRECY

As pointed out with the Hidden Valley Ranch Research Snapshot in the last chapter, one drawback to actual field experimentation is that the marketplace is a public forum. Therefore, secrets no longer exist. In the case of a new product, not only does the competition know about the new product, but a competitor can sometimes benefit from the test-market by monitoring the same dependent variables as is the sponsoring firms. This may cause them to launch a competing product. In some cases, the competitor can even beat the originating company to the national marketplace.

While Clorox Super Detergent with Bleach remained in the test-market stage, P&G introduced Tide with Bleach across the country. Fab 1 Shot, a pouch laundry from Colgate-Palmolive, preempted Cheer Power Pouches by Procter & Gamble, but P&G wasn't sorry. Fab 1 Shot was not a commercial success. Perhaps Colgate-Palmolive should have observed the test-market results more closely. Food companies also are notorious for buying new food products and breaking down the recipe.

During the 1980s, soft, "homestyle" cookies were a market success. However, only one company perfected the recipe. The rest simply purchased the cookies and had their chemists determine how to make them. This resulted in legal actions that lasted for years.

When Not to Test-market

Not all product introductions are test-marketed. Expensive durables, such as refrigerators, automobiles, or heavy equipment, are rarely test-marketed because of the prohibitive cost of producing test units. Products that involve very little investment to get to market also are not appropriate for test-marketing. This may be the case with small modifications to existing products. In other cases, test-marketing is used as a last resort because a new concept might be easily imitated by competitors. Secrecy is more important than research in these cases.

Bacardi recently decided not to test-market a line of low calorie spirits. One important reason was the loss of secrecy and the fear that competitors would hasten a similar product to market.[9] Also, Bacardi believes it is riding the crest of a strong consumer trend toward lower calorie options. Thus, the calorie-conscious segment may be growing as consumers turn away from beer toward something less damaging to the waistline.

Many times, the decision whether to test-market or not is difficult. If a company chooses to forgo test-marketing, millions may be saved, but perhaps even more millions are lost when a product fails. Anheuser-Busch's Catalina Blonde beer (a "super light" beer targeted at women), Frito-Lay's Max Snax, and P&G's Pampers Rash Guard all failed in test-markets. However, the mistakes would have been even more costly had the brands immediately been introduced nationally. Like all research, test-marketing should only be conducted when the potential benefit exceeds the likely costs.

Selecting a Test-Market

Selecting test-markets is, for the most part, a sampling problem. The researcher seeks a sample of test-market cities that is representative of the population comprised of all consumers in the relevant marketing area. If a new product is being launched throughout Australia, for example, the researcher must choose cities that are typical of all Australians.

Thus, test-market cities should represent the entire competitive marketplace. For companies wishing to market a product through the United States, there is no single ideal test-market city. Nevertheless, the researcher must usually avoid cities that are not representative of the nation. Regional or urban differences, atypical climates, unusual ethnic compositions, or different lifestyles may dramatically affect a marketing program. Sometimes, although the researchers may wish to sell a product throughout the entire region of the United States, they may have a certain benefit segment in mind. Food companies may introduce a product that is intended for segments that enjoy spicy food, for example. In this case, they may choose cities known to favor spicier, more flavor-filled foods, such as New Orleans and San Antonio. In this case, those test-market cites have populations that fit the benefit segment to which the product is aimed.

U.S. Test-market Cities

Researchers who wish to select representative U.S. test-markets have a more complex problem because it is usually necessary to use three or four cities. Cities are selected as experimental units, and one or more additional cities may be used as control markets. The experimental and control markets should be similar in population size, income, ethnic composition, and so on. Differences in these demographic factors and other characteristics among the experimental or control markets affect the test results. Using the terminology introduced in the last chapter, these factors represent extraneous variables that can produce potential confounds.

Because of the importance of having representative markets for comparisons, certain cities are used repeatedly for test-market operations. Whereas some larger cities like Tampa; Peoria, Illinois; and San Antonio are attractive test-markets, many test-markets are conducted in smaller cities. Exhibit 12.2 lists several of the most popular U.S. test-markets.[10] Their popularity lies in how close they come to

EXHIBIT 12.2
Popular Test-Markets and Selected Demographic Characteristics

City	2000 Population	Median Age	Percent of Households w/Children	Hispanic Proportion (Percent)
Cedar Rapids, IA	191,701	35.2	31.8	1.4
Eau Claire, WI	148,337	34.7	31.4	0.8
Grand Junction, CO	116,255	38.1	31.4	10.0
Odessa-Midland, TX	237,132	33.0	38.4	35.8
Pittsfield, MA	84,699	40.6	27.6	1.7
Wichita Falls, TX	140,518	33.6	33.8	11.8
Entire U.S.	281,000,000	35.3	32.8	12.5
Wichita, KS	344,284	34.1	34.6	7.4

©RICHARD CUMMINS/CORBIS

While Tampa is a more commonly used test-market city, Miami is very appropriate for products aimed at Hispanic markets.

duplicating the average U.S. demographic profile. Researchers may find that some cities, like Wichita, Kansas and Cedar Rapids, Iowa, are particularly representative of the United States based on median age and households with children. On the other hand, they have very small percentage of Hispanic population. This may not pose a problem if the product is not thought to have any strong ethnic identification. Conversely, if a product is expected to have appeal based on ethnicity, then the test-market may be better conducted in Grand Junction, Colorado, and Wichita Falls, Texas. Because of this, Wichita Falls, Texas is considered by many to be the most typical U.S. city.[11]

International Test-markets

More and more companies become international companies every day. As a result, they may be test-marketing in foreign lands. The principles are still the same: "What cities represent the larger market best?"

Americans and Canadians are similar in many respects. However, one shouldn't assume that a product that is successful in the United States will be successful in Canada. Thus, even after a successful American launch, a company may wish to conduct a test-market in Canada. In addition, even if a new product is liked by the Canadian market, a unique marketing approach may be in order. Generally, Calgary, Alberta, is considered a prime test-market location for the Canadian market. When Italy's Podere Castorani Winery wished to expand to Canada, the product was tested in Calgary. Likewise, when Shell introduced a fast-pay charge system, Calgary again proved a suitable test-market.[12]

Like the United States, Canada is comprised of many different ethnic segments. Companies should also be aware that French Canada is quite different from the rest of the country. Thus, companies may consider a test-market in Quebec City, Quebec, to see how French Canadian consumers will react.

Test-marketing in Europe can be particularly difficult. While companies can test their products country by country, the sheer costs involved with test-marketing motivate firms to look for cities more representative of large parts of Europe. Copenhagen, Denmark, is one such city. While the population is somewhat homogenous demographically, it is also multilingual and receptive to new ideas.[13] Copenhagen is particularly representative of northern Europe. Other cities to be considered include Frankfurt, Germany, Birmingham, England, and Madrid, Spain.

One benefit of test-marketing in the United States is the large ethnic population base. For instance, some companies considering expansion to Brazil have test-marketed the ideas in Provo, Utah. Provo, better known for the Church of the Latter-Day Saints and Brigham Young University, contains a large percentage of Brazilians and Americans who have spent time in Brazil. Students at Brigham Young are required to do missionary work, and many do so in Brazil.[14] Therefore, the way a product performs in Provo may indicate to some degree the way a product would perform in San Paulo.

Companies may sometimes test-market a product in one country with plans of introducing it in another. Singapore has been used to test products made for the U.S. market. While Singapore may not be as representative of the United States as is Wichita Falls, Texas, competitors are less likely to spot the new product and take some kind of action aimed at spoiling the test-market results or piggy-backing on these results and launching their own product. As Singapore is sometimes used for products intended for the United States, European cities are sometimes used to project how well a product will do in China.

Factors to Consider in Test-market Selection

Obtaining a representative test-market requires considering many factors that may not be obvious to the inexperienced researcher. Consider the observation of a vice president of ITT Continental Banking:

When I started in the business, I thought people picked cities like Columbus, Ohio, because their populations were typical. But I found the main reasons were that they were isolated media markets and the distribution patterns were such that they didn't have to worry about the chain warehouse shipping outside of Columbus. It's difficult to translate information from a city which represents 0.1 percent of the United States and multiply that to get 99.9 percent. I think it is much more important to get control of the distribution and the advertising message.[15]

As with all decisions, the objectives of the decision makers will influence the choice of alternative. The following factors should be considered in the selection of a test-market.

POPULATION SIZE

No one size represents the best population for a test-market city. Practically all metropolitan areas in the United States are large enough. The population simply should be large enough to provide meaningful results with respect to the larger population, yet small enough to ensure that costs are not prohibitive. New York City is far too large to be a popular test-market, as is Chicago and Los Angeles in the United States. Likewise, Tokyo and Mexico City are considered too large for practical test-markets. Conversely, notice that the attractive test-market cities shown in Exhibit 12.2 are all well under 1 million in population. This allows far greater control at a far lower price than using the largest U.S. cities.

DEMOGRAPHIC COMPOSITION AND LIFESTYLE CONSIDERATIONS

Ethnic backgrounds, incomes, age distributions, lifestyles, and so on within the market should be representative of the market segment to which an offering is targeted. If a product is intended to be equally targeted toward the entire U.S. market, the product should then be test-marketed in cities that most closely match the entire U.S. population, like Wichita Falls, Texas. Test-marketing on the West Coast may not be representative because people residing in metropolitan areas along the Pacific tend to be unique in some ways. For instance, West Coast consumers are quick to accept innovations that might not ever be adopted on a large scale elsewhere. Additionally, most of these cities have large percentages of either Hispanic and/or Asian populations, making them less appropriate for representing the entire country.

In contrast, if an offering is targeted only toward a specific geographic segment, then the test-markets should have profiles that reflect that particular segment. Many products have demand patterns that vary regionally. In the United States, alcoholic beverage consumption varies by region. While spirit sales (i.e., whiskey) dominate in the Northeast, Southerners consume the most beer per capita. Thus, beer companies may favor the South whereas whiskey companies would do better to emphasize New England in their test-marketing.

Products geared toward ethnic markets should likewise emphasize cities with high proportions of the respective consumer group. Mobile phone companies realize that Hispanics have different usage habits on average than many other consumer groups.[16] Thus, test-market cities may include Miami, Florida, or Midland, Texas, where very large numbers of Hispanic consumers reside.

COMPETITIVE SITUATION

Competitive market shares, competitive advertising, and distribution patterns should be typical so that test-markets will represent other geographic regions. If they are not representative, it will be difficult to project the test-market results to other markets.

Consider a firm that test-markets a new product in a specific geographical area in which the company has a dominant market share. Here, the sales force may have a much easier time getting shelf space than in an area where market share is low. The result is a higher acceptance level among retailers, lower cost of sell-in (obtaining initial distribution), and a greater upside potential for test-market results. Hence, projecting the results of this particular test-market into those where the same level of past success is not enjoyed proves difficult.

MEDIA COVERAGE AND EFFICIENCY

Local media (television spots, newspapers) will never exactly replicate national media. However, duplicating the national media plan or using one similar to it is important. Sunday newspaper supplements are sometimes used as a substitute for national magazine advertising. This does not duplicate a national plan, but may provide a rough estimate of the plan's impact. Ideally, a market should be represented by the major television networks, typical cable television programming, and newspaper coverage. Some magazines have regional editions or advertising inserts.

MEDIA ISOLATION

Advertising in communities outside of the test-market may contaminate the test-market. Furthermore, advertising money is wasted when it reaches consumers who cannot buy the advertised product because they live outside the test area. Markets such as Tulsa, Oklahoma, and Green Bay, Wisconsin, are highly desirable because advertising does not spill over into other areas. Notice how the cities in Exhibit 12.2 would also seem to share this characteristic.

SELF-CONTAINED TRADING AREA

Distributors should sell primarily or exclusively in the test-market area. Shipments in and out of markets from chain warehouses can produce confusing shipping figures. Frito-Lay test-marketed Olean-based versions of Ruffles, Lay's, Doritos, and Tostitos under the Max name in Cedar Rapids, Iowa. However, large amounts of the chips were purchased by droves of consumers in markets far from the test site.[17] Publicity about the no-fat chips had retailers fielding telephone orders from as far away as California, Texas, and New Jersey. Had the company relied solely on shipment information, the plants it built for what became WOW! Chips would have been much larger than needed.

OVERUSED TEST-MARKETS

If consumers or retailers become aware of the tests, they will react in a manner different from their norm. Thus, it is not a good idea to establish one great test-market and use it time and time again. Tucson, Arizona, is one area now used less frequently than in the past because Tuscsonian consumers now display atypical reactions to new-product introductions. Perhaps they are so accustomed to in-store promotion and advertising of new products that the reaction to innovative marketing is now below average.

Estimating Sales Volume: Some Problems

As mentioned above, an important use of test-marketing is estimating how well some product will do in the marketplace. This means that sales projections must be made based on how well a product performs in a test-market. Numerous methodological factors cause problems in estimating national sales results based on regional tests. Often, these problems result from mistakes in the design or execution of the test-market itself.

Overattention

If too much attention is paid to testing a new product, the product may be more successful than it would be under more normal marketing conditions. In the test-market, the firm's advertising agency may make sure that the test-markets have excellent television coverage (which may or may not be representative of the national television coverage). If salespeople are aware that a test is being conducted in their territory, they may spend unusual amounts of time making sure the new product is available or displayed better.

Unrealistic Store Conditions

Store conditions may be set at the level of the market leader rather than at the national level. For example, extra shelf facings, eye-level stocking, and other conditions resulting from artificial distribution may be obtained in the test-market.

This situation may result from research design problems or overattention, as previously described. For example, if retailers are made aware that someone is paying more attention to their efforts with a given product, they may give it artificially high distribution and extra retail support.

Reading the Competitive Environment Incorrectly

Another common mistake is to assume that the competitive environment will be the same nationally as in the test-market. If competitors are unaware of a test-market, the results will not measure competitors' reactions to company strategy. Competitors' responses after a national introduction may differ substantially from the way they reacted in the test-market. On the other hand, competitors may react to a test-market by attempting to undermine it. If they know that a firm is testing, they may attempt to disrupt test-market results with increased promotions and lower prices for their own products, among other potential acts of **test-market sabotage**.

When Starbucks test-marketed its supermarket brand coffee in Chicago, Procter & Gamble broadcast television commercials touting Millstone coffee's victory over Starbucks in taste tests. The commercials lampooned Starbucks for being more interested in selling T-shirts and novelties than coffee. P&G also offered free samples of Millstone to disrupt the result of Starbucks' test-market.[18] Similarly, Heineken competitors may launch heavy price cutting or other acts, which, whether they are intentionally meant to or not, may disrupt the test-market.

Test-market sabotage
Intentional attempts to disrupt the results of a test-market being conducted by another firm.

Incorrect Volume Forecasts

In the typical test-market, unit sales volume or market share is a focus of attention. Shipments, warehouse withdrawals, or store scanner data may be the major basis for projecting sales. Forecasted volume for test-markets should be adjusted to reflect test distribution levels, measurement problems with store data, and other differences between test-markets and national markets.

Smooth and Easy Sauce ("the gravy stick with all the gravy basics in one refrigerated bar") had a short product life. Test-market sales volume projections were inaccurate because the sauce was initially sold in what turned out to be an eight-month supply. At one point in the test-market, more bars were returned and discarded due to spoilage (372,000) than were sold (207,000).

Initial penetration, if projected directly, may overstate the situation. Many consumers who make a trial purchase may not repurchase the product. Researchers must be concerned with repurchase rates as well as with initial trial purchases. Supplementing retail store scanner data with purchase diaries and panel data will help indicate what sales volume will be over time.

Time Lapse

One relatively uncontrolled problem results from the time lapse between the test-market experiment and the national introduction of the product. Often, the time period between the test-market and national introduction is a year or more. Given the time needed to build production capacity, develop channels of distribution, and gain initial sales acceptance, this may be unavoidable. However, the longer the time between the test-market and the actual selling market, the less accurate one should expect the results to be.

Projecting Test-Market Results

Consumer Surveys

Most researchers support sales data with consumer survey data during test-markets. These help monitor consumer awareness and attitudes toward the test-marketed product as well as the repeat purchase likelihood. Frequently this information is acquired via consumer panels.

Straight Trend Projections

Sales can be identified and the market share for the test area calculated. The simplest method of projecting test-market results involves straight trend projections. Suppose the market share is 3.5 percent in a test-market region. A straight-line projection assumes that the true actual market share after launch will be 3.5 percent. Researchers using straight-line projections assume that the test-market is representative of the larger target market. Often, this assumption is based on the fact that there is no good reason to provide a different projection. After all, the test-market is supposed to be set up to represent the entire market.

Ratio of Test Product Sales to Total Company Sales

A measure of the company's competitive strength in the test-market region might be used as a basis for adjusting test-market results. Calculating a ratio of test product sales to total company sales in the area may provide a benchmark for modifying projections into other markets. In other words, if a new product accounts for 5 percent of the total company sales in a test-market area(s), then the projection is that the new product will account for 5 percent of total company sales in all markets.

Market Penetration x Repeat-Purchase Rate

A third way that sales projections can be taken into account is the likelihood of repeat purchases. To calculate market share for products that are subject to repeat purchases, the following formula is used:

market penetration (trial buyers) $\times$ *repeat purchase rate* $=$ *market share*

For example, suppose a product is tried by 30 percent of the population and the repeat purchase rate is 25 percent. Market share will then be 7.5 percent (30 percent $\times$ 25 percent = 7.5 percent).

Market penetration
The percentage of target market customers who purchased the product—often measured early in a test-market.

The repeat-purchase rate must be obtained from longitudinal research that establishes some form of historical record. Traditionally, a consumer panel has been necessary for recording purchases over time. Thus, panel data may indicate a cumulative product class buying rate, or **market penetration**, in the early weeks of the test-market. One way to look at market penetration is as the percentage of target market customers who purchased the product. As the test-market continues, repeat purchases from these buyers can be recorded until the number of trial purchases has leveled off. Exhibit 12.3 indicates typical purchase and repurchase patterns for a new product in a test-market.

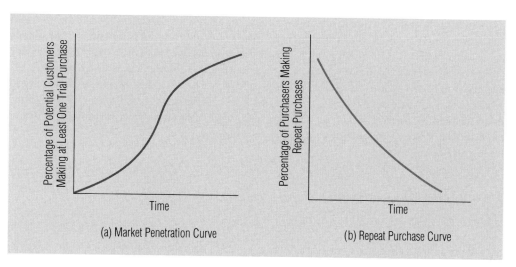

EXHIBIT 12.3
New-Product Trial Purchase Curve and Repeat-Purchase Curve

Alternative Test-Market Methods

Standard and Control Methods

The discussion so far has focused on the *standard method* of test-marketing. This means that the firm chooses test-markets and then obtains distribution within those markets using members of its own sales force. External validity is very high with this approach. Everything is just as it would be in a full-scale introduction.

In recent years, researchers have reduced test-market costs and the probability of competitive interference by using controlled store tests that simulate actual retail conditions. The **control method of test-marketing** involves a "minimarket test" in a small city, using *control store distribution,* or forced distribution. A marketing research company that specializes in test-marketing performs the entire test-marketing task, including the initial sale to retailers (referred to as *sell-in*), warehousing, distribution, and shelving of the test product. The research company pays retailers for shelf space and therefore can guarantee distribution to stores that represent a predetermined percentage of the market's all-commodity volume (the total dollar sales for that product in a defined market). Thus, the firm is guaranteed distribution in stores that represent a predetermined percentage of the market.

Control method of test-marketing
A "minimarket test" using forced distribution in a small city; retailers are paid for shelf space so that the test-marketer can be guaranteed distribution.

The warehousing function and portions of the retailer's stocking function are performed by the research agency. Therefore, the retailer may be more willing to cooperate with the research because selling the product will be effortless. However, this raises the question of whether the retailer would react to the product in the same fashion if the product were going through its normal distribution channels. With controlled store testing, out-of-stocks—a potential problem in the traditional channel of distribution—rarely occur. The research agency monitors the sales results without the use of an outside auditing firm.

For example, Market Facts, which conducts controlled store tests in metropolitan areas including Orlando, Florida; Erie, Pennsylvania; and Fort Wayne, Indiana, has auditors in test cities visit cooperating stores a minimum of two times each week during controlled store tests, minimizing out-of-stock conditions and ensuring maintenance of desired shelf conditions, location, facings, price, and so on. Thus, the experimental error that often interferes with sales tests is controlled.

Using the control method of test-marketing has several advantages:

1. Reduced costs
2. Shorter time period needed for reading test-market results
3. Increased secrecy from competitors
4. No distraction of company salespeople from regular product lines

Lower costs result from the smaller market tests. Distribution is guaranteed. Secrecy is increased and monitoring the test product's movement is increasingly difficult for competitors. One potential problem with a controlled store test is that distribution may be abnormally high. Also, retailers' complete cooperation with promotions, such as ensuring that the product is never out of stock, may result in higher-than-normal sales. This type of study becomes more like a laboratory study, in which factors are increasingly controlled. Thus, if a firm's objective is to test distribution for a product, a standard test-market will be much more appropriate. However, when the problem is to test a specific set of alternatives and determine which is best for a particular segment, controlled store testing may be superior.

High-Technology Systems Using Scanner Data

Electronic test-markets
A system of test-marketing that measures dependent variables with scanner-based consumer panels and manipulates advertising based on a special delivery system that can swap out one television commercial or advertisement for another.

Several research suppliers offer test-marketing systems that combine scanner-based consumer panels (discussed in Chapter 10) with high-technology broadcasting systems. This allows experimentation with different advertising messages via split-cable broadcasts or other technology. These systems, sometimes called **electronic test-markets**, enable researchers to measure the immediate impact of commercial television viewing of specific programs on unit sales volume.

A household's barcoded identification number is entered into a store's computer when a household member makes a purchase. The computer links the household's item-by-item purchases with television viewing data during extensive test-marketing programs. For example, Information Resources Incorporated (IRI) has selected certain medium-sized cities, such as Pittsfield, Massachusetts, to serve as scanner-based test-markets. The company installs an electronic device on every television in selected households that become scanner-based panel members. In these electronically wired households, the device measures television viewing habits in five-second increments to determine whether a particular television commercial was viewed.

However, IRI's system also allows the researcher to manipulate what advertising the panel households see. The electronic device on the television set allows the researcher to cut into the regularly scheduled broadcasts and substitute a test commercial (introducing a new product, for example) for the commercial that is transmitted nationally over the television network. Furthermore, IRI has arranged with local newspapers and national magazines to print special editions for the test households. One household may find a cents-off coupon for a test product in the morning paper, whereas the house next door receives a regular newspaper without even a mention of the product. In this way experimental and control groups may be established and scanner-based sales data used as the dependent variable.

Needless to say, the high-tech electronic test-marketing systems increase the speed and accuracy of test-marketing. But they also can be expensive. A full IRI test costs several million dollars per year.

Simulated Test-markets

Simulated test-market
A research laboratory in which the traditional shopping process is compressed into a shot timespan.

Marketing research program strategies often include plans for simulated test-markets because managers wish to minimize the number of products that go through the lengthy and costly process of full-scale marketing. A **simulated test-market** is a research laboratory in which the traditional shopping process is compressed into a short timespan. Consumers visit a research facility, where they are exposed to advertisements (usually as part of a television program shown in a theater setting). They then shop in a room that resembles a supermarket aisle. Researchers estimate trial purchase rates and how frequently consumers will repurchase the product based on their simulated purchases in the experimental store.

Simulated test-markets almost always use a computer model of sales to produce estimates of sales volume. For example, M/A/R/C Inc. offers the ASSESSOR modeling system. Simulated test-markets cannot replace full-scale test-marketing, but they allow researchers to make early predictions about the likelihood of success of a go/no-go decision. These results become significant information for determining which products ultimately will be introduced into real test-markets.

RESEARCHSNAPSHOT

Testing in a Virtual World

Modern technologies are offering alternatives to conventional test-markets. These come in several different forms. High-tech firms have developed web-based software that allows consumers to enter virtual worlds where they can select, among other things, what types of clothes to wear to certain events, or what kind of shoes to wear to get there. Companies like Levi's can provide a virtual world through their website and include some new jean designs for consumers to try out virtually. Certainly much cheaper than a conventional test-market, the company can get a sense for what types of consumers are turned on by which types of jeans.

Video-game-type test-markets can also be conducted. These work much like the popular simulation games in which consumers control the daily lives of virtual families. However, these simulated people are programmed to act like real consumers.

Among other things, a soft-drink company can use these to estimate how vending machine usage is affected by different arrangements of pop machines within a given building. Pepsi and Coke have both taken advantage of virtual test-markets of this type. The simulated test-market has even been a basis for pricing and promotion budgets in North Africa. The simulated consumers were programmed based on brand and media preferences for several thousand actual Moroccan consumers.

Only time will tell whether these virtual test-markets have accuracy approaching actual test-markets or not. Certainly, the cost advantages will make them attractive to many companies.

Sources: Elkin, Tobi (2003), "Virtual Test-Markets," Advertising Age, 74 (10/27), 74 (43), 6; Fass, Allison (2005), "Game Theory," Forbes, 176 (11/14), 93–99.

A major problem with simulated test-marketing occurs when the marketer does not execute the marketing plan that was tested during the simulated test. If the marketer changes the advertising copy, price, or another variable, the model used to measure product acceptance will no longer be accurate.

Virtual-Reality Simulations

The Research Snapshot box above illustrates how computer-based simulations can be used to mimic actual consumer behavior. In some cases, virtual consumers can be programmed using complex mathematical derivations. The math is intended to represent consumer decisions. Virtual consumers can then react to virtual markets with virtual new stores and virtual new products. Although high-tech, this can be a less expensive method of testing than an actual test-market.

Other virtual test-markets have consumers actually logging on to simulated shopping environments and selecting different products for different situations. At http://www.threadless.com, consumers can choose their favorite T-shirt design from among several concepts. The designs that are selected most often are then taken from the virtual market to the real market.[19] Consumers can even participate in the design process.

Retailers can also test-market the way consumers may react in a new retail store environment. A **virtual-reality simulated test-market** attempts to reproduce the atmosphere of an actual retail store with visually compelling images appearing on a computer screen.[20] Real consumers can virtually shop by moving through the store using a computer mouse. They can even click on things to place them in a virtual shopping cart. In this way, retailers can estimate how long consumers spend in certain parts of the store and where it is that their attention may be attracted.

Virtual-reality simulated test-markets have many potential uses. For example, managers for a chain of fast-food restaurants noticed that customers would stand at registers, staring at the menu board, and take a long time to place an order. Often this created long lines and customers waiting in these lines became frustrated and walked away. Managers speculated that the menu boards were too extensive and confusing. A virtual-reality simulated test-market with multiple virtual menu boards was easily designed on a computer. The research findings revealed that grouping products together into meals with a small discount increased ordering speed and total order size for most research subjects. This issue would have been very difficult to study with another research design. Manipulations can be implemented much more easily in virtual environments compared to actual retail environments.

Virtual-reality simulated test-market
An experiment that attempts to reproduce the atmosphere of an actual retail store with visually compelling images appearing on a computer.

Complex Experimental Designs

The previous chapter focused on simple experimental designs. Most discussion centered on experiments manipulating a single variable. Here, the focus shifts to more complex experimental designs involving multiple experimental variables. Most laboratory marketing experiments involve complex experimental designs and even test-markets can involve multiple experimental manipulations. Chapter 22 will then examine the statistical analysis of such experiments.

Completely Randomized Design

Completely randomized design
An experimental design that uses a random process to assign subjects (test units) to treatment levels to investigate the effects of an experimental variable.

A **completely randomized design** is an experimental design that uses a random process to assign subjects to treatment levels of an experimental variable. Randomization of experimental units is the researcher's attempt to control extraneous variables while manipulating potential causes. A one-variable experimental design can be completely randomized, so long as subjects are assigned in a random way to a particular experimental treatment level.

Consider an experiment to examine the effects of various incentives on response rate in a mail survey. Thus, the experimental variable is the incentive. This can be manipulated over three treatment levels:

1. no incentive to the control group
2. a one dollar personal incentive
3. a one dollar charity incentive

Suppose the sample frame is divided into three groups of fifteen each ($n_1 + n_2 + n_3 = 45$). Assigning treatments to groups is a simple random process. Exhibit 12.4 illustrates the experiment and provides a dummy table of hypothetical results.

A random number process could be used to assign subjects to one of the three groups. Suppose each of the forty-five subjects is assigned a number ranging from 1 to 45. If a random number is selected between 1 and 45 (i.e., 12), that person can be assigned to the first group, with every

EXHIBIT 12.4
Experiment Examining Effect of Incentive on Response Rate

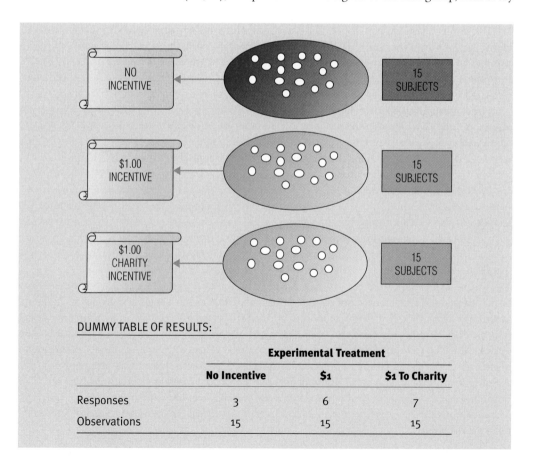

DUMMY TABLE OF RESULTS:

	Experimental Treatment		
	No Incentive	$1	$1 To Charity
Responses	3	6	7
Observations	15	15	15

third person afterward and before also assigned to the first group (12, 15, 18, . . . 45 and 9, 6, 3). The process can be repeated with the remaining thirty subjects by selecting a random number between 1 and 30, and then selecting every other subject. At this point, only 15 subjects remain and will comprise the third group. All 45 subjects are now assigned to one of three groups. Each group corresponds to one of the three levels of incentive. A variable representing which group a subject belongs to becomes the independent variable. The dependent variable is measured for each of the three treatment groups to determine which method of increasing response was the best. In this example, if the results turn out as indicated in the dummy table, the conclusion would be that the one-dollar incentive to charity would cause the highest response rate.

Randomized-block Design

The **randomized-block design** is an extension of the completely randomized design. A form of randomization is used to control for *most* extraneous variation; however, the researcher has identified a single extraneous variable that might affect subjects' responses systematically. The researcher will attempt to isolate the effects of this single variable by blocking out its effects.

A **blocking variable** is a categorical variable that is expected to be associated with different values of a dependent variable for each group. For instance, gender is a common blocking variable. Many potential dependent variables are expected to be different for men and women. For instance, women are more price-conscious than men. So, if a researcher is studying the effect of price and package design on purchase, they may want to also record a person's gender and include it as an extra explanatory variable over and above the experimental variable's price and packaging.

The term *randomized block* originated in agricultural research that applied several levels of a treatment variable to each of several blocks of land. Systematic differences in agricultural yields due to the quality of the blocks of land may be controlled in the randomized-block design. In marketing research the researcher may wish to isolate block effects such as store size, territory location, market shares of the test brand or its major competition, per capita consumption levels for a product class, city size, and so on. Suppose that a manufacturer of Mexican food is considering two packaging alternatives. Marketers suspect that geographic region might confound the experiment. They have identified three regions where attitudes toward Mexican food may differ (Midland, Texas; Normal, Illinois; and Naples, Florida). In a randomized-block design, each block must receive every treatment level. Assigning treatments to each block is a random process. In this example the two treatments will be randomly assigned to different cities within each region.

Sales results such as those in Exhibit 12.5 might be observed. The logic behind the randomized-block design is similar to that underlying the selection of a stratified sample rather than a simple random one. By isolating the block effects, one type of extraneous variation is partitioned out and a more efficient experimental design therefore results. This is because experimental error is reduced with a given sample size.

Randomized-block design
An extension of the completely randomized design in which a single, categorical extraneous variable that might affect test units' responses to the treatment is identified and the effects of this variable are isolated by being blocked out.

Blocking variable
A categorical variable that is expected to be associated with different values of a dependent variable for each group. It effectively controls for an extraneous cause in experimental analysis.

Factorial Designs

Suppose a brand manager believes that an experiment that only manipulates a price factor is too limited because price changes have to be communicated with increased promotional support. The brand manager suggests that more than one independent variable must be incorporated into the

EXHIBIT 12.5 **Randomized Block Design**

| Treatment | Percentage Who Purchase Product | | | |
	Mountain	North Central West	North Central East	Mean for Treatments
Package A	14.0% (Phoenix)	12.0% (St. Louis)	7.0% (Milwaukee)	11.0%
Package B	16.0% (Albuquerque)	15.0% (Kansas City)	10.0% (Indianapolis)	13.6%
Mean for cities	15.0%	13.5%	8.5%	

EXHIBIT 12.6
Factorial Design — Toy Robots

Price	Package Design	
	Red	**Gold**
$25	Cell 1	Cell 4
$30	Cell 2	Cell 5
$35	Cell 3	Cell 6

Factorial design
An experiment that investigates the interaction of two or more independent variables on a single dependent variable.

research design. Even though the single-factor experiments considered so far may have one specific variable blocked and other confounding sources controlled, they are still limited. A **factorial design** allows for the testing of the effects of two or more treatments (factors) at various levels.

Recall from the last chapter that experiments produce main effects and interactions. Main effects are differences (in the dependent variable) between treatment levels. Interactions produce differences (in the dependent variable) between experimental cells based on combinations of variables.

To further explain the terminology of experimental designs, let us use the example of a manufacturer of toy robots that wishes to measure the effect of different prices and packaging designs on consumers' perceptions of product quality. Exhibit 12.6 indicates three experimental treatment levels of price ($25, $30, and $35) and two levels of packaging design (Red and Gold). The table shows that every combination of treatment levels requires a separate experimental group. In this experiment, with three levels of price and two levels of packaging design, we have a 3×2 (read "three by two") factorial design because the first factor (variable) is varied in three ways and the second factor is varied in two ways. A 3×2 design requires six cells, or six experimental groups ($3 \times 2 = 6$). If the subjects each receive only one combination of experimental variables, then we use the term 3×2 between-subjects design to describe the experiment.

The number of treatments (factors) and the number of levels of each treatment identify the factorial design. A 3×3 design incorporates two factors, each having three levels; a $2 \times 2 \times 2$ design has three factors, each having two levels. The treatments need not have the same number of levels; for example, a $3 \times 2 \times 4$ factorial design is possible. The important idea is that in a factorial experiment, each treatment level is combined with every other treatment level.

In addition to the advantage of investigating two or more independent variables simultaneously, factorial designs allow researchers to measure interaction effects. In a 2×2 experiment the interaction is the effect produced by treatments A and B combined. If the effect of one treatment differs at various levels of the other treatment, interaction occurs.

To illustrate the value of a factorial design, suppose a researcher is comparing two magazine ads. The researcher is investigating the believability of ads on a scale from 0 to 100 and wishes to consider the gender of the reader as a blocking factor. The experiment has two independent variables: gender and ads. This 2×2 factorial experiment permits the experimenter to test three hypotheses. Two hypotheses yield main effects:

- Ad A is more believable than Ad B.
- Men believe ads more than women.

However, the primary research question may deal with the interaction hypothesis:

- Ad A is more believable than Ad B among women, but Ad B is more believable than Ad A among men.

A high score indicates a more believable ad. Exhibit 12.7 shows that the mean believability score for both genders is 65. This suggests that there is no main sex effect. Men and women evaluate believability of the advertisements equally. The main effect for ads indicates that ad A is more believable than ad B (70 versus 60), supporting the first hypothesis. However, if we inspect the data and look within the levels of the factors, we find that men find ad B more believable and women find ad A more believable. This is an interaction effect because the believability score of the advertising factor differs at different values of the other independent variable, sex. Thus, the interaction hypothesis is supported.

RESEARCHSNAPSHOT

A Lethal Interaction

In pharmacology, the interaction effect is usually called a *synergistic effect*.[21] An example is the lethal combination of barbiturate sleeping pills and alcohol. Each of these is a drug, and each reduces the number of heartbeats per minute. Their combined effect, however, is a much more severe reduction than one would expect knowing their individual effects. These two treatments together are not merely additive—their combined effect is much more than the sum of their individual effects. Another way of phrasing the synergistic effect is the following: The effect of one treatment differs depending on the level of the other treatment; that is, the reduction in pulse due to alcohol differs depending on whether or not barbiturates are in a person's system.

©ICONICA/GETTY IMAGES

	Ad A	Ad B		
Men	60	70	65	Main effects of gender
Women	80	50	65	
	70	60		
	Main effects of ad			

EXHIBIT 12.7
A 2 × 2 Factorial Design That Illustrates the Effects of Gender and Ad Content on Believability

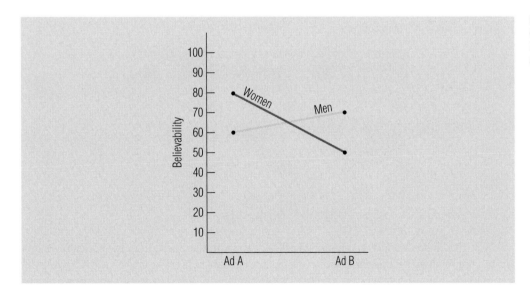

EXHIBIT 12.8
Graphic Illustration of Interaction between Gender and Advertising Copy

Exhibit 12.8 graphs the results of the believability experiment. The line for men represents the two mean believability scores for ads A and B. The other line represents the same relationship for women. Notice the difference between the slopes of the two lines. This also illustrates support for the interaction of the ad copy with biological sex. The difference in the slopes means that the believability of the advertising copy depends on whether a man or a woman is reading the advertisement.

Latin Square Design

The **Latin square design** attempts to control or block out the effect of two or more confounding extraneous factors. This design is so named because of the layout of the table that represents the design. A Latin square is a balanced, two-way classification scheme.[22] In the following 3×3 matrix, each letter occurs only once in each row and in each column:

		Order of Usage		
		1	**2**	**3**
	1	A	B	C
Subject	2	B	C	A
	3	C	A	B

The letters A, B, and C identify the three treatments; the rows and columns of the table identify the confounding factors. For example, a taste test might be confounded by the order of tasting; the first taste may seem better than the last. The taste test might also be confounded by individual taste preferences. To control for these factors, each subject is exposed to every treatment. If all the subjects receive three tastes and the order in which they taste is randomized, neither individual preference nor order effects can confound the experiment; thus, the order of treatment may be randomized under the restriction of balance required for the Latin square. The same type of balance is required for the second confounding factor. The end result of this design is that each treatment will be administered under conditions that involve all levels of both confounding factors. In summary, the Latin square design manipulates one independent variable and controls for two additional sources of extraneous variation by restricting randomization with respect to the row and column effects.

A major assumption of the Latin square design is that interaction effects are expected to be minimal or nonexistent. Thus, it is assumed that the first subject does not have a strong preference for the first product tasted, and the third subject does not have a strong preference for the last product tasted.

A Latin square may have any number of treatments; for example, the matrix for a five-treatment experiment is as follows:

	1	**2**	**3**	**4**	**5**
1	A	B	C	D	E
2	B	C	D	E	A
3	C	D	E	A	B
4	D	E	A	B	C
5	E	A	B	C	D

Note that this 5×5 matrix requires 25 cells. It also indicates that the number of treatment levels for confounding both factor 1 and factor 2 must be equal. This may present certain problems. For example, suppose a retail grocery chain wishes to control for shelf space and city where the product is sold. The chain may be limited in its experiment because it markets in only three cities, but wishes to experiment with four levels of shelf height.

Having an unequal number of levels for each factor may be one drawback that will eliminate the Latin square design as a possibility. A second limitation is the assumption that there is no interaction effect. However, making this assumption allows the experiment to be conducted with fewer subjects than would be required for a comparable factorial design. Like most other forms of marketing research, the Latin square design has its drawbacks, but in certain situations it has advantages.

Summary

1. Know the basics of test-marketing. Test-marketing is an experimental procedure providing an opportunity to test a new product or marketing plan under realistic conditions. Test-markets maximize external validity because the conditions closely approximate reality. Test-marketing provides the opportunity to estimate the outcomes of alternative courses of action. Test-market cities are selected based on how well they represent the consumer market of interest. Also, medium-sized cities are often used for test-markets because it is less expensive than using a big city.

2. Recognize the appropriate uses of test-marketing. Major uses of test-marketing include forecasting the success of a newly developed product, testing hypotheses about different options for marketing mix elements, and identifying weaknesses in product designs or marketing strategies. Whereas the first two reasons are usually intentional results in that they are the reason a test-market is implemented in the first place, the last reason often occurs when results from a test-market are less favorable than expected.

3. List the advantages and disadvantages of test-marketing. The two major advantages of test-markets discussed in the chapter are the real-world setting and the ease in interpretation and communication of results. These advantages have to be weighed against several key disadvantages. These include the great amount of money that it costs to conduct a test-market, the length of time it takes to design, implement, and analyze a test-market, and the loss of secrecy that comes when the product is marketed publicly. A full test-market can cost millions of dollars and take well over a year, and the competitors will know most of your strategic thinking.

4. Use manipulations to implement a completely randomized experimental design, a randomized-block design, and a factorial experimental design. The key to randomization is to assign subjects to experimental cells in a way that spreads extraneous variables out evenly across every condition. Blocking variables can be added to simple randomized experimental designs to control for categorical variables that are expected to be related to the dependent variable. Finally, a factorial design results when multiple experimental and/or blocking variables are included in a single model. Both main effects and interactions result.

5. Display experimental results using graphical charts. The graphical charts show main effects when there are differences in the height of the lines connecting points that indicate an experimental treatment condition. Interactions are indicated when lines have different slopes.

Key Terms and Concepts

Cannibalize	Electronic test-markets	Randomized-block design
Test-market sabotage	Simulated test-market	Blocking variable
Market penetration	Virtual-reality simulated test-market	Factorial design
Control method of test-marketing	Completely randomized design	Latin square design

Questions for Review and Critical Thinking

1. Why is a test-market usually considered an experiment?
2. What are the advantages and disadvantages of test-marketing?
3. List three typical uses of test-markets.
4. When is test-marketing likely to be conducted? When is it unlikely?
5. Which of the following products or marketing strategies are likely to be test-marketed? Why or why not?
   a. A computerized robot lawn mower
   b. A line of 8-ounce servings of vegetarian dishes for senior citizens
   c. A forklift truck
   d. A new brand of eye drops especially for brown-eyed people
   e. A new, heavy-duty KitchenAid mixer
   f. An advertising campaign to get people to drink a cola drink in the morning
6. Suppose a new golf ball is introduced by a major manufacturer. It is called "Hi-Ball." The company introduces the product in four cities: Tampa, Florida; Baton Rouge, Louisiana; Fort Worth, Texas; and Minneapolis, Minnesota. They test four different prices using a different price in each city. They also use coupons in Minneapolis and Fort Worth but not in Tampa and Baton Rouge. The plan is for the test-market to start in September 2006 and run through December 2007.
   a. Critique this test-market design.
   b. How can the design be improved?

c. If this design has problems, why might a company sometimes use some design very much like this one?

d. **ETHICS** In what ways could a competitor sabotage this test-market?

e. How long should the test-market periods last for golf balls?

7. What are six popular U.S. test-market cities? What makes them popular? Is there such a thing as a bad test-market city?

8. What is the difference between standard test-marketing and controlled test-marketing?

9. How are the results of a test-market projected to a national level? What problems arise in making such projections? What factors are important in selecting test-markets?

10. What advantages does simulated test-marketing have over traditional test-marketing? What limitations does it have?

Research Activities

1. **'NET** Use the *Wilson Business Index* or a library search engine to search for stories about "test-markets." Read a couple and write a brief report.

2. In a 2 × 2 factorial design, there are eight possible patterns of effects. Assume that independent variable A and independent variable B have significant main effects, but there is no interaction between them. Another combination might be no effects of variable A, but a significant effect of variable B with a significant interaction effect between them. Diagram each of these eight possible effects.

3. **ETHICS** A mouthwash manufacturer learns that a competitor is test-marketing a new lemon-flavored mouthwash in an Arizona city. The marketing research department of the competing firm is told to read the results of the test-market, and the marketing manager is told to lower the price of the company's brand to disrupt the test-market. Is this ethical?

Case 12.1 Bueno Chiles Rellenos

Mike Gavagan and Kathy Parker were discussing their test-market plans for a new item, frozen chiles rellenos for the microwave oven. Chiles rellenos, a traditional Mexican dish, are roasted poblano chile peppers filled with Monterey Jack cheese and encrusted in a cornmeal batter.

The idea to develop a microwavable chiles rellenos meal had struck Parker, manager of new product development, the day after she dined in a Mexican restaurant and enjoyed her first chiles rellenos. She thought that Mexican food was a lot of fun and that adults should have it more often. Of course, working for a large grocery product firm had helped direct her thinking toward the frozen meal. The product had passed the concept stages and was now ready for the big step. Parker wanted a test either in Cedar Rapids, Iowa, or in Eau Claire, Wisconsin.

Gavagan said, "Let's go to Texas. They love Mexican food there. If it goes over well there, it will go over anywhere. If we were testing a new soup, Eau Claire would be fine. The nation's eating habits change ever so slowly. A conservative market like that would be great for soup, but not for our new Mexican meal. We should test in Wichita Falls, Texas."

Questions

1. What factors should be considered when selecting a test-market? Are there any special demographic considerations for this product?

2. Where could you find demographic and retail sales information about the three locations being considered as test-markets? Find some information about these markets that would help to determine which area should be used as a test-market.

3. Which test-market should the company select?

Part 4
Measurement
Concepts

©BRAND X PICTURES/JUPITER IMAGES

CHAPTER 13
Measurement

CHAPTER 14
Attitude Measurement

CHAPTER 15
Questionnaire Design

APPENDIX 15A
Question Wording and Measurement
Scales for Commonly Researched
Topics

CHAPTER 13
MEASUREMENT

After studying this chapter, you should be able to

1. Determine what needs to be measured to address a research question or hypothesis
2. Distinguish levels of scale measurement
3. Know how to form an index or composite measure
4. List the three criteria for good measurement
5. Perform a basic assessment of scale reliability and validity

Chapter Vignette—Money Matters?

Griff Mitchell is the Vice President of Customer Relationship Management (CRM) for one of the world's largest suppliers of industrial heavy equipment. In this role, he oversees all sales and service operations. This year, for the first time, the company has decided to perform a CRM employee evaluation process that will allow an overall ranking of all CRM employees. Griff

©ASSOCIATED PRESS/AP

knows this will be a difficult task for many reasons, not the least of which is that he oversees over a thousand employees worldwide.

The ranking will be used to single out the best performers. These employees will be recognized at the company's annual CRM conference. The rankings will also be used to identify the lowest 20 percent of performers. These employees will be put on a probationary list with specific targeted improvement goals that will have to be met within twelve months or they will be fired. Griff becomes really stressed out trying to define the performance ranking process.

Griff's key question is, What is performance? Although these employees are now often referred to as CRM employees, they have traditionally performed the sales function. Griff calls a meeting of senior CRM managers to discuss how ranking decisions should be made.

One manager simply argues that sales volume should be the sole criteria. She believes that "sales figures provide an objective performance measure that will make the task easy and difficult to refute." Another counters that for the past twenty-two years, he has simply used his opinion of each employee's performance to place each of them into one of three groups: top performers, good performers, and underperformers. "I think about who is easy to work with and doesn't cause much trouble. It has worked for twenty-two years, why won't it work now?" Another responds curtly, "It's margin! It's margin! I don't care about sales volume; I want my guys selling things that improve my division's profit!" One of the newer managers sits silently through most of the meeting and finally summons up the courage to speak. "Aren't we CRM? That means performance should not be tied to sales, profits, or convenience, it should be based on how well a salesperson builds and maintains relationships with customers. So, we should see how satisfied the customers assigned to the employee are and use this in the evaluation process!" After this, the meeting disintegrates into a shouting match with each manager believing the others' ideas are flawed.

Griff feels like he is back to square one. "How do I make sure I have a valid performance measure so that all of our people are treated fairly?" He decides to seek out an opinion from a long-time friend in the research business, Robin Donald. Robin suggests that a research project may be needed to define a reliable and valid measure. She also brings up the fact that because employees from all over the world will be considered, the measure will have to maintain its reliability and validity anywhere it is used! Griff agrees to the project. He also feels good about letting someone outside the company develop the measure.

What Do I Measure?

Not every cook or chef needs to follow a recipe to create a great dish, but most amateur chefs find one very useful. Look at Exhibit 13.1. The recipe shows ingredients that can produce a tasty chicken dish. However, many readers, even those with some cooking ability, may have a difficult time following this recipe. Why? First, many may have difficulty translating all the French terms. Second, even when this is done, many will have difficulty knowing just what amounts of what ingredients should be included. How many could easily deal with the different measures listed by the ingredients? "How much is 50 ml?" "What is 454 g?" "How much is a pinch?" "Can I use my normal measuring utensils (scales)?"

If one tries to follow the recipe, one will certainly realize that even common things like weights and amounts can be measured multiple ways. If a mistake is made in measuring something, the dish

(a) Recette de la Jour		(b) Dogtes de Poulet Faibles avec Crackers
454 g	Poitrine de Poulet	
50 ml	Farine Tout Usage	
2 ml	De Poudre D'ail	
2 ml	De Poudre D'oignon	
1 ml	De Sel	
2	Blancs d'oeuf	
50 ml	De Lait Écrémé	
Pincée	De le Poivre Rouge	
36	Crackers (Tout Crounche)	

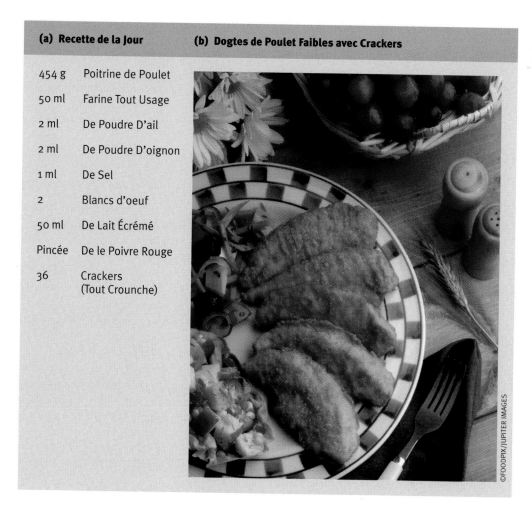

©FOODPIX/JUPITER IMAGES

EXHIBIT 13.1
More Ways Than 1 to Measure Ingredients

may be completely ruined. Just as in the culinary arts, business and marketing concepts can often be measured in more than one way. Also, researchers often may have to use imperfect measurement devices. When a concept is measured poorly, the "recipe" is a likely disaster. Only in this case, the "recipe" is usually an important business decision poorly made instead of a ruined dish.

The chapter vignette describes a situation in which Griff must develop a "recipe" for distinguishing employees based on job performance. Before the measurement process can be defined, he will have to decide exactly what it is that needs to be produced. In this case, the outcome should be a valid job performance measure.

The decision statement, corresponding research questions, and research hypotheses can be used to decide what concepts need to be measured in a given project. **Measurement** is the process of describing some property of a phenomenon of interest, usually by assigning numbers in a reliable and valid way. The numbers convey information about the property being measured. When numbers are used, the researcher must have a rule for assigning a number to an observation in a way that provides an accurate description.

Measurement can be illustrated by thinking about the way instructors assign students' grades. A grade represents a student's performance in a class. Students with higher performance should receive a different grade than do students with lower performance. Even the apparently simple concept of student performance is measured in many different ways. Consider the following options:

1. A student can be assigned a letter corresponding to his/her performance.
    a.   A — Represents excellent performance
    b.   B — Represents good performance
    c.   C — Represents average performance
    d.   D — Represents poor performance
    e.   F — Represents failing performance
2. A student can be assigned a number from 1 to 20.
    a.   20 — Represents outstanding performance
    b.   11–20 — Represent differing degrees of passing performance
    c.   Below 11 — Failing performance
3. A student can be assigned a number corresponding to a percentage performance scale.
    a.   100 percent — Represents a perfect score. All assignments are performed correctly.
    b.   60–99 percent — Represents differing degrees of passing performance, each number representing the proportion of correct work.
    c.   0–59 percent — Represents failing performance but still captures proportion of correct work.
4. A student can be assigned one of two letters corresponding to performance.
    a.   P — Represents a passing mark
    b.   F — Represents a failing mark

Actually, this is not terribly different than a manager who must assign performance scores to employees. In each case, students with different marks are distinguished in some way. However, some scales may better distinguish students. Each scale also has the potential of producing error or some lack of validity. Exhibit 13.2 illustrates a common measurement application.

Often, instructors may use a percentage scale all semester long and then be required to assign a letter grade for a student's overall performance. Does this produce any measurement problems? Consider two students who have percentage scores of 79.4 and 70.0, respectively. The most likely outcome when these scores are translated into "letter grades" is that each receives a C (the common ten-point spread would yield a 70–80 percent range for a C). Consider a third student who finishes with a 69.0 percent average and a fourth student who finishes with a 79.9 percent average.

Which students are happiest with this arrangement? The first two students receive the same grade, even though their scores are 9.4 percent apart. The third student gets a grade lower (D) performance than the second student, even though their percentage scores are only 1.0 percentage point different. The fourth student, who has a score only 0.5 percent higher than the first student, would receive a B. Thus, the measuring system (final grade) suggests that the fourth student outperformed the first (assuming that 79.9 is rounded up to 80) student (B versus C), but the first student did not outperform the second (each gets a C), even though the first and second students have the greatest difference in percentage scores.

Measurement
The process of describing some property of a phenomenon of interest, usually by assigning numbers in a reliable and valid way.

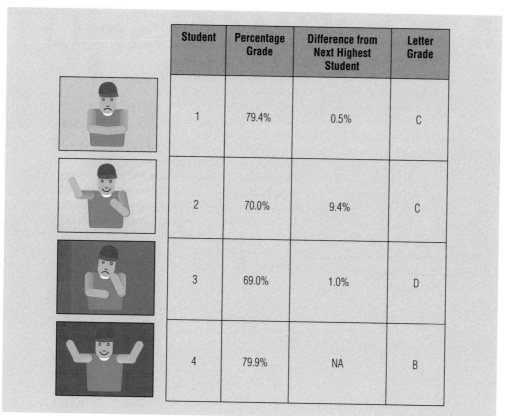

Student	Percentage Grade	Difference from Next Highest Student	Letter Grade
1	79.4%	0.5%	C
2	70.0%	9.4%	C
3	69.0%	1.0%	D
4	79.9%	NA	B

EXHIBIT 13.2
Are There Any Validity Issues with This Measurement?

A strong case can be made that error exists in this measurement system. All measurement, particularly in the social sciences, contains error. Researchers, if we are to represent concepts truthfully, must make sure that the measures used, if not perfect, are accurate enough to yield correct conclusions. Ultimately, research and measurement are tied closely together.

Concepts

A researcher has to know what to measure before knowing how to measure something. The problem definition process should suggest the concepts that must be measured. A **concept** can be thought of as a generalized idea that represents something of meaning. Concepts such as *age, sex, education,* and *number of children* are relatively concrete properties. They present few problems in either definition or measurement. Other concepts are more abstract. Concepts such as *loyalty, personality, channel power, trust, corporate culture, customer satisfaction, value,* and so on are more difficult to both define and measure. For example, *loyalty* has been measured as a combination of customer share, the relative proportion of a person's purchases going to one competing brand/store and commitment, or the degree to which a customer will sacrifice to do business with a brand/store.[1] The first component is a behavioral measure and the second is attitudinal.

Concept
A generalized idea that represents something of meaning.

Operational Definitions

Researchers measure concepts through a process known as **operationalization**. This process involves identifying scales that correspond to variance in the concept. **Scales**, just as a scale you may use to check your weight, provide a range of values that correspond to different values in the concept being measured. In other words, scales provide **correspondence rules** that indicate that a certain value on a scale corresponds to some true value of a concept. Hopefully, they do this in a truthful way.

Here is an example of a correspondence rule: "Assign the numerals 1 through 7 to individuals according to how much trust that person has in a sales representative. If the sales representative is completely trustworthy, assign a 7. If the sales rep is perceived as completely untrustworthy, assign the numeral 1."

Operationalization
The process of identifying scales that correspond to variance in a concept to be involved in a research process.

Scales
A device providing a range of values that correspond to different values in a concept being measured.

Correspondence rules
Indicate the way that a certain value on a scale corresponds to some true value of a concept.

RESEARCHSNAPSHOT

Measuring Yahoo! Impact

Earlier in the book, the concept of marketing metrics was introduced. The whole idea behind marketing metrics is measurement of key characteristics that indicate business performance in some way. Billions of dollars are being spent on Internet advertising in the United States, and those numbers are rising every year. In 2007, over $15 billion will be spent. Does this make sense? Even though Internet advertising and promotion is hardly over a decade old, most firms struggle with ways to measure the effectiveness of an ad placed on a web page.

The key question is, "What is the impact of an Internet ad?" Companies seem fixated with sales as a measure of impact. However, this overlooks other potential ways an ad can have impact, such as changing attitudes or creating awareness. Companies like Yahoo!, Google, and Ask try to base

advertising rates on "impact." Marketing Management Analytics is a research company in Wilton, Connecticut, that will soon offer research to advertisers (for a fee) to measure the impact of Internet ads. This research will examine what happens when somebody clicks on an ad. How often does it eventually lead to a sale or to one of the business goals motivating the ad? A reliable and valid measure of Internet ad effectiveness will probably involve multiple items assessing both online behavior (like click-through data and what path people take once they click on an ad) and offline behavior (whether consumers arriving in stores attribute their shopping to an Internet ad). When the ads are successful, firms will really Yahoo!

Sources: Aaron, Patrick O. (2005), "Yahoo to Track Impact of Internet Ads," Wall Street Journal, December 15, B4; Marketing Management Analytics, Inc. (2005), "Yahoo! And MMA to Offer measurement Service to Enable Marketers to Optimize Advertising Spending Across Media," press release (12/16), http://biz.yahoo.com/prnews

©SUSAN VAN ETTEN

VARIABLES

Researchers use variance in concepts to make diagnoses. Therefore, when we defined variables in an earlier chapter, we really were suggesting that variables capture different concept values. Scales capture variance in concepts and, as such, the scales provide the researcher's variables. Thus, for practical purposes, once a research project is underway, there is little difference between a concept and a variable. Consider the following hypothesis:

H1: Experience *is positively related to* job performance.

The hypothesis implies a relationship between two variables, experience and job performance. The variables capture variance in the experience and performance concepts. One employee may have fifteen years of experience and be a top performer. A second may have ten years experience and be a good performer. The scale used to measure experience is quite simple in this case and would involve simply providing the number of years an employee has been with the company. Job performance is captured by a scale in which a supervisor places the employee into a category as described in the vignette.

TOTHEPOINT

Not everything that can be counted counts, and not everything that counts can be counted.

—Albert Einstein

CONSTRUCTS

Sometimes, a single variable cannot capture a concept alone. Using multiple variables to measure one concept can often provide a more complete account of some concept than could any single variable. Even in the physical sciences, multiple measurements are often used to make sure an accurate representation is obtained. In social science, many concepts are measured with multiple measurements.

Construct
A term used to refer to concepts measured with multiple variables.

A **construct** is a term used for concepts that are measured with multiple variables. For instance, when a marketing researcher wishes to measure the customer orientation of a salesperson, several variables like these may be used, each captured on a 1–5 scale:

1. I offer the product that is best suited to a customer's problem.
2. A good employee has to have the customer's best interests in mind.
3. I try to find out what kind of products will be most helpful to a customer.[2]

Constructs can be very helpful in operationalizing a concept.

EXHIBIT 13.3 **Media Skepticism: An Operational Definition**

Concept	Conceptual Definition	Operational Definition
Media skepticism	*Media skepticism* is the degree to which individuals are skeptical of the reality presented in the mass media. Media skepticism varies across individuals, from those who are mildly skeptical and accept most of what they see and hear in the media to those who completely discount and disbelieve the facts, values, and portrayal of reality in the media.	Please tell me how true each statement is about the media. Is it very true, not very true, or not at all true? 1. The program was *not* very accurate in its portrayal of the problem. 2. Most of the story was staged for entertainment purposes. 3. The presentation was slanted and unfair. 4. I think the story was fair and unbiased. 5. I think important facts were purposely left out of the story. Individual items were scored on a 4-point scale with values from 1 to 4; higher scores represented greater skepticism. Media skepticism is defined as the sum of these five scores.

Source: Michael D. Cozzens and Noshir S. Contractor, "The Effects of Conflicting Information on Media Skepticism," Communications Research, August 1987, pp. 437–451.

An operational definition is like a manual of instructions or a recipe: Even the truth of a statement like "Gaston Gourmet likes key lime pie" depends on the recipe. Different instructions lead to different results.[3]

An operational definition tells the investigator, "Do such-and-such in so-and-so manner."[4] Exhibit 13.3 presents a concept definition and an operational definition from a study on a construct called *media skepticism*.

Levels of Scale Measurement

Marketing researchers use many scales or number systems. Not all scales capture the same richness in a measure. Not all concepts require a rich measure. Traditionally, the level of scale measurement is seen as important because it determines the mathematical comparisons that are allowable. The four levels or types of scale measurement are *nominal, ordinal, interval,* and *ratio level scales.* Each type offers the researcher progressively more power in analyzing and testing the validity of a scale.

Nominal Scale

Nominal scales represent the most elementary level of measurement. A nominal scale assigns a value to an object for identification or classification purposes. The value can be, but does not have to be, a number because no quantities are being represented. In this sense, a nominal scale is truly a qualitative scale. Nominal scales are extremely useful even though they can be considered elementary.

Marketing researchers use nominal scales quite often. For instance, suppose Barq's Root Beer was experimenting with three different types of sweeteners (cane sugar, corn syrup, or fruit extract). The researchers would like the experiment to be blind, so when subjects are asked to taste one of the three root beers, the drinks are labeled A, B, or C, not cane sugar, corn syrup, or fruit extract.

Nominal scales
Represent the most elementary level of measurement in which values are assigned to an object for identification or classification purposes only.

Nominal scaling is arbitrary in the sense that each label can be assigned to any of the categories without introducing error; for instance, in the rootbeer example above, the researcher can assign the letter C to any of the three options without damaging scale validity. The researcher could just as easily use numbers instead of letters. If so, cane sugar, corn syrup, and fruit extract might be identified with the numbers 1, 2, and 3, respectively, or even 543, 26, and 2010, respectively. Either set of numbers is equally valid since the numbers are not representing different quantities. They are simply identifying the type of sweetener.

We encounter nominal numbering systems all the time. Uniform numbers are nominal numbers. Brett Favre is identified on the football field by his jersey number. What is his number? Airport terminals are identified with a nominal numbering system. In the Atlanta airport, a departing traveler has to go through terminals T, A, B, C, and D in order before reaching an international departure gate at terminal E. School bus numbers are nominal in that they simply identify a bus. Elementary school buses sometimes use both a number and an animal designation to help small children get on the right bus. So, bus number "8" may also be the "tiger" bus.

The first drawing in Exhibit 13.4 depicts the number 7 on a horse's colors. This is merely a label to allow bettors and racing enthusiasts to identify the horse. The assignment of a 7 to this horse does not mean that it is the seventh fastest horse or that it is the seventh biggest, or anything else meaningful. But, the 7 does let you know when you have won or lost your bet!

Exhibit 13.5 lists some nominal scales commonly used by marketing researchers. Nominal scale properties mean the numbering system simply identifies things.

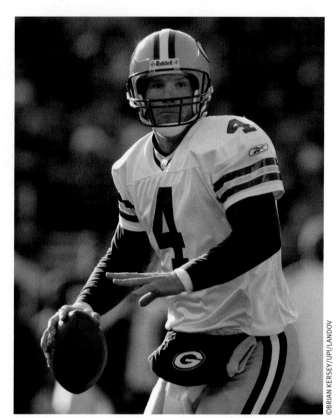
Athletes wear nominal numbers on their jerseys.
©BRIAN KERSEY/UPI/LANDOV

EXHIBIT 13.4
Nominal, Ordinal, Interval, and Ratio Scales Provide Different Information

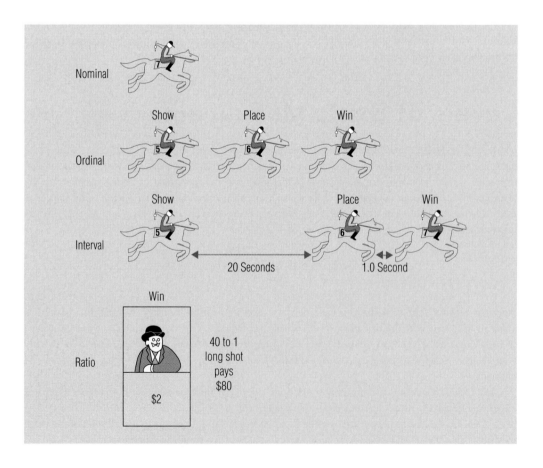

Ordinal Scale

Ordinal scales have nominal properties, but they also allow things to be arranged based on how much of some concept they possess. In other words, an ordinal scale is a ranking scale. When a professor assigns an A, B, C, D, or F to a student at the end of the semester, he or she is using an ordinal scale.

Research participants often are asked to *rank order* things based on preference. So, preference is the concept, and the ordinal scale lists the options from most to least preferred, or vice versa. In this sense, ordinal scales are somewhat arbitrary, but not nearly as arbitrary as a nominal scale. Five objects can be ranked from 1–5 (least preferred to most preferred) or 1–5 (most preferred to least preferred) with no loss of meaning.

Without nominal scales, how would you know which terminal to go to at this airport?

Ordinal scales
Ranking scales allowing things to be arranged based on how much of some concept they possess.

When business professors take some time off and go to the race track, even they know that a horse finishing in the "show" position has finished after the "win" and "place" horses (see the second drawing in Exhibit 13.4). The order of finish can be accurately represented by an ordinal scale using an ordered number rule:

- Assign 1 to the "win" position
- Assign 2 to the "place" position
- Assign 3 to the "show" position

Perhaps the winning horse defeated the place horse by a nose, but the place horse defeated the show horse by twenty seconds. The ordinal scale does not tell by how much a horse won, but it is good enough to let someone know the result of a wager. Typical ordinal scales in marketing research ask respondents to rate brands, companies, and the like as excellent, good, fair, or poor. Researchers know excellent is higher than good, but they do not know by how much.

Interval Scale

Interval scales have both nominal and ordinal properties, but they also capture information about differences in quantities of a concept. So, not only would a sales manager know that a particular salesperson outperformed a colleague, but the manager would know by how much. If a professor assigns grades to term papers using a numbering system ranging from 1.0–20.0, not only does the scale represent the fact that a student with a 16.0 outperformed a student with 12.0, but the scale would show by how much (4.0).

Interval scales
Scales that have both nominal and ordinal properties, but that also capture information about differences in quantities of a concept from one observation to the next.

The third drawing in Exhibit 13.4 depicts a horse race in which the win horse is one second ahead of the place horse, which is 20 seconds ahead of the show horse. Not only are the horses identified by the order of finish, but the difference between each horse's performance is known. So, horse number 7 and horse number 6 performed similarly, but horse number 5 performed not nearly as well.

The classic example of an interval scale is the Fahrenheit temperature scale. Consider the following weather:

- June 6 was 80° F
- December 7 was 40° F

The interval Fahrenheit scale lets us know that December 7 was 40° F colder than June 6. But, we cannot conclude that December 7 was twice as cold as June 6. Although the actual numeral 80 is indeed twice as great as 40, remember that this is a scaling system. In this case, the scale is not iconic, meaning that it does not exactly represent some phenomenon. These temperatures can be converted to the more common Celsius scale. Then, the following would result:

- June 6 was 26.7° C
- December 7 was 4.4° C

Obviously, now we can see that December 7 was not twice as cold as June 6. December 7 was 40° F or 22.3° C cooler, depending upon your thermometer. Interval scales are very useful because they capture relative quantities in the form of distances between observations. No matter what thermometer is used, December 7 was colder than June 6.

Ratio Scale

Ratio scales
Represent the highest form of measurement in that they have all the properties of interval scales with the additional attribute of representing absolute quantities; characterized by a meaningful absolute zero.

Ratio scales represent the highest form of measurement in that they have all the properties of interval scales with the additional attribute of representing absolute quantities. Interval scales represent only relative meaning whereas ratio scales represent absolute meaning. In other words, ratio scales provide iconic measurement. Zero, therefore, has meaning in that it represents an absence of some concept.

An absolute zero is a defining characteristic in determining between ratio and interval scales. For example, money is a way to measure economic value. Consider the following items offered for sale in an online auction:

- Antique railroad pocket watch circa 1910—sold for $50
- Authentic Black Forest cuckoo clock—sold for $75
- Antique gold-filled Elgin wristwatch circa 1950—sold for $100
- "Antique" 1970s digital watch—did not sell and there were no takers for free

We can make the ordinal conclusions that the cuckoo clock was worth more than the pocket watch and that the wristwatch was worth more than the cuckoo, all of which were worth more than the 1970s digital watch. We can make interval conclusions such as that the cuckoo was worth $25 more than the pocket watch. We can also conclude that the wristwatch was worth twice as much as the pocket watch and that the 1970s watch was worthless (selling price = $0.00). The latter two conclusions are possible because money price represents a ratio scale.

Temperature can also be captured by a ratio scale. The Kelvin scale begins at 0 K, corresponding to −273.2° on the Celsius scale (an interval scale). This temperature is known as absolute zero. Zero K is the point at which the kinetic energy of atoms in a water molecule approaches 0, meaning that they are moving as slowly as possible. This is as cold as water can get since there is no way of slowing the molecules further (they never completely stop). Thus, 0 K indeed has absolute meaning.

When a manager assigns a performance commission based directly on the amount of sales produced, the bonus is based on a ratio scale. Zero has an absolute meaning, particularly if you are the one without a bonus! Griff could decide to use a ratio sales measure to rank performance for the CRM division. This would be valid only if performance was truly equal to sales.

Mathematical and Statistical Analysis of Scales

While it is true that mathematical operations can be performed with numbers from nominal scales, the result may not have a great deal of meaning. For instance, a school district may perform mathematical operations on the nominal school bus numbers. With this, they may find that the average

RESEARCHSNAPSHOT

Football Follies

The subject of whether or not certain mathematical properties can be conducted with certain types of scales has been debated in the social science literature for decades. One famous statistician used a funny parable about a football folly to make a point about this very well. The story goes something like this:

A football coach purchased a vending machine that would assign numbers (0 to 99) to the school's football players randomly. Over the years, then, all numbers should be equally used. By randomly assigning the numbers in this way, no players were treated unequally because no one could choose one of their favorite numbers. Everybody simply got the number the machine spit out.

Professor Aaron Urd, naturally curious about anything having to do with numbers, became suspicious that the football players had secretly been breaking into the machine to select more preferred numbers. Professor Urd believed that football had no place in college and would have loved to show how unscrupulous the football players really are—stealing numbers no less! However, Professor Urd had a problem. Football numbers are nominal numbers; all they do is identify! Therefore, as all good statisticians knew, you cannot compute averages with nominal numbers. In fact, all you can do is count nominal numbers. This problem tormented Professor Urd for years. He desperately wanted to test his hypothesis about the football number theft. Many times he entered the football numbers into a spreadsheet but could not bring himself to add, multiply, or divide them. It just wouldn't be right!

One fall, Aleck Smart, a star defensive tackle on the football team, wrote a term paper for Professor Aaron Urd entitled "A Statistical Treatment of the Football Team Numbering System." Aleck, not being the brightest student, missed the day when Professor Urd taught students that you could not do arithmetic with nominal numbers. So, Aleck Smart computed all manner of statistics with data consisting of the last ten years of football numbers worn by the team. Among these, he showed that the average football number over those years was 40.1. Professor Aaron Urd was conflicted with this result. How can this be? If the numbers were assigned randomly, then shouldn't the average be 50? This must confirm his suspicion about the football number theft. But even to think this troubled him because it meant his brain was unintentionally computing the average of nominal numbers!

A few days later, Aleck dropped by Professor Aaron Urd's office to pick up his paper (after office hours of course). Professor Urd lit into Aleck: "I have given you a failing grade, Mr. Smart. Numbers from football jerseys are nominal numbers! Don't you know that you cannot take the average of nominal numbers?"

Aleck thought about that a while and answered, "Professor Urd, the numbers don't know where they came from."

Professor Urd decided to change Aleck's grade to a B−. He then used Aleck's calculations to try and show the faculty senate that the football team was indeed breaking into the machine.

Sources: Lord, F.M. (1953), "On the Statistical Treatment of Football Numbers," American Psychologist, 8, 750–751; Cohen, Jacob (1990), "Things I Have Learned (So Far)," American Psychologist, 45 (December), 1304–1312.

©DAVE KAUP/CORBIS

school bus number is 77.7 with a standard deviation of 20.5. Will this help them use the buses more efficiently or better assign bus routes? Probably not. Thus, although you can put numbers into formulas and perform calculations with almost any numbers, the researcher has to know the meaning behind the numbers before useful conclusions can be drawn.[5]

▧ DISCRETE MEASURES

Discrete measures are those that take on only one of a finite number of values. A discrete scale is most often used to represent a classificatory variable. Therefore, discrete scales do not represent intensity of measures, only membership. Common discrete scales include any yes-or-no response, matching, color choices, or practically any scale that involves selecting from among a small number of categories. Thus, when someone is asked to choose from the following responses

- Disagree
- Neutral
- Agree

the result is a discrete value that can be coded 1, 2, or 3, respectively. This is also an ordinal scale to the extent that it represents an ordered arrangement of agreement. Nominal and ordinal scales are discrete measures.

TOTHEPOINT

When you can measure what you are talking about and express it in numbers, you know something about it.

—William Thompson, Lord Kelvin

Discrete measures
Measures that take on only one of a finite number of values.

Certain statistics are most appropriate for discrete measures. Exhibit 13.5 shows statistics for each scale level. The largest distinction is between statistics used for discrete versus continuous measures. For instance, the central tendency of discrete measures is best captured by the mode. When a student wants to know what the most likely grade is for MKT4311, the mode will be very useful. Observe the results below from the previous semester:

The mode is a "B" since more students obtained that value than any other value. Therefore, the "average" student would expect a B in MKT4311.

A	5 Students	D	6 Students
B	20 Students	F	6 Students
C	12 Students		

■ CONTINUOUS MEASURES

Continuous measures are those assigning values anywhere along some scale range in a place that corresponds to the intensity of some concept. Ratio measures are continuous measures. Thus, when we measure sales for each salesperson using the dollar amount sold, we are assigning continuous measures. A number line could be constructed ranging from the least amount sold to the most and a spot on the line would correspond exactly to a salesperson's performance.

Continuous measures Measures that reflect the intensity of a concept by assigning values that can take on any value along some scale range.

Strictly speaking, interval scales are not necessarily continuous. Consider the following common type of survey question:

	Strongly Disagree	Disagree	Neutral	Agree	Strongly Agree
I enjoy participating in online auctions	1	2	3	4	5

This is a discrete scale because only the values 1, 2, 3, 4, or 5 can be assigned. Furthermore, it is an ordinal scale because it only orders based on agreement. We really have no way of knowing that the difference in agreement of somebody marking a 5 instead of a 4 is the same as the difference in agreement of somebody marking a 2 instead of a 1. Therefore, the mean is not an appropriate way of stating central tendency, and we really shouldn't use many common statistics on these responses.

However, as a scaled response of this type takes on more values, the error introduced by assuming that the differences between the discrete points are equal becomes smaller. This may be seen by imagining a *Likert scale* with a thousand levels of agreement rather than three or four. The differences between the different levels become so small with a thousand levels that only tiny errors could be introduced by assuming each interval is the same. Therefore, marketing researchers generally treat interval scales containing five or more categories of response as interval. When fewer than five categories are used, this assumption is inappropriate. So, interval scales are treated as continuous when five or more categories are used.

The researcher should keep in mind, however, the distinction between ratio and interval measures. Errors in judgment can be made when interval measures are treated as ratio. For example, attitude is usually measured with an interval scale. An attitude of zero means nothing. In fact, attitude would only have meaning in a relative sense. Therefore, attitude takes on meaning when one person's response is compared to another or through some other comparison. A single attitude score alone contains little meaning.

The mean and standard deviation may be calculated from continuous data. Using the actual quantities for arithmetic operations is permissible with ratio scales. Thus, the ratios of scale values are meaningful. A ratio scale has all the properties of nominal, ordinal, and interval scales. However, the same cannot be said in reverse. An ordinal scale, for example, has nominal properties, but it does not have interval or ratio properties (see Exhibit 13.5).

Chapters 19 through 23 further explore the limitations scales impose on the mathematical analysis of data.

EXHIBIT 13.5 **Facts About the Four Levels of Scales**

Level	Examples	Numerical Operations	Descriptive Statistics
Nominal	Yes – No Female – Male Buy – Did Not Buy Postal Code: ____	Counting	• Frequencies • Mode
Ordinal	Rankings Choose from the Following: • Dissatisfied • Satisfied • Very Satisfied • Delighted Indicate Your Level of Education: • HS Diploma • Some College • Bachelor's Degree • Graduate Degree	Counting and Ordering	• Frequencies • Mode • Median • Range
Interval	100-Point Job Performance Ratings Assigned by Supervisors: 0% = Worst Performers 100% = Best Performers Temperature-Type Attitude Scales: Low Temperature = Bad Attitude High Temperature = Good Attitude	Common Arithmetic Operations	• Mean • Median • Variance • Standard Deviation
Ratio	Amount Purchased Salesperson Sales Volume Likelihood of performing some act: • 0%=No Likelihood to • 100%=Certainty Number of stores visited Time spent viewing a particular web page Number of web pages viewed	All Arithmetic Operations	• Mean • Median • Variance • Standard Deviation

Index Measures

Earlier, we distinguished constructs as concepts that require multiple variables to measure them adequately. Looking back to the chapter vignette, could it be that multiple items will be required to adequately represent job performance? Likewise, a consumer's attitude toward some product is usually a function of multiple attributes. An **attribute** is a single characteristic or fundamental feature of an object, person, situation, or issue.

Attribute
A single characteristic or fundamental feature of an object, person, situation, or issue.

Indexes and Composites

Multi-item instruments for measuring a construct are called *index measures,* or *composite measures.* An **index measure** assigns a value based on how much of the concept being measured is associated with an observation. Indexes often are formed by putting several variables together. For example, a social class index is based on three weighted variables: income, occupation, and education. Usually, occupation is seen as the single best indicator and would be weighted highest. With an index, the different attributes may not be strongly correlated with each other. A person's income does not always relate strongly to their education. The American Consumer Satisfaction Index shows how satisfied American consumers are based on an index of satisfaction scores. Readers are likely not surprised to know that Americans appear more satisfied with soft drinks than they are with cable TV companies based on this index.[6]

Index measure
An index assigns a value based on how much of the concept being measured is associated with an observation. Indexes often are formed by putting several variables together.

Composite measures
Assign a value to an observation based on a mathematical derivation of multiple variables.

Composite measures also assign a value based on a mathematical derivation of multiple variables. For example, salesperson satisfaction may be measured by combining questions such as "How satisfied are you with your job? How satisfied are you with your territory? How satisfied are you with the opportunity your job offers?" For most practical applications, composite measures and indexes are computed in the same way.[7]

Computing Scale Values

Exhibit 13.6 demonstrates how a composite measure can be created from common rating scales. This particular scale can be used to assess how much a consumer trusts a website.[8] This particular composite represents a **summated scale**. A summated scale is created by simply summing the response to each item making up the composite measure. In this case, the consumer would have a trust score of 13 based on responses to five items. A researcher may sometimes choose to average the scores rather than summing them. The advantage to this is that the composite measure is expressed on the same scale as are the items that make it up. So, instead of a 13, the consumer would have a score of 2.6. The information content is the same.

Summated scale
A scale created by simply summing (adding together) the response to each item making up the composite measure.

Sometimes, a response may need to be reverse-coded before computing a summated or averaged scale value. **Reverse coding** means that the value assigned for a response is treated oppositely from the other items. If a sixth item was included on the trust scale that said, "I do not trust this website," reverse coding would be necessary to make sure the composite made sense. The content of this item is the reverse of trust (distrust), so the scale itself should be reversed. Thus, on a 5-point scale, the values are reversed as follows:

Reverse coding
Means that the value assigned for a response is treated oppositely from the other items.

- 5 becomes 1
- 4 becomes 2
- 3 stays 3
- 2 becomes 4
- 1 becomes 5

Therefore, if this same consumer described in Exhibit 13.6 responded to this new item with a 5, it would be reverse coded as a 1 before computing the summated scale. Thus, the summated scale value would become 14.

EXHIBIT 13.6
Computing a Composite Scale

Item	Strongly Disagree (SD) → Strongly Agree (SA)				
This site appears to be more trustworthy than other sites I have visited.	SD	⒟	N	A	SA
My overall trust in this site is very high.	SD	D	Ⓝ	A	SA
My overall impression of the believability of the information on this site is very high.	SD	⒟	N	A	SA
My overall confidence in the recommendations on this site is very high.	SD	⒟	N	A	SA
The company represented in this site delivers on its promises.	SD	D	N	Ⓐ	SA

Computation:
Scale Values: SD = 1, D = 2, N = 3, A = 4, SA = 5

Thus, the Trust score for this consumer is
$$2 + 3 + 2 + 2 + 4 = 13$$

RESEARCHSNAPSHOT

Recoding Made Easy

Most computer statistical software makes scale recoding easy. The screenshot shown here is from SPSS, perhaps the most widely used statistical software in business-related research. All that needs to be done to reverse-code a scale is to go through the right click-through sequence. In this case, the following steps would be followed:

1. Click on transform.
2. Click on recode.
3. Choose to recode into the same variable.
4. Select the variable(s) to be recoded.
5. Click on old and new values.
6. Use the menu that appears to enter the old values and the matching new values. Click add after entering each pair.
7. Click continue.

This would successfully recode variable X13 in this case.

©ROYALTY FREE/CORBIS

Three Criteria for Good Measurement

The three major criteria for evaluating measurements are reliability, validity, and sensitivity.

Reliability

Reliability is an indicator of a measure's internal consistency. Consistency is the key to understanding reliability. A measure is reliable when different attempts at measuring something converge on the same result. If a professor's marketing research tests are reliable, a student should tend toward consistent scores on all tests. In other words, a student that makes an 80 on the first test should make scores close to 80 on all subsequent tests. Another way to look at this is that the student who makes the best score on one test will exhibit scores close to the best score in the class on the other tests. If it is difficult to predict what students would make on a test by examining their previous test scores, the tests probably lack reliability. When a measuring process provides reproducible results, the measuring instrument is reliable.

Reliability
An indicator of a measure's internal consistency.

■ INTERNAL CONSISTENCY

Internal consistency represents a measure's homogeneity. An attempt to measure trust may require asking several similar but not identical questions, as shown above. The set of items that make up a measure are referred to as a *battery* of scale items. *Internal consistency* of a multiple-item measure can be measured by correlating scores on subsets of items making up a scale.

Internal consistency
Represents a measure's homogeneity or the extent to which each indicator of a concept converges on some common meaning.

Split-half method
A method for assessing internal consistency by checking the results of one-half of a set of scaled items against the results from the other half.

Coefficient alpha (α)
The most commonly applied estimate of a multiple item scale's reliability. It represents the average of all possible split-half reliabilities for a construct.

The **split-half method** of checking reliability is performed by taking half the items from a scale (for example, odd-numbered items) and checking them against the results from the other half (even-numbered items). The two scale *halves* should correlate highly. They should also produce similar scores.

Coefficient alpha (α) is the most commonly applied estimate of a multiple item scale's reliability.[9] Coefficient α represents internal consistency by computing the average of all possible split-half reliabilities for a multiple-item scale. The coefficient demonstrates whether or not the different items converge. Although coefficient α does not address validity, many researchers use α as the sole indicator of a scale's quality. Coefficient alpha ranges in value from 0, meaning no consistency, to 1, meaning complete consistency (all items yield matching values). Generally speaking, scales with a coefficient α between 0.80 and 0.95 are considered to have very good reliability. Scales with a coefficient α between 0.70 and 0.80 are considered to have good reliability, and an α value between 0.60 and 0.70 indicates fair reliability. When the coefficient α is below 0.6, the scale has poor reliability.[10] Most statistical software such as SPSS will easily compute coefficient α.

▓ TEST-RETEST RELIABILITY

Test-retest method
Administering the same scale or measure to the same respondents at two separate points in time to test for stability.

The **test-retest method** of determining reliability involves administering the same scale or measure to the same respondents at two separate times to test for stability. If the measure is stable over time, the test, administered under the same conditions each time, should obtain similar results. Test-retest reliability represents a measure's repeatability.

Suppose a researcher at one time attempts to measure buying intentions and finds that 12 percent of the population is willing to purchase a product. If the study is repeated a few weeks later under similar conditions, and the researcher again finds that 12 percent of the population is willing to purchase the product, the measure appears to be reliable. High stability correlation or consistency between two measures at time 1 and time 2 indicates high reliability.

Assume that a person does not change his or her attitude about dark beer. Attitude might be measured with an item like the one shown below:

I prefer dark beer to all other types of beer.

If repeated measurements of that individual's attitude toward dark beer are taken with the same scale, a reliable instrument will produce the same results each time the scale is measured. Thus one's attitude in March 2007 should tend to be the same as one's attitude in October 2007. When a measuring instrument produces unpredictable results from one testing to the next, the results are said to be unreliable because of error in measurement.

As another example, consider these remarks by a Gillette executive made about the reliability problems in measuring reactions to razor blades:

There is a high degree of noise in our data, a considerable variability in results. It's a big mish-mash, what we call the night sky in August. There are points all over the place. A man will give a blade a high score one day, but the next day he'll cut himself a lot and give the blade a terrible score. But on the third day, he'll give the same blade a good score. What you have to do is try to see some pattern in all this. There are some gaps in our knowledge.[11]

Measures of test-retest reliability pose two problems that are common to all longitudinal studies. First, the pre-measure, or first measure, may sensitize the respondents to their participation in a research project and subsequently influence the results of the second measure. Furthermore, if the time between measures is long, there may be an attitude change or other maturation of the subjects. Thus, a reliable measure can indicate a low or a moderate correlation between the first and second administration, but this low correlation may be due to an attitude change over time rather than to a lack of reliability.

Reliability is a necessary but not sufficient condition for validity. A reliable scale may not be valid. For example, a purchase intention measurement technique may consistently indicate that 20 percent of those sampled are willing to purchase a new product. Whether the measure is valid depends on whether 20 percent of the population indeed purchases the product. A reliable but invalid instrument will yield consistently inaccurate results.

Validity

Good measures should be both precise and accurate. Reliability represents how precise a measure is in that the different attempts at measuring the same thing converge on the same point. Accuracy deals more with how a measure assesses the intended concept. **Validity** is the accuracy of a measure or the extent to which a score truthfully represents a concept.

Achieving validity is not a simple matter. The opening vignette describes this point. The job performance measure should truly reflect job performance. If a supervisor's friendship affects the performance measure, then the scale's validity is diminished. Likewise, if the performance scale is defined as effort, the result may well be a reliable scale but not one that maximizes validity. Effort may well lead to performance but effort probably does not equal performance.

Another example of a validity question might involve a media researcher who wonders what it means when respondents indicate they have been *exposed* to a magazine. The researcher wants to know if the measure is valid. The question of validity expresses the researcher's concern with accurate measurement. Validity addresses the problem of whether a measure (for example, an attitude measure used in marketing) indeed measures what it is supposed to measure. When a measure lacks validity, any conclusions based on that measure are also likely to be faulty.

Students should be able to empathize with the following validity problem. Consider the controversy about highway patrol officers using radar guns to clock speeders. A driver is clocked at 75 mph in a 55 mph zone, but the same radar gun aimed at a house registers 28 mph. The error occurred because the radar gun had picked up impulses from the electrical system of the squad car's idling engine. The house wasn't speeding—and the test was not completely valid.

■ ESTABLISHING VALIDITY

Researchers have attempted to assess validity in many ways. They attempt to provide some evidence of a measure's degree of validity by answering a variety of questions. Is there a consensus among my colleagues that my attitude scale measures what it is supposed to measure? Does my measure correlate with other measures of the same concept? Does the behavior expected from my measure predict actual observed behavior? The three basic approaches to establishing validity are *face* or *content validity, criterion validity,* and *construct validity.*

Face (content) validity refers to the subjective agreement among professionals that a scale logically reflects the concept being measured. Simply, do the test items make sense given a concept's definition? When an inspection of the test items convinces experts that the items match the definition, the scale is said to have face validity.

Clear, understandable questions such as "How many children do you have?" generally are agreed to have face validity. In scientific studies, however, researchers generally prefer stronger evidence because of the elusive nature of attitudes and other marketing phenomena. For example, the ACNielsen television rating system is based on the PeopleMeter system, which mechanically records whether a sample household's television is turned on and records the channel selection. If one of the viewers leaves the room or falls asleep, the measure is not a valid measure of audience.

Criterion validity addresses the question, "Does my measure correlate with measures of the similar concepts or known quantities?" Criterion validity may be classified as either *concurrent validity* or *predictive validity* depending on the time sequence in which the new measurement scale and the criterion measure are correlated. If the new measure is taken at the same time as the criterion measure and is shown to be valid, then it has concurrent validity. Predictive validity is established when a new measure predicts a future event. The two measures differ only on the basis of a time dimension—that is, the criterion measure is separated in time from the predictor measure.

A practical example of predictive validity is illustrated by a commercial research firm's test of the relationship between a rough commercial's effectiveness (as determined, for example, by recall scores) and a finished commercial's effectiveness (also by recall scores). Ad agencies often test animatic rough, photomatic rough, or live-action rough commercials before developing actual finished commercials. One marketing research consulting firm suggests that this testing has high predictive validity. Rough commercial recall scores provide correct estimates of the final finished commercial recall scores more than 80 percent of the time.[12] While face (content) validity is a subjective evaluation, criterion validity provides a more rigorous empirical test.

Validity
The accuracy of a measure or the extent to which a score truthfully represents a concept.

Face (content) validity
A scale's content logically appears to reflect what was intended to be measured.

Criterion validity
The ability of a measure to correlate with other standard measures of similar constructs or established criteria.

Construct validity
Exists when a measure reliably measures and truthfully represents a unique concept; consists of several components including face validity, convergent validity, criterion validity, and discriminant validity.

Convergent validity
Another way of expressing internal consistency; highly reliable scales contain convergent validity.

Discriminant validity
Represents how unique or distinct is a measure; a scale should not correlate too highly with a measure of a different construct.

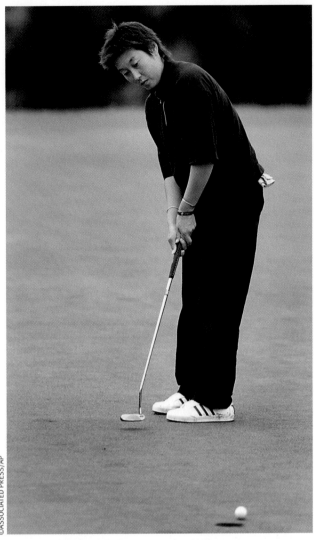

©ASSOCIATED PRESS/AP

A golfer can hit reliable but not valid putts. Notice that this putt converges to the left of the hole.

Construct validity exists when a measure reliably measures and truthfully represents a unique concept. Construct validity consists of several components, including

- Face or Content validity
- Convergent validity
- Criterion or validity
- Discriminant validity

Convergent validity is another way of expressing internal consistency. Highly reliable scales contain convergent validity. Criterion validity and face validity were discussed above. **Discriminant validity** represents how unique or distinct is a measure. A scale should not correlate too highly with a measure of a different construct. For example, a customer satisfaction measure should not correlate too highly with a cognitive dissonance scale if the two concepts are truly different. As a rough rule of thumb, when two scales are correlated above 0.75, discriminant validity may be questioned. Multivariate procedures like factor analysis can be useful in establishing construct validity. The reader is referred to other sources for a more detailed discussion.[13]

Reliability versus Validity

The differences between reliability and validity can be illustrated by the rifle targets in Exhibit 13.7. Suppose an expert sharpshooter fires an equal number of rounds with a century-old rifle and a modern rifle.[14] The shots from the older gun are considerably scattered, but those from the newer gun are closely clustered. The variability of the old rifle compared with that of the new one indicates it is less reliable. The target on the right illustrates the concept of a systematic bias influencing validity. The new rifle is reliable (because it has little variance), but the sharpshooter's vision is hampered by glare. Although shots are consistent, the sharpshooter is unable to hit the bull's-eye.

Sensitivity

Sensitivity
A measurement instrument's ability to accurately measure variability in stimuli or responses.

The sensitivity of a scale is an important measurement concept, particularly when *changes* in attitudes or other hypothetical constructs are under investigation. **Sensitivity** refers to an instrument's ability to accurately measure variability in a concept. A dichotomous response category, such as

EXHIBIT 13.7
Reliability and Validity on Target

Old Rifle	New Rifle	New Rifle Sunglare
Low Reliability	High Reliability	Reliable but not Valid
(Target A)	(Target B)	(Target C)

"agree or disagree," does not allow the recording of subtle attitude changes. A more sensitive measure with numerous categories on the scale may be needed. For example, adding "strongly agree," "mildly agree," "neither agree nor disagree," "mildly disagree," and "strongly disagree" will increase the scale's sensitivity.

The sensitivity of a scale based on a single question or single item can also be increased by adding questions or items. In other words, because composite measures allow for a greater range of possible scores, they are more sensitive than single-item scales. Thus, sensitivity is generally increased by adding more response points or adding scale items.

Summary

1. Determine what needs to be measured. Researchers can determine what concepts must be measured by examining research questions and hypotheses. A hypothesis often states that one concept is related to another. Therefore, the concepts listed in the hypotheses must have operational measures if the research is to be performed.

2. Distinguish levels of scale measurement. Four levels of scale measurement can be identified. Each level is associated with increasingly more complex properties. Nominal scales assign numbers or letters to objects for identification or classification. Ordinal scales arrange objects based on relative magnitude of a concept. Thus, ordinal scales represent rankings. Interval scales also represent an ordering based on relative amounts of a concept, but they also capture the differences between scale values. Thus, interval scales allow stimuli to be compared to each other based on the difference in their scale scores. Ratio scales are absolute scales, starting with absolute zeros at which there is a total absence of the attribute. Nominal and ordinal scales are discrete. The mode is the best way to represent central tendency for discrete measures. Ratio measures are continuous and interval scales are generally treated as continuous. For continuous measures, the mean represents a valid representation of central tendency.

3. Forming a composite measure. Indexes and composite measures are formed by combining scores from multiple items. For instance, a composite score can be formed by adding the scores to multiple items, each intended to represent the same concept.

4. List the criteria for good measurement. Good measurement exists when a measure is reliable, valid, and sensitive. Thus, reliability, validity, and sensitivity are characteristics of good measurement. Reliability represents the consistency and repeatability of a measure. Validity refers to the degree to which the instrument measures the concept the researcher wants to measure. Sensitivity is the instrument's ability to accurately measure variability in stimuli or responses.

5. Provide a basic assessment of scale reliability and validity. Reliability is most often assessed using coefficient alpha. Coefficient alpha should be above 0.6 for a scale to be considered as acceptably reliable. Validity is assessed in components. A measure that has adequate construct validity is one that is likely to be well measured. Construct validity consists of face or content validity, convergent validity (internal consistency), discriminant validity, and criterion validity. Statistical procedures like factor analysis can be helpful in providing evidence of construct validity.

Key Terms and Concepts

Measurement	Discrete measures	Coefficient alpha (α)
Concept	Continuous measures	Test-retest method
Operationalization	Attribute	Validity
Scales	Index measure	Face (content) validity
Correspondence rules	Composite measures	Criterion validity
Construct	Summated scale	Construct validity
Nominal scales	Reverse coding	Convergent validity
Ordinal scales	Reliability	Discriminant validity
Interval scales	Internal consistency	Sensitivity
Ratio scales	Split-half method	

Questions for Review and Critical Thinking

1. Define *measurement*. How is your performance in a marketing research class being measured?
2. What is the difference between a *concept* and a *construct?*
3. Suppose a researcher takes over a project only after a proposal has been written by another researcher. Where will the researcher find the things that need to be measured?
4. Describe the four different levels of scale measurement.
5. Consider the different grading measuring scales described at the beginning of the chapter. Describe what level of measurement is represented by each. Which method do you think contains the least opportunity for error?
6. Look at the responses to the following survey items that describe how stressful consumers believed a Christmas shopping trip was using a ten-point scale ranging from 1 (= no stress at all) to 10 (= extremely stressful):
   a. How stressful was finding a place to park? _7_
   b. How stressful was the checkout procedure? _5_
   c. How stressful was trying to find exactly the right product? _8_
   d. How stressful was finding a store employee? _6_
      i. What would be the stress score for this respondent based on a summated scale score?
      ii. What would be the stress score for this respondent based on an average composite scale score?
      iii. Do any items need to be reverse-coded? Why or why not?
7. How is it that marketing researchers can justify treating a seven-point Likert scale as interval?
8. What are the components of construct validity? Describe each.
9. Why might a researcher wish to use more than one question to measure satisfaction with a particular aspect of retail shopping?
10. How can a researcher assess the reliability and validity of a multi-item composite scale?
11. Comment on the validity and reliability of the following:
    a. A respondent's report of an intention to subscribe to *Consumer Reports* is highly reliable. A researcher believes this constitutes a valid measurement of dissatisfaction with the economic system and alienation from big business.
    b. A general-interest magazine claimed that it was a better advertising medium than television programs with similar content. Research had indicated that for a soft drink and other test products, recall scores were higher for the magazine ads than for thirty-second commercials.
    c. A respondent's report of frequency of magazine reading consistently indicates that she regularly reads *Good Housekeeping* and *Gourmet* and never reads *Cosmopolitan*.
12. Indicate whether the following measures use a nominal, ordinal, interval, or ratio scale:
    a. Prices on the stock market
    b. Marital status, classified as "married" or "never married"
    c. Whether a respondent has ever been unemployed
    d. Professorial rank: assistant professor, associate professor, or professor
    e. Grades: A, B, C, D, or F

Research Activities

1. Go to the library and find out how *Sales and Marketing Management* magazine constructs its buying-power index.
2. Define each of the following concepts, and then operationally define each one by providing correspondence rules between the definition and the scale:
   a. A good bowler
   b. The television audience for *The Tonight Show*
   c. Purchasing intention for a palm-sized computer
   d. Consumer involvement with cars
   e. A workaholic
   f. Fast-food restaurant
   g. The American Dream
3. 'NET Use the ACSI scores found at http://www.theacsi.org to respond to this question. Using the most recent two years of data, test the following two hypotheses:
   a. American consumers are more satisfied with breweries than they are with wireless telephone services.
   b. 'NET American consumers are more satisfied with discount and department stores than they are with automobile companies.
4. Refer back to the opening vignette. Use the *Business Resource Center* to search for stories dealing with job performance. In particular, pay attention to stories that may be related to CRM. Make a recommendation to Griff concerning a way that job performance should be measured. Would your scale be nominal, ordinal, interval, or ratio?
5. 'NET Go to http://www.queendom.com/tests. Click on the lists of personality tests. Take the hostility test. Do you think this is a reliable and valid measure of how prone someone is to generally act in a hostile manner?

Case 13.1 FlyAway Airways

 Wesley Shocker, research analyst for FlyAway Airways, was asked by the director of research to make recommendations regarding the best approach for monitoring the quality of service provided by the airline.[15] FlyAway Airways is a national air carrier that has a comprehensive route structure consisting of long-haul, coast-to-coast routes and direct, nonstop routes between short-haul metropolitan areas. Current competitors include Midway and Alaska Airlines. FlyAway Airlines is poised to surpass the billion-dollar revenue level required to be designated as a major airline. This change in status brings a new set of competitors. To prepare for this move up in competitive status, Shocker was asked to review the options available for monitoring the quality of FlyAway Airways service and the service of its competitors. Such monitoring would involve better understanding the nature of service quality and the ways in which quality can be tracked for airlines.

After some investigation, Shocker discovered two basic approaches to measuring quality of airline service that can produce similar ranking results. His report must outline the important aspects to consider in measuring quality as well as the critical points of difference and similarity between the two approaches to measuring quality.

Some Background on Quality

In today's competitive airline industry, it's crucial that an airline do all it can do to attract and retain customers. One of the best ways to do this is by offering quality service to consumers. Perceptions of service quality vary from person to person, but an enduring element of service quality is the consistent achievement of customer satisfaction. For customers to perceive an airline as offering quality service, they must be satisfied, and that usually means receiving a service outcome that is equal to or greater than what they expected.

An airline consumer usually is concerned most with issues of schedule, destination, and price when choosing an airline. Given that most airlines have competition in each of these areas, other factors that relate to quality become important to the customer when making a choice between airlines. Both subjective aspects of quality (that is, food, pleasant employees, and so forth) and objective aspects (that is, on-time performance, safety, lost baggage, and so forth) have real meaning to consumers. These secondary factors may not be as critical as schedule, destination, and price, but they do affect quality judgments of the customer.

There are many possible combinations of subjective and objective aspects that could influence a customer's perception of quality at different times. Fortunately, since 1988, consumers of airline services have had access to objective information from the Department of Transportation regarding service performance in some basic categories. Unfortunately, the average consumer is most likely unaware of or uninterested in these data on performance; instead, consumers rely on personal experience and subjective opinion to judge quality of service. Periodic surveys of subjective consumer opinion regarding airline service experience are available through several sources. These efforts rely on contact with a sample of consumers who may or may not have informed opinions regarding the quality of airline service for all airlines being compared.

A Consumer Survey Approach

In his research, Shocker discovered a recent study conducted to identify favorite airlines of frequent fliers. This study is typical of the survey-based, infrequent (usually only annually), subjective efforts conducted to assess airline quality. A New York firm, Research & Forecasts, Inc., published results of a consumer survey of frequent fliers that used several criteria to rate domestic and international airlines. Criteria included comfort, service, reliability, food quality, cost, delays, routes served, safety, and frequent-flier plans. The questionnaire was sent to 25,000 frequent fliers.

The 4,462 people who responded were characterized as predominantly male (59 percent) professional managers (66 percent) whose average age was 45 and who traveled an average of at least 43 nights a year for both business and pleasure. This group indicated that the most important factors in choosing an airline were 1) route structure (46 percent), 2) price (42 percent), 3) reliability (41 percent), 4) service (33 percent), 5) safety (33 percent), 6) frequent-flier plans (33 percent), and 7) food (12 percent). When asked to rate twenty different airlines, respondents provided the rankings in Case Exhibit 13.1–1.

CASE EXHIBIT 13.1–1 **Ranking of Major Airlines: Consumer Survey Approach**

1. American	11. Lufthansa
2. United	12. USAir
3. Delta	13. KLM
4. TWA	14. America West
5. SwissAir	15. JAL
6. Singapore	16. Alaska
7. British Airways	17. Qantas
8. Continental	18. Midway
9. Air France	19. Southwest
10. Pan Am	20. SAS

A Weighted Average Approach

Shocker also discovered a newer, more objective approach to measuring airline quality in a study recently published by the National Institute for Aviation Research at the Wichita State University in Wichita, Kansas. The Airline Quality Rating (AQR) is a weighted average of nineteen factors that have relevance when judging the quality of airline services (see Case Exhibit 13.2–2). The AQR is based on data that are readily obtainable (most of the data are updated monthly) from published sources for each major airline operating in the United States. Regularly published data on such factors as consumer complaints, on-time performance, accidents, number of aircraft, and financial performance are available from the Department of Transportation, the National Transportation Safety Board, Moody's Bond Record, industry trade publications, and annual reports of individual airlines.

To establish the nineteen weighted factors, an opinion survey was conducted with a group of sixty-five experts in the aviation field. These experts included representatives of most major airlines, air travel experts, Federal Aviation Administration (FAA) representatives, academic researchers, airline manufacturing and support firms,

Factor	Weight
1. Average age of fleet	−5.85
2. Number of aircraft	+4.54
3. On-time performance	+8.63
4. Load factor	−6.98
5. Pilot deviations	−8.03
6. Number of accidents	−8.38
7. Frequent-flier awards	−7.35
8. Flight problems[b]	−8.05
9. Denied boardings[b]	−8.03
10. Mishandled baggage[b]	−7.92
11. Fares[b]	−7.60
12. Customer service[b]	−7.20
13. Refunds	−7.32
14. Ticketing/boarding[b]	−7.08
15. Advertising[b]	−6.82
16. Credit[b]	−5.94
17. Other[b]	−7.34
18. Financial stability	−6.52
19. Average seat-mile cost	−4.49

$$AQR = \frac{w_1F_1 - w_2F_2 + w_3F_3 + \cdots - w_{19}F_{19}}{w_1 + w_2 + w_3 + \cdots + w_{19}}$$

a. The 19-item rating has a reliability coefficient (Cronbach's Alpha) of 0.87.
b. Data for these factors come from consumer complaints registered with the Department of Transportation.

and individual consumers. Each expert was asked to rate the importance that each individual factor might have to a consumer of airline services using a scale of 0 (no importance) to 10 (great importance). The average importance ratings for each of the nineteen factors were then used as the weights for those factors in the AQR. Case Exhibit 13.1-2 shows the factors included in the Airline Quality Rating, the weight associated with each factor, and whether the factor has a positive or negative impact on quality from the consumer's perspective.

Rank	Airline	AQR Score
1	American	+0.328
2	Southwest	+0.254
3	Delta	+0.209
4	United	+0.119
5	USAir	+0.054
6	Pan Am	+0.003
7	Northwest	−0.063
8	Continental	−0.346
9	America West	−0.377
10	TWA	−0.439

Using the Airline Quality Rating formula and recent data, produce AQR scores and rankings for the 10 major U.S. airlines shown in Case Exhibit 13.1–3.

What Course to Chart?

Shocker has discovered what appear to be two different approaches to measuring quality of airlines. One relies on direct consumer opinion and is mostly subjective in its approach to quality and the elements considered. The other relies on performance data that are available through public sources and appear to be more objective. Both approaches incorporate pertinent elements that could be used by consumers to judge the quality of an airline. Shocker's recommendation must consider the comprehensiveness and usefulness of these approaches for FlyAway Airways as it moves into a more competitive environment. What course of action should he recommend?

Questions
1. How comparable are the two different methods? In what ways are they similar? In what ways are they different?
2. What are the positive and negative aspects of each approach that Shocker should consider before recommending a course of action for FlyAway Airways?
3. What aspects of service quality does each approach address well and not so well?
4. Considering the two methods outlined, what types of validity would you consider to be demonstrated by the two approaches to measuring quality? Defend your position.
5. Which of the methods should Shocker recommend? Why?

CHAPTER 14
ATTITUDE
MEASUREMENT

After studying this chapter, you should be able to

1. Describe how marketing researchers think of attitudes
2. Identify basic approaches to measuring attitudes
3. Discuss the use of rating scales for measuring attitudes
4. Represent a latent construct by constructing a summated scale
5. Summarize ways to measure attitudes with ranking and sorting techniques and randomized response questions
6. Discuss major issues involved in the selection of a measurement scale

Chapter Vignette: Sharing the Road with Trucks: Motorists' Nightmare?

The more than $800 billion U.S. consumers spend each year to buy, maintain, and operate automobiles far outstrips spending on any other kind of transportation.[1] But whether on interstate highways, city streets, or country lanes, these cars must share the road with trucks hauling freight. This everyday fact is a business issue for the logistics companies involved in trucking, because motorists' attitudes about trucks can shape their driving behavior and potentially affect accident rates and associated costs. And attitudes can also affect public support for laws related to the trucking industry—and freight transportation costs as a result. With trucks carrying a greater volume of freight than any transportation mode except rail, and with spending on this mode far higher than for the others, logistics companies benefit from knowing—and eventually shaping—motorists' attitudes.

©LESTER LEFKOWITZ/CORBIS

A team of researchers at Mississippi State University measured these attitudes with a survey. To reach a large sample economically, they inserted questions on this topic in a yearly survey of drivers conducted by the university's Social Science Research Center (SSRC). They asked subjects to indicate their agreement or disagreement with six statements:

1. Large trucks present a safety hazard on highways.
2. Driving beside or near large trucks makes me nervous.
3. Truck drivers often drive in ways that are dangerous to passenger cars.
4. During a rainstorm, the water from large trucks creates dangerous conditions for other vehicles.
5. Drivers of large trucks frequently drive too fast.
6. Large trucks frequently create dangerous conditions by trying to pass each other.

For each statement, subjects used a five-point scale to indicate whether they stongly agreed, agreed, were neutral (or didn't know), disagreed, or strongly disagreed.

The researchers combined their answers with other responses on the standard SSRC survey to see whether the attitudes were associated with categories of drivers or driving experiences, such as amount of driving and accidents. The drivers had a negative impression of trucks' impact on their safety. Over half agreed with every statement but the first, with 80 percent concerned about the road spray from trucks driving in the rain. Perceptions were somewhat less negative among males and those who drive most often.

Measurement of attitudes is a common objective in marketing research. Just as logistics companies can apply this study's results to craft practical responses—for example, educating inexperienced drivers and equipping trucks with better splash protection—other marketers explore attitudes to answer questions that range from identifying needs to evaluating satisfaction with after-sales service. This chapter describes various methods of attitude measurement.

Attitudes in Marketing Research

Attitude
An enduring disposition to consistently respond in a given manner to various aspects of the world, composed of affective, cognitive, and behavioral components.

For social scientists, an attitude is as an enduring disposition to respond consistently in a given manner to various aspects of the world, including persons, events, and objects. One way to understand attitudes is to think of their components. Consider this brief statement: "Sally loves shopping at Sam's. She believes the store is clean and conveniently located and that it has the lowest prices. She intends to shop there every Thursday." As in this example, an attitude has three components: affective, cognitive, and behavioral. The affective component refers to an individual's general feelings or emotions toward an object. Statements such as "I love my Chevrolet Corvette," "I enjoyed reading *A Corporate Bestiary,*" and "I hate cranberry juice" reflect the emotional character of attitudes. The way a person feels about a product, an advertisement, or an object is usually tied to his or her *beliefs* or *cognitions.* This cognitive component represents an individual's awareness of and knowledge about an object. One person might feel happy about the purchase of an automobile because she believes the car "gets great gas mileage" or knows that the dealer is "the best in New Jersey." The behavioral component of an attitude reflects a predisposition to action by reflecting a consumer's buying or purchase intentions.

Hypothetical constructs
Variables that are not directly observable but are measurable through indirect indicators, such as verbal expression or overt behavior.

Attitudes as Hypothetical Constructs

Generally, consumers act in a way consistent with their attitudes. Therefore, attitudes are a popular marketing research topic.

©DON MASON/CORBIS

Many variables that marketing researchers wish to investigate are psychological variables that cannot be observed directly. For example, someone may have an attitude toward a particular brand of shaving cream, but we cannot observe this attitude. To measure an attitude, we make an inference based on the way a person responds to multiple individual scale items. Unobserved or latent variables are known as **hypothetical constructs** or just constructs. Common constructs include consumer commitment, value, feelings, organizational commitment, salesperson orientation, role stress, and many more.

Importance of Measuring Attitudes

Most marketing managers hold the intuitive belief that changing consumers' or prospects' attitudes toward a product is a major marketing goal. At the individual level, this issue is complicated, but aggregate attitude change has been shown to be related to aggregate sales volume changes. Because modifying attitudes plays a pervasive role in marketing strategies, the measurement of attitudes is an important task. For example, after Whiskas cat food had been

RESEARCHSNAPSHOT

This Hypothetical Construct Is a Four-Letter Word

Love is a four-letter word. And a hypothetical construct—that is, a term that psychologists use to describe or explain consistent patterns of human behavior. Love, hate, thirst, learning, intelligence—all of these are hypothetical constructs. They are hypothetical in that they do not exist as physical entities; therefore, they cannot be seen, heard, felt, or measured directly. There is no love center in the brain that, if removed, would leave a person incapable of responding positively and affectionately toward other people and things. Love and hate are constructs in that we invent these terms to explain why, for instance, a young man spends all his time with one young woman while completely avoiding another. From a scientific point of view, we might be better off if we said that this young man's behavior suggested that he had a relatively enduring, positive-approach attitude toward the first woman and a negative-avoidance attitude toward the second.

Source: *Psychology Today: An Introduction* (Del Mar, CA: CRM Books, 1970), p. 613.

©ROYALTY-FREE/CORBIS

sold in Europe for decades, the brand faced increased competition from new premium brands, and consumers had difficulty identifying with the brand. The company conducted attitude research to determine how people felt about their cats and their food alternatives. The study revealed that cat owners see their pets both as independent and as dependent fragile beings.[2] Cat owners held the attitude that cats wanted to enjoy their food but needed nutrition. This attitude research was directly channeled into managerial action. Whiskas marketers begin positioning the product as having "Catisfaction," using advertisements that featured a purring silver tabby—a pedigreed cat—which symbolizes premium quality but also presents the image of a sweet cat. The message: "Give cats what they like with the nutrition they need. If you do, they'll be so happy that they'll purr for you." This effort reversed the sales decline the brand had been experiencing.

©BRAND X PICTURES/JUPITER IMAGES

While cats' attitudes may be difficult to measure, we can easily measure how consumers feel about different types of cat food.

Techniques for Measuring Attitudes

A remarkable variety of techniques has been devised to measure attitudes. This variety stems in part from lack of consensus about the exact definition of the concept. In addition, the affective, cognitive, and behavioral components of an attitude may be measured by different means. For example, sympathetic nervous system responses may be recorded using physiological measures to quantify affect, but they are not good measures of behavioral intentions. Direct verbal statements concerning

Ranking
A measurement task that requires respondents to rank order a small number of stores, brands, or objects on the basis of overall preference or some characteristic of the stimulus.

Rating
A measurement task that requires respondents to estimate the magnitude of a characteristic or quality that a brand, store, or object possesses.

Sorting
A measurement task that presents a respondent with several objects or product concepts and requires the respondent to arrange the objects into piles or classify the product concepts.

Choice
A measurement task that identifies preferences by requiring respondents to choose between two or more alternatives.

affect, belief, or behavior are used to measure behavioral intent. However, attitudes may also be interpreted using qualitative techniques like those discussed in Chapter 6.

Research may assess the affective (emotional) components of attitudes through physiological measures such as galvanic skin response (GSR), blood pressure, and pupil dilation (see Chapter 10). These measures provide a means of assessing attitudes without verbally questioning the respondent. In general, they can provide a gross measure of likes or dislikes, but they are not extremely sensitive to the different gradients of an attitude.

Obtaining verbal statements from respondents generally requires that the respondents perform a task such as ranking, rating, sorting, or making choices. A **ranking** task requires the respondent to rank order a small number of stores, brands, feelings, or objects on the basis of overall preference or some characteristic of the stimulus. **Rating** asks the respondent to estimate the magnitude or the extent to which some characteristic exists. A quantitative score results. The rating task involves marking a response indicating one's position using one or more attitudinal or cognitive scales. A **sorting** task might present the respondent with several product concepts printed on cards and require the respondent to classify the concepts by placing the cards into groups (stacks of cards). Another type of attitude measurement is **choice** between two or more alternatives. If a respondent chooses one object over another, the researcher assumes that the respondent prefers the chosen object, at least in this setting. The following sections describe the most popular techniques for measuring attitudes.

Attitude Rating Scales

Perhaps the most common practice in marketing research is using rating scales to measure attitudes. This section discusses many rating scales designed to enable respondents to report the intensity of their attitudes.

Simple Attitude Scales

In its most basic form, attitude scaling requires that an individual agree or disagree with a statement or respond to a single question. For example, respondents in a political poll may be asked whether they agree or disagree with the statement "The president should run for re-election." Or, an individual might indicate whether he or she likes or dislikes jalapeño bean dip. This type of self-rating scale merely classifies respondents into one of two categories, thus having only the properties of a nominal scale, and the types of mathematical analysis that may be used with this basic scale are limited.

Despite the disadvantages, simple attitude scaling may be used when questionnaires are extremely long, when respondents have little education, or for other specific reasons. A number of simplified scales are merely checklists: A respondent indicates past experience, preference, and the like merely by checking an item. In many cases the items are adjectives that describe a particular object. In a survey of small-business owners and managers, respondents indicated whether they found working in a small firm more rewarding than working in a large firm, as well as whether they agreed with a series of attitude statements about small businesses. For example, 77 percent said small and mid-sized businesses "have less bureaucracy," and 76 percent said smaller companies "have more flexibility" than large ones.[3]

Most attitude theorists believe that attitudes vary along continua. Early attitude researchers pioneered the view that the task of attitude scaling is to measure the distance from "good" to "bad," "low" to "high," "like" to "dislike," and so on. Thus, the purpose of an attitude scale is to find an individual's position on the continuum. However, simple scales do not allow for fine distinctions between attitudes. Several other scales have been developed for making more precise measurements.

Category Scales

The simplest rating scale contains only two response categories: agree/disagree. Expanding the response categories provides the respondent with more flexibility in the rating task. Even more

RESEARCHSNAPSHOT

Attitudes of the Rich

Testing that old saying about the rich being "different from you and me," the Harrison Group, a marketing research firm, conducted a survey of five hundred rich households—those with at least $5 million in liquid assets, placing them in the top 0.5 percent of the United States in terms of their economic status. The interviews asked members of these households about their habits and attitudes. What they learned about attitudes might surprise you, at least if your ideas about wealth come from the fabulous misbehavior displayed in soap operas and supermarket tabloids.

The survey asked respondents to agree or disagree with statements on a variety of topics. It found that a sizable share of this group does not care to show off with a lavish lifestyle. Only 11 percent said they want others to "know they are wealthy," and almost half said luxury items like fancy watches, jewelry, and cars are a "waste of money." Many stand firm on ethical grounds. Less than 10 percent admitted they had more than once "compromised their values" to make money, and only half expressed concern that living in comfort may interfere with their children's work ethic.

If some of these responses surprise you, you have company, including people who should know better. The Harrison Group also teamed up with advertising firm AgencySacks to ask marketers specializing in luxury products to predict how wealthy people would answer the same questions. The marketers expected that few rich people would see luxury goods as a waste and that most would worry about their children's work ethic.

Source: Based on Sandra O'Loughlin, "Luxe Marketing: Perception vs. Reality," Brandweek, 46 (September 19, 2005), 22–28; Harrison Group, "About Us" and "Wealth Study Methodology," http://www.harrisongroup.com, accessed March 6, 2006.

©NATIONAL GEOGRAPHIC/GETTY IMAGES

information is provided if the categories are ordered according to a particular descriptive or evaluative dimension. Consider the following question:

How often do you disagree with your spouse about how much to spend on vacation?

☐ *Never*   ☐ *Rarely*   ☐ *Sometimes*   ☐ *Often*   ☐ *Very often*

This **category scale** is a more sensitive measure than a scale that has only two response categories. By having more choices for a respondent, the potential exists to provide more information. However, if the researcher tries to represent something that is truly bipolar (yes/no, female/male, member/non-member, and so on) with more than two categories, error may be introduced.

Question wording is an extremely important factor in the usefulness of these scales. Exhibit 14.1 shows some common wordings used in category scales. The issue of question wording is discussed in Chapter 15.

Category scale
A rating scale that consists of several response categories, often providing respondents with alternatives to indicate positions on a continuum.

Method of Summated Ratings: The Likert Scale

A method that is simple to administer and therefore extremely popular is marketing researchers' adaptation of the method of summated ratings, developed by Rensis Likert.[4] With the **Likert scale**, respondents indicate their attitudes by checking how strongly they agree or disagree with carefully constructed statements, ranging from very positive to very negative attitudes toward some object. Individuals generally choose from approximately five response alternatives—strongly agree, agree, uncertain, disagree, and strongly disagree—although the number of alternatives may range from three to nine. In the following example, from a study of food-shopping behavior, there are five alternatives:

In buying food for my family, price is no object.

Strongly Disagree	Disagree	Uncertain	Agree	Strongly Agree
☐	☐	☐	☐	☐
(1)	(2)	(3)	(4)	(5)

Likert scale
A measure of attitudes designed to allow respondents to rate how strongly they agree or disagree with carefully constructed statements, ranging from very positive to very negative attitudes toward some object.

Researchers assign scores, or weights, to each possible response. In this example, numerical scores of 1, 2, 3, 4, and 5 are assigned to each level of agreement, respectively. The numerical scores, shown in parentheses, may not be printed on the questionnaire or computer screen. Strong agreement

EXHIBIT 14.1 **Selected Category Scales**

Quality				
Excellent	Good	Fair	Poor	
Very good	Fairly good	Neither good nor bad	Not very good	Not good at all
Well above average	Above average	Average	Below average	Well below average

Importance				
Very important	Fairly important	Neutral	Not so important	Not at all important

Interest				
Very interested		Somewhat interested		Not very interested

Satisfaction				
Completely satisfied	Somewhat satisfied	Neither satisfied nor dissatisfied	Somewhat dissatisfied	Completely dissatisfied
Very satisfied	Quite satisfied	Somewhat satisfied	Not at all satisfied	

Frequency				
All of the time	Very often	Often	Sometimes	Hardly ever
Very often	Often	Sometimes	Rarely	Never
All of the time	Most of the time	Some of the time	Just now and then	

Truth				
Very true	Somewhat true	Not very true	Not at all true	
Definitely yes	Probably yes	Probably no	Definitely no	

Uniqueness				
Very different	Somewhat different	Slightly different	Not at all different	
Extremely unique	Very unique	Somewhat unique	Slightly unique	Not at all unique

indicates the most favorable attitude on the statement, and a numerical score of 5 is assigned to this response.

▦ REVERSE RECODING

The statement given in this example is positively framed. If a statement is framed negatively (such as "I carefully budget my food expenditures"), the numerical scores would need to be reversed. This is done by **reverse recoding** the negative item so that a strong agreement really indicates an un-favorable response rather than a favorable attitude. In the case of a five-point scale, the recoding is done as follows:

Reverse recoding
A method of making sure all the items forming a composite scale are scored in the same direction. Negative items can be recoded into the equivalent responses for a non-reverse coded item.

Old Value	New Value
1	5
2	4
3	3
4	2
5	1

1. My doctor's office staff takes a warm and personal interest in me.
2. My doctor's office staff is friendly and courteous.
3. My doctor's office staff is more interested in serving the doctor's needs than in serving my needs.
4. My doctor's office staff always acts in a professional manner.

Source: Journal of Marketing by Stephen W. Brown & Teresa Swarts. Copyright 1989 by Am. Marketing Assn (AMA (Chic). Reproduced with permission of Am. Marketing Assn (AMA (Chic) in the format Textbook via Copyright Clearance Center.

Recoding in this fashion turns agreement with a negatively worded item into a mirror image, meaning the result is the same as disagreement with a positively worded item. SPSS has a recode function that allows simple recoding to be done by entering "old" and "new" scale values. Alternatively, a simple mathematical formula can be entered. In this case, the formula

$$X_{new\ value} = 6 - X_{old\ value}$$

would result in the same recoding.

COMPOSITE SCALES

A Likert scale may include several scale items to form a **composite scale**. Each statement is assumed to represent an aspect of a common attitudinal domain. For example, Exhibit 14.2 shows the items in a Likert scale for measuring attitudes toward patients' interaction with a physician's service staff. The total score is the summation of the numerical scores assigned to an individual's responses. Here the maximum possible score for the composite would be 20 if a 5 were assigned to "strongly agree" responses for each of the positively worded statements and a 5 to "strongly disagree" responses for the negative statement. Item 3 is negatively worded and therefore it is reverse coded.

In Likert's original procedure, a large number of statements are generated, and an *item analysis* is performed. The purpose of the item analysis is to ensure that final items evoke a wide response and discriminate among those with positive and negative attitudes. Items that are poor because they lack clarity or elicit mixed response patterns are eliminated from the final statement list. Scales that use multiple items can be analyzed for reliability and validity. Only a set of items that shows good reliability and validity should be summed or averaged to form a composite scale representing a hypothetical construct. Unfortuantely, not all researchers are willing or able to thoroughly assess reliability and validity. Without this test, the use of Likert scales can be disadvantageous because there is no way of knowing exactly what the items represent or how well they represent anything of interest.

Composite scale
A way of representing a latent construct by summing or averaging respondents' reactions to multiple items each assumed to indicate the latent construct.

Semantic Differential

The **semantic differential** is actually a series of attitude scales. This popular attitude measurement technique consists of getting respondents to react to some concept using a series of seven-point bipolar rating scales. Bipolar adjectives—such as "good" and "bad," "modern" and "old-fashioned," or "clean" and "dirty"—anchor the beginning and the end (or poles) of the scale. The subject makes repeated judgments about the concept under investigation on each of the scales. Exhibit 14.3 shows seven of eighteen scales used in a research project that measured attitudes toward supermarkets.

The scoring of the semantic differential can be illustrated using the scale bounded by the anchors "modern" and "old-fashioned." Respondents are instructed to check the place that indicates the nearest appropriate adjective. From left to right, the scale intervals are interpreted as "extremely modern," "very modern," "slightly modern," "both modern and old-fashioned," "slightly old-fashioned," "very old-fashioned," and "extremely old-fashioned":

Modern __ __ __ __ __ __ __ *Old-fashioned*

The semantic differential technique originally was developed as a method for measuring the meanings of objects or the "semantic space" of interpersonal experience.[5] Marketing researchers have found the semantic differential versatile and useful in business applications. The validity of the

Semantic differential
A measure of attitudes that consists of a series of seven-point rating scales that use bipolar adjectives to anchor the beginning and end of each scale.

Semantic Differential Scales for Measuring Attitudes toward Supermarkets

Inconvenient location _ _ _ _ _ _ _ _ _ Convenient location

Low prices _ _ _ _ _ _ _ _ _ High prices

Pleasant atmosphere _ _ _ _ _ _ _ _ _ Unpleasant atmosphere

Modern _ _ _ _ _ _ _ _ _ Old-fashioned

Cluttered _ _ _ _ _ _ _ _ _ Spacious

Fast checkout _ _ _ _ _ _ _ _ _ Slow checkout

Dull _ _ _ _ _ _ _ _ _ Exciting

Source: Julie H. Yu, Gerald Albaum, and Michael Swenson, "Is a Central Tendency Error Inherent in the Use of Semantic Differential Scales in Different Cultures?" International Journal of Market Research, Summer 2003, downloaded from Business & Company Resource Center, http://galenet.galegroup.com.

semantic differential depends on finding scale anchors that are semantic opposites. This can sometimes prove difficult. However, in attitude or image studies simple anchors such as very unfavorable and very favorable work well.

For scoring purposes, a numerical score is assigned to each position on the rating scale. Traditionally, scores are 1, 2, 3, 4, 5, 6, 7 or $-3, -2, -1, 0, +1, +2, +3$. Many marketing researchers find it desirable to assume that the semantic differential provides interval data. This assumption, although widely accepted, has its critics, who argue that the data have only ordinal properties because the numerical scores are arbitrary. Practically, marketing researchers treat semantic differential scales as metric (at least interval). This is because the amount of error introduced by assuming the intervals between choices are equal (even though this is uncertain) is fairly small.

Exhibit 14.4 illustrates a typical **image profile** based on semantic differential data. Because the data are assumed to be interval, either the arithmetic mean or the median will be used to compare the profile of one product, brand, or store with that of a competing product, brand, or store.

Image profile
A graphic representation of semantic differential data for competing brands, products, or stores to highlight comparisons.

Image Profile of Commuter Airlines versus Major Airlines

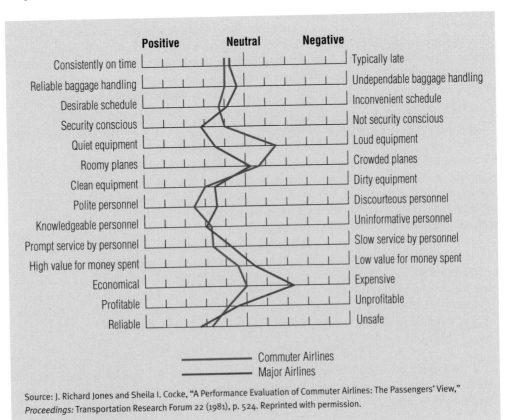

Source: J. Richard Jones and Sheila I. Cocke, "A Performance Evaluation of Commuter Airlines: The Passengers' View," Proceedings: Transportation Research Forum 22 (1981), p. 524. Reprinted with permission.

Numerical Scales

In a **numerical scale**, numbers, rather than semantic space or verbal descriptions, serve as the response options to identify categories (response positions). For example, if scale items have five response positions, the scale is called a five-point numerical scale. A six-point scale has six positions and a seven-point scale seven positions, and so on. Consider the following numerical scale:

> *Now that you've had your automobile for about one year, please tell us how*
> *satisfied you are with your Ford Taurus.*
> *Extremely Dissatisfied   1   2   3   4   5   6   7   Extremely Satisfied*

This numerical scale uses bipolar adjectives in the same manner as the semantic differential.

In practice, researchers have found that a scale with numerical labels for intermediate points on the scale is as effective a measure as the true semantic differential.

Numerical scale
An attitude rating scale similar to a semantic differential except that it uses numbers, instead of verbal descriptions, as response options to identify response positions.

Stapel Scale

The **Stapel scale** was originally developed in the 1950s to measure simultaneously the direction and intensity of an attitude. Modern versions of the scale, with a single adjective, are used as a substitute for the semantic differential when it is difficult to create pairs of bipolar adjectives. The modified Stapel scale places a single adjective in the center of an even number of numerical values (ranging, perhaps, from +3 to −3). The scale measures how close to or distant from the adjective a given stimulus is perceived to be. Exhibit 14.5 illustrates a Stapel scale item used in measurement of a retailer's store image.

The advantages and disadvantages of the Stapel scale are very similar to those of the semantic differential. However, the Stapel scale is markedly easier to administer, especially over the telephone. Because the Stapel scale does not require bipolar adjectives, it is easier to construct than the semantic differential. Research comparing the semantic differential with the Stapel scale indicates that results from the two techniques are largely the same.[6]

Stapel scale
A measure of attitudes that consists of a single adjective in the center of an even number of numerical values.

Constant-Sum Scale

With a **constant-sum scale**, respondents are asked to divide a fixed number of points among several attributes to indicate their relative importance. Suppose United Parcel Service (UPS) wishes to determine the importance of the attributes of accurate invoicing, delivery as promised, and price to

Constant-sum scale
A measure of attitudes in which respondents are asked to divide a constant sum to indicate the relative importance of attributes; respondents often sort cards, but the task may also be a rating task.

EXHIBIT 14.5

A Stapel Scale for Measuring a Store's Image

Bloomingdale's

+3
+2
+1

Wide Selection

−1
−2
−3

Select a *plus* number for words that you think describe the store accurately. The more accurately you think the word describes the store, the larger the plus number you should choose. Select a *minus* number for words you think do not describe the store accurately. The less accurately you think the word describes the store, the larger the minus number you should choose. Therefore, you can select any number from +3 for words that you think are very accurate all the way to −3 for words that you think are very inaccurate.

Source: Dennis Menezes and Norbert F. Elbert, "Alternative Semantic Scaling Formats for Measuring Store Image: An Evaluation," Journal of Marketing Research, February 1979, pp. 80–87. Reprinted by permission of the American Marketing Association.

RESEARCHSNAPSHOT

A Measuring Stick for Website Usability

Two technology experts looking for a standard way to measure websites' usability developed metrics emphasizing attitudes. Rather than, say, measuring how long it took users to accomplish a particular task, they asked users to rate their experiences using each site. Each rater evaluated the site's content (information and transactions), ease of use, promotion (advertising on the site), "made for the medium" (features that make the site fit the user's particular needs), and emotions (sense of accomplishment, interest in the site's content, credibility, and control over the flow of content).

Of course, what is very important on one site may be minor on another. A prospective investor looking for information about an airline would likely seek a different online experience than a consumer visiting the same site to plan a vacation, and they both would have still different expectations for an online bookstore. As a result, the usability assessment begins by asking respondents to rate each category being evaluated in terms of how important it is for a particular kind of company, assuming the rater is either a consumer or an investor. For example, a user might rate an airline website's content, ease of use, and so on for a consumer. These ratings use a 100-point constant-sum scale.

Each rater divides 100 points among the five categories. The rater then evaluates, on a scale of 1 to 10, how well the site performs in each category. The importance ratings weight those scores. So, if a rater assigns 5 points to the emotion category and thinks the site performs at a 6 on the 1-to-10 scale, the weighted score is 30. By combining all the ratings for a website, a site can earn between 0 and 1,000 points. In the researchers' test of this rating system, it delivered helpful insights.

Source: Based on Ritu Agarwal and Viswanath Venkatesh, "Assessing a Firm's Web Presence: A Heuristic Evaluation Procedure for the Measurement of Usability," Information Systems Research, June 2002, downloaded from Business & Company Resource Center at http://galenet.galegroup.com; and G.A. Buchholz, "Losability vs. Usability," Digital Web, http://www.digital-web.com, July 11, 2005,

organizations that use its service in business–to-business marketing. Respondents might be asked to divide a constant sum of 100 points to indicate the relative importance of those attributes:

Divide 100 points among the following characteristics of a delivery service according to how important each characteristic is to you when selecting a delivery company.
Accurate invoicing _____
Delivery as promised _____
Lower price _____

The constant-sum scale works best with respondents who have high educational levels. If respondents follow the instructions correctly, the results will approximate interval measures. As the number of stimuli increases, this technique becomes increasingly complex.

This technique may be used for measuring brand preference. The approach, which is similar to the paired-comparison method, is as follows:

Divide 100 points among the following brands according to your preference for each brand:
Brand A _____
Brand B _____
Brand C _____

In this case, the constant-sum scale is a rating technique. However, with minor modifications, it can be classified as a sorting technique. Although the constant sum scale is widely used, strictly speaking, the scale is flawed because the last response is completely determined by the way the respondent has scored the other choices. Although this is probably somewhat complex to understand, the fact is that practical reasons often outweigh this concern.

Graphic Rating Scales

Graphic rating scale
A measure of attitude that allows respondents to rate an object by choosing any point along a graphic continuum.

A **graphic rating scale** presents respondents with a graphic continuum. The respondents are allowed to choose any point on the continuum to indicate their attitude. Exhibit 14.6 shows a traditional graphic scale, ranging from one extreme position to the opposite position. Typically a

EXHIBIT 14.6
Graphic Rating Scale

Please evaluate each attribute in terms of how important it is to you by placing an X at the position on the horizontal line that most reflects your feelings.

Seating comfort   Not important _____ Very important

In-flight meals   Not important _____ Very important

Airfare   Not important _____ Very important

respondent's score is determined by measuring the length (in millimeters) from one end of the graphic continuum to the point marked by the respondent. Many researchers believe that scoring in this manner strengthens the assumption that graphic rating scales of this type are interval scales. Alternatively, the researcher may divide the line into predetermined scoring categories (lengths) and record respondents' marks accordingly. In other words, the graphic rating scale has the advantage of allowing the researcher to choose any interval desired for scoring purposes. The disadvantage of the graphic rating scale is that there are no standard answers.

Graphic rating scales are not limited to straight lines as sources of visual communication. Picture response options or another type of graphic continuum may be used to enhance communication with respondents. A variation of the graphic ratings scale is the ladder scale. This scale also includes numerical options:

Here is a ladder scale [response scale is shown Exhibit 14.7]. It represents the "ladder of life." As you see, it is a ladder with eleven rungs numbered 0 to 10. Let's suppose the top of the ladder represents the best possible life for you as you describe it, and the bottom rung represents the worst possible life for you as you describe it.

On which rung of the ladder do you feel your life is today?

0   1   2   3   4   5   6   7   8   9   10

Research to investigate children's attitudes has used happy-face scales (see Exhibit 14.8). The children are asked to indicate which face shows how they feel about candy, a toy, or some other concept. Research with the happy-face scale indicates that children tend to choose the faces at the

EXHIBIT 14.7
A Ladder Scale

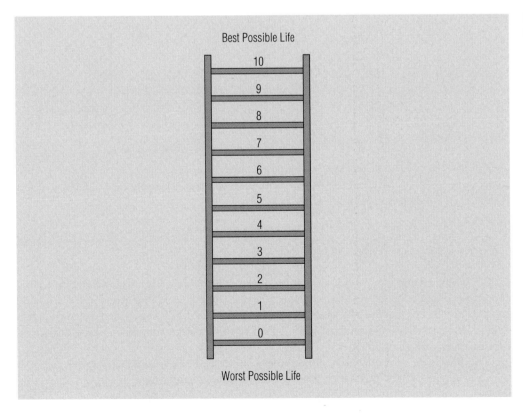

Best Possible Life

10
9
8
7
6
5
4
3
2
1
0

Worst Possible Life

RESEARCHSNAPSHOT

How Much Is a Healthy Home Worth?

Homebuilders need to know what consumers like, but before they invest in a lot of expensive features, they should know what consumers will pay for. If consumers' budgets require some hard choices, the homebuilder needs to know which features are extremely valued, which are nice but not important, and which are difficult to trade off because they are so close in buyer's minds. When a group of researchers at the University of British Columbia wanted to measure attitudes toward features of "healthy houses," they

compared the scores with a Thurstone scale.

A *healthy house* refers to one built with materials and a design affording superior indoor air quality, lighting, and acoustics. The researchers mailed a survey asking respondents whether they would be willing to pay extra if the

builder could guarantee better indoor air quality, lighting systems, and acoustics. The survey also presented nine attributes associated with superior indoor air quality and energy efficiency. These were presented in every combination of pairs, and the respondents were directed to choose which item in each pair they considered more important. Responses to the paired-comparison questions generated a ranking, which the researchers used to create a Thurstone scale. The highest-ranked attribute (energy efficiency) appears at the top of the scale, with the next attribute (natural light) significantly below it. Thicker insulation, anti-allergic materials, and airtightness are grouped close together below natural light, and artificial light falls noticeably below the other features.

Source: Wellington Spetic, Robert Kozak, and David Cohen, "Willingness to Pay and Preferences for Healthy Home Attributes in Canada," Forest Products Journal, 55 (October), 19–24; and Bower, John (1999), Healthy House Building for the New Millennium, Healthy House Institute.

EXHIBIT 14.8

Graphic Rating Scale with Picture Response Categories Stressing Visual Communication

ends of the scale. Although this may be because children's attitudes fluctuate more widely than adults' or because they have stronger feelings both positively and negatively, the tendency to select the extremes is a disadvantage of the scale.

Thurstone Interval Scale

Thurstone scale
An attitude scale in which judges assign scale values to attitudinal statements and subjects are asked to respond to these statements.

In 1927 attitude research pioneer Louis Thurstone developed the concept that attitudes vary along continua and should be measured accordingly. The construction of a **Thurstone scale** is a fairly complex process that requires two stages. The first stage is a ranking operation, performed by judges who assign scale values to attitudinal statements. The second stage consists of asking subjects to respond to the attitudinal statements.

The Thurstone method is time-consuming and costly. From a historical perspective, it is valuable, but its current popularity is low. This method is rarely used in applied marketing research.

EXHIBIT 14.9 **Summary of Advantages and Disadvantages of Rating Scales**

Rating Measure	Subject Must	Advantages	Disadvantages
Category scale	Indicate a response category	Flexible, easy to respond to	Items may be ambiguous; with few categories, only gross distinctions can be made
Likert scale	Evaluate statements on a scale of agreement	Easiest scale to construct	Hard to judge what a single score means
Semantic differential and numerical scales	Choose points between bipolar adjectives on relevant dimensions	Easy to construct; norms exist for comparison, such as profile analysis	Bipolar adjectives must be found; data may be ordinal, not interval
Stapel scale	Choose points on a scale with a single adjective in the center	Easier to construct than semantic differential, easy to administer	Endpoints are numerical, not verbal, labels
Constant-sum scale	Divide a constant sum among response alternatives	Approximates an interval measure	Difficult for respondents with low education levels
Graphic scale	Choose a point on a continuum	Visual impact, unlimited scale points	No standard answers
Graphic scale with picture response categories	Choose a visual picture	Visual impact, easy for poor readers	Hard to attach a verbal explanation to a response

Exhibit 14.9 summarizes the attitude-rating techniques discussed in this section.

Measuring Behavioral Intention

The behavioral component of an attitude involves the behavioral expectations of an individual toward an attitudinal object. Typically, the component of interest to marketers is a buying intention, a tendency to seek additional information, or plans to visit a showroom. Category scales for measuring the behavioral component of an attitude ask about a respondent's likelihood of purchase or intention to perform some future action, using questions such as the following:

How likely is it that you will purchase an mp3 player?

- *I definitely will buy*
- *I probably will buy*
- *I might buy*
- *I probably will not buy*
- *I definitely will not buy*

I would write a letter to my representative in Congress or other government official in support of this company if it were in a dispute with government.

- *Extremely Likely*
- *Very Likely*
- *Somewhat Likely*
- *Likely, about a 50–50 chance*
- *Somewhat Unlikely*
- *Very Unlikely*
- *Absolutely Unlikely*

The wording of statements used in these scales often includes phrases such as "I would recommend," "I would write," or "I would buy" to indicate action tendencies.

Expectations also may be measured using a scale of subjective probabilities, ranging from 100 for "absolutely certain" to 0 for "absolutely no chance." Researchers have used the following subjective probability scale to estimate the chance that a job candidate will accept a sales position:

_____	100%	(Absolutely certain) I will accept
_____	90%	(Almost sure) I will accept
_____	80%	(Very big chance) I will accept
_____	70%	(Big chance) I will accept
_____	60%	(Not so big a chance) I will accept
_____	50%	(About even) I will accept
_____	40%	(Smaller chance) I will accept
_____	30%	(Small chance) I will accept
_____	20%	(Very small chance) I will accept
_____	10%	(Almost certainly not) I will accept
_____	0%	(Certainly not) I will accept

Behavioral Differential

Behavioral differential
A rating scale instrument similar to a semantic differential, developed to measure the behavioral intentions of subjects toward future actions.

A general instrument, the **behavioral differential**, is used to measure the behavioral intentions of subjects toward an object or category of objects. As in the semantic differential, a description of the object to be judged is followed by a series of scales on which subjects indicate their behavioral intentions toward this object. For example, one item might be something like this:

A 25-year-old female sales representative

Would __ __ __ __ __ __ __ __ __ Would not

Ask this person for advice.

Ranking

TOTHEPOINT

My tastes are very simple. I only want the best.

—Oscar Wilde

Consumers often *rank order* their preferences. An ordinal scale may be developed by asking respondents to rank order (from most preferred to least preferred) a set of objects or attributes. Respondents easily understand the task of rank ordering the importance of product attributes or arranging a set of brand names according to preference. Like the constant sum scale, technically the ranking scale also suffers from inflexibility in that if we know how some ranked five out of six alternatives, we know the answer to the sixth.

Paired Comparisons

Paired comparison
A measurement technique that involves presenting the respondent with two objects and asking the respondent to pick the preferred object; more than two objects may be presented, but comparisons are made in pairs.

Consider a situation in which a chainsaw manufacturer learned that a competitor had introduced a new lightweight (6-pound) chain saw. The manufacturer's lightest chain saw weighed 9 pounds. Executives wondered if they needed to introduce a 6-pound chain saw into the product line. The research design chosen was a **paired comparison**. A 6-pound chain saw was designed, and a prototype built. To control for color preferences, the competitor's chain saw was painted the same color as the 9- and 6-pound chain saws. Respondents were presented with two chain saws at a time and asked to pick the one they preferred. Three pairs of comparisons were required to determine the most preferred chain saw.

The following question illustrates the typical format for asking about paired comparisons.

I would like to know your overall opinion of two brands of adhesive bandages. They are Curad and Band-Aid. Overall, which of these two brands—Curad or Band-Aid—do you think is the better one? Or are both the same?

Curad is better   _____
Band-Aid is better   _____
They are the same   _____

If researchers wish to compare four brands of pens on the basis of attractiveness or writing quality, six comparisons $[(n)(n - 1)/2]$ will be necessary.

When comparing only a few items, such as products or advertisements, ranking objects with respect to one attribute is not difficult. As the number of items increases, the number of comparisons increases geometrically. If the number of comparisons is too large, respondents may become fatigued and no longer carefully discriminate among them.

Sorting

Sorting tasks requires that respondents indicate their attitudes or beliefs by arranging items on the basis of perceived similarity or some other attribute. One advertising agency has had consumers sort photographs of people to measure their perceptions of a brand's typical user. Another agency used a sorting technique in which consumers used a deck of fifty-two cards illustrating elements from advertising for the brand name being studied. The study participants created a stack of cards showing elements they recalled seeing or hearing, and the interviewer then asked the respondent to identify the item on each of those cards. National City Corporation, a banking company, has used sorting as part of its research into the design of its website. Consumers participating in the research were given a set of cards describing various parts of processes that they might engage in when they are banking online. The participants were asked to arrange the cards to show their idea of a logical way to complete these processes. This research method showed the website designers how consumers go about doing something—sometimes very differently from the way the bankers expected.[7]

A variant of the constant-sum technique uses physical counters (for example, poker chips or coins), to be divided among the items being tested. In an airline study of customer preferences, the following sorting technique could be used:

Here is a sheet that lists several airlines. Next to the name of each airline is a pocket. Here are ten cards. I would like you to put these cards in the pockets next to the airlines you would prefer to fly on your next trip. Assume that all of the airlines fly to wherever you would choose to travel. You can put as many cards as you want next to an airline, or you can put no cards next to an airline.

Cards

American Airlines	_____
Delta Airlines	_____
United Airlines	_____
Southwest Airlines	_____
Northwest Airlines	_____

Randomized Response Questions

In special cases, such as when respondents are being asked to provide sensitive or embarrassing information in a survey, the researcher may use **randomized response questions**. To understand this procedure, we can consider a portion of a questionnaire from an Internal Revenue Service survey on income tax cheating:

In this section you will be asked some questions about different things you might have done when filling out your tax return. A flip of a coin will determine which questions you are to answer. All that we will know is your answer of either "yes" or "no"; we will not know which question you are answering. I'll show you how it works in a minute, but the important thing to know is that your answers are completely anonymous. Using special kinds of statistics we will never know what you do. So, we hope you will be completely honest with us. Only in this way will this survey be of help to us.

For example, let's flip the coin. (HAVE EXAMPLE CARD READY.) Let's say it comes up heads. Then you will respond to the "heads" statement: "I had scrambled eggs for breakfast this morning." If you did have scrambled eggs, you would say "yes." If you did not have scrambled eggs, you would say "no." Now, the coin could come up tails and you would respond to the "tails" question: "I had potatoes for dinner last night." You would say "yes" if you did and "no" if you didn't.

Randomized response questions
A research procedure used for dealing with sensitive topics, in which a random procedure determines which of two questions a respondent will be asked to answer.

1. Heads *Sometime in the past, I have failed to file a tax return when I think I should have.*
   Tails *I have lived in this community for over five years.*
      Yes...1
      No...2

2. Heads *Sometime in the past, I purposely listed more deductions than I was entitled to.*
   Tails *I voted in the last presidential election.*
      Yes...1
      No...2

3. Heads *Sometime in the past, I purposely failed to report some income on my tax return—even just a minor amount.*
   Tails *I own a car.*
      Yes...1
      No...2

4. Heads *On at least one occasion, I have added a dependent that I wasn't entitled to.*
   Tails *I have been to a movie within the last year.*
      Yes...1
      No...2

5. Heads *To the best of my knowledge, my tax return for [year] was filled out with absolute honesty.*
   Tails *I have eaten out in a restaurant within the last 6 months.*
      Yes...1
      No...2

6. Heads *I stretched the truth just a little in order to pay fewer taxes for [year].*
   Tails *Generally, I watch one hour or more of television each day.*
      Yes...1
      No...2

This Is the End of the Interview.
Thank You Very Much for Your Cooperation.

The coin flipping randomly determines which of the two questions the respondent answers. Thus, the interviewer does not know whether the sensitive question about income tax cheating or the meaningless question is being answered, because the responses ("yes" or "no") are identical for both questions.

The proportion of "yes" answers to the income tax question is calculated by a formula that includes previous estimates of the proportion of respondents who answer "yes" to the meaningless question and the probability (*Pr*) that the meaningless question is being answered:

$$Pr(\text{"yes" answer}) = Pr(\text{"yes" on question A}) + Pr(\text{"yes" on question B})$$
$$= Pr(\text{question A is chosen}) \times Pr(\text{"yes" on question A})$$
$$+ Pr(\text{question B is chosen}) \times Pr(\text{"yes" on question B})$$

Although estimates are subject to error, the respondent remains anonymous, and response bias is thereby reduced.

The randomized response method originally was applied in personal interview surveys. However, randomized response questions in a slightly modified format have been successfully applied in other situations.

Other Methods of Attitude Measurement

Attitudes, as hypothetical constructs, cannot be observed directly. We can, however, infer one's attitude by the way he or she responds to multiple attitude indicators. A summated rating scale can be made up of three indicators of attitude. Consider the following three semantic differential items that may capture a consumer's attitude toward Microsoft Word:

very good ___ ___ ___ ___ ___ ___ ___ *very bad*
very unfavorable ___ ___ ___ ___ ___ ___ ___ *very favorable*
very positive ___ ___ ___ ___ ___ ___ ___ *very negative*

The terminology is such that now attitude would be represented as a latent (unobservable) construct indicated by a consumer's response to these items. How do you feel about Microsoft Word?

Selecting a Measurement Scale: Some Practical Decisions

Now that we have looked at a number of attitude measurement scales, a natural question arises: "Which is most appropriate?" As in the selection of a basic research design, there is no single best answer for all research projects. The answer to this question is relative, and the choice of scale will depend on the nature of the attitudinal object to be measured, the manager's problem definition, and the backward and forward linkages to choices already made (for example, telephone survey versus mail survey). However, several questions will help focus the choice of a measurement scale:

1. Is a ranking, sorting, rating, or choice technique best?
2. Should a monadic or a comparative scale be used?
3. What type of category labels, if any, will be used for the rating scale?
4. How many scale categories or response positions are needed to accurately measure an attitude?
5. Should a balanced or unbalanced rating scale be chosen?
6. Should a scale that forces a choice among predetermined options be used?
7. Should a single measure or an index measure be used?

We will discuss each of these issues.

Ranking, Sorting, Rating, or Choice Technique?

The decision whether to use ranking, sorting, rating, or a choice technique is determined largely by the problem definition and especially by the type of statistical analysis desired. For example, ranking provides only ordinal data, limiting the statistical techniques that may be used.

Monadic or Comparative Scale?

If the scale to be used is not a ratio scale, the researcher must decide whether to include a standard of comparison in the verbal portion of the scale. Consider the following rating scale:

Now that you've had your automobile for about one year, please tell us how satisfied you are with its engine power and pickup.

Completely Dissatisfied	Dissatisfied	Somewhat Satisfied	Satisfied	Completely Satisfied
☐	☐	☐	☐	☐

This is a **monadic rating scale**, because it asks about a single concept (the brand of automobile the individual actually purchased) in isolation. The respondent is not given a specific frame of reference. A **comparative rating scale** asks a respondent to rate a concept, such as a specific brand, in comparison with a benchmark—perhaps another similar concept, such as a competing brand—explicitly used as a frame of reference. In many cases, the comparative rating scale presents an ideal situation as a reference point for comparison with the actual situation. For example:

Please indicate how the amount of authority in your present position compares with the amount of authority that would be ideal for this position.

Too much ☐   About right ☐   Too little ☐

Monadic rating scale
Any measure of attitudes that asks respondents about a single concept in isolation.

Comparative rating scale
Any measure of attitudes that asks respondents to rate a concept in comparison with a benchmark explicitly used as a frame of reference.

RESEARCHSNAPSHOT

Skip the Pâté, We're Ordering Thai Food

To get an idea of worldwide attitudes toward foods of different cultures, *The Wall Street Journal* worked with GfK Custom Research Worldwide to conduct a survey that boiled down what might have been complex opinions into a few simple choices. The research firm interviewed more than twenty thousand people in the United States, Russia, Turkey, and seventeen European countries. The first question asked for a single rating: "National cuisines (typical dishes of a country) around the world are often thought to have different characteristics and are appreciated for different reasons. In your opinion, which is the most fatten-

ing?" Then the researcher asked, "Which is the least fattening in your opinion?" and "Which is the most overrated cuisine (in other words, does-n't live up to its reputation)?"

These questions were meant to generate ideas; they were hardly specific enough to pinpoint a new product idea or

solve global food debates. In this context, the researchers asked for a simple rating (most fattening, least fattening, most overrated), rather than challenging respondents to rank or sort a variety of cuisines. In addition, the survey did not force a choice. Many respondents indicated only that it was "difficult to say."

As simple as the survey was, it did generate at least one surprising result: By a noteworthy margin, the cuisine identified as "most overrated" was the prestigious cuisine of France. The overall response rate was 39 percent choosing French, and even 22 percent of the French respondents selected their own cuisine for this dubious honor. Could the reason be that French cuisine is so expensive or has such a strong reputation to live up to? Unfortunately, the simple measurement scale does not provide an explanation.

Source: Based on Jennifer Howze, "Survey: French Food Flambéed," The Wall Street Journal, January 6, 2006, http://online.wsj.com; and "Cuisine Survey," The Wall Street Journal, http://online.wsj.com , accessed January 6, 2006.

What Type of Category Labels, If Any?

We have discussed verbal labels, numerical labels, and unlisted choices. Many rating scales have verbal labels for response categories because researchers believe they help respondents better understand the response positions. The maturity and educational levels of the respondents will influence this decision. The semantic differential, with unlabeled response categories between two bipolar adjectives, and the numerical scale, with numbers to indicate scale positions, often are selected because the researcher wishes to assume interval-scale data.

How Many Scale Categories or Response Positions?

Should a category scale have four, five, or seven response positions or categories? Or should the researcher use a graphic scale with an infinite number of positions? The original developmental research on the semantic differential indicated that five to eight points is optimal. However, the researcher must determine the number of meaningful positions that is best for the specific project. This issue of identifying how many meaningful distinctions respondents can practically make is basically a matter of sensitivity, but at the operational rather than the conceptual level.

Balanced or Unbalanced Rating Scale?

Balanced rating scale
A fixed-alternative rating scale with an equal number of positive and negative categories; a neutral point or point of indifference is at the center of the scale.

The fixed-alternative format may be balanced or unbalanced. For example, the following question, which asks about parent-child decisions relating to television program watching, is a **balanced rating scale**:

Who decides which television programs your children watch?

Child decides all of the time. ☐

Child decides most of the time. ☐

Child and parent decide together.   ☐

Parent decides most of the time.   ☐

Parent decides all of the time.   ☐

This scale is balanced because a neutral point, or point of indifference, is at the center of the scale.

Unbalanced rating scales may be used when responses are expected to be distributed at one end of the scale. Unbalanced scales, such as the following one, may eliminate this type of "end piling":

Completely Dissatisfied	*Dissatisfied*	*Somewhat Satisfied*	*Satisfied*	*Completely Satisfied*
☐	☐	☐	☐	☐

Notice that there are three "satisfied" responses and only two "dissatisfied" responses above. The choice of a balanced or unbalanced scale generally depends on the nature of the concept or the researcher's knowledge about attitudes toward the stimulus to be measured.

Use a Scale That Forces a Choice among Predetermined Options?

In many situations, a respondent has not formed an attitude toward the concept being studied and simply cannot provide an answer. If a **forced-choice rating scale** compels the respondent to answer, the response is merely a function of the question. If answers are not forced, the midpoint of the scale may be used by the respondent to indicate unawareness as well as indifference. If many respondents in the sample are expected to be unaware of the attitudinal object under investigation, this problem may be eliminated by using a **non-forced-choice scale** that provides a "no opinion" category, as in the following example:

How does the Bank of Commerce company compare with the First National Bank?

☐ *Bank of Commerce is better than First National Bank.*

☐ *Bank of Commerce is about the same as First National Bank.*

☐ *Bank of Commerce is worse than First National Bank.*

☐ *Can't say.*

Asking this type of question allows the investigator to separate respondents who cannot make an honest comparison from respondents who have had experience with both banks. The argument for forced choice is that people really do have attitudes, even if they are unfamiliar with the banks, and should be required to answer the question. Still, the use of forced-choice questions is associated with higher incidences of "no answer." Internet surveys make forced-choice questions easy to implement because the delivery can be set up so that a respondent cannot go to the next question until the previoius question is answered. Realize, however, if a respondent truly has no opinion, and the no opinion option is not included, he or she may simply quit responding to the questionnaire.

Single Measure or an Index Measure?

Whether to use a single measure or an index measure depends on the complexity of the issue to be investigated, the number of dimensions the issue contains, and whether individual attributes of the stimulus are part of a holistic attitude or are seen as separate items. The researcher's conceptual definition will be helpful in making this choice.

The researcher has many scaling options. Generally, the choice is influenced by plans for the later stages of the research project. Again, problem definition becomes a determining factor influencing the research design.

Unbalanced rating scale
A fixed-alternative rating scale that has more response categories at one end than the other resulting in an unequal number of positive and negative categories.

Forced-choice rating scale
A fixed-alternative rating scale that requires respondents to choose one of the fixed alternatives.

Non-forced-choice scale
A fixed-alternative rating scale that provides a "no opinion" category or that allows respondents to indicate that they cannot say which alternative is their choice.

TOTHEPOINT

Refusing to have an opinion is a way of having one, isn't it?

—Luigi Pirandello

Summary

1. Describe how marketing researchers think of attitudes. Attitudes are enduring dispositions to consistently respond in a given manner to various aspects of the world, including persons, events, and objects. Attitudes consist of three components: the affective, or the emotions or feelings involved; the cognitive, or awareness or knowledge; and the behavioral, or the predisposition to action. Attitudes are latent constructs and because of this, they are not directly observable.

2. Identify basic approaches to measuring attitudes. Many methods for measuring attitudes have been developed for attitude measurement. Most fall into the categories of ranking, rating, sorting, and choice techniques.

3. Discuss the use of rating scales for measuring attitudes. One class of rating scales, category scales, provides several response categories to allow respondents to indicate the intensity of their attitudes. The Likert scale uses a series of statements with which subjects indicate agreement or disagreement. The levels of agreement with some statement are assigned numerical scores. A semantic differential uses a series of attitude scales anchored by bipolar adjectives. The respondent indicates where his or her attitude falls between the polar attitudes. Variations on this method, such as numerical scales and the Stapel scale, are also used. The Stapel scale puts a single adjective in the center of a range of numerical values from $+3$ to -3. Constant-sum scales require the respondent to divide a constant sum into parts, indicating the weights to be given to various attributes of the item being studied.

4. Represent a latent construct by constructing a summated scale. Researchers use composite scales to represent latent constructs. An easy way to create a composite scale is to add the responses to multiple items together to form a total. Thus, a respondent's scores to four items can be simply added together to form a summated scale. The researcher must check to make sure that each scale item is worded positively, or at least all in the same direction. For example, if multiple items are used to form a satisfaction construct, a higher score for each item should lead to higher satisfaction. If one of the items represents dissatisfaction, such that a higher score represents lower satisfaction, this item must be reverse recoded prior to creating the composite scale.

5. Summarize ways to measure attitudes with ranking and sorting techniques and randomized response questions. People often rank order their preferences. Thus, ordinal scales that ask respondents to rank order a set of objects or attributes may be developed. In the paired-comparison technique, two alternatives are paired and respondents are asked to pick the preferred one. Sorting requires respondents to indicate their attitudes by arranging items into piles or categories.

6. Discuss major issues involved in the selection of a measurement scale. The researcher can choose among a number of attitude scales. Choosing among the alternatives requires considering several questions, each of which is generally answered by comparing the advantages of each alternative to the problem definition. A monadic rating scale asks about a single concept. A comparative rating scale asks a respondent to rate a concept in comparison with a benchmark used as a frame of reference. Scales may be balanced or unbalanced. Unbalanced scales may prevent responses from piling up at one end. Forced-choice scales require the respondent to select an alternative; non-forced-choice scales allow the respondent to indicate an inability to select an alternative.

Key Terms and Concepts

Attitude	Composite scale	Paired comparison
Hypothetical constructs	Semantic differential	Randomized response questions
Ranking	Image profile	Monadic rating scale
Rating	Numerical scale	Comparative rating scale
Sorting	Stapel scale	Balanced rating scale
Choice	Constant-sum scale	Unbalanced rating scale
Category scale	Graphic rating scale	Forced-choice rating scale
Likert scale	Thurstone scale	Non-forced-choice scale
Reverse recoding	Behavioral differential	

Questions for Review and Critical Thinking

1. What is an *attitude*? Is there a consensus concerning its definition?
2. Distinguish between *rating* and *ranking*. Which is a better attitude measurement technique? Why?
3. Assume the researcher wanted to create a summated scale indicating a respondent's attitude toward the trucking industry. What would the result be for the respondent whose response is as indicated below?
4. How would you perform reverse recoding using statistical software like SAS or SPSS?
5. What advantages do numerical scales have over semantic differential scales?
6. Identify the issues a researcher should consider when choosing a measurement scale.
7. Name some situations in which a semantic differential might be useful.

	Strongly Disagree	Disagree	Somewhat Disagree	Somewhat Agree	Agree	Strongly Agree
6. I feel the trucking industry in Canada is very important to our economy.	☐	☐	☐	☒	☐	☐
7. Truck drivers go out of their way to help make the roads safer.	☐	☐	☐	☐	☒	☐
8. The trucking industry is harmful to Canadians in more ways than one.	☐	☒	☐	☐	☐	☐
9. Without the trucking industry, our communities would be much better off.	☐	☐	☒	☐	☐	☐
10. Truck drivers are among the most courteous drivers.	☐	☐	☐	☐	☐	☒

8. Should a Likert scale ever be treated as though it had ordinal properties?
9. In each of the following, identify the type of scale and evaluate it:
   a. A U.S. representative's questionnaire sent to constituents:

   Do you favor or oppose the Fair Tax Proposal?

In Favor	Opposed	No Opinion
☐	☐	☐

   b. How favorable are you toward the Fair Tax Proposal?

   Very Unfavorable ☐ ☐ ☐ ☐ ☐ ☐ *Very Favorable*

   c. A psychographic statement asking the respondent to circle the appropriate response:

   I shop a lot for specials.

Strongly Disagree	Disagree	Neutral	Agree	Strongly Agree
1	2	3	4	5

10. What is the difference between a measured variable and a latent construct?
11. If a Likert summated scale has ten scale items, do all ten items have to be phrased as either positive or negative statements, or can the scale contain a mix of positive and negative statements?
12. If a semantic differential has ten scale items, should all the positive adjectives be on the right and all the negative adjectives on the left?
13. **ETHICS** A researcher thinks many respondents will answer "don't know" or "can't say" if these options are printed on an attitude scale along with categories indicating level of agreement. The researcher does not print either "don't know" or "can't say" on the questionnaire because the resulting data would be more complicated to analyze and report. Is this proper?
14. **'NET** SRI International investigates U.S. consumers by asking questions about their attitudes and values. It has a website so people can VALS-type themselves. To find out your VALS type, go to http://www.sric-bi.com/VALS/presurvey.shtml.

Research Activities

1. A researcher wishes to compare two hotels on the following attributes:
   Convenience of location
   Friendly personnel
   Value for money

   a. Design a Likert scale to accomplish this task.
   b. Design a semantic differential scale to accomplish this task.
   c. Design a graphic rating scale to accomplish this task.

Case 14.1 Roeder-Johnson Corporation

A decade ago, the talk in business circles was all about the central role of technology, especially the Internet, in the success of new businesses. Some investors seemed eager to back almost any start-up with "dot-com" in its name or its business plan. Although the go-go investment climate of the 1990s seems far away, entrepreneurs still start companies every year, and they are still making their case to the investment community. What business ideas do investors like? Is high-tech still important? Public relations firm Roeder-Johnson Corporation, which specializes in start-up companies and those involved in technology innovation, conducted an online survey into the attitudes of seventy subjects, including venture capitalists, entrepreneurs, journalists, and company analysts.[8] The central question was this:

Do you believe that unique technology is crucial to the success of start-up companies today?

1. Rarely
2. Occasionally
3. Frequently
4. Usually
5. Always

The remainder of the survey asked for reasons why technology is important to start-ups and invited comments from the respondents.

In its news release, Roeder-Johnson reported that 91 percent of respondents consider technology to be important at least frequently. The breakdown was 39 percent frequently, 39 percent usually, and 13 percent always. The remaining 9 percent of respondents cited technology as important only occasionally, and none said it is rarely important.

Questions

1. Evaluate the rating scale used for the question in this survey. Is it balanced? Are the category labels clear? Is the number of categories appropriate?
2. Suggest three ways that Roeder-Johnson could improve this survey without a major cost increase.
3. Based on the information given here, what do you think the research objectives for this survey might have been? Do you think the survey met its objectives? Explain.

Case 14.2 Ha-Pah-Shu-Tse

Raymond RedCorn is an Osage Indian. The Ha-Pah-Shu-Tse (Osage for "red corn") restaurant in Pawhuska, Oklahoma, is the only authentic Native American restaurant in the state and one of few in the country.

The Ha-Pah-Shu-Tse restaurant opened in 1972 with a seating capacity of eight; today, after expansion, crowds of up to ninety keep RedCorn and his wife busy. They are currently marketing an Indian fry bread mix, and they are planning on increased sales for their only packaged good. Indian fry bread mix has long been a staple of the Native American diet. The bread is sweet and contains basic ingredients such as flour, shortening, and sugar.

The Restaurant

Waltina RedCorn married into the Osage tribe forty-seven years ago and learned how to cook from two women named Grandma Baconrind and Grandma Lookout. They must have taught her well, because customers of the Ha-Pah-Shu-Tse are not content just to eat there—they often have the RedCorns mail them fry bread mix. Raymond RedCorn finds that people who eat the unusual native dish usually request the recipe. He says, "I have not found anyone who does not like the bread." Customers aren't limited to local fans of Indian food. Because the fry bread is sold or served in restaurants and stores in Oklahoma as well as at a museum, people from as far away as Europe have tried it.

According to RedCorn, "About once a week, someone from England comes in." He serves these British customers fry bread or the restaurant's "best-sellers," Indian Meat Pie or Navaho Taco, and tells them the story of fry bread and how it got him an invitation to Buckingham Palace. When he was eighteen years old, he was in London for a Boy Scout Jamboree. One evening he was frying the Indian bread when the British Boy Scout organizer approached with two young men. It was only after everyone had tasted RedCorn's culinary effort that the Prince of Wales was introduced. "The Indian delegation from Oklahoma was invited to set up their tents on the ground at the palace and spend the weekend being entertained by the young royalty," RedCorn says.

The Product

The product as it is today took several years to perfect. The Red-Corns wanted a mix that would need only the addition of water. Each batch was sent to relatives and friends for judgment on the taste until everyone was convinced it was the best it could be.

The mix, consisting of Indian flour, is already distributed in Tulsa, Bartlesville, and surrounding towns under the Ha-Pah-Shu-Tse brand name. It is packaged in 2- and 5-pound silver bags with Raymond RedCorn in Osage tribal costume pictured on the front. Directions for making the fry bread are listed on the back of the package.

The Research Problem

When planning the marketing for the Indian fry bread mix, student consultants working with the Small Business Administration suggested some attitude research. They felt that successfully marketing the Ha-Pah-Shu-Tse product depended on knowing what consumer reactions to Indian foods would be. They believed that if the image of Indian foods and consumers' awareness of them were measured, RedCorn would have a better chance of marketing his product. In addition, the student consultants felt that the name Ha-Pah-Shu-Tse violated many of the requirements for a good brand name—it was not short, simple, or easy to recall, and was difficult to pronounce and spell.

Questions

1. What marketing questions must be answered as Ha-Pah-Shu-Tse plans for expansion? How can marketing research help answer those questions?
2. What type of attitude scale would you recommend? How would you generate a set of items (attributes) to be measured?
3. Does an image profile seem appropriate in this case?

Case 14.3 Attitudes toward Technology and Lifestyle

A marketing research company sent the attitude scales in Case Exhibit 14.3–1 to members of its consumer panel. Other questions on the questionnaire were about ownership and/or use of computers, consumer electronic devices, satellite TV ownership, cellular phones, and Internet activity.

Questions

1. What type of attitude scale appears in the case study?
2. Evaluate the list of statements. Do the statements appear to measure a single concept?
3. What do they appear to be measuring?

EXHIBIT 14.3-1 **Attitude Scale**

Below is a list of statements that may or may not be used to describe your attitudes toward technology and your lifestyle. Please indicate to what extent each statement describes your attitudes by placing an X in a box from 1 to 10, where 10 means that statement "Describes your attitudes completely" and a 1 means that statement "Does not describe your attitudes at all." (X ONE BOX ACROSS FOR EACH STATEMENT.)

	Does Not Describe Your Attitudes At All								Describes Your Attitudes Completely	
	1	2	3	4	5	6	7	8	9	10
I like to impress people with my lifestyle.	☐	☐	☐	☐	☐	☐	☐	☐	☐	☐
Technology is important to me.	☐	☐	☐	☐	☐	☐	☐	☐	☐	☐
I am very competitive when it comes to my career.	☐	☐	☐	☐	☐	☐	☐	☐	☐	☐
Having fun is the whole point of life.	☐	☐	☐	☐	☐	☐	☐	☐	☐	☐
Family is important, but I have other interests that are just as important to me.	☐	☐	☐	☐	☐	☐	☐	☐	☐	☐
I am constantly looking for new ways to entertain myself.	☐	☐	☐	☐	☐	☐	☐	☐	☐	☐
Making a lot of money is important to me.	☐	☐	☐	☐	☐	☐	☐	☐	☐	☐
I spend most of my free time doing fun stuff with my friends.	☐	☐	☐	☐	☐	☐	☐	☐	☐	☐
I like to spend time learning about new technology products.	☐	☐	☐	☐	☐	☐	☐	☐	☐	☐
I like to show off my taste and style.	☐	☐	☐	☐	☐	☐	☐	☐	☐	☐
I like technology.	☐	☐	☐	☐	☐	☐	☐	☐	☐	☐
My family is by far the most important thing in my life.	☐	☐	☐	☐	☐	☐	☐	☐	☐	☐
I put a lot of time and energy into my career.	☐	☐	☐	☐	☐	☐	☐	☐	☐	☐
I am very likely to purchase new technology products or services.	☐	☐	☐	☐	☐	☐	☐	☐	☐	☐
I spend most of my free time working on improving myself.	☐	☐	☐	☐	☐	☐	☐	☐	☐	☐

CHAPTER 15
QUESTIONNAIRE DESIGN

After studying this chapter, you should be able to

1. Explain the significance of decisions about questionnaire design and wording
2. Define alternatives for wording open-ended and fixed-alternative questions
3. Summarize guidelines for questions that avoid mistakes in questionnaire design
4. Describe how the proper sequence of questions may improve a questionnaire
5. Discuss how to design a questionnaire layout
6. Describe criteria for pretesting and revising a questionnaire and for adapting it to global markets

Chapter Vignette: J.D. Power Asks Consumers to Get Real

Are you driving your dream car? Most of us can't, because we bump up against the practical reality that we can't pay for every great new feature. As car makers consider adding new features, they have to evaluate not only which ones appeal to consumers but also which ones will actually sell, considering their likely cost. J.D. Power and Associates recently addressed this issue in a survey of about seventeen thousand consumers.[1]

In the J.D. Power survey, consumers were asked whether they were familiar with twenty-two different emerging technologies. Then they were asked about their interest in each technology, rating their interest using a scale ("definitely interested," "probably interested," and so on). Next, the study indicated the likely price of each technology, and consumers were asked their interest, given the price. The results ranked the features according to interest level, based on the percentage who indicated they were either definitely or probably interested in the feature.

Learning price information often changed consumers' interest levels. Night vision systems appealed to 72 percent of consumers, placing it in second place in the rankings. But when consumers learned the systems would likely add $1,500 to the price of a car, this technology dropped to a rank of 17, near the bottom. In contrast, HD radio ranked in sixteenth place until consumers saw a price tag of just $150. That price pushed the feature up to third place. Still, two features remained in the top five even with pricing information: run-flat tires and stability control. And three of the bottom-five features—a reconfigurable cabin, lane departure warning system, and smart sensing power-swing front doors—stayed in the bottom rankings. Automakers can use findings such as these to determine which features are price-sensitive and which might be appealing even at a higher price.

In the J.D. Power survey, answers changed when respondents were given more information. This chapter outlines a procedure for questionnaire design, which addresses concerns such as the wording and order of questions and the layout of the questionnaire.

©ROYALTY FREE/CORBIS

Questionnaire Quality and Design: Basic Considerations

Each stage in the interdependent marketing research process is important. Yet a marketing research survey is only as good as the questions it asks. The importance of question wording is easily overlooked, but questionnaire design is one of the most critical stages in the survey research process.

Businesspeople who are inexperienced at marketing research frequently believe that constructing a questionnaire is a simple task. Amateur researchers think a short questionnaire can be written in minutes. Unfortunately, newcomers who naively believe that good grammar is all a person needs to construct a questionnaire generally end up with useless results. Ask a bad question, get bad results.

Good questionnaire design requires far more than correct grammar. People don't understand questions just because they are grammatically correct. Respondents simply may not know what is being asked. They may be unaware of the product or topic of interest. They may confuse the subject with something else. The question may not mean the same thing to everyone interviewed. Finally, people may refuse to answer personal questions. Most of these problems can be minimized, however, if a skilled researcher composes the questionnaire.

For a questionnaire to fulfill a researcher's purposes, the questions must meet the basic criteria of *relevance* and *accuracy*. To achieve these ends, a researcher who is systematically planning a questionnaire's design will be required to make several decisions—typically, but not necessarily, in the following order:

1. What should be asked?
2. How should questions be phrased?
3. In what sequence should the questions be arranged?
4. What questionnaire layout will best serve the research objectives?
5. How should the questionnaire be pretested? Does the questionnaire need to be revised?

This chapter provides guidelines for answering each question.

TOTHEPOINT

How often misused words generate misleading thoughts.

—Herbert Spencer

What Should Be Asked?

Certain decisions made during the early stages of the research process will influence the questionnaire design. The preceding chapters stressed good problem definition and clear research questions. This leads to specific research hypotheses that in turn, clearly indicate what must be measured. Different types of questions may be better at measuring certain things than are others. In addition, the communication medium used for data collection—that is, telephone interview, personal interview, or self-administered questionnaire—must be determined. This decision is another forward linkage that influences the structure and content of the questionnaire. The specific questions to be asked will be a function of the previous decisions.

The latter stages of the research process will have an important impact on questionnaire wording. The questions that should be asked will, of course, take the form of data analysis into account. When designing the questionnaire, the researcher should consider the types of statistical analysis that will be conducted.

Questionnaire Relevancy

A questionnaire is *relevant* to the extent that all information collected addresses a research question that will help the decision maker address the current marketing problem. Asking a wrong question or an irrelevant question is a common pitfall. If the marketing task is to pinpoint store image problems, questions asking for political opinions may be irrelevant. The researcher should be specific about data needs and have a rationale for each item requesting information. Irrelevant questions are more than a nuisance because they make the survey needlessly long. In a study where two samples of the same group of businesses received either a one-page or a three-page questionnaire, the response rate was nearly twice as high for the one-page survey.[2]

Conversely, many researchers, after conducting surveys, find that they omitted some important questions. Therefore, when planning the questionnaire design, researchers must think about possible omissions. Is information on the relevant demographic and psychographic variables being collected? Would certain questions help clarify the answers to other questions? Will the results of the study provide the answer to the marketing manager's problem?

Questionnaire Accuracy

Once a researcher decides what should be asked, the criterion of accuracy becomes the primary concern. *Accuracy* means that the information is reliable and valid. While experienced researchers generally believe that questionnaires should use simple, understandable, unbiased, unambiguous, and nonirritating words, no step-by-step procedure for ensuring accuracy in question writing can be generalized across projects. Obtaining accurate answers from respondents depends strongly on the researcher's ability to design a questionnaire that will facilitate recall and motivate respondents to cooperate. Respondents tend to be more cooperative when the subject of the research interests them. When questions are not lengthy, difficult to answer, or ego threatening, there is a higher probability of obtaining unbiased answers.

Question wording and sequence also substantially influence accuracy, which can be particularly challenging when designing a survey for technical audiences. The Department of Treasury commissioned a survey of insurance companies to evaluate their offering of terrorism insurance as required by the government's terrorism reinsurance program. But industry members complained that the survey misused terms such as "contract" and "high risk," which have precise meanings for insurers, and asked for policy information "to date," without specifying which date. These questions caused confusion and left room for interpretation, calling the survey results into question.[3]

How Should Questions Be Phrased?

There are many ways to phrase questions, and many standard question formats have been developed in previous research studies. This section presents a classification of question types and provides some helpful guidelines for writing questions.

Open-Ended Response versus Fixed-Alternative Questions

Two basic types of questions can be identified based on the amount of freedom respondents have in answering. Thus, they call for responses that are either open-ended or closed (from a fixed set of choices).

Open-ended response questions pose some problem or topic and ask respondents to answer in their own words. If the question is asked in a personal interview, the interviewer may probe for more information, as in the following examples:

What names of local banks can you think of offhand?
What comes to mind when you look at this advertisement?
In what way, if any, could this product be changed or improved? I'd like you to tell me anything you can think of, no matter how minor it seems.
What things do you like most about Federal Express's service?
Why do you buy more of your clothing in Nordstrom than in other stores?
How can our stores better serve your needs?
Please tell me anything at all that you remember about the BMW commercial you saw last night.

Open-ended response questions are free-answer questions. They may be contrasted with **fixed-alternative questions**—sometimes called *closed questions*—which give respondents specific

Open-ended response questions
Questions that pose some problem and ask respondents to answer in their own words.

Fixed-alternative questions
Questions in which respondents are given specific, limited-alternative responses and asked to choose the one closest to their own viewpoint.

limited-alternative responses and ask them to choose the one closest to their own viewpoints. For example

Did you use any commercial feed or supplement for livestock or poultry in 2006?

- *Yes*
- *No*

As compared with ten years ago, would you say that the quality of most products made in Japan is higher, about the same, or not as good?

- *Higher*
- *About the same*
- *Not as good*

Do you think the Renewable Energy Partnership Program has affected your business?

- *Yes, for the better*
- *Yes, for the worse*
- *Not especially*

In which type of bookstore is it easier for you to shop—a regular bookstore or a bookstore on the Internet?

- *Regular bookstore*
- *Internet bookstore*

How much of your shopping for clothes and household items do you do in wholesale club stores?

- *All of it*
- *Most of it*
- *About one-half of it*
- *About one-quarter of it*
- *Less than one-quarter of it*

USING OPEN-ENDED RESPONSE QUESTIONS

Open-ended response questions are most beneficial when the researcher is conducting exploratory research, especially when the range of responses is not known. Such questions can be used to learn which words and phrases people spontaneously give to the free-response question. Respondents are free to answer with whatever is uppermost in their minds. By obtaining free and uninhibited responses, the researcher may find some unanticipated reaction toward the product. Such responses will reflect the flavor of the language that people use in talking about goods or services and thus may provide a source of new ideas for advertising copywriting. Also, open-ended response questions are valuable at the beginning of an interview. They are good first questions because they allow respondents to warm up to the questioning process.

The cost of administering open-ended response questions is substantially higher than that of administering fixed-alternative questions because the job of editing, coding, and analyzing the data is quite extensive. As each respondent's answer is somewhat unique, there is some difficulty in categorizing and summarizing the answers. The process requires that an editor go over a sample of questions to develop a classification scheme. This scheme is then used to code all answers according to the classification scheme.

Another potential disadvantage of the open-ended response question is the possibility that interviewer bias will influence the answer. While most interviewer instructions state that answers are to be recorded verbatim, rarely does even the best interviewer get every word spoken by the respondent. Interviewers have a tendency to take shortcuts. When this occurs, the interviewer may well introduce error because the final answer may reflect a combination of the respondent's and interviewer's ideas.

Also, articulate individuals tend to give longer answers to open-ended response questions. Such respondents often are better educated and from higher income groups and therefore may not be representative of the entire population, and yet they may give a large share of the responses.

RESEARCHSNAPSHOT

©ASSOCIATED PRESS, AP

Corporate Reputations: Consumers Put Johnson & Johnson on Top

To report the reputations of well-known companies, *The Wall Street Journal* sponsors an annual research project, the Corporate Reputation Survey. The idea is to see what U.S. adults think about corporations, not to rate a predetermined set of companies, so the study has two phases.

In the first phase, the researchers identified the companies that were most "visible," meaning companies that people were most likely to think about—and therefore have an attitude toward. This phase avoided the problem of asking individuals to rate the qualities of a company they have never heard of. This research used open-ended questions asking respondents to name two companies they felt had the best reputation and two that had the worst. Because of the open-ended format, some respondents mistakenly gave names that were subsidiaries or brands of the same company. The researchers counted those responses as mentions of the parent company so that all responses would be included. The researchers determined the number of times each company was mentioned and selected the sixty named most often for the second phase of the study.

The second phase was aimed at generating rankings of the corporations, so questions and answer choices needed to be more specific. The researchers identified six dimensions of a corporate reputation: products and services, financial performance, workplace environment, social responsibility, vision and leadership, and emotional appeal. Within these categories, they identified twenty attributes, such as whether respondents would trust the company if they had a problem with its goods or services and how sincere its corporate communications were. In an online survey, each respondent was asked to rate one company on all twenty attributes. Then the respondent was invited (not required) to rate a second company. More than 250 ratings were generated for each company. These responses were combined to create an overall rating for the company.

The top-ranked company for two years running was Johnson & Johnson, followed by Coca-Cola and Google. On the six dimensions of reputation, J&J was tops in emotional appeal and its goods and services, and it made the top five on the other dimensions. This honor is more than just good publicity; J&J also was the firm from which the largest share of people said they would "definitely purchase" products.

Source: Based on Ronald Alsop, "Ranking Corporation Reputations," The Wall Street Journal, December 6, 2005, http://online.wsj.com; "Corporate Reputation Survey Methodology," The Wall Street Journal, December 5, 2005, http://online.wsj.com; "2005 Reputation Quotient Rankings," The Wall Street Journal, December 6, 2005, http://online.wsj.com; "Corporate Reputation Survey," The Wall Street Journal, December 6, 2005, http://online.wsj.com.

■ USING FIXED-ALTERNATIVE QUESTIONS

In contrast, fixed-alternative questions require less interviewer skill, take less time, and are easier for the respondent to answer. This is because answers to closed questions are classified into standardized groupings prior to data collection. Standardizing alternative responses to a question provides comparability of answers, which facilitates coding, tabulating, and ultimately interpreting the data.

However, when a researcher is unaware of the potential responses to a question, fixed-alternative questions obviously cannot be used. If the researcher assumes what the responses will be but is in fact wrong, he or she will have no way of knowing the extent to which the assumption was incorrect. Sometimes this type of error comes to light after the questionnaire has been used. Researchers found cross-cultural misunderstandings in a survey of mothers called the Preschooler Feeding Questionnaire. By talking to a group of African-American mothers, a researcher at the University of Chicago determined that they had experiences with encouraging children to eat more and using food to calm children, but they used different language for these situations than the questionnaire used, so they misinterpreted some questions.[4]

Unanticipated alternatives emerge when respondents believe that closed answers do not adequately reflect their feelings. They may make comments to the interviewer or write additional answers on the questionnaire indicating that the exploratory research did not yield a complete array of responses. After the fact, little can be done to correct a closed question that does not provide enough alternatives. Therefore, a researcher may find exploratory research with open-ended responses valuable before writing a descriptive questionnaire. The researcher should strive to ensure that there are sufficient response choices to include almost all possible answers.

Respondents may check off obvious alternatives, such as price or durability, if they do not see the choice they would prefer. Also, a fixed-alternative question may tempt respondents to check an answer that is more prestigious or socially acceptable than the true answer. Rather than stating that they do not know why they chose a given product, they may select an alternative among those presented, or as a matter of convenience, they may select a given alternative rather than think of the most correct response.

Most questionnaires mix open-ended and closed questions. As we have discussed, each form has unique benefits. In addition, a change of pace can eliminate respondent boredom and fatigue.

Types of Fixed-Alternative Questions

Earlier in the chapter a variety of fixed-alternative questions were presented. We will now identify and categorize the various types.

The **simple-dichotomy (dichotomous-alternative) question** requires the respondent to choose one of two alternatives. The answer can be a simple "yes" or "no" or a choice between "this" and "that." For example:

Did you make any long-distance calls last week?

☐ *Yes*　　☐ *No*

Simple-dichotomy (dichotomous-alternative) question
A fixed-alternative question that requires the respondent to choose one of two alternatives.

Several types of questions provide the respondent with *multiple-choice alternatives*. The **determinant-choice question** requires the respondent to choose one—and only one—response from among several possible alternatives. For example:

Please give us some information about your flight. In which section of the aircraft did you sit?

- *First class*
- *Business class*
- *Coach class*

Determinant-choice question
A fixed-alternative question that requires the respondent to choose one response from among multiple alternatives.

The **frequency-determination question** is a determinant-choice question that asks for an answer about the general frequency of occurrence. For example:

How frequently do you watch the MTV television channel?

- *Every day*
- *5–6 times a week*
- *2–4 times a week*
- *Once a week*
- *Less than once a week*
- *Never*

Frequency-determination question
A fixed-alternative question that asks for an answer about general frequency of occurrence.

Attitude rating scales, such as the Likert scale, semantic differential, Stapel scale, and so on, are also fixed-alternative questions. These scales were discussed in Chapter 14.

The **checklist question** allows the respondent to provide multiple answers to a single question. The respondent indicates past experience, preference, and the like merely by checking off items. In many cases the choices are adjectives that describe a particular object. A typical checklist question might ask the following:

Please check which of the following sources of information about investments you regularly use, if any.

- *Personal advice of your broker(s)*
- *Brokerage newsletters*
- *Brokerage research reports*
- *Investment advisory service(s)*
- *Conversations with other investors*
- *Web page(s)*
- *None of these*
- *Other (please specify)* _____

Checklist question
A fixed-alternative question that allows the respondent to provide multiple answers to a single question by checking off items.

A major problem in developing dichotomous or multiple-choice alternatives is the framing of the response alternatives. There should be no overlap among categories. Alternatives should be *mutually exclusive,* meaning only one dimension of an issue should be related to each alternative. The following listing of income groups illustrates a common error:

- *Under $15,000*
- *$15,000–$30,000*
- *$30,000–$55,000*
- *$55,000–$70,000*
- *Over $70,000*

How many people with incomes of $30,000 will be in the second group, and how many will be in the third group? Researchers have no way to determine the answer. Grouping alternatives without forethought about analysis is likely to diminish accuracy.

　　Also, few people relish being in the lowest category. To negate the potential bias caused by respondents' tendency to avoid an extreme category, researchers often include a category lower than the lowest expected answers.

Phrasing Questions for Self-Administered, Telephone, and Personal Interview Surveys

The means of data collection—telephone interview, personal interview, self-administered questionnaire—will influence the question format and question phrasing. In general, questions for mail, Internet, and telephone surveys must be less complex than those used in personal interviews. Questionnaires for telephone and personal interviews should be written in a conversational style. Exhibit 15.1 illustrates how a question may be revised for a different medium.

　　In a telephone survey about attitudes toward police services, the questionnaire not only asked about general attitudes such as how much respondents trust their local police officers and whether the police are "approachable," "dedicated," and so on, but also provided basic scenarios to help respondents put their expectations into words. For example, the interviewer asked respondents to imagine that someone had broken into their home and stolen items, and that the respondent called

EXHIBIT 15.1
Reducing Question Complexity by Providing Fewer Responses

Mail Form:

How satisfied are you with your community?

1. Very satisfied
2. Quite satisfied
3. Somewhat satisfied
4. Slightly satisfied
5. Neither satisfied nor dissatisfied
6. Slightly dissatisfied
7. Somewhat dissatisfied
8. Quite dissatisfied
9. Very dissatisfied

Revised for Telephone:

How satisfied are you with your community? Would you say you are very satisfied, somewhat satisfied, neither satisfied nor dissatisfied, somewhat dissatisfied, or very dissatisfied?

Very satisfied	1
Somewhat satisfied	2
Neither satisfied nor dissatisfied	3
Somewhat dissatisfied	4
Very dissatisfied	5

Source: Don A. Dillman, *Mail and Telephone Surveys: The Total Design Method* (New York: John Wiley & Sons, 1978), p. 209. Reprinted with permission.

the police to report the crime. The interviewer asked how quickly or slowly the respondent expected the police to arrive.[5]

When a question is read aloud, remembering the alternative choices can be difficult. Consider the following question from a personal interview:

There has been a lot of discussion about the potential health risks to nonsmokers from tobacco smoke in public buildings, restaurants, and business offices. How serious a health threat to you personally is the inhaling of this secondhand smoke, often called passive smoking: *Is it a very serious health threat, somewhat serious, not too serious, or not serious at all?*

1. *Very serious*
2. *Somewhat serious*
3. *Not too serious*
4. *Not serious at all*
5. *(Don't know)*

The last portion of the question was a listing of the four alternatives that serve as answers. This listing at the end is often used in interviews to remind the respondent of the alternatives, since they are not presented visually. The fifth alternative, "Don't know," is in parentheses because, although the interviewer knows it is an acceptable answer, it is not read. The researcher only uses this response when the respondent truly cannot provide an answer.

The data collection technique also influences the layout of the questionnaire. Layout will be discussed later in the chapter.

The Art of Asking Questions

No hard-and-fast rules determine how to develop a questionnaire. Fortunately, research experience has yielded some guidelines that help prevent the most common mistakes.

Avoid Complexity: Use Simple, Conversational Language

Words used in questionnaires should be readily understandable to all respondents. The researcher usually has the difficult task of adopting the conversational language of people at the lower education levels without talking down to better-educated respondents. Remember, not all people have the vocabulary of a college graduate. Many consumers, for instance, have never gone beyond a high school education.

Respondents can probably tell an interviewer whether they are married, single, divorced, separated, or widowed, but providing their *marital status* may present a problem. The technical jargon of top corporate executives should be avoided when surveying retailers or industrial users. "Brand image," "positioning," "marginal analysis," and other corporate language may not have the same meaning for or even be understood by a store owner-operator in a retail survey. The vocabulary used in the following question from an attitude survey on social problems probably would confuse many respondents:

When effluents from a paper mill can be drunk and exhaust from factory smokestacks can be breathed, then humankind will have done a good job in saving the environment. . . . Don't you agree that what we want is zero toxicity: no effluents?

Besides being too long and confusing, this question is leading.

Avoid Leading and Loaded Questions

Leading and loaded questions are a major source of bias in question wording. A **leading question** suggests or implies certain answers. A study of the dry cleaning industry asked this question:

TOTHEPOINT

I don't know the rules of grammar. . . . If you're trying to persuade people to do something, or buy something, it seems to me you should use their language, the language they use every day, the language in which they think. We try to write in the vernacular.

—David Ogilvy

Leading question
A question that suggests or implies certain answers.

RESEARCHSNAPSHOT

What to Do with the Clubhouse?

Mathematician Jennifer Lewis Priestley helps the managers of golf and country clubs collect and interpret data. One club showed her a member survey containing the following question:

We need to make some decisions about our clubhouse. The clubhouse itself is too small and requires substantial physical improvement, and it's been a long time since we undertook a major redecorating project. Do you favor

a. remodeling the current clubhouse?
b. building a new clubhouse?
c. doing nothing?

The wording of the question and the answer choices are biased in favor of action. The question criticizes the current clubhouse and places the question in the context of "a long time since we undertook a major redecorating project." To select

©JEFF GREENBERG/PHOTOEDIT

choice c, the respondent would have to disregard the premise of the question.

To eliminate the bias and include neutral wording so that the responses could more accurately represent the members' opinions, Priestley recommended some changes:

Considering the current clubhouse, which of the following statements most closely reflects your views?

a. The current clubhouse should remain the same.
b. The current clubhouse should be remodeled (size will remain the same).
c. The current clubhouse should be remodeled and expanded.
d. The club needs a new clubhouse (current clubhouse torn down).

Source: Based on Jennifer Lewis Priestley, "Determining What Your Marketing Members Want," Club Management, October 2004, downloaded from InfoTrac at http://infotrac.galegroup.com.

Many people are using dry cleaning less because of improved wash-and-wear clothes. How do you feel wash-and-wear clothes have affected your use of dry cleaning facilities in the past 4 years?

☐ *Use less*　　　☐ *No change*　　　☐ *Use more*

The potential "bandwagon effect" implied in this question threatens the study's validity. *Partial mention of alternatives* is a variation of this phenomenon:

Do small imported cars, such as Volkswagens, get better gas mileage than small U.S. cars?
How do you generally spend your free time, watching television or what?

Loaded question
A question that suggests a socially desirable answer or is emotionally charged.

A **loaded question** suggests a socially desirable answer or is emotionally charged. Consider the following question from a survey about media influence on cooking and home-decorating behavior:[6]

What most influences you to buy food equipment?

• *My own need for equipment at the time*
• *Salesperson at store*
• *Food magazines*
• *Food shows on TV*
• *Internet food sites*
• *Family or friends*
• *Food/dining section of newspaper*
• *Other*
• *I rarely/never buy food preparation equipment*

Over half the respondents chose the first alternative. Although this question is not emotionally loaded, many people could be reluctant to say they are swayed by the media rather than making purchases out of their own, independently experienced need.

A television station produced the following 10-second spot asking for viewer feedback:

We are happy when you like programs on Channel 7. We are sad when you dislike programs on Channel 7. Write us and let us know what you think of our programming.

Few people wish to make others sad. This question is likely to elicit only positive comments.

Certain answers to questions are more socially desirable than others. For example, a truthful answer to the following classification question might be painful:

Where did you rank academically in your high school graduating class?

- *Top quarter*
- *2nd quarter*
- *3rd quarter*
- *4th quarter*

When taking personality or psychographic tests, respondents frequently can interpret which answers are most socially acceptable even if those answers do not portray their true feelings. For example, which are the socially desirable answers to the following questions on a self-confidence scale?

I feel capable of handling myself in most social situations.

☐ *Agree*   ☐ *Disagree*

I seldom fear my actions will cause others to have low opinions of me.

☐ *Agree*   ☐ *Disagree*

Invoking the status quo is a form of loading that results in bias because most people tend to resist change.[7] An experiment conducted in the early days of polling illustrates the unpopularity of change.[8] Comparable samples of respondents were simultaneously asked two questions about the presidential succession. One sample was asked, **"Would you favor or oppose adding a law to the Constitution preventing a president from succeeding himself more than once?"** The other sample was asked, **"Would you favor or oppose changing the Constitution in order to prevent a president from succeeding himself more than once?"** Fifty percent of respondents answered negatively to the first question. For the second question, 65 percent of respondents answered negatively. Thus, the public would rather add to than change the Constitution.

Asking respondents "how often" they use a product or visit a store leads them to generalize about their habits, because there usually is some variance in their behavior. In generalizing, a person is likely to portray an *ideal* behavior rather than an *average* behavior. For instance, brushing your teeth after each meal may be ideal, but busy people may skip a brushing or two. An introductory **counterbiasing statement** or preamble to a question that reassures respondents that their "embarrassing" behavior is not abnormal may yield truthful responses:

Counterbiasing statement
An introductory statement or preamble to a potentially embarrassing question that reduces a respondent's reluctance to answer by suggesting that certain behavior is not unusual.

Some people have the time to brush three times daily but others do not. How often did you brush your teeth yesterday?

If a question embarrasses the respondent, it may elicit no answer or a biased response. This is particularly true with respect to personal or classification data such as income or education. The problem may be mitigated by introducing the section of the questionnaire with a statement such as this:

To help classify your answers, we'd like to ask you a few questions. Again, your answers will be kept in strict confidence.

A question statement may be leading because it is phrased to reflect either the negative or the positive aspects of an issue. To control for this bias, the wording of attitudinal questions may be reversed for 50 percent of the sample. This **split-ballot technique** is used with the expectation that two alternative phrasings of the same question will yield a more accurate total response than will a single phrasing. For example, in a study on small-car buying behavior, one-half of a sample of imported-car purchasers received a questionnaire in which they were asked to agree or disagree with the statement **"Small U.S. cars are cheaper to maintain than small imported cars."** The other half of the import-car owners received a questionnaire in which the statement read **"Small imported cars are cheaper to maintain than small U.S. cars."**

Split-ballot technique
Using two alternative phrasings of the same question for respective halves of a sample to elicit a more accurate total response than would a single phrasing.

Avoid Ambiguity: Be as Specific as Possible

Items on questionnaires often are ambiguous because they are too general. Consider such indefinite words as *often, occasionally, regularly, frequently, many, good,* and *poor.* Each of these words has many different meanings. For one consumer *frequent* reading of *Fortune* magazine may be reading six or seven issues a year. Another consumer may think reading two issues a year is frequent.

Questions such as the following one, used in a study measuring the reactions of consumers to a television boycott, should be interpreted with care:

Please indicate the statement that best describes your family's television viewing during the boycott of Channel 7.

- *We did not watch any television programs on Channel 7.*
- *We watched hardly any television programs on Channel 7.*
- *We occasionally watched television programs on Channel 7.*
- *We frequently watched television programs on Channel 7.*

Some marketing scholars have suggested that the rate of diffusion of an innovation is related to the perception of product attributes such as *divisibility,* which refers to the extent to which the innovation may be tried or tested on a limited scale.[9] An empirical attempt to test this theory using semantic differentials was a disaster. Pretesting found that the bipolar adjectives *divisible–not divisible* were impossible for consumers to understand because they did not have the theory in mind as a frame of reference. A revision of the scale used these bipolar adjectives:

Testable   ____ ____ ____ ____ ____ ____   *Not testable*
(sample use possible)   *(sample use not possible)*

However, the question remained ambiguous because the meaning was still unclear.

A brewing industry study on point-of-purchase advertising (store displays) asked:

What degree of durability do you prefer in your point-of-purchase advertising?

- *Permanent (lasting more than 6 months)*
- *Semipermanent (lasting from 1 to 6 months)*
- *Temporary (lasting less than 1 month)*

Here the researchers clarified the terms *permanent, semipermanent,* and *temporary* by defining them for the respondent. However, the question remained somewhat ambiguous. Beer marketers often use a variety of point-of-purchase devices to serve different purposes—in this case, what is the purpose? In addition, analysis was difficult because respondents were merely asked to indicate a preference rather than a *degree* of preference. Thus, the meaning of a question may not be clear because the frame of reference is inadequate for interpreting the context of the question.

A student research group asked this question:

What media do you rely on most?

- *Television*
- *Radio*
- *Internet*
- *Newspapers*

This question is ambiguous because it does not ask about the content of the media. "Rely on most" for what—news, sports, entertainment?

Avoid Double-Barreled Items

Double-barreled question
A question that may induce bias because it covers two issues at once.

A question covering several issues at once is referred to as a **double-barreled question** and should always be avoided. Making the mistake of asking two questions rather than one is easy—for example, **"Please indicate your degree of agreement with the following statement: 'Wholesalers and retailers are responsible for the high price of meat.'"** Which intermediaries are responsible, the wholesalers or the retailers? When multiple questions are asked in one question, the results may be exceedingly difficult to interpret. Consider the following question from a magazine's survey entitled "How Do You Feel about Being a Woman?":

Between you and your husband, who does the housework (cleaning, cooking, dishwashing, laundry) over and above that done by any hired help?

- *I do all of it.*
- *I do almost all of it.*
- *I do over half of it.*
- *We split the work fifty-fifty.*
- *My husband does over half of it.*

The answers to this question do not tell us if the wife cooks and the husband washes the dishes.

A survey by a consumer-oriented library asked,

Are you satisfied with the present system of handling "closed-reserve" and "open-reserve" readings? (Are enough copies available? Are the required materials ordered promptly? Are the borrowing regulations adequate for students' use of materials?)

☐ *Yes*   ☐ *No*

A respondent may feel torn between a "yes" to one part of the question and a "no" to another part. The answer to this question does not tell the researcher which problem or combination of problems concerns the library user.

The following comment offers good advice regarding double-barreled questions:

Generally speaking, it is hard enough to get answers to one idea at a time without complicating the problem by asking what amounts to two questions at once. If two ideas are to be explored, they deserve at least two questions. Since question marks are not rationed, there is little excuse for the needless confusion that results [from] the double-barreled question.[10]

Avoid Making Assumptions

Consider the following question:

Should Macy's continue its excellent gift-wrapping program?

☐ *Yes*   ☐ *No*

This question has a built-in assumption: that people believe the gift-wrapping program is excellent. By answering "yes," the respondent implies that the program is, in fact, excellent and that things are fine just as they are. When a respondent answers "no," he or she implies that the store should discontinue the gift wrapping. The researchers should not place the respondent in that sort of bind by including an implicit assumption in the question.

Another frequent mistake is assuming that the respondent had previously thought about an issue. For example, the following question appeared in a survey concerning Jack-in-the-Box: **"Do you think Jack-in-the-Box restaurants should consider changing their name?"** Respondents have not likely thought about this question beforehand. Most respondents answered the question even though they had no prior opinion concerning the name change. Research that induces people to express attitudes on subjects they do not ordinarily think about is meaningless.

Avoid Burdensome Questions That May Tax the Respondent's Memory

A simple fact of human life is that people forget. Researchers writing questions about past behavior or events should recognize that certain questions may make serious demands on the respondent's memory. Writing questions about prior events requires a conscientious attempt to minimize the problems associated with forgetting.

RESEARCHSNAPSHOT

Who's *Really* Doing the Housework?

Married women have been a large part of the workforce for decades, but wives continue to complain that when both spouses hold jobs, women bear the heavier responsibility for housework. Researchers have recently considered whether the problem is one of fairness or misperception.

Some evidence suggests that the difference in estimates depends partly on data gathering. First, it matters whom the researchers question and when they ask. If the study asks men and women to recall how they used their time at home, both groups tend to overestimate the time they devote to housework.

Also, defining time spent on housework turns out to be more complex than you might guess. Why? People often combine activities. For example, someone might grab an armload of dirty clothes to shove into the washing machine on the way to the den to use the computer. Is that housework?

Detailed data from the long-term Sloan 500 Family Study provide some insights. This study used the Experi-

ence Sampling Method (ESM) to overcome problems associated with asking people to remember how they used their time. With ESM, participants wear programmed wristwatches that beep at randomly chosen times. Whenever the watch beeps, participants are supposed to answer a short questionnaire indicating what their primary and secondary activities are and what they are thinking about at that time. With regard to housework, researchers found that if they count time spent on housework as either a primary or secondary activity, the overreporting of housework time shrinks. If the definition of housework is further expanded to include time spent thinking about it—not necessarily procrastinating, but maybe planning or managing household tasks—the overreporting shrinks again. The way housework is defined also affects the size of the gap between husbands' and wives' contributions.

Source: Based on Yun-Suk Lee and Linda J. Waite, "Husbands' and Wives' Time Spent on Housework: A Comparison of Measures," Journal of Marriage and Family 67(2) (2005): 328–36, abstract downloaded from OCLC FirstSearch, http://firstsearch.oclc.org; Barbara Schneider and Linda Waite, "Timely and Timeless: Working Parents and Their Children," Conference on Work, Family, Health and Well-Being, Washington, DC, June 16–18, 2003, downloaded from Maryland Population Research Center Web site, http://www.popcenter.umd.edu; Alfred P. Sloan Center on Parents, Children and Work, "Overview of Center Research," http://www.sloanworkingfamilies.org, accessed March 8, 2006.

©ROYALTY-FREE/CORBIS

In many situations, respondents cannot recall the answer to a question. For example, a telephone survey conducted during the 24-hour period following the airing of the Super Bowl might establish whether the respondent watched the Super Bowl and then ask, "Do you recall any commercials on that program?" If the answer is positive, the interviewer might ask, "What brands were advertised?" These two questions measure *unaided recall,* because they give the respondent no clue as to the brand of interest.

If the researcher suspects that the respondent may have forgotten the answer to a question, he or she may rewrite the question in an *aided-recall* format—that is, in a format that provides a clue to help jog the respondent's memory. For instance, the question about an advertised beer in an aided-recall format might be "Do you recall whether there was a brand of beer advertised on that program?" or "I am going to read you a list of beer brand names. Can you pick out the name of the beer that was advertised on the program?" While aided recall is not as strong a test of attention or memory as unaided recall, it is less taxing to the respondent's memory.

Telescoping and squishing are two additional consequences of respondents' forgetting the exact details of their behavior. *Telescoping* occurs when respondents believe that past events happened more recently than they actually did. The opposite effect, *squishing,* occurs when respondents think that recent events took place longer ago than they really did. A solution to this problem may be to refer to a specific event that is memorable—for example, "How often have you gone to a sporting event since the World Series?" Because forgetting tends to increase over time, the question may concern a recent period: "How often did you watch HBO on cable television last week?" (During the editing stage, the results can be transposed to the appropriate time period.)

In situations in which "I don't know" or "I can't recall" is a meaningful answer, simply including a "don't know" response category may solve the question writer's problem.

What Is the Best Question Sequence?

The order of questions, or the question sequence, may serve several functions for the researcher. If the opening questions are interesting, simple to comprehend, and easy to answer, respondents' cooperation and involvement can be maintained throughout the questionnaire. Asking easy-to-answer questions teaches respondents their role and builds their confidence.

A mail survey among department store buyers drew an extremely poor return rate. A substantial improvement in response rate occurred, however, when researchers added some introductory questions seeking opinions on pending legislation of great importance to these buyers. Respondents completed all the questions, not only those in the opening section.

In their attempt to "warm up" respondents toward the questionnaire, student researchers frequently ask demographic or classificatory questions at the beginning. This generally is not advisable, because asking for personal information such as income level or education may embarrass or threaten respondents. Asking potentially embarrassing questions at the middle or end of the questionnaire usually is better, after rapport has been established between respondent and interviewer.

Order bias can result from a particular answer's position in a set of answers or from the sequencing of questions. In political elections in which candidates lack high visibility, such as elections for county commissioners and judges, the first name listed on the ballot often receives the highest percentage of votes. For this reason, many election boards print several ballots so that each candidate's name appears in every possible position on the ballot.

Order bias can also distort survey results. For example, suppose a questionnaire's purpose is to measure levels of awareness of several charitable organizations. If Big Brothers and Big Sisters is always mentioned first, the American Red Cross second, and the American Cancer Society third, Big Brothers and Big Sisters may receive an artificially high awareness rating because respondents are prone to yea-saying (by indicating awareness of the first item in the list).

Asking specific questions before asking about broader issues is a common cause of order bias. For example, bias may arise if questions about a specific clothing store are asked prior to those concerning the general criteria for selecting a clothing store. Suppose a respondent indicates in the first portion of a questionnaire that she shops at a store where parking needs to be improved. Later in the questionnaire, to avoid appearing inconsistent, she may state that parking is less important than she really believes it is. Specific questions may thus influence the more general ones. As a result, it is advisable to ask general questions before specific questions to obtain the freest of open-ended responses. This procedure, known as the **funnel technique**, allows the researcher to understand the respondent's frame of reference before asking more specific questions about the level of the respondent's information and the intensity of his or her opinions.

Consider how later answers might be biased by previous questions in this questionnaire on environmental pollution:

Circle the number on the following table that best expresses your feelings about the severity of each environmental problem:

Problem	Not a Problem				Very Severe Problem
Air pollution from automobile exhausts	1	2	3	4	5
Air pollution from open burning	1	2	3	4	5
Air pollution from industrial smoke	1	2	3	4	5
Air pollution from foul odors	1	2	3	4	5
Noise pollution from airplanes	1	2	3	4	5
Noise pollution from cars, trucks, motorcycles	1	2	3	4	5
Noise pollution from industry	1	2	3	4	5

Not surprisingly, researchers found that the responses to the air pollution questions were highly correlated—in fact, almost identical.

Order bias
Bias caused by the influence of earlier questions in a questionnaire or by an answer's position in a set of answers.

Funnel technique
Asking general questions before specific questions in order to obtain unbiased responses.

RESEARCHSNAPSHOT

What Citizens (Don't) Know about Climate Change

Climate change as a result of global warming has frequently been featured in the news, especially in stories related to science and technology. Scientists at the Massachusetts Institute of Technology's Laboratory for Energy and the Environment (LFEE) have dedicated themselves to researching a variety of approaches to slow down climate change. The scientists recognize, however, that these innovations have a cost, so their use will depend partly on public interest in the problem and demand for solutions. As a result, LFEE conducted an online survey, which it sent to a national panel.

One challenge for the study was that before researchers could gauge citizens' willingness to pay for new technologies, they needed to know whether most people were even aware of the energy alternatives. They asked, "Have you heard of or read about any of the following in the past year? Check all that apply," followed by a list of ten technologies for mitigating climate change. Only three technologies—more efficient cars, solar energy, and nuclear energy— were checked by a majority of

respondents. Seventeen percent admitted to not hearing about any of the technologies, a number that the researchers acknowledge may be too low, because some people might want to appear better informed than they are.

Perhaps lack of interest is a factor as well. Another question gave respondents a list of twenty-two issues and asked them to choose the most important. The environment was ranked thirteenth. In a question asking respondents to rank the importance of specific environmental problems, "global warming" was in sixth place, trailing water pollution, destruction of ecosystems, and toxic waste.

All of these questions presented respondents with a list of alternatives to check. What precautions should the survey have taken to minimize the chance that the order of alternatives influenced respondents' opinions that some items were familiar or important?

Source: Based on "U.S. Public in the Dark on Climate Change Issues," Bulletin of the American Meteorological Society 86(6) (June 2005), downloaded from FirstSearch at http://firstsearch.oclc.org; and Howard J. Herzog, Thomas E. Curry, David M. Reiner, and Stephen Ansolabehere, "Climate Change Poorly Understood, Not a High Priority, Shows MIT Public Survey," Energy and Environment (Massachusetts Institute of Technology Laboratory for Energy and the Environment), December 2004, pp. 7–8, accessed at http://lfee.mit.edu.

With attitude scales, there also may be an *anchoring effect*. The first concept measured tends to become a comparison point from which subsequent evaluations are made. Randomization of items on a questionnaire susceptible to the anchoring effect helps minimize order bias.

A related problem is bias caused by the order of alternatives on closed questions. To avoid this problem, the order of these choices should be rotated if producing alternative forms of the questionnaire is possible. However, marketing researchers rarely print alternative questionnaires to eliminate problems resulting from order bias. A more common practice is to pencil in Xs or check marks on printed questionnaires to indicate where the interviewer should start a series of repetitive questions. For example, the capitalized phrases in the following question provide instructions to the interviewer to "rotate" brands, starting with the one checked:

I would like to determine how likely you would be to buy certain brands of candy in the future. Let's start with (X'ED BRAND). (RECORD BELOW UNDER APPROPRIATE BRAND. REPEAT QUESTIONS FOR ALL REMAINING BRANDS.)

Start Here:	( ) Mounds	(X) Almond Joy	( ) Snickers
Definitely would buy	−1	−1	−1
Probably would buy	−2	−2	−2
Might or might not buy	−3	−3	−3
Probably would not buy	−4	−4	−4
Definitely would not buy	−5	−5	−5

One advantage of Internet surveys is the ability to reduce order bias by having the computer randomly order questions and/or response alternatives. With complete randomization, question order is random and respondents see response alternatives in different random positions.

Asking a question that does not apply to the respondent or that the respondent is not qualified to answer may be irritating or cause a biased response because the respondent wishes to please the interviewer or to avoid embarrassment. Including a **filter question** minimizes the chance of asking questions that are inapplicable. Asking **"Where do you generally have check-cashing problems in Springfield?"** may elicit a response even though the respondent has had no check-cashing

Filter question
A question that screens out respondents who are not qualified to answer a second question.

problems. He or she may wish to please the interviewer with an answer. A filter question such as **"Do you ever have a problem cashing a check in Springfield? — Yes — No"** would screen out the people who are not qualified to answer.

Another form of filter question, the **pivot question**, can be used to obtain income information and other data that respondents may be reluctant to provide. For example,

Pivot question
A filter question used to determine which version of a second question will be asked.

"Is your total family income over or under $50,000?" IF UNDER, ASK, "Is it over or under $25,000?" IF OVER, ASK, "Is it over or under $75,000?"

Under $25,000	$50,001–$75,000
$25,001–$50,000	Over $75,000

Exhibit 15.2 gives an example of a flowchart plan for a questionnaire. Structuring the order of the questions so that they are logical will help to ensure the respondent's cooperation and eliminate

EXHIBIT 15.2 Flow of Questions to Determine the Level of Prompting Required to Stimulate Recall

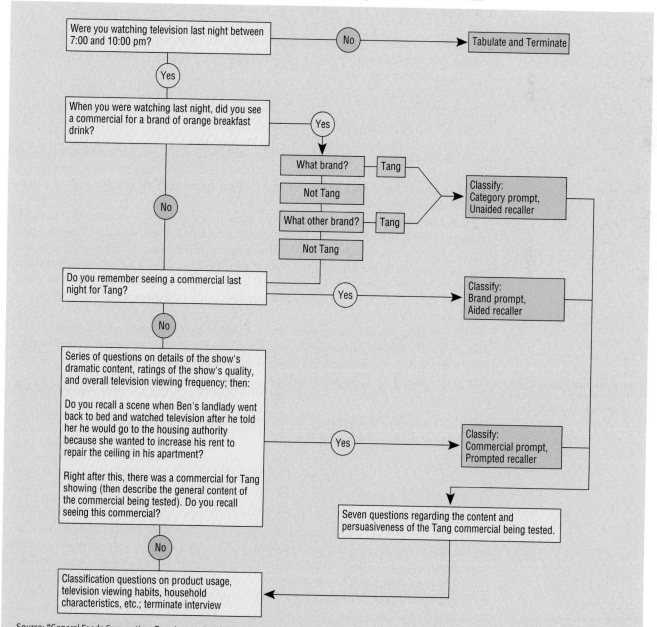

Source: "General Foods Corporation: Tang Instant Breakfast Drink (B)," © 1978 F. Stewart DeBruicker and Harvey N. Singer, The Wharton School, University of Pennsylvania. Reprinted with permission.

confusion or indecision. The researcher maintains legitimacy by making sure that the respondent can comprehend the relationship between a given question (or section of the questionnaire) and the overall purpose of the study. Furthermore, a logical order may aid the individual's memory. Transitional comments explaining the logic of the questionnaire may ensure that the respondent continues. Here are two examples:

We have been talking so far about general shopping habits in this city. Now I'd like you to compare two types of grocery stores—regular supermarkets and grocery departments in wholesale club stores.

So that I can combine your answers with those of other farmers who are similar to you, I need some personal information about you. Your answers to these questions—as to all of the others you've answered—are confidential, and you will never be identified to anyone without your permission. Thanks for your help so far. If you'll answer the remaining questions, it will help me analyze all your answers.

What Is the Best Layout?

Good layout and physical attractiveness are crucial in mail, Internet, and other self-administered questionnaires. For different reasons, a good layout in questionnaires designed for personal and telephone interviews is also important.

Traditional Questionnaires

Exhibit 15.3 shows a page from a telephone questionnaire. The layout is neat and attractive, and the instructions for the interviewer (all boldface capital letters) are easy to follow. The responses "It depends," "Refused," and "Don't Know" are enclosed in a box to indicate that these answers are acceptable but responses from the five-point scale are preferred.

Often rate of return can be increased by using money that might have been spent on an incentive to improve the attractiveness and quality of the questionnaire. Mail questionnaires should never be overcrowded. Margins should be of decent size, white space should be used to separate blocks of print, and the unavoidable columns of multiple boxes should be kept to a minimum. A question should not begin on one page and end on another page. Splitting questions may cause a respondent to read only part of a question, to pay less attention to answers on one of the pages, or to become confused.

Questionnaires should be designed to appear as short as possible. Sometimes it is advisable to use a booklet form of questionnaire rather than stapling a large number of pages together. In situations in which it is necessary to conserve space on the questionnaire or to facilitate data entry or tabulation of the data, a multiple-grid layout may be used. The **multiple-grid question** presents several similar questions and corresponding response alternatives arranged in a grid format. For example,

Multiple-grid question
Several similar questions arranged in a grid format.

Airlines often offer special fare promotions. On a vacation trip would you take a connecting flight instead of a nonstop flight if the connecting flight were longer?

	Yes	No	Not sure
One hour longer?	☐	☐	☐
Two hours longer?	☐	☐	☐
Three hours longer?	☐	☐	☐

Experienced researchers have found that the title of a questionnaire should be phrased carefully. In self-administered and mail questionnaires, a carefully constructed title may capture the respondent's interest, underline the importance of the research ("Nationwide Study of Blood Donors"), emphasize the interesting nature of the study ("Study of Internet Usage"), appeal to the respondent's ego ("Survey among Top Executives"), or emphasize the confidential nature of the study ("A Confidential Survey among . . . "). The researcher should take steps to ensure that the wording of the title will not bias the respondent in the same way that a leading question might.

EXHIBIT 15.3 Layout of a Page from a Telephone Questionnaire

5. Now I'm going to read you some types of professions. For each one, please tell me whether you think the work that profession does, on balance, has a very positive impact on society, a somewhat positive impact, a somewhat negative impact, a very negative impact, or not much impact either way on society. First . . . **(START AT X'D ITEM. CONTINUE DOWN AND UP THE LIST UNTIL ALL ITEMS HAVE BEEN READ AND RATED.)**

START HERE:	Very Positive Impact	Some-what Positive Impact	Some-what Negative Impact	Very Negative Impact	Not Much Impact	(DO NOT READ)		
						It Depends	Refused	Don't Know
[ ] Members of Congress	1	2	3	4	5	0	X	Y (24)
[ ] Business executives	1	2	3	4	5	0	X	Y (25)
[ ] Physicians	1	2	3	4	5	0	X	Y (26)
[ ] Political pollsters—that is, people who conduct surveys for public officials or political political candidates	1	2	3	4	5	0	X	Y (27)
[ ] Researchers in the media—that is, people in media such as television, newspapers, magazines and radio, who conduct surveys about issues later reported in the media	1	2	3	4	5	0	X	Y (28)
[ ] Telemarketers—that is, people who sell products or services over the phone	1	2	3	4	5	0	X	Y (29)
[ ] Used car salesmen	1	2	3	4	5	0	X	Y (30)
[ ] Market researchers—that is, people who work for commercial research firms who conduct surveys to see what the public thinks about certain kinds of consumer products or services	1	2	3	4	5	0	X	Y (31)
[ ] Biomedical researchers	1	2	3	4	5	0	X	Y (32)
[ ] Public-opinion researchers—that is, people who work for commercial research firms who conduct surveys to see what the public thinks about important social issues	1	2	3	4	5	0	X	Y (33)
[ ] College and university professors	1	2	3	4	5	0	X	Y (34)
[ ] Attorneys	1	2	3	4	5	0	X	Y (35)
[ ] Members of the clergy	1	2	3	4	5	0	X	Y (36)
[ ] Journalists	1	2	3	4	5	0	X	Y (37)

By using several forms, special instructions, and other tricks of the trade, the researcher can design the questionnaire to facilitate the interviewer's job of following interconnected questions. Exhibits 15.4 and 15.5 illustrate portions of telephone and personal interview questionnaires. Note how the layout and easy-to-follow instructions for interviewers in Questions 1, 2, and 3 of Exhibit 15.4 help the interviewer follow the question sequence.

EXHIBIT 15.4 **Telephone Questionnaire with Skip Questions**

1. Did you take the car you had checked to the Standard Auto Repair Center for repairs?

   –1 Yes   **(SKIP TO Q. 3)**   –2 No

2. **(IF NO, ASK:)** Did you have the repair work done?

   –1 Yes   –2 No

   ⬇   ⬇

   1. Where was the repair work done? _____   1. Why didn't you have the car repaired?
   _____   _____
   2. Why didn't you have the repair work done   _____
   at the Standard Auto Repair Center? _____   _____
   _____
   _____
   _____

3. **(IF YES TO Q. 1, ASK:)** How satisfied were you with the repair work? Were you . . .

   –1 Very satisfied

   –2 Somewhat satisfied

   –3 Somewhat dissatisfied

   –4 Very dissatisfied

   (IF SOMEWHAT OR VERY DISSATISFIED:) In what way were you dissatisfied?
   _____
   _____
   _____

4. **(ASK EVERYONE:)** Do you ever buy gas at the 95th Street Standard Center?

   –1 Yes   –2 No   **(SKIP TO Q. 6)**

5. **(IF YES, ASK:)** How often do you buy gas there?

   –1 Always

   –2 Almost always

   –3 Most of the time

   –4 Part of the time

   –5 Hardly ever

6. Have you ever had your car washed there?

   –1 Yes   –2 No

7. Have you ever had an oil change or lubrication done there?

   –1 Yes   –2 No

EXHIBIT 15.5 **Personal Interview Questionnaire**

"Hello, my name is _____. I'm a Public Opinion Interviewer with Research Services, Inc. We're making an opinion survey about banks and banking, and I'd like to ask you . . ."

1. What are the names of local banks you can think of offhand? (INTERVIEWER: List names in order mentioned.)
   a. _____
   b. _____
   c. _____
   d. _____
   e. _____
   f. _____
   g. _____

2. Thinking now about the experiences you have had with the different banks here in Boulder, have you ever talked to or done business with . . . (INTERVIEWER: Insert name of bank checked in red below.)
   a. Are you personally acquainted with any of the employees or officers at _____?
   b. (If YES) Who is that? _____
   c. How long has it been since you have been inside _____?
      (INTERVIEWER: Now go back and repeat 2–2c for all other banks listed.)

	(2) Talked		(2a and 2b) Know Employee Or Officer		(2c) Been in Bank in:				
	Yes	No	No	Name	Last Year	1–5	5-Plus	No	DK
Arapahoe National Bank	1	2	1	_____	1	2	3	4	5
First National Bank	1	2	1	_____	1	2	3	4	5
Boulder National Bank	1	2	1	_____	1	2	3	4	5
Security Bank	1	2	1	_____	1	2	3	4	5
United Bank of Boulder	1	2	1	_____	1	2	3	4	5
National State Bank	1	2	1	_____	1	2	3	4	5

3. (HAND BANK RATING CARD) On this card there are a number of contrasting phrases or statements—for example, "Large" and "Small." We'd like to know how you rate (NAME OF BANK CHECKED IN RED BELOW) in terms of these statements or phrases. Just for example, let's use the terms "fast service" and "slow service." If you were to rate a bank #1 on this scale, it would mean you find their service "very fast." On the other hand, a 7 rating would indicate you feel their service is "very slow," whereas a 4 rating means you don't think of them as being either "very fast" or "very slow." Are you ready to go ahead? Good! Tell me then how you would rate (NAME OF BANK CHECKED IN RED) in terms of each of the phrases or statements on that card. How about (READ NEXT BANK NAME)? . . . (INTERVIEWER: Continue on until respondent has evaluated all six banks.)

	Arapahoe National	First National	Boulder National	Security Bank	United Bank	National State
a. Service	_____	_____	_____	_____	_____	_____
b. Size	_____	_____	_____	_____	_____	_____
c. Business vs. Family	_____	_____	_____	_____	_____	_____
d. Friendliness	_____	_____	_____	_____	_____	_____
e. Big/Small Business	_____	_____	_____	_____	_____	_____
f. Rate of Growth	_____	_____	_____	_____	_____	_____
g. Modernness	_____	_____	_____	_____	_____	_____
h. Leadership	_____	_____	_____	_____	_____	_____
i. Loan Ease	_____	_____	_____	_____	_____	_____
j. Location	_____	_____	_____	_____	_____	_____
k. Hours	_____	_____	_____	_____	_____	_____
l. Ownership	_____	_____	_____	_____	_____	_____
m. Community Involvement	_____	_____	_____	_____	_____	_____

(continued)

EXHIBIT 15.5 **Personal Interview Questionnaire** (*Continued*)

4. Suppose a friend of yours who has just moved to Boulder asked you to recommend a bank. Which local bank would you recommend? Why would you recommend that particular bank?

Arapahoe National	1
First National	2
Boulder National	3
Security Bank	4
United Bank of Boulder	5
National State Bank	6
Other (Specify) _____	
DK/Wouldn't	9

5. Which of the local banks do you think of as: (INTERVIEWER: Read red-checked item first, then read each of the other five.)

the newcomer's bank? _____

the student's bank? _____

the Personal Banker bank? _____

the bank where most C.U. faculty and staff bank? _____

the bank most interested in this community? _____

the most progressive bank? _____

6. Which of these financial institutions, if any, (HAND CARD 2) are you or any member of your immediate family who lives here in this home doing business with now?

Bank	1
Credit Union	2
Finance Company	3
Savings and Loan	4
Industrial Bank	5
None of these	6
DK/Not sure	7

(IF NONE, Skip to 19.)

7. If a friend asked you to recommend a place where he or she could get a loan with which to buy a home, which financial institution would you probably recommend? (INTERVIEWER: Probe for specific name.) Why would you recommend (INSTITUTION NAMED)?

Would Recommend: _____

_____

Wouldn't	0
DK/Not Sure	9

Source: Reprinted with permission from the Council of American Survey Research, http://www.casro.org.

Instructions are often capitalized or printed in bold to alert the interviewer that it may be necessary to proceed in a certain way. For example, if a particular answer is given, the interviewer or respondent may be instructed to skip certain questions or go to a special sequence of questions. To facilitate coding, question responses should be precoded when possible, as in Exhibit 15.4.

Exhibit 15.5 illustrates some other useful techniques that are possible with personal interviews. Questions 3 and 6 instruct the interviewer to hand the respondent a card bearing a list of alternatives. Cards may help respondents grasp the intended meaning of the question and remember all the brand names or other items they are being asked about. Also, Questions 2, 3, and 6 instruct the interviewer that rating of the banks will start with the bank that has been checked in red pencil on the printed questionnaire. The name of the red-checked bank is not the same on every questionnaire. By rotating the order of the check marks, the researchers attempted to reduce order bias caused by respondents' tendency to react more favorably to the first set of questions.

Exhibit 15.6 illustrates a series of questions that includes a *skip question*. Either skip instructions or an arrow drawn pointing to the next question informs the respondent which question comes next.

EXHIBIT 15.6
Example of a Skip Question

1. If you had to buy a computer tomorrow, which of the following three types of computers do you think you would buy?

    1 Desktop—Go to Q. 3
    2 Laptop—Go to Q. 3
    3 Palm-sized (PDA)

2. (If "Palm-sized" on Q. 1, ask): What brand of computer do you think you would buy?

3. What is your age?

Layout is extremely important when questionnaires are long or require the respondent to fill in a large amount of information. In many circumstances, using headings or subtitles to indicate groups of questions will help the respondent grasp the scope or nature of the questions to be asked. Thus, at a glance, the respondent can follow the logic of the questionnaire.

Internet Questionnaires

Layout is also an important issue for questionnaires appearing on the Internet. A questionnaire on a website should be easy to use, flow logically, and have a graphic look and overall feel that motivate the respondent to cooperate from start to finish. Many of the guidelines for layout of paper questionnaires apply to Internet questionnaires. There are, however, some important differences.

With *graphical user interface (GUI) software,* the researcher can exercise control over the background, colors, fonts, and other visual features displayed on the computer screen so as to create an attractive and easy-to-use interface between the computer user and the Internet survey. GUI software allows the researcher to design questionnaires in which respondents click on the appropriate answer rather than having to type answers or codes.

Researchers often use web publishing software, such as WebSurveyor, FrontPage, or Netscape Composer, to format a questionnaire so that they will know how it should appear online. Questionnaire publishing also is available through survey host sites such as www.zoomerang.com. However, several features of a respondent's computer may influence the appearance of an Internet questionnaire. For example, discrepancies between the designer's and the respondent's computer settings for screen configuration (e.g., 640×480 pixels versus 800×600 pixels) may result in questions not being fully visible on the respondent's screen, misaligned text, or other visual problems. The possibility that the questionnaire the researcher/designer constructs on his or her computer may look different from the questionnaire that appears on the respondent's computer should always be considered when designing Internet surveys. One sophisticated remedy is to use the first few questions on an Internet survey to ask about operating system, browser software, and other computer configuration issues so that the questionnaire that is delivered is as compatible as possible with the respondent's computer. A simpler solution is to limit the horizontal width of the questions to seventy characters or less, to decrease the likelihood of wrap-around text.

LAYOUT ISSUES

Even if the questionnaire designer's computer and the respondents' computers are compatible, a web questionnaire designer should consider several layout issues. The first decision is whether the questionnaire will appear page by page, with individual questions on separate screens (web pages), or on a scrolling basis, with the entire questionnaire appearing on a single web page that the respondent scrolls from top to bottom. The *paging layout* (going from screen to screen) greatly facilitates skip patterns. Based on a respondent's answers to filter questions, the computer can automatically insert relevant questions on subsequent pages. If the entire questionnaire appears on one page (the *scrolling layout*), the display should advance smoothly, as if it were a piece of paper being moved up or down. The scrolling layout gives the respondent the ability to read any portion of the questionnaire at any time, but the absence of page boundaries can cause problems. For example, suppose a Likert scale consists of fifteen statements in a grid-format layout, with the response categories **Strongly Agree, Agree, Disagree,** and **Strongly Disagree** at the beginning of the questionnaire. Once the respondent has scrolled down beyond the first few statements, he or she may not be able to see both the statements at the end of the list and the response categories at the top of the grid simultaneously. Thus, avoiding the problems associated with splitting questions and response categories may be difficult with scrolling questionnaires.

When a scrolling questionnaire is long, category or section headings are helpful to respondents. It is also a good idea to provide links to the top and bottom parts of each section, so that users can navigate through the questionnaire without having to scroll through the entire document.[11]

Whether a web survey is page-by-page or scrolling format a **push button** with a label should clearly describe the actions to be taken. For example, if the respondent is to go to the next page, a large arrow labeled "NEXT" might appear in color at the bottom of the screen.

Decisions must be made about the use of color, graphics, animation, sound, and other special features that the Internet makes possible. One point to remember is that, although sophisticated graphics are not a problem for people with very powerful computers, many respondents' computers are not powerful enough to deliver complex graphics at a satisfactory speed, if at all. A textured background, colored headings, and small graphics can make a questionnaire more interesting and appealing, but they may present problems for respondents with older computers and/or low-bandwidth Internet connections.

With a paper questionnaire, the respondent knows how many questions he or she must answer. Because many Internet surveys offer no visual clues about the number of questions to be asked, it is important to provide a **status bar** or some other visual indicator of questionnaire length. For example, including a partially filled rectangular box as a visual symbol and a statement such as "The status bar at top right indicates approximately what portion of the survey you have completed" increases the likelihood that the respondent will finish the entire sequence of questions. Exhibit 15.7 shows a question from a online survey that uses a simple and motivating design. The survey presents one question at a time for simplicity. So that respondents can see their progress toward the end of the questionnaire, a gauge in the upper right corner fills from left to right as the respondent proceeds from Start to Finish.

An Internet questionnaire uses windows known as dialog boxes to display questions and record answers. Exhibit 15.8 portrays four common ways of displaying questions on a computer screen. Many Internet questionnaires require the respondent to activate his or her answer by clicking on the **radio button** for a response. Radio buttons work like push buttons on automobile radios: Clicking on an alternative response deactivates the first choice and replaces it with the new response. A **drop-down box**, such as the one shown in Exhibit 15.8, is a space-saving device that allows the researcher to provide a list of responses that are hidden from view until they are needed. A general statement, such as "Please select" or "Click here," is shown initially. Clicking on the downward-facing arrow makes the full range of choices appear. If the first choice in a list, such as "Strongly Agree," is shown while the other responses are kept hidden, the chance that response bias will occur is increased. Drop-down boxes may present a problem

Push button
In a dialog box on an Internet questionnaire, a small outlined area, such as a rectangle or an arrow, that the respondent clicks on to select an option or perform a function, such as submit.

Status bar
In an Internet questionnaire, a visual indicator that tells the respondent what portion of the survey he or she has completed.

Radio button
In an Internet questionnaire, a circular icon, resembling a button, that activates one response choice and deactivates others when a respondent clicks on it.

Drop-down box
In an Internet questionnaire, a space saving device that reveals responses when they are needed but otherwise hides them from view.

EXHIBIT 15.7
Question in an Online Screening Survey for Joining a Consumer Panel

Source: J.D. Power and Associates, "JDPowerPanel," https://ia.jdpa.com/20/survey/onsurvey.phtml, accessed March 9, 2006.

EXHIBIT 15.8
**Alternative Ways of
Displaying Internet Questions**

Radio button

Last month, did you purchase products or services over the Internet?

○ Yes

○ No

How familiar are you with Microsoft's Xbox video game player?

Know Extremely Well	Know Fairly Well	Know a Little	Know Just Name	Never Heard of
○	○	○	○	○

Drop-down box, closed position

In which country or region do you currently reside?

Click Here ▼

Drop-down box, open position

In which country or region do you currently reside?

Click Here ▼

Click Here
United States
Asia/Pacific (excluding Hawaii)
Africa
Australia or New Zealand
Canada
Europe
Latin America, South America, or Mexico
Middle East
Other

Check box

From which location(s) do you access the Internet? Select all that apply.
☐ Home
☐ Work
☐ Other Location

**Please indicate which of the following Web sites you have
ever visited or used. (CHOOSE ALL THAT APPLY.)**
☐ E*Trade's Web site
☐ Waterhouse's Web site
☐ Merrill Lynch's Web site
☐ Fidelity's Web site
☐ Schwab's Web site
☐ Powerstreet
☐ Yahoo! Finance
☐ Quicken.com
☐ Lycos Investing
☐ AOL's Personal Finance
☐ None of the above

Open-ended, one-line box

What company do you think is the most visible sponsor of sports?

Open-ended, scrolling text box

What can we do to improve our textbook?

for individuals with minimal computer skills, as they may not know how to reveal hidden responses behind a drop-down menu or how to move from one option to another in a moving-bar menu.

Check boxes

In an Internet questionnaire, small graphic boxes, next to answers, that a respondent clicks on to choose an answer; typically, a check mark or an **X** appears in the box when the respondent clicks on it.

Open-ended boxes

In an Internet questionnaire, boxes where respondents can type in their own answers to open-ended questions.

Pop-up boxes

In an Internet questionnaire, boxes that appear at selected points and contain information or instructions for respondents.

Checklist questions may be followed by check boxes, several, none, or all of which may be checked by the respondent. Open-ended boxes are boxes in which respondents type their answers to open-ended questions. Open-ended boxes may be designed as *one-line text boxes* or *scrolling text boxes,* depending on the breadth of the expected answer. Of course, open-ended questions require that respondents have both the skill and the willingness to keyboard lengthy answers on the computer. Some open-ended boxes are designed so that respondents can enter numbers for frequency response, ranking, or rating questions. For example,

Below you will see a series of statements that might or might not describe how you feel about your career. Please rate each statement using a scale from 1 to 4, where 4 means "Totally Agree," 3 means "Somewhat Agree," 2 means "Somewhat Disagree," and 1 means "Totally Disagree." Please enter your numeric answer in the box provided next to each statement. Would you say that . . .

A lack of business knowledge relevant to my field/career could hurt my career advancement.
My career life is an important part of how I define myself.

Pop-up boxes are message boxes that can be used to highlight important information. For example, pop-up boxes may be use to provide a privacy statement, such as the following:

IBM would like your help in making our website easier to use and more effective. Choose to complete the survey now or not at all.

Clicking on Privacy Statement opens the following pop-up box:

Survey Privacy Statement
This overall Privacy Statement verifies that IBM is a member of the TRUSTe program and is in compliance with TRUSTe principles. This survey is strictly for market research purposes. The information you provide will be used only to improve the overall content, navigation, and usability of ibm.com.

In some cases, respondents can learn more about how to use a particular scale or get a definition of a term by clicking on a link, which generates a pop-up box. One of the most common reasons for using pop-up boxes is *error trapping,* a topic discussed in the next section.

Chapter 14 described graphic rating scales, which present respondents with a graphic continuum. On the Internet, researchers can take advantage of scroll bars or other GUI software features to make these scales easy to use. For example, the graphic continuum may be drawn as a measuring rod with a plus sign on one end and a minus sign on the other. The respondent then moves a small rectangle back and forth between the two ends of the scale to scroll to any point on the continuum. Scoring, as discussed in Chapter 14, is in terms of some measure of the length (millimeters) from one end of the graphic continuum to the point marked by the respondent.

Finally, researchers often include a customized thank-you page at the end of an Internet questionnaire, so that a brief thank-you note pops onto respondents' screens when they click on the Submit push button.[12]

■ SOFTWARE THAT MAKES QUESTIONNAIRES INTERACTIVE

Computer code can be written to make Internet questionnaires interactive and less prone to errors. The writing of software programs is beyond the scope of this discussion. However, several of the interactive functions that software makes possible should be mentioned here.

As discussed in Chapter 9, Internet software allows the branching off of questioning into two or more different lines, depending on a particular respondent's answer, and the skipping or filtering of questions. Questionnaire-writing software with Boolean skip and branching logic is readily available. Most of these programs have *hidden skip logic* so that respondents never see any evidence of skips. It is best if the questions the respondent sees flow in numerical sequence. However, some programs number all potential questions in numerical order, and the respondent sees only the numbers on the questions he or she answers. Thus, a respondent may answer questions 1 through 11 and then next see a question numbered 15 because of the skip logic.

Software can systematically or randomly manipulate the questions a respondent sees. **Variable piping software** allows variables, such as answers from previous questions, to be inserted into unfolding questions. Other software can randomly rotate the order of questions, blocks of questions, and response alternatives from respondent to respondent.

Researchers can use software to control the flow of a questionnaire. Respondents can be blocked from backing up, or they can be allowed to stop in mid-questionnaire and come back later to finish. A questionnaire can be designed so that if the respondent fails to answer a question or answers it with an incorrect type of response, an immediate error message appears. This is called **error trapping**. With **forced answering software**, respondents cannot skip over questions as they do in mail surveys. The program will not let them continue if they fail to answer a question. The software may insert a boldfaced error message on the question screen or insert a pop-up box instructing the respondent how to continue. For example, if a respondent does not answer a question and tries to proceed to another screen, a pop-up box might present the following message:

You cannot leave a question blank. On questions without a "Not sure" or "Decline to answer" option, please choose the response that best represents your opinions or experiences.

The respondent must close the pop-up box and answer the question in order to proceed to the next screen.

Some designers include an **interactive help desk** in their web questionnaire so that respondents can solve problems they encounter in completing a questionnaire. A respondent might e-mail questions to the survey help desk or get live, interactive, real-time support via an online help desk.

Some respondents will leave the questionnaire website, prematurely terminating the survey. In many cases sending an e-mail message to these respondents at a later date, encouraging them to revisit the website, will persuade them to complete the questionnaire. Through the use of software and cookies, researchers can make sure that the respondent who revisits the website will be able to pick up at the point where he or she left off.

Once an Internet questionnaire has been designed, it is important to pretest it to ensure that it works with Internet Explorer, Netscape, AOL, WebTV, and other browsers. Some general-purpose programming languages, such as Java, do not always work with all browsers. Because different browsers have different peculiarities, a survey that works perfectly well with one may not function at all with another.[13]

Variable piping software
Software that allows variables to be inserted into an Internet questionnaire as a respondent is completing it.

Error trapping
Using software to control the flow of an Internet questionnaire—for example, to prevent respondents from backing up or failing to answer a question.

Forced answering software
Software that prevents respondents from continuing with an Internet questionnaire if they fail to answer a question.

Interactive help desk
In an Internet questionnaire, a live, real-time support feature that solves problems or answers questions respondents may encounter in completing the questionnaire.

How Much Pretesting and Revising Are Necessary?

Many novelists write, rewrite, revise, and rewrite again certain chapters, paragraphs, or even sentences. The researcher works in a similar world. Rarely does he or she write only a first draft of a questionnaire. Usually the questionnaire is tried out on a group, selected on a convenience basis, that is similar in makeup to the one that ultimately will be sampled. Although the researcher should not select a group too divergent from the target market—for example, selecting business students as surrogates for businesspeople—pretesting does not require a statistical sample. The pretesting process allows the researcher to determine whether respondents have any difficulty understanding the questionnaire and whether there are any ambiguous or biased questions. This process is exceedingly beneficial. Making a mistake with twenty-five or fifty subjects can avoid the potential disaster of administering an invalid questionnaire to several hundred individuals. For a questionnaire investigating teaching students' experience with web-based instruction, the researcher had the questionnaire reviewed first by university faculty members to ensure the questions were valid, then asked twenty teaching students to try answering the questions and indicate any ambiguities they noticed. Their feedback prompted changes in the format and wording. Pretesting was especially helpful because the English-language questionnaire was used in a school in the United Arab Emirates, where English is spoken but is not the primary language.[14]

RESEARCHSNAPSHOT

Pretesting the CAHPS Hospital Survey

The federal government's Centers for Medicare and Medicaid Services (CMS) is supposed to make information about hospital performance available to the public so that patients can compare hospitals and make informed choices about health-care services. An important aspect of hospital performance is whether patients feel satisfied with the care they receive. Many hospitals have used surveys to measure patient satisfaction, but comparing hospitals requires that all facilities use the same survey. So, CMS has spent several years creating and modifying a questionnaire, the Consumer Assessment of Health Providers and Systems (CAHPS) Hospital Survey, and similar questionnaires for other health-care providers.

Considering that the CAHPS Hospital Survey is being made available to all U.S. hospitals and the data will be made public, the researchers developing the survey have put it through extensive

pretesting, with public comment invited at each stage of the process. The first version of the survey, consisting of 68 questions, was given to a sample of 18 individuals drawn from the general population, who were then interviewed to discuss how they interpreted the questions. Based on their

reactions, the researchers modified the survey to make it clearer and then tested it on 13 more people. Almost half the interviews were conducted in Spanish. This process resulted in a draft survey with 66 items.

Next, the 66-item survey underwent pilot testing with almost 50,000 patients at hospitals in three states. Hospitals were selected to represent a cross-section of hospital types in those states. The researchers verified that a representative sample of the population completed the survey, and they analyzed the data to assess which questions best predicted satisfaction levels. Based on these analyses, the questionnaire was reduced to 32 items. That questionnaire was tested at several more hospitals and reviewed by the National Quality Forum. Based on this feedback, seven items were deleted and then two items were restored to the quesionnaire. Finally, the resulting 27-item survey was ready for use nationwide.

Source: Elizabeth Goldstein, Marybeth Farquhar, Christine Crofton, Charles Darby, and Steven Garfinkel, "Measuring Hospital Care from the Patients' Perspective: An Overview of the CAHPS Hospital Survey Development Process," Health Services Research, December 2005, downloaded from Business & Company Resource Center, http://galenet.galegroup.com; U.S. Department of Health and Human Services, Agency for Healthcare Research and Quality (AHRQ), "CAHPS Surveys and Tools to Advance Patient-Centered Care" http://www.cahps.ahrq.gov, last updated February 28, 2006; AHRQ, "CAHPS Survey Products," http://www.cahps.ahrq.gov, last updated March 6, 2006; Ron D. Hays and Julie Brown, "Field Testing: What It Is and How We Do It," CAHPS Connection, December 2005, http://www.cahps.ahrq.gov.

Preliminary tabulation
A tabulation of the results of a pretest to help determine whether the questionnaire will meet the objectives of the research.

Tabulating the results of a pretest helps determine whether the questionnaire will meet the objectives of the research. A **preliminary tabulation** often illustrates that, although respondents can easily comprehend and answer a given question, that question is inappropriate because it does not provide relevant information to help solve the marketing problem. Consider the following example from a survey among distributors of powder-actuated tools such as stud drivers concerning the percentage of sales to given industries:

Please estimate what percentage of your fastener and load sales go to the following industries:

- *% heating, plumbing, and air conditioning*
- *% carpentry*
- *% electrical*
- *% maintenance*
- *% other (please specify)*

The researchers were fortunate to learn that asking the question in this manner made it virtually impossible to obtain the information actually desired. Most respondents' answers did not total 100 percent, and the question had to be revised. In general, getting respondents to add everything correctly is a problem. Pretesting difficult questions such as these is essential.

What administrative procedures should be implemented to maximize the value of a pretest? Administering a questionnaire exactly as planned in the actual study often is not possible. For example, mailing out a questionnaire might require several weeks that simply cannot be spared. Pretesting a questionnaire in this manner would provide important information on response rate but may not point out why questions were skipped or what questions are ambiguous or confusing. Personal interviewers can record requests for additional explanation or comments that indicate respondents' difficulty with question sequence or other factors. This is the primary reason why interviewers are often used for pretest work. Self-administered questionnaires are not reworded to be personal interviews, but interviewers are instructed to observe respondents and ask for their comments after they complete the questionnaire. When pretesting personal or telephone interviews, interviewers may test alternative wordings and question sequences to determine which format best suits the intended respondents.

No matter how the pretest is conducted, the researcher should remember that its purpose is to uncover any problems that the questionnaire may cause. Thus, pretests typically are conducted to answer questions about the questionnaire such as the following:

- Can the questionnaire format be followed by the interviewer?
- Does the questionnaire flow naturally and conversationally?
- Are the questions clear and easy to understand?
- Can respondents answer the questions easily?
- Which alternative forms of questions work best?

Pretests also provide means for testing the sampling procedure—to determine, for example, whether interviewers are following the sampling instructions properly and whether the procedure is efficient. Pretests also provide estimates of the response rates for mail surveys and the completion rates for telephone surveys.

Usually a questionnaire goes through several revisions. The exact number of revisions depends on the researcher's and client's judgment. The revision process usually ends when both agree that the desired information is being collected in an unbiased manner.

Designing Questionnaires for Global Markets

Now that marketing research is being conducted around the globe, researchers must take cultural factors into account when designing questionnaires. The most common problem involves translating a questionnaire into other languages. A questionnaire developed in one country may be difficult to translate because equivalent language concepts do not exist or because of differences in idiom and vernacular. Although Spanish is spoken in both Mexico and Venezuela, one researcher found out that the Spanish translation of the English term *retail outlet* works in Mexico but not in Venezuela. Venezuelans interpreted the translation to refer to an electrical outlet, an outlet of a river into an ocean, or the passageway onto a patio.

Counting on an international audience to speak a common language such as English does not necessarily bridge these gaps, even when the respondents actually do speak more than one language. Cultural differences incorporate many shades of meaning that may not be captured by a survey delivered in a language used primarily for, say, business transactions. In a test of this idea, undergraduate students in twenty-four countries completed questionnaires about attitudes toward school and career. Half received the questionnaire in English, and half in their native language. The results varied, with country-to-country differences being smaller when students completed the questionnaire in English.[15]

International marketing researchers often have questionnaires back translated. **Back translation** is the process of taking a questionnaire that has previously been translated from one language to another and having it translated back again by a second, independent translator. The back translator is often a person whose native tongue is the language that will be used for the questionnaire. This process can reveal inconsistencies between the English version and the translation. For example, when a soft-drink company translated its slogan "Baby, it's cold inside" into Cantonese for research in Hong Kong, the result read "Small Mosquito, on the inside, it is very cold." In Hong Kong, *small mosquito* is a colloquial expression for a small child. Obviously the intended meaning of the advertising message had been lost in the translated questionnaire.[16]

As indicated in Chapter 8, literacy influences the designs of self-administered questionnaires and interviews. Knowledge of the literacy rates in foreign countries, especially those that are just developing modern economies, is vital.

Back translation
Taking a questionnaire that has previously been translated into another language and having a second, independent translator translate it back to the original language.

Summary

1. Explain the significance of decisions about questionnaire design and wording. Good questionnaire design is a key to obtaining accurate survey results. The specific questions to be asked will be a function of the type of information needed to answer the manager's questions and the communication medium of data collection. Relevance and accuracy are the basic criteria for judging questionnaire results. A questionnaire is *relevant* if no unnecessary information is collected and the information needed for solving the marketing problem is obtained. *Accuracy* means that the information is reliable and valid.

2. Define alternatives for wording open-ended and fixed-alternative questions. Knowing how each question should be phrased requires some knowledge of the different types of questions possible. Open-ended response questions pose some problem or question and ask the respondent to answer in his or her own words. Fixed-alternative questions require less interviewer skill, take less time, and are easier to answer. In fixed-alternative questions the respondent is given specific limited alternative responses and asked to choose the one closest to his or her own viewpoint. Standardized responses are easier to code, tabulate, and interpret. Care must be taken to formulate the responses so that they do not overlap. Respondents whose answers do not fit any of the fixed alternatives may be forced to select alternatives that do not communicate what they really mean. Open-ended response questions are especially useful in exploratory research or at the beginning of a questionnaire. They make a questionnaire more expensive to analyze because of the uniqueness of the answers. Also, interviewer bias can influence the responses to such questions.

3. Summarize guidelines for questions that avoid mistakes in questionnaire design. Some guidelines for questionnaire construction have emerged from research experience. The language should be simple to allow for variations in educational level. Researchers should avoid leading or loaded questions, which suggest answers to the respondents, as well as questions that induce them to give socially desirable answers. Respondents have a bias against questions that suggest changes in the status quo. Their reluctance to answer personal questions can be reduced by explaining the need for the questions and by assuring respondents of the confidentiality of their replies. The researcher should carefully avoid ambiguity in questions. Another common problem is the double-barreled question, which asks two questions at once.

4. Describe how the proper sequence of questions may improve a questionnaire. Question sequence can be very important to the success of a survey. The opening questions should be designed to capture respondents' interest and keep them involved. Personal questions should be postponed to the middle or end of the questionnaire. General questions should precede specific ones. In a series of attitude scales the first response may be used as an anchor for comparison with the other responses. The order of alternatives on closed questions can affect the results. Filter questions are useful for avoiding unnecessary questions that do not apply to a particular respondent. Such questions may be put into a flowchart for personal or telephone interviewing.

5. Discuss how to design a questionnaire layout. The layout of a mail or other self-administered questionnaire can affect its response rate. An attractive questionnaire encourages a response, as does a carefully phrased title. Internet questionnaires present unique design issues. Decisions must be made about the use of color, graphics, animation, sound, and other special layout effects that the Internet makes possible.

6. Describe criteria for pretesting and revising a questionnaire and for adapting it to global markets. Pretesting helps reveal errors while they can still be corrected easily. A preliminary tabulation may show that, even if respondents understand questions, the responses are not relevant to the marketing problem. Often, the most efficient way to conduct a pretest is with interviewers to generate quick feedback. International marketing researchers must take cultural factors into account when designing questionnaires. The most widespread problem involves translation into another language. International questionnaires are often back translated.

Key Terms and Concepts

Open-ended response questions
Fixed-alternative questions
Simple-dichotomy
    (dichotomous-alternative) question
Determinant-choice question
Frequency-determination question

Checklist question
Leading question
Loaded question
Counterbiasing statement
Split-ballot technique
Double-barreled question

Order bias
Funnel technique
Filter question
Pivot question
Multiple-grid question
Push button

Status bar　　　　　　　　　　Open-ended boxes　　　　　　　Forced answering software
Radio button　　　　　　　　　Pop-up boxes　　　　　　　　　Interactive help desk
Drop-down box　　　　　　　　Variable piping software　　　　Preliminary tabulation
Check boxes　　　　　　　　　Error trapping　　　　　　　　　Back translation

Questions for Review and Critical Thinking

1. Evaluate and comment on the following questions, taken from several questionnaires:

   a. A university computer center survey on SPSS usage:

      How often do you use SPSS statistical software? Please check one.

      - *Infrequently (once a semester)*
      - *Occasionally (once a month)*
      - *Frequently (once a week)*
      - *All the time (daily)*

   b. A survey of advertising agencies:

      Do you understand and like the Federal Trade Commission's new corrective advertising policy?

      ——*Yes*　　——*No*

   c. A survey on a new, small electric car:

      Assuming 90 percent of your driving is in town, would you buy this type of car?

      ——*Yes*　　——*No*

      If this type of electric car had the same initial cost as a current "Big 3" full-size, fully equipped car, but operated at one-half the cost over a five-year period, would you buy one?

      ——*Yes*　　——*No*

   d. A student survey:

      Since the beginning of this semester, approximately what percentage of the time do you get to campus using each of the forms of transportation available to you per week?

      Walk ——　*Bicycle* ——
      Public transportation ——　*Motor vehicle* ——

   e. A survey of motorcycle dealers:

      Should the company continue its generous cooperative advertising program?

   f. A survey of media use by farmers:

      Thinking about yesterday, put an X in the box below for each quarter-hour time period during which, so far as you can recall, you personally listened to radio. Do the same for television.

      6:00 to 10:00 A.M. by quarter-hours

      Radio →　TV →

      (columns: 6:00–6:15, 6:15–6:30, 6:30–6:45, 6:45–7:00, 7:00–7:15, 7:15–7:30, 7:30–7:45, 7:45–8:00)

      Radio →　TV →

      (columns: 8:00–8:15, 8:15–8:30, 8:30–8:45, 8:45–9:00, 9:00–9:15, 9:15–9:30, 9:30–9:45, 9:45–10:00)

   If you did not watch TV any time yesterday, X here ☐
   If you did not listen to radio any time yesterday, X here ☐

   g. A government survey of gasoline retailers:

      Suppose the full-service pump selling price for regular gasoline is 232.8 cents per gallon on the first day of the month. Suppose on the 10th of the month the price is raised to 234.9 cents per gallon, and on the 25th of the month it is reduced to 230.9 cents per gallon. In order to provide the required data you should list the accumulator reading on the full-service regular gasoline pump when the station opens on the 1st day, the 10th day, and the 25th day of the month and when the station closes on the last day of the month.

   h. An anti-gun-control group's survey:

      Do you believe that private citizens have the right to own firearms to defend themselves, their families, and their property from violent criminal attack?

      ——*Yes*　　——*No*

   i. A survey of the general public:

      In the next year, after accounting for inflation, do you think your real personal income will go up or down?

      1. *Up*
      2. *(Stay the same)*
      3. *Down*
      4. *(Don't know)*

   j. **ETHICS** A survey of the general public:

      Some people say that companies should be required by law to label all chemicals and substances that the government states are potentially harmful. The label would tell what the chemical or substance is, what dangers it might pose, and what safety procedures should be used in handling the substance. Other people say that such laws would be too strict. They say the law should require labels on only those chemicals and substances that the companies themselves decide are potentially harmful. Such a law, they say, would be less costly for the companies and would permit them to exclude those chemicals and substances they consider to be trade secrets. Which of these views is closest to your own?

      1. *Require labels on all chemicals and substances that the government states are potentially harmful.*
      2. *(Don't know)*
      3. *Require labels on only those chemicals and substances that companies decide are potentially harmful.*

   k. A survey of voters:

      Since agriculture is vital to our state's economy, how do you feel about the administration's farm policies?

      Strongly favor
      Somewhat favor
      Somewhat oppose
      Strongly oppose
      Unsure

2. The following question was asked of a sample of television viewers:

   We are going to ask you to classify the type of fan you consider your-self to be for different sports and sports programs.

   - **Diehard Fan: Watch games, follow up on scores and sports news multiple times a day**
   - **Avid Fan: Watch games, follow up on scores and sports news once a day**
   - **Casual Fan: Watch games, follow up on scores and sports news occasionally**
   - **Championship Fan: Watch games, follow up on scores and sports news only during championships or playoffs**
   - **Non-Fan: Never watch games or follow up on scores**
   - **Anti-Fan: Dislike, oppose, or object to a certain sport**

   Does this question do a good job of avoiding ambiguity?

3. How might the wording of a question about income influence respondents' answers?

4. What is the difference between a *leading question* and a *loaded question?*

5. Design one or more open-ended response questions to measure reactions to a magazine ad for a Xerox photocopier.

6. Design one or more questions to measure how a person who has just been shown a television commercial might describe the commercial.

7. Evaluate the layout of the filter question that follows:

   Are you employed either full time or part time?

   Mark (x) one.   ☐ Yes   ☐ No

   If yes: How many hours per week are you usually employed? *Mark (x) one.*

   ☐ Less than 35   ☐ 35 or more

   What is the zip code at your usual place of work?

   _____

8. It has been said that surveys show that consumers hate advertising, but like specific ads. Comment.

9. Design a complete questionnaire to evaluate a new fast-food fried chicken restaurant.

10. Design a short but complete questionnaire to measure consumer satisfaction with an airline.

11. Develop a checklist of things to consider in questionnaire construction.

12. Design a complete personal interview questionnaire for a zoo that wishes to determine who visits the zoo and how they evaluate it.

13. Design a complete self-administered questionnaire for a bank to give to customers immediately after they open new accounts.

14. Design a questionnaire for your local Big Brothers and Big Sisters organization to investigate awareness of and willingness to volunteer time to this organization.

15. Design a questionnaire for a bank located in a college town to investigate the potential for attracting college students as checking account customers.

16. The Apple Assistance Center is a hotline to solve problems for users of Macintosh computers and other Apple products. Design a short (postcard-size) consumer satisfaction/service quality questionnaire for the Apple Assistance Center.

17. 'NET Visit the following website: http://www.history.org. What type of questions might be asked in a survey to evaluate the effectiveness of this website in terms of being informative and in terms of being an effective sales medium?

18. A client tells a researcher that she wants a questionnaire that evaluates the importance of thirty product characteristics and rates her brand and ten competing brands on these characteristics. The researcher believes that this questionnaire will induce respondent fatigue because it will be far too long. Should the researcher do exactly what the client says or risk losing the business by suggesting a different approach?

19. **ETHICS** A lobbying organization designs a short questionnaire about its political position. It also includes a membership solicitation with the questionnaire. Is this approach ethical?

20. 'NET Visit Mister Poll at http://www.misterpoll.com, where you will find thousands of user-contributed polls on every imaginable topic from the controversial to the downright zany. What you find will depend on when you visit the site. However, you might find something such as a Movie Poll, where you pick your favorite film of the season. Evaluate the questions in the poll.

21. 'NET Try to find two friends that know the same foreign language. Write ten Likert questions that measure how exciting a retail store environment is to shop in. Have one of your friends interpret the question into the foreign language. Have the other take the translation and state each question in English. How similar is the translated English to the original English? Comment.

Research Activity

1. Design eight questions that assess how effective an undergraduate college business course has been.

Case 15.1 Agency for Healthcare Research and Quality

At the U.S. Department of Health and Human Services, the Agency for Healthcare Research and Quality (AHRQ) developed a survey to measure hospital employees' attitudes about patient safety in their facilities.[17] The survey is designed to help hospitals ensure safety by creating an environment in which employees share information, improve safety when problems are identified, and if necessary, change the way employees deliver care. The AHRQ suggests that hospitals use the survey to identify areas needing improvement and repeat its use to track changes over time.

The survey is shown in Case Exhibit 15.1–1.

Questions

1. Evaluate the questionnaire. Can you suggest any improvements?

2. Will this survey meet its objectives? Explain.

CASE EXHIBIT 15.1–1 **AHRQ Hospital Questionnaire**

INSTRUCTIONS

This survey asks for your opinions about patient safety issues, medical error, and event reporting in your hospital and will take about 10 to 15 minutes to complete.

> • An *"event"* is defined as any type of error, mistake, incident, accident, or deviation, regardless of whether or not it results in patient harm.
>
> • *"Patient safety"* is defined as the avoidance and prevention of patient injuries or adverse events resulting from the processes of health care delivery.

SECTION A: Your Work Area/Unit

In this survey, think of your "unit" as the work area, department, or clinical area of the hospital where you spend *most* of your work time or provide *most* of your clinical services.

What is your primary work area or unit in this hospital? Mark ONE answer by filling in the circle.

O a. Many different hospital units/No specific unit

O b. Medicine (non-surgical)	O g. Intensive care unit (any type)	O l. Radiology
O c. Surgery	O h. Psychiatry/mental health	O m. Anesthesiology
O d. Obstetrics	O i. Rehabilitation	O n. Other, please specify:
O e. Pediatrics	O j. Pharmacy	
O f. Emergency department	O k. Laboratory	

Please indicate your agreement or disagreement with the following statements about your work area/unit. Mark your answer by filling in the circle.

Think about your hospital work area/unit...	Strongly Disagree ▼	Disagree ▼	Neither ▼	Agree ▼	Strongly Agree ▼
1. People support one another in this unit	①	②	③	④	⑤
2. We have enough staff to handle the workload	①	②	③	④	⑤
3. When a lot of work needs to be done quickly, we work together as a team to get the work done	①	②	③	④	⑤
4. In this unit, people treat each other with respect	①	②	③	④	⑤
5. Staff in this unit work longer hours than is best for patient care	①	②	③	④	⑤
6. We are actively doing things to improve patient safety	①	②	③	④	⑤
7. We use more agency/temporary staff than is best for patient care	①	②	③	④	⑤
8. Staff feel like their mistakes are held against them	①	②	③	④	⑤
9. Mistakes have led to positive changes here	①	②	③	④	⑤
10. It is just by chance that more serious mistakes don't happen around here	①	②	③	④	⑤
11. When one area in this unit gets really busy, others help out	①	②	③	④	⑤
12. When an event is reported, it feels like the person is being written up, not the problem	①	②	③	④	⑤

(continued)

CASE EXHIBIT 15.1-1 **AHRQ Hospital Questionnaire** (*continued*)

SECTION A: Your Work Area/Unit (continued)

Think about your hospital work area/unit...

	Strongly Disagree ▼	Disagree ▼	Neither ▼	Agree ▼	Strongly Agree ▼
13. After we make changes to improve patient safety, we evaluate their effectiveness	①	②	③	④	⑤
14. We work in "crisis mode" trying to do too much, too quickly	①	②	③	④	⑤
15. Patient safety is never sacrificed to get more work done	①	②	③	④	⑤
16. Staff worry that mistakes they make are kept in their personnel file	①	②	③	④	⑤
17. We have patient safety problems in this unit	①	②	③	④	⑤
18. Our procedures and systems are good at preventing errors from happening	①	②	③	④	⑤

SECTION B: Your Supervisor/Manager
Please indicate your agreement or disagreement with the following statements about your immediate supervisor/manager or person to whom you directly report. Mark your answer by filling in the circle.

	Strongly Disagree ▼	Disagree ▼	Neither ▼	Agree ▼	Strongly Agree ▼
1. My supervisor/manager says a good word when he/she sees a job done according to established patient safety procedures	①	②	③	④	⑤
2. My supervisor/manager seriously considers staff suggestions for improving patient safety	①	②	③	④	⑤
3. Whenever pressure builds up, my supervisor/manager wants us to work faster, even if it means taking shortcuts	①	②	③	④	⑤
4. My supervisor/manager overlooks patient safety problems that happen over and over	①	②	③	④	⑤

SECTION C: Communications
How often do the following things happen in your work area/unit? Mark your answer by filling in the circle.

Think about your hospital work area/unit...

	Never ▼	Rarely ▼	Some-times ▼	Most of the time ▼	Always ▼
1. We are given feedback about changes put into place based on event reports	①	②	③	④	⑤
2. Staff will freely speak up if they see something that may negatively affect patient care	①	②	③	④	⑤
3. We are informed about errors that happen in this unit	①	②	③	④	⑤
4. Staff feel free to question the decisions or actions of those with more authority	①	②	③	④	⑤
5. In this unit, we discuss ways to prevent errors from happening again	①	②	③	④	⑤
6. Staff are afraid to ask questions when something does not seem right	①	②	③	④	⑤

(*continued*)

CASE EXHIBIT 15.1-1 AHRQ Hospital Questionnaire (*continued*)

SECTION D: Frequency of Events Reported
In your hospital work area/unit, when the following mistakes happen, *how often are they reported?* Mark your answer by filling in the circle.

	Never ▼	Rarely ▼	Some-times ▼	Most of the time ▼	Always ▼
1. When a mistake is made, but is *caught and corrected before affecting the patient*, how often is this reported?	①	②	③	④	⑤
2. When a mistake is made, but has *no potential to harm the patient*, how often is this reported?	①	②	③	④	⑤
3. When a mistake is made that *could harm the patient*, but does not, how often is this reported?	①	②	③	④	⑤

SECTION E: Patient Safety Grade
Please give your work area/unit in this hospital an overall grade on patient safety. Mark ONE answer.

A	B	C	D	E
○	○	○	○	○
Excellent	Very Good	Acceptable	Poor	Failing

SECTION F: Your Hospital
Please indicate your agreement or disagreement with the following statements about your hospital. Mark your answer by filling in the circle.

Think about your hospital...	Strongly Disagree ▼	Disagree ▼	Neither ▼	Agree ▼	Strongly Agree ▼
1. Hospital management provides a work climate that promotes patient safety	①	②	③	④	⑤
2. Hospital units do not coordinate well with each other	①	②	③	④	⑤
3. Things "fall between the cracks" when transferring patients from one unit to another	①	②	③	④	⑤
4. There is good cooperation among hospital units that need to work together	①	②	③	④	⑤
5. Important patient care information is often lost during shift changes	①	②	③	④	⑤
6. It is often unpleasant to work with staff from other hospital units .	①	②	③	④	⑤
7. Problems often occur in the exchange of information across hospital units	①	②	③	④	⑤
8. The actions of hospital management show that patient safety is a top priority...	①	②	③	④	⑤
9. Hospital management seems interested in patient safety only after an adverse event happens	①	②	③	④	⑤
10. Hospital units work well together to provide the best care for patients...	①	②	③	④	⑤
11. Shift changes are problematic for patients in this hospital............	①	②	③	④	⑤

SECTION G: Number of Events Reported
In the past 12 months, how many event reports have you filled out and submitted? Mark ONE answer.

○ a. No event reports
○ b. 1 to 2 event reports
○ c. 3 to 5 event reports

○ d. 6 to 10 event reports
○ e. 11 to 20 event reports
○ f. 21 event reports or more

(*continued*)

CASE EXHIBIT 15.1-1 **AHRQ Hospital Questionnaire** (*continued*)

SECTION H: Background Information
This information will help in the analysis of the survey results. Mark ONE answer by filling in the circle.

1. How long have you worked in this <u>hospital</u>?
    - O a. Less than 1 year
    - O b. 1 to 5 years
    - O c. 6 to 10 years
    - O d. 11 to 15 years
    - O e. 16 to 20 years
    - O f. 21 years or more

2. How long have you worked in your current hospital <u>work area/unit</u>?
    - O a. Less than 1 year
    - O b. 1 to 5 years
    - O c. 6 to 10 years
    - O d. 11 to 15 years
    - O e. 16 to 20 years
    - O f. 21 years or more

3. Typically, how many <u>hours per week</u> do you work in this hospital?
    - O a. Less than 20 hours per week
    - O b. 20 to 39 hours per week
    - O c. 40 to 59 hours per week
    - O d. 60 to 79 hours per week
    - O e. 80 to 99 hours per week
    - O f. 100 hours per week or more

4. What is your staff position in this hospital? Mark ONE answer that best describes your staff position.
    - O a. Registered Nurse
    - O b. Physician Assistant/Nurse Practitioner
    - O c. LVN/LPN
    - O d. Patient Care Assistant/Hospital Aide/Care Partner
    - O e. Attending/Staff Physician
    - O f. Resident Physician/Physician in Training
    - O g. Pharmacist
    - O h. Dietician
    - O i. Unit Assistant/Clerk/Secretary
    - O j. Respiratory Therapist
    - O k. Physical, Occupational, or Speech Therapist
    - O l. Technician (e.g., EKG, Lab, Radiology)
    - O m. Administration/Management
    - O n. Other, please specify:

5. In your staff position, do you typically have direct interaction or contact with patients?
    - O a. YES, I typically have direct interaction or contact with patients.
    - O b. NO, I typically do NOT have direct interaction or contact with patients.

6. How long have you worked in your current specialty or profession?
    - O a. Less than 1 year
    - O b. 1 to 5 years
    - O c. 6 to 10 years
    - O d. 11 to 15 years
    - O e. 16 to 20 years
    - O f. 21 years or more

SECTION I: Your Comments
Please feel free to write any comments about patient safety, error, or event reporting in your hospital.

THANK YOU FOR COMPLETING THIS SURVEY.

Source: Agency for Healthcare Research and Quality, "Hospital Survey on Patient Safety Culture," http://www.ahrq.gov/qual/hospculture/.

Case 15.2 Canterbury Travels

Hometown, located in the northcentral United States, had a population of about fifty thousand. There were two travel agencies in Hometown before Canterbury Travels opened its doors.

Canterbury Travels was in its second month of operations. Owner Roxanne Freeman had expected to have more business than she actually had. She decided that she needed to conduct a survey to determine how much business Hometown offered. She also wanted to learn whether people were aware of Canterbury Travels. She thought that this survey would determine the effectiveness of her advertising.

The questionnaire that Roxanne Freeman designed is shown in Case Exhibit 15.2–1.

Questions

1. Critically evaluate the questionnaire.
2. Will Canterbury Travels gain the information it needs from this survey?
3. Design a questionnaire to satisfy Roxanne Freeman's information needs.

CASE EXHIBIT 15.2-1 **Travel Questionnaire**

The following questionnaire pertains to a project being conducted by a local travel agency. The intent of the study is to better understand the needs and attitudes of Hometown residents toward travel agencies. The questionnaire will take only 10 to 15 minutes to fill out at your convenience. Your name will in no way be connected with the questionnaire.

1. Have you traveled out of state?   _____Yes _____No
2. If yes, do you travel for:
   Business   Both
   Pleasure
3. How often do you travel for the above?
   0–1 times per month   0–1 times per year
   2–3 times per month   2–3 times per year
   4–5 times per month   4–5 times per year
   6 or more times per month   6 or more times per year
4. How do you make your travel arrangements?
   Airline   Travel agency
   Other (please specify) _____
5. Did you know that travel agencies do not charge the customer for their services?
   _____Yes _____No
6. Please rate the following qualities that would be most important to you in the selection of a travel agency:

	Good				Bad
Free services (reservations, advice, and delivery of tickets and literature)	___	___	___	___	___
Convenient location	___	___	___	___	___
Knowledgeable personnel	___	___	___	___	___
Friendly personnel	___	___	___	___	___
Casual atmosphere	___	___	___	___	___
Revolving charge account	___	___	___	___	___
Reputation	___	___	___	___	___
Personal sales calls	___	___	___	___	___

7. Are you satisfied with your present travel agency?

	Very satisfied				Very dissatisfied
Holiday Travel	___	___		___	___
Leisure Tours	___	___		___	___
Canterbury Travels	___	___		___	___
Other _____	___	___		___	___

(continued)

8. If not, what are you dissatisfied with about your travel agency?

	Good				**Bad**
Free services (reservations, advice, and delivery of tickets and literature)	_____	_____	_____	_____	_____
Convenient location	_____	_____	_____	_____	_____
Knowledgeable personnel	_____	_____	_____	_____	_____
Friendly personnel	_____	_____	_____	_____	_____
Casual atmosphere	_____	_____	_____	_____	_____
Revolving charge account	_____	_____	_____	_____	_____
Reputation	_____	_____	_____	_____	_____
Personal sales calls	_____	_____	_____	_____	_____

9. Did you know that there is a new travel agency in Hometown?

    _____Yes   _____No

10. Can you list the travel agencies in Hometown and their locations?

    _____
    _____
    _____

11. Do you use the same travel agency repeatedly?

	0–1 times per month	2–3 times per month	4–5 times per month	6 or more times per month	0–1 times per year	2–3 times per year	4–5 times per year	6 or more times per year
Holiday Travel								
Leisure Tours								
Canterbury Travels								
Other (please specify)								

12. Have you visited the new travel agency in Hometown?

    _____Yes   _____No

13. If yes, what is its name? _____

14. How do you pay for your travel expenses?

    Cash   Company charge

    Check   Personal charge

    Credit card   Other _____

15. Which of these have you seen advertising for?

    Holiday Travel

    Canterbury Travels

    Other _____

16. Where have you seen or heard the advertisement you describe above?

17. Would you consider changing travel agencies?

    _____Yes   _____No

The following are some personal questions about you that will be used for statistical purposes only. Your answers will be held in the strictest confidence.

18. What is your age?

    19–25   46–55

    26–35   56–65

    36–45   Over 65

19. What is your sex?

    Male   Female

(*continued*)

CASE EXHIBIT 15.2-1 **Travel Questionnaire** (*continued*)

20. What is your marital status?

Single   Divorced

Married   Widowed

21. How long have you lived in Hometown?

0–6 months   5–10 years

7–12 months   11–15 years

1–4 years   Over 15 years

22. What is your present occupation?

Business and professional   Laborer

Salaried and semiprofessional   Student

Skilled worker

23. What is the highest level of education you have completed?

Elementary school   1–2 years of college

Junior high school   3–4 years of college

Senior high school   More than 4 years of college

Trade or vocational school

24. What is your yearly household income?

$0–$5,000 $25,001–$40,000

$5,001–$10,000 $40,001–$60,000

$10,001–$15,000 $60,000 and above

$15,001–$25,000

Case 15.3 McDonald's Spanish Language Questionnaire

The questions in Case Exhibit 15.3–1, about a visit to McDonald's, originally appeared in Spanish and were translated into English.

Questions

1. What is the typical process for developing questionnaires for markets where consumers speak a language other than English?

2. Find someone who speaks Spanish and have him or her back translate the questions that appear in Case Exhibit 15.3–1. Are these Spanish-language questions adequate?

CASE EXHIBIT 15.3-1 **McDonald's Questionnaire**

AQUI → SE EMPIEZA

1. **En general, ¿qué tan satisfecho/a quedó con su visita a este McDonald's hoy?** .... NADA SATISFECHO/A ☹ ① ② ③ ④ ⑤ MUY SATISFECHO/A ☺

2. **Su visita fue.......** Adentro (**A**) o en el Drive-thru (**DT**) Ⓐ Adentro   Ⓓⓣ Drive-thru

3. **Su visita fue.......** Durante el Desayuno (**D**), Almuerzo (**A**), Cena (**C**) Ⓓ Desayuno   Ⓐ Almuerzo   Ⓐ Cena

4. **Su visita fue.......** Entre semana (**E**) o Fin de semana (**F**) Ⓔ Entre semana   Ⓕ Fin de semana

COMIDA

5. ¿Quedó satisfecho/a con la comida que recibio hoy? Ⓢ Si   Ⓝ No

Si NO, ¿cuál fue el problema?

Favor de rellenar el(los) círculo(s) apropiado(s).

Sandwich / platillo frío

Apariencia desagradable

Mal sabor de la comida

Pocas papas en la bolsa / caja

Papas / tortitas de papa frías

Papas no bien saladas

Bebida aguada / de mal sabor

Case 15.4 Schönbrunn Palace in Vienna

The Schönbrunn Palace in Vienna was constructed in the eighteenth century during the reign of the Hapsburgs. Today this former summer residence of the imperial family is one of Austria's top tourist attractions.

The questions in Case Exhibit 15.4–1, about a visit to the Schönbrunn Palace, originally appeared in German and were translated into English.

Questions

1. What is the typical process for developing questionnaires for markets where consumers speak a different language?
2. Find someone who speaks German and have him or her back translate the questions that appear in Case Exhibit 15.4–1. Are these German questions adequate?

CASE EXHIBIT 15.4–1 **Schönbrunn Palace Questionnaire**

Befragung der Besucher   **Schloß Schönbrunn**

Land/Staat _____ Bundesland (nur für Ö) _____

Alter _____ Jahre   Geschlecht ◻ männlich ◻ weiblich

Heutiges Datum ___ . ___ . 199__   Uhrzeit _____

• **Waren Sie heute zum ersten Mal im Schloß Schönbrunn?**
◻ ja   ◻ nein, zum ___ . Mal

• **Welche Tour haben Sie gemacht?**
◻ *Grand Tour* (40 Räume)
◻ *Imperial Tour* (22 Räume)

• **Welche Art von Führung haben Sie gewählt?**
◻ *Schönbrunn Führung (Angebot des Schlosses)*
◻ *eigener Reiseführer (Reisegruppe, Fremdenführer)*
◻ *Tonbandführer (Audioguide) in* _____ *Sprache*
◻ *keinerlei Führung*

• **Falls Sie an einer Führung teilgenommen haben:**
Wie finden Sie Ihren Führer bzw. Ihre Führerin?
◻ sehr freundlich   ◻ eher freundlich   ◻ eher unfreundlich   ◻ sehr unfreundlich
weil ... _____

• **Bei Verwendung eines Tonbandführers (Audioguide):**
Wie finden Sie die angebotenen Audioguides?
◻ sehr gut   ◻ eher gut   ◻ eher schlecht   ◻ sehr schlecht
weil ... _____

• **Wie ist Ihr Gesamteindruck vom Schloß Schönbrunn alles in allem?**
◻ sehr gut   ◻ eher gut   ◻ eher schlecht   ◻ sehr schlecht
weil ... _____

• **Wie ist Ihr Eindruck vom Personal im Schloß?**
◻ sehr gut   ◻ eher gut   ◻ eher schlecht   ◻ sehr schlecht
weil ... _____

• **Wie gut finden Sie sich im Schloß Schönbrunn/Park zurecht (Hinweisschilder, kennt man sich gut aus, findet man die Kassen, Toiletten, den Ausgang, etc.)?**
◻ sehr gut   ◻ eher gut   ◻ eher schlecht   ◻ sehr schlecht
weil ... _____

• **Fühlten Sie sich nach dem Besuch gut informiert über das Schloß und seine Geschichte?**
◻ sehr gut   ◻ eher gut   ◻ eher schlecht   ◻ sehr schlecht

• **Wurden Sie bei der Besichtigung gestört?**
durch (andere) Gruppen:
◻ sehr stark   ◻ etwas   ◻ kaum   ◻ gar nicht
durch Einzelbesucher:
◻ sehr stark   ◻ etwas   ◻ kaum   ◻ gar nicht

• **Wie finden Sie die Art, wie die Räume dargestellt werden (Einrichtung, Möblierung, Beleuchtung, Dekoration, etc.)?**
◻ sehr gut   ◻ eher gut   ◻ eher schlecht   ◻ sehr schlecht
weil ... _____

• **Haben Sie nach dem Besuch im Schloß Schönbrunn eine lebendige Vorstellung vom einstigen Leben bei Hof?**
◻ ja   ◻ etwas   ◻ kaum   ◻ nein
weil ... _____

• **Was würden Sie noch gerne über das Schloß erfahren?**
_____

• **Wie finden Sie die Eintrittspreise?**
◻ viel zu teuer   ◻ etwas zu teuer   ◻ angemessen   ◻ günstig

• **Wie finden Sie das Angebot im Museumshop?**
◻ sehr gut   ◻ eher gut   ◻ eher schlecht   ◻ sehr schlecht
weil ... _____

• **Was könnte Ihrer Meinung nach noch verbessert werden?**
_____
_____
_____
_____

Vielen Dank für Ihren Besuch und Ihre Anregungen!

As Chapters 13, 14, and 15 explain, problem definitions and research objectives determine the nature of the questions to be asked. In most cases researchers construct custom questions for their specific projects. However, in many instances different research projects have some common research objectives. This appendix compiles question wordings and measurement scales frequently used by marketing researchers. It is by no means exhaustive. It does not repeat every question already discussed in the text. For example, it does not include the hundreds of possible semantic differential items or Likert scale items discussed in Chapter 14.

The purpose of this appendix is to provide a bank of questions and scales for easy reference. It can be used when marketing research objectives dictate investigation of commonly researched issues.

Questions About Advertising

Awareness

Have you ever seen any advertising for (brand name)?
☐ *Yes*   ☐ *No*

Are you aware of (brand name)?
☐ *Yes*   ☐ *No*

If yes, how did you first become aware of (brand name)?

- *In-flight airline magazine*
- *Poster or billboard at airport*
- *Television at airport*
- *Card in the seatback pocket*
- *Other (please specify)* _____

Unaided Recall/Top of the Mind Recall

Can you tell me the names of any brands of (product category) for which you have seen or heard any advertising recently?

_____
_____
_____

(After reading a magazine or viewing a TV program with commercials) Please try to recall all the brands you saw advertised on/in (name of program or magazine). (DO NOT PROBE. WRITE BRAND NAMES IN ORDER MENTIONED BY RESPONDENT.)

(After establishing that the respondent watched a certain television program) Do you recall seeing a commercial for any (product category)? (IF YES) What brand of (product category) was advertised?

Aided Recall

(After establishing that the respondent watched a certain television program or read a certain magazine) Now, I'm going to read you a list of brands. Some of them were advertised on/in (name of program or magazine); others were not. Please tell me which ones you remember seeing, even if you mentioned them before.

Brand A (Advertised)
Brand B (Not advertised)
Brand C (Advertised)

Do you remember seeing a commercial for (specific brand name)?

☐ *Yes*   ☐ *No*

Recognition

(Show advertisement to respondent) Did you see or read any part of this advertisement?

☐ *Yes*   ☐ *No*

Message Communication/Playback (Sales Point Playback)

These questions require that the researcher first qualify awareness with a question such as **"Have you ever seen any advertising for (brand name)?"** The interviewer then asks message playback questions.

(If yes) What did the advertising tell you about (brand name or product category)?

_____

_____

Other than trying to sell you the product, what do you think was the main idea in the description you just read (commercial you just saw)?

_____

_____

What was the main thing it was trying to communicate about the product?
What did the advertising for (brand name) say about the product?

_____

_____

What did you learn about (brand name) from this advertisement?

_____

_____

Attitude Toward the Advertisement

Please choose the statement below that best describes your feelings about the commercial you just saw.

- *I liked it very much.*
- *I liked it.*
- *I neither liked nor disliked it.*
- *I disliked it.*
- *I disliked it very much.*

Was there anything in the commercial you just saw that you found hard to believe?

☐ *Yes*   ☐ *No*

What thoughts or feelings went through your mind as you watched the advertisement?

Attitude Toward Advertised Brand (Persuasion)

Based on what you've seen in this commercial, how interested would you be in trying the product?

- *Extremely interested*
- *Very interested*
- *Somewhat interested*
- *Not very interested*
- *Not at all interested*

The advertisement tried to increase your interest in (brand). How was your buying interest affected?

- *Increased considerably*
- *Increased somewhat*
- *Not affected*
- *Decreased somewhat*
- *Decreased considerably*

Based on what you've just seen in this commercial, how do you think (brand name) might compare to other brands you've seen or heard about?

- *Better*
- *As good as*
- *Not as good as*

Readership/Viewership

Have you ever read (seen) a copy of (advertising medium)?

☐ *Yes*   ☐ *No*

How frequently do you (watch the evening news on channel X)?

- *Every day*
- *5–6 times a week*
- *2–4 times a week*
- *Once a week*
- *Less than once a week*
- *Never*

Several of the questions about products or brands in the following section are also used to assess attitudes toward advertised brands.

Questions About Ownership and Product Usage

Ownership

Do you own a (product category)?

☐ *Yes*   ☐ *No*

Purchase Behavior

Have you ever purchased a (product category or brand name)?

☐ *Yes*   ☐ *No*

Regular Usage

Which brands of (product category) do you regularly use?

- *Brand A*
- *Brand B*
- *Brand C*
- *Do not use _____*

Which brands of (product category) have you used in the past month?

- *Brand A*
- *Brand B*
- *Brand C*
- *Do not use _____*

In an average month, how often do you buy (product category or brand name)?

Record Number of Times per Month _____

How frequently do you buy (product category or brand name)?

- *Every day*
- *5–6 times a week*
- *2–4 times a week*
- *Once a week*
- *Less than once a week*
- *Never*

Would you say you purchase (product category or brand name) more often than you did a year ago, about the same as a year ago, or less than a year ago?

- *More often than a year ago*
- *About the same as a year ago*
- *Less than a year ago*

Questions About Goods and Services

Ease of Use

How easy do you find using (brand name)?

- *Very easy*
- *Easy*
- *Neither easy nor difficult*
- *Difficult*
- *Very difficult*

Uniqueness

How different is this brand from other brands of (product category)?

- *Very different*
- *Somewhat different*
- *Slightly different*
- *Not at all different*

How would you rate this product (brand name) on uniqueness?

- *Extremely unique*
- *Very unique*
- *Somewhat unique*
- *Slightly unique*
- *Not at all unique*

Please form several piles of cards so that statements that are similar to each other or say similar things are in the same pile. You may form as many piles as you like, and you may put as many or as few cards as you want in a pile. You can set aside any statements that you feel are unique or different and are not similar to any of the other statements.

Attribute Ratings/Importance of Characteristics

Measurement scales such as the semantic differential and Likert scales are frequently used to assess product attributes, especially when measuring brand image or store image. See Chapter 15.

How important is (specific attribute), as far as you are concerned?

- *Very important*
- *Of some importance*
- *Of little importance*
- *Of absolutely no importance*

We would like you to rate (brand name or product category) on several different characteristics. (For concept tests, add: Since you may not have used this product before, please base your answers on your impressions from what you've just read.)

Characteristic A

- *Excellent*
- *Good*
- *Fair*
- *Poor*

Interest

In general, how interested are you in trying a new brand of (product category)?

- *Very interested*
- *Somewhat interested*
- *Not too interested*
- *Not at all interested*

Like/Dislike

What do you like about (brand name)?

_____

_____

What do you dislike about (brand name)?

_____

_____

How do you like the taste of (brand name)?

- *Like it very much*
- *Like it*
- *Neither like nor dislike it*
- *Dislike it*
- *Strongly dislike it*

Preference

Which credit card do you prefer to use?

- *American Express*
- *MasterCard*
- *Visa*
- *No preference*

Expectations

How would you compare the way (company's) service was actually delivered with the way you had anticipated that (company) would provide the service?

- *Much better than expected*
- *Somewhat better than expected*
- *About the same as expected*
- *Somewhat worse than expected*
- *Much worse than expected*

Satisfaction

How satisfied were you with (brand name)?

- *Very satisfied*
- *Somewhat satisfied*
- *Very dissatisfied*

How satisfied were you with (brand name)?

- *Very satisfied*
- *Very dissatisfied*
- *Somewhere in between*

(If somewhere in between) On balance, would you describe yourself as leaning toward being more satisfied or more dissatisfied with (brand name) than with the brand you normally use?

- *Satisfied*
- *Dissatisfied*

Now that you have owned (brand name) for 6 months, please tell us how satisfied you are with it.

- *Completely satisfied*
- *Very satisfied*
- *Fairly well satisfied*
- *Somewhat dissatisfied*
- *Very dissatisfied*

Quality

How would you rate the quality of (brand name)?

- *Excellent*
- *Good*
- *Fair*
- *Poor*

Please indicate how the quality of (Brand A) compares with the quality of (Brand B).

- *Better*
- *About the same*
- *Worse*

Problems

Have you experienced problems with (company's) service?

☐ *Yes*   ☐ *No*

When attempting to contact (company's) representative, how much of a problem, if any, was each of the following:

Phones busy

☐ *No problem at all*   ☐ *Slight problem*   ☐ *Somewhat of a problem*   ☐ *Major problem*

Put on hold too long or too often

☐ *No problem at all*   ☐ *Slight problem*   ☐ *Somewhat of a problem*   ☐ *Major problem*

What are the major shortcomings of (brand name)? (PROBE: What other shortcomings are there?)

Benefits

Do you think (product concept) would have major benefits, minor benefits, or no benefits at all?

- *Major benefits*
- *Minor benefits*
- *No benefits at all*

Improvements

In what ways, if any, could (brand name) be changed or improved? We would like you to tell us anything you can think of, no matter how minor it seems.

Buying Intentions for Existing Products

Do you intend to buy a (brand name or product category) in the next month (3 months, year, etc.)?

☐ *Yes*   ☐ *No*

If a free (product category) were offered to you, which would you select?

- *Brand A*
- *Brand B*
- *Brand C*
- *Do not use*

Buying Intentions Based on Product Concept

(Respondent is shown a prototype or asked to read a concept statement.) Now that you have read about (product concept), if this product were available at your local store, how likely would you be to buy it?

- *Would definitely buy it*
- *Would probably buy it*
- *Might or might not buy it*
- *Would probably not buy it*
- *Would definitely not buy it*

(Hand response card to respondent.) Which phrase on this card indicates how likely you would be to buy this product the next time you go shopping for a product of this type?

- *Would definitely buy it*
- *Would probably buy it*
- *Might or might not buy it*
- *Would probably not buy it*
- *Would definitely not buy it*

Now that you have read about (product concept), if this product were available at your local store for (price), how likely would you be to buy it?

- *Would definitely buy it*
- *Would probably buy it*
- *Might or might not buy it*
- *Would probably not buy it*
- *Would definitely not buy it*

How often, if ever, would you buy (product concept)?

- *Once a week or more*
- *Once every 2 to 3 weeks*
- *Once a month / every 4 weeks*
- *Once every 2 to 3 months*
- *Once every 4 to 6 months*
- *Less than once a year*
- *Never*

Based on your experience, would you recommend (company) to a friend who wanted to purchase (product concept)?

- *Recommend that the friend buy from (company)*
- *Recommend that the friend not buy from (company)*
- *Offer no opinion either way*

Reason for Buying Intention

Why do you say that you would (would not) buy (brand name)? (PROBE: What other reason do you have for feeling this way?)

Questions About Demographics

Age

What is your age, please?
What year were you born?

Education

What is your level of education?

- *Some high school or less*
- *Completed high school*
- *Some college*
- *Completed college*
- *Some graduate school*
- *Completed graduate school*

What is the highest level of education you have obtained?

- *Some high school or less*
- *High school graduate*
- *Some college*
- *College graduate*
- *Postgraduate school*
- *Completed graduate school*

Marital Status

What is your marital status?'

- *Married*
- *Divorced/separated*
- *Widowed*
- *Never married/single*

Children

Are there any children under the age of 6 living in your household?

☐ *Yes*   ☐ *No*

If yes, how many?

Income

Which group describes your annual family income?

- *Under $20,000*
- *$20,000–$39,000*
- *$40,000–$59,999*
- *$60,000–$79,999*
- *$80,000–$99,999*
- *$100,000–$149,999*
- *$150,000 or more*

Please check the box that describes your total household income before taxes in (year). Include income for yourself as well as for all other persons who live in your household.

- *Less than $10,000*
- *$10,000–$14,999*
- *$15,000–$19,999*
- *$20,000–$24,999*
- *$25,000–$29,999*
- *$30,000–$34,999*
- *$35,000–$39,999*
- *$40,000–$49,999*
- *$50,000–$59,999*
- *$60,000–$74,999*
- *$75,000 or more*

Occupation

What is your occupation?

- *Professional*
- *Executive*
- *Managerial*
- *Administrative*
- *Sales*

- *Technical*
- *Labor*
- *Secretarial*
- *Clerical*
- *Other*

What is your occupation?

- *Homemaker*
- *Professional/technical*
- *Upper management/executive*
- *Middle management*
- *Sales/marketing*

- *Clerical or service worker*
- *Tradesperson/machine operator*
- *Laborer*
- *Retired*
- *Student*

Part 5
Sampling and Fieldwork

©MATTHIAS CLAMER/STONE+/GETTY IMAGES

CHAPTER 16
Sampling Designs and Sampling Procedures

CHAPTER 17
Determination of Sample Size: A Review of Statistical Theory

CHAPTER 18
Fieldwork

CHAPTER 16
SAMPLING DESIGNS AND SAMPLING PROCEDURES

LEARNING OUTCOMES

After studying this chapter, you should be able to

1. Explain reasons for taking a sample rather than a complete census
2. Describe the process of identifying a target population and selecting a sampling frame
3. Compare random sampling and systematic (nonsampling) errors
4. Identify the types of nonprobability sampling, including their advantages and disadvantages
5. Summarize the advantages and disadvantages of the various types of probability samples
6. Discuss how to choose an appropriate sample design, as well as challenges for Internet sampling

Chapter Vignette: At Cadbury, Gum Chewing Takes Expertise

After Cadbury Schweppes acquired Pfizer's candy brands, including Bubbaloo, Dentyne, and Trident, new technology and marketing research pointed the company to a new product idea.[1] From a consumer survey, Cadbury knew that most Americans chew gum, and more than two-thirds of those gum chewers said one reason was to avoid snacking. Looking for a product that would serve as a junk-food alternative, company researchers identified gum pellets with liquid centers as a possible new product. Pfizer's sale to Cadbury had included a manufacturing technology that used different flavors for the candy coating and liquid filling. By delivering two flavors and three textures (crunchy, chewy, and liquid), Cadbury hoped the new gum would satisfy customers' cravings for more substantial snacks. And the small pellets of gum seemed more adult-friendly than other liquid-center gums, which were sold under the Freshen Up and Bubbaloo brands.

The developers' next step was to come up with appealing flavor combinations. Peppermint was one obvious choice since most gum has a mint flavor, which tends to maintain a good taste in the chewer's mouth. Another idea came from consumer testing showing that the most popular fruit flavor is strawberry. Cadbury worked with food scientists to select a strawberry flavoring that was less like the jam-sweet flavor popular with children and more like the taste of a fresh strawberry. Then company marketers selected vanilla centers for the mint gum and lime centers for the strawberry gum.

Finally, the new products were ready for consumer testing. Here, Cadbury faced a problem typically associated with testing foods: Most consumers don't pay enough attention to tastes and smells to give helpful feedback. Their comments are vague, so a truly random sample of the consumer population would not give the company the information it needed. Instead, Cadbury recruited a sample from a sensory panel. Panel members passed tests rating their sense of smell and even the rate at which they salivate. Cadbury trained the panelists for the gum-chewing job, teaching them to chew steadily along with the beats of a metronome.

Testers chewed samples of the gum for precisely three minutes, timing themselves with electronic clocks. At the end of each chewing period, a panel leader asked for comments. Panelists cleared their palates with crackers and water before trying the next sample. Eventually, the panelists provided enough feedback for the company to pinpoint winning flavor combinations and move on to engineering the production process.

Just as Cadbury needed a sample of gum chewers to make judgments about its products, sampling is a familiar part of daily life. A customer in a bookstore picks up a book, looks at the cover, and skims a few pages to get a sense of the writing style and content before deciding whether to buy. A high school student visits a college classroom to listen to a professor's lecture. Selecting a university on the basis of one classroom visit may not be scientific sampling, but in a personal situation, it may be a practical sampling experience. When measuring every item in a population is impossible, inconvenient, or too expensive, we intuitively take a sample.

Although sampling is commonplace in daily activities, these familiar samples are seldom scientific. For researchers, the process of sampling can be quite complex. Sampling is a central aspect of marketing research, requiring in-depth examination. This chapter explains the nature of sampling and ways to determine the appropriate sample design.

Sampling Terminology

The process of sampling involves using a a portion of a population to make conclusions about the whole population. A **sample** is a subset, or some part, of a larger population. The purpose of sampling is to estimate an unknown characteristic of a population.

Sampling is defined in terms of the population being studied. A **population (universe)** is any complete group—for example, of people, sales territories, stores, or college students—that shares some common set of characteristics. The term **population element** refers to an individual member of the population.

Researchers could study every element of a population to draw some conclusion. A **census** is an investigation of all the individual elements that make up the population—a total enumeration rather than a sample. Thus, if we wished to know whether more adult Texans drive pickup trucks than sedans, we could contact every adult Texan and find out whether or not they drive a pickup truck or a sedan. We would then know the answer to this question definitively.

Sample
A subset, or some part, of a larger population.

Population (universe)
Any complete group of entities that share some common set of characteristics.

Population element
An individual member of a population.

Census
An investigation of all the individual elements that make up a population.

Why Sample?

At a wine-tasting party, guests sample wine by having a small taste from each of a number of bottles of wine. From this, the consumer decides if he or she likes a particular wine. If an entire bottle were consumed to decide, the guest may end up too inebriated to care about the next bottle. However, in a scientific study in which the objective is to determine an unknown population value, why should a sample rather than a complete census be taken?

Pragmatic Reasons

Applied marketing research projects usually have budget and time constraints. If Ford Motor Corporation wished to take a census of past purchasers' reactions to the company's recalls of defective models, the researchers would have to contact millions of automobile buyers. Some of them would be inaccessible (for example, out of the country), and it would be impossible to contact all these people within a short time period.

A researcher who wants to investigate a population with an extremely small number of population elements may elect to conduct a census rather than a sample because the cost, labor, and time drawbacks would be relatively insignificant. For a company that wants to assess salespersons' satisfaction with its computer networking system, circulating a questionnaire to all twenty-five of its employees is practical. In most situations, however, many practical reasons favor sampling. Sampling cuts costs, reduces labor requirements, and gathers vital information quickly. These advantages may be sufficient in themselves for using a sample rather than a census, but there are other reasons.

Accurate and Reliable Results

Another major reason for sampling is that most properly selected samples give results that are reasonably accurate. If the elements of a population are quite similar, only a small sample is necessary to accurately portray the characteristic of interest. Thus, a population consisting of 10,000 eleventh grade students in all-boys Catholic high schools will require a smaller sample than a broader population consisting of 10,000 high school students from coeducational secondary schools.

A visual example of how different-sized samples produce generalizable conclusions is provided in Exhibit 16.1. All are JPEG images that contain different numbers of "dots." More dots mean

EXHIBIT 16.1
A Photographic Example of How Sampling Works

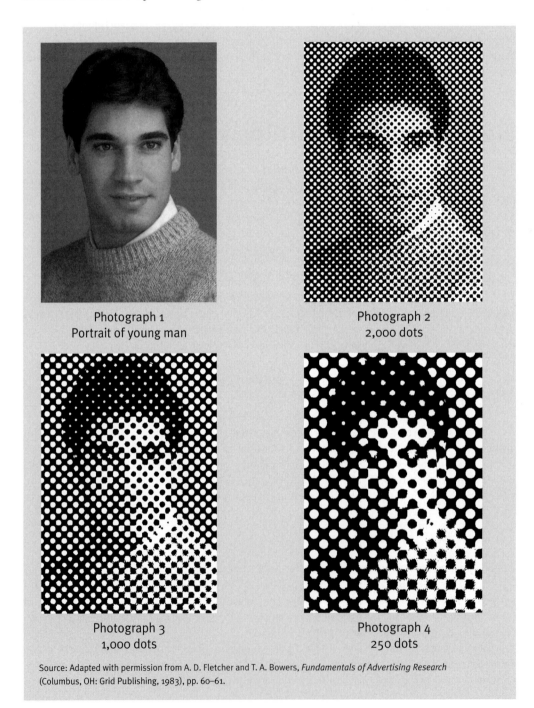

Photograph 1
Portrait of young man

Photograph 2
2,000 dots

Photograph 3
1,000 dots

Photograph 4
250 dots

Source: Adapted with permission from A. D. Fletcher and T. A. Bowers, *Fundamentals of Advertising Research* (Columbus, OH: Grid Publishing, 1983), pp. 60–61.

RESEARCHSNAPSHOT

William's Census Was Ahead of Its Time

After William the Conqueror took over England, he wanted to see what his conquest had netted him. Monarchs back then lacked basic information such as the number of estates or livestock in the kingdom. So in 1086, William ordered a unique survey. Every village and fief was counted to the last building, netting detailed data on how much land and wealth each person owned. He used the data to levy taxes. The result was "The Domesday Book," a corruption of "Doomsday," the Day of Judgment. The king's taxes were considered as inescapable as divine judgment. No other king of the Middle Ages conducted such a thorough inventory.

Today, governments conduct censuses, keep our names and birthdates on file, and zealously document everything that can be taxed. It's difficult to imagine an age when people were not an entry in the government's books.

Source: Reprinted with permission from "Millennium Milestones: William's Census Was Ahead of Its Time," Tulsa World, March 27, 1999, p. A–3. © Associated Press.

©PHILIP MOULD, HISTORICAL PORTRAITS LTD, LONDON, UK/BRIDGEMAN ART LIBRARY

more memory is required to store the photo. In this case, the dots can be thought of as sampling units representing the population which can be thought of as all the little pieces of detail that form the actual image.

The first photograph is comprised of thousands of dots resulting in a very detailed photograph. Very little detail is lost and the face can be confidently recognized. The other photographs provide less detail. Photograph 2 consists of approximately 2,000 dots. The face is still very recognizable, but less detail is retained than in the first photograph. Photograph 3 is made up of 1,000 dots, constituting a sample that is only half as large as that in photograph 2. The 1,000-dot sample provides an image that can still be recognized. Photograph 4 consists of only 250 dots. Yet, if you look at the picture at a distance, you can still recognize the face. The 250-dot sample is still useful, although some detail is lost and under some circumstances (such as looking at it from a short distance) we have less confidence in judging the image using this sample. *Precision* has suffered, but *accuracy* has not.

A sample may on occasion be more accurate than a census. Interviewer mistakes, tabulation errors, and other nonsampling errors may increase during a census because of the increased volume of work. In a sample, increased accuracy may sometimes be possible because the fieldwork and tabulation of data can be more closely supervised. In a field survey, a small, well-trained, closely supervised group may do a more careful and accurate job of collecting information than a large group of nonprofessional interviewers who try to contact everyone. An interesting case in point is the use of samples by the Bureau of the Census to check the accuracy of the U.S. Census. If the sample indicates a possible source of error, the census is redone.

Destruction of Test Units

Many research projects, especially those in quality-control testing, require the destruction of the items being tested. If a manufacturer of firecrackers wished to find out whether each unit met a specific production standard, no product would be left after the testing. This is the exact situation in many marketing strategy experiments. For example, if an experimental sales presentation were presented to every potential customer, no prospects would remain to be contacted after the experiment. In other words, if there is a finite population and everyone in the population participates in the research and cannot be replaced, no population elements remain to be selected as sampling units. The test units have been destroyed or ruined for the purpose of the research project.

Practical Sampling Concepts

Before taking a sample, researchers must make several decisions. Exhibit 16.2 presents these decisions as a series of sequential stages, but the order of the decisions does not always follow this sequence. These decisions are highly interrelated. The issues associated with each of these stages, except for fieldwork, are discussed in this chapter and Chapter 17. Fieldwork is examined in Chapter 18.

Defining the Target Population

Once the decision to sample has been made, the first question concerns identifying the target population. What is the relevant population? In many cases this question is easy to answer. Registered voters may be clearly identifiable. Likewise, if a company's 106-person sales force is the population of concern, there are few definitional problems. In other cases the decision may be difficult. One survey concerning organizational buyer behavior incorrectly defined the population as purchasing agents whom sales representatives regularly contacted. After the survey, investigators discovered that industrial engineers within the customer companies rarely talked with the salespeople but substantially affected buying decisions. For consumer research, the appropriate population element frequently is the household rather than an individual member of the household. This presents some problems if household lists are not available.

At the outset of the sampling process, the target population must be carefully defined so that the proper sources from which the data are to be collected can be identified. The usual technique

EXHIBIT 16.2
Stages in the Selection of a Sample

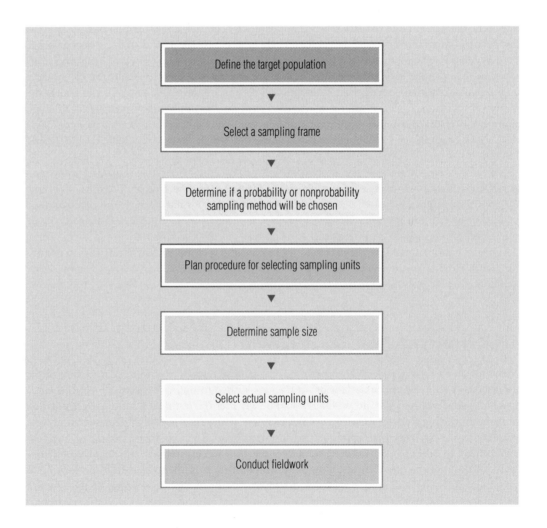

RESEARCHSNAPSHOT

George Gallup's Nation of Numbers

George H. Gallup . . . born in 1901 . . . left [his] hometown, Jefferson, [Iowa,] as soon as he could find his way in a bigger world. The first step was Iowa City and the State University of Iowa. Then in 1922, between his junior and senior years, George answered an advertisement for summer employment in St. Louis. The Post-Dispatch *hired fifty students to survey the city, questioning readers about what they liked and didn't like in the newspaper.*

Each and every reader was to be surveyed. The students were hired to go to every door in St. Louis—there were 55,000 homes in the city then—and ask the same questions. Gallup, one hot day, knocked on one door too many, got the same answers one time too many, and decided, there's got to be a better way.

"A New Technique for Objective Methods for Measuring Reader Interest in Newspapers" was the way, and the title of Gallup's doctoral thesis at Iowa. Working with the Des Moines *Register* and *Tribune* and the 200-year-old statistical theory probabilities of the Swiss mathematician Jakob Bernoulli, Gallup developed "sampling" techniques. You didn't have to talk to everybody, he said, as long as you randomly selected interviews according to a sampling plan that took into account whatever diversity was relevant in the universe of potential respondents—geographic, ethnic, economic, and so on.

Well, it seemed to work for newspapers, and George Gallup, instructor, was in great demand around the country. He became head of the journalism department at Drake University and then switched to a professorship at Northwestern University—all the while doing readership surveys for papers in Chicago, Cleveland, Buffalo, and points east and west. He was hot, and in that summer of 1932, a new advertising agency, Young & Rubicam, invited him to New York to create a research department and procedures for evaluating the effectiveness of advertising. He did that, too. One of his first Y&R surveys, based on newspaper experience, indicated that the number of readers of advertisements was proportional to the length of the paragraphs in a piece of copy.

Source: Excerpted from "George Gallup's Nation of Numbers," Esquire, December 1983, pp. 91–92.

©BETTMANN/CORBIS

for defining the target population is to answer questions about the crucial characteristics of the population. Does the term *comic book reader* include children under six years of age who do not actually read the words? Does *all persons west of the Mississippi* include people in east bank towns that border the river, such as East St. Louis, Illinois? The question to answer is, "Whom do we want to talk to?" The answer may be users, nonusers, recent adopters, or brand switchers.

To implement the sample in the field, tangible characteristics should be used to define the population. A baby food manufacturer might define the population as all women still capable of bearing children. However, a more specific *operational definition* would be women between the ages of twelve and fifty. While this definition by age may exclude a few women who are capable of childbearing and include some who are not, it is still more explicit and provides a manageable basis for the sample design.

The Sampling Frame

In practice, the sample will be drawn from a list of population elements that often differs somewhat from the defined target population. A list of elements from which the sample may be drawn is called a **sampling frame**. The sampling frame is also called the *working population* because these units will eventually provide units involved in analysis. A simple example of a sampling frame would be a list of all members of the American Medical Association.

In practice, almost every list excludes some members of the population. For example, would a university e-mail directory provide an accurate sampling frame for a given university's student population? Perhaps the sampling frame excludes students who registered late and includes students who have resigned from the university. The e-mail directory also will likely list only the student's official university e-mail address. However, many students may not ever use this address, opting to use a private e-mail account instead. Thus, the university e-mail directory could not be expected to perfectly represent the student population. However, a perfect representation isn't always possible or needed.

Sampling frame
A list of elements from which a sample may be drawn; also called working population.

EXHIBIT 16.3 Mailing List Directory Page

Lists Available - *Alphabetical*

S.I.C. Code	List Title	United States Total Count	United States State Count Page	Canadian Count
	A			
5122-02	Abdominal Supports	201	‡	28
8399-03	Abortion Alternatives Organizations`	946	‡	*
8093-04	Abortion Information & Services	551	‡	*
5085-23	Abrasives	1811	‡	277
5169-04	Absorbents	145	‡	*
6541-03	Abstracters	4057	58	*
6411-06	Accident & Health Insurance	2113	‡	9
8748-52	Accident Reconstruction Service	125	‡	*
8721-01	Accountants	127392	64	6933
8721-02	Accounting & Bookkeeping General Svc	27996	64	2072
5044-08	Accounting & Bookkeeping Machines/Supls	889	‡	50
5044-01	Accounting & Bookkeeping Systems	624	‡	1230
8711-02	Acoustical Consultants	381	‡	91
1742-02	Acoustical Contractors	3063	47	433
1742-01	Acoustical Materials	878	‡	210
8999-10	Actuaries	1185	‡	*
8049-13	Acupuncture (Acupuncturists)	2921	62	493
5044-02	Adding & Calculating Machines/Supplies	5524	49	648
5044-09	Addressing Machines & Supplies	345	‡	29
5169-01	Adhesives & Glues	1187	‡	4
3579-02	Adhesives & Gluing Equipment	170	‡	204
6411-02	Adjusters	6164	57	8357
6411-01	Adjusters-Public	161	‡	*
8322-07	Adoption Agencies	1621	‡	32
8059-03	Adult Care Facilities	596	‡	*
8361-08	Adult Congregate Living Facilities	170	‡	*
7319-03	Advertising-Aerial	337	‡	26
7311-01	Advertising-Agencies & Counselors	27753	59	2552
7336-05	Advertising-Art Layout & Production Svc	457	‡	101
7331-05	Advertising-Direct Mail	6347	59	540
7311-03	Advertising-Directory & Guide	2465	‡	124
7319-01	Advertising-Displays	3441	59	571
7319-11	Advertising-Indoor	209	‡	63
7311-05	Advertising-Motion Picture	143	‡	11
7311-06	Advertising-Newspaper	4274	59	404
7312-01	Advertising-Outdoor	3052	59	297
7311-08	Advertising-Periodical	817	‡	78
7313-03	Advertising-Radio	2866	59	247
7311-07	Advertising-Shoppers' Guides	392	‡	4
5199-17	Advertising-Specialties	12827	52	1648
7389-12	Advertising-Telephone	120	‡	*
7313-05	Advertising-Television	1746	‡	102
7319-02	Advertising-Transit & Transportation	179	‡	38
0721-03	Aerial Applicators (Service)	1479	‡	61
3999-01	Aerosols	158	‡	*
3812-01	Aerospace Industries	426	‡	*
	Affluent Americans		73	
5191-04	Agricultural Chemicals	549	‡	210
8748-20	Agricultural Consultants	1047	‡	474
9999-32	Air Balancing	353	‡	*
5084-64	Air Brushes	219	‡	*
4512-02	Air Cargo Service	6005	48	*
5075-01	Air Cleaning & Purifying Equipment	2055	‡	342
5084-02	Air Compressors	4358	50	717
	(See Compressors Air & Gas)			
1711-17	Air Conditioning Contractors & Systems	50951	47	2667
	Available By Brands Sold			
	Airtemp (A)	187		
	Amana (B)	1450		
	Arco Aire (2)	673		
	Armstrong/Magic Chef (C)	395		
	Arvin (4)	106		
	Bryant (D)	2223		
	Carrier (E)	5927		
	Coleman (5)	1176		
	Comfortmaker/Singer (O)	989		
	Day & Night (Z)	749		
	Fedders (H)	318		
	Heli/Quaker (3)	1977		
	Janitrol (7)	587		
	Kero-Sun (W)	2		
	Lennox (K)	4390		
	Luxaire (L)	510		
	Payne (M)	553		

Some firms, called *sampling services* or *list brokers,* specialize in providing lists or databases that include the names, addresses, phone numbers, and e-mail addresses of specific populations. Exhibit 16.3 shows a page from a mailing list company's offerings. Lists offered by companies such as this are compiled from subscriptions to professional journals, credit card applications, warranty card registrations, and a variety of other sources. One sampling service obtained its listing of households with children from an ice cream retailer who gave away free ice cream cones on children's birthdays. The children filled out cards with their names, addresses, and birthdays, which the retailer then sold to the mailing list company.

A valuable source of names is Equifax's series of city directories. Equifax City Directory provides complete, comprehensive, and accurate business and residential information. The city directory records the name of each resident over eighteen years of age and lists pertinent information about each household. The reverse directory pages offer a unique benefit. A **reverse directory** provides, in a different format, the same information contained in a telephone directory. Listings may be by city and street address or by phone number, rather than alphabetical by last name. Such a directory is particularly useful when a retailer wishes to survey only a certain geographical area of a city or when census tracts are to be selected on the basis of income or another demographic criterion.

A **sampling frame error** occurs when certain sample elements are excluded or when the entire population is not accurately represented in the sampling frame. Election polling that used a

Reverse directory
A directory similar to a telephone directory except that listings are by city and street address or by phone number rather than alphabetical by last name.

Sampling frame error
An error that occurs when certain sample elements are not listed or are not accurately represented in a sampling frame.

telephone directory as a sampling frame would be contacting households with listed phone numbers, not households whose members are likely to vote. A better sampling frame might be voter registration records. Another potential sampling frame error involving phone records is the possibility that a phone survey could underrepresent people with disabilities. Some disabilities, such as hearing and speech impairments, might make telephone use impossible. However, when researchers in Washington State tested for this possible sampling frame error by comparing Census Bureau data on the prevalence of disability with the responses to a telephone survey, they found the opposite effect. The reported prevalence of a disability was actually higher in the phone survey.[2] These findings could be relevant for research into a community's health status or the level of demand for services for disabled persons.

As in this example, population elements can be either under- or overrepresented in a sampling frame. A savings and loan defined its population as all individuals who had savings accounts. However, when it drew a sample from the list of accounts rather than from the list of names of individuals, individuals who had multiple accounts were overrepresented in the sample.

SAMPLING FRAMES FOR INTERNATIONAL MARKETING RESEARCH

The availability of sampling frames around the globe varies dramatically. Not every country's government conducts a census of population. In some countries telephone directories are incomplete, no voter registration lists exist, and accurate maps of urban areas are unobtainable. However, in Taiwan, Japan, and other Asian countries, a researcher can build a sampling frame relatively easily because those governments release some census information. If a family changes households, updated census information must be reported to a centralized government agency before communal services (water, gas, electricity, education, and so on) are made available.[3] This information is then easily accessible in the local *Inhabitants' Register*.

Sampling Units

During the actual sampling process, the elements of the population must be selected according to a certain procedure. The **sampling unit** is a single element or group of elements subject to selection in the sample. For example, if an airline wishes to sample passengers, it may take every twenty-fifth name on a complete list of passengers. In this case the sampling unit would be the same as the element. Alternatively, the airline could first select certain flights as the sampling unit and then select certain passengers on each flight. In this case the sampling unit would contain many elements.

If the target population has first been divided into units, such as airline flights, additional terminology must be used. A unit selected in the first stage of sampling is called a **primary sampling unit (PSU)**. A unit selected in a successive stages of sampling is called a **secondary sampling unit** or (if three stages are necessary) **tertiary sampling unit**. When there is no list of population elements, the sampling unit generally is something other than the population element. In a random-digit dialing study, the sampling unit will be telephone numbers.

Sampling unit
A single element or group of elements subject to selection in the sample.

Primary sampling unit (PSU)
A term used to designate a unit selected in the first stage of sampling.

Secondary sampling unit
A term used to designate a unit selected in the second stage of sampling.

Tertiary sampling unit
A term used to designate a unit selected in the third stage of sampling.

Random Sampling and Nonsampling Errors

An advertising agency sampled a small number of shoppers in grocery stores that used Shopper's Video, an in-store advertising network. The agency hoped to measure brand awareness and purchase intentions. Investigators expected this sample to be representative of the grocery-shopping population. However, if a difference exists between the value of a sample statistic of interest (for example, the sample group's average willingness to buy the advertised brand) and the value of the corresponding population parameter (the population's average willingness to buy), a *statistical error* has occurred. Chapter 8 classified two basic causes of differences between statistics and parameters:

1. random sampling errors
2. systematic (nonsampling) error

An estimation made from a sample is not the same as a census count. **Random sampling error** is the difference between the sample result and the result of a census conducted using identical procedures. Of course, the result of a census is unknown unless one is taken, which is rarely done. Other sources of error also can be present. Random sampling error occurs because of chance variation in the scientific selection of sampling units. The sampling units, even if properly selected according to sampling theory, may not perfectly represent the population, but generally they are reliable estimates. Our discussion on the process of randomization (a procedure designed to give everyone in the population an equal chance of being selected as a sample member) will show that, because random sampling errors follow chance variations, they tend to cancel one another out when averaged. This means that properly selected samples generally are good approximations of the population. Still, the true population value almost always differs slightly from the sample value, causing a small random sampling error. Every once in a while, an unusual sample is selected because too many atypical people were included in the sample and a large random sampling error occurred.

Random Sampling Error

The theories behind the concept of sample reliability and other basic statistical concepts are reviewed in detail in Chapter 17, which discusses sample size. At this point, simply recognize that *random sampling error* is a technical term that refers *only* to statistical fluctuations that occur because of chance variations in the elements selected for the sample.

Random sampling error is a function of sample size. As sample size increases, random sampling error decreases. Of course, the resources available will influence how large a sample may be taken. It is possible to estimate the random sampling error that may be expected with various sample sizes. Suppose a survey of approximately 1,000 people has been taken in Fresno to determine the feasibility of a new soccer franchise. Assume that 30 percent of the respondents favor the idea of a new professional sport in town. The researcher will know, based on the laws of probability, that 95 percent of the time a survey of slightly fewer than 900 people will produce results with an error of approximately plus or minus 3 percent. If the survey were conducted with only 325 people, the margin of error would increase to approximately plus or minus 5 percentage points. This example illustrates random sampling errors.

Systematic Sampling Error

Systematic (nonsampling) errors result from nonsampling factors, primarily the nature of a study's design and the correctness of execution. These errors are *not* due to chance fluctuations. For example, highly educated respondents are more likely to cooperate with mail surveys than poorly educated ones, for whom filling out forms is more difficult and intimidating. Sample biases such as these account for a large portion of errors in marketing research. The term *sample bias* is somewhat unfortunate, because many forms of bias are not related to the selection of the sample.

We discussed nonsampling errors in Chapter 8. Errors due to sample selection problems, such as sampling frame errors, are systematic (nonsampling) errors and should not be classified as random sampling errors.

Less than Perfectly Representative Samples

Random sampling errors and systematic errors associated with the sampling process may combine to yield a sample that is less than perfectly representative of the population. Exhibit 16.4 illustrates two nonsampling errors (sampling frame error and nonresponse error) related to sample design. The total population is represented by the area of the largest square. Sampling frame errors eliminate some potential respondents. Random sampling error (due exclusively to random, chance fluctuation) may cause an imbalance in the representativeness of the group. Additional errors will occur if individuals refuse to be interviewed or cannot be contacted. Such nonresponse error may also cause the sample to be less than perfectly representative. Thus, the actual sample is drawn from a population different from (or smaller than) the ideal.

EXHIBIT 16.4 **Errors Associated with Sampling**

Source: Adapted from Keith K. Cox and Ben M. Enis, *The Marketing Research Process* (Pacific Palisades, CA: Goodyear, 1972); and Danny N. Bellenger and Barnet A. Greenberg, *Marketing Research: A Management Information Approach* (Homewood, IL: Richard D. Irwin, 1978), pp. 154–155.

Probability versus Nonprobability Sampling

Several alternative ways to take a sample are available. The main alternative sampling plans may be grouped into two categories: probability techniques and nonprobability techniques.

In **probability sampling**, every element in the population has a *known, nonzero probability* of selection. The simple random sample, in which each member of the population has an equal probability of being selected, is the best-known probability sample.

In **nonprobability sampling**, the probability of any particular member of the population being chosen is unknown. The selection of sampling units in nonprobability sampling is quite arbitrary, as researchers rely heavily on personal judgment. Technically, no appropriate statistical techniques exist for measuring random sampling error from a nonprobability sample. Therefore, projecting the data beyond the sample is, technically speaking, statistically inappropriate. Nevertheless, researchers sometimes find nonprobability samples best suited for a specific researcher purpose. As a result, nonprobability samples are pragmatic and are used in market research.

Probability sampling
A sampling technique in which every member of the population has a known, nonzero probability of selection.

Nonprobability sampling
A sampling technique in which units of the sample are selected on the basis of personal judgment or convenience; the probability of any particular member of the population being chosen is unknown.

Nonprobability Sampling

Although probability sampling is preferred, we will discuss nonprobability sampling first to illustrate some potential sources of error and other weaknesses in sampling.

Convenience Sampling

As the name suggests, **convenience sampling** refers to sampling by obtaining people or units that are conveniently available. A research team may determine that the most convenient and economical method is to set up an interviewing booth from which to intercept consumers at a shopping center. Just before elections, television stations often present person-on-the-street interviews that

Convenience sampling
The sampling procedure of obtaining those people or units that are most conveniently available.

are presumed to reflect public opinion. (Of course, the television station generally warns that the survey was "unscientific and random" [*sic*].) The college professor who uses his or her students has a captive sample—convenient, but perhaps not so representative.

Researchers generally use convenience samples to obtain a large number of completed questionnaires quickly and economically, or when obtaining a sample through other means is impractical. For example, many Internet surveys are conducted with volunteer respondents who, either intentionally or by happenstance, visit an organization's website. Although this method produces a large number of responses quickly and at a low cost, selecting all visitors to a website is clearly convenience sampling. Respondents may not be representative because of the haphazard manner by which many of them arrived at the website or because of self-selection bias.

Similarly, research looking for cross-cultural differences in organizational or consumer behavior typically uses convenience samples. Rather than selecting cultures with characteristics relevant to the hypothesis being tested, the researchers conducting these studies often choose cultures to which they have access (for example, because they speak the language or have contacts in that culture's organizations). Further adding to the convenience, cross-cultural research often defines "culture" in terms of nations, which are easier to identify and obtain statistics for, even though many nations include several cultures and some people in a given nation may be more involved with the international business or academic community than with a particular ethnic culture.[4] Here again, the use of convenience sampling limits how well the research represents the intended population.

The user of research based on a convenience sample should remember that projecting the results beyond the specific sample is inappropriate. Convenience samples are best used for exploratory research when additional research will subsequently be conducted with a probability sample.

Judgment Sampling

Judgment (purposive) sampling
A nonprobability sampling technique in which an experienced individual selects the sample based on personal judgment about some appropriate characteristic of the sample member.

Judgment (purposive) sampling is a nonprobability sampling technique in which an experienced individual selects the sample based on his or her judgment about some appropriate characteristics required of the sample member. Researchers select samples that satisfy their specific purposes, even if they are not fully representative. The consumer price index (CPI) is based on a judgment sample of market-basket items, housing costs, and other selected goods and services expected to reflect a representative sample of items consumed by most Americans. Test-market cities often are selected because they are viewed as typical cities whose demographic profiles closely match the national profile. A fashion manufacturer regularly selects a sample of key accounts that it believes are capable of providing information needed to predict what may sell in the fall. Thus, the sample is selected to achieve this specific objective.

Judgment sampling often is used in attempts to forecast election results. People frequently wonder how a television network can predict the results of an election with only 2 percent of the votes reported. Political and sampling experts judge which small voting districts approximate overall state returns from previous election years; then these *bellwether precincts* are selected as the sampling units. Of course, the assumption is that the past voting records of these districts are still representative of the political behavior of the state's population.

Quota Sampling

Suppose a firm wishes to investigate consumers who currently subscribe to an HDTV (high definition television) service. The researchers may wish to ensure that each brand of HDTV televisions is included proportionately in the sample. Strict probability sampling procedures would likely underrepresent certain brands and overrepresent other brands. If the selection process were left strictly to chance, some variation would be expected.

Quota sampling
A nonprobability sampling procedure that ensures that various subgroups of a population will be represented on pertinent characteristics to the exact extent that the investigator desires.

The purpose of **quota sampling** is to ensure that the various subgroups in a population are represented on pertinent sample characteristics to the exact extent that the investigators desire. Stratified sampling, a probability sampling procedure described in the next section, also has this objective, but it should not be confused with quota sampling. In quota sampling, the interviewer has a quota to achieve. For example, an interviewer in a particular city may be assigned 100 interviews, 35 with owners of Sony TVs, 30 with owners of Samsung TVs, 18 with owners of Panasonic

RESEARCHSNAPSHOT

American Kennel Club Tries to Keep Pet Owners Out of the Doghouse

The Amercian Kennel Club (AKC) is an organization dedicated to promoting purebred dogs and their health and well-being as family companions. So, the organization commissioned a study to investigate dog ownership and the acceptance of dogs in their neighborhoods. The AKC used quota sampling in its recent Dog Ownership Study, which set out to compare attitudes of dog owners and nonowners, based on a sample of one thousand people. In such a small sample of the U.S. population, some groups might not be represented, so the study design set quotas for completed interviews in age, sex, and geographic categories. The primary sampling units for this phone survey were selected with random-digit dialing. In the next phase of selection, the researchers ensured that respondents filled the quotas for each group. They further screened respondents so that half owned dogs and half did not.

An objective of the survey was to help dog owners understand concerns of their neighbors so that the AKC can provide better education in responsible dog ownership, contributing to greater community harmony. The study found that people without dogs tended to be most concerned about dogs jumping and barking and owners not "picking up after their dogs." Lisa Peterson, director of club communications for AKC, commented, "Anyone considering bringing a dog home should realize that it's a 10- to 15-year commitment of time, money, and love that should not be taken lightly."

The study addressed the pleasures of a pet's companionship, as well as the duties. A benefit of ownership was that dog owners were somewhat more likely than nonowners to describe themselves as laid back and happy.

Source: American Kennel Club, "AKC Mission Statement" and "History of the American Kennel Club," AKC Web site, http://www.akc.org, accessed March 20, 2006; American Kennel Club, "AKC Responsible Dog Ownership Day Survey Reveals Rift between Dog and Non-Dog Owners," news release, http://www.akc.org, September 7, 2005.

©ICONICA/GETTY IMAGES

TVs, and the rest with owners of other brands. The interviewer is responsible for finding enough people to meet the quota. Aggregating the various interview quotas yields a sample that represents the desired proportion of each subgroup.

POSSIBLE SOURCES OF BIAS

The logic of classifying the population by pertinent subgroups is essentially sound. However, because respondents are selected according to a convenience sampling procedure rather than on a probability basis (as in stratified sampling), the haphazard selection of subjects may introduce bias. For example, a college professor hired some of his students to conduct a quota sample based on age. When analyzing the data, the professor discovered that almost all the people in the "under twenty-five years" category were college-educated. Interviewers, being human, tend to prefer to interview people who are similar to themselves.

Quota samples tend to include people who are easily found, willing to be interviewed, and middle class. Fieldworkers are given considerable leeway to exercise their judgment concerning selection of actual respondents. Interviewers often concentrate their interviewing in areas with heavy pedestrian traffic such as downtowns, shopping malls, and college campuses. Those who interview door-to-door learn quickly that quota requirements are difficult to meet by interviewing whoever happens to appear at the door. People who are more likely to stay at home generally share a less active lifestyle and are less likely to be meaningfully employed. One interviewer related a story of working in an upper-middle-class neighborhood. After a few blocks, he arrived in a neighborhood of mansions. Feeling that most of the would-be respondents were above his station, the interviewer skipped these houses because he felt uncomfortable knocking on doors that would be answered by these people or their hired help.

ADVANTAGES OF QUOTA SAMPLING

The major advantages of quota sampling over probability sampling are speed of data collection, lower costs, and convenience. Although quota sampling has many problems, carefully supervised data collection may provide a representative sample of the various subgroups within a population.

Quota sampling may be appropriate when the researcher knows that a certain demographic group is more likely to refuse to cooperate with a survey. For instance, if older men are more likely to refuse, a higher quota can be set for this group so that the proportion of each demographic category will be similar to the proportions in the population. A number of laboratory experiments also rely on quota sampling because it is difficult to find a sample of the general population willing to visit a laboratory to participate in an experiment.

Snowball Sampling

Snowball sampling
A sampling procedure in which initial respondents are selected by probability methods and additional respondents are obtained from information provided by the initial respondents.

A variety of procedures known as **snowball sampling** involve using probability methods for an initial selection of respondents and then obtaining additional respondents through information provided by the initial respondents. This technique is used to locate members of rare populations by referrals. Suppose a manufacturer of sports equipment is considering marketing a mahogany croquet set for serious adult players. This market is certainly small. An extremely large sample would be necessary to find 100 serious adult croquet players. It would be much more economical to survey, say, 300 people, find 15 croquet players, and ask them for the names of other players.

Reduced sample sizes and costs are clearcut advantages of snowball sampling. However, bias is likely to enter into the study because a person suggested by someone also in the sample has a higher probability of being similar to the first person. If there are major differences between those who are widely known by others and those who are not, this technique may present some serious problems. However, snowball sampling may be used to locate and recruit heavy users, such as consumers who buy more than fifty compact disks per year, for focus groups. As the focus group is not expected to be a generalized sample, snowball sampling may be appropriate.

Probability Sampling

All probability sampling techniques are based on chance selection procedures. Because the probability sampling process is random, the bias inherent in nonprobability sampling procedures is eliminated. Note that the term *random* refers to the procedure for selecting the sample; it does not describe the data in the sample. *Randomness* characterizes a procedure whose outcome cannot be predicted because it depends on chance. Randomness should not be thought of as unplanned or unscientific—it is the basis of all probability sampling techniques. This section will examine the various probability sampling methods.

Simple Random Sampling

Simple random sampling
A sampling procedure that assures each element in the population of an equal chance of being included in the sample.

The sampling procedure that ensures each element in the population will have an equal chance of being included in the sample is called **simple random sampling**. Examples include drawing names from a hat and selecting the winning raffle ticket from a large drum. If the names or raffle tickets are thoroughly stirred, each person or ticket should have an equal chance of being selected. In contrast to other, more complex types of probability sampling, this process is simple because it requires only one stage of sample selection.

Although drawing names or numbers out of a fishbowl, using a spinner, rolling dice, or turning a roulette wheel may be an appropriate way to draw a sample from a small population, when populations consist of large numbers of elements, sample selection is based on tables of random numbers (see Table A.1 in the Appendix) or computer-generated random numbers.

TOTHEPOINT

Make everything as simple as possible, but not simpler.

—Albert Einstein

Suppose a researcher is interested in selecting a simple random sample of all the Honda dealers in California, New Mexico, Arizona, and Nevada. Each dealer's name is assigned a number from 1 to 105. The numbers can be written on paper slips, and all the slips can be placed in a bowl. After the slips of paper have been thoroughly mixed, one is selected for each sampling unit. Thus, if the sample size is 35, the selection procedure must be repeated 34 times after the first slip has been selected. Mixing the slips after each selection will ensure that those at the bottom of the bowl will continue to have an equal chance of being selected in the sample.

To use a table of random numbers, a serial number is first assigned to each element of the population. Assuming the population is 99,999 or fewer, five-digit numbers may be selected from the table of random numbers merely by reading the numbers in any column or row, moving up, down, left, or right. A random starting point should be selected at the outset. For convenience, we will assume that we have randomly selected as our starting point the first five digits in columns 1 through 5, row 1, of Table A.1 in the Appendix. The first number in our sample would be 37751; moving down, the next numbers would be 50915, 99142, and so on.

The random-digit dialing technique of sample selection requires that the researcher identify the exchange or exchanges of interest (the first three numbers) and then use a table of numbers to select the next four numbers. In practice, the exchanges are not always selected randomly. Researchers who wanted to find out whether Americans of African descent prefer being called "black" or "African-American" narrowed their sampling frame by selecting exchanges associated with geographic areas where the proportion of the population (African-Americans/blacks) was at least 30 percent. The reasoning was that this made the survey procedure far more efficient, considering that the researchers were trying to contact a group representing less than 15 percent of U.S. households. This initial judgment sampling raises the same issues we discussed regarding nonprobability sampling. In this study, the researchers found that respondents were most likely to prefer the term *black* if they had attended schools that were about half black and half white.[5] If such experiences influence the answers to the question of interest to the researchers, the fact that blacks who live in predominantly white communities are underrepresented may introduce bias into the results.

Systematic Sampling

Suppose a researcher wants to take a sample of 1,000 from a list of 200,000 names. With **systematic sampling**, every 200th name from the list would be drawn. The procedure is extremely simple. A starting point is selected by a random process; then every n^{th} number on the list is selected. To take a sample of consumers from a rural telephone directory that does not separate business from residential listings, every 23rd name might be selected as the *sampling interval.* In the process, Mike's Restaurant might be selected. This unit is inappropriate because it is a business listing rather than a consumer listing, so the next eligible name would be selected as the sampling unit, and the systematic process would continue.

While systematic sampling is not actually a random selection procedure, it does yield random results if the arrangement of the items in the list is random in character. The problem of *periodicity* occurs if a list has a systematic pattern—that is, if it is not random in character. Collecting retail sales information every seventh day would result in a distorted sample because there would be a systematic pattern of selecting sampling units—sales for only one day of the week (perhaps Monday) would be sampled. If the first 50 names on a list of contributors to a charity were extremely large donors, periodicity bias might occur in sampling every 200th name. Periodicity is rarely a problem for most sampling in marketing research, but researchers should be aware of the possibility.

Systematic sampling
A sampling procedure in which a starting point is selected by a random process and then every n^{th} number on the list is selected.

Stratified Sampling

The usefulness of dividing the population into subgroups, or *strata,* whose members are more or less equal with respect to some characteristic was illustrated in our discussion of quota sampling. The first step is the same for both stratified and quota sampling: choosing strata on the basis of existing information—for example, classifying retail outlets based on annual sales volume. However, the process of selecting sampling units within the strata differs substantially. In **stratified sampling**, a subsample is drawn using simple random sampling within each stratum. This is not true of quota sampling.

The reason for taking a stratified sample is to obtain a more efficient sample than would be possible with simple random sampling. Suppose, for example, that urban and rural groups have widely different attitudes toward energy conservation, but members within each group hold very similar attitudes. Random sampling error will be reduced with the use of stratified sampling, because each group is internally homogeneous but there are comparative differences between

Stratified sampling
A probability sampling procedure in which simple random subsamples that are more or less equal on some characteristic are drawn from within each stratum of the population.

groups. More technically, a smaller standard error may result from this stratified sampling because the groups will be adequately represented when strata are combined.

Another reason for selecting a stratified sample is to ensure that the sample will accurately reflect the population on the basis of the criterion or criteria used for stratification. This is a concern because occasionally simple random sampling yields a disproportionate number of one group or another and the sample ends up being less representative than it could be.

A researcher can select a stratified sample as follows. First, a variable (sometimes several variables) is identified as an efficient basis for stratification. A stratification variable must be a characteristic of the population elements known to be related to the dependent variable or other variables of interest. The variable chosen should increase homogeneity within each stratum and increase heterogeneity between strata. The stratification variable usually is a categorical variable or one easily converted into categories (that is, subgroups). For example, a pharmaceutical company interested in measuring how often physicians prescribe a certain drug might choose physicians' training as a basis for stratification. In this example the mutually exclusive strata are MDs (medical doctors) and ODs (osteopathic doctors).

Next, for each separate subgroup or stratum, a list of population elements must be obtained. (If such lists are not available, they can be costly to prepare, and if a complete listing is not available, a true stratified probability sample cannot be selected.) Using a table of random numbers or some other device, a *separate* simple random sample is then taken within each stratum. Of course, the researcher must determine how large a sample to draw for each stratum. This issue is discussed in the following section.

Proportional versus Disproportional Sampling

Proportional stratified sample

A stratified sample in which the number of sampling units drawn from each stratum is in proportion to the population size of that stratum.

If the number of sampling units drawn from each stratum is in proportion to the relative population size of the stratum, the sample is a **proportional stratified sample**. Sometimes, however, a disproportional stratified sample will be selected to ensure an adequate number of sampling units in every stratum. Sampling more heavily in a given stratum than its relative population size warrants is not a problem if the primary purpose of the research is to estimate some characteristic separately for each stratum and if researchers are concerned about assessing the differences among strata. Consider, however, the percentages of retail outlets presented in Exhibit 16.5. A proportional sample would have the same percentages as in the population. Although there is a small percentage of warehouse club stores, the average store size, in dollar volume, for the warehouse club store stratum is quite large and varies substantially from the average store size for the smaller independent stores. To avoid overrepresenting the chain stores and independent stores (with smaller sales volume) in the sample, a disproportional sample is taken.

EXHIBIT 16.5
Disproportional Sampling: Hypothetical Example

	Percentage in Population	Proportional Sample	Disproportional Sample
Warehouse Clubs	20%	20%	50%
Chain Stores	57%	57%	38%
Small Independents	23%	23%	12%

In a **disproportional stratified sample** the sample size for each stratum is not allocated in proportion to the population size but is dictated by analytical considerations, such as variability in store sales volume. The logic behind this procedure relates to the general argument for sample size: As variability increases, sample size must increase to provide accurate estimates. Thus, the strata that exhibit the greatest variability are sampled more heavily to increase sample efficiency—that is, produce smaller random sampling error. Complex formulas (beyond the scope of an introductory course in marketing research) have been developed to determine sample size for each stratum. A simplified rule of thumb for understanding the concept of optimal allocation is that the stratum sample size increases for strata of larger sizes with the greatest relative variability. Other complexities arise in determining population estimates. For example, when disproportional stratified sampling is used, the estimated mean for each stratum has to be weighed according to the number of elements in each stratum in order to calculate the total population mean.

Disproportional stratified sample
A stratified sample in which the sample size for each stratum is allocated according to analytical considerations.

Cluster Sampling

The purpose of **cluster sampling** is to sample economically while retaining the characteristics of a probability sample. Consider a researcher who must conduct five hundred personal interviews with consumers scattered throughout the United States. Travel costs are likely to be enormous because the amount of time spent traveling will be substantially greater than the time spent in the interviewing process. If an aspirin marketer can assume the product will be equally successful in Phoenix and Baltimore, or if a frozen pizza manufacturer assumes its product will suit the tastes of Texans equally as well as Oregonians, cluster sampling may be used to represent the United States.

In a cluster sample, the primary sampling unit is no longer the individual element in the population (for example, grocery stores) but a larger cluster of elements located in proximity to one another (for example, cities). The *area sample* is the most popular type of cluster sample. A grocery store researcher, for example, may randomly choose several geographic areas as primary sampling units and then interview all or a sample of grocery stores within the geographic clusters. Interviews are confined to these clusters only. No interviews occur in other clusters. Cluster sampling is classified as a probability sampling technique because of either the random selection of clusters or the random selection of elements within each cluster. Some examples of clusters appear in Exhibit 16.6.

Cluster sampling
An economically efficient sampling technique in which the primary sampling unit is not the individual element in the population but a large cluster of elements; clusters are selected randomly.

Population Element	Possible Clusters in the United States
U.S. adult population	States Counties Metropolitan Statistical Areas Census Tracts Blocks Households
College seniors	Colleges
Manufacturing firms	Counties Metropolitan Statistical Areas Localities Plants
Airline travelers	Airports Planes
Sports fans	Football Stadiums Basketball Arenas Baseball Parks

EXHIBIT 16.6
Examples of Clusters

RESEARCHSNAPSHOT

Who's at Home? Different Ways to Select Respondents

A carefully planned telephone survey often involves multistage sampling. First the researchers select a sample of households to call, and then they select someone within each household to interview—not necessarily whoever answers the phone. Cecilie Gaziano, a researcher with Research Solutions in Minneapolis, conducted an analysis of various selection procedures used in prior research, looking for the methods that performed best in terms of generating a representative sample, achieving respondent cooperation, and minimizing costs.

Gaziano found several methods worth further consideration. One of these was full enumeration, in which the interviewer requests a list of all the adults living in the household, generates a random number, uses the number to select a name from that list, and asks to speak with that person. In a variation of this approach, called the *Kish method,* the interviewer

requests the number of males by age and the number of females by age, and then uses some form of randomization to select either a male or a female and a number—say, the oldest male or the third oldest female. A third method is to interview the person who last had a birthday.

In the studies Gaziano examined, the Kish method did not seem to discourage respondents by being too intrusive. That method was popular because it came close to being random. The last-birthday method generated somewhat better cooperation rates, which may have made that method more efficient in terms of costs. However, some question whether the person on the phone accurately knows the birthdays of every household member, especially in households with several adults. Methods that request the gender of household members also address a challenge of getting a representative phone survey sample: females tend to answer the phone more often than males.

Source: Cecilie Gaziano, "Comparative Analysis of Within-Household Respondent Selection Techniques," Public Opinion Quarterly, 69 (Spring 2005), 124–157; "Communication Researchers and Policy-Making," Journal of Broadcasting & Electronic Media, March 2004, accessed at http://www.allbusiness.com, accessed March 19, 2006.

Cluster samples frequently are used when lists of the sample population are not available. For example, when researchers investigating employees and self-employed workers for a downtown revitalization project found that a comprehensive list of these people was not available, they decided to take a cluster sample, selecting organizations (business and government) as the clusters. A sample of firms within the central business district was developed, using stratified probability sampling to identify clusters. Next, individual workers within the firms (clusters) were randomly selected and interviewed concerning the central business district.

Ideally a cluster should be as heterogeneous as the population itself—a mirror image of the population. A problem may arise with cluster sampling if the characteristics and attitudes of the elements within the cluster are too similar. For example, geographic neighborhoods tend to have residents of the same socioeconomic status. Students at a university tend to share similar beliefs. This problem may be mitigated by constructing clusters composed of diverse elements and by selecting a large number of sampled clusters.

Multistage Area Sampling

Multistage area sampling
Sampling that involves using a combination of two or more probability sampling techniques.

So far we have described two-stage cluster sampling. **Multistage area sampling** involves two or more steps that combine some of the probability techniques already described. Typically, geographic areas are randomly selected in progressively smaller (lower-population) units. For example, a political pollster investigating an election in Arizona might first choose counties within the state to ensure that the different areas are represented in the sample. In the second step, precincts within the selected counties may be chosen. As a final step, the pollster may select blocks (or households) within the precincts, then interview all the blocks (or households) within the geographic area. Researchers may

EXHIBIT 16.7 Illustration of Multistage Area Sampling

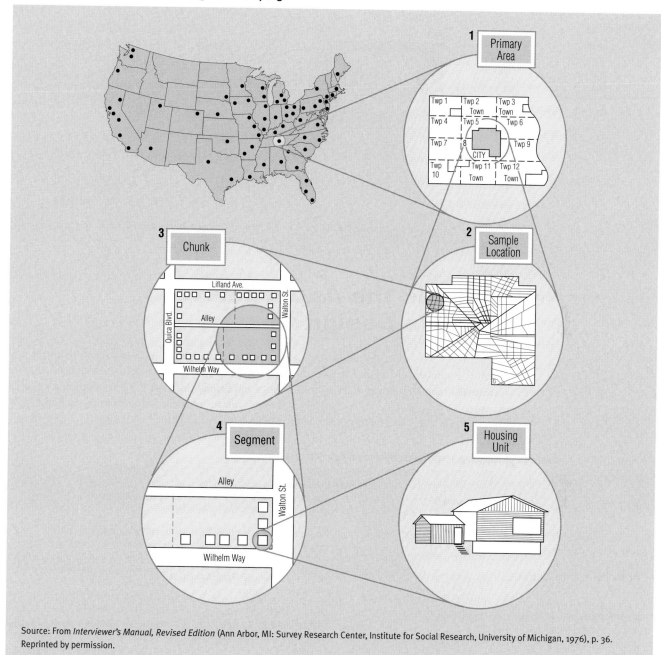

Source: From *Interviewer's Manual, Revised Edition* (Ann Arbor, MI: Survey Research Center, Institute for Social Research, University of Michigan, 1976), p. 36. Reprinted by permission.

take as many steps as necessary to achieve a representative sample. Exhibit 16.7 graphically portrays a multistage area sampling process frequently used by a major academic research center. Progressively smaller geographic areas are chosen until a single housing unit is selected for interviewing.

The Bureau of the Census provides maps, population information, demographic characteristics for population statistics, and so on, by several small geographical areas; these may be useful in sampling. Census classifications of small geographic areas vary, depending on the extent of urbanization within Metropolitan Statistical Areas (MSAs) or counties. Exhibit 16.8 illustrates the geographic hierarchy inside urbanized areas.

EXHIBIT 16.8
**Geographic Hierarchy inside
Urbanized Areas**

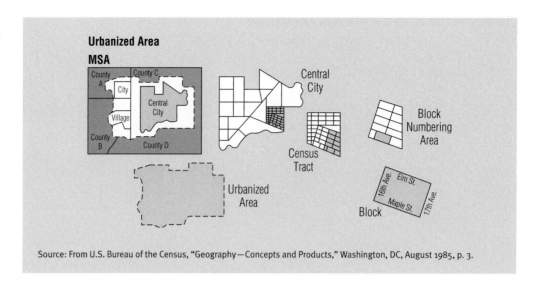

Source: From U.S. Bureau of the Census, "Geography—Concepts and Products," Washington, DC, August 1985, p. 3.

What Is the Appropriate Sample Design?

A researcher who must decide on the most appropriate sample design for a specific project will identify a number of sampling criteria and evaluate the relative importance of each criterion before selecting a sampling design. This section outlines and briefly discusses the most common criteria. Exhibit 16.9 summarizes the advantages and disadvantages of each nonprobability sampling technique, and Exhibit 16.10 does the same for the probability sampling techniques.

EXHIBIT 16.9 Comparison of Sampling Techniques: Nonprobability Samples

| | Nonprobability Samples | | |
Description	**Cost and Degree of Use**	**Advantages**	**Disadvantages**
1. *Convenience:* The researcher uses the most convenient sample or economical sample units.	Very low cost, extensively used	No need for list of population	Unrepresentative samples likely; random sampling error estimates cannot be made; projecting data beyond sample is relatively risky
2. *Judgment:* An expert or experienced researcher selects the sample to fulfill a purpose, such as ensuring that all members have a certain characteristic.	Moderate cost, average use	Useful for certain types of forecasting; sample guaranteed to meet a specific objective	Bias due to expert's beliefs may make sample unrepresentative; projecting data beyond sample is risky
3. *Quota:* The researcher classifies the population by pertinent properties, determines the desired proportion to sample from each class, and fixes quotas for each interviewer.	Moderate cost, very extensively used	Introduces some stratification of population; requires no list of population	Introduces bias in researcher's classification of subjects; nonrandom selection within classes means error from population cannot be estimated; projecting data beyond sample is risky
4. *Snowball:* Initial respondents are selected by probability samples; additional respondents are obtained by referral from initial respondents.	Low cost, used in special situations	Useful in locating members of rare populations	High bias because sample units are not independent; projecting data beyond sample is risky

EXHIBIT 16.10 Comparison of Sampling Techniques: Probability Samples

| Description | Probability Samples | | |
	Cost and Degree of Use	Advantages	Disadvantages
1. *Simple random:* The researcher assigns each member of the sampling frame a number, then selects sample units by random method.	High cost, moderately used in practice (most common in random digit dialing and with computerized sampling frames)	Only minimal advance knowledge of population needed; easy to analyze data and compute error	Requires sampling frame to work from; does not use knowledge of population that researcher may have; larger errors for same sampling size than in stratified sampling; respondents may be widely dispersed, hence cost may be higher
2. *Systematic:* The researcher uses natural ordering or the order of the sampling frame, selects an arbitrary starting point, then selects items at a preselected interval.	Moderate cost, moderately used	Simple to draw sample; easy to check	If sampling interval is related to periodic ordering of the population, may introduce increased variability
3. *Stratified:* The researcher divides the population into groups and randomly selects subsamples from each group. Variations include proportional, disproportional, and optimal allocation of subsample sizes.	High cost, moderately used	Ensures representation of all groups in sample; characteristics of each stratum can be estimated and comparisons made; reduces variability for same sample size	Requires accurate information on proportion in each stratum; if stratified lists are not already available, they can be costly to prepare
4. *Cluster:* The researcher selects sampling units at random, then does a complete observation of all units or draws a probability sample in the group.	Low cost, frequently used	If clusters geographically defined, yields lowest field cost; requires listing of all clusters, but of individuals only within clusters; can estimate characteristics of clusters as well as of population	Larger error for comparable size than with other probability samples; researcher must be able to assign population members to unique cluster or else duplication or omission of individuals will result
5. *Multistage:* Progressively smaller areas are selected in each stage by some combination of the first four techniques.	High cost, frequently used, especially in nationwide surveys	Depends on techniques combined	Depends on techniques combined

Degree of Accuracy

Selecting a representative sample is important to all researchers. However, the degree of accuracy required or the researcher's tolerance for sampling and nonsampling error may vary from project to project, especially when cost savings or another benefit may be a trade-off for a reduction in accuracy.

For example, when the sample is being selected for an exploratory research project, a high priority may not be placed on accuracy because a highly representative sample may not be necessary. For other, more conclusive projects, the sample result must precisely represent a population's characteristics, and the researcher must be willing to spend the time and money needed to achieve accuracy.

Resources

The cost associated with the different sampling techniques varies tremendously. If the researcher's financial and human resources are restricted, certain options will have to be eliminated. For a graduate student working on a master's thesis, conducting a national survey is almost always out of the

RESEARCHSNAPSHOT

Reactions to Handbills in Hong Kong

On busy city sidewalks, pedestrians often encounter a form of advertising called *handbills,* leaflets handed to passersby, informing them of a new store, a theater event, or some other nearby product or service. In highly populated urban centers, handbills are a common and successful method of direct marketing promotion—reaching tens of thousands of potential customers. Two marketing researchers in Hong Kong recently decided that this form of advertising had received little research attention, so they conducted exploratory research into consumer attitudes about handbills.

The selection of a sample design started with advance knowledge of the researchers' population. They decided to interview people in Hong Kong because the city has an extremely dense population—6 million people within 419 square miles. As a result, pedestrian traffic is heavy, and handbill distribution is a common sight on Hong Kong streets. A sample drawn from the Hong Kong population would be likely to include many people

who have experiences with and attitudes toward handbills. The Hong Kong population provided another advantage. The researchers wished to use a telephone question-

naire, and the majority of households in Hong Kong have a telephone line with a registered number. Finally, language was unlikely to be a problem; the survey was conducted in Chinese, spoken by all but a small percentage of Hong Kong's population.

In a sense, this survey involved a convenience sample, drawn from a population where the researchers live and work, rather than other parts of the world, where perhaps opinions would have been more diverse. Nevertheless, for an exploratory study into a formerly unexplored topic, the greater resources required for a more complex sampling method might not have been justified. The researchers were able to find response patterns for further investigation: People who accepted handbills were more likely to be female, relatively young, and have the equivalent of a high school education. Most of them took the handbills to help the distributor finish his or her work, and most read the handbills.

Source: Gerard Prendergast and Yuen Sze Man, "Perceptions of Handbills as a Promotional Medium: An Exploratory Study," Journal of Advertising Research, 45 (March 2005), 124–131; "Direct Delivery," Direct Marketing of Asia, Limited, http://www.dm-asia.com, accessed March 20, 2006.

question because of limited resources. Managers concerned with the cost of the research versus the value of the information often will opt to save money by using a nonprobability sampling design rather than make the decision to conduct no research at all.

Time

A researcher who needs to meet a deadline or complete a project quickly will be more likely to select a simple, less time-consuming sample design. A telephone survey that uses a sample based on random-digit dialing takes considerably less time than a survey that uses an elaborate disproportional stratified sample.

Advance Knowledge of the Population

Advance knowledge of population characteristics, such as the availability of lists of population members, is an important criterion. In many cases, however, no list of population elements will be available to the researcher. This is especially true when the population element is defined by ownership of a particular product or brand, by experience in performing a specific job task, or on a qualitative dimension. A lack of adequate lists may automatically rule out systematic sampling, stratified sampling, or other sampling designs, or it may dictate that a preliminary study, such as a short telephone survey using random digit dialing, be conducted to generate information to build a sampling frame for the primary study. In many developing countries, things like reverse directories are rare. Thus, researchers planning sample designs have to work around this limitation.

National versus Local Project

Geographic proximity of population elements will influence sample design. When population elements are unequally distributed geographically, a cluster sample may become much more attractive.

Internet Sampling Is Unique

Internet surveys allow researchers to reach a large sample rapidly—both an advantage and a disadvantage. Sample size requirements can be met overnight or in some cases almost instantaneously. A researcher can, for instance, release a survey during the morning in the Eastern Standard Time zone and have all sample size requirements met before anyone on the West Coast wakes up. If rapid response rates are expected, the sample for an Internet survey should be metered out across all time zones. In addition, people in some populations are more likely to go online during the weekend than on a weekday. If the researcher can anticipate a day-of-the-week effect, the survey should be kept open long enough so that all sample units have the opportunity to participate in the research project.

The ease and low cost of an Internet survey also has contributed to a flood of online questionnaires, some more formal than others. As a result, frequent Internet users may be more selective about which surveys they bother answering. Researchers investigating college students' attitudes toward environmental issues found that those who responded to an e-mail request that had been sent to all students tended to be more concerned about the environment than students who were contacted individually through systematic sampling. The researchers concluded that students who cared about the issues were more likely to respond to the online survey.[6]

Another disadvantage of Internet surveys is the lack of computer ownership and Internet access among certain segments of the population. A sample of Internet users is representative only of Internet users, who tend to be younger, better educated, and more affluent than the general population. This is not to say that all Internet samples are unrepresentative of all target populations. Nevertheless, when using Internet surveys, researchers should be keenly aware of potential sampling problems that can arise due to systematic characteristics of heavy computer users.

Website Visitors

As noted earlier, many Internet surveys are conducted with volunteer respondents who visit an organization's website intentionally or by happenstance. These *unrestricted samples* are clearly convenience samples. They may not be representative because of the haphazard manner by which many respondents arrived at a particular website or because of self-selection bias.

A better technique for sampling website visitors is to randomly select sampling units. SurveySite, a company that specializes in conducting Internet surveys, collects data by using its "pop-up survey" software. The software selects web visitors at random and "pops up" a small javascript window asking the person if he or she wants to participate in an evaluation survey. If the person clicks "Yes," a new window containing the online survey opens up. The person can then browse the site at his or her own pace and switch to the survey at any time to express an opinion.[7]

Randomly selecting website visitors can cause a problem. It is possible to overrepresent frequent visitors to the site and thus represent site visits rather than visitors. Several programming techniques and technologies (using cookies, registration data, or prescreening) are available to help accomplish more representative sampling based on site traffic.[8] Details of these techniques are beyond the scope of this discussion.

This type of random sampling is most valuable if the target population is defined as visitors to a particular website. Evaluation and analysis of visitors' perceptions and experiences of the website would be a typical survey objective with this type of sample. Researchers who have broader interests may obtain Internet samples in a variety of other ways.

Panel Samples

Drawing a probability sample from an established consumer panel or other prerecruited membership panel is a popular, scientific, and effective method for creating a sample of Internet users. Typically, sampling from a panel yields a high response rate because panel members have already agreed to cooperate with the research organization's e-mail or Internet surveys. Often panel members are compensated for their time with a sweepstakes, a small cash incentive, or redeemable points. Further, because the panel has already supplied demographic characteristics and other information from previous questionnaires, researchers are able to select panelists based on product ownership, lifestyle, or other characteristics. A variety of sampling methods and data transformation techniques can be applied to assure that sample results are representative of the general public or a targeted population.

Consider Harris Interactive Inc., an Internet survey research organization that maintains a panel of more than 6.5 million individuals in the United States. In the early twenty-first century, Harris plans to expand this panel to between 10 million and 15 million and to include an additional 10 million people internationally.[9] A database this large allows the company to draw simple random samples, stratified samples, and quota samples from its panel members.

Harris Interactive finds that two demographic groups are not fully accessible via Internet sampling: people ages 65 and older—a group that is rapidly growing—and those with annual incomes of less than $15,000. In contrast, 18- to 25-year-olds—a group that historically has been very hard to reach by traditional research methods—are now extremely easy to reach over the Internet.[10]

To ensure that survey results are representative, Harris Interactive uses a *propensity-weighting* scheme. The research company does parallel studies—by phone as well as over the Internet—to test the accuracy of its Internet data-gathering capabilities. Researchers look at the results of the telephone surveys and match those against the Internet-only survey results. Next, they use propensity weighting to adjust the results, taking into account the motivational and behavioral differences between the online and offline populations. (How propensity weighting adjusts for the difference between the Internet population and the general population is beyond the scope of this discussion.)

Recruited Ad Hoc Samples

Another means of obtaining an Internet sample is to obtain or create a sampling frame of e-mail addresses on an *ad hoc* basis. Researchers may create the sampling frame offline or online. Databases containing e-mail addresses can be compiled from many sources, including customer/client lists, advertising banners on pop-up windows that recruit survey participants, online sweepstakes, and registration forms that must be filled out in order to gain access to a particular website. Researchers may contact respondents by "snail mail" or by telephone to ask for their e-mail addresses and obtain permission for an Internet survey. Using offline techniques, such as random-digit dialing and short telephone screening interviews, to recruit respondents can be a very practical way to get a representative sample for an Internet survey. Companies anticipating future Internet research can develop a valuable database for sample recruitment by including e-mail addresses in their customer relationship databases (by inviting customers to provide that information on product registration cards, in telephone interactions, through on-site registration, etc.).[11]

Opt-in Lists

Opt in
To give permission to receive selected e-mail, such as questionnaires, from a company with an Internet presence.

Survey Sampling International specializes in providing sampling frames and scientifically drawn samples. The company offers more than 3,500 lists of high-quality, targeted e-mail addresses of individuals who have given permission to receive e-mail messages related to a particular topic of interest. Survey Sampling International's database contains millions of Internet users who **opt in** for limited participation. An important feature of Survey Sampling International's database is that the company has each individual confirm and reconfirm interest in communicating about a topic before the person's e-mail address is added to the company's database.[12]

By whatever technique the sampling frame is compiled, it is important *not* to send unauthorized e-mail to respondents. If individuals do not *opt in* to receive e-mail from a particular organization, they may consider unsolicited survey requests to be spam. A researcher cannot expect high response rates from individuals who have not agreed to be surveyed. Spamming is not tolerated by experienced Internet users and can easily backfire, creating a host of problems—the most extreme being complaints to the Internet service provider (ISP), which may shut down the survey site.

Summary

1. Explain reasons for taking a sample rather than a complete census. Sampling is a procedure that uses a small number of units of a given population as a basis for drawing conclusions about the whole population. Sampling often is necessary because it would be practically impossible to conduct a census to measure characteristics of all units of a population. Samples also are needed in cases where measurement involves destruction of the measured unit.

2. Describe the process of identifying a target population and selecting a sampling frame. The first problem in sampling is to define the target population. Incorrect or vague definition of this population is likely to produce misleading results. A sampling frame is a list of elements, or individual members, of the overall population from which the sample is drawn. A sampling unit is a single element or group of elements subject to selection in the sample.

3. Compare random sampling and systematic (nonsampling) errors. There are two sources of discrepancy between the sample results and the population parameters. One, random sampling error, arises from chance variations of the sample from the population. Random sampling error is a function of sample size and may be estimated using the central-limit theorem, discussed in Chapter 17. Systematic, or nonsampling, error comes from sources such as sampling frame error, mistakes in recording responses, or nonresponses from persons who are not contacted or who refuse to participate.

4. Identify the types of nonprobability sampling, including their advantages and disadvantages. The two major classes of sampling methods are probability and nonprobability techniques. Nonprobability techniques include convenience sampling, judgment sampling, quota sampling, and snowball sampling. They are convenient to use, but there are no statistical techniques with which to measure their random sampling error.

5. Summarize the advantages and disadvantages of the various types of probability samples. Probability samples are based on chance selection procedures. These include simple random sampling, systematic sampling, stratified sampling, and cluster sampling. With these techniques, random sampling error can be accurately predicted.

6. Discuss how to choose an appropriate sample design, as well as challenges for Internet sampling. A researcher who must determine the most appropriate sampling design for a specific project will identify a number of sampling criteria and evaluate the relative importance of each criterion before selecting a design. The most common criteria concern accuracy requirements, available resources, time constraints, knowledge availability, and analytical requirements. Internet sampling presents some unique issues. Researchers must be aware that samples may be unrepresentative because not everyone has a computer or access to the Internet. Convenience samples drawn from website visitors can create problems. Drawing a probability sample from an established consumer panel or an ad hoc sampling frame whose members opt in can be effective.

Key Terms and Concepts

Sample
Population (universe)
Population element
Census
Sampling frame
Reverse directory
Sampling frame error
Sampling unit
Primary sampling unit (PSU)

Secondary sampling unit
Tertiary sampling unit
Random sampling error
Probability sampling
Nonprobability sampling
Convenience sampling
Judgment (purposive) sampling
Quota sampling
Snowball sampling

Simple random sampling
Systematic sampling
Stratified sampling
Proportional stratified sample
Disproportional stratified sample
Cluster sampling
Multistage area sampling
Opt in

Questions for Review and Critical Thinking

1. If you decide whether you want to see a new movie or television program on the basis of the "coming attractions" or television commercial previews, are you using a sampling technique? A scientific sampling technique?

2. Name some possible sampling frames for the following:
   a. Electrical contractors
   b. Tennis players
   c. Dog owners
   d. Foreign-car owners
   e. Wig and hair goods retailers
   f. Minority-owned businesses
   g. Men over six feet tall

3. Describe the difference between a probability sample and a nonprobability sample.

4. In what types of situations is conducting a census more appropriate than sampling? When is sampling more appropriate than taking a census?

5. Comment on the following sampling designs:
   a. A citizen's group interested in generating public and financial support for a new university basketball arena prints a questionnaire in area newspapers. Readers return the questionnaires by mail.
   b. A department store that wishes to examine whether it is losing or gaining customers draws a sample from its list of credit card holders by selecting every tenth name.
   c. A motorcycle manufacturer decides to research consumer characteristics by sending one hundred questionnaires to each of its dealers. The dealers will then use their sales records to track down buyers of this brand of motorcycle and distribute the questionnaires.
   d. An advertising executive suggests that advertising effectiveness be tested in the real world. A one-page ad is placed in a magazine. One-half of the space is used for the ad itself. On the other half, a short questionnaire requests that readers comment on the ad. An incentive will be given for the first thousand responses.
   e. A research company obtains a sample for a focus group through organized groups such as church groups, clubs, and schools. The organizations are paid for securing respondents; no individual is directly compensated.
   f. A researcher suggests replacing a consumer diary panel with a sample of customers who regularly shop at a supermarket that uses optical scanning equipment. The burden of recording purchases by humans will be replaced by computerized longitudinal data.
   g. A banner ad on a business-oriented website reads, "Are you a large company Sr. Executive? Qualified execs receive $50 for under 10 minutes of time. Take the survey now!" Is this an appropriate way to select a sample of business executives?

6. When would a researcher use a judgment, or purposive, sample?

7. A telephone interviewer asks, "I would like to ask you about race. Are you Native American, Hispanic, African-American, Asian, or white?" After the respondent replies, the interviewer says, "We have conducted a large number of surveys with people of your background, and we do not need to question you further. Thank you for your cooperation." What type of sampling is likely being used?

8. If researchers know that consumers in various geographic regions respond quite differently to a product category, such as tomato sauce, is area sampling appropriate? Why or why not?

9. What are the benefits of stratified sampling?

10. What geographic units within a metropolitan area are useful for sampling?

11. Marketers often are particularly interested in the subset of a market that contributes most to sales (for example, heavy beer drinkers or large-volume retailers). What type of sampling might be best to use with such a subset? Why?

12. Outline the step-by-step procedure you would use to select the following:
    a. A simple random sample of 150 students at your university
    b. A quota sample of 50 light users and 50 heavy users of beer in a shopping mall intercept study
    c. A stratified sample of 50 mechanical engineers, 40 electrical engineers, and 40 civil engineers from the subscriber list of an engineering journal

13. Selection for jury duty is supposed to be a totally random process. Comment on the following computer selection procedures, and determine if they are indeed random:
    a. A program instructs the computer to scan the list of names and pick names that were next to those from the last scan.
    b. Three-digit numbers are randomly generated to select jurors from a list of licensed drivers. If the weight information listed on the license matches the random number, the person is selected.
    c. The juror source list is obtained by merging a list of registered voters with a list of licensed drivers.

14. **ETHICS** To ensure a good session, a company selects focus group members from a list of articulate participants instead of conducting random sampling. The client did not inquire about sample selection when it accepted the proposal. Is this ethical?

15. **'NET** Go to http://www.reversephonedirectory.com and put in your phone number. How accurate is this database?

16. **'NET** Go to the U.S. Census Bureau's home page at http://www.census.gov, click on M in Subjects A to Z, and then click on Metropolitan Area and State Data Book. You can find profiles of every state from this website. Suppose a representative sample of the state of Louisiana is used to represent the current U.S. population. How well does Louisiana represent the United States overall? How well does Louisiana represent California or Maine? Use the profiles of the states and of the country to form your opinion.

Case 16.1 Who's Fishing?

Washington Times columnist Gene Mueller writes about fishing and other outdoor sporting activities.[13] Mueller commented recently that although interest groups express concerns about the impact of saltwater fishers on the fish population, no one really knows how many people fish for recreation or how many fish they catch. This situation would challenge marketers interested in the population of anglers.

How could a marketer get an accurate sample? One idea would be to contact residents of coastal counties using random-digit dialing. This sampling frame would include many, if not all, of the people who fish in the ocean, but it would also include many people who do not fish—or who fish for business rather than recreation. A regional agency seeking to gather statistics on anglers, the Atlantic Coastal Cooperative Statistics Program, prefers to develop a sampling frame more related to people who fish.

Another idea would be to use state fishing license records. Privacy would be a drawback, however. Some people might not want their records shared, and they might withhold phone numbers. Further complicating this issue for Atlantic fishing is that most states in the Northeast do not require a license for saltwater fishing. Also exempt in some states are people who fish from the shore and from piers.

A political action group called the Recreational Fishing Alliance suggests that charter fishing businesses collect data.

Questions

1. Imagine that an agency or business has asked for help in gathering data about the number of sports anglers who fish off the coast of Georgia. What advice would you give about sampling? What method or combination of methods would generate the best results?
2. What other criteria besides accuracy would you expect to consider? What sampling methods could help you meet those criteria?

Case 16.2 Scientific Telephone Samples

Scientific Telephone Samples (STS), located in Santa Ana, California, specializes in selling sampling frames for marketing research.[14] The STS sampling frame is based on a database of all working residential telephone exchanges in the United States. Thus, STS can draw from any part of the country—no matter how large or how small. The information is updated several times per year and cross-checked against area code and assigned exchange lists furnished by telephone companies. Exchange and/or working blocks designated for business or governmental telephones, mobile phones, and other commercial services are screened out.

STS can furnish almost any type of random digit sample desired, including

- National samples (continental United States only, or with Alaska and Hawaii)
- Stratified national samples (by census region or division)
- Census region or division samples
- State samples
- Samples by MSA
- County samples
- Samples by zip code
- City samples by zip code
- Exchange samples generated from lists of three-digit exchanges
- Targeted random-digit dialing samples (including over forty variables and special databases for high-income areas, Hispanics, African-Americans, and Asians)

STS offers two different methods for pulling working blocks. Either method can be used regardless of the geographic sampling unit (for example, state, county, zip). The two versions are Type A (unweighted) and Type B (weighted/efficient).

Type A samples are pulled using a strict definition of randomness. They are called "unweighted" samples because each working block has an equal chance of being selected to generate a random digit number. Completed interviews from a Type A sample that has been dialed to exhaustion should be highly representative of the population under study.

Type B, or "efficient," samples are preweighted, so random digit dialing numbers are created from telephone working blocks in proportion to the number of estimated household listings in each working block. Working blocks that are more filled with numbers will be more prevalent in a sample. For example, a working block that had fifty known numbers in existence would have twice the probability of being included as one that had just twenty-five numbers.

Type B samples are most useful when a researcher is willing to overlook a strict definition of randomness in favor of slightly more calling efficiency because of fewer "disconnects." In theory, completed interviews from Type B samples may tend to overrepresent certain types of working blocks, but many researchers feel there is not much difference in representativeness.

Questions

1. Evaluate the geographic options offered by STS. Do they seem to cover all the bases?
2. Evaluate the STS method of random-digit dialing.

Case 16.3 Action Federal Savings and Loan Corporation

Steve Miles made a big move six months ago. He quit his job as director of retail marketing at the largest bank in the state to become marketing manager for Action Federal Savings and Loan. It had been only three-and-a-half years since he received his bachelor's degree in marketing at the largest university in the state, but he was bright, personable, and ambitious. Now, after several months of orientation at Action Federal (Steve called it "Mickey Mouse"), he was beginning his own marketing operations, hiring Roberta Nimoy from City University as his marketing research assistant.

Steve wanted to do an image study of each of the thirteen branches of Action Federal located throughout the state. The main branch and three others were located in tall office buildings in the capital city and nearby suburbs. The other branches were located in rural areas, and their architecture was designed to fit into the surroundings. One was located in a restored colonial home. Another, the Old Mill branch, located next to a park with a historic windmill, was designed to be compatible with the nearby river and mill.

Steve asked Roberta to develop the sampling plan for the study. After some investigation, she learned that all the accounts were listed alphabetically in the main branch's computer. She thought that a list of names and addresses could be generated by taking a sample of 1,300. The computer would be programmed to randomly select every nth name. Since the savings and loan had approximately 112,000 customers, every 86th name would be selected.

Questions
1. Evaluate Action Federal's sampling plan.
2. What alternative sampling plans might be used?

CHAPTER 17
DETERMINATION OF SAMPLE SIZE: A REVIEW OF STATISTICAL THEORY

After studying this chapter, you should be able to

1. Implement descriptive and inferential statistics
2. Interpret frequency distributions, proportions, and measures of central tendency and dispersion
3. Distinguish among population, sample, and sampling distributions
4. Explain the central-limit theorem
5. Summarize the use of confidence interval estimates
6. Discuss major issues in specifying sample size

Chapter Vignette: Federal Reserve Finds Cards Are Replacing Cash

Payment options have gone high-tech. Businesses that sell to consumers—and even charities that seek donations from individuals—need to plan for a wide range of choices beyond traditional cash or checks. Today's spenders are more likely to pay with a debit or credit card or through a variety of methods for electronic transfer of funds. To measure this trend in more detail, researchers at the Federal Reserve conducted surveys of depository institutions (banks, savings and loan institutions, and credit unions), asking them to report the number of each type of payment the institutions processed.[1]

In planning this survey, the Fed's researchers carefully designed the sample, including the number of institutions to contact. The total number of depository institutions in the United States was already known: 14,117. The researchers had to select enough institutions from this population to be confident that the answers would be representative of transactions nationwide.

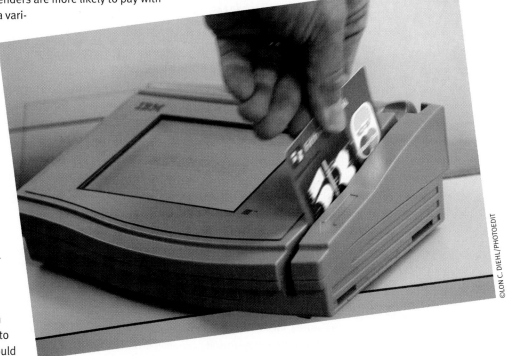

©LON C. DIEHL/PHOTOEDIT

A stratified random sample was used so that each type of institution would be included. The researchers had conducted a similar survey three years earlier and obtained a 54 percent response rate, so they assumed the rate would be similar. Using techniques such as those described in this chapter, the researchers determined that, given the total number of institutions and the response rate, they would need to sample 2,700 depository institutions to obtain results that they could say, with 95 percent confidence, were accurate to within ±5 percent of the responses.

With a response rate just above that of the prior survey, 1,500 institutions reponded, giving data on the number of transactions processed in each payment category. Their responses confirmed earlier analysis showing that the number of checks paid in the United States is declining while the number of electronic payments is increasing. Because this survey measured institutional transactions, it could not count the number of purchases made with cash.

Formally identifying the proper sample size requires applied statistical theory. Statistics often inspires dread among students. However, when a would-be researcher learns a few tricks of the trade, using statistics can become second nature. Many of these "tricks" involve learning the specialized language of statisticians. Simply put, if you do not understand the basics of the language, you will have problems in conversation. Statistics is the language of the researcher. This chapter reviews some of the basic terminology of statistical analysis and applies statistical principles to the process of determining a sample size.

Review of Basic Terminology

The first six sections of this chapter summarize key statistical concepts necessary for understanding the theory that underlies the derivation of sample size. These sections are intended for students who need to review the basic aspects of statistics theory. Even those students who received good grades in their elementary statistics classes probably will benefit from a quick review of the basic statistical concepts. Some students will prefer to just skim this material and proceed to page 449, where the discussion of the actual determination of sample size begins. Others need to study these sections carefully to acquire an understanding of statistics.

Descriptive and Inferential Statistics

The *Statistical Abstract of the United States* presents table after table of figures associated with numbers of births, number of employees in each county of the United States, and other data that the average person calls "statistics." They are descriptive statistics. Another type of statistics, inferential statistics, is used to make inferences about a whole population from a sample. For example, when a firm test-markets a new product in Sacramento and Birmingham, it wishes to make an inference from these sample markets to predict what will happen throughout the United States. So, two applications of statistics exist: (1) to describe characteristics of the population or sample and (2) to generalize from a sample to a population.

Sample Statistics and Population Parameters

The primary purpose of inferential statistics is to make a judgment about a population, or the total collection of all elements about which a researcher seeks information. A sample is a subset or relatively small portion of the total number of elements in a given population. Data from a sample are always uncertain but when data come from all elements of a population, certainty is possible.

Sample statistics are measures computed from sample data. **Population parameters** are measured characteristics of a specific population. Sample statistics are used to make inferences (guesses) about population parameters.[2] In our notation, we will generally represent population parameters with Greek lowercase letters—for example, μ or σ—and sample statistics with English letters, such as X or S.

Sample statistics
Variables in a sample or measures computed from sample data.

Population parameters
Variables in a population or measured characteristics of the population.

Making Data Usable

Suppose a telephone survey has been conducted for a savings and loan association. The data have been recorded on a large number of questionnaires. To make the data usable, this information must be organized and summarized. Methods for doing this include frequency distributions, proportions, and measures of central tendency and dispersion.

Amount	Frequency (Number of People Who Hold Deposits in Each Range)
Under $3,000	499
$3,000–$4,999	530
$5,000–$9,999	562
$10,000–$14,999	718
$15,000 or more	811
	3,120

EXHIBIT 17.1
Frequency Distribution of Deposits

Frequency Distributions

One of the most common ways to summarize a set of data is to construct a *frequency table,* or frequency distribution. The process begins with recording the number of times a particular value of a variable occurs. This is the frequency of that value. Continuing the example of a telephone survey for a savings and loan association, Exhibit 17.1 represents a frequency distribution of respondents' answers to a question that asked how much money customers had deposited in the institution.

A similar method that is also simple is to construct a distribution of relative frequency, or a percentage distribution. To develop a frequency distribution of percentages, divide the frequency of each value by the total number of observations, and multiply the result by 100. Based on the data in Exhibit 17.1, Exhibit 17.2 shows the percentage distribution of deposits; that is, the percentage of people holding deposits within each range of values.

Probability is the long-run relative frequency with which an event will occur. Inferential statistics uses the concept of a probability distribution, which is conceptually the same as a percentage distribution except that the data are converted into probabilities. Exhibit 17.3 shows the probability distribution of the savings and loan deposits.

Frequency distribution
A set of data organized by summarizing the number of times a particular value of a variable occurs.

Percentage distribution
A frequency distribution organized into a table (or graph) that summarizes percentage values associated with particular values of a variable.

Probability
The long-run relative frequency with which an event will occur.

Proportions

When a frequency distribution portrays only a single characteristic in terms of a percentage of the total, it defines the proportion of occurrence. A proportion, such as the proportion of tenured professors at a university, indicates the percentage of population elements that successfully meet some standard concerning the particular characteristic. A proportion may be expressed as a percentage, a fraction, or a decimal value.

Proportion
The percentage of elements that meet some criterion.

Amount	Percent (Percentage of People Who Hold Deposits in Each Range)
Under $3,000	16
$3,000–$4,999	17
$5,000–$9,999	18
$10,000–$14,999	23
$15,000 or more	26
	100

EXHIBIT 17.2
Percentage Distribution of Deposits

Amount	Probability
Under $3,000	.16
$3,000–$4,999	.17
$5,000–$9,999	.18
$10,000–$14,999	.23
$15,000 or more	.26
	1.00

Measures of Central Tendency

On a typical day, a sales manager counts the number of sales calls each sales representative makes. He or she wishes to inspect the data to find the center, or middle area, of the frequency distribution. Central tendency can be measured in three ways—the mean, median, or mode—each of which has a different meaning.

◼ THE MEAN

Mean
A measure of central tendency; the arithmetic average.

We all have been exposed to the average known as the **mean**. The mean is simply the arithmetic average, and it is a common measure of central tendency. To express this mathematically, we use the summation symbol, the capital Greek letter *sigma* (Σ). A typical use might look like this:

$$\sum_{i=1}^{n} X_i$$

which is a shorthand way to write the sum

$$X_1 + X_2 + X_3 + X_4 + X_5 + \cdots + X_n$$

Below the Σ is the initial value of an index, usually, i, j, or k, and above it is the final value, in this case n, the number of observations. The shorthand expression says to replace i in the formula with the values from 1 to 8 and total the observations obtained. Without changing the basic formula, the initial and final index values may be replaced by other values to indicate different starting and stopping points.

Suppose a sales manager supervises the eight salespeople listed in Exhibit 17.4. To express the sum of the salespeople's calls in Σ notation, we just number the salespeople (this number becomes the index number) and associate subscripted variables with their numbers of calls:

Index		Salesperson	Variable		Number of Calls
1	=	Mike	X_1	=	4
2	=	Patty	X_2	=	3
3	=	Billie	X_3	=	2
4	=	Bob	X_4	=	5
5	=	John	X_5	=	3
6	=	Frank	X_6	=	3
7	=	Chuck	X_7	=	1
8	=	Samantha	X_8	=	5

RESEARCHSNAPSHOT

The Well-Chosen Average

When you read an announcement by a corporate executive or a business proprietor that the average pay of the people who work in his or her establishment is so much, the figure may mean something or it may not. If the average is a median, you can learn something significant from it: Half of the employees make more than that; half make less. But if it is a mean (and believe me, it may be, if its nature is unspecified), you may be getting nothing more revealing than the average of one $450,000 income—the proprietor's—and the salaries of a crew of lower wage workers. "Average annual pay of $57,000" may conceal both the $20,000 salaries and the owner's profits taken in the form of a whopping salary.

Let's take a longer look at this scenario. This table shows how many people get how much. The boss might like to express the situation as "average wage $57,000," using that deceptive mean. The mode, however, is more revealing: The most common rate of pay in this business is $20,000 a year. As usual, the median tells more about the situation than any other single figure. Half of the people get more than $30,000 and half get less.

Number of People	Title	Salary
1	Proprietor	$450,000
1	President	150,000
2	Vice presidents	100,000

1	Controller	57,000	♦ Mean (arithmetical average)
3	Directors	50,000	
4	Managers	37,000	
1	Supervisor	30,000	♦ Median (the one in the middle; 12 above, 12 below)
12	Workers	20,000	♦ Mode (occurs most frequently)

Imagine what would happen to your hometown's average income if Ross Perot and Bill Gates moved into town.

Do politicians use statistics to lie or do the statistics lie? Politicians sometimes try to play one class of people against another in trying to get elected. One political claim is that the "rich do not pay taxes" or the "rich do not pay their fair share of taxes." If you are curious about this, some facts are available at http://www.taxfoundation.org or http://www.irs.gov/pub/irs-soi/03in05tr.xls. Do the top 1 percent of wage earners pay taxes? Do the top 5 percent of wage earners pay taxes?

Sources: Darrell Huff and Irving Geis, *How to Lie with Statistics* (New York: W.W. Norton, 1954), p. 33; Jackson, Brooks and Kathleen H. Jamieson (2004), "Finding Fact in Political Debate," *American Behavioral Scientist*, 48 (October 1), 233–247.

We then write an appropriate Σ formula and evaluate it:

$$\sum_{i=1}^{8} X_i = X_1 + X_2 + X_3 + X_4 + X_5 + X_6 + X_7 + X_8$$
$$= 4 + 3 + 2 + 5 + 3 + 3 + 1 + 5$$
$$= 26$$

EXHIBIT 17.4

Number of Sales Calls per Day by Salesperson

Salesperson	Number of Sales Calls
Mike	4
Patty	3
Billie	2
Bob	5
John	3
Frank	3
Chuck	1
Samantha	5
Total	26

This notation is the numerator in the formula for the arithmetic mean:

$$\text{Mean} = \frac{\sum_{i=1}^{n} X}{n} = \frac{26}{8} = 3.25$$

The sum $\sum_{i=1}^{n} X$ tells us to add all the Xs whose subscripts are between 1 and n inclusive, where n equals the number of observations. The formula shows that the mean number of sales calls in this example is 3.25.

Researchers generally wish to know the population mean, μ (lowercase Greek letter *mu*), which is calculated as follows:

$$\mu = \frac{\sum_{i=1}^{n} X}{N}$$

where

  N = number of all observations in the population

Often we will not have enough data to calculate the population mean, μ, so we will calculate a sample mean, $\overline{X}$ (read "X bar"), with the following formula:

$$\overline{X} = \frac{\sum_{i=1}^{n} X}{n}$$

where

  n = number of observations made in the sample

More likely than not, you already know how to calculate a mean. However, knowing how to distinguish among the symbols Σ, μ, and X is helpful to understand statistics.

In this introductory discussion of the summation sign (Σ), we have used very detailed notation that includes the subscript for the initial index value (i) and the final index value (n). However, from this point on, references to Σ will sometimes omit the subscript for the initial index value (i) and the final index value (n).

▨ THE MEDIAN

Median
A measure of central tendency that is the midpoint; the value below which half the values in a distribution fall.

The next measure of central tendency, the **median**, is the midpoint of the distribution, or the 50th percentile. In other words, the median is the value below which half the values in the sample fall. In the sales manager example, 3 is the median because half the observations are greater than 3 and half are less than 3.

▨ THE MODE

Mode
A measure of central tendency; the value that occurs most often.

In apparel *mode* refers to the most popular fashion. In statistics the **mode** is the measure of central tendency that identifies the value that occurs most often. In our example of sales calls, Patty, John, and Frank each made three sales calls. The value 3 occurs most often, so 3 is the mode. The mode is determined by listing each possible value and noting the number of times each value occurs.

Measures of Dispersion

The mean, median, and mode summarize the central tendency of frequency distributions. Accurate analysis of data also requires knowing the tendency of observations to depart from the central tendency. Thus, another way to summarize the data is to calculate the dispersion of the data, or how

RESEARCHSNAPSHOT

Are Incomes Growing? It Depends What You Measure

When marketers investigate demand, they often are interested in income levels. And if the income of a population is growing, marketers hope that trend signals potential growth in demand. So, marketers may have been pleased to hear the former U.S. Treasury Secretary, John Snow, comment on the strength of the national economy. Snow mentioned data showing that income had grown 8.2 percent between January 2001 and January 2006.

In evaluating these numbers, it's important to consider what is being measured. The growth Snow reported was in per capita after-tax income. Because he measured income after taxes, he was looking at taxation as well as pay rates, which certainly would affect the amount of funds available to consumers. By using *per capita* income, he referred to the total earnings divided by the population—in other words, the statistical mean.

When measuring income, statisticians generally look at the median. Data available for changes in median income paint a less rosy picture. Between 2000 and 2005, the median hourly wage rose by only 2.9 percent. Growth among salaried employees was even stronger. Similarly, marketers are interested in buying power. During the last few years, income and energy prices have increased. However, buying power has increased faster than energy prices leading to an increase in buying power and good news for American retailers. Thus, if one focused on only energy prices or only income, the picture of the economy could be fuzzy.

Sources: Based on Greg Ip, "Snow Defends President's Handling of Economy," The Wall Street Journal, March 20, 2006, http://online.wsj.com; Chain Store Age (2006), "$468 Billion: Disposable Income Growth," 82 (January), 141.

©JOE TREE/ALAMY

the observations vary from the mean. Consider, for instance, the twelve-month sales patterns of the two products shown in Exhibit 17.5. Both have a mean monthly sales volume of 200 units, but the dispersion of observations for product B is much greater than that for product A. There are several measures of dispersion.

EXHIBIT 17.5

Sales Levels for Two Products with Identical Average Sales

	Units Product A	Units Product B
January	196	150
February	198	160
March	199	176
April	200	181
May	200	192
June	200	200
July	200	201
August	201	202
September	201	213
October	201	224
November	202	240
December	202	261
Average	**200**	**200**

EXHIBIT 17.6
**Low Dispersion versus
High Dispersion**

THE RANGE

The simplest measure of dispersion is the range. It is the distance between the smallest and the largest values of a frequency distribution. In Exhibit 17.5, the range for product A is between 196 units and 202 units (6 units), whereas for product B the range is between 150 units and 261 units (111 units). The range does not take into account all the observations; it merely tells us about the extreme values of the distribution.

Just as people may be fat or skinny, distributions may be fat or skinny. While we do not expect all observations to be exactly like the mean, in a skinny distribution they will lie a short distance from the mean. Product A is an example; the observations are close together and reasonably close to the mean. In a fat distribution, such as the one for Product B, they will be spread out. Exhibit 17.6 illustrates this concept graphically with two frequency distributions that have identical modes, medians, and means but different degrees of dispersion.

The interquartile range is the range that encompasses the middle 50 percent of the observations—in other words, the range between the bottom quartile (lowest 25 percent) and the top quartile (highest 25 percent).

DEVIATION SCORES

A method of calculating how far any observation is from the mean is to calculate individual deviation scores. To calculate a deviation from the mean, use the following formula:

$$d_{i_i} = X_i - \overline{X}$$

For the value of 150 units for product B for the month of January, the deviation score is -50; that is, $150 - 200 = -50$. If the deviation scores are large, we will have a fat distribution because the distribution exhibits a broad spread.

WHY USE THE STANDARD DEVIATION?

Statisticians have derived several quantitative indexes to reflect a distribution's spread, or variability. The *standard deviation* is perhaps the most valuable index of spread, or dispersion. Students often have difficulty understanding it. Learning about the standard deviation will be easier if we first look at several other measures of dispersion that may be used. Each of these has certain limitations that the standard deviation does not.

First is the average deviation. We compute the average deviation by calculating the deviation score of each observation value (that is, its difference from the mean), summing these scores, and then dividing by the sample size (n):

$$\text{Average deviation} = \frac{\sum (X_i - \overline{X})}{n}$$

While this measure of spread seems interesting, it is never used. Positive deviation scores are canceled out by negative scores with this formula, leaving an average deviation value of zero no matter how wide the spread may be. Hence, the average deviation is a useless spread measure.

One might correct for the disadvantage of the average deviation by computing the absolute values of the deviations. In other words, we ignore all the positive and negative signs and use only the absolute value of each deviation. The formula for the mean absolute deviation is

$$\text{Mean absolute deviation} = \frac{\sum |X_i - \overline{X}|}{n}$$

While this procedure eliminates the problem of always having a zero score for the deviation measure, some technical mathematical problems make it less valuable than some other measures.

Variance

Another means of eliminating the sign problem caused by the negative deviations canceling out the positive deviations is to square the deviation scores. The following formula gives the mean squared deviation:

$$\text{Mean squared deviation} = \frac{\sum \left(X_i - \overline{X} \right)^2}{n}$$

This measure is useful for describing the sample variability. However, we typically wish to make an inference about a population from a sample, and so the divisor $n - 1$ is used rather than n in most pragmatic marketing research problems.[3] This new measure of spread, called **variance**, has the following formula:

$$\text{Variance} = S^2 = \frac{\sum \left(X_i - \overline{X} \right)^2}{n - 1}$$

Variance
A measure of variability or dispersion. Its square root is the standard deviation.

Variance is a very good index of dispersion. The variance, S^2, will equal zero if and only if each and every observation in the distribution is the same as the mean. The variance will grow larger as the observations tend to differ increasingly from one another and from the mean.

Standard Deviation

While the variance is frequently used in statistics, it has one major drawback. The variance reflects a unit of measurement that has been squared. For instance, if measures of sales in a territory are made in dollars, the mean number will be reflected in dollars, but the variance will be in squared dollars. Because of this, statisticians often take the square root of the variance. Using the square root of the variance for a distribution, called the **standard deviation**, eliminates the drawback of having the measure of dispersion in squared units rather than in the original measurement units. The formula for the standard deviation is

Standard deviation
A quantitative index of a distribution's spread, or variability; the square root of the variance for a distribution.

$$S = \sqrt{S^2} = \sqrt{\frac{\sum \left(X_i - \overline{X} \right)^2}{n - 1}}$$

Exhibit 17.7 illustrates that the calculation of a standard deviation requires the researcher to first calculate the sample mean. In the example with eight salespeople's sales calls (Exhibit 17.4), we calculated the sample mean as 3.25. Exhibit 17.7 illustrates how to calculate the standard deviation for these data.

At this point we can return to thinking about the original purpose for measures of dispersion. We want to summarize the data from survey research and other forms of marketing research. Indexes of central tendency, such as the mean, help us interpret the data. In addition, we wish to calculate a measure of variability that will give us a quantitative index of the dispersion of the distribution. We have looked at several measures of dispersion to arrive at two very adequate means of measuring dispersion: the variance and the standard deviation. The formula given is for the sample standard deviation, S.

The formula for the population standard deviation, σ, which is conceptually very similar, has not been given. Nevertheless, you should understand that σ measures the dispersion in the population and S measures the dispersion in the sample. These concepts are crucial to understanding statistics. Remember, the student must learn the language of statistics to use it in a research project. If you do not understand the language at this point, review this material now.

X	(X − X̄)	(X − X̄)²
4	(4 − 3.25) = .75	.5625
3	(3 − 3.25) = −.25	.0625
2	(2 − 3.25) = −1.25	1.5625
5	(5 − 3.25) = 1.75	3.0625
3	(3 − 3.25) = −.25	.0625
3	(3 − 3.25) = −.25	.0625
1	(1 − 3.25) = −2.25	5.0625
5	(5 − 3.25) = 1.75	3.0625
Σᵃ	a	13.5000

$$n = 8 \quad \bar{X} = 3.25$$

$$S = \sqrt{\frac{\sum(X-\bar{X})^2}{n-1}} = \sqrt{\frac{13.5}{8-1}} = \sqrt{\frac{13.5}{7}} = \sqrt{1.9286} = 1.3887$$

ᵃThe summation of this column is not used in the calculation of the standard deviation.

The Normal Distribution

Normal distribution
A symmetrical, bell-shaped distribution that describes the expected probability distribution of many chance occurrences.

One of the most common probability distributions in statistics is the **normal distribution**, commonly represented by the *normal curve*. This mathematical and theoretical distribution describes the expected distribution of sample means and many other chance occurrences. The normal curve is bell shaped, and almost all (99 percent) of its values are within ±3 standard deviations from its mean. An example of a normal curve, the distribution of IQ scores, appears in Exhibit 17.8. In this example, 1 standard deviation for IQ equals 15. We can identify the proportion of the curve by measuring a score's distance (in this case, standard deviation) from the mean (100).

EXHIBIT 17.8
Normal Distribution: Distribution of Intelligence Quotient (IQ) Scores

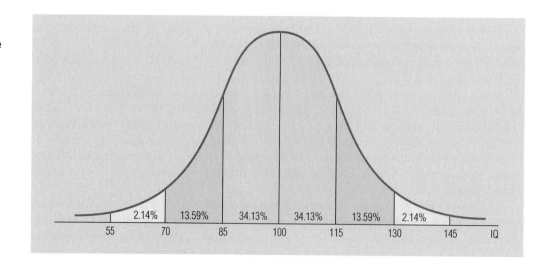

EXHIBIT 17.9
**Standardized Normal
Distribution**

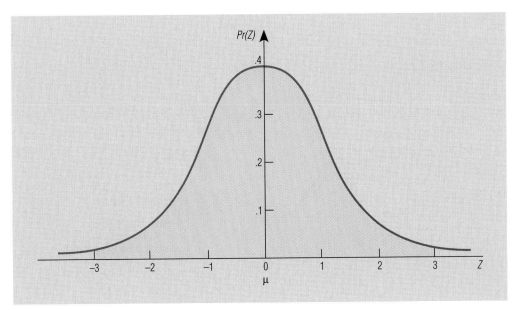

EXHIBIT 17.10   **Standardized Normal Table: Area under Half of the Normal Curve[a]**

Z Standard Deviations from the Mean (Units)	Z Standard Deviations from the Mean (Tenths of Units)									
	.0	.1	.2	.3	.4	.5	.6	.7	.8	.9
0.0	.000	.040	.080	.118	.155	.192	.226	.258	.288	.315
1.0	.341	.364	.385	.403	.419	.433	.445	.455	.464	.471
2.0	.477	.482	.486	.489	.492	.494	.495	.496	.497	.498
3.0	.499	.499	.499	.499	.499	.499	.499	.499	.499	.499

[a]Area under the segment of the normal curve extending (in one direction) from the mean to the point indicated by each row-column combination. For example, about 68 percent of normally distributed events can be expected to fall within 1.0 standard deviation on either side of the mean (0.341 × 2). An interval of almost 2.0 standard deviations around the mean will include 95 percent of all cases.

The **standardized normal distribution** is a specific normal curve that has several characteristics:

1. It is symmetrical about its mean.
2. The mean identifies the normal curve's highest point (the mode) and the vertical line about which this normal curve is symmetrical.
3. The normal curve has an infinite number of cases (it is a continuous distribution), and the area under the curve has a probability density equal to 1.0.
4. The standardized normal distribution has a mean of 0 and a standard deviation of 1.

Exhibit 17.9 illustrates these properties. Exhibit 17.10 is a summary version of the typical standardized normal table found at the end of most statistics textbooks. A more complex table of areas under the standardized normal distribution appears in Table A.2 in the appendix.

The standardized normal distribution is a purely theoretical probability distribution, but it is the most useful distribution in inferential statistics. Statisticians have spent a great deal of

Standardized normal distribution
A purely theoretical probability distribution that reflects a specific normal curve for the standardized value, z.

TOTHEPOINT

Order is heaven's law.

—Alexander Pope

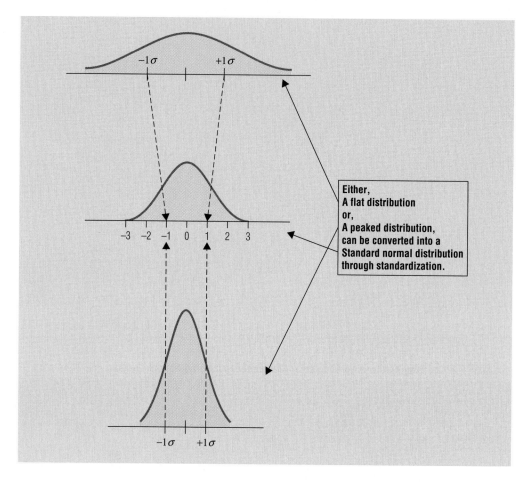

Either,
A flat distribution
or,
A peaked distribution,
can be converted into a
Standard normal distribution
through standardization.

time and effort making it convenient for researchers to find the probability of any portion of the area under the standardized normal distribution. All we have to do is transform, or convert, the data from other observed normal distributions to the standardized normal curve. In other words, the standardized normal distribution is extremely valuable because we can translate, or transform, any normal variable, X, into the standardized value, Z. Exhibit 17.11 illustrates how either a skinny distribution or a fat distribution can be converted into the standardized normal distribution. This ability to transform normal variables has many pragmatic implications for the marketing researcher. The standardized normal table in the back of most statistics and marketing research books allows us to evaluate the probability of the occurrence of many events without any difficulty.

Computing the standardized value, Z, of any measurement expressed in original units is simple: Subtract the mean from the value to be transformed, and divide by the standard deviation (all expressed in original units). The formula for this procedure and its verbal statement follow. In the formula, note that σ, the population standard deviation, is used for calculation.[4]

$$\text{Standardized value} = \frac{\text{Value to be transformed} - \text{Mean}}{\text{Standard deviation}}$$

$$Z = \frac{X - \mu}{\sigma}$$

where

μ = hypothesized or expected value of the mean

Suppose that in the past a toy manufacturer has experienced mean sales, μ, of 9,000 units and a standard deviation, σ, of 500 units during September. The production manager wishes to know whether wholesalers will demand between 7,500 and 9,625 units during September of the upcoming year. Because no tables are available showing the distribution for a mean of 9,000 and a standard deviation of 500, we must transform our distribution of toy sales, X, into the standardized form using our simple formula. The following computation shows that the probability (Pr) of

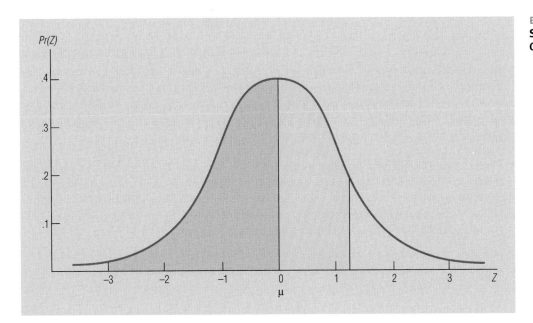

EXHIBIT 17.12
Standardized Distribution Curve

obtaining sales in this range is equal to .893:

$$Z = \frac{X - \mu}{\sigma} = \frac{7,500 - 9,000}{500} = -3.00$$

$$Z = \frac{X - \mu}{\sigma} = \frac{9,625 - 9,000}{500} = 1.25$$

Using Exhibit 17.10 (or Table A.2 in the appendix), we find that

When $Z = -3.00$, the area under the curve (probability) equals 0.499.

When $Z = 1.25$, the area under the curve (probability) equals 0.394.

Thus, the total area under the curve is .499 + .394 = .893. (The area under the curve corresponding to this computation is the shaded area in Exhibit 17.12.) The sales manager, therefore, knows there is a .893 probability that sales will be between 7,500 and 9,625.

At this point, it is appropriate to repeat that understanding statistics requires an understanding of the language that statisticians use. Each concept discussed so far is relatively simple, but a clear-cut command of this terminology is essential for understanding what we will discuss later on.

Population Distribution, Sample Distribution, and Sampling Distribution

Before we outline the technique of statistical inference, three additional types of distributions must be defined: population distribution, sample distribution, and sampling distribution. When conducting a research project or survey, the researcher's purpose is not to describe the sample of respondents, but to make an inference about the population. As defined previously, a population, or universe, is the total set, or collection, of potential units for observation. The sample is a smaller subset of this population.

A frequency distribution of the population elements is called a **population distribution**. The mean and standard deviation of the population distribution are represented by the Greek letters μ and σ. A frequency distribution of a sample is called a **sample distribution**. The sample mean is designated $\overline{X}$, and the sample standard deviation is designated S.

Population distribution
A frequency distribution of the elements of a population.

Sample distribution
A frequency distribution of a sample.

The concepts of population distribution and sample distribution are relatively simple. However, we must now introduce another distribution, which is the crux of understanding statistics: the *sampling distribution of the sample mean*. The sampling distribution is a theoretical probability distribution that in actual practice would never be calculated. Hence, practical, business-oriented students have difficulty understanding why the notion of the sampling distribution is important. Statisticians, with their mathematical curiosity, have asked themselves, "What would happen if we were to draw a large number of samples (say, 50,000), each having n elements, from a specified population?" Assuming that the samples were randomly selected, the sample means, $\overline{X}$s, could be arranged in a frequency distribution. Because different people or sample units would be selected in the different samples, the sample means would not be exactly equal. The shape of the sampling distribution is of considerable importance to statisticians. If the sample size is sufficiently large and if the samples are randomly drawn, we know from the central-limit theorem that the sampling distribution of the mean will be approximately normally distributed.

A formal definition of the sampling distribution is as follows:

Sampling distribution
A theoretical probability distribution of sample means for all possible samples of a certain size drawn from a particular population.

A sampling distribution is a theoretical probability distribution that shows the functional relation between the possible values of some summary characteristic of n cases drawn at random and the probability (density) associated with each value over all possible samples of size n from a particular population.[5]

The sampling distribution's mean is called the *expected value* of the statistic. The expected value of the mean of the sampling distribution is equal to μ. The standard deviation of a sampling distribution of $\overline{X}$ is called **standard error of the mean** ($S_{\overline{X}}$) and is approximately equal to

Standard error of the mean
The standard deviation of the sampling distribution.

$$S_{\overline{X}} = \frac{\sigma}{\sqrt{n}}$$

To review, for us to make an inference about a population from a sample, we must know about three important distributions: the population distribution, the sample distribution, and the sampling distribution. They have the following characteristics:

	Mean	Standard Deviation
Population distribution	μ	σ
Sample distribution	$\overline{X}$	S
Sampling distribution	$\mu_{\overline{X}} = \mu$	$S_{\overline{X}}$

We now have much of the information we need to understand the concept of statistical inference. To clarify why the sampling distribution has the characteristic just described, we will elaborate on two concepts: the standard error of the mean and the central-limit theorem. You may be wondering why the standard error of the mean, $S_{\overline{X}}$, is defined as $S_{\overline{X}} = \sigma/\sqrt{n}$. The reason is based on the notion that the variance or dispersion within the sampling distribution of the mean will be less if we have a larger sample size for independent samples. We can see intuitively that a larger sample size allows the researcher to be more confident that the sample mean is closer to the population mean. In actual practice, the standard error of the mean is estimated using the sample's standard deviation. Thus, $S_{\overline{X}}$ is estimated using $S/\sqrt{n}$.

Exhibit 17.13 shows the relationship among a population distribution, the sample distribution, and three sampling distributions for varying sample sizes. In part (a) the population distribution is not a normal distribution. In part (b) the sample distribution resembles the distribution of the population; however, there may be some differences. In part (c) each sampling distribution is normally distributed and has the same mean. Note that as sample size increases, the spread of the sample means around μ decreases. Thus, with a larger sample size we will have a skinnier sampling distribution.

EXHIBIT 17.13
Fundamental Types of Distributions

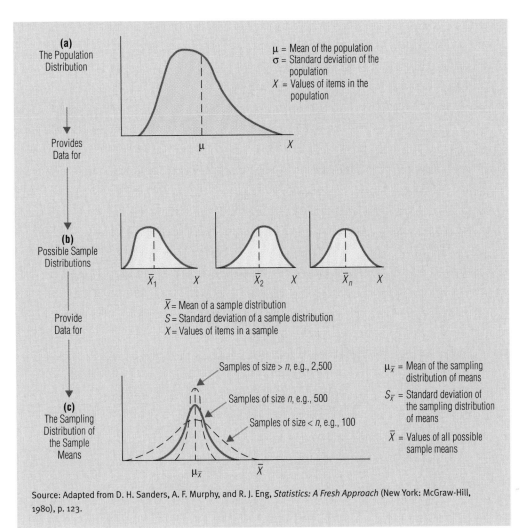

(a)
The Population Distribution

μ = Mean of the population
σ = Standard deviation of the population
X = Values of items in the population

Provides Data for

(b)
Possible Sample Distributions

$\overline{X}_1$ X $\overline{X}_2$ X $\overline{X}_n$ X

$\overline{X}$ = Mean of a sample distribution
S = Standard deviation of a sample distribution
X = Values of items in a sample

Provide Data for

Samples of size > n, e.g., 2,500

Samples of size n, e.g., 500

Samples of size < n, e.g., 100

$\mu_{\overline{X}}$ = Mean of the sampling distribution of means

$S_{\overline{X}}$ = Standard deviation of the sampling distribution of means

$\overline{X}$ = Values of all possible sample means

(c)
The Sampling Distribution of the Sample Means

$\mu_{\overline{X}}$ $\overline{X}$

Source: Adapted from D. H. Sanders, A. F. Murphy, and R. J. Eng, *Statistics: A Fresh Approach* (New York: McGraw-Hill, 1980), p. 123.

Central-Limit Theorem

Finding that the means of random samples of a sufficiently large size will be approximately normal in form and that the mean of the sampling distribution will approach the population mean is very useful. Mathematically, this is the assertion of the **central-limit theorem**, which states, as the sample size, n, increases, the distribution of the mean, $\overline{X}$, of a random sample taken from practically any population approaches a normal distribution (with a mean μ and a standard deviation $\sigma/\sqrt{n}$).[6] The central-limit theorem works regardless of the shape of the original population distribution (see Exhibit 17.14).

A simple example will demonstrate the central-limit theorem. Assume that a consumer researcher is interested in the number of dollars children spend on toys each month. Assume further that the population the consumer researcher is investigating consists of eight-year-old children in a certain school. In this example, the population consists of only six individuals. (This is a simple and perhaps somewhat unrealistic example; nevertheless, assume that the population size is only six elements.) Exhibit 17.15 shows the population distribution of toy expenditures. Alice, a relatively deprived child, has only $1 per month, whereas Freddy, the rich kid, has $6 to spend. The average expenditure on toys each month is $3.50, so the population mean, μ, equals 3.5 (see Exhibit 17.16).

Central-limit theorem
The theory that, as sample size increases, the distribution of sample means of size n, randomly selected, approaches a normal distribution.

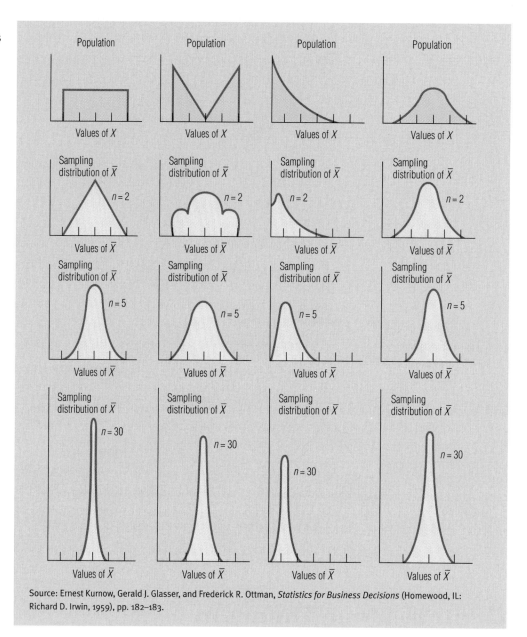

Source: Ernest Kurnow, Gerald J. Glasser, and Frederick R. Ottman, *Statistics for Business Decisions* (Homewood, IL: Richard D. Irwin, 1959), pp. 182–183.

Child	Toy Expenditures
Alice	$1.00
Becky	2.00
Noah	3.00
Tobin	4.00
George	5.00
Freddy	6.00

EXHIBIT 17.16
Calculation of Population Mean

X
$1.00
2.00
3.00
4.00
5.00
6.00
$\sum$ $21.00

Calculations: $\mu = \dfrac{\sum X}{n} = \dfrac{21}{6} = 3.5 = \mu_{\bar{X}}$

Now assume that we do not know everything about the population, and we wish to take a sample size of two, to be drawn randomly from the population of the six individuals. How many possible samples are there? The answer is 15, as follows:

```
1, 2
1, 3    2, 3
1, 4    2, 4    3, 4
1, 5    2, 5    3, 5    4, 5
1, 6    2, 6    3, 6    4, 6    5, 6
```

Exhibit 17.17 lists the sample mean for each of the possible fifteen samples and the frequency distribution of these sample means with their appropriate probabilities. These sample means comprise a sampling distribution of the mean, and the distribution is *approximately* normal. If we increased the sample size to three, four, or more, the distribution of sample means would more closely approximate a normal distribution. While this simple example is not a proof of the central-limit theorem, it should give you a better understanding of the nature of the sampling distribution of the mean.

This theoretical knowledge about distributions can be used to solve two practical marketing research problems: estimating parameters and determining sample size.

Estimation of Parameters

A catalog retailer, such as Horchow, may rely on sampling and statistical estimation to prepare for Christmas orders. The company can expect that twenty-eight days after mailing a catalog, it will have received X percent of the orders it will get. With this information, the company can tell within 5 percent how many ties it will sell by Christmas. Making a proper inference about population parameters is highly practical for a marketer that must have the inventory appropriate for a short selling season.

Suppose you are a product manager for Beatrice Foods and you recently conducted a taste test to measure intention to buy a reformulated Swiss Miss Lite Cocoa Mix. The results of the research indicate that when the product was placed in eight hundred homes and a callback was made two weeks later, 80 percent of the respondents said they would buy it: 76 percent of those who had not previously used low-calorie cocoa and 84 percent of those who had. How can you be sure there were no statistical errors in this estimate? How confident can you be of these figures?

Students often wonder whether statistics are really used in the business world. The two situations just described provide contemporary examples of the need for statistical estimation of parameters and the value of statistical techniques as managerial tools.

EXHIBIT 17.17
Arithmetic Means of Samples and Frequency Distribution of Sample Means

	Sample Means		
Sample	**ΣX**	**$\bar{X}$**	**Probability**
$1, $2	$3.00	$1.50	1/15
1, 3	4.00	2.00	1/15
1, 4	5.00	2.50	1/15
1, 5	6.00	3.00	1/15
1, 6	7.00	3.50	1/15
2, 3	5.00	2.50	1/15
2, 4	6.00	3.00	1/15
2, 5	7.00	3.50	1/15
2, 6	8.00	4.00	1/15
3, 4	7.00	3.50	1/15
3, 5	8.00	4.00	1/15
3, 6	9.00	4.50	1/15
4, 5	9.00	4.50	1/15
4, 6	10.00	5.00	1/15
5, 6	11.00	5.50	1/15

	Frequency Distribution	
Sample Mean	**Frequency**	**Probability**
$1.50	1	1/15
2.00	1	1/15
2.50	2	2/15
3.00	2	2/15
3.50	3	3/15
4.00	2	2/15
4.50	2	2/15
5.00	1	1/15
5.50	1	1/15

Point Estimates

Our goal in using statistics is to make an estimate about population parameters. A population mean, μ, and standard deviation, σ, are constants, but in most instances of marketing research, they are unknown. To estimate population values, we are required to sample. As we have discussed, $\bar{X}$ and S are random variables that will vary from sample to sample with a certain probability (sampling) distribution.

RESEARCHSNAPSHOT

Measuring Viewership . . . with Confidence

Media research firms like Arbitron and Nielsen provide data on audience sizes after programs have aired, but can advertisers predict audiences ahead of time? One way to get an estimate is to ask people about their intended media behavior. For example, Harris Interactive used an online poll to ask people whether they intended to watch the Winter Olympics held in Turin, Italy, and if so, which events they planned to watch.

The Harris poll obtained responses from 1,002 adults. The data represented percentages who planned to watch any of the television coverage of the Olympics and percentages who planned to watch specific events. Results were segmented by age, sex, and other demographics. According to the researchers, the confidence level was 95 percent that the sampling error was not greater than ±3 percentage points.

The poll found that 61 percent of men and 69 percent of women planned to watch the Winter Olympics. Given the confidence interval, we can say with 95 percent confidence that more women than men planned to watch, because the true value for men would be within the range of 58 percent to 64 percent and the true value for women would be between 66 percent and 72 percent. However, we cannot say from this poll whether more men or women actually watched the games. For that, advertisers had to wait for the after-the-fact data from the media researchers.

Source: Based on "Two-Thirds of U.S. Adults Plan to Watch the Winter Olympics," The Wall Street Journal, February 10, 2006, http://online.wsj.com; Liz Clarke, "2006 Winter Olympic Games," Washington Post, February 21, 2006, http://www.washingtonpost.com.

©KAI PFAFFENBACH/REUTERS/LANDOV

Our previous example of statistical inference was somewhat unrealistic because the population had only six individuals. Consider the more realistic example of a prospective racquetball entrepreneur who wishes to estimate the average number of days players participate in this sport each week. When statistical inference is needed, the population mean, μ, is a constant but unknown parameter. To estimate the average number of playing days, we could take a sample of three hundred racquetball players throughout the area where our entrepreneur is thinking of building club facilities. If the sample mean, $\overline{X}$, equals 2.6 days per week, we might use this figure as a **point estimate**. This single value, 2.6, would be the best estimate of the population mean. However, we would be extremely lucky if the sample estimate were exactly the same as the population value. A less risky alternative would be to calculate a confidence interval.

Point estimate
An estimate of the population mean in the form of a single value, usually the sample mean.

Confidence Intervals

If we specify a range of numbers, or interval, within which the population mean should lie, we can be more confident that our inference is correct. A **confidence interval estimate** is based on the knowledge that $\mu = \overline{X} \pm$ a small sampling error. After calculating an interval estimate, we can determine how probable it is that the population mean will fall within this range of statistical values. In the racquetball project, the researcher, after setting up a confidence interval, would be able to make a statement such as "With 95 percent confidence, I think that the average number of days played per week is between 2.3 and 2.9." This information can be used to estimate market demand because the researcher has a certain confidence that the interval contains the value of the true population mean.

The crux of the problem for a researcher is to determine how much random sampling error to tolerate. In other words, what should the confidence interval be? How much of a gamble should be taken that μ will be included in the range? Do we need to be 80 percent, 90 percent, or 99 percent sure? The **confidence level** is a percentage or decimal that indicates the long-run probability that the results will be correct. Traditionally, researchers have used the 95 percent confidence level. While there is nothing magical about the 95 percent confidence level, it is useful to select this confidence level in our examples.

As mentioned, the point estimate gives no information about the possible magnitude of random sampling error. The confidence interval gives the estimated value of the population

Confidence interval estimate
A specified range of numbers within which a population mean is expected to lie; an estimate of the population mean based on the knowledge that it will be equal to the sample mean plus or minus a small sampling error.

Confidence level
A percentage or decimal value that tells how confident a researcher can be about being correct; it states the long-run percentage of confidence intervals that will include the true population mean.

parameter, plus or minus an estimate of the error. We can express the idea of the confidence interval as follows:

$$\mu = \bar{X} \pm \text{ a small sampling error}$$

More formally, assuming that the researchers select a large sample (more than thirty observations), the small sampling error is given by

$$\text{Small sampling error} = Z_{c.l.} S_{\bar{X}}$$

where

$Z_{c.l.}$ = value of Z, or standardized normal variable, at a specified confidence level (*c.l.*)

$S_{\bar{X}}$ = standard error of the mean

The precision of our estimate is indicated by the value of $Z_{c.l.} S_{\bar{X}}$. It is useful to define the range of possible error, E, as follows:

$$E = Z_{c.l.} S_{\bar{X}}$$

Thus,

$$\mu = \bar{X} \pm E$$

where

$\bar{X}$ = sample mean

E = range of sampling error

or

$$\mu = \bar{X} \pm Z_{c.l.} S_{\bar{X}}$$

The confidence interval $\pm E$ is always stated as one-half of the total confidence interval.

The following step-by-step procedure can be used to calculate confidence intervals:

1. Calculate $\bar{X}$ from the sample.
2. Assuming σ is unknown, estimate the population standard deviation by finding S, the sample standard deviation.
3. Estimate the standard error of the mean, using the following formula:

$$S_{\bar{X}} = \frac{S}{\sqrt{n}}$$

4. Determine the Z-value associated with the desired confidence level. The confidence level should be divided by 2 to determine what percentage of the area under the curve to include on each side of the mean.
5. Calculate the confidence interval.

The following example shows how calculation of a confidence interval can be used in preparing a demographic profile, a useful tool for market segmentation. Suppose you plan to open a sporting goods store to cater to working women who golf. In a survey of 100 women in your market area, you find that the mean age ($\bar{X}$) is 37.5 years, with a standard deviation (S) of 12.0 years. Even though 37.5 years is the "expected value" and the best guess for the true mean age in the population (μ), the likelihood is that the mean is not exactly 37.5. Thus, a confidence interval around the sample mean computed using the steps just given will be useful:

1. $\bar{X}$ = 37.5 years
2. S = 12.0 years
3. $S_{\bar{X}} = \dfrac{12.0}{\sqrt{100}} = 1.2$
4. Suppose you wish to be 95 percent confident—that is, assured that 95 times out of 100, the estimates from your sample will include the population parameter. Including 95 percent of the area requires that 47.5 percent (one-half of 95 percent) of the distribution on each side be included. From the Z-table (Table A.2 in the appendix), you find that 0.475 corresponds to the Z-value 1.96.

5. Substitute the values for $Z_{c.l.}$ and $S_{\bar{X}}$ into the confidence interval formula:

$$\mu = 37.5 \pm (1.96)(1.2)$$
$$= 37.5 \pm 2.352$$

You can thus expect that μ is contained in the range from 35.148 to 39.852 years. Intervals constructed in this manner will contain the true value of μ 95 percent of the time.

Step 3 can be eliminated by entering S and n directly in the confidence interval formula:

$$\mu = \bar{X} \pm Z_{c.l.} \frac{S}{\sqrt{n}}$$

Remember that $S/\sqrt{n}$ represents the standard error of the mean, $S_{\bar{X}}$. Its use is based on the central-limit theorem.

If you wanted to increase the probability that the population mean will lie within the confidence interval, you could use the 99 percent confidence level, with a Z-value of 2.57. You may want to calculate the 99 percent confidence interval for the preceding example; you can expect that μ will be in the range between 34.416 and 40.584 years.

We have now examined the basic concepts of inferential statistics. You should understand that sample statistics such as the sample means, $\bar{X}$s, can provide good estimates of population parameters such as μ. You should also realize that there is a certain probability of being in error when you estimate a population parameter from sample statistics. In other words, there will be a random sampling error, which is the difference between the survey results and the results of surveying the entire population. If you have a firm understanding of these basic terms and ideas, which are the essence of statistics, the remaining statistics concepts will be relatively simple for you. Several ramifications of the simple ideas presented so far will permit you to make better decisions about populations based on surveys or experiments.

Sample Size

Random Error and Sample Size

When asked to evaluate a marketing research project, most people, even those with little marketing research training, begin by asking, "How big was the sample?" Intuitively we know that the larger the sample, the more accurate the research. This is in fact a statistical truth; random sampling error varies with samples of different sizes. In statistical terms, increasing the sample size decreases the width of the confidence interval at a given confidence level. When the standard deviation of the population is unknown, a confidence interval is calculated using the following formula:

$$\text{Confidence interval} = \bar{X} \pm Z \frac{S}{\sqrt{n}}$$

Observe that the equation for the plus or minus error factor in the confidence interval includes n, the sample size:

$$E = Z \frac{S}{\sqrt{n}}$$

If n increases, E is reduced. Exhibit 17.18 illustrates that the confidence interval (or magnitude of error) decreases as the sample size, n, increases.

We already noted that it is not necessary to take a census of all elements of the population to conduct an accurate study. The laws of probability give investigators sufficient confidence regarding the accuracy of data collected from a sample. Knowledge of the characteristics of the sampling distribution helps researchers make reasonably precise estimates.

Students familiar with the law of diminishing returns in economics will easily grasp the concept that increases in sample size reduce sampling error at a *decreasing rate*. For example, doubling a sample of 1,000 will reduce random sampling error by 1 percentage point, but doubling the sample from 2,000 to 4,000 will reduce random sampling error by only another half percentage point.

RESEARCHSNAPSHOT

Target and Wal-Mart Shoppers Really Are Different

Scarborough Research conducts ongoing consumer research that combines a telephone interview on media behavior with a mail survey about shopping habits and lifestyle and a television diary for detailed data about television viewing. Scarborough recognizes the importance of sample size for minimizing errors. Its sample includes over 200,000 adults so that it can make estimates of the U.S. population.

An example is a recent comparison of consumers who shop exclusively at either Target or Wal-Mart. When respondents were asked to identify the stores at which they had shopped during the preceding three months, the largest share (40 percent) named both Target and Wal-Mart. However, 31 percent shopped at Wal-Mart but not Target, and 12 percent shopped at Target but not Wal-Mart. Scarborough compared

the consumer behavior of the latter two groups.

Target shoppers who shunned Wal-Mart were more likely to shop at more upscale stores, including Macy's and Nordstrom. They also were more likely than the average shopper to visit many different stores. Wal-Mart shoppers who stayed away from Target were more likely to shop at discounters such as Dollar General and Kmart, and they were more likely to be at least fifty years old. Target-only shoppers tended to be younger and were more likely to have a high household income.

Given a U.S. adult population of approximately 220 million, do you think the sample size was adequate to make these comparisons?

Source: Based on Scarborough Research, "In the Battle for Discount Shoppers, Target and Wal-Mart Find Brand Loyalty in Different Customer Groups," news release, September 19, 2005, http://www.scarborough.com; Scarborough Research, "About Scarborough: Methodology," http://www.scarborough.com, accessed March 16, 2006; U.S. Census Bureau, *Statistical Abstract of the United States*, 2006, table 11, p. 13.

More technically, random sampling error is inversely proportional to the square root of *n*. (Exhibit 17.18 gives an approximation of the relationship between sample size and error.) Thus, the main issue becomes one of determining the optimal sample size.

Factors in Determining Sample Size for Questions Involving Means

Three factors are required to specify sample size: (1) the variance, or heterogeneity, of the population; (2) the magnitude of acceptable error; and (3) the confidence level. Suppose a researcher wishes to find out whether nine-year-old boys are taller than four-year-old boys. Intuitively we

EXHIBIT 17.18
Relationship between Sample Size and Error

Source: From Foundations of Behavioral Research 3rd edition by Kerlinger. © 1986. Reprinted with permission of Wadsworth, a division of Thomson Learning: http://www.thomsonrights.com. Fax 800-730-2215.

EXHIBIT 17.19 **Statistical Information Needed to Determine Sample Size for Questions Involving Means**

Variable	Symbol	Typical Source of Information
Standard deviation	S	Pilot study or rule of thumb
Magnitude of error	E	Managerial judgment or calculation ($Z S_{\bar{x}}$)
Confidence level	$Z_{c.l.}$	Managerial judgment

know that even with a very small sample size, the correct information probably will be obtained. This is based on the fact that the determination of sample size depends on the research question and the variability within the sample.

The *variance,* or *heterogeneity,* of the population is the first necessary bit of information. In statistical terms, this refers to the *standard deviation* of the population. Only a small sample is required if the population is homogeneous. For example, predicting the average age of college students requires a smaller sample than predicting the average age of people who visit the zoo on a given Sunday afternoon. As *heterogeneity* increases, so must sample size. Thus, to test the effectiveness of an acne medicine, the sample must be large enough to cover the range of skin types.

The *magnitude of error,* or the confidence interval, is the second necessary bit of information. Defined in statistical terms as *E,* the magnitude of error indicates how precise the estimate must be. It indicates a certain precision level. From a managerial perspective, the importance of the decision in terms of profitability will influence the researcher's specifications of the range of error. If, for example, favorable results from a test-market sample will result in the construction of a new plant and unfavorable results will dictate not marketing the product, the acceptable range of error probably will be small; the cost of an error would be too great to allow much room for random sampling errors. In other cases, the estimate need not be extremely precise. Allowing an error of $\pm\$1,000$ in total family income instead of $E = \pm 50$ may be acceptable in most market segmentation studies.

The third factor of concern is the *confidence level.* In our examples, we will typically use the 95 percent confidence level. This, however, is an arbitrary decision based on convention; there is nothing sacred about the 0.05 chance level (that is, the probability of 0.05 of the true population parameter being incorrectly estimated). Exhibit 17.19 summarizes the information required to determine sample size.

Estimating Sample Size for Questions Involving Means

Once the preceding concepts are understood, determining the actual size for a simple random sample is quite easy. The researcher must follow three steps:

1. Estimate the standard deviation of the population.
2. Make a judgment about the allowable magnitude of error.
3. Determine a confidence level.

The only problem is estimating the standard deviation of the population. Ideally, similar studies conducted in the past will give a basis for judging the standard deviation. In practice, researchers who lack prior information conduct a pilot study to estimate the population parameters so that another, larger sample of the appropriate sample size may be drawn. This procedure is called *sequential sampling* because researchers take an initial look at the pilot study results before deciding on a larger sample to provide more precise information.

A rule of thumb for estimating the value of the standard deviation is to expect it to be one-sixth of the range. If researchers conducting a study on television purchases expected the price paid to range from $100 to $700, a rule-of-thumb estimate for the standard deviation would be $100.

For the moment, assume that the standard deviation has been estimated in some preliminary work. If our concern is to estimate the mean of a particular population, the formula for sample size is

$$n = \left(\frac{ZS}{E} \right)^2$$

where

Z = standardized value that corresponds to the confidence level

S = sample standard deviation or estimate of the population standard deviation

E = acceptable magnitude of error, plus or minus error factor (range is one-half of the total confidence interval)[7]

Suppose a survey researcher studying annual expenditures on lipstick wishes to have a 95 percent confidence level ($Z = 1.96$) and a range of error (E) of less than $2. If the estimate of the standard deviation is $29, the sample size can be calculated as follows:

$$n = \left(\frac{ZS}{E} \right)^2 = \left(\frac{(1.96)(29)}{2} \right)^2 = \left(\frac{56.84}{2} \right)^2 = 28.42^2 = 808$$

If a range of error (E) of $4 is acceptable, sample size can be reduced:

$$n = \left(\frac{ZS}{E} \right)^2 = \left(\frac{(1.96)(29)}{4} \right)^2 = \left(\frac{56.84}{4} \right)^2 = 14.21^2 = 202$$

Thus, doubling the range of acceptable error reduces sample size to approximately one-quarter of its original size. Stated conversely in a general sense, doubling sample size will reduce error by only approximately one-quarter.

The Influence of Population Size on Sample Size

The ACNielsen Company estimates television ratings. Throughout the years, it has been plagued with questions about how it is possible to rate 98 million or more television homes with such a small sample (approximately 5,000 households). The answer to that question is that in most cases the size of the population does not have a major effect on the sample size. As we have indicated, the variance of the population has the largest effect on sample size. However, a finite correction factor may be needed to adjust a sample size that is more than 5 percent of a finite population. If the sample is large relative to the population, the foregoing procedures may overestimate sample size, and the researcher may need to adjust sample size. The finite correction factor is $\sqrt{(N-n)(N-1)}$, where N = population size and n = sample size.

Factors in Determining Sample Size for Proportions

Researchers frequently are concerned with determining sample size for problems that involve estimating population proportions or percentages. When the question involves the estimation of a proportion, the researcher requires some knowledge of the logic for determining a confidence interval around a sample proportion estimation (p) of the population proportion (π). For a confidence interval to be constructed around the sample proportion (p), an estimate of the standard error of the proportion (S_p) must be calculated and a confidence level specified.

The precision of the estimate is indicated by the value $Z_{c.l.}S_p$. Thus, the plus-or-minus estimate of the population proportion is

$$\text{Confidence interval} = p \pm Z_{c.l.}S_p$$

RESEARCHSNAPSHOT

Slone Survey Finds That Most of Us Use Medications

Companies that sell medicines, vitamins, or herbal remedies can obtain detailed sales data. However, sales figures do not tell what consumers do with those products. Is that bottle of Tylenol capsules shared among a large household with people who have a variety of pains? Does one person with a nagging headache take all of them? Or does the bottle sit on the shelf for months "just in case"?

To investigate the actual use of medications, Boston University's Slone Epidemiology Center contacted consumers by telephone and asked about their medications. The Slone Survey identified subjects through random-digit dialing. Then the interviewer used a computer-generated random number to select a household member to respond. If the individual was between ages fourteen and seventeen, the interviewer obtained permission from an adult. If the person was younger or otherwise unable to respond to the questions, the interviewer spoke to someone with knowledge of that person's medications.

The interviewer asked each respondent to gather the packages or bottles containing all the medications the person took within the preceding seven days. To help respondents think of every medication, the interviewer read a list of common reasons for using medications and a list of trade names. The interviewer gathered a list of all medications the respondent used and the reasons for using each.

The 3,667 subjects included 625 children. The researchers compared demographic data from the subject population with Census Bureau data on the U.S. population. For most characteristics, the survey population matched the U.S. population. The reported 95 percent confidence intervals for the data from adults ranged from ±0.2 percent for estimates of 1 percent to ±0.7 percent for estimates of 20 percent. For the smaller sample population of children, the confidence intervals were roughly twice as large.

The study found that 82 percent of U.S. adults take at least one medication during the course of a week, with 30 percent taking at least five. The most commonly used medications among adults were painkillers, and 42 percent of adults take vitamins. Pain relievers are also the most common medications among the 56 percent of children who take medications in a given week.

Source: Based on "Patterns of Medication Use in the United States, 2004: The Slone Survey," Medical Benefits, 22 (7/30/2005), 1–2; and Slone Epidemiology Center, Boston University, "Patterns of Medication Use in the United States: A Report from the Slone Survey," 2004, downloaded at http://http://www.bu.edu/slone/, accessed March 22, 2006.

If the researcher selects a 95 percent probability for the confidence interval, $Z_{c.l.}$ will equal 1.96 (see Table A.2 in the appendix). The formula for S_p is

$$S_p = \sqrt{\frac{pq}{n}} \text{ or } S_p = \sqrt{\frac{p(1-n)}{n}}$$

where

S_p = estimate of the standard error of the proportion

p = proportion of successes

$q = 1 - p$, or proportion of failures

Suppose that 20 percent of a sample of 1,200 television viewers recall seeing an advertisement. The proportion of successes (p) equals 0.2, and the proportion of failures (q) equals 0.8. We estimate the 95 percent confidence interval as follows:

$$\text{Confidence interval} = p \pm Z_{c.l.}S_p$$
$$= 0.2 \pm 1.96 S_p$$
$$= 0.2 \pm 1.96 \sqrt{\frac{p(1-n)}{n}}$$
$$= 0.2 \pm 1.96 \sqrt{\frac{(0.2)(0.8)}{1,200}}$$
$$= 0.2 \pm 1.96(0.0115)$$
$$= 0.2 \pm 0.022$$

Thus, the population proportion who see an advertisement is estimated to be included in the interval between 0.178 and 0.222, or roughly between 18 and 22 percent, with a 95 percent confidence coefficient.

To determine *sample size* for a proportion, the researcher must make a judgment about confidence level and the maximum allowance for random sampling error. Furthermore, the size of the proportion influences random sampling error, so an estimate of the expected proportion of successes must be made, based on intuition or prior information. The formula is

$$n = \frac{Z_{c.l.}^2 pq}{E^2}$$

where

n = number of items in sample

$Z_{c.l.}^2$ = square of the confidence level in standard error units

p = estimated proportion of successes

q = $1 - p$, or estimated proportion of failures

E^2 = square of the maximum allowance for error between the true proportion and the sample proportion, or $Z_{c.l.} S_p$ squared

Suppose a researcher believes that a simple random sample will show that 60 percent of the population (p) recognizes the name of an automobile dealership. The researcher wishes to estimate with 95 percent confidence ($Z_{c.l.} = 1.96$) that the allowance for sampling error is not greater than 3.5 percentage points (E). Substituting these values into the formula gives

$$n = \frac{(1.96)^2 (0.6)(0.4)}{0.035^2}$$

$$= \frac{(3.8416)(0.24)}{0.001225}$$

$$= \frac{0.922}{0.001225}$$

$$= 753$$

Calculating Sample Size for Sample Proportions

In practice, a number of tables have been constructed for determining sample size. Exhibit 17.20 illustrates a sample size table for problems that involve sample proportions (p).

The theoretical principles underlying calculation of sample sizes of proportions are similar to the concepts discussed in this chapter. Suppose we wish to take samples in two large cities, New Orleans and Miami. We wish no more than 2 percentage points of error, and we will be satisfied with a 95 percent confidence level (see Exhibit 17.20). If we assume all other things are equal, then in the New Orleans market, where 15 percent of the consumers favor our product and 85 percent prefer competitors' brands, we need a sample of 1,222 to get results with only 2 percentage points of error. In the Miami market, however, where 30 percent of the consumers favor our brand and 70 percent prefer other brands (a less heterogeneous market), we need a sample size of 2,009 to get the same sample reliability.

Exhibit 17.21 shows a sampling error table typical of those that accompany research proposals or reports. Most studies will estimate more than one parameter. Thus, in a survey of 100 people in which 50 percent agree with one statement and 10 percent with another, the sampling error is expected to be 10 and 6 percentage points of error, respectively.

EXHIBIT 17.20 Selected Tables for Determining Sample Size When the Characteristic of Interest Is a Proportion

Sample Size for a 95 Percent Confidence Level when Parameter in Population Is Assumed to Be over 70 Percent or under 30 Percent

Size of Population	Reliability			
	±1% Point	±2% Points	±3% Points	±5% Points
1,000	a	a	473	244
2,000	a	a	619	278
3,000	a	1,206	690	291
4,000	a	1,341	732	299
5,000	a	1,437	760	303
10,000	4,465	1,678	823	313
20,000	5,749	1,832	858	318
50,000	6,946	1,939	881	321
100,000	7,465	1,977	888	321
500,000 to ∞	7,939	2,009	895	322

Sample Size for a 95 Percent Confidence Level when Parameter in Population Is Assumed to Be over 85 Percent or under 15 Percent

Size of Population	Reliability			
	±1% Point	±2% Points	±3% Points	±5% Points
1,000	a	a	353	235
2,000	a	760	428	266
3,000	a	890	461	278
4,000	a	938	479	284
5,000	a	984	491	289
10,000	3,288	1,091	516	297
20,000	3,935	1,154	530	302
50,000	4,461	1,195	538	304
100,000	4,669	1,210	541	305
500,000 to ∞	4,850	1,222	544	306

[a] In these cases, more than 50 percent of the population is required in the sample. Since the normal approximation of the hypergeometric distribution is a poor approximation in such instances, no sample value is given.

Source: Nan Lin, *Foundations of Social Research* (New York: McGraw-Hill, 1976), p. 447. Copyright © 1976 by Nan Lin. Used with permission.

Determining Sample Size on the Basis of Judgment

Just as sample units may be selected to suit the convenience or judgment of the researcher, sample size may also be determined on the basis of managerial judgments. Using a sample size similar to those used in previous studies provides the inexperienced researcher with a comparison with other researchers' judgments.

EXHIBIT 17.21 **Allowance for Random Sampling Error (Plus and Minus Percentage Points) at 95 Percent Confidence Level**

Response	Sample Size						
	2,500	**1,500**	**1,000**	**500**	**250**	**100**	**50**
10 (90)	1.2	1.5	2.0	3.0	4.0	6.0	8.0
20 (80)	1.6	2.0	2.5	4.0	5.0	8.0	11.0
30 (70)	1.8	2.5	3.0	4.0	6.0	9.0	13.0
40 (60)	2.0	2.5	3.0	4.0	6.0	10.0	14.0
50 (50)	2.0	2.5	3.0	4.0	6.0	10.0	14.0

Source: Nan Lin, *Foundations of Social Research* (New York: McGraw-Hill, 1976).

Another judgmental factor that affects the determination of sample size is the selection of the appropriate item, question, or characteristic to be used for the sample size calculations. Several different characteristics affect most studies, and the desired degree of precision may vary for these items. The researcher must exercise some judgment to determine which item will be used. Often the item that will produce the largest sample size will be used to determine the ultimate sample size. However, the cost of data collection becomes a major consideration, and judgment must be exercised regarding the importance of such information.

Another consideration stems from most researchers' need to analyze various subgroups within the sample. For example, suppose an analyst wishes to look at differences in retailers' attitudes by geographic region. The analyst will want to make sure to sample an adequate number of retailers in the New England, Mid-Atlantic, and South Atlantic regions to ensure that subgroup comparisons are reliable. There is a judgmental rule of thumb for selecting minimum subgroup sample size: Each subgroup to be separately analyzed should have a minimum of 100 units in each category of the major breakdowns. With this procedure, the total sample size is computed by totaling the sample sizes necessary for these subgroups.

Determining Sample Size for Stratified and Other Probability Samples

Stratified sampling involves drawing separate probability samples within the subgroups to make the sample more efficient. With a stratified sample, the sample variances are expected to differ by strata. This makes the determination of sample size more complex. Increased complexity may also characterize the determination of sample size for cluster sampling and other probability sampling methods. The formulas are beyond the scope of this book. Students interested in these advanced sampling techniques should investigate advanced sampling textbooks.

A Reminder about Statistics

Learning the terms and symbols defined in this chapter will provide you with the basics of the language of statisticians and researchers. As you learn more about the pragmatic use of statistics in marketing research, do not forget these concepts. Rules are important in learning a foreign language and when the rules are forgotten, being understood becomes very difficult. The same is true for the student who forgets the basics of the "foreign language" of statistics.

Summary

1. Implement descriptive and inferential statistics. Determination of sample size requires a knowledge of statistics. Statistics is the language of the researcher, and this chapter introduced its vocabulary. Descriptive statistics describe characteristics of a population or sample. Thus, calculating a mean and a standard deviation to "describe" or profile a sample is a commonly applied descriptive statistical approach. Inferential statistics investigate samples to draw conclusions about entire populations. If a mean is computed and then compared to some preconceived standard, then inferential statistics are being implemented.

2. Interpret frequency distributions, proportions, and measures of central tendency and dispersion. A frequency distribution shows how frequently each response or classification occurs. A simple tally count illustrates a frequency distribution. A proportion indicates the percentage of group members that have a particular characteristic. Three measures of central tendency are commonly used: the mean, or arithmetic average; the median, or halfway value; and the mode, or most frequently observed value. These three values may differ, and care must be taken to understand distortions that may arise from using the wrong measure of central tendency. Measures of dispersion further describe a distribution. The range is the difference between the largest and smallest values observed. The most useful measures of dispersion are the variance (the summation of each observation's deviation from the mean, divided by one less than the number of observations) and standard deviation, which is the square root of the variance.

3. Distinguish among population, sample, and sampling distributions. The techniques of statistical inference are based on the relationship among the population distribution, the sample distribution, and the sampling distribution. The population distribution is a frequency distribution of the elements of a population. The sample distribution is a frequency distribution of a sample. A sampling distribution is a theoretical probability distribution of sample means for all possible samples of a certain size drawn from a particular population. The sampling distribution's mean is the expected value of the mean, which equals the population's mean. The standard deviation of the sampling distribution is the standard error of the mean, approximately equal to the standard deviation of the population, divided by the square root of the sample size.

4. Explain the central-limit theorem. The central-limit theorem states that as sample size increases, the distribution of sample means of size n, randomly selected, approaches a normal distribution. This theoretical knowledge can be used to estimate parameters and determine sample size.

5. Summarize the use of confidence interval estimates. Estimating a population mean with a single value gives a point estimate. The confidence interval estimate is a range of numbers within which the researcher is confident that the population mean will lie. The confidence level is a percentage that indicates the long-run probability that the confidence interval estimate will be correct. Many research problems involve the estimation of proportions. Statistical techniques may be used to determine a confidence interval around a sample proportion.

6. Discuss the major issues in specifying sample size. The statistical determination of sample size requires knowledge of (1) the variance of the population, (2) the magnitude of acceptable error, and (3) the confidence level. Several computational formulas are available for determining sample size. Furthermore, a number of easy-to-use tables have been compiled to help researchers calculate sample size. The main reason a large sample size is desirable is that sample size is related to random sampling error. A smaller sample makes a larger error in estimates more likely. Calculation of sample size for a sample proportion is not difficult. However, most researchers use tables that indicate predetermined sample sizes.

Key Terms and Concepts

Sample statistics	Median	Sample distribution
Population parameters	Mode	Sampling distribution
Frequency distribution	Variance	Standard error of the mean
Percentage distribution	Standard deviation	Central-limit theorem
Probability	Normal distribution	Point estimate
Proportion	Standardized normal distribution	Confidence interval estimate
Mean	Population distribution	Confidence level

Questions for Review and Critical Thinking

1. What is the difference between descriptive and inferential statistics?
2. Suppose the speed limits in thirteen countries in miles per hour are as follows:

Country	Highway Miles per Hour
Italy	87
France	81
Hungary	75
Belgium	75
Portugal	75
Great Britain	70
Spain	62
Denmark	62
Netherlands	62
Greece	62
Japan	62
Norway	56
Turkey	56

   What is the mean, median, and mode for these data? Feel free to use your computer (statistical software or spreadsheet) to get the answer.
3. Prepare a frequency distribution for the data in question 2.
4. Why is the standard deviation rather than the average deviation typically used?
5. Calculate the standard deviation for the data in question 2.
6. Draw three distributions that have the same mean value but different standard deviation values. Draw three distributions that have the same standard deviation value but different mean values.
7. A manufacturer of MP3 players surveyed one hundred retail stores in each of the firm's sales regions. An analyst noticed that in the South Atlantic region the average retail price was $165 (mean) and the standard deviation was $30. However, in the Mid-Atlantic region the mean price was $170, with a standard deviation of $15. What do these statistics tell us about these two sales regions?
8. What is the sampling distribution? How does it differ from the sample distribution?
9. What would happen to the sampling distribution of the mean if we increased sample size from 5 to 25?
10. Suppose a fast-food restaurant wishes to estimate average sales volume for a new menu item. The restaurant has analyzed the sales of the item at a similar outlet and observed the following results:

   $\bar{X} = 500$ (mean daily sales)
   $S = 100$ (standard deviation of sample)
   $n = 25$ (sample size)

The restaurant manager wants to know into what range the mean daily sales should fall 95 percent of the time. Perform this calculation.

11. In the example on page 452 of research on lipstick, where $E = \$2$ and $S = \$29$, what sample size would we require if we desired a 99 percent confidence level?
12. Suppose you are planning to sample cat owners to determine the average number of cans of cat food they purchase monthly. The following standards have been set: a confidence level of 99 percent and an error of less than five units. Past research has indicated that the standard deviation should be 6 units. What is the required sample size?
13. In a survey of 500 people, 60 percent responded positively to an attitude question. Calculate a confidence interval at 95 percent to get an interval estimate for a proportion.
14. What is a standardized normal curve?
15. A researcher expects the population proportion of Cubs fans in Chicago to be 80 percent. The researcher wishes to have an error of less than 5 percent and to be 95 percent confident of an estimate to be made from a mail survey. What sample size is required?
16. **ETHICS** Using the formula in this chapter, a researcher determines that at the 95 percent confidence level, a sample of 2,500 is required to satisfy a client's requirements. The researcher actually uses a sample of 1,200, however, because the client has specified a budget cap for the survey. What are the ethical considerations in this situation?
17. **'NET** Go to http://www.dartmouth.edu/~chance/ to visit the Chance course. The Chance course is an innovative program to creatively teach introductory materials about probability and statistics. The Chance course is designed to enhance quantitative literacy. Numerous videos can be played online.
18. **'NET** Go to http://www.researchinfo.com. Click on "Marketing Research Calculators." Which of the calculators can be used to help find the sample size required? How big of a sample is needed to make an inference about the U.S. population $+/- 5$ percent? How large a sample is needed to make an inference about the population of Norway $+/- 5$ percent? Remember, population statistics can be found in the *CIA World Factbook* online. Comment.
19. **'NET** A random number generator and other statistical information can be found at http://www.random.org. Flip some virtual coins. Perform twenty flips with an Aurelian coin. Perform twenty flips with a Constatius coin. Perform frequency tables for each result. What conclusion might you draw? Would the result change if you flipped the coins 200 times or 2,000 times?

Research Activities

1. **'NET** Go to http://www.surveypro.com. Click on pricing. Write a brief report that describes how prices are charged to someone wishing to use this service to host a survey. What happens as the desired sample size increases? Why is this?
2. **'NET** Use an online library service to find basic business research studies that report a "response rate" or number of respondents compared to number of contacts. You may wish to consult

journals such as the *Journal of Business Research,* the *Journal of Marketing,* or the *Journal of Personal Selling and Sales Management.* Find at least 25 such studies. What is the average response rate across all of these studies? Do there appear to be any trends or factors that are associated with lower response rates? Write a brief report on your findings.

Case 17.1 Pointsec Mobile Technologies

When salespeople, construction supervisors, managers, and other employees are away from the workplace, many of them carry mobile devices such as laptop computers and PDAs, often containing valuable, private data related to their jobs. Pointsec provides security systems to protect such data. To bring home the vulnerability of mobile devices, Pointsec decided to share information about the number of such devices left behind on taxis.[8]

The research involved conducting a survey of taxi drivers. Staff members at Pointsec's public relations firm called major taxi companies in nine cities in Australia, Denmark, Finland, France, Germany, Norway, Sweden, Great Britain, and the United States. Each of the cooperating companies put these interviewers in touch with about one hundred drivers. Drivers were asked how many devices of each type—cell phones, PDAs, computers, and so on—had been left in their cab over the preceding six months. From these numbers, they came up with the rate of items left behind. Multiplying by the size of

taxi fleets in each city, the researchers came up with city-by-city numbers: 3.42 cell phones per cab yielded 85,619 cell phones left behind in Chicago, for example. In London, the researchers concluded 63,135 cell phones were left in cabs, a startling increase of 71 percent compared to four years earlier.

Questions

1. Discuss why the sampling method and sample size make these results questionable, even though the numbers were reported as if they were precise.
2. The simple survey method described in the case may have been sufficient as a way to draw attention to the issue of data security. However, if the company were using data on lost mobile devices to predict demand for a product, accuracy might be more significant. Imagine that you have been asked to collect data on mobile devices left in cabs, and you wish to be able to report results with a 95 percent confidence level. How can you improve the sample design and select an appropriate sample size?

Case 17.2 Coastal Star Sales Corporation (A)

Download the data sets for this case from www.thomsonedu.com/marketing/zikmund or request them from your instructor.

Coastal Star Sales Corporation is a West Coast wholesaler that markets leisure products from several manufacturers. Coastal Star has an eighty-person sales force that sells to wholesalers in a six-state area, which is divided into two sales regions. Case Exhibit 17.2–1 shows the names of a sample of eleven salespeople, some descriptive information about each person, and sales performance for each of the last two years.

Questions

1. Calculate a mean and a standard deviation for each variable.

2. Set a 95 percent confidence interval around the mean for each variable.
3. Calculate the median, mode, and range for each variable.
4. Organize the data for current sales into a frequency distribution with three classes: (a) under $500,000, (b) $500,001 to $999,999, and (c) $1,000,000 and over.

   Organize the data for years of selling experience into a frequency distribution with two classes: (a) less than five years and (b) five or more years.
6. Convert the frequency distributions from question 5 to percentage distributions.

CASE EXHIBIT 17.2-1 **Salesperson Data: Coastal Star Sales Corporation**

Region	Salesperson	Age	Years of Experience	Sales Previous Year	Sales Current Year
Northern	Jackson	40	7	$ 412,744	$ 411,007
Northern	Gentry	60	12	1,491,024	1,726,630
Northern	La Forge	26	2	301,421	700,112
Northern	Miller	39	1	401,241	471,001
Northern	Mowen	64	5	448,160	449,261
Southern	Young	51	2	518,897	519,412
Southern	Fisk	34	1	846,222	713,333
Southern	Kincaid	62	10	1,527,124	2,009,041
Southern	Krieger	42	3	921,174	1,030,000
Southern	Manzer	64	5	463,399	422,798
Southern	Weiner	27	2	548,011	422,001

CHAPTER 18
FIELDWORK

After studying this chapter, you should be able to

1. Describe the role and job requirements of fieldworkers
2. Summarize the skills to cover when training inexperienced interviewers
3. List principles of good interviewing
4. Describe the activities involved in the management of fieldworkers
5. Discuss how supervisors should minimize errors in the field

Chapter Vignette: Census Takers Get Electronic Gadgets

The Census Bureau tries to count every person living in the United States, but to do so, the bureau cannot rely solely on surveys mailed to known addresses.[1] Besides the mail questionnaires, the agency sends out legions of census takers, called *enumerators,* to make sure all residences have been identified and to follow up on households that have not responded by mail. Among the many issues that complicate this job is the simple fact that new housing is constantly being constructed. New housing developments involve new streets and new addresses developed since the previous census.

©LLOYD WOLF FOR THE U.S. CENSUS BUREAU

In the past, whenever enumerators discovered streets and housing units that did not exist in their records, they took out a pencil and sketched a map. Back at the agency's offices, staffers in the Geography Division would scan these drawings, refine them, and then transfer the map data to its mapping database, called TIGER, for Topologically Integrated Geographic Encoding and Referencing. When TIGER was introduced for the 1990 census, the system was a tremendous breakthrough as a source of comprehensive geographical data, including streets, rivers, and railroads. However, keeping the database up-to-date is difficult. To meet this challenge for the 2010 census, the Census Bureau has been developing and testing new technology—handheld computers equipped with global positioning system (GPS) devices. Under the plan being tested, enumerators carry handheld computers containing electronic maps to help them locate addresses. If they encounter new addresses that are not in the database, the enumerators enter the new locations by walking or driving the street and recording their GPS coordinates along the way. These data should be more accurate than the rough sketches were.

In addition to the mapping system, the census takers' handheld computers contain the census questionnaire. Enumerators will travel to households that did not respond to the mailed census, and at each home, they will ask the census questions and enter the responses directly into their computers. The responses can then be submitted electronically for tabulation at the Census Bureau's Maryland headquarters. Interviewers such as the Census Bureau's enumerators are a cornerstone of the marketing research business. This chapter discusses the nature of their work and the practices managers can use to maximize interviewers' effectiveness.

RESEARCHSNAPSHOT

Interviewing for Horizon Research Services

Along with the big-name national and international research firms like Yankelovich, Nielsen, and Gallup, many smaller research companies offer interviewing and other services to clients in their city or region. An example is Horizon Research Services, located in Columbia, Missouri. Founded by Kathleen Anger, a psychologist with a deep sense of curiosity, Horizon has served local organizations including Columbia's banks and hospitals. The company conducts focus groups, telephone surveys, and other research projects.

Horizon uses part-time employees to staff its dozen computer workstations whenever a client requests a telephone survey. One of those interviewers is Jennifer Hill, who holds a full-time position as a researcher at the University of Missouri–Columbia. When Horizon needs her to make calls, she works a six- to nine-o'clock shift in the evening.

According to Hill, one of the most significant challenges of the interviewer's job is simply to keep the respondent from hanging up. In the first few seconds of the phone call, she quickly reassures the person that the call is for research, not to sell them something. After that, retaining respondents becomes a matter of reinforcing that they are "doing a good service [because] it's for research."

Horizon's telephone interviewers also recruit people to participate in focus groups. Typically, the company needs four interviewers to spend about three hours just to fill a twelve-person focus group. The reason is that finding willing individuals who meet the project's specifications may require up to six hundred phone calls.

Source: Based on Kevin Coleman, "Research Firm Reflects Consumer Trends," Columbia (Missouri) Daily Tribune, May 21, 2005, downloaded at http://www.columbiatribune.com; and Horizon Research Services website, http://www.horizonresearch.com, accessed March 27, 2006.

The Nature of Fieldwork

A personal interviewer administering a questionnaire door to door, a telephone interviewer calling from a central location, an observer counting pedestrians in a shopping mall, and others involved in the collection of data and the supervision of that process—each of these people is a **fieldworker**. The activities they perform vary substantially. The supervision of data collection for a mail survey differs from that for an observation study as much as the factory production process for cereal differs from that for a pair of ski boots. Yet, just as quality control is basic to each production operation, the same basic issues arise in the various types of fieldwork. For ease of presentation, this chapter focuses on the interviewing process conducted by personal interviewers. However, many of the issues apply to all fieldworkers, no matter what their specific settings.

Fieldworker
An individual who is responsible for gathering data in the field.

Who Conducts the Fieldwork?

The actual data collection process is rarely carried out by the person who designs the research. However, the data-collecting stage is crucial, because the marketing research project is no better than the data collected in the field. So, the marketing research administrator must select capable people and trust them to gather the data. An irony of marketing research is that highly educated and trained individuals design the research, but when typical surveys are conducted, the people who gather the data usually have little research training or experience. Knowing that research is no better than the data collected in the field, research administrators must concentrate on carefully selecting fieldworkers.

Much fieldwork is conducted by research suppliers that specialize in data collection. When a second party is subcontracted, the job of the study designer at the parent firm is not only to hire a research supplier but also to build in supervisory controls over the field service. In some cases a third-party firm is employed. For example, a company may contact a marketing research firm that in turn subcontracts the fieldwork to a **field interviewing service**.

Various field interviewing services and full-service marketing research agencies perform all manner of personal surveys including central location telephone interviewing, mall-intercepts, and

Field interviewing service
A research supplier that specializes in gathering data.

other forms of fieldwork for a fee. These agencies typically employ field supervisors who supervise and train interviewers, edit completed questionnaires in the field, and telephone or recontact respondents to confirm that interviews have been conducted.

Whether the research administrator hires an **in-house interviewer** or selects a field interviewing service, fieldworkers should ideally meet certain job requirements. Although the job requirements for different types of surveys vary, normally interviewers should be healthy, outgoing, and of pleasing appearance—that is, well groomed and tailored. People who enjoy talking with strangers usually make better interviewers. An essential part of the interviewing process is establishing rapport with the respondent. An outgoing nature may help interviewers ensure respondents' full cooperation. Interviewer bias may occur if the fieldworker's clothing or physical appearance is unattractive or unusual. One exception to this would be ethnographic research. In ethnographic research, the interviewer should dress to blend in with the group being studied. So, if holey jeans and a dirty T-shirt are the dress *du jour,* then the interviewer should dress likewise.

Survey interviewers generally are paid hourly rates or per-interview fees. Often interviewers are part-time workers from a variety of backgrounds—homemakers, graduate students, schoolteachers, and others. Some research projects require special knowledge or skills, such as familiarity with the topic they are asking about. In a survey investigating whether health education improves the likelihood that people who have suffered a stroke will quit smoking, the researchers used trained nurses to administer questionnaires that included each patient's medical history.[2] Taking an accurate medical history is a skill that requires more training than most interviewers would likely have.

In-House Training for Inexperienced Interviewers

After personnel are recruited and selected, they must be trained.[3] Suppose a woman who has just sent her youngest child off to first grade is hired by a marketing research interviewing firm. She has decided to become a professional interviewer. The training she will receive after being hired may vary from virtually no training to an extensive, three-day program if she is selected by one of the larger marketing research agencies. Almost always, trainees will receive a **briefing session** on the particular project.

The objective of training is to ensure that the data collection instrument will be administered in a uniform fashion by all fieldworkers. The goal of training sessions is to ensure that each respondent is provided with common information. If the data are collected in a uniform manner from all respondents, the training session will have succeeded.

More extensive training programs are likely to cover the following topics:

- How to make initial contact with the respondent and secure the interview
- How to ask survey questions
- How to probe
- How to record responses
- How to terminate the interview

Typically, recruits record answers on a practice questionnaire during a simulated training interview.

Making Initial Contact and Securing the Interview

■ PERSONAL INTERVIEWS

Interviewers are trained to make appropriate opening remarks that will convince the respondent that his or her cooperation is important, as in this example:

Good afternoon, my name is _____, and I'm with [insert name of firm], an international marketing research company. We are conducting a survey concerning _____. I would like to get a few of your ideas. It will take [insert accurate time estimate] minutes.

TELEPHONE INTERVIEWS

For the initial contact in a telephone interview, the introduction might be something like this:

Good evening, my name is _____. I am not trying to sell anything. I'm calling from [insert name of firm] in Mason, Ohio. We are seeking your opinions on some important matters and it will only take [insert accurate time estimate] minutes of your time.

Giving the interviewer's name personalizes the call. Personal interviewers may carry a letter of identification or an ID card to indicate that the study is a *bona fide* research project and not a sales call. The name of the research agency is used to imply that the caller is trustworthy. The respondent must be given an accurate estimate of the amount of time participating in the interview will take. If someone is told that only three minutes will be required for participation, and the questionning proceeds to five mintues or more, the respondent will tend to quit before completing the interview. Providing an accurate estimate of the time not only helps gain cooperation, but it is also the ethically correct thing to do.

INTERNET SURVEYS

A similar approach may be used to an Internet survey. The potential respondent may receive an email requesting assistance, as in the following example:

We are contacting you because of your interest in [subject matter inserted here]. We would like to invite you to participate in a survey that asks your opinion on matters related to [subject matter inserted here]. In return for your participation, we will [insert incentive here]. To participate, click on this url: http://www.clickhere.com.

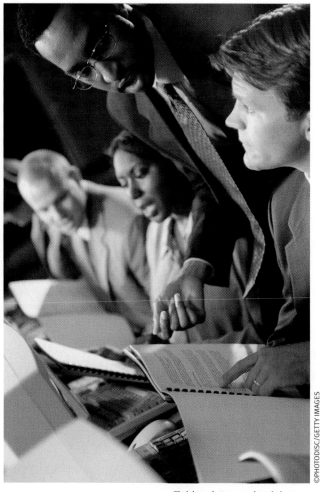

Fieldworkers need training both in the basics and required practices or good interviewing principles.

GAINING PARTICIPATION

The Interviewer's Manual from the Survey Research Center at the University of Michigan recommends avoiding questions that ask permission for the interview, such as "May I come in?" and "Would you mind answering some questions?" Some people will refuse to participate or object to being interviewed. Interviewers should be instructed on handling objections. For example, if the respondent says, "I'm too busy right now," the interviewer might be instructed to respond, "Will you be in at four o'clock this afternoon? I would be happy to schedule a time with you." In other cases, client companies will not wish to offend any individual. In this case, the interviewer will be instructed to merely say, "Thank you for your time."

The **foot-in-the-door compliance technique** and the **door-in-the-face compliance technique** are useful in securing interviews. Foot-in-the-door theory attempts to explain compliance with a large or difficult task on the basis of respondents' earlier compliance with a smaller initial request. One experiment has shown that compliance with a minor telephone interview (that is, a small request that few people refuse) will lead to greater compliance with a second, larger request to fill out a long mail questionnaire. An interviewer employing door-in-the-face technique begins by making an initial request so large that nearly everyone will react negatively (that is, slams the door in his or her face). When this happens, the interviewer can then request a smaller favor, such as asking a respondent to participate in a "short" survey. However, this technique presents an ethical issue if the respondent is deceived. Thus, the initial request should also be a legitimate request.

Foot-in-the-door compliance technique
A technique for obtaining a high response rate, in which compliance with a large or difficult task is induced by first obtaining the respondent's compliance with a smaller request.

Door-in-the-face compliance technique
A two-step process for securing a high response rate. In step 1 an initial request, so large that nearly everyone refuses it, is made. Next, a second request is made for a smaller favor; respondents are expected to comply with this more reasonable request.

RESEARCHSNAPSHOT

Questioning and Probing on an Electronic Bulletin Board

Online research often involves self-administered questionnaires with little role for an interviewer. An exception is interviewing with electronic bulletin boards, in which the interviewer posts comments and participants submit their responses for all the participants to read. Generally, the research firm screens and invites a sample of participants via e-mail, and those who accept receive a password to access the bulletin board for several days. The resulting small-group discussion takes place online, rather than in a meeting room.

Typically, the interviewer, or moderator, works from a discussion guide that specifies the questions to cover each day. The guide may indicate when each question is to be posted in order to spread the questions out and give participants time to visit the bulletin board and reply. Because the online format allows some time for reading and reflection, questions can be complex. The following question, for example, encourages participants to ponder several dimensions of a company's reputation:

"Could you now do the same for Dell: What are your perceptions of the company? What adjectives would you use to describe your image of the company? Why? How would you describe Dell's advertising?"

Such a complex question would be difficult to answer in a phone interview. But in the context of a bulletin board, one respondent might address one aspect of Dell's reputation, while another thinks of a different aspect, and the moderator then probes for more reaction to each line of thought as responses are posted to the bulletin board.

Because the moderator cannot see or hear participants, word choice is critical. The moderator should encourage participation. Often the moderator must seek clarification because messages are harder to interpret without clues from body language and vocal tones. Occasionally, someone makes inappropriate remarks, and bulletin boards allow this situation to be handled with private messages. Those messages should not only indicate the kind of information that is needed from the respondent, but also mention that his or her continued participation is valuable.

Source: Based on Adam Blunt, "Bulletin Boards—a Tool for B2B Qualitative Research," NOP World, June 30, 2005, originally posted on http://www.nopworld.com, accessed at http://www.gfkamerica.com; and "Frequently Asked Questions: Participation in Surveys," HarrisPollOnline, http://www.harrispollonline.com, accessed March 28, 2006.

Asking the Questions

The purpose of an interview is, of course, to record a respondent's answers. Training in the art of asking questions can be extremely beneficial, because interviewer bias can be a source of considerable error in survey research.

There are five major rules for asking questions:

1. Ask questions exactly as they are worded in the questionnaire.
2. Read each question very carefully and clearly.
3. Ask the questions in the specified order.
4. Ask every question specified in the questionnaire.
5. Repeat questions that are misunderstood or misinterpreted.[4]

Interviewers are generally trained to know these rules, but when working in the field, many do not follow these procedures exactly. Inexperienced interviewers may not understand the importance of strict adherence to the instructions. Even professional interviewers take shortcuts when the task becomes monotonous. Interviewers may shorten questions or rephrase unconsciously when they rely on their memory of the question rather than reading the question as it is worded. Even the slightest change in wording may inject some bias into a study. By reading the question, the interviewer may be reminded to concentrate on avoiding slight variations in tone of voice on particular words or phrases.

If respondents do not understand a question, they usually will ask for some clarification. The recommended procedure is to repeat the question. If the person does not understand a word such as HDTV (high definition television) in the question "Do you feel HDTV should be the standard delivery for television networks?" the interviewer should respond with the full name of the acronym. If the respondent still doesn't understand, then the interviewer may say, "Just whatever it

RESEARCHSNAPSHOT

Probing for Deeper Meaning at Olson Zaltman Associates

At Olson Zaltman Associates, highly trained interviewers probe for the deeper thinking that underlies attitudes toward brands or product categories. The research firm's method, called ZMET (for Zaltman Metaphor Elicitation Technique), begins by asking each respondent to come to a one-on-one interview, bringing along a set of eight to ten photographs related to their thoughts and feelings about the interview's topic. The interviewer uses the photos as nonverbal clues about the associations the person makes with the product or brand.

A typical interview lasts two hours. The interviewer's challenge is to ask questions that reveal what is behind the selection of the photographs without actually suggesting the interviewer's own ideas. The interviewer begins by asking the respondent to describe the topic-related thoughts and feelings that each picture illustrates. The interviewer then probes to uncover a deeper meaning by asking the respondent to elaborate on the initial statements. This process requires skill based on training in fields such as psychotherapy and sociology. Finally, the respondent works with an associate to create a computerized collage that illustrates the respondent's thoughts and feelings about the topic.

Researchers then use computer software to identify response patterns that suggest "metaphors" for the product—a general theme that describes respondents' attitudes. In a study of air fresheners, people want to avoid having odors in their home alienate them from visitors (an underlying desire for connection with others); they also want an air freshener to seem natural, rather than masking something (an underlying desire to evoke nature). Based on these ideas, the client developed Breeze air freshener. In another project, Motorola hired Olson Zaltman to help it market a high-tech security system. Many research participants brought in images of dogs, signifying the protection that dogs give their owners. As a result, Motorola avoided brand names emphasizing technology, instead calling the new system the Watchdog.

Source: Based on Robert Wielaard, "What People Don't Know They Know," America's Intelligence Wire, December 8, 2005, downloaded at http://www.accessmylibrary.com; Olson Zaltman Associates, home page and "What We Do," http://www.olsonzaltman.com, accessed March 23, 2006; Glenn L. Christensen and Jerry C. Olson, "Mapping Consumers' Mental Models with ZMET," Psychology and Marketing 19(6) (June 2002): 477–502.

©GARY EDWARDS/ZEFA/CORBIS

means to you." However, interviewers often supply their own personal definitions and ad lib clarifications, and they may include words that are not free from bias. One reason interviewers do this is that field supervisors tend to reward people for submitting completed questionnaires and to be less tolerant of interviewers who leave questions blank because of alleged misunderstandings.

Often respondents volunteer information relevant to a question that is supposed to be asked at a later point in the interview. In this situation the response should be recorded under the question that deals specifically with that subject. Then, rather than skip the question that was answered out of sequence, the interviewer should be trained to say something like "We have briefly discussed this, but let me ask you . . . ." By asking every question, the interviewer can be sure that complete answers are recorded. If the partial answer to a question answered out of sequence is recorded on the space reserved for the earlier question and the subsequent question is skipped, an omission error will occur when the data are tabulated.

Probing When No Response Is Given

Similar to the approach discussed for qualitative interviews, interviewers should be provided instructions on how to probe when respondents give no answer, incomplete answers, or answers that require clarification. First, probing is necessary when a respondent must be motivated to expand on, clarify, explain, or complete his or her answer. Interviewers must encourage respondents to clarify or expand on answers by providing a stimulus that will not suggest their own ideas or attitudes. An ability to probe with neutral stimuli is a mark of an experienced and effective interviewer. Second, probing may be necessary when a respondent begins to ramble or lose track. In such cases, a respondent must be led to focus on the specific content of the interview and to avoid irrelevant and unnecessary information.

Interviewers have several possible probing tactics to choose from, depending on the situation:

- *Repeating the question.* When the respondent remains completely silent, he or she may not have understood the question or decided how to answer it. Mere repetition may encourage the

EXHIBIT 18.1
Commonly Used Probes and Their Abbreviations

Interviewer's Probe	Standard Abbreviation
Repeat question	(RQ)
Anything else?	(AE or Else?)
Any other reason?	(AO?)
Any others?	(Other?)
How do you mean?	(How mean?)
Could you tell me more about your thinking on that?	(Tell more)
Would you tell me what you have in mind?	(What in mind?)
What do you mean?	(What mean?)
Why do you feel that way?	(Why?)
Which would be closer to the way you feel?	(Which closer?)

Source: Survey Research Center, *Interviewer's Manual*, rev. ed. (Ann Arbor, MI: Institute for Social Research, University of Michigan, 1976), p. 16.

respondent to answer in such cases. For example, if the question is "What do you not like about Guiness?" and the respondent does not answer, the interviewer may probe: "Just to check, is there anything that you do not like about Guiness?"

- *Using a silent probe.* If the interviewer believes that the respondent has more to say, a silent probe—that is, an expectant pause or look—may motivate the respondent to gather his or her thoughts and give a complete response.
- *Repeating the respondent's reply.* As the interviewer records the response, he or she may repeat the respondent's reply verbatim. This may stimulate the respondent to expand on the answer.
- *Asking a neutral question.* Asking a neutral question may specifically indicate the type of information that the interviewer is seeking. For example, if the interviewer believes that the respondent's motives should be clarified, he or she might ask, "Tell me about this feeling." If the interviewer feels that there is a need to clarify a word or phrase, he or she might say, "What do you mean by _____?" Exhibit 18.1 lists some common interview probes and the standard abbreviations that are recorded on the questionnaire with the respondent's answers.

The purpose of asking questions as probes is to encourage responses. Such probes should be neutral and not leading. Probes may be general (such as "Anything else?") or they may be questions specifically designed by the interviewer to clarify a particular statement by the respondent.

Recording the Responses

An analyst who fails to instruct fieldworkers in the techniques of properly recording survey answers rarely forgets to do so a second time. Although recording an answer seems extremely simple, mistakes can occur in this phase of the research. Each fieldworker should use the same recording process.

Rules for recording responses to fixed-alternative questions vary with the specific questionnaire. A general rule, however, is to place a check mark in the box that correctly reflects the respondent's answer. All too often interviewers don't bother recording the answer to a filter question because they believe the subsequent answer will make the answer to the filter question obvious. However, editors and coders do not know how the respondent actually answered a question.

The general instruction for recording open-ended questions is to record the response verbatim, a task that is difficult for most people. Inexperienced interviewers should be given an opportunity to practice verbatim recording of answers before being sent into the field. Some suggestions for recording open-ended answers include

- Record responses during the interview.
- Use the respondent's own words.
- Do not summarize or paraphrase the respondent's answer.
- Include everything that pertains to the question objectives.
- Include all of your probes.[5]

Especially for sensitive topics, decisions about how to record responses may be more difficult than these guidelines suggest. For a survey that included open-ended questions about sexual behavior, researchers found that some decisions about how to record answers affected the way responses were later interpreted. For example, they defined notation that would indicate pauses and vocal emphasis, which helped researchers identify answers that involved confusion or strong emotions. However, recording every nonverbal behavior led researchers to speculate about whether one respondent was crying or using drugs (he had a cold). Likewise, when transcriptions recorded the respondent's exact words and pronunciation, including dialects and mistakes in grammar and word usage, researchers were tempted to speculate about demographic characteristics, such as a speaker's race or educational level. As the researchers evaluated the effects of these decisions about how to record answers, they concluded that such decisions should be made carefully in light of the research objectives.[6]

Exhibit 18.2 shows an example of a completed questionnaire page. Note how the interviewer adds supplementary comments to the fixed-alternative questions and indicates probing questions by placing them in parentheses. Answers have been recorded without paraphrasing. In this case, the interviewer has resisted the temptation to conserve time and space by filtering comments. The *RQ* recorded in question A4a indicates a repeat-question probe.

Terminating the Interview

The final aspect of training is to instruct interviewers on how to close the interview. Fieldworkers should wait to close the interview until they have secured all pertinent information. The interviewer who departs hastily will be unable to record the spontaneous comments respondents sometimes offer after all formal questions have been asked. Merely recording one of these comments may result in a new product idea or creative marketing campaign. Avoiding hasty departures is also a matter of courtesy. The fieldworker should also answer any respondent questions concerning the nature and purpose of the study to the best of his or her ability.

Finally, it is extremely important to thank the respondent for his or her time and cooperation. The fieldworker may be required to reinterview the respondent at some future time. So, the respondent should be left with a positive feeling about having cooperated in a worthwhile operation.

Principles of Good Interviewing

Yankelovich Partners is one of the nation's top marketing research organizations.[7] One reason for its success is its careful attention to fieldwork. This section presents this organization's principles of good interviewing. These principles apply no matter what the nature of the specific assignment; they are universal and represent the essence of sound data collection for marketing research purposes. For clarity, they have been divided into two categories: *the basics* (the interviewing point of view) and *required practices* (standard inquiry premises and procedures).

The Basics

Interviewing is a skilled occupation so not everyone can do it, and even fewer can do it extremely well. A good interviewer observes the following basic principles:

1. *Have integrity, and be honest.* This is the cornerstone of all professional inquiry, regardless of its purpose.

EXHIBIT 18.2

Example of a Completed Questionnaire Page

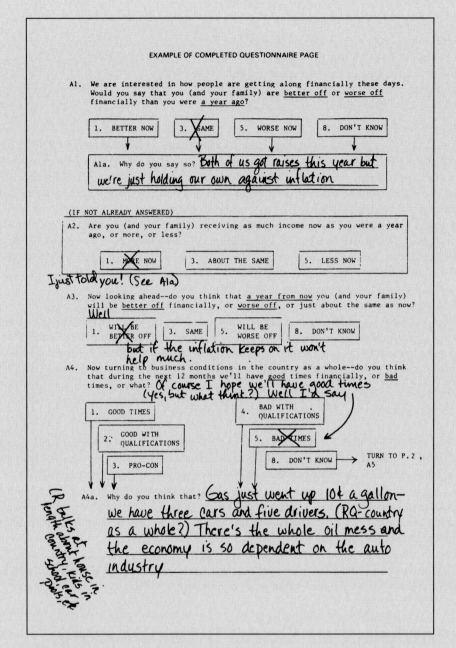

Source: Survey Research Center, *Interviewer's Manual*, rev. ed. (Ann Arbor, MI: Institute for Social Research, University of Michigan, 1976), p. 26. Reprinted by permission.

2. *Have patience and tact.* Interviewers ask for information from people they do not know. Thus, all the rules of human relations that apply to inquiry situations—patience, tact, and courtesy—apply even more to interviewing. You should at all times follow the standard business conventions that control communications and contact.

3. *Pay attention to accuracy and detail.* Among the greatest interviewing "sins" are inaccuracy and superficiality, for the professional analyst can misunderstand, and in turn mislead, a client. A good rule to follow is not to record a response unless you fully understand it yourself. Probe for clarification and rich, full answers. Record responses verbatim: Never assume you know what a respondent is thinking or jump to conclusions as to what he or she might have said but did not.

RESEARCHSNAPSHOT

Interviewers at Work: Jerusalem and Canberra

The principles of good interviewing are the same on every continent. Interviewers working in Jerusalem, Israel, and Canberra, Australia, share similar objectives: gathering responses tactfully and with a commitment to meet the survey's requirements.

In Jerusalem, a research firm called Dialog conducts political polls. Interviewer Oded Blech says he encounters a variety of challenges in trying to convince people to be surveyed. Some claim they will be out shopping for the entire night so calling back will be futile. He has heard lies, such as the father hissing at the child on the phone to say that he isn't at home. Blech and his colleagues know they must continue to be polite anyway. One coworker, Inbal Bracha, an engineering student, says refusals are less likely when she smiles as she talks, which makes her voice more pleasant. Her other technique for obtaining compliance is to speak rapidly but politely, telling the person that the survey will be brief and giving him or her "the feeling that he [or she] is very important."

In Canberra, field interviewer Genevieve Power works for the Australian Bureau of Statistics. Rather than phoning subjects,

she has to travel to their homes to ask them demographic questions and inquire about topics such as literacy and spending. Power needs strong interpersonal skills to speak with people from a variety of backgrounds. Her presence of mind carried her through an unusual situation. Power was working near the city of Darwin, traveling to a home with a forbidding gate at the end of a long, narrow driveway bordered by closely planted trees. Power entered the gate, closed it carefully behind her, and drove to the house. There she found a man seated in a bathtub in the front yard, enjoying a quiet bath. Though he was naked, he rose and shook Powers's hand politely. She conducted the interview as he replied from the bathtub. When she finished, her nude subject rose again to say goodbye.

Source: Based on Hilary Leila Krieger, "Even the Pollsters Take Some of Their Surveys with a Grain of Salt," Jerusalem Post, December 30, 2005, p. 1; and "Fielding Answers All in a Day's Work for Interviewers," Canberra Times, December 8, 2005, http://web1.infotrac.galegroup.com.

4. *Exhibit a real interest in the inquiry at hand, but keep your own opinions to yourself.* Impartiality is imperative—if your opinions were wanted, you would be asked, not your respondent. You are an asker and a recorder of other people's opinions, not a contributor to the study data.
5. *Be a good listener.* Too many interviewers talk too much, wasting time when respondents could be supplying more pertinent facts or opinions on the study topic.
6. *Keep the inquiry and respondents' responses confidential.* Do not discuss the studies you are doing with relatives, friends, or associates; it is unacceptable to both the research agency and its clients. Above all, *never* quote one respondent's opinion to another—that is the greatest violation of privacy.
7. *Respect others' rights.* Marketing research depends on people's willingness to provide information. In obtaining this information, you must follow a happy medium path. Between the undesirable extremes of failure to get it all and unnecessary coercion, this middle road is one of clear explanation, friendliness, and courtesy, offered in an interested and persuasive tone. Impress upon prospective respondents that their cooperation is important and valuable.

Required Practices

Here are practical rules of marketing research inquiry that should be followed and used without exception:

1. *Complete the number of interviews according to the sampling plan assigned to you.* Both are calculated with the utmost precision so that when assignments are returned, the study will benefit from having available the amount and type of information originally specified.
2. *Follow the directions provided.* Remember that many other interviewers are working on the same study in other places. Lack of uniformity in procedure can only spell disaster for later analysis. Each direction has a purpose, even though it may not be completely evident to you.

3. *Make every effort to keep schedules.* Schedules range from "hurry up" to "there should be plenty of time," but there is always a good reason, and you should be as responsive as possible. If you foresee problems, call and explain.

4. *Keep control of each interview you do.* It is up to you to determine the pace of a particular interview, keeping several points in mind:

   a. There is an established *average* length of an interview from the time you start to talk to the respondent to the time you finish. It represents a *guideline,* but some interviews will be shorter and some longer.

   b. Always get the whole story from the respondent, and write it all down in the respondent's own words. Also, remember to keep the interview focused on the subject at hand and prevent it from wandering off into unnecessary small talk.

   c. Avoid offending the respondent by being too talkative yourself.

5. *Complete the questionnaires meticulously.*

   a. Follow exactly all instructions that appear directly on the questionnaire. Before you start interviewing, learn what these instructions direct you to do.

   b. Ask the questions from the first to the last in the exact numerical order (unless directed to do otherwise in some particular instances). Much thought and effort go into determining the order of the questioning to avoid bias or to set the stage for subsequent questions.

   c. Ask each question exactly as it is written. There is never a justifiable reason for rephrasing a question. The cost of doing so is lack of uniformity; the research agency would never know whether all respondents were replying to the same question or replying to fifty different interviewers' interpretations of the question.

   d. Never leave a question blank. It will be difficult to tell whether you failed to ask it, whether the respondent could not answer it because of lack of knowledge or certainty, or whether the respondent refused to answer it for personal reasons. If none of the answer categories provided prove suitable, write in what the respondent said, in his or her own words.

   e. Use all the props provided to aid both interviewers and respondents: show cards, pictures, descriptions, sheets of questions for the respondents to answer themselves, and so on. All have a specific interview purpose. Keys to when and how to use them appear on the questionnaire at the point at which they are to be used.

6. *Check over each questionnaire you have completed.* This is best done directly after it has been completed. If you find something you did wrong or omitted, correct it. Often you can call a respondent back, admit you missed something (or are unclear about a particular response), and then straighten out the difficulty.

7. *Compare your sample execution and assigned quota with the total number of questionnaires you have completed.* Do not consider your assignment finished until you have done this.

8. *Clear up any questions with the research agency.* At the start of an assignment or after you have begun, if you have questions for which you can find no explanatory instructions, call the agency to get the matter clarified. (Many agencies provide toll-free numbers so that there will be no expense to you.)

Fieldwork Management

Marketing managers preparing for the fieldwork stage should consider the meaning of the following stanza from Robert Burns's poem "To a Mouse":

The best laid schemes o' mice and men
Gang aft a—gley;
An' lea'e us nought but grief and pain,
For promis'd joy.

The best plans of mice, men, and marketing researchers may go astray. An excellent research plan may go astray if the field operations are performed incorrectly. A proper research design will eliminate numerous sources of error, but careful execution of the fieldwork is necessary to produce results without substantial error. For these reasons fieldwork management is an essential part of the marketing research process.

Managers of field operations select, train, supervise, and control fieldworkers. Our discussion of fieldwork principles mentioned selection and training. This section investigates the tasks of the fieldwork managers in greater detail.

Briefing Session for Experienced Interviewers

Whether interviewers have just completed their training in fundamentals or are already experienced, they always need to be informed about the individual project. Both experienced and inexperienced fieldworkers must be briefed on the background of the sponsoring organization, sampling techniques, asking of questions, callback procedures, and other matters specific to the particular project.

If there are any special instructions—for example, about using show cards or video equipment or restricted interviewing times—they should also be covered during the training session. Instructions for handling certain key questions are always important. For example, the following fieldworker instructions appeared in a survey of institutional investors who make buy-and-sell decisions about stocks for banks, pension funds, and so on:

Questions 13a, 13b
These questions will provide verbatim comments for the report to the client. Probe for more than one- or two-word answers and record verbatim. Particularly, probe for more information when respondent gives a general answer—e.g., "Poor management," "It's in a good industry." Ask, In what ways is management poor? What's good about the industry? And so on.

A training session for experienced interviewers might go something like this: All interviewers report to the central office, where they receive a brief explanation of the firm's background and the general aims of the study. Interviewers are provided with minimal information about the purpose of the study to ensure that they will not transmit any preconceived notions to respondents. For example, in a survey about the banks in a community, the interviewers would be told that the research is a banking study but not the name of the sponsoring bank. To train the interviewers about the questionnaire, a field supervisor conducts an interview with another field supervisor who acts as a respondent. The trainees observe the interviewing process, after which they each interview and record the responses of another field supervisor who acts as a respondent. After the practice interview, the trainees receive additional instructions.

Training to Avoid Procedural Errors in Sample Selection

The briefing session also covers the sampling procedure. A number of research projects allow the interviewer to be at least partially responsible for selecting the sample. These sampling methods offer the potential for selection bias. This potential for bias is obvious in the case of quota sampling but less obvious in other cases. For example, in probability sampling in which every n^{th} house is selected, the fieldworker uses his or her discretion in identifying housing units. Avoiding selection bias may be more difficult than it sounds. For example, in an old, exclusive neighborhood, a mansion's coach house or servants' quarters may have been converted into an apartment that should be identified as a housing unit. This type of dwelling and other unusual housing units (apartments with alley entrances only, lake cottages, or rooming houses) may be overlooked, giving rise to selection error. Errors may also occur in the selection of random-digit dialing samples. Considerable effort should be expended in training and supervisory control to minimize these errors.

Another selection problem is the practice of contacting a respondent when and where it is convenient for both parties. Consider the following anecdote from an industrial marketing research interviewer:

Occasionally getting to the interview is half the challenge and tests the interviewer's ingenuity. Finding your way around a huge steel mill is not easy. Even worse is trying to find a correct turn-off to gravel pit D when it's snowing so hard that most direction signs are obliterated. In arranging an appointment with an executive at

RESEARCHSNAPSHOT

Total Quality Management for Interviewing

Interviewers and their supervisors can improve the process of data collection to minimize errors. One popular method, total quality management (TQM), seeks continuous improvement by getting everyone involved in measuring performance and looking for ways to improve processes:

- *Measure response rates, and improve interviewer training to improve response rates.* To do this, researchers must describe the procedure for contacting subjects and consider alternatives, such as letters of introduction, the timing of contacts, and the number of attempts to make before

a subject is classified as a nonrespondent. Interviewers should be taught about the impact on research quality of interviewing only the people who are easiest to contact, and they should be trained to persuade people to participate.

- *Measure defects in terms of measurement errors and improve interviewer techniques and respondent behavior.* Researchers should measure the

pattern of response rates by interviewer, looking for interviewer variance (a tendency for different interviewers to obtain different answers). To measure respondent behavior, researchers can ask interviewers for objective information such as the presence of a third person, as well as for an evaluation of each interview's success; the data may signal respondent behaviors with a potential to bias responses from certain segments.

- *Measure the interview process, including the training provided, the application of principles from training, and feedback about the interviewer.* The training should be aimed at specific, measurable objectives, with a plan for measuring whether the interviewers' performance shows that training objectives were met. For a standardized interview, one way to tell whether the interviews are following the guidelines is to measure whether they all last about the same amount of time. Verification by reinterviewing a subsample provides insight into the accuracy of recording responses. Where variances occur, the supervisor and interviewers should investigate the cause, looking for ways to improve training and interviewing.

Source: Based on Geert Loosveldt, Ann Carton, and Jaak Billiet, "Assessment of Survey Data Quality: A Pragmatic Approach Focused on Interviewer Tasks," *International Journal of Market Research,* Spring 2004, downloaded from Business & Company Resource Center, http://galenet.galegroup.com.

a rock quarry outside Kansas City, he told me his office was in "Cave Number 3." It was no joke. To my surprise, I found a luxurious executive office in a cave, which had long ago been hollowed by digging for raw material.[8]

In that case, finding the sample unit was half the battle.

Supervision of Fieldworkers

Although briefing and training interviewers will minimize the probability of their interviewing the wrong households or asking biased questions, there is still considerable potential for errors in the field. Direct supervision of personal interviewers, telephone interviewers, and other fieldworkers is necessary to ensure that the techniques communicated in the training sessions are implemented in the field.

Supervision of interviewers, like other forms of supervision, refers to controlling the efforts of workers. Field supervision of interviewers requires checking to see that field procedures are being properly followed. A supervisor checks field operations to ensure that the interviewing schedule is being met. Supervisors collect the questionnaires or other instruments daily and edit them for completeness and legibility. (See Chapter 19 for more details on editing.) If problems arise, supervisors discuss them with the fieldworkers, providing training when necessary.

In addition to quality control, continual training may be provided. For example, if a telephone supervisor notices that interviewers are allowing the phone to ring more than eight times before considering the call a "no answer," the supervisor can instruct interviewers not to do so, as the person who eventually answers is likely to be annoyed.

Sampling Verification

Another important job of a supervisor is to verify that interviews are being conducted according to the sampling plan rather than with the sampling units most accessible to the interviewer. An interviewer might be tempted to go to the household next door for an interview rather than record the sampling unit as not at home, which would require a callback. Carefully recording the number of completed interviews will help ensure that the sampling procedure is being properly conducted. Supervisors are responsible for motivating interviewers to follow the sampling plan carefully.

Closer supervision of the interviewing procedure can occur in central-location telephone interviewing. Supervisors may be able to listen to the actual interview by switching onto the interviewer's line. Of course, this is harder to do when interviewers call from their own homes.

Supervisors must also make sure that the right people within the household or sampling unit are being contacted. One research project for a children's cereal required that several products be placed in the home and that children record their daily consumption and reactions to each cereal in a diary. Although the interviewers were supposed to contact the children to remind them to fill out the diaries, a field supervisor observed that in almost half the cases the mothers were filling out the diaries after the children left for school because their children had not done so. The novelty of the research project had worn off after a few days; eating a specific cereal each day was no longer fun after the first few times, and the children had stopped keeping the diaries. Similar situations may occur with physicians, executives, and other busy people. The interviewer may find it easier to interview a nurse, secretary, or other assistant rather than wait to speak with the right person.

Interviewer Cheating

The most blatant form of **interviewer cheating** occurs when an interviewer falsifies interviews, merely filling in fake answers rather than contacting respondents. This is sometimes refered to as **curb-stoning**. Although this situation does occur, it is not common if the job of selection has been properly accomplished. However, less obvious forms of interviewer cheating occur with greater frequency. Interviewers often consider quota sampling to be time consuming, so an interviewer may stretch the requirements a bit to obtain seemingly qualified respondents. In the interviewer's eyes, a young-looking 36-year-old may be the same as a 30-year-old who fits the quota requirement; checking off the under-30 category thus isn't really cheating. Consider the fieldworker who must select only heavy users of a certain brand of hand lotion that the client says is used by 15 percent of the population. If the fieldworker finds that only 3 percent qualify as heavy users, he or she may be tempted to interview an occasional user to stretch the quota somewhat. All of these approaches are unethical.

An interviewer may fake part of a questionnaire to make it acceptable to the field supervisor. In a survey on automobile satellite radio systems, suppose an interviewer is requested to ask for five reasons why consumers have purchased this product. If he or she finds that people typically give two or perhaps three reasons and even with extensive probing cannot think of five reasons, the interviewer might be tempted to cheat. Rather than have the supervisor think he or she was goofing off on the probing, the interviewer may fill in five reasons based on past interviews. In other cases, the interviewer may cut corners to save time and energy.

Interviewers may fake answers when they find questions embarrassing or troublesome to ask because of sensitive subjects. Thus, the interviewer may complete most of the questionnaire but leave out a question or two because he or she found it troublesome or time-consuming. For example, in a survey among physicians, an interviewer might find questions about artificial-insemination donor programs embarrassing, skip these questions, and fill in the gaps later.

What appears to be interviewer cheating often is caused by improper training or fieldworkers' inexperience. A fieldworker who does not understand the instructions may skip or miss a portion of the questionnaire.

Interviewer cheating
The practice by fieldworkers of filling in fake answers or falsifying interviews.

Curb-stoning
A form of interviewer cheating in which an interviewer makes up the responses instead of conducting an actual interview.

Interviewers may be reluctant to interview sampling units who they feel may be difficult or undesirable to interview. Sometimes fieldworkers are instructed to say at the conclusion of each interview, "Thank you for your time—and by the way, my supervisor may call you to ask about my work. Please say whatever you wish." This or a similar statement not only increases the number of respondents willing to cooperate with the verification process but also improves the quality of fieldwork.

Verification by Reinterviewing

Verification
Quality-control procedures in fieldwork intended to ensure that interviewers are following the sampling procedures and to determine whether interviewers are cheating.

Supervision for quality control attempts to ensure that interviewers are following the sampling procedure and to detect falsification of interviews. Supervisors verify approximately 15 percent of the interviews by reinterviewing. Normally the interview is not repeated; rather, supervisors recontact respondents and ask about the length of the interview and their reactions to the interviewer; then they collect basic demographic data to check for interviewer cheating. Such **verification** does not detect the more subtle form of cheating in which only portions of the interview have been falsified. A validation check may simply point out that an interviewer contacted the proper household but interviewed the wrong individual in that household—which, of course, can be a serious error.

Fieldworkers should be aware of supervisory verification practices. Knowing that there may be a telephone or postcard validation check often reminds interviewers to be conscientious in their work. The interviewer who is conducting quota sampling and needs an upper-income Hispanic male will be less tempted to interview a middle-income Hispanic man and falsify the income data in this situation.

Certain information may allow for partial verification without recontacting the respondent. Computer-assisted telephone interviewers often do not know the phone number dialed by the computer or other basic information about the respondent. Thus, answers to questions added to the end of the telephone interview to identify a respondent's area code, phone number, city, zip code, and so on may be used to verify the interview. The computer can also record every attempted call, the time intervals between calls, and the time required to conduct each completed interview—data that may help in identifying patterns related to cheating by interviewers.

Summary

1. Describe the role and job requirements of fieldworkers. Fieldworkers are responsible for gathering data in the field. These activities may be performed by the organization that needs the information, by research suppliers, or by third-party field service organizations. Proper execution of fieldwork is essential to produce research results without substantial error. Proper control of fieldwork begins with interviewer selection. Fieldworkers generally should be healthy, outgoing, and well groomed.

2. Summarize the skills to cover when training inexperienced interviewers. New fieldworkers must be trained in opening the interview, asking the questions, probing for additional information, recording the responses, and terminating the interview.

3. List principles of good interviewing. Good interviewers have integrity, patience, and tact. They are attentive to detail and interested in the inquiry at hand. They behave impartially, listen carefully, and maintain confidentiality. They respect the rights of others. Interviewing should adhere to several required practices. Interviewers should complete all interviews according to the sample plan and follow the directions provided. They should try to meet schedules and maintain control of the interview. They should fill in answers meticulously and then check over the questionnaire to make sure it is complete. Before finishing an assignment, they should verify that the number of completed questionnaires matches the sampling plan and assigned quotas. If they have questions, they should check with the agency conducting the research.

4. Describe the activities involved in the management of fieldworkers. Experienced fieldworkers are briefed for each new project to familiarize them with its specific requirements. A particular concern of the briefing session is reminding fieldworkers to adhere closely to the prescribed sampling procedures.

5. Discuss how supervisors should minimize errors in the field. Careful supervision of fieldworkers also is necessary. Supervisors gather and edit questionnaires each day. They check to see that field procedures are being properly followed and that interviews are on schedule. They also check to ensure that the correct sampling units are being used and that the proper people are responding in the study. Finally, supervisors check for interviewer cheating and verify portions of the interviews by reinterviewing a certain percentage of each fieldworker's respondents.

Key Terms and Concepts

Fieldworker	Briefing session	Interviewer cheating
Field interviewing service	Foot-in-the-door compliance technique	Curb-stoning
In-house interviewer	Door-in-the-face compliance technique	Verification

Questions for Review and Critical Thinking

1. What qualities should fieldworkers possess?
2. **ETHICS** An interviewer has a rather long telephone interview. The estimate suggests that fully completing the survey will take thirty minutes. However, what do you think the response rate will be if people are told ahead of time that it will take thirty minutes to finish participating in the survey? Should the interviewer fudge a little and state that the survey will take only fifteen minutes? Explain.
3. What should the interviewer do if a question is misunderstood? If a respondent answers a question before encountering it in the questionnaire?
4. When should interviewers probe? Give some examples of how probing should be done.
5. How should respondents' answers to open-ended questions be recorded?
6. How should the fieldworker terminate the interview?
7. Why is it important to ensure that fieldworkers adhere to the sampling procedure specified for a project?
8. **ETHICS** What forms does interviewer cheating take? How can such cheating be prevented or detected?
9. **ETHICS** Two interviewers are accused of curb-stoning. What have they done?
10. Comment on the following field situations.
    a. After conducting a survey with ten people, an interviewer noticed that many of the respondents were saying "Was I right?" after a particular question.
    b. A questionnaire asking about a new easy-opening can has the following instructions to interviewers:

    (Hand respondent can and matching instruction card.)

"Would you please read the instructions on this card and then open this can for me?" *(Interviewer: Note any comments respondent makes. Do not under any circumstances help him or her to open the can or offer any explanation as to how to open it. If respondent asks for help, tell him that the instructions are on the card. Do not discuss the can or its contents.)*

   c. A researcher gives balloons to children of respondents to keep the children occupied during the interview.
   d. An interviewer tells the supervisor, "With the price of gas, this job isn't paying as well as before!"
   e. When a respondent asks how much time the survey will take, the interviewer responds, "fifteen to twenty minutes." The respondent says, "I'm sorry, I have to refuse. I can't give you that much time right now."
11. Write some interviewer instructions for a telephone survey.
12. A fieldworker conducting a political poll is instructed to interview registered voters. The fieldworker interviews all willing participants who are eligible to vote (those who may register in the future) because allowing their opinions to be recorded is part of her patriotic duty. Is she doing the right thing?
13. An interviewer finds that when potential respondents ask how much time the survey will take, most refuse if they are told fifteen minutes. The interviewer now says ten minutes and finds that most respondents enjoy answering the questions. Is this the right thing to do?
14. A fieldworker asks respondents whether they will answer a few questions. However, the interviewer also observes the respondent's race and approximate age. Is this ethical?

Research Activity

1. **'NET** Go to http://www.quirks.com and look at the menu in the left margin. In the list, you should find a hyperlink labeled "telephone facilities." Click here. Using the resulting window, investigate the following.

   Suppose you were interested in conducting telephone interviews in a number of places. List telephone facilities in Denmark, Mexico, South Korea, and Alabama (United States). Is CATI available in every county?

Case 18.1 Thomas and Dorothy Leavey Library

The Thomas and Dorothy Leavey Library serves the students and faculty of the University of Southern California. Staff at the busy library wanted to know more about its patrons, what library resources they find helpful, and whether they are satisfied with the library's services. However, like many libraries, this organization had a tiny budget for marketing research. As a result, the goal was to conduct exploratory research while spending less than $250.[9]

Staff members studied surveys conducted by other libraries to get ideas for a one-page printed questionnaire. Colleagues on the library staff provided suggestions, and a few undergraduates tested the survey for clarity. Next, the survey schedule was chosen: thirty-six continuous hours that did not conflict with any holidays or exams.

The fieldwork involved setting up and staffing a table offering the survey and then inviting library patrons to stop and fill out a questionnaire. Possible locations included space near an elevator, stairs, or computers, but the lobby area offered the greatest opportunity, because everyone passed through the lobby when using the facility's only entrance. The survey's planners divided the time into sixty slots and recruited students with jobs at the library to serve as the fieldworkers. Other members of the library staff also volunteered to fill time slots. The students in particular were enthusiastic about inviting library patrons to complete questionnaires. A bowl of candy for participants was a small incentive, combined with a raffle for donated prizes.

Questions

1. Imagine that you were asked to help prepare for this survey. What fieldwork challenges would you expect to arise in a survey such as this, to be carried out by inexperienced fieldworkers?
2. What training would you recommend for the students and other library staffers conducting this survey? Suggest topics to cover and advice to give these fieldworkers.

Case 18.2 Margaret Murphy O'Hara

Margaret Murphy O'Hara was fatigued. As she wiped the perspiration from her brow, she felt that the Massachusetts summer sun was playing a trick on her. It was her first day at work, and the weather was hot. She had no idea that being a field interviewer required so much stamina. Even though she was tired, she was happy with her new job. She didn't yet have the knack of holding her purse, questionnaires, and clipboard while administering the show cards, but she knew she'd get the hang of it. The balancing act can be learned, she thought.

When she met her supervisor, Mary Zagorski, at the end of her first day, Margaret described her day. Margaret said she thought the questionnaire was a bit too long. She laughed, saying that an elderly lady had fallen asleep after about twenty minutes of interviewing.

Margaret mentioned that a number of people had asked why they were selected. Margaret said she did not know exactly what to say when somebody asked, "Why did you pick me?"

She said that the nicest person she had interviewed was a man whose wife wasn't home to be surveyed. He was very friendly and didn't balk at being asked about his income and age like some of the other people she had interviewed.

She said she had one problem that she needed some help with resolving. Four or five people refused to grant the interview. Margaret explained that one woman answered the door and said she was too busy because her son, an army private, was leaving the country. The woman was throwing a little party for him before he went off to the airport. Margaret didn't want to spoil their fun with the survey. Another lady said that she was too busy and really didn't know anything about the subject anyway. However, she did suggest her next-door neighbor, who was very interested in the subject. Margaret was able to interview this person to make up for the lost interview. It actually went quite well.

Margaret said another woman wouldn't be interviewed because she didn't know anything about the Zagorski interviewing service, and Margaret didn't know quite what to tell her. Finally, she couldn't make one interview because she didn't understand the address: 9615 South Francisco Rear. Margaret told Mary it was quite a day, and she looked forward to tomorrow.

Questions

1. Is Margaret going to be a good professional interviewer?
2. What should Mary Zagorski tell Margaret?

Part 6
Data Analysis and Presentation

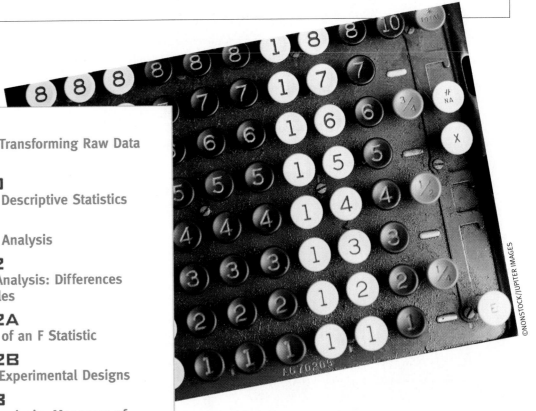

©NONSTOCK/JUPITER IMAGES

CHAPTER 19
Editing and Coding: Transforming Raw Data into Information

CHAPTER 20
Basic Data Analysis: Descriptive Statistics

CHAPTER 21
Univariate Statistical Analysis

CHAPTER 22
Bivariate Statistical Analysis: Differences Between Two Variables

CHAPTER 22A
Manual Calculations of an F Statistic

CHAPTER 22B
ANOVA for Complex Experimental Designs

CHAPTER 23
Bivarate Statistical Analysis: Measures of Association

APPENDIX 23A
Arithmetic Behind OLS

CHAPTER 24
Introducing Multivariate Statistical Analysis

APPENDIX 24A
Getting Factor Results with SAS or SPSS

CHAPTER 25
Communicating Research Results: Research Report, Oral Presentation, and Research Follow-Up

CHAPTER 19
EDITING AND CODING:
TRANSFORMING RAW DATA INTO INFORMATION

After studying this chapter, you should be able to

1. Know when a response is really an error and should be edited
2. Appreciate coding of pure qualitative research
3. Understand the way data are represented in a data file
4. Understand the coding of structured responses including a dummy variable approach
5. Appreciate the ways that technological advances have simplified the coding process

Chapter Vignette: I Hate My Boss!

Elizabeth Aimee, a private research consultant, has been pouring through employee "suggestions" all day. Her firm has been hired to try and improve company performance and morale at Chop-Mart, a local mega-store. Employees can fill out a form that contains a few open-ended questions, including

1. How do you feel about your job?
2. Is the company meeting expectations?
3. What feelings do you experience when you are at work?

The form also contains a few closed-ended questions, including

1. How clear are your job responsibilities?

   - Always clear _____
   - Sometimes clear _____
   - Completely unclear _____

2. Do you like your job?

   - Yes _____
   - No _____

Among the responses to the first question she finds the following:

- I hate my boss!
- Miserable, just like my coworkers.
- My boss is an ogre!!
- The job's fine, my supervisors are jerks.
- I love my boss—not!
- I like coming to work.
- I have mixed feelings about my job.
- Terrified
- Ashamed

Also, among the closed-ended questions, she finds that many people failed to answer the question about job responsibilities and that about 75 percent of employees say they like their jobs. A few employees checked both "sometimes clear" and "always clear" in responding to their job responsibilities.

"How can I possibly make sense of this?" Ms. Aimee knows she must code the open-ended responses. Since this is difficult, she asks an assistant to help with the task. What does it mean when someone says "I hate my boss"? How should the response be coded when someone says, "The job's fine, my supervisors are jerks"? She recalls reading a paper indicating that emotions are important drivers of performance.[1] Perhaps employees are experiencing too much fear in the workplace and this is tied to managerial behavior? However, more detailed analysis of these responses is needed. The results from this analysis will only be as good as the coding.

This chapter deals with coding and editing raw data. Researchers must pay careful attention to their coding because poor coding leads directly to nonresponse error.[2]

Stages of Data Analysis

Once the fieldwork is completed, the researcher will be anxious to begin data analysis. This will complete the transformation from data into intelligence. However, the **raw data** may not be in a form that lends itself well to data analysis. Raw data are recorded just as the respondent indicated. For an oral response, the raw data are in the words of the respondent, whereas for a questionnaire response, the actual number checked is the number stored. Raw data will often also contain errors both in the form of respondent errors and nonrespondent errors. Whereas a respondent error, as discussed in Chapter 8, is a mistake made by the respondent, a **nonrespondent error** is a mistake made by an interviewer or by a person responsible for creating an electronic data file representing the responses.

Exhibit 19.1 provides an overview of data analysis. The first two stages result in an electronic file suitable for data analysis. This file can then be used in the application of various statistical routines including those associated with descriptive, univariate, bivariate, or multivariate analysis. Each of these data analysis approaches will be discussed in the subsequent chapters. An important part of the editing, coding, and filing stages is checking for errors. As long as error remains in the data, the process of transformation from raw data to intelligence will be made more risky and more difficult. Editing and coding are the first two stages in the data analysis process.

Data integrity refers to the notion that the data file actually contains the information that the researcher promised the decision maker he or she would obtain. Additionally, data integrity extends to the fact that the data have been edited and properly coded so that they are useful to the decision

Raw data
The unedited responses from a respondent exactly as indicated by that respondent.

Nonrespondent error
Error that the respondent is not responsible for creating, such as when the interviewer marks a response incorrectly.

Data integrity
The notion that the data file actually contains the information that the researcher promised the decision maker he or she would obtain, meaning in part that the data have been edited and properly coded so that they are useful to the decision maker.

EXHIBIT 19.1
Overview of the Stages of Data Analysis

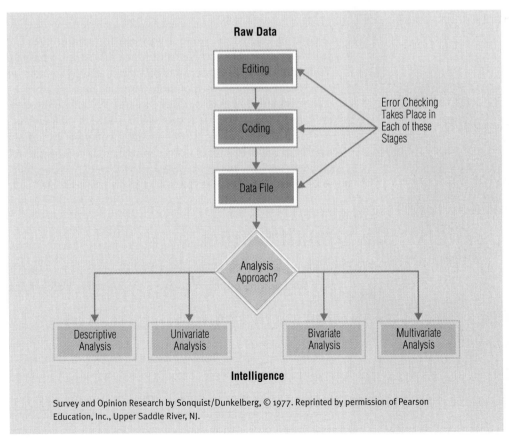

Survey and Opinion Research by Sonquist/Dunkelberg, © 1977. Reprinted by permission of Pearson Education, Inc., Upper Saddle River, NJ.

maker. Any errors in this process, just as with errors or shortcuts in the interview process itself, harm the integrity of the data.

Editing

Fieldwork often produces data containing mistakes. For example, consider the following simple questionnaire item and response:

How long have you lived at your current address? __48__

The researcher had intended the response to be in years. Perhaps the respondent has indicated the number of months rather than years he or she has lived at this address? Alternatively, if this was an interviewer's form, he or she may have marked the response in months without indicating this on the form. How should this be treated? Sometimes, responses may be contradictory. What if the same respondent above gives this response?

What is your age? __32 years__

This answer contradicts the earlier response. If the respondent is 32 years of age, then how could he or she have lived at the same address for 48 years? Therefore, an adjustment should be made to accommodate this information. The most likely case is that this respondent has lived at the current address for four years.

This example illustrates data **editing**. Editing is the process of checking and adjusting data for omissions, consistency, and legibility. In this way, the data become ready for analysis by a computer. So, the editor's task is to check for errors and omissions on questionnaires or other data collection forms. When the editor discovers a problem, he or she adjusts the data to make them more complete, consistent, or readable.

At times, the editor may need to reconstruct data. In the example above, the researcher can guess with some certainty that the respondent entered the original questions in months instead of years. Therefore, the probable true answer can be reconstructed. While the editor should try to make adjustments in an effort to represent as much information from a respondent as possible, reconstructing responses in this fashion should be done only when the probable true response is very obvious. Had the respondent's age been 55 years, filling in the response with years would not have been advisable barring other information. Perhaps the respondent has lived in the house since childhood? That possibility would seem real enough to prevent changing the response.

Field Editing

Field supervisors often are responsible for conducting preliminary **field editing** on the same day as the interview. Field editing is used to

1. Identify technical omissions such as a blank page on an interview form
2. Check legibility of handwriting for open ended responses
3. Clarify responses that are logically or conceptually inconsistent.

Field editing is particularly useful when personal interviews have been used to gather data. In these cases, a daily field edit allows supervisors to deal with some questions by asking interviewers,

Editing
The process of checking the completeness, consistency, and legibility of data and making the data ready for coding and transfer to storage.

Field editing
Preliminary editing by a field supervisor on the same day as the interview to catch technical omissions, check legibility of handwriting, and clarify responses that are logically or conceptually inconsistent.

Field edits allow supervisors to spot errors before the data file is created.

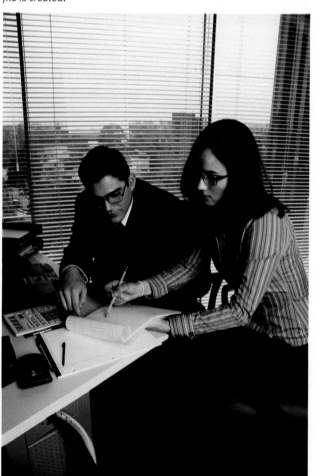

RESEARCHSNAPSHOT

Do you Have Integrity?

Data integrity is essential to successful research and decision making. Sometimes, this is a question of ethics. Whereas data integrity can suffer when an interviewer or coder simply makes up data, other things can occur that limit data integrity. For instance, data with a large portion of non-response has lower integrity than data without so much missing data. However, if respondents have truly left questions blank, the editor should not feel compelled to just "make up" responses.

Data integrity can also suffer simply because the data are edited or coded poorly. For example, the data coder should be aware that data may be used by other downstream users. Therefore, consistent coding should exist. For example, if a coder sometimes uses 1 for women and 2 for men, while on another data set uses 0 for men and 1 for women, the possibility exists that analyses using these categories will be confused. Who exactly are the men and who are the women? This is particularly true if the coder does not enter value labels for the variable.

Consider how important consistent coding is for companies that share or sell secondary data. Occupations need a common coding just as do product classes, industries, and numerous other potential data values. Fortunately, industries have standard codes such as NAICS (North American Industrial Classification System) and SIC (Standardized Industrial Classification) codes. Some professional coders have adopted postal service guidelines for coding things like states and addresses. A search of the U.S. Post Office website should come to a page with these guidelines (http://pe.usps.gov). Without a standardized approach, analysts may never be quite sure what they are looking at from one data set to another. Thus, research firms need to carefully maintain information coding systems that help maximize data integrity.

©ROYALTY-FREE/CORBIS

Sources: Dubberly, Hugh (2004), "The Information Loop," CIOInsight, 43 (September), 55–61; Shonerd, René (2003), "Data Integrity Rules," Association Management, 55 (9), 14.

who may still be able to remember the interviews, about facts that may allow errors to be identified and perhaps corrected. In addition, the number of unanswered questions or incomplete responses can be reduced with rapid follow-up. A daily field edit allows fieldworkers to identify respondents who should be recontacted to fill in omissions in a timely fashion.

The supervisor may also use field edits to spot the need for further interviewer training or to correct faulty procedures. For example, if an interviewer did not correctly follow skip patterns, training may be indicated. The supervisor may also notice that an interviewer is not properly probing some open-ended responses.

In-House Editing

Although simultaneous field editing is highly desirable, in many situations (particularly with mail questionnaires) early reviewing of the data is not always possible. **In-house editing** rigorously investigates the results of data collection. The research supplier or research department normally has a centralized office staff perform the editing and coding function.

For example, Arbitron measures radio audiences by having respondents record their listening behavior—time, station, and place (home or car)—in diaries. After the diaries are returned by mail, in-house editors perform usability edits in which they check that the postmark is after the last day of the survey week, verify the legibility of station call letters (station WKXY could look like KWXY), look for completeness of entries on each day of the week, and perform other editing activities. If the respondent's age or sex is not indicated, the respondent is called to ensure that this information is included.

In-house editing
A rigorous editing job performed by a centralized office staff.

TOTHEPOINT

Excellence is to do a common thing in an uncommon way.

—Booker T. Washington

Editing for Consistency

The chapter vignette describes some research responses that appear contradictory at first glance. For instance, can employees hate their bosses but still like their jobs? Ms. Aimee is performing an in-house editing task and may need to adjust for inconsistent or contradictory responses. Did the respondent make a mistake or can someone really experience these two opposing reactions?

ILLUSTRATING INCONSISTENCY—FACT OR FICTION?

Consider another situation in which a telephone interviewer has been instructed to interview only registered voters in a state that requires voters to be at least eighteen years old. If the editor's review of a questionnaire indicates that the respondent was only seventeen years old, the editor's task is to correct this mistake by deleting this response because this respondent should never have been considered as a sampling unit. The sampling units (respondents) should all be consistent with the defined population.

The editor also should check for consistency within the data collection framework. For example, a survey on out-shopping behavior (shopping in towns other than the one in which the person resides) might have a question such as the following:

In which of the following cities have you shopped for clothing during the last year?

- *San Francisco*
- *Sacramento*
- *San José*
- *Los Angeles*
- *Other* _____

Please list the clothing stores where you have shopped during the last two months.

Suppose a respondent checks Sacramento and San Francisco to the first question. If the same respondent lists a store that has a location only in Los Angeles in the second question, an error is indicated. Either the respondent failed to list Los Angeles in the first question or listed an erroneous store in the second question. These answers are obviously inconsistent.

TAKING ACTION WHEN RESPONSE IS OBVIOUSLY AN ERROR

What should the editor do? If solid evidence exists that points to the fact that the respondent simply failed to check Los Angeles, then the response to the first question can be changed to indicate that the person shopped in that city as well. Since Los Angeles is not listed next to Sacramento or San Francisco, it is unlikely that the respondent checked the wrong city inadvertently. Perhaps the question about the stores triggered a memory that did not come to the respondent when checking off the cities. This seems quite possible, and if another question can also point strongly to the fact that the respondent actually shopped at the store in Los Angeles, then the change should be made.

However, perhaps the respondent placed a mail order with the store in Los Angeles and simply did not physically shop in the store. If other evidence suggests this possibility, then the researcher should not make an adjustment to the first question. For example, a later question may have the respondent list any clothing orders placed via mail order (or by telephone or Internet order).

Responses should be logically consistent, but the researcher should not jump to the conclusion that a change should be made at the first site of an inconsistency. In all but the most obvious situations, a change should only be made when multiple pieces of evidence exist that some response is in error and when the likely true response is obvious. In the chapter vignette, Ms. Aimee will be looking for multiple pieces of evidence that a respondent really does *not like* his or her job among those respondents who report being sick of the boss but who have marked *liking* the job. Without multiple pieces of evidence, the responses should be left as they are. Look back at the responses listed for the first question. Since several of the open-ended questions express mixed feelings, she should probably not make any changes. Maybe employees really do hate their bosses but like their jobs!

Many surveys use filter or "skip" questions that direct a respondent to a specific set of questions depending on how the filter question is answered according to the respondent's answers. Common filter questions involve age, sex, home ownership, or product usage. A survey might involve different questions for a home owner than for someone who does not own a home. A data record may sometimes contain data on variables that the respondent should never have been asked. For example, if someone indicated that he or she did not own a home, yet responses for the home questions are provided, a problem is indicated. The editor may check other responses to make sure that the screening question was answered accurately. For instance, if the respondent left the question about home value unanswered, then the editor will be confident that the person truly does not own a home. In cases like this, the editor should adjust these answers by considering all answers to the irrelevant questions as "no response" or "not applicable."

EDITING TECHNOLOGY

Today, computer routines can check for inconsistencies automatically. Thus, for electronic questionnaires, rules can be entered which prevent inconsistent responses from ever being stored in the file used for data analysis. These rules should represent the conservative judgment of a trained data analyst. Some online survey services can assist in providing this service. In fact, the rules can even be pre-programmed to prevent many inconsistent responses. Thus, if a person who is twenty-five indicates that he or she has lived in the same house for forty-eight years, a pop-up window can appear requiring the respondent to go back and fix an earlier incorrect response. Electronic questionnaires can also prevent a respondent from being directed to the wrong set of questions based on a screening question response.

Editing for Completeness

In some cases the respondent may have answered only the second portion of a two-part question. The following question creates a situation in which an in-house editor may have to adjust answers for completeness:

Does your organization have more than one computer network server?

☐ *Yes*   ☐ *No*

If yes, how many? _____

If the respondent checked neither yes nor no but indicated three computer installations, the editor should change the first response to a "Yes" as long as other information doesn't indicate otherwise. Here again, a computerized questionnaire may either not allow a response to the "how many" question if someone checked yes or require the respondent to go back to the previous question once he or she tries to enter a number for the "how many" question.

Item nonresponse is the technical term for an unanswered question on an otherwise complete questionnaire. Missing data results from item nonresponse. Specific decision rules for handling this problem should be meticulously outlined in the editor's instructions. In many situations the decision rule is to do nothing with the missing data and simply leave the item blank. However, when the relationship between two questions is important, such as that between a question about job satisfaction and one's pay, the editor may be tempted to insert a **plug value**. The decision rule may be to plug in an average or neutral value in each instance of missing data. Several choices are available:

1. Leave the response blank. Because the question is so important, the risk of creating error by plugging a value is too great.
2. Plug in alternate choices for missing data ("yes" the first time, "no" the second time, "yes" the third time, and so forth).
3. Randomly select an answer. The editor may flip a coin with heads for "yes" and tails for "no."
4. The editor can **impute** a missing value based on the respondent's choices to other questions. Many different techniques exist for imputing data. Some involve complex statistical estimation approaches that use the available information to forecast a best guess for the missing response.[3]

This issue used to be a bigger deal when many statistical software programs required complete data for an analysis to take place. Other routines may require that an entire sampling unit be eliminated from analysis if even a single response is missing (list-wise deletion). Today, most statistical programs can accommodate an occasional missing response through the use of pair-wise deletion. Pair-wise deletion means the data that the respondent did provide can still be used in statistical analysis. As a result, pair-wise deletion produces a larger effective sample size than list-wise deletion.

Option one above is not a bad option unless a response for that particular respondent is crucial, which would rarely be the case. Option four could also be a good option if the response is important or if the effective sample size would be too small if all missing responses are deleted. As long

Item nonresponse
The technical term for an unanswered question on an otherwise complete questionnaire resulting in missing data.

Plug value
An answer that an editor "plugs in" to replace blanks or missing values so as to permit data analysis; choice of value is based on a predetermined decision rule.

Impute
To fill in a missing data point through the use of a statistical algorithm that provides a best guess for the missing response based on available information.

as the researcher is confident that the imputation methods are providing good guesses, this method may allow a response to this item to be salvaged.

The editor must decide whether an entire questionnaire is usable. When a questionnaire has too many missing answers, it may not be suitable for the planned data analysis. While no exact answer exists for this question, a questionnaire with a quarter of the responses or more missing is suspect. In such a situation the editor can record that a particular incomplete questionnaire has been dropped from the sample.

Editing Questions Answered Out of Order

Another task an editor may face is rearranging the answers given to open-ended questions such as may occur in a focus group interview. The respondent may have provided the answer to a subsequent question in his or her comments to an earlier open-ended question. Because the respondent already had clearly identified the answer, the interviewer may not have asked the subsequent question, wishing to avoid hearing "I already answered that earlier" and to maintain interview rapport. If the editor is asked to list answers to all questions in a specific order, the editor may move certain answers to the section related to the skipped question.

Facilitating the Coding Process

While all of the previously described editing activities will help coders, several editing procedures are designed specifically to simplify the coding process. For example, the editor should check written responses for any stray marks. Respondents are often asked to circle responses. Sometimes, a respondent may accidentally draw a circle that overlaps two numbers. For example, the circle may include both 3 and 4. The editor may be able to decide which is the most accurate response and indicate that on the form. Occasionally, a respondent may do this to indicate indecision between the 3 and the 4. Again, if the editor sees that the circle is carefully drawn to include both responses, he or she may indicate a 3.5 on the form. Such ambiguity is impossible with an electronic questionnaire.

▓ EDITING AND TABULATING "DON'T KNOW" ANSWERS

In many situations, respondents answer "don't know." On the surface, this response seems to indicate unfamiliarity with the subject matter at question. A *legitimate* "don't know" response is the same as "no opinion." However, there may be reasons for this response other than the legitimate "don't know." A *reluctant* "don't know" is given when the respondent simply does not want to answer a question. For example, asking an individual who is not the head of the household about family income may elicit a "don't know" answer meaning, "This is personal, and I really do not want to answer the question." If the individual does not understand the question, he or she may give a *confused* "I don't know" answer.

In some situations the editor can separate the legitimate "don't knows" ("no opinion") from the other "don't knows." The editor may try to identify the meaning of the "don't know" answer from other data provided on the questionnaire. For instance, the value of a home could be derived from knowledge of the zip code and the average value of homes within that area.

In structured questionnaires, the researcher has to decide whether to provide the respondent with a "don't know" or "no opinion" option. If neither of these is offered, the respondents may simply choose not to answer when they honestly don't know how or don't want to respond to a question. A computerized questionnaire can be set up to require a response to every question. Here, if a "no opinion" or "don't know" opinion is not made available, the result is a forced choice design. The advantages and disadvantages of forced choice questioning were discussed in Chapter 14.

Pitfalls of Editing

Subjectivity can enter into the editing process. Data editors should be intelligent, experienced, and *objective*. A *systematic procedure* for assessing the questionnaires should be developed by the research analyst so that the editor has clearly defined decision rules to follow. Any inferences such as imputing missing values should be done in a manner that limits the chance for the data editor's subjectivity to influence the response.

Pretesting Edit

Editing questionnaires during the pretest stage can prove very valuable. For example, if respondents' answers to open-ended questions were longer than anticipated, the fieldworkers, respondents, and analysts would benefit from a change to larger spaces for the answers. Answers will be more legible because the writers have enough space, answers will be more complete, and answers will be verbatim rather than summarized. Examining answers to pretests may identify poor instructions or inappropriate question wording on the questionnaire.

Coding ◀

Editing may be differentiated from **coding**, which is the assignment of numerical scores or classifying symbols to previously edited data. Careful editing makes the coding job easier. Codes are meant to represent the meaning in the data.

Assigning numerical symbols permits the transfer of data from questionnaires or interview forms to a computer. **Codes** often, but not always, are numerical symbols. However, they are more broadly defined as rules for interpreting, classifying, and recording data. In qualitative research, numbers are seldom used for codes.

Coding
The process of assigning a numerical score or other character symbol to previously edited data.

Codes
Rules for interpreting, classifying, and recording data in the coding process; also, the actual numerical or other character symbols assigned to raw data.

Coding Qualitative Responses

▓ UNSTRUCTURED QUALITATIVE RESPONSES (LONG INTERVIEWS)

Qualitative coding was introduced in Chapter 6. In qualitative research, the codes are usually words or phrases that represent themes. Exhibit 19.2 shows a hermeneutic unit in which a qualitative researcher is applying a code to a text describing in detail a respondent's reactions to several different

EXHIBIT 19.2
Coding Qualitative Data with Words

glasses of wine. The researcher is trying to understand in detail what defines the wine drinking experience. In this case, coding is facilitated by the use of qualitative software.

After reading through the text several times, and applying a word-counting routine, the researcher realizes that appearance, the nose (aroma), and guessing (trying to guess what the wine will be like or what type of wine is in the glass) are important themes. A code is assigned to these categories. Similarly, other codes are assigned as shown in the *code manager window*. The density column shows how often a code is applied. After considerable thought and questioning of the experience, the researcher builds a network, or grounded theory, that suggests how a wine may come to be associated with feelings of romance. This theory is shown in the network view. The reader interested in learning more about using software to help with qualitative coding should refer to the software sources provided in Chapter 6.

▦ STRUCTURED QUALITATIVE RESPONSES

Qualitative responses to structured questions such as "yes" or "no" can be stored in a data file with letters such as "Y" or "N." Alternatively, they can be represented with numbers, one each to represent the respective category. So, the number 1 can be used to represent "Yes" and 2 can be used to represent "No." Since this represents a nominal numbering system, the actual numbers used are arbitrary. Even though the codes are numeric, the variable is classificatory, simply separating the positive from the negative responses.

Dummy coding
Numeric "1" or "0" coding where each number represents an alternate response such as "female" or "male."

For reasons that should become increasingly apparent in later chapters, the research may consider adopting **dummy coding** for dichotomous responses like yes or no. Dummy coding assigns a 0 to one category and a 1 to the other. So, for yes/no responses, a 0 could be "no" and a 1 would be "yes." Similarly, a "1" could represent a female respondent and a "0" would be a male respondent. Dummy coding provides the researcher with more flexibility in how structured, qualitative responses are analyzed statistically.

Dummy coding can be used when more than two categories exist, but because a dummy variable can only represent two categories, multiple dummy variables are needed to represent a single qualitative response that can take on more than two categories. In fact, the rule is that if k is the number of categories for a qualitative variable, $k-1$ dummy variables are needed to represent the variable.

Dummy coding is a simple (dummy-proof) way to represent classification variables.

▦ DATA FILE TERMINOLOGY

Once structured, qualitative responses are coded, they are stored in an electronic data file. Here, both the qualitative responses and quantitative responses are likely stored for every respondent involved in a survey or interview. A terminology exists that helps describe this process and the file that results.

Some of the terminology seems strange these days. For instance, what does a "card" have to do with a simple computer file? Most of the terminology describing files goes back to the early days of computers. In those days, data and the computer programs that produced results were stored on actual computer cards. Hopefully,

EXHIBIT 19.3
Data Storage Terminology in SPSS

readers will no longer have to use physical cards to store data. Much easier and more economical ways exist.

Researchers organize coded data into cards, fields, records, and files. Cards are the collection of records that make up a file. A **field** is a collection of characters (a *character* is a single number, letter, or special symbol such as a question mark) that represents a single piece of data, usually a variable. Some variables may require a large field, particularly for text data; other variables may require a field of only one character. Text variables are represented by **string characters**, which is computer terminology for a series of alphabetic characters (non-numeric characters) that may form a word. String characters often contain long fields of eight or more characters. In contrast, a dummy variable is a numeric variable that needs only one character to form a field.

A **record** is a collection of related fields. A record was the way a single, complete computer card was represented. Researchers may use the term *record* to refer to one respondent's data. A **data file** is a collection of related records that make up a data set.

Exhibit 19.3 shows the SPSS variable view used to describe an SPSS file storing a data set. Most of the headings are straightforward, beginning with the name of the variable, the type of variable (numeric or string), the size, the label, and so forth. Notice toward the bottom that the variable *country* is a string variable. The values for this variable are words that correspond to the country from which the specific record originates (Unites States, United Kingdom, Canada, or Australia). All of the remaining variables are numeric.

The coder will sometimes like to associate a label with specific values of a numeric variable. Exhibit 19.3 shows the value labels dialog box that opens when the "Values" column is clicked. Notice that the variable *dummy* contains an entry in this column. **Value labels** are extremely useful and allow a word or short phrase to be associated with a numeric coding. In this case, the value label helps describe whether or not someone has an MBA degree. The labels are matched to the numeric code as follows:

- If dummy = 0, the value label is "no degree"
- If dummy = 1, the value label is "MBA"

The analysts will no doubt appreciate the coder's value labeling. Now, when frequencies or other statistical output is created for this variable, the value label will appear instead of simply a number. The advantage is that the analyst will not have to remember what coding was used. In other words, he or she won't have to remember that a "1" meant an MBA. Other statistical programs accommodate value labels in similarly easy fashions. With SAS, the coder could create a format statement as follows:

```
proc format;
value labels
    0 = 'none'
    1 = 'mba';
```

Field
A collection of characters that represents a single type of data—usually a variable.

String characters
Computer terminology to represent formatting a variable using a series of alphabetic characters (nonnumeric characters) that may form a word.

Record
A collection of related fields that represents the responses from one sampling unit.

Data file
The way a data set is stored electronically in spreadsheet-like form in which the rows represent sampling units and the columns represent variables.

Value labels
Unique labels assigned to each possible numeric code for a response.

```
data chap19;
input dummy perf sales;
format dummy labels.;
```

This sequence reads three variables: dummy, perf (performance), and sales. Just as in the SPSS example, the sequence assigns the label "none" to a value of 0 for dummy and a label of "mba" to a value of 1 for dummy.

The Data File

Data are generally stored in a matrix that resembles a common spreadsheet file. A data file stores the data from a research project and is typically represented in a rectangular arrangement (matrix) of data in rows and columns. Typically, each row represents a respondent's scores on each variable and each row represents a variable for which there is a value for every respondent. Exhibit 19.4 illustrates a data matrix corresponding to the variable view in Exhibit 19.3. In this case, data exist for forty respondents. No doubt, the data file appears to be a spreadsheet. A spreadsheet like Excel is an acceptable way to store a data file, and increasingly, statistical programs like SPSS, SAS, and others can work easily with an Excel spreadsheet.

Each column in Exhibit 19.4 represents a particular variable. The first two columns are ratio variables representing hours worked and labor costs, respectively. The next seven columns are variables taken from survey questions. Six of these are semantic differential scales that are scored from 1 to 10 based on the respondent's opinion. The next variable is a variable indicating likelihood of quitting, also using a ten-point scale. Finally, the last two variables, dummy and country, represent whether or not the respondent has an MBA and in which country he or she works, respectively.

Code Construction

There are two basic rules for code construction. First, the coding categories should be *exhaustive,* meaning that a coding category should exist for all possible responses. With a categorical variable such as sex, making categories exhaustive is not a problem. However, trouble may arise when the

EXHIBIT 19.4
A Data File Stored in SPSS

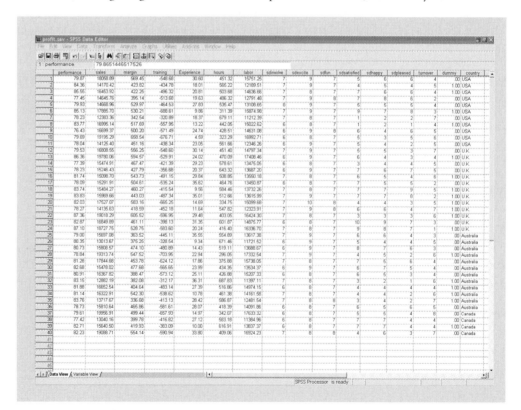

RESEARCHSNAPSHOT

I Ain't Missing You

Researchers used to sorely miss the data left blank by respondents. However, there are new alternatives to dealing with missing data. Most notably, various imputation methods exist that can provide educated guesses for missing data. Researchers have analyzed the accuracy of using these techniques. These studies have examined the effect of using statistical imputation methods when as much as 60 percent of some data is missing.

The results are interesting and encouraging. Researchers examining this issue begin with some known mean and standard deviation for a variable. They then remove the desired proportion to represent missing data (30 or 60 percent). Imputation methods are then used to try to recover the missing values. Various computer programs exist which can be used to perform these imputations. Results suggest that with 30 percent data, these simple routines can accurately recover the missing data parameters. In particular, the estimation techniques available

with the NORM program for missing data appear to be quite accurate. Similar techniques for imputation also exist within standard statistical packages such as SAS. Many of these techniques use an estimation method known as maximum likelihood to project missing values. With these kinds of techniques, researchers won't be missing missing data for long!

Sources: Vriens, Marco and Eric Melton (2002), "Multiple Imputation Can Improve Managing Missing Data," Marketing Research, 14 (Fall), 12–17. Ball, Dwayne (2003), "Review of Statistical Analysis with Missing Data, 2d," Journal of Marketing Research, (August), 374; Little, R.A. and D. B. Rubin (2002), Statistical Analysis with Missing Data, 2d, John Wiley & Sons, Hoboken, NJ.

response represents a small number of subjects or when responses might be categorized into a class not typically found. For example, when questioned about automobile ownership, an antique car collector might mention that he drives a Packard Clipper. This may present a problem if separate categories have been developed for all possible makes of cars. Solving this problem frequently requires inclusion of an "other" code category to ensure that the categories are all-inclusive. For example, household size might be coded 1, 2, 3, 4, and 5 or more. The "5 or more" category assures all subjects of a place in a category.

Missing data should also be represented with a code. In the "good old days" of computer cards, a numeric value such as 9 or 99 was used to represent missing data. Today, most software will understand that either a period or a blank response represents missing data.

Second, the coding categories should be *mutually exclusive* and *independent*. This means that there should be no overlap among the categories to ensure that a subject or response can be placed in only one category.

Precoding Fixed-Alternative Questions

When a questionnaire is highly structured, the categories may be precoded before the data are collected. Exhibit 19.5 presents a questionnaire for which the precoded response categories were determined before the start of data collection. The codes in the data file will correspond to the small numbers beside each choice option. In most instances, the codes will not actually appear on the questionnaire.

The questionnaire in Exhibit 19.5 shows several demographic questions classifying individuals' scores. Question 29 has three possible answers, and they are precoded 1, 2, 3. Question 30 asks a person to respond "yes" (1) or "no" (2) to the question "Are you the male or female head of the household?" Once again, technology is making things easier and much of this type of coding is automated. For users of web-based survey services, all that one need do is submit a questionnaire and in return he or she will receive a coded data file in the software of his or her choice.

Telephone interviews are still widely used. The partial questionnaire in Exhibit 19.6 shows a precoded format for a telephone interview. In this situation the interviewer circles the coded numerical score as the answer to the question.

EXHIBIT 19.5 Precoding Fixed-Alternative Responses

29. Do you—or does anyone else in your immediate household—belong to a labor union?

¹☐ <u>Yes</u>, I personally belong to a labor union.
²☐ <u>Yes</u>, another member of my household belongs to a labor union.
³☐ <u>No</u>, no one in my household belongs to a labor union.

30. Are you the male or female head of the household—that is, <u>the person whose income is the chief source of support of the household?</u>

¹☐ Yes   ²☐ No

31. Would you please check the appropriate combined yearly income *(before income taxes and any other payroll deductions)* from <u>all sources of all those</u> in your immediate household? *(Please include income from salaries, investments, dividends, rents, royalties, bonuses, commissions, etc.)* <u>Please remember that your individual answers will not be divulged.</u>

¹☐ Less than $4,000	⁷☐ $8,000–$8,999	¹³☐ $25,000–$29,999
²☐ $4,000–$4,999	⁸☐ $9,000–$9,999	¹⁴☐ $30,000–$39,999
³☐ $5,000–$5,999	⁹☐ $10,000–$12,499	¹⁵☐ $40,000–$49,999
⁴☐ $6,000–$6,999	¹⁰☐ $12,500–$14,999	¹⁶☐ $50,000–$74,999
⁵☐ $7,000–$7,499	¹¹☐ $15,000–$19,999	¹⁷☐ $75,000–$99,999
⁶☐ $7,500–$7,999	¹²☐ $20,000–$24,999	¹⁸☐ $100,000 or more

32 a. Do you personally own corporate stocks?   ¹☐ Yes   ²☐ No

   b. Do you own stocks in the corporation for which you work?
   Do you own them in a corporation for which you do <u>not</u> work?
   (Please check as many as apply.)

   Own <u>STOCK</u> in:

   ¹☐ Company for which I work   ²☐ Other company

   <u>THANK YOU VERY MUCH FOR YOUR COOPERATION</u>

   If you would like to make any comments on any of the subjects covered in this study, please use the space below:

   _____

   _____

Precoding can be used if the researcher knows what answer categories exist before data collection occurs. Once the questionnaire has been designed and the structured (or closed-form) answers identified, coding then becomes routine. In some cases, predetermined responses are based on standardized classification schemes. A coding framework that standardizes occupation follows:

What is your occupation? (PROBE: What kind of work is that?)

01	Professional, technical, and kindred workers	08	Service workers
		09	Laborers, except farm and mine
02	Farmers	10	Retired, widow, widower
03	Managers, officials, and proprietors	11	Student
		12	Unemployed, on relief, laid off
04	Clerical	13	Homemaker
05	Sales workers	14	Other (specify)
06	Craftsmen, foremen, and kindred workers	99	No occupation given
07	Operatives and kindred workers		

Computer-assisted telephone interviewing (CATI) requires precoding. Changing the coding framework after the interviewing process has begun is extremely difficult because it requires changes in the computer programs. In any event, coding closed-ended structured responses is a straightforward process of entering the code into the data file.

More on Coding Open-Ended Questions

Surveys that are largely structured will sometimes contain some semi-structured open-ended questions. These questions may be exploratory or they may be potential follow-ups to structured

EXHIBIT 19.6 **Precoded Format for Telephone Interview**

Study #45641   For office use only
Travel (Telephone Screening)   Respondent #_____
City:
Chicago
Gary
Ft. Wayne
Bloomington

Hello, I'm _____ from_____, a national survey research company. We are conducting a study and would like to ask you a few questions.

A. Before we begin, do you—or any member of your family—work for ...
   1 A travel agency   2 An advertising agency   3 A marketing research company
  (If "yes" to any of the above, terminate and tally on contact sheet)

B. By the way, have you been interviewed as part of a survey research study within the past month?
   1 Yes—(Terminate and tally on contact sheet)
   2 No—(Continue)

  1. Have you yourself made any trips of over 100 miles within the continental 48 states in the past 3 months?
    1 Yes
    2 No—(Skip to Question 10)

  2. Was the trip for business reasons (paid for by your firm), vacation, or personal reasons?

	Last Trip	Second Last Trip	Other Trips
Business	1	1	1
Vacation	2	2	2
Personal (excluding a vacation)	3	3	3

questions. The purpose of coding such questions is to reduce the large number of individual responses to a few general categories of answers that can be assigned numerical codes.

Similar answers should be placed in a general category and assigned the same code much as the codes are assigned in the qualitative sample involving wine consumption above. Except in this case, a small amount of data may be obtained from a large number of respondents, whereas in the hermeneutic unit above, a large amount of data is obtained from one or a small number of respondents. For example, a consumer survey about frozen food also asked why a new microwaveable product would not be purchased:

- We don't buy frozen food very often.
- I like to prepare fresh food.
- Frozen foods are not as tasty as fresh foods.
- I don't like that freezer taste.

All of these answers could be categorized under "dislike frozen foods" and assigned the code 1. Code construction in these situations reflects the judgment of the researcher.

A major objective in the code-building process is to accurately transfer the meanings from written responses to numeric codes. Experienced researchers recognize that the key idea in this process is that code building is based on thoughts, not just words. The end result of code building should be a list, in an abbreviated and orderly form, of all comments and thoughts given in answers to the questions.

Developing an appropriate code from the respondent's exact comments is somewhat of an art. Researchers generally perform a test tabulation to identify verbatim responses from approximately 20 percent of the completed questionnaires and then establish coding categories reflecting the judgment of the person constructing the codes. **Test tabulation** is the tallying of a small sample of the total number of replies to a particular question. The purpose is to preliminarily identify the stability and distribution of answers that will determine a coding scheme. Exhibit 19.7 illustrates open-ended responses and preliminary open-ended codes generated for the question "Why does the chili you just tasted taste closer to homemade?" During the coding procedure, the respondent's opinions are

Test tabulation
Tallying of a small sample of the total number of replies to a particular question in order to construct coding categories.

EXHIBIT 19.7 **Coding Open-Ended Questions about Chili**

You don't get that much meat in a can.	1.	Don't get that much meat in a can
The beans are cooked just right.	2.	Beans are cooked just right
It just (doesn't look) like any canned chili I've had. I can see spices;		
I've never seen it in any canned chili.	3.	I can see spices
It is not too spicy,	4.	Not too spicy
but it is tasty—savory.	5.	It is tasty
It's not (loaded with beans)—just enough beans.	6.	Has just enough beans
It's moist—not too chewy.	7.	Moist
	8.	Not too chewy
Tastes (fresh).	9.	Fresh taste
The canned stuff is too (soft). Too overcooked usually.	10.	Canned is usually overcooked
It doesn't have a lot of filler and not too many beans.	11.	Not a lot of filler
	12.	Not too many beans
It's not too spicy. It's not too hot, it's mild.	13.	Not too hot, it's mild
Has enough spice to make it tastier.	14.	Has enough spice
It seems to have a pretty good gravy. Some are watery.	15.	Gravy not watery

Walker Research, "Coding Open Ends Based on Thoughts," *The Marketing Researcher*, December 1979, pp.1–3.

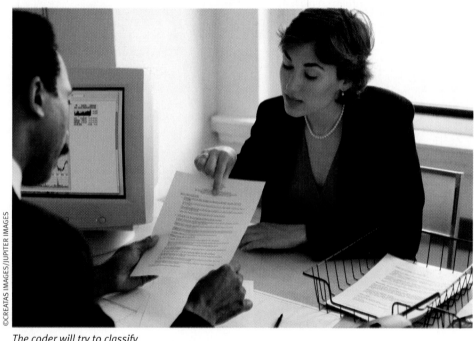

©CREATAS IMAGES/JUPITER IMAGES

The coder will try to classify all of the comments from the interviewer in a code that facilitates analysis.

divided into mutually exclusive thought patterns. These separate divisions may consist of a single word, a phrase, or a number of phrases, but in each case represent only one thought. Each separate thought is coded once. When a thought is composed of more than one word or phrase, only the most specific word or phrase is coded.

After tabulating the basic responses, the researcher must determine how many answer categories will be acceptable. This will be influenced by the purpose of the study and the limitations of the computer program or plan for data entry. For example, if only one single-digit field is assigned to a particular survey question, the number of possible categories is limited. If an "other" or "miscellaneous" code category appears along with a "don't know/no answer" category, the code construction will be further limited.

Devising the Coding Scheme

A coding scheme should not be too elaborate. The coder's task is only to summarize the data. Exhibit 19.8 shows a test tabulation of airport visitors' responses to a question that asked for comments about the Honolulu Airport. After the first pass at devising the coding scheme, the researcher must decide whether to revise it and whether the codes are appropriate for answering management's questions. A preliminary scheme with too many categories can always be collapsed or reduced later in the analysis. If initial coding is too abstract and only a few categories are established, revising the codes to more concrete statements will be difficult unless the raw data were recorded.

In the Honolulu Airport example, the preliminary tabulation contained too many codes, but it could be reduced to a smaller number of categories. For example, the heading "Friendly/ Attractive Personnel" could include the responses "Friendly staff/people," "Polite VIP/friendly/ helpful," and "Cute VIP." Experienced coders group answers under generalized headings that are pertinent to the research question. Individual coders should give the same code to similar

	Number
Prices high: restaurant/coffee shop/snack bar	90
Dirty—filthy—smelly restrooms/airport	65
Very good/good/excellent/great	59
Need air-conditioning	52
Nice/beautiful	45
Gift shops expensive	32
Too warm/too hot	31
Friendly staff/people	25
Airport is awful/bad	23
Long walk between terminal/gates	21
Clean airport	17
Employees rude/unfriendly/poor attitude	16
More signs/maps in lobby/streets	16
Like it	15
Love gardens	11
Need video games/arcade	10
More change machines/different locations	8
More padded benches/comfortable waiting area	8
More security personnel including HPD	8
Replace shuttle with moving walkways	8
Complaint: flight delay	7
Cool place	7
Crowded	7
Provide free carts for carry-on bags	7
Baggage storage inconvenient/need in different locations	6
Floor plan confusing	6
Mailbox locations not clear/more needed	6
More restaurants and coffee shops/more variety	6
Need a place to nap	6
Polite VIP/friendly/helpful	6
Poor help in gift shops/rude/unfriendly	6
Slow baggage delivery/service	6
Very efficient/organized	6
Excellent food	5
Install chilled water drinking fountains	5
Love Hawaii	5
More TV sets	5
Noisy	5
People at sundries/camera rude	5
Shuttle drivers rude	5
Something to do for passengers with long waits	5
Airport too spread out	4
Better information for departing/arriving flights	4
Better parking for employees	4
Better shuttle service needed	4
Cute VIP	4

EXHIBIT 19.8

Open-Ended Responses to a Survey about the Honolulu Airport

responses. The categories should be sufficiently unambiguous that coders will not classify items in different ways.

Coding open-ended questions is a very complex issue. Certainly, this task cannot be mastered simply from reading this chapter. However, the reader should have a feel for the art of coding responses into similar categories. With practice, and by using multiple coders so that consistency can be examined, one can become skilled at this task.

RESEARCHSNAPSHOT

Verbastat

Traditional coding of open-ended responses is an expensive, labor-intensive task. For surveys with several open-ended questions, coding can cause the overall cost of research to skyrocket. Verbastat by SPSS provides a fast, reliable way to automate as much of the process as possible—without compromising quality.

Instead of waiting for all questionnaires to come back from the field, researchers can import data while interviewing is in progress. Verbastat leads the coder through the process screen by screen for fast, efficient, and reliable coding. Researchers can reuse code frames to further automate coding—enabling the completion of more surveys in less time, for faster turnaround and lower costs.

Verbastat is not a handwriting recognition scanner or content analysis package; it does not try to decipher the semantic content of sentences and automatically assign values. Rather, it greatly enhances the classification decision-making process by showing the coder which responses are likely to be classified together. The coder retains control over the process, but Verbastat helps by providing counts, key word lists, and a user-friendly interface. All decisions are easily reversible, and the entire process is reduced to just three broad steps: data entry, classification, and generation of coded data files that can be used with virtually any analysis package.

Source: Adapted with permission form http://www.spss.com/training/pub_desc.cfm?courseID=100000385, downloaded June 26, 2001.

©ROYALTY-FREE/CORBIS

Code Book

Code book
A book that identifies each variable in a study and gives the variable's description, code name, and position in the data matrix.

A **code book** gives each variable in the study and its location in the data matrix. In essence, the code book provides a quick summary that is particularly useful when a data file becomes very large. Exhibit 19.9 illustrates a portion of a code book from the telephone interview illustrated in Exhibit 19.6. Notice that the first few fields record the study number, city, and other information used for identification purposes. Researchers commonly identify individual respondents by giving each an identification number or questionnaire number. When each interview is identified with a number entered into each computer record, errors discovered in the tabulation process can be checked on the questionnaire to verify the answer.

Editing and Coding Combined

Frequently the person coding the questionnaire performs certain editing functions, such as translating an occupational title provided by the respondent into a code for socioeconomic status. A question that asks for a description of the job or business often is used to ensure that there will be no problem in classifying the responses. For example, respondents who indicate "salesperson" as their occupation might write their job description as "selling shoes in a shoestore" or "selling IBM supercomputers to the defense department." Generally, coders are instructed to perform this type of editing function, seeking the help of a tabulation supervisor if questions arise.

Computerized Survey Data Processing

In most studies with large sample sizes, a computer is used for data processing. The process of transferring data from a research project, such as answers to a survey questionnaire, to computers is referred to as **data entry**. Several alternative means exist for entering data into a computer. In studies involving highly structured paper and pencil questionnaires, an **optical scanning system** may be used to read material directly into the computer's memory from *mark-sensed questionnaires*. The form may look similar to the type a student uses to take a multiple-choice test.

Data entry
The activity of transferring data from a research project to computers.

Optical scanning system
A data processing input device that reads material directly from mark-sensed questionnaires.

In a research study using computer-assisted telephone interviewing or a self-administered Internet questionnaire, responses are automatically stored and tabulated as they are collected. Direct data capture substantially reduces clerical errors that occur during the editing and coding

Question Number	Field or Column Number	Description and Meaning of Code Values
		Study #45641
		January 20__
		***N* = 743**
—	1–5	Study number (45641)
—	6	City
		1. Chicago
		2. Gary
		3. Ft. Wayne
		4. Bloomington
—	7–9	Interview number (3 digits on upper left-hand corner of questionnaire)
A	Not entered	Family, work for
		1. Travel agency
		2. Advertising agency
		3. Marketing research company
B	Not entered	Interviewed past month
		1. Yes
		2. No
1.	10	Traveled in past 3 months
		1. Yes
		2. No
2.	11	Purpose last trip
		1. Business
		2. Vacation
		3. Personal
	12	Purpose second last trip
		1. Business
		2. Vacation
		3. Personal
	13	Purpose other trips
		1. Business
		2. Vacation
		3. Personal

EXHIBIT 19.9
Portion of a Code Book from a Travel Study

process. If researchers have security concerns, the data collected in an Internet survey should be encrypted and protected behind a firewall.

When data are not optically scanned or directly entered into the computer the moment they are collected, data processing begins with keyboarding. A data entry process transfers coded data from the questionnaires or coding sheets onto a hard drive or floppy disk. As in every stage of the research process, there is some concern about whether the data entry job has been done correctly. Data entry workers, like anyone else, may make errors. To ensure 100 percent accuracy in transferring the codes, the job should be *verified* by a second data entry worker. If an error has been made, the verifier corrects the data entry. This process of verifying the data is never performed by the same person who entered the original data. A person who misread the coded questionnaire during the keyboarding operation might make the same mistake during the verifying process, and the mistake might go undetected.

Error Checking

The final stage in the coding process is error checking and verification, or *data cleaning,* to ensure that all codes are legitimate. For example, computer software can examine the entered data and identify coded values that lie outside the range of acceptable answers. For example, if "sex" is coded 1 for "male" and 2 for "female" and a 3 code is found, a mistake obviously has occurred and an adjustment must be made.

Summary

1. Know when a response is really an error and should be edited. Data editing is necessary before coding and storing the data file. The data editor must sometimes alter a respondent's answer. Often, this situation arises because of inconsistent responses; that is, responses to different questions that contradict each other. The editor should be cautious in altering a respondent's answer. Only when a certain response is obviously wrong and the true response is easily determined should the coder substitute a new value for the original response. Ideally, multiple pieces of evidence would suggest the original response as inaccurate and also suggest the accurate response before the respondent takes such a step. Missing data should generally be left as missing although imputation methods exist to provide an educated guess for missing values. These imputation methods can be used when the sample size is small and the researcher needs to retain as many responses as possible.

2. Appreciate coding of pure qualitative research. Qualitative research such as typified by depth interviews, conversations, or other responses are coded by identifying the themes underlying some interview. The codes become a key component of a hermeneutic unit that ultimately can be linked to one another to form a grounded theory. The frequency with which some thought is expressed helps to identify appropriate coding for unstructured qualitative data.

3. Understand the way data are represented in a data file. A survey provides an overview of respondents based on their answers to questions. These answers are edited, coded, and then stored in a data file. The data file is structured as a data matrix in which the rows represent respondents and the columns represent variables. Thus, a survey in which 200 respondents are asked 50 structured questions would result in a data matrix consisting of 200 rows and 50 columns.

4. Understand the coding of structured responses including a dummy variable approach. Quantitative structured responses are generally coded simply by marking the number corresponding to the choice selected by the respondent. Qualitative structured responses must also be coded. Dichotomous variables lend themselves well to dummy coding. With dummy coding, the two possible choices to a question are coded with a "1" for one response and a "0" for the other. Short-answer or list questions are coded by assigning a number to all responses that seem to suggest the same theme even if different words are used.

5. Appreciate the ways that technological advances have simplified the coding process. Throughout the chapter, technological advances in data collection were mentioned. These advances have automated a great deal of data coding and reduced the chances of respondent error. For instance, some inconsistent responses can be automatically screened and the respondent can be prompted to go back and correct a response that seems inconsistent. Also, if a respondent fails to answer a question, a pop-up window can take that respondent back to the question and force him or her to respond in order to continue through the rest of the questionnaire.

Key Terms and Concepts

Raw data	Plug value	Record
Nonrespondent error	Impute	Data file
Data integrity	Coding	Value labels
Editing	Codes	Test tabulation
Field editing	Dummy coding	Code book
In-house editing	Field	Data entry
Item nonresponse	String characters	Optical scanning system

Questions for Review and Critical Thinking

1. What is the purpose of editing? Provide some examples of questions that might need editing.
2. When should the raw data from a respondent be altered by a data editor?
3. Ms. Aimee, the data editor from the opening vignette, is going through responses. After reviewing the first eight responses each indicating the respondent has very negative feelings about his or her supervisors, she comes across a response that suggests the employee believes his or her boss is the best possible boss in the world. Ms. Aimee is tempted to dismiss this as a potentially misleading response. What evidence might she look to in making the decision to alter or delete this response?

4. How is data coding different from data editing?

5. A 25-year-old respondent indicates that she owns her own house in Springfield, Illinois, and it is valued at $990 million. Later in the interview, she indicates that she didn't finish high school and that she drives a 1993 Buick Century. Should the editor consider altering any of these responses? If so, how?

6. What role might a word counter play in coding qualitative research results?

7. A survey respondent from Florida has been asked to respond as to whether or not he or she owns a boat, and if so, whether he or she stores the boat at a marina. Over two hundred respondents are included in this sample. What suggestions do you have for coding the information provided?

8. How would a dummy variable be used to represent whether or not a respondent in a restaurant ordered dessert after their meal?

9. List at least three ways in which recent technological advances (within the last fifteen years) have changed the way data are coded?

10. **ETHICS** A large retail company implements an employee survey that ostensibly is aimed at customer satisfaction. The survey includes a yes or no question that asks whether or not the employee has ever stolen something from the workplace. How could this data be coded? What steps could be attempted to try and ensure that the employee's response is honest? Do you believe it is fair to ask this question? Should the employee take action against employees who have indicated that they have stolen something?

11. A researcher asks, "What do you remember about advertising for Gillette Turbo razors?" A box with enough room for 100 words is provided in which the respondent can answer the question. The survey involves responses from 250 consumers. How should the code book for this question be structured? What problems might it present?

12. **'NET** Use http://www.naicscode.com to help with this response. What is the NAICS code for golf (country) clubs? What is the NAICS code for health clubs? How can these codes be useful in creating data files?

13. **'NET** Explore the advantages of computerized software such as Atlas-Ti. The website is at http://www.atlasti.com. How do you think it might assist in coding something like a depth interview or a collage created by a respondent?

Research Activity

1. Design a short questionnaire with fewer than five fixed-alternative questions to measure student satisfaction with your college bookstore. Interview five classmates and then arrange the database into a data matrix.

2. **'NET** The web page of the Research Triangle Institute (http://www.rti.org) describes its research tools and methods in some detail. Click on *tools and methods* and explore the surveys and survey tools described there. How might these methods assist in coding?

Case 19.1 U.S. Department of the Interior Heritage Conservation and Recreation Service

Some years ago the U.S. Department of the Interior conducted a telephone survey to help plan for future outdoor recreation. A nine-page questionnaire concerning participation in outdoor recreational activities and satisfaction with local facilities was administered by the Opinion Research Corporation of Princeton, New Jersey, to 4,029 respondents. The last two pages of the questionnaire appear in Case Exhibit 19.1–1.

Assume the data will be entered into a data file in which each data entry should include the following information:
- Respondent number
- State code (all fifty states)

Question

Design the coding for this portion of the questionnaire. Assume that the data from previous pages of the questionnaire will follow these data.

CASE EXHIBIT 19.1-1 **Sample Page from Questionnaire**

The following questions are for background purposes.

32. Do you live in an . . .
☐ Urban location
☐ Suburban location
☐ Rural location

33. Counting yourself, how many members of your family live here? (If "1" on Q.33, go to Q.35) ____

34. How many family members are . . .
Over 65 years _____
40 to 65 years _____
21 to 39 years _____
12 to 20 years _____
5 to 11 years _____
Under 5 years _____

35. What is your age? (Years) _____

36. In school, what is the highest grade (or year) you have completed? (Circle response)

Elementary school	01	02	03	04	05	06
Junior high school	07	08				
High school	09	10	11	12		
College	13	14	15	16		
Graduate school	17	18	19	20	21	

(continued)

37. What is your occupation? What kind of work is that?
    □ Professional, technical, and kindred workers
    □ Farmers
    □ Managers, officials, and proprietors
    □ Clerical and kindred workers
    □ Sales workers
    □ Craftspersons, forepersons, and kindred workers
    □ Operatives and kindred workers
    □ Service workers
    □ Laborers, except farm and mine

    □ Retired, widow, widower
    □ Student
    □ Unemployed, on relief, laid off → Go to Q.43
    □ Housewife

    □ Other (specify) _____

38. How many hours a week do you work at your place of employment? _____ (hours)

39. How many days of vacation do you get in a year?
    _____ (days)

40. Please tell me which of the following income categories most closely describe the total family income for the year before taxes, including wages and all other income. Is it . . .

    □ Under $12,000
    □ $12,000–$20,000
    □ $20,001–$30,000
    □ $30,001–$50,000
    □ $50,001–$100,000
    □ Over $100,001

41. Sex of respondent . . .
    □ Male
    □ Female

42. What is the zip code at your place of employment?

This concludes the interview; thank you very much for your cooperation and time.

Case 19.2 Shampoo 9-10

A shampoo, code named "9–10" was given to women for trial use.[4] The respondents were asked what they liked and disliked about the product. Some sample codes are given in Case Exhibits 19.2–1 and 19.2–2.

There were two separate sets of codes: the codes in Case Exhibit 19.2–1 were for coding the respondents' likes, and the codes in Case Exhibit 19.2–2 were for coding their dislikes. The headings identify fields in the data matrix and the different attributes of shampoo. The specific codes are listed under each attribute. The coding instructions were first to look for the correct heading, and then to locate the correct comment under that heading and use that number as the code.

For example, if, in response to a "like" question, a respondent had said, "The shampoo was gentle and mild," a coder would look in field 10, the "gentleness" field, and find the comment "Gentle/mild/not harsh"; then the coder would write "11" next to the comment. If, under "dislikes," someone had said, "I would rather have a shampoo with a crème rinse," the coder would look in field 16 for comparison to other shampoos and write "74" ("Prefer one with a crème rinse") beside that response.

The sample questionnaires appear in Case Exhibit 19.2–3.

Questions

1. Code each of the three questionnaires.
2. Evaluate this coding scheme.

CASE EXHIBIT 19.2-1 **Sample Codes for "Like" Questions**

Test No. <u>Shampoo</u>
Question: Likes

Field 10 Gentleness	**Field 11 Result on Hair**
11 Gentle/mild/not harsh	21 Good for hair/helps hair
12 Wouldn't strip hair of natural oils	22 Leaves hair manageable/no tangles/no need for crème rinse
13 Doesn't cause/helps flyaway hair	23 Gives hair body
14 Wouldn't dry out hair	24 Mends split ends
15 Wouldn't make skin/scalp break out	25 Leaves hair not flyaway
16 Organic/natural	26 Leaves hair silky/smooth
17	27 Leaves hair soft
18	28 Leaves hair shiny
19	29 Hair looks/feels/good/clean
20	30
1–	2–
1+ Other gentleness	2+ Other results on hair

(*continued*)

CASE EXHIBIT 19.2-1 Sample Codes for "Like" Questions (*continued*)

Field 12 Cleaning

31	Leaves no oil/keeps hair dry
32	It cleans well
33	Lifts out oil/dirt/artificial conditioners
34	Don't have to scrub as much
35	No need to wash as often/keeps hair cleaner longer
36	Doesn't leave a residue on scalp
37	Good lather
38	Good for oily hair
39	
40	
3−	
3+	Other cleaning

Field 13 Miscellaneous

41	Cheaper/economical/good price
42	Smells good/nice/clean
43	Hairdresser recommended
44	Comes in different formulas
45	Concentrated/use only a small amount
46	Good for whole family (unspecified)
47	
48	
49	
50	
4−	Other miscellaneous
4+	Don't know/nothing

CASE EXHIBIT 19.2-2 Sample Codes for "Dislike" Questions

Test No. Shampoo
Question: Dislikes

Field 14 Harshness

51	Too strong
52	Strips hair/takes too much oil out
53	Dries hair out
54	Skin reacts badly to it
55	
56	
57	
58	
59	
60	
5−	
5+	Other harshness

Field 15 Cleaning

61	Doesn't clean well
62	Leaves a residue on scalp
63	Poor lather
64	Not good for oily hair
65	
66	
67	
68	
69	
70	
6−	
6+	Other cleaning

Field 16 Comparison to Others

71	Prefer herbal/organic shampoo
72	Prefer medicated/dandruff shampoo
73	Same as other shampoos—doesn't work any differently
74	Prefer one with a crème rinse
75	Prefer another brand (unspecified)
76	
77	
78	
79	
80	
7−	
7+	Other comparison to others

Field 17 Miscellaneous

81	Don't like the name
82	Too expensive
83	Not economical for long hair
84	Use what hairdresser recommends
85	
86	
87	
88	
89	
90	
8−	Other miscellaneous
8+	Don't know what/disliked/nothing

1. What, if anything, did you particularly like about this shampoo?

    My hairdresser recommends it, so it must be good for your hair. It smells good too.

2. What, if anything, did you particularly dislike about this shampoo?

    It's too expensive. It doesn't have a cream rinse, so you still have to buy that too. It really doesn't work any better than other shampoos for the amount of money you pay for it.

---

1. What, if anything, did you particularly like about this shampoo?

    There are different kinds for different types of hair. I use the one for dry hair. It doesn't dry out my hair. It leaves it soft & shiny. It works so well I only have to use a little bit for each shampoo.

2. What, if anything, did you particularly dislike about this shampoo?

    Nothing. I liked it.

---

1. What, if anything, did you particularly like about this shampoo?

    I have limp, oily hair and have to wash it real often. With this shampoo I found it stayed cleaner longer, so I don't have to shampoo as often and my hair has more body.

2. What, if anything, did you particularly dislike about this shampoo?

    I like the shampoo but I don't think the name is very appealing.

CHAPTER 20
BASIC DATA ANALYSIS: DESCRIPTIVE STATISTICS

After studying this chapter, you should be able to
1. Know what descriptive statistics are and why they are used
2. Create and interpret simple tabulation and cross-tabulation tables
3. Understand how cross-tabulations can reveal relationships
4. Perform basic data transformations
5. List different computer software products designed for descriptive statistical analysis

Chapter Vignette: Choose Your "Poison"

Most Americans enjoy an adult beverage occasionally. But not all Americans like the same drink. Many decision makers are interested in what Americans like to drink. Retailers need to have the correct product mix for their particular customers if profits are to be increased and customers made more satisfied. Restaurants need to know what their customers like to have with the types of food they serve. Policy makers need to know what types of restrictions should be placed on what types of products to prevent underage drinking and alcohol abuse. Researchers could apply sophisticated statistics to address questions related to Americans' drinking preferences, but a lot can be learned from just counting what people are buying.

A grocery store built in 1975 in Chicago allocates 15 percent of their floor space to adult beverage products. Out of this 15 percent, 60 percent is allocated to beer, 25 percent to spirits, and 15 percent to wine. Since the products are not merchandised the same way (different types of shelving, aisles, and racking are needed), adjusting the floor space to change these percentages is not an easy task. Over the three decade history of the store, the customer base has changed. Originally, stay-at-home moms buying groceries for the family best characterized the customer base. During the 1990s, empty-nesters, including retirees with high disposable incomes, characterized the customer base. More recently, younger singles just starting careers have moved into the nearby neighborhoods. Should the store reconsider its adult beverage merchandising?

©STEPHEN OLIVER/DORLING KINDERSLEY/GETTY IMAGES

In 1992, American consumers showed a heavy preference toward beer. Among American adults who drank adult beverages,[1]

- 47 percent drank beer
- 21 percent drank spirits
- 27 percent drank wine

By 2005, Americans had changed their drinking preferences. Now,

- 36 percent drink beer
- 21 percent drink spirits
- 39 percent drink wine

A couple of other facts have become clear. A count of the preferred beverages among American adult consumers twenty-nine and younger shows the following preferences:[2]

- 48 percent drink beer
- 32 percent drink liquor
- 17 percent drink wine

Across America, grocers account for 35 percent of all beer sales, but convenience stores, where younger consumers tend to shop, account for 45 percent.[3] If the grocery store is converting more to a convenience store, maybe a continued emphasis on beer is wise. However, wine consumers are more *attractive* from several perspectives. Wine now ranks among the top ten food categories in America, based on grocery store dollar sales volume. Forty-five percent of all wine is sold in grocery stores. What we find is that the consumer who buys wine is also more likely to buy products like prime or choice beef and imported cheeses, instead of lower quality and lower priced meat and cheese products. As a result, the average $13.44 spent on wine in a grocery store (as opposed to $11.94 on beer) is only part of the story in explaining why wine customers may be *grape* customers![4]

What should the grocer emphasize in marketing adult beverages? Perhaps the research based on counting can address this decision.

The Nature of Descriptive Analysis

Descriptive analysis
The elementary transformation of raw data in a way that describes the basic characteristics such as central tendency, distribution, and variability.

Perhaps the most basic statistical analysis is descriptive analysis. **Descriptive analysis** is the elementary transformation of data in a way that describes the basic characteristics such as central tendency, distribution, and variability. A researcher takes responses from 1,000 American consumers and tabulates their favorite soft drink brand and the price they expect to pay for a six-pack of that product. The mode for favorite soft drink and the average price across all 1,000 consumers would be descriptive statistics that describe central tendency in two different ways. Averages, medians, modes, variance, range, and standard deviation typify widely applied descriptive statistics.

Descriptive statistics can summarize responses from large numbers of respondents in a few simple statistics. When a sample is used, the sample descriptive statistics are used to make inferences about characteristics of the entire population of interest. Descriptive statistics are simple but powerful. The researcher enters the area of univariate statistical analysis when this is the case. Chapter 21 will focus on this extension of basic descriptive statistics. Because they are so simple, descriptive statistics are used very widely.

Chapter 13 indicated that the level of scale measurement helps the researcher choose the most appropriate form of statistical analysis. Exhibit 20.1 shows how the level of scale measurement influences the choice of descriptive statistics. Remember that all statistics appropriate for lower-order scales (nominal is the lowest) are suitable for higher-order scales (ratio is the highest).

Consider the following data. Sample consumers were asked where they most often purchased beer. The result is a nominal variable which can be described with a frequency distribution (see the bar chart in Exhibit 20.1). Ten percent indicated they most often purchased beer in a drug store, 45 percent indicated a convenience store, 35 percent indicated a grocery store, and 7 percent indicated a specialty store. Three percent listed "other" (not shown in the bar chart). The mode is convenience store since more respondents chose this than any other category. A similar distribution may have been obtained if the chart plotted the number of respondents ranking each store as their favorite type of place to purchase beer.

The bottom part of Exhibit 20.1 displays example descriptive statistics for interval and ratio variables. In this case, the chart displays results of a question asking respondents how much they typically spend on a bottle of wine purchased in a store. The mean and standard deviation are displayed beside the chart as 11.7 and 4.5, respectively. Additionally, a frequency distribution is shown with a histogram. A **histogram** is graphical way of showing a frequency distribution in which the height of a bar corresponds to the frequency of a category. Histograms are useful for any type of data, but with continuous variables (interval or ratio) the histogram is useful for providing a quick assessment of the distribution of the data. A normal distribution line is superimposed over the histogram providing an easy comparison to see if the data are skewed or multi-modal.

Histogram
A graphical way of showing a frequency distribution in which the height of a bar corresponds to the observed frequency of the category.

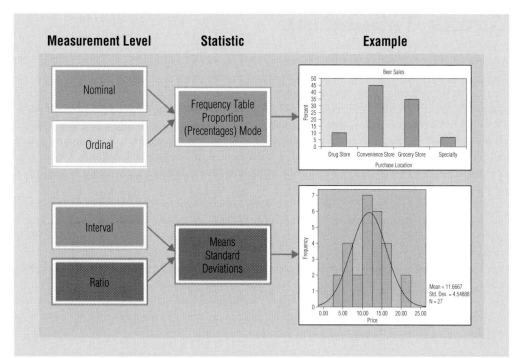

Tabulation

Tabulation refers to the orderly arrangement of data in a table or other summary format. When this tabulation process is done by hand the term *tallying* is used. Counting the different ways respondents answered a question and arranging them in a simple tabular form yields a **frequency table**. The actual number of responses to each category is a variable's frequency distribution. A simple tabulation of this type is sometimes called a *marginal tabulation*.

Simple tabulation tells the researcher how frequently each response occurs. This starting point for analysis requires the researcher to count responses or observations for each category or code assigned to a variable. A frequency table showing where consumers generally purchase beer can be computed easily. The tabular results that correspond to the chart would appear as follows:

Tabulation
The orderly arrangement of data in a table or other summary format showing the number of responses to each response category; tallying.

Frequency table
A table showing the different ways respondents answered a question.

Response	Frequency	Percent	Cumulative Percentage
Drug Store	50	10	10
Convenience Store	225	45	55
Grocery Store	175	35	90
Specialty	35	7	97
Other	15	3	100

The frequency column shows the tally result or the number of respondents listing each store, respectively. The percent column shows the total percentage in each category. The cumulative percentage shows the percentage indicating either a particular category or any preceding category as their preferred place to purchase beer. From this chart, the mode indicates that the typical consumer buys beer at the convenience store since more people indicated this as their top response.

Similarly, a recent tabulation of Americans' responses to the simple question of "Who is your favorite TV personality?" revealed the response varied by age. For respondents aged 18–24, Conan O'Brien was listed first. For respondents aged 30–39, Bill O'Reilly was the preferred TV personality, and among consumers 65 and older, Oprah Winfrey was the modal response.[5] The idea that age may influence choice of favorite celebrity brings us to cross-tabulation.

Cross-Tabulation

Cross-tabulation
The appropriate technique for addressing research questions involving relationships among multiple less-than interval variables; results in a combined frequency table displaying one variable in rows and another in columns.

A frequency distribution or tabulation can address many research questions. As long as a question deals with only one categorical variable, tabulation is probably the best approach. Although frequency counts, percentage distributions, and averages summarize considerable information, simple tabulation may not yield the full value of the research. **Cross-tabulation** is the appropriate technique for addressing research questions involving relationships among multiple less-than interval variables. A cross-tabulation is a combined frequency table. Cross-tabulation allows the inspection and comparison of differences among groups based on nominal or ordinal categories. One key to interpreting a cross-tabulation table is comparing the observed table values with hypothetical values that would result from pure chance.

Exhibit 20.2 summarizes several cross-tabulations from consumers' responses to a questionnaire on ethical behavior in the United States.[6] Panel A suggests how two questionable behaviors (variables—taking home supplies, calling in sick) may vary with basic demographic variables. A researcher interested in the relative ethical perspectives of business executives and the general public can inspect panel B and compare the two groups. If business executives and the general public have the same ethical attitudes, the observed percentages should be equal for each question. This does not appear to be the case. The data lead to the conclusion that business executives participate in these behaviors more than the general public. However, before reaching the conclusion that business executives are less ethical than the general public, one must carefully scrutinize this finding for possible extraneous variables.

Contingency table
A data matrix that displays the frequency of some combination of possible responses to multiple variables; cross-tabulation results.

Contingency Tables

Exhibit 20.3 shows example cross-tabulation results using contingency tables. A **contingency table** is a data matrix that displays the frequency of some combination of possible responses to multiple

EXHIBIT 20.2 Cross-Tabulation Tables from a Survey on Ethics in America

(A) Reported Behavior (Percentage of General Public Who Have Ever Done Each Activity)

Activity	Age — Under 50 Years Old	Age — Over 50 Years Old	Gender — Men	Gender — Women	Education — College Graduate	Education — High School Graduate
Taken home work supplies	50	26	47	33	58	21
Called in sick to work when not ill	40	18	Not reported		36	21

(B) Reported Behavior (Percentage Who Have Ever Done Each Activity)

Activity	Business Executives	General Public
Taken home work supplies	74	40
Called in sick to work when not ill	14	31
Used company telephone for personal long-distance calls	78	15
Overstated deductions somewhat on tax forms	35	13
Driven while drunk	80	33
Saw a fellow employee steal something at work and did not report it	7	26

From Roger Ricklefs, "Ethics in America," The Wall Street Journal, October 31, 1983, p. 33, 42; November 1, 1983, p. 33; November 2, 1983, p. 33; and November 3, 1983, pp. 33, 37.

EXHIBIT 20.3
Possible Cross-Tabulations of One Question

(A) Cross-Tabulation of Question "Do you shop at Target?" by Sex of Respondent

	Yes	No	Total
Men	150	75	225
Women	180	45	225
Total	330	120	450

(B) Percentage Cross-Tabulation of Question "Do you shop at Target?" by Sex of Respondent, Row Percentage

	Yes	No	Total (Base)
Men	66.7%	33.3%	100% (225)
Women	80.0%	20.0%	100% (225)

(C) Percentage Cross-Tabulation of Question "Do you shop at Target?" by Sex of Respondent, Column Percentage

	Yes	No
Men	45.5%	62.5%
Women	54.5%	37.5%
Total	100%	100%
(Base)	(330)	(120)

variables. Two-way contingency tables, meaning they involve two less-than interval variables, are used most often. A three-way contingency table involves three less-than interval variables. Beyond three variables, contingency tables become difficult to analyze and explain easily.

Two variables are depicted in the contingency table shown in panel A:

- Row Variable: Biological Sex _____M _____F
- Column Variable: "Do you shop at Target? YES or NO"

Several conclusions can be drawn initially by examining the row and column totals:

1. 225 men and 225 women responded as can be seen in the row totals column.
2. Out of 450 total consumers responding, 330 consumers indicated that "yes" they do shop at Target and 120 indicated "no," they do not shop at Target. This can be observed in the column totals at the bottom of the table. These row and column totals often are called **marginals** because they appear in the table's margins.

Researchers usually are more interested in the inner cells of a contingency table. The inner cells display conditional frequencies (combinations). Using these values, we can draw some more specific conclusions:

3. Out of 330 consumers who shop at Target, 150 are male and 180 are female.
4. Alternatively, out of the 120 respondents not shopping at Target, 75 are male and 45 are female.

This finding helps us know whether the two variables are related. If men and women equally patronized Target, we would expect that hypothetically 165 of the 330 shoppers would be female and 165 would be female. Because we have equal numbers of men and women, the 330 would be equally male and female. The hypothetical expectations (165m/165f) are not observed. What is the implication? Target shoppers are more likely to be female than male. Notice that the same meaning could be drawn by analyzing non-Target shoppers.

Marginals
Row and column totals in a contingency table, which are shown in its margins.

RESEARCHSNAPSHOT

Contingent Personalities

Who is the world's favorite celebrity? This is an important question because the answer helps to determine how much a celebrity endorsement is worth. Sports stars like Tiger Woods are effective in shaping consumers' product preferences worldwide. Pop stars like the Spice Girls have been effectively used to increase soft drink sales in the United Kingdom. In other parts of the world, perhaps Sharon Cumeta could do the same. Perhaps some celebrities are effective nearly everywhere, but others may only be effective in a

given country. Their effectiveness is contingent upon region.

Television personalities also influence the public's opinion by giving their own. But, all opinions may not be equal. Polling agencies like the Harris interactive poll (http://www.harrisinteractive.com) monitor the popularity of celebrities. Who is America's favorite television personality? Oprah Winfrey has achieved the top rating by Americans for several years. But, is Oprah's likeability contingent upon other factors? Cross-tabulations can help answer this question. Consider the following 2-by-2 contingency table showing results of 1,000 respondents asked to choose

whether they prefer Oprah Winfrey or David Letterman:

	Oprah Winfrey	David Letterman	Totals
Men	150	350	500
Women	380	120	500
	530	470	1,000

Or, consider the 3 by 3 contingency table:

	Oprah Winfrey	Bill O'Reilly	Jon Stewart	Totals
Conservatives	60	260	20	340
Liberals	100	20	200	320
Moderates	210	70	60	340
	370	350	280	1000

In either case, opinions about the preferred celebrity seem to be contingent, or to depend on some characteristic. Results like these would suggest that although Oprah is preferred overall, men prefer David Letterman over Oprah. Also, one's favorite celebrity depends on political orientation. Thus, marketing managers should consider the contingencies when trying to identify preferred celebrities.

Sources: Erdogan, B. Zater, Michael J. Baker, and Stephen Tagg (2001), "Selecting Celebrity Endorsers: The Practitioner's Perspective," Journal of Advertising Research, 41 (May/June), 39–48; Goetzl, David and Wayne Friedman (2002), "What We're Talking About," Advertising Age, 73 (12/2), 51–57; The Wall Street Journal Online (2006), "Harris Poll: Oprah Again Tops America's List of Favorite TV Personalities," (February 3), http://online.wsj.com/article/SB113889692780763347-search.html?KEYWORDS=Oprah&COLLECTION=wsjie/6month.

A two-way contingency table like the one shown in part A is referred to as a *2 × 2 table* because it has two rows and two columns. Each variable has two levels. A two-way contingency table displaying two variables one (the row variable) with three levels and the other with four levels would be referred to as a *3 × 4 table*. Any cross-tabulation table may be classified according to the number of rows by the number of columns (*R by C*).

Percentage Cross-Tabulations

When data from a survey are cross-tabulated, percentages help the researcher understand the nature of the relationship by making relative comparisons simpler. The total number of respondents or observations may be used as a **statistical base** for computing the percentage in each cell. When the objective of the research is to identify a relationship between answers to two questions (or two variables), one of the questions is commonly chosen to be the source of the base for determining percentages. For example, look at the data in parts A, B, and C of Exhibit 20.3. Compare part B with part C. Selecting either the row percentages or the column percentages will emphasize a particular comparison or distribution. The nature of the problem the researcher wishes to answer will determine which marginal total will serve as a base for computing percentages.

Fortunately, a conventional rule determines the direction of percentages. The rule depends on which variable is identified as an independent variable and which is a dependent variable. Simply

Statistical base
The number of respondents or observations (in a row or column) used as a basis for computing percentages.

put, independent variables should form the rows in a contingency table. The marginal total of the independent variable should be used as the base for computing the percentages. Although survey research does not establish cause-and-effect evidence, one might argue that it would be logical to assume that a variable such as biological sex might predict beverage preference. This makes more sense than thinking that beverage preference would determine biological sex.

Elaboration and Refinement

The *Oxford Universal Dictionary* defines *analysis* as "the resolution of anything complex into its simplest elements." Once a researcher has examined the basic relationship between two variables, he or she may wish to investigate this relationship under a variety of different conditions. Typically, a third variable is introduced into the analysis to elaborate and refine the researcher's understanding by specifying the conditions under which the relationship between the first two variables is strongest and weakest. In other words, a more elaborate analysis asks, "Will interpretation of the relationship be modified if other variables are simultaneously considered?"

Elaboration analysis involves the basic cross-tabulation within various subgroups of the sample. The researcher breaks down the analysis for each level of another variable. If the researcher has cross-tabulated shopping preference by sex (see Exhibit 20.3) and wishes to investigate another variable (say, marital status), a more elaborate analysis may be conducted. Exhibit 20.4 breaks down the responses to the question "Do you shop at Target?" by sex and marital status. The data show women display the same preference whether married or single. However, married men are much more likely to shop at Target than are single men. The analysis suggests that the original conclusion about the relationship between sex and shopping behavior for women be retained. However, a relationship that was not discernible in the two-variable case is evident. Married men more frequently shop at Target than do single men.

The finding is consistent with an interaction effect. The combination of the two variables, sex and marital status, is associated with differences in the dependent variable. Interactions between variables examine moderating variables. A moderator variable is a third variable that changes the nature of a relationship between the original independent and dependent variables. Marital status is a moderator variable in this case. The interaction effect suggests that marriage changes the relationship between sex and shopping preference.

In other situations the addition of a third variable to the analysis may lead us to reject the original conclusion about the relationship. When this occurs, the elaboration analysis suggests the relationship between the original variables is spurious (see Chapter 3).

The chapter vignette described data suggesting a relationship between the type of store in which a consumer shops and beverage preference. Convenience store shoppers seem to choose beer over wine while grocery store shoppers choose wine over beer. Does store type drive drinking preference? Perhaps age determines both the type of store consumers choose to buy in and their preference for adult beverages. Younger consumers both disproportionately shop in convenience stores and drink beer.

How Many Cross-Tabulations?

Surveys may ask dozens of questions and hundreds of categorical variables can be stored in a data warehouse. Computer-assisted marketing researchers can "fish" for relationships by cross-tabulating

TOTHEPOINT

The more we study, the more we discover our ignorance.

—Percy Bysshe Shelley

Elaboration analysis
An analysis of the basic cross-tabulation for each level of a variable not previously considered, such as subgroups of the sample.

Moderator variable
A third variable that changes the nature of a relationship between the original independent and dependent variables.

	Single		Married	
	Men	Women	Men	Women
"Do you shop at Target?"				
Yes	55%	80%	86%	80%
No	45%	20%	14%	20%

EXHIBIT 20.4
Cross-Tabulation of Marital Status, Sex, and Responses to the Question "Do You Shop at Target?"

every categorical variable with every other categorical variable. Thus, every possible response becomes a possible explanatory variable. A researcher addressing an exploratory research question may find some benefit in such a fishing expedition. Software exists that can automatically search through volumes of cross-tabulations. These may even provide some insight into the market segment structure for some product. Alternatively, the program may flag the cross-tabulations suggesting the strongest relationship. CHAID (chi-square automatic interaction detection) software exemplifies software that makes searches through large numbers of variables possible.[7] Data-mining can be conducted in a similar fashion and may suggest relationships that are worth considering further.

Outside of exploratory research, researchers should conduct cross-tabulations that address specific research questions or hypotheses. When hypotheses involve relationships among two categorical variables, cross-tabulations are the right tool for the job.

Quadrant Analysis

Quadrant analysis
An extension of cross-tabulation in which responses to two rating-scale questions are plotted in four quadrants of a two-dimensional table.

Importance-performance analysis
Another name for quadrant analysis.

Quadrant analysis is a variation of cross-tabulation in which responses to two rating scale questions are plotted in four quadrants of a two-dimensional table. Most quadrant analysis in marketing research portrays or plots relationships between average responses about a product attribute's importance and average ratings of a company's (or brand's) performance on that product feature. The term **importance-performance analysis** is sometimes used because consumers rate perceived importance of several attributes and rate how well the company's brand performs on that attribute. Generally speaking, the marketer would like to end up in the quadrant indicating high performance on an important attribute.

Exhibit 20.5 illustrates a quadrant analysis for an international, mid-priced hotel chain.[8] The chart shows the importance and the performance ratings provided by business travelers. After plotting the scores for each of eight attributes, the analysis suggests areas for improvement. The arrows indicate attributes that the hotel firm should concentrate on to move from quadrant three, which means the performance on those attributes is low but business consumers rate those attributes as important, to quadrant four, where attributes are both important and rated highly for performance.

EXHIBIT 20.5
An Imortance-Performance or Quadrant Analysis of Hotels

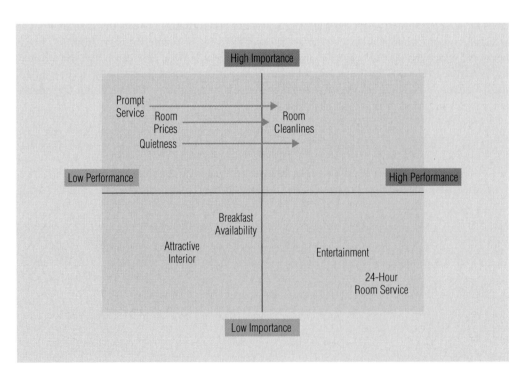

Data Transformation

Simple Transformations

Data transformation (also called *data conversion*) is the process of changing the data from their original form to a format suitable for performing a data analysis that will achieve research objectives. Researchers often modify the values of scalar data or create new variables. For example, many researchers believe that less response bias will result if interviewers ask respondents for their year of birth rather than their age. This presents no problem for the research analyst, because a simple data transformation is possible. The raw data coded as birth year can easily be transformed to age by subtracting the birth year from the current year.

In earlier chapters, we discussed recoding and creating summated scales. These also are common data transformations.

Collapsing or combining adjacent categories of a variable is a common form of data transformation used to reduce the number of categories. A Likert scale may sometimes be collapsed into a smaller number of categories. For instance, consider the following Likert item administered to a sample of state university seniors:

Data transformation
Process of changing the data from their original form to a format suitable for performing a data analysis addressing research objectives.

TO THE POINT

All that we do is done with an eye to something else.

—Aristotle

	Strongly Disagree	Disagree	Neutral	Agree	Strongly Agree
I am satisfied with my college experience at this university	☐	☐	☐	☐	☐

The following frequency table describes results for this survey item:

Strongly Disagree	Disagree	Neutral	Agree	Strongly Agree
110	30	15	35	210

Exhibit 20.6 shows an example of a bimodal distribution.

The distribution of responses suggests the responses are bimodal. That is, two peaks exist in the distribution, one at either end of the scale. Since the vast majority of respondents (80 percent = (110 + 210)/400) indicated either strongly disagree or strongly agree, the variable closely resembles a categorical variable. Customers either strongly disagreed or strongly agreed with the statement. So, the research may wish to collapse the responses into two categories. While multiple ways exist to accomplish this, the researcher may assign the value of one to all respondents who either strongly disagreed or disagreed and the value two to all respondents who either agreed or strongly agreed. Respondents marking neutral would be deleted from analysis.

Problems with Data Transformations

Researchers often perform a median split to collapse a scale with multiple response points into two categories. The **median split** means respondents below the observed median go into one category and respondents above the median go into another. Although this is common, the approach is best applied only when the data do indeed exhibit bimodal characteristics. When the data are unimodal, such as would be the case with normally distributed data, a median split will lead to error.

Exhibit 20.7 illustrates this problem. Clearly, most respondents either slightly agree or slightly disagree with this statement. The central tendency could be represented by the median of 3.5, a mean of 3.5, or the mode of 3.5 (3 and 4 each have the same number of responses). The "outliers," if any,

Median split
Dividing a data set into two categories by placing respondents below the median in one category and respondents above the median in another.

EXHIBIT 20.6
Bimodal Distributions Are Consistent with Transformations into Categorical Values.

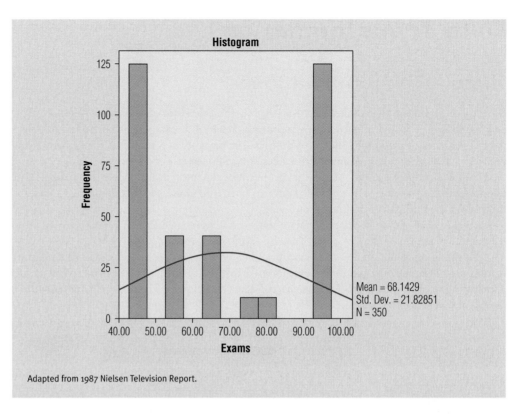

Adapted from 1987 Nielsen Television Report.

EXHIBIT 20.7 **The Problem with Median Splits with Unimodal Data**

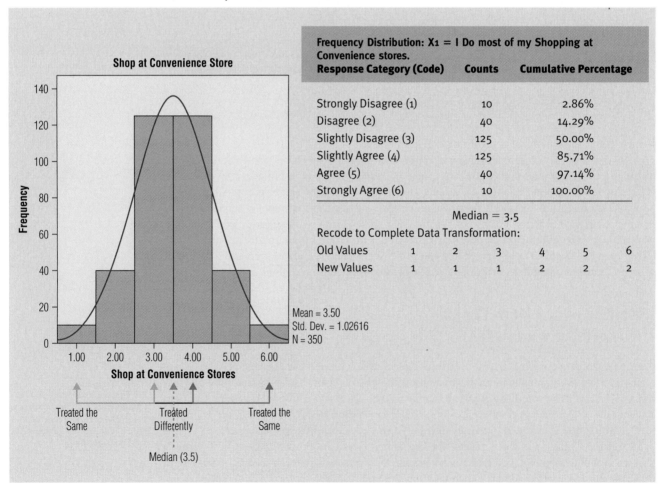

appear to be those not indicating something other than slight agreement/disagreement. A case can be made that the respondents indicating slight disagreement are more similar to those indicating slight agreement than they are to those respondents indicating strong disagreement. Yet, the recode places values 1 and 3 in the same new category, but places values 3 and 4 in a different category (see the recoding scheme in Exhibit 20.7). The data distribution does not support a median split into two categories and so a transformation collapsing these values into agreement and disagreement is inappropriate.

When a sufficient number of responses exist and a variable is ratio, the researcher may choose to delete one-fourth to one-third of the responses around the median to effectively ensure a bimodal distribution. Median splits should always be performed only with great care, though, as the inappropriate collapsing of continuous variables into categorical variables ignores the information contained within the untransformed values.

Index Numbers

The consumer price index and wholesale price index are secondary data sources that are frequently used by marketing researchers. Price indexes, like other **index numbers**, represent simple data transformations that allow researchers to track a variable's value over time and compare a variable(s) with other variables. Recalibration allows scores or observations to be related to a certain base period or base number.

Index numbers
Scores or observations recalibrated to indicate how they relate to a base number.

Consider the information in Exhibit 20.8. Weekly television viewing statistics are shown grouped by household size. Index numbers can be computed for these observations in the following manner:

1. A base number is selected. The United States household average of 52 hours and 36 minutes represents the central tendency and will be used.
2. Index numbers are computed by dividing the score for each category by the base number and multiplying by 100. The index reflects percentage changes from the base:

$$\text{1 person hh:} \quad \frac{41:01}{52:36} = 0.7832 \times 100 = 78.32$$

$$\text{2 person hh:} \quad \frac{47:58}{52:36} = 0.9087 \times 100 = 90.87$$

$$\text{3+ person hh:} \quad \frac{60:49}{52:36} = 1.1553 \times 100 = 115.53$$

$$\text{Total U.S. average:} \quad \frac{52:36}{52:36} = 1.0000 \times 100 = 100.00$$

If the data are time-related, a base year is chosen. The index numbers are then computed by dividing each year's activity by the base-year activity and multiplying by 100. Index numbers require ratio measurement scales. Marketing managers may often chart consumption in some category over time. Relating back to the chapter vignette, grocers may wish to chart the United States wine consumption index. Using 1968 as a base year, the current U.S. wine consumption index is just over 2.0, meaning that the typical American consumer drinks just over 8.7 liters of wine per year.[9]

Household Size	Hours:Minutes
1	41:01
2	47:58
3+	60:49
Total U.S. average	52:36

Adapted from 1987 Nielsen Television Report.

EXHIBIT 20.8
Hours of Television Usage per Week

RESEARCHSNAPSHOT

Wine Index Can Help Retailers

Indexes can be very useful, and researchers are sometimes asked to create index values from secondary data. The chapter vignette described a situation where a retailer was making decisions about merchandising based on the consumption habits of store customers. If a U.S. grocer is considering wine merchandising in another country, he/she may be interested to know wine indexes of other countries.

Using 1968 U.S. wine consumption as a base, the current wine consumption index for the United Kingdom is 4.1, South Africa's index value is 2.2 (almost the same as the United States), Israel's index is 0.4, and Luxembourg's wine index is 14.1 (59.2 liters/person/year)! This information would be helpful in making decisions about the amount of space and attention given to wine in different countries. Similarly, the retailer could compute wine or beer indices by state. Policy agencies could also chart indices on alcohol consumption that may be helpful in regulating underage consumption.

Sources: http://www.wineinstitute.com.

Calculating Rank Order

Survey respondents are often asked to rank order brand or store preferences. Employee respondents may provide rankings of several different employee benefit plans. Ranking data can be summarized by performing a data transformation. The transformation involves multiplying the frequency by the ranking score for each choice to result in a new scale.

For example, suppose a manager of a frequent-flier program had ten executives rank their preferences for locations in which to hold the company's annual conference. Exhibit 20.9 shows how executives ranked each of four locations: Hawaii, Paris, Greece, and Hong Kong. Exhibit 20.10 tabulates frequencies for these rankings. A ranking summary can be computed by assigning the destination with the highest preference the lowest number (1) and the least preferred destination the highest consecutive number (4). The summarized rank orderings were obtained with the following calculations:

$$
\begin{aligned}
\text{Hawaii:} \quad & (3 \times 1) + (5 \times 2) + (1 \times 3) + (1 \times 4) = 20 \\
\text{Paris:} \quad & (3 \times 1) + (1 \times 2) + (3 \times 3) + (3 \times 4) = 26 \\
\text{Greece:} \quad & (2 \times 1) + (2 \times 2) + (4 \times 3) + (2 \times 4) = 26 \\
\text{Hong Kong:} \quad & (2 \times 1) + (2 \times 2) + (2 \times 3) + (4 \times 4) = 28
\end{aligned}
$$

Three executives chose Hawaii as the best destination (ranked "1"), five executives selected Hawaii as the second best destination, and so forth. The lowest total score indicates the first (highest)

EXHIBIT 20.9
Executive Rankings of Potential Conference Destinations

Executive	Hawaii	Paris	Greece	Hong Kong
1	1	2	4	3
2	1	3	4	2
3	2	1	3	4
4	2	4	3	1
5	2	1	3	4
6	3	4	1	2
7	2	3	1	4
8	1	4	2	3
9	4	3	2	1
10	2	1	3	4

EXHIBIT 20.10
Frequencies of Conference
Destination Rankings

	Preference Rankings			
Destination	1st	2nd	3rd	4th
Hawaii	3	5	1	1
Paris	3	1	3	3
Greece	2	2	4	2
Hong Kong	2	2	2	4

preference ranking. The results show the following rank ordering: (1) Hawaii, (2) Paris, (3) Greece, and (4) Hong Kong. Company employees may be glad to hear their conference will be in Hawaii.

Tabular and Graphic Methods of Displaying Data

Tables, graphs, and charts may simplify and clarify data. Graphical representations of data may take a number of forms, ranging from a computer printout to an elaborate pictograph. Tables, graphs, and charts, however, all facilitate summarization and communication. For example, see how the simple frequency table and histogram shown in Exhibit 20.7 provide a summary that quickly and easily communicates meaning that would be more difficult to see if all 350 responses were viewed separately.

Today's researcher has many convenient tools to quickly produce charts, graphs, or tables. Even basic word processing programs like Word include chart functions that can construct the chart within the text document. Bar charts (histograms), pie charts, curve/line diagrams, and scatter plots are among the most widely used tools. Some choices match well with certain types of data and analyses.

Bar charts and pie charts are very effective in communicating frequency tabulations and simple cross-tabulations. Exhibit 20.11 displays frequency data from the chapter vignette with pie charts. Each pie summarizes preference in the respective year. The size of each pie slice corresponds to a frequency value associated with that choice. When the two pie charts are compared, the result communicates a cross-tabulation. Here, the comparison clearly communicates that wine preference has increased at the expense of beer preference. In other words, the relative slice of pie for wine has become larger.

Chapter 25 discusses how these and other graphic aids may improve the communication value of a written report or oral presentation.

EXHIBIT 20.11
Pie Charts Work Well with
Tabulations and Cross-
Tabulations

Computer Programs for Analysis

Statistical Packages

Just fifty years ago, the thought of a typical U.S. company performing even basic statistical analyses like cross-tabulations on a thousand or more observations was unrealistic. The personal computer brought this capability not just to average companies, but even to small companies with limited resources. Today, computing power is seldom a barrier to completing a research project.

In the 1980s and early 1990s, when the PC was still a relatively novel innovation, specialized statistical software formerly used on mainframe computers made their way into the personal computing market. Today, most spreadsheet packages can perform a wide variety of basic statistical options. Excel's basic data analysis tool will allow descriptive statistics including frequencies and measures of central tendency to be easily computed.[10] Most of the basic statistical features are now menu driven, reducing the need to memorize function labels. Spreadsheet packages like Excel continue to evolve and become more viable for performing many basic statistical analyses (see Exhibit 20.12).

Despite the advances in spreadsheet applications, commercialized statistical software packages remain extremely popular among researchers. They continue to become easier to use and more compatible with other data interface tools including spreadsheets and word processors. Like any specialized tool, statistical packages are more tailored to the types of analyses performed by statistical analysts, including marketing researchers. Thus, any serious business or social science researcher should still become familiar with at least one general computer software package.

Two of the most popular general statistical packages are SAS (http://www.sas.com) and SPSS (http://www.spss.com). SAS revenues exceed $1.4 billion and its software can be found on computers worldwide. SAS was founded in 1976, and its statistical software historically has been widely used in engineering and other technical fields. SPSS sales exceed $224 million and the company was founded in 1968. SPSS stands for *Statistical Package for the Social Sciences.* SPSS is commonly used by university business and social science students. Marketing researchers have traditionally used SPSS

EXHIBIT 20.12
The Basic Data Analysis Window

more than any other statistical software tool. SPSS has been viewed as more user-friendly in the past. However, today's versions of both SPSS and SAS are very user friendly and give the user the option of using drop-down menus to conduct analysis rather than writing computer code.

Excel, SAS, and SPSS account for most of the statistical analysis conducted in marketing research. University students are sometimes exposed to MINITAB. MINITAB's revenues are approximately $10 million per year. Economists sometimes favor MINITAB; however, it has traditionally been viewed as being less user-friendly than other choices.

In the past, data entry was an issue as specific software required different types of data input. Today, however, all the major software packages including SAS and SPSS can work from data entered into a spreadsheet. The spreadsheets can be imported into the data windows or simply read by the program. Most conventional online survey tools will return data to the user in the form of either an SPSS data file, an Excel spreadsheet, or a plain text document.

Exhibit 20.13 shows a printout of descriptive statistics generated by SAS for two variables: EMP (number of employees working in an MSA, or Metropolitan Statistical Area) and SALES (sales volume in dollars in an MSA) for ten MSAs. The number of data elements (N), mean, standard deviation, and other descriptive statistics are displayed. SAS output is generally simple and easy to read.

As an example of SPSS output, each histogram shown in the exhibits on page 510 was created by SPSS. By clicking on "charts" in the SPSS tool menu, one can see the variety of charts that can be created. The key place to click to generate statistical results in tabular form is "analyze." Here, one can see the many types of analysis that can be created. In this chapter, the choices found by clicking on "analyze" and then "descriptive statistics" are particularly relevant.

Exhibit 20.14 shows an SPSS cross-tabulation of two variables, class status and smoking behavior. The data come from a sample intercepted on an urban university campus. It addresses the research question, "Does smoking on campus vary across groups?" More non-smokers than smokers are found. However, the results show that graduate students, and to a lesser extent instructors, smoke more than the norm. The SPSS user can ask for any number of statistics and percentages to be included with this output by clicking on the corresponding options.

EXHIBIT 20.13 **SAS Computer Output of Descriptive Statistics**

State = NY Variable	N	Mean	Standard Deviation	Minimum Value	Maximum Value	Std Error of Mean	Sum	Variance	C.V.
EMP	10	142.930	232.665	12.800	788.800	73.575	1429.300	54133.0	162.782
SALES	10	5807.800	11905.127	307.000	39401.000	3764.732	58078.000	141732049.1	204.985

Key: EMP = number of employees (000)   SALES = Sales (000)

EXHIBIT 20.14

Examples of SPSS Output for Cross-Tabulation

CLASS * SMOKING Cross-Tabulation				
		Smoking		
Count		**Smoker**	**Non-smoker**	**Total**
Class	high school	7	9	16
	undergraduate	9	22	31
	graduate	15	10	25
	career	6	6	12
Total		37	47	84

Computer Graphics and Computer Mapping

Graphic aids prepared by computers have practically replaced graphic presentation aids drawn by artists. Computer graphics are extremely useful for descriptive analysis. As mentioned in Chapter 2, decision support systems can generate two- or three-dimensional computer maps to portray data about sales, demographics, lifestyles, retail stores, and other features. Exhibit 20.15 shows a computer graphic depicting how fast-food consumption varies from state to state. The chart shows the relative frequencies of eating fast-food burgers, chicken, tacos, or other types of fast-food across several states. Computer graphics like these have become more common as common applications have introduced easy ways of generating 3-D graphics. Many 3-D maps are also available. Many computer maps are used by marketers to show locations of high-quality customer segments. Competitors' locations are often overlaid for additional quick and easy visual reference. Scales that show miles, population densities, and other characteristics can be highlighted in color, with shading, and with symbols.

Box and whisker plots
Graphic representations of central tendencies, percentiles, variabilities, and the shapes of frequency distributions.

Many computer programs can draw **box and whisker plots**, which provide graphic representations of central tendencies, percentiles, variabilities, and the shapes of frequency distributions. Exhibit 20.16 shows a computer-drawn box and whisker plot for 100 responses to a question measured on a ten-point scale. The response categories are shown on the vertical axis. The small box inside the plot represents responses for half of all respondents. Thus, half of respondents marked 4, 5, or 6. This gives a measure of variability called the **interquartile range**, but the term *midspread* is less complex and more descriptive. The location of the line within the box indicates the median. The dashed lines that extend from the top and bottom of the box are the whiskers. Each whisker extends either the length of the box (the midspread in our example is 2 scale points) or to the most extreme observation in that direction.

Interquartile range
A measure of variability.

Outlier
A value that lies outside the normal range of the data.

An **outlier** is a value that lies outside the normal range of the data. In Exhibit 20.16 outliers are indicated by either a 0 or an asterisk. Box and whisker plots are particularly useful for spotting outliers or comparing group categories (e.g., men versus women).

EXHIBIT 20.15

A 3-D Graph Showing Fast-Food Consumption Patterns around the United States

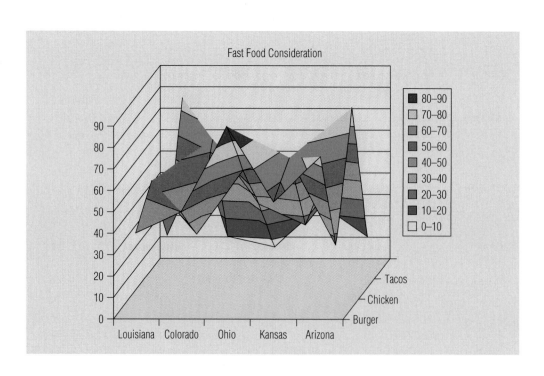

EXHIBIT 20.16
Computer Drawn Box and Whisker Plot

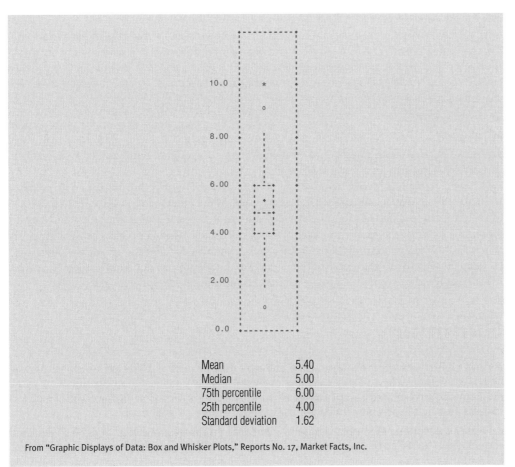

Mean	5.40
Median	5.00
75th percentile	6.00
25th percentile	4.00
Standard deviation	1.62

From "Graphic Displays of Data: Box and Whisker Plots," Reports No. 17, Market Facts, Inc.

Interpretation

An interpreter at the United Nations translates a foreign language into another language to explain the meaning of a foreign diplomat's speech. In marketing research, the interpretation process explains the meaning of the data. After the statistical analysis of the data, inferences and conclusions about their meaning are developed.

A distinction can be made between *analysis* and *interpretation*. **Interpretation** is drawing inferences from the analysis results. Inferences drawn from interpretations lead to managerial implications. In other words, each statistical analysis produces results that are interpreted with respect to insight into a particular decision. The logical interpretation of the data and statistical analysis are closely intertwined. When a researcher calculates a cross-tabulation of a demographic variable with brand choice, an interpretation is drawn suggesting that one segment may be more or less likely to choose a given brand. This interpretation of the statistical analysis may lead to a suggestion that a brand be withdrawn from certain demographic markets.

From a management perspective, however, the qualitative meaning of the data and their managerial implications are an important aspect of the interpretation. Consider the crucial role played by interpretation of research results in investigating one new product, a lip stain that could color the lips a desired shade semi-permanently and last for about a month at a time:

The lip stain idea, among lipstick wearers, received very high scores on a rating scale ranging from "excellent" to "poor," presumably because it would not wear off. However, it appeared that even among routine wearers of lipstick the idea was being rated highly more for its interesting, even ingenious, nature than for its practical

Interpretation
The process of drawing inferences from the analysis results.

appeal to the consumer's personality. They liked the idea, but for someone else, not themselves. . . . [Careful interpretation of the data] revealed that not being able to remove the stain for that length of time caused most women to consider the idea irrelevant in relation to their own personal needs and desires. Use of the product seems to represent more of a "permanent commitment" than is usually associated with the use of a particular cosmetic. In fact, women attached overtly negative meaning to the product concept, often comparing it with hair dyes instead of a long-lasting lipstick.[11]

TOTHEPOINT

The thing to do is to supply light.

—Woodrow Wilson

This example shows that interpretation is crucial. However, the process is difficult to explain in a textbook because there is no one best way to interpret data. Many possible interpretations of data may be derived from a number of thought processes. Experience with selected cases will help you develop your own interpretative ability.

Data are sometimes merely reported and not interpreted. Research firms may provide reams of computer output that do not state what the data mean. At the other extreme, some researchers tend to analyze every possible relationship between each and every variable in the study. Such an approach is a sign that the research problem was not adequately defined prior to beginning the research and the researcher really doesn't know what business decision the research is addressing. Researchers who have a clear sense of the purpose of the research do not request statistical analysis of data that have little or nothing to do with the primary purpose of the research.

Summary

1. Know what descriptive statistics are and why they are used. Descriptive analyses provide descriptive statistics. These include measures of central tendency and variation. Statistics such as the mean, mode, median, range, variance, and standard deviation are all descriptive statistics. These statistics provide a basic summary describing the basic properties of a variable.

2. Create and interpret simple tabulation and cross-tabulation tables. Statistical tabulation is another way of saying that we count the number of observations in each possible response category. In other words, tabulation is the same as tallying. Tabulation is an appropriate descriptive analysis for less-than interval variables. Frequency tables and histograms are used to display tabulation results.

3. Understand how cross-tabulations can reveal relationships. Cross-tabulation is the appropriate technique for assessing relationships among multiple less-than interval variables. The key to interpreting a cross-tabulation result is to compare actual observed values with hypothetical values that would result from pure chance. When observed results vary from these values, a relationship is indicated.

4. Perform basic data transformations. Data transformations are often needed to assist in data analysis and involve changing the mathematical form of data in some systematic way. Basic data transformations include reverse coding, summating scales, creating index numbers, and collapsing a variable based on a median split.

5. List different computer software products designed for descriptive statistical analysis. While spreadsheets have improved with respect to their ability to conduct basic statistical analyses, marketing researchers still rely heavily on specialized statistical software. SAS and SPSS are two of the best known statistical packages. Each is available for even the most basic modern PC and can be used with a drop-down window interface, practically eliminating the need for writing computer code.

Key Terms and Concepts

Descriptive analysis	Statistical base	Index numbers
Histogram	Elaboration analysis	Box and whisker plots
Tabulation	Moderator variable	Interquartile range
Frequency table	Quadrant analysis	Outlier
Cross-tabulation	Importance-performance analysis	Interpretation
Contingency table	Data transformation	
Marginals	Median split	

Questions for Review and Critical Thinking

1. What are five descriptive statistics used to describe the basic properties of variables?
2. What is a *histogram?* What is the advantage of overlaying a normal distribution over a histogram?
3. A survey asks respondents to respond to the statement "My work is interesting." Interpret the frequency distribution shown here (taken from an SPSS output):
   a. My work in interesting:

Category Label	Code	Abs. Freq.	Rel. Freq. (Pct.)	Adj. Freq. (Pct.)	Cum. Freq. (Pct.)
Very true	1	650	23.9	62.4	62.4
Somewhat true	2	303	11.2	29.1	91.5
Not very true	3	61	2.2	5.9	97.3
Not at all true	4	28	1.0	2.7	100.0
	•	1,673	61.6	Missing	
	Total	2,715	100.0	100.0	
Valid cases	1,042		Missing cases	1,673	

4. Use the data in the following table to
   a. prepare a frequency distribution of the respondents' ages
   b. cross-tabulate the respondents' genders with cola preference
   c. identify any outliers

Individual	Gender	Age	Cola Preference	Weekly Unit Purchases
John	M	19	Coke	2
Al	M	17	Pepsi	5
Bill	M	20	Pepsi	7
Mary	F	20	Coke	2
Jim	M	18	Coke	4
Karen	F	16	Coke	4
Tom	M	17	Pepsi	12
Sassi	F	22	Pepsi	6
Amie	F	20	Pepsi	2
Dawn	F	19	Pepsi	3

5. Data on the average size of a soda (in ounces) at all thirty major league baseball parks are as follows: 14, 18, 20, 16, 16, 12, 14, 16, 14, 16, 16, 16, 14, 32, 16, 20, 12, 16, 20, 12, 16, 16, 24, 16, 16, 14, 14, 12, 14, 20. Compute descriptive statistics for this variable including a box and whisker plot. Comment on the results.

6. The following computer output shows a cross-tabulation of frequencies and provides frequency number (N) and row (R) percentages.
   a. Interpret this output including a conclusion about whether or not the row and column variables are related.
   b. Critique the way the analysis is presented.
   c. Draw a pie chart indicating percentages for having read a book in the past three month for those with and those without high school diplomas.

Have You Read a Book in Past 3 Months?	Have High School Diploma?		Total
	Yes	No	
Yes	489	174 :	663
	73.8	26.2 :	
No	473	378 :	851
	55.6	44.4 :	
	......	......	......
TOTAL	962	552 :	1514

7. List and describe at least three basic data transformations.
8. What conditions suggest that a ratio variable should be transformed into a dichotomous (two group) variable represented with dummy coding?
9. A data processing analyst for a research supplier finds that preliminary computer runs of survey results show that consumers love a client's new product. The employee buys a large block of the client's stock. Is this ethical?

Research Activities

1. **'NET** Go the website for the Chicago Cubs baseball team (http://chicago.cubs.mlb.com). Use either the schedule listing or the stats information to find their record in the most recent season. Create a data file with a variable indicating whether each game was won or lost and a variable indicating whether the game was played at home in Wrigley Field or away from home. Using computerized software like SPSS or SAS,
   a. Compute a frequency table and histogram for each variable.
   b. Use cross-tabulations to examine whether a relationship exists between where the game is played (home or away) and winning.
   c. Extra Analysis: Repeat the analyses for the Houston Astros baseball team (http://www.astros.com). What does this suggest for the relationship between playing at home and winning?

2. **'NET** Go to http://www.spss.com and click on Industries and Market Research. What services does the company provide?

Case 20.1 Body on Tap

A few years ago Vidal Sassoon, Inc., took legal action against Bristol-Myers over a series of TV commercials and print ads for a shampoo that had been named Body on Tap because of its beer content.[12] The prototype commercial featured a well-known high fashion model saying, "In shampoo tests with over 900 women like me, Body on Tap got higher ratings than Prell for body. Higher than Flex for conditioning. Higher than Sassoon for strong, healthy-looking hair."

The evidence showed that several groups of approximately 200 women each tested just one shampoo. They rated it on a six-step qualitative scale, from "outstanding" to "poor," for twenty-seven separate attributes, such as body and conditioning. It became clear that 900 women did not, after trying both shampoos, make product-to-product comparisons between Body on Tap and Sassoon or between Body on Tap and any of the other brands mentioned. In fact, no woman in the tests tried more than one shampoo.

The claim that the women preferred Body on Tap to Sassoon for "strong, healthy-looking hair" was based on combining the data for the "outstanding" and "excellent" ratings and discarding the lower four ratings on the scale. The figures then were 36 percent for Body

on Tap and 24 percent (of a separate group of women) for Sassoon. When the "very good" and "good" ratings were combined with the "outstanding" and "excellent" ratings, however, there was only a difference of 1 percent between the two products in the category of "strong, healthy-looking hair."

The research was conducted for Bristol-Myers by Marketing Information Systems, Inc. (MISI), using a technique known as blind monadic testing. The president of MISI testified that this method typically is employed when what is wanted is an absolute response to a product "without reference to another specific product." Although he testified that blind monadic testing was used in connection with comparative advertising, that was not the purpose for which Bristol-Myers retained MISI. Rather, Bristol-Myers wished to determine consumer reaction to the introduction of Body on Tap. And Sassoon's in-house research expert stated flatly that blind monadic testing cannot support comparative advertising claims.

Question
Comment on the professionalism of the procedures used to make the advertising claim. Why do you believe the researchers performed the data transformations described?

Case 20.2 Downy-Q Quilt

The research for Downy-Q is an example of a commercial test that was conducted when an advertising campaign for an established brand had run its course.[13] The revised campaign, "Fighting the Cold," emphasized that Downy-Q was an "extra-warm quilt"; previous research had demonstrated that extra warmth was an important and deliverable product quality. The commercial test was requested to measure the campaign's ability to generate purchase interest.

The marketing department had recommended this revised advertising campaign and was now anxious to know how effectively this commercial would perform. The test concluded that "Fighting the Cold" was a persuasive commercial. It also demonstrated that the new campaign would have greater appeal to specific market segments.

Method

Brand choices for the same individuals were obtained before and after viewing the commercial. The commercial was tested in thirty-second, color-moving, storyboard form in a theater test. Invited viewers were shown programming with commercial inserts. Qualified respondents were women who had bought quilts in outlets that carried Downy-Q. The results are shown in Case Exhibits 20.2–1 through 20.2–4.

Question

Interpret the data in these tables. What recommendations and conclusions would you offer to Downy-Q management?

CASE EXHIBIT 20.2–1 Shifts in Brand Choice Before and After Showing of Downy-Q Quilt Commercial

Question: We are going to give away a series of prizes. If you are selected as one of the winners, which of the following would you truly want to win?

Brand Choice after Commercial	Brand Choice before Commercial (%)	
	Downy-Q (n = 23)	Other Brand (n = 237)
Downy-Q	78	19
Other brand	22	81

CASE EXHIBIT 20.2–2 Pre/Post Increment in Choice of Downy-Q

Question: We are going to give away a series of prizes. If you are selected as one of the winners, which of the following would you truly want to win? (Check list.)

Demographic Group	"Fighting the Cold"		Norm: All Quilt Commercials	
	Base	Score	Average	Range
Total audience	(260)	+15	+10	6–19
By marital status				
Married	(130)	+17		
Not married	(130)	+12		
By age				
Under 35	(130)	+14		
35 and over	(130)	+15		
By employment status				
Not employed	(90)	+13		
Employed	(170)	+18		

CASE EXHIBIT 20.2-3 **Adjective Checklist for Downy-Q Quilt Commercial**

Question: Which of these words do you feel come closest to describing the commercial you've just seen? (Check all the apply.)
(Check list.)

Adjective	"Fighting the Cold" (%)	Norm: All Quilt Commercials (%)
Positive		
Appealing	18	24
Clever	11	40
Convincing	20	14
Effective	19	23
Entertaining	5	24
Fast moving	12	21
Genuine	7	4
Imaginative	7	21
Informative	24	18
Interesting	13	17
Original	7	20
Realistic	8	3
Unusual	3	8
Negative		
Amateurish	9	11
Bad Taste	4	4
Dull	33	20
Repetitious	17	16
Silly	8	19
Slow	8	7
Unbelievable	3	5
Unclear	3	2
Unimportant	14	14
Uninteresting	32	19

CASE EXHIBIT 20.2-4 **Product Attribute Checklist for Downy-Q**

Question: Which of the following statements do you feel apply to Downy-Q?
(Mark as many or as few as you feel apply.)

Attributes	"Fighting the Cold" (%)
Extra warm	56
Lightweight	48
Pretty designs	45
Durable fabrics	28
Nice fabrics	27
Good construction	27

CHAPTER 21
UNIVARIATE STATISTICAL ANALYSIS

After studying this chapter, you should be able to

1. Implement the hypothesis-testing procedure
2. Use p-values to assess statistical significance
3. Test a hypotheses about an observed mean compared to some standard
4. Know the difference between Type I and Type II errors
5. Know when a univariate χ^2 test is appropriate and how to conduct one

Chapter Vignette: Pizza Targets

We all have trouble deciding where to eat or shop sometimes. Consumers have some idea in mind about the type of food they wish to eat, the atmosphere they want to experience, and the price they wish to pay. They use these *benchmarks* in the decision-making process.

Consider the other side of the coin. Companies like Domino's, Papa John's, and Pizza Hut each operate thousands of stores and have to decide which locations will remain open and where new locations are needed. Domino's operates over 6,000 stores in the United States and over 2,000 internationally.[1] Recently, Domino's closed over 400 stores around the United States in a single year.[2]

Location decisions are very important in retailing, and an important part of the marketing strategy for these firms involves rules that help make these decisions. Restaurants and retailers with thousands of locations can establish benchmarks based on historical performance trends. Restaurants like Pizza Hut and Domino's can use demographic data to help identify potentially good restaurant locations, and they can use demographics along with profitability and sales growth statistics to help decide when a restaurant should close.

Families and college students eat a lot of pizza. Researchers may be asked to perform research to determine if enough families live within a ten-minute drive to support a restaurant. Location rules may involve comparing a sample's demographic characteristics to demographic benchmarks. For instance, if historical data indicated that a successful restaurant generally was surrounded by families with an average of 1.4 children or more, the research may sample prospective locations and compare the observed average family size to this benchmark. Similarly, the company may have benchmarks for household income. Benchmarks like these can help make difficult decisions like these manageable.

©ROYALTY-FREE/CORBIS

Hypothesis Testing

Descriptive research and causal research designs often climax with hypotheses tests. Hypotheses were defined in Chapter 3 as formal statements of explanations stated in a testable form. Generally, hypotheses should be stated in concrete fashion so that the method of empirical testing seems almost obvious. Types of hypotheses tested commonly in marketing research include the following:

1. Relational hypotheses—examine how changes in one variable vary with changes in another. This is usually tested by assessing covariance in some way, very often with regression analysis.
2. Hypotheses about differences between groups—examine how some variable varies from one group to another. Very common in causal designs.
3. Hypotheses about differences from some standard—examine how some variable differs from some preconceived standard. The preconceived standard sometimes represents the true value of the variable in a population. These tests can involve either a test of a mean for better-than ordinal variables or a test of frequencies if the variable is ordinal or nominal. These tests typify univariate statistical tests.

Empirical testing typically involves inferential statistics. This means that an inference will be drawn about some population based on observations of a sample representing that population. Statistical analysis can be divided into several groups:

- **Univariate statistical analysis** tests hypotheses involving only one variable.
- **Bivariate statistical analysis** tests hypotheses involving two variables.
- **Multivariate statistical analysis** tests hypotheses and models involving multiple (three or more) variables or sets of variables.

Univariate statistical analysis
Tests of hypotheses involving only one variable.

Bivariate statistical analysis
Tests of hypotheses involving two variables.

Multivariate statistical analysis
Statistical analysis involving three or more variables or sets of variables.

The focus in this chapter is on univariate statistics. Thus, we examine statistical tests appropriate for drawing inferences about a single variable. In the chapter vignette, the restaurant may wish to test hypotheses about a single variable—family size. A sample will be drawn from the relevant population and tested against a benchmark of 1.4.

The Hypothesis-Testing Procedure

PROCESS

Hypotheses are tested by comparing the researcher's educated guess with empirical reality. The process can be described as follows:

- First, the hypothesis is derived from the research objectives. The hypothesis should be stated as specifically as possible.
- Next, a sample is obtained and the relevant variable is measured.
- The measured value obtained in the sample is compared to the value either stated explicitly or implied in the hypothesis. If the value is consistent with the hypothesis, the hypothesis is supported. If the value is not consistent with the hypothesis, the hypothesis is not supported.

A univariate hypothesis consistent with the chapter vignette would be

H1: The average number of children per family in zip code 70360-9238 is greater than 1.4.

If a sample is drawn from this zip code and the average number of children per family is 0.075, the hypothesis is not supported. If the average number of children is 3.3, the hypothesis is supported.

Univariate hypotheses are typified by tests comparing some observed sample mean against a benchmark value. The test addresses the question, Is the sample mean truly different from the benchmark? But, how different is really different? If the observed sample mean is 1.45 and the benchmark is 1.40, would the hypothesis still be supported? Probably not! When the observed mean is so close to the benchmark, we do not have sufficient confidence that a second set of data using a new sample taken from the same population might not produce a finding conflicting

RESEARCHSNAPSHOT

F-22 Target Tests

In January 2006, the F-22 Raptor fighter plane, jointly produced by Boeing and Lockheed-Martin, flew its first operational missions in support of operation Noble Eagle. In 2007, the U.S. Air Force has allocated over $100 billion to purchase more F-22 Raptors as it becomes the fifth generation U.S. fighter plane. Imagine all the tests that must be conducted before a fighter plane with a price tag somewhere in the neighborhood of $160–$350 million each goes into service.

Many of the tests involve statistical analyses comparing actual performance against benchmarks. In this sense, they are not entirely different than traditional business research tests comparing sample performance against some target. These tests involve how much stress some component can take before failing, how much acceleration the jet can achieve, how much maintenance is required, how accurate the plane's weapons systems are in hitting air to air targets, and the accuracy of the plane's air to ground weapons systems. Many tests like these can be analyzed with univariate statistical tests.

Imagine a test involving the accuracy of the plane's air-to-air defense systems. An F-22 pilot is asked to practice evasive maneuvers while trying to hit multiple moving targets playing the role of an enemy aircraft. Designers of the plane claim that with equally qualified pilots, an F-22 could defend itself in combat against six F-15 fighters, the plane it is making obsolete. After considering these claims, suppose the Air Force performed a test requiring that the F-22 would be able to shoot down more than five targets per flight during this test. The diagram below depicts the hypothesized case and the contrasting case (statistically, this would be the null).

The test is conducted fifty times with the results shown below:

The hypothesized result —
more than five targets hit.

If the hypothesis is wrong — less
than 5 targets are hit.

	N	Mean	Std. Deviation	Std. Error Mean
targets	50	7.1000	2.35822	.33350

The F-22 averaged 7.1 targets hit per test flight. The fewest targets hit was 2 and the most hit was 12. Is this performance good enough to support the hypothesis? The univariate statistic testing this result suggests the answer to this question is yes. The p-value for this test is less than .001 which supports the premise that the mean number of hits will be greater than 5.

			Test Value = 5			
					95% Confidence Interval of the Difference	
	T	d.f.	p-value (2-tailed)	Mean Difference	Lower	Upper
targets	6.297	49	.000	2.10000	1.4298	2.7702

Sources: Scott, William B. (2000), "F-22 Flight Tests Paced by Aircraft Availability," Aviation Week and Space Technology, 153 (Oct. 16), 53; Scott, William B. (2001), "F-22 Raptor Scores First Air-to-Air Kill During Test," Aviation Week and Space Technology, 155 (October 1), 5; http://www.f-22raptor.com; Nelson, Melissa (2005), "Pilot Says U.S. Stealth Fighter has no Equal," HeraldToday.com, December 21, accessed Feb. 7, 2006.

©ASSOCIATED PRESS/U.S. AIR FORCE

with the benchmark. In contrast, when the mean turns out well above 1.40, perhaps 3.3, then we could more easily trust that another sample would not produce a mean equal to or less than 1.40.

In statistics classes, students are exposed to hypothesis testing as a contrast between a *null* and an *alternative* hypothesis. A "null" hypothesis can be thought of as the expectation of findings as if no hypothesis existed (i.e., "no" or "null" hypothesis). In other words, the state implied by the null hypothesis is the opposite of the state represented by the actual hypothesis. A null to the hypothesis listed above is

H_n: *The average number of children per family in zip code 70360-9238 is equal to 1.4 (not greater than).*

The alternative hypothesis states the opposite of the null, which normally conforms to one of the common types of relationships above. So, the researcher's hypothesis is generally stated in the form of an "alternative" hypothesis. Are you confused?

While this terminology is common in statistical theory, the idea of a null hypothesis can be confusing. Therefore, the use of the term *null hypothesis* will be avoided when at all possible. The reader should instead focus on what the findings should look like if the proposed hypothesis is true. If the hypothesis above is true, an observed sample's mean should be noticeably greater than 1.40. We test to see if this idea can be supported by the empirical evidence.

Empirical evidence is provided by test results comparing the observed mean against some sampling distribution. The variance in observations also plays a role because with greater variance, there is more of a chance that the range of values includes 1.40. A statistical test's significance level or p-value becomes a key indicator of whether or not a hypothesis can be supported.

Significance level
A critical probability associated with a statistical hypothesis test that indicates how likely an inference supporting a difference between an observed value and some statistical expectation is true. The acceptable level of Type I error.

p-value
Probability value, or the observed or computed significance level; p-values are compared to significance levels to test hypotheses.

■ SIGNIFICANCE LEVELS AND p-VALUES

A **significance level** is a critical probability associated with a statistical hypothesis test that indicates how likely it is that an inference supporting a difference between an observed value and some statistical expectation is true. **p-value** stands for probability-value and is essentially another name for an *observed* or *computed* significance level. Exhibit 21.1 discusses interpretations of p-values in different kinds of statistical tests. The probability in a p-value is that the statistical expectation (null) for a given test is true. So, low p-values mean there is little likelihood that the statistical expectation

EXHIBIT 21.1
p-Values and Statistical Tests

Test Description	Test Statistic	
Compare an Observed Frequency with a Predetermined Value	X^2—Low p-values Indicate that Observed Frequency Is Different than Predetermined Value	df = 1
Compare an Observed Mean with Some Predetermined Value	Z or t-test—Low p-values Indicate the Observed Mean Is Different than Some Predetermined Value (Often 0)	$\alpha = .025$ $\alpha = .025$ m = 3.0 $\bar{X}$
Compare an Observed Proportion with Some Predetermined Value	Z or t-test for Proportions—Low p-values Indicate that the Observed Proportion Is Different than the Predetermined Value	50%
Bivariate Tests:		
Compare Whether Two Observed Means Are Different from One Another.	Z or t-test—Low p-values Indicate the Means Are Different	$\mu = 0$
Compare Whether Two Less-than Interval Variables Are Related Using Cross-tabs	X^2—Low p-values Indicate the Variables Are Related to One Another	df = 3
Compare Whether Two Interval or Ratio Variables Are Correlated to One Another	t-test for Correlation—Low p-values Indicate the Variables Are Related to One Another	r = 0

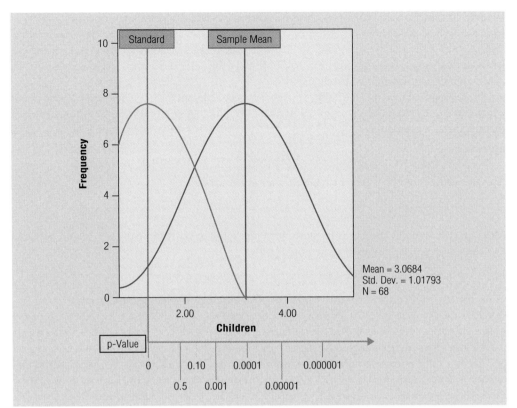

EXHIBIT 21.2
As the observed mean gets
further from the standard
(proposed population mean),
the p-value decreases.
The lower the p-value, the
more confidence you have
that the sample mean is
different.

is true. This means the researcher's hypothesis positing (suggesting) a difference between an observed mean and a population mean, or between an observed frequency and a population frequency, or for a relationship between two variables, is likely supported.

Traditionally, researchers have specified an acceptable significance level for a test prior to the analysis. Later, we will discuss this as an acceptable amount of Type I error. For most applications, the acceptable amount of error, and therefore the acceptable significance level, is $0.1, 0.05$, or 0.01. If the p-value resulting from a statistical test is less than the pre-specified significance level, then a hypothesis about differences is supported.

Exhibit 21.2 illustrates an important property of p-values. In this case, the comparison standard of 1.4 is shown as a red line. The sample result is shown as a blue line (3.1). The normal curve illustrates what other sample results would likely be. What is most important to realize is that as the observed value gets further from 1.4, the p-value gets smaller, meaning that the chance of the mean actually equaling 1.4 also is smaller. With the observed mean of 3.1 and the observed standard deviation of 1.02, there is very little chance that the researcher would be wrong in concluding the actual number of children per family is greater than 1.4.

Consider the test in the Research Snapshot box on page 525. The statistical test is whether or not the mean computed from the fifty observations is different from 5. Given the risk associated with being wrong, the researcher uses a most conservative acceptable significance level of 0.01. After computing the appropriate test, the research observes a computed significance level or p-value that is less than 0.001. Therefore, the hypothesis is supported.

In discussing confidence intervals, statisticians use the term *confidence level,* or *confidence coefficient,* to refer to the level of probability associated with an interval estimate. However, when discussing hypothesis testing, statisticians change their terminology and call this a *significance level, α* (the Greek letter *alpha*).

An Example of Hypothesis Testing

The example described here illustrates the conventional statistical approach to testing a univariate hypothesis with an interval or ratio variable. Suppose the Pizza-In restaurant is concerned about store image before deciding whether to expand. Pizza-In managers are most interested in how friendly customers perceive the service to be. A sample of 225 customers was obtained and asked to indicate their perceptions of service on a five-point scale, where 1 indicates "very unfriendly" service and 5 indicates "very friendly" service. The scale is assumed to be an interval scale, and experience has shown that the previous distribution of this attitudinal measurement assessing the service dimension was approximately normal.

Now, suppose Pizza-In believes the service has to be different from 3.0 before a decision about expansion can be made. In conventional statistical terminology, the null hypothesis for this test is that the mean is equal to 3.0:

$$H_0: \mu = 3.0$$

The alternative hypothesis is that the mean does not equal 3.0:

$$H_1: \mu \neq 3.0$$

More practically, the researcher is likely to write the substantive hypotheses (as it would be stated in a research report or proposal) something like this:

H_1: Customer perceptions of friendly service are significantly greater than three.

Note that the substantive hypothesis matches the "alternative" phrasing. In practical terms, researchers do not state null and alternative hypotheses. Only the substantive hypothesis implying what is expected to be observed in the sample is formally stated.

Next, the researcher must decide on a significance level. This level corresponds to a region of rejection on a normal sampling distribution as shown in Exhibit 21.1. The peak of the distribution is the theoretical expected value for the population mean. In this case it would be three. If the acceptable significance level is 0.05, then the 0.025 on either side of the mean that is furthest away from the mean forms the rejection zone (shaded blue in Exhibit 21.1). The values within the unshaded area are called *acceptable at the 95 percent confidence level* (or 5 percent significance level, or 0.05 alpha level), and if we find that our sample mean lies within this region we conclude that the means are not different from the expected value, 3 in this case. More precisely, we fail to reject the null hypothesis. In other words, the range of acceptance (1) identifies those acceptable values that reflect a difference from the hypothesized mean in the null hypothesis and (2) shows the range within which any difference is so minuscule that we would conclude that this difference was due to random sampling error rather than to a false null hypothesis. H_1 would not be supported.

In our example, the Pizza-In restaurant hired research consultants who collected a sample of 225 interviews. The mean friendliness score on a five-point scale equaled 3.78. (If σ is known, it is used in the analysis; however, this is rarely true and was not true in this case.[3]) The sample standard deviation was $S = 1.5$. Now we have enough information to test the hypothesis.

The researcher has decided that the acceptable significance level will be set at 0.05. This means that the researcher wishes to draw conclusions that will be erroneous 5 times in 100 (0.05) or fewer. From the table of the standardized normal distribution, the researcher finds that the Z score of 1.96 represents a probability of 0.025 that a sample mean will be above 1.96 standard errors from μ. Likewise, the table shows that 0.025 of all sample means will fall below -1.96 standard errors from μ. Adding these two "tails" together, we get 0.05.

Critical values
The values that lie exactly on the boundary of the region of rejection.

The values that lie exactly on the boundary of the region of rejection are called **critical values** of μ. Theoretically, the critical values are $Z = -1.96$ and $+1.96$. Now we must transform these critical Z-values to the sampling distribution of the mean for this image study. The critical values are

$$\text{Critical value} - \text{lower limit} = \mu - ZS_{\bar{X}} \quad \text{or} \quad \mu - Z\frac{S}{\sqrt{n}}$$

$$= 3.0 - 1.96\left(\frac{1.5}{\sqrt{225}}\right)$$

$$= 3.0 - 1.96(.1)$$

$$= 3.0 - 0.196$$

$$= 2.804$$

EXHIBIT 21.3
A Hypothesis Test Using the Sampling Distribution of $\overline{X}$ under the Hypothesis $\mu = 3.0$

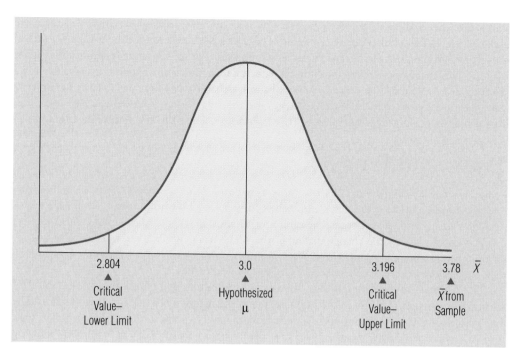

$$\text{Critical value} - \text{upper limit} = \mu + ZS_{\overline{X}} \quad \text{or} \quad \mu + Z\frac{S}{\sqrt{n}}$$

$$= 3.0 + 1.96 \left(\frac{1.5}{\sqrt{225}}\right)$$

$$= 3.0 + 1.96(.1)$$

$$= 3.0 + 0.196$$

$$= 3.196$$

Based on survey results, the sample mean ($\overline{X}$) is 3.78. The sample mean is contained in the region of rejection (see the dark shaded areas of Exhibit 21.3). Since the sample mean is greater than the critical value of 3.196, falling in one of the tails (regions of rejection), the researcher concludes that the sample result is statistically significant beyond the 0.05 level. A region of rejection means that the thought that the observed sample mean equals the predetermined value of 3.0 will be rejected when the computed value takes a value within the range. Here is another way to express this result: If we took 100 samples from this population and the mean were actually 3.0, fewer than five will show results that deviate this much.

What does this mean to the management of the Pizza-In? The results indicate that customers believe the service is pretty friendly. The probability is less than 5 in 100 that this result ($\overline{X} = 3.78$) would occur because of random sampling error. This suggests that friendliness of the service personnel may not be problem. However, perhaps Pizza-In should compare its friendliness rating with the friendliness rating of a key competitor. That analysis will have to wait until we cover bivariate tests.

An alternative way to test the hypothesis is to formulate the decision rule in terms of the Z-statistic. Using the following formula, we can calculate the observed value of the Z-statistic given a certain sample mean, $\overline{X}$:

$$Z_{\text{obs}} = \frac{\overline{X} - \mu}{S_{\overline{X}}}$$

$$= \frac{3.78 - \mu}{S_{\overline{X}}}$$

$$= \frac{3.78 - 3.0}{.1}$$

$$= \frac{.78}{.1}$$

$$= 7.8$$

In this case, the Z-value is 7.8 and we find that we have met the criterion of statistical significance at the 0.05 level. This result produces a p-value of 0.000001. Once again, since the p-value is less than the acceptable significance level, the hypothesis is supported. The service rating is significantly higher than 3.0. This example used the conventional statistical terminology involving critical values and a statistical null hypothesis. Once again, it is rare that researchers have to look up tabled values for critical values anymore since the statistical packages will usually return a p-value for a given test. Thus, the p-value, or a confidence interval associated with the p-value, is the key to interpretation.

Type I and Type II Errors

Hypothesis testing using sample observations is based on probability theory. We make an observation of a sample and use it to infer the probability that some observation is true within the population the sample represents. Because we cannot make any statement about a sample with complete certainty, there is always the chance that an error will be made. When a researcher makes the observation using a census, meaning that every unit (person or object) in a population is measured, then conclusions are certain. Researchers very rarely use a census.

The researcher using sampling runs the risk of committing two types of errors. Exhibit 21.4 summarizes the state of affairs in the population and the nature of Type I and Type II errors. The four possible situations in the exhibit result because the null hypothesis (using the example above, $\mu = 3.0$) is actually either true or false and the observed statistics ($\overline{X} = 3.78$) will result in acceptance or rejection of this null hypothesis.

▦ TYPE I ERROR

Suppose the observed sample mean described above leads to the conclusion that the mean is greater than 3.0 when in fact the true population mean is equal to 3.0. A **Type I error** has occurred. A Type I error occurs when a condition that is true in the population is rejected based on statistical observations. When a researcher sets an acceptable significance level a priori (α), he or she is determining tolerance for a Type I error. Simply put, a Type I error occurs when the researcher concludes that there is a statistical difference when in reality one does not exist. When testing for relationships, a Type I error occurs when the researcher concludes a relationship exists when in fact one does not exist.

▦ TYPE II ERROR

If the alternative condition is in fact true (in this case the mean is not equal to 3.0) but we conclude that we should not reject the null hypothesis (accept that the mean is equal to 3.0), we make what is called a **Type II error**. A Type II error is the probability of failing to reject a false null hypothesis. This incorrect decision is called beta (β). In practical terms, a Type II error means that we fail to reach the conclusion that some difference between an observed mean and a benchmark exists when in fact the difference is very real. In terms of a bivarate correlation, a Type II error would mean the idea that a relationship exists between two variables is rejected when in fact the relationship does indeed exist.

Unfortunately, without increasing sample size the researcher cannot simultaneously reduce Type I and Type II errors. They are inversely related. Thus, reducing the probability of a Type II error increases the probability of a Type I error. In marketing problems, Type I errors generally are considered more serious than Type II errors. Thus more emphasis is placed on determining the significance level, α, than in determining β.[4]

Type I error
An error caused by rejecting the null hypothesis when it is true; has a probability of alpha. Practically, a Type I error occurs when the researcher concludes that a relationship or difference exits in the population when in reality it does not exist.

Type II error
An error caused by failing to reject the null hypothesis when the alternative hypothesis is true; has a probability of beta. Practically, a Type II error occurs when a researcher concludes that no relationship or difference exists when in fact one does exist.

EXHIBIT 21.4
Type I and Type II Errors in Hypothesis Testing

	Decision	
Actual State in the Population	**Accept H_o**	**Reject H_o**
H_o is true	Correct—no error	Type I error
H_o is false	Type II error	Correct—no error

RESEARCHSNAPSHOT

The Law and Type I and Type II Errors

Although most attorneys and judges do not concern themselves with the statistical terminology of Type I and Type II errors, they do follow this logic. For example, our legal system is based on the concept that a person is innocent until proven guilty. Assume that the null hypothesis is that the individual is innocent. If we make a Type I error, we will send an innocent person to prison. Our legal system takes many precautions to avoid Type I errors. A Type II error would occur if a guilty party were set free (the null hypothesis would have been accepted).

Our society places such a high value on avoiding Type I errors that Type II errors are more likely to occur.

©ROYALTY-FREE/CORBIS

Choosing the Appropriate Statistical Technique

Numerous statistical techniques are available to assist the researcher in interpreting data. Choosing the right tool for the job is just as important to the researcher as to the mechanic. Making the correct choice can be determined by considering

1. The type of question to be answered
2. The number of variables involved
3. The level of scale measurement

Today, the researcher rarely has to perform a paper and pencil calculation. Hypotheses are tested by using a correct click-through sequence in a statistical software package. The mathematics of these packages is highly reliable. Therefore, if the researcher can choose the right statistic, know the right click-through sequence, and read the output that results, the right statistical conclusion should be easy to reach.

Type of Question to Be Answered

The type of question the researcher is attempting to answer is a consideration in the choice of statistical technique. For example, a researcher may be concerned simply with the central tendency of a variable or with the distribution of a variable. Comparison of different business divisions' sales results with some target level will require a one-sample *t*-test. Comparison of two salespeople's average monthly sales will require a *t*-test of two means, but a comparison of quarterly sales distributions will require a chi-square test.

The researcher should consider the method of statistical analysis before choosing the research design and before determining the type of data to collect. Once the data have been collected, the initial orientation toward analysis of the problem will be reflected in the research design.

Number of Variables

The number of variables that will be simultaneously investigated is a primary consideration in the choice of statistical technique. A researcher who is interested only in the average number of times a prospective home buyer visits financial institutions to shop for interest rates can concentrate on investigating only one variable at a time. However, a researcher trying to measure multiple

RESEARCHSNAPSHOT

Living in a Statistical Web

Having trouble learning statistical concepts? Do a little surfing and the concepts may become clear. Many sources exist that illustrate statistical problems and provide data for practice. Here are just a few:

STATLIB

http://lib.stat.cmu.edu/

StatLib is a system for distributing statistical software, datasets, and information by electronic mail, FTP, and the World Wide Web.

SURFSTAT.AUSTRALIA

http://www.anu.edu.au/nceph/surfstat/surfstat-home/
surfstat.html

SurfStat.australia is an online text in introductory statistics from the University of Newcastle.

GLOBALLY ACCESSIBLE STATISTICAL PROCEDURES

http://www.stat.sc.edu/
rsrch/gasp/

The Globally Accessible Statistical Procedures initiative is designed to make statistical routines easily available via the World Wide Web.

ELECTRONIC ENCYCLOPEDIA OF STATISTICAL EXAMPLES AND EXERCISES

http://www.stat.ohio-state.edu/~eesee/

The Electronic Encyclopedia of Statistical Examples and Exercises is a resource for the study of statistics that includes real-world examples of the uses and abuses of statistics and statistical inference.

THE RICE VIRTUAL LAB IN STATISTICS

http://www.ruf.rice.edu/~lane/rvls.html

http://www.ruf.rice.edu/~lane/hyperstat/contents.html

The Rice Virtual Lab in Statistics provides hypertext materials such as HyperStat Online.

StatCrunch

http://www.statcrunch.com/

STATCRUNCH is a statistical software package via the World Wide Web.

complex organizational variables cannot do the same. Simply put, univariate, bivariate, and multivariate statistical procedures are distinguished based on the number of variables involved in an analysis.

Level of Scale of Measurement

The scale measurement level helps choose the most appropriate statistical techniques and appropriate empirical operations. Testing a hypothesis about a mean, as we have just illustrated, is appropriate for interval scaled or ratio scaled data. Suppose a researcher is working with a nominal scale that identifies users versus nonusers of bank credit cards. Because of the type of scale, the researcher may use only the mode as a measure of central tendency. In other situations, where data are measured on an ordinal scale, the median may be used as the average or a percentile may be used as a measure of dispersion. For example, ranking brand preferences generally employs an ordinal scale. Nominal and ordinal data are often analyzed using frequencies or cross-tabulation.

Parametric versus Nonparametric Hypothesis Tests

Parametric statistics
Involve numbers with known, continuous distributions; when the data are interval or ratio scaled and the sample size is large, parametric statistical procedures are appropriate.

Nonparametric statistics
Appropriate when the variables being analyzed do not conform to any known or continuous distribution.

The terms **parametric statistics** and **nonparametric statistics** refer to the two major groupings of statistical procedures. The major distinction between them lies in the underlying assumptions about the data to be analyzed. Parametric statistics involve numbers with known, continuous distributions. When the data are interval or ratio scaled and the sample size is large, parametric statistical procedures are appropriate. Nonparametric statistics are appropriate when the numbers do not conform to a known distribution.

Parametric statistics are based on the assumption that the data in the study are drawn from a population with a normal (bell-shaped) distribution and/or normal sampling distribution. For

EXHIBIT 21.5 **Univariate Statistical Choice Made Easy**

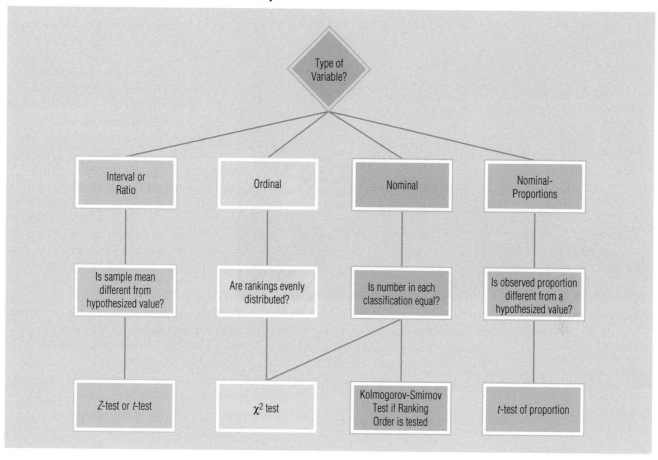

example, if an investigator has two interval-scaled measures, such as gross national product (GNP) and industry sales volume, parametric tests are appropriate. Possible statistical tests might include product-moment correlation analysis, analysis of variance, regression, or a *t*-test for a hypothesis about a mean.

Nonparametric methods are used when the researcher does not know how the data are distributed. Making the assumption that the population distribution or sampling distribution is normal generally is inappropriate when data are either ordinal or nominal. Thus, nonparametric statistics are referred to as distribution free.[5] Data analysis of both nominal and ordinal scales typically uses nonparametric statistical tests.

Exhibit 21.5 provides illustrates how an appropriate univariate statistical method can be selected. The exhibit illustrates how statistical techniques vary according to scale properties and the type of question being asked. More univariate statistical tests exist than are shown in Exhibit 21.5, but these basic options address the majority of univariate analyses in marketing research. A complete discussion of all univariate techniques is beyond the scope of this text.

t-test
A hypothesis test that uses the *t*-distribution. A univariate *t*-test is appropriate when the variable being analyzed is interval or ratio.

The *t*-Distribution

A univariate **t-test** is appropriate for testing hypotheses involving some observed mean against some specified value. The **t-distribution**, like the standardized normal curve, is a symmetrical, bell-shaped distribution with a mean of 0 and a standard deviation of 1.0. When sample size (*n*) is larger than 30, the *t*-distribution and *Z*-distribution are almost identical. Therefore, while the *t*-test is strictly appropriate for tests involving small sample sizes with unknown standard deviations,

t-distribution
A symmetrical, bell-shaped distribution that is contingent on sample size; has a mean of 0 and a standard deviation equal to 1.

Ultra-luxury car makers have sales goals that may involve selling 1,000 cars or fewer a year worldwide. What questions are asked in marketing a car like this that might involve a univariate analysis?[6]

Degrees of freedom (d.f.)
The number of observations minus the number of constraints or assumptions needed to calculate a statistical term.

researchers commonly apply the *t*-test for comparisons involving the mean of an interval or ratio measure. The precise height and shape of the *t*-distribution vary with sample size. More specifically, the shape of the *t*-distribution is influenced by its **degrees of freedom (d.f.).** The degrees of freedom are determined by the number of distinct calculations that are possible given a set of information. In the case of a univariate *t*-test, the degrees of freedom are equal to the sample size (*n*) minus one.

Exhibit 21.6 illustrates *t*-distributions for 1, 2, 5, and an infinite number of degrees of freedom. Notice that the *t*-distribution approaches a normal distribution rapidly with increasing sample size. This is why, in practice, marketing researchers usually apply a *t*-test even with large samples. The practical effect is that the conclusion will be the same since the distributions are so similar with large samples and the correspondingly larger numbers of degrees of freedom.

Another way to look at degrees of freedom is to think of adding four numbers together when you know their sum—for example,

$$
\begin{array}{r}
4 \\
2 \\
1 \\
+X \\
\hline
12
\end{array}
$$

The value of the fourth number has to be 5. The values of the first three digits could change to any value (freely vary), but the fourth value would have to be determined for the mean to still equal to 12. In this example there are three degrees of freedom. Degrees of freedom can be a difficult

EXHIBIT 21.6
The *t*-Distribution for Various Degrees of Freedom

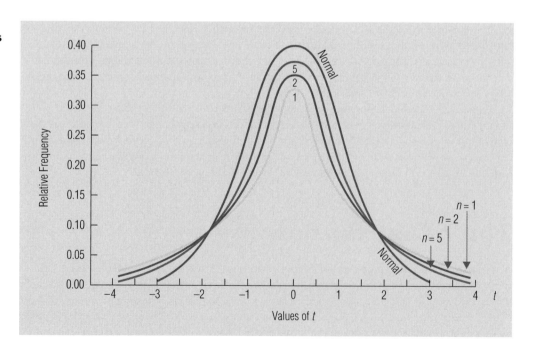

concept to understand fully. For most basic statistical analyses, the user only needs to remember the rule for determining the number of degrees of freedom for a given test. Today, with computerized software packages, even that number is provided automatically for most tests.

The calculation of t closely resembles the calculation of the Z-value. To calculate t, use the formula

$$t = \frac{\overline{X} - \mu}{S_{\overline{X}}}$$

with $n - 1$ degrees of freedom.

The Z-distribution and the t-distribution are very similar, and thus the Z-test and t-test will provide much the same result in most situations. However, when the population standard deviation (σ) is known, the Z-test is most appropriate. When σ is unknown (the situation in most marketing research studies), and the sample size greater than 30, the Z-test also can be used. When σ is unknown and the sample size is small, the t-test is most appropriate. Since the two distributions are similar with larger sample sizes, the two tests often yield the same conclusion.

Calculating a Confidence Interval Estimate Using the *t*-Distribution

Suppose a business organization is interested in finding out how long newly hired MBA graduates remain on their first jobs. On the basis of a small sample of employees with MBAs, the researcher wishes to estimate the population mean with 95 percent confidence. The data from the sample are presented below.

Number of years on first job: 3 5 7 1 12 1 2 2 5
4 2 3 1 3 4 2 6

To find the confidence interval estimate of the population mean for this small sample, we use the formula

$$\mu = \overline{X} \pm t_{c.l.} S_{\overline{X}}$$

or

$$\text{Upper limit} = \overline{X} + t_{c.l.} \left(\frac{S}{\sqrt{n}} \right)$$

$$\text{Lower limit} = \overline{X} - t_{c.l.} \left(\frac{S}{\sqrt{n}} \right)$$

where

μ = population mean
$\overline{X}$ = sample mean
$t_{c.l.}$ = critical value of t at a specified confidence level
$S_{\overline{X}}$ = standard error of the mean
S = sample standard deviation
n = sample size

More specifically, the step-by-step procedure for calculating the confidence interval is as follows:

1. We calculate $\overline{X}$ from the sample. Summing our data values yields $\Sigma X = 63$, and $\overline{X} = \Sigma X / n = 63/17 = 3.7$.
2. Since σ is unknown, we estimate the population standard deviation by finding S, the sample standard deviation. For our example, $S = 2.66$.
3. We estimate the standard error of the mean using the formula $S_{\overline{X}} = S/\sqrt{n}$ Thus, $S_{\overline{X}} = 2.66/\sqrt{17}$ or $S_{\overline{X}} = 0.645$.
4. We determine the t-values associated with the desired confidence level. To do this, we go to Table A.3 in the appendix. Although the t-table provides information similar to that in the

Z-table, it is somewhat different. The *t*-table format emphasizes the chance of error, or significance level (α), rather than the 95 percent chance of including the population mean in the estimate. Our example is a two-tailed test. Since a 95 percent confidence level has been selected, the significance level equals $0.05(1.00 - 0.95 = 0.05)$. Once this has been determined, all we have to do to find the *t*-value is look under the 0.05 column for *two-tailed tests* at the row in which degrees of freedom (*d.f.*) equal the appropriate value ($n - 1$). Below 16 degrees of freedom ($n - 1 = 17 - 1 = 16$), the *t*-value at the 95 percent confidence level (0.05 level of significance) is $t = 2.12$.

5. We calculate the confidence interval:

$$\text{Lower limit} = 3.7 - 2.12\left(\frac{2.66}{\sqrt{17}}\right) = 2.33$$

$$\text{Upper limit} = 3.7 + 2.12\left(\frac{2.66}{\sqrt{17}}\right) = 5.07$$

In our hypothetical example it may be concluded with 95 percent confidence that the population mean for the number of years spent on the first job by MBAs is between 2.33 and 5.07.

ONE AND TWO-TAILED *t*-TESTS

Univariate Z-tests and *t*-tests can be one or two-tailed. A two-tailed test is one that tests for differences from the population mean that are either greater or less. Thus, the extreme values of the normal curve (or tails) on both the right and the left are considered. In practical terms, when a research question does not specify whether a difference should be greater than or less than, a two-tailed test is most appropriate. For instance, the following research question could be examined using a two-tailed test:

The number of take-out pizza restaurants within a postal-code in Germany is not equal to 5.

A one-tailed univariate test is appropriate when a research hypothesis implies that an observed mean can only be greater than or less than a hypothesized value. Thus, only one of the "tails" of the bell-shaped normal curve is relevant. For instance, the following hypothesis could be appropriately examined with a one-tailed test:

H1: The number of pizza restaurants with a postal code in Florida is greater than five.

In this case, if the observed value is significantly less than five, the hypothesis is still not supported. Practically, a one-tailed test can be determined from a two-tailed test result by taking half of the observed p-value. When the researcher has any doubt about whether a one- or two-tailed test is appropriate, he or she should opt for the less conservative two-tailed test. Most computer software will assume a two-tailed test unless otherwise specified.

Univariate Hypothesis Test Using the *t*-Distribution

The step-by-step procedure for a *t*-test is conceptually similar to that for hypothesis testing with the Z-distribution. Suppose a Pizza-In store manager believes that the average number of customers who return a pizza or ask for a refund is twenty per day. The store records the number of returns and exchanges for each of the twenty-five days it was open during a given month. Are the return/complaint observations different than twenty per day? The substantive hypothesis is

$$H_1 : \mu \neq 20$$

1. The researcher calculates a sample mean and standard deviation. In this case, $\overline{X} = 22$ and S (sample standard deviation) $= 5$.

2. The standard error is computed ($S_{\bar{X}}$):

$$S_{\bar{X}} = \frac{S}{\sqrt{n}}$$

$$= \frac{5}{\sqrt{25}}$$

$$= 1$$

3. The researcher then finds the *t*-value associated with the desired level of confidence level or statistical significance. If a 95 percent confidence level is desired, the significance level is 0.05.

4. The critical values for the *t*-test are found by locating the upper and lower limits of the confidence interval. The result defines the regions of rejection. This requires determining the value of *t*. For 24 degrees of freedom ($n = 25$, $d.f. = n - 1$), the *t*-value is 2.064. The critical values are

$$\text{Lower limit} = \mu - t_{c.l.} S_{\bar{X}} = 20 - 2.064 \left(\frac{5}{\sqrt{25}} \right)$$

$$= 20 - 2.064(1)$$

$$= 17.936$$

$$\text{Upper limit} = \mu + t_{c.l.} S_{\bar{X}} = 20 + 2.064 \left(\frac{5}{\sqrt{25}} \right)$$

$$= 20 + 2.064(1)$$

$$= 22.064$$

Finally, the researcher makes the statistical decision by determining whether the sample mean falls between the critical limits. For the pizza store sample, $\bar{X} = 22$. The sample mean is *not* included in the region of rejection. Even though the sample result is only slightly less than the critical value at the upper limit, the null hypothesis cannot be rejected. In other words, the pizza store manager's assumption appears to be correct.

As with the *Z*-test, there is an alternative way to test a hypothesis with the *t*-statistic. This is by using the formula

$$t_{\text{obs}} = \frac{\bar{X} - \mu}{S_{\bar{X}}}$$

$$t_{\text{obs}} = \frac{22 - 20}{1} = \frac{2}{1} = 2$$

We can see that the observed *t*-value is less than the critical *t*-value of 2.064 at the 0.05 level when there are $25 - 1 = 24$ degrees of freedom. As a result, the p-value is greater than .05 and the hypothesis is not supported. We cannot conclude with 95 percent confidence that the mean is not 20.

The Chi-Square Test for Goodness of Fit

A **chi-square (χ^2) test** is one of the most basic tests for statistical significance and is particularly appropriate for testing hypotheses about frequencies arranged in a frequency or contingency table. Univariate tests involving nominal or ordinal variables are examined with a χ^2. More generally, the χ^2 test is associated with **goodness-of-fit (GOF)**. GOF can be thought of as how well some matrix (table) of numbers matches or *fits* another matrix of the same size. Most often, the test is between a table of observed frequency counts and another table of expected values (central tendency) for those counts.

Consider the following hypothesis that relates back to the chapter vignette:

H1: Papa John's Pizza stores are more likely to be located in a stand-alone location than in a shopping center.

A competitor may be interested in this hypothesis as part of the competitor analysis in a marketing plan. A researcher for the competitor gathers a random sample of 100 Papa John's locations in

Chi-square (χ^2) test
One of the most basic tests for statistical significance that is particularly appropriate for testing hypotheses about frequencies arranged in a frequency or contingency table.

Goodness-of-fit (GOF)
A general term representing how well some computed table or matrix of values matches some population or predetermined table or matrix of the same size.

California (where the competitor is located). The sample is selected from phone directories and the locations are checked by having an assistant drive to each location. The following observations are recorded in a frequency table.

Location	One-Way Frequency Table
Stand-Alone	60 stores
Shopping Center	40 stores
Total	100 stores

These observed values (O_i) can be compared to the expected values for this distribution (E_i) to complete a χ^2 test. The χ^2 value will reflect the likelihood that the observed values come from a distribution reflected by the expected values. The higher the value of the χ^2 test, the less likely it is that the expected and observed values are the same.

In statistical terms, a χ^2 test determines whether the difference between an observed frequency distribution and the corresponding expected frequency distribution is due to sampling variation. Computing a χ^2 test is fairly straightforward and easy. Students who master this calculation should have little trouble understanding future significance tests since the basic logic of the χ^2 test underlies these tests as well.

The steps in computing a χ^2 test are as follows:

1. Gather data and tally the observed frequencies for the categorical variable.
2. Compute the expected values for each value of the categorical variable.
3. Calculate the χ^2 value, using the observed frequencies from the sample and the expected frequencies.
4. Find the degrees of freedom for the test.
5. Make the statistical decision by comparing p-value associated with the calculated χ^2 against the predetermined significance level (acceptable Type I error rate).

These steps can be illustrated with the pizza store location example.

- The data for the location variable (stand-alone or shopping center) are provided in the frequency table above.
- The next step asks, "What are the expected frequencies for the location variable? This is another way of asking the central tendency for each category. Since the sample size is 100, finding the expected values is easy. If no pattern exists in the locations, they should be distributed randomly across the two categories. We would expect that half (50) of the locations would be stand-alone and half (50) would be in a shopping center. This is another way of saying that the expected probability of being one type of location is 50 percent. The expected values also can be placed in a frequency table:

Location	Expected Frequencies
Stand-Alone	100/2 = 50 stores
Shopping Center	100/2 = 50 stores
Total	100 stores

- The actual χ^2 value is computed using the following formula:

$$\chi^2 = \sum \frac{(O_i - E_i)^2}{E_i}$$

where,

χ^2 = chi-square statistic
O_i = observed frequency in the ith cell
E_i = expected frequency in the ith cell

Sum the squared differences:

$$\chi^2 = \frac{(O_1 - E_1)^2}{E_i} + \frac{(O_2 - E_2)^2}{E_2}$$

RESEARCHSNAPSHOT

Art for Girls and Boys

Chi-square tests are used often in marketing research. Consider a private art museum that sponsors a program of summer art classes for children. They need to plan the number and types of activities and exhibits that should be included in the museum. One question is whether or not an equal number of boys and girls will come to the museum. A random sample from its list of students shows more girls than boys. They decide to observe the relative frequencies of boys and girls for the first 1,000 visitors under the age of sixteen. The results are shown in the bar charts below:

Therefore, the acceptable level of Type I error is set at 0.01. Rather than referring to a critical value table, the p-value associated with a χ^2 value and the associated degrees of freedom can be found on any one of several statistical calculators found on the Internet. In this case, the researcher uses the calculator found at http://faculty.vassar.edu/lowry/tabs.html#csq. By simply plugging in the observed value of 38.4 and the number of degrees of freedom as indicated, 1 in this case, the calculator returns a p-value. In this case, the p-value returned is less than 0.0001. Therefore, since the p-value is less than the acceptable level of risk, the researcher reaches the conclusion that the

The χ^2 value can be computed as shown below:

	Expected	Observed	$O - E$	$(O - E)^2$	$(O - E)^2/E$
Boys	500	402	−98	9604	19.208
Girls	500	598	98	9604	19.208
	1000	1000			38.416

The museum managers want to be sure a difference exists before investing resources into activities designed for girls or boys only.

children visiting the museum are not equally distributed between boys and girls. Clearly, more girls visit than boys.

Thus, the museum can go about designing features that appeal to boys and girls proportionately to the observed frequency distribution.

Thus, we determine that the chi-square value equals 4:

$$\chi^2 = \frac{(60 - 50)^2}{50} + \frac{(40 - 50)^2}{50}$$
$$= 4$$

Alternatively, the calculation can be followed in tabular form:

Location:	O_i	E_i	$(O_i - E_i)$	$\dfrac{(O_i - E_i)^2}{E_i}$
Stand-Alone	60	50	10	100/50 = 2.0
Shopping Center	40	50	−10	100/50 = 2.0
Total	100	100	0	$\chi^2 = 4.0$

- Like many other probability distributions, the χ^2 distribution is not a single probability curve, but a family of curves. These curves vary slightly with the degrees of freedom. In this case, the degrees of freedom can be computed as

$$d.f. = k - 1$$

where

k = number of cells associated with column or row data.

Thus, the degrees of freedom equal $1 (d.f. = 2 - 1 = 1)$.

- Now the computed χ^2 value needs to be compared with the critical chi-square values associated with the 0.05 probability level with 1 degree of freedom. In Table A.4 of the appendix the critical χ^2 value is 3.84. Since the calculated χ^2 is larger than the tabular chi-square, the conclusion is that the observed values do not equal the expected values. Therefore, the hypothesis is supported. More Papa John's restaurants are located in stand-alone locations.

We discuss the chi-square test further in Chapter 22, as it is also frequently used to analyze contingency tables.

Hypothesis Test of a Proportion

Hypothesis test of a proportion
A test that is conceptually similar to the one used when the mean is the characteristic of interest but that differs in the mathematical formulation of the standard error of the proportion.

Researchers often test univariate statistical hypotheses about population proportions. The population proportion (π) can be estimated on the basis of an observed sample proportion (p). Conducting a **hypothesis test of a proportion** is conceptually similar to hypothesis testing when the mean is the characteristic of interest. Mathematically the formulation of the standard error of the proportion differs somewhat, though.

Consider the following example. A state legislature is considering a proposed right-to-work law. One legislator has hypothesized that more than 50 percent of the state's labor force is unionized. In other words, the hypothesis to be tested is that the proportion of union workers in the state is greater than 0.5.

The researcher formulates the hypothesis that the population proportion (π) exceeds 50 percent (0.5):

$$H_1 : \pi > 0.5$$

Suppose the researcher conducts a survey with a sample of 100 workers and calculates $p = 0.6$. Even though the population proportion is unknown, a large sample allows use of a Z-test (rather than the t-test). If the researcher decides that the decision rule will be set at the 0.01 level of significance, the critical Z-value of 2.57 is used for the hypothesis test. Using the following formula, we can calculate the observed value of Z given a certain sample proportion:

$$Z_{obs} = \frac{p - \pi}{S_p}$$

where

p = sample proportion
π = hypothesized population proportion
S_p = estimate of the standard error of the proportion

The formula for S_p is

$$S_p = \sqrt{\frac{pq}{n}} \quad \text{or} \quad S_p = \sqrt{\frac{p(1-p)}{n}}$$

where

S_p = estimate of the standard error of the proportion
p = proportion of successes
$q = 1 - p$, proportion of failures

In our example,

$$S_p = \sqrt{\frac{(0.6)(0.4)}{100}}$$

$$= \sqrt{\frac{0.24}{100}}$$

$$= \sqrt{0.0024}$$

$$= 0.04899$$

Z_{obs} can now be calculated:

$$Z_{obs} = \frac{p - \pi}{S_p}$$

$$= \frac{0.6 - 0.5}{0.04899}$$

$$= \frac{0.1}{0.04899}$$

$$= 2.04$$

The Z_{obs} value of 2.04 is less than the critical value of 2.57, so the hypothesis is not supported.

Additional Applications of Hypothesis Testing

The discussion of statistical inference in this chapter has been restricted to examining the difference between an observed sample mean and a population or pre-specified mean, a $\chi 2$ test examining the difference between an observed frequency and the expected frequency for a given distribution and Z-tests to test hypotheses about sample proportions when sample sizes are large. Other hypothesis tests for population parameters estimated from sample statistics exist but are not mentioned here. Many of these tests are no different conceptually in their methods of hypothesis testing. However, the formulas are mathematically different. The purpose of this chapter has been to discuss basic statistical concepts. Once you have learned the basic terminology in this chapter, you should have no problem generalizing to other statistical problems.

As we emphasized in Chapter 17, the key to understanding statistics is learning the basics of the language. This chapter has presented verbs, nouns, and some of the rules of the grammar of statistics. Here, we begin to adopt a more practical perspective by focusing on the p-values to determine whether a hypothesis is supported rather than discussing null and alternative hypotheses. In more cases than not, low p-values (below the specified α) support researchers' hypotheses.[7] It is hoped that some of the myths about statistics have been shattered and that they are becoming easier to use.

Summary

1. **Implement the hypothesis testing procedure.** Hypothesis testing can involve univariate, bivariate, or multivariate statistics. In this chapter, the focus is on univariate statistics. These are tests that involve one variable. Usually, this means that the observed value for one variable will be compared to some benchmark or standard. Statistical analysis is needed to test hypotheses when sample observations are used to draw an inference about some corresponding population. The research establishes an acceptable significance level, representing the chance of a Type I error, and then computes the statistic that applies to the situation. The exact statistic that must be computed depends largely on the level of scale measurement.

2. Use p-values to test statistical significance. A p-value is the probability value associated with a statistical test. The probability in a p-value is the probability that the expected value for some test distribution is true. In other words, for a t-test, the expected value of the t-distribution is 0. If a researcher is testing whether or not a variable is significantly different from 0, then the p-value that results from the corresponding computed t-value represents the probability that the true population mean is actually 0. For most marketing research hypotheses, a low p-value supports the hypothesis. If a p-value is lower than the researcher's acceptable significance level (α), then the hypothesis is usually supported.

3. Test a hypothesis about an observed mean. Researchers often have to compare an observed sample mean with some specified value. The appropriate statistical test to compare an interval or ratio level variable's mean with some value is either the Z- or t-test. The Z-test is most appropriate when the sample size is large or the population standard deviation is known. The t-test is most appropriate when the sample size is small or the population standard deviation is not known. In most practical applications the t-test and Z-test will result in the same conclusion. The t-test is used more often in practice.

4. Know the difference between Type I and Type II errors. A Type I error occurs when a researcher reaches the conclusion that some difference or relationship exists within a population when in fact none exists. In the context of a univariate t-test, the researcher may conclude that some mean value for a variable is greater than 0 when in fact the true value for that variable in the population being considered is 0. A Type II error is the opposite situation. When the researcher reaches the conclusion that no difference exists when one truly does exist in the population, the researcher has committed a Type II error. More attention is usually given to Type I errors. Type II errors are very sensitive to sample size.

5. Know the univariate χ^2 test. A χ^2 test is one of the most basic tests for statistical significance. The test is particularly appropriate for testing hypotheses about frequencies arranged in a frequency or contingency table. The χ^2 test value is a function of the observed value for a given entry in a frequency table minus the statistical expected value for that cell. The observed statistical value can be compared to critical values to determine the p-value with any test. The χ^2 test is often considered a goodness-of-fit test because it can test how well an observed matrix represents some theoretical standard.

Key Terms and Concepts

Univariate statistical analysis	Type I error	Degrees of freedom (d.f.)
Bivariate statistical analysis	Type II error	Chi-square (χ^2) test
Multivariate statistical analysis	Parametric statistics	Goodness-of-fit (GOF)
Significance level	Nonparametric statistics	Hypothesis test of a proportion
p-value	t-test	
Critical valuesz	t-distribution	

Questions for Review and Critical Thinking

1. What is the purpose of a statistical hypothesis?
2. What is a *significance level*? How does a researcher choose a significance level?
3. What is the difference between a *significance level* and a *p-value*?
4. How is a p-value used to test a hypothesis?
5. Distinguish between a *Type I* and *Type II error*.
6. What are the factors that determine the choice of the appropriate statistical technique?
7. A researcher is asked to determine whether or not a sales objective of better than $75,000 per salesperson is possible. A market test is done involving twenty salespeople. What conclusion

would you reach? The sales results are as follows:

a	28,000	105,000	58,000	93,000	96,000
b.	67,000	82,500	75,000	81,000	59,000
c.	101,000	60,500	77,000	72,500	48,000
d.	99,000	78,000	71,000	80,500	78,000

8. Assume you have the following data: $H1 : \mu \neq 200$, $S = 30$, $n = 64$, and $Xbar = 218$. Conduct a two-tailed hypothesis test at the 0.05 significance level.
9. If the data in question 8 had been generated with a sample of 25 ($n = 25$), what statistical test would be appropriate?

10. The answers to a researcher's question will be nominally scaled. What statistical test is appropriate for comparing the sample data with hypothesized population data?

11. A researcher plans to ask employees whether they favor, oppose, or are indifferent about a change in the company retirement program. Formulate a hypothesis for a chi-square test and the way the variable would be created.

12. Give an example in which a Type I error may be more serious than a Type II error.

13. Refer to the pizza store location χ^2 data on pages 537–540. What statistical decisions could be made if the 0.01 significance level were selected rather than the 0.05 level?

14. Determine a hypothesis that the following data may address and perform a χ^2 test on the survey data.

a. *American Idol* should be broadcast before 9 p.m.

Agree	40
Neutral	35
Disagree	25
	100

b. Political affiliation of a group indicate

Republicans	102
Democrats	98
	200

15. A researcher hypothesizes that 15 percent of the people in a test-market will recall seeing a particular advertisement. In a sample of 1,200 people, 20 percent say they recall the ad. Perform a hypothesis test.

Research Activities

1. 'NET What is the ideal climate? Fill in the following blanks: The lowest temperature in January should be no lower than _____ degrees. At least _____ days should be sunny in January.

   a. List at least 15 places where you would like to live. Using the Internet, find the average low temperature in January for each place. This information is available through various weather related websites such as http://www.weather.com or through each community's local news website. Record the data in a spreadsheet or statistical package such as SPSS. Using the benchmark (preferred population low temperature) you filled in above, test whether the sample places that you would like to live have an ideal January minimum temperature.

   b. Using the same website, record how many days in January are typically sunny. Test whether or not the number of sunny days meets your standard.

   c. For each location, record whether or not there was measurable precipitation yesterday. Test the following hypothesis: H1: Among places you would like to live, there is less than a 33.3 percent chance of rain/snow on a given day (five days out of fifteen).

2. ETHICS Examine the statistical choices under "analyze" in SPSS. Click on compare means. To compare an observed mean to some benchmark or hypothesized population mean, the available choice is a one-sample *t*-test. A researcher is preparing a report and finds the following result testing a hypothesis that suggested the sample mean did not equal 14:

   a. What is the p-value? Is the hypothesis supported?

   b. Write the 95% confidence interval which corresponds to an α of 0.05.

   c. Technically, since the sample size is greater than 30, a *Z*-test might be more appropriate. However, since the *t*-test result is readily available with SPSS, the research presents this result. Is there an ethical problem in using the one-sample *t*-test?

One-Sample Statistics

	N	Mean	Std. Deviation	Std. Error Mean
1997–2000	67	14.5337	16.02663	1.95796

Test Value = 14

	t	d.f.	Sig. (two-tailed)	Mean Difference	95% Confidence Interval of the Difference	
					Lower	Upper
1997–2000	0.273	66	0.786	0.53373	−3.3755	4.4429

Case 21.1 Quality Motors

Download the data sets for this case from http://zikmund.swcollege.com or request them from your instructor.

Quality Motors is an automobile dealership that regularly advertises in its local market area. It claims that a certain make and model of car averages 30 miles to a gallon of gas and mentions that this figure may vary with driving conditions. A local consumer group wishes to verify the advertising claim. To do so, it selects a sample of recent purchasers of this make and model of automobile. It asks them to drive their cars until two tanks of gasoline have been used up and to record the mileage. The group then calculates and records the miles per gallon for each year. The data in Case Exhibit 21.1–1 portray the results of the tests.

Questions

1. Formulate a statistical hypothesis appropriate for the consumer group's purpose.
2. Calculate the mean average miles per gallon. Compute the sample variance and sample standard deviation.
3. Construct the appropriate statistical test for your hypothesis, using a 0.05 significance level.

CASE EXHIBIT 21.1–1 **Miles per Gallon Information**

Purchaser	Miles per Gallon	Purchaser	Miles per Gallon
1	30.9	14	27.0
2	24.5	15	26.7
3	31.2	16	31.0
4	28.7	17	23.5
5	35.1	18	29.4
6	29.0	19	26.3
7	28.8	20	27.5
8	23.1	21	28.2
9	31.0	22	28.4
10	30.2	23	29.1
11	28.4	24	21.9
12	29.3	25	30.9
13	24.2		

Case 21.2 Coastal Star Sales Corporation (B)

Download the data sets for this case from http://zikmund.swcollege.com or request them from your instructor.

See Coastal Star Sales Corporation (A), Case 17.1, for a description of the data.

Questions

1. Develop a hypothesis concerning the average age of the sales force at Coastal Star and test the hypothesis.
2. Calculate the mean for the previous year's sales, and use it as the basis for forming a hypothesis concerning the current year's sales. Test the hypothesis concerning the current year's sales.

CHAPTER 22
BIVARIATE STATISTICAL ANALYSIS: DIFFERENCES BETWEEN TWO VARIABLES

LEARNING OUTCOMES

After studying this chapter, you should be able to

1. Recognize when a particular bivariate statistical test is appropriate
2. Calculate and interpret a χ^2 test for a contingency table
3. Calculate and interpret an independent samples *t*-test comparing two means
4. Understand the concept of analysis of variance (ANOVA)
5. Interpret an ANOVA table

Chapter Vignette: Is the Price Right?

The objective in most of the pricing games on *The Price is Right* is knowing the right price. When consumers know the right price, they save money, and saving money can be very exciting. Perhaps *The Price is Right* is ready for a new pricing game called "Bricks or Clicks." ? "Bricks or Clicks" would involve examining several products and then letting Bob Barker know whether or not a specific product is priced lower on the Internet (clicks) or at a traditional retailer (bricks).

Are prices lower on the Internet? This has been a subject of much debate over the last decade. In the early days of Internet retailing, so-called experts made many grand predictions about how e-tailing would evolve. A few predictions may have been correct, but most have proved wrong. For instance, many predicted that e-tailing would make many traditional retailers obsolete. Almost all predictions involving price forecast that the wide availability of price information on the Internet would force prices to their lowest level. Smart software systems called *bots* would quickly search the Internet and inform the consumer where an item could be purchased at the lowest price. However, consumers that think the Internet is always the avenue to the lowest price may not be right.[1]

Are prices offered by e-tailers really lower? Are the price discounts greater on the Internet? The answers depend on what a consumer is trying to buy. A 2001 study of the prices of DVDs showed the following average prices:[2]

© FRED PROUSER/REUTERS/LANDOV

Retail Type	Average Price	Percentage-Price
E-tailers	$19.92	72.0%
Traditional (Multi-Channel Retailers)	$23.19	83.9%

A comparison of the prices suggests that dot-com retailers offer better prices.

Case closed? Not so fast! If consumers need a DVD player instead of a DVD, they may have better luck with a more traditional retailer, or at least one that offers both real and virtual retail shopping opportunities (multi-channel). In consumer electronics, the following results are seen:

Retail Type	DVD Player Average Price	Percentage-Price
E-tailers	$371.95	75.6%
Multi-Channel Retailers	$360.30	74.8%

A comparison of these prices suggests that the multi-channel retailers offer better prices. Even though they may never appear on a television game show, consumers and businesses alike find many occasions to compare prices.

What Is the Appropriate Test of Difference?

Researchers commonly test hypotheses stating that two groups differ. In marketing research, differences in behavior, characteristics, beliefs, opinions, emotions, or attitudes are commonly examined. For example, in the most basic experimental design, the researcher tests differences between subjects assigned to an experimental group and subjects assigned to the control group. A survey researcher may be interested in whether male and female consumers purchase a product in the same amount. Business researchers may also test whether or not business units in Europe are as profitable as business units in the United States. Such tests are bivariate **tests of differences** when they involve only two variables: a variable that acts like a dependent variable and a variable that acts as a classification variable.

Exhibit 22.1 illustrates that the type of measurement, the nature of the comparison, and the number of groups to be compared influence the statistical choice. Often researchers are interested in testing differences in mean scores between groups or in comparing how two groups' scores are distributed across possible response categories. We will focus our attention on these issues.[3] The rest of the chapter focuses on how to choose the right statistic for two-group comparisons and perform the corresponding test. Exhibit 22.1 provides a frame of reference for the rest of the chapter by illustrating various possible comparisons involving a few golfers.

Construction of contingency tables for χ^2 analysis gives a procedure for comparing observed frequencies of one group with the frequencies of another group. This is a good starting point from which to discuss testing of differences.

Test of differences
An investigation of a hypothesis stating that two (or more) groups differ with respect to measures on a variable.

Cross-Tabulation Tables: The χ^2 Test for Goodness-of-Fit

TOTHEPOINT

You got to be careful if you don't know where you're going, because you might not get there.

—Yogi Berra

Cross-tabulation is among the most widely used statistical techniques among marketing researchers. Cross-tabulations are intuitive and easily understood. They also lend themselves well to graphical analysis using tools like bar charts.

A cross-tabulation, or contingency table, is a joint frequency distribution of observations on two more variables. Researchers generally rely on two-variable cross-tabulations the most since the results can be easily communicated. Cross-tabulations are much like tallying. When two variables exist, each with two categories, four cells result. The χ^2 distribution provides a means for testing the statistical significance of contingency table. In other words, the bivariate χ^2 test examines statistical significance of relationships among two less than interval variables.

EXHIBIT 22.1 **Choosing the Right Statistic**

	Dolly	Lori	Measurement Levels Involved	Statistic Comment
Driver Distance	203.1 meters	185.0 meters	Distance = Ratio Golfer = Nominal, creating 2 groups	An independent samples *t*-test could be used to compare the average distance (ratio variable) by golfer (nominal variable) assuming we had observed 28 drives for each.
3-Wood Distance	185 meters	179.5 meters	Distance = Ratio Club = Nominal, creating 2 groups	As above, we could compare distance between the two with an independent samples *t*-test, but suppose we wished to know whether or not Lori's distance with the 3-Wood is different than her distance with her driver. When we compare one ratio variable observed on one person grouped by a nominal variable (club type—driver/3-wood), a paired-samples *t*-test would be used.
Nationality	Brazil	New Zealand	Nationality = Nominal Rank = Ordinal	If we wished to know whether nationality affected a golfer's ranking in some competition, we could use a cross-tab with χ^2.
Favorite Brand	Mizuno	Callaway	Brand = Nominal Nationality = Nominal	If we observed 50 women golfers, and wished to know whether nationality affected whether they were more likely to prefer Mizuno to Callaway, again the appropriate analysis would be a cross-tab with χ^2.
	Driver Distance = 220 meters		Dependent Variable is Distance = Ratio Independent Variable is Nominal (Golfer) and results in 3 groups (distance for Dolly, Lori, and now Mel)	If we add a 3rd golfer (Mel), and we wished to test for differences in driver distance, we would move to one way ANOVA.

The χ^2 test for a contingency table involves comparing the observed frequencies (O_i) with the expected frequencies (E_i) in each cell of the table. The goodness- (or closeness-) of-fit of the observed distribution with the expected distribution is captured by this statistic. Remember that the convention is that the row variable is considered the independent variable and the column variable is considered the dependent variable.

Recall that in Chapter 21 we used a χ^2 test to examine whether or not Papa John's restaurants in California were more likely to be located in a stand-alone location or in a shopping center. The univariate (one-dimensional) analysis suggests that the majority of the locations (60 percent) are stand-alone units:

Location	One-Way Frequency Table
Stand-alone	60 stores
Shopping Center	40 stores
Total	100 stores

Recall that the $\chi^2 = 4.0$ with 1 degree of freedom (p < 0.01).

Is there any effect of location of Papa John's restaurants? Suppose the researcher wishes to examine the following hypothesis:

Stand-alone locations are more likely to be profitable than are shopping center locations.

While the researcher is unable to obtain the dollar figures for profitability of each unit, a press release indicates which Papa John's units were profitable and which were not. Cross-tabulation using a χ^2 test is appropriate because

- The independent variable (location) is less-than interval.
- The dependent variable (profitable/not profitable) is less-than interval.

The data can be recorded in the following 2 × 2 contingency table:

Location	Profitable	Not Profitable	Total
Stand-alone	50	10	60
Shopping Center	15	25	40
Totals	65	35	100

Several conclusions appear evident. One, it seems that more stores are profitable than not profitable (65 versus 35, respectively). Secondly, more of the profitable restaurants seem to be in stand-alone locations (50/65). However, is the difference strong enough to be statistically significant?

Is the observed difference between stand-alone and shopping center locations the result of chance variation due to random sampling? Is the discrepancy more than sampling variation? The χ^2 test allows us to conduct tests for significance in the analysis of the $R \times C$ contingency table (where R = row and C = column). The formula for the χ^2 statistic is the same as that for one-way frequency tables (see Chapter 21):

$$\chi^2 = \sum \frac{(O_i - E_i)^2}{E_i}$$

where

χ^2 = chi-square statistic

O_i = observed frequency in the ith cell

E_i = expected frequency in the ith cell

Again, as in the univariate χ^2 test, a frequency count of data that nominally identify or categorically rank groups is acceptable.

If the researcher's hypothesis is true, the frequencies shown in the contingency table should not resemble a random distribution. In other words, if location has no effect on profitability, the profitable and unprofitable stores would be spread evenly across the two location categories. This is really the logic of the test in that it compares the observed frequencies with the theoretical expected values for each cell.

After obtaining the observations for each cell, the expected values for each cell must be obtained. The expected values for each cell can be computed easily using this formula:

$$E_{ij} = \frac{R_i\,C_j}{n}$$

where

$R_i =$ total observed frequency count in the ith row

$C_j =$ total observed frequency count in the jth column

$n =$ sample size

Only the total column and total row values are needed for this calculation. Thus, the calculation could be performed before the data are even tabulated. The following values represent the expected values for each cell:

Location	Profitable	Not Profitable	Total
Stand-alone	$(60 \times 65)/100 = 39$	$(60 \times 35)/100 = 21$	60
Shopping Center	$(65 \times 40)/100 = 26$	$(40 \times 35)/100 = 14$	40
Totals	65	35	100

Notice that the row and column totals are the same for both the observed and expected contingency matrices. These values also become useful in providing the substantive interpretation of the relationship. Variance from the expected value indicates a relationship.

The actual bivariate χ^2 test value can be calculated in the same manner as for the univariate test. The one difference is that the degrees of freedom are now obtained by multiplying the number of rows minus one $(R - 1)$ times the number of columns minus one $(C - 1)$:

$$\chi^2 = \sum \frac{(O_i - E_i)^2}{E_i}$$

with $(R - 1)(C - 1)$ degrees of freedom. The observed and expected values can be plugged into the formula as follows:

$$\chi^2 = \frac{(50 - 39)^2}{39} + \frac{(10 - 21)^2}{21} + \frac{(15 - 26)^2}{26} + \frac{(25 - 14)^2}{14}$$

$$= 3.102 + 5.762 + 4.654 + 8.643$$

$$= 22.16$$

The number of degrees of freedom equals 1:

$$(R - 1)(C - 1) = (2 - 1)(2 - 1) = 1$$

From Table A.4 in the appendix, we see that the critical value at the 0.05 probability level with 1 d.f. is 3.84. Thus, we are very confident that the observed values do not equal the expected values. Before the hypothesis can be supported, however, the researcher must check and see that the deviations from the expected values are in the hypothesized direction. Since the difference

RESEARCHSNAPSHOT

Chi-Training

When is a cross-tabulation with a χ^2 test appropriate? The answer to this question can be determined by answering these questions:

- Are multiple variables expected to be related to one another?
- Is the independent variable nominal or ordinal?
- Is the dependent variable nominal or ordinal?

When the answer to all of these questions is yes, cross-tabulation with a χ^2 test will address the research question. One common application involves the effect of some workplace change. For instance, this might involve the adoption of a new technology or the effect of training. For instance, consider the following contingency data represented in bar charts to the right.

The data show whether or not the adoption of a new information system produced accurate or inaccurate information. The 2-by-2 contingency table underlying this bar chart produces a χ^2 value of 5.97 with 1 degree of freedom. The p-value is less than 0.05; thus,

the new technology does seem to have changed accuracy. However, we must examine the actual cell counts to see exactly what this effect has been. In this case, the bar chart indicates that the new technology is associated with more incidences of accurate rather than inaccurate information.

Sources: For examples of research involving this type of analysis, see Gohmann, S.E., R.M. Barker, D.J. Faulds, and J. Guan (2005), "Salesforce Automation, Perceived Information Accuracy and User Satisfaction," Journal of Business and Industrial Marketing, 20, 23–32; Makela, C.J. and S. Peters (2004), "Consumer Education: Creating Consumer Awareness Among Adolescents in Botswana," International Journal of Consumer Studies, 28 (September), 379–387.

between the stand-alone locations' observed profitability and the expected values for that cell are positive, the hypothesis is supported. Location is associated with profitability. Thus, testing the hypothesis involves two key steps:

1. Examine the statistical significance of the observed contingency table.
2. Examine whether the differences between the observed and expected values are consistent with the hypothesized prediction.

Proper use of the χ^2 test requires that each expected cell test requires that each expected cell frequency (E_{ij}) have a value of at least 5. If this sample size requirement is not met, the researcher should take a larger sample or combine (collapse) response categories.

The *t*-Test for Comparing Two Means

Independent Samples *t*-Test

When a researcher needs to compare means for a variable grouped into two categories based on some less than interval variable, a *t*-test is appropriate. One way to think about this is as testing the way a dichotomous (two-level) independent variable is associated with changes in a continuous dependent variable. Several variations of the *t*-test exist.

Most typically, the researcher will apply the **independent samples *t*-test**, which tests the differences between means taken from two independent samples or groups. So, for example, if we measure the price for some designer jeans at thirty different retail stores, of which fifteen are Internet-only stores (pure clicks) and fifteen are traditional stores, we can test whether or not the prices are different based on store type with an independent samples *t*-test. The *t*-test for difference of means assumes the two samples (one Internet and one traditional store) are drawn from normal distributions and that the variances of the two populations are approximately equal (homoscedasticity).

Independent samples *t*-test
A test for hypotheses stating that the mean scores for some interval- or ratio-scaled variable grouped based on some less than interval classificatory variable.

▦ INDEPENDENT SAMPLES *t*-TEST CALCULATION

The *t*-test actually tests whether or not the differences between two means is zero. Not surprisingly, this idea can be expressed as the difference between two population means:

$$\mu_1 = \mu_2, \text{ which is equivalent to, } \mu_1 - \mu_2 = 0$$

However, since this is inferential statistics, we test the idea by comparing two sample means $(\overline{X}_1 - \overline{X}_2)$.

A verbal expression of the formula for *t* is

$$t = \frac{\text{Sample Mean 1} - \text{Sample Mean 2}}{\text{Variability of random means}}$$

Thus, the *t*-value is a ratio with information about the difference between means (provided by the sample) in the numerator and the standard error in the denominator. The question is whether the observed differences have occurred by chance alone. To calculate *t*, we use the following formula:

$$t = \frac{\overline{X}_1 - \overline{X}_2}{S_{\overline{X}_1 - \overline{X}_2}}$$

where

$$\overline{X}_1 = \text{mean for group 1}$$
$$\overline{X}_2 = \text{mean for group 2}$$
$$S_{\overline{X}_1 - \overline{X}_2} = \text{pooled, or combined, standard error of difference between means}$$

A **pooled estimate of the standard error** is a better estimate of the standard error than one based on the variance from either sample. The pooled standard error of the difference between means of independent samples can be calculated using the following formula:

Pooled estimate of the standard error
An estimate of the standard error for a *t*-test of independent means that assumes the variances of both groups are equal.

$$S_{\overline{X}_1 - \overline{X}_2} = \sqrt{\left(\frac{(n_1 - 1)\, S_1^2 + (n_2 - 1)\, S_2^2}{n_1 + n_2 - 2} \right) \left(\frac{1}{n_1} + \frac{1}{n_2} \right)}$$

where

$$S_1^2 = \text{variance of group 1}$$
$$S_2^2 = \text{variance of group 2}$$
$$n_1 = \text{sample size of group 1}$$
$$n_2 = \text{sample size of group 2}$$

Are business majors or sociology majors more positive about a career in business? A *t*-test can be used to test the difference between sociology majors and business majors on scores on a scale measuring attitudes toward business. We will assume that the attitude scale is an interval scale. The result of the simple random sample of these two groups of college students is shown below:

Business Students	Sociology Students
$\bar{X}_1 = 16.5$	$\bar{X}_2 = 12.2$
$S_1 = 2.1$	$S_2 = 2.6$
$n_1 = 21$	$n_2 = 14$

A high score indicates a favorable attitude toward business. This particular t-test tests whether the difference in attitudes between sociology and business students is significant. A higher t-value is associated with a lower p-value. As the t gets higher and the p-value gets lower, the researcher has more confidence that the means are truly different. The relevant data computation is

$$S_{\bar{X}_1 - \bar{X}_2} = \sqrt{\left(\frac{(n_1 - 1)S_1^2 + (n_2 - 1)S_2^2}{n_1 + n_2 - 2}\right)\left(\frac{1}{n_1} + \frac{1}{n_2}\right)}$$

$$= \sqrt{\left(\frac{(20)(2.1)^2 + (13)(2.6)^2}{33}\right)\left(\frac{1}{21} + \frac{1}{14}\right)}$$

$$= 0.797$$

The calculation of the t-statistic is

$$t = \frac{\bar{X}_1 - \bar{X}_2}{S_{\bar{X}_1 - \bar{X}_2}}$$

$$= \frac{16.5 - 12.2}{0.797}$$

$$= \frac{4.3}{0.797}$$

$$= 5.395$$

In a test of two means, degrees of freedom are calculated as follows:

$$d.f. = n - k$$

where

$n = n_1 + n_2$

k = number of groups

In our example d.f. equals 33. If the 0.01 level of significance is selected, reference to Table A.3 in the appendix yields the critical t-value. The t-value of 2.75 must be surpassed by the observed t-value if the hypothesis test is to be statistically significant at the 0.01 level. The calculated value of t, 5.39, far exceeds the critical value of t for statistical significance, so it is significant at $\alpha = 0.01$. The p-value is less than 0.01. In other words, this research shows that business students have significantly more positive attitudes toward business than do sociology students.

PRACTICALLY SPEAKING

In practice, computer software is used to compute the t-test results. Exhibit 22.2 displays a typical t-test printout. These particular results examine the following research question:

RQ: Does religion relate to price sensitivity?

This question was addressed in the context of restaurant and wine consumption by allowing 100 consumers to sample a specific wine and then tell the researcher how much they would be willing to pay for a bottle of the wine. The sample included 57 Catholics and 43 Protestants. Because no direction of the relationship is stated (no hypotheses is offered), a two-tailed test is

RESEARCHSNAPSHOT

Expert "T-eeze"

When is an independent samples *t*-test appropriate? Once again, we can find out by answering some simple questions:

- Is the dependent variable interval or ratio?
- Can the dependent variable scores be grouped based upon some categorical variable?
- Does the grouping result in scores drawn from independent samples?
- Are two groups involved in the research question?

When the answer to all questions is yes, an independent samples *t*-test is appropriate. Often, business researchers may wish to examine how some process varies between novices and experts. Consider the following example.

Researchers looked at the difference in decision speed for expert and novice salespeople faced with the same situation. Decision speed is a ratio dependent variable and the scores are grouped based on whether or not the salesperson is an expert or a novice. Thus, this categorical variable produces two groups. The results across forty respondents, twenty experts, and twenty novices, are shown at the top right.

The average difference in decision time is 38 seconds. Is this significantly different from 0? The calculated *t*-test is 2.76 with 38 d.f. The one-tailed p-value is 0.0045; thus the conclusion is reached that experts do take less time to make a decision than do novices.

Decision Time (seconds)

©IMAGES SOURCE/JUPITER IMAGES

Source: Shepherd, D.G., S.F. Gardial, M.G. Johnson, and J.O. Rentz (2006), "Cognitive Insights into the Highly Skilled or Expert Salesperson," Psychology and Marketing, 23 (February), 115–138. Reprinted with permission of John Wiley & Sons, Inc.

EXHIBIT 22.2 Independent Samples *t*-Test Results

Group Statistics

	rel	N	Mean	Std. Deviation	Std. Error Mean	
price	Catholic	57	61.00	43.381	5.746	1. Shows mean, standard deviation, and standard error for each group (Catholic and Protestant)
	Protestant	43	50.27	64.047	9.767	

Independent Samples Test

NOTE: Top row shows results assuming equal variances. Bottom row assumes variance is different in each.

		Levene's Test for Equality of Variances		t-Test for Equality of Means						95% Confidence Interval of the Difference	
		F	Sig.	t	d.f.	Sig. (2-tailed)	Mean Difference	Std. Error Difference		Lower	Upper
price	Equal variances assumed	.769	.383	.998	98	.321	10.734	10.752		−10.603	32.070
	Equal variances not assumed			.947	69.829	.347	10.734	11.332		−11.868	33.336

2. Computed *t*-test value shown in this column (*t* = 0.998).

3. P-value for *t*-value and associated degrees of freedom (*t* = 0.998, 98 d.f.)

4. Confidence intervals for α = 0.05 (100% − 95%). In this case, it includes 0.

appropriate. Although instructors still find some value in having students learn to perform the *t*-test calculations, this is the procedure by which *t*-test results are most often generated and interpreted today.

The interpretation of the *t*-test is made simple by focusing on either the p-value or the confidence interval and the group means. Here are the basic steps:

1. Examine the difference in means to find the "direction" of any difference. In this case, Catholics are willing to pay nearly $9 more than Protestants.
2. Compute or locate the computed *t*-test value. In this case, $t = 0.998$.
3. Find the p-value associated with this *t* and the corresponding degrees of freedom. Here, the p-value (two-tailed significance level) is 0.321. This suggest a 32 percent chance that the means are actually equal given the observed sample means. Assuming a 0.05 acceptable Type I error rate (α), the appropriate conclusion is that the means are not significantly different.
4. The difference can also be examined using the 95 percent confidence interval ($-10.603 < \overline{X}_1 - \overline{X}_2 < 32.070$). Since the confidence interval includes 0, we lack sufficient confidence that the true difference between the population means is 0.

A few points are worth noting about this particular result. First, strictly speaking, the *t*-test assumes that the two population variances are equal. A slightly more complicated formula exists which will compute the *t*-statistic assuming the variances are not equal.[4] SPSS provides both results when an independent samples *t*-test is performed. The sample variances appear considerably different in this case (43.4, 64.0). Nonetheless, the conclusions are the same using either assumption. In marketing research, we often deal with values that have variances close enough to assume equal variance. This isn't always the case in the physical sciences where variables may take on values of drastically different magnitude. Thus, the rule of thumb in marketing research is to use the equal variance assumption. In the vast majority of cases, the same conclusion will be drawn using either assumption.

Second, notice that even though the means appear to be not so close to each other, the statistical conclusion is that they are the same. The substantive conclusion is that Catholics and Protestants would not be expected to pay different prices. Why is it that means do not appear to be similar, yet that is the conclusion? The answer lies in the variance. Respondents tended to provide very wide ranges of acceptable prices. Notice how large the standard deviations are compared to the mean for each group. Since the *t*-statistic is a function of the standard error, which is a function of the standard deviation, a lot of variance means a smaller *t*-value for any given observed difference. When this occurs, the researcher may wish to double check for outliers. A small number of wild price estimates could be inflating the variance for one or both groups. An additional consideration would be to increase the sample size and test again.

Third, a *t*-test is used even though the sample size is greater than 30. Strictly speaking, a *Z*-test could be used to test this difference. Researchers often employ a *t*-test even with large samples. As samples get larger, the *t*-test and *Z*-test will tend to yield the same result. Although a *t*-test can be used with large samples, a *Z*-test should not be used with small samples. Also, a *Z*-test can be used in instances where the population variance is known ahead of time.

As another example, consider eleven sales representatives categorized as either young (1) or old (2) on the basis of their ages in years, as shown in Exhibit 22.3. The exhibit presents a SAS computer output that compares the mean sales volume for these two groups.

EXHIBIT 22.3 SAS *t*-Test Output

t-Test Procedure Variable: CR Sales										
Age	*n*	Mean	Standard Deviation	Standard Error	Minimum	Maximum	Variances	*t*	DF	Prob > |*T*|
1	6	61879.33333	22356.20845	9126.88388	41152.00000	103059.0000	Unequal	−0.9758	5.2	0.3729
2	5	86961.80000	53734.45098	24030.77702	42775.00000	172530.0000	Equal	−1.0484	9.0	0.3218
For *Ho*: Variances are equal, $F = 5.78$ with 4 and 5 *DF*, Prob. $> F = 0.0815$.										

Paired-Samples *t*-Test

What happens when means need to be compared that are not from independent samples? Such might be the case when the same respondent is measured twice; for instance, when the respondent is asked to rate both how much he or she likes shopping on the Internet and how much he or she likes shopping in traditional stores. Since the liking scores are both provided by the same person, the assumption that they are independent is not realistic. Additionally, if one compares the prices the same retailers charge in their stores with the prices they charge on their websites, the samples cannot be considered independent because each pair of observations is from the same sampling unit.

A **paired-samples *t*-test** is appropriate in this situation. The idea behind the paired-samples *t*-test can be seen in the following computation:

$$t = \frac{\bar{d}}{s_d \sqrt{n}}$$

Paired-samples *t*-test
An appropriate test for comparing the scores of two interval variables drawn from related populations.

where $\bar{d}$ is the difference between means, s_d is the standard deviation of the observed differences, and n is the number of observations. Researchers also can compute the paired-samples *t*-test using statistical software. For example, using SPSS, the click through sequence would be:

Analyze → Compare Means → Paired-Samples t-*test*

A dialog box then appears in which the "paired variables" should be entered. When a paired-samples *t*-test is appropriate, the two numbers being compared are usually scored as separate variables.

Exhibit 22.4 displays a paired samples *t*-test result. A sample of 143 young adult consumers was asked to rate how likely they would be consider purchasing an engagement ring (or want their ring

EXHIBIT 22.4 **Example Results for a Paired-Samples *t*-Test**

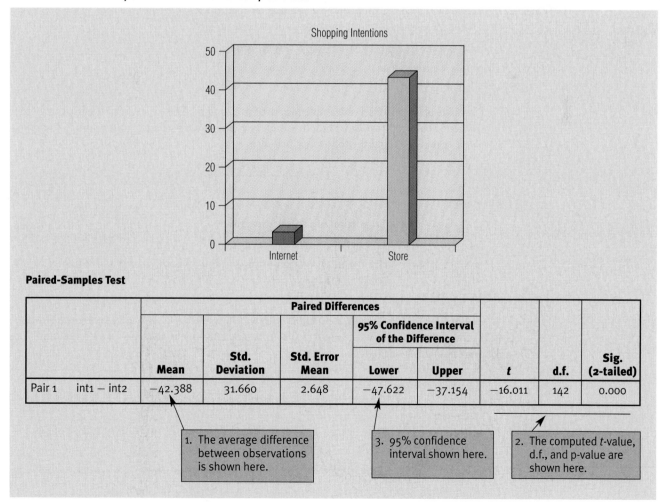

Paired-Samples Test

		Paired Differences						
				95% Confidence Interval of the Difference				
	Mean	**Std. Deviation**	**Std. Error Mean**	**Lower**	**Upper**	**t**	**d.f.**	**Sig. (2-tailed)**
Pair 1 int1 − int2	−42.388	31.660	2.648	−47.622	−37.154	−16.011	142	0.000

1. The average difference between observations is shown here.

3. 95% confidence interval shown here.

2. The computed *t*-value, d.f., and p-value are shown here.

purchased) via (a) an Internet retailer and (b) a well-known jewelry store. Each respondent provided two responses much as in a within-subjects experimental design. The bar chart depicts the means for each variable (Internet purchase likelihood and store purchase likelihood). The t-test results suggest that average difference of -42.4 is associated with a t-value of -16.0. As can be seen using either the p-value (0.000 rounded to 3 decimals) or the confidence interval $-47.6 < \bar{d} < -37.1$), which does not include 0, the difference is significantly different from 0. Therefore, the results suggest a higher likelihood to buy a wedding ring in a well-known real retail store than via an Internet merchant. Maybe that is a good idea!

Management researchers have used paired-samples t-tests to examine the effect of downsizing on employee morale. For instance, job satisfaction for a sample of employees can be measured immediately after the downsizing. Some months later, employee satisfaction can be measured again. The difference between the satisfaction scores can be compared using a paired-samples t-test. Results suggest that the employee satisfaction scores increase within a few months of the downsizing as evidenced by statistically significant paired-samples t-values.[5]

The Z-Test for Comparing Two Proportions

What type of statistical comparison can be made when the observed statistics are proportions? Suppose a researcher wishes to test the hypothesis that wholesalers in the northern and southern United States differ in the proportion of sales they make to discount retailers. Testing whether the population proportion for group 1 (p_1) equals the population proportion for group 2 (p_2) is conceptually the same as the t-test of two means. This section illustrates a **Z-test for differences of proportions**, which requires a sample size greater than thirty.

The test is appropriate for a hypothesis of this form:

Z-test for differences of proportions
A technique used to test the hypothesis that proportions are significantly different for two independent samples or groups.

$$H_0: \pi_1 = \pi_2$$

which may be restated as

$$H_0: \pi_1 - \pi_2 = 0$$

Comparison of the observed sample proportions p_1 and p_2 allows the researcher to ask whether the difference between two *large* random samples occurred due to chance alone. The Z-test statistic can be computed using the following formula:

$$Z = \frac{(p_1 - p_2) - (\pi_1 - \pi_2)}{S_{p_1-p_2}}$$

where

p_1 = sample proportion of successes in group 1

p_2 = sample proportion of successes in group 2

$\pi_1 - \pi_2$ = hypothesized population proportion 1 minus hypothesized population proportion 2

$S_{p_1-p_2}$ = pooled estimate of the standard error of differences in proportions

The statistic normally works on the assumption that the value of $\pi_1 - \pi_2$ is zero, so this formula is actually much simpler than it looks at first inspection. Readers also may notice the similarity between this and the paired-samples t-test.

To calculate the standard error of the differences in proportions, use the formula

$$S_{p_1-p_2} = \sqrt{\bar{p}\bar{q}\left(\frac{1}{n_1} + \frac{1}{n_2}\right)}$$

where

$\bar{p}$ = pooled estimate of proportion of successes in a sample

$\bar{q} = 1 - \bar{p}$, or pooled estimate of proportion of failures in a sample

n_1 = sample size for group 1

n_2 = sample size for group 2

To calculate the pooled estimator, $\bar{p}$, use the formula

$$\bar{p} = \frac{n_1 p_1 + n_2 + p_2}{n_1 + n_2}$$

Suppose the survey data are as follows:

Northern Wholesalers	Southern Wholesalers
$p_1 = 0.35$	$p_2 = 0.40$
$n_1 = 100$	$n_2 = 100$

First, the standard error of the difference in proportions is

$$S_{p_1-p_2} = \sqrt{\bar{p}\bar{q}\left(\frac{1}{n_1} + \frac{1}{n_2}\right)}$$

$$= \sqrt{(0.375)(0.625)\left(\frac{1}{100} + \frac{1}{100}\right)} = 0.068$$

where

$$\bar{p} = \frac{(100)(0.35) + (100)(0.40)}{100 + 100} = 0.375$$

If we wish to test the two-tailed question of no difference, we must calculate an observed Z-value. Thus,

$$Z = \frac{(p_1 - p_2) - (\pi_1 - \pi_2)}{S_{p_1-p_2}}$$

$$= \frac{(0.35 - 0.40) - (0)}{0.068}$$

$$= -0.73$$

In this example the idea that the proportion of sales differs by region is not supported. The calculated Z-value is less than the critical Z-value of 1.96. Therefore, the p-value associated with the test is greater than 0.05.

Analysis of Variance (ANOVA)

What Is ANOVA?

When the means of more than two groups or populations are to be compared, one-way **analysis of variance (ANOVA)** is the appropriate statistical tool. ANOVA involving only one grouping variable is often referred to as *one-way* ANOVA because only one independent variable is involved. Another way to define ANOVA is as the appropriate statistical technique to examine the effect of a less-than interval independent variable on an at-least interval dependent variable. Thus, a categorical independent variable and a continuous dependent variable are involved. An independent samples *t*-test can be thought of as a special case of ANOVA in which the independent variable has only two levels. When more levels exist, the *t*-test alone cannot handle the problem.

The statistical null hypothesis for ANOVA is stated as follows:

$$\mu_1 = \mu_2 = \mu_3 = \cdots = \mu_k$$

Analysis of variance (ANOVA)
Analysis involving the investigation of the effects of one treatment variable on an interval-scaled dependent variable—a hypothesis-testing technique to determine whether statistically significant differences in means occur between two or more groups.

The symbol k is the number of groups or categories for an independent variable. In other words, all group means are equal. The substantive hypothesis tested in ANOVA is[6]

At least one group mean is not equal to another group mean.

As the term *analysis of variance* suggests, the problem requires comparing variances to make inferences about the means.

The chapter vignette discussed how a sample of prices taken from the Internet could be explained by the source of the price. Specifically, the independent variable could be thought of as "source," meaning either Internet or multi-channel retailer. The dependent variable is price. Since only two groups exist for the independent variable, either an independent samples *t*-test or one-way ANOVA could be used. The results would be identical.

However, assume that source involved three group levels. Prices would now be compared based on whether the retailer was a bricks-and-clicks retailer (multi-channel, meaning real and virtual stores), a bricks-only store (only physical stores) or a clicks-only retailer (virtual or Internet stores only). One-way ANOVA would be the choice for this analysis.

Simple Illustration of ANOVA

ANOVA's logic is fairly simple. Look at the data table below that describes how much coffee respondents report drinking each day based on which shift they work (GY stands for Graveyard shift).

Day	1
Day	3
Day	4
Day	0
Day	2
GY	7
GY	2
GY	1
GY	6
Night	6
Night	8
Night	3
Night	7
Night	6

The following table displays the means for each group and the overall mean:

Shift	Mean	Std. Deviation	N
Day	2.00	1.58	5
GY	4.00	2.94	4
Night	6.00	1.87	5
Total	4.00	2.63	14

Exhibit 22.5 plots each observation with a bar. The long blue vertical line illustrates the total range of observations. The lowest is 0 cups and the highest is 8 cups of coffee for a range of 8. The overall mean is 4 cups. Each group mean is shown with a different colored line that matches the bars corresponding to the group. The day shift averages 2 cups of coffee a day, the graveyard shift 4 cups, and the night shift 6 cups of coffee per day.

Here is the basic idea of ANOVA. Look at the dark double-headed arrow in Exhibit 22.5. This line represents the range of the differences between group means. In this case, the lowest mean is 2 cups and the highest mean is 6 cups. Thus, the blue vertical line corresponds to the total variation (range) in the data and the thick double-headed black line corresponds to the variance accounted

EXHIBIT 22.5 **Illustration of ANOVA Logic**

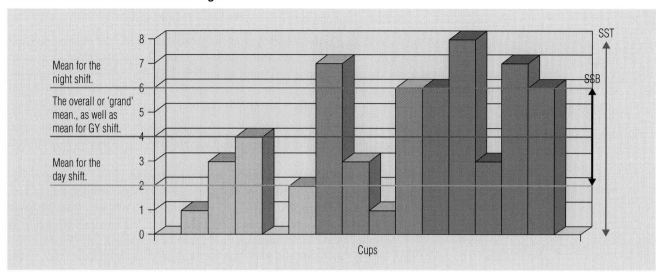

for by the group differences. As the thick black line accounts for more of the total variance, then the ANOVA model suggests that the group means are not all the same, and in particular, not all the same as the overall mean. This also means that the independent variable, in this case work shift, explains the dependent variable. Here, the results suggest that knowing when someone works explains how much coffee they drink. Night-shift workers drink the most coffee.

Partitioning Variance in ANOVA

TOTAL VARIABILITY

An implicit question with the use of ANOVA is, "How can the dependent variable best be predicted?" Absent any additional information, the error in predicting an observation is minimized by choosing the central tendency, or mean for an interval variable. For the coffee example, if no information was available about the work shift of each respondent, the best guess for coffee drinking consumption would be four cups. The total error (or variability) that would result from using the **grand mean**, meaning the mean over all observations, can be thought of as

$$SST = \text{Total of (observed value} - \text{grand mean)}^2$$

Grand mean
The mean of a variable over all observations.

Although the term error is used, this really represents how much total variation exists among the measures.

Using the first observation, the error of observation would be

$$(1 \text{ cup} - 4 \text{ cups})^2 = 9$$

The same squared error could be computed for each observation and these squared errors totaled to give SST.

BETWEEN-GROUPS VARIANCE

ANOVA tests whether "grouping" observations explains variance in the dependent variable. In Exhibit 22.5, the three colors reflect three levels of the independent variable, work shift. Given this additional information about which shift a respondent works, the prediction changes. Now, instead of guessing the grand mean, the group mean would be used. So, once we know that someone works the day shift, the prediction would be that he or she consumes 2 cups of coffee per day. Similarly, the graveyard and night-shift predictions would be 4 and 6 cups, respectively. Thus, the **between-groups variance** can be found by taking the total sum of the weighted difference

Between-group variance
The sum of differences between the group mean and the grand mean summed over all groups for a given set of observations.

between group means and the overall mean as shown:

$$\text{SSB} = \text{Total of } n_{\text{group}}(\text{Group Mean} - \text{Grand Mean})^2$$

The weighting factor (n_{group}) is the specific group sample size. Let's consider the first observation once again. Since this observation is in the day shift, we predict 2 cups of coffee will be consumed. Looking at the day shift group observations in Exhibit 22.5, the new error in prediction would be

$$(2 \text{ cups} - 4 \text{ cups})^2 = (2)^2 = 4$$

The error in prediction has been reduced from 3 using the grand mean to 2 using the group mean. This squared difference would be weighted by the group sample size of 5, to yield a contribution to SSB of 20.

Next, the same process could be followed for the other groups yielding two more contributions to SSB. Because the graveyard shift group mean is the same as the grand mean, that group's contribution to SSB is 0. Notice that the night-shift group mean is also 2 different than the grand mean, like the day shift, so this group's contribution to SSB is likewise 20. The total SSB then represents the variation explained by the experimental or independent variable. In this case, total SSB is 40. The reader may look at the statistical results shown in Exhibit 22.6 to find this value in the sums of squares column.

WITHIN-GROUP ERROR

Finally, error within each group would remain. Whereas the group means explain the variation between the total mean and the group mean, the distance from the group mean and each individual observation remains unexplained. This distance is called **within-group error or variance**. The values for each observation can be found by

Within-group error or variance
The sum of the differences between observed values and the group mean for a given set of observations; also known as total error variance.

$$\text{SSE} = \text{Total of } (\text{Observed Mean} - \text{Group Mean})^2$$

Again, looking at the first observation, the SSE component would be

$$\text{SSE} = (1 \text{ cup} - 2 \text{ cups})^2 = 1 \text{ cup}$$

This process could be computed for all observations and then totaled. The result would be the total error variance—a name sometimes used to refer to SSE since it is variability not accounted for by the group means. These three components are used in determining how well an ANOVA model explains a dependent variable.

The *F*-Test

F-test
A procedure used to determine whether there is more variability in the scores of one sample than in the scores of another sample.

The **F-test** is the key statistical test for an ANOVA model. The *F*-test determines whether there is more variability in the scores of one sample than in the scores of another sample. The key question is whether the two sample variances are different from each other or whether they are from the same population. Thus, the test breaks down the variance in a total sample and illustrates why ANOVA is *analysis of variance*.

The *F*-statistic (or *F*-ratio) can be obtained by taking the larger sample variance and dividing by the smaller sample variance. Using Table A.5 or A.6 in the appendix is much like using the tables of the *Z*- and *t*-distributions that we have previously examined. These tables portray the *F*-distribution, which is a probability distribution of the ratios of sample variances. These tables indicate that the distribution of *F* is actually a family of distributions that change quite drastically with changes in sample sizes. Thus, degrees of freedom must be specified. Inspection of an *F*-table allows the researcher to determine the probability of finding an *F* as large as a calculated *F*.

USING VARIANCE COMPONENTS TO COMPUTE *F*-RATIOS

In ANOVA, the basic consideration for the *F*-test is identifying the relative size of variance components. The three forms of variation described briefly above are:

1. SSE—variation of scores due to random error or within-group variance due to individual differences from the group mean. This is the error of prediction.

RESEARCHSNAPSHOT

More than One-Way

An independent samples *t*-test is a special case of one-way ANOVA. When the independent variable in ANOVA has only two groups, the results for an independent samples *t*-test and ANOVA will be the same. The two sets of statistical results below demonstrate this fact. Both outputs are taken from the same data. The test considers whether men or women are more excited about a new Italian restaurant in their town. Sex2 is dummy coded so that 0 = men and 1 = women. Excitement was measured on a scale ranging from 0 to 6.

Independent Samples *t*-test Results:

Group Statistics

	Sex2	N	Mean	Std. Deviation	Std. Error Mean
excitement	0.00	69	2.64	2.262	0.272
	1.00	73	2.32	2.140	0.250

Independent Samples Test

		Levene's Test for Equality of Variances		*t*-Test for Equality of Means					95% Confidence Interval of the Difference	
		F	Sig.	t	d.f.	Sig. (two-tailed)	Mean Difference	Std. Error Difference	Lower	Upper
excitement	Equal variances assumed	1.768	.186	.873	140	.384	.323	.369	−.408	1.053
	Equal variances not assumed			.872	138.265	.385	.323	.370	−.409	1.054

In this case, we would conclude that men and women are equally excited—or unexcited as the case may be. The *t* of 0.873 with 140 d.f. is not significant (p = 0.384).

ANOVA Results:

Descriptives

		N	Mean	Std. Deviation	Std. Error	95% Confidence Interval for Mean		Minimum	Maximum
						Lower Bound	Upper Bound		
excitement	0.00	69	2.64	2.262	0.272	2.09	3.18	0	7
	1.00	73	2.32	2.140	0.250	1.82	2.81	0	7
	Total	142	2.47	2.198	0.184	2.11	2.84	0	7

ANOVA

		Sum of Squares	d.f.	Mean Square	F	Sig.
excitement	Between Groups	3.692	1	3.692	0.763	0.384
	Within Groups	677.695	140	4.841		
	Total	681.387	141			

Notice that the *F*-ratio shown in the ANOVA table is associated with the same p-value as is the *t*-value above. This is no accident since the *F* and *t* are mathematical functions of one another. So, when two groups are involved, the researcher can skin the cat either way!

2. SSB—systematic variation of scores between groups due to manipulation of an experimental variable or group classifications of a measured independent variable or between-group variance.
3. SST—the total observed variation across all groups and individual observations.

Thus, we can partition **total variability** into *within-group variance* and *between-group variance*. The *F*-distribution is a function of the ratio of these two sources of variances:

$$F = f\left(\frac{SSB}{SSE}\right)$$

A larger ratio of variance between groups to variance within groups implies a greater value of *F*. If the *F*-value is large, the results are likely to be statistically significant.

A DIFFERENT BUT EQUIVALENT REPRESENTATION

F also can be thought of as a function of the between-group variance and total variance.

$$F = f\left(\frac{SSB}{SST - SSB}\right)$$

In this sense, the ratio of the thick black line to the blue line representing the total range of data presents the basic idea of the *F*-value. Appendix 22A explains the calculations in more detail with an illustration.

Practically Speaking

Exhibit 22.6 displays the ANOVA result for the coffee-drinking example. Again, one advantage of living in modern times is that even a simple problem like this one need not be hand computed.

EXHIBIT 22.6 **Interpreting ANOVA**

Tests of Between-Subjects Effects   (Dependent Variable: Coffee)

Source	Type III Sum of Squares	d.f.	Mean Square	F	Sig.
Corrected Model	40.000[a]	2	20.000	4.400	.039
Intercept	221.538	1	221.538	48.738	.000
Shift	40.000	2	20.000	4.400	.039
Error	50.000	11	4.545		
Total	314.000	14			

[a]R Squared = .444 (Adjusted R Squared = .343)

1. This row shows overall *F*-value testing whether all group means are equal. The sums of squares column calculates the SST, SSE, and SSB (shift row).

Shift	Mean	Std. Error	95% Confidence Interval	
			Lower Bound	Upper Bound
Day	2.000	.953	−.099	4.099
GY	4.000	1.066	1.654	6.346
Night	6.000	.953	3.901	8.099

2. This column shows the group means for each level of the independent variable.

Even though this example presents a small problem, one-way ANOVA models with more observations or levels would be interpreted similarly.

The first thing to check is whether or not the overall model F is significant. In this case, the computed $F = 4.40$ with 2 and 11 degrees of freedom. The p-value associated with this value is 0.039. Thus, we have high confidence in concluding that the group means are not all the same. Second, the researcher must remember to examine the actual means for each group to properly interpret the result. Doing so, the conclusion reached is that the night-shift people drink the most coffee, followed by the graveyard-shift workers, and then lastly, the day-shift workers.

As there are three groups, we may wish to know whether or not group 1 is significantly different than group 3 or group 2, and so on. In a later chapter, we will describe ways of examining specifically which group means are different from one another. In this particular example, the answer is fairly obvious.

Summary

1. Recognize when a particular bivariate statistical test is appropriate. Bivariate statistical techniques analyze scores on two variables at a time. Tests of difference investigate hypotheses stating that two (or more) groups differ with respect to a certain behavior, characteristic, or attitude. Both the type of measurement and the number of groups to be compared influence researchers' choices of the type of statistical test.

2. Calculate and interpret a χ^2 test for a contingency table. A χ^2 test is used in conjunction with cross-classification or cross-tabulations. Thus, when an independent variable is ordinal or nominal and a dependent variable is likewise ordinal or nominal, a χ^2 test can examine whether a relationship exists between the row variable and column variable. A χ^2 test is computed by examining the squared differences between observed cell counts and the expected value for each cell in a contingency table. Higher χ^2 values are generally associated with lower p-values, meaning a greater chance that the relationship between the row and column variable is statistically significant.

3. Calculate and interpret an independent samples t-test comparing two means. When a researcher needs to compare means for a variable grouped into two categories based on some less-than interval variable, a t-test is appropriate. An independent samples t-test examines whether a dependent variable like price differs based on a grouping variable like biological sex. Statistically, the test examines whether the difference between the mean for men and women is different from 0. A paired-samples t-test examines whether or not the means from two variables that are not independent are different. A common situation calling for this test is when the two observations are from the same respondent. A simple before-and-after test calls for a paired-sample t-test so long as the dependent variable is continuous.

4. Understand the concept of analysis of variance (ANOVA). ANOVA is the appropriate statistical technique to examine the effect of a less-than interval independent variable on an at-least interval dependent variable. Conceptually, ANOVA partitions the total variability into three types: total variation, between-group variation, and within-group variation. As the explained variance represented by SSB becomes larger relative to SSE or SST, the ANOVA model is more likely to be significant, indicating that at least one group mean is different from another group mean.

5. Interpret an ANOVA table. An ANOVA table provides essential information. Most importantly, the ANOVA table contains the model F-ratio. The researcher should examine this value along with the corresponding p-value. Generally, as F increases, p decreases, meaning that a statistically significant ANOVA model is more likely.

Key Terms and Concepts

Test of differences

Independent samples t-test

Pooled estimate of the standard error

Paired-samples t-test

Z-test for differences of proportions

Analysis of variance (ANOVA)

Grand mean

Between-group variance

Within-group error or variance

F-test

Questions for Review and Critical Thinking

1. What tests of difference are appropriate in the following situations?
   a. Average campaign contributions (in $) of Democrats, Republicans, and Independents are to be compared.
   b. Advertising managers and brand managers have responded "yes," "no," or "not sure" to an attitude question. The advertising and brand managers' responses are to be compared.
   c. One-half of a sample received an incentive in a mail survey while the other half did not. A comparison of response rates is desired.
   d. A researcher believes that married men will push the grocery cart when grocery shopping with their wives. How would the hypothesis be tested?
   e. A manager wishes to compare the job performance of a salesperson before ethics training with the performance of that same salesperson after ethics training.

2. Perform a χ^2 test on the following data:
   a. Regulation is the best way to ensure safe products.

	Agree	**Disagree**	**No Opinion**
Managers	58	66	8
Line Employees	34	24	10
Totals	92	90	18

   b. Ownership of residence

	Yes	**No**
Male	25	20
Female	16	14

3. Interpret the following computer cross-tab output including a χ^2 test. Variable COMMUTE is "How did you get to work last week?" Variable GENDER is "Are you male or female?" Comment on any particular problems with the analysis.

COMMUTE * GENDER Cross-Tabulation

			GENDER		
			Female	**Male**	**Total**
COMMUTE	at home	Count	6	10	16
		% within COMMUTE	37.5%	62.5%	100.0%
		% within GENDER	7.0%	17.9%	11.3%
		% of Total	4.2%	7.0%	11.3%
	Bus	Count	16	16	32
		% within COMMUTE	50.0%	50.0%	100.0%
		% within GENDER	18.6%	28.6%	22.5%
		% of Total	11.3%	11.3%	22.5%
	Drive	Count	32	17	49
		% within COMMUTE	65.3%	34.7%	100.0%
		% within GENDER	37.2%	30.4%	34.5%
		% of Total	22.5%	12.0%	34.5%
	Passenger	Count	24	9	33
		% within COMMUTE	72.7%	27.3%	100.0%
		% within GENDER	27.9%	16.1%	23.2%
		% of Total	16.9%	6.3%	23.3%
	Walk	Count	8	4	12
		% within COMMUTE	66.7%	33.3%	100.0%
		% within GENDER	9.3%	7.1%	8.5%
		% of Total	5.6%	2.8%	8.5%
Total		Count	86	56	142
		% within COMMUTE	60.6%	39.4%	100.0%
		% within GENDER	100.0%	100.0%	100.0%
		% of Total	60.6%	39.4%	100.0%

χ^2 Tests

	Value	**Df**	**Asymp. Sig. (two-sided)**
Pearson Chi-Square	7.751[a]	4	0.101
Likelihood Ratio	7.725	4	0.102
N of Valid Cases	142		

[a]1 cells (10.0%) have expected count less than 5. The minimum expected count is 4.73.

4. A store manager's computer-generated list of all retail sales employees indicates that 70 percent are full-time employees, 20 percent are part-time employees, and 10 percent are furloughed or laid-off employees. A sample of fifty employees from the list indicates that there are forty full-time employees, six part-time employees, and four furloughed/laid-off employees. Conduct a statistical test to determine whether the sample is representative of the population.

5. Test the following hypothesis using the data summarized in the table below. Interpret your result:

   H1: Internet retailers offer lower prices for DVD players than do traditional in-store retailers.

Retail Type	DVD Player Average Price	Standard Deviation	n
E-tailers	$371.95	$50.00	25
Multi-Channel Retailers	$360.30	$45.00	25

6. The territories in a company's eastern and western regions were rated for sales potential based on the company's evaluation system. A sales manager wishes to conduct a *t*-test of means to determine whether there is a difference between the two regions. Conduct this test preferably using a statistical software package:

Region	Territory	Rating	Region	Territory	Rating
West	1	74	East	8	81
West	2	88	East	9	63
West	3	78	East	10	56
West	4	85	East	11	68
West	5	100	East	12	80
West	6	114	East	13	79
West	7	98	East	14	69

7. How does an independent sample *t*-test differ from the following?
   a. one-way ANOVA
   b. paired-samples *t*-test
   c. a χ^2 test
   d. a *Z*-test for differences

8. Are *t*-tests or *Z*-tests used more often in marketing research? Why?

9. A sales force received some management-by-objectives training. Are the before/after mean scores for salespeople's job performance statistically significant at the 0.05 level? The results from a sample of employees are as follows (use your computer and statistical software to solve this problem):

Skill	Before	After	Skill	Before	After
Carlos	4.84	5.43	Tommy	4.00	5.00
Sammy	5.24	5.51	Laurie	4.67	4.50
Melanie	5.37	5.42	Ronald	4.95	4.40
Philippe	3.69	4.50	Amanda	4.00	5.95
Cargill	5.95	5.90	Brittany	3.75	3.50
Dwight	4.75	5.25	Mathew	3.85	4.00
Amy	3.90	4.50	Alice	5.00	4.10

10. Using the "CAR" data that accompanies the text (see website), consider the following problem. The data describe attitudes of car owners from Germany and the United States toward their automobiles. The variable "ATT" is how much respondents like their current car (attitude), "ATTNEW" is their attitude toward a new car called the Cycle. The "COUNTRY" variable is self-explanatory. The "SPEND" variable is how much the respondents spend on average on products to keep their cars clean (in Euros). Using SPSS or other statistical software, test the following hypotheses:

    The owners' attitudes toward the Cycle are more favorable than attitudes toward their current cars.
    Germans like their cars more than Americans.

11. Conduct a *Z*-test to determine whether the following two samples indicate that the population proportions are significantly different at the 0.05 level:

	Sample 1	Sample 2
Sample proportion	0.77	0.68
Sample size	55	46

12. In an experiment with wholesalers, a researcher manipulated perception of task difficulty and measured level of aspiration for performing the task a second time. Group 1 was told the task was very difficult, group 2 was told the task was somewhat difficult but attainable, and group 3 was told the task was easy. Perform an ANOVA on the resulting data:

Level of Aspiration (10-Point Scale)

Subjects	Group 1	Group 2	Group 3
1	6	5	5
2	7	4	6
3	5	7	5
4	8	6	4
5	8	7	2
6	6	7	3
Cases	6	6	6

13. Interpret the following output examining group differences for purchase intentions. The three groups refer to consumers from three states: Florida, Minnesota, and Hawaii.

Tests of Between-Subjects Effects
Dependent Variable: int2

Source	Type III Sum of Squares	d.f.	Mean Square	F	Sig.
Corrected Model	6681.746[a]	2	3340.873	3.227	.043
Intercept	308897.012	1	308897.012	298.323	.000
State	6681.746	2	3340.873	3.227	.043
Error	148068.543	143	1035.444		
Total	459697.250	146			
Corrected Total	154750.289	145			

[a]R Squared = 0.043 (Adjusted R Squared = 0.030)

Law
Dependent Variable: int2

State	Mean	Std. Error	95% Confidence Interval	
			Lower Bound	**Upper Bound**
F	37.018	4.339	28.441	45.595
M	50.357	4.965	40.542	60.172
H	51.459	4.597	42.373	60.546

Research Activities

1. **ETHICS/NET** How ethical is it to do business in different countries around the world? An international organization, Transparency International, keeps track of the perception of ethical practices in different countries. Visit the website and search for the latest corruption indices (http://www.transparency.org/policy_and_research/surveys_indices/cpi/2005). Using the data found here, test the following research questions.
    a. Are Nations from Europe and North America perceived to be more ethical than nations from Asia, Africa, and South America? Include Australia and New Zealand with Europe.

    b. Are there differences among the corruption indices between 2003 and 2005?
2. **NET** The Federal Reserve Bank of St. Louis maintains a database called FRED (Federal Reserve Economic Data). Navigate to the FRED database at http://research.stlouisfed.org/fred. Randomly select a five-year period between 1970 and 2005 and then compare average figures for U.S. employment in retail trade with those for U.S. employment in wholesale trade. What statistical tests are appropriate?

Case 22.1 Old School versus New School Sports Fans

Download the data sets for this case from http://www.thomsonedu.com/marketing/zikmund or request them from your instructor.

Three academic researchers investigated the idea that, in American sports, there are two segments with opposing views about the goal of competition (i.e., winning versus self-actualization) and the acceptable/desirable way of achieving this goal.[7] Persons who believe in "winning at any cost" are proponents of sports success as a product and can be labeled new school (NS) individuals. The new school is founded on notions of the player before the team, loyalty to the highest bidder, and high-tech production and consumption of professional sports. On the other hand, persons who value the process of sports and believe that "how you play the game matters" can be labeled old school (OS) individuals. The old school emerges from old-fashioned American notions of the team before the player,

sportsmanship, and loyalty above all else, and competition simply for "love of the game."

New School/Old School was measured by asking agreement with ten attitude statements. The scores on these statements were combined. Higher scores represent an orientation toward old school values. For purposes of this case study, individuals who did not answer every question were eliminated from the analysis. Based on their summated scores, respondents were grouped into low score, middle score, and high score groups. Case Exhibit 22.1–1 shows the SPSS computer output of a cross-tabulation to relate the gender of the respondent (GENDER) with the New School/Old School grouping (OLDSKOOL).

Questions

Is this form of analysis appropriate?
Interpret the computer output and critique the analysis.

CASE EXHIBIT 22.1-1 **SPSS Output**

OLDSKOOL * GENDER Crosstabulation

| | | | GENDER | | |
			women	men	Total
OLDSKOOL	high	Count	9	17	26
		% within OLDSKOOL	34.6%	65.4%	100.0%
		% within GENDER	10.6%	9.2%	9.6%
		% of Total	3.3%	6.3%	9.6%
	low	Count	45	70	115
		% within OLDSKOOL	39.1%	60.9%	100.0%
		% within GENDER	52.9%	37.8%	42.6%
		% of Total	16.7%	25.9%	42.6%
	middle	Count	31	98	129
		% within OLDSKOOL	24.0%	76.0%	100.0%
		% within GENDER	36.5%	53.0%	47.8%
		% of Total	11.5%	36.3%	47.8%
Total		Count	85	185	270
		% within OLDSKOOL	31.5%	68.5%	100.0%
		% within GENDER	100.0%	100.0%	100.0%
		% of Total	31.5%	68.5%	100.0%

Chi-Square Tests

	Value	df	Asymp. Sig. (2-sided)
Pearson Chi-Square	6.557[a]	2	.038
Likelihood Ratio	6.608	2	.037
N of Valid Cases	270		

[a] 0 cells (.0%) have expected count less than 5. The minimum expected count is 8.19.

APPENDIX 22A
MANUAL CALCULATION OF AN *F*-STATISTIC

Manual calculations are almost unheard of these days. However, understanding the calculations can be very useful in gaining a thorough understanding of ANOVA. The data in Exhibit 22A.1 are from a hypothetical packaged-goods company's test-market experiment on pricing. Three pricing treatments were administered in four separate areas (12 test areas, A–L, were required). These data will be used to illustrate ANOVA.

Terminology for the variance estimates is derived from the calculation procedures, so an explanation of the terms used to calculate the *F*-ratio should clarify the meaning of the analysis of variance technique. The calculation of the *F*-ratio requires that we partition the total variation into two parts:

$$\underset{(SST)}{\text{Total sum of squares}} = \underset{(SSE)}{\substack{\text{Within-group} \\ \text{sum of squares}}} + \underset{(SSB)}{\substack{\text{Between-group} \\ \text{sum of squares}}}$$

or

$$SST = SSE + SSB$$

SST is computed by squaring the deviation of each score from the grand mean and summing these squares:

$$SST = \sum_{i=1}^{n} \sum_{j=1}^{c} \left(X_{ij} - \overline{\overline{X}} \right)^2$$

where

X_{ij} = individual score—that is, the ith observation or test unit in the jth group

$\overline{\overline{X}}$ = grand mean

n = number of all observations or test units in a group

c = number of jth groups (or columns)

	Sales in Units (thousands)		
	Regular Price, $.99	Reduced Price, $.89	Cents-Off Coupon, Regular Price
Test-Market A, B, or C	130	145	153
Test-Market D, E, or F	118	143	129
Test-Market G, H, or I	87	120	96
Test-Market J, K, or L	84	131	99
Mean	$\overline{X}_1 = 104.75$	$\overline{X}_2 = 134.75$	$\overline{X}_3 = 119.25$
Grand mean	$\overline{\overline{X}} = 119.58$		

In our example,

$$
\begin{aligned}
SST = \; & (130 - 119.58)^2 + (118 - 119.58)^2 + (87 - 119.58)^2 \\
& + (84 - 119.58)^2 + (145 - 119.58)^2 + (143 - 119.58)^2 \\
& + (120 - 119.58)^2 + (131 - 119.58)^2 + (153 - 119.58)^2 \\
& + (129 - 119.58)^2 + (96 - 119.58)^2 + (99 - 119.58)^2 \\
= \; & 5,948.93
\end{aligned}
$$

SSE, the variability that we observe within each group, or the error remaining after using the groups to predict observations, is calculated by squaring the deviation of each score from its group mean and summing these scores:

$$
SSE = \sum_{i=1}^{n} \sum_{j=1}^{c} \left(X_{ij} - \overline{X}_{j} \right)^2
$$

where

X_{ij} = individual score

$\overline{X}_{j}$ = group mean for the *j*th group

n = number of observations in a group

c = number of *j*th groups

In our example,

$$
\begin{aligned}
SSE = \; & (130 - 104.75)^2 + (118 - 104.75)^2 + (87 - 104.75)^2 \\
& + (84 - 104.75)^2 + (145 - 134.75)^2 + (143 - 134.75)^2 \\
& + (120 - 134.75)^2 + (131 - 134.75)^2 + (153 - 119.25)^2 \\
& + (129 - 119.25)^2 + (96 - 119.25)^2 + (99 - 119.25)^2 \\
= \; & 4,148.25
\end{aligned}
$$

SSB, the variability of the group means about a grand mean, is calculated by squaring the deviation of each group mean from the grand mean, multiplying by the number of items in the group, and summing these scores:

$$
SSB = \sum_{j=1}^{c} n_{j} \left(\overline{X}_{j} - \overline{\overline{X}} \right)^2
$$

where

$\overline{X}_{j}$ = group mean for the *j*th group

$\overline{\overline{X}}$ = grand mean

n_{j} = number of items in the *j*th group

In our example,

$$
\begin{aligned}
SSB = \; & 4(104.75 - 119.58)^2 + 4(134.75 - 119.58)^2 \\
& + 4(119.25 - 119.58)^2 \\
= \; & 1,800.68
\end{aligned}
$$

The next calculation requires dividing the various sums of squares by their appropriate degrees of freedom. These divisions produce the variances, or *mean squares*. To obtain the mean square between groups, we divide *SSB* by $c - 1$ degrees of freedom:

$$
MSB = \frac{SSB}{c - 1}
$$

In our example,

$$
MSB = \frac{1,800.68}{3 - 1} = \frac{1,800.68}{2} = 900.34
$$

To obtain the mean square within groups, we divide SSE by $cn - c$ degrees of freedom:

$$MSE = \frac{SSE}{cn - c}$$

In our example,

$$MSE = \frac{4,148.25}{12 - 3} = \frac{4,148.25}{9} = 460.91$$

Finally, the F-ratio is calculated by taking the ratio of the mean square between groups to the mean square within groups. The between-groups mean square is the numerator and the within-groups mean square is the denominator:

$$F = \frac{MSB}{MSE}$$

In our example,

$$F = \frac{900.34}{460.91} = 1.95$$

There will be $c - 1$ degrees of freedom in the numerator and $cn - c$ degrees of freedom in the denominator:

$$\frac{c - 1}{cn - c} = \frac{3 - 1}{3(4) - 3} = \frac{2}{9}$$

In Table A.5 in the text appendix, the critical value of F at the 0.05 level for 2 and 9 degrees of freedom indicates that an F of 4.26 would be required to reject the null hypothesis.

In our example we conclude that we cannot reject the null hypothesis. It appears that all the price treatments produce approximately the same sales volume.

The information produced from an analysis of variance is traditionally summarized in table form. Exhibits 22A.2 and 22A.3 summarize the formulas and data from our example.

EXHIBIT 22A.2
ANOVA Summary Table

Source of Variation	Sum of Squares	Degrees of Freedom	Mean Square	F-Ratio
Between groups	$SSB = \sum_{j=1}^{c} n_j(\bar{X}_j - \bar{\bar{X}})^2$	$c - 1$	$MSB = \dfrac{SSB}{c - 1}$	—
Within groups	$SSE = \sum_{i=1}^{n} \sum_{j=1}^{c} (X_{ij} - \bar{X}_j)^2$	$cn - c$	$MSE = \dfrac{SSE}{cn - c}$	$F = \dfrac{MSB}{MSE}$
Total	$SST = \sum_{i=1}^{n} \sum_{j=1}^{c} (X_{ij} - \bar{\bar{X}})^2$	$cn - 1$	—	—

where c = number of groups
n = number of observations in a group

EXHIBIT 22A.3
Pricing Experiment ANOVA Table

Source of Variation	Sum of Squares	Degrees of Freedom	Mean Square	F-Ratio
Between groups	1,800.68	2	900.34	—
Within groups	4,148.25	9	460.91	1.953
Total	5,948.93	11	—	—

To test for statistical significance in a randomized block design, or RBD (see Chapter 12), another version of analysis of variance is utilized. The linear model for the RBD for an individual observation is[*]

$$Y_{ij} = \mu + \alpha_j + \beta_i + \varepsilon_{ij}$$

where

Y_{ij} = individual observation on the dependent variable

μ = grand mean

α_j = jth treatment effect

β_i = ith block effect

ε_{ij} = random error or residual

The statistical objective is to determine whether significant differences exist among treatment means and block means. This is done by calculating an F-ratio for each source of effects.

The same logic that applies in single-factor ANOVA—using variance estimates to test for differences among means—applies in ANOVA for randomized block designs. Thus, to conduct the ANOVA, we partition the total sum of squares (SS_{total}) into non-overlapping components.

$$SS_{total} = SS_{treatments} + SS_{blocks} + SS_{error}$$

The sources of variance are defined as follows.

Total sum of squares:

$$SS_{total} = \sum_{i=1}^{r} \sum_{j=1}^{c} \left(Y_{ij} - \overline{\overline{Y}} \right)^2$$

where

Y_{ij} = individual observation

$\overline{\overline{Y}}$ = grand mean

r = number of blocks (rows)

c = number of treatments (columns)

Treatment sum of squares:

$$SS_{treatments} = \sum_{i=1}^{r} \sum_{j=1}^{c} \left(\overline{Y}_j - \overline{\overline{Y}} \right)^2$$

where

$\overline{Y}_j$ = jth treatment mean

$\overline{\overline{Y}}$ = grand mean

Block sum of squares:

$$SS_{blocks} = \sum_{i=1}^{r} \sum_{j=1}^{c} \left(\overline{Y}_i - \overline{\overline{Y}} \right)^2$$

where

$\overline{Y}_i$ = ith block mean

$\overline{\overline{Y}}$ = grand mean

---

[*]We assume no interaction effect between treatments and blocks.

Source of Variation	Sum of Squares	Degrees of Freedom	Mean Squares
Between blocks	SS_{blocks}	$r-1$	$\dfrac{SS_{blocks}}{r-1}$
Between treatments	$SS_{treatments}$	$c-1$	$\dfrac{SS_{treatments}}{c-1}$
Error	SS_{error}	$(r-1)(c-1)$	$\dfrac{SS_{error}}{(r-1)(c-1)}$
Total	SS_{total}	$rc-1$	—

Sum of squares error:

$$SS_{error} = \sum_{i=1}^{r}\sum_{j=1}^{c}\left(Y_{ij} - \bar{Y}_i - \bar{Y}_j - \bar{\bar{Y}}\right)^2$$

The SS_{error} may also be calculated in the following manner:

$$SS_{error} = SS_{total} - SS_{treatments} - SS_{blocks}$$

The degrees of freedom for $SS_{treatments}$ are equal to $c-1$ because $SS_{treatments}$ reflects the dispersion of treatment means from the grand mean, which is fixed. Degrees of freedom for blocks are $r-1$ for similar reasons. S_{Serror} reflects variations from both treatment and block means. Thus, $d.f. = (r-1)(c-1)$.

Mean squares are calculated by dividing the appropriate sum of squares by the corresponding degrees of freedom.

Exhibit 22B.1 is an ANOVA table for the randomized block design. It summarizes what has been discussed and illustrates the calculation of mean squares.

F-ratios for treatment and block effects are calculated as follows:

$$F_{treatment} = \frac{\text{Mean square treatment}}{\text{Mean square error}}$$

$$F_{blocks} = \frac{\text{Mean square blocks}}{\text{Mean square error}}$$

Factorial Designs

There is considerable similarity between the factorial design (see Chapter 12) and the one-way analysis of variance. The sum of squares for each of the treatment factors (rows and columns) is similar to the between-groups sum of squares in the single-factor ANOVA model. Each treatment sum of squares is calculated by taking the deviation of the treatment means from the grand mean. Determining the sum of squares for the interaction is a new calculation because this source of variance is not attributable to the treatment sum of squares or the error sum of squares.

ANOVA for a Factorial Experiment

In a two-factor experimental design the linear model for an individual observation is

$$Y_{ijk} = \mu + \beta_i + \alpha_j + I_{ij} + \varepsilon_{ijk}$$

where

$Y_{ijk} =$ individual observation on the dependent variable

$\mu =$ grand mean

$\beta_i = i$th effect of factor B—row treatment

$\alpha_j = j$th effect of factor A—column treatment

$I_{ij} = $ interaction effect of factors A and B

$\varepsilon_{ijk} = $ random error or residual

Partitioning the Sum of Squares for a Two-Way ANOVA

Again, the total sum of squares can be allocated into distinct and overlapping portions:

Sum of squares total	=	Sum of squares rows (treatment B)	+	Sum of squares columns (treatment A)	+	Sum of squares interaction	+	Sum of squares error

or

$$SS_{\text{total}} = SSR_{\text{treatment B}} + SSC_{\text{treatment A}} + SS_{\text{interaction}} + SS_{\text{error}}$$

Sum of squares total:

$$SS_{\text{total}} = \sum_{i=1}^{r}\sum_{j=1}^{c}\sum_{k=1}^{n}\left(Y_{ijk} - \bar{\bar{Y}}\right)^2$$

where

$Y_{ijk} = $ individual observation on the dependent variable

$\bar{\bar{Y}} = $ grand mean

$j = $ level of factor A

$i = $ level of factor B

$k = $ number of an observation in a particular cell

$r = $ total number of levels of factor B (rows)

$c = $ total number of levels of factor A (columns)

$n = $ total number of observations in the sample

Sum of squares rows (treatment B):

$$SSR_{\text{treatment B}} = \sum_{i=1}^{r}\left(\bar{Y}_i - \bar{\bar{Y}}\right)^2$$

where

$\bar{Y}_i = $ mean of ith treatment—factor B

Sum of squares columns (treatment A):

$$SSC_{\text{treatment A}} = \sum_{j=1}^{c}\left(Y_j - \bar{\bar{Y}}\right)^2$$

where

$\bar{Y}_j = $ mean of jth treatment—factor A

Sum of squares interaction:

$$SS_{\text{interaction}} = \sum_{i=1}^{r}\sum_{j=1}^{c}\sum_{k=1}^{n}\left(Y_{ij} - \bar{Y}_i - \bar{Y}_j - \bar{\bar{Y}}\right)^2$$

The above is one form of calculation. However, $SS_{\text{interaction}}$ generally is indirectly computed in the following manner:

$$SS_{\text{interaction}} = SS_{\text{total}} - SSR_{\text{treatment B}} - SSC_{\text{treatment A}} - SS_{\text{error}}$$

EXHIBIT 22B.2
ANOVA Table for Two-Factor Design

Source of Variation	Sum of Squares	Degrees of Freedom	Mean Square	F-Ratio
Treatment B	$SSR_{treatment\,B}$	$r-1$	$MSR_{treatment\,B} = \dfrac{SSR_{treatment\,B}}{r-1}$	$\dfrac{MSR_{treatment\,B}}{MS_{error}}$
Treatment A	$SSC_{treatment\,A}$	$c-1$	$MSC_{treatment\,A} = \dfrac{SSC_{treatment\,A}}{c-1}$	$\dfrac{MSC_{treatment\,A}}{MS_{error}}$
Interaction	$SS_{interaction}$	$(r-1)(c-1)$	$MS_{interaction} = \dfrac{SS_{interaction}}{(r-1)(c-1)}$	$\dfrac{MS_{interaction}}{MS_{error}}$
Error	SS_{error}	$rc(n-1)$	$MS_{error} = \dfrac{SS_{error}}{rc(n-1)}$	
Total	SS_{total}	$rcn-1$		

Sum of squares error:

$$SS_{error} = \sum_{i=1}^{r}\sum_{j=1}^{c}\sum_{k=1}^{n}\left(Y_{ijk} - \bar{Y}_{ij}\right)^2$$

where

$\bar{Y}_{ij}$ = mean of the interaction effect

These sums of squares, along with their respective degrees of freedom and mean squares, are summarized in Exhibit 22B.2.

CHAPTER 23
BIVARIATE STATISTICAL ANALYSIS:
MEASURES OF ASSOCIATION

After studying this chapter, you should be able to

1. Apply and interpret simple bivariate correlations
2. Interpret a correlation matrix
3. Understand simple (bivariate) regression
4. Understand the least-squares estimation technique
5. Interpret regression output including the tests of hypotheses tied to specific parameter coefficients

Chapter Vignette: What's for Lunch?

Why do some people eat more than others? What an interesting question! In fact, many, many people have an interest in explaining what we eat and how much of it we eat. Policy makers are concerned with public obesity. Nutritionists are concerned with the extent to which our diets provide necessary nutrients without unnecessary or harmful ingredients. Restaurants are concerned with providing attractive menu choices that satisfy consumers. While some companies benefit when we eat more, others benefit when we eat less.

What makes someone eat more? The list of factors that correlate with food intake is wide-ranging and includes personality variables, cultural variables, and demographics. Some more basic findings suggest food intake can be easily controlled. Consider what happens when less food is placed on a plate. Guess what? Consumers eat less! More food on the plate and consumers eat more![1] This works both ways. For overweight consumers, the finding suggests that putting less on your plate or ordering smaller size portions in restaurants is a way to control calorie intake. However, other results suggest that consumers who place too little on their plate may show signs of malnutrition.[2]

Who benefits when people eat more? Well, consumers need a certain minimum number of calories each day for a healthy lifestyle. Interestingly, as fast-food companies have moved into third world nations, the dietary health of some of these communities has actually improved. So, consumers sometimes benefit. Fast-food companies can benefit. Fast-food employees highly encourage customers to "super-size" their meals because, frankly, the more consumers eat, the more profit the restaurants make. However, as tastes change, so do the types of foods that are successful. While McDonald's has had success with salads, a typical Burger King restaurant offering salads sells about three a day.[3]

This short story about our eating habits illustrates how important measures of association can be. The story shows how researchers would be asked to demonstrate the strength of association for each of the following:

- Menu choice and customer satisfaction
- Food portion size and consumption
- Food consumption and health

- Portion size and restaurant profitability
- Personal taste and restaurant patronage

Knowing the relationships among these factors can mean the difference between winning and losing for many decision makers.

The Basics

In marketing, sales volume is often *the* dependent variable managers want to predict. Independent variables including marketing-mix elements such as price, number of salespeople, and the amount of advertising relate to sales volume. Uncontrollable variables including population, economic conditions, and competitive intensity also affect sales. Most managers would not be surprised to find that sales of baby strollers are associated with the number of babies born in each sales period. In this case the dependent variable is the sales volume of baby strollers, and the independent variable is the number of babies born. The mathematical symbol X is commonly used for an independent variable, and Y typically denotes a dependent variable.

The chi-square (χ^2) test provides information about whether two or more less-than interval variables are interrelated. For example, a χ^2 test between a measure of package color and product choice provides information about the independence or interrelationship of the two variables. Over the years, psychological statisticians have developed several other techniques that demonstrate empirical association.

Exhibit 23.1 shows that measurement characteristics influence which **measure of association** is most appropriate. This chapter describes simple correlation (Pearson's product-moment correlation

Measure of association
A general term that refers to a number of bivariate statistical techniques used to measure the strength of a relationship between two variables.

EXHIBIT 23.1
Bivariate Analysis—Common Procedures for Testing Association

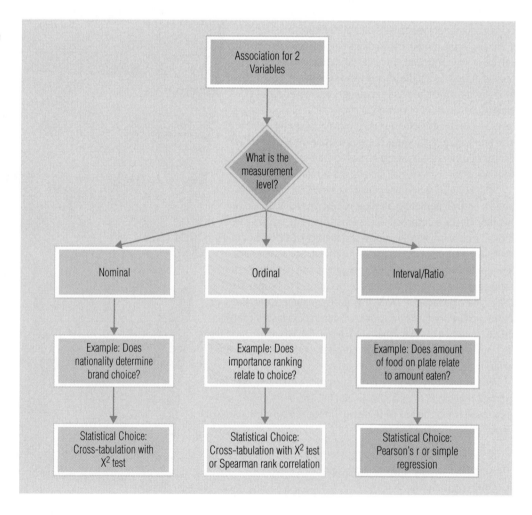

coefficient, r) and bivariate or simple regression analysis. Correlation analysis is most appropriate for interval or ratio variables. Regression can accommodate either less-than interval independent variables, but the dependent variable must be continuous. Other techniques mentioned are for advanced students who have specific needs.[4]

Simple Correlation Coefficient

The most popular technique for indicating the relationship of one variable to another is correlation. A **correlation coefficient** is a statistical measure of covariation, or association between two variables. **Covariance** is the extent to which a change in one variable corresponds systematically to a change in another. Correlation can be thought of as a standardized covariance.

When correlations estimate relationships between continuous variables, the Pearson product-moment correlation is appropriate. The correlation coefficient, r, ranges from -1.0 to $+1.0$. If the value of r equals $+1.0$, a perfect positive relationship exists. Perhaps the two variables are one and the same! If the value of r equals -1.0, a perfect negative relationship exists. The implication is that one variable is a mirror image of the other. As one goes up, the other goes down in proportion and vice versa. No correlation is indicated if r equals 0. A correlation coefficient indicates both the magnitude of the linear relationship and the direction of that relationship. For example, if we find that $r = -0.92$, we know we have a very strong inverse relationship—that is, the greater the value measured by variable X, the lower the value measured by variable Y.

The formula for calculating the correlation coefficient for two variables X and Y is as follows:

$$r_{xy} = r_{yx} = \frac{\sum_{i=1}^{n}(X_i - \overline{X})(Y_i - \overline{Y})}{\sqrt{\sum_{i=1}^{n}(X_i - \overline{X})^2 \sum_{i=1}^{n}(Y_i - \overline{Y})^2}}$$

where the symbols $\overline{X}$ and $\overline{Y}$ represent the sample averages of X and Y, respectively. An alternative way to express the correlation formula is

$$r_{xy} = r_{yx} = \frac{\sigma_{xy}}{\sqrt{\sigma_x^2 \sigma_y^2}}$$

where

$\sigma_x^2 = $ variance of X

$\sigma_y^2 = $ variance of Y

$\sigma_{xy} = $ covariance of X and Y

with

$$\sigma_{xy} = \frac{\sum_{i=1}^{n}(X_i - \overline{X})(Y_i - \overline{Y})}{n}$$

If associated values of X_i and Y_i differ from their means in the same direction, their covariance will be positive. If the values of X_i and Y_i tend to deviate in opposite directions, their covariance will be negative.

The Pearson correlation coefficient is a standardized measure of covariance. Covariance coefficients retain information about the absolute scale ranges so that the strength of association for scales of different possible values cannot be compared directly. Researchers find the correlation coefficient useful because they can compare two correlations without regard for the amount of variance exhibited by each variable separately.

Exhibit 23.2 illustrates the correlation coefficients and scatter diagrams for several sets of data. Notice that in the no correlation condition the observations are scattered rather evenly about the space. In contrast, when correlations are strong and positive, the observations lie mostly in quadrants II and IV formed by inserting new axes though $\overline{X}$ and $\overline{Y}$. If correlation was strong and negative, the observations would lie mostly in quadrants I and III.

Correlation coefficient
A statistical measure of the covariation, or association, between two at-least interval variables.

Covariance
Extent to which two variables are associated systematically with each other.

EXHIBIT 23.2
**Scatter Diagram to Illustrate
Correlation Patterns**

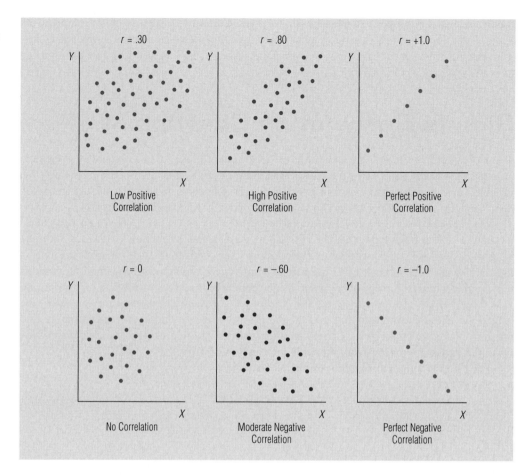

**EXHIBIT 23.2
Scatter Diagram to Illustrate
Correlation Patterns**

An Example

The correlation coefficient can be illustrated with a simple example. Today, researchers do not need to calculate correlation manually. However, the calculation process helps illustrate exactly what is meant by correlation and covariance. Consider an investigation made to determine whether the average number of hours worked in manufacturing industries is related to unemployment. A correlation analysis of the data is carried out in Exhibit 23.3.

The correlation between the two variables is -0.635, indicating an **inverse (negative) relationship**. When number of hours goes up, unemployment comes down. This makes intuitive sense. If factories are increasing output, regular workers will typically work more overtime and new employees will be hired (reducing the unemployment rate). Both variables are probably related to overall economic conditions.

Inverse (negative) relationship
Covariation in which the association between variables is in the opposite direction. As one goes up, the other goes down.

Correlation, Covariance, and Causation

TOTHEPOINT

Statistics are like a bikini. What they reveal is suggestive, but what they conceal is vital.

—Aaron Levenstein

Recall from Chapter 3 that concomitant variation is one condition needed to establish a causal relationship between two variables. When two variables covary, they display concomitant variation. This systematic covariation does not in and of itself establish causality. Remember that the relationship would also need to be nonspurious and that any hypothesized "cause" would have to occur before any subsequent effect. Work experience displays a significant correlation with job performance.[5] However, in a retail context, workers with more experience often get assigned to newer stores. Thus, the researcher would need to sort out to what extent age of the store may also be responsible for *causing* store performance.

EXHIBIT 23.3 Correlation Analysis of Number of Hours Worked in Manufacturing Industries with Unemployment Rate

Unemployment Rate (X_i)	Number of Hours Worked (Y_i)	$X_i - \bar{X}$	$(X_i - \bar{X})^2$	$Y_i - \bar{Y}$	$(Y_i - \bar{Y})^2$	$(X_i - \bar{X})(Y_i - \bar{Y})$
5.5	39.6	.51	.2601	−.71	.5041	−.3621
4.4	40.7	−.59	.3481	.39	.1521	−.2301
4.1	40.4	−.89	.7921	.09	.0081	−.0801
4.3	39.8	−.69	.4761	−.51	.2601	.3519
6.8	39.2	1.81	3.2761	−1.11	1.2321	−2.0091
5.5	40.3	.51	.2601	−.01	.0001	−.0051
5.5	39.7	.51	.2601	−.61	.3721	−.3111
6.7	39.8	1.71	2.9241	−.51	.2601	−.8721
5.5	40.4	.51	.2601	.09	.0081	.0459
5.7	40.5	.71	.5041	.19	.0361	.1349
5.2	40.7	.21	.0441	.39	.1521	.0819
4.5	41.2	−.49	.2401	.89	.7921	−.4361
3.8	41.3	−1.19	1.4161	.99	.9801	−1.1781
3.8	40.6	−1.19	1.4161	.29	.0841	−.3451
3.6	40.7	−1.39	1.9321	.39	.1521	−.5421
3.5	40.6	−1.49	2.2201	.29	.0841	−.4321
4.9	39.8	−.09	.0081	−.51	.2601	.0459
5.9	39.9	.91	.8281	−.41	.1681	−.3731
5.6	40.6	.61	.3721	.29	.0841	.1769

$$\bar{X} = 4.99$$
$$\bar{Y} = 40.31$$
$$\sum(X_i - \bar{X})^2 = 17.8379$$
$$\sum(Y_i - \bar{Y})^2 = 5.5899$$
$$\sum(X_i - \bar{X})(Y_i - \bar{Y}) = -6.3389$$

$$r = \frac{\sum(X_i - \bar{X})(Y_i - \bar{Y})}{\sqrt{\sum(X_i - \bar{X})^2 \sum(Y_i - \bar{Y})^2}} = \frac{-6.3389}{\sqrt{(17.8379)(5.5899)}} = \frac{-6.3389}{\sqrt{99.712}} = -.635$$

Coefficient of Determination

If we wish to know the proportion of *variance* in Y that is explained by X (or vice versa), we can calculate the **coefficient of determination (R^2)** by squaring the correlation coefficient:

$$R^2 = \frac{\text{Explained variance}}{\text{Total variance}}$$

Coefficient of determination (R^2)
A measure obtained by squaring the correlation coefficient; the proportion of the total variance of a variable accounted for by another value of another variable.

The coefficient of determination, R^2, measures that part of the total variance of Y that is accounted for by knowing the value of X. In the example about unemployment and hours worked, $r = -0.635$; therefore, $R^2 = 0.403$. About 40 percent of the variance in unemployment can be explained by the variance in hours worked, and vice versa. As can be seen, R-*squared* really is just r squared!

Correlation Matrix

Correlation matrix
The standard form for reporting correlation coefficients for more than two variables.

A **correlation matrix** is the standard form for reporting observed correlations among multiple variables. Although any number of variables can be displayed in a correlation matrix, each entry represents the bivariate relationship between a pair of variables. Exhibit 23.4 shows a correlation matrix that relates some measures of salesperson job performance to characteristics of the sales force.[6]

Note that the main diagonal consists of correlations of 1.00. Why is this? Simply put, any variable is correlated with itself perfectly. Had this been a covariance matrix, the diagonal would display the variance for any given variable.

Performance (S) was measured by identifying the salesperson's actual annual sales volume in dollars. Notice that the performance variable has a 0.45 correlation with the workload variable (WL), which was measured by recording the number of accounts in a sales territory. Notice also that the salesperson's perception of job-related tension (JT) as measured by an attitude scale has a -0.48 correlation with performance (S). Thus, when perceived job tension is high, performance is low.

Researchers are also concerned with statistical significance. The procedure for determining statistical significance is the t-test of the significance of a correlation coefficient. Typically it is hypothesized that $r = 0$, and then a t-test is performed. The logic behind the test is similar to that for the significance tests already considered. Statistical programs usually indicate the p-value associated with each correlation and/or star significant correlations using asterisks. The Research Snapshot box on the following page displays the way correlation matrices are often reported.

EXHIBIT 23.4 Pearson Product-Moment Correlation Matrix for Salesperson Example[a]

Variables	S	JS	GE	SE	OD	VI	JT	RA	TP	WL
Performance (S)	1.00									
Job satisfaction (JS)	.45[b]	1.00								
Generalized self-esteem (GE)	.31[b]	.10	1.00							
Specific self-esteem (SE)	.61[b]	.28[b]	.36[b]	1.00						
Other-directedness (OD)	.05	−.03	−.44[b]	−.24[c]	1.00					
Verbal intelligence (VI)	−.36[b]	−.13	−.14	−.11	−.18[d]	1.00				
Job-related tension (JT)	−.48[b]	−.56[b]	−.32[b]	−.34[b]	.26[b]	−.02	1.00			
Role ambiguity (RA)	−.26[c]	−.24[c]	−.32[b]	−.39[b]	.38[b]	−.05	−.44[b]	1.00		
Territory potential (TP)	.49[b]	.31[b]	.04	.29[b]	.09	−.09	−.38[b]	−.26[b]	1.00	
Workload (WL)	.45[b]	.11	.29[c]	.29[c]	−.04	−.12	−.27[c]	−.22[d]	.49[b]	1.00

[a]Numbers below the diagonal are for the sample; those above the diagonal are omitted.
[b]$p < .001$.
[c]$p < .01$.
[d]$p < .05$.

RESEARCHSNAPSHOT

What Makes Attractiveness?

What are the things that make someone attractive? Many people are interested in this question. Among these are companies that hire people to sell fashion. The correlation matrix below was computed with SPSS. The correlations show how different characteristics related to each other. Variables include a measure of fit, meaning how well the person matches a fashion retail concept, attractiveness, weight (how overweight someone appears), age, manner of dress, and personality. Thus, a sample of consumers rated a model shown in a photograph on those characteristics. The results reveal the following:

Correlations

		Fit	Attract	Fat	Age	Modern	Cold
Fit	Pearson Correlation	1	0.831**	−0.267*	0.108	−0.447**	−0.583**
	Sig. (2-tailed)		0.000	0.036	0.404	0.000	0.000
	N	62	62	62	62	62	62
Attract	Pearson Correlation	0.831**	1	−0.275*	0.039	−0.428**	−0.610**
	Sig. (2-tailed)	0.000		0.030	0.766	0.001	0.000
	N	62	62	62	62	62	62
Fat	Pearson Correlation	−0.267*	−0.275*	1	0.082	0.262*	0.058
	Sig. (2-tailed)	0.036	0.030		0.528	0.040	0.653
	N	62	62	62	62	62	62
Age	Pearson Correlation	0.108	0.039	0.082	1	−0.019	0.104
	Sig. (2-tailed)	0.404	0.766	0.528		0.882	0.423
	N	62	62	62	62	62	62
Modern	Pearson Correlation	−0.447**	−0.428**	0.262*	−0.019	1	0.603**
	Sig. (2-tailed)	0.000	0.001	0.040	0.882		0.000
	N	62	62	62	62	62	62
Cold	Pearson Correlation	−0.583**	−0.610**	0.058	0.104	0.603**	1
	Sig. (2-tailed)	0.000	0.000	0.653	0.423	0.000	
	N	62	62	62	62	62	62

**Correlation is significant at the 0.01 level (2-tailed)   *Correlation is significant at the 0.05 level (2-tailed).

Thus, if the model seems to "fit" the store concept, she seems attractive. If she is too big, she is seen as less attractive. Age is unrelated to attractiveness or fit. Modernness and perceived coldness also are associated with lower attractiveness. Using these correlations, a retailer can help determine what employees should look like!

Correlations can be found using SPSS by navigating as shown below:

©JILL WENDELL/JUPITER IMAGES

Regression Analysis

Regression analysis is another technique for measuring the linear association between a dependent and an independent variable. Although simple regression and correlation are mathematically equivalent in most respects, regression is a dependence technique where correlation is an interdependence technique. A dependence technique makes a distinction between dependent and independent variables. An interdependence technique does not make this distinction and simply is concerned with how variables relate to one another.

Thus, with simple regression, a dependent (or criterion) variable, Y, is linked to an independent (or predictor) variable, X. Regression analysis attempts to predict the values of a continuous, interval-scaled dependent variable from specific values of the independent variable.

The Regression Equation

Simple (bivariate) linear regression
A measure of linear association that investigates straight-line relationships between a continuous dependent variable and an independent variable that is usually continuous, but can be a categorical dummy variable.

The discussion here concerns **simple (bivariate) linear regression**. Simple regression investigates a *straight-line relationship* of the type

$$Y = \alpha + \beta X,$$

where Y is a continuous dependent variable and X is an independent variable that is usually continuous, although dichotomous nominal or ordinal variables can be included in the form of a dummy variable. Alpha (α) and beta (β) are two parameters that must be estimated so that the equation best represents a given set of data. These two parameters determine the height of the regression line and the angle of the line relative to horizontal. When these parameters change, the line changes. Regression techniques have the job of estimating values for these parameters that make the line *fit* the observations the best.

The result is simply a linear equation, or the equation for a line, just as in basic algebra! α represents the Y intercept (where the line crosses the y-axis) and β is the slope coefficient. The slope is the change in Y associated with a change of one unit in X. Slope may also be thought of as rise over run. That is, how much Y rises (or falls if negative) for every one unit change in the X-axis.

Parameter Estimate Choices

The estimates for α and β are the key to regression analysis. In most business research, the estimate of β is most important. The explanatory power of regression rests with β because this is where the direction and strength of the relationship between the independent and dependent variable is explained.

A Y-intercept term is sometimes referred to as a constant because α represents a fixed point. An estimated slope coefficient is sometimes referred to as a regression weight, regression coefficient, parameter estimate, or sometimes even as a *path* estimate. The term path estimate is a descriptive term adapted because of the way hypothesized causal relationships are often represented in diagrams:

$$\boxed{X} \xrightarrow{\beta_1} \boxed{Y}$$

For all practical purposes, these terms are used interchangeably.

Parameter estimates can be presented in either raw or standardized form. One potential problem with raw parameter estimates is due to the fact that they reflect the measurement scale range. So, if a simple regression involved distance measured with miles, very small parameter estimates may indicate a strong relationship. In contrast, if the very same distance is measured with centimeters, a very large parameter estimate would be needed to indicate a strong relationship.

Exhibit 23.5 provides an illustration. Suppose a researcher was interested in how much space was allocated to a specific snack food on a shelf and how it related to sales. Fifteen observations are taken from 15 different stores. The blue line represents a typical distance showing shelf space

EXHIBIT 23.5
The Advantage of Standardized Regression Weights

12.5 cm

Estimated Regression Line: $\hat{Y} = 22 + .07X_1$

0.000078 miles

Estimated Regression Line: $\hat{Y} = 0.00014 + .0000004X_1$

measured in cm. The green line is the same distance shown in miles. The top frame shows hypothetical regression results if the independent variable is measured in centimeters. The bottom frame shows the very same regression results if the independent variable is measured in miles. Even though these two regression lines are the same, the parameter coefficients do not seem comparable.

Thus, researchers often explain regression results by referring to a **standardized regression coefficient (β)**. A standardized regression coefficient provides a common metric allowing regression results to be compared to one another no matter what the original scale range may have been. Due to the mathematics involved in standardization, the standardized Y-intercept term is always 0.[7] The regression equation for the shelf space example would then become:

$$\hat{Y} = 0 + 0.16X_1$$

Even if the distance measures for the fifteen observations were converted to some other metric (feet, meters, and so on), the standardized regression weight would still be 0.16.

Researchers use shorthand to label regression coefficients as either "raw" or "standardized." The most common shorthand is as follows:

- $\mathbf{B}_0$ or $\mathbf{b}_0$ = raw (unstandardized) Y-intercept term; what was referred to as α above.
- $\mathbf{B}_1$ or $\mathbf{b}_1$ = raw regression coefficient or estimate.
- $\boldsymbol{\beta}_1$ = standardized regression coefficients.

Standardized regression coefficient (β)
The estimated coefficient indicating the strength of relationship between an independent variable and dependent variable expressed on a standardized scale where higher absolute values indicate stronger relationships (range is from -1 to 1).

RAW REGRESSION ESTIMATES (b_1)

Raw regression weights have the advantage of retaining the scale metric—which is also their key disadvantage. Where should the researcher focus then? Should the standardized or unstandardized coefficients be interpreted? The answer to this question is fairly simple.

- If the purpose of the regression analysis is forecasting, then raw parameter estimates must be used. This is another way of saying that the researcher is interested only in prediction.

Thus, when the researcher above wants to predict how much will be consumed based on the amount of shelf space, raw regression coefficients must be used. For instance, the forecast for 14 cm of shelf space can be found as follows:

$$\hat{Y} = 22 + 0.07(14) = 23.0$$

The same result can be found by using the equation representing the distance in miles.

STANDARDIZED REGRESSION ESTIMATES (β_1)

Standardized regression estimates have the advantage of a constant scale. No matter what range of values the independent variables take on, β will not be affected. When should standardized regression estimates be used?

- Standardized regression estimates should be used when the researcher is testing explanatory hypotheses; in other words, when the purpose of the research is more explanation than prediction.

Visual Estimation of a Simple Regression Model

As mentioned above, simple regression involves finding a best-fit line given a set of observations plotted in two-dimensional space. Many ways exist to estimate where this line should go. Estimation techniques involve terms such as instrumental variables, maximum likelihood, visual estimation and ordinary least squares (OLS). We focus on the latter two in this text.

Suppose a researcher is interested in forecasting sales for a construction distributor (wholesaler) in Florida. The distributor believes a reasonable association exists between sales and building permits issued by counties. Using bivariate linear regression on the data in Exhibit 23.6, the researcher will be able to explain sales potential (Y) in various counties based on the number of building permits (X).

The data are plotted in a scatter diagram in Exhibit 23.7. In the diagram the vertical axis indicates the value of the dependent variable, Y, and the horizontal axis indicates the value of the independent variable, X. Each single point in the diagram represents an observation of X and Y at a given point in time. The values are simply points in a Cartesian plane.

One way to determine the relationship between X and Y is to simply visually draw the best-fit straight line through the points in the figure. That is, try to draw a line that goes through the center of the plot of points. If the points are thought of as bowling pins, the best-fit line can be thought of as the path that would on average knock over the most bowling pins. For any given value of the independent variable, a prediction can be made by selecting the dependent variable that goes along with that value. For example, if we want to forecast sales if building permits are 150, we simply follow the dotted green lines shown in the exhibit to yield a prediction of about 112. The better one can estimate where the best-fit line should be, the less will be the error in prediction.

EXHIBIT 23.6

Relationship of Sales Potential to Building Permits Issued

Dealer	Y Dealer's Sales Volume (Thousands)	X Building Permits
1	77	86
2	79	93
3	80	95
4	83	104
5	101	139
6	117	180
7	129	165
8	120	147
9	97	119
10	106	132
11	99	126
12	121	156
13	103	129
14	86	96
15	99	108

EXHIBIT 23.7
The Best Fit Line or Knocking Out the Pins

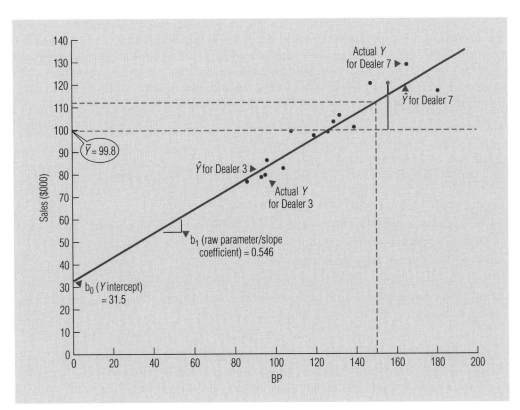

ERRORS IN PREDICTION

Any method of drawing a line can be used to perform regression. However, some methods will obviously have more error than others. Consider our bowling ball line above. One person may be better at guessing where it should be than another. We would know who was better by determining the total error of prediction.

Let's consider error by first thinking about what value of sales would be the best guess if we had no information about any other variable. In that case, our univariate best guess would be the mean sales of 99.8. If the green spot corresponding to 156 building permits ($X = 156$) were predicted with the mean, the resulting error in prediction would be represented by the distance of the blue and red vertical line.

Once information about the independent variable is provided, we can then use the prediction provided by the best-fit line. In this case, our best-fit line is the "bowling ball" line shown in the exhibit. The error in prediction using this line would be indicated by the red vertical line extending from the regression line to the actual observation. Thus, it appears that at least for this observation, our prediction using the regression line has reduced the error in prediction that would result from guessing with the mean. Statistically, this is the goal of regression analysis. We would like an estimation technique that would place our line so that the total sum of all errors over all observations is minimized. In other words, no line fits better. Although with good guess work, visual estimation may prove somewhat accurate, perhaps there is a more certain way.

Ordinary Least-Squares Method of Regression Analysis (OLS)

The researcher's task is to find the best means for fitting a straight line to the data. OLS is a relatively straightforward mathematical technique that guarantees that the resulting straight line will produce the least possible total error in using X to predict Y. The logic is based on how much better a regression line can predict values of Y compared to simply using the mean as a prediction for all observations no matter what the value of X may be.

Unless the dependent and independent variables are perfectly related, no straight line can connect all observations. More technically, the procedure used in the least-squares method generates a straight line that minimizes the sum of squared deviations of the actual values from this predicted regression line. With the symbol e representing the deviations of the observations from the regression line, no other line can produce less error. The deviations are squared so that positive and negative misses do not cancel each other out. The OLS criterion is as follows:

$$\sum_{i=1}^{n} e_i^2 \text{ is minimum}$$

where

$e_i = Y_i - \hat{Y}_i$ (the residual)

$Y_i =$ actual observed value of the dependent variable

$\hat{Y}_i =$ estimated value of the dependent variable (pronounced "Y-hat")

$n =$ number of observations

$i =$ number of the particular observation

The general equation for any straight line can be represented as $Y = b_0 + b_1 X$. If we think of this as the true hypothetical line that we try to estimate with sample observations, the regression equation will represent this with a slightly different equation:

$$Y_i = b_0 + b_1 X_1 + e_i$$

The equation means that the predicted value for any value of X (X_i) is determined as a function of the estimated slope coefficient, plus the estimated intercept coefficient + some error.

The raw parameter estimates can be found using the following formulas:

$$b_1 = \frac{n(\sum X_i Y_i) - (\sum X_i)(\sum Y_i)}{n(\sum X_i^2) - (\sum X_i)^2}$$

and

$$b_0 = \bar{Y} - b_1 \bar{X}$$

where

$Y_i = i$th observed value of the dependent variable

$X_i = i$th observed value of the independent variable

$\bar{Y} =$ mean of the dependent variable

$X =$ independent variable

$\bar{X} =$ mean of the independent variable

$n =$ number of observations

$b_0 =$ intercept estimate

$b_1 =$ slope estimate (regression weight)

The careful reader may notice some similarity between the correlation calculation and the equation for b_1. In fact, the standardized regression coefficient from a simple regression equals the Pearson correlation coefficient for the two variables. Once the estimates are obtained, a predicted value for the dependent variable can be found for any value of X_i with this equation:

$$\hat{Y}_i = b_0 + b_i X_i$$

Appendix 23A demonstrates the arithmetic necessary to calculate the parameter estimates.

STATISTICAL SIGNIFICANCE OF REGRESSION MODEL

As with ANOVA, the researcher needs a way of testing the statistical significance of the regression model. Also like ANOVA, an F-test provides the answer to this question.

The overall F-test for regression can be illustrated with Exhibit 23.7. Once again examine the multicolored line showing the predicted value for $X = 156$.

1. The total line including the blue and red line represents the *total deviation* of the observation from the mean:

$$Y_i - \bar{Y}$$

2. The blue portion represents how much of the total deviation is *explained* by the *regression* line:

$$\hat{Y}_i - \bar{Y}$$

3. The red portion represents how much of the total deviation is not explained by the regression line (also equal to e_i):

$$Y_i - \hat{Y}_i$$

These three components are mathematically related because the total deviation is a sum of what is explained by the regression line and what is not explained by the regression line. This can be expressed mathematically as

$$(Y_i - \bar{Y}) \;=\; (\hat{Y}_i - \bar{Y}) \;+\; (Y_i - \hat{Y}_i)$$

	Deviation	Deviation
Total	explained by	unexplained by
Deviation =	the regression +	the regression
(SST)	(SSR)	(SSE)

Just as in ANOVA, the total deviation represents the total variation to be explained. Thus, the partitioning of the variation into components allows us to form a ratio of the explained variation versus the unexplained variation. The corresponding abbreviation for this partitioning is

$$SST = SSR + SSE$$

An **F-test (regression)**, or an *analysis of variance,* can be applied to a regression to test the relative magnitudes of the *SSR* (Sums of Squares − Regression) and *SSE* (Sums of Squared Errors) with their appropriate degrees of freedom. The equation for the *F*-test is

$$F_{(k-1)(n-k)} = \frac{SSR/(k-1)}{SSE/(n-k)} = \frac{MSR}{MSE}$$

F-test (regression)
A procedure to determine whether more variability is explained by the regression or unexplained by the regression.

where,

MSR is an abbreviation for Mean Squared Regression

MSE is an abbreviation for Mean Squared Error

k is the number of independent variables (always 1 for simple regression)

n is the sample size

Once again, researchers today need not calculate this by hand. Regression programs will produce an "ANOVA" table, which will provide the *F*-value and a p-value (significance level), and will generally show the partitioned variation in some form. For the sales example, the following table is obtained:

ANOVA

	df	SS	MS	F	p-value
Regression (SSR)	1	3398.48911	3398.489	91.29854	0.0000003
Residual (SSE)	13	483.910892	37.22391		
Total	14	3882.4			

Thus, building permits explains a significant portion of the variation in sales as evidenced by the very low p-value.

R^2

The *coefficient of determination*, R^2, reflects the proportion of variance explained by the regression line. In this example, R^2 can be found with this formula:

$$R^2 = \frac{SSR}{SST} = \frac{3398.5}{3882.4} = 0.875$$

The coefficient of determination may be interpreted to mean that 87.5 percent of the variation in sales was explained by associating the variable with building permits.

What is an "acceptable" R^2 value? This question is asked frequently. However, guidelines for R^2 values are neither simple nor straightforward. Indeed, good and bad values for the coefficient of determination depend on so many factors that a single precise guideline is considered inappropriate. The focus should be on the *F*-test. However, in practice, do not expect to often see a simple regression result with an R^2 anywhere near the value in this example. They will normally be considerably lower.[8]

INTERPRETING REGRESSION OUTPUT

Exhibit 23.8 displays output for the building permit problem. Most computerized software provides similar output for regression analysis. Interpreting simple regression output is a simple two-step process.

1. Interpret the overall significance of the model.
   a. The output will include the "model *F*" and a significance value. When the model *F* is significant (low p-value), the independent variable explains a significant portion of the variation in the dependent variable.
   b. The coefficient of determination or R^2 can be interpreted. As mentioned earlier, this is the percentage of total variation in the dependent variable accounted for by the independent variable. Another way to think of this is as the extent to which the variances of the independent and dependent variable overlap.

EXHIBIT 23.8
Simple Regression Results for Building Permit Example

R	R Square	Adjusted R Square	Std. Error of the Estimate
.936(a)	.875	.866	6.10114

a Predictors: (Constant), Permits

ANOVA(b)

1. Is model significant?

	Sum of Squares	df	Mean Square	F	Sig.
Regression	3398.489	1	3398.489	91.299	.000(a)
Residual	483.911	13	37.224		
Total	3882.400	14			

a Predictors: (Constant), Permits
b Dependent Variable: Sales

2. Interpret parameter estimates?

Coefficients[a]

Model	Unstandardized Coefficients: B	Std. Error	Standardized Coefficient: Beta (β)	t	Sig.
1.000 (Constant)	31.502	7.319		4.304	0.001
Permits	0.546	0.057	0.936	9.555	0.000

a   Dependent Variable: Sales

2. The individual parameter coefficient is interpreted.
    a. The *t*-value associated with the slope coefficient can be interpreted. In this case, the *t* of 9.555 is associated with a very low p-value (0.000 to 3 decimal places). Therefore, the slope coefficient is significant. For simple regression, the p-value for the model *F* and for the *t*-test of the individual regression weight will be the same.
    b. A *t*-test for the intercept term (constant) is also provided. However, this is seldom of interest since the explanatory power rests in the slope coefficient.
    c. If a need to forecast sales exists, the estimated regression equation is needed. Using the raw coefficients, the estimated regression line is

$$\hat{Y} = 31.5 + 0.546X$$

    d. The regression coefficient (slope) indicates that for every building permit issued, sales increase 0.546. Moreover, the standardized regression coefficient of 0.936 would allow the researcher to compare the explanatory power of building permits versus some other potential independent variable. For simple regression, β_1 equals *r*.

PLOTTING THE OLS REGRESSION LINE

To draw a regression line on the scatter diagram, only two predicted values of *Y* need to be plotted. The data for two dealers is used to illustrate how this is done:

$$\text{Dealer 7 (actual Y value} = 129\text{): } \hat{Y}_7 = 31.5 + 0.546(165)$$
$$= 121.6$$

$$\text{Dealer 3 (actual Y value} = 80\text{): } \hat{Y}_3 = 31.5 + 0.546(95)$$
$$= 83.4$$

Using the data for Dealer 7 and Dealer 3, we can draw a straight line connecting the points 121.6 and 83.4. Exhibit 23.9 shows the regression line.

To determine the error (residual) of any observation, the predicted value of *Y* is first calculated. The predicted value is then subtracted from the actual value. For example, the actual observation

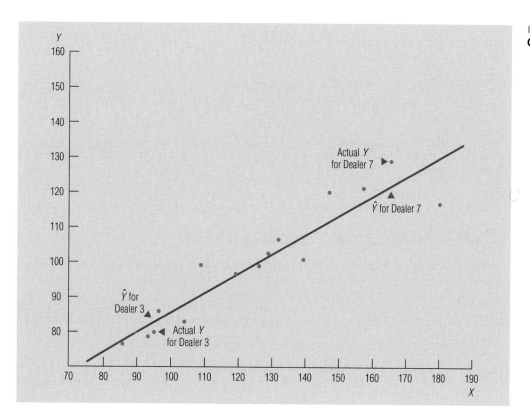

EXHIBIT 23.9
OLS Regression Line

RESEARCHSNAPSHOT

Size and Weight

America seems obsessed with weight control. Thin seems to stay in and the fight to get thin is a multibillion dollar business. Recall in an earlier Research Snapshot correlations between factors related to attractiveness were discussed. What if the following hypothesis were tested?

H1: Perceptions that a female model is overweight are related negatively to perceptions of attractiveness.

Using the scales from the earlier Snapshot, this can be tested with a simple regression. The results can be summarized as shown here:

Model	Sum of Squares	d.f.	Mean Square	F	Sig.
1　Regression	9.228	1	9.227	4.914	0.030
Residual	112.660	60	1.877		
Total	121.8870968	61			

| | Unstandardized Coefficients | | | Standardized Coefficients | | |
Model	B	Std. Error		β	t	Sig.
1　(Constant)	4.413	0.952			4.636	0.00002
X113	−0.582	0.262		−0.275	−2.216	0.030

The results support the hypothesis. The $\beta = -0.275$ is both in the expected direction (negative) and significant ($p < 0.05$). Therefore, if respondents perceived someone as "too fat," they likewise saw the person as less attractive.

©PHOTODISC/GETTY IMAGES

---

for Dealer 9 is 97, and the predicted value is 96.5; thus only a small margin of error, $e = 0.5$, is involved in this regression line:

$$e_9 = Y_9 - \hat{Y}_9$$
$$= 97 - 96.5$$
$$= 0.5$$

where

$$\hat{Y}_9 = 31.5 + .546(119)$$

TOTHEPOINT

Forecasting is like trying to drive a car blindfolded and following directions given by a person who is looking out the back window.

—Anonymous

SIMPLE REGRESSION AND HYPOTHESIS TESTING

The explanatory power of regression lies in hypothesis testing. Regression is often used to test relational hypotheses. For example, from the chapter vignette, simple regression could be used to test the hypothesis relating food quantity to food consumption.

H1: The amount of food eaten during a meal is related positively to the amount of food placed on a plate.

In the sales example, the regression addresses a hypothesis linking permits to sales.

H1: Sales are positively related to the number of building permits.

The outcome of the hypothesis test involves two conditions that must both be satisfied.

1. The regression weight must be in the hypothesized direction. Positive relationships require a positive coefficient and negative relationships require a negative coefficient.
2. The t-test associated with the regression weight must be significant.

In the sales example, both of these conditions are satisfied and the hypothesis would be supported.

Summary

1. Apply and interpret simple bivariate correlations. This chapter covers two approaches for studying relationships among two at-least interval variables. A bivariate correlation is an index that displays how much two variables covary. Another way to think of correlation is as a standardized measure of covariance. When two variables display a correlation of 1.0, they are perfectly correlated. That means that they have no unique variance. In most ways, they are one and the same. When two variables are correlated −1.0 they are perfectly negatively correlated. In this sense they are mirror images of one another. Thus, correlations can range between −1.0 and 1.0. Correlations near 0 indicate a lack of relationship between two variables.

2. Interpret a correlation matrix. A correlation matrix presents all possible bivariate correlations among a set of variables. The statistical significance of each variable can be tested with a t-test. Low p-values for this test indicate significant correlations. Patterns of strong correlations among variables indicate variables that share variance in common.

3. Understand simple (bivariate) regression. Simple linear regression investigates a straight-line relationship between one dependent variable and one independent variable. The regression can be done intuitively by plotting a scatter diagram of the X and Y points and drawing a line to fit the observed relationship. OLS estimation mathematically determines the best-fitting regression line for the observed data. The line determined by this method may be used to forecast values of the dependent variable, given a value for the independent variable. The line's goodness-of-fit may be evaluated with a variant of the ANOVA (analysis of variance) technique or by calculating the coefficient of determination.

4. Understand the least-squares estimation technique. OLS is an estimation technique that minimizes the least-squared error for all observations. Regression models are evaluated based on how much variance they explain. Models with a high SSR relative to SST or SSE explain more variance in the dependent variable. SSR represents the proportion of total deviation from the mean among observations that can be explained by the regression line. SSE, the sums of square error, represents the amount of deviation from the mean for observations that is not accounted for by the regression line. OLS fits the line to minimize SSE.

5. Interpret regression output including the tests of hypotheses tied to specific parameter coefficients. Regression results are interpreted in a two-step process. First, the model's significance is evaluated. The model F-ratio, which is a ratio of SSR to SSE, is a key statistic. A significant F-ratio means that the independent variable explains a significant portion of the variance in the dependent variable. Second, the individual parameter coefficients are evaluated. When the regression is run for forecasting purposes, the raw parameter coefficients are most useful. When the regression is run for explanatory purposes, the standardized regression weight (β) is most useful.

Key Terms and Concepts

Measure of association	Inverse (negative) relationship	Simple (bivariate) linear regression
Correlation coefficient	Coefficient of determination (R^2)	Standardized regression coefficient (β)
Covariance	Correlation matrix	F-test (regression)

Questions for Review and Critical Thinking

1. What is *covariance?*
2. How are covariance and correlation different?
3. How does a researcher determine if a correlation coefficient is significant?
4. The management of a regional bus line thought the company's cost of gas might be correlated with its passenger/mile ratio. The data and a correlation matrix follow. Comment.

Year	Average Wholesale Cost of Gas	Passengers/Miles
1	56.5	8.37
2	59.4	8.93
3	63.0	9.15
4	65.6	9.79
5	89.0	11.20

	Year	Price	Mile
Year (r)	1.00000	0.87016	0.95127
p-value	0.00000	0.05510	0.01280
Price (r)	0.87016	1.00000	0.97309
p-value	0.05510	0.00000	0.00530
Mile (r)	0.95127	0.97309	1.00000
p-value	0.01280	0.00530	0.00000

5. Interpret the following data:
   a. $\hat{Y} = 5.0 + .30X_1$
      i. Where the dependent variable equals turnover intentions for line managers and the independent variable equals number of employees supervised.
   b. $\hat{Y} = 250 - 4.0X_1$
      i. **'NET** Where the dependent variable is the number of hits on a new banner ad and the independent variable is the number of weeks the ad has run.
6. What are some different terms used to refer to the slope coefficient estimated in regression analysis?
7. The following ANOVA summary table is the result of a regression of sales on year of sales. Is the relationship statistically significant at the 0.95 significance level? Fill in the value for Sums of Squares in the SST row. Comment.

8.

Source of Variation	Sum of Squares	d.f.	Mean Square	F-Value	p-value
SSR	605,370,750	1	605,370,750	3.12	0.115
SSE	1,551,381,712	8	193,922,714		
SST		9			

9. Address the following questions about regression analysis:
   a. Define *simple linear regression.*
   b. When it is most appropriate to rely on raw parameter coefficients and when is it most appropriate to rely on standardized parameter coefficients?
   c. Why is the Y-intercept estimate equal to 0 for standardized estimates?
   d. What are the steps in interpreting a regression model?
10. The following table gives a football team's season-ticket sales, percentage of games won, and number of active alumni for the years 1996–2005.

Year	Season-Ticket Sales	Percentage of Games Won	Number of Active Alumni
1996	4,995	40	NA
1997	8,599	54	3,450
1998	8,479	55	3,801
1999	8,419	58	4,000
2000	10,253	63	4,098
2001	12,457	75	6,315
2002	13,285	36	6,860
2003	14,177	27	8,423
2004	15,730	63	9,000
2005	15,805	70	9,500

   a. Compute a correlation matrix for the variables. A software statistical package is recommended. Interpret the correlation between each pair of variables.
   b. Estimate a regression model for sales = Percentage of games won.
   c. Estimate a regression model for sales = Number of active alumni.
   d. If *sales* is the dependent variable, which of the two independent variables do you think explains sales better? Explain.
11. Are the different forms of consumer installment credit in the following table highly correlated?

Debt Outstanding (millions of dollars)

Year	Gas Cards	Travel and Entertainment Cards	Bank Credit Cards	Retail Cards	Total Credit Cards	Total Installment Credit
1	$ 939	$ 61	$ 828	$ 9,400	$ 11,228	$79,428
2	1,119	76	1,312	10,200	12,707	87,745
3	1,298	110	2,639	10,900	14,947	98,105
4	1,650	122	3,792	11,500	17,064	102,064
5	1,804	132	4,490	13,925	20,351	111,295
6	1,762	164	5,408	14,763	22,097	127,332
7	1,832	191	6,838	16,395	25,256	147,437
8	1,823	238	8,281	17,933	28,275	156,124
9	1,893	273	9,501	18,002	29,669	164,955
10	1,981	238	11,351	19,052	32,622	185,489
11	2,074	284	14,262	21,082	37,702	216,572

12. A manufacturer of disposable washcloths/wipes told a retailer that sales for this product category closely correlated with sales of disposable diapers. The retailer thought he would check this out for his own sales-forecasting purposes. The researcher says, "Disposable washcloths/wipes sales can be predicted with knowledge of disposable diaper sales." Is this the right thing to say?

13. Explain how OLS determines where a regression line should be placed among a plot of observations?

Research Activities

1. **'NET** The Federal Reserve Bank of St. Louis maintains a database called FRED (Federal Reserve Economic Data). Navigate to the FRED database at http://www.stls.frb.org/fred/index.html. Randomly select a five-year period between 1970 and 2000 and then find the correlation between average U.S. employment in retail trade and U.S. employment in wholesale trade. Which statistical test is appropriate?

2. **'NET/ETHICS** Go to http://www.transparency.org. Find the corruption perception indices for 2005. Go to http://www.geert-hofstede.com/hofstede_dimensions.php. Create a data set that includes the corruption perception indices for at least fifteen countries and the score for one of the Hofstede cultural valued dimensions. Conduct a regression and interpret the relationship between cultural values and corruption perceptions.

Case 23.1 International Operations at CarCare Inc.

CarCare is considering expanding its operations beyond the United States. The company wants to know whether it should target countries with consumers who tend to have a positive attitude toward their current cars. It has gathered data on U.S. and German car owners. The data are included in the "car" data set that can be viewed on the website at http://www.thomsonedu.com/marketing/zikmund (car.sav or car.xls) or available from your instructor. Using the data, conduct a correlation and simple regression analysis using spending as the dependent variable and attitude toward the current car as the independent variable.

1. Test the hypothesis: Attitude toward one's car is related positively to spending for car-care products.

2. Would you recommend they do more research to identify nations with relatively favorable attitudes toward the cars they own?

[NOTE: This data set was referred to for the first time in Chapter 22.]

APPENDIX 23A
ARITHMETIC
BEHIND OLS

With simple arithmetic we can solve for the parameter estimates using the OLS equations. Here, the data from Exhibit 23.6 are used. The different pieces of the equations are calculated and shown in Exhibit 23A.1. To estimate the relationship between the distributor's sales to a dealer and the number of building permits, we insert values from the table as shown below:

$$b_1 = \frac{n(\sum X_i Y_i) - (\sum X_i)(\sum Y_i)}{n(\sum X_i^2) - (\sum X_i)^2}$$

$$b_1 = \frac{15(193,345) - 2,806,875}{15(245,759) - 3,515,625}$$

$$= 0.546$$

$$b_o = \bar{Y} - b_1 \bar{X}$$

$$= 99.8 - 0.546(125)$$

$$= 31.5$$

EXHIBIT 23A.1 **Least-Squares Computation**

	Y	Y²	X	X²	XY
1	77	5,929	86	7,396	6,622
2	79	6,241	93	8,649	7,347
3	80	6,400	95	9,025	7,600
4	83	6,889	104	10,816	8,632
5	101	10,201	139	19,321	14,039
6	117	13,689	180	32,400	21,060
7	129	16,641	165	27,225	21,285
8	120	14,400	147	21,609	17,640
9	97	9,409	119	14,161	11,543
10	106	11,236	132	17,424	13,992
11	99	9,801	126	15,876	12,474
12	121	14,641	156	24,336	18,876
13	103	10,609	129	16,641	13,287
14	86	7,396	96	9,216	8,256
15	99	9,801	108	11,664	10,692
	$\Sigma Y = 1,497$ $\bar{Y} = 99.8$	$\Sigma Y^2 = 153,283$	$\Sigma X = 1,875$ $\bar{X} = 125$	$\Sigma X^2 = 245,759$	$\Sigma XY = 193,345$

The formula $\hat{Y}_1 = 31.5 + 0.546X_1$ is the regression equation used for the prediction of the dependent variable. Suppose the wholesaler is considering opening a new dealership in an area where the number of building permits equals 89. We would need to compute a predicted value for $X = 89$. Sales in this area may be forecasted as

$$\hat{Y} = 31.5 + 0.546(X)$$
$$= 31.5 + 0.546(89)$$
$$= 31.5 + 48.6$$
$$= 80.1$$

Thus, the distributor may expect sales of 80.1 (or \$80,100) in this new area★.

Calculation of the correlation coefficient gives an indication of how accurate the predictions are. In this example the correlation coefficient is $r = 0.94$ and the coefficient of determination is $R^2 = 0.88$.

★This is a point estimate. A confidence interval can be calculated for this sales estimate; however, the topic is beyond the scope of the book.

CHAPTER 24
INTRODUCING MULTIVARIATE STATISTICAL ANALYSIS

After studying this chapter, you should be able to

1. Understand what multivariate statistical analysis involves and know the two types of multivariate analysis
2. Interpret results from multiple regression analysis
3. Interpret results from multivariate analysis of variance (MANOVA)
4. Interpret basic exploratory factor analysis results
5. Know what multiple discriminant analysis can be used to do
6. Understand how cluster analysis can identify market segments

Chapter Vignette: Cow-A-Bunga Never Goes Out of Style

As humans, we long to relive the past. This yearning to hold on to the past is a common psychological experience.[1] The psychology of consumption is of interest to many people who are not psychologists, however. The fact is, nostalgia sells, and marketing researchers are very interested in understanding exactly what nostalgia is, who is most prone to react to it, and how it contributes to business success.

When a Boomer or Gen-Xer walks through the toy store, he or she is likely to feel right at home. Toy companies like Hasbro have realized that adults buy toys for kids to enjoy. Grown-up consumers like to buy things they feel good about. Thus, the toy shelves are filled with throwback versions of GI Joe, Barbie, and even the Teenage Mutant Ninja Turtles.[2] The game shelves are filled with classic versions of familiar games like Risk, Stratego, and Monopoly.[3]

Not to be outdone, other marketers are also counting on nostalgic consumers. Appliance companies have recently turned to retro designs with classic 1950s versions of toasters, blenders, and even ovens.[4] Advertisers are also turning to nostalgia as they try to produce more effective sales appeals. Among others, Coca-Cola has used nostalgic advertising to help consumers relive the past.[5]

How can marketers better integrate nostalgia into their business plans? Researchers are working on numerous issues related to nostalgia:

- How can nostalgia be measured?
- What emotions is nostalgia associated with?[6]
- Can market segments be defined based on the type and amount of nostalgia experienced?
- What happens to consumers when they experience nostalgia?
- What makes a nostalgic consumer different from one who does not experience nostalgia?
- What are the positive outcomes for the business when consumer nostalgia increases?

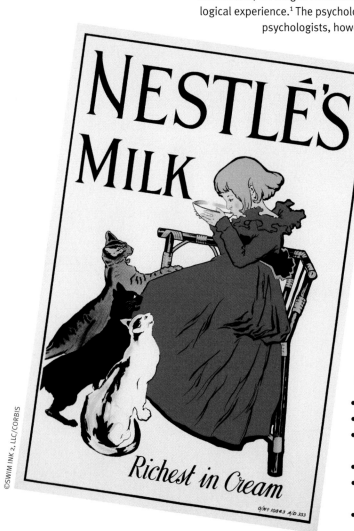

Nostalgia is a complex experience involving multiple thoughts and feelings. The complexity makes nostalgia somewhat difficult to study. Multivariate research procedures can help address these questions as they consider the effects of multiple variables simultaneously. However, it seems that nostalgic thoughts mean good vibes for the marketer.[7] Cow-a-bunga!

The Nature of Multivariate Analysis

What Is Multivariate Data Analysis?

If only business problems were really as simple as most textbook examples. Most coursework involves solving problems that have a definite answer. They are relatively well-defined problems in which the information provided in the problem can be used to produce *one* solution.

Unfortunately, in the real world, most business problems are ill-defined. Not only do they not have a definite answer, but generally information needs to be massaged and generated before any solution can be obtained. Therefore, most business research studies involve many variables that must be organized for meaning. As researchers become increasingly aware of the multidimensional nature of business problems, they gain a greater appreciation for multivariate data analysis.

The proceeding chapters have addressed univariate and bivariate analyses. Research that involves three or more variables, or that is concerned with underlying dimensions among multiple variables, will involve multivariate statistical analysis. Multivariate statistical methods analyze multiple variables or even multiple sets of variables simultaneously. How do we know when someone has experienced nostalgia and whether or not the experience has altered behavior? Nostalgia itself is a latent factor that involves multiple indicators that together represent nostalgia. As such, the measurement and outcomes of nostalgia lend themselves well to multivariate analysis.[8] Likewise, many other marketing problems involve multivariate data analysis including most psychographic research and most research that seeks to identify viable market segments.

TOTHEPOINT

The essence of mathematics is not to make simple things complicated, but to make complicated things simple.

—S. Gudder

The "Variate" in Multivariate

Another distinguishing characteristic of multivariate analysis is the **variate**. The variate is a mathematical way in which a set of variables can be represented with one equation. Variates are formed as a linear combination of variables, each contributing to the overall meaning of the variate based upon an empirically derived weight. Mathematically, the variate is a function of the measured variables involved in an analysis:

$$V_k = f(X_1, X_2, \ldots, X_m)$$

Variate
A mathematical way in which a set of variables can be represented with one equation.

V_k is the kth variate. Every analysis could involve multiple sets of variables, each represented by a variate. X_1 to X_m represent the measured variables.

Here is a simple illustration. Recall that constructs are distinguished from variables by the fact that multiple variables are needed to measure a construct. If we measured nostalgia with five variables, a variate of the following form could be created:

$$V_k = L_1 X_1 + L_2 X_2 + L_3 X_3 + L_4 X_4 + L_5 X_5$$

V_k represents the score for nostalgia, X_1 to X_5 represent the observed scores on the five scale items that are expected to indicate nostalgia, and L_1 to L_5 are parameter estimates much like regression weights that suggest how highly related each variable is to the overall nostalgia score.

Don't worry! We do not have to manually calculate these scores anymore. We'll rely on the computer to do the heavy lifting. However, this type of relationship is common to multivariate procedures.

EXHIBIT 24.1
**Which Multivariate Approach
Is Appropriate?**

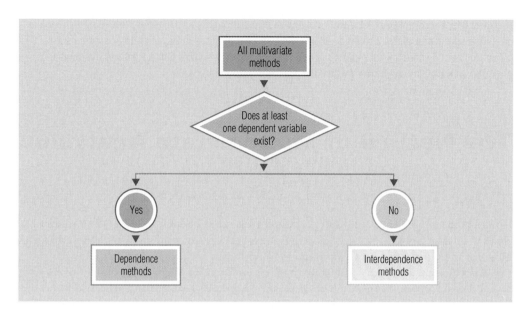

Classifying Multivariate Techniques

Exhibit 24.1 presents a very basic classification of multivariate data analysis procedures. Two basic groups of multivariate techniques are *dependence methods* and *interdependence methods.*

Dependence Techniques

Dependence techniques
Multivariate statistical techniques that explain or predict one or more dependent variables.

When hypotheses involve distinction between independent and dependent variables, **dependence techniques** are needed. For instance, when we hypothesize that nostalgia is related positively to purchase intentions, nostalgia takes on the character of an independent variable and purchase intentions take on the character of a dependent variable. Predicting the dependent variable "sales" on the basis of numerous independent variables is a problem frequently investigated with dependence techniques. *Multiple regression analysis, multiple discriminant analysis, multivariate analysis of variance,* and *structural equations modeling* are all dependence methods.

Interdependence Techniques

Interdependence techniques
Multivariate statistical techniques that give meaning to a set of variables or seek to group things together; no distinction is made between dependent and independent variables.

When researchers examine questions that do not distinguish between independent and dependent variables, **interdependence techniques** are used. No one variable or variable subset is to be predicted from or explained by the others. The most common interdependence methods are *factor analysis, cluster analysis,* and *multidimensional scaling.* A marketing manager might utilize these techniques to identify profitable market segments or clusters or to classify cities on the basis of population size, income distribution, race and ethnic distribution, and consumption of a manufacturer's product to select comparable test-markets. Interdependence techniques can also be useful in examining the validity of multiple item measures.

Influence of Measurement Scales

As in other forms of data analysis, the nature of the measurement scales will determine which multivariate technique is appropriate for the data. Exhibits 24.2 and 24.3 show that selection of a multivariate technique requires consideration of the types of measures used for both independent and dependent sets of variables. These exhibits refer to nominal and ordinal scales as *nonmetric* and interval and ratio scales as *metric.*

Chapter 24: Introducing Multivariate Statistical Analysis

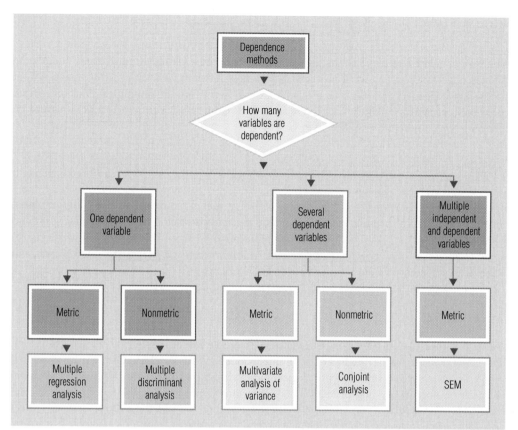

EXHIBIT 24.2
Which Multivariate
Dependence Technique
Should I Use?

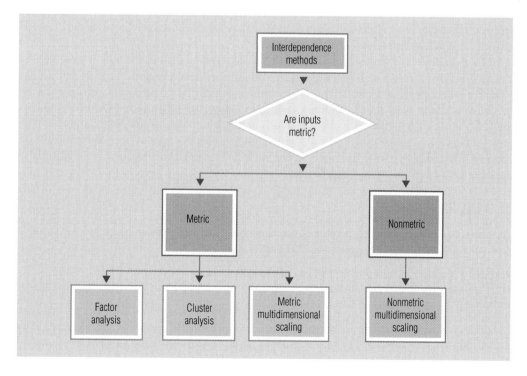

EXHIBIT 24.3
Which Multivariate
Interdependence Technique
Should I Use?

Analysis of Dependence

Multivariate dependence techniques are variants of the **general linear model (GLM)**. Simply, the GLM is a way of modeling some process based on how different variables cause fluctuations from the average dependent variable. Fluctuations can come in the form of group means that differ from the overall mean as is in ANOVA or in the form of a significant slope coefficient as in regression. The basic idea can be thought of as follows:

$$\hat{Y}_i = \mu + \Delta X + \Delta F + \Delta XF$$

Here, μ represents a constant, which can be thought of as the overall mean of the dependent variable, ΔX and ΔF represent changes due to main effect independent variables (such as experimental variables) and blocking independent variables (such as covariates or grouping variables), respectively, and ΔXF represents the change due to the combination (interaction effect) of those variables. Realize that Y_i in this case could represent multiple dependent variables, just as X and B could represent multiple independent variables. Multiple regression analysis, n-way ANOVA, and MANOVA represent common forms that the GLM can take.

Multiple Regression Analysis

Multiple regression analysis is an extension of simple regression analysis allowing a metric dependent variable to be predicted by multiple independent variables. Chapter 23 illustrated simple linear regression analysis with an example explaining a construction dealer's sales volume with the number of building permits issued. Thus, one dependent variable is explained by one independent variable. Yet reality is more complicated and several additional factors probably affect sales. The other plausible independent variables include prices, economic factors, advertising intensity, and consumers' incomes in the area. The simple regression equation can be expanded to represent multiple regression analysis:

$$Y_i = b_0 + b_1X_1 + b_2X_2 + b_3X_3 + \cdots + b_nX_n + e_i$$

Thus, as a form of the GLM, dependent variable predictions ($\hat{Y}$) are made by adjusting the constant (b_0, which would be equal to the mean if all slope coefficients are 0) based on the slope coefficients associated with each independent variable.[9]

Less than interval (nonmetric) independent variables can be used in multiple regression. This can be done by implementing dummy variable coding. A **dummy variable** is a variable that uses a 1 and a 0 to code the different levels of dichotomous variable. Multiple dummy variables can be included in a regression model. Dummy coding is appropriate when data from two countries are being compared. Suppose the average labor rate for automobile production is included in a sample taken from respondents in Mexico and in South Korea. A response from Mexico could be assigned a 0 and responses from South Korea could be assigned 1 to create a country variable appropriate for use with multiple regression.

▦ A SIMPLE EXAMPLE

Assume that a toy manufacturer wishes to explain store sales (dependent variable) using a sample of stores from Canada and Europe. Several hypotheses are offered:

- H1: *Competitor's sales* are related negatively to sales.
- H2: Sales are higher in communities with a *sales office* than when no sales office is present.
- H3: *Grammar school enrollment* in a community is related positively to sales.

Competitor's sales is how much the primary competitor sold in the same stores over the same time period. Both the dependent variable and the competitor's sales are ratio variables measured in Euros (Canadian sales were converted to Euros). The presence of a sales office is a categorical variable that can be represented with dummy coding (0 = no office in this particular region, 1 = office in this region). Grammar school enrollment is also a ratio variable simply represented by the number of students enrolled in elementary schools in each community (in thousands).[10] A sample of twenty-four communities is gathered and the data are entered into a regression program to produce the following results:

Regression equation: $\hat{Y} = 102.18 + 0.387X_1 + 115.2X_2 + 6.73X_3$

Coefficient of multiple determination $(R^2) = 0.845$

F-value $= 14.6$; $p < 0.05$

The regression equation indicates that sales are positively related to X_1, X_2, and X_3. The coefficients show the effect on the dependent variable of a 1-unit increase in any of the independent variables. The value $b_2 = 115.2$ indicates that an increase of \$115,200 (115.2 thousands) in toy sales is expected with each additional unit of X_2. Thus, it appears that having a company sales office in a community is associated with a very positive effect on sales. Grammar school enrollments also may help predict sales. An increase of 1 unit of enrollment (1,000 students) indicates a sales increase of \$6,730. A one-unit increase in competitors' sales volume (X_1) in the territory adds little to the toy manufacturer's sales (\$387).

Because the effect associated with X_1 is positive, H1 is not supported because the sign of the regression coefficient is opposite the prediction. Instead of losing sales to the competition, as competitors' sales go up, so do the sales of this toy company. The effects associated with H2 and H3 are in the hypothesized direction. Thus, if the coefficients are statistically significant, each will be supported.

REGRESSION COEFFICIENTS IN MULTIPLE REGRESSION

Recall that in simple regression, the coefficient $\mathbf{b}_1$ represents the slope of X on Y. Multiple regression involves multiple slope estimates, or regression weights. One challenge in regression models is to understand how one independent variable affects the dependent variable considering the effect of other independent variables. As long as the independent variables are related to each other, the regression weight associated with one independent variable is affected by the regression weight of another. Regression coefficients are unaffected by each other only when independent variables are independent.

Conventional regression programs can provide standardized parameter estimates, β_1, β_2, and so on, that can be thought of as *partial* regression coefficients. The correlation between Y and X_1, controlling for the correlation that X_2 has with the Y, is called **partial correlation**. Consider a standardized regression model with only two independent variables:[11]

Partial correlation
The correlation between two variables after taking into account the fact that they are correlated with other variables too.

$$Y = \beta_1 X_1 + \beta_2 X_2 + e_i$$

The coefficients β_1 and β_2 are partial regression coefficients, which express the relationship between the independent variable and dependent variable taking into consideration that the other variable also is related to the dependent variable. As long as the correlation between independent variables is modest, partial regression coefficients adequately represent the relationships. When the correlation between two independent variables becomes high, the regression coefficients may not be reliable. We return to this issue later in the chapter.

When researchers want to know which independent variable is most predictive of the dependent variable, the standardized regression coefficient (β) is used. One huge advantage of β is that it provides a constant scale. Therefore, the greater the absolute value of the standardized regression coefficient, the more that particular independent variable is responsible for explaining the dependent variable. For example, suppose in the toy example above, the following standardized regression coefficients were found:

$$\beta_1 = 0.10$$
$$\beta_2 = 0.30$$
$$\beta_3 = 0.10$$

The resulting standardized regression equation would be

$$Y = 0.10X_1 + 0.30X_2 + 0.10X_3 + e_i$$

Using standardized coefficients, the researcher concludes that the relationship between competitor's sales (X_1) and company sales (Y) is the same strength as is the relationship between grammar school enrollment (X_3) and company sales. Perhaps more importantly, though, the conclusion can also be reached that the relationship between having a sales office in the area (X_2) and sales is three

RESEARCHSNAPSHOT

Too Much of a Good Thing!

Researchers often test hypotheses by examining regression coefficients. Thus, we are often looking for correlations, sometimes in all the wrong places. Financial data can be problematic to analyze. Consider the case of a financial manager trying to analyze gross margin (dependent variable = margin per employee) using the following independent variables:

- Average sales per square foot per quarter
- Average labor costs per week

- Years of experience for the manager
- Job performance rating for the previous year (100-point scale)

Regression results can be obtained in SPSS by clicking on ANALYZE, REGRESSION, and then LINEAR. The VIF column must be requested by clicking on STATISTICS and then checking COLINEARITY DIAGNOSTICS. After doing so, the following results are obtained. For the overall model,

ANOVA(b)

Model		Sum of Squares	d.f.	Mean Square	F	Sig.
1	Regression	142566.5332	4	35641.6333	13.56899	.0000008
	Residual	91934.43848	35	2626.698242		
	Total	234500.9717	39			

A   Predictors: (constant), performance, experience, labor, sales
B   Dependent Variable: margin

The F of 13.57 is highly significant (<.001), so the variables explain a large portion of the variance in the dependent variable.

The model R^2 is .61 also supporting this conclusion. The results for the independent variable tests show the following:

Coefficients(a)

Model		Unstandardized Coefficients B	Std. Error	Standardized Coefficients Beta	t	Sig.	VIF
1	(Constant)	171.242614	235.9374392		0.725797	0.47279	
	Sales	0.090784631	0.030835442	2.339759409	2.944165	0.00572	56.3836
	Labor	−0.070267446	0.035014493	−1.587938574	−2.00681	0.05254	55.8971
	Experience	−0.488078747	0.955764142	−0.054331204	−0.51067	0.61279	1.0105
	Performance	−1.856084354	3.034080822	−0.068978263	−0.61175	0.54466	1.1351

a   Dependent Variable: margin

©PHOTODISC/GETTY IMAGES

Even though the model results appear strong, only one independent variable is significant at a Type I error rate of 0.050 – sales. However, the β coefficients do not make sense. The β coefficients for both sales and labor are beyond the range that β should theoretically take (−1.0 to 1.0). Nothing can be correlated with something more than perfectly (which would be a correlation of 1.0 or −1.0). Notice also that the two VIF factors for sales and labor are in the 50s. Generally, when multiple VIF factors approach 5 or greater, problems with multicollinearity can be expected. The high correlation between sales and labor are a problem.

As often occurs with financial data, they can be difficult to use as independent variables. In this case, the researcher may wish to rerun the model after dropping one of the offending variables.

times as strong as the other two relationships. Thus, management may wish to place more emphasis on locating sales offices in major markets.

■ R^2 IN MULTIPLE REGRESSION

The coefficient of multiple determination in multiple regression indicates the percentage of variation in Y explained by *all* independent variables. A value of $R^2 = 0.845$ means that 84.5 percent of the variance in the dependent variable is explained by the independent variables. If two independent variables are truly independent (uncorrelated with each other), the R^2 for a multiple regression model is equal to the separate R^2 values that would result from two separate simple regression models. More typically, the independent variables are related to one another, meaning that the model R^2 from a multiple regression model will be less than the separate R^2 values resulting from individual simple regression models. This reduction in R^2 is proportionate to the extent to which the independent variables are interrelated or *collinear*.

STATISTICAL SIGNIFICANCE IN MULTIPLE REGRESSION

Following from simple regression, an *F*-test is used to test statistical significance by comparing the variation explained by the regression equation to the residual error variation. The *F*-test allows for testing of the relative magnitudes of the sum of squares due to the regression (*SSR*) and the error sum of squares (*SSE*).

$$F = \frac{(SSR)/k}{(SSE)/(n - k - 1)} = \frac{MSR}{MSE}$$

where

k = number of independent variables

n = number of observations

MSR = Mean Squares Regression

MSE = Mean Squares Error

Degrees of freedom for the *F*-test (*d.f.*) are:

$d.f.$ for the numerator $= k$

$d.f.$ for the denominator $= n - k - 1$

For the example above,

$d.f.$ (numerator) $= 3$

$d.f.$ (denominator) $= 12 - 3 - 1 = 8$

A table of critical *F*-values shows that for 3 and 8 d.f., and a 0.05 Type I error rate, a value of 4.07 or more is necessary for the regression model to be considered significant, meaning that it explains a significant portion of the total variation in the dependent variable. In practice, statistical programs will report the p-value associated with the *F*-test directly. Similarly, the programs report the statistical test for each individual independent variable. Independent variables with p-values below the acceptable Type I error rate are considered significant predictors of the dependent variable.

STEPS IN INTERPRETING A MULTIPLE REGRESSION MODEL

Multiple regression models often are used to test some proposed theoretical model. For instance, a researcher may be asked to develop and test a model explaining business unit performance. Why do some business units outperform others? Multiple regression models can be interpreted using these steps:

1. Examine the model *F*-test. If the test result is not significant, the model should be dismissed and there is no need to proceed to further steps.
2. Examine the individual statistical tests for each parameter estimate. Independent variables with significant results can be considered a significant explanatory variable.
3. Examine the model R^2. No cutoff values exist that can distinguish an acceptable amount of explained variation across all regression models. However, the absolute value of R^2 is more important when the researcher is more interested in prediction than explanation. In other words, the regression is run for pure forecasting purposes. When the model is more oriented toward explaining which variables are most important in explaining the dependent variable, cutoff values for the model R^2 are inappropriate.

EXHIBIT 24.4 **Interpreting Multiple Regression Results**

```
                              The SAS System      21:52 Wednesday, March 1, 2006    2

                                 The REG Procedure
                                  Model: MODEL1
                               Dependent Variable:     Paid

                         Number of Observations Read    28
                         Number of Observations Used    28

                               Analysis of Variance

                                    Sum of      Mean
          Source            DF      Squares     Square      F Value     Pr > F

          Model             3      1770668      590223       19.38      <.0001
          Error            24       731035       30460
          Corrected Total  27      2501703

                  Root MSE              174.52738    R-Square     0.7078
                  Dependent Mean        654.03571    Adj R-Sq     0.6713
                  Coeff Var              26.68469

                               Parameter Estimates

                    Parameter     Standard                          Standardized
  Variable   DF     Estimate        Error    t Value   Pr > |t|       Estimate      VIF

  Intercept   1    -109.90538    217.46253    -0.51     0.6179            0
  Hours       1       0.99438      0.27688     3.59     0.0015         0.55433      1.96
  Budget      1       6.60121      3.54784     1.86     0.0751         0.28210      1.89
  State       1     -66.36397     84.82434    -0.78     0.4416        -0.11073      1.65
```

1. Interpret model *F*-test. Test is significant (p < .05).

3. The model R² is interpreted. The IVs explain over 70% of variation in the dependent variable.

2. Interpret individual parameter estimates. In this case, only hours is significant based on a p-value below .05 (0.0015).

4. VIFs are checked for multicollinearity problems. None are indicated here.

Multicollinearity
The extent to which independent variables in a multiple regression analysis are correlated with each other; high multicollinearity can make interpreting parameter estimates difficult or impossible.

4. Examine collinearity diagnostics. **Multicollinearity** in regression analysis refers to how strongly interrelated the independent variables in a model are. When multicollinearity is too high, the individual parameter estimates become difficult to interpret. Most regression programs can compute variance inflation factors (VIF) for each variable. As a rule of thumb, VIF above 5.0 suggests problems with multicollinearity.[12]

Exhibit 24.4 illustrates these steps. The regression model explains business unit profitability for a sample of twenty-eight business units for a Fortune 500 company. The independent variables are hours (average hours spent in training for the workforce), budget (the percentage of the promotional budget used), and state (a dummy variable indicating whether the business unit is in Arizona and coded 0, or in Ohio and coded 1). In this case, the researcher is using a maximum acceptable Type I error rate of 0.05. The conclusion reached from this analysis is that hours spent in training seem to pay off in increased business unit profitability as evidenced by the significant, positive regression coefficient ($\beta = 0.55$, p < 0.05).

ANOVA (n-way) and MANOVA

An ANOVA or MANOVA model also represents a form of the GLM. ANOVA can be extended beyond one-way ANOVA to predict a dependent variable with multiple categorical independent variables. Multivariate analysis of variance (MANOVA), is a multivariate technique that predicts multiple continuous dependent variables with multiple independent variables. The independent variables are categorical, although a continuous control variable can be included in the form of a covariate. MANOVA stands for multivariate analysis of variance. Statistical programs usually refer to any ANOVA with only one dependent variable as univariate analysis of variance or simply by ANOVA.

> **Multivariate analysis of variance (MANOVA)**
> A multivariate technique that predicts multiple continuous dependent variables with multiple categorical independent variables.

▓ N-WAY (UNIVARIATE) ANOVA

The interpretation of an n-way ANOVA model follows closely from the regression results described above. The steps involved are essentially the same with the addition of interpreting differences between means:

1. Examine the overall model *F*-test result. If significant, proceed.
2. Examine individual *F*-tests for individual independent variables.
3. For each significant categorical independent variable, interpret the effect by examining the group means (see Chapter 11).
4. For each significant, continuous covariate, interpret the parameter estimate (**b**).
5. For each significant interaction, interpret the means for each combination. A graphical representation as illustrated in Chapter 11 can greatly assist in this interpretation.

▓ INTERPRETING MANOVA

MANOVA models produce an additional layer of testing. The first layer of testing involves the multivariate *F*-test, which is based on a statistic called Wilke's Lambda (Λ). This test examines whether or not an independent variable explains significant variation among the dependent variables within the model. If this test is significant, then the *F*-test results from individual univariate regression models nested within the MANOVA model are interpreted. The rest of the interpretation results follow from the one-way ANOVA or multiple regression model results above. See the Research Snapshot box on the following page for a guide to interpretation.

Discriminant Analysis

Researchers often need to produce a classification of sampling units. This process may involve using a set of independent variables to decide if a sampling unit belongs in one group or another. A physician might record a person's blood pressure, weight, and blood cholesterol level and then categorize that person as having a high or low probability of a heart attack. A researcher interested in retailing failures might be able to group firms as to whether they eventually failed or did not fail on the basis of independent variables such as location, financial ratios, or management changes. A bank might want to discriminate between potentially successful and unsuccessful sites for electronic fund transfer system machines. A sales manager might want to distinguish between applicants to hire and those not to hire. The challenge is to find the discriminating variables to use in a predictive equation that will produce better than chance assignment of the individuals to the two groups.

Discriminant analysis is a multivariate technique that predicts a categorical dependent variable (rather than a continuous, interval-scaled variable, as in multiple regression) based on a linear combination of independent variables. In each problem above, the researcher determines which variables explain why an observation falls into one of two or more groups. A linear combination of independent variables that explains group memberships is known as a discriminant function. Discriminant analysis is a statistical tool for determining such linear combinations. The researcher's task is to derive the coefficients of the discriminant function (a straight line).

> **Discriminant analysis**
> A statistical technique for predicting the probability that an object will belong in one of two or more mutually exclusive categories (dependent variable), based on several independent variables.

RESEARCHSNAPSHOT

How to Get MANOVA Results

A department store developer gathered data looking at the effect of nostalgia on customer impressions. A field experiment was set up in which a key department was either given a modern design or a retro design. The retro design was hoped to create feelings of nostalgia. Several hundred consumers were interviewed. Since two related dependent variables are involved (y_1 = interest and y_2 = excitement), MANOVA is the appropriate technique.

MANOVA can be conducted using SPSS by clicking on ANALYZE, then GENERAL LINEAR MODEL, and then MULTIVARIATE (if only one dependent variable was involved, the choice would be UNIVARIATE). This opens a dialog box as shown here:

The dialog box includes places to enter dependent variables, fixed factors (between-subjects categorical independent variables), and covariates. In this case, the fixed factors are

1. Experimental variable (0 = modern, 1 = retro)
2. Respondent sex (0 = male, 1 = female)

Respondent age is included as a covariate or control variable (years). SPSS provided output that can be summarized briefly:

1. Multivariate Results:
   a. Wilke's Lambda = 0.964
   b. Overall multivariate F = 9.6 with 2 and 510 d.f.
   c. The p-value associated with this result is less than 0.001. Thus, the multivariate results are significant so the research proceeds to interpret the individual univariate ANOVA results for each dependent variable (SPSS provides these results automatically).
2. The univariate model F statistics for each dependent variable are both significant ($p < 0.001$) so the researcher moves on to the next step.
3. The individual effects associated with y_1 (interest) are interpreted. For example, for the experimental variable, the result is,

a. $F = 0.4$, with 1 and 511 d.f. for interest ($p = 0.531$).
b. Age is not significant.
c. The interaction is not significant.
4. The individual effects associated with y_2 (excitement) are interpreted. For example, for the experimental variable, the result is,
a. $F = 13.4$, with 1 and 511 d.f. for excitement ($p < 0.001$).
b. Sex and age are both significant predictors too ($p < 0.001$).
c. The interaction of sex and the retro/modern experimental variable is also significant.
5. After carefully reviewing the means for each experimental cell as well as the covariate results, the researcher reaches the following conclusions:
a. The retro look produced more excitement but not necessarily more interest.
b. Women are more interested and more excited about shopping.
c. The effect of the retro condition was stronger for men than women. That is, the difference in means between the retro and modern condition is larger for men than for women.
d. Younger consumers are more excited about shopping.

We will consider an example of the two-group discriminant analysis problem where the dependent variable, Y, is measured on a nominal scale. (Although n-way discriminant analysis is possible, it is beyond the scope of this discussion.) Suppose a personnel manager for an electrical wholesaler has been keeping records on successful versus unsuccessful sales employees. The personnel manager believes it is possible to predict whether an applicant will succeed on the basis of age, sales aptitude test scores, and mechanical ability scores. As stated at the outset, the problem is to find a linear function of the independent variables that shows large differences in group means. The first task is to estimate the coefficients of the applicant's discriminant function. To calculate the individuals' discriminant scores, the following linear function is used:

$$Z_i = b_1 X_{1i} + b_2 X_{2i} + \cdots + b_n X_{ni}$$

where

$Z_i =$ ith applicant's discriminant score

$b_n =$ discriminant coefficient for the nth variable

$X_{ni} =$ ith applicant's value on the nth independent variable

Using scores for all the individuals in the sample, a discriminant function is determined based on the criterion that the groups be maximally differentiated on the set of independent variables.

Returning to the example with three independent variables, suppose the personnel manager finds the standardized weights in the equation to be

$$Z = b_1 X_1 + b_2 X_2 + b_3 X_3$$
$$= 0.069 X_1 + 0.013 X_2 + 0.0007 X_3$$

This means that age (X_1) is much more important than sales aptitude test scores (X_2). Mechanical ability (X_3) has relatively minor discriminating power.

In the computation of the linear discriminant function, weights are assigned to the variables to maximize the ratio of the difference between the means of the two groups to the standard deviation within groups. The standardized discriminant coefficients, or weights, provide information about the relative importance of each of these variables in discriminating between the two groups.

A major goal of discriminant analysis is to perform a classification function. The purpose of classification in our example is to predict which applicants will be successful and which will be unsuccessful and to group them accordingly. To determine whether the discriminant analysis can be used as a good predictor of applicant success, information provided in the "confusion matrix" is used. Suppose the personnel manager has 40 successful and 45 unsuccessful employees in the sample. The confusion matrix shows that the number of correctly classified employees (72 out of 85) is much higher than would be expected by chance:

Confusion Matrix

Actual Group	Predicted Group		
	Successful	Unsuccessful	
Successful	34	6	40
Unsuccessful	7	38	45

Tests can be performed to determine whether the rate of correct classification is statistically significant.

Exhibit 24.5 summarizes multivariate dependence techniques.

EXHIBIT 24.5 **Multivariate Dependence Techniques Summary**

Technique	Purpose	Number of Dependent Variables	Number of Independent Variables	Type of Measurement	
				Dependent	Independent
Multiple regression	To investigate simultaneously the effects of several independent variables on a dependent variable	1	2 or more	Interval	Interval
Discriminant analysis	To predict the probability that an object or individual will belong in one of two or more mutually exclusive categories, based on several independent variables	1	2 or more	Nominal	Interval
MANOVA	To determine simultaneously whether statistically significant mean differences occur between groups on several variables	2 or more	1 or more	Interval	Nominal

Analysis of Interdependence

Suppose we wished to identify the factors that are associated with pleasant shopping experiences,[13] identify factors that would allow better flexibility and control of logistics programs,[14] or identify groups of students each associated with a unique learning style.[15] All of these are problems that have been addressed through the use of a multivariate interdependence technique. Rather than attempting to predict a variable or set of variables from a set of independent variables, we use techniques like *factor analysis, cluster analysis,* and *multidimensional scaling* to better understand the structure of a set of variables or objects.

Factor Analysis

Factor analysis
A prototypical multivariate, interdependence technique that statistically identifies a reduced number of factors from a larger number of measured variables.

Factor analysis is a prototypical multivariate, interdependence technique. Factor analysis is a technique of statistically identifying a reduced number of factors from a larger number of measured variables. The factors themselves are not measured, but instead, they are identified by forming a variate using the measured variables. Factors are usually latent constructs like attitude or satisfaction or an index like social class. A researcher need not distinguish between independent and dependent variables to conduct factor analysis. Factor analysis can be divided into two types:

1. Exploratory factor analysis (EFA)—performed when the researcher is uncertain about how many factors may exist among a set of variables. The discussion here concentrates primarily on EFA.
2. Confirmatory factor analysis (CFA)—performed when the researcher has strong theoretical expectations about the factor structure before performing the analysis. CFA is a good tool for assessing construct validity because it provides a test of how well the researcher's "theory" about the factor structure fits the actual observations. Many books exist on CFA alone and the reader is referred to any of those sources for more on CFA.

609

EXHIBIT 24.6
A Simple Illustration of Factor Analysis

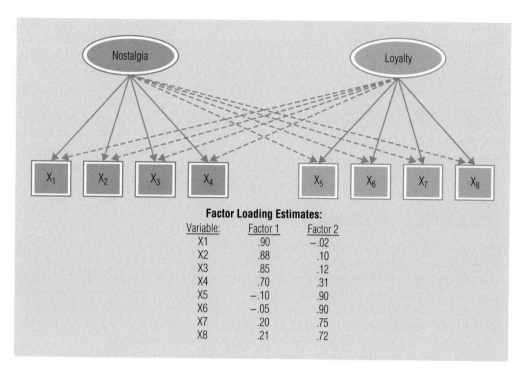

Factor Loading Estimates:

Variable:	Factor 1	Factor 2
X1	.90	−.02
X2	.88	.10
X3	.85	.12
X4	.70	.31
X5	−.10	.90
X6	−.05	.90
X7	.20	.75
X8	.21	.72

Exhibit 24.6 illustrates factor analysis graphically. Suppose a researcher is asked to examine the effectiveness of creating feelings of nostalgia in a restaurant on customer loyalty. Three hundred fifty customers at themed restaurants around the country are interviewed and asked to respond to the following Likert scales (1 = Strongly Disagree to 7 = Strongly Agree):

X_1—I feel a strong connection to the past when I am in this place.
X_2—This place evokes memories of the past.
X_3—I feel a yearning to relive past experiences when I dine here.
X_4—This place looks like a page out of the past.
X_5—I am willing to pay more to dine in this restaurant.
X_6—I feel very loyal to this establishment.
X_7—I enjoy recommending this place to others.
X_8—I will go out of my way to dine here.

Factor analysis can summarize the information in the eight variables in a smaller number of variables, perhaps two in this case. More than one technique exists for estimating the variates that form the factors. However, the general idea is to mathematically produce variates that explain the most total variance among the set of variables being analyzed. If the factor results suggested two factors, Exhibit 24.6 would represent the results. Thus, EFA provides two important pieces of information:

1. How many factors exist among a set of variables?
2. What variables match up or "load on" which factors?

FACTOR LOADINGS

Each arrow connecting a factor (represented by an oval in the Exhibit) to a variable (represented by a box in the Exhibit) is associated with a **factor loading**. A factor loading indicates how strongly correlated a factor is with a measured variable. In other words, to what extent does a variable "load" on a factor? EFA depends on the loadings for proper interpretation. A latent construct can be interpreted based on the pattern of loadings and the content of the variables. In this way, the latent construct is measured indirectly by the variables.

Factor loading
Indicates how strongly a measured variable is correlated with a factor.

Loading estimates are provided by factor analysis programs. In Exhibit 24.6, the factor loading estimates are shown beneath the factor diagram. The thick arrows indicate high loading estimates and the thin dotted lines correspond to weak loading estimates. Factors are interpreted by examining any patterns that emerge from the factor results. Here, a clear pattern emerges. The first four variables produce high loadings on factor 1 and the last four variables produce high loadings on factor 2.

When a clear pattern of factor loadings emerges, interpretation is easy. Because the first four variables all have content consistent with nostalgia and the second four variables all have content consistent with customer loyalty, the two factors can easily be labeled. Factor one represents the latent construct nostalgia and factor 2 represents the latent construct customer loyalty.

DATA REDUCTION TECHNIQUE

Data reduction technique

Multivariate statistical approaches that summarize the information from many variables into a reduced set of variates formed as linear combinations of measured variables.

Factor analysis is considered a **data reduction technique**. Data reduction techniques allow a researcher to summarize information from many variables into a reduced set of variates or composite variables. Data reduction is advantageous for many reasons. In general, the rule of parsimony suggests an explanation involving fewer components is better than one involving many more. Factor analysis accomplishes data reduction by capturing variance from many variables with a single variate. Data reduction is also a way of identifying which variables among a large set might be important in some analysis. Thus, data reduction simplifies decision making.

In our example, the researcher can now form two composite factors representing the latent constructs nostalgia and customer loyalty. These can be formed using factor equations of this form:

$$F_k = L_1 X_1 + L_2 X_2 + L_3 X_3 + L_4 X_4 + L_5 X_5 + L_6 X_6 + L_7 X_7 + L_8 X_8$$

where

F_k is the factor score for the kth factor—in this case there are two factors

L represents factor loadings (ith) 1 through 8 for the corresponding factor

X represents the value of the corresponding measured variable

Using this type of equation, the scores for variables X_1–X_8 can be summarized by two scores, one for factor 1 and one for factor 2. If the researcher wanted to analyze the correlation among these variables, now all that needs to be done is to analyze the bivariate correlation between factor 1 (nostalgia) and factor 2 (loyalty). This should prove much easier than analyzing an 8×8 correlation matrix. Statistical programs like SPSS and SAS will produce factor scores automatically if requested (see Appendix 24A).

We can see that because F_1 is associated with high values for L_1 through L_4 (and low values for L_5, L_6, L_7, and L_8) and F_2 is associated with high values for L_5 through L_8 (and low for L_1, L_2, L_3, and L_4), F_1 is determined almost entirely by the nostalgia items and F_2 is determined almost entirely by the customer loyalty items. The factor pattern of high and low loadings can be used to match measured variables to factors in this way.

CREATING COMPOSITE SCALES WITH FACTOR RESULTS

When a clear pattern of loadings exists as in this case, the researcher may take a simpler approach. F1 could be created simply by summing the four variables with high loadings and creating a summated scale representing nostalgia. F2 could be created by summing the second four variables (those loading highly on F2) and creating a second summated variable. This would introduce very little error given the pattern of loadings. In other words, very low loadings suggest a variable does not contribute much to the factor. The researcher could test the reliability of each summated scale by computing a coefficient alpha estimate. Then, the research could conduct a bivariate regression analysis that would test how much nostalgia contributed to loyalty.

COMMUNALITY

A researcher may wish to know how much a single variable has in common with all factors. Communality is a measure of the percentage of a variable's variation that is explained by the factors. A relatively high communality indicates that a variable has much in common with the other variables taken as a group. Communality for any variable is equal to the sum of the squared loadings for that variable. The communality for X1 is

$$0.90^2 - 0.02^2 = 0.8104$$

These values are shown on factor analysis printouts.

TOTAL VARIANCE EXPLAINED

Along with the factor loadings, the percentage of total variance of original variables explained by the factors can be useful. Recall that variance is correlation squared. Thus, if each loading is squared and totaled, that total divided by the number of factors provides an estimate of the variance in a set of variables explained by a factor. This explanation of variance is much the same as R^2 in multiple regression. Again, these values are computed by the statistics program so there is seldom a need to compute them manually. In this case, though, the variance accounted for among the eight variables by the nostalgia factor is 0.36 and the variance among the eight variables explained by the loyalty factor is 0.35. Thus, the two factors explain 71 percent of the variance in the eight variables:

$$0.36 + 0.35 = 0.71$$

An extension of this idea is sometimes used to help validate composite factors. Simply put, if only four items are used to create a summated scale, then the average variance explained for each of the four items can be used to indicate convergent validity for a factor. This is one statistic that is sometimes necessary to compute manually. If four items are used to form a composite scale and they have loadings of 0.7, −0.7, 0.8, and 0.9, respectively, the variance explained for the scale is

$$\frac{0.7^2 + (-0.7)^2 + 0.8^2 + 0.9^2}{4} = 0.61$$

Ideally, the researcher would like scales to explain at least half of the total variation among the measured variables.

HOW MANY FACTORS?

Oftentimes, the researcher asks the question, "How many factors will exist among a large number of variables?" While a detailed discussion is beyond the scope of this text, the question is usually addressed based on the eigenvalues for a factor solution. Eigenvalues are a measure of how much variance is explained by each factor. The most common rule is to base the number of factors on the number of eigenvalues greater than 1.0. This is the default rule for most statistical programs. So, unless some other rule is specified, the number of factors shown in a factor solution is based on this rule.

FACTOR ROTATION

Factor rotation is a mathematical way of simplifying factor results. The most common type of factor rotation is a process called varimax. A discussion of the technical aspects of the concept of factor rotation is far beyond the scope of this book. However, it involves creating new reference axes for a given set of variables. An initial factor solution is often difficult to interpret. Rotation clears things up by producing more obvious patterns of loadings. Users should experiment with this by looking at unrotated and rotated solutions.

Factor rotation
A mathematical way of simplifying factor analysis results to better identify which variables "load on" which factors; the most common procedure is varimax.

Cluster Analysis

Cluster analysis
A multivariate approach for
grouping observations based
on similarity among measured
variables.

Cluster analysis is a multivariate approach for identifying objects or individuals that are similar to one another in some respect. Thus, cluster analysis is an important tool for identifying market segments. Cluster analysis classifies individuals or objects into a small number of mutually exclusive and exhaustive groups. Objects or individuals are assigned to groups so that there is great similarity within groups and much less similarity between groups. The cluster should have high internal (within-cluster) homogeneity and external (between-cluster) heterogeneity.

Cluster analysis facilitates market segmentation by identifying subjects or individuals who have similar needs, lifestyles, or responses to marketing promotions. Clusters, or subgroups, of recreational vehicle owners may be identified on the basis of their similarity with respect to recreational vehicle usage and the benefits they want from recreational vehicles. Alternatively, the researcher might use demographic or lifestyle variables to group individuals into clusters identified as market segments.

We will illustrate cluster analysis with a hypothetical example relating to the types of vacations taken by twelve individuals. Vacation behavior is represented on two dimensions: number of vacation days and dollar expenditures on vacations during a given year. Exhibit 24.7 is a scatter diagram that represents the geometric distance between each individual in two-dimensional space. The diagram portrays three clear-cut clusters. The first subgroup, consisting of individuals L, H, and B, suggests a group of individuals who have many vacation days but do not spend much money on their vacations. The second cluster, represented by individuals A, I, K, G, and F, represents intermediate values on both variables—average amounts of vacation days and average dollar expenditures on vacations. The third group, individuals C, J, E, and D, consists of individuals who have relatively few vacation days but spend large amounts on vacations.

In this example, individuals are grouped on the basis of their similarity or proximity to one another. The logic of cluster analysis is to group individuals or objects by their similarity to or distance from each other. The mathematical procedures for deriving clusters will not be dealt with here, as our purpose is only to introduce the technique.

A classic study provides a very pragmatic example of the use of cluster analysis.[8] Marketing managers frequently are interested in finding test-market cities that are very similar so that no

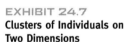

EXHIBIT 24.7
**Clusters of Individuals on
Two Dimensions**

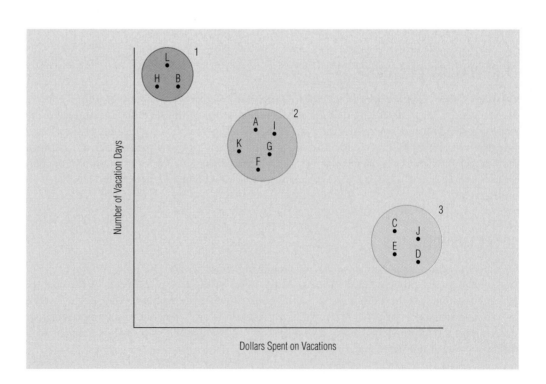

EXHIBIT 24.8 **Cluster Analysis of Test-Market Cities**

Cluster Number	City	Cluster Number	City	Cluster Number	City
1	Omaha Oklahoma City Dayton Columbus Fort Worth	7	Sacramento San Bernardino San Jose Phoenix Tucson	13	Allentown Providence Jersey City York Louisville
2	Peoria Davenport Binghamton Harrisburg Worcester	8	Gary Nashville Jacksonville San Antonio Knoxville	14	Paterson Milwaukee Cincinnati Miami Seattle
3	Canton Youngstown Toledo Springfield Albany	9	Indianapolis Kansas City Dallas Atlanta Houston	15	San Diego Tacoma Norfolk Charleston Fort Lauderdale
4	Bridgeport Rochester Hartford New Haven Syracuse	10	Mobile Shreveport Birmingham Memphis Chattanooga	16	New Orleans Richmond Tampa Lancaster Minneapolis
5	Wilmington Orlando Tulsa Wichita Grand Rapids	11	Newark Cleveland Pittsburgh Buffalo Baltimore	17	San Francisco Detroit Boston Philadelphia
6	Bakersfield Fresno Flint El Paso Beaumont	12	Albuquerque Salt Lake City Denver Charlotte Portland	18	Washington St. Louis

Note: Points not in a cluster—Honolulu, Wilkes-Barre.

Source: Reprinted by permission, Paul E. Green, Ronald E. Frank, and Patrick J. Robinson, "Cluster Analysis in Test-Market Selection," *Management Science*, Vol. 13, P.B393 (Table 2), April 1967. Copyright © 1967, the Institute for Operations Research and the Management Sciences (INFORMS), 7240 Parkway Drive, Suite 310, Hanover, MD 21076 USA

extraneous variation will cause differences between the experimental and control markets. In this study the objects to be clustered were cities. The characteristics of the cities, such as population, retail sales, number of retail outlets, and percentage of nonwhites, were used to identify the groups. Cities such as Omaha, Oklahoma City, Dayton, Columbus, and Fort Worth were similar and cities such as Newark, Cleveland, Pittsburgh, Buffalo, and Baltimore were similar, but individual cities within each group were dissimilar to those within other groups or clusters. (See Exhibit 24.8 for additional details.)

This example should help to clarify the difference between factor analysis and cluster analysis. In factor analysis the researcher might search for constructs that underlie the variables (population, retail sales, number of retail outlets); in cluster analysis the researcher would seek constructs that underlie the objects (cities).

Cluster analysis differs from multiple discriminant analysis in that the groups are not predefined. The purpose of cluster analysis is to determine how many groups really exist and to define their composition.

Multidimensional Scaling

Multidimensional scaling
A statistical technique that measures objects in multidimensional space on the basis of respondents' judgments of the similarity of objects.

Multidimensional scaling provides a means for measuring objects in multidimensional space on the basis of respondents' judgments of the similarity of objects. The perceptual difference among objects is reflected in the relative distance among objects in the multidimensional space.

Traditionally, attitudes have been measured by using a scale for each component of an attitude and then combining the individual scores into an aggregate score. In the most common form of multidimensional scaling, subjects are asked to evaluate an object's similarity to other objects. For example, a sports car study may ask respondents to rate the similarity of an Acura TSX to a Chevrolet Corvette. The analyst then attempts to explain the difference in objects on the basis of the components of attitudes. The unfolding of the attitude components helps explain why objects are judged to be similar or dissimilar.

In one study MBA students were asked to provide their perceptions of relative similarities among six graduate schools. Next, the overall similarity scores for all possible pairs of objects were aggregated for all individual respondents and arranged in a matrix. With the aid of a computer program, the judgments about similarity were statistically transformed into distances by placing the graduate schools into a specified multidimensional space. The distance between similar objects on the perceptual map was small for similar objects; dissimilar objects were farther apart.

Exhibit 24.9 shows a perceptual map in two-dimensional space. Inspection of the map illustrates that Harvard and Stanford were perceived as quite similar to each other. MIT and Carnegie also were perceived as very similar. MIT and Chicago, on the other hand, were perceived as dissimilar. The researchers identified the two axes as "quantitative versus qualitative curriculum" and "less versus more prestige." The labeling of the dimension axes is a task of interpretation for the researcher and is not statistically determined. As with other multivariate techniques in the analysis of interdependence, there are several alternative mathematical techniques for multidimensional scaling. Likewise, there are multiple ways of using multivariate

How similar are these cars? This is the input to multidimensional scaling.

procedures to generate a perceptual map. For example, factor scores resulting from factor analysis can be plotted along the factor dimensions. Such an approach may show the competitive positioning of several retailers along dimensions related to value and quality.

Exhibit 24.10 summarizes the multivariate techniques for analysis of interdependence.

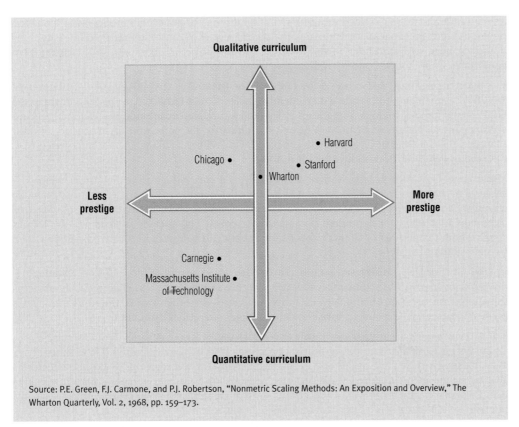

Source: P.E. Green, F.J. Carmone, and P.J. Robertson, "Nonmetric Scaling Methods: An Exposition and Overview," The Wharton Quarterly, Vol. 2, 1968, pp. 159–173.

EXHIBIT 24.10 **Summary of Multivariate Techniques for Analysis of Interdependence**

Technique	Purpose	Type of Measurement
Factor analysis	To summarize into a reduced number of factors the information contained in a large number of variables	Interval
Cluster analysis	To classify individuals or objects into a small number of mutually exclusive and exhaustive groups, ensuring that there will be as much likeness within groups and as much difference among groups as possible	Interval
Multidimensional scaling	To measure objects in multidimensional space on the basis of respondents' judgments of their similarity	Varies depending on technique

Summary

1. Understand what multivariate statistical analysis involves and know the two types of multivariate analysis. Multivariate statistical methods analyze multiple variables or even multiple sets of variables simultaneously. They are particularly useful for identifying latent constructs using multiple individual measures. Multivariate techniques represent data through the use of variates. Variates are mathematical combinations of variables. The two major types of multivariate procedures are interdependence and dependence techniques. Interdependence techniques do not distinguish dependent and interdependent variables, whereas dependence techniques to do make this distinction.

2. Interpret results from multiple regression analysis. Multiple regression analysis predicts a continuous dependent variable with multiple independent variables. The independent variables can be either continuous or categorical. Categorical variables must be coded as dummy variables. Multiple regression results are analyzed by examining the significance of the overall model using the F-test results, the individual parameter estimates, the overall model R^2, and the model collinearity diagnostics. Standardized regression coefficients have the advantage of a common scale making them comparable from model to model and variable to variable.

3. Interpret results from multivariate analysis of variance (MANOVA). MANOVA is an extension of ANOVA involving multiple related dependent variables. Thus, MANOVA represents a form of the GLM predicting that multiple categorical independent variables affect multiple, related dependent variables. Interpretation of a MANOVA model is similar to interpretation of a regression model. However, the multivariate F-test results associated with Wilke's Lambda (Λ) are interpreted first, followed by interpretation of the individual ANOVA results.

4. Interpret basic exploratory factor analysis results. EFA is a data reduction technique in which the variance in multiple variables is represented by a smaller number of factors. The factors generally represent latent factors or indexes. Factor loadings resulting from rotated factor solutions are important in properly interpreting factor analysis results. The pattern of loadings that results suggests both the number of latent factors that may exist and helps validate scales that may be used in other statistical analysis.

5. Know what multiple discriminant analysis can be used to do. Another dependence technique is discriminant analysis. Discriminant analysis uses multiple independent variables to classify observations into one of a set of mutually exclusive categories. In other words, discriminant analysis predicts a categorical dependent variable with multiple independent variables.

6. Understand how cluster analysis can identify market segments. Cluster analysis classifies multiple observations into a smaller number of mutually exclusive and exhaustive groups. These should have as much similarity within groups and as much difference between groups as possible. In cluster analysis the groups are not predefined. However, clusters can be used to represent market segments because market segments also represent consumers that are similar to each other within a segment, but who are different from consumers in other segments.

Key Terms and Concepts

Variate
Dependence techniques
Interdependence techniques
General linear model (GLM)
Multiple regression analysis
Dummy variable

Partial correlation
Multicollinearity
Multivariate analysis of variance
   (MANOVA)
Discriminant analysis
Factor analysis

Factor loading
Data reduction technique
Factor rotation
Cluster analysis
Multidimensional scaling

Questions for Review and Critical Thinking

1. Define *multivariate statistical analysis.*
2. What is the *variate* in multivariate? What is an example of a variate in multiple regression and in factor analysis?
3. What is the distinction between *dependence techniques* and *interdependence techniques?*
4. What is *GLM?* How can multiple regression and n-way ANOVA be described as GLM approaches?
5. What are the steps in interpreting a multiple regression analysis result? Can the same steps be used to interpret a univariate ANOVA model?
6. A researcher dismisses a regression result because the model R^2 was under 0.70. Do you think this was necessarily wise? Explain.
7. Return to the simple example of regression results for the toy company presented in the chapter. Since the data come equally from Europe and Canada, does this represent a potential source of variation that is not accounted for in the researcher's model?

How could the researcher examine whether or not sales may be dependent upon country?
8. What is a *factor loading?*
9. How does factor analysis allow for data reduction?
10. How is the number of factors decided in most EFA programs?
11. Give an example of a situation in which each of the techniques mentioned in question 5 might be used.
12. What is *multidimensional scaling?* When might a researcher use this technique?
13. What is *cluster analysis?* When might a researcher use this technique?
14. Name at least two multivariate techniques that can be useful in constructing perceptual maps.
15. A researcher uses multiple regression to predict a client's sales volume based on gross domestic product, personal income, disposable personal income, unemployment, and the consumer price index. What problems might be anticipated with this multiple regression model?

Research Activities

1. Use the multistep process to interpret the regression results below. This model has been run by a researcher trying to explain customer loyalty to a restaurant. The independent variables are customer perceptions of value, atmosphere, quality, and a location variable labeled center. This is a dummy variable that takes the value of 1 if the restaurant is in a shopping center and 0 if it is a stand-alone location. What substantive conclusions would you recommend to the restaurant company?

Model Summary

Model	R	R Square	Adjusted R Square	Std. Error of the Estimate
1	0.176	0.031	0.027	0.996

DV = Loyalty

ANOVA(b)

Model		Sum of Squares	df	Mean Square	F	Sig.
1	Regression	27.9731	4	6.9933	7.049	0.0000138
	Residual	876.0469	883	0.9921		
	Total	904.0200	887			

Coefficients(a)

Model		Unstandardized Coefficients B	Std. Error	Standardized Coefficients Beta	t	Sig.	VIF
1	(Constant)	−0.306	0.229		−1.338	0.181	
	Value	0.104	0.036	0.099	2.877	0.004	1.087
	Atmosphere	0.048	0.026	0.067	1.883	0.060	1.144
	Quality	0.044	0.028	0.054	1.590	0.112	1.038
	Center	−0.250	0.071	−0.124	−3.508	0.000	1.132

2. Interpret the following GLM results. Following from an example in the chapter, *Performance* is the performance rating for a business unit manager. *Sales* is a measure of the average sales for that unit. *Experience* is the number of years the manager has been in the industry. The variable *dummy* has been added. This variable is 1 if the manager has no advanced college degree and a 1 if the manager has an MBA. Do you have any recommendations?

```
                        The SAS System        21:06 Saturday, March 4, 2006  3
                          The GLM Procedure
                     Dependent Variable: performance

                                      Sum of
        Source             DF         Squares      Mean Square    F Value    Pr > F

        Model               3      173.6381430     57.8793810      13.87     <.0001
        Error              36      150.2341040      4.1731696
        Corrected Total    39      323.8722470


               R-Square     Coeff Var      Root MSE     performance Mean
               0.536132     2.514731       2.042834          81.23468


        Source             DF      Type III SS     Mean Square    F Value    Pr > F
        dummy               1      136.9511200     136.9511200     32.82     <.0001
        sales               1       22.4950649      22.4950649      5.39     0.0260
        Experience          1        2.2356995       2.2356995      0.54     0.4689

Level of     -------performance------- -----------sales---------- ----Experience--------
dummy   N    Mean     Std Dev     Mean       Std Dev     Mean       Std Dev
0       22   79.4848842 1.78987031 15979.7723 2008.32604 23.8984087 8.27327485
1       18   83.3733171 2.50773844 16432.0080 2015.18863 20.6788050 8.96324112
```

3. Interpret the following regression results. All of the variables are the same as in number 2. These results are produced with a regression program instead of the GLM-univariate ANOVA program.
   a. What do you notice when the results are compared to those in number 2? Comment.
   b. List the independent variables in order from greatest to least in terms of how strong the relationship is with performance.
   c. When might one prefer to use an ANOVA program instead of a multiple regression program?

```
                         The SAS System        21:06 Saturday, March 4, 2006    5
                         The REG Procedure
                             Model: MODEL1
                     Dependent Variable: performance

                 Number of observations Read        40
                 Number of observations Used        40

                            Analysis of Variance

                                    Sum of         Mean
         Source              DF     Squares        Square     F Value    Pr > F

         Model         3         173.6381457.87938   13.87     <.0001
         Error              36     150.23410       4.17317
         Corrected Total    39     323.87225

                    Root MSE              2.04283   R-Square    0.5361
                    Dependent Mean       81.23468   Adj R-Sq    0.4975
                    Coeff Var             2.51473

                            Parameter Estimates

                             Parameter      Standard                        Standardized
   Variable     Label      DF   Estimate       Error    t Value   Pr > |t|     Estimate

   Intercept   Intercept   1    72.68459     2.88092     25.23    <.0001            0
   dummy       dummy       1     3.80621     0.66442      5.73    <.0001      0.66546
   sales       sales       1  0.00038324  0.00016507      2.32    0.0260      0.26578
   Experience  Experience  1     0.02829     0.03866      0.73    0.4689      0.08475
```

4. Interpret the following factor analysis results. The variables represent sample results of self-reported emotions while viewing a film. What two summated scales might be produced based on these results?

Total Variance Explained

Component	Initial Eigenvalues Total	% of Variance	Cumulative %	Extraction Sums of Squared Loadings Total	% of Variance	Cumulative %
1	2.94	36.74	36.74	2.94	36.74	36.74
2	2.51	31.34	68.08	2.51	31.34	68.08
3	0.71	8.84	76.92			
4	0.60	7.53	84.45			
5	0.42	5.20	89.65			
6	0.29	3.67	93.32			
7	0.29	3.64	96.96			
8	0.24	3.04	100.00			

Extraction Method: Principal Component Analysis.

Component Matrix(a)

	Factor 1	Factor 2
Interesting	0.664	−0.327
Anxious	0.444	0.511
Enthusiastic	0.842	−0.332
Worried	0.295	0.828
Exciting	0.812	−0.206
Tired	0.269	0.835
Happy	0.784	−0.383
Guilty	0.398	0.675

Extraction Method: Principal Component Analysis.

A   2 components extracted.

Rotated Component Matrix(a)

	Component Factor 1	Factor 2
Interesting	0.739	−0.024
Anxious	0.194	0.648
Enthusiastic	0.904	0.044
Worried	−0.073	0.876
Exciting	0.825	0.147
Tired	−0.100	0.872
Happy	0.872	−0.025
Guilty	0.084	0.779

Extraction Method: Principal Component Analysis.

Rotation Method: Varimax with Kaiser Normalization.

A   Rotation converged in 3 iterations.

5. **'NET** Go to http://www.census.gov and examine some of the tables for your area. Cut and paste the table into a spreadsheet or statistical program. Run one dependence and one interdependence technique on the data. Interpret the results.

6. **'NET** Use http://www.ask.com to find an *F*-ratio calculator that will return a p-value given a calculated *F*-ratio and the degrees of freedom associated with the test.

7. **'NET** The Federal Reserve Bank of St. Louis maintains a database called FRED (Federal Reserve Economic Data). Navigate to the FRED database at http://www.stls.frb.org/fred/index.html. Use the consumer price index, exchange rates, interest rates, and one other variable to predict the consumer price index for the same time period. The data can either be downloaded or cut and pasted into another file.

Case 24.1 The Utah Jazz

The Utah Jazz are interested in understanding the market for the National Basketball Association. A study is conducted as described here.

Data Collection

Data came from a survey of adult residents of a large western metropolitan area. Respondents were selected in accordance with a quota sample of the area that was based on the age and sex characteristics reported in the most recent census. Six age categories for both males and females were used to gain representation of these characteristics in the market. In addition, interviewers were assigned to various parts of the area to ensure representation of the market with respect to socioeconomic characteristics. A total of 225 respondents age 18 and over provided data for the study.

Interviews were conducted by trained interviewers using a self-completion questionnaire. The presence of the interviewers served to answer any questions that might arise as well as to ensure compliance with the instructions.

Measures for the variables in the three categories of AIO (attitudes, interest, and opinions) were obtained using six-point rating scales. For example, the item for price proneness asked, "When you are buying a product such as food, clothing, and personal care items, how important is it to get the lowest price?" This item was anchored with "Not at all important" and "Extremely important."

The broadly defined category of demographics included standard socioeconomic characteristics as well as media preferences and attendance at professional hockey matches and university basketball games. Demographics were obtained using a variety of forced-choice and free-response measures, the natures of which are indicated in the variable information presented in Case Exhibit 24.1–1. The categorical measures of type of dwelling and preferred type of radio programming were coded as dummy variables for analysis. The

criterion measure of patronage came from an open-ended question asking how many NBA games the respondent had attended during the past season.

Data Analysis

The distribution of responses to the attendance item was skewed, as might be expected. Thus, 57.3 percent of the respondents reported having attended none of the 41 possible games. Those who attended at least one game were recorded in accordance with specification of the light half and the heavy half of the market. This category of patrons was split as nearly as possible at the median, *giving 20.9 percent who attended one or two games* and *21.8 percent who attended three or more*. The three patronage categories thus used for analysis were subsequently termed the *none, low,* and *high* segments.

Given the categorical nature of the criterion measure and the continuous nature of the predictor variables, both univariate analysis of variance and discriminant analysis were employed for the survey. Each of the four categories of predictor variables was subjected to a *separate discriminant* analysis to test the multivariate hypothesis of relationship between patronage and the predictor set in question. The univariate ANOVAs were used to provide complementary information about the nature of the segments.

Results

Case Exhibit 24.1–1 gives the results of the analyses conducted on the four sets of predictor variables. Each set produced at least one variable that was significant in univariate analysis. Three of the four discriminant analyses were significant.

The first predictor set involving AIOs, "marketing orientation," provided only a single variable that ANOVA showed to differentiate among the members of the three patronage segments. The discriminant analysis was nonsignificant.

Source: Courtesy of the American Marketing Association. Adapted from paper presented at AMA conference, 1984.

"Interests in leisure pursuits" emerged as more predictive. By univariate ANOVA, four variables were found significant at the 0.05 level. The discriminant analysis was significant at $p = 0.004$.

"Opinions about professional sports" provided significant prediction of patronage. Seven of the nine variables reached significance at the 0.05 level in univariate analysis. The discriminant analysis was significant beyond $p = 0.001$, and it produced two significant functions. The first significant function provided 79.8 percent of the explained variance, and the second function provided 20.2 percent.

Finally, the set "demographics" was also found to be related to patronage. Counting the four dummy-coded measures of dwelling type and the five similar preferences for radio programming as separate variables, 7 of the 22 demographics reached significance in univariate analysis. The discriminant analysis was significant at $p = 0.004$.

Question

Interpret the managerial significance of the ANOVA and multiple discriminant analysis results.

CASE EXHIBIT 24.1-1 **Characteristics of the Market for Professional Basketball**

Variables	Means None (n = 129)	Means Low (n = 47)	Means High (n = 49)	F-Ratio	p	Loading I	Loading II
Market Orientation[a]							
Price proneness	3.99	4.04	3.63	1.31	.271		
Quality proneness	4.95	4.74	4.82	.74	.480		
Product awareness	4.45	4.02	4.00	3.71	.026		
Product involvement	4.34	4.43	4.14	.66	.517		
Prepurchase planning	4.21	3.85	3.82	2.03	.134		
Brand loyalty	3.95	4.39	3.92	.96	.384		
Information search	3.83	3.55	3.96	1.06	.347		
Interests in Leisure Pursuits[b]							
Need for change from work routine	4.11	4.34	4.55	1.92	.150	.34	
Need for independence in leisure choice	4.88	4.94	4.96	.09	.911	.08	
Need for companionship during leisure	4.85	5.13	4.88	1.16	.317	.10	
Preference for passive versus active pursuits	3.64	4.15	4.57	7.28	.001	.70	
Self-image as athletic	3.67	4.38	4.47	5.89	.003	.60	
Childhood attendance at sporting events	3.38	3.89	4.18	5.41	.005	.60	
Pleasure from sporting events	3.14	3.66	4.27	10.62	.000	.84	
Opinions about Professional Sports[c]							
Athletes as a reference group	3.51	3.64	4.18	3.90	.022	.30	−.19
Excitement from enthusiastic crowd	4.27	4.72	4.73	2.70	.069	.24	.20
Excitement from animosity between teams	3.29	3.28	4.27	6.94	.001	.36	−.41
Acceptance of alcoholic beverages at games	2.60	3.64	3.39	6.88	.001	.34	.46
Enjoyment from large crowds	3.91	3.85	4.49	3.22	.042	.23	−.32
Enjoyment when standing at games	3.37	3.44	3.90	2.25	.108	.22	−.17
Excitement of professional basketball	4.09	3.91	4.67	5.34	.005	.27	−.49
Satisfaction from professional basketball	3.17	3.70	4.80	24.98	.000	.78	−.26
Importance of a winning team	4.26	4.69	5.07	6.12	.003	.39	.02
Demographics[d]							
Years in local area (number of years)	24.47	23.51	19.04	2.02	.135	−.24	
Sex (0 = female, 1 = male)	.40	.55	.65	5.45	.006	.39	
Marital status (0 = single, 1 = married)	.60	.62	.45	2.00	.138	−.21	
Household size (number of persons)	3.13	3.27	3.14	.11	.896	.01	
Rents apartment (0 = no, 1 = yes)	.18	.32	.35	3.70	.026	.30	
Rents a house (0/1)	.09	.09	.08	.03	.967	−.03	
Owns a house (0/1)	.60	.49	.41	3.08	.048	−.29	
Owns a condominium (0/1)	.05	.02	.06	.50	.607	.01	
Head of household (0/1)	.52	.64	.67	2.19	.115	.24	

(*continued*)

CASE EXHIBIT 24.1-1 **Characteristics of the Market for Professional Basketball** (*continued*)

Variables	Means None (n = 129)	Low (n = 47)	High (n = 49)	F-Ratio	p	Loading I	II
Demographics[d]							
Occupational prestige of self (NORC scale)	68.05	69.36	70.63	1.27	.284	.19	
Job leaves evenings free for entertainment (0/1)	.87	.85	.92	.57	.567	.10	
Prefers easy-listening music radio programming (0/1)	.39	.34	.29	.83	.438	−.15	
Prefers contemporary popular music radio (0/1)	.16	.28	.27	1.96	.143	.20	
Prefers rock music radio (0/1)	.14	.11	.27	2.76	.066	.23	
Prefers country-western music radio (0/1)	.15	.19	.08	1.22	.299	−.12	
Prefers talk and news radio programming (0/1)	.09	.04	.06	.52	.597	−.08	
Education (years of schooling)	13.08	13.66	13.56	5.11	.007	.38	
Age (years)	41.51	39.79	33.59	4.21	.016	−.34	
Annual household income (7-point scale)	4.88	5.11	5.16	.65	.523	.13	
Monthly personal expenditures on entertainment for household (dollars)	85.10	112.45	101.29	1.38	.254	.13	
Attendance at university basketball (games last year)	.92	1.89	4.14	15.29	.000	.66	
Attendance at professional hockey (matches last year)	.69	2.28	2.78	5.33	.006	.37	

[a]Canonical discriminant analysis not significant at $p = .189$; therefore, no loadings are given.

[b]Canonical discriminant analysis significant at $p = .004$, first function significant. Centroids for the market segment groups are as follows: none, −.29; low, .19; high, .59.

[c]Canonical discriminant analysis significant at $p = .000$, both functions significant. Centroids for the market segment groups on the first function are as follows: none, −.47; low, .26; high, 1.00. Centroids on the second function are as follows: none, −.10; low, .57; high, −.27.

[d]Canonical discriminant analysis significant at $p = .004$, first function significant. Centroids for the market segment groups are as follows: none, −.41; low, .14; high, .97.

Case 24.2 How Do We Keep Them?

Download the data sets for this case from http://www.thomsonedu.com/marketing/zikmund or request them from your instructor.

Use the data labeled profit for this case. The data go along with the Research Snapshot box on page 602. In addition, management has collected several semantic differential scales from the managers asking them to use emotions to describe the way they feel about their jobs. The emotions include

involved   exciting   fun   satisfied   happy   pleased

The managers want to understand turnover. So, another variable is included that gives the likelihood a manger will quit within twelve

months (labeled turnover in data). After running some initial regression models with eight independent variables predicting turnover, management was confused. They complained that there were too many variables to make sense of.

Thus, the researcher turned to a data reduction technique. Afterwards, a regression model with fewer independent variables gave some clear direction regarding emotions and turnover:

1. Perform the appropriate multivariate technique to identify underlying dimensions that may exist among the emotion ratings.
2. Create scales for any underlying dimensions.
3. Use these scales as independent variables in a regression model.
4. Interpret the results.

APPENDIX 24A
GETTING FACTOR RESULTS WITH SAS OR SPSS

Although researchers may choose to use a spreadsheet to produce simple or even multiple regression results, they will almost always turn to a specialized program for procedures like factor analysis. As a way of familiarizing readers with the mechanics involved, here are some instructions for getting factor results in each program.

SAS is most typically interfaced by writing short computer programs. SAS can read EXCEL spreadsheets quite easily. The data simply need to be "imported" into SAS by using the File dialog box (click on File to begin this process—see SAS documentation contained in the help files for more on how to do this). Once the data are set up, a factor program can be easily produced. Suppose we wished to run a factor program including a varimax rotation on twelve variables labeled X1–X12. The program would be

$$\text{proc factor rotate} = v;$$
$$\text{var X1–X12;}$$

After clicking "run," the results appear in the output window.

In SPSS, the click-through sequence is as follows:

- ANALYZE
- DATA REDUCTION
- FACTOR ANALYSIS

This produces a dialog box. Now follow the following steps to get results that would match those above:

- Highlight variables X1 to X12 (either individually or in multiples).
- Click the ▶ to move them into the "Variables" window.
- Click "ROTATION."
  - Select VARIMAX.
- Optional: Click "OPTIONS."
  - Select "SORT BY SIZE."
  - Select "SUPPRESS ABSOLUTE VALUES LESS THAN."
    - These two options make the output easier to read by organizing the output around the size of the loadings on each factor and by not showing loadings below some specified absolute value (0.1 by default). For factor analyses involving many variables, this is particularly helpful.
- Click "CONTINUE."
- Click "OK."

The results will appear in the output window.

CHAPTER 25
COMMUNICATING RESEARCH RESULTS:
RESEARCH REPORT, ORAL PRESENTATION, AND RESEARCH FOLLOW-UP

After studying this chapter, you should be able to

1. Discuss the research report from the perspective of the communications process
2. Define the parts of a research report following a standard format
3. Explain how to use tables for presenting numerical information
4. Summarize how to select and use the types of research charts
5. Describe how to give an effective oral presentation
6. Discuss the importance of Internet reporting and research follow-up

Chapter Vignette: What the World Needs Now Is . . . Mathematicians Who Can Write

As computing power has placed analytical tools into the hands of every manager, the need for people who understand what these tools can do and what the results mean is greater than ever.[1] Think about the power of search engines such as Google, which operate based on mathematical formulas. These programs can track the sites consumers visit, the links they click on, and even what they buy. Using such data for several large companies that agreed to participate in a study, the Interactive Advertising Bureau used mathematics-based analysis to measure the effectiveness of each company's advertising. For example, the bureau told Ford Motor Company that it could have earned $625 million more from the sale of trucks if its advertising budget had been 6 percent rather than 2.5 percent of its total ad spending.

©MEDIOIMAGES/JUPITER IMAGES

The ability to provide such practical information makes employees with quantitative skills extremely valuable. Harrah's Entertainment, for example, has analyzed data to develop detailed customer profiles, segmenting customers by age, gender, zip code, the amount of time spent gambling, and the value of their winnings or losses. Using mathematical modeling, Harrah's can select groups and match them with special offers—not just to draw in more customers but to maximize the company's profits.

To apply the power of mathematics, organizations need managers who can understand the data—but also numbers experts who can effectively communicate what they have learned. If understanding math adds value to an organization, being able to share that knowledge multiplies the value. Effectively communicating quantitative information is all the more valuable because the skill is, unfortunately, rare. A survey of major corporations found that in seven out of ten companies, at least two-thirds of their employees have writing responsibility, and more than half said their employees frequently produced technical reports. Over three-fourths of the companies said their employees also prepare oral reports incorporating presentation software such as PowerPoint. But more than four out of ten companies said they had to provide training for employees with deficient writing skills.

Why should a careful researcher have to be a good writer, too? After the researcher has spent days, weeks, or even months working on a project, preparation of the report may feel like an anticlimactic formality. All the "real" work has been done; it just has to be put on paper. This attitude can be disastrous, however. Even if the project was well designed, the data carefully obtained and analyzed by sophisticated statistical methods, and important conclusions reached, unless the reporting is effective, all of the earlier efforts will have been wasted. Often the research report is the only part of the project that others ever see. If people who need to use the research results have to wade through a disorganized presentation, are confused by technical jargon, or find sloppiness of language or thought, they will probably discount the report and make decisions without it, just as if the project had never been done. So, the research report is a crucial means for communicating the whole project. This chapter explains the communication of research results with written reports, oral presentations, and follow-up conversations.[2]

Insights from the Communications Model

Some insights from the theory of communications help to clarify the importance of the research report. Exhibit 25.1 illustrates one view of the **communication process**. Several elements influence successful communication.

- The *communicator*—the source or sender of the message (the writer of the report)
- The *message*—the set of meanings being sent to or received by the audience (the *findings* of the research project)
- The *medium*—the way in which the message is delivered to the audience (the oral or written report itself)
- The *audience*—the receiver or destination of the message (the manager who will make a decision based—we hope—on the report findings)
- *Feedback*—a communication, also involving a message and channel, that flows in the reverse direction (from the audience to the original communicator) and that may be used to modify subsequent communications (the manager's response to the report)

Communication process
The process by which one person or source sends a message to an audience or receiver and then receives feedback about the message.

TOTHEPOINT

It is a luxury to be understood.

—Ralph Waldo Emerson

EXHIBIT 25.1
The Communication Process

RESEARCHSNAPSHOT

Sloppy Numbers in the Crosshairs of Dow Jones Newspaper Fund's Director

As executive director of the Dow Jones Newspaper Fund, former *Wall Street Journal* editor Richard Holden has a mission to improve the quality of journalism education. His formal role emphasizes high school and college students, but Holden finds that even the professionals can use some education in reporting data. He has gathered examples of newspaper reports that present numbers in ways that are confusing, misleading, or even incorrect.

Consider the following examples, taken from a seminar Holden presented to journalists. See if you can identify the problem with each statement:

"Visa announced that its new credit card will carry an adjustable rate set monthly at four percent above the prime rate, in line with other variable-rate cards."

This is a common mistake: confusing *percentage* and *percentage points*. A rate set so slightly above the prime rate would be an unusually good bargain. For example, at the time of this writing, the prime rate is 7.5 percent; prime plus 4 percent would be just 7.8 percent, far below the rates charged for most credit cards. The writer probably meant Visa would charge prime rate plus four percentage points, which in this example would be 11.5 percent.

"Battling Hunger, a food pantry, said it delivered 110,000 tons of food to Detroit last Thanksgiving. The food was delivered to help residents there overcome the effects of a severe economic slump, particularly in the automobile industry."

This example shows that it is important to check whether numbers themselves, including the units of measure, are logical. In this case, 110,000 tons equals 220 million pounds of food. Can that be reasonable? Even if the food pantry served a million people—all of Detroit plus some suburbanites—it would have distributed 220 pounds of food to each individual. Not likely. When numbers are this unrealistic, the writer should check the calculations, including the decimal point's location, and the units. Perhaps this writer meant 110,000 pounds or 110 tons.

Source: Based on Carl Bialik, "Monitoring Numbers in the News," The Wall Street Journal, January 20, 2006, http://online.wsj.com; Carl Bialik, "The Results Are In," The Wall Street Journal, January 27, 2006, http://online.wsj.com; and Dow Jones Newspaper Fund, "About DJNF," http://djnewspaperfund.dowjones.com, accessed March 29, 2006.

©BASSOULS SOPHIE/CORBIS SYGMA

This model may make communication seem simple. Perhaps communication is simple when the message flows smoothly from writer to reader, and then in return, from reader to writer to provide feedback. Actually, communication is more complex. Exhibit 25.2 illustrates one key difficulty. The communicator and the audience each have individual fields of experience. These overlap to some extent; otherwise no communication would be possible. Still, a great deal of experience is not common to both parties. As communicators send a message, they encode it in terms that make sense to them based on their fields of experience. As the individuals in the audience receive the message, they decode it based on their own fields of experience. The message is successfully communicated only if the parties share enough common experience for it to be encoded, transmitted, and decoded with roughly the same meaning.

In the research setting, the communicator (the researcher) has spent a great deal of time studying a problem. He or she has looked at secondary sources, gathered primary data, used statistical techniques to analyze the data, and reached conclusions. When the report on the project is written,

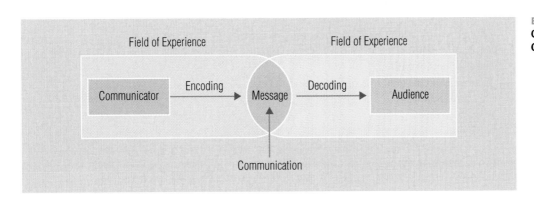

EXHIBIT 25.2
Communication Occurs in a Common Field of Experience

all this "baggage" will affect its contents. On the assumption that the reader has a lot of background information on the project, the researcher may produce pages and pages of unexplained tables, expecting the reader to unearth from them the same patterns that the researcher has observed. The report may contain technical terms such as *parameter estimate, F-distribution, statistical significance, correlations,* and *eigenvalue,* on the assumption that the reader will understand them. Another researcher may assume that the reader does not have a lot of background information and may go overboard explaining everything in the report in sixth-grade terms. Although the researcher's intent is to ensure that the reader will not get lost, this effort may insult the reader.

Usually when readers receive a report, they have not thought much about the project. They may not know anything about statistics and may have many other responsibilities. If they cannot understand the report quickly, they may put it on a stack of things to do someday.

Simply delivering a report to its audience is not sufficient to ensure that it gets attention. The report needs to be written so as to draw on the common experience of the researcher and the reader. And the person responsible for making sure that it does so is the writer—not the reader. Unless a report is really crucial, a busy reader will not spend time and effort struggling through an inadequate or difficult-to-read document.

The Report in Context

Research report
An oral presentation or written statement of research results, strategic recommendations, and/or other conclusions to a specific audience.

A **research report** is an oral presentation and/or written statement whose purpose is to communicate research results, strategic recommendations, and/or other conclusions to management or other specific audiences. Although this chapter deals primarily with the final *written* report required by an extensive research project, remember that the final report may not be the only kind prepared. For a small project, a short oral or written report on the results may be all that is needed. Extensive projects may involve many written documents, interim reports, a long final written report, and several oral presentations. In addition, technical materials may be posted on an organization's Intranet.

The chapter's emphasis on the final report should not be taken to mean that other communications, such as progress reports during the course of the project, are any less important to the project's eventual success. The chapter's suggestions can be easily adapted to apply to these additional communications and shorter, less formal reports.

Report Format

Report format
The makeup or arrangement of parts necessary to a good research report.

Although every research report is custom-made for the project it represents, some conventions of **report format** are universal. They represent a consensus about the parts necessary for a good research report and how they should be ordered. This consensus is not a law, however. Every book on report writing suggests the use of its own unique format, and every report writer has to pick and choose the section and order that will work best for the project at hand. Many companies and universities also have in-house report formats or writing guides for writers to follow. The format described in this section serves as a starting point from which a writer can shape his or her own appropriate format. It includes seven major elements:

1. Title page (sometimes preceded by a title fly page)
2. Letter of transmittal
3. Letter of authorization
4. Table of contents (and lists of figures and tables)
5. Executive Summary
   a. Objectives
   b. Results
   c. Conclusions
   d. Recommendations

EXHIBIT 25.3 **Report Format**

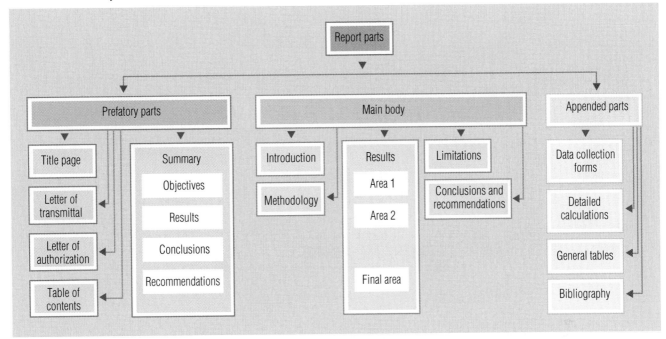

6. Body
    a. Introduction
        1. Background
        2. Objectives
    b. Methodology
    c. Results
    d. Limitations
    e. Conclusions and recommendations
7. Appendix
    a. Data collection forms
    b. Detailed calculations
    c. General tables
    d. Bibliography
    e. Other support material

This format is illustrated graphically in Exhibit 25.3.

Tailoring the Format to the Project

The format of a research report may need to be adjusted for two reasons: (1) to obtain the proper level of formality and (2) to decrease the complexity of the report. The format given here is for the most formal type of report, such as one for a large project done within an organization or one done by a research agency for a client company. This type of report is usually bound in a permanent cover and may be hundreds of pages long.

In less formal reports, each part is shorter, and some parts are omitted. Exhibit 25.4 illustrates how the format is adapted to shorter, less formal reports. The situation may be compared to the way people's clothing varies according to the formality of the occasion. The most formal report is dressed, so to speak, in a tuxedo or long evening gown. It includes the full assortment of prefatory parts—title fly page, title page, letters of transmittal and authorization, and table of contents. Like changing into an everyday business suit, dropping down to the next level of formality involves eliminating parts of the prefatory material that are not needed in this situation and reducing the

EXHIBIT 25.4 Adapting Report Format to Required Formality

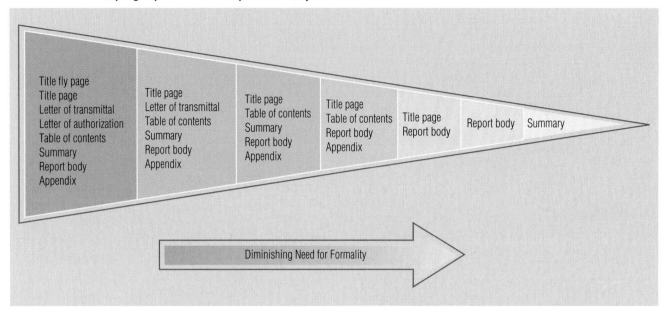

complexity of the report body. In general, as the report moves down through the sport coat and slacks and then blue jeans stages, more prefatory parts are dropped, and the complexity and length of the report body are reduced.

How does the researcher decide on the appropriate level of formality? The general rule is to include all the parts needed for effective communication in the particular circumstances—and no more. This depends on how far up in management the report is expected to go and how routine the matter is. A researcher's immediate supervisor does not need a 100-page, "black-tie" report on a routine project. However, the board of directors does not want a one-page "blue jeans" report on a big project that backs a major expansion program. The formal report to top management may later be stripped of some of the prefatory parts (and thus reduced in formality) for wider circulation within the company.

The Parts of the Report

The guidelines that call for each element of the research report also dictate the content of each part.

TITLE PAGE

The *title page* should state the title of the report, for whom the report was prepared, by whom it was prepared, and the date of release or presentation. The title should give a brief but complete indication of the purpose of the research project. Addresses and titles of the preparer and recipient may also be included. On confidential reports, the title page may list the people to whom the report should be circulated. For the most formal reports, the title page is preceded by a title fly page, which contains only the report's title.

LETTER OF TRANSMITTAL

Relatively formal and very formal reports include a *letter of transmittal*. Its purpose is to release or deliver the report to the recipient. It also serves to establish some rapport between the reader and the writer. This is the one part of the formal report in which a personal or even slightly informal tone should be used. The transmittal should not dive into the report findings except in the broadest terms.

Exhibit 25.5 presents a sample letter of transmittal. Note that the opening paragraph releases the report and briefly identifies the factors of authorization. The letter comments generally on

EXHIBIT 25.5
Sample Letter of Transmittal

```
                    SOFTPROOF LEATHER PRODUCTS COMPANY, INC.
                              KENT, OHIO 44240


                               December 1, 20XX


        Mr. Carl M. Wheeler
        Vice President for Marketing
        Home Office

        Subject:  Presentation of Report on Study of Small-Volume Customers

        Dear Mr. Wheeler:

        Here is my report on the study of small-volume customers.  This report, the
        subject of our conference today, was prepared according to your authorization
        memorandum dated April 21, 20XX.

        As we suspected would be the case when we started the study, the report
        recommends that we take a very careful new look at our present attitude toward
        serving customers whose volumes are less than $20,000 per year.  Some of the
        experienced salespeople whom we contacted in personal interviews gave us some
        excellent suggestions about what our new attitude should be.

        The returns from our mail survey of small-volume customers were not as high
        as we wanted them to be.  We do believe, though, that the questionnaires
        returned are representative of the customers involved in the study.  The
        follow-up survey of a sample of customers who did not return the first
        questionnaire was most reassuring on this point.

        As is perhaps typical of a research department, we discovered during this
        study another problem area which might bear investigation.  This area is
        that of redefining the boundaries of our sales territories.  We are now doing
        some preliminary thinking about this problem.  Should we decide research is
        warranted, we later will make our recommendations to you.

        We are grateful to you, Mr. Wheeler, for your cooperation in this important
        study.  Your keeping the president informally up to date on our progress
        should pave the way toward his accepting the recommendations made in the
        report.

                                      Sincerely,

                                      Harold M Johnson

                                      Harold M. Johnson
        Approved:                     Associate Analyst
        December 1, 20XX              Sales Analysis Section

        T. T. Landham
        Director and Senior Analyst
        Sales Analysis Section
```

Source: Adapted from David M. Robinson, *Writing Reports for Management Decisions* (Columbus, OH: Merrill, 1969), p. 340. Reprinted with permission.

findings and matters of interest regarding the research. The closing section expresses the writer's personal interest in the project just completed and in doing additional, related work.

LETTER OF AUTHORIZATION

The *letter of authorization* is a letter to the researcher that approves the project, details who has responsibility for it, and describes the resources available to support it. Because the researcher would not write this letter personally, writing guidelines will not be discussed here. In many situations, simply referring to the authorization in the letter of transmittal is sufficient. If so, the letter of authorization need not be included in the report. In some cases, though, the reader may be unfamiliar with the authorization or may need detailed information about it. In such cases, the report should include this letter, preferably an exact copy of the original.

THE TABLE OF CONTENTS

A *table of contents* is essential to any report more than a few pages long. It should list the divisions and subdivisions of the report with page references. The table of contents is based on the final outline of the report, but it should include only the first-level subdivisions. For short reports it is sufficient to include only the main divisions. If the report includes many figures or tables, a list of these should immediately follow the table of contents.

RESEARCHSNAPSHOT

Research ROI

The research summary, like the original research design, should be based on the marketing problem to be solved and the resulting insight into how to address that problem. In today's competitive business environment, companies cannot afford to do research just because it is interesting. They need marketing research that helps them compete.

Logically, this should mean that companies are measuring whether research helps their bottom line. In practice, however, measuring the return on investment (ROI) for marketing research is still a relatively new idea. Marketing research consultants at a firm called A. Dawn Lesh International surveyed companies to find out how they measure the effectiveness of their marketing

research projects. The firm discovered that only 10 to 15 percent of the companies measured research effectiveness at all. Some of those that did measure it simply looked at whether the project's client was satisfied or whether the quality of the work was high. In other cases, researchers determined the expected value of each idea uncovered by the research project.

Lesh International proposes measures that put a dollar value on the research. One of these, which the firm calls ROI Lite, is the dollar value of the marketing decision multiplied by the client's estimate of the increased confidence that the right alternative will be selected, divided by the cost of the research. The second measure, ROI Complete, incorporates the likelihood that the research client will act on the information.

Sources: Based on Kate Maddox, "Market Research Charges Online," B to B, April 4, 2005, Maddox, Kate (2005), "The ROI of Research," B to B, 89 (April 5), 25–26; Maddox, Kate (2005), "Market Research Charges Online," B to B, 90 (April 4), 28–31; Brent Hieggelke, "Marketing & ROI," iMediaConnection, October 19, 2004, http://www.imediaconnection.com, accessed April 1, 2006.

THE SUMMARY

The *summary*, also known as executive summary, briefly explains why the research project was conducted, what aspects of the problem were considered, what the outcome was, and what should be done. It is a vital part of the report. Studies have indicated that nearly all managers read a report's summary, while only a minority read the rest of the report. Thus, the writer's only chance to produce an impact may be in the summary.

The summary should be written only after the rest of the report has been completed. It represents the essence of the report. It should be one page long (or, at most, two pages), so the writer must carefully sort out what is important enough to be included in it. Several pages of the full report may have to be condensed into one summarizing sentence. Some parts of the report may be condensed more than others; the number of words in the summary need not be in proportion to the length of the section being discussed. The summary should be written to be self-sufficient. In fact, the summary is often detached from the report and circulated by itself.

The summary contains four elements. First, it states the objectives of the report, including the most important background information and the specific purposes of the project. Second, it presents the methodology and the major results. Next come the conclusions. These are opinions based on the results and constitute an interpretation of the results. Finally come recommendations, or suggestions for action, based on the conclusions. In many cases, managers prefer not to have recommendations included in the report or summary. Whether or not recommendations are to be included should be clear from the particular context of the report.

THE BODY

Introduction section
The part of the body of a research report that discusses background information and the specific objectives of the research.

The *body* constitutes the bulk of the report. It begins with an **introduction section** setting out the background factors that made the project necessary as well as the objectives of the report. It continues with discussions of the methodology, results, and limitations of the study and finishes with conclusions and recommendations based on the results.

The introduction explains why the project was done and what it aimed to discover. It should include the basic authorization and submittal data. The relevant background comes

RESEARCHSNAPSHOT

Dr. Zemel's Valuable Data

What do you think about a research design that includes paying for the right to include secondary data? This would be part of your design if you were using some of the data collected by Michael Zemel, a professor of nutrition and medicine at the University of Tennessee. Research he conducted found a correlation between eating dairy products and losing weight. Food companies including Kraft and Dannon saw those results as a potential selling point for their products. Zemel, in turn, concluded that if his results would profit the companies, he should share in the returns. He began charging dairy food companies a licensing fee in exchange for the right to refer to his research.

Some observers, including the Center for Science in the Public Interest, object that payments to researchers interfere with their objectivity. Zemel responds that his arrangement is essentially the

same as the long-accepted practice of pharmaceutical companies paying for research into possible new drug treatments.

In the meantime, another research project found that among a group of children aged nine to fourteen, those who drank more milk wound up weighing *more* than the others. Until scientific research can arrive at a definitive conclusion about dairy consumption and weight, dairy marketers face some difficult decisions about using such data in their marketing research and advertising.

Source: Based on Stephanie Thompson, "Dairy Scientist Decides to Milk His Research for All It's Worth," Advertising Age, 76 (June 20, 2005), 3–38; and Jerry Markton, "Dairy Industry Sued over Weight Loss Claims," The Washington Post, June 29, 2005, http://www.washingtonpost.com, accessed April 1, 2006.

©FOODPIX/JUPITER IMAGES

---

next. Enough background should be included to explain why the project was worth doing, but unessential historical factors should be omitted. The question of how much is enough should be answered by referring to the needs of the audience. A government report that will be widely circulated requires more background than a company's internal report on customer satisfaction. The last part of the introduction explains exactly what the project tried to discover. It discusses the statement of the problem and research questions as they were stated in the research proposal. Each purpose presented here should have a corresponding entry in the results section later in the report.

The second part of the body is the **research methodology section**. This part is a challenge to write because it must explain technical procedures in a manner appropriate for the audience. The material in this section may be supplemented with more detailed explanations in the appendix or a glossary of technical terms. This part of the report should address four topics:

1. *Research design.* Was the study exploratory, descriptive, or causal? Did the data come from primary or secondary sources? Were results collected by survey, observation, or experiment? A copy of the survey questionnaire or observation form should be included in the appendix. Why was this particular design suited to the study?
2. *Sample design.* What was the target population? What sampling frame was used? What sample units were used? How were they selected? How large was the sample? What was the response rate? Detailed computations to support these explanations should be saved for the appendix.
3. *Data collection and fieldwork.* How many and what types of fieldworkers were used? What training and supervision did they receive? Was the work verified? This section is important for establishing the degree of accuracy of the results.
4. *Analysis.* This section should outline the general statistical methods used in the study, but the information presented here should not overlap with what is presented in the results section.

The **results section** should make up the bulk of the report and should present, in some logical order, those findings of the project that bear on the objectives. The results should be organized as a continuous narrative, designed to be convincing but not to oversell the project. Summary tables and charts should be used to aid the discussion. These may serve as points of reference to the data being discussed and free the prose from excessive facts and figures. Comprehensive or detailed charts, however, should be saved for the appendix.

Because no research is perfect, its limitations should be indicated. If problems arose with nonresponse error or sampling procedures, these should be discussed. However, the discussion of

Research methodology section
The part of the body of a report that presents the findings of the project. It includes tables, charts, and an organized narrative.

Results section
The part of the body of a report that presents the findings of the project. It includes tables, charts, and an organized narrative.

limitations should avoid overemphasizing the weaknesses; its aim should be to provide a realistic basis for assessing the results.

The last part of the body is the **conclusions and recommendations section**. As mentioned earlier, conclusions are opinions based on the results, and recommendations are suggestions for action. The conclusions and recommendations should be presented in this section in more detail than in the summary, and the text should include justification as needed.

◼ THE APPENDIX

The *appendix* presents the "too . . ." material. Any material that is too technical or too detailed to go in the body should appear in the appendix. This includes materials of interest only to some readers or subsidiary materials not directly related to the objectives. Some examples of appendix materials are data collection forms, detailed calculations, discussions of highly technical questions, detailed or comprehensive tables of results, and a bibliography (if appropriate). Since the advent of company Intranets, much appendix material is posted on internal web pages.

◼ BASIC MARKETING RESEARCH REPORT

The outline described applies especially to applied market research projects. When basic research reports are written, such as might be submitted and potentially published in an academic business journal, the outline changes slightly since some components become irrelevant. A common outline used in basic marketing research proceeds as follows:

1. Abstract
2. Introduction
3. Background
   a. Literature Review
   b. Hypotheses
4. Research Methods
5. Results
6. Discussion
   a. Implications
   b. Limitations
   c. Future Research
7. Conclusions
8. References
9. Appendices

The material in the sections does not change very much between market and marketing research. So, the elements within each section are the same with only the noted exceptions. The basic research report will place a greater emphasis on how the current research is integrated into the previous literature dealing with the research topic. This section finishes with a specific set of theoretical hypotheses. The research methodology and results section may contain more statistical detail and jargon since the reader is expected to be knowledgeable in basic research methodology. A quick look at an academic business journal like the *Journal of Business Research,* the *Journal of Marketing,* the *Journal of the Academy of Marketing Science,* or the *Journal of Management* will give a reader a feel for this type of writing. Overall, though, both basic and applied marketing research reports involve technical writing and the principles of good technical writing apply.

Effective Use of Graphic Aids

Used properly, **graphic aids** can clarify complex points or emphasize a message. Used improperly or sloppily, they can distract or even mislead a reader. Graphical aids work best when they are an integral part of the text. The graphics should always be interpreted in the text. This does not mean that the writer should exhaustively explain an obvious chart or table, but it *does* mean that the text should point out the key elements of any graphic aid and relate them to the discussion in progress.

Several types of graphic aids may be useful in research reports including tables, charts, maps, and diagrams. The following discussion briefly covers the most common ones, tables and charts. The reader interested in other types of graphic material should consult more specialized sources.

Tables

Tables are most useful for presenting numerical information, especially when several pieces of information have been gathered about each item discussed. For example, consider how hard following the information in Exhibit 25.6 might be with only narrative text and no graphical aids. Using tables allows a writer to point out significant features without getting bogged down in detail. The body of the report should include only relatively short summary tables, with comprehensive tables reserved for an appendix.

Each table should include the following elements:

- *Table number.* This allows for simple reference from the text to the table. If the text includes many tables, a list of tables should be included just after the table of contents.
- *Title.* The title should indicate the contents of the table and be complete enough to be intelligible without referring to the text.
- *Stubheads and bannerheads.* The stubheads contain the captions for the rows of the table, and the bannerheads (or boxheads) contain those for the columns.
- *Footnotes.* Any explanations or qualifications for particular table entries or sections should be given in footnotes.
- *Source notes.* If a table is based on material from one or more secondary sources rather than on new data generated by the project, the sources should be acknowledged, usually below the table.

Tables in a survey research report typically follow the format shown in Exhibit 25.7. This example cross-tabulates demographics with survey responses. Data from a statistical test also might be reported in table form, as shown in Exhibit 25.8.

Suppose an airline asks a question about customers' satisfaction with its baggage-handling service. In addition to showing the simple frequency for each category, most research analysts would cross-tabulate answers to the baggage-handling questions with several demographic variables such as gender, income, education, and age. To present multiple cross-tabulations individually in separate tables requires considerable space. Thus, many research reports use a space-saving format, with either stubheads for rows or bannerheads for columns, to allow the reader to view several cross-tabulations at the same time. Exhibit 25.9 presents several cross-tabulations in a single table with stubheads.

Charts

Charts translate numerical information into visual form so that relationships may be easily grasped. The accuracy of the numbers is reduced to gain this advantage. Each chart should include the following elements:

- *Figure number.* Charts (and other illustrative material) should be numbered in a separate series from tables. The numbers allow for easy reference from the text. If there are many charts, a list of them should be included after the table of contents.
- *Title.* The title should describe the contents of the chart and be independent of the text explanation. The number and title may be placed at the top or bottom of the chart.
- *Explanatory legends.* Enough explanation should be put on the chart to spare the reader a need to look at the accompanying text. Such explanations should include labels for axes, scale numbers, and a key to the various quantities being graphed.

EXHIBIT 25.6 **Parts of a Table**

Table number →   Title →

Table 1024. Retail Sales—New Passenger Cars: 1990 to 2003

[In thousands 9,300 represents 9,300, 000, except as indicated. Retail new car sales include both sales to individuals and to corporate fleets. It also includes leased cars.]

Item	1990	1995	1997	1998	1999	2000	2001	2002	2003
Total retail new passenger car sales	9,300	8,635	8,272	8,142	8,698	8,847	8,423	8,103	7,510
Domestic[1]	6,897	7,129	6,917	6,762	6,979	6,831	6,325	5,676	5,527
Imports	2,403	1,506	1,355	1,380	1,719	2,016	2,098	2,226	2,083
Japan	1,719	982	726	691	758	863	837	923	817
Germany	265	207	297	367	467	517	523	547	544
Other	419	317	332	322	494	637	798	756	722

Stubheads (left margin)   Bannerheads (right margin)

[1] Includes cars produced in Canada and Mexico.

Source: U.S. Bureau of Transportation Statistics, *National Transportation Statistics 2004*, Data Supplied by following source: *Motor Vehicle Facts & Figures, 1997*. Southfield, MI: *Ward's Motor Vehicle Facts & Figures, 2002*. Southfield, MI: 2002. See also <http://www.bts.gov>.

↑   Source

Footnote (left margin)

— Represents zero.   [1]Change from prior year.

Source: U.S. Census Bureau, *Statistical Abstract of the United States*, 2006, table 1024, p. 678.

EXHIBIT 25.7 **Reporting Format for a Typical Cross-Tabulation**

Online Activity	Age Group						
	12–17	18–28	29–40	41–50	51–59	60–69	70+
E-mail	89%	88%	92%	90%	94%	90%	89%
Online games	81%	54%	37%	29%	25%	25%	32%
Instant messaging	75%	66%	52%	38%	42%	33%	14%
Downloading music	51%	45%	28%	16%	14%	8%	5%
Job hunting	30%	62%	51%	40%	36%	17%	2%
Job research	—	44%	59%	59%	54%	31%	13%

Source: Excerpted from Susannah Fox and Mary Madden, "Generations Online," Pew Internet and American Life Project, December 2005, p. 3, http://www.pewinternet.org.

EXHIBIT 25.8 **Reporting Format for a Typical Statistical Test**

Will investors be more cautious about buying stock in companies with questionable advertising?

	Business	Advertising Management
Yes	57%	46%
No	27	35
Not sure	16	19
	$n = 177$	$n = 154$

$$x^2 = 4.933 \qquad d.f. = 2 \qquad p < .08$$

Source: Report to the Federal Trade Commission on the Effects of the STP "Public Notice" Advertising Campaign, June 1979.

EXHIBIT 25.9 **Using a Stubhead Format to Include Several Cross-Tabulations in One Table**

| Characteristic | Total Persons | Level of Highest Degree | | | | | | | |
		Not a High School Graduate	High School Graduate Only	Some College, No Degree	Associate's	Bachelor's	Master's	Professional	Doctorate
All persons*	$37,046	$18,734	$27,915	$29,533	$35,958	$51,206	$62,514	$115,212	$88,471
Age:									
25 to 34 years old	33,212	18,920	26,073	28,954	32,276	43,794	51,040	74,120	62,109
35 to 44 years old	42,475	22,123	31,479	36,038	38,442	57,438	66,264	126,165	101,382
45 to 54 years old	45,908	23,185	32,978	40,291	41,511	59,208	68,344	132,180	92,229
55 to 64 years old	45,154	23,602	31,742	38,131	39,147	57,423	66,760	138,845	98,433
65 years old and over	28,918	17,123	20,618	28,017	23,080	41,323	42,194	77,312	56,724
Sex:									
Male	44,726	21,447	33,286	36,419	43,462	63,084	76,896	136,128	95,894
Female	28,367	14,214	21,659	22,615	29,537	38,447	48,205	72,445	73,516

*For persons 18 years old and over with earnings.

Source: Excerpted from U.S. Census Bureau, *Statistical Abstract of the United States*, 2006, table 217, p. 148.

EXHIBIT 25.10
Distortion by Alternating Scales

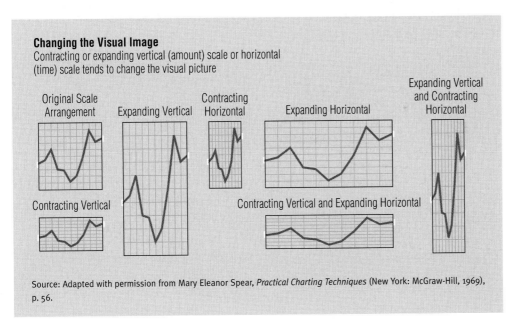

Changing the Visual Image
Contracting or expanding vertical (amount) scale or horizontal (time) scale tends to change the visual picture

Original Scale Arrangement
Expanding Vertical
Contracting Horizontal
Expanding Horizontal
Expanding Vertical and Contracting Horizontal
Contracting Vertical
Contracting Vertical and Expanding Horizontal

Source: Adapted with permission from Mary Eleanor Spear, *Practical Charting Techniques* (New York: McGraw-Hill, 1969), p. 56.

- *Source and footnotes.* Any secondary sources for the data should be acknowledged. Footnotes may be used to explain items, although they are less common for charts than for tables.

Charts are subject to distortion, whether unintentional or deliberate. Exhibit 25.10 shows how altering the scale changes the reader's impression of the data. A particularly severe kind of distortion comes from treating unequal intervals as if they were equal; this generally results from a deliberate attempt to distort data. Exhibit 25.11 shows this type of distortion. In this example, someone has attempted to make the rise on the chart more dramatic by compressing the portion in which the data show little real change.

Another common way of introducing distortion is to begin the vertical scale at some value larger than zero. Exhibit 25.12 shows how this exaggerates the amount of change in the period

EXHIBIT 25.11
Distortion from Treating Unequal Time Intervals as Equal

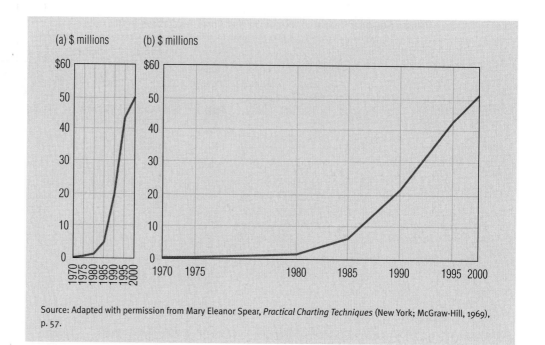

Source: Adapted with permission from Mary Eleanor Spear, *Practical Charting Techniques* (New York; McGraw-Hill, 1969), p. 57.

EXHIBIT 25.12
Distortion of Charts Using Broken Vertical Scales

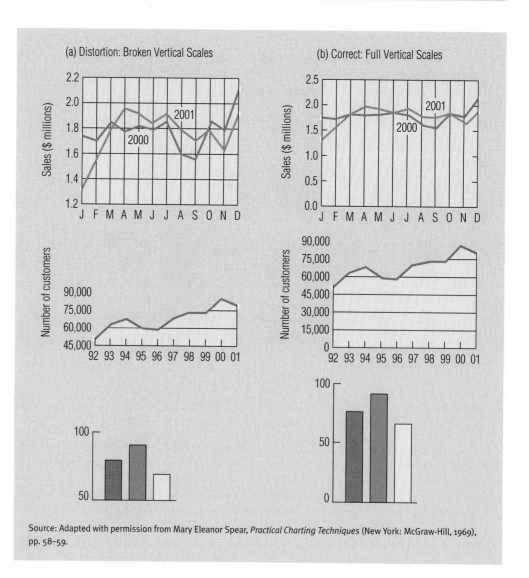

Source: Adapted with permission from Mary Eleanor Spear, *Practical Charting Techniques* (New York: McGraw-Hill, 1969), pp. 58–59.

EXHIBIT 25.13 **Pie Charts**

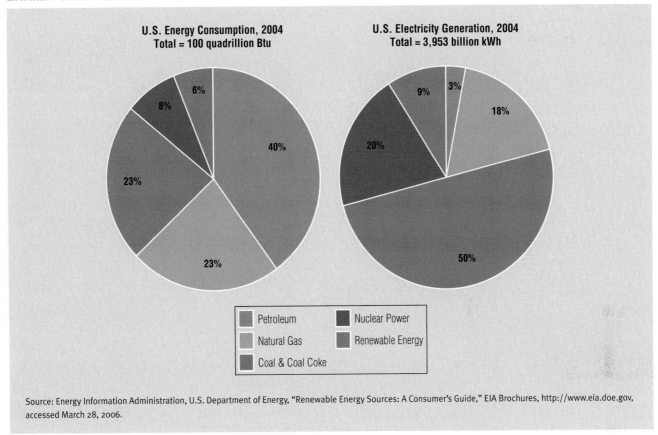

Source: Energy Information Administration, U.S. Department of Energy, "Renewable Energy Sources: A Consumer's Guide," EIA Brochures, http://www.eia.doe.gov, accessed March 28, 2006.

covered. This type of broken scale is often used in published reports of stock price movements. In this case, it is assumed that the reader is interested mostly in the changes and is aware of the exaggeration. For most research reports, however, this assumption is not valid. The vertical axis of a graph should start at zero.

PIE CHARTS

One of the most useful kinds of charts is the pie chart, which shows the composition of some total quantity at a particular time. As shown in the example in Exhibit 25.13, each angle, or "slice," is proportional to its percentage of the whole. Companies often use pie charts to show how revenues were used or the composition of their sales. Each of the segments should be labeled with its description and percentage. The writer should not try to include too many small slices; about six slices is a typical maximum.

LINE GRAPHS

Line graphs are useful for showing the relationship of one variable to another. The dependent variable generally is shown on the vertical axis, and the independent variable on the horizontal axis. The most common independent variable for such charts is time, but it is by no means the only one. Exhibit 25.14 depicts a *simple line graph.*

Variations of the line graph also are useful. The *multiple-line graph,* such as the example in Exhibit 25.15, shows the relationship of more than one dependent variable to the independent variable. The line for each dependent variable should be in a different color or pattern and should be clearly labeled. The writer should not try to squeeze in too many variables; this can quickly lead to confusion rather than clarification.

EXHIBIT 25.14
Simple Line Graph

EXHIBIT 25.15
Multiple-Line Graph

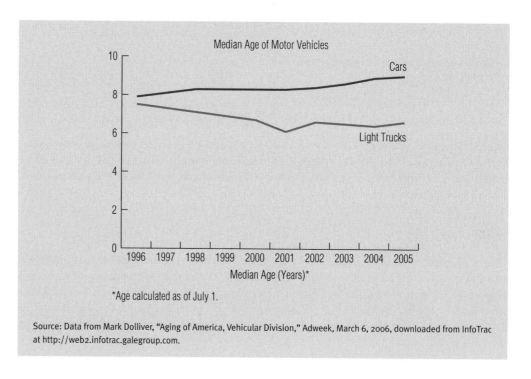

A second variation is the *stratum chart,* which shows how the composition of a total quantity changes as the independent variable changes. Exhibit 25.16 provides an example. The same cautions mentioned in connection with multiple-line graphs apply to stratum charts.

■ BAR CHARTS

A bar chart shows changes in the value of a dependent variable (plotted on the vertical axis) at discrete intervals of the independent variable (on the horizontal axis). A simple bar chart is shown in Exhibit 25.17.

EXHIBIT 25.16
Stratum Chart

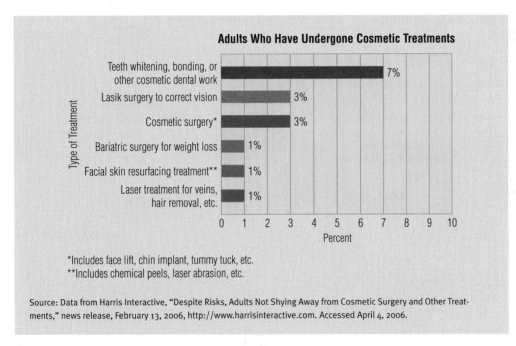

*Includes face lift, chin implant, tummy tuck, etc.
**Includes chemical peels, laser abrasion, etc.

Source: Data from Harris Interactive, "Despite Risks, Adults Not Shying Away from Cosmetic Surgery and Other Treatments," news release, February 13, 2006, http://www.harrisinteractive.com. Accessed April 4, 2006.

EXHIBIT 25.17
Simple Bar Chart

Like the line graph, the bar chart format has variations. A common variant is the *subdivided-bar chart* (see Exhibit 25.18). It is much like a stratum chart, showing the composition of the whole quantity. The *multiple-bar chart* (see Exhibit 25.19) shows how multiple variables are related to the primary variable. In each of these cases, each bar or segment of the bar needs to be clearly identified with a different color or pattern. The writer should not use too many divisions or dependent variables. Too much detail obscures the essential advantage of charts, which is to make relationships easy to grasp.

Oral presentation
A spoken summary of the major findings, conclusions, and recommendations, given to clients or line managers to provide them with the opportunity to clarify any ambiguous issues by asking questions.

The Oral Presentation

The conclusions and recommendations of most research reports are presented orally as well as in writing. The purpose of an **oral presentation** is to highlight the most important findings of a research project and provide clients or line managers with an opportunity to ask questions. The oral presentation may be as simple as a short video conference with a manager at the client organization's location or as formal as a report to the company board of directors.

RESEARCHSNAPSHOT

Noah's Law of Slide Presentations

During oral presentations of research reports, many presenters use slides that viewers in the back row cannot read. In fact, some presenters use slides that viewers in the front row cannot read.

All viewers would be much happier if all presenters were to follow Noah's Law of Slide Presentations. Noah's Law says, Never, ever, under any circumstances whatsoever, put more than forty words on a single slide. A number counts as a word. Noah's Law is called Noah's Law because when God made it rain for forty days and forty nights, He flooded the whole world, and no presenter should attempt that with one overhead.

Note that, in Noah's Law, forty is the absolute upper limit. Twenty is a good average. Seven is even better. If seven words look lonely,

presenters can always MAKE THE LETTERS BIGGER.

Advertising legendary David Ogilvy was a devout follower of Noah's Law. He thought so highly of it that he invented and enforced Ogilvy's Corollary. Ogilvy's Corollary says, Never put anything on a slide that you don't intend to read out loud to your audience word for word. He reasoned that when one message comes in on the visual channel while another comes in on the auditory channel, the audience will probably neglect one message or the other.

Source: Adapted with permission from William D. Wells, University of Minnesota, "Noah's Law of Overhead Transparencies," ACR Newsletter, June 1993, p. 10. Published by the Association for Consumer Research, Peter Bloch, 222 Middlebush Hall, University of Missouri, Columbia, MO 65211.

©DAVID YOUNG-WOLFF/PHOTOEDIT

EXHIBIT 25.18
Subdivided Bar Chart

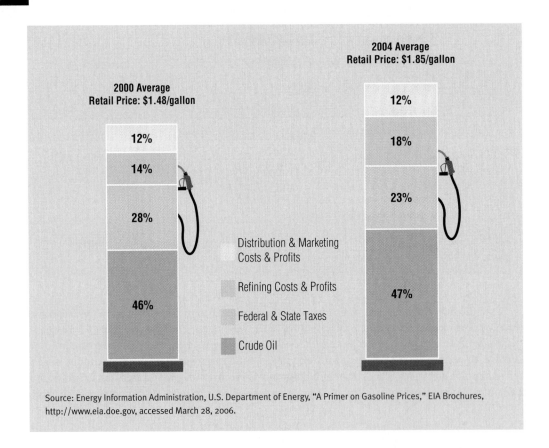

Source: Energy Information Administration, U.S. Department of Energy, "A Primer on Gasoline Prices," EIA Brochures, http://www.eia.doe.gov, accessed March 28, 2006.

In either situation, the key to effective presentation is preparation. Communication specialists often suggest that a person preparing an oral presentation begin at the end.[3] In other words, while preparing a presentation, a researcher should think about what he or she wants the client to know when it has been completed. The researcher should select the three or four most important findings for emphasis and rely on the written report for a full summary. The researcher also needs to be ready to defend the results of the research. This is not the same as being defensive; instead, the researcher should be prepared to deal in a confident, competent manner with the questions that

EXHIBIT 25.19
Multiple-Bar Chart

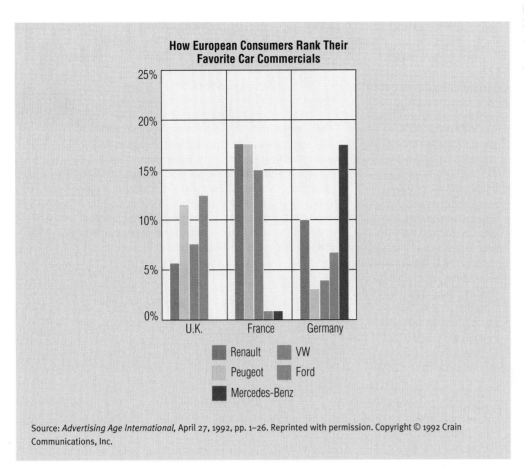

How European Consumers Rank Their Favorite Car Commercials

Legend: Renault, Peugeot, Mercedes-Benz, VW, Ford

Source: *Advertising Age International*, April 27, 1992, pp. 1–26. Reprinted with permission. Copyright © 1992 Crain Communications, Inc.

arise. Remember that even the most reliable and valid research project is worthless if the managers who must act on its results are not convinced of its importance.

As with written reports, a key to effective oral presentation is adapting to the audience. Delivering an hour-long formal speech when a ten-minute discussion is called for (or vice versa) will reflect poorly on both the presenter and the report.

Lecturing or reading to the audience is sure to impede communication at any level of formality. The presenter should refrain from reading prepared text word for word. By relying on brief notes, familiarity with the subject, and as much rehearsal as the occasion calls for, the presenter will foster better communication. He or she should avoid research jargon and use short, familiar words. The presenter should maintain eye contact with the audience and repeat the main points. Because the audience cannot go back and replay what the speaker has said, an oral presentation often is organized around a standard format: "Tell them what you are going to tell them, tell them, and tell them what you just told them."

Graphic and other visual aids can be as useful in an oral presentation as in a written one. Presenters can choose from a variety of media. Slides, overhead-projector acetates, and on-screen computer-generated graphics are useful for larger audiences. For smaller audiences, the researcher may put the visual aids on posters or flip charts. Another possibility is to make copies of the charts for each participant, possibly as a supplement to one of the other forms of presentation.

Whatever medium is chosen, each visual aid should be designed to convey a simple, attention-getting message that supports a point on which the audience should focus its thinking. As they do in written presentations, presenters should interpret graphics for the audience. The best slides are easy to read and interpret. Large typeface, multiple colors, bullets that highlight, and other artistic devices can enhance the readability of charts.

Using gestures during presentations also can help convey the message and make presentations more interesting. Here are some tips on how to gesture:[4]

- Open up your arms to embrace your audience. Keep your arms between your waist and shoulders.
- Drop your arms to your sides when not using them.

RESEARCHSNAPSHOT

Online Reports: Easy to Get, Easy to Ignore

A variety of commercially available computer programs provide detailed data on website usage. Among these titles are ClickTracks

Analytics, Fireclick, Sane Solutions, Urchin, WebSideStore, WebtrafficIQ, and WebTrends. These programs can gather details and generate reports about the behavior of various customer segments who visit a website (for example, new visitors, returning visitors, and subscribers to the company's e-mail newsletter). Behaviors that can be tracked include the links that visitors click on, the purchases they make, and the amount of time they spend at the website.

With reports so easy to obtain whenever they are needed or as frequently as every day, marketers can quickly accumulate mounds of data. But what do they do with the reports? Ideally, someone should be analyzing the reports and acting on the information. However, when reporters for *Network Computing* recently asked two hundred web administrators about their use of web analytics software, the responses indicated a widespread lack of follow-up. Almost all the administrators used the software, but not a single one could think of a change they had made to their websites in response to information they obtained from the resulting reports.

Source: Based on Jeffrey Rubin and Ravind Budhiraja, "Intelligence Services," Network Computing, July 7, 2005, downloaded from Business & Company Resource Center, http://galenet.galegroup.com; Joshua Kaufman, "Practical Usability Testing," Digital Web, February 13, 2006, http://www.digital-web.com, accessed April 2, 2006.

- Avoid quick and jerky gestures, which make you appear nervous. Hold gestures longer than you would in normal conversation.
- Vary gestures. Switch from hand to hand and at other times use both hands or no hands.
- Don't overuse gestures.

Some gestures are used to draw attention to points illustrated by visual aids. For these, gesturing with an open hand can seem more friendly and can even release tension related to nervousness. In contrast, a nervous speaker who uses a laser pointer may distract the audience as the pointer jumps around in the speaker's shaky hand.[5]

Reports on the Internet

Many clients want numerous employees to have access to research findings. One easy way to share data is to make executive summaries and reports available on a company Intranet. In addition, a company can use information technology on the Internet to design questionnaires, administer surveys, analyze data, and share the results in a presentation-ready format. Real-time data capture allows for beginning-to-end reporting. A number of companies offer fully web-based research management systems—for example, WebSurveyor's online solution for capturing and reporting research findings.

The Research Follow-Up

Research follow-up
Recontacting decision makers and/or clients after they have had a chance to read over a research report in order to determine whether additional information or clarification is necessary.

Research reports and oral presentations should communicate research findings so that managers can make business decisions. In many cases, the manager who receives the research report is unable to interpret the information and draw conclusions relevant to managerial decisions. For this reason, effective researchers do not treat the report as the end of the research process. They conduct a **research follow-up**, in which they recontact decision makers and/or clients after the latter have had a chance to read over the report. The purpose is to determine whether the researchers need to provide additional information or clarify issues of concern to management. Just as marketing research may help an organization learn about its customers' satisfaction, the research follow-up can help marketing research staffers ensure the satisfaction of their customers, marketing managers.

Summary

1. Discuss the research report from the perspective of the communications process. A research report is an oral or written presentation of research findings directed to a specific audience to accomplish a particular purpose. Report preparation is the final stage of the research project. It is important because the project can guide management decisions only if it is effectively communicated. The theory of communications emphasizes that the writer (communicator) must tailor the report (message) so that it will be understood by the manager (audience), who has a different field of experience.

2. Define the parts of a research report following a standard format. The consensus is that the format for a research report should include certain prefatory parts, the body of the report, and appended parts. The report format should be varied to suit the level of formality of the particular situation. The prefatory parts of a formal report include a title page, letters of transmittal and authorization, a table of contents, and a summary. The summary is the part of a report most often read and should include a brief statement of the objectives, results, conclusions, and (depending on the research situation) recommendations. The report body includes an introduction that gives the background and objectives, a statement of methodology, and a discussion of the results, their limitations, and appropriate conclusions and recommendations. The appendix includes various materials too specialized to appear in the body of the report.

3. Explain how to use tables for presenting numerical information. Tables present large amounts of numerical information in a concise manner. They are especially useful for presenting several pieces of information about each item discussed. Short tables are helpful in the body of the report; long tables are better suited for an appendix. Each table should include a number, title, stubheads and bannerheads, footnotes for any explanations or qualifications of entries, and source notes for data from secondary sources.

4. Summarize how to select and use the types of research charts. Charts present numerical data in a way that highlights their relationships. Each chart should include a figure number, title, explanatory legends, and a source note for secondary sources. Pie charts show the composition of a total (the parts that make up a whole). Line graphs show the relationship of a dependent variable (on the vertical axis) to an independent variable (horizontal axis). Most commonly, the independent variable is time. Bar charts show changes in a dependent variable at discrete intervals of the independent variable—for example, comparing one year with another or one subset of the population with another. Variants of these charts are useful for more complex situations.

5. Describe how to give an effective oral presentation. Most research projects are reported on orally as well as in writing, so the researcher needs to prepare an oral presentation. The presentation should defend the results without being defensive. The presentation must be tailored to the situation and the audience. The presenter should practice delivering the presentation in a natural way, without reading to the audience. Graphic aids are useful supplements when they are simple and easy to read. Gestures also add interest and emphasis.

6. Discuss the importance of Internet reporting and research follow-up. Posting a summary of results online gives clients ready access to that information. Some online survey software processes the data and displays results in a presentation-ready format. In the follow-up stage of a research project, the researchers recontact decision makers after submitting the report. This helps the researchers determine whether they need to provide further information or clarify any issues of concern to management.

Key Terms and Concepts

Communication process

Research report

Report format

Introduction section

Research methodology section

Results section

Conclusions and recommendations section

Graphic aids

Oral presentation

Research follow-up

Questions for Review and Critical Thinking

1. Why is it important to think of the research report from a communications perspective?
2. As a manager, what degree of formality would you want from your research department?
3. What types of tables might be used to describe some of the various statistical tests discussed in previous chapters?
4. What is the difference between a *basic marketing research paper* and *an applied market research report*?
5. What is a *pie chart?* What is a *bar chart?* When might one be preferable over the other?
6. What are some basic business research journals? Find some published research reports in these journals. How do they meet the standards set forth in this chapter?
7. What rules should be followed when preparing slides for computer-generated presentations?
8. **ETHICS** What ethical concerns arise when you prepare (or read) a report?
9. **ETHICS** A researcher working for Hi Time prepares a bar chart comparing the number of customers visiting two competing booths at a fashion trade show. One booth is the Hi Time booth, the other is for a competing company, So Cool. First, the chart is prepared as shown here:

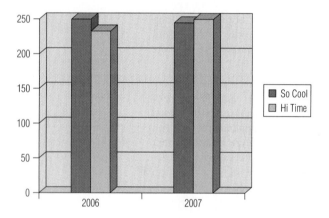

In preparing for a presentation to the Hi Time Board, the client tells the researcher that the chart doesn't seem to reflect the improvements made since 2006. Therefore, the researcher prepares the chart as shown here:

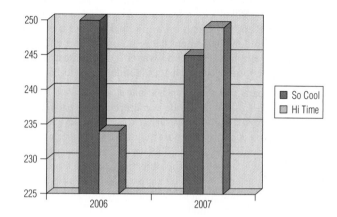

a. What has reformatting the bar chart accomplished?
b. Was it ethical for the client to ask for the bar chart to be redrawn?
c. Would it be ethical for the researcher to use the new chart in the presentation?

Research Activity

1. **'NET** Go to the Business & Company Resource Center which you can access through the publisher of this text (see www.thomsonedu.com/marketing/zikmund). Put "Starbucks" or "McDonald's" in the company search engine. Look at the news and articles for that company. Limit the search by using the word "report." Find one of the articles that actually presents some research reports, such as consumer reactions to a new product. Prepare power point slides that contain appropriate charts to present the results.

Case 25.1 Annenberg Public Policy Center

A recent study by the Annenberg Public Policy Center investigated one major area of marketing decisions: pricing practices.[6] Specifically, the study addressed consumer knowledge and attitudes about the practice of online retailers adjusting their prices according to customer characteristics, such as how frequently they buy from the retailer. For example, a website selling cameras charged different prices for the same model depending on whether the visitor to the site had previously visited sites that supply price comparisons. In general, charging different prices is called price discrimination and is legal unless it discriminates by race or sex or involves antitrust or price-fixing laws (such as two competitors agreeing to charge certain prices).

The Annenberg study consisted of telephone interviews conducted with a sample of 1,500 adults, screened to find persons who had used the Internet in the preceding thirty days. The questionnaire gathered demographic data and data about Internet usage. In addition, the interviewer read seventeen statements about basic laws and practices related to price discrimination and the targeting of consumers according to their shopping behaviors. Respondents were asked whether each of these statements was true or false. Case Exhibits 25.1–1 through 25.1–4 summarize some of the results from this study.

Questions

1. The information provided here is not detailed enough for a formal report, but assume that you are making an informal report in a preliminary stage of the reporting process. Which of these findings do you want to emphasize as your main points? Why?
2. Prepare a written summary of the findings, using at least two tables or charts.
3. Prepare two tables or charts that would be suitable to accompany an oral presentation of these results. Are they different from the visual aids you prepared for question 2? Why or why not?

CASE EXHIBIT 25.1-1 Selected Information about the Sample

Sex

Male	48%
Female	52%

Online Connection at Home

Dial-up connection only	31%
Cable modem (with/without dial-up)	18%
DSL (with/without dial-up)	25%
Cable or DSL with another method	13%
Don't know	4%
No connection at home	9%

Self-Ranked Expertise Navigating the Internet

Beginner	14%
Intermediate	40%
Advanced	34%
Expert	12%

Source: Joseph Turow, Lauren Feldman, and Kimberly Meltzer, "Open to Exploitation: American Shoppers Online and Offline," APPC report, June 2005, p. 15, downloaded at http://www.annenbergpublicpolicycenter.org.

CASE EXHIBIT 25.1-2 Responses to Selected Knowledge Questions

Statement	Response*		
	True	False	Don't Know
Companies today have the ability to follow my activity across many sites on the web.	**80%**	8%	12%
It is legal for an *online* store to charge different people different prices at the same time of day.	**38%**	29%	33%
By law, a site such as Expedia or Orbitz that compares prices on different airlines must include the lowest airline prices.	37%	**32%**	31%
It is legal for an *offline* store to charge different people different prices at the same time of day.	**29%**	42%	29%
When a website has a privacy policy, it means the site will not share my information with other websites or companies.	59%	**25%**	16%

*When the numbers do not add up to 100%, it is because of a rounding error. **Boldface** type indicates the correct answer.

Source: Joseph Turow, Lauren Feldman, and Kimberly Meltzer, "Open to Exploitation: American Shoppers Online and Offline," APPC report, June 2005, p. 20, downloaded at http://www.annenbergpublicpolicycenter.org. Accessed April 5, 2006.

CASE EXHIBIT 25.1-3 **Responses to Selected Attitude Questions**

	Response*			
Statement	Agree	Disagree	Neutral	Don't Know
It's okay if a store charges me a price based on what it knows about me.	8%	91%	—	1%
It's okay if an *online* store I use charges different people different prices for the same products during the same hour.	11%	87%	1%	1%
It would bother me to learn that other people pay less than I do for the same products.	76%	22%	1%	1%
It would bother me if websites I shop at keep detailed records of my buying behavior.	57%	41%	2%	1%
It's okay if a store I shop at frequently uses information it has about me to create a picture of me that improves the services it provides for me.	50%	47%	2%	1%

*When the numbers do not add up to 100%, it is because of a rounding error.

Source: Joseph Turow, Lauren Feldman, and Kimberly Meltzer, "Open to Exploitation: American Shoppers Online and Offline," APPC report, June 2005, p. 22, downloaded at http://www.annenbergpublicpolicycenter.org. Accessed April 7, 2006.

CASE EXHIBIT 25.1-4 **Predicting Knowledge Score from Selected Demographics**

	Unstandardized Regression Coefficient (B)	Standardized Regression Coefficient (β)
Education	0.630*	0.200
Income	0.383*	0.150
Self-perceived ability to navigate Internet	0.616*	0.149
Constant	2.687	
R^2	0.148	

*Significance <0.001 level.

Source: Joseph Turow, Lauren Feldman, and Kimberly Meltzer, "Open to Exploitation: American Shoppers Online and Offline," APPC report, June 2005, p. 29, downloaded at http://www.annenbergpublicpolicycenter.org. Accessed April 6, 2006.

A Final Note on Marketing Research

We began by drawing an analogy between research and a needle in a haystack. Hopefully, after reading and studying the material in this book, you can now understand and apply basic processes that help identify key information needs and turn raw data into intelligence. Thus, after sifting through a vast sea of information, this intelligence helps someone make a better decision, which, in turn, helps make someone's life better. Thus, marketing research is a very important and useful area of knowledge that can lead to meaningful skills. The set of cases that follow provide the reader with one last chance to gain experience through real-world applications of marketing research. If you are still hungry for more about marketing research, there are many more advanced topics that can increase your skills in one of the specialized areas of research!

Part 7
Comprehensive Cases with Computerized Databases

©MARK HARWOOD/ICONICA/GETTY IMAGES

CASE 1
Running the Numbers: Does It Pay?

CASE 2
Employees Federal Credit Union

CASE 3
University Van Pool

CASE 4
Values and the Automobile Market

CASE 5
Say It Ain't So! Is This the Real Thing?

CASE 6
TABH, INC., Automotive Consulting

CASE 7
Survey on Americans and Dietary Supplements

COMPREHENSIVE CASES

Case 1: Running the Numbers: Does It Pay?

Dr. William Ray, a research consultant, has received a government grant to fund research examining how aspects of a student's college experiences relate to his or her job performance. Senator B.G. Shot is being lobbied by his constituents that employers are discriminating against people who do not like math by giving them lower salaries. Senator Shot has obtained $50,000 to fund the project, and Dr. Ray has been awarded this government grant. The Senator hopes the research supported by the grant will help provide a basis to support the proposed legislation making discrimination against those people who do not like math illegal.

The research questions that this particular grant propose include:

RQ1: Does a student's liking of quantitative coursework in college affect his or her future earnings?

RQ2: Do people with an affinity for quantitative courses get promoted more quickly than those who do not?

Dr. Ray has gained the cooperation of a Fortune 500 service firm that employs over 20,000 employees across eight locations. The company allows Dr. Ray to survey employees who have been out of college for three years. Three hundred responses were obtained by sending an e-mail invitation to participate to approximately 1,000 employees who fit this profile. The e-mail provided a click-through questionnaire which directed respondents to a website where the survey was conducted. Each invitation was coded so that the actual respondents could be identified. Dr. Ray, however, kept this information confidential so the company could not identify any particular employee's response.

The following table describes the variables that were collected.

Variables Available from Company Records

Variable Name	Variable Type	Coding
PROM	Nominal indicating whether the employee has been promoted	1 = "Promoted" 0 = "Not Promoted"
GPA	Self-Reported GPA in Last Year of College	0 (lowest) to 4 (highest)
Sex	Nominal	1 = "Female" 0 = "Male"
School	Nominal	School Initials
Salary	Ratio	Actual annual salary from last year

Questions from Survey

	Coding	Strongly Disagree (1)	Disagree (2)	Neutral (3)	Agree (4)	Strongly Agree (5)
X1	The quantitative courses I took in school were the most useful courses.	☐	☐	☐	☐	☐
X2	Very few topics can be understood if you do not understand the arithmetic.	☐	☐	☐	☐	☐
X3	I hated going to math classes in college.	☐	☐	☐	☐	☐
X4	I learned a great deal from the quantitative projects assigned to me in college.	☐	☐	☐	☐	☐
X5	Students do not need to study quantitative topics in college to succeed in their careers.	☐	☐	☐	☐	☐

Please use the following items to describe your undergraduate college experience. For each pair of items, choose the check box closest to the adjective that best describes your experience.

Coding		(−3)	(−2)	(−1)	(0)	(1)	(2)	(3)	
S1	Dull	☐	☐	☐	☐	☐	☐	☐	Exciting
S2	Laborious	☐	☐	☐	☐	☐	☐	☐	Playful
S3	Stressful	☐	☐	☐	☐	☐	☐	☐	Relaxing
S4	Boring	☐	☐	☐	☐	☐	☐	☐	Fun
S5	Carefree	☐	☐	☐	☐	☐	☐	☐	Responsible

Questions:

1. Does this grant present Dr. Ray with an ethical dilemma?
2. Derive at least one hypothesis for each research question listed above.
3. Use the data that corresponds to this case to perform an adequate test of each hypothesis. Interpret the results.
4. Is there evidence supporting the discrimination claim? Explain.
5. List another hypothesis (unrelated to the research questions in the grant) that could be tested with this data.
6. Test that hypothesis.
7. Considering employees' attitudes about their college experience, does the amount of fun that students had in college or the degree to which they thought quantitative classes were a positive experience relate more strongly to salary?
8. Would the "problem" that led to the grant be a candidate for ethnographic research? Explain.

Case 2: Employees Federal Credit Union

(Download the data sets for this case from http://www. thomsonedu.com/marketing/zikmund or request them from your instructor.) Employees Federal Credit Union (EFCU) is the credit union for a Fortune 500 firm. Any employee of the organization is eligible for membership in the employees' credit union.

Over the past few years, the Employees Federal Credit Union has accumulated a large amount of surplus funds, which have been invested in certificates of deposit. It has also experienced a lower loan/share ratio than other credit unions of similar size. Because of these factors, the credit union's average earnings on its investments have slowly declined and its profit margins are being squeezed. The EFCU Board of Directors decided that a research project should be conducted to determine why its members are not borrowing money from the credit union. More specifically, the research project was mandated to answer the question of why members are borrowing money from other alternative sources instead of from the credit union.

In addition to the above, the EFCU Board of Directors expressed its desire to determine what the members' attitudes were toward the overall management and operations of the credit union. It was determined that the following questions should be addressed, as well:

- How informed is the membership about the services provided by the credit union?
- Are there any differences between members who live in the area of the firm's headquarters and members who live outside of the area in opinion toward borrowing funds and the services provided by the credit union?

RESEARCH OBJECTIVES

To respond to the questions raised by the board, the following objectives were developed. The research design was formulated to address each of the objectives stated below:

- To determine the reasons why people join the credit union
- To determine the reasons why members use other financial institutions when they need to borrow funds

- To measure member attitudes and beliefs about the proficiencies of credit union employees
- To determine whether there are any perceived differences between members who live in the area of the firm's headquarters and members who live elsewhere
- To determine member awareness of the services offered by the credit union
- To measure member attitudes and beliefs about how effectively the credit union is operated

RESEARCH DESIGN AND DATA COLLECTION METHOD

The research data were collected using a mail questionnaire survey. This technique was determined to be the best method for collecting the research data for the following reasons:

- The credit union members were widely dispersed geographically.
- The board wanted to minimize the cost of conducting the research.
- Several of the questions asked in the questionnaire were of a sensitive nature.
- The board had the flexibility of being able to wait for the survey results before taking any action.

A copy of the questionnaire used to gather the research data is provided in Case Exhibit 2.1. Most of the questions were designed as structured questions because of the variation in the educational backgrounds, job functions, and interests of the members surveyed. However, the respondents were given the flexibility to answer several key questions in an unstructured format. The Likert scale was principally used where attitude measurements were requested.

SAMPLING PROCEDURES

The population of the EFCU is well-defined; consequently, a simple random sample of the membership was selected. A sample size of 300 was calculated using the estimated population standard deviation

CASE EXHIBIT 2.1 EFCU Member Opinion Survey

1. Are you currently a member of the Employees Federal Credit Union (EFCU)?
   Yes ( )   No ( )

   If no, please have the member of your household who is a member of the EFCU complete the questionnaire. If no one in your household is a member, please return the questionnaire in the enclosed prepaid envelope.

2. Why did you join the credit union? (Check as many answers as are applicable.)
   ___ Convenience
   ___ Higher interest rates on my savings than other financial institutions pay
   ___ More personal than other facilities
   ___ Wanted a readily available source for borrowing money
   ___ Advertisements prompted me to join
   ___ Other—please explain: _____
   _____

Statements 3 through 6 ask for your opinion of the credit union employees. Check the response that best describes your rating of the credit union employees in each category. Please check only one response for each statement.

3. The credit union employees are courteous.

Strongly disagree	Disagree	Uncertain	Agree	Strongly agree
( )	( )	( )	( )	( )

4. The credit union employees are helpful.

Strongly disagree	Disagree	Uncertain	Agree	Strongly agree
( )	( )	( )	( )	( )

5. The credit union employees are professional.

Strongly disagree	Disagree	Uncertain	Agree	Strongly agree
( )	( )	( )	( )	( )

6. The credit union employees are always available.

Strongly disagree	Disagree	Uncertain	Agree	Strongly agree
( )	( )	( )	( )	( )

7. What is your opinion about the rates the credit union is paying on its share (members/savings) accounts?
   A. Very high ___   B. High ___   C. Average ___
   D. Low ___   E. Very low ___   F. No opinion ___

8. What is your opinion about the rates the credit union is charging its members to borrow funds?
   A. Very high ___   B. High ___   C. Average ___
   D. Low ___   E. Very low ___   F. No opinion ___

9. How often do you receive a financial statement of your account activity?

Too often	Very often	About right	Not often enough	Never
( )	( )	( )	( )	( )

10. How would you rate the accuracy of your statements?

Excellent	Good	Fair	Poor
( )	( )	( )	( )

11. Are they easy to understand?
    Yes ( ) No ( )

12. Do you feel that the credit union maintains your account information in a confidential manner?
    Yes ( ) No ( )

The questions in the next set are important in determining how effective the credit union has been in communicating its different services to the members. Please answer each question honestly—remember, there are no right or wrong answers.
   Circle the response that best describes your awareness of the services offered by the credit union.

   Circle 1—If you were aware of the service and have used it.
   Circle 2—If you were aware of the service but have not used it.
   Circle 3—If you did not know this service was offered by the credit union.

(Continued)

CASE EXHIBIT 2.1 EFCU Member Opinion Survey (*Continued*)

	Aware and Have Used	Aware but Have Not Used	Unaware of Service
13. Regular share accounts	1	2	3
14. Special subaccounts	1	2	3
15. Christmas club accounts	1	2	3
16. Individual retirement accounts	1	2	3
17. MasterCard credit cards	1	2	3
18. Signature loans	1	2	3
19. New car loans	1	2	3
20. Late model car loans	1	2	3
21. Older model car loans	1	2	3
22. Household goods/appliance loans	1	2	3
23. Recreational loans	1	2	3
24. Share collateralized loans	1	2	3
25. IRA loans	1	2	3
26. Line of credit loans	1	2	3

27. Do you currently have a loan with the credit union?
Yes ( )   No ( )

28. During the past year, have you borrowed money from a bank or other lending source other than the credit union?
Yes ( )   No ( )
If no, go to question 30.

29. Why did you go to a source other than the credit union?
___ My loan application at the credit union was not approved.
___ The credit union did not offer this type of credit.
___ I found better loan rates elsewhere.
___ I have an established credit line elsewhere.
___ I prefer to use a local financial institution.
___ Other: _____

For statements 30 through 34, check the response that best describes your feelings about the statements. Check only one response for each statement given.

30. The credit union's loan rates are lower than those offered by other institutions.

Strongly disagree	Disagree	Uncertain	Agree	Strongly agree
( )	( )	( )	( )	( )

31. The credit union personnel will keep my personal financial information confidential.

Strongly disagree	Disagree	Uncertain	Agree	Strongly agree
( )	( )	( )	( )	( )

32. The credit union is prompt in processing loan applications.

Strongly disagree	Disagree	Uncertain	Agree	Strongly agree
( )	( )	( )	( )	( )

33. The current financial services provided by the credit union meet the needs of its members.

Strongly disagree	Disagree	Uncertain	Agree	Strongly agree
( )	( )	( )	( )	( )

34. The loan applications used by the credit union are simple and easy to complete.

Strongly disagree	Disagree	Uncertain	Agree	Strongly agree
( )	( )	( )	( )	( )

35. Which of the services provided by the credit union do you like best?

_____

36. Which of the services provided by the credit union do you like least?

_____

37. Overall, how do you feel the credit union is being managed and operated?
A. Excellent___   B. Good___   C. Average___
D. Poor___   E. Very poor___   F. No opinion___

(Continued)

CASE EXHIBIT 2.1 EFCU Member Opinion Survey (*Continued*)

38. Do you live in the headquarters area?
    Yes ( )   No ( )
    If yes, go to question 40.
39. Do you feel the credit union meets your needs as well as those of members who live in the headquarters area?
    Yes ( )   No ( )
    If no, please explain:_____
    _____

40. If you were managing the credit union, what changes would you make and what additional services, if any, would you provide?
    _____
    _____
    _____
    _____
    _____
    _____

We sincerely appreciate the time and effort you made in completing this questionnaire. Thank you for your help.

---

based on the responses from 15 members to question 37 of the questionnaire. Question 37 was used because it capsulized the essence of the research project.

The random numbers used in making the selection of the sampling units were generated with the help of a personal computer. The sampling frame used was the January 31 trial balance listing of the EFCU membership. According to the sampling frame, EFCU had 3,531 members on that date. As a result, the 300 random numbers were generated within the range of 1 to 3,531. Each random number was matched to a corresponding number in the sampling frame, and those individuals were selected to receive copies of the survey questionnaire.

FIELDWORK

Most of the fieldwork for the research project, including all of the editing and coding of the survey data, was performed by the Supervisory Committee Chairperson. The following is a list of the (much-appreciated) assistance received during the field procedures:

- Bob Perkins obtained a copy of the most currently available listing of the membership of the EFCU.
- The payroll department prepared mailing labels for all the members in the sample who were having withholding for the credit union taken out of their payroll checks.
- The credit union clerks obtained the addresses and prepared mailing labels for all the remaining individuals selected in the sample.
- Administrative assistants helped copy and collate the survey questionnaires and prepare them for mailing.
- Ron Walker mailed all of the survey questionnaires.

The survey data from the structured questions were coded based on classifications established by the researcher. The codes were input into a series of databases using an IBM personal computer and a statistical software package.

Of the 125 returned questionnaires, two were not included in the survey results. One of the questionnaires was returned without the first two pages attached, and the other questionnaire appeared to be deliberately falsified; not only were all the responses on this

questionnaire at the extremes, but a number of contradictions were noted as well.

ADDITIONAL INFORMATION

Several of the questions will require the use of a computerized database. Each variable name is represented by its question number. Q1 is the variable name for question 1, "Are you a member of the Employees Federal Credit Union?" Q2 is the variable name for question 2, etc. Case Exhibit 2.2 presents the coding. Your instructor will provide information about obtaining the EFCU's data set if this material is part of the case assignment. (The data are available in SPSS or Excel format.)

CASE EXHIBIT 2.2 Codes for Questionnaire

strongly disagree = 1, strongly agree = 5
very high = 1, very low = 5, no opinion = 6
too often = 1, never = 5
excellent = 1, poor = 4
excellent = 1, very poor = 5, no answer = 6
yes = 1, no = 2, no answer = 3
aware and have used = 1, unaware = 3

Questions
1. Evaluate the research objectives.
2. Evaluate the research design in light of the stated research objectives.
3. Using the computerized database, obtain simple frequencies for the answers to each question (the answers to the open-ended questions are not included in the database).
4. Perform the appropriate cross-tabulations.
5. Perform the appropriate univariate and bivariate statistical tests after you develop hypotheses for these particular tests.

This case was prepared by John H. Walkup, senior project manager, Mapco, Inc.

Case 3: University Van Pool

Oklahoma State University is a major university. Its main campus in Stillwater is located an equal distance (approximately 75 miles) from Oklahoma City and Tulsa, the state's two largest metropolitan areas. Almost 20,000 students are enrolled in classes on the Stillwater campus.

Because many OSU students commute from Oklahoma City (approximately 500) or Tulsa (approximately 700), it was suggested that a van pooling system could be a viable operation. The basic concept was to have central locations in both Tulsa and Oklahoma City where students could board vans (or buses) and ride to the university campus. Students would be dropped off at the same location on the return trip. A commuter student would be the driver of the van, which would substantially reduce the cost of operating the service. Case Exhibit 3.1 provides additional information about the cost associated with operating this service.

THE SURVEY RESEARCH PROJECT

A telephone survey was conducted to determine how many OSU students were regular commuters and to estimate the demand for the commuting service. The questionnaire used in the study appears in Case Exhibit 3.2. The student directory served as a sampling frame. Initially, pages from the directory were randomly selected. For each page selected as a primary sampling unit, an interviewer was instructed to call every name that listed Tulsa or Oklahoma City as the student's address. The first question on the questionnaire determined whether the student was actually commuting. This resulted in a sample size of 224 commuting students.

The data from the survey were edited and coded to be analyzed using the SPSS computer program. The variables from the data set entitled Commuter are listed in Case Exhibit 3.3. A missing value is represented by a period. (The data are also available in Microsoft Excel.)

Questions

1. Evaluate the research design.
2. What variables in the available data set will be most important to solve the problem? Identify which of these are dependent variables and which are independent variables.
3. Using the computerized data base called Commuter, demonstrate that you can perform descriptive analyses such as calculation of frequency distributions and calculation of means.
4. Using cross-tabulation analysis, determine which market segment is most likely to use the van pool.
5. Is the van pool economically feasible in Tulsa? In Oklahoma City?
6. Perform an in-depth interview with a commuter student at your local university. Choose a student who has to commute over fifty miles or at least one hour to get to school. Begin by having the student discuss his or her feelings about the commute and why it is he or she is willing to do this rather than take some option at another school or via the Internet. Also, get his or her reaction to a "van" approach such as discussed here. How do his or her comments shape your opinion of this idea?

CASE EXHIBIT 3.1 **Cost Associated with Van-Pooling**

An example of a cost analysis on a per-trip basis for vans is presented below. This analysis assumes that a van can carry fifteen people but on the average will be carrying ten people (two-thirds load factor) plus the driver. We also assume that we don't have to pay for the driver; in other words, he or she is a student and will drive instead of paying for the ride.

Cost of Used Van	$20,000		
Less Resale Value	$4,000		
Net Cost	$16,000		
Useful life of van (miles)		100,000	
Net cost per mile			$0.16
Gas costs per gallon	$2.90		
Mileage of van (mpg)		10	
Cost of gas per mile			$0.29
Maintenance per mile			$0.25
Total Costs/Mile			$0.70
Miles per round trip		150	
Cost per trip			$105.00
Average number of passengers		10	
Cost per passenger			$10.50

CASE EXHIBIT 3.2 Marketing Research Questionnaire: Commuting Service to Stillwater, Oklahoma

Hello, I'm _____[your name]_____. We are conducting a survey to find out if it would be feasible for OSU to establish a van or bus commuting service for students commuting to school in Stillwater.

1. Do you commute to OSU to attend classes? _____Yes _____No
    [If yes, continue with the interview.
    If no, terminate and try again.]

2. How many times a week do you travel to Stillwater to attend classes?
    _____times per week.

3. How do you get to Stillwater—drive your own car, pool with other students, or some other method?
    __1__ Drives own car
    __2__ Rides in pool
    __3__ Other

    [If student rides in a pool]
4. What percentage of the time are you the driver in your car pool? _____%

5. What mileage does your car get on the road? _____ mpg

6. What do you think is your total cost per month to commute to OSU? $_____

   Two alternative methods available for providing a service to OSU are providing a van or a bus. A bus would be similar to riding commercially in that it would depart early in the morning to be at school by 8:00 A.M. and return after 12:00 noon. A second bus would depart so as to arrive by 12:30 P.M. and would return after 5:00 P.M. A licensed driver would be hired by the university to drive the bus. A van would have similar departure times, but arrangements would be made so that the commuters would do the driving on a rotating basis.
   I am going to make a number of statements about these possible methods of commuting and would like you to indicate your agreement or disagreement with each of the statements. When I read each statement, I would like you to either strongly agree, agree, slightly agree, indicate no feeling, slightly disagree, disagree, or strongly disagree.
   [Go over this with the respondent to be sure he or she understands what you are trying to do.]

7. The inconvenience of commuting by bus or van outweighs the advantages.
    __7__SA __6__A __5__SA __4__N __3__SD __2__D __1__SD

8. I could use the time riding over to Stillwater to study.
    __7__SA __6__A __5__SA __4__N __3__SD __2__D __1__SD

9. I would rather be able to come and go as I please.
    __7__SA __6__A __5__SA __4__N __3__SD __2__D __1__SD

10. Having to wait for the van or bus coming home would take too much time.
    __7__SA __6__A __5__SA __4__N __3__SD __2__D __1__SD

11. I don't like riding buses because they are so uncomfortable.
    __7__SA __6__A __5__SA __4__N __3__SD __2__D __1__SD

12. Riding a van would be better than riding a bus.
    __7__SA __6__A __5__SA __4__N __3__SD __2__D __1__SD

13. If I were in a van pool, I would be willing to do some of the driving.
    __7__SA __6__A __5__SA __4__N __3__SD __2__D __1__SD

14. Having to drive to the pickup point is too much of a bother.
    __7__SA __6__A __5__SA __4__N __3__SD __2__D __1__SD

15. Driving myself is getting too expensive.
    __7__SA __6__A __5__SA __4__N __3__SD __2__D __1__SD

16. I would worry too much about the dependability of a van or bus.
    __7__SA __6__A __5__SA __4__N __3__SD __2__D __1__SD

(Continued)

17. I could save money by taking a van or bus.
    _7_ SA _6_ A _5_ SA _4_ N _3_ SD _2_ D _1_ SD

18. If a bus were available, I would use it.
    _7_ SA _6_ A _5_ SA _4_ N _3_ SD _2_ D _1_ SD

19. If a van were available, I would use it.
    _7_ SA _6_ A _5_ SA _4_ N _3_ SD _2_ D _1_ SD

20. I don't like riding a van because they are so uncomfortable.
    _7_ SA _6_ A _5_ SA _4_ N _3_ SD _2_ D _1_ SD

21. I would be concerned about the driving by others in a van.
    _7_ SA _6_ A _5_ SA _4_ N _3_ SD _2_ D _1_ SD

22. Taking a van or bus is too much of a hassle.
    _7_ SA _6_ A _5_ SA _4_ N _3_ SD _2_ D _1_ SD

Finally, I have some questions about you as a student. This survey is strictly confidential, and your name will never be used in any results.

23. What is your class status? _1_ Fresh _2_ Soph _3_ Jr _4_ Sr _5_ Grad

24. Do you consider yourself full or part time? _1_ Full _2_ Part

25. Are you also employed? _1_ Yes _2_ No

    [If yes]
26. Full or part time? _1_ Full _2_ Part

27. Your age? _____

28. Sex _1_ Male _2_ Female [You should be able to figure that out.]

29. Are you married? _1_ Yes _2_ No

30. How are you financing your education?
    _1_ Own funds _2_ Parents _3_ Scholarship _4_ GI Bill _5_ Other

31. What percentage savings would you need to realize before you would be interested in riding a bus?
    ____ % ____ Wouldn't ride a bus.

32. What percentage savings would you need to realize before you would be interested in riding a van?
    ____ % ____ Wouldn't ride a van.

Thank you very much for your time in answering this survey.

CASE EXHIBIT 3.3 Commuter Data Set Variables

ID	Identification number	STATUS	1 = freshman, 5 = grad student
—	Question 1 not coded	FULLTIME	1 = full time, 2 = part time
FREQ	Frequency per week (Question 2)	EMPLOYED	1 = yes, 2 = no
METHOD	1 = own car, 2 = pool, 3 = other	AGE	Age
PDRIVE	% drive own car	SEX	1 = male, 2 = female
MILEAGE	Car mileage, mpg	MARRIED	1 = yes, 2 = no
ESTCOST	Estimated cost per month	FINANCE	1 = own, 2 = parents, 3 = school,
INCONV	Inconvenience		4 = GI bill, 5 = other
STUDY	I could study	PSAVBUS	% savings bus
COMEGO	Come and go	RBUS	1 = wouldn't ride bus at all
TIME	Too much time	PSAVVAN	% savings van
BUSCOMF	Bus is uncomfortable	RVAN	1 = wouldn't ride van at all
VANBUS	Van better than bus	ASAVBUS*	Amount bus savings needed
DRIVEV	Would drive van	ASAVVAN	Amount van savings needed
PICKUP	Pickup is a bother	GASCOST	Computed gas cost
EXPENSE	Driving is expensive	DIFF	Estimate − computed gas cost
DEPEND	Worry about dependability	COSTT	Cost per trip
SAVE	I could save money	BUSSAVT	Bus savings needed per trip
USEBUS	I would use a bus	VANSAVT	Van savings needed per trip
USEVAN	I would use a van	MAXBUS	Maximum price for bus
VANCOMF	Van is uncomfortable	MAXVAN	Maximum price for van
CONCERN	Concern about drivers	VRIDER	Van rider; 1 = yes, 0 = no
HASSLE	Van or bus too much hassle		

*Variables from the beginning of the list through RVAN were taken directly from the raw data on the questionnaire. The rest of the variables were calculated from the original variables as follows:

ASAVBUS	= PSAVBUS × ESTCOST
ASAVVAN	= PSAVVAN × ESTCOST
GASCOST	= FREQ × PDRIVE/100 × 52/12 × 150 ×1.25/MILEAGE
DIFF	= ESTCOST − GASCOST
COSTT	= ESTCOST/(FREQ × 52/12)
BUSSAVT	= ASAVBUS/(FREQ × 52/12)
VANSAVT	= ASAVVAN/(FREQ × 52/12)
MAXBUS	= COSTT − BUSSAVT
MAXVAN	= COSTT − VANSAVT

IF MAXVAN>4.5 THEN VRIDER = 1, ELSE IF MAXVAN ≠ 1 THEN VRIDER = 2
GASCOST is an estimate of what the marginal cost of the trip to Stillwater from Tulsa or Oklahoma City and back would be for gasoline alone. It assumes a gasoline price of $2.90 per gallon and a 150-mile round trip (75 miles to the pick-up location in the heart of each city).

This case was prepared by Clifford E. Young, University of Colorado—Denver, and William G. Zikmund.

Case 4: Values and the Automobile Market

(Download the data sets for this case from http://www.thomsonedu.com/marketing/zikmund or request them from your instructor.) In the last decade, the luxury car segment became one of the most competitive in the automobile market. Many American consumers who purchase luxury cars prefer imports from Germany and Japan.

A marketing vice president with General Motors once commented, "Import-committed buyers have been frustrating to us." This type of thinking has led industry analysts to argue that to successfully compete in the luxury car segment, U.S. carmakers need to develop a better understanding of the consumers so that they can better segment the market and better position their products via more effective advertising. Insight into the foreign-domestic luxury car choice may result from examining owners' personal values in addition to their evaluations of car attributes, because luxury cars, like many other conspicuously consumed luxury products, may be purchased mainly for value-expressive reasons.

Industry analysts believe it would be important to assess whether personal values of consumers could be used to explain ownership of

American, German, and Japanese luxury cars. Further, they believe they should also assess whether knowledge of owners' personal values provides any additional information useful in explaining ownership of American, German, and Japanese luxury cars beyond that obtained from their evaluations of the cars' attributes.

Personal values are likely to provide insights into reasons for ownership of luxury cars for at least two reasons. First, Americans have always had a very personal relationship with their cars and have used them as symbols of their self-concept. For instance, people who value a *sense of accomplishment* are quite likely to desire a luxury car that they feel is an appropriate symbol of their achievement, whereas people who value *fun, enjoyment, and excitement* are likely to desire a luxury car that they perceive as fun and exciting to drive. An advertiser trying to persuade the former segment to purchase a luxury car should position the car as a status symbol that will help its owners demonstrate their accomplishments to others. Similarly, an advertiser trying to persuade the latter segment to purchase a luxury car should position the car as a fun and exciting car to drive. In other words, effective advertising shows consumers how purchasing a given product will help them achieve their valued state, because brands tied to values will be perceived more favorably than brands that deliver more mundane benefits.

Second, when a market is overcrowded with competing brands offering very similar options—as is the case with the luxury car market—consumers are quite likely to choose between brands on the basis of value-expressive considerations.

METHOD

Data were collected via a mail survey sent to 498 consumers chosen at random from a list obtained from a syndicated research company located in an affluent county in a southern state. The list contained names of people who had purchased either a luxury American car (Cadillac or Lincoln Mercury), a luxury German car (Mercedes or BMW), or a luxury Japanese car (Infiniti or Lexus) within the last year. A cover letter explained that the survey was part of an academic research project. People were asked to return the questionnaires anonymously to a university address (a postage-paid envelope was provided with each survey). Beyond an appeal to help the researchers, respondents were not offered any other incentive to complete the surveys. Of the 498 questionnaires originally sent, 17 were returned by the post office as undeliverable. One hundred fifty-five completed surveys were received, for a response rate of 32.2 percent.

The Survey Instrument

The survey included questions on (1) various issues that people consider when purchasing new cars, (2) importance of car attributes, (3) importance of different values, and (4) demographics (sex, age, education, and family income). Questions relating to the issues that people consider when purchasing new cars were developed through initial interviews with consumers and were measured with a 7-point

Likert scale with end anchors of "strongly agree" and "strongly disagree." (See Case Exhibit 4.1.) A list of 12 car attributes was developed from the initial interviews with consumers and by consulting *Consumer Reports*. (See Case Exhibit 4.2.) The importance of each attribute was measured with a 7-point numerical scale with end points labeled "very important" and "very unimportant." The List of Values (LOV) scale in Case Exhibit 4.3 was used to measure the importance of values. Respondents were asked to rate each of the eight values (we combined fun, enjoyment, and excitement into one value) on a 7-point numerical scale with end points labeled "very important" and "very unimportant."

The Sample

Of the 155 respondents in the sample, 58 (37.4 percent) owned an American luxury car, 38 (24.5 percent) owned a European luxury car, and 59 (38.1 percent) owned a Japanese luxury car. The majority of the sample consisted of older (85 percent were 35 years of age or above), more educated (64 percent were college graduates), and economically well-off (87.2 percent earned $65,000 or more) consumers.

THE CODE BOOK

Case Exhibit 4.4 lists the SPSS variable names and identifies codes for these variables. (Note that this data set is also available in Microsoft Excel.)

ADDITIONAL INFORMATION

Several of the questions will require the use of a computerized database. Your instructor will provide information about obtaining the VALUES data set if the material is part of the case assignment.

CASE EXHIBIT 4.1 **Issues That Consumers Consider When Buying Luxury Atomobiles**

Having a luxury car is a major part of my fun and excitement.[a] (Issue 1)

Owning a luxury car is a part of "being good to myself." (Issue 2)

When I was able to buy my first luxury car, I felt a sense of accomplishment. (Issue 3)

I enjoy giving my friends advice about luxury cars. (Issue 4)

Getting a good deal when I buy a luxury car makes me feel better about myself. (Issue 5)

I seek novelty and I am willing to try new innovations in cars. (Issue 6)

I tend to buy the same brand of the car several times in a row. (Issue 7)

I tend to buy from the same dealer several times in a row. (Issue 8)

I usually use sources of information such as *Consumer Reports* in deciding on a car. (Issue 9)

I usually visit three or more dealerships before I buy a car. (Issue 10)

I would read a brochure or watch a video about defensive driving. (Issue 11)

When buying a new luxury car, my family's opinion is very important to me. (Issue 12)

My family usually accompanies me when I am shopping for a new luxury car. (Issue 13)

I usually rely upon ads and salespersons for information on cars. (Issue 14)

I usually rely upon friends and acquaintances for information on cars. (Issue 15)

When shopping for a car, it is important that the car dealer make me feel at ease. (Issue 16)

Most of my friends drive luxury import cars. (Issue 17)

Most of my friends drive luxury domestic cars. (Issue 18)

I think celebrity endorsers in ads influence people's choices of luxury cars. (Issue 19)

I would not buy a luxury car if I felt that my debt level is higher than usual. (Issue 20)

[a] Note: Subjects' responses were measured with 1 as "strongly agree" and 7 as "strongly disagree."

CASE EXHIBIT 4.2 **Car Attributes**

Attribute	Code	Attribute	Code
Comfort	Comfort	Low maintenance cost	Lomc
Safety	Safety	Reliability	Rely
Power	Power	Warranty	Warrant
Speed	Speed	Nonpolluting	Nonpol
Styling	Styling	High gas mileage	Gasmle
Durability	Durabil	Speed of repairs	Repairs

CASE EXHIBIT 4.3 **List of Values**

Value	Code	Value	Code
Fun-Enjoyment-Excitement	Fun	Sense of accomplishment	Accomp
Sense of belonging	Belong	Warm relationship	Warm
Being well respected	Respect	Security	Security
Self-fulfillment	Selfful	Self-respect	Selfres

CASE EXHIBIT 4.4 **List of Variables and Computer Codes**

ID—Identification number

AGE (categories are 2 = 35 years and under, 3 = 36–45 yrs, 4 = 46–55 yrs, 5 = 56–65 yrs, 6 = 65+ yrs)

SEX (1 = male, 0 = female)

EDUC—Education (1 = less than high school, 2 = high school grad, 3 = some college, 4 = college grad, 5 = graduate degree)

INCOME (1 = less than $35,000, 2 = $35–50,000, 3 = $50–65,000, 4 = $65,000+)

CAR—Type of luxury car (American car, European car, Japanese car)

ISSUES—The sequence of issues listed in Case Exhibit 4.1. (Strongly agree = 1; strongly disagree = 7)

ATTRIBUTES—The sequence of car attributes listed in Case Exhibit 4.2. (Very important to you = 1; very unimportant to you = 7)

VALUES—The sequence of values listed in Case Exhibit 4.3. (Very important = 1; very unimportant = 7)

Questions

1. Is the sampling method adequate? Is the attitude measuring scale sound? Explain.
2. Using the computerized database with a statistical software package, calculate the means of the three automotive groups for the values variables. Do any of the values variables show significant differences between American, Japanese, and European car owners?
3. Are there any significant differences on importance of attributes?
4. Write a short statement interpreting the results of this research.

Advanced Questions

5. Are any of the value scale items highly correlated?
6. Should multivariate analysis be used to understand the data?

Case materials based on research by Ajay Sukhdial and Goutam Chakraborty, Oklahoma State University.

Case 5: Say It Ain't So! Is This the Real Thing?

INTRODUCTION

David Ortega is the lead researcher for an upscale restaurant group hoping to add another chain that would compete directly with the upscale Smith and Wollensky restaurants (http://www.smithandwollensky.com). The average check for a customer at Smith and Wollensky is approximately $80 to $90.[1] Whenever a new venture of this type is planned, one has to wonder whether there are enough customers willing to pay premium prices given the large number of lesser priced alternatives. In fact, Smith and Wollensky is considering opening a lesser priced "Grill" that would be positioned so that the average customer check would be about half that of the original. What is it that people are willing to pay for and what sacrifices can be made to deliver a satisfying if not luxurious experience? How can he create a unique experience at a lower price? These are the questions facing David Ortega.

[1]MacNealy, Jeremy (2006), "Smith and Wollensky on the Grill," The Motley Fool, http://www.fool.com/News/mft/2006/mft06040425.htm, accessed April 28, 2006.

RESEARCH APPROACH

After considering how to study the issue, David decides a qualitative research approach will be useful. He hopes to develop a deep understanding of how the fine dining experience offers value—and perhaps some insights into what intangibles create value for consumers in general. After considering the different options, he decides on a phenomenological approach. The primary tool of investigation is conversational interviewing. David plans to enter into casual conversations with businesspeople in the lounge of the downtown Ritz Carlton. He begins the conversation by commenting on the wine he

is sipping—something like, "It isn't bad, but it's hard to believe they get $14 for a glass of this stuff."

RESULTS

Two weeks later, David has conducted "conversations" with five consumers. He found them very willing and free to talk about the things they indulge in. He develops a field log of notes from the consumers' comments. The notes are recorded verbatim.[2] The following field notes are highlighted:

Respondent	Date/Time	Text
Joe, wm, 55, attorney	12/5/06 – 10:15 PM	Well, wine doesn't have to be expensive to be good. Beyond some basic price point . . . maybe $12 a bottle . . . I find a lot of good wines. But, the wine has to fit the situation. It has to add something. A fake Rolex will tell time; but a real Rolex tells you about you. I don't mind paying for something that's unique—even though it might not be my cup of tea. Chateau Masur is like that. It's from Lebanon! It isn't always elegant or delicious, but it is always real. You always know it comes from some place very unique and is made under the most trying circumstances.
Sally, hf, 45, medical sales	12/7/06 – 5:45 PM	We pay too much for a lot of stuff though. I like things to be genuine. When you ask for crab you get crab—not Krab with a "K." It's made of fish you know!
		. . .
		I love old neighborhood Italian restaurants. They aren't always expensive. But, they have character. I think that it is very easy to spoil. I might not want a checkered red and white table cloth at home, but the Italian restaurant has to have one. I have to smell the garlic from the parking lot. And, that cheap Chianti, the kind with the basket cradle—it had better be from Italy—it tastes sooo good there. You know, you could pay more, but a nice dinner there with a couple of friends is worth a lot.
		You know, the people who make great wine or who have great restaurants kind of luck into it. I don't think they really ever sent out a survey asking what the restaurant or the wine should be like. I think they said I am going to make this the way that I want it to be . . . and it just happens to be right! They are so committed to the product that it works—no matter the price. But commitment like that costs a little more usually—although they aren't in it for the money.
Hebert, wm, 40, oil executive	12/8/06 – 11:00 PM	How old is it? The older it is, the more it is worth—yeah! I like this French wine that has "depuis 1574," maybe its name is Hugel (trying to recall). Imagine the same family running that company for hundreds of years. I like to think about the family in the vineyards—the old man on a tractor with his sons running around the sides. Their kids are hanging around the barn.
		. . .
		You know, you can buy cheap things and get cheated too. We are free to be cheated at any price point! (laughter) I remember bringing home a bottle of "Louisiana Hot Sauce." Man, that stuff didn't have any heat to it at all. When I looked at the bottle, do you know where it was from? . . . Man, it was from Tennessee . . . can you believe that, Louisiana Hot Sauce from Tennessee!! What a scam.
		. . . .
		When I buy something nice, I want it to be real. Burgundy should be from Burgundy. Bordeaux should be from Bordeaux. Champagne should be from Champagne—not Texas or California! (laughter) Because I know in Champagne, they know how to make Champagne—sparkling wine. They have perfected the methods over hundreds of years. A good glass of Champagne is worth what you pay!
Angela, bf, 60, insurance executive	12/9/06 – 6:45 PM	Look at this hotel . . . when you just look at the price you think 'this is crazy!' But, look at the attention to detail. Cleaning the floor is a production. Have you noticed the way they turn down your bed? Taking care of the plants is serious business to these people. I've stayed at a place like this in Florida—I loved it. At first, I couldn't put my finger on it. Then, it hit me. The place smelled like Florida. They have a way of giving everything the smell of sweet grass and citrus. It's terrific. Another one in California smelled of sandalwood and cypress. You have to be willing to pay more for people that care so much about what they do. Maybe that's your wine? Those smells make me think of those special places. When I drink a wine, I think about where it comes from too.
Burt, wm, 35, sales	12/9/06 – 9:30 PM	It's okay for something to be cheap . . . even fake! As long as I know it's fake. I've got three fake Rolexes. This one looks pretty good . . . looks genuine . . . but look at the way the second hand moves . . . it's jumping. A real one wouldn't do that!!
		I ate with this guy the other night who sent back a bottle of wine after ordering it. When the waiter pulled the cork, it didn't have Domaine Mas Blanc written on it—that's the name of the wine. He said, "How do I know it is real?" You know, he was right. When you spend $80 for a bottle, you want the real stuff. But, if you spend $10 for a bottle of wine in a restaurant, who the hell cares?

---

[2]For more comments along this same line, see Beverland, M. (2006), "The Real Thing: Branding Authenticity in the Luxury Wine Trade," Journal of Business Research, 59 (Feb), 251-258; Beverland, M. (2005), "Crafting Brand Authenticity: The Case of Luxury Wines," Journal of Management Studies, 42 (July), 103-129; and Wolff, C. (2005), "Blending High Style and Authenticity," Lodging Hospitality, 61 (11/1), 72-76.

RESULTS

David decides to use a word count to try to identify the main themes. Hopefully, these themes can help clarify the business problem. Perhaps if the information can't answer the questions above, it will point him in the right direction. Whatever the case, David feels the project has helped him better understand the total value proposition offered by restaurants, wines, hotels, and other products.

Questions:

1. Comment on the research approach. Do you feel it was an appropriate choice?

2. **ETHICS** David did not inform these respondents that he was doing marketing research during these conversations. Why do you think he withheld this information and was appropriate to do so?

3. **'NET** Using the Internet, try to identify at least three restaurants that Smith and Wollensky competes with and three with whom the new S&W Grill may compete.

4. Try to interpret the discussions above. You may use one of the approaches discussed in the text. What themes should be coded? What themes occur most frequently? Can the different themes be linked together to form a unit of meaning?

5. What is the result of this research? What should David report back to the restaurant group?

Case 6: TABH, INC., Automotive Consulting

(Download the data sets for this case from http://www. thomsonedu.com/marketing/zikmund or request them from your instructor.) TABH consulting specializes in research for automobile dealers in the United States, Canada, Mexico, and Europe. Although much of their work is done on a pay-for fee basis with customers such as dealerships and dealership networks selling all major makes of automobiles, they also produce a monthly "white paper" that is sold via their website. This off-the-shelf research is purchased by other research firms and by companies within the auto industry itself. This month, they would like to produce a white paper analyzing the viability of college students attending schools located in small college towns as a potentially underserved market segment.

TABH management assigns a junior analyst named Michel Gonzalez to the project. Lacking time for a more comprehensive study, Michel decides to contact the traffic department at Cal Poly University in Pomona, California, and at Central Missouri State University in Warrensburg, Missouri. Michel wishes to obtain data from the students' automobile parking registration records. Although both schools are willing to provide anonymous data records for a limited number of students, Cal Poly offers Michel a chance to visit during the registration period, which just happens to be next week. As a result, not only can Michel get data from students' registration forms, but a small amount of primary data can be obtained by intercepting students near the registration window. In return, Michel is asked to purchase a booth at the Cal Poly career fair.

As a result, Michel obtains some basic information from students. The information results in a small data set consisting of the follow observations for 100 undergraduate college students in Pomona, California:

Variable	Description
Sex	Student's sex dummy coded with 1 = female and 0 = male
Color	Color of a student's car as listed on his or her registration form
Major	Student's major field of study (Business, Liberal Arts (LA), or Engineering (ENG))
Grade	Student's grade record reported as the mode (A, B or C)
Finance	Whether the student financed the car he or she is driving or paid for it with cash coded 0 = cash payment and 1 = financed
Residence	Whether the student lives on campus or commutes to school coded 0 = commute and 1 = on campus
Animal	Michel asks each student to quickly draw a cartoon about the type of car they would like to purchase. Students are told to depict the car as an animal in the cartoon. Although Michel expects to interpret these cartoons more deeply when time allows, the initial coding specifies what type of animal was drawn by each respondent. When Michel was unsure of what animal was drawn, a second researcher was conferred with to determine what animal was depicted. Some students depicted the car as a dog, some as a cat, and some as a mule.

The purpose of the white paper is to offer car dealers considering new locations a comparison of the profile of a small town university with the primary market segments for their particular automobile. For instance, a company specializing in small pickup trucks appeals to a different market segment than does a company specializing in two-door economy sedans. Many small towns currently do not have dealerships, particularly beyond the "big 3." Although TABH cannot predict with certainty who may purchase the white paper, it particularly wants to appeal to companies with high sales growth in the United States, such as Kia (http://www.kia.com), Hyundai (http://www.hyundai.com), and potentially European auto dealerships currently without significant U.S. distribution, such as Smart (http://www.smart.com), among others. TABH also hopes the white paper may eventually lead to a customized project for one of these companies. Thus, the general research question is

What are the automobile market segment characteristics of students attending U.S. universities in small towns?

This question can be broken down into a series of more specific questions:

- What segments can be identified based on identifiable characteristics of students?
- How do different segments view a car?
- What types of automobiles would be most in demand?

Questions:

1. What types of tests can be performed using the data that may at least indirectly address the primary research question?
2. What do you think the primary conclusions of the white paper will be based on the data provided?
3. Assuming a small college town lacked an auto dealership (beyond Ford, GM, and Chrysler), what two companies should be most interested in this type of location? Use the Internet if

necessary to perform some cursory research on different car companies.
4. What are the weaknesses in basing decisions on this type of research?
5. Are there key issues that may diminish the usefulness of this research?
6. What kinds of themes might emerge from the cartoon drawings?
7. Are there any ethical dilemmas presented in this case?

Case 7: Survey on Americans and Dietary Supplements

The NPR/Kaiser/Kennedy School Poll is a project of National Public Radio, the Henry J. Kaiser Family Foundation, and Harvard University's Kennedy School of Government. These organizations collaborated to conduct a Survey on Americans and Dietary Supplements. The results of this survey are based on telephone interviews conducted between February 19 and February 25, 1999, with

1,200 adults 18 years or older nationwide. Case Exhibits 7.1 through 7.6 summarize some of the results of this survey.

Question

Analyze these data and write up a report on your conclusions.

CASE EXHIBIT 7.1 Knowledge of and Attitudes about Dietary Supplements by Frequency of Use

	Total	Frequency of Use		
		Regularly	Sometimes	Hardly Ever/Never
Follow news reports about dietary supplements very/fairly closely	35%	56%	49%	27%
Very/somewhat familiar with supplements	55%	88%	83%	40%
Give supplements to kids (have kids < 18)	18%	42%	40%	8%
Important to have access to supplements	60%	91%	84%	46%
Good for health/well-being	52%	85%	76%	38%
Supplements can help people with at least 4 of 6 illnesses	36%	57%	47%	27%
Supplements are inadequately tested	48%	39%	44%	52%
Many supplements don't do what ads claim	49%	29%	36%	58%
Boosting immune system means:				
Prevents illness	64%	73%	63%	62%
Helps people when sick	43%	48%	45%	41%
People who use supplements are hurt/sick often/sometimes	47%	38%	45%	50%
Know that government doesn't regulate supplements	53%	58%	46%	54%
Should be more government regulation of:				
Safety	59%	55%	55%	62%
Purity/dosage	60%	55%	58%	62%
Ad claims	63%	62%	62%	65%
Extra regulation for supplements produced for children	77%	78%	77%	77%
If government said supplements were ineffective, would continue to use	72%	71%	72%	NA

CASE EXHIBIT 7.2 Knowledge of and Attitudes about Dietary Supplements by Age

	Total	Sum				
		18–29	30+	30–49	50–64	65+
Very/somewhat familiar with supplements	55%	63%	53%	58%	57%	37%
Know that government doesn't regulate supplements	53%	45%	56%	58%	57%	47%
Use supplements regularly	18%	16%	19%	15%	24%	22%
Good for health/well-being	52%	56%	51%	53%	54%	43%
Supplements can help people with at least 4 of 6 illnesses	36%	35%	36%	38%	37%	29%
Supplements are inadequately tested	48%	43%	50%	51%	53%	45%
Many supplements don't do what ads claim	49%	44%	50%	50%	56%	44%
Extra regulation for supplements produced for children	77%	82%	76%	79%	73%	70%

CASE EXHIBIT 7.3 **Knowledge of and Attitudes about Dietary Supplements by Education**

	Total	College Graduate	Some College	High School Graduate or Less
Follow news reports about dietary supplements very/fairly closely	35%	46%	39%	30%
Very/somewhat familiar with supplements	55%	64%	64%	49%
Know that government doesn't regulate supplements	53%	67%	56%	46%
Supplements are inadequately tested	48%	62%	49%	43%
Many supplements don't do what ads claim	49%	55%	47%	47%
Boosting immune system means:				
Prevents illness	64%	68%	69%	60%
Helps people when sick	43%	42%	43%	43%
Should be more government regulation of:				
Safety	59%	62%	61%	58%
Purity/dosage	60%	65%	64%	57%
Ad claims	63%	68%	63%	62%
Use supplements regularly	18%	22%	20%	16%
Good for health/well-being	52%	53%	59%	49%
Supplements can help people with at least 4 of 6 illnesses	36%	37%	38%	34%

CASE EXHIBIT 7.4 **Demographic Profile of Regular Users of Dietary Supplements**

This table gives the percent of regular users who are in each category.

Men	46%
Women	55%
18–29	20%
30–49	34%
50–64	25%
65+	19%
Household income:	
<$20K	20%
$20–29.9K	16%
$30–49.9K	15%
$50–74.9K	13%
$75K+	10%
Refused	20%
Don't Know	5%
Education:	
<High-School Graduate	4%
High-School Graduate	27%
Some College	32%
College Graduate	27%
Region:	
East	22%
Midwest	20%
South	32%
West	26%
Urban/rural:	
Urban	31%
Suburban	48%
Rural	21%
Party ID:	
Republican	24%
Democrat	27%
Independent	42%
Think they promote health:	
Yes	85%
No	3%
Belief in their health benefits:	
High	57%
Medium	34%
Low	9%

CASE EXHIBIT 7.5 **Regular Users of Dietary Supplements**

This table gives the percent of each specific group who are regular users.

National	18%
By gender:	
Men	18%
Women	19%
By age:	
18–29	16%
30–49	15%
50–64	24%
65+	22%
By race/ethnicity:	
White (non-Hispanic)	20%
Black (non-Hispanic)	8%
Hispanic	14%
By household income:	
<$20K	20%
$20c29.9K	20%
$30–49.9K	16%
$50–74.9K	17%
$75K+	16%
By education:	
<High-School Graduate	16%
High-School Graduate	17%
Some College	20%
College Graduate	22%
By region:	
East	20%
Midwest	15%
South	17%
West	23%
By urban/rural:	
Urban	18%
Suburban	19%
Rural	18%
By party ID:	
Republican	17%
Democrat	16%
Independent	21%
By think they promote health:	
Yes	30%
No	3%
By belief in their health benefits:	
High	30%
Medium	14%
Low	8%

CASE EXHIBIT 7.6 **Believers in Benefits of Dietary Supplements**

This table gives the percent of each group who believe dietary supplements are good for people's health and well-being.

National	52%
By gender:	
Men	51%
Women	53%
By age:	
18–29	56%
30–49	53%
50–64	54%
65+	43%
By race/ethnicity:	
White (non-Hispanic)	53%
Black (non-Hispanic)	40%
Hispanic	57%
By household income:	
<$20K	54%
$20–29.9K	56%
$30–49.9K	53%
$50–74.9K	58%
$75K+	45%
By education:	
<High-School Graduate	46%
High-School Graduate	50%
Some College	59%
College Graduate	53%
By region:	
East	54%
Midwest	51%
South	49%
West	56%
By urban/rural:	
Urban	49%
Suburban	52%
Rural	56%
By party ID:	
Republican	54%
Democrat	48%
Independent	54%
By use of supplements:	
Regular	85%
Sometimes	76%
Hardly ever/never	38%

NPR/Kaiser/Kennedy School Poll is a project of National Public Radio, the Henry J. Kaiser Foundation, & Harvard University's Kennedy School of Government.

APPENDIX
APPENDIX

Statistical Tables

TABLE A.1 **Random Digits**

37751	04998	66038	63480	98442	22245	83538	62351	74514	90497
50915	64152	82981	15796	27102	71635	34470	13608	26360	76285
99142	35021	01032	57907	80545	54112	15150	36856	03247	40392
70720	10033	25191	62358	03784	74377	88150	25567	87457	49512
18460	64947	32958	08752	96366	89092	23597	74308	00881	88976
65763	41133	60950	35372	06782	81451	78764	52645	19841	50083
83769	52570	60133	25211	87384	90182	84990	26400	39128	97043
58900	78420	98579	33665	10718	39342	46346	14401	13503	46525
54746	71115	78219	64314	11227	41702	54517	87676	14078	45317
56819	27340	07200	52663	57864	85159	15460	97564	29637	27742
34990	62122	38223	28526	37006	22774	46026	15981	87291	56946
02269	22795	87593	81830	95383	67823	20196	54850	46779	64519
43042	53600	45738	00261	31100	67239	02004	70698	53597	62617
92565	12211	06868	87786	59576	61382	33972	13161	47208	96604
67424	32620	60841	86848	85000	04835	48576	33884	10101	84129
04015	77148	09535	10743	97871	55919	45274	38304	93125	91847
85226	19763	46105	25289	26714	73253	85922	21785	42624	92741
03360	07457	75131	41209	50451	23472	07438	08375	29312	62264
72460	99682	27970	25632	34096	17656	12736	27476	21938	67305
66960	55780	71778	52629	51692	71442	36130	70425	39874	62035
14824	95631	00697	65462	24815	13930	02938	54619	28909	53950
34001	05618	41900	23303	19928	60755	61404	56947	91441	19299
77718	83830	29781	72917	10840	74182	08293	62588	99625	22088
60930	05091	35726	07414	49211	69586	20226	08274	28167	65279
94180	62151	08112	26646	07617	42954	22521	09395	43561	45692
81073	85543	47650	93830	07377	87995	35084	39386	93141	88309
18467	39689	60801	46828	38670	88243	89042	78452	08032	72566
60643	59399	79740	17295	50094	66436	92677	68345	24025	36489
73372	61697	85728	90779	13235	83114	70728	32093	74306	08325
18395	18482	83245	54942	51905	09534	70839	91073	42193	81199
07261	28720	71244	05064	84873	68020	39037	68981	00670	86291
61679	81529	83725	33269	45958	74265	87460	60525	42539	25605
11815	48679	00556	96871	39835	83055	84949	11681	51687	55896
99007	35050	86440	44280	20320	97527	28138	01088	49037	85430
06446	65608	79291	16624	06135	30622	56133	33998	32308	29434

TABLE A.2 **Area under the Normal Curve**

z	.00	.01	.02	.03	.04	.05	.06	.07	.08	.09
0.0	.0000	.0040	.0080	.0120	.0160	.0199	.0239	.0279	.0319	.0359
0.1	.0398	.0438	.0478	.0517	.0557	.0596	.0636	.0675	.0714	.0753
0.2	.0793	.0832	.0871	.0910	.0948	.0987	.1026	.1064	.1103	.1141
0.3	.1179	.1217	.1255	.1293	.1331	.1368	.1406	.1443	.1480	.1517
0.4	.1554	.1591	.1628	.1664	.1700	.1736	.1772	.1808	.1844	.1879
0.5	.1915	.1950	.1985	.2019	.2054	.2088	.2123	.2157	.2190	.2224
0.6	.2257	.2291	.2324	.2357	.2389	.2422	.2454	.2486	.2518	.2549
0.7	.2580	.2612	.2642	.2673	.2704	.2734	.2764	.2794	.2823	.2852
0.8	.2881	.2910	.2939	.2967	.2995	.3023	.3051	.3078	.3106	.3133
0.9	.3159	.3186	.3212	.3238	.3264	.3289	.3315	.3340	.3365	.3389
1.0	.3413	.3438	.3461	.3485	.3508	.3531	.3554	.3577	.3599	.3621
1.1	.3643	.3665	.3686	.3708	.3729	.3749	.3770	.3790	.3810	.3830
1.2	.3849	.3869	.3888	.3907	.3925	.3944	.3962	.3980	.3997	.4015
1.3	.4032	.4049	.4066	.4082	.4099	.4115	.4131	.4147	.4162	.4177
1.4	.4192	.4207	.4222	.4236	.4251	.4265	.4279	.4292	.4306	.4319
1.5	.4332	.4345	.4357	.4370	.4382	.4394	.4406	.4418	.4429	.4441
1.6	.4452	.4463	.4474	.4484	.4495	.4505	.4515	.4525	.4535	.4545
1.7	.4554	.4564	.4573	.4582	.4591	.4599	.4608	.4616	.4625	.4633
1.8	.4641	.4649	.4656	.4664	.4671	.4678	.4686	.4693	.4699	.4706
1.9	.4713	.4719	.4726	.4732	.4738	.4744	.4750	.4756	.4761	.4767
2.0	.4772	.4778	.4783	.4788	.4793	.4798	.4803	.4808	.4812	.4817
2.1	.4821	.4826	.4830	.4834	.4838	.4842	.4846	.4850	.4854	.4857
2.2	.4861	.4864	.4868	.4871	.4875	.4878	.4881	.4884	.4887	.4890
2.3	.4893	.4896	.4898	.4901	.4904	.4906	.4909	.4911	.4913	.4916
2.4	.4918	.4920	.4922	.4925	.4927	.4929	.4931	.4932	.4934	.4936
2.5	.4938	.4940	.4941	.4943	.4945	.4946	.4948	.4949	.4951	.4952
2.6	.4953	.4955	.4956	.4957	.4959	.4960	.4961	.4962	.4963	.4964
2.7	.4965	.4966	.4967	.4968	.4969	.4970	.4971	.4972	.4973	.4974
2.8	.4974	.4975	.4976	.4977	.4977	.4978	.4979	.4979	.4980	.4981
2.9	.4981	.4982	.4982	.4983	.4984	.4984	.4985	.4985	.4986	.4986
3.0	.49865	.4987	.4987	.4988	.4988	.4989	.4989	.4989	.4990	.4990
4.0	.49997									

Chaiho Kim, *Statistical Analysis for Induction and Decision*. Copyright © 1973 by The Dryden Press, a division of Holt, Rinehart and Winston, Inc. Reprinted with permission of Holt, Rinehart and Winston.

TABLE A.3 **Distribution of _t_ for Given Probability Levels**

	Level of Significance for One-Tailed Test					
	.10	.05	.025	.01	.005	.0005
	Level of Significance for Two-Tailed Test					
_d.f._	.20	.10	.05	.02	.01	.001
1	3.078	6.314	12.706	31.821	63.657	636.619
2	1.886	2.920	4.303	6.965	9.925	31.598
3	1.638	2.353	3.182	4.541	5.841	12.941
4	1.533	2.132	2.776	3.747	4.604	8.610
5	1.476	2.015	2.571	3.365	4.032	6.859
6	1.440	1.943	2.447	3.143	3.707	5.959
7	1.415	1.895	2.365	2.998	3.499	5.405
8	1.397	1.860	2.306	2.896	3.355	5.041
9	1.383	1.833	2.262	2.821	3.250	4.781
10	1.372	1.812	2.228	2.764	3.169	4.587
11	1.363	1.796	2.201	2.718	3.106	4.437
12	1.356	1.782	2.179	2.681	3.055	4.318
13	1.350	1.771	2.160	2.650	3.012	4.221
14	1.345	1.761	2.145	2.624	2.977	4.140
15	1.341	1.753	2.131	2.602	2.947	4.073
16	1.337	1.746	2.120	2.583	2.921	4.015
17	1.333	1.740	2.110	2.567	2.898	3.965
18	1.330	1.734	2.101	2.552	2.878	3.922
19	1.328	1.729	2.093	2.539	2.861	3.883
20	1.325	1.725	2.086	2.528	2.845	3.850
21	1.323	1.721	2.080	2.518	2.831	3.819
22	1.321	1.717	2.074	2.508	2.819	3.792
23	1.319	1.714	2.069	2.500	2.807	3.767
24	1.318	1.711	2.064	2.492	2.797	3.745
25	1.316	1.708	2.060	2.485	2.787	3.725
26	1.315	1.706	2.056	2.479	2.779	3.707
27	1.314	1.703	2.052	2.473	2.771	3.690
28	1.313	1.701	2.048	2.467	2.763	3.674
29	1.311	1.699	2.045	2.462	2.756	3.659
30	1.310	1.697	2.042	2.457	2.750	3.646
40	1.303	1.684	2.021	2.423	2.704	3.551
60	1.296	1.671	2.000	2.390	2.660	3.460
120	1.289	1.658	1.980	2.358	2.617	3.373
∞	1.282	1.645	1.960	2.326	2.576	3.291

TABLE A.4 Chi-Square Distribution

Degrees of Freedom (d.f.)	Area in Shaded Right Tail (α)		
	.10	.05	.01
1	2.706	3.841	6.635
2	4.605	5.991	9.210
3	6.251	7.815	11.345
4	7.779	9.488	13.277
5	9.236	11.070	15.086
6	10.645	12.592	16.812
7	12.017	14.067	18.475
8	13.362	15.507	20.090
9	14.684	16.919	21.666
10	15.987	18.307	23.209
11	17.275	19.675	24.725
12	18.549	21.026	26.217
13	19.812	22.362	27.688
14	21.064	23.685	29.141
15	22.307	24.996	30.578
16	23.542	26.296	32.000
17	24.769	27.587	33.409
18	25.989	28.869	34.805
19	27.204	30.144	36.191
20	28.412	31.410	37.566
21	29.615	32.671	38.932
22	30.813	33.924	40.289
23	32.007	35.172	41.638
24	33.196	36.415	42.980
25	34.382	37.652	44.314
26	35.563	38.885	45.642
27	36.741	40.113	46.963
28	37.916	41.337	48.278
29	39.087	42.557	49.588
30	40.256	43.773	50.892

Example of how to use this table: In a chi-square distribution with 6 degrees of freedom (d.f.), the area to the right of a critical value of 12.592 — i.e., the α area — is .05.

TABLE A.5 Critical Values of F_{v_1,v_2} for $\alpha = .05$

v_1 = Degrees of Freedom for Numerator

v_2	1	2	3	4	5	6	7	8	9	10	12	15	20	24	30	40	60	120	∞
1	161	200	216	225	230	234	237	239	241	242	244	246	248	249	250	251	252	253	254
2	18.5	19.0	19.2	19.2	19.3	19.3	19.4	19.4	19.4	19.4	19.4	19.4	19.5	19.5	19.5	19.5	19.5	19.5	19.5
3	10.1	9.55	9.28	9.12	9.01	8.94	8.89	8.85	8.81	8.79	8.74	8.70	8.66	8.64	8.62	8.59	8.57	8.55	8.53
4	7.71	6.94	6.59	6.39	6.26	6.16	6.09	6.04	6.00	5.96	5.91	5.86	5.80	5.77	5.75	5.72	5.69	5.66	5.63
5	6.61	5.79	5.41	5.19	5.05	4.95	4.88	4.82	4.77	4.74	4.68	4.62	4.56	4.53	4.50	4.46	4.43	4.40	4.37
6	5.99	5.14	4.76	4.53	4.39	4.28	4.21	4.15	4.10	4.06	4.00	3.94	3.87	3.84	3.81	3.77	3.74	3.70	3.67
7	5.59	4.74	4.35	4.12	3.97	3.87	3.79	3.73	3.68	3.64	3.57	3.51	3.44	3.41	3.38	3.34	3.30	3.27	3.23
8	5.32	4.46	4.07	3.84	3.69	3.58	3.50	3.44	3.39	3.35	3.28	3.22	3.15	3.12	3.08	3.04	3.01	2.97	2.93
9	5.12	4.26	3.86	3.63	3.48	3.37	3.29	3.23	3.18	3.14	3.07	3.01	2.94	2.90	2.86	2.83	2.79	2.75	2.71
10	4.96	4.10	3.71	3.48	3.33	3.22	3.14	3.07	3.02	2.98	2.91	2.85	2.77	2.74	2.70	2.66	2.62	2.58	2.54
11	4.84	3.98	3.59	3.36	3.20	3.09	3.01	2.95	2.90	2.85	2.79	2.72	2.65	2.61	2.57	2.53	2.49	2.45	2.40
12	4.75	3.89	3.49	3.26	3.11	3.00	2.91	2.85	2.80	2.75	2.69	2.62	2.54	2.51	2.47	2.43	2.38	2.34	2.30
13	4.67	3.81	3.41	3.18	3.03	2.92	2.83	2.77	2.71	2.67	2.60	2.53	2.46	2.42	2.38	2.34	2.30	2.25	2.21
14	4.60	3.74	3.34	3.11	2.96	2.85	2.76	2.70	2.65	2.60	2.53	2.46	2.39	2.35	2.31	2.27	2.22	2.18	2.13
15	4.54	3.68	3.29	3.06	2.90	2.79	2.71	2.64	2.59	2.54	2.48	2.40	2.33	2.29	2.25	2.20	2.16	2.11	2.07
16	4.49	3.63	3.24	3.01	2.85	2.74	2.66	2.59	2.54	2.49	2.42	2.35	2.28	2.24	2.19	2.15	2.11	2.06	2.01
17	4.45	3.59	3.20	2.96	2.81	2.70	2.61	2.55	2.49	2.45	2.38	2.31	2.23	2.19	2.15	2.10	2.06	2.01	1.96
18	4.41	3.55	3.16	2.93	2.77	2.66	2.58	2.51	2.46	2.41	2.34	2.27	2.19	2.15	2.11	2.06	2.02	1.97	1.92
19	4.38	3.52	3.13	2.90	2.74	2.63	2.54	2.48	2.42	2.38	2.31	2.23	2.16	2.11	2.07	2.03	1.98	1.93	1.88
20	4.35	3.49	3.10	2.87	2.71	2.60	2.51	2.45	2.39	2.35	2.28	2.20	2.12	2.08	2.04	1.99	1.95	1.90	1.84
21	4.32	3.47	3.07	2.84	2.68	2.57	2.49	2.42	2.37	2.32	2.25	2.18	2.10	2.05	2.01	1.96	1.92	1.87	1.81
22	4.30	3.44	3.05	2.82	2.66	2.55	2.46	2.40	2.34	2.30	2.23	2.15	2.07	2.03	1.98	1.94	1.89	1.84	1.78
23	4.28	3.42	3.03	2.80	2.64	2.53	2.44	2.37	2.32	2.27	2.20	2.13	2.05	2.01	1.96	1.91	1.86	1.81	1.76
24	4.26	3.40	3.01	2.78	2.62	2.51	2.42	2.36	2.30	2.25	2.18	2.11	2.03	1.98	1.94	1.89	1.84	1.79	1.73
25	4.24	3.39	2.99	2.76	2.60	2.49	2.40	2.34	2.28	2.24	2.16	2.09	2.01	1.96	1.92	1.87	1.82	1.77	1.71
30	4.17	3.32	2.92	2.69	2.53	2.42	2.33	2.27	2.21	2.16	2.09	2.01	1.93	1.89	1.84	1.79	1.74	1.68	1.62
40	4.08	3.23	2.84	2.61	2.45	2.34	2.25	2.18	2.12	2.08	2.00	1.92	1.84	1.79	1.74	1.69	1.64	1.58	1.51
60	4.00	3.15	2.76	2.53	2.37	2.25	2.17	2.10	2.04	1.99	1.92	1.84	1.75	1.70	1.65	1.59	1.53	1.47	1.39
120	3.92	3.07	2.68	2.45	2.29	2.18	2.09	2.02	1.96	1.91	1.83	1.75	1.66	1.61	1.55	1.50	1.43	1.35	1.25
∞	3.84	3.00	2.60	2.37	2.21	2.10	2.01	1.94	1.88	1.83	1.75	1.67	1.57	1.52	1.46	1.39	1.32	1.22	1.00

v_2 = Degrees of Freedom for Denominator

TABLE A.8 Critical Values of F_{v_1,v_2} for $\alpha = .01$

v_1 = Degrees of Freedom for Numerator

	1	2	3	4	5	6	7	8	9	10	12	15	20	24	30	40	60	120	∞
1	4,052	5,000	5,403	5,625	5,764	5,859	5,928	5,982	6,023	6,056	6,106	6,157	6,209	6,235	6,261	6,287	6,313	6,339	6,366
2	98.5	99.0	99.2	99.2	99.3	99.3	99.4	99.4	99.4	99.4	99.4	99.4	99.4	99.5	99.5	99.5	99.5	99.5	99.5
3	34.1	30.8	29.5	28.7	28.2	27.9	27.7	27.5	27.3	27.2	27.1	26.9	26.7	26.6	26.5	26.4	26.3	26.2	26.1
4	21.2	18.0	16.7	16.0	15.5	15.2	15.0	14.8	14.7	14.5	14.4	14.2	14.0	13.9	13.8	13.7	13.7	13.6	13.5
5	16.3	13.3	12.1	11.4	11.0	10.7	10.5	10.3	10.2	10.1	9.89	9.72	9.55	9.47	9.38	9.29	9.20	9.11	9.02
6	13.7	10.9	9.78	9.15	8.75	8.47	8.26	8.10	7.98	7.87	7.72	7.56	7.40	7.31	7.23	7.14	7.06	6.97	6.88
7	12.2	9.55	8.45	7.85	7.46	7.19	6.99	6.84	6.72	6.62	6.47	6.31	6.16	6.07	5.99	5.91	5.82	5.74	5.65
8	11.3	8.65	7.59	7.01	6.63	6.37	6.18	6.03	5.91	5.81	5.67	5.52	5.36	5.28	5.20	5.12	5.03	4.95	4.86
9	10.6	8.02	6.99	6.42	6.06	5.80	5.61	5.47	5.35	5.26	5.11	4.96	4.81	4.73	4.65	4.57	4.48	4.40	4.31
10	10.0	7.56	6.55	5.99	5.64	5.39	5.20	5.06	4.94	4.85	4.71	4.56	4.41	4.33	4.25	4.17	4.08	4.00	3.91
11	9.65	7.21	6.22	5.67	5.32	5.07	4.89	4.74	4.63	4.54	4.40	4.25	4.10	4.02	3.94	3.86	3.78	3.69	3.60
12	9.33	6.93	5.95	5.41	5.06	4.82	4.64	4.50	4.39	4.30	4.16	4.01	3.86	3.78	3.70	3.62	3.54	3.45	3.36
13	9.07	6.70	5.74	5.21	4.86	4.62	4.44	4.30	4.19	4.10	3.96	3.82	3.66	3.59	3.51	3.43	3.34	3.25	3.17
14	8.86	6.51	5.56	5.04	4.70	4.46	4.28	4.14	4.03	3.94	3.80	3.66	3.51	3.43	3.35	3.27	3.18	3.09	3.00
15	8.68	6.36	5.42	4.89	4.56	4.32	4.14	4.00	3.89	3.80	3.67	3.52	3.37	3.29	3.21	3.13	3.05	2.96	2.87
16	8.53	6.23	5.29	4.77	4.44	4.20	4.03	3.89	3.78	3.69	3.55	3.41	3.26	3.18	3.10	3.02	2.93	2.84	2.75
17	8.40	6.11	5.19	4.67	4.34	4.10	3.93	3.79	3.68	3.59	3.46	3.31	3.16	3.08	3.00	2.92	2.83	2.75	2.65
18	8.29	6.01	5.09	4.58	4.25	4.01	3.84	3.71	3.60	3.51	3.37	3.23	3.08	3.00	2.92	2.84	2.75	2.66	2.57
19	8.19	5.93	5.01	4.50	4.17	3.94	3.77	3.63	3.52	3.43	3.30	3.15	3.00	2.92	2.84	2.76	2.67	2.58	2.49
20	8.10	5.85	4.94	4.43	4.10	3.87	3.70	3.56	3.46	3.37	3.23	3.09	2.94	2.86	2.78	2.69	2.61	2.52	2.42
21	8.02	5.78	4.87	4.37	4.04	3.81	3.64	3.51	3.40	3.31	3.17	3.03	2.88	2.80	2.72	2.64	2.55	2.46	2.36
22	7.96	5.72	4.82	4.31	3.99	3.76	3.59	3.45	3.35	3.26	3.12	2.98	2.83	2.75	2.67	2.58	2.50	2.40	2.31
23	7.88	5.66	4.76	4.26	3.94	3.71	3.54	3.41	3.30	3.21	3.07	2.93	2.78	2.70	2.62	2.54	2.45	2.35	2.26
24	7.82	5.61	4.72	4.22	3.90	3.67	3.50	3.36	3.26	3.17	3.03	2.89	2.74	2.66	2.58	2.49	2.40	2.31	2.21
25	7.77	5.57	4.68	4.18	3.86	3.63	3.46	3.32	3.22	3.13	2.99	2.85	2.70	2.62	2.53	2.45	2.36	2.27	2.17
30	7.58	5.39	4.51	4.02	3.70	3.47	3.30	3.17	3.07	2.98	2.84	2.70	2.55	2.47	2.39	2.30	2.21	2.11	2.01
40	7.31	5.18	4.31	3.83	3.51	3.29	3.12	2.99	2.89	2.80	2.66	2.52	2.37	2.29	2.20	2.11	2.02	1.92	1.80
60	7.08	4.98	4.13	3.65	3.34	3.12	2.95	2.82	2.72	2.63	2.50	2.35	2.20	2.12	2.03	1.94	1.84	1.73	1.60
120	6.85	4.79	3.95	3.48	3.17	2.96	2.79	2.66	2.56	2.47	2.34	2.19	2.03	1.95	1.86	1.76	1.66	1.53	1.38
∞	6.63	4.61	3.78	3.32	3.02	2.80	2.64	2.51	2.41	2.32	2.18	2.04	1.88	1.79	1.70	1.59	1.47	1.32	1.00

v_2 = Degrees of Freedom for Denominator

TABLE A.7 **Critical Values of the Pearson Correlation Coefficient**

	Level of Significance for One-Tailed Test			
	.05	.025	.01	.005
	Level of Significance for Two-Tailed Test			
d.f.	.10	.05	.02	.01
1	.988	.997	.9995	.9999
2	.900	.950	.980	.990
3	.805	.878	.934	.959
4	.729	.811	.882	.917
5	.669	.754	.833	.874
6	.622	.707	.789	.834
7	.582	.666	.750	.798
8	.549	.632	.716	.765
9	.521	.602	.685	.735
10	.497	.576	.658	.708
11	.576	.553	.634	.684
12	.458	.532	.612	.661
13	.441	.514	.592	.641
14	.426	.497	.574	.623
15	.412	.482	.558	.606
16	.400	.468	.542	.590
17	.389	.456	.528	.575
18	.378	.444	.516	.561
19	.369	.433	.503	.549
20	.360	.423	.492	.537
21	.352	.413	.482	.526
22	.344	.404	.472	.515
23	.337	.396	.462	.505
24	.330	.388	.453	.496
25	.323	.381	.445	.487
26	.317	.374	.437	.479
27	.311	.367	.430	.471
28	.306	.361	.423	.463
29	.301	.355	.416	.486
30	.296	.349	.409	.449
35	.275	.325	.381	.418
40	.257	.304	.358	.393
45	.243	.288	.338	.372
50	.231	.273	.322	.354
60	.211	.250	.295	.325
70	.195	.232	.274	.303
80	.183	.217	.256	.283
90	.173	.205	.242	.267
100	.164	.195	.230	.254

TABLE A.8 **Critical Values of *T* in the Wilcoxon Matched-Pairs Signed-Ranks Test**

	Level of Significance for Two-Tailed Test		
N	.05	.02	.01
6	1	—	—
7	2	0	—
8	4	2	0
9	6	3	2
10	8	5	3
11	11	7	5
12	14	10	7
13	17	13	10
14	21	16	13
15	25	20	16
16	30	24	19
17	35	28	23
18	40	33	28
19	46	38	32
20	52	43	37
21	59	49	43
22	66	56	49
23	73	62	55
24	81	69	61
25	90	77	68

Adapted from Table 2 of Frank Wilcoxon and Roberta A. Wilcoxon, *Some Rapid Approximate Statistical Procedures* (New York: American Cynamid Company, 1964), p. 28.

Glossary of frequently used symbols

Greek Letters

α (alpha)	level of significance or probability of a Type I error
β (beta)	probability of a Type II error or slope of the regression line
μ (mu)	population mean
ρ (rho)	population Pearson correlation coefficient
Σ (summation)	take the sum of
π (pi)	population proportion
σ (sigma)	population standard deviation
χ^2	chi–square statistic

English Letters

$d.f.$	number of degrees of freedom
F	F-statistic
n	sample size
p	sample proportion
$Pr(\ )$	probability of the outcome in the parentheses
r	sample Pearson correlation coefficient
r^2	coefficient of determination (squared correlation coefficient)
R^2	coefficient of determination (multiple regression)
S	sample standard deviation (inferential statistics)
$S_{\overline{X}}$	estimated standard error of the mean
S_p	estimated standard error of the proportion
S^2	sample variance (inferential statistics)
t	t-statistic
X	variable or any unspecified observation
$\overline{X}$	sample mean
Y	any unspecified observation on a second variable, usually the dependent variable
$\hat{Y}$	predicted dependent variable score
Z	standardized score (descriptive statistics) or Z-statistic

GLOSSARY

GLOSSARY

A

Absolute causality Means the cause is necessary and sufficient to bring about the effect.

Acquiescence bias A tendency for people to agree or give positive responses.

Administrative error An error caused by the improper administration or execution of the research task.

Advocacy research Research undertaken to support a specific claim in a legal action or represent some advocacy group.

Analysis of variance (ANOVA) Analysis involving the investigation of the effects of one treatment variable on an interval-scaled dependent variable—a hypothesis-testing technique to determine whether statistically significant differences in means occur between two or more groups.

Applied marketing research Research conducted to address a specific marketing decision for a specific firm or organization.

At-home scanning system A system that allows consumer panelists to perform their own scanning after taking home products, using handheld wands that read UPC symbols.

Attitude An enduring disposition to consistently respond in a given manner to various aspects of the world, composed of affective, cognitive, and behavioral components.

Attribute A single characteristic or fundamental feature of an object, person, situation, or issue.

B

Back translation Taking a questionnaire that has previously been translated into another language and having a second, independent translator translate it back to the original language.

Backward linkage Implies that later steps influence earlier stages of the research process.

Balanced rating scale A fixed-alternative rating scale with an equal number of positive and negative categories; a neutral point or point of indifference is at the center of the scale.

Basic experimental design An experimental design in which only one variable is manipulated.

Basic marketing research Research conducted without a specific decision in mind that usually does not address the needs of a specific organization. It attempts to expand the limits of marketing knowledge in general and is not aimed at solving a particular pragmatic problem.

Behavioral differential A rating scale instrument similar to a semantic differential, developed to measure the behavioral intentions of subjects toward future actions.

Between-group variance The sum of differences between the group mean and the grand mean summed over all groups for a given set of observations.

Between-subjects design Each subject receives only one treatment combination.

Bivariate statistical analysis Tests of hypotheses involving two variables.

Blocking variable A categorical variable that is expected to be associated with different values of a dependent variable for each group. It effectively controls for an extraneous cause in experimental analysis.

Box and whisker plots Graphic representations of central tendencies, percentiles, variabilities, and the shapes of frequency distributions.

Briefing session A training session to ensure that each interviewer is provided with common information.

C

Callbacks Attempts to recontact individuals selected for a sample who were not available initially.

Cannibalize When consumers choose a new offering as a replacement for another product offered by the same company.

Case studies The documented history of a particular person, group, organization, or event.

Categorical variable A variable that indicates membership in some group.

Category scale A rating scale that consists of several response categories, often providing respondents with alternatives to indicate positions on a continuum.

Causal inference A conclusion that when one thing happens, another specific thing will follow.

Causal research Allows causal inferences to be made; seeks to identify cause-and-effect relationships.

Cell Refers to a specific treatment combination associated with an experimental group.

Census A survey in which every member of a population is measured. Statistical inference is not needed when a census is conducted.

Central-limit theorem The theory that, as sample size increases, the distribution of sample means of size n, randomly selected, approaches a normal distribution.

Central location interviewing Telephone interviews conducted from a central location using wats lines at fixed charges.

Check boxes In an Internet questionnaire, small graphic boxes, next to answers, that a respondent clicks on to choose an answer; typically, a check mark or an **X** appears in the box when the respondent clicks on it.

Checklist question A fixed-alternative question that allows the respondent to provide multiple answers to a single question by checking off items.

Chi-square (χ^2) test One of the most basic tests for statistical significance which is particularly appropriate for testing hypotheses about frequencies arranged in a frequency or contingency table.

Choice A measurement task that identifies preferences by requiring respondents to choose between two or more alternatives.

Classificatory variable Another term for a categorical variable because it classifies units into categories.

Click-through rate Proportion of people who are exposed to an internet ad who actually click on its hyperlink to enter the website. Click-through rates are generally very low.

Cluster analysis A multivariate approach for grouping observations based on similarity among measured variables.

Cluster sampling An economically efficient sampling technique in which the primary sampling unit is not the individual element in the population but a large cluster of elements; clusters are selected randomly.

Code book A book that identifies each variable in a study and gives the variable's description, code name, and position in the data matrix.

Codes Rules for interpreting, classifying, and recording data in the coding process; also, the actual numerical or other character symbols assigned to raw data.

Coding The process of assigning a numerical score or other character symbol to previously edited data.

Coefficient alpha (α) The most commonly applied estimate of a multiple item scale's reliability. It represents the average of all possible split-half reliabilities for a construct.

Coefficient of determination (R^2) A measure obtained by squaring the correlation coefficient. The proportion of the total variance of a variable accounted for by another value of another variable.

Cohort effect Refers to a change in the dependent variable that occurs because members of one experimental group experienced different historical situations than members of other experimental groups.

Communication process The process by which one person or source sends a message to an audience or receiver and then receives feedback about the message.

Comparative rating scale Any measure of attitudes that asks respondents to rate a concept in comparison with a benchmark explicitly used as a frame of reference.

Completely randomized design An experimental design that uses a random process to assign subjects (test units) to treatment levels to investigate the effects of an experimental variable.

Composite measures Assign a value to an observation based on a mathematical derivation of multiple variables.

Composite scale A way of representing a latent construct by summing or averaging respondents' reactions to multiple items, each assumed to indicate the latent construct.

Computer-assisted telephone interviewing (CATI) Technology that allows answers to telephone interviews to be entered directly into a computer for processing.

Concept A generalized idea that represents something of meaning.

Concept testing A frequently performed type of exploratory research representing many similar research procedures all having the same purpose: to screen new, revised, or repositioned ideas.

Conclusions and recommendations section The part of the body of a report that provides opinions based on the results and suggestions for action.

Concomitant variation One of three criteria for causality; occurs when two events "covary," meaning they vary systematically.

Conditional causality Means that a cause is necessary but not sufficient to bring about an effect.

Confidence interval estimate A specified range of numbers within which a population mean is expected to lie; an estimate of the population mean based on the knowledge that it will be equal to the sample mean plus or minus a small sampling error.

Confidence level A percentage or decimal value that tells how confident a researcher can be about being correct. It states the long-run percentage of confidence intervals that will include the true population mean.

Confidentiality The information involved in a research will not be shared with others.

Conflict of interest Occurs when one researcher works for two competing companies.

Confound An experiment means that there is an alternative explanation beyond the experimental variables for any observed differences in the dependent variable.

Constancy of conditions Means that subjects in all experimental groups are exposed to identical conditions except for the differing experimental treatments.

Constant Something that does not change; is not useful in addressing research questions.

Constant-sum scale A measure of attitudes in which respondents are asked to divide a constant sum to indicate the relative importance of attributes; respondents often sort cards, but the task may also be a rating task.

Construct A term used to refer to concepts measured with multiple variables.

Construct validity Exists when a measure reliably measures and truthfully represents a unique concept. Construct validity consists of several components including face validity, convergent validity, criterion validity, and discriminant validity.

Consumer panel A longitudinal survey of the same sample of individuals or households to record their attitudes, behavior, or purchasing habits over time.

Content analysis The systematic observation and quantitative description of the manifest content of communication.

Content providers Parties that furnish information on the World Wide Web.

Contingency table A data matrix that displays the frequency of some combination of possible responses to multiple variables; cross-tabulation results.

Continuous measures Measures that reflect the intensity of a concept by assigning values that can take on any value along some scale range.

Continuous variable A variable that can take on a range of values that correspond to some quantitative amount.

Contributory causality Means that a cause need be neither necessary nor sufficient to bring about an effect.

Contrived observation Observation in which the investigator creates an artificial environment in order to test a hypothesis.

Control group A group of subjects to whom no experimental treatment is administered.

Control method of test-marketing A "minimarket test" using forced distribution in a small city. Retailers are paid for shelf space so that the test-marketer can be guaranteed distribution.

Convenience sampling The sampling procedure of obtaining those people or units that are most conveniently available.

Convergent validity Another way of expressing internal consistency. Highly reliable scales contain convergent validity.

Conversations An informal qualitative data-gathering approach in which the researcher engages a respondent in a discussion of the relevant subject matter.

Cookies Small computer files that a content provider can save onto the computer of someone who visits its website.

Correlation coefficient A statistical measure of the covariation, or association, between two at least interval variables.

Correlation matrix The standard form for reporting correlation coefficients for more than two variables.

Correspondence rules Indicate the way that a certain value on a scale corresponds to some true value of a concept.

Counterbalancing Attempts to eliminate the confounding effects of order of presentation by requiring that one-fourth of the subjects be exposed to treatment A first, one-fourth to treatment B first, one-fourth to treatment C first, and finally one-fourth to treatment D first.

Counterbiasing statement An introductory statement or preamble to a potentially embarrassing question that reduces a respondent's reluctance to answer by suggesting that certain behavior is not unusual.

Covariance Extent to which two variables are associated systematically with each other.

Cover letter Letter that accompanies a questionnaire to induce the reader to complete and return the questionnaire.

Criterion validity The ability of a measure to correlate with other standard measures of similar constructs or established criteria.

Critical values The values that lie exactly on the boundary of the region of rejection.

Cross-checks The comparison of data from one source with data from another source to determine the similarity of independent projects.

Cross-functional teams Employee teams composed of individuals from various functional areas, such as engineering, production, finance, and marketing, who share a common purpose.

Cross-sectional study A study in which various segments of a population are sampled and data are collected at a single moment in time.

Cross-tabulation The appropriate technique for addressing research questions involving relationships among multiple less than interval variables. It results in a combined frequency table displaying one variable in rows and another in columns.

Cross-validate To verify that the empirical findings from one culture also exist and behave similarly in another culture.

Curb-stoning A form of interviewer cheating in which an interviewer makes up the responses instead of conducting an actual interview.

Customer discovery Involves mining data to look for patterns identifying who is likely to be a valuable customer.

Customer-oriented Describes a firm in which all decisions are made with a conscious awareness of their effect on the consumer.

Customer relationship management (CRM) Part of the DSS that addresses exchanges between the firm and its customers.

Custom research Research projects that are tailored specifically to a client's unique needs.

D

Data Facts or recorded measures of certain phenomena (things).

Data analysis The application of reasoning to understand the data that have been gathered.

Data conversion The process of changing the original form of the data to a format suitable to achieve the research objective; also called data transformation.

Data entry The activity of transferring data from a research project to computers.

Data file The way a data set is stored electronically in spreadsheet-like form in which the rows represent sampling units and the columns represent variables.

Data integrity The notion that the data file actually contains the information that the researcher promised the decision maker he or she would obtain, meaning in part that the data have been edited and properly coded so that they are useful to the decision maker.

Data mining The use of powerful computers to dig through volumes of data to discover patterns about an organization's customers and products; applies to many different forms of analysis.

Data quality The degree to which data represent the true situation.

Data reduction technique Multivariate statistical approaches that summarize the information from many variables into a reduced set of variates formed as linear combinations of measured variables.

Data transformations Process of changing the data from their original form to a format suitable for performing a data analysis addressing research objectives.

Data warehouse The multitiered computer storehouse of current and historical data.

Data warehousing The process allowing important day-to-day operational data to be stored and organized for simplified access.

Data-processing error A category of administrative error that occurs because of incorrect data entry, incorrect computer programming, or other procedural errors during data analysis.

Data wholesalers Companies that put together consortia of data sources into packages that are offered to municipal, corporate, and university libraries for a fee.

Database A collection of raw data arranged logically and organized in a form that can be stored and processed by a computer.

Database marketing The use of customer databases to promote one-to-one relationships with customers and create precisely targeted promotions.

Debriefing Research subjects are fully informed and provided with a chance to ask any questions they may have about the experiment.

Decision making The process of developing and deciding among alternative ways of resolving a problem or choosing from among alternative opportunities.

Decision statement A written expression of the key question(s) that the research user wishes to answer.

Decision support system (DSS) A computer-based system that helps decision makers confront problems through direct interaction with databases and analytical software programs.

Degrees of freedom The number of observations minus the number of constraints or assumptions needed to calculate a statistical term.

Deliverables The term used often in consulting to describe research objectives to a research client.

Demand characteristic Experimental design elements or procedures that unintentionally provide subjects with hints about the research hypothesis.

Demand effect Occurs when demand characteristics actually affect the dependent variable.

Dependence techniques Multivariate statistical techniques that explain or predict one or more dependent variables.

Dependent variable A process outcome or a variable that is predicted and/or explained by other variables.

Depth interview A one-on-one interview between a professional researcher and a research respondent conducted about some relevant business or social topic.

Descriptive analysis The elementary transformation of raw data in a way that describes the basic characteristics such as central tendency, distribution, and variability.

Descriptive research Describes characteristics of objects, people, groups, organizations, or environments; tries to "paint a picture" of a given situation.

Determinant-choice question A fixed-alternative question that requires the respondent to choose one response from among multiple alternatives.

Diagnostic analysis Seeks to diagnose reasons for market outcomes and focuses specifically on the beliefs and feelings consumers have about and toward competing products.

Dialog boxes Windows that open on a computer screen to prompt the user to enter information.

Direct observation A straightforward attempt to observe and record what naturally occurs; the investigator does not create an artificial situation.

Director of marketing research This person provides leadership in research efforts and integrates all staff-level research activities into one effort. The director plans, executes, and controls the firm's marketing research function.

Discrete measures Measures that take on only one of a finite number of values.

Discriminant analysis A statistical technique for predicting the probability that an object will belong in one of two or more mutually exclusive categories (dependent variable), based on several independent variables.

Discriminant validity Represents how unique or distinct is a measure. A scale should not correlate too highly with a measure of a different construct.

Discussion guide A focus group outline that includes written introductory comments informing the group about the focus group purpose and rules and then outlines topics or questions to be addressed in the group session.

Disguised questions Indirect questions that assume the purpose of the study must be hidden from the respondent.

Disproportional stratified sample A stratified sample in which the sample size for each stratum is allocated according to analytical considerations.

Do Not Call legislation Restricts any telemarketing effort from calling consumers who either register with a no-call list or who request not to be called.

Door-in-the-face compliance technique A two-step process for securing a high response rate. In step 1 an initial request, so large that nearly everyone refuses it, is made. Next, a second request is made for a smaller favor; respondents are expected to comply with this more reasonable request.

Door-to-door interviews Personal interviews conducted at respondents' doorsteps in an effort to increase the participation rate in the survey.

Double-barreled question A question that may induce bias because it covers two issues at once.

Drop-down box In an Internet questionnaire, a space-saving device that reveals responses when they are needed but otherwise hides them from view.

Drop-off method A survey method that requires the interviewer to travel to the respondent's location to drop off questionnaires that will be picked up later.

Dummy coding Numeric "1" or "0" coding where each number represents an alternate response such as "female" or "male."

Dummy tables Tables placed in research proposals that are exact representations of the actual tables that will show results in the final report with the exception that the results are hypothetical (fictitious).

Dummy variable The way a dichotomous (two group) independent variable is represented in regression analysis by assigning a 0 to one group and a 1 to the other.

E

Editing The process of checking the completeness, consistency, and legibility of data and making the data ready for coding and transfer to storage.

Elaboration analysis An analysis of the basic cross-tabulation for each level of a variable not previously considered, such as subgroups of the sample.

Electronic data interchange (EDI) Type of exchange that occurs when one company's computer system is integrated with another company's system.

Electronic test-markets A system of test-marketing that measures dependent variables with scanner-based consumer panels and manipulates advertising based on a special delivery system that can swap out one television commercial or advertisement for another.

E-mail surveys Surveys distributed through electronic mail.

Empirical testing Means that something has been examined against reality using data.

Environmental scanning Entails all information gathering designed to detect changes in the external operating environment of the firm.

Error trapping Using software to control the flow of an Internet questionnaire—for example, to prevent respondents from backing up or failing to answer a question.

Ethical dilemma Refers to a situation in which one chooses from alternative courses of actions, each with different ethical implications.

Ethnography Represents ways of studying cultures through methods that involve becoming highly active within that culture.

Experiment A carefully controlled study in which the researcher manipulates a proposed cause and observes any corresponding change in the proposed effect.

Experimental condition One of the possible levels of an experimental variable manipulation.

Experimental group A group of subjects to whom an experimental treatment is administered.

Experimental treatment The term referring to the way an experimental variable is manipulated.

Experimental variable Represents the proposed cause and is controlled by the researcher by manipulating it.

Exploratory research Conducted to clarify ambiguous situations or discover ideas that may be potential business opportunities.

External data Data created, recorded, or generated by an entity other than the researcher's organization.

External validity Is the accuracy with which experimental results can be generalized beyond the experimental subjects.

Extremity bias A category of response bias that results because some individuals tend to use extremes when responding to questions.

Eye-tracking monitor A mechanical device used to observe eye movements. Some eye monitors use infrared light beams to measure unconscious eye movements.

F

F-test A procedure used to determine whether there is more variability in the scores of one sample than in the scores of another sample.

F-test (regression) A procedure to determine whether more variability is explained by the regression or unexplained by the regression.

Face (content) validity A scale's content logically appears to reflect what was intended to be measured.

Factor analysis A prototypical multivariate, interdependence technique that statistically identifies a reduced number of factors from a larger number of measured variables.

Factor loading Indicates how strongly a measured variable is correlated with a factor.

Factor rotation A mathematical way of simplifying factor analysis results to better identify which variables "load on" which factors. The most common procedure is varimax.

Factorial design An experiment that investigates the interaction of two or more independent variables on a single dependent variable.

Fax survey A survey that uses fax machines as a way for respondents to receive and return questionnaires.

Field A collection of characters that represents a single type of data—usually a variable.

Field editing Preliminary editing by a field supervisor on the same day as the interview to catch technical omissions, check legibility of handwriting, and clarify responses that are logically or conceptually inconsistent.

Field experiments Research projects involving experimental manipulations that are implemented in a natural environment.

Field interviewing service A research supplier that specializes in gathering data.

Field notes The researcher's descriptions of what actually happens in the field; these notes then become the text from which meaning is extracted.

Fieldworker An individual who is responsible for gathering data in the field.

Filter question A question that screens out respondents who are not qualified to answer a second question.

Fixed-alternative questions Questions in which respondents are given specific, limited-alternative responses and asked to choose the one closest to their own viewpoint.

Focus blog A type of informal, "continuous" focus group established as an Internet blog for the purpose of collecting qualitative data from participant comments.

Focus group A small group discussion about some research topic led by a moderator who guides discussion among the participants.

Focus group interview An unstructured, free-flowing interview with a small group of around six to ten people. Focus groups are led by a trained moderator who follows a flexible format encouraging dialogue among respondents.

Foot-in-the-door compliance technique A technique for obtaining a high response rate, in which compliance with a large or difficult task is induced by first obtaining the respondent's compliance with a smaller request.

Forced answering software Software that prevents respondents from continuing with an Internet questionnaire if they fail to answer a question.

Forced-choice rating scale A fixed-alternative rating scale that requires respondents to choose one of the fixed alternatives.

Forecast analyst Employee who provides technical assistance such as running computer programs and manipulating data to generate a sales forecast.

Forward linkage Implies that the earlier stages of the research process influence the later stages.

Free-association techniques Record respondents' first (top-of-mind) cognitive reactions to some stimulus. The Rorschach or inkblot test typifies a free-association method.

Frequency distribution A set of data organized by summarizing the number of times a particular value of a variable occurs.

Frequency-determination question A fixed-alternative question that asks for an answer about general frequency of occurrence.

Frequency table A table showing the different ways respondents answered a question.

Funded marketing research Refers to basic research usually performed by academic researchers that is financially supported by some public or private institution, as in federal government grants.

Funnel technique Asking general questions before specific questions in order to obtain unbiased responses.

G

General linear model (GLM) A way of explaining and predicting a dependent variable based on fluctuations (variation) from its mean. The fluctuations are due to changes in independent variables.

Geo-demographics Refers to information describing the demographic profile of consumers in a particular geographic region.

Global information system An organized collection of computer hardware, software, data, and personnel designed to capture, store, update, manipulate, analyze, and immediately display information about worldwide business activity.

Goodness-of-fit (GOF) A general term representing how well some computed table or matrix of values matches some population or predetermined table or matrix of the same size.

Graphic aids Pictures or diagrams used to clarify complex points or emphasize a message.

Graphic rating scale A measure of attitude that allows respondents to rate an object by choosing any point along a graphic continuum.

Grounded theory Represents an inductive investigation in which the researcher poses questions about information provided by respondents or taken from historical records; the researcher asks the questions to him or herself and repeatedly questions the responses to derive deeper explanations.

H

Hawthorne effect People will perform differently from normal when they know they are experimental subjects.

Hermeneutics An approach to understanding phenomenology that relies on analysis of texts through which a person tells a story about him or herself.

Hermeneutic unit Refers to a text passage from a respondent's story that is linked with a key theme from within this story or provided by the researcher.

Hidden observation Observation in which the subject is unaware that observation is taking place.

Histogram A graphical way of showing a frequency distribution in which the height of a bar corresponds to the observed frequency of the category.

History effect Occurs when some change other than the experimental treatment occurs during the course of an experiment that affects the dependent variable.

Host Where the content for a particular website physically resides and is accessed.

Human subjects review committee Carefully reviews proposed research design to try to make sure that no harm can come to any research participant.

Hypothesis A formal statement explaining some outcome.

Hypothesis test of a proportion A test that is conceptually similar to the one used when the mean is the characteristic of interest but that differs in the mathematical formulation of the standard error of the proportion.

Hypothetical constructs Variables that are not directly observable but are measurable through indirect indicators, such as verbal expression or overt behavior.

I

Idealism A term that reflects the degree to which one bases one's morality on moral standards.

Image profile A graphic representation of semantic differential data for competing brands, products, or stores to highlight comparisons.

Importance-performance analysis Another name for quadrant analysis.

Impute To fill in a missing data point through the use of a statistical algorithm that provides a best guess for the missing response based on available information.

In-house editing A rigorous editing job performed by a centralized office staff.

In-house interviewer A fieldworker who is employed by the company conducting the research.

In-house research Research performed by employees of the company that will benefit from the research.

Independent samples *t*-test A test for hypotheses stating that the mean scores for some interval- or ratio-scaled variable grouped based on some less than interval classificatory variable.

Independent variable A variable that is expected to influence the dependent variable in some way.

Index measure An index assigns a value based on how much of the concept being measured is associated with an observation. Indexes often are formed by putting several variables together.

Index numbers Scores or observations recalibrated to indicate how they relate to a base number.

Index of retail saturation A calculation that describes the relationship between retail demand and supply.

Information Data formatted (structured) to support decision making or define the relationship between two facts.

Information completeness Having the right amount of information.

Informed consent When an individual understands what the researcher wants him or her to do and consents to the research study.

Instrumentation effect A nuisance that occurs when a change in the wording of questions, a change in interviewers, or a change in other procedures causes a change in the dependent variable.

Integrated marketing communication Means that all promotional efforts (advertising, public relations, personal selling, event marketing, and so forth) should be coordinated to communicate a consistent image.

Integrated marketing mix The effects of various combinations of marketing-mix elements on important outcomes.

Interaction effect Differences in dependant variable means due to a specific combination of independent variables.

Interactive help desk In an Internet questionnaire, a live, real-time support feature that solves problems or answers questions respondents may encounter in completing the questionnaire.

Interactive medium A medium, such as the Internet, that a person can use to communicate with and interact with other users.

Interdependence techniques Multivariate statistical techniques that give meaning to a set of variables or seek to group things together. No distinction is made between dependent and independent variables.

Internal consistency Represents a measure's homogeneity or the extent to which each indicator of a concept converges on some common meaning.

Internal and proprietary data Secondary data that originate inside the organization.

Internal validity Exists to the extent that an experimental variable is truly responsible for any variance in the dependent variable.

Internet A worldwide network of computers that allows users access to information from distant sources.

Internet survey A self-administered questionnaire posted on a website.

Interpretation The process of drawing inferences from the analysis results.

Interrogative techniques Asking multiple what, where, who, when, why, and how questions.

Interquartile range A measure of variability.

Interval scales Scales that have both nominal and ordinal properties, but that also capture information about differences in quantities of a concept from one observation to the next.

Interviewer bias A response bias that occurs because the presence of the interviewer influences respondents' answers.

Interviewer cheating The practice by fieldworkers of filling in fake answers or falsifying interviews.

Interviewer error Mistakes made by interviewers failing to record survey responses correctly.

Intranet A company's private data network that uses Internet standards and technology.

Introduction section The part of the body of a research report that discusses background information and the specific objectives of the research.

Inverse (negative) relationship Covariation in which the association between variables is in the opposite direction. As one goes up, the other goes down.

Item nonresponse Failure of a respondent to provide an answer to a survey question.

J

Judgment (purposive) sampling A nonprobability sampling technique in which an experienced individual selects the sample based on personal judgment about some appropriate characteristic of the sample member.

K

Keyword search Takes place as the search engine searches through millions of web pages for documents containing the keywords.

Knowledge A blend of previous experience, insight, and data that forms organizational memory.

Knowledge management The process of creating an inclusive, comprehensive, easily accessible organizational memory, which is often called the organization's *intellectual capital*.

L

Laboratory experiment The researcher has more complete control over the research setting and extraneous variables.

Laddering A particular approach to probing, asking respondents to compare differences between brands at different levels that produces distinctions at the attribute level, the benefit level, and the value or motivation level.

Latin square design A balanced, two-way classification scheme that attempts to control or block out the effect of two or more extraneous factors by restricting randomization with respect to the row and column effects.

Leading question A question that suggests or implies certain answers.

Likert scale A measure of attitudes designed to allow respondents to rate how strongly they agree or disagree with carefully constructed statements, ranging from very positive to very negative attitudes toward some object; several scale items may be used to form a summated index.

Literature review A directed search of published works, including periodicals and books, that discusses theory and presents empirical results that are relevant to the topic at hand.

Loaded question A question that suggests a socially desirable answer or is emotionally charged.

Longitudinal study A survey of respondents at different times, thus allowing analysis of response continuity and changes over time.

M

Mail survey A self-administered questionnaire sent to respondents through the mail.

Main effect Differences in a dependent variable by an experimental variable treatment level.

Mall intercept interviews Personal interviews conducted in a shopping mall.

Manager of decision support systems Employee who supervises the collection and analysis of sales, inventory, and other periodic customer relationship management (CRM) data.

Managerial action standard A specific performance criterion upon which a decision can be based.

Manipulation Means that the researcher alters the level of the variable in specific increments.

Manipulation check A validity test of an experimental manipulation to make sure that the manipulation does produce differences in the independent variable.

Marginals Row and column totals in a contingency table which are shown in its margins.

Market intelligence The subset of data and information that actually has some explanatory power enabling effective decisions to be made.

Market opportunity A situation that makes some potential competitive advantage possible.

Market penetration The percentage of target market customers who purchased the product—often measured early in a test-market.

Market problem A situation that makes some significant negative consequence more likely.

Market tracking The observation and analysis of trends in industry volume and brand share over time.

Market-based analysis A form of data mining that analyzes anonymous point-of-sale transaction databases to identify coinciding purchases or relationships between products purchased and other retail shopping information.

Marketing channel A network of interdependent institutions that perform the logistics necessary for consumption to occur.

Marketing concept A central idea in modern marketing thinking that focuses on how the firm provides value to customers more than on the physical product or production process.

Marketing ethics The application of morals to behavior related to the exchange environment.

Marketing metrics Quantitative ways of monitoring and measuring marketing performance.

Marketing orientation The corporate culture existing for firms adopting the marketing concept. It emphasizes customer orientation, long-term profitability over short-term profits, and a cross-functional perspective.

Marketing research The application of the scientific method in searching for the truth about marketing phenomena. These activities include defining marketing opportunities and problems, generating and evaluating marketing ideas, monitoring performance, and understanding the marketing process.

Maturation effects Effects that are a function of time and the naturally occurring events that coincide with growth and experience.

Mean A measure of central tendency; the arithmetic average.

Measure of association A general term that refers to a number of bivariate statistical techniques used to measure the strength of a relationship between two variables.

Measurement The process of describing some property of a phenomenon of interest, usually by assigning numbers in a reliable and valid way.

Median A measure of central tendency that is the midpoint; the value below which half the values in a distribution fall.

Median split Dividing a data set into two categories by placing respondents below the median in one category and respondents above the median in another.

Mixed-mode survey Study that employs any combination of survey methods.

Mode A measure of central tendency; the value that occurs most often.

Model building The use of secondary data to help specify relationships between two or more variables; can involve the development of descriptive or predictive equations.

Moderator A person who leads a focus group interview and ensures that everyone gets a chance to speak and contribute to the discussion.

Moderator variable A third variable that changes the nature of a relationship between the original independent and dependent variables.

Monadic rating scale Any measure of attitudes that asks respondents about a single concept in isolation.

Moral standards Principles that reflect beliefs about what is ethical and what is unethical.

Mortality effect (sample attrition) Occurs when some subjects withdraw from the experiment before it is completed.

Multicollinearity The extent to which independent variables in a multiple regression analysis are correlated with each other. High multicollinearity can make interpreting parameter estimates difficult or impossible.

Multidimensional scaling A statistical technique that measures objects in multidimensional space on the basis of respondents' judgments of the similarity of objects.

Multiple regression analysis An analysis of association in which the effects of two or more independent variables on a single, interval-scaled dependent variable are investigated simultaneously.

Multiple-grid question Several similar questions arranged in a grid format.

Multistage area sampling Sampling that involves using a combination of two or more probability sampling techniques.

Multivariate analysis of variance (MANOVA) A statistical technique that provides a simultaneous significance test of mean difference between groups for two or more dependent variables. A truly multivariate form of the GLM.

Multivariate statistical analysis Statistical analysis involving three or more variables or sets of variables.

Mystery shoppers Employees of a research firm who are paid to pretend to be actual shoppers.

N

Neural network A form of artificial intelligence in which a computer is programmed to mimic the way that human brains process information.

No contacts People who are not at home or who are otherwise inaccessible on the first and second contact.

Nominal scales Represent the most elementary level of measurement in which values are assigned to an object for identification or classification purposes only.

Non-forced-choice scale A fixed-alternative rating scale that provides a "no opinion" category or that allows respondents to indicate that they cannot say which alternative is their choice.

Nonparametric statistics Appropriate when the variables being analyzed do not conform to any known or continuous distribution.

Nonprobability sampling A sampling technique in which units of the sample are selected on the basis of personal judgment or convenience; the probability of any particular member of the population being chosen is unknown.

Nonrespondent error Error that the respondent is not responsible for creating, such as when the interviewer marks a response incorrectly.

Nonrespondents People who are not contacted or who refuse to cooperate in the research.

Nonresponse error The statistical differences between a survey that includes only those who responded and a perfect survey that would also include those who failed to respond.

Nonspurious association One of three criteria for causality; means any covariation between a cause and an effect is true and not simply due to some other variable.

Normal distribution A symmetrical, bell-shaped distribution that describes the expected probability distribution of many chance occurrences.

Numerical scale An attitude rating scale similar to a semantic differential except that it uses numbers, instead of verbal descriptions, as response options to identify response positions.

O

Observation The systematic process of recording the behavioral patterns of people, objects, and occurrences as they are witnessed.

Observer bias A distortion of measurement resulting from the cognitive behavior or actions of a witnessing observer.

Online focus group A qualitative research effort in which a group of individuals provides unstructured comments by entering their remarks into an electronic Internet display board of some type.

Open-ended boxes In an Internet questionnaire, boxes where respondents can type in their own answers to open-ended questions.

Open-ended response questions Questions that pose some problem and ask respondents to answer in their own words.

Operationalization The process of identifying scales that correspond to variance in a concept to be involved in a research process.

Opt in To give permission to receive selected e-mail, such as questionnaires, from a company with an Internet presence.

Optical scanning system A data processing input device that reads material directly from mark-sensed questionnaires.

Oral presentation A spoken summary of the major findings, conclusions, and recommendations, given to clients or line managers to provide them with the opportunity to clarify any ambiguous issues by asking questions.

Order bias Bias caused by the influence of earlier questions in a questionnaire or by an answer's position in a set of answers.

Ordinal scales A ranking scale allowing things to be arranged based on how much of some concept they possess.

Outlier A value that lies outside the normal range of the data.

Outside agency An independent research firm contracted by the company that actually will benefit from the research.

P

p-value Probability value; or the observed or computed significance level. P-values are compared to significance levels to test hypotheses.

Paired comparison A measurement technique that involves presenting the respondent with two objects and asking the respondent to pick the preferred object. More than two objects may be presented, but comparisons are made in pairs.

Paired-samples *t*-test An appropriate test for comparing the scores of two interval variables drawn from related populations.

Parametric statistics Involve numbers with known, continuous distributions. When the data are interval or ratio scaled and the sample size is large, parametric statistical procedures are appropriate.

Partial correlation The correlation between two variables after taking into account the fact that they are correlated with other variables too.

Participant-observation Ethnographic research approach where the researcher becomes immersed within the culture that he or she is studying and draws data from his or her observations.

Percentage distribution A frequency distribution organized into a table (or graph) that summarizes percentage values associated with particular values of a variable.

Performance-monitoring research Refers to research that regularly, sometimes routinely, provides feedback for evaluation and control of marketing activity.

Personal interview Face-to-face communication in which an interviewer asks a respondent to answer questions.

Phenomenology A philosophical approach to studying human experiences based on the idea that human experience itself is inherently subjective and determined by the context in which people live.

Picture frustration A version of the TAT using a cartoon drawing in which the respondent suggests a dialogue in which the characters might engage.

Piggyback A procedure in which one respondent stimulates thought among the others; as this process continues, increasingly creative insights are possible.

Pilot study A small-scale research project that collects data from respondents similar to those to be used in the full study.

Pivot question A filter question used to determine which version of a second question will be asked.

Placebo A false experimental effect used to create the perception that some effect has been administered.

Placebo effect The effect in a dependent variable associated with the psychological impact that goes along with knowledge of that some treatment is being administered.

Plug value An answer that an editor "plugs in" to replace blanks or missing values so as to permit data analysis; choice of value is based on a predetermined decision rule.

Point estimate An estimate of the population mean in the form of a single value, usually the sample mean.

Pooled estimate of the standard error An estimate of the standard error for a t-test of independent means that assumes the variances of both groups are equal.

Pop-up boxes In an Internet questionnaire, boxes that appear at selected points and contain information or instructions for respondents.

Population (universe) Any complete group of entities that share some common set of characteristics.

Population distribution A frequency distribution of the elements of a population.

Population element An individual member of a population.

Population parameters Variables in a population or measured characteristics of the population.

Preliminary tabulation A tabulation of the results of a pretest to help determine whether the questionnaire will meet the objectives of the research.

Pretest A small-scale study in which the results are only preliminary and intended only to assist in design of a subsequent study.

Pretesting Screening procedure that involves a trial run with a group of respondents to iron out fundamental problems in the survey design.

Pricing Involves finding the amount of monetary sacrifice that best represents the value customers perceive in a product after considering various market constraints.

Primary sampling unit (PSU) A term used to designate a unit selected in the first stage of sampling.

Probability The long-run relative frequency with which an event will occur.

Probability sampling A sampling technique in which every member of the population has a known, nonzero probability of selection.

Probing An interview technique that tries to draw deeper and more elaborate explanations from the discussion.

Problem Occurs when there is a difference between the current conditions and a more preferable set of conditions.

Problem definition The process of defining and developing a decision statement and the steps involved in translating it into more precise research terminology, including a set of research objectives. If this process breaks down at any point, the research will almost certainly be useless or even harmful.

Product-oriented Describes a firm that prioritizes decision making in a way that emphasizes technical superiority in the product.

Production-oriented Describes a firm that prioritizes efficiency and effectiveness of the production processes in making decisions.

Projective technique An indirect means of questioning enabling respondents to project beliefs and feelings onto a third party, an inanimate object, or a task situation.

Promotion The communication function of the firm responsible for informing and persuading buyers.

Promotion research Investigates the effectiveness of advertising, premiums, coupons, sampling, discounts, public relations, and other sales promotions.

Proportion The percentage of elements that meet some criterion.

Proportional stratified sample A stratified sample in which the number of sampling units drawn from each stratum is in proportion to the population size of that stratum.

Proprietary marketing research The gathering of new data to investigate specific problems.

Pseudo-research Conducted not to gather information for marketing decisions but to bolster a point of view and satisfy other needs.

Psychogalvanometer A device that measures galvanic skin response, a measure of involuntary changes in the electrical resistance of the skin.

Pull technology Consumers request information from a web page and the browser then determines a response; the consumer is essentially asking for the data.

Pupilometer A mechanical device used to observe and record changes in the diameter of a subject's pupils.

Push button In a dialog box on an Internet questionnaire, a small outlined area, such as a rectangle or an arrow, that the respondent clicks on to select an option or perform a function, such as submit.

Push poll Telemarketing under guise of research.

Push technology Sends data to a user's computer without a request being made; software is used to guess what information might be interesting to consumers based on the pattern of previous responses.

Q

Quadrant analysis An extension of cross-tabulation in which responses to two rating-scale questions are plotted in four quadrants of a two-dimensional table.

Qualitative data Data that are not characterized by numbers, and instead are textual, visual, or oral; focus is on stories, visual portrayals, meaningful characterizations, interpretations, and other expressive descriptions.

Qualitative marketing research Research that addresses marketing objectives through techniques that allow the researcher to provide elaborate interpretations of market phenomena without depending on numerical measurement; its focus is on discovering true inner meanings and new insights.

Quantitative data Represent phenomena by assigning numbers in an ordered and meaningful way.

Quantitative marketing research Marketing research that addresses research objectives through empirical assessments that involve numerical measurement and analysis.

Quasi-experimental designs Experimental designs that do not involve random allocation of subjects to treatment combinations.

Quota sampling A nonprobability sampling procedure that ensures that various subgroups of a population will be represented on pertinent characteristics to the exact extent that the investigator desires.

R

Radio button In an Internet questionnaire, a circular icon, resembling a button, that activates one response choice and deactivates others when a respondent clicks on it.

Random digit dialing Use of telephone exchanges and a table of random numbers to contact respondents with unlisted phone numbers.

Random sampling error A statistical fluctuation that occurs because of chance variation in the elements selected for a sample.

Random sampling error The difference between sample result and the result of a census conducted using identical procedures; a statistical fluctuation that occurs because of chance variations in the elements selected for a sample.

Randomization The random assignment of subject and treatments to groups; it is one device for equally distributing the effects of extraneous variables to all conditions.

Randomized response questions A research procedure used for dealing with sensitive topics, in which a random procedure determines which of two questions a respondent will be asked to answer.

Randomized-block design An extension of the completely randomized design in which a single, categorical extraneous variable that might affect test units' responses to the treatment is identified and the effects of this variable are isolated by being blocked out.

Ranking A measurement task that requires respondents to rank order a small number of stores, brands, or objects on the basis of overall preference or some characteristic of the stimulus.

Rating A measurement task that requires respondents to estimate the magnitude of a characteristic or quality that a brand, store, or object possesses.

Ratio scales Represent the highest form of measurement in that they have all the properties of interval scales with the additional attribute of representing absolute quantities. Ratio scales are characterized by a meaningful absolute zero.

Raw data The unedited responses from a respondent exactly as indicated by that respondent.

Record A collection of related fields that represents the responses from one sampling unit.

Refusals People who are unwilling to participate in a research project.

Relationship marketing Communicates the idea that a major goal of marketing is to build long-term relationships with the customers contributing to their success.

Relativism A term that reflects the degree to which one rejects moral standards in favor of the acceptability of some action. This way of thinking rejects absolute principles in favor of situation-based evaluations.

Relevance The characteristics of data reflecting how pertinent these particular facts are to the situation at hand.

Reliability An indicator of a measure's internal consistency.

Repeated measures Experiments in which an individual subject is exposed to more than one level of an experimental treatment.

Replicable When the same conclusion is reached based on another researcher's interpretation.

Report format The makeup or arrangement of parts necessary to a good research report.

Research analyst A person responsible for client contact, project design, preparation of proposals, selection of research suppliers, and supervision of data collection, analysis, and reporting activities.

Research assistants Research employees who provide technical assistance with questionnaire design, data analyses, and similar activities.

Research design A master plan that specifies the methods and procedures for collecting and analyzing the needed information.

Research follow-up Recontacting decision makers and/or clients after they have had a chance to read over a research report in order to determine whether additional information or clarification is necessary.

Research generalist An employee who serves as a link between management and research specialists. The research generalist acts as a problem definer, an educator, a liaison, a communicator, and a friendly ear.

Research methodology section The part of the body of a report that presents the findings of the project. It includes tables, charts, and an organized narrative.

Research objectives The goals to be achieved by conducting research.

Research program Numerous related studies that come together to address multiple, related research objectives.

Research project A single study that addresses one or a small number of research objectives.

Research proposal A written statement of the research design.

Research questions Express the research objectives in terms of questions that can be addressed by research.

Research report An oral presentation or written statement of research results, strategic recommendations, and/or other conclusions to a specific audience.

Research suppliers Commercial providers of marketing research services.

Researcher-dependent Research in which the researcher must extract meaning from unstructured responses such as text from a recorded interview or a collage representing the meaning of some experience.

Respondents People who verbally answer an interviewer's questions or provide answers to written questions.

Respondent error A category of sample bias resulting from some respondent action or inaction such as nonresponse or response bias.

Response bias A bias that occurs when respondents either consciously or unconsciously tend to answer questions with a certain slant that misrepresents the truth.

Response latency The amount of time it takes to make a choice between two alternatives; used as a measure of the strength of preference.

Response rate The number of questionnaires returned or completed divided by the number of eligible people who were asked to participate in the survey.

Results section The part of the body of a report that presents the findings of the project. It includes tables, charts, and an organized narrative.

Reverse coding Means that the value assigned for a response is treated oppositely from the other items.

Reverse directory A directory similar to a telephone directory except that listings are by city and street address or by phone number rather than alphabetical by last name.

Reverse recoding A method of making sure all the items forming a composite scale are scored in the same direction. Negative items can be recoded into the equivalent responses for a non-reverse coded item.

S

Sample A subset, or some part, of a larger population.

Sample bias A persistent tendency for the results of a sample to deviate in one direction from the true value of the population parameter.

Sample distribution A frequency distribution of a sample.

Sample selection error An administrative error caused by improper sample design or sampling procedure execution.

Sample statistics Variables in a sample or measures computed from sample data.

Sample survey A more formal term for a survey.

Sampling distribution A theoretical probability distribution of sample means for all possible samples of a certain size drawn from a particular population.

Sampling frame A list of elements from which a sample may be drawn; also called working population.

Sampling frame error An error that occurs when certain sample elements are not listed or are not accurately represented in a sampling frame.

Sampling Involves any procedure that draws conclusions based on measurements of a portion of the population.

Sampling unit A single element or group of elements subject to selection in the sample.

Scales A device providing a range of values that correspond to different values in a concept being measured.

Scanner data The accumulated records resulting from point of sale data recordings.

Scanner-based consumer panel A type of consumer panel in which participants' purchasing habits are recorded with a laser scanner rather than a purchase diary.

Search engine A computerized directory that allows anyone to search the World Wide Web for information using a keyword search.

Secondary data Data that have been previously collected for some purpose other than the one at hand.

Secondary sampling unit A term used to designate a unit selected in the second stage of sampling.

Self-administered questionnaires Surveys in which the respondent takes the responsibility for reading and answering the questions.

Self-selection bias A bias that occurs because people who feel strongly about a subject are more likely to respond to survey questions than people who feel indifferent about it.

Semantic differential A measure of attitudes that consists of a series of seven-point rating scales that use bipolar adjectives to anchor the beginning and end of each scale.

Sensitivity A measurement instrument's ability to accurately measure variability in stimuli or responses.

Significance level A critical probability associated with a statistical hypothesis test that indicates how likely an inference supporting a difference between an observed value and some statistical expectation is true. The acceptable level of Type I error.

Simple (bivariate) linear regression A measure of linear association that investigates straight-line relationships between a continuous dependent variable and an independent variable that is usually continuous, but can be a categorical dummy variable.

Simple random sampling A sampling procedure that assures each element in the population of an equal chance of being included in the sample.

Simple-dichotomy (dichotomous-alternative) question A fixed-alternative question that requires the respondent to choose one of two alternatives.

Simulated test-market A research laboratory in which the traditional shopping process is compressed into a short time span.

Single-source data Diverse types of data offered by a single company; usually integrated on the basis of a common variable such as geographic area or store.

Site analysis techniques Techniques that use secondary data to select the best location for retail or wholesale operations.

Situation analysis The gathering of background information to familiarize researchers and managers with the decision-making environment.

Smart agent software Software capable of learning an Internet user's preferences and automatically searching out information in selected websites and then distributing it.

Snowball sampling A sampling procedure in which initial respondents are selected by probability methods and additional respondents are obtained from information provided by the initial respondents.

Social desirability bias Bias in responses caused by respondents' desire, either conscious or unconscious, to gain prestige or appear in a different social role.

Sorting A measurement task that presents a respondent with several objects or product concepts and requires the respondent to arrange the objects into piles or classify the product concepts.

Split-ballot technique Using two alternative phrasings of the same questions for respective halves of a sample to elicit a more accurate total response than would a single phrasing.

Split-half method A method for assessing internal consistency by checking the results of one-half of a set of scaled items against the results from the other half.

Spyware Software placed on a computer without consent or knowledge of the user.

Standard deviation A quantitative index of a distribution's spread, or variability; the square root of the variance for a distribution.

Standard error of the mean The standard deviation of the sampling distribution.

Standardized normal distribution A purely theoretical probability distribution that reflects a specific normal curve for the standardized value, z.

Standardized regression coefficient (β) The estimated coefficient indicating the strength of relationship between an independent variable and dependent variable expressed on a standardized scale where higher absolute values indicate stronger relationships (range is from -1 to 1).

Standardized research service Companies that develop a unique methodology for investigating a business specialty area.

Stapel scale A measure of attitudes that consists of a single adjective in the center of an even number of numerical values.

Statistical base The number of respondents or observations (in a row or column) used as a basis for computing percentages.

Status bar In an Internet questionnaire, a visual indicator that tells the respondent what portion of the survey he or she has completed.

Stratified sampling A probability sampling procedure in which simple random subsamples that are more or less equal on some characteristic are drawn from within each stratum of the population.

Streaming media Consist of multimedia content such as audio or video that is made available in real time over the Internet or a corporate intranet.

String characters Computer terminology to represent formatting a variable using a series of alphabetic characters (nonnumeric characters) that may form a word.

Structured question A question that imposes a limit on the number of allowable responses.

Subjective Results are researcher-dependent, meaning different researchers may reach different conclusions based on the same interview.

Subjects The sampling units for an experiment, usually human respondents who provide measures based on the experimental manipulation.

Summated scale A scale created by simply summing (adding together) the response to each item making up the composite measure.

Supply chain Another term for a channel of distribution, meaning the link between suppliers and customers.

Survey A research technique in which a sample is interviewed in some form or the behavior of respondents is observed and described in some way.

Symptoms Observable cues that serve as a signal of a problem because they are caused by that problem.

Syndicated service A marketing research supplier that provides standardized information for many clients in return for a fee.

Systematic error Error resulting from some imperfect aspect of the research design that causes respondent error or from a mistake in the execution of the research.

Systematic or nonsampling error Occurs if the sampling units in an experimental cell are somehow different than the units in another cell, and this difference affects the dependent variable.

Systematic sampling A sampling procedure in which a starting point is selected by a random process and then every n^{th} number on the list is selected.

T

t-distribution A symmetrical, bell-shaped distribution that is contingent on sample size. It has a mean of 0 and a standard deviation equal to 1.

t-test A hypothesis test that uses the t-distribution. A univariate t-test is appropriate when the variable being analyzed is interval or ratio.

Tabulation The orderly arrangement of data in a table or other summary format showing the number of responses to each response category; tallying.

Tachistoscope Device that controls the amount of time a subject is exposed to a visual image.

Telephone interviews Personal interviews conducted by telephone, the mainstay of commercial survey research.

Television monitoring Computerized mechanical observation used to obtain television ratings.

Temporal sequence One of three criteria for causality; deals with the time order of events—the cause must occur before the effect.

Tertiary sampling unit A term used to designate a unit selected in the third stage of sampling.

Test of differences An investigation of a hypothesis stating that two (or more) groups differ with respect to measures on a variable.

Test tabulation Tallying of a small sample of the total number of replies to a particular question in order to construct coding categories.

Test units The subjects or entities whose responses to the experimental treatment are measured or observed.

Test-market An experiment that is conducted within actual market conditions.

Test-market sabotage Intentional attempts to disrupt the results of a test-market being conducted by another firm.

Test-retest method Administering the same scale or measure to the same respondents at two separate points in time to test for stability.

Testing effects A nuisance effect occurring when the initial measurement or test alerts or primes subjects in a way that affects their response to the experimental treatments.

The scientific method The way researchers go about using knowledge and evidence to reach objective conclusions about the real world.

Thematic apperception test (TAT) A test that presents subjects with an ambiguous picture(s) in which consumers and products are the center of attention; the investigator asks the subject to tell what is happening in the picture(s) now and what might happen next.

Themes Identified by the frequency with which the same term (or a synonym) arises in the narrative description.

Theory A formal, logical explanation of some events that includes predictions of how things relate to one another.

Thurstone scale An attitude scale in which judges assign scale values to attitudinal statements and subjects are asked to respond to these statements.

Time series design Used for an experiment investigating long-term structural changes.

Timeliness Means that the data are current enough to still be relevant.

Total quality management A business philosophy that emphasizes market-driven quality as a top organizational priority.

Total value management Trying to manage and monitor the entire process by which consumers receive benefits from a company.

Total variation The sum of within-group variance and between-group variance. The sum of the differences between a set of observed values and the grand mean of all observations.

Tracking study A type of longitudinal study that uses successive samples to compare trends and identify changes in variables such as consumer satisfaction, brand image, or advertising awareness.

Type I error An error caused by rejecting the null hypothesis when it is true. It has a probability of alpha. Practically, a Type I error occurs when the researcher concludes that a relationship or difference exits in the population when in reality it does not exist.

Type II error An error caused by failing to reject the null hypothesis when the alternative hypothesis is true. It has a probability of beta. Practically, a Type II error occurs when a researcher concludes that no relationship or difference exists when in fact one does exist.

U

Unbalanced rating scale A fixed-alternative rating scale that has more response categories piled up at one end and an unequal number of positive and negative categories.

Undisguised questions Straightforward questions that assume the respondent is willing to answer.

Uniform resource locator (URL) A website address that web browsers recognize.

Unit of analysis A study indicates what or who should provide the data and at what level of aggregation.

Univariate statistical analysis Tests of hypotheses involving only one variable.

Unobtrusive methods Methods in which research respondents do not have to be disturbed for data to be gathered.

Unstructured question A question that does not restrict the respondents' answers.

V

Validity The accuracy or a measure or the extent to which a score truthfully represents a concept.

Value labels Unique labels assigned to each possible numeric code for a response.

Variable Anything that varies or changes from one instance to another; can exhibit differences in value, usually in magnitude or strength, or in direction.

Variable piping software Software that allows variables to be inserted into an Internet questionnaire as a respondent is completing it.

Variance A measure of variability or dispersion. Its square root is the standard deviation.

Variate Variate is a mathematical way in which a set of variables can be represented with one equation.

Verification Quality-control procedures in fieldwork intended to ensure that interviewers are following the sampling procedures and to determine whether interviewers are cheating.

Virtual-reality simulated test-market An experiment that attempts to reproduce the atmosphere of an actual retail store with visually compelling images appearing on a computer.

Visible observation Observation in which the observer's presence is known to the subject.

Voice-pitch analysis A physiological measurement technique that records abnormal frequencies in the voice that are supposed to reflect emotional reactions to various stimuli.

W

Welcome screen The first web page in an internet survey, which introduces the survey and requests that the respondent enter a password or pin.

Within-group error or variance The sum of the differences between observed values and the group mean for a given set of observations; also known as total error variance.

Within-subjects design Involves repeated measures because with each treatment the same subject is measured.

World Wide Web (WWW) A portion of the Internet that is a system of computer servers that organize information into documents called web pages.

Z

Z-test for differences of proportions A technique used to test the hypothesis that proportions are significantly different for two independent samples or groups.

ENDNOTES

ENDNOTES

Chapter 1

1 Grapetime, Terry (2004), "Vote for Me," Marketing Research, 16 (Winter), 5; Best Review 2004), "AFLAC's Quacking Duck Selected One of America's Favorite Icons," 105 (October), 119; Gage, Jack (2005), "Waddling Through," Forbes, 176 (8/15), 90.

2 Keyo, Michelle (1996), "Web Site of the Week: Jelly Belly: Using Sampling to Build a Customer Database," Inc. Online, http://www.inc.com, December 9, 1996.

3 Penn, Catherine (2005), "New Drinks Include a Health Benefit for 05," Beverage Industry, 96 (January), 45–54.

4 "U.S. Coffee Makers Perky as Consumption Increases," Nations Restaurant Business, 36 (4/22/2002), 34; "U.S. Specialty Coffee Market in 30 Year Renaissance," http://www.cnn.com, December 15, 2000.

5 Kafka, Peter (2005), "Bean-Counter," Forbes, 175 (2/28), 78–80.

6 Garvin, Andrew P. (2005), "Evolve Approach to Serve Complex Market," Marketing News (September 15), p. 22.

7 Thomas, Jerry W. (2002), "Skipping MR a Major Error," Marketing News (March 4), 50.

8 Gibson, Lawrence D. (2000), "Quo Vadis Marketing Research?" Marketing Research, 12 (Spring), 36–41.

9 Matthew, Arnold (2004), "FDA Delays DTC Draft Guidance to Study How Consumers Use Brief Summaries," Medical Marketing and Media, 39 (November), 10.

10 See, for example, Babin, Barry J., Chebat, J.C. and Richard Michon (2004), "Perceived Appropriateness and its Effect on Quality, Affect and Behavior," Journal of Retailing and Consumer Services, 11 (September), 287–298.

11 Leo Y. M. Sin; Alan C. B. Tse, Oliver H. M. Yau, Raymond P. M. Chow, Jenny S.Y. Lee, Lorett B.Y. Lau (2005), "Relationship Marketing Orientation: Scale Development and Cross-Cultural Validation," Journal of Business Research, 58 (February), 185–194; Nakata, Cheryl and K. Sivakumar (2001), "Instituting the Marketing Concept in a Multinational Setting: The Role of National Culture," Journal of the Academy of Marketing Science, 29 (Summer), 255–275; Day, George (1994), "The Capabilities of Market-Driven Organizations," Journal of Marketing, 58 (October), 37–52; Ward, James C., M. D. Hutt and Peter H. Reingen (1994), "Evolving Patterns of Organizational Beliefs in the Formation of Strategy," Journal of Marketing, 58 (April), 96–110.

12 Reyes, Sonia (2000), "Ian Friendly: Groove Tube," BrandWeek (October 16), M111–M116.

13 Gelb, Betsy D. and Gabriel M. Gelb (1991), "What Research Inside the Organization Can Accomplish," Marketing Research (December), 44.

14 Marketing News (1990), "Burger King Opens Customer Hot Line" (May 28), 7.

15 Professional Builder (2004), "David Weekley Homes Reign in Fort Worth Market," 69 (December), 31–34.

16 Professional Builder (2004), "Builder POV: David Weekley," 69 (January), 69, 31–32.

17 Sharman, G. K. (1997), "Sessions Challenge Status Quo," Marketing News (November 10), p. 18.

18 Schwartz, David, Concept Testing: How to Test Product Ideas Before You Go to Market (New York: AMACOM, 1987), p. 91.

19 Wyner, Gordon A. (2005), "Biz Problems Can Get Solved With Research," Marketing News (September 15), 33–34.

20 Benezra, Karen (1994), "Fritos Around the World," BrandWeek (March 27), 32; USA Today, "Cheetos Make Debute in China But Lose Cheese in Translation" (September 2), B-1.

21 See Allenby, Greg M., Thomas S. Shively, Yang Sha and Mark J. Garratt (2004), "A Choice Model for Packaged Goods: Dealing with Discrete Quantities and Quantity Discounts," Marketing Science, 23 (Winter), 14–21.

22 Mohn, N. Carroll (1995), "Pricing Research for Decision Making," Marketing Research (Winter), 11–12.

23 See Allenby, Greg M., Thomas S. Shively, Yang Sha and Mark J. Garratt (2004), "A Choice Model for Packaged Goods: Dealing with Discrete Quantities and Quantity Discounts," Marketing Science, 23 (Winter), 14–21.

24 Mohn, N. Carroll (1995), "Pricing Research for Decision Making," Marketing Research (Winter), 11–12.

25 Ofir, Chezy (2004), "Reexamining Latitude of Price Acceptability and Price Thresholds: Predicting Basic Consumer Reaction to Price," Journal of Consumer Research, 30 (March), 612–621.

26 Bonamici, Kate (2004), "Big-Foot Dips Toe in Coffee," Fortune, 149 (January 26), 70.

27 Gardyn, Rebecca (2001), "Same Name, New Number: AT&T's Brand Image Gets a Needed Boost from a Well-Rounded Hero," American Demographics (March), 56.

28 Schneider, Lars-Peter and Bettina T. Cornwell (2005), "Cashing in on Crashes via Brand Placement in Computer Games," International Journal of Advertising, 24 (3), 321–342.

29 Low, George S. (2000), "Correlates of Integrated Marketing Communications," Journal of Advertising Research (May).

30 Hein, Kenneth (2004), "Best Buy Calls the 'Odd' Squad: Group of Tech 'Geeks' gets Spotlight in National Branding Spot," Brandweek, 45 (October 18), 11; DSN Retailing Today (2004), "Best Buy Turns On the Geek Appeal. (CE & Entertainment)," 42 (February 24), 22.

31 Garretson, Judith and Scot Burton (2005), "The Role of Spokescharacters as Advertisement and Package Cues in Integrated Marketing Communications," Journal of Marketing, 69 (October), 118–132.

32 Clancy, Kevin J. and Randy L. Stone (2005), "Don't Blame the Metrics," Harvard Business Review, 83 (June), 26–28.

33 Honomichl, Jack (2001), "Growth Stunt," Marketing News (June 4), 144.

34 Express Magazine, "You Say Tomato, I say Tomahto," (Spring), 19.

35 Information from Ben & Jerry's web page at http://www.benjerry.com; LearNet's Video Ben & Jerry's; and a press release from Ben & Jerry's, February 20, 1997.

Chapter 2

1 Collett, Stacy (2002), "External Business Intelligence Can be a Powerful Addition to your Data Warehouse, but Beware of Data Overload," Computerworld, (April 15), 34.

2   See Albers, Brad (2001), "Home Depot's Special Projects Support Team Powers Information Management for Business Needs," Journal of Organizational Excellence, 21 (Winter), 3–15; Songini, Marc L. (2002), "Home Depot's Next IT Project: Data Warehouse," Computerworld, 36 (October 7), 1–2.

3   LaBahn, Douglass W. and Robert Krapfel (2000), "Early Supplier Involvement in Customer New Product Development: A Contingency Model of Component Supplier Intentions," Journal of Busines Research, 47 (March), 173–190.

4   Tay, Nicholas S. P. and Robert F. Lusch (2005), "A Preliminary Test of Hunt's General Theory of Competition: Using Artificial Adaptive Agents to Study Complex and Ill-Defined Environments," Journal of Business Research, 58 (September), 1155–1168.

5   Knapp, Ellen M. (1998), "Knowledge Management," Business and Economic Review (July–September), 3–6.

6   Sherman, D. J., D. Berkowitz, and W. E. Soulder (2005), "New Product Development Performance and the Interaction of Cross-Functional Integration and Knowledge Management," Journal of Product Innovation Management, 22 (September), 399–411.

7   Chonko, L. B., A. J. Dubinsky, E. Jones, and J. A. Roberts (2003), "Organizational and Individual Learning in the Sales Force: An Agenda for Sales Research," Journal of Business Research, 56 (December), 935–946.

8   DSN Retailing Today (2005), "Beneifs of RFID Becoming More Visible" (August 8), 22.

9   Hall, Mark (2002), "Seeding for Data Growth," Computerworld, 36 (April 15), 52.

10 Angwein, J. and Delaney, K. J. (2005), "Top Web Sites Build Up Ad Backlog, Raise Rates," Wall Street Journal (November 16), A1.

11 Gale Annual Directory of Databases, Gale Research Inc.: Detroit.

12 Patrick A. Moore and Ronald Milliman (1995), "Application of the Internet in Marketing Education," paper presented at the Southwest Marketing Association, Houston, Texas.

13 Geng, X., M. B. Stinchcombe, and A. B. Whinston (2001), "Radically New Product Introduction Using On-Line Auctions," Journal of Electronic Commerce, 5 (Spring), 169–189.

14 Business Week Online (2002), "A Better Web Through Higher Math" (January 22), http://www.businessweek.com (accessed November 12, 2005).

15 Rangaswamy, Arvind and G. Lilien (1997), "Software Tools for New Product Development," Journal of Marketing Research, 34 (February), 177–184.

16 Desouza, Kevin and Yukika Awazu (2005), "Maintaining Knowledge Management Systems: A Strategic Imperative," Journal of the American Society for Information Science and Technology, 56 (May), 765–768.

17 Rangaswamy, Arvind and G. Lilien (1997).

18 Close, A. G., A. Dixit and N. Malhotra (2005), "Chalkboards to Cybercourses: The Internet and Marketing Education," Marketing Education Review, 15 (Summer), 81–94.

19 Adopted with permission from deJony, Jennifer (1995), "View from the Top," Technology, 1, downloaded from the Internet July 3, 1998.

20 Excerpt reprinted with permission from http://houns54.clearlake.ibm.com/solutions/erp/erppub.nsf/detailcontacts/Stage_1_ERPLifecycle_Solution_Inquirywhat, downloaded June 21, 2001.

21 Wells, H.G. (1940), "The Brain: Organization of the Modern World."

Chapter 3

1   This section is based in part on Richard Draft, Management (Hillsdale, IL: Dryden Press, 1994).

2   Zahay, Debra, Abbie Griffin and Elisa Fredericks (2004), "Sources, Uses, and Forms of Data in the New Product Development Process," Industrial Marketing Management, 33 (October), 658–666.

3   Hara, Yoshika (2002), "New Industry Awaits Human-Friendly Bipeds—'Personal Robots' get Ready to Walk on the Human Side," Electronic Engineering Times (September 16), 157–159.

4   Bocchi, Joe, Jacqueline K. Eastman, and Cathy Owens Swift (2004), "Retaining the Online Learner: Profile of Students in an Online MBA Program and Implications for Teaching Them," Journal of Education for Business (March/April), 245–253.

5   Janoff, Barry (2001), "Brands of the Land," BrandWeek (April 20), 28.

6   Bocchi, Eastman and Swift (2004); Carr, S. (2000), "As Distance Education Comes of Age, the Challenge is Keeping the Students," Chronicle of Higher Education, 23, A1.; Moskal and Dziuban (2001), "Present and Future Directions for Assessing Cybereduation: The Changing Research Paradigm," in L. R.Vandervert, L.V. Chavinina and R. A. Cornell, Eds., Cybereducation: The Future of Long-Distance Learning, New York: P. D. Moskal and C. G. Dziuban, Liebert, 157–184.

7   Thomas, Jerry W. (2005), "Skipping MR a Major Error," Marketing News (March 4), 50.

8   A. Einstein and L. Infeld, The Evolution of Physics (New York: Simon and Schuster, 1942), p. 95.

9   Perdue, B.C. and J.O. Summers (1986), "Checking the Success of Manipulations in Marketing Experiments," Journal of Marketing Research, 23 (November), 317–326.

10 See, for example, Kwok, S. and M. Uncles (2005), "Sales Promotion Effectiveness: The Impact of Consumer Differences at An Ethnic-Group Level," Journal of Product and Brand Management, 14 (3), 170–186.

11 Approximate currency rates as of November, 2005.

12 Babin, B.J., D.M. Hardesty and T.A. Suter (2003), "Color and Shopping Intentions: The Effect of Price Fairness and Perceived Affect," Journal of Business Research, 56 (July), 541–551.

13 Crowley, Michael (2004), "Conservatives (Finally) Rejoice," New Republic, 231, 13–14.

Chapter 4

1   Wood, Charles M. and Tracy A. Suter (2004), "Making Marketing Principles Tangible: Online Auctions as Living Case Studies," Journal of Marketing Education, 26 (August), 137–144; Weinberg, Bruce D. and Lenita Davis (2005), "Exploring the WOW in Online-Auction Feedback," Journal of Business Research, 58 (November), 1609–1621.

2   Fellman, M. W. (1998), "Mesmerizing Method Gets Results," Marketing News, 32 (7/20), 1–38; McDonald, W. J. (1998), "Consumer Decision Making and Altered States of Consciousness: A Study of Dualities," Journal of Business Research, 42 (July), 287–294.

3   Henderson, Naomi R. (2005), "Good Research Tools Never go out of Style and Don't Shift in the Winds of Whatever is New and Trendy," Marketing Research, 17 (Spring), 39–40.

4   Thomas C. Kinnear and Ann Root, Eds., Survey of Marketing Research (Chicago: American Marketing Association, 1994).

5   Kinnear and Root (1994).

6   Blembach, J. and K. Clancy (2000), "Boy, Oh Boy!" Adweek—Southeastern Edition, 21 (9/25), 16.

7   See Armstrong, J. S. (1989), "Why Do We Know? Predicting the Interests and Opinions of the American Consumer," Journal of Forecasting, 5 (September), 464.

8   See John, Joby and Mark Needel (1989), "Entry-Level Marketing Research Recruits: What do Recruiters Need?" Journal of Marketing Education (Spring), 68–73.

9   Ryman, Anne (2005), "Top 25 Global Research," Marketing News, 39 (August 15), H4–H38.

10 See Izzo, G. Martin and Scott J. Vitell (2003), "Exploring the Effects of Professional Education on Salespeople: The Case of Autonomous Agents," Journal of Marketing Theory & Practice, 11 (Fall), 26–38; Loe, Terry and William A. Weeks (2000), "An Empirical Investigation of Efforts to Improve Sales Students' Moral Reasoning," Journal of Personal Selling and Sales Management, 20 (Fall), 243–252.

11 Barnett, Tim and Sean Valentino (2004), "Issue Contingencies and Marketers' Recognition of Ethical Issues, Ethical Judgments and Behavioral Intentions," Journal of Business Research, 57 (April), 338–346.

12 Robin, D. P., R. E. Reidenbach and B. J. Babin (1997), "The Nature, Measurement and Stability of Ethical Judgements in the Workplace," Psychological Reports, 80, 563–580.

13 Gillin, Donna L. (2001), "The Evolution of Privacy Legislation: How Privacy Issues are Changing Research," Marketing Research, 13 (Winter), 6–7.

14 Jarvis, Steve (2002), "CMOR Finds Survey Refusal Rate Still Rising," Marketing News, 36 (2/4), 4.

15 Gillin, Donna (2001).

16 Spangenberg, E., B. Grohmann and D. E. Sprott (2005), "It's Beginning to Smell (and Sound) a lot Like Christmas: The Interactive Effects of Ambient Scent and Music in a Retail Setting," The Journal of Business Research, 58 (November), 582–589; Michon, Richard, Jean-Charles Chebat and L.W. Turley (2005), "Mall Atmospherics: The Interaction Effects of the Mall Environment on Shopping Behavior," Journal of Business Research, 58 (May), 576–583.

17 Carrigan, M. and M. Kirkup (2001), "The Ethical Responsibilities of Marketers in Retail Observational Research: Protecting Stakeholders through the 'Ethical Research' Covenant," International Journal of Retail, Distribution and Consumer Research, 11 (October), 411–435.

18 Marketing News (1995), "Marketers Value Honesty in Marketing Researchers," 29 (6/5), 27.

19 Brennan, M., S. Benson and Z. Kearns (2005), "The Effect of Introductions on Telephone Survey Participation Rates," International Journal of Market Research, 47 (1), 65–74.

20 Mack, Beth (2002), "Online Privacy Critical to Research Success," Marketing News, 36 (11/25), 21.

Chapter 5

1 Gibson, Lawrence D. (1998), "Defining Marketing Problems: Don't Spin Your Wheels Solving the Wrong Puzzle," Marketing Research, 10 (Spring), 4–12.

2 Moon, M., J. T. Mentzer and D. E. Thomas, Jr. (2000), "Customer Demand Planning at Lucent Technologies: A Case Study in Continuous Improvement through Sales Forecast Auditing," Industrial Marketing Management, 29 (January), 19–26.

3 Business China (2004), "What's New in Your Industry," 30 (2/16), 8–9.

4 Waters, C. L. (2005), "The United States Launch of Sony PlayStation 2," Journal of Business Research, 58 (July), 995–998. Provides a discussion of research issues associated with launching a game console in today's competitive environment.

5 Chapman, Randall G. (1989), "Problem Definition in Marketing Research Studies," Journal of Consumer Marketing, 6 (Spring), 51–59; Yang, Yoo S., Robert P. Leone and Dala L. Aldaen (1992), "A Market Expansion Ability Approach to Identify Potential Exporters," Journal of Marketing, 56 (January), 84–96.

6 Ackoff, Russell L., The Scientific Method (New York: Wiley, 1962), p. 71.

7 Majchrzak, A., L. P. Cooper and O. E. Neece (2004), "Knowledge Reuse for Innovation," Management Science, 50 (February), 174–188.

8 Gibson, Lawrence D. (1988).

9 Gibson, Lawrence D. (1988).

10 Chapman, Randall G. (1989).

11 Holbert, N. B. (1976), "Research: The Ways of Academe and Business," Business Horizons (February), 38.

12 Honomichl, Jack (2002), "ICR/International Communications Research," Marketing News, 36 (6/11), 47.

13 Excerpt reprinted with permission from Paul E. Green, Abba M. Krieger and Terry G. Varra (1997), "Evaluating New Products," Marketing Research: A Magazine of Management and Applications (Winter), 17–18.

Chapter 6

1 Cassidy, Hilary (2005), "Many Paths to Cool, But Big Gains for All," Brandweek, 46 (June 20), S53.

2 Niemi, Wayne (2004), "Schoenfeld to Leave as Vans CEO; As Its Deal with VF Corp. Closes, The Skate Brand Gains a New President and A New Focus on Apparel," Footwear News (July 5), 2.

3 McLaughlin, Lisa (2004), "The New Roll Model," Time, 164 (7/26), 74.

4 Sayre, Shay, Qualitative Methods for Marketplace Research (Sage: Thousand Oaks, CA, 2001).

5 Sayre, Shay (2001); Morse, Janice M. and Lyn Richards, Readme First for a User's Guide to Qualitative Methods (Sage: Thousand Oaks, CA, 2002).

6 See, for example, May, Carl (2005), "Methodological Pluralism: British Sociology and the Evidence-Based State: A Reply to Payne et al.," Sociology, 39 (July), 519–528; Achenbaum, A. A. (2001), "When Good Research Goes Bad," Marketing Research, 13 (Winter), 13–15. Wade, K. R. (2002), "We Have Come Upon the Enemy: And They are Us," Marketing Research, 14 (Summer), 39.

7 Babin, Barry J., William R. Darden and Mitch Griffin (1994), "Work and/or Fun: Measuring Hedonic and Utilitarian Shopping Value," Journal of Consumer Research, 20 (March), 644–656.

8 Stengal, J. R., A. L. Dixon and C. T. Allen (2003), "Listening Begins at Home," Harvard Business Review (November), 106–116.

9 Semon, Thomas T. (2002), "You Get What You Pay for: It May be Bad MR," Marketing News, 36 (April 15), 7.

10 The NPD process in the Exhibit is similar to that described in Lamb, C., J. Hair and C. McDaniel, Essentials of Marketing, 5th Edition (Thompson: Mason, Ohio, 2005), 297.

11 Hamel, G. and C. K. Prahalad (1991), "Corporate Imagination and Expeditionary Marketing," Harvard Business Review (July–August), 85.

12 Martens, Claire (2004), "Sometimes a Great Notion Isn't Yet a Great Product," Harvard Management Update (March), 3–4.

13 Thompson, Craig J. (1997), "Interpreting Consumers: A Hermeneutical Framework for Deriving Marketing Insights from the Tests of Consumers' Consumption Stories," Journal of Marketing Research, 34 (November), 438–455 (see pp. 443–444 for quotation).

14 Thompson, Craig J. (1997), "Interpreting Consumers: A Hermeneutical Framework for Deriving Marketing Insights from the Tests of Consumers' Consumption Stories," Journal of Marketing Research, 34 (November), 438–455; Woodside, Arch G., H. M. Pattinson and K. E. Miller (2005), "Advancing Hermeneutic Research for Interpreting Interfirm New Product Development," Journal of Business and Industrial Marketing, 20, 364–379.

15 While we refer to a hermeneutic unit as being text-based here for simplicity, they can actually also be developed using pictures, videotapes, or artifacts as well. Software such as Atlas-TI will allow files containing pictures, videos, and text to be combined into a hermeneutic unit.

16 Morse, Janice M. and Lyn Richards (2002).

17 See Feldman, Stephen P. (1998), "Playing with the Pieces: Deconstruction and the Loss of Moral Culture," Journal of Management Studies, 35 (January), 60–80.

18 American Demographics (2004), "Futurespeak," 26 (April), 44.

19 Louella, Miles (2003), "Living their Lives," Marketing (UK) (12/11), 27–28.

20 Reid, D. M. (1999), "Changes in Japan's Post-Bubble Business Environment: Implications for Foreign-Affiliated Companies," Journal of International Marketing, 7 (3), 38–63.

21 Morse, Janice M. and Lyn Richards (2002).

22 Strauss, A. L. and J. Corbin, Basics of Qualitative Research (Newbury Park, CA: Sage Publications, 1990).

23 Geiger, S. and D. Turley (2005), "Personal Selling as a Knowledge-Based Activity: Communities of Practice in the Sales Force," Irish Journal of Management, 26, 61–70.

24 Beverland (2005), "The Components of Prestige Brands," Journal of Business Research, forthcoming; Beverland, Michael (2004), "Brand Value, Convictions, Flexibility and New Zealand Wine," Business Horizons, 47 (September/October), 53–61.

25 Harwood, Jonathan (2005), "Philip Morris Develops Smokeless Cigarette," Marketing Week, 28 (3/31), 5.

26 Heather, R. P. (1994), "Future Focus Groups," American Demographics (January 1), 6.

27 Creamer, Mathew (2005), "Slowly, Marketers Learn How to Let Go and Let Blog," Advertising Age, 76 (10/31), 1–35.

28 Fass, Allison (2005), "Collective Opinion," Forbes, 176 (11/28), 76–79.

29 O'Loughlin, Sandra (2005), "Real Women Have Lingerie," Brandweek, 46 (11/14), 22–24.

30 See Palan, K. M. and R. E. Wilkes (1997), "Adolescent-Parent Interaction in Family Decision Making," Journal of Consumer Research, 24 (September), 159–170; Haytko, Diana L. and Julie Baker (2004), "It's All at the Mall: Exploring Adolescent Girls' Experiences," Journal of Retailing, 80 (Spring), 67–83.

31 Godes, David and Dina Mayzlin (2004), "Using On-Line Conversations to Study Word-of-Mouth Communications," Marketing Science, 23, 545–560.

32 Babin, Barry J., William R. Darden and James S. Boles (1995), "Salesperson Stereotypes, Consumer Emotions, and Their Impact on Information Processing," Journal of the Academy of Marketing Science, 23 (Spring, 1995), 94–105.

33 Murphy, Ian (1996), "Aided by Research, Harley Goes Whole Hog," Marketing News, 30 (12/02), 16–17.

34 Philip Kotler, "Behavioral Models for Analyzing Buyers," Journal of Marketing (October 1965), pp. 37–45.

35 Alsop, Ronald (1998), "Advertisers Put Consumers on the Couch," The Wall Street Journal (May 13), 19.

36 Grimm, Matthew (2002), "Wine Ads: A New Sobriety," American Demographics (February), 42–43.

37 Boone, Louis E. and David L. Kurtz, Contemporary Marketing (Fort Worth: Dryden, 1995).

38 van Manen, M., Researching Lived Experience: Human Science for an Action-Sensitive Pedagogy (London, ON: Althouse, 1990).

Chapter 7

1 Joint Advertising, Market Research & Studies, "Market Research and Studies," JAMRS website, http://www.jamrs.org, accessed February 8, 2006; Arndorfer, James B., "Target Practice," Advertising Age, November 28, 2005, 76 (11/28), 1–41; Margolis, Emanuel, "Building a Database of Potential Soldiers," Connecticut Law Tribune, October 24, 2005, http://www.ctlawtribune.com; and James B. Arndorfer, "Army Looking for a Direct Hit," Advertising Age, July 11, 2005, 76 (7/11), 4–36.

2 "Breakfast Sandwich Boom," Chain Leader, November 2005, downloaded from InfoTrac at http://web2.infotrac.galegroup.com; and Perlik, Allison, "Fast Starts," Restaurants & Institutions, January 15, 2006, http://web2.infotrac.galegroup.com.

3 Grow, Brian, "Yes, Ma'am, That Part Is in Stock," BusinessWeek, August 1, 2005, downloaded from InfoTrac at http://web2.infotrac.galegroup.com; and Servigistics, "Servigistics Pricing: Maximizing the Profitability of Your Service Network," http://www.servigistics.com, accessed February 7, 2006.

4 Prasso, Sheridan, "Battle for the Face of China," Fortune, December 12, 2005, downloaded from InfoTrac at http://web2.infotrac.galegroup.com.

5 Charles, Susan K., "Custom Content Delivery," Online, March–April 2004, downloaded from Business & Company Resource Center at http://galenet.galegroup.com; Fleming, Lee, "Digital Delivery: Pushing Content to the Desktop," Digital Information Group, January 31, 1997; and "How Smart Agents Will Change Selling," Forbes ASAP, August 28, 1995, p. 95.

6 "Seeking New Beer Drinkers in the High Andes," Global Agenda, July 20, 2005, downloaded from Business &

Company Resource Center, http://galenet.galegroup.com; and "China Ranked Largest Beer Consumer in 2004," Kyodo News International, December 15, 2005, http://galenet.galegroup.com.

7 This section is based on Levy, Michael and Barton Weitz, *Retail Management* (Homewood, IL: Richard D. Irwin, 1992), pp. 357–358.

8 Data from the "About Us" section of the Capital One website, http://www.capitalone.com, accessed February 9, 2006.

9 Rao, Srikumar S., "Technology: The Hot Zone," Forbes, November 18, 1996.

10 IBM Business Intelligence Data Mining Product Discovery, http://www.ibm.com.

11 Wasserman, Todd, Gerry Khermouch and Jeff Green, "Mining Everyone's Business," Brandweek, February 28, 2000, p. 34.

12 DataMind, "Clients: Case Studies," DataMind website, http://www.datamind.com, accessed February 6, 2006.

13 Totty, Michael, "Making Searches Work at Work," The Wall Street Journal, December 19, 2005, http://online.wsj.com.

14 "Hispanic-Owned Businesses: Growth Projections, 2004–2010," HispanicBusiness.com Store, http://www.hbinc.com, accessed February 7, 2006.

15 Neff, Jack, "Wal-Mart Takes Stock in RetailLink System," Advertising Age, May 21, 2001, p. 6.

16 See Federal Grants Wire, "National Trade Data Bank (NTDB)," http://www.federalgrantswire.com, accessed February 6, 2006; and STAT-USA, "What Information Is Available under GLOBUS and NTBD?" and "GLOBUS & NTDB," http://www.stat-usa.gov, accessed February 6, 2006.

17 Based on Brown, Warren, "Pain at the Pump Doesn't Faze New-Car Buyers," Washington Post, January 29, 2006, http://www.washingtonpost.com; Wells, Melanie, "Snowboarding Secrets," Forbes, February 14, 2005, downloaded from InfoTrac at http://web5.infotrac.galegroup.com; and Halliday, Jean, "Automakers Scrap SUVs, Tout Hybrids," Advertising Age, September 26, 2005, http://web5.infotrac.galegroup.com.

Chapter 8

1 Darlin, Damon, "The Only Question That Matters," Business 2.0, September 2005, downloaded from InfoTrac at http://web2.infotrac.galegroup.com; Kirkpatrick, David, "Throw It at the Wall and See if It Sticks," Fortune, December 12, 2005, http://web2.infotrac.galegroup.com; and McGregor, Jena, "Would You Recommend Us?" Business Week,

January 30, 2006, http://web5.infotrac.galegroup.com.

2 Vascellaro, Jessica E. "Who'll Give Me $50 for This Purse from Nana?" The Wall Street Journal, December 28, 2005, http://online.wsj.com; and Survey.com, "Survey Reveals Majority of Americans Receive Unwanted Gifts," news release, December 19, 2005, http://www.survey.com.

3 Excerpts from Arlen, Michael J. *Thirty Seconds* (New York: Farrar, Straus and Giroux, Inc., 1979, 1980), pp. 185–186. This material first appeared in The New Yorker.

4 However, the popularity of marketing research has affected the willingness of respondents to participate in surveys. People are increasingly refusing to participate.

5 Tuckel, Peter and Harry O'Neill, "The Vanishing Respondent in Telephone Surveys," a paper presented at the 56th annual conference of the American Association of Public Opinion Research (AAPOR) in Montreal on May 17–20, 2001.

6 Cull, William L., Karen G. O'Connor, Sanford Sharp, and Suk-fong S. Tang, "Response Rates and Response Bias for 50 Surveys of Pediatricians," Health Services Research, February 2005, downloaded from Business & Company Resource Center, http://galenet.galegroup.com.

7 Lee, Eunkyu, Michael Y. Hu and Rex S. Toh, "Respondent Non-cooperation in Surveys and Diaries: An Analysis of Item Non-response and Panel Attrition," International Journal of Market Research, Autumn 2004, downloaded from InfoTrac at http://web7.infotrac.galegroup.com.

8 Douglas Aircraft, Consumer Research (undated), p. 13.

9 For an interesting study of extremity bias, see Baumgartner, Hans and Jan-Benedict E. M. Steekamp, "Response Styles in Marketing Research: A Cross-National Investigation," Journal of Marketing Research, May 2001, pp. 143-156.

10 Turner, Charles F., Maria A. Villarroel, James R. Chromy, Elizabeth Eggleston and Susan M. Rogers, "Same-Gender Sex among U.S. Adults: Trends across the Twentieth Century and during the 1990s," Public Opinion Quarterly, Fall 2005, downloaded from InfoTrac at http://web7.infotrac.galegroup.com.

11 The term *questionnaire* technically refers only to mail and self-administered surveys, and the term *interview schedule* is used for interviews by telephone or face-to-face. However, we will use *questionnaire* to refer to all three forms of communications in this book.

12 Bright, Beckey "Nearly Half of Americans Resolve to Get Healthy in 2006, Poll Shows," The Wall Street Journal, January 17, 2006, http://online.wsj.com.

13 Ohlemacher, Stephen "Study Finds that Marriage Builds Wealth," Yahoo! News, January 18, 2006, http://news.yahoo.com; and Charles Pierret, "The National Longitudinal Survey of Youth: 1979 Cohort at 25," Monthly Labor Review, February 2005, pp. 3–7.

14 The Bureau of Business Practice, *Profiles in Quality: Blueprints for Action from 50 Leading Companies* (Boston: Allyn and Bacon, 1991), p. 113.

15 Weisberg, Karen "Change Maker," Food Service Director, January 15, 2006, downloaded from InfoTrac at http://web7.infotrac.galegroup.com.

16 Gavin, David A. "Competing on the Eight Dimensions of Quality," Harvard Business Review, November–December 1987, pp. 101-8.

17 Forelle, Charles, "Many Colleges Ignore New SAT Writing Test," The Wall Street Journal, December 7, 2005, http://online.wsj.com; and Kaplan Inc., "Kaplan's New SAT Survey Results," College Admissions, Kaplan website, http://www.kaptest.com, accessed February 14, 2006.

Chapter 9

1 Based on Ellyn Spragins, "Ask Them Yourself: How to Survey Customers on the Cheap," Fortune, December 12, 2005, downloaded from InfoTrac at http://web2.infotrac.galegroup. com; Debbie Bardon, "Online Social Networking for Business," Online, November–December 2004, downloaded from Business & Company Resource Center at http://galenet.galegroup.com; LinkedIn home page, http://www.linkedin.com, accessed February 22, 2006; and Zoomerang home page, http://info.zoomerang.com, accessed February 22, 2006.

2 Warwick, Donald T. and Charles A. Lininger, The Sample Survey: Theory and Practice (New York: McGraw-Hill, 1975), p. 2.

3 Lockley, L. C. "Notes on the History of Marketing Research," Journal of Marketing, April 1950, p. 733.

4 Hof, Robert D. "The Power of Us," BusinessWeek, June 20, 2005, downloaded from InfoTrac at http://web2.infotrac.galegroup.com.

5 For a complete discussion of conducting surveys in Hispanic neighborhoods, see Hernandes, Sigfredo A. and Carol J. Kaufman, "Marketing Research in Hispanic Barrios: A Guide to Survey Research," Marketing Research, March 1990, pp. 11–27.

6 Curtin, Richard, Stanley Presser and Eleanor Singer, "Changes in Telephone Survey Nonresponse over the Past Quarter Century," Public Opinion Quarterly, Spring 2005, downloaded from InfoTrac at http://web3.infotrac.galegroup.com.

7 Cuneo, Alice Z. "Researchers Flail as Public Cuts the Cord," Advertising Age, November 15, 2004, downloaded from InfoTrac at http://web3.infotrac.galegroup.com.

8 See ibid.; and Jon Kamman, "Cell Phones Put Pollsters 'in a Muddle,'" USA Today, December 31, 2003, http://www.usatoday.com.

9 Hembroff, Larry A. Debra Rusz, Ann Rafferty, Harry McGee and Nathaniel Ehrlich, "The Cost-Effectiveness of Alternative Advance Mailings in a Telephone Survey," Public Opinion Quarterly, Summer 2005, downloaded from InfoTrac at http://web3.infotrac.galegroup.com.

10 Brennan, Mike, Susan Benson and Zane Kearns (2005), "The Effect of Introductions on Telephone Survey Participation Rates," International Journal of Market Research, 47 (1), 65–74.

11 Dillman, Don A. Mail and Internet Surveys: The Tailored Design Method (New York: John Wiley and Sons, 2000), p. 173.

12 Schaefer, David R. and Don A. Dillman, "Development of a Standard E-Mail Methodology: Results of an Experiment," Public Opinion Quarterly 62(3) (Fall 1998), p. 378.

13 Ibid.

14 For a complete discussion of fax surveys, see the excellent article by Dickson, John P. and Douglas L. Maclachlan, "Fax Surveys: Return Patterns and Comparison with Mail Surveys," Journal of Marketing Research, February 1996, pp. 108–113.

15 Merriman, Joyce A. "Your Feedback Is Requested," American Family Physician, October 1, 2005, downloaded from InfoTrac at http://web3.infotrac.galegroup.com.

16 Dillmann, D. A. (2000), Mail and Internet Surveys, The Tailored Design Method, NY: Wiley. pp. 369–372.

17 Göritz, Anja S. (2004), "Recruitment for On-Line Access Panels," International Journal of Market Research, 46 (4), 411–425.

18 Fricker, Scott, Mirta Galesic, Roger Tourangeau and Ting Yan, "An Experimental Comparison of Web and Telephone Surveys," Public Opinion Quarterly, Fall 2005, downloaded from InfoTrac at http://web3.infotrac.galegroup.com.

19 See Nielsen, Jakob "Keep Online Surveys Short," Alertbox, February 2, 2004, http://www.useit.com; "About Jakob Nielsen," http://www.useit.com, accessed February 21, 2006; and Nielsen Norman Group, "About Nielsen Norman Group," http://www.nngroup.com, accessed February 21, 2006.

20 See Kilbourne, Lawrene "Avoid the Field of Dreams Fallacy," Quirk's Marketing Research Review, January 2005, pp. 70, 72–73.

21 Mary Lisbeth D'Amico, "Call Security," The Wall Street Journal, February 13, 2006, http://online.wsj.com.

22 For an interesting empirical study, see Akaah, Ishmael P. and Edward A. Riordan, "The Incidence of Unethical Practices in Marketing Research: An Empirical Investigation," Journal of the Academy of Marketing Sciences, Spring 1990, pp. 143–152.

23 Based on "Do-Not-Call List Reduces Telemarketing, Poll Finds," The Wall Street Journal, January 12, 2006, http://online.wsj.com.

Chapter 10

1 Based on Thomas Mucha, "This Is Your Brain on Advertising," Business 2.0, August 2005, downloaded from InfoTrac at http://web2.infotrac.galegroup.com; and Peter Laybourne and David Lewis, "Neuromarketing: The Future of Consumer Research?" Admap, May 2005, pp. 28–30.

2 Selltiz, Claire, Lawrence S. Wrightsman and Stuart W. Cook, Research Methods in Social Relations (New York: Holt, Rinehart and Winston, 1976), p. 251.

3 Campbell, Angus, Philip E. Converse and Willard L. Rodgers, The Quality of American Life (New York: Russell Sage Foundation, 1976), p. 112. Although weather conditions did not correlate with perceived quality of life, the comfort variable did show a relationship with the index of well-being. This association might be confounded by the fact that ventilation and/or air-conditioning equipment is less common in less affluent homes. Income was previously found to correlate with quality of life.

4 Abrams, Bill The Observational Research Handbook (Chicago: NTC Business Books, 2000), pp. 2, 105.

5 Adapted with permission from the April 30, 1980 issue of Advertising Age. Copyright © 1980 by Crain Communications, Inc.

6 Nielsen Media Research, "About Nielsen Media Research," http://www.nielsenmedia.com, accessed February 24, 2006.

7 Arbitron, "The Portable People Meter System," http://www.arbitron.com, accessed February 24, 2006.

8 PreTesting Company, "About the PreTesting Company" and "Television," http://www.pretesting.com, accessed February 24, 2006.

9 Jupiter Media, "Accurate Web Site Visitor Measurement Crippled by Cookie Blocking and Deletion," news release, March 14, 2005, http://www.jupitermedia.com. See also Steve Johnson, "Who's in Charge of the Web Site Ratings Anyway?" Chicago Tribune, February 26, 2006, sec. 1, p. 18.

10 Kiley, David "Google: Searching for an Edge in Ads," Business Week, January 30, 2006, downloaded from InfoTrac at http://web3.infotrac.galegroup.com. See also Pieter Sanders and Bram Lebo, "Click Tracking: A Fool's Paradise?" Brandweek, June 6, 2005, http://web3.infotrac.galegroup.com.

11 Neff, Jack "Aging Population Brushes Off Coloring," Advertising Age, July 25, 2005, downloaded from InfoTrac at http://web5.infotrac.galegroup.com.

12 Stringer, Kortney "Eye-Tracking Technology for Marketers," Detroit Free Press, August 1, 2005, downloaded from Business & Company Resource Center, http://galenet.galegroup.com.

13 Krugman's, Herbert B. statement as quoted in "Live, Simultaneous Study of Stimulus, Response Is Physiological Measurement's Great Virtue," Marketing News, May 15, 1981, pp. 1, 20.

14 Based on "Mazda Turns to Eye-Tracking to Assist Revamp of European Site," New Media Age, November 3, 2005, downloaded from Business & Company Resource Center, http://galenet.galegroup.com; and "Persuasion Is the New Focus," Revolution, February 21, 2006, downloaded from the Media Coverage page of the Syzygy website, http://www.syzygy.co.uk.

15 Adapted with permission from Bruce Rayner, "Product Development, Now Hear This!" Electronic Business, August 1997.

Chapter 11

1 Like Dragnet, the story is true but the brand names are fictitious.

2 Babin, Barry J., David M. Hardesty and Tracy A. Suter (2003), "Color and Shopping Intentions: The Intervening Effect of Price Fairness and Perceived Affect," Journal of Business Research, 56 (July), 541–551.

3 Shadish, William R., Thomas D. Cook and Donald T. Campbell, Experimental and Quasi Experimental Designs for Generalized Causal Inference. (Geneva, IL: Houghton Mifflin, 2002).

4 Ellingstad, Vernon and Norman W. Heimstra, Methods in the Study of Human Behavior (Monterey, CA: Brooks/Cole, 1974).

5 Anderson, Barry F., The Psychological Experiment: An Introduction to the Scientific Method. (Belmont, CA: Brooks/Cole, 1971), p. 28, 42–44.

6 Reitter, Robert N. (2003), "Comment: American Media and the Smoking-Related Behaviors of Asian Adolescents," Journal of Advertising Research, 43 (March), 12–13.

7 Lach, Jennifer (2000), "Up in Smoke," American Demographics, 22 (March), 26.

8 Mitchell, Vincent-Wayne and Sarah Haggett (1997), "Sun-Sign Astrology in Market Segmentation: An Empirical Investigation," Journal of Consumer Marketing, 14 (2), 113–131.

9 Roethlisberger, F. J. and W. J. Dickson, Management and the Worker: (Harvard University Press: Cambridge, MA, 1939).

10 Shiv, Baba, Ziv Carmon and Dan Aneley (2005), "Placebo Effects of Marketing Actions: Consumers May Get What they Pay for," Journal of Marketing Research, 42 (November), 383–393.

11 Tybout, Alice M. and Gerald Zaltman (1974), "Ethics in Marketing Research: Their Practical Relevance," Journal of Marketing Research, 21 (November), 357–368.

12 Peterson, Robert A. (2001), "On the Use of Students in Social Science Research: Evidence from a Second Order Meta Analysis," Journal of Consumer Research, 28 (December), 450–461.

13 Shadish, William R., Thomas D. Cook, and Donald T. Campbell (2002).

14 Reprinted with permission from Lee Martin, Geoffrey "Drinkers Get Court Call," Advertising Age, May 20, 1991. Copyright © 1991 Crain Communications, Inc.

Chapter 12

1 This vignette drawn from multiple sources: Sampey, Kathleen (2005), "Heineken Test Marketing New Light Beer," Adweek, 46 (11/7), 7; Beirne, Mike (2005), "Heineken Green Lights $40M," Brandweek, 46 (40), 9; Beirne, Mike (2005), "Brewers Face Hard Questions about Luxury Light Beers," Brandweek, 46 (11/14), 7; Sampey, Kathleen (2005), "Heineken Seeks 'Light-Line' Ideas," Adweek, 46 (11/7), 7.

2 Market Testing Consumer Products (New York: National Industrial Conference Board, 1967), p. 13.

3 Riste, Christine (2002), La suprématie contée des prospectus, "Libre Service Actualité-LSA," (January 17), 1751.

4 Babin, B. J. and Adilson Borges (2005), "Product Category and Promotional Theme Congruency: Its Effect on Preference and Retail Store Image," in Development in Marketing Science, H. Spotts, Ed., Academy of Marketing Science, Coral Gables, FL.

5 Wilson, M. (2005), "Solution Makes it Simple," Chain Store Age, 81 (June), 69.

6 Ding, Ming and Jehoshua Eliashberg (2002), "Structuring the New Product Development Pipeline," Management Science, 48 (March), 343–363.

7 Heller, Laura. (2001), "Circuit City Saves on New Look," DSN Retailing Today, 40 (10/22), 3–4.

8 Cadbury, N. D. (1975), "When, Where, and How to Test Market,"

Harvard Business Review, (May–June), 96–105.

9 Drug Store News (2005), "Spirit Category Expected to See Robust Growth," 27 (May 2), 60.

10 Neff, Jack (2001), "Average City, USA," Advertising Age, 72 (7/9), 12.

11 Neff, Jack (2001).

12 Ramage, Norma (2005), "Testing, Testing 1, 2, 3," Marketing Magazine, 110 (July), 1196.

13 U.S. Commercial Service Denmark (2006), "How to Open the Northern European Market," http://www.buyusa.gov/denmark, accessed January 22, 2006.

14 Berta, Dina (2003), "Utah City Turns Out to be Best Test Market for Brazilian Concept," Nation's Restaurant News," (September 22), 192.

15 Sally Scanlon (1979), "The True Test," Sales and Marketing Management, March, 57.

16 Vence, Deborah L. (2005), "Net Serves as Best Tool to Connect with Hispanics," Marketing News (9/1), 29–37.

17 Pollack, Jodham (1996), "Price Issues Dog Frito Olean Tests," Advertising Age (November 25), 4.

18 Neff, Jack (1998), "Millstone," Advertising Age (June 29), S16.

19 LaVallee, Andrew (2005), "Road Testing T-Shirts," Women's Wear Daily, 189 (4/27), 8.

20 Burke, Raymond R. (1996), "New Technology Helps Managers Envision the Future," Harvard Business Review, March–April 1996, 120–131.

21 Chou, Ya-Lun, Statistical Analysis with Business and Economics Applications, (Ft. Worth: Holt, Rinehart and Winston, 1975).

22 Winer, B. J., Statistical Principles in Experimental Design, 2nd ed. (New York: McGraw-Hill, 1971).

Chapter 13

1 Babin, Barry J. and Jill Attaway (2000), "Atmospheric Affect as a Tool for Creating Value and Gaining Share of Customer," Journal of Business Research, 49 (August), 91–99; Verhoef, P.C. (2003), "Understanding the Effect of Customer Relationship Management Efforts on Customer Retention and Customer Share Development," Journal of Marketing 67 (October), 30–45.

2 Periatt, J. A., S. A. LeMay and S. Chakrabarty (2004), "The Selling Orientation-Customer Orientation (SOCO) Scale: Cross-Validation of the Revised Version," Journal of Personal Selling and Sales Management," 24 (Winter), 49–54.

3 Anderson, Barry F., The Psychology Experiment. (Monterey, CA: Brooks/Cole, 1971), p. 26.

4 Kerlinger, Fred N., Foundations of Behavioral Research. (New York: Holt, Rinehart and Winston, 1973).

5 Cohen, Jacob (1990), "Things I Have Learned (So Far)," American Psychologist, 45 (December), 1304–1312.

6 Arnold, Catherine (2004), "Satisfaction's the Name of the Game," Marketing News, 38 (10/15), 39–45. Also, see http://www.theacsi.org.

7 In more advanced applications such as those involving structural equations analysis, a distinction can be made between reflective composites and formative indexes. See Hair, J. F., W. C. Black, B. J. Babin, R. Anderson and R. Tatham, Multivariate Data Analysis, 6th Edition (Upper Saddle River, NJ: Prentice Hall, 2006).

8 Bart, Yakov, Venkatesh Shankar, Fareena Sultan and Glen L. Urban (2005), "Are the Drivers and Role of Online Trust the Same for All Web Sites and Consumers? A Large-Scale Exploratory Study," Journal of Marketing, 69 (October), 133–152.

9 Cronbach, Lee J. (2004), "My Current Thoughts on Coefficient Alpha and Successor Procedures," Center for the Study of Evaluation Report 643, http://epm.sagepub.com/cgi/content/short/64/3/391.

10 Hair et al. (2006).

11 Wells, Chris (1980), "The War of the Razors," Esquire (February), 3.

12 Burke Marketing Research, "Rough Commercial Recall Testing," Cincinnati, OH; undated.

13 Hair et al. (2006).

14 Cox, Keith K. and Ben M. Enis, The Marketing Research Process. (Pacific Palisades, CA: Goodyear, 1972); Kerlinger, Fred N., Foundations of Behavioral Research, 3rd ed. (Ft. Worth: Holt, Rinehart and and Winston, 1986).

15 Headley, Dean E., Brent D. Bowen and Jacqueline R. Liedtke. This case, originally titled "Navigating through Airline Quality," was reviewed and accepted for publication by the Society for Case Research.

Chapter 14

1 Data from U.S. Census Bureau, Statistical Abstract of the United States, 2006, pp. 694, 718, 725, accessed at http://www.census.gov/prod/www/statistical-abstract.html. Research reported in Moore, Robert S., Stephen LeMay, Melissa L. Moore, Pearson Lidell, Brian Kinard and David McMillen, "An Investigation of Motorists' Perceptions of Trucks on the Highways," Transportation Journal, Winter 2005, downloaded from InfoTrac at http://web3.infotrac.galegroup.com.

2 Karen Nickel Anhalt, "Whiskas Campaign Recruits a Tiny Tiger," Advertising Age International, October 19, 1998, p. 41.

3 Breeden, Richard, "Owners, Executives Cite Small Firms' Advantages," The Wall Street Journal, January 3, 2006, http://online.wsj.com; and AllBusiness.com, "SMB State of the Union Study," Winter 2005, News and Press page, http://www.allbusiness.com/press/barometer.pdf.

4 Likert, Rensis "A Technique for the Measurement of Attitudes," Archives of Psychology 19 (1931), pp. 44–53.

5 Osgood, Charles, George Suci and Percy Tannenbaum, The Measurement of Meaning (Urbana: University of Illinois Press, 1957). Seven-point scales were used in the original work; however, subsequent researchers have modified the scale to have five points, nine points, and so on.

6 Menezes, Dennis and Norbert F. Elbert, "Alternative Semantic Scaling Formats for Measuring Store Image: An Evaluation," Journal of Marketing Research, February 1979, pp. 80–87.

7 Costanzo, Chris "How Consumer Research Drives Web Site Design," American Banker, April 19, 2005, downloaded from Business & Company Resource Center, http://galenet.galegroup.com.

8 Roeder-Johnson Corp., "Technology Still Matters to Start-Ups Say Venture Capitalists and Other Industry Influencers," news release, January 24, 2006, http://finance.yahoo.com; and Roeder-Johnson Corp., "Importance of Unique Technology to Start-Up Companies: A Survey," January 2006, downloaded at http://www.roeder-johnson.com.

Chapter 15

1 White, Joseph B. "The Price of Safety," The Wall Street Journal, December 5, 2005, http://online.wsj.com; and J. D. Power and Associates, "J. D. Power and Associates Reports: Premium Surround Sound Systems and HD Radio Garner High Consumer Interest Based on Their Market Price, while Consumers Prefer One-Time Fee over the Monthly Fee Associated with Satellite Radio," news release, http://www.jdpower.com, August 18, 2005.

2 Smith, Robert, David Olah, Bruce Hansen and Dan Cumbo, "The Effect of Quesionnaire Length on Participant Response Rate: A Case Study in the U.S. Cabinet Industry," Forest Products Journal, November–December 2003, downloaded from Business & Company Resource Center, http://galenet.galegroup.com.

3 "Insurers Question Methods in U.S. Treasury Survey on Terror Backstop," A. M. Best Newswire, April 12, 2005, downloaded from Business & Company Resource Center, http://galenet.galegroup.com.

4 "Mothers Misunderstand Questions on Feeding Questionnaire," Medical Letter on the CDC and FDA, September 5, 2004, downloaded from Business & Company Resource Center, http://galenet.galegroup.com.

5 Donahue, Amy K. and Joanne M. Miller, "Citizen Preferences and Paying for Police," Journal of Urban Affairs 27(4) (2005): 419–35.

6 Nathan Weber, "Research: A Survey Shows How Media Influence Our Decorating and Cooking Choices," HFN, the Weekly Newspaper for the Home Furnishing Network, December 5, 2005, downloaded from Business & Company Resource Center, http://galenet.galegroup.com.

7 Stanley L. Payne, The Art of Asking Questions (Princeton, NJ: Princeton University Press, 1951), p. 185. The reader who wants a more detailed account of question wording is referred to this classic book on that topic.

8 Roll, Charles W., Jr. and Albert H. Cantril, Polls: Their Use and Misuse in Politics (New York: Basic Books, 1972), pp. 106–7.

9 Other product attributes are relative advantage, compatibility, complexity, and communicability.

10 Payne, Stanley L. (1951), pp. 102–3.

11 Dillman, Don A. Mail and Internet Surveys: The Tailored Design Method (New York: John Wiley and Sons, 2000), pp. 357–61.

12 Young, Sarah J. and Craig M. Ross, "Web Questionnaires: A Glimpse of Survey Research in the Future," Parks & Recreation, Vol. 35, No. 6 (June 2000), p. 30.

13 Michel, Matt "Controversy Redux," CASRO Journal, http://www.decisionanalyst.com/publ_art/contredux.htm, downloaded February 8, 2001.

14 Ghaleb Almekhlafi, Abdurrahman "Preservice Teachers' Attitudes and Perceptions of the Utility of Web-Based Instruction in the United Arab Emirates," International Journal of Instructional Media 32(3) (2005): 269–84.

15 Harzing, Anne-Wil "Does the Use of English-Language Questionnaires in Cross-National Research Obscure National Differences?" International Journal of Cross Cultural Management 5(2) (2005): 213–24.

16 Cateora, Philip R. International Marketing (Homewood, IL: Richard D. Irwin, 1990), pp. 387–89.

17 "Hospitals, Feds Design Survey to Identify Culture That Encourages Patient Safety," Health Care Strategic Management, February 2005, downloaded from Business & Company Resource Center, http://galenet.galegroup.com; and Agency for Healthcare Research and Quality, "Hospital Survey on Patient Safety Culture," accessed at http://www.ahrq.gov/qual/hospculture, March 7, 2006.

Chapter 16

1 Based on Deborah Ball, "As Chocolate Sags, Cadbury Gambles on a Piece of Gum," The Wall Street Journal, January 12, 2006, http://online.wsj.com; Cadbury Schweppes, "Products: Trident Splash," Gumopolis, http://www.tridentgum.com, accessed March 16, 2006; Cadbury Schweppes, "New Cadbury Schweppes Americas Confectionary Facility Holds Future Gum Innovation: New Jersey Based Science & Technology Center to Meet Demands of Growing Gum Market," news release, http://www.cadburyschweppes.com, February 6, 2006.

2 Kinne, Susan and Tari D. Topolski, "Inclusion of People with Disabilities in Telephone Health Surveillance Surveys," American Journal of Public Health 95(3) (March 2005): 512–517.

3 Brock, Sabra E. "Marketing Research in Asia: Problems, Opportunities, and Lessons," Marketing Research, September 1989, p. 47.

4 Yeganeh, Hamid, Zhan Su, Elie Virgile and M. Chrysostome, "A Critical Review of Epistemological and Methodological Issues in Cross-Cultural Research," Journal of Comparative International Management, December 2004, downloaded from InfoTrac at http://web2.infotrac.galegroup.com.

5 Sigenman, Lee, Steven A. Tuch and Jack K. Martin, "What's in a Name? Preference for 'Black' versus 'African-American' among Americans of African Descent," Public Opinion Quarterly, Fall 2005, downloaded from InfoTrac at http://web2.infotrac.galegroup.com.

6 Rideout, Bruce E. Katherine Hushen, Dawn McGinty, Stephanie Perkins and Jennifer Tate, "Endorsement of the New Ecological Paradigm in Systematic and E-Mail Samples of College Students," Journal of Environmental Education, Winter 2005, downloaded from InfoTrac at http://web2.infotrac.galegroup.com.

7 SurveySite, "What We Do: Quantitative Research," http://www.surveysite.com, accessed March 15, 2006.

8 Council of American Survey Research Organizations (CASRO), "Frequently Asked Questions about Conducting Online Research: New Methodologies for Traditional Techniques," 1998, http://www.casro.org.

9 Mellinger, Gloria "Harris Interactive Inc.," World Opinion Research Profiles, July 18, 2000.

10 Ibid.

11 CASRO, "Frequently Asked Questions about Conducting Online Research."

12 Survey Sampling International, "Internet Sampling Solutions," http://www.ssisamples.com, accessed March 15, 2006.

13 Based on Gene Mueller, "It's Hard to Figure Number of Anglers," Washington Times, March 20, 2005, downloaded from InfoTrac at http://web3.infotrac.galegroup.com; Atlantic Coastal Cooperative Statistics Program, "About Us: Committees," http://www.accsp.org, accessed March 16, 2006; Atlantic States Marine Fisheries Commission, "About Us," http://www.asmfc.org, accessed March 16, 2006.

14 Material for this case is from *Scientific Telephone Samples User's Manual,* Scientific Telephone Samples, Santa Ana, CA.

Chapter 17

1 Based on Gerdes, Geoffrey R., Jack K. Walton II, May X. Liu, Darrel W. Parke and Namirembe Mukasa, "Trends in the Use of Payment Instruments in the United States," Federal Reserve Bulletin, Spring 2005, downloaded from InfoTrac at http://web2.infotrac.galegroup.com.

2 Most of the statistical material in this book assumes that the population parameters are unknown, which is the typical situation in most applied research projects.

3 The reasons for this are related to the concept of degrees of freedom, which will be explained later. At this point, disregard the intuitive notion of division by n, because it produces a biased estimate of the population variance.

4 In practice, most survey researchers will not use this exact formula. A modification of the formula, $Z = (X - \mu)/S$, using the sample standard deviation in an adjusted form, is frequently used.

5 Hayes, William L. *Statistics* (New York: Holt, Rinehart and Winston, 1963), p. 193.

6 Wonnacott, Thomas H. and Ronald J. Wonnacott, *Introductory Statistics,* 2nd ed. (New York: Wiley, 1972), p. 125.

7 Note that the derivation of this formula is (1) $E = ZS_{\bar{x}}$; (2) $E = ZS/\sqrt{n}$; (3) $\sqrt{n}\ ZS/E$; (4) $(n) = (ZS/E)^2$.

8 Based on Bialik, Carl "A Survey Probes the Back Seats of Taxis, with Dubious Results," The Wall Street Journal, January 28, 2005, http://online.wsj.com; and Pointsec Mobile Technologies, "Taxis Hailed as Black Hole for Lost Cell Phones and PDAs, as Confidential Data Gets Taken for a Ride," news release, January 24, 2005, http://www.pointsec.com.

Chapter 18

1 Based on Tillett, Scott L. "Up for the Count: Census Bureau Continues Technology Tradition," Geo World, April 2005, downloaded from InfoTrac at http://web1.infotrac.galegroup.com; Census Bureau, "Census Bureau Selects Sites for Census Dress Rehearsal," news release, January 19, 2006, http://www.census.gov; Census Bureau, "Census Bureau to Test Handheld Computers in Southwest Georgia" news release, April 16, 2004, http://www.census.gov; and Census Bureau, "Census Bureau to Test Handheld Computers in Northwest Queens," news release, April 23, 2004, http://www.census.gov.

2 Sauerbeck, Laura R., Jane C. Khoury, Daniel Woo, Brett M. Kissela, Charles J. Moomaw and Joseph P. Broderick, "Smoking Cessation after Stroke: Education and Its Effect on Behavior," Journal of Neuroscience Nursing, December 2005, downloaded from InfoTrac at http://web1.infotrac.galegroup.com.

3 This section relies heavily on *Interviewer's Manual,* rev. ed. (Ann Arbor, MI: Survey Research Center, Institute for Social Research, University of Michigan, 1976).

4 Ibid., p. 11.

5 Ibid., pp. 11–13. Reprinted by permission.

6 Oliver, Daniel G., Julianne M. Serovich and Tina L. Mason, "Constraints and Opportunities with Interview Transcription: Towards Reflection in Qualitative Research," Social Forces, December 2005, downloaded from InfoTrac at http://web1.infotrac.galegroup.com.

7 www.viewpointlearning.com

8 Ripley, Birch G. "Confessions of an Industrial Marketing Research Executive Interviewer," Marketing News, September 10, 1976, p. 20.

9 Based on Susanna Eng and Susan Gardner, "Conducting Surveys on a Shoestring Budget," American Libraries 36(2) (February 2005), downloaded from OCLC FirstSearch at http://firstsearch.oclc.org; and "Thomas and Dorothy Leavey Library," University of Southern California Information Services Division, http://www.usc.edu/isd, accessed March 28, 2006.

Chapter 19

1 Hareli, Shiomo, Noga Shomrat and Haum Biger (2005), "The Role of Emotions in Employees' Explanations for Failure in the Workplace," Journal of Managerial Psychology, 20 (8) 663–680.

2 Braunsberger, Karin, B. R. Buckler and David J. Ortinau (2005), "Categorizing Cognitive Responses: An Empirical Investigation of the Cognitive Intent Congruency Between Independent Raters and Original Subject Raters," Journal of the Academy of Marketing Science, 33 (Fall), 620–632.

3 These imputation methods are beyond the scope of this text. For more see Hair et al., *Multivariate Data Analysis,* (Upper Saddle River, NJ: Prentice Hall, 2006), pp. 39–73, 709–740.

4 Pope, Jeffrey L., Practical *Marketing Research,* (New York: AMACOM, 1981), p. 22 © 1998–1999 VNU Business Media Inc. Used with permission.

Chapter 20

1 Dolliver, Mark (2005), "Plow Under Your Hops and Plant Some Vines," Adweek, 46 (7/25), 36–38.

2 Dolliver, Mark (2005).

3 Kirsche, M.L. (2005), "Targeting Boomers Could Boost Fizzling Out Beer Sales," Drug Store News, 27 (6/6), 81.

4 Longo, Don (2005), "Drink Up," Progressive Grocer, 84 (10/15), 52–58.

5 The Wall Street Journal (2006), "Oprah Again Tops American's List of Favorite Personalities" (2/3), http://online.wsj.com/article_print/SB113889692780763347.html, accessed February 2, 2006.

6 Ricklefs, Roger (1983), "Ethics in America," The Wall Street Journal (October 31), 33–42; November 1, 1983, p. 33; November 2, 1983, p. 33; November 3, 1983, 33–37.

7 See Dubinsky, Alan J., Rajan Nataraajan and Wen-Yeh Huang (2005), "Consumers' Moral Philosophies: Identifying the Idealist and the Relativist," Journal of Business Research, 58 (December), 1690–1701. Deal, Ken (2005), "Deeper Into the Trees," Marketing Research, 17 (Summer), 38–40.

8 Adapted from Yavas, Ugur and Emin Babakus (2003), "What Do Guests Look for in a Hotel? A Multi-Attribute Approach," Services Marketing Quarterly, 25 (2), 6–14.

9 http://www.wineinstitute.org/communications/statistics, accessed February 6, 2006.

10 The data analysis tool must be added to the conventional Excel install by unpacking the data tool. This can be done by clicking on tools and then clicking on ad-ins and following the instructions. See http://www.microsoft.com for more instructions on how to accomplish this.

11 Iuso, Bill (1975), "Concept Testing: An Appropriate Approach," Journal of Marketing Research, 12 (May), 230.

12 Diamon, Sidney (1982), "Market Research Latest Target in Ad Claim," Advertising Age (January 25), 52. Reprinted with Perimission by Crain Communications, Inc.

13 Adapted with permission from Melvin Prince, *Consumer Research for Management Decisions* (New York: John Wiley and Sons, 1982), pp. 163–166.

Chapter 21

1 Thomson, Gale Research Database.

2 Garber, Amy (2003), "Pizza Players Eye New Products, Demographics to Increase Sales," Nation's Restaurant Business (September 8), 4–6.

3 Technically the t-distribution should be used when the population variance is unknown and the standard deviation is estimated from sample data. However, with large samples, the t-distribution approximates the Z-distribution, so the two will generally yield the same result.

4 See a comprehensive statistics text for a more detailed explanation.

5 A more complex discussion of the differences between parametric and nonparametric statistics appears in Appendix 22A.

6 Kranz, Rick (2004), "Maybach, Rolls Models are Far Below Predictions," 79 Automotive News (10/18).

7 In most cases, low p-values support hypotheses. However, if the hypothesis is that the observations will be equal to the theoretical expectations for a given distribution (this would be the null case), then a high p-value would be desired to support the hypothesis. Generally, this is not good form for a hypothesis. Exceptions to this rule exist. One of the most common is when a researcher compares some matrix of values with some alternative matrix of values with a goodness-of-fit test. Particularly in advanced applications (beyond the scope of this book), the researcher may wish to test whether or not the two matrices are the same within sampling error. In this case, the researcher would need an insignificant p-value (above α) to support the hypothesis.

Chapter 22

1 Murphy, Victoria (2003), "The Revolution that Wasn't," Chain Store Age, 172 (10/27), 210.

2 Tang, F. F. and X. Xing (2001), "Will the Growth of Multi-Channel Retailing Diminsh the Pricing Efficiency of the Web?," Journal of Retailing, 77, 319–333.

3 Three nonparametric tests—the Wilcoxon matched-pairs signed-ranks test, the Kruskal-Wallis test, and the Mann-Whitney U test—and ANOVA for complex experimental designs are covered in appendixes to this chapter.

4 The formula is not shown here but it can be found in most basic statistics books.

5 See, for example, Armstrong-Stassen, M. (2002), "Designated Redundant but Escaping Lay-Off: A Special Group of Lay-Off Survivors," Journal

of Occupational and Organizational Psychology, 75 (March), 1–13.

6 This is the "statistical alternative" hypothesis.

7 Sukhdial, Ajay, Damon Aiken and Lynn Kahle (2002), "Are You Old School? A Scale for Measuring Sports Fans' Old-School Orientation," Journal of Advertising Research, 42 (July/August), 71–81.

Chapter 23

1 Levitsky, David L. and Trisha Youn (2004), "The More Food Young Adults Are Served, the More They Overeat," Journal of Nutrition, 134 (October), 2546–2549.

2 Rolls, B. J., L. S. Roe and J. S. Meengs (2006), "Reductions in Portion Size and Energy Density of Foods are Additive and Lead to Sustained Decreases in Energy Intake," American Journal of Clinical Nutrition, 83 (January), 11–17.

3 Gray, Stephen (2006), "McDonald's Menu Upgrade Boosts Meal Prices and Results," The Wall Street Journal, February 18, A1.

4 For a discussion of the other measures of association, see the appendix to this chapter and Jean Dickinson Gibbons, Nonparametric Methods for Quantitative Analysis (New York: Holt, Rinehart and Winston, 1976).

5 Bott, Jennifer P., Daniel J. Svyantek, Scott A. Goodman and David S. Bernal (2003), "Expanding the Performance Domain: Who Says Nice Guys Finish Last?" International Journal of Organizational Analysis, 11 (2), 137–152.

6 Bagozzi, Richard P. (1978), "Salesforce Performance and Satisfaction as a Function of Individual Difference, Interpersonal and Situational Factors," Journal of

Marketing Research, November, 517–531.

7 Recall that the mean for a standardized variable is equal to 0.

8 For more on this topic, see Hair, J. F., W. C. Black, B. J. Babin, R. Tathum and R. Anderson, Multivariate Data Analysis, 6th Edition (Upper Saddle River, NJ: Prentice Hall, 2006).

Chapter 24

1 Goulding, Christina (2001), "Romancing the Past: Heritage Visitors and the Nostalgic Consumer," Psychology and Marketing, 18 (June), 565–592.

2 Tesoriero, H. W. (2002), "Babes in 80s Toyland," Time, 160 (November 11), 14.

3 MMR (2004), "Nostalgia, Education Hot Trends in Toys," 21 (February 23), 47, Thomson-Gale Database.

4 Betts, Kate (2004), "A 1950s State of Mind," Time (April 15), 4.

5 Osborn, Suzanne Barry (2001), "It's Yesterday Once More: Companies Use Nostalgia to Entice Consumers," Chain Store Age (June), 32.

6 See Holak, S. L. and W. Havlena (1998), "Feelings, Fun and Memories: An Examination of the Emotional Components of Nostalgia," Journal of Business Research, 42 (3), 217–226.

7 Muehling, Darrel D. and David E. Sprott (2004), "The Power of Reflection," Journal of Advertising, 33 (Fall), 25–35.

8 Holak, S. L. and W. Havlena (1998).

9 When the actual regression model is illustrated as an explanation of the actual dependent variable in a population, Y_i is used and an error term (e_i) is included because the sample parameters cannot be expected to perfectly predict and explain the actual value of the

dependent variable in the population. When we use a regression equation to represent its ability to predict sample values of the dependent variable from the estimated parameter coefficients, $\hat{Y}_i$ is used to represent predicted values of Y_i and no error term is included since the actual amount of error in any given observation is unknown.

10 School enrollment statistics can often be found using the Internet and either searching through government statistics or examining the website for the local school district or school board.

11 The constant term has disappeared since it is equal to 0 when the regression coefficients are standardized.

12 See Hair et al. (2006) for more on this topic.

13 Cox, A. D., D. Cox and R. D. Anderson (2005), "Reassessing the Pleasures of Store Shopping," Journal of Business Research, 58 (March), 250–259.

14 Closs, D. J., M. Swink and A. Nair (2005), "The Role of Information Connectivity in Making Flexible Logistics Programs Successful," International Journal of Physical Distribution & Logistics Management, 35 (4), 258–277.

15 Morrison, Mark, A. Sweeney and T. Heffernan (2003), "Learning Styles of On-Campus and Off-Campus Marketing Students: The Challenge for Marketing Educators," Journal of Marketing Education, 25 (December), 208–217.

Chapter 25

1 Based on Baker, Stephen "Math Will Rock Your World," Business Week, January 23, 2006, downloaded from

InfoTrac at http://web5. infotrac.galegroup.com; Natalie Canavor and Claire Meirowitz, "Good Corporate Writing: Why It Matters, and What to Do," Communication World, July–August 2005, http://web1.infotrac. galegroup.com; and National Commission on Writing, "Writing: A Ticket to Work . . . or a Ticket Out," September 2004, http://www. writingcommission.org.

2 The original version of this chapter was written by John Bush, Oklahoma State University, and appeared in William G. Zikmund, Business Research Methods (Hinsdale, IL: Dryden Press, 1984).

3 "A Speech Tip," Communication Briefings 14(2), p. 3.

4 These guidelines, adapted with permission from Marjorie Brody (President, Brody Communications, 1200 Melrose Ave., Melrose Park, PA 19126), appeared in "How to Gesture When Speaking," Communication Briefings 14(11), p. 4.

5 "Tips of the Month," Communication Briefings 24(7) (May 2005), p. 1.

6 Based on Bridis, Ted "Study: Shoppers Naïve about Online Pricing," Information Week, June 1, 2005, downloaded from InfoTrac at http://web2.infotrac.galegroup.com; Annenberg Public Policy Center (APPC), "Annenberg Study Shows Americans Vulnerable to Exploitation in the Online and Offline Marketplace," June 1, 2005, http://www. annenbergpublicpolicycenter.org; and Joseph Turow, Lauren Feldman and Kimberly Meltzer, "Open to Exploitation: American Shoppers Online and Offline," APPC report, June 2005, downloaded at http://www.annenbergpublicpolicy center.org.

INDEX

INDEX

A

ABI/INFORM database, 36
absolute causality, 55
accessing available data, 39
accuracy
  in descriptive research, 53
  of questionnaire, 354
  of sampling, 404–405, 421
ACNielsen Company
  BASES system of, 83–84
  data of, 35, 178
  MovieTickets.com and, 177
  people meter of, 65
  sample size and, 452
  TV monitoring system, 244–246
acquiescence bias, 192
ACT, Inc., 205
active data warehousing, 32
active research, 88
ad hoc sample, 424
administrative error, 193–194
advertising, questions about, 391–393
advocacy research, 97–98
AFLAC Insurance, 2–3
Agency for Healthcare Research and
    Quality (AHRQ) survey, 382–386
aided recall, 364, 392
alcohol abuse, causes of, 260
Alien Technology Corporation, 30
alternative hypothesis, 526
ambiguity
  decision making and, 49–50
  in question phrasing, 362
  of symptoms, 107
American Kennel Club, 413
American Marketing Association, Code of
    Ethics of, 93, 96–97
analysis, definition of, 507
analysis of dependence
  discriminant analysis, 605, 607
  general linear model, 600
  MANOVA, 605
  multiple regression analysis, 600–604
  n-way (univariate) ANOVA, 605
analysis of interdependence
  cluster analysis, 612–613
  factor analysis, 608–611
  multidimensional scaling, 614–615
  overview of, 608, 615

analysis of variance (ANOVA)
  complex designs, 571–572
  description of, 557–558
  example of, 558–559, 562
  factorial designs, 572–574
  F-test, 560–562
  manual calculations of, 568–570
  multivariate (MANOVA), 605, 606
  n-way, 605
  partitioning variance in, 559–560
  regression and, 587
analyzing data, 67–68
anchoring effect, 366
Anheuser-Busch, 56–57
Annenberg Public Policy Center, 645–646
ANOVA. *See* analysis of variance
appendix to report, 632
applied marketing research, 6
archives, computerized data, 35–38
area sample, 417
asking questions, 464–465
assumptions, avoiding, 363
at-home scanning system, 249
Atlas-Ti, 137, 152, 497
AT&T, 17–18
attitude, 330
attitude measurement
  behavioral intention, 341–342
  example of, 329–330
  importance of, 330–331
  other methods of, 344–345
  questionnaire wording for, 391–398
  randomized response questions,
    343–344
  ranking, 342–343
  rating scales, 332–341
  selecting scale for, 345–347
  sorting, 343
  techniques for, 331–332
attribute, 319
auctions, online, 72–73
audience, 624
Australian Bureau of Statistics, 469

B

back translation, 379
backward linkage, 58
balanced rating scales, 346–347
bar charts, 638, 639

basic experimental design, 269
basic marketing research, 6
basic marketing research report, 632
basketball, market for, 619–621
behavioral differential, 342
behavioral intention, 341–342,
    397–398, 447
behavioral tracking, 34–35
benchmarks, 523
Ben & Jerry's Homemade, Inc., 25
Best Buy, 18
between-groups variance, 559–560, 562
between-subjects designs, 271–272
bias
  of experimenter, 265–266
  in personal interview, 211–212
  in quota sampling, 413
  self-selection, 190
bivariate statistical analysis, 524, 526
Black Forest Motors, 71
blind monadic testing, 520
blocking variable, 301
blogs, data mining, 169
body of report, 630–632
box and whisker plots, 516
Brawny man, 52
Brazil, 292
briefing session, 462, 471
Bristol-Myers, 520
Brown-Forman, 22
budget, 78, 155
burdensome questions, 363–364
Burger King, 288
business-class travel, 15
business decision making
  intuitive, 79–80
  problem definition and, 108–109
  research-based, 48–50
business ethics, 91, 97
business marketing orientations, 7–8

C

Cadbury gum testers, 402–403
calculating
  confidence interval estimate, 535–536
  F-ratio manually, 568–570
  rank order, 512–513
callbacks, 212–213, 216, 228
Canada, 292

cannibalize, 286
Carson, Johnny, 132
cases
  Employees Federal Credit Union,
    650–653
  Running the Numbers, 649–650
  Say It Ain't So, 659–661
  Survey on Americans and Dietary
    Supplements, 662–664
  TABH, Inc., Automotive Consulting,
    661–662
  University Van Pool, 654–657
  Values and Automobile Market,
    657–659
case studies, 138–140
categorical variables, 115, 259
category scales, 332–333, 346
causal inference, 54–55
causal research, 53–57, 58
causal research design, 256
causation, 578
cell, 261
cellphones, 215, 273
census, 403
Census Bureau enumerators, 460
central-limit theorem, 443–445, 446
central location interviews, 217
central tendency, measures of, 432–434
certainty and decision making, 49
CHAID (chi-square automatic interaction
    detection) software, 508
change interview, 111
character, 487
charts, use of in reports, 633, 635–639,
    640, 641
check box, 375, 376
checklist questions, 357
Cheetos, 14
children, research with, 90
Children's Online Privacy Protection Act
    (COPPA), 89
chi-square distribution, 668
chi-square (χ^2) test, 537–540,
    546–550, 576
choice, 332, 345, 347
Circuit City, 290
classificatory variables, 115
click-through rate, 246–247
client sponsors, rights and obligations
    of, 97–98

cluster analysis, 612–613
cluster sampling, 417–418
code book, 494, 495
codes, 485
codes of ethics, 91, 93, 96–97
coding data
    construction of codes, 488–489
    editing and, 484, 494
    error checking, 495
    file, terminology for, 486–488
    open-ended questions, 490–493
    overview of, 67, 485
    precoding fixed-alternative questions,
        489–490, 491
    qualitative responses, 485–488
    scheme for, 492–493
    standard codes, 481
coefficient alpha (α), 322
coefficient of determination (R^2),
    579–580, 588, 602–603
coffee industry, 3–4
cohort effect, 274
Coke, 105
collages, 151–152
collecting data, 39–40
communality, 611
communication
    importance of, 623–624
    language, using, 359
    nonverbal, 239
    oral presentation, 639–642
    as process, 624–626
    technologies of, 21
    See also report
communicator, 624
comparative rating scales, 345
complementary evidence, 239–240
completely randomized design, 300–301
completeness of information, 29, 483–484
complex experimental designs, 280
complexity, avoiding, 359
composite measures, 319–320
composite scales, 335, 610
compromise design, 279
computer, 38, 152. See also Internet
computer-assisted telephone
    interviewing, 217–218, 490
computer graphics, 516
computerized survey data processing,
    494–495
computer programs. See software
computing scale values, 320
concept, 311
concept testing, 133–135
conclusions, faulty, 96–97
conclusions and recommendations section
    of report, 632
concomitant variation, 54, 578
conditional causality, 55
confidence interval estimate, 447–449,
    535–536
confidence level, 447, 451
confidentiality, 87, 96
confirmatory factor analysis, 608
conflict of interest, 96
confound, 264
consistency, editing for, 481–482
constancy of conditions, 268
constants, 115
constant-sum scales, 337–338
constructs, 312–313
construct validity, 323, 324
Consumer Assessment of Health Providers
    and Systems (CAHPS) Hospital
    Survey, 378

consumer panel, 197–198
consumption, psychology of, 596
content analysis, 244
content providers, 40
content validity, 323
contingency tables, 504–505, 546–550
continuous measures, 318–319
continuous variables, 115, 261
contract, proposal as, 121–123
contributory causality, 55–56
contrived observation, 241–242
control group, 261
control method of test-marketing,
    297–298
convenience sampling, 411–412
convergent validity, 323, 324
conversations, 150
cookies, 42
COPPA (Children's Online Privacy
    Protection Act), 89
Corporation Reputation Survey, 356
correlation, regression compared to, 582
correlation coefficient, 577–581
correlation matrix, 580–581
correspondence rules, 311
counterbalancing, 268
counterbiasing statement, 361
covariance, 577, 578
cover letter, 221, 222
criterion validity, 323
critical values, 528
criticism, research that implies, 77–78
CRM (customer relationship
    management), 31, 169–170
cross-checks of data, 161–162
cross-functional effort, 9–10
cross-functional teams, 82–83
cross-sectional studies, 196
cross-tabulation, 504–508
cross-tabulation tables, 546–550, 634, 635
cross-validate, 22
curb-stoning, 473
customer discovery, 169
customer-oriented firm, 8–9
customer relationship management
    (CRM), 31, 169–170
customer satisfaction survey, 189, 198–202
custom research, 84–85

D

data
    characteristics of, 28–29
    collecting, 39–40
    editing, 67, 480–485, 494
    gathering, and analyzing, 67–68
    integrating, 27
    qualitative and quantitative, 133
    raw, 479
    scanner, 34–35, 37
    single-source, 35
    See also coding data; displaying data;
        secondary data
data analysis, 68, 479–480
database marketing, 169–170
databases, 32, 36–38
data cleaning, 495
data conversion, 161
data entry process, 494–495
data file, 486–488
data integrity, 479–480, 481
data mining, 168–169
data-processing error, 193
data reduction technique, 610
data specialist companies, 35

data transformation, 509–511
data warehouse/data warehousing, 32
data wholesalers, 36, 37
David Weekley homes, 12
DDB SignBank, 238
debriefing, 89, 268–269
deception in research designs, 89–90
decision making, 49, 154–155. See also
    business decision making; strategic
    decision making
decision statement, 104, 112–114,
    118–119
decision support system (DSS), 26,
    31–38, 76
Defense Department, 39
defining
    problem, 104, 107–108
    research objectives, 59–62
    target population, 406–407
degrees of freedom, 534
deliverables, 59
demand characteristics, 265–267
demand effect, 265
demographics, questions about, 398–400
dependence techniques, 598, 608. See also
    analysis of dependence
dependent variable (Y), 115–116,
    261–262
depth interviews, 149–150
descriptive analysis, 502–503
descriptive research, 51–53, 57–58, 90
descriptive statistics, 430
design. See research design
determinant-choice questions, 357
deviation scores, 436
diagnostic analysis, 53
diagramming experimental designs, 276
DIALOG, 36, 37
dialog boxes, 229
Dialog research firm, 469
diary product intake, 631
dichotomous-alternative questions, 357
direct observation, 240–242
director of marketing research, 75, 76–82
discrete measures, 317–318
discriminant analysis, 605, 607
discriminant validity, 323, 324
discussion guide, 145–146
disguised questions, 196
Disney, 16
dispersion, measures of, 434–438
displaying data, methods of, 513–517,
    632–639, 640, 641
disproportional stratified sampling, 417
dissemination of faulty conclusions, 96–97
distorting charts, 635–637
distribution channels for secondary data,
    171–177
distribution research, 15–17
distributors, 35
Do Not Call legislation, 88
"don't know" answers, 484
door-in-the-face compliance
    technique, 463
door-to-door interviews, 212
double-barreled questions, 362–363
Dow Jones News Retrieval, 36, 37
drawing conclusions, 68
drop-down box, 374, 375, 376
drop-off method, 225
DSS (decision support system), 26,
    31–38, 76
dummy coding, 486
dummy tables, 123–124
dummy variable, 600

E

editing data, 67, 480–485, 494
educational market, 47–48
E-Lab, LLC, 252
elaboration analysis, 507
electronic bulletin boards, 464
electronic data interchange (EDI), 38
Electronic Encyclopedia of Statistical
    Examples and Exercises, 532
electronic interactive media, 208
electronic test-markets, 298
e-mail surveys, 225–226
emotion, and research, 155
empirical testing, 64
environmental scanning, 41, 164–165
Equifax City Directory, 408
errors
    in prediction of regression, 585
    reporting, 96
    in survey research, 187–195
error trapping, 377
estimating
    parameters, 445–449
    sales volume, 294–296
    systematic error, 194–195
e-tailing, 545–546
ethical dilemma, 86
ethical issues
    in experimentation, 268–269
    with focus groups, 144
    in human observation, 242
    overview of, 85–86
    privacy, 98
    professionalism, 98–99
    with research with children, 90
    in survey research, 232
    See also rights and obligations
ethnography, 137–138
Europe, 292
European Union, 22
Excel (Microsoft), 514, 515
Experience Sampling Method, 364
experimental condition, 257
experimental designs
    basic vs. factorial, 269
    classification of, 276
    complex, 280, 300–304
    compromise, 279
    deception in, 89–90
    dependent variable and, 261–262
    factorial, 269, 301–303, 572–574
    independent variable and, 259, 261
    posttest-only control group, 278–279
    pretest-posttest control group, 278
    quasi-experimental, 276–277
    test units, 262–265, 405
    time series, 279–280
experimental group, 261
experimental outcome, 258
experimental research
    color and preference, 256–259
    demand characteristics, 265–267
    establishing control, 268
    ethical issues in, 268–269
    nature of, 256
    See also experimental designs
experimental treatment, 259
experimental variable, 56
experimenter bias, 265–266
experiments, 56–57
exploratory factor analysis, 608
exploratory research
    characteristics of, 57
    description of, 51

misuse of, 153–155
objectives of, 61–62
qualitative research and, 132–133
external data, 171
external validity, 275
extraneous variables, 264–265, 268
extremity bias, 192
eye-tracking monitor, 249
E-ZPass, 126

F

face validity, 323
fact-finding, 163–165
factor analysis, 608–611
factorial designs, 269, 301–303, 572–574
factor loading, 609–610
factor rotation, 611
Fairfax County Public Library, 199
Fandango, 177
fax surveys, 225
FDA, 5, 6
Federal Reserve survey, 429–430
Federal Trade Commission, 91
FedEx, 182–183
feedback, 210, 624
field, 487
field editing, 480–481
field experiment, 270–271, 291
field interviewing service, 461–462
field notes, 151
fieldwork, 461–462, 470–472
fieldworker, 461–467, 471–474
filter questions, 366–367
financial databases, 37
Fisher-Price Rescue Heroes, 71
fixed-alternative questions, 354–355,
356–358, 489–490, 491
focus blog, 147
focus group, 62
focus group interview, 141–149
follow-up, research, 642–643
Food and Drug Administration, 5, 6
food intake, 575, 631
foot-in-the-door compliance
technique, 463
forced answering software, 377
forced-choice rating scales, 347
Ford Motor Company, 41, 105, 623
forecast analyst, 76
forecasting product success, 285–286
format of report, 626–632
forward linkage, 58
F-ratio, calculating, 568–570
free-association technique, 151
frequency-determination
questions, 357
frequency distribution, 431
frequency table, 503
F-test, 560–562, 587
F-22 Raptor fighter plane, 525
full enumeration, 418
funded marketing research, 122
funnel technique, 365

G

Gallup, George H., 407
gas prices and SUVs, 182
gathering data, 67
Geeks, 18
general linear model, 600
General Social Survey (National Opinion
Research Center), 210
geo-demographics, 14

geographical databases, 36–37
Georgia-Pacific products, 287
global information systems, 30
global issues
in mail surveys, 224
in personal interviews, 214
in questionnaire design, 379
in sampling frames, 409
in telephone interviews, 218
Globally Accessible Statistical
Procedures, 532
global marketing research, 21–22
global sources of secondary
data, 178–180
Golden Books, 17
goodness-of-fit, 537–540, 546–550
goods and services, questions about,
394–398
Google, 40–41
GPS (Global Positioning Systems), 34,
101, 460
grading and measurement, 310–311
grand mean, 559
graphical user interface (GUI)
software, 373
graphic methods of displaying data
charts, 633, 635–639, 640, 641
computer graphics and
mapping, 516
overview of, 513
tables, 633, 634
use of, 632–633
graphic rating scales, 338–340
grounded theory, 138

H

Häagen-Dazs ice cream, 84
handbills, 422
Hardi Plank, 287
Harley-Davidson, 11
harm, protection from, 90–91
Harrah's Entertainment, 623
Harris Interactive Inc., 424, 447, 506
Harrison Group, 333
Harvard Cooperative Society, 45
Hawthorne effect, 266
healthy house, rating, 340
Heineken Premium Light, 284–285
hermeneutic approach, 136, 137
heterogeneity, 451
hidden observation, 238
hidden skip logic, 376
Hidden Valley Ranch, 271
histogram, 502–503
history effect, 273–274
home building industry, 11–12
Home Depot, 27, 35
home theaters, 17
Horizon Research Services, 461
host, 39
human interactive media, 208
human subjects review committee, 91, 92
hypnosis, 72–73, 91
hypothesis, 63–64, 118
hypothesis testing
applications of, 541
example of, 527–530
process, 524–526
of proportion, 540–541
significance levels and p-values,
526–527
simple regression and, 590–591
Type I and Type II errors, 530
hypothetical construct, 330

I

IBM, 27, 46
idea generation, 133, 134
idealism, 86
identifying product weakness, 286–287
image profile, 336
importance-performance analysis, 508
impute, 483, 489
incentives to participate, 216, 221
independent samples t-test, 550–554, 561
independent variable (X), 115,
257–259, 261
index measures, 319–320, 347
index numbers, 511
index of retail saturation, 167
inferential statistics, 430
information, valuable, characteristics
of, 27–29
Information Resources, Inc., 248
informed, right to be, 89–90
informed consent, 87, 90–91
in-house editing, 481
in-house interviewer, 462
in-house research, 73–74
input management, 32–35
instrumentation effect, 274
integrated marketing communication, 18
integrated marketing mix, 18
integrity of data, 479–480, 481
interaction effect, 258, 302–303
interactive help desk, 377
interactive medium, 40–41
interdependence techniques, 598,
615. See also analysis of
interdependence
internal and proprietary data, 170–171
internal consistency, 321–322
internal validity, 272–275
international test-markets, 292–293
Internet
overview of, 39–42
privacy on, 98
questionnaires for, 373–377
report on, 642
sampling and, 423–424
secondary data and, 173, 174
surveys using, 226–230
Internet, 2, 42
interpretation, 517–518
interquartile range, 516
interrogative techniques, 109
interval scales, 314, 315–316, 319
interviewer bias, 192–193
interviewer cheating, 194, 473–474
interviewer error, 194
interviews
coding, 485–488
combining observation with, 242
depth, 149–150
focus group, 141–149
personal, 209–214
principles of good, 467–469
probing after no response, 465–466
questions, asking, 464–465
recording responses, 466–467, 468
rules for, 469–470
semi-structured, 150–151
situation analysis and, 108–110
telephone, 214–218
terminating, 467
verification by reinterviewing, 474
intranets, 42
introduction section of report, 630–631
Intuit, 185–186

inverse (negative) relationship, 578
item nonresponse, 211, 483

J

J. D. Power and Associates, 83
Jelly Belly brand, 3
jobs, 75–76, 77, 78
Joint Advertising, Market Research &
Studies (Department of Defense),
159–160
judgment sampling, 412, 455

K

Kaplan, Inc., 205
keyword search, 40
kiosk interactive surveys, 230
Kish method, 418
Klipmart, 247
knowledge, 29
knowledge management, 29–30
Krispy Kreme, 24, 26–27

L

laboratory experiment, 269
laddering, 149
language, using, 359
Latin square design, 304
layout of questionnaires
Internet, 373–377
traditional, 368–373
leading questions, 359–360
letter of authorization, 629
letter of transmittal, 628–629
level of scale measurement, 532
libraries, 171–173
licensing fee for research, 631
Likert scales, 318, 333–335
limited research service, 84–85
line graphs, 637–638
LinkedIn service, 207
list brokers, 408
listening, 132
literature review, 62
loaded questions, 360–361
location decisions, 523
longitudinal studies, 196–197

M

magnitude of error, 451
mail survey, 219–224
main effect, 258
mall intercept interviews, 213–214
management, 76, 77–82, 470–472. See also
director of marketing research
managerial action standard, 118
manipulation, 56
manipulation checks, 273
MANOVA (multivariate analysis of
variance), 605, 606
mapping system, 460
marginals, 505
market-basket analysis, 168–169
marketing channel, 15
marketing concept, 8, 11–12
marketing ethics, 86
Marketing Information Systems, Inc., 520
Marketing Management Analytics, 312
marketing metrics, 19, 312
marketing mix, 14–18, 286
marketing orientation, 8–10
marketing-oriented firm, 8

marketing research
applied and basic, 6
categories of, 31
definition of, 5
determining need for, 19–21
funded, 122
innovation and, 3–4
Internet and, 39–40
nature of, 4–5
proprietary, 34
in twenty-first century, 21–22
types of, 50–57
uncertainty and, 57–58
marketing strategy. *See* strategic decision
making
market intelligence, 27
market opportunity, 48
market penetration, 296
market problem, 48
market share, 296–297
market tracking, 164
Marriott Corporation, 76
matching, 263
mathematical analysis of scales, 316–319
maturation effect, 274
Mazda Motor Europe, 252
MBA degree, market for, 47–48, 52–53
McDonald's, 38, 287, 288, 389
means
overview of, 432–434, 450–452
standard error of, 442
t-test for comparing, 550–556
mean squares
between groups, 569
within groups, 570
measurement
of central tendency, 432–434
concepts and, 311
of dispersion, 434–438
index, 319–320
operational definitions and, 311–314
overview of, 309–311
reliability of, 321–322, 324
scale, 313–319, 532, 598–599
sensitivity of, 324–325
validity of, 323–324
See also attitude measurement; scale
measurement
measures of association, 575–577
mechanical observation
physiological reactions, 249–250
scanner-based research, 247–249
television monitoring, 244–246
traffic cameras, 245
Website traffic monitoring, 246–247
media, using to communicate, 208
median, 434
median split, 509–510
medium, 624
memory, questions that tax, 363–364
Mercedes-Benz, 71
mere-measurement effect, 195
message, 624
metaphor elicitation technique, 465
metric scales, 598
MINITAB, 515
misrepresentation of research, 95–96
missing data, 489
misuses of research, 153–155
mixed-mode survey, 230
M&M characters, 52
M:Metrics, 209
Mobiltrak, 245
model building, 165–168, 434
moderator, 143
moderator variables, 507

monadic rating scales, 345
moral standards, 86
mortality effect, 275
Mr. Peanut, 52
multicollinearity, 604
multidimensional scaling, 614–615
multiple-bar charts, 639, 641
multiple-grid questions, 368
multiple regression analysis, 600–604
multistage area sampling, 418–420
multivariate analysis of variance
(MANOVA), 605, 606
multivariate statistical analysis, 524,
597–599
mystery shoppers, 90

N

NAICS (North American Industrial
Classification System), 481
National Do Not Call Registry, 234
National Trade Data Bank, 179–180
navigating Internet, 40
neural network, 168
Neuroco, 236
Noah's Law of Slide Presentations, 640
no contact, in survey research, 189
nominal scales, 313–314, 319
non-forced-choice rating scales, 347
noninteractive media, 208
nonmetric scales, 598
nonparametric statistics, 532–533
nonprobability sampling, 411–414, 420
nonrespondent error, 479
nonresponse error, 189–190, 221
nonsampling error, 262, 410–411
nonspurious association, 54–55
nonverbal communication, 239
normal curve, area under, 666
normal distribution, 438–441
Norman Estates, 53
nostalgia, marketing of, 596–597
null hypothesis, 525–526
numerical scales, 337
nutrition labels, 6
n-way analysis of variance (ANOVA), 605

O

objectives. *See* research objectives
objectivity, 94, 97
observation technique
combining with interviews, 242
complementary evidence, 239–240
content analysis, 244
definition of, 237
direct, 240–242
ethnography and, 137–138
field notes and, 151
human behavior and, 238–239
mechanical, 244–250
phenomena for, 237
physical objects and, 243–244
purpose of, 65
visible and hidden, 238
observer bias, 241
Ogilvy's Corollary, 640
OLS. *See* ordinary least-squares method
Olson Zaltman Associates, 465
one-group pretest-posttest design, 277
one-shot design, 276–277
one-tailed tests, 536
one-way ANOVA, 561
online auctions, 72–73
online focus groups, 147–148
open-ended box, 375, 376

open-ended questions, coding, 490–493
open-ended response questions, 354–355
operational definition, 311–314
Opinion Research Corporation, 497
optical scanning system, 494
opt-in list, 424
oral presentation, 639–642
order bias, 365
ordinal scales, 314, 315, 319
ordinary least-squares method (OLS)
arithmetic behind, 594–595
coefficient of determination (R^2)
and, 588
hypothesis testing and, 590–591
interpreting regression output,
588–589
overview of, 585–586
plotting regression line, 589–590
statistical significance and, 586–587
organizational structure
conflict and, 77–82
cross-functional teams, 82–83
director, 76–77
jobs, 75–76, 77
overview of, 74
outcomes, anticipating, 123–124
outlier, 516
outside research agency, 73. *See also*
research suppliers
ownership, questions about, 393–394

P

paging layout, 373
paired comparison, 342
paired-samples *t*-test, 555–556
panel sample, 423–424
parameters, estimation of, 445–449,
582–583
parametric statistics, 532–533
partial correlation, 601
participant-observation, 137
participants, rights and obligations of,
87–91
participation, gaining, 463
partitioning sum of squares, 573–574
passive research, 88–89
Pearson correlation coefficient, 577, 671
Pearson product-moment correlation
matrix, 580
peer review process, 91, 92
percentage cross-tabulations, 506–507
percentage distribution, 431
performance function of marketing
research, 31
performance-monitoring research, 18–19
personal interviews
layout for, 371–372
phrasing questions for, 358–359
pros and cons of, 209–212
training to make, 462
types of, 212–214
phenomenological approach, 136
phrasing of questions, 354–359
physical-trace evidence, 243–244
physiological reactions, measuring,
249–250
picture frustration, 152–153
pie charts, 513, 637
piggyback, 141
pilot studies, 62
pitfalls of editing, 484–485
pivot questions, 367
placebo, 89, 267
placebo effect, 267
place marketing, 80

planning
research design, 64–65
research proposal and, 119–120
plotting OLS regression line, 589–590
plug value, 483
point estimates, 446–447
Pointsec Mobile Technologies, 459
pooled estimate of the standard error, 551
population distribution, 441–443
population element, 403
population parameters, 430
population size and sample size, 452
population (universe), 403
pop-up box, 376
posttest-only control group design,
278–279, 300
precoding fixed-alternative questions,
489–490, 491
preliminary tabulation, 378
preparing report, 68
presenting results, 95–96
pretest-posttest control group design, 278
pretests
definition of, 62
editing questionnaires during, 485
for questionnaire, 377–379
for survey research, 323
pricing, definition of, 14
pricing research, 14–15
primary sampling unit, 409
privacy issues, 88–89, 98
Prizm data, 159–160, 178
probability, 431, 432
probability sampling, 411, 414–420, 421
probability theory, 530
probing respondents, 110, 465–466
problem
business decision and, 108–117
complexity of, 104–107
with data transformations, 509–511
defining, 104, 107–108
writing objectives and questions,
117–118
problem-focused decision making, 50
processing data, 67
Procter & Gamble, 19, 131
producers, and secondary data, 173–178
product development, 51, 290
production-oriented firm, 7, 8
product-oriented firm, 7, 8
product research, 14
product usage, questions about, 393–394
professionalism, 98–99
profitability, 9, 12
projecting test-market results, 296–297
projective techniques, 153
promotion, definition of, 17
promotion research, 17–18
propensity-weighting, 424
proportion
description of, 431
hypothesis test of, 540–541
sample size for, 452–455
Z-test for comparing, 556–557
proportional stratified sampling, 416
proposal, 119–124
proprietary marketing research, 34
protection from harm, 90–91
pseudo-research, 92–94
psychogalvanometer, 250
public opinion surveys, 191
pull technology, 41
Pulte Homes, 171
pupilometer, 249–250
purpose of research, 91–94
push button, 374

push polls, 94
push technology, 41, 94
p-value, 526–527

Q

quadrant analysis, 508
qualitative research
    case studies, 138–139
    concept testing and, 133–135
    conversation, 150–151
    depth interview, 149–150
    description of, 129–130
    ethnography, 137–138
    exploratory research and, 132–133
    focus group interview, 141–149
    free-association/sentence completion,
        151–153
    grounded theory, 138
    misuse of, 153–155
    orientations, 135–136
    phenomenology, 136–137
    quantitative compared to, 130–132
    techniques of, 140
qualitative responses, coding, 485–488
quality
    of data, 28–29
    definition of, 198
    dimensions of, 202
quantified electroencephalography, 236
quantitative research, 130–132
quasi-experimental designs, 276–277
questionnaire design
    deciding what to ask, 353–354
    example of, 352
    global issues in, 379
    guidelines for, 359–364
    layout, 368–377
    phrasing, 354–359
    pretesting and revising, 377–379
    sequence, 365–368
    wording and measurement scales
        for, 391–400
questionnaires. See self-administered
    questionnaires
questions
    asking, 464–465
    editing, when answered out of
        order, 484
    type of, and statistical technique, 531
    writing, 117–119
    See also specific types
quota sampling, 412–414

R

R^2 (coefficient of determination),
    579–580, 588, 602–603
radio button, 374, 375
radio frequency identification (RFID)
    tags, 30
random digit dialing, 216
random digits, table of, 665
randomization, 263
randomized-block design, 301,
    571–572
randomized response questions, 343–344
random sampling error
    confidence intervals and, 447
    description of, 188, 409–410
    sample size and, 449–450
    table of, 454, 456
range, 436
ranking, 332, 342–343, 345
rank order, 315, 512–513
rating, 332, 345

rating scales, attitude
    category, 332–333
    constant-sum, 337–338
    graphic, 338–340
    Likert scale, 333–335
    numerical, 337
    semantic differential, 335–336
    simple, 332
    Stapel, 337
    summary of, 341
    Thurstone, 340
ratio scales, 314, 316, 319
raw data, 479
raw regression estimates, 583
real time, 36
recording responses, 466–467, 468
records, 33, 487
refusal, in survey research, 189
regression analysis, 582–591
reinterviewing, verification by, 474
relational hypothesis, 524
relationship marketing, 10–11
relativism, 86
relevance
    of data, 28
    of questionnaire, 353–354
relevant variables, 116
reliability
    of sampling, 404–405
    types of, 321–322
    validity compared to, 324
repeated measures, 263–264
replicable results, 154
report
    appendix, 632
    of basic marketing research, 632
    body of, 630–632
    editing, 625
    formality of, 627–628
    format of, 626–632
    graphic aids in, 632–639
    on Internet, 642
    letter of authorization, 629
    letter of transmittal, 628–629
    oral presentation, 639–642
    preparing, 68
    research report, 626
    summary, 630
    table of contents, 629
    title page, 628
reporting errors, 96
representative sample, 216, 227–228
research analyst, 76
research assistant, 76
research design
    causal, 256
    planning, 64–65
    selecting, for survey research, 230–231
researcher-dependent research, 129
research follow-up, 642–643
research generalist, 81–82
research methodology section of
    report, 631
research objectives
    defining, 59–62, 109
    stating, 62–63
    for survey research, 186–187
    writing, 112–114, 117
research process. See stages in research
    process
research program, 68
research project, 68
research proposal. See proposal
research questions. See questions
research report, 626. See also report
research suppliers, 83–85, 97

respondent error, 189–193
respondents, 186
response bias, 190–193
response error, editing, 482–483
response latency, 240
response rates
    for Internet surveys, 229
    for mail surveys, 220–224
results, presenting, 95–96, 639–642. See
    also graphic methods of displaying
    data; report
results section of report, 631–632
Retail Forward, 83, 84
reverse coding, 320
reverse directory, 408
reverse recoding, 334–335
revising questionnaire, 377–379
RFID (radio frequency identification)
    tags, 30
Rice Virtual Lab in Statistics, 532
rights and obligations
    of client sponsors, 97–98
    of concerned parties, 86–87
    interaction of, 86–87
    of participants, 87–91
    of researchers, 91–97
ringtones, 164
RJR smokeless cigarette, 105
Roeder-Johnson Corporation, 350
Rolling Rock beer, 66

S

sabotage, test-market, 295
salaries, 78
sales and research, mixing, 91–92, 94
sales volume, estimating, 294–296
sample, definition of, 403
sample attrition, 275
sample bias, 188
sample distribution, 441–443
sample selection error, 194
sample size
    determining, 450–456
    population size and, 452
    random error and, 447–450
sample statistics, 430
sample survey, 186
sampling
    description of, 65–67
    design for, 420–422
    example of, 402–403
    Internet and, 423–424
    nonprobability, 411–414, 420
    probability, 411, 414–420, 421
    procedure for, 406–409
    purpose of, 403–405
    random, and nonsampling errors,
        409–411
    training in procedures for, 471–472
    verification of, 473
    See also sample size
sampling distribution of sample mean,
    442–443
sampling frame, 407–409
sampling frame error, 408–409
sampling services, 408
sampling unit, 409
SAS, 514–515, 622
scale measurement
    influence of, 598–599
    level of, 532
scales
    category, 332–333, 346
    composite, 335, 610
    interval, 314, 315–316, 319

Likert, 318, 333–335
    metric, 598
    nominal, 313–314, 319
    nonmetric, 598
    ordinal, 314, 315, 319
    overview of, 311, 313–319
    for questionnaire design, 391–400
    ratio, 314, 316, 319
    statistical analysis of, 316–319
    summated, 320
    See also rating scales, attitude
scanner-based consumer panel, 247
scanner data
    electronic test-markets and, 298
    purchase behavior and, 34–35
    statistical databases and, 37
Scarborough Research, 450
Schönbrunn Palace questionnaire, 390
Schwinn, 139
scientific method, 7
Scientific Telephone Samples, 427
scrolling layout, 373–374
search engines, 40
seat-of-the-pants decision making, 80
secondary data
    database marketing and customer
        relationship management, 169–170
    data mining, 168–169
    fact-finding and, 163–165
    global sources, 178–180
    model building, 165–168
    pros and cons of, 160–162
    single-source, 178
    sources of, 170–177
secondary sampling unit, 409
secrecy, 291
selection effect, 274
self-administered questionnaires
    distribution of, 218–219, 224–225
    e-mail survey, 225–226
    fax survey, 225
    Internet survey, 226–230
    kiosk interactive survey, 230
    mail survey, 219–220
    phrasing questions for, 358–359
    response rates, 220–224
self-selection bias, 190
semantic differential, 335–336, 344–345
semi-structured interviews, 150–151
sensitivity, 324–325
sequence of questions, 365–368
sequential sampling, 451
service monitoring, 94
SIC (Standardized Industrial
    Classification), 481
significance level, 526–527, 603, 669, 670
simple (bivariate) linear regression, 582
simple correlation coefficient, 577–581
simple data transformation, 509
simple-dichotomy questions, 357
simple random sampling, 414–415
simulated test-markets, 298–299
Singapore, 292–293
single-source data, 35, 178
site analysis techniques, 167
situation analysis, 108
situation frequency, 105–106
size of sample, 67
skip questions, 370, 372–373
Slone Epidemiology Center, 453
smart agent software, 41–42
snowball sampling, 414
social desirability bias, 193
software
    CHAID, 508
    graphical user interface (GUI), 373

software (continued)
   for interactive questionnaires, 376–377
   smart agent, 41–42
   spyware, 89
   for statistical analysis, 514–516
   web publishing, 373
   Website usage data, 642
Sony PlayStation, 108
sorting, 332, 343, 345
split-ballot technique, 361
split-half method, 322
SPSS (Statistical Package for the Social
      Sciences), 514–515, 606, 622
spyware, 89
squishing, 364
stages in research process
   alternatives, choosing among, 59
   defining objectives, 59–64
   drawing conclusions and preparing
      report, 68
   gathering data, 67
   overview of, 58–59
   planning design, 64–65
   processing and analyzing data, 67–68
   sampling, 65–67
standard deviation, 436–438, 451, 535
standard error of the mean, 442
standardized normal distribution,
      439–440
standardized regression coefficient, 583
standardized regression estimates, 583
standardized research service, 83–84
Stapel scale, 337
Starbucks, 4, 9
STATCRUNCH, 532
static group design, 277
stating research objectives, 62–63
Statistical Abstract of the United States, 35
statistical analysis
   computer programs for, 514–516
   descriptive, 502–503
   of scales, 316–319
   types of, 524
statistical base, 506
statistical databases, 36–37
statistical inference, 442
statistical technique, choosing
   bivariate, 546, 547
   level of scale measurement and, 532
   multivariate, 598, 599
   number of variables and, 531–532
   overview of, 531
   parametric vs. nonparametric, 532–533
   type of question and, 531
statistical test, reporting format for, 634
statistical theory
   central-limit theorem, 443–445, 446
   estimation of parameters, 445–449
   making data usable, 431–438
   normal distribution, 438–441
   population, sample, and sampling
      distributions, 441–443
   terminology, 430–431
StatLib, 532
status bar, 374
status quo, invoking, 361
straight trend projections, 296
strategic decision making
   marketing mix and, 14–18
   marketing performance and, 18–19
   opportunities and, 13
   overview of, 12–13
   target markets and, 13–14
stratified sampling, 415–416, 456
stratum charts, 638, 639

streaming media, 147
string characters, 487
structural equations modeling (SEM), 598
structuration theory, 63
structured qualitative responses,
      coding, 486
structured questions, 196
students, as subjects, 275
sub-divided bar charts, 639, 640
subjective results, 132
subjects, 256, 267
summary of report, 630
summated scales, 320
sum of squares, partitioning, 573–574
supervision of fieldworkers, 472–474
supply chain, 15
SurfStat.australia, 532
survey, definition of, 186
survey research
   administrative error, 193–194
   advantages of, 187
   communicating using media, 208
   description of, 64–65
   as descriptive research, 53
   errors in, 187–188
   ethical issues in, 232
   methods of, 195–198
   objectives of, 186–187
   personal interviews, 209–214
   pretesting, 232
   respondent error, 189–193
   selecting design for, 230–231
   self-administered questionnaires,
      218–230
   systematic error, 194–195
   telephone interviews, 214–218
   Total quality management and customer
      satisfaction surveys, 198–202
Survey Sampling International, 424
symptoms
   identifying, 110
   of problem, 48
   problem definition and, 106–107
   relevant issues and, 112
syndicated service, 83
synergistic effect, 303
systematic error, 188, 194–195, 262
systematic sampling, 415
systematic sampling error, 410–411
Syzygy, 252

T

table of contents, 629
tables, 513–515, 546–550, 633, 634
tabulation, 503
tachistoscope, 269
target markets, 13–14
target population, defining, 66–67,
      406–407
t-distribution, 533–537, 667
telemarketing, 88
telephone interviews
   characteristics of, 214–217
   layout of page from, 369
   phrasing questions for, 358–359
   precoded format for, 489–490, 491
   skip questions, 370
   training to make, 463
   types of, 217–218
telescoping, 364
temporal sequence, 54
terminating interviews, 467
tertiary sampling unit, 409
testing effect, 274

test markets
   advantages of, 287–288
   alternative methods, 297–299
   complex experimental designs,
      300–304
   decision to use, 290–291
   description of, 56
   disadvantages of, 288–290
   estimating sales volume, 294–296
   example of, 284–285
   projecting results, 296–297
   selecting, 291–294
   uses of, 285–287
test-retest reliability, 322
tests of difference, 546
test tabulation, 491–492
test units, 262–265, 405
Texas Instruments, 252
thematic apperception test, 152–153
themes, 138, 139
theory, 63
Thomas and Dorothy Leavey
      Library, 476
3 × 4 tables, 506
Thurstone interval scale, 340
time
   consciousness of, 36
   exploratory research and, 155
   management, staff, and, 78–79
   for problem definition, 119
   timeliness of data, 29
time series designs, 279–280
title page, 628
total quality management, 11,
      198–202, 472
total value management, 18
tracking study, 197
traffic cameras, 245
training for interviewers, 462–467,
      471–472
trend spotting, 238
truthful, obligation to be, 87
t-tests, 533–535, 550–556
two-tailed tests, 536
2 × 2 tables, 506
Type I error, 530–531
Type II error, 530–531

U

unaided recall, 364, 391–392
unbalanced rating scales, 347
uncertainty, 49, 57–58
undisguised questions, 196
Uniform Resource Locator (URL), 40
United Parcel Service (UPS), 30
unit of analysis, 114
units, sampling, 67
univariate hypothesis test, 524–525, 533,
      536–537
univariate statistical analysis, 524
Universal Product Code (UPC), 37
unobtrusive method, 67
unrestricted sample, 423
unstructured qualitative responses,
      coding, 485–486
unstructured questions, 196
UPC (Universal Product Code), 37
Upjohn Company, Rogaine, 157
UPS (United Parcel Service), 30
URL (Uniform Resource Locator), 40
U.S. Department of the Interior
      survey, 497–498
U.S. test-market cities, 291–292
users, rights and obligations of, 97–98

V

validity, 272–276, 323–324
value labels, 487
Vans shoes, 128
variable piping software, 377
variables
   blocking, 301
   dependent (Y), 115–116, 261–262
   dummy, 600
   experimental, 56
   extraneous, 264–265, 268
   independent (X), 115, 257–259, 261
   moderator, 507
   number of, and statistical technique,
      531–532
   overview of, 114–116, 312
variance, 437, 451
variance components, using to compute
      F-ratios, 560, 562
variate, 597
vendors, 35, 173
Verbastat (SPSS), 494
verification by reinterviewing, 474
Vidal Sassoon, Inc., 520
videoconferencing, 147
virtual-reality simulated test-market, 299
visible observation, 238
visual estimation of simple regression
      model, 584–585
voice-pitch analysis, 250

W

Walker Information Group, 206
Wal-Mart, 30, 38
web publishing software, 373
Website
   MovieTickets.com, 177
   resources, 532
   traffic monitoring, 246–247
   Wine.com, 45
welcome screen, 227
Wendy's, 288
Wilcoxon matched-pairs signed-ranks
      test, 672
Wine.com, 45
wine consumers, 53
within-group error or variance, 560, 562
within-subjects designs, 271–272
working population, 407
Wrangler, 38
writing decision statements and
      objectives, 112–114, 117
WWW (World Wide Web), 40

X

X (independent variable), 115, 257–259,
      261
χ^2 (chi-square) test, 537–540,
      546–550, 576

Y

Y (dependent variable), 115–116, 261–262
Yandelovich Partners, 467
Yoplait Go-Gurt, 8–9

Z

Zales, 17
Z-distribution, 533, 535
Z-statistic, 528–530
Z-test, 535, 536, 556–557